DETAIL FROM "MID DAY
AT THE BELL INN" BY
GEORGE MORLAND

MASTERS OF THE ART

Not only successful brewers, the Morlands also boasted an
illustrious painter in the family. George Morland (1763-1804), became
a noted painter of rustic Georgian English life. Indeed, he was a
welcome and frequent guest at the
family's pubs - often settling his
bill with a masterly-drawn sketch.
It was in tribute to him that the
now familiar "sign of the artist"

DOG HOUSE HOTEL, FRILFORD HEATH, OXON

was originated, honouring both the painter's and the brewer's art.

AN OUTSTANDING PORTFOLIO OF BEERS

From our flagship ale "Old Speckled Hen" to
the distinctive "Morland Original Bitter," our fine
family of beers are brewed with exceptional care
and great enthusiasm by people proud to carry
on the tradition begun so many years ago.

You'll find several Morland pubs in this Guide. Pay one
a visit for a real taste of English history.

Egon Ronay's Guides
Richbell House
77 St John St
London EC1M 4AN

Managing Director **Simon Tattersall**
Editorial Director **Andrew Eliel**
Publishing Director **Angela Nicholson**
Editor **Nigel Edmund-Jones**

Leading Guides Ltd
Part of the Richbell NewMedia Ltd Group of Companies

The contents of this book are believed correct at the time of printing. Nevertheless, the publisher can accept no responsibility for errors or omissions or changes in the details given.

Designed and typeset in Great Britain by Paul Fry and Carl Pandy for Bookman Projects Ltd.
Printed in Italy.

First published 1996 by Bookman Projects Ltd.
Floor 22
1 Canada Square
Canary Wharf
London E14 5AP

Establishments are independently researched or inspected. Inspections are anonymous and carried out by Egon Ronay's Guides team of professional inspectors. They may reveal their identities at pubs in order to check all the rooms and other facilities. The Guide is independent in its editorial selection and does not accept advertising, payment or hospitality from listed establishments.

Egon Ronay's Pubs & Inns Awards 1997

This year's award winners are presented here. Full details of the recipients can be found on the pages indicated.

14 Inn at Whitewell
Whitewell
**Pub of
the Year**

16 White Hart
Crowborough
**Family Pub
of the Year**

18 Ramsholt Arms
Ramsholt
**Pub Newcomer
of the Year**

20 The Bull Inn
Charlbury
**Pub Hosts
of the Year**

22 The Angel
Long Crendon
**Seafood Pub
of the Year**

26 The Lamb
London WC1
**Cheese Pub
of the Year**

Full Contents: Page 4

1997 AWARDS

CONTENTS

Introduction
by Nigel Edmund-Jones

After 32 years, we still endeavour to seek out the very best in independently-run 'free houses' (pubs free of 'tie' to a brewery) throughout the country, though there is always room for well-run managed houses in this Guide (after all, we're sponsored by a brewery). Food has always been our main interest but it may surprise many readers to learn that Egon Ronay's Guides have recommended pubs in completely separate 'Food', 'B&B' and 'Atmosphere' categories ever since the publication of our first Guide in 1964. For this reason we urge those readers who write to us complaining about food in pubs where we do not recommend it to check clearly our specific recommendation for that pub.

In this Guide our recommendation is clearly categorised on each entry; for the last few years we have also distributed window stickers to every establishment featured in that year's Guide – these clearly distinguish between the categories. Those pubs that try to pull the wool over their patrons' eyes (by, say, a pub recommended for 'Atmosphere' only advertising a special dining night in their local paper as 'Egon Ronay recommended') should be avoided and be reported to their local Trading Standards Office. We endeavour to keep track of those landlords who wish to abuse our good name and every year the list of recommended establishments in the Guide changes quite significantly.

Our recommendations are not for typically-average, 7-day-a-week drinkers' pubs – we have every eccentric variation, with some pubs clearly trying to trade as restaurants, and some even closing for one or two days a week. Nevertheless, the traditional pub atmosphere is retained and good cask-conditioned ale is often a major attraction. The enormous success of pub food in recent years is surely down to the very informality of the British pub: diners are attracted by familiar surroundings, ordering drinks at the bar, choosing as little (or as much) as they like from a familiar menu, and expecting straightforward service without any airs and graces.

Fish finds favour
We are happy to welcome the Sea Fish Industry Authority as new sponsors in this Guide. Early last year we invited pubs to send us details of their piscatorial offerings; once we had trawled through all their menus it became clear (not least because of the BSE scare earlier in the year) that fish was now a major attraction at pubs right across the country – from sensationally fresh shellfish platters in Scotland to milky-fresh cod and chips on the East Coast, and mussels, monkfish and more in the West Country. We found an exciting range of fresh fish and shellfish on offer and so we have highlighted every pub that makes the effort to serve up good fish dishes with our new Seafood Symbol:

Finding our 1997 Seafood Pub of the Year was a hard choice. Eventually, after several visits, *The Angel* in Long Crendon, Buckinghamshire emerged as a very worthy winner - you can read about it further on page 22. Among the Regional Winners (listed on page 24) you will find the aptly-named *Crab & Lobster* at Asenby and *The Fishers* in Edinburgh. Also in the Guide are *The Sea Trout Inn* in Staverton and *The Fish* in land-locked Sutton Courtenay, a stellar new re-entry in this Guide. Both pubs live up to their fishy names splendidly.

Landlords do it their way
So many pubs appear to be run for the benefit of their landlord rather than for the benefit of their customers. We regularly receive complaints about pubs where the chef has gone home early or where there are variations to the opening or bar food hours. Seasonal variations are common throughout the land but we urge not only landlords to be consistent but also our readers to be understanding. It may not be the easiest of tasks running a seven-days-a-week business but a little flexibility goes a long way towards creating customer satisfaction. The trade press often features pubs for sale that are described as 'having great potential' due to being recently 'traded for lifestyle'. Need we say more?

Credit where credit is due

As consumers, we should also take some landlords to task for steadfastly refusing to take credit cards. Prices of food in pubs continue to rise along with the increased demand and, at the top end of the market, pub food prices are certainly on a par with those in the local restaurants with which they compete. Since the vast majority of pubs recommended in this Guide clearly do not provide the same level of service as that of a restaurant it seems rather one-sided that customers are not given the convenience of paying by credit cards in so many etablishments These days, with on-line multi-credit-card machines and other time-saving systems, there is much less paperwork involved and it seems churlish of landlords not to accept that credit card company charges are a small price to pay for the convenience (and security) of not handling so much cash. Wake up, landlords, there's a retail revolution going on outside your cosy tavern doors; this kind of service convenience (as well as good food) is what customers are looking for if they are to part with more of their hard-earned cash in pubs.

Irish Bars

The 'rise and rise of Irishness' (as Guinness's marketing department will have it) continues apace with Irish-themed bars opening at an alarming speed: Bass's *O'Neill's*, Allied Domecq Leisure's *Scruffy Murphy's*, Greene King's *Sean O'Grady's*, Whitbread's *JJ Murphy's* and *O'Hagan's*, and Greenalls' pubs like *Shifty O'Shea's* and *Daisy O'Brien's* are multiplying.

Only recently one of this writer's London 'locals' (admittedly a rather un-loved pub called the *Queen Victoria*) was transmogrified by Scottish Courage into *Finnegan's Wake*; this was undoubtedly due to the fact that there was an all-singing *Yates's Wine Lodge* (a loud, clubby pub), the *Photographer & Firkin* and a *Rat & Parrot* (another Scottish Courage themed pub) all within one minute's walk. Competition is everything with the big brewers, market share a Holy Grail ... but if you want the real thing then you need look no further than the *O'Conor Don* in London's Marylebone Lane where, unlike the mass of these themed 'Irish' pubs, the food is the genuine article (and a million miles away from 'Ma O'Grady's taste of Ireland' or Mother Kelly's doorstep sandwiches!).

Along with this inexorable rise in popularity of all things Irish is the phenomenal success of Bass's Caffrey's nitro-keg, draught-flow, so-called-Irish chilled 'ale'. Where one succeeds, others follow: almost every major brewery in the country now makes this style of beer, from Kilkenny, John Smith's Smooth, Greene King Wexford Cream Ale and Alloa Calder's Cream Ale to Morland Original Smooth. Smooth, cold and creamy it may be, designed to win lager drinkers back to beer, but is it the equal of a tip-top 'real', cask-conditioned ale like Morland Old Speckled Hen?

The stars above

Newcomers to our list of Pub Bar Food Star winners (see page 12) include *The White Hart* in Great Yeldham (Essex), *The Drewe Arms* in Broadhembury (Devon), *The Woodchester Inn* in Woodchester and *The Fox* in Lower Oddington (both in Gloucestershire), *The Feathers* in Brockton, *The Bull Inn* in Charlbury (also winner of our 1997 Pub Hosts of the Year) and *The Fish* in Sutton Courtenay (both in Oxfordshire), *The Montague Inn* in Shepton Mallet (Somerset) and *The White Hart* in Nayland (Suffolk). Also a winner of a new star this year is *The Inn at Whitewell*, which wins our 1997 Pub of the Year award (see page 14); Richard Bowman's wonderful inn embodies all that we look for in a good pub or inn: good food, 'real' beer, hospitable atmosphere, friendly welcome and comfortable overnight accommodation. Long may it prosper.

Good pub grub

The humble 'banger' plays an important part in the tradition of pub food - where would we be without bangers 'n'mash with onion gravy? There is surely nowhere better to sample the butcher's art - specifically those of Bill O'Hagan, 'Britain's best sausage maker' (according to the British Sausage Appreciation Society) - than at the *Sussex Brewery* in Hermitage (see entry) near Emsworth, West Sussex. Here you will find up to 40 varieties – from the Chichester Sausage with rolled oats, Ballard's bitter and Sussex herbs to lamb and mint, South African boerewors, chorizo and skinless vegetarian patties. The kitchen at *The Inn at Whitewell* gives their Cumberland bangers a nice little Irish twist by serving them with champ, while *The Fox* in Lower Oddington offers a rather upmarket hot sausage and Meaux mustard French bread sandwich - now who can deny that's not good pub grub?

Old Speckled Hen

Finally, we are indebted to brewers Morland & Co as sponsors of this Guide with their 'renowned Old Speckled Hen' brand – one of the country's leading cask-conditioned and bottled ales. Morland's involvement reflects the importance of real ale as a major attraction in the vast majority of pubs and inns that we recommend within these pages, and also the growing popularity of Old Speckled Hen as one of the most widely stocked guest beers. Morland's marketing for Old Speckled Hen features a gentlemanly fox hunting for perfection as its motif – entirely appropriate, as our inspectors act as bell-wethers, tirelessly hunting down the very best pubs and inns across the country. Look out for Old Speckled Hen – you'll find it regularly available in pubs in this Guide all around Britain (particularly near Morland's brewery in Abingdon, Oxfordshire, even outside the gates – see the *Brewery Tap* entry). This year's most northern sighting of the Old Hen herself has been at the *Ardvasar Hotel* on the Isle of Skye in Scotland – let's hope she nestles there permanently!

Speak up

The last word has to go to the menu at *Cubley Hall* in Penistone: 'If you have a problem, so do we'. If only all landlords realised that it *is* as simple as that ... and that the answer is not to be found in the local cash and carry. If you have a problem at any of the pubs recommended in this Guide we urge you to make your voice heard at the time of your visit; trying to sort out a problem after the event invariably produces an unsatisfactory result. If you still find any part of the experience not worthy of our recommendation then please write to us (or fax) on one of the Readers Comments' forms at the back of the Guide.

"OLD SPECKLED HEN"

Foreword

Welcome to Egon Ronay's "Old Specked Hen" Guide, 1997 Pubs & Inns, the definitive guide to the best pubs and inns in Great Britain and Ireland.

For the second year running the guide is being sponsored by Morland plc, brewers of the famous "Old Speckled Hen."

As a regional brewer who is extremely well supported by pubs nationwide, Morland is delighted to be associated with a guide which promotes such a wonderful selection of the UK's treasured pubs and inns. In seeking out the pleasures and traditional qualities which are to be found in Britain's finest pubs, you will discover the delightful uniqueness of our country's heritage and hospitality.

What could be more fitting than to celebrate the best of British pubs with the help of one of the country's celebrated ales? Morland's "Old Speckled Hen" is an established leader in its market, and is appreciated as a truly classic beer with a unique smoothness and subtle blend of flavours. Our advertising encourages drinkers to *hunt for perfection* in their choice of ale. When using Egon Ronay's "Old Speckled Hen" Guide, 1997 Pubs & Inns, you too will find perfection, pub perfection.

As the second oldest independent brewer in the country, Morland has spent nearly 300 years producing fine traditional ales which provide pubs with an essential ingredient to offer you, the pub enthusiast – quality British beer. By supporting this year's Guide, we hope we can also help you discover quality pubs in which to enjoy, among other things, some of the world's finest beers.

Happy hunting.

Mike Watts

Michael Watts, Chief Executive
MORLAND PLC

Combine quality pubs with

The story behind "Old Speckled Hen."

"Old Speckled Hen" was destined to be associated with the best things Britain has to offer. The history of its name stretches back to 1927. In that year, MG produced a unique prototype saloon car. Canvas covered, painted gold and flecked with black, it was eventually used as a factory run-around vehicle – fondly called the

"old speckled 'un" by locals in the town of Abingdon. Typical of names passed by word of mouth, this changed over time to the "old speckled hen".

As the 50th anniversary of the Abingdon factory approached, MG asked Morland, the established brewers in the town, to produce a special traditional ale to celebrate the occasion. Morland linked their ale to MG by naming it "Old Speckled Hen".

"Old Speckled Hen" is a pale ale which owes its distinctive character and dry taste to a unique strain of yeast first used in 1896. The individual blend of flavours reflects skills developed over 285 years of independent brewing history.

Today "Old Speckled Hen" is an established premium traditional ale in Britain's beer market – an ale with a flavour as unique as the vintage car it is named after.

The brand is supported by a distinctive national advertising campaign. The advertisements are drawn in 19th century "Punch" magazine style, and feature a robust, yet very gentlemanly, fox – hunting for perfection!

quality beer, and find perfection.

How To Use This Guide

Order of Entries

London appears first and is in alphabetical order by establishment name. Listings outside London are in alphabetical order by location within divisions of England, Scotland, Wales, Channel Islands (inc the Isle of Man) and Northern Ireland. See contents page and the index for specific page numbers.

Map References

Map references alongside each pub entry are to the map section at the back of the Guide. Use this to select establishments in the area that you wish to visit.

Good Bar Food

We include establishments where our team of professional inspectors found good-quality **Bar Food**. Such pubs and inns are indicated by the symbol **FOOD** printed in the margin alongside the entry. No mention is made of a pub's separate restaurant operation unless one menu is served throughout the pub's dining areas or if the restaurant is also recommended in *Egon Ronay's Visa Guide 1997 Hotels & Restaurants*.

Dishes listed are meant to be typical of the pub's style and not a definitive menu description. We indicate when bar food is served and also any times when food is not available. Meal times in recommended restaurants may differ from bar food times. If there is an outdoor eating area we include this information in the statistics. Pubs serving outstanding bar food are indicated by a ★ alongside their name (see additional list of Starred Pubs on page 12).

Good Accommodation

We also inspect accommodation, and those pubs and inns recommended for an overnight stay are indicated by the symbol **B&B** in the margin alongside the entry. We list the number of bedrooms, the price for an en-suite double bedroom (with bath rather than shower where available) and a full cooked breakfast for two, and whether children are welcome overnight. Very occasionally the price of a cooked breakfast is not included but we have indicated where this is the case. 'Single' room prices do not always refer to single rooms as they may often refer to single occupancy of a double room.

We assume that it is possible to check-in all day; where this is not the case (and thus advisable to arrange a time when booking) we print check-in by arrangement. General accommodation closures around Christmas are not mentioned as these are so variable; however, if there is a regular period during the year that a pub is traditionally closed (say for staff holidays) then we list that information.

We have assigned a 'Sleep' symbol **Zzz**... to those pubs and inns that we consider offer particularly comfortable and/or quiet accommodation.

Pubs with Atmosphere

Pubs recommended for being particularly atmospheric, pleasant or interesting places in which to enjoy a drink (rather than the bar food or accommodation) are indicated by the symbol **A** alongside their entry. Interestingly-located pubs and those with particularly good real ales (micro-brewery pubs, for example) are also highlighted by the **A** symbol. All the pubs are clearly recommended for either Food **FOOD**, Accommodation **B&B** or Atmosphere **A**. Every year we get dozens of complaints about the food served in pubs where we do not recommend it; we urge readers to clearly differentiate between our recommendations.

Opening Hours

We have tried to ascertain from landlords their general opening hours; however, these should not be taken as firm times and readers should certainly assume that longer hours might apply in summer and shorter in winter. In particular, following the recent change in Sunday Licensing laws, Sunday opening hours may change from those times we have listed.

Beer

We indicate whether an establishment is a Free House (ie not owned by a brewery), and list the names of a number of regular real ales that were being offered when we last contacted the pub. These are often likely to change and should not be taken as permanent offers. Our Beer symbol ▼ indicates that an unusual or interesting range of beers is usually on offer – these may be micro-brewery pubs or 'brewery taps'.

Children Welcome

Entries indicate whether the pub has facilities suitable for families; those that offer a good combination of the facilities (perhaps where children are allowed in the bar to eat or where there's a special children's menu, a family room or an indoor/outdoor play area) are marked by the 'Family' symbol ☺. See also listings in the Regional Round-Up at the back of the Guide. If there is no mention of family facilities then readers should assume that the pub does not welcome children. Children may well be charged extra for breakfast if sharing their parents' bedroom free of charge overnight.

Credit Cards

We list credit cards accepted and also note those pubs which accept none. Occasionally, credit cards may only be accepted for accommodation and not for bar food.

Symbols

★	**Outstanding Bar Food**
🐟	**Good seafood served – sponsored by the Sea Fish**
	Industry Authority
🍺	**Good selection of British Cheeses**
▼	**Particularly good or unusual range of real ales**
🍷	**Half a dozen or more wines served by the glass in the bar**
Zzz...	**Particularly comfortable and/or quiet Accommodation**
☺	**Suitable for families**
Ilchester	**Serves Ilchester Cheese**

Starred Pubs 1997

London
EC1, Farringdon **The Eagle**
EC1, Clerkenwell **The Peasant**
NW1, Primrose Hill **The Engineer**
NW1, Primrose Hill **The Lansdowne**
SW10, Chelsea **Chelsea Ram**
W2, Westbourne Grove
The Westbourne

England
Berkshire, West Ilsley **Harrow Inn**
Buckinghamshire, Long Crendon
The Angel
Cambridgeshire, Keyston,
Pheasant Inn
Cambridgeshire, Madingley
Three Horseshoes
Cambridgeshire, Wansford-in-England
The Haycock
Cornwall, Gunwalloe **Halzephron Inn**
Cumbria, Cartmel Fell **Masons Arms**
Cumbria, Crosthwaite **Punch Bowl**
Cumbria, Ulverston **Bay Horse Inn**
Devon, Broadhembury **Drewe Arms**
Devon, Kingsteignton **Old Rydon Inn**
Devon, Rockbeare **Jack in the Green**
Dorset, Corscombe **Fox Inn**
Durham, Romaldkirk **Rose & Crown**
Essex, Great Yeldham **White Hart**
Essex Horndon-on-the-Hill **Bell Inn**
Gloucestershire, Coln St Aldwyns
New Inn
Gloucestershire, Lower Oddington
The Fox
Gloucestershire, Woodchester
Woodchester Inn
Hampshire, Winchester
Wykeham Arms
Hereford & Worcester, Brimfield
The Roebuck & Poppies
Hereford & Worcester, Winforton
Sun Inn
Kent, Ightham Common **Harrow Inn**
Kent, Ivy Hatch **The Plough**
Kirklees, Shelley **Three Acres**
Lancashire, Lydgate **White Hart**
Lancashire, Whitewell
Inn at Whitewell
Norfolk, Burnham Market **Hoste Arms**
Northumberland, Warenford
Warenford Lodge
Oxfordshire, Bledington
King's Head Inn
Oxfordshire, Charlbury **Bull Inn**

Oxfordshire, Cumnor
Bear & Ragged Staff
Oxfordshire, Sutton Courtenay
The Fish
Shropshire, Brockton **The Feathers**
Somerset, Batcombe **Batcombe Inn**
Somerset, Beckington **Woolpack Inn**
Somerset, Monksilver **Notley Arms**
Somerset, Shepton Montague
Montague Inn
Suffolk, Nayland **White Hart**
Suffolk, Southwold **The Crown**
Suffolk, Stoke-by-Nayland **Angel Inn**
Surrey, Grayswood **Wheatsheaf Inn**
West Sussex, Lower Beeding
Jeremy's at The Crabtree
West Sussex, Midhurst **Angel Hotel**
Wiltshire, North Newnton
Woodbridge Inn
Wiltshire, Rowde **George & Dragon**
North Yorkshire, Hetton **Angel Inn**
North Yorkshire, Saxton **Plough Inn**
North Yorkshire, Wass
Wombwell Arms

Scotland
Argyll & Bute, Kilberry **Kilberry Inn**
Fife, Kirkcaldy **Hoffmans**

Wales
Powys, Llyswen **Griffin Inn**

Channel Islands
Alderney, St Anne **Georgian House**

Northern Ireland
Lisburn, Hillsborough **Hillside Bar**

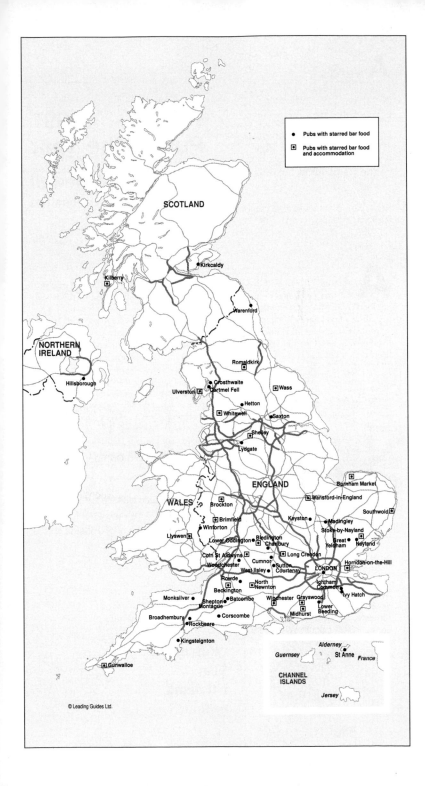

Pubs with starred bar food

Pubs with starred bar food and accommodation

SCOTLAND

Kirkcaldy

Kilberry

Warenford

NORTHERN
IRELAND

Hillsborough

Romaldkirk

Crosthwaite
Cartmel Fell
Ulverston

Wass

Hetton

Whitewell

Saxton

Shelley

Lydgate

ENGLAND

Burnham Market

WALES

Brockton

Wansford-in-England

Brimfield

Keyston

Madingley

Southwold

Winforton

Stoke-by-Nayland

Llyswen

Lower Oddington

Bledington

Great
Yeldham

Nayland

Charlbury

Coln St Aldwyns

Long Crendon

Horndon-on-the-Hill

Woodchester

Cumnor

Sutton

West Ilsley

Courtenay

LONDON

Rowde

North

Newnton

Ightham
Common

Beckington

Ivy Hatch

Monksilver

Batcombe

Winchester

Grayswood

Shepton
Montague

Lower
Beeding

Broadhembury

Corscombe

Midhurst

Rockbeare

Kingsteignton

Gunwalloe

Alderney

Guernsey

St Anne

France

CHANNEL
ISLANDS

Jersey

© Leading Guides Ltd.

Awards

1997
Pub of the Year

Inn at Whitewell
Whitewell, Lancashire

A real one-off, Richard Bowman's inn is delightfully individual (but not easy to find on a dark night – persevere and you'll find it delightfully set by the River Hodder amid the outstanding, but little-known, beauty of the Vale of Bowland). It is neither a hotel nor pub nor restaurant but all these rolled into a true 'inn' with every attribute (and more) that one might wish for in such an establishment: warm hospitality, good food in both the atmospheric bar and friendly restaurant (overlooking

the river), comfortable and cosseting bedrooms, a wine shop, art gallery and even trout, salmon and grayling fishing for overnight guests. A charming, eccentric air and seemingly-haphazard furnishing arrangements cleverly combine to bring the whole operation together in a most unusual way – where else would one find reading stands beside the bedroom WCs or cricket balls as key fobs, not to mention Bang & Olufson music systems, videos, binoculars and the odd peat fire in the accommodation? Head chef Breda Murphy brings a beguiling Irish angle to the food that encompasses a wide spectrum, from carefully-prepared, home-made soups and ice creams to good local meats, fresh fish and Irish cheeses. Even children and dogs ('with kind natures') are welcomed.

"Pub of the Year ... I'll drink to that!"

Awards

PAST WINNERS
1995 **The Hoste Arms** Burnham Market, Norfolk
1995 **The Angel** Hetton, North Yorkshire
1994 **The Lamb** Great Rissington, Gloucestershire
1993 **Rose & Crown** Romaldkirk, Durham
1992 **The Roebuck** Brimfield, Hereford & Worcester

MORLAND PLC
(brewers of Old Speckled Hen)

**CONGRATULATE EGON RONAY'S GUIDES
PUB OF THE YEAR**
INN AT WHITEWELL

Awards

1997
Family Pub of the Year
The White Hart
Crowborough, East Sussex

Two years ago, the run-down White Hart – a large, mock-Tudor pub with a twin-gabled facade on the top of Crowborough Hill – was in a sorry state but Carl and Judith Martin spotted the pub's potential as an independently-run family pub. So they started work on providing every conceivable family facility, from an indoor play area, complete with kitchen playhouse, video, chalkboards, multiplication tables and books, to a well-equipped outdoor play area (with bouncy castle, wooden fort, climbing rope, sandpit and baby swing) in the large garden. There is now much to satisfy the demands of today's parents: good bar food, and

particularly good ales for the adults, along with baby food, a children's menu (including picnic boxes), vegetarian dishes, sugar-free drinks, high-chairs and a baby-changing area in the disabled toilet. The Wibbly Wobbly Farmyard mini zoo houses a menagerie of pygmy goats, rabbits, ducks, chickens, guinea-pigs and a pot-bellied pig. Dad, however, may be more interested in the Old Hen served at the bar! Summer barbecues and special holiday events are all geared towards entertaining the whole family.

"It's my independent view that family pubs are very Good News!"

Awards

PAST WINNERS	
1996	**Olde Coach House**
	Ashby St Ledgers,
	Northamptonshire
1995	**Batcombe Inn**
	Batcombe, Somerset

MORLAND PLC

(brewers of Old Speckled Hen)

CONGRATULATE EGON RONAY'S GUIDES
FAMILY PUB OF THE YEAR

THE WHITE HART

Awards

1997
Pub Newcomer of the Year
The Ramsholt Arms
Ramsholt, Suffolk

In a glorious riverside setting, right by an old barge quay, with an unusual pink-painted exterior, the Ramsholt Arms is well worth the drive through remote countryside to find. It's a friendly pub, with a superbly positioned terrace that makes the most of the views over the fields and marshes across the sweeping River Deben, an open-plan interior with a curving bar that leads round from an airy dining-room with picture windows to a 'snug' area, first-rate bar food, comfortable overnight accommodation, and ample parking. Michael and Kirsten Bartholemew have brought a new lease of life to this delightful pub, creating a thriving hostelry that encompasses many of the concepts that make today's modern pubs so successful: real ales, a good selection of wines served by the glass, proper fresh food and a welcome for families. It may sound a simple equation but Michael and Kirsten Bartholemew make it all add up with style. Whether you come to watch the bird life (of all sorts), to sample the offerings from Kirsten's kitchen, to savour a pint of Adnams while listening to the rattling of boat mast stays, the cry of gulls or lapping of water on the shore or to stay overnight and enjoy walks the riverbank, the Ramsholt Arms has a great deal to offer.

"Always on the lookout for a rising star!"

Awards

PAST WINNERS	
1996	**Carrington Arms,** Moulsoe.
1995	**Cridford Inn,** Trusham
	Halzephron Inn, Gunwalloe
1994	**Five Arrows,** Waddesdon
	Fox Inn, Lower Oddington
1993	**Fox & Hounds**, Starbotton
	Woodbridge Inn, North Newnton

MORLAND PLC
(brewers of Old Speckled Hen)

CONGRATULATE EGON RONAY'S GUIDES
PUB NEWCOMER OF THE YEAR
THE RAMSHOLT ARMS

Awards

1997
Pub Hosts of the Year
Roy & Suzanne Flynn
The Bull Inn
Charlbury, Oxfordshire

Roy and Suzanne Flynn took over The Bull early in 1995. They spent the summer refurbishing the interior and even rebuilding some areas, eventually re-opening in September of the same year. Set in a busy little Cotswold town, the handsome, atmospheric inn dates back to the 16th century and the splendid refurbishment has been done with good taste. There is much to catch (and please) the eye – from old baskets hanging from beams in the bar to a collection of china in a corner cupboard and old weighing scales on a fine dresser. Roy Flynn is very personable, a natural front man

for a modern pub/restaurant such as this, with a friendly and helpful manner; he is always pleased to advise on the menu that his wife Suzanne oversees in the kitchen. The Bull is not only a new entry in this year's Guide but it also gains a star for Suzanne's exceptional bar food. Roy's and Suzanne's attention to detail (warm French bread, butter in pots, interesting salad dressings, comfortable sofas, fruit pot pourri) and keenness to please are clearly evident to all who walk through the doors of their welcoming inn.

"Hosts of the Year, eh? That deserves a few rounds!"

Awards

PAST WINNERS	
1995	**The Macleod Family** **The Pierhouse & Seafood** **Restaurant** Port Appin, Argyll & Bute, Scotland
1995	**Robert & Sally Hughes** **Penhelig Arms Hotel** Aberdovey, Gwynedd, Wales

MORLAND PLC
(brewers of Old Speckled Hen)

CONGRATULATE EGON RONAY'S GUIDES
PUB HOSTS OF THE YEAR
ROY & SUZANNE FLYNN

Awards

1997
Seafood Pub of the Year
The Angel
Long Crendon, Buckinghamshire

Deliveries of fresh fish come from all corners of the country (Scotland, Cornwall and Billingsgate – mostly via local fish and game dealer Richard Parker) to satisfy chef-proprietor Mark Jones's search for the finest fresh seafood. His pub/restaurant (call it what you will, but you can still enjoy a good pint of Braskpear's ale with your fish 'n' chips) deservedly nets the big one, catering admirably for both those who want to eat informally and those who want to dine restaurant-style. Snackers can fill the gap with Provençal-style fish soup, taglierini with mixed seafood or a platter of Scottish smoked fishes with a whisky and horsradish relish, while diners may push the boat out

for a seafood platter (prawns, scallops, salmon, squid, halibut and monkfish, according to availability), lobsters, crabs, tuna or a more involved dish like monkfish roasted with bacon and served with chargrilled vegetables and chili oil. It may be a cliché, but the ingredients really are left to speak for themselves – and when they're as fresh as you'll find here that's clearly the best way. The choice of seafood is extensive, the cooking accurate and the passion in the kitchen evident.

Awards

See page 24 for Seafood Pub of the Year Regional Winners

SEA FISH INDUSTRY AUTHORITY

CONGRATULATES EGON RONAY'S GUIDES
SEAFOOD PUB OF THE YEAR
THE ANGEL

Awards

Seafood Pub of the Year
1997 Regional Winners

London – The Cow London, W2
Tom Conran's 'Saloon Bar' offerings include Irish rock oysters, Cornish crab, Dublin Bay prawns and moules marinière – undoubtedly the finest shellfish available in a London pub.

South of England – Dering Arms Pluckley, Kent
An impressive, manorial building with a baronial interior and a relaxing atmosphere; fine, fresh fish from Hythe dominates the imaginative menus in both bar and restaurant.

West Country – Drewe Arms Broadhembury, Devon
'Seafood' is the watchword in Nigel and Kerstin Burge's pretty, thatched pub. From open prawn sandwiches and dressed crab to fancier fish dishes with complementary sauces, everything is consistently superb – be sure to book.

East of England – Ratcatchers Eastgate, Norfolk
An enthusiastic kitchen produces a long menu, of which seafood is only one section (but undoubtedly the best). Fresh fish comes from Lowestoft and shellfish from the North Norfolk coast. Once again, booking is recommended.

Midlands/Heart of England – Peacock Inn
Redmile, Nottinghamshire
Landlord Colin Crawford knows his market and his market knows what it likes – seafood. Chef Frank Garbez's daily-changing blackboard menus encompass crab mousse, scallops, red snapper and fresh tuna.

North of England – Crab & Lobster
Asenby, North Yorkshire
An exceptional selection of superb seafood at a very out-of-the-ordinary pub. Crab ravioli, lobster risotto, oysters, Oriental-spiced sea bass, roast monkfish, moules marinière – you name it and it's on the menu (there's even a fish club sandwich).

Scotland – Fishers Edinburgh (Leith), Lothian
Outstanding, all-day seafood speciality bar where the whiff of salty sea air is obviously inspirational. Sardines, smokies, squid, turbot – if it's out there in the sea the Fishers will land it on your plate with style.

Wales – Clytha Arms Clytha, Monmouthshire
Enticing Manx kippers, smoked sewin (sea trout grilse), mussels, scallops and prawns with laverbread pasta, John Dory and monkfish with oyster mushrooms may be among the attractions at Andrew and Beverley Canning's delightful little pub near Abergavenny.

Northern Ireland – The Plough Hillsborough, Lisburn
Chef-proprietor Derek Patterson's enthusiasm for seafood knows no bounds. His annual oyster festival is an enormous success and the inspiration for dishes throughout his 'restaurant/bistro/wine bar' (it's still a pub as well!) is worldly: look out for seafood céviche, Oriental monkfish, Swedish gravad lax, Cajun-spiced shark steaks or surf 'n' turf.

TREAT YOURSELF TO A
Feast
OF *Fish*

You've found the perfect pub now choose the best from the menu...

Go For Fish

Awards

1997
Ilchester Cheese Pub of the Year
The Lamb
London WC1

The winning dish 'Alliteration Pie' (a chicken, cheese, and cider crumble) owes part of its origin to the time when the pub used to be a cider house, frequented by Charles Dickens who lived round the corner. Actually, in the strictest sense chef Lionel Trattles' dish is not really a pie at all – the chicken in cider is baked in the oven, with a topping of cheese crumble made with Applewood smoked (cheddar) – hardly a traditional pie crust! Nevertheless, it's a hearty and scrumptious meal that would have gone down well with the Victorian and Edwardian music-hall stars from the Holborn Empire, whose sepia photographs adorn the walls.

Awards

The Ilchester Cheese Co, a supporter of this Guide in 'all things cheese' for several years, has introduced this year's awards to encourage pub chefs to find out for themselves the tremendous versatility of Ilchester speciality cheeses for use in cooking, as well as for use in cold dishes and cheeseboards.

Lionel Trattles receives £1,000 worth of Virgin vouchers, which can be spent on a whole range of options including Virgin flights, balloon rides, Megastore items, or even a stay at Raymond Blanc's *Le Manoir au Quat' Saisons*. The two runners-up (see next page) each receive £250 worth of vouchers.

To participate next year, just create an imaginative dish using Ilchester cheese, send us the recipe, and you too could be on your way to New York!

See page 28 for runners-up

THE ILCHESTER CHEESE CO.

CONGRATULATES EGON RONAY'S GUIDES
CHEESE PUB OF THE YEAR
THE LAMB

Awards

Ilchester Cheese Pub of the Year
1997 Runners-up

Rabbit Victoriana, pan-fried and topped
with a fondue of grated Ilchester sage Derby
and white wine

Warenford Lodge Warenford, Northumberland

Ilchester Double Gloucester onion & chive cheese and bacon soup

White Hart Cadnam, Hampshire

Ilchester Cheese Co. Ltd.

Somerton Road, Ilchester, Somerset, BA22 8JL
Telephone 01935 840531   Fax 01935 841223

Hunting for Perfection~

THE ELUSIVE ALE AT LAST IN VIEW

(and thought of the heady pleasures that await
spurs them on).

On finding
The Coveted Ale.

Happy thought. ~ "Our exhausting foxtrot through the fields, those daring leaps over thorny hedges, that close encounter with an Alsatian... all worthwhile. What a pint! See that colour, as rich as autumn leaves. Now savour that unique smoothness, the subtle blend of flavours."

"Our dogged pursuit of perfection has been amply rewarded in – of all places – The Farmer's Arms!"

BREWED BY MORLAND OF ABINGDON. EST'D. 1711.

MORLAND
"OLD
SPECKLED
HEN"
Strong Fine Ale

**FOUND! THE ALE THAT MAKETH
THE MEAL.**

Savouring the Subtle Blend of Flavours.

Happy thought. ~ "Such a richness of flavours! Complex, but not cluttered. A hint of nuttiness perhaps... a suggestion of plump, ripe autumn fruit? Beautifully seasoned, too ... so mellow and mature. Excellent body, superbly smooth and, I daresay, wickedly more-ish.

"As I've always said, my friend, why settle for sponge when one can have fruitcake!"

BREWED BY MORLAND OF ABINGDON. EST'D. 1711.

MORLAND
"OLD SPECKLED HEN"
Strong Fine Ale

THIS PIECE C

OPENS THE D

THE BEST HC

PLASTIC
OORS OF
TEL ROOMS.

MAKING LIFE EASIER

WHEREVER

BE SURE T

THE BEST F

YOU GO,
O EAT OFF
ASTIC.

MAKING LIFE EASIER

Egon Ronay's *VISA* Guide 1997
HOTELS & RESTAURANTS

The CD-ROM version of Egon Ronay's VISA Guide 1997 Hotels & Restaurants provides the fastest and most user-friendly way to access information about 3,200 recommended UK establishments. You can search via location, price, name, type of accommodation, type of cuisine and many speciality services.

From the editorial screens you can take an interactive tour, viewing photographs, menus and other information about your selected establishment.*

You can also visit Egon Ronay's Guides on the Internet. Our own web site gives you access to many innovative features, including frequent updating of hotel and restaurant reviews.

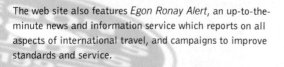

The web site also features *Egon Ronay Alert*, an up-to-the-minute news and information service which reports on all aspects of international travel, and campaigns to improve standards and service.

*Participating establishments only.

To find out more, visit our web site at:
http://www.egon-ronay.infocomint.com

London

N1   The Albion   A

Tel 0171-607 7450   Map 16 C2
10 Thornhill Road Islington N1 1HW

Once a coaching inn, this Georgian pub is in the middle of a quiet residential part of Islington. The front is welcoming with creeping ivy, tables and benches outside and an old-fashioned illustrated sign of a coach. The front room has plenty of tables, settles and chairs around a large wooden bar. The top part of the bar and the walls are decorated with coaching and horse-related bric-a-brac. At the back, there is a dark-panelled bar and a homely pinkish non-smoking and non-dining lounge. The lovely paved garden (unusual for London) has a weeping willow, a trellis covered with creepers and plenty of tables and chairs. The Albion was recommended for its all-day food last year but as we went to press Scottish & Newcastle's chef/manager was about to leave. *Open 11-11 (Sun 12-10.30).* **Beer** *Courage Best, Theakston XB & Best. Garden. Amex, Diners, MasterCard,* **VISA**

SW18   The Alma   FOOD

Tel 0181-870 2537   Fax 0181-874 9055   Map 17 B5
499 Old York Road Wandsworth SW18 1FT

Conveniently located across from Wandsworth station and close to the Young's brewery, the Alma is part of Charles Gotto's well-run group of atmospheric pubs, all of which have a strong emphasis on food (see also entries for *The Ship, The Castle* and *The Coopers Arms).* The Victorian tavern's bright, green-tiled facade and hanging flower baskets are distinctive enough but you may have more difficulty finding your way round the Wandsworth one-way system if arriving by car). In the darkwood interior of the airy central room, cast-iron tables and pinball and slot-machines range around an island bar counter. At the back, the dining-room has yellow-painted walls, framed cartoons, illustrations and beautiful pieces of antique kitchen and restaurant equipment. Daylight coming through the ceiling gives a soft and comfortable feel. The bar menu offers the likes of Toulouse sausage, eggs Benedict, mussels in cider, pasta du jour and sandwiches. Other dishes might include fresh mackerel fillets hollandaise and vegetable couscous. Besides the Young's on handpump, you'll find a superb selection of wines offered by the glass. Espresso and regular coffee are also available. *Open 11-10.30 (Sun 12-10).* **Bar Food** *12-3 (Sun till 4), 7-10.30.* **Beer** *Young's. Amex, Diners, MasterCard,* **VISA**

SE1   The Anchor   A

Tel 0171-407 1577   Fax 0171-407 0741   Map 17 D4
34 Park Street Bankside SE1 9DN

Located south-east of Southwark Bridge, with a bankside terrace overlooking the River Thames and the City beyond. The original Anchor was burnt down ten years after the Great Fire but the present Georgian building that replaced it is atmospheric, with a rambling interior that has rooms on several levels, intimate corners, old beams, darkwood panelling and leather seating. Good selection of draught beers – look out for the Old Speckled Hen herself, who seems to have flown from her regular nest on to a guest perch. *Open 11-11 (Sun 12-10.30).* **Beer** *Courage Best & Directors, Greenalls Bitter, Anchor Bitter (John Smith's), Flowers Original, up to four guest beers. Riverview patio. Family room. Pub closed 25, 26 Dec & 1 Jan. Amex, Diners, MasterCard,* **VISA**

SW3   The Australian   FOOD

Tel 0171-589 3114   Map 19 C5
29 Milner Street Chelsea SW3 2QD

The name and theme of this ivy-covered Nicholson's pub celebrate a very early game of cricket (back in the days of WG Grace) played by an Australian touring team in what is now Lennox Gardens. The walls are covered with pictures of famous British and Australian players, and in the evening there tends to be a young and lively clientele. During the daytime it's also useful to know that it's a short walk from Harrods and Peter Jones and that there are a few outside tables facing south and taking in the sun (the locals demand that drinkers are inside after sunset). A straightforward bar snack menu ranges from Antipodean egg and bacon pie and ploughman's lunches to deep-fried cod, Cumberland sausage with Welsh rarebit and chili con carne, plus daily specials and freshly-cut sandwiches (eg the Australian steak sandwich with 'special secret sauce' and an enormous BLT). *Open 11-11 (Sun 12-10.30).* **Bar Food** *12-3 only (Sun only in summer).* **Beer** *Tetley, Adnams, Brakspear, Eldridge Pope Thomas Hardy, guest beers. MasterCard,* **VISA**

W4   Bell & Crown   A

Tel 0181-994 4164   Map 17 A5
Strand on the Green Chiswick W4 3PF

Strand on the Green is a lovely place for a stroll along the Thames river bank, but you'll have to get to the pub early at weekends for a table outside. Never fear, if you can't find a table or bench on the two-level terrace then walk on along the towpath and work up a thirst. Where better to sample a pint of London Pride or one of Fuller's seasonal ales? – the brewery is only about a mile and a half west of here. To one side of the terrace is a conservatory with cane furniture; this is suitable for families. *Open 11-11 (Sun 12-10.30).* **Beer** *Fuller's. Patio, outdoor eating. Amex, MasterCard,* **VISA**

EC4   Black Friar   A

Tel 0171-236 5650   Map 17 D4
174 Queen Victoria Street Blackfriars EC4V 8DB

The Black Friar has one of London's most extraordinary pub interiors – students of architecture should soak it all in before getting too soaked on the particularly good cask-conditioned ales on offer. Built in 1875 on the site of the Black Friar monastery, it has a dazzlingly distinctive art nouveau interior that dates back to 1905. Bas-relief bronze representations of monks in various stages of drunkenness adorn the outside walls; inside, they are represented going about their daily tasks and indulging their habits alongside astonishing marble arches, mirrors and extravagant gold and coloured mosaics. It is difficult to tire of the busy decor, which constantly reveals previously unnoticed hints, inscriptions and monk figures. The pub attracts a mix of tourists (architectural enthusiasts among them) and City clientele – 'Silence is Golden' but you won't find much of it here! Snacks at lunchtime only. Nicholson's. *Open 11-11 Mon-Fri.* **Beer** *Tetley Bitter, Brakspear, Adnams, guest beer. Pub closed all day Sat & Sun. MasterCard,* **VISA**

SW18   Brewers Inn   FOOD

Tel 0181-874 4128   Fax 0181-877 1953   Map 17 B6   B&B
147 East Hill Wandsworth SW18 2QB

At the edge of Wandsworth's one-way system, the new flagship of local brewers Young's is a revelation on both the food and accommodation fronts. It's very popular for midweek lunches when quick snacks include filled baked potatoes and baguettes, though the more adventurous might favour chargrilled chicken and avocado salad, salmon and haddock fishcakes with parsley sauce (priced as starter or main course) or vegetable tempura with sweet chili dip. Main courses such as Toulouse sausage with mash and onion gravy and cod in beer batter with fries feature on a daily special board. The 65-seat candlelit dining-room is much more intimate at night and main courses may include salmon fillet with spinach and tarragon beurre blanc and sirloin steak with Roquefort cheese butter and watercress. There's a good selection of home-made nursery puddings to follow, and two dozen wines (including bubbly) by the glass to accompany; the service is up-beat, friendly and well organised. Following conversion from a derelict state two years ago, the bedrooms are a real find (but already regularly booked). Tall, double-glazed Georgian front windows are effectively insulated against traffic noise and the spacious rooms have either easy chairs or a sofa-bed. Appointments include satellite TV and a trouser press; the brightly-lit bathrooms sport spotless white ceramic washbasins and baths with powerful fitted showers. *Open 11-11 (Sun 12-3, 7-10.30).* ***Bar Food*** *12-2.30, 6-10 (Sun 12-2, 7-9).* ***Beer*** *Young's.* ***Accommodation*** *16 bedrooms, all en suite, £80 (£60 Fri & Sat, £70/£50 single). Children welcome overnight, extra bed & cot supplied (under-12s share free, third person sharing £15). MasterCard,* ***VISA***

W8 The Britannia A

Tel 0171-937 1864 Map 19 A4
1 Allen Street Kensington W8 6UX

In spite of its street number, you have to walk a hundred yards south from Kensington High Street before you find this old girl opposite a church. It's a cheering and often surprisingly peaceful old pub that can be a pleasant respite from the rigours of shopping on Kensington High Street. At the front, public and saloon bars are divided by a partition, and share a horseshoe bar; wood-panelling, settles and other seats, some in the bow windows. At the back, beyond the narrow saloon, a spacious (but less characterful) room has its own bar and food servery. The conservatory/ family room is no-smoking at lunchtime. *Open 11-11, Sun 12-10.30.* ***Beer*** *Youngs, guest beer. No credit cards.*

SW1 Buckingham Arms FOOD

Tel 0171-222 3386 Map 19 D4
62 Petty France St James's SW1H 9EU

The Buckingham Arms has an elegant feel, with chintzy curtains and etched mirrors behind the long bar. Within the spacious bar area is the dining-room and food counter. The menu may offer such deep-fried delights as mozzarella sticks with tomato relish, whitebait or Camembert with hot redcurrant sauce. Hot sandwiches include the Buckingham burger, big chicken ciabatta and a croque madame. In addition, there are ever-popular pub grub favourites like chili, lasagne, shepherd's pie and jacket potatoes. 15 or so wines by the glass. Very busy at lunch time, it quietens down in the evening. *Open 11-11 (Sun 12-5.40).* ***Bar Food*** *12-2.30, 6-9 (Sun 12-4).* ***Beer*** *Young's. Pub closed Sun evening. MasterCard,* ***VISA***

SW11 The Castle FOOD

Tel 0171-228 8181 **Fax 0171-924 5887** Map 17 B5
115 Battersea High Street SW11 3JR

Tucked away in 'Battersea Village', a little off the beaten track, with a simple frontage almost consumed by ivy. Inside is a successful combination of bare boards and rugs and an eclectic mix of furniture plus a large open fire. Three rooms are all served by one bar and include a separate dining area, an open-plan main bar room and a high-ceilinged conservatory to the rear, opening on to a paved garden edged with plants. Food is taken seriously and the weekly-changing blackboard menu offers the likes of a freshly-made soup, roast leeks with egg and caper vinaigrette, corned beef hash, pumpkin and ricotta lasagne with salad, cod in beer batter with chips and tartare sauce, roast lamb with caponata, and poached salmon with ginger butter. Calvados-stewed plums with custard, grilled banana with chocolate sauce or cheeses from Neal's Yard Dairy to finish. The Sunday menu is simpler but still offers a good choice. An espresso coffee machine is another little touch that distinguishes the Castle from so many of London's more mundane pubs. Friendly staff serve well-kept Young's ales and around a dozen wines by the glass. Sister pub to *The Ship, The Alma* and *The Coopers Arms* (see entries). *Open 11-11 (Sun 12-10.30).* ***Bar Food*** *12-3, 7-10 (no food Sun eve).* ***Beer*** *Young's. Paved garden, outdoor eating, occasional summer weekend barbecue. Amex, MasterCard,* ***VISA***

SW10   Chelsea Ram   ★   FOOD

Tel 0171-351 4008   Fax 0171-349 0885   Map 19 B6
32 Burnaby Street Chelsea SW10 0PL

Tucked away in the shadow of the Lotts Road power station, Young's tenant Nick Elliot's former backstreet local is one of the new breed of pub/restaurants, although it has definitely not lost its roots as a pub. The interior is airy and 'modern pubby' with rustic tables, a mix of tweed-covered chairs, shelves covered with everything from dried flowers to a sculpted foot and a token display of books. There's a strong emphasis on food, with a short menu supplemented by a handful of daily blackboard specials (usually a varying pasta dish, fresh fish, one meat dish and a couple of baguette sandwiches). A daily soup, roasted vegetable salad with tomato salsa, bangers and mash with onion gravy, warm salads, club sandwich, a 'cheese of the moment' served with home-made oatcakes, and chocolate truffle torte are typical dishes; large plates add a touch of style. Young's ales are supplemented by a range of very drinkable wines, all on display and around ten sold by the glass, sensibly-priced champagne and Spanish cava by the glass. A few tables are set out on the pavement under awnings in summer. Upstairs is a small function room that seats 12. The rear area of the pub was brightened up last year with the addition of a conservatory roof, but the rear can still be stuffy if occupied by smokers. *Open 11-3, 5.30-11 (Sat from 6.30, Sun 12-3, 7-10.30).* **Bar Food** *12-2.30, 7-9.45 (Sun to 9.30).* **Beer** *Young's.* MasterCard, **VISA**

W8   Churchill Arms   FOOD

Tel 0171-727 4242   Map 18 A3
119 Kensington Church Street W8 4LN

Loquacious Irish landlord Gerry O'Brien takes great pride in and is to a great degree responsible for the wonderful atmosphere, charm and originality which characterises this pub near Notting Hill tube station. Among many other things he is a collector par excellence; the walls of the attractive conservatory restaurant exhibit his impressive collection of 1600 butterflies and the ceiling of the bar is covered with chamber pots, brasses and copper ornaments. The 'Thai-rish' food operation mixes standard pub fare like beef and Guinness pie, moussaka and plaice and chips with a popular Thai restaurant in the rear of the pub serving 20 Thai dishes like green beef curry or fried rice with chicken, spring onions and Thai spices. Both chef and staff are Thai. Sandwiches and ploughman's lunches are also offered. *Open 11-11 (Sun 12-10.30).* **Bar Food** *12-3, 6-11 (not Sun eve).* **Beer** *Fuller's.* MasterCard, **VISA**

WC1   Cittie of Yorke   FOOD

Tel 0171-242 7670   Fax 0171-405 6371   Map 16 C3
22 High Holborn WC1V 6BS

A fine piece of Victorian architecture with ornate ceilings, a Grade II listing and recently-improved toilets. The back room is the most impressive, with high ceilings, a coal-burning stove dating back to the year of Waterloo, and intimate little booths across the very long bar. The gantry above is stacked with thousand-gallon wine vats. The Vaulted Bar downstairs is a long room with low, vaulted ceilings and a cellar atmosphere; tradition has it that during the Gordon Riots in the mid-18th century (described by Dickens in *Barnaby Rudge*), some of the refugees took shelter here by descending a staircase that used to lead down from Gray's Inn. Food is available on both floors. The regular menu covers a range from black pudding and egg to chicken wings, burgers, fish and chips, steaks and homely puds (jam roly poly, sponge pudding, sherry trifle). Daily specials extend the range further. Sandwiches are made to order. The Vaulted Bar tends to be quieter and the queue at its food counter is usually shorter. *Open 11.30-11. Pub closed Sun.* **Bar Food** *12-3, 5.30-10 (smaller menu 2.30-5).* **Beer** *Sam Smith's.* Amex, MasterCard, **VISA**

We endeavour to be as up-to-date as possible but inevitably some changes to landlords, chefs and other key staff occur after the Guide has gone to press.

W4 | City Barge | A

Tel & Fax 0181-994 2148   Map 17 A5
27 Strand on the Green Chiswick W4 3PH

A riverside pub dating back to the 15th century; charming original, intimate bar at towpath level, plus a modern extension and a warm, bright conservatory upstairs. The food offering appears to be improving (but sticking to popular pub favourites like jacket potatoes, chargrills and interesting baguette sandwiches) with a new chef/manager. The pub took a starring part in The Beatles' 1965 film *Help;* opposite the pub, in the middle of the Thames, is Oliver's Island where Cromwell hid from the Cavalier Army. During high tides a floodgate is used to prevent water from entering the lower bar. Scottish Courage. *Open 11.30-11 (Sun 12-10.30).* **Beer** *Wadworth 6X, Theakston Best & Old Peculier, Courage Directors. Pub closed 25 Dec eve.* MasterCard, **VISA**

EC1 | Cock Tavern | FOOD

Tel 0171-248 2918   Map 16 D3
East Poultry Avenue Central Markets EC1A 9LH

Popular among food-hoovering meat traders, City folk and medics from Bart's Hospital, this is a large basement restaurant hidden away in a pub at the very heart of Smithfield market. The animation and cheerful atmosphere start at 6.30am with a generous breakfast – choose from black pudding, kidneys, smoked haddock with poached egg, hash browns, bubble and squeak, eggs any way and so on ... The choice is extensive: seven set breakfasts, omelettes, rolls or sandwiches, all at competitive prices. The lunch menu concentrates on meat with prime Scotch 8oz steaks done a dozen ways (including an 18oz T-bone steak) plus occasional larger versions going up to 40oz (record eating time 13 minutes – and then he had a pudding!). Roast rib of beef, salt brisket, trout, Dover sole and a table d'hote lunch at £9.50 complete the picture. It's not an establishment known for its decor but nonetheless it is a fun place, enlivened by the banter of serious trenchermen! *Open 6.30am-3.30pm.* **Bar Food** *6.30-10.30am, 12-3. Free House.* **Beer** *Courage Best, Young's. Pub closed Sat, Sun & Bank Holidays. Amex, MasterCard,* **VISA**

SW3 | Coopers Arms | FOOD

Tel 0171-376 3120   Fax 0171-352 9187   Map 19 B5
Flood Street Chelsea SW3 5TB

A small, lively Young's pub on two floors, the ground floor of which is a single room with a large, solid table on which newspapers are laid for perusal; the upstairs has waitress service and is useful if you want to get away from the general hustle and bustle of the bar. It's the same blackboard menu throughout, though, offering a mix of traditional and more modern pub fare at lunchtimes only: perhaps a home-made soup like split pea and ham, salmon fillet with hollandaise and new potatoes, Creole fish stew, lamb steak with 'deep-fried spuds', gammon steak with honey mustard sauce and salad (no sandwiches). Flambéed bananas with brandy and cream, chocolate kumquat cake with whipped cream or apple and blackberry crumble to finish. Around 16 wines served by the glass. Under the same tenancy as *The Ship, The Alma* and *The Castle* (see entries). *Open 11-11 (Sun 12-10.30).* **Bar Food** *12.30-3 only.* **Beer** *Young's. Amex, MasterCard,* **VISA**

W2 | The Cow | FOOD

Tel 0171-221 5400   Map 18 A2
89 Westbourne Park Road W2 5QH

Despite the name, shellfish is the name of the game in this often-crowded pub owned by Tom Conram. The eating area is confined to a few small round polished tables in the narrow rear section, and, in fine weather, pavement tables outside. Order and pay at the bar for excellent moules marinière, whole Cornish crab (for which nut crackers are required – but the effort is worthwhile); oyster, mussel and Dublin Bay prawn gratin and The Cow Special – half a dozen Irish rock oysters and a pint of Guinness or a glass of white wine. The shellfish display is impressive, particularly at the weekend whenm a Seafood Platter is offered (£19.80 for two). There are a few dishes for vegetarians and meat-eaters, maybe fusilli with tomato, aubergine and walnuts, spinach, bacon and blue cheese salad and Cumberland sausages, onion gravy and mash. 1997 London Regional Winner of our Seafood Pub of the Year award. Upstairs, the Cow Dining Room (Tel 0171-221 0021) is now a separately-owned restaurant run by chef Francesca Melman. Fish (rather than shellfish) features among the half dozen or so dishes at each stage: perhaps baked sardines, Caesar salad with fresh anchovies, sea bass with fennel purée or cod fritura mista. *Open 12-11 (Sun 12-10.30).* **Bar Food** *12.30-3, 6.30-10.30.* **Beer** *Fuller's London Pride, guest beer. Closed 25, 26 Dec & 1 Jan. MasterCard,* **VISA**

NW8   Crockers Folly   FOOD

Tel 0171-286 6608   Fax 0171-266 1543   Map 18 B1
24 Aberdeen Place Maida Vale NW8 8JR

Built in 1898 and originally designed as a luxury hotel to accommodate passengers from Marylebone station (which, rather sadly for the Victorian owner, was eventually built somewhat further away than he had hoped for!). Nowadays, it's a 'Genuine Freehouse and Dining Room'. The Victorian design creates an extravagant atmosphere and the entrance hosts a beautiful two-tone marble counter and a large fireplace. High, arched doors open on to two rooms: one mainly used by drinkers and game-lovers (bar billiards and fruit machines), the second, characterised by etched windows and a high, baroque ceiling, for dining. There's a selection of four home-made pies (Somerset pork with cider and celery or fisherman's), freshly-baked filled baguettes and particularly good sausages (pork and leek, lamb and rosemary, Tewkesbury beef, chicken and herb or hot Windies hurricane), the latter served with mash (or chips) and onion gravy, plus wonderful cheese platters from a choice of some 20 cheeses, and a daily roast. Daily specials extend the range and busy Sunday lunches offer a choice of four traditional roasts. Nursery-style desserts. Just off Edgware Road, a short walk from Lord's cricket ground – on Test Match days there may be an outdoor barbecue on the pavement. *Open 11-11 (Sun 12-10.30).* **Bar Food** *12-2.30, 6-9.30 (hot), sandwiches served all day. Free House.* **Beer** *Brakspear, Bass, Adnams, Theakston Best, Young's Bitter, Gale's HSB, Greene King Abbot Ale, guest beer. Amex, Diners, MasterCard,* **VISA**

SW3   Cross Keys   FOOD

Tel 0171-349 9111   Fax 0171-349 9333   Map 19 C6
1 Lawrence Street Chelsea SW3 5NB

Last year, Carmel Azzopardi (formerly of the *Beach Blanket Babylon* bar), Rudy Weller and Michael Bertorelli took the dear old Cross Keys by the scruff of its neck, turned it upside down, re-fashioned it with a total makeover and re-invented it as another of London's new-wave pubs. What was lost was one of London's lovely, but presumably unprofitable, little 'local' pubs (whose unusual bar-in-the-round was once reproduced as a setting for a TV series) and in its place comes a hopefully profitable, modern pub/bar/bistro/restaurant. Call it what you will, but you can still enjoy cask-conditioned ales from Scottish Courage and straightforward, all-day bar snacks like nachos, soup of the day, bangers and mash (£6), and baguettes with warm tomato and Brie, tuna and sweetcorn or chicken (served with coleslaw, £3.50-£5.50) in the very modern little front bar. The pub sign still swings outside and it still says 'bar' on one of the lead-windowed front doors, so you know you're still in a pub, albeit transmogrified into a more modern beast. Flagstone floors and a modern chandelier hanging from the double-height ceiling (there's a first-floor private function room for 150, with a balcony overlooking the bar) help give the bar a spacious feel; the flat wall sculpture of a man that surrounds the fireplace is another clever and most unusual touch, clearly showing the designer's hand at work. Through a mock garden arch, a delightful rear dining-room with a conservatory roof is dominated by a full-height tree (lit by fairy lights at night) and an extraordinary wall collage of bric a brac;

slatted birch-branch wall decorations, wonderful, custom-made wooden benches and tables plus chef Taofik Feshitan's open-plan kitchen complete the informal setting. During regular meal times (around 12-3.30, 7-11) one may orders, say, just a dish from the restaurant menu in the bar: perhaps salad niçoise with chargrilled salmon, home-made fishcakes with rocket salad, sweet chili jelly and pickled cucumber or grilled chicken breast with sautéed Chinese leaves, mushrooms and black bean vinaigrette. Additional charges for vegetables and an 'optional' 12 ½ % service charge can push the prices up from Kings Road to Cheyne Walk (high to higher), but the quality of cooking is not in doubt. Sunday lunch is a fixed-price menu at £12/£15 (+12 ½ %) for 2/3 courses. *Open 12-12 (Sun 12-10.30).* **Bar Food** *12-9 (Sun 12-10.30).* **Beer** *Ruddles Best, Theakston Best, Webster's Yorkshire. Amex, MasterCard,* **VISA**

W6	The Dove	FOOD

Tel 0181-748 5405   Map 17 A4
19 Upper Mall Hammersmith W6 9TA

'Rule, Britannia, rule the waves; Britons never will be slaves' was said to be written here by James Thomson in 1740 and a manuscript of *Rule Britannia* is affixed to a wall of this lovely old riverside pub in commemoration. In fact, the pub dates back even further – to the 17th century – and, thankfully, it has escaped the blitz of modernization. It boasts the world's smallest public bar but there's plenty of room elsewhere, including a cosy, flagstoned river terrace for fine weather. Lunchtimes see well-cooked traditional dishes; braised steak in Guinness, stuffed baked potatoes and various ploughman's platters. In the evenings (Sun to Thu only) Thai food is on offer, individually cooked to a standard which rivals many of London's better-known Thai restaurants. A selection of mixed starters, chicken satay, stir-fries of squid, beef or prawns (all including carefully-cooked egg fried rice). Both red, yellow and green curries are usually available, a green of beef with bamboo shoots being particularly delicious. Good Fuller's beers and friendly service. Not suitable for children under the age of 14. *Open 11-11 (Sun 12-10.30).* **Bar Food** *12-3, 7-10.* **Beer** *Fuller's. Riverside patio/terrace, outdoor eating. No credit cards.*

EC1	The Eagle	★	FOOD

Tel 0171-837 1353   Map 16 C3
159 Farringdon Road EC1R 3AL

🍷

Pub, bar and restaurant all rolled into one, but without the service of the latter (ie no bookings, no table ordering and a menu that diminishes towards the end of each meal time). David Eyre's and Michael Belben's food-led pub is open during pub drinking hours (except at weekends) and offers pub food that is decidedly out of the ordinary and good enough to gain a recommendation in our *1997 Hotels & Restaurants Guide.* There is no doubting that Eyre and Belben set the standard to which at least a dozen other London pubs now aspire. As many people must come here for the food as for the busy bar atmosphere – and it does get busy (don't go looking for a quiet table for two)! With its sanded hardwood floor, magnolia walls and a vibrant atmosphere, the pub setting makes it all the more surprisinig when one encounters such a high standard of food. No bookings are taken, but persevere, share a table, order your food at the top of your voice and enjoy the robust Mediterranean dishes cooked in an open-plan kitchen. Around eight options are marked up on a blackboard, often changing twice daily; however, one stalwart, *bife ana* (a marinated rump steak sandwich), is a permanent fixture. Other recent offerings have included pea soup with chorizo and mint, butternut and sage risotto, red mullet with tomatoes, capers, olives and basil, *fabada* (Asturian butter beans and pork stew), roast duck with sweet roast onions and sherry vinegar and rocket salad, and grilled Italian sausages with garlic mash and spinach with lemon and olive oil. There's always a cheese plate (Spanish Manchego with *dulce de membrillo* – quince paste – or soft Italian with focaccia and rocket) and a simple dessert like Portuguese custard tarts. Dish prices are around £7-£9.50 for main courses and there's a range of a dozen or so wines by the glass. The first floor is an art gallery. *Open 12-11.* **Bar Food** *12.30-2.30 (Sat till 4), 6.30-10.30.* **Beer** *Charles Wells Eagle Bombardier & Eagle IPA, Ruddles County. Pub closed Sun, Bank Holidays, Easter Saturday, 2 weeks Christmas. No credit cards.*

N1   Eagle Tavern   A

Tel 0171-253 4715   Map 16 D3
2 Shepherdess Walk off City Road N1 7LB

'Up and down the City Road, in and out the Eagle, that's the way the money goes, pop goes the weasel'. Probably better known through the song (which celebrates the music hall of that name that stood on this site until 1901) than for the pub itself. Memories of the theatre adorn the walls of the large comfortable bar, which has plenty of seating. The second bar has a simpler atmosphere with bare wooden floors and darkwood furniture. Background music and busy throughout the day. Back patio with picnic tables. Bass Taverns. *Open 12-11 (Sun 12-5 only). Pub closed all Sat & Sun eve.* **Beer** *Bass, Charles Wells Eagle IPA, 4-8 guest beers. Paved garden. MasterCard,* **VISA**

NW1   The Engineer   ★   FOOD

Tel 0171-722 0950   Fax 0171-483 0592   Map 16 C3
65 Gloucester Avenue NW1 8JH

Once upon a time this was a quiet, sleepy pub in a very residential part of Primrose Hill, where Princess Road joins Gloucester Avenue. It was built in 1846 by Isambard Kingdom Brunel, who is rather better known for his engineering feats of building more major projects such as railways, tunnels, bridges and steamships than for pubs. Standing on a corner site across from the London Filmmakers' Co-op its renaissance has created a new focal point for the area and now attracts a discerning dining crowd both from near and far. Run by Abigail Osbourne and Tamsin Olivier, the place buzzes with activity. A walled, paved garden to the rear is extremely popular in fine weather and tables there are offered on a first-come, first-seated basis. The interior is brightly and very simply decorated in a fashionably rustic manner with a spacious, often crowded bar area and separate dining area (bookings essential) occupying the side and rear sections – a long narrow part and a couple of more intimate rooms, all set up for eating. The food is both imaginative and well prepared. The first-class menu changes fortnightly and an eclectic mix of dishes might include antipasti (with charcuterie or vegetarian), a daily fresh soup, smoked haddock fishcakes, a daily fresh egg pasta dish, rocket, pear and Serrano ham salad, or avocado, fennel and little gem salad – all these types of dishes may be dual-priced for small or large portions. Continue with chargrilled vegetables timable with ricotta pesto and a sweet and sour tomato sauce, sesame free-range chicken salad with red cabbage and crispy won ton leaves, breast of duck with grilled spring onion, aubergine, roasted sweet potato and chick pea purée, pan-fried pork loin chop with porcini mushroom sauce and creamy polenta or a daily fresh fish dish (perhaps roast halibut with frisée, braised vegetables and plum tomato vinaigrette). Sunday brunch. There's a short, relatively inexpensive wine list with good wines served by the glass and good-value house champagne. The Engineer has a very friendly, laid-back atmosphere and the staff are right on the ball. Every London neighbourhood should have a modern-style 'local' as good as this! Plans are afoot for a new conservatory. *Open 11-11 (Tue 6-11 only), Sun 12-10.30.* **Bar Food** *12-3 (not Tue), 6.30-11 (Sun 12-3, 6-10.30). Closed Tuesday lunchtime.* **Beer** *Fuller's London Pride, guest beer. Garden, outside eating. MasterCard,* **VISA**

NW3   The Flask   A

Tel 0171-435 4580   Map 16 B2
14 Flask Walk Hampstead NW3 1HE

Located in a pedestrian street off Hampstead High Street, the Flask is a favourite, friendly rendezvous for comedians, artists and drinkers alike. It has a proper public bar, separated from the saloon bar by the original Victorian panelling. The back room opens up on to a conservatory mainly used as a dining-room but also as a set up for charity events and music hall nights which the landlords frequently organise. Around 16 wines are served by the glass. Not to be confused with the other *Flask* pub at the top of Highgate West Hill. *Open 11-11 (Sun 12-10.30).* **Beer** *Young's. Conservatory. MasterCard,* **VISA**

SE1   Founders Arms   A

Tel 0171-928 1899   Map 17 D4
52 Hopton Street Bankside SE1 9JH

♀

A large, modern building (built in 1979) with a riverside terrace – a wonderful
location with panoramic views. Located near Blackfriars Bridge and – for those
prepared to wait until the year 2000 – the new Tate Gallery (currently a building site
– but you may be reading this in the year 2001!). The bar is airy and bright with
large picture windows looking out over the city and St Paul's Cathedral. The front
terrace is large enough to cater for crowds of drinkers on busy, sunny days. Up to a
dozen wines are served by the glass. Convenient for the new Globe theatre. *Open 11-
11 (Sun 12-10.30).* **Beer** *Young's. Amex, MasterCard,* **VISA**

EC1   Fox & Anchor   FOOD

Tel 0171-253 4838   Fax 0171-250 0696   Map 16 D3
115 Charterhouse Street EC1M 6AA

♀

Traditional Victorian London pub on the north side of Charterhouse Street (opposite
Fox & Knot Street), with an atmosphere that can scarcely have changed in the last
100 years. Being across the road from Smithfield meat market, a special charter allows
breakfast to be washed down with strong liquid refreshment. Breakfast (served until
3pm Mon-Fri) can be a gargantuan affair complete with black pudding or steak and
kidneys if you so require, but smaller (and vegetarian) appetites are equally happily
assuaged. Lunch brings Welsh rarebit, steak and kidney pie (the house speciality),
omelettes and a selection of good-quality steaks. Deep-fried plaice and salads are also
offered. Hardly gourmet fare, but an interesting pub (and there's certainly nothing
wrong with the quality of the meat!). Over a dozen wines are served by the glass.
Booking is advisable, particularly for breakfast – when you should expect to share
a table. Upstairs is a private room seating 22. Nicholson's. *Open 7am-9pm (Fri till
10pm). Closed Sun & Bank Holidays.* **Bar Food** *7am-3pm (Mon-Fri).* **Beer** *Tetley Bitter,
Nicholson's Best, Wadworth 6X, guest beers. Amex, Diners, MasterCard,* **VISA**

SW19   Fox & Grapes   A

Tel 0181-946 5599   Map 17 B6
Camp Road Wimbledon SW19 4UN

♀

Once a gin shop, converted with the next door stables into a pub in 1956, you'll find
no TV or machines here, indeed, in their words: 'no anything made after 1950'.
Strictly speaking, that's not true as the exterior (fronting Wimbledon Common) was
given a facelift last year and the inside redecorated – but it captures the atmosphere of
this friendly, reliable, community pub perfectly. Dog walkers, dogs and golfers are all
welcome. *Open 11-11 (Sun 12-10.30).* **Beer** *Courage Best & Directors, Wadworth 6X.
Amex, MasterCard,* **VISA**

W1   French House   FOOD

Tel 0171-437 2799   Map 18 D3
49 Dean Street Soho W1V 5HL

♀

Formerly The York Minster (but known as 'Frenchie's' since having been the
unofficial meeting place for the Free French during the war), this last of Soho's
bohemian pubs only gained its present name about ten years ago and long been the
haunt of actors, writers and artists. The walls of the single, small room are a photo-
montage of the more (and less) famous habitués both past and present, although room
is also found in summer for a team list for the pub's next cricket match. Owners Noel
Botham (himself a writer) and his wife Lesley Lewis have happily kept things exactly
as they have always been, without music, fruit machines or other modern intrusions.
The bar is mainly for drinking rather than eating (especially at night when it gets
pretty busy and it's then largely a case of drinking standing up), so bar food is limited

to just two items: a sandwich made with home-made bread (perhaps cheese and salad) and something like duck liver paté with toast, both made by the folk who run the pub's first-floor restaurant (French House Dining Room – reservations on 0171-437 2477 – also recommended in our *1997 Hotels & Restaurants Guide);* here, the short lunch and dinner menus (you can have just a single dish) offer main dishes like chicken soup with polenta dumplings, duck leg confit with pickled pear and a cucumber and watercress salad, steamed mussels, lamb's sweetbreads with broad beans, peas and Jersey Royal potatoes, fennel and thyme tart, Welsh rarebit, double lemon pudding and hazelnut and white chocolate ice cream. On the drinks front there is an unusually good range of around 18 wines served by the glass, all at very realistic prices. *Open 12-11. Bar Food 12.30-3, 6.30-10.30 (no food Sun). Restaurant 12.30-2.45, 6.30-11.30. Closed Sun, Bank Holidays & 10 days Christmas/New Year. Amex, Diners, MasterCard, VISA*

| SW3 | Front Page | FOOD |

Tel & Fax 0171-352 290   Map 19 B6
35 Old Church Street Chelsea SW3 5BS

Just moments from the crush of the Kings Road and its array of busier, less welcoming places, on a prime corner site in a quiet residential area of Chelsea, stands the smart and stylish Front Page (previously known, for at least 300 years, as the *Black Lion).* Its white-painted exterior is decked with colourful hanging baskets and large, attractive gas lamps; inside is spacious, extremely light and airy, thanks to high ceilings and large windows which let in plenty of natural daylight. Rich navy blue curtains are matched by painted ceiling borders, and whirling ceiling fans help keep the room fresh. Part-panelled, it's furnished in informal rustic style with solid stripped wood tables, round-back chairs and long benches on well-worn floorboards; walls have minimal covering, save some Victorian-style nudes. At either end of the bar, two large blackboards display the day's food choice, which is light and interesting, in a bistro style: perhaps chicken liver and brandy paté with herb toasts, grilled avocado filled with crab, smoked salmon and cream cheese, pan-fried pork fillet with mustard sauce, and spaghetti tossed with mussels, chilis, garlic and tomato salsa. Young, friendly and keen staff provide good service with a smile. Upstairs is a 24-seat function/private dining-room. See also entries for *The Sporting Page* and *The Chequers* in Well, Hampshire. *Open 11-11 (Sun 12-10.30). Bar Food 12-2.30, 7-10 (Sun to 9.30). Beer Webster's Yorkshire Bitter, Ruddles County, Boddingtons, guest beer. MasterCard, VISA*

> We only recommend food (Bar Food) in those establishments highlighted with the **FOOD** symbol.

| SE1 | George Inn | A |

Tel 0171-407 2056   Fax 0171-403 6613   Map 17 D4
77 Borough High Street Southwark SE1 1NH

After almost 400 years of history this pub was rescued by the National Trust in the 1930s and is now run by Whitbread. It's London's only surviving original coaching inn, dating back to when London Bridge was the only way into the city, and is certainly one of the capital's most celebrated pub landmarks. A large cobbled courtyard terrace overlooks the beautiful black and white frontage with its galleried section and hanging flower baskets. A series of bars is interlinked: the wine bar contains a food counter, the George Bar has low ceilings, dark beams, latticed windows and lantern lamps and the Old Bar has a dark, quiet atmosphere and an open fireplace. A popular pub with city types (until mid-evening), tourists and beer fans alike – a beer festival is held during the third week of each month; ask about Bishops ales, a truly local ale. Eight wines are served by the glass. *Open 11-11 (Sun 12-10.30). Beer Bishops Cathedral Bitter, Whitbread Castle Eden, Flowers Original, Boddingtons, Brakspear Bitter, guest beers. Family room. Amex, Diners, MasterCard, VISA*

E14   The Grapes   A

Tel & Fax **0171-987 4396**   Map 17 D4
76 Narrow Street Limehouse E14 8BP

Over 300 years old, the Grapes probably hasn't changed much since Charles Dickens, a frequent visitor, used it as the model for the Six Jolly Fellowship Porters in *Our Mutual Friend*. In this narrow riverside pub, squeezed in between buildings that used to house ship chandlers, block- and tackle-makers, barge-builders and the like, it's easy to imagine Thames watermen drinking in the downstairs bar, with its bare floorboards and boarded, nicotine-stained ceiling. Prime position for watching the passing traffic is from the new teak deck overlooking the river, whose murky water laps at the stilts of the building. Since the opening of the Limehouse tunnel there's no direct access from the Highway – as you approach the tunnel turn left up Butchers Row, right into Commercial Road, first right down Branch Road and keep your wheels in the left-hand gutter leading round to Narrow Street. The pub is on the Thames Path, a walkway along the river leading to Canary Wharf. Nearest public transport is the Docklands Light Railway, alighting at either Limehouse or West Ferry. *Open 12-3, 5.30-11 (Sat 7-11 only, Sun 12-3.30, 7-10.30). Beer Ind Coope Burton Ale, Tetley Bitter, Friary Meux, guest ale. Amex, Diners, MasterCard, VISA*

SW1   The Grenadier   FOOD

Tel 0171-235 3074   Fax 0171-235 3400   Map 19 C4
18 Wilton Row Belgravia SW1 7NR

Not far from Hyde Park Corner, tucked away in the curve of cobbled Wilton Row mews, the bright red, white and blue frontage of this patriotic pub can't be missed. The bijou, intimate dark bar and restaurant were once used as a mess by the Duke of Wellington's Grenadiers and the place is full of historical atmosphere with even a few sabres, daggers and bugles hanging from the ceiling. The dark, panelled bar is small and customers spread outside on to the quiet cul-de-sac. Two candle-lit dining-rooms at the back are intimate with seats for just 21; try smoked Scottish salmon, Stilton puffs, beef Wellington or straightforward fish 'n' chips served with mushy peas. A set menu offers a traditional roast. Good snacks in the bar – from ploughman's lunches to sausage, beans and chips or scampi and chips. Scottish Courage. *Open 12-11 (Sun 12-3, 7-10.30). Bar Food 12-2.30, 6-10 (Sun till 9.30). Beer Young's Special, Theakston Best, Young's Special, guest beer. Pub closed 24 Dec eve-26 Dec, 31 Dec eve & 1 Jan. Amex, MasterCard, VISA*

W1   The Guinea   FOOD

Tel 0171-409 1728   Fax 0171-491 1442   Map 18 C3
30 Bruton Place off Berkeley Square W1X 7AA

Y

Tucked away in a mews between Bruton Street and Berkeley Square, this Mayfair institution continues to gain acclaim for its charcoal-grilled prime Scotch Highland steaks along with Rossmore oysters and Scottish smoked salmon in its expensive rear restaurant. The bar menu offers a considerably cheaper alternative to eating in the restaurant, with enduring classics like their superior steak and kidney pie and grilled sausages (at lunchtimes only). An interesting selection of hot ciabatta bread sandwiches is also out of the ordinary: try the Siciliano made with free-range chicken, smoked bacon, sun-dried tomatoes, mascarpone and chopped olives; or the Mirabeau with Aberdeen sirloin steak, lettuce, tarragon, anchovies, olives, tomatoes and mayonnaise; sandwiches are made to order (often with at least a ten-minute wait) and well worth the struggle through the Mayfair regulars who pack the small bar at lunchtime, when getting a seat is nigh on impossible. *The Windmill* in Mill Street (close to Regent Street) is run by the same landlord. *Open 11-11 (Sat 6.30-11 only). Bar Food 12-3. Beer Young's. Pub closed lunch Sat & all Sun. Amex, Diners, MasterCard, VISA*

EC1   The Hope, Sir Loin   FOOD

Tel 0171-253 8525   Map 16 D3
94 Cowcross Street Smithfield EC1M 6BH

A restaurant above a traditional Smithfield pub that is well known for its enormous breakfasts. Gourmands can start the day with the whole works: egg, bacon, sausage, black pudding, kidneys, liver, baked beans, tomatoes, mushrooms and toast. Less voracious appetites might settle for kippers or eggs-any-way. Roasts are the lunchtime specialities in the pub downstairs, while upstairs you'll find scampi, an enormous mixed grill (order in advance), roast rack of lamb, calf's liver and bacon, and steaks. Booking advised. **Bar Food** *7am-9.30am, 12-2 (no food Sat or in evenings).* **Beer** *Courage, Webster's, Young's, Ruddles. Pub closed from 3.30pm Mon-Fri, all Sat, Sun, Bank Holidays & 25 Dec-5 Jan. Amex, MasterCard,* **VISA**

SE1   Horniman at Hay's   FOOD

Tel 0171-407 3611   Fax 0171-357 6449   Map 17 D4
Hay's Galleria Tooley Street London Bridge SE1 2HD

Right at the entrance of Hay's Galleria on the south bank overlooking the Thames by London Bridge, Horniman's is a modern interpretation of Victorian style in the premises of the family's tea-packing company. The tribute to Frederick John Horniman's travels is discreetly paid through a painted mural on top of the bar. It's part pub, part café and the tables on the gallerias have views of the river and the City in the background. The Pantry restaurant offers hot and cold English pub fare (steak and kidney pie, turkey and ricotta pasta, curries) at lunchtime. *Open 10-11 (Sat 10-4, Sun 10-3).* **Bar Food** *12-3 only.* **Beer** *Burton, Timothy Taylor's Landlord, Eldridge Pope Traditional, Tetley Bitter, Adnams Broadside, guest beers. Pub closed weekend evenings. Amex, MasterCard,* **VISA**

SW6   Imperial Arms   FOOD

Tel 0171-736 9179   Map 19 A6
577 Kings Road Chelsea SW6 2EH

At the back of the Imperial Arms, on Kings Road between World's End and Parsons Green is a paved terrace where tables and chairs are set out in summer. It's very much an eating pub, specialising in crustacea, shellfish and the barbecue. Rossmore oysters are served just as they are (rock or native) or cooked à la mornay, Rockefeller (on a bed of spinach with a dash of Pernod and cheese sauce) or Kilpatrick (an Aussie variant involving bacon strips and Worcester sauce). Cromer crabs and Scottish lobster also appear in their season, as does some truly wild Irish smoked salmon (in a platter or a sandwich). From the barbecue, overseen by larger-than-life landlord Cornelius O'Grady, come beefburgers, gammon steak, rump steak and wild boar sausages. In addition there's a daily curry, seasonal stews and summer salads; all come at reasonable prices. Lighter snacks, too, like sandwiches and a good platter of cheeses, but the oysters are really the thing to shell out on. Opening times may be affected when Chelsea football team play at home. *Open 11-11 (Sun 12-4, 7.30-10.30).* **Bar Food** *breakfast from 10, 12-3, 7.30-11 (Sun till 10).* **Beer** *Morland Old Speckled Hen, Marston's Pedigree, Wadworth 6X, Courage Best. Patio, outdoor eating. Amex, Diners, MasterCard,* **VISA**

We endeavour to be as up-to-date as possible but inevitably some changes to landlords, chefs and other key staff occur after the Guide has gone to press.

NW3   Jack Straw's Castle   A

Tel 0171-435 8885   Fax 0171-794 4805   Map 16 B2
North End Way Hampstead NW3 7ES

♇

The Inn was built in 1721 on the site of what used to be the hay wagon from which
Jack Straw addressed the peasants during the 1381 revolt. Damaged during the
Second World War, it was rebuilt in the early sixties. It has a clean country pub look
with a cream and white weatherboard frontage, and an agreeable paved-and-cobbled
courtyard where barbecues and an arts and craft fair takes place at weekends. Being
one of the highest points in London, the second-floor restaurant has beautiful
panoramic views over Hampstead Heath. *Open 11-11 (Sun 12-10.30).* **Beer** *Bass,
Fuller's London Pride, guest beer. Courtyard, outdoor eating area. Amex, Diners,
MasterCard,* **VISA**

SW6   Jim Thompson's   FOOD

Tel 0171-731 0999   Fax 0171-736 8421   Map 19 A6
617 Kings Road SW6 2EF

East meets West in a self-styled Oriental bar/restaurant and bazaar – Jim Thompson's
is hardly your normal London pub! Named after the renowned American who
opened up the Thai silk industry and then disappeared without trace in the Malaysian
jungle, the pub is themed to the hilt, with Oriental artefacts galore scattered around
the pub's interior, each bearing its own (high) price tag. There are two food
operations within: to the rear is a surprisingly spacious, high-ceilinged dining-room
draped with floating silks, while to the front is a more usual bare brick-walled pub
bar. In both, the menus offer a list of dishes that have been inspired by countries from
the whole of IndoChina and the Spice Islands. Bar snacks on the one-plate Oriental
Express menu (served to 7.30pm) might range from Singaporean spring rolls, Thai
salads, Malaysian stir-fried chicken, Burmese prawns and Indonesian *mee goreng* (egg
noodles with chicken, bean sprouts, spring onions and chili); toasted sandwiches and
burgers are also offered (ah! – so this is still a pub). Sunday night see live jazz. To the
rear is a patio garden area. JT's is on the bend of Kings Road where it joins New
Kings Road – it's unusual and it's fun. Also at: 34 Surrey Street, Croydon (Tel 0181-
256 0007). *Open 12-11 (Sun till 10.30).* **Bar Food** *12-7.30. Restaurant 12-2.30, 7-11
(Sun to 10.30).* **Beer** *Tetley, Marston's Pedigree. Amex, Diners, MasterCard,* **VISA**

W11   Ladbroke Arms   A

Tel & Fax 0171-727 6648   Map 18 A3
54 Ladbroke Road Notting Hill Gate W11 3NW

Opposite Notting Hill police station, on the corner of Ladbroke Road and the
charming Willby Mews. The front terrace is resplendent with flowers in summer and
welcomes you with open arms; built a few steps above street level, it is well stocked
with tables, benches and parasols (and thus very popular in good weather). Inside is a
traditional mixture of mahogany panelling, yellow velvet-covered banquettes, large
etched mirrors, a semi-circular bar with pillars and a split-level area at the back.
There's a very civilised atmosphere with smiling faces and classical music softly
playing in the background. Scottish Courage. *Open 11-3, 5.30-11 (Sat 11-11, Sun
12-3, 7-10.30).* **Beer** *Courage Best & Directors, John Smith's, Wadworth 6X, guest beer.
Closed 25 Dec eve. MasterCard,* **VISA**

WC1   The Lamb   FOOD

Tel 0171-405 0713   Map 16 C3
94 Lamb's Conduit Street off Theobalds Road WC1N 3LZ

One of London's most atmospheric pubs, an unspoilt Victorian gem that retains
some wonderful original features like a beautiful U-shaped counter with gantry and
swivelling snob screens. On the walls hang sepia photographs from the Holborn
Empire, a Victorian music hall destroyed during the war. The pub gets very busy in
the evenings with a jolly and friendly atmosphere. At lunchtime, home-cooked daily
specials are worth a stop: beef stew in red wine, meat loaf, pork and Guinness pie and
well prepared salads. Chef Lionel Trattles' tasty 'Alliteration Pie' (a cheese crumble-

topped chicken and cider dish) wins The Lamb the 1997 Ilchester Cheese Pub of the Year Award (see page 26). Traditional roasts on Sundays. There is a small dining area and a few tables are set outside on the rear yard, where barbecues take place in good weather. On Sundays, the Carvery restaurant is open on the first floor.
Open 11-11 (Sun 12-4, 7-10.30). **Bar Food** *12-2.30 (Sun to 3.30).*
Beer Young's. MasterCard, **VISA**

WC2   Lamb & Flag   FOOD

Tel 0171-497 9504   Map 18 D3
33 Rose Street (off Garrick St) Covent Garden WC2E 9EV

A busy Georgian pub steeped in history (Dryden was famously mugged here in 1679 – and they still celebrate Dryden night) and retaining an atmosphere from Dickens's time with low ceilings, darkwood panelling and built-in benches on the ground floor. The two small, separate bars downstairs have limited seating areas and customers tend to spread out on to the paved area in front of the pub or in the quieter dining-room upstairs. The bar serves good ploughman's lunches and doorstep sandwiches; hot dishes include the ubiquitous bangers and mash with fried onions, shepherd's pie and beans, cod chips and peas, boiled bacon, pepperoni pasta salad, chili con carne and curries. No children under 14. Scottish Courage. *Open 11-11 (Fri & Sat till 10.45, Sun 12-10.30).* **Bar Food** *12-5 (Sun till 3) only.* **Beer** *Courage Best & Directors, John Smith's, Morland Old Speckled Hen, Wadworth 6X. No credit cards.*

EC3   Lamb Tavern   FOOD

Tel 0171-626 2454   Map 17 D4
10-12 Leadenhall Market EC3V 1LR

In contrast to Richard Rodgers' ultra-modern Lloyds building next door is Leadenhall market, known for its Victorian cast-iron and glass-covered cobbled lanes, as well as being home to the Lamb Tavern. A characterful place, with engraved glass windows, cast iron pillars, a tiled picture panel depicting Dick Whittington, and a spiral staircase leading up to a mezzanine floor. The pub was used as a location for the filming of *Brannigan* with John Wayne (as a photo of the 'Duke' together with landlady Linda Morris testifies) as well as a scene from the *Winds of War* with Robert Mitchum. Foodwise, there's not a great deal of choice because they do just one thing and do it well – a succulent hot roast beef sandwich carved to order from the wing rib and served in lengths of French bread. There are a few other sandwiches (perhaps hot roast pork) but the beef is the best and by far the most popular. A delicious spin-off from all this beef-roasting is the dripping it generates, which can be had with a piece of French bread – a real treat. *Open 11-9. Pub closed Sat, Sun & Bank Holidays.* **Bar Food** *11-2.30 only.* **Beer** *Young's. Amex, Diners, MasterCard,* **VISA**

NW1   The Lansdowne   ★   FOOD

Tel 0171-483 0409   Map 16 C3
90 Gloucester Avenue Primrose Hill NW1 8HX

Old Victorian pub converted a few years ago into the new style of bare-boards London pub with a strong emphasis on food. Inside, there's a motley collection of tables and chairs, vases of fresh flowers and a few magazines piled up on an old chest. Amanda Pritchett can be seen at work in the small, spick-and-span kitchen where she cooks up the likes of minestrone soup, country terrine with relish and pickles, marinated chicken salad, sirloin steak with mash and peas and roast hake with aïoli and poached vegetables. The shortness of the menu – just five starters, five main courses and a few desserts written up on the blackboard daily – goes a long way to explain the excellence of the results. Not suitable for children under the age of 14. *Open 11-11 (Sun 12-3, 7-10.30, Mon 6-11 only).* **Bar Food** *12-2.30 (except Mon, Sun from 1), 7-10 (Sun 7.30-9.30).* **Beer** *Bass, guest beer. Six outside tables. Pub closed Mon lunch. No credit cards.*

N1   Marquess Tavern   FOOD

Tel 0171-354 2975   Map 16 D3
32 Canonbury Street off Essex Road Islington N1 2TB

Built in 1850 and named after the Marquess of Northampton who owned large swaithes of Islington at the time. Tables set outside look out on to the green scenery of the canal running just yards away from this imposing Young's pub at the corner of Canonbury Street and Arran Walk. The bar inside is roomy and comfortable with elegant fireplaces and oil portraits. Food is served in the high-ceilinged dining-room at the back (unfortunately not as bright as the rest of the rooms). Lamb chops provençale, boiled bacon and parsley sauce or 'Marquess Red Pie' (corned beef, potato and onion) are examples of the typical daily specials that are prepared to order and come straight out of the kitchen. The selection of cold dishes is equally tempting: cheese- or paté-stuffed mushrooms, chips and salads and quiches are home-made. A daily roast and other pies, vegetarian dishes and regular pub favourites complete the picture. *Open 11-11 (Sun 12-10.30). **Bar Food** 12-9.30 (no food Sun). **Beer** Young's. Front patio, outdoor eating. No credit cards.*

W2   Monkey Puzzle   A

Tel 0171-723 0143   Map 18 B2
30 Southwick Street off Sussex Gardens W2 1JQ

Situated on the ground floor of a modern building, the Monkey Puzzle is owned by Dorset brewery Hall & Woodhouse, so the beers are not the ubiquitous London brews. There's a flowery open-air terrace at the front which has been recently spruced up; a small monkey puzzle tree (replacing the original that blew down at the end of the 80s) in a corner by the road struggles to live up to the impression made by its predecessor. Hardly one of London's more characterful pubs but it is ideally situated for a quick pint before heading over the road to Paddington Station. *Open 11-11 (Sun 12-10.30). Free House. **Beer** Hall & Woodhouse. Terrace. Amex, Diners, MasterCard, **VISA***

SW1   Morpeth Arms   FOOD

Tel 0171-834 6442   Map 19 D5
58 Millbank SW1P 4RW

🍷

Located at the corner of Ponsonby Place and overlooking the river this is the perfect stop for Tate Gallery visitors. An impressive collection of law books graces the walls – the pub was purpose-built in Victorian times for the Wardens of the old Millbank prison and an escaped prisoner still haunts it today. Home-made daily specials like steak and kidney pie, home-made curries and pies, and good wild boar and venison sausages served with creamed or new potatoes, onion gravy and peas. Quick service from a food counter. Braised oxtail with red wine and onion sauce is a regular favourite and deep-fried fish is prepared to order. 15 or so wines are served by the glass. Tables are set outside to the front and side of the pub, but it certainly isn't the quietest spot in town! A perfect stop for Tate Gallery visitors. *Open 11-11, Sun usual hours. Bar Food 12-8.30. **Beer** Young's. Patio, outdoor eating. MasterCard, **VISA***

SW1   Nag's Head   FOOD

Tel 0171-235 1135   Map 19 C4
53 Kinnerton Street Belgravia SW1X 8ED

Probably the smallest pub in London but certainly not the least interesting. The front was built in 1780, when the horses used on the Grosvenor Estate provided the inspiration for the name (the pub was the haunt of the ostlers). The low-ceilinged, panelled bar and dining-room communicate through a narrow stairway; the lower back bar was recently extended with a York stone floor and now incoporates a salad bar. A 1930s' what-the-butler-saw machine and a fortune-telling machine taking old pennies are popular features, with takings going to Queen Charlotte's Hospital. Personal bric-a-brac and photographs give a homely and intimate feel. The home-made cooking covers ever-popular pub favourites like steak and mushroom pie, shepherd's pie, chili con carne and real-ale sausage mash and beans; in addition, there is a daily roast, cheese melts, 'Irish crusties and champ', ploughman's lunches, sandwiches and baked potatoes. Death by chocolate cake only for pudding in the summer; spotted Dick and sponge puddings in the winter. A cover charge of £1 is made for evening meal service. Kinnerton Street runs between Motcomb Street and Wilton Place (off Knightsbridge). *Open 11-11 (Sun 12-7)*. **Bar Food** *served 'all day' (from noon until it's all gone). Free House*. **Beer** *Adnams, Tetley Bitter, guest beer. No credit cards.*

| W1 | Newman Arms | FOOD |

Tel 0171-636 1127   Map 18 D2
23 Rathbone Street off Oxford Street W1P 1AG

Just north of Oxford Street, a 260-year-old building on the site of an old ale house; inside, there's a cosy, panelled bar and an upstairs dining-room with a pleasant, homely feel: red velvet curtains and wall seats, blue and white chequered tablecloths and a gas fire in winter. Home-baked English pies and puddings are landlady Tracy Bird's specialities. The selection might include steak and kidney, spicy shepherd's, fisherman's, vegetarian, and chicken and broccoli – all baked to order. In addition, three is salmon en croute (with dill and fromage frais), a cheese platter with crusty bread, club sandwich, vegetarian salad platter, and home-made quiche with buttered Jersey potatoes. Rhubarb crumble, trifle and apple pie for the sweet-toothed. No children under 14. Bass Charrington. *Open 11.30-11 (Sat 5.30-11 only). Pub closed Sun*. **Bar Food** *12-3.30 (sandwiches all day)*. **Beer** *Bass, Fuller's London Pride, Hancock's*. MasterCard, **VISA**

| W1 | O'Conor Don | FOOD |

Tel 0171-935 9311   Fax 0171-486 6706   Map 18 C2
88 Marylebone Lane W1M 5FJ

The O'Callaghans' family-run Irish pub offers a warm welcome and wholesome fare: 'true Irish geniality in the heart of London's West End'. It's named after Don, Prince of Connacht, the chief of the Royal House of O'Conor out of which came 11 High Kings of Ireland and 26 successive Kings of Connacht. The building, on a corner site where Bentinck Street meets Marylebone Lane, has stained-glass windows on two sides. Within, the bar has bare floorboards and dark panelled walls decorated with polished Victorian mirrors and a series of Guinness advertisements. A collection of odd carver chairs and gate-legged tables add to the homely feel. Chef Conor Fitzpatrick's bar food shows that there is real enthusiasm and skill in the kitchen and includes excellent sandwiches (1½ rounds of smoked salmon or Cavan ham), colcannon with breast of turkey or roast rib-eye of beef, a daily soup, fresh Irish Atlantic oysters, fishcakes, ham and colcannon with swede, turnip and mustard sauce, and excellent Irish stew with pearl barley. Vegetarians can enjoy spinach and mixed cheeses dumplings with tomato and basil sauce. Seats fill up quickly, so get there early for food (particularly at lunchtime). Don't expect any real ale, but you can, of course, get a great pint of Guinness. If you're worried about which door to take for the conveniences then ladies should head for *fir* and gents for *mná!* The airy restaurant (Ard Ri – Gaelic for 'High King' – Dining Room) has its own entrance and is recommended in our *1997 Hotels & Restaurants Guide*; its menu changes weekly (table d'hote £15 lunch, £18 dinner), but you can expect the likes of good soda bread, butternut squash and sage soup, beef and Guinness casserole, grilled rib steak with artichoke mash, armagnac and prune parfait with Earl Grey syrup, and Irish cheeses on both the set menu and à la carte. Charming, friendly service. Minimum £10 spend for credit cards. As we went to press a new bar was being built in the basement. *Open 11-11 (Sat 12-11, Sun 12-6)*. **Bar Food** *12-10 (no food 25, 26 Dec or Bank Holidays). Restaurant 12-2.30 (not Sat or Sun), 6-10 (not Sun)*. Amex, MasterCard, **VISA**

EC4 — Old Bell Tavern — A

Tel 0171-583 0070   Map 17 D4
95 Fleet Street EC4Y 1DH

The tavern was built by Sir Christopher Wren during the reconstruction of St Bride's church (after the Great Fire) nearby and features darkwood half-panelled walls with ochre sponge paint and cast-iron gas fireplaces. The bar is cosy and characterful. Solid wooden bar stools are set along the rear window with a selection of daily papers and more seating is available near the entrance. Food is limited to sandwiches made to order and there's an interesting selection of beers. Nicholson's. *Open 11-11. Pub closed Sat & Sun.* **Beer** *Tetley, Marston's Pedigree, Brakspear, guest beer. Amex, MasterCard,* **VISA**

EC2 — Old Dr Butler's Head — FOOD

Tel 0171-606 3504 Fax 0171-606 4967   Map 16 D3
Mason's Avenue Coleman Street Moorgate EC2V 5BT

Built originally in 1610, it was destroyed during the Great Fire and rebuilt in 1666. Today, under the direction of Whitbread, it retains its beamed and panelled 17th-century atmosphere. Extremely busy at lunchtime, they prepare some of the City's best sandwiches and ploughman's lunches with thick, delicious crusty bread filled with carved turkey, ham, roast beef, sausages or cheese. The old Doctor himself was court physician to King James I; he developed a medicinal ale for curing gastric ailments, which led to his acquiring a number of alehouses. These days, a pint of 'Boddies' and a hearty steak and kidney pudding should keep one in fine fettle; bang up-to-date (and keeping the pub ahead in the pub food stakes) offerings include balti mushroom curry, swordfish steak and tortelloni pasta with garlic bread. To finish, perhaps Spotted Dick or treacle sponge and custard. *Open 11-11.* **Bar Food** *11.30-3 only.* **Beer** *Boddingtons, Flowers, Marston's Pedigree, Brakspear, two guest beers. Closed Sat, Sun & Bank Holidays. Amex, Diners, MasterCard,* **VISA**

WC2 — Opera Tavern — A

Tel 0171-836 7321   Map 17 C4
23 Catherine Street WC2B 5JS

Friendly Victorian pub right across from the Drury Lane Theatre Royal. Original gas lamps remain above the bar and the walls are covered with theatre memorabilia. The small upstairs bar, cosily furnished with tables, chairs and a sofa, is used as a dining-room. Taylor Walker (Allied Domecq). *Open 12-11.* **Beer** *Tetley Bitter, Burton Ale, Adnams Bitter. Pub closed Sun. Amex, Diners, MasterCard,* **VISA**

SW1 — Orange Brewery — A

Tel 0171-730 5984   Map 19 C5
37 Pimlico Road SW1W 8NE

On a corner site overlooking paved Orange Square, which is now graced by a Philip Jackson bronze statue of a youthful Wolfgang Leopold Mozart (who stayed nearby for a short while in 1764 when aged eight), the rather imposing, cream-painted Orange Brewery was revamped a couple of years ago. You'll still find plenty of wood inside – although now the tables, chairs and bar stools are carefully sprayed to make them look old – plus an eclectic mix of bric-a-brac (old beer jugs, a glass yard of ale) and bright blackboards proclaiming mediocre bar food, a good range of bottled beers and the merits of their in-house brews. A viewing window in the panelled room at one end of the long, curving bar gives just the merest glimpse down into the cellar where they brew their own ales: *SW1* (3.8% ABV), *SW2* (4.8%), dark, silky *Pimlico Porter* (4.5%) and seasonal ales like a heady winter brew. Suspended Victorian gas lamps give an unusual, old-London feel to the high-ceilinged, open-plan interior. 'Free House' it proclaims over the door, but the pub is part of a carefully-themed Scottish Courage group (but none the worse for it). Sloane Square tube station and Victoria Coach station are a short walk away. *Open 11-11 (Sun 12-10.30).* **Beer** *own brews. Amex, MasterCard,* **VISA**

EC1 | The Peasant | ★ | FOOD

Tel 0171-336 7726 Fax 0171-251 4476   Map 16 C3
240 St John Street EC1V 4PH

Built in 1890 as a Victorian gin palace, the former George & Dragon was transformed by Craig Schorn and Michael Kittos into one of the select band of London's new-wave dining pubs whose raison d'etre is really food. Last year we said that the pub hadn't lost its pub identity as three real ales were offered; well, even though there are no more cask-conditioned ales it's still a pub! The Peasant is no secret and booking is essential; as we went to press the first floor was being redeveloped into a restaurant, *Room 240*, in order to increase the main bar area (which will remain essentially the same with plain wooden tables, darkwood bench seating and a mix of old-fashioned dining chairs) on the ground floor and give diners a little more comfort and space. The bright, modern extension will include a conservatory extension on the first floor and good use will be made of the high Victorian ceiling, tall windows and cornicing. John O'Carroll and Caroline Hamlin will be running the kitchen and continue to produce a regularly-changing menu with interesting and unusual dishes: artichoke, broad bean, pea, mint and cos salad; chicken tabbouleh with tomato, red onion and cucumber; antipasti; grilled swordfish with chick peas, preserved lemon, peppers and rocket; smoked trout with buckwheat bread, French beans and crème fraiche, and rib-eye steak with courgettes, aubergines, tomatoes and chili. Warm basmati rice pudding with mango and paw-paw, rhubarb fool with biscotti or Irish cheddar with poached figs and walnut bread to finish. A short selection of wines is carefully chosen and several are available by the glass. '12½% service on all bills'. Easy parking. *Open 12-11 (Sat 6-11).* **Bar Food** *12.30-2.30 & 6.30-10.45. Closed all Sun, Bank Holidays, 10 days Christmas.* Amex, MasterCard, **VISA**

SW3 | Phene Arms | FOOD

Tel 0171-352 3294 Fax 0171-352 7026   Map 19 B6
9 Phene Street off Oakley Street Chelsea SW3 5NY

Carmen and Wesley Davis's unassuming neighbourhood pub is tucked away in a quiet Chelsea cul-de-sac, with the added attraction of having a terrace and quite a large garden for alfresco eating. There's a new chef here and the menu now covers a much wider and more imaginative range, from sandwiches, baguettes and ploughman's to bar snacks like tempura squid, ciabatta with chargrilled chicken breast, Gruyère and fries, and deep-fried potato skins with sour cream and salsa. In addition, there are fancier dishes like toasted goat's cheese with almonds, Parma ham-wrapped roast monkfish, magret of duck with orange-candied sweet potatoes offered in the dining areas. Daily blackboard specials extend the range even further, perhaps with half a dozen Rossmore oysters, roast wildboar with redcurrant jus or medallion of kangaroo with Savoy cabbage and juniperberry sauce. *Open 11-11 (Sun 12-10.30).* **Bar Food** *12-3 (Sat & Sun to 4), 7-10.30 (Sun to 10).* **Beer** Morland Old Speckled Hen, Courage Best & Directors, Webster's Yorkshire, guest beer. *Garden, terrace, outdoor eating.* Amex, Diners, MasterCard, **VISA**

SE5 | Phoenix & Firkin | A

Tel 0171-701 8282   Map 17 D5
5 Windsor Walk Denmark Hill SE5 8BB

Denmark Hill station was destroyed by a fire in 1980; the Phoenix & Firkin rose from its ashes thanks to Bruce's Brewery and public support. Nowadays, under the ownership of Taylor Walker (part of the Allied Domecq), the group of Firkin pubs stretches right across the country, with its house-brewed beers (three permanent, three seasonal) still the major attraction. The interior structure of the station remains, with an extremely high ceiling allowing enough room for a comfortable mezzanine level. An enormous double-faced clock stands near the door. The decor is of brick, green paint and bare wood and there is live music on Thursday nights (quite loud 'background' music at other times). *Open 11-11, Sun 12-10.30.* **Beer** *Own brews: Rail Ale, Phoenix, Dogbolter, Golden Glory, guest beer. No credit cards.*

W2 — Prince Bonaparte — FOOD

Tel 0171-229 5912
80 Chepstow Road W2 5BE

Map 18 A2

For many years this was a large, undistinguished Victorian public house occupying a corner site with Talbot Road and attracting undiscriminating drinkers. Transformed a couple of years ago by Beth Coventry, Mark Harris and Phillip Wright, it now attracts a very different crowd who expect roast garlic in their mash, tapénade on their crostini, pesto with their pasta. Where once there were three separate bars and an off-licence there is now just one very spacious, almost cavernous, L-shaped room with an extensive area towards the rear set out for diners. The decor is rather rough and ready, and the atmosphere very laid-back and non-intimidating. Plain wooden tables and all manner of wooden chairs are set out facing the open-plan kitchen, itself an extension of the central, U-shaped bar counter where all-day tapas-style snacks are served. The twice-daily-changing blackboard menu is the main attraction; a snap-shot menu might offer field mushroom and parsley soup, Caesar salad, sausage or Scotch rib-eye steak sandwich, mozzarella, basil and roast tomato bruschetta with rocket and olives, blackened Cajun chicken breast with refried beans and avocado salad, lamb steak with parsnip mash and roast onions, chargrilled wild salmon with chili rice and a roast tomato and mint salsa. All is generally well prepared and imaginatively put together. There's little in the way of desserts, but always ice cream and perhaps just one cheese, sticky toffee pudding or a crumble. Good espresso coffee. Arrive early to ensure a table (no bookings). *Open 11-11, (Tue 6-11 only, Sun 12-10.30). Pub closed Tue lunchtime.* **Bar Food** *12-3, 6.30-10 (Sun 12-10).* **Beer** *Bass, Fuller's London Pride, guest beer. No credit cards.*

WC1 — Princess Louise — A

Tel 0171-405 8816   Fax 0171-430 2544
208 High Holborn WC1V 7BW

Map 16 C3

A remarkable Victorian pub which has changed little since being named after Queen Victoria's fourth daughter and still boasts original mirrors surrounded by decorated floral tiles and ornate plasterwork. A minimum of eight cask-conditioned 'real' ales are gathered from around the country and are the major attraction, along with the impressive U-shaped bar that threads through the main room with its bare floorboards. In summer, despite the attractions of the listed interior, drinkers appear to enjoy sampling the London 'smoke' on the pavement outside. The more comfortable upstairs lounge bar, whose bamboo plants and ceiling fans suggest a colonial feel (albeit with up-to-date, not-so-background music) serves rather average Thai food at lunchtimes. Owned by Regent Inns. *Open 11-11 (Sat 12-3, 6-11). Pub closed Sun & Bank Holiday Mondays. Free House.* **Beer** *Brakspear Bitter, Gale's HSB, Young's, Greene King IPA, four guest beers. MasterCard, VISA*

WC2 — The Salisbury — A

Tel 0171-836 5863
90 St Martin's Lane WC2N 4AP

Map 18 D3

A Victorian pub, built in 1830 and named after the Marquess of Salisbury (Robert Arthur Talbot Gascoyne-Cecil, no less, who was thrice Prime Minister), whose Art Nouveau bronze nymph lamps dividing the semi-circle benches are a classic design. Original etched-glass partitions still remain but some walls have been plastered with theatre ads. One of London's oldest theatre pubs, it is still a popular meeting place for the theatrical fraternity and often 'standing room only'. Landlord Kevin Lee keeps a good pint of Bass and his wife Patsy looks after the pub grub; in 1997 they will have been at The Salisbury for 10 years – we raise a glass to them. *Open 11-11 (Sun 12-10.30).* **Beer** *Burton Ale, Wadworth 6X, Theakston Best Bitter, Eldridge Pope Dorchester Bitter. Family Room. Amex, Diners, MasterCard, VISA*

SW18 The Ship FOOD

Tel 0181-870 9667
41 Jews Row Wandsworth SW18 1TB

Map 17 B5

Tucked away by the river behind Wandsworth bus garage, the MacDonalds drive-thru and by a ready-mix concrete plant, The Ship's setting doesn't sound in the least bit inviting. Nevertheless, once you've made your way round the one-way maze (the slip-road turning off the Wandsworth Bridge is from the south side heading north), thing do begin to look up! A delightful terrace, complete with rose-covered rustic trellis, stretches on several levels all the way to the riverside; an outside bar helps cater for the drinkers who horde here on fine days. The conservatory bar makes a pleasant, airy, most un-London-like venue, with its motley collection of old wooden tables, benches, chairs and pews; there's also a public bar, very much a locals' haunt. A recent extension (45 seats, bookings taken, waiter service) to one side is where you'll find an open kitchen and the food servery, with one menu served throughout. Last year a new chef took over – along with a new management team – and the menu now offers the likes of New Zealand green-lipped mussels in a rich cheese and brandy sauce, smoked haddock and Red Leicester fishcakes with a tangy orange and fennel coulis, and chargrilled burgers alongside steaks (sirloin, lamb, tuna) and perhaps sautéed chicken breast with a blue cheese sauce, glazed walnuts and mace-spiced apple potato. However, they're not too grand to serve just a bowl of chips or cheese-topped garlic bread. When weather permits, a spit-roast or barbecue on the terrace is very, very popular (chicken and fig kebabs, chargrilled lamb steak). The Ship is a Young's pub, under a joint tenancy with the nearby *The Alma, The Coopers Arms* in Chelsea and *The Castle* in Battersea (see entries). The beer is always good – it's about as close to the brewery as you'll get – and there are lots of wines sold by the glass. Bonfire Night (November 5th) and the Last Night of The Proms (early September) are celebrated in style. London pubs are generally unsuitable for children but The Ship is a rare exception, particularly in summer – just outside the pub's gate is an enormous old ship's anchor on a safe riverside walkway. *Open 11-11 (Sun 12-10.30).* **Bar Food** *12.30-3 (Sat & Sun till 4), 7-10.30 (Sun till 10).* **Beer** *Young's. Riverside terrace, outdoor eating, summer barbecue.* Amex, MasterCard, **VISA**

NW3 Spaniards Inn A

Tel 0181-455 3276 Fax 0181-201 9710
Spaniards Road Hampstead NW3 7JJ

Map 16 B2

A comfortable pub with a warm, friendly atmosphere, very popular at weekends; it has been both a toll house and the home of a Spanish ambassador in its long history. The ground-floor bar overlooks the garden and has lovely old settles, open fires and intimate corners, while upstairs (Turpin's Bar) is quieter. The vast garden is split in two by a narrow walkway covered with climbing ivy; one side has wooden tables and benches, the other white iron garden furniture with table umbrellas. Budgies happily sing in the background aviary. Perfect refreshment stop for Hampstead Heath walkers. No children under 18 in bar areas. Parking for 42 cars. *Open 11-11 (Sun 12-10.30).* **Beer** *Bass, Fuller's London Pride, Hancock's HB, Adnams Extra, guest beers in winter. Garden.* Amex, MasterCard, **VISA**

SW10 Sporting Page FOOD

Tel 0171-352 6465 Fax 0171-352 8162
6 Camera Place Chelsea SW10 0BH

Map 19 B6

The former Red Anchor attracts a mainly younger Chelsea set with its wine bar atmosphere, but the ales are 'real' enough and the prices at pub levels (albeit Chelsea-high). There are dark blue walls above pale wood dado panelling, with decorative tiled panels depicting famous sporting events (the Boat Race among them) and sporting figures like W G Grace. Seating is largely made up of upholstered benches around solid rosewood tables. Typical bar food dishes include home-made soups (apple and parsnip), chicken and leek pie with new potatoes, Thai chicken curry with jasmine rice, Cumberland sausages with herb mash and baked beans, Arbroath smokies and king scallops on vegetable rösti with herb vinaigrette. Hot chicken salad and home-made salmon fishcakes are regular favourites. *Open 11-11 (Sun 12-10.30). Bar Food 12-2.30, 7-10 (Sun till 9.30). Beer Wadworth 6X, Webster's Yorkshire, Boddingtons. Patio, outdoor eating. Closed 25 & 26 Dec. MasterCard, VISA*

SW1   The Star   A

Tel 0171-235 3019   Map 19 C4
6 Belgrave Mews West SW1X 8HT

Bruce and Kathleen Taylor have been running the delightfully different (for London) Star since 1984. It's tucked away in a cobbled mews between Halkin Place (itself off West Halkin Street) and Chesham Place, near Belgrave Square; the pub's exterior is resplendent with hanging baskets and flower tubs in summer. Visit when it's not packed (at weekday lunchtimes or early evening) and you'll find the atmosphere of a small, friendly local rather than that of a busy city pub. There are stools along the bar counter, stripped wood tables and chairs, cushioned settles and colonial ceiling fans; upstairs is a cosy bar, often used for private parties. A straightforward weekday pub lunch menu (corned beef hash, chicken curry) is extended slightly in the evening. Friendly staff. Opening hours are extended for the two weeks before Christmas. *Open 11.30-11 (Sat 11.30-3, 6.30-11, Sun 12-3, 7-10.30). Beer Fuller's. Closed 25 & 26 Dec. No credit cards.*

EC1   Thomas Wethered   A

Tel 0171-278 9983   Map 16 D3
33 Rosoman Street Northampton Road Clerkenwell EC1R 0HU

Country-themed Whitbread pub which was the first in London to serve Wethered Bitter. The U-shape is laid out into different bars and lounges and the comfortable Directors Lounge at the back is used as a family room. *Open 11-11 (Sun 12-10.30). Beer Brakspear, Boddingtons, Flowers Original, three guest beers. Family room. Amex, MasterCard, VISA*

W9   The Warrington, Ben's Thai   FOOD

Tel 0171-266 3134   Map 18 A1
The Warrington 93 Warrington Crescent Maida Vale W9 1EH

Ben's Thai is a popular venue on the first floor of *The Warrington* pub – a grand Victorian landmark in Maida Vale. Staff work at a frenetic pace, ensuring a speedy throughput of diners; nevertheless, booking is essential. The menu lists a selection of enjoyable Thai dishes that range from the mild to the hot: chicken or beef satay, deep-fried prawns in rice pastry, and minced pork and prawns on toast with a sweet and sour sauce feature among the starters. *Boh Tak*, a spicy, hot and sour seafood soup flavoured with lemon grass includes squid, prawns and chunks of fish and comes in an earthenware pot warmed by a small burner; other specialities include Thai-style duck salad and fillets of chicken in batter with chili and soy sauce. Incidentally, the lively pub downstairs (Tel 0171-266 2929) is open all day and offers good real ales. *Bar Food 12-2.30 (ring to confirm), D 6-10 (Sun from 7). MasterCard, VISA*

W2   The Westbourne   ★   FOOD

Tel 0171-221 1332 Fax 0181-969 8407   Map 18 A2
101 Westbourne Park Villas Notting Hill W2 5ED

The mish-mash of tables and chairs reflects the eclectic mix of clientele at Oliver Daniaud's and Sebastian Boyle's recently-converted, new-wave pub/restaurant. The pavement outside is a heaving throng of Notting Hill's bohemian crowd in the heat of the summer, while in the evenings it may take a while to secure a table for eating. However, the wait is well worth while. The twice-daily-changing menu is chalked up on a board behind the bar along with the wines and beers available. The food choice is short, with only six or so dishes on offer at any one time, but the quality of the food is excellent. Typical dishes from a recent menu included watercress soup, pork rillettes with toast and cornichons, half a lobster with mayonnaise, grilled mackerel with pak choy Chinese greens, roast quail with lentils, fennel and mint, and fruit and sherry trifle. The style is that of a modern bistro, the execution usually spot on, service is cheerful and resulting satisfaction levels are high. You order and pay for everything at the bar and the food is then delivered to your table. *Open 12-11 (Sat 11-11, Sun 12-10.30). Closed Monday lunchtime. Bar Food 1-3.30, 7-10 (Sun till 9.30). Free House. Beer Boddingtons, guest beer. MasterCard, VISA*

SW6   White Horse   FOOD

Tel 0171-736 2115   Fax 0171-610 6091   Map 17 B5
1-3 Parson's Green Fulham SW6 4UL

A substantial part-red sandstone Victorian pub standing at the northern end of Parsons Green, with a large, triangular walled terrace overlooking Parson's Green to its front. The interior is hugely spacious – emphasising the decidedly pubby character of the place. On the periphery of the high-ceilinged, U-shaped room (the bar occupies the centre of the U) is a selection of leather chesterfield sofas and a few round tables with bentwood chairs. The food counter along one side of the bar has a series of booths (children may accompany their parents here), each of which seats six. Whether you're eating or just drinking, seating at peak times can be at a premium and this can rather detract from full and proper enjoyment of the food. Bar snacks encompass potato skins, quesadillas with chicken, chorizo or vegetables, a plate of charcuterie and cheese, New Zealand green-lipped mussels in a tomato and basil sauce, and home-made duck and chicken liver paté. In the evenings a different kitchen team produce more bistro-style dishes: grilled goat's cheese, Caesar salad, chili con carne, salmon fishcakes with parsley cream sauce or medallions of pork in a cider and apple sauce. The liquid offerings are put to good use in the kitchen in lamb cutlets in a Highgate mild sauce and sauté chicken cooked in Frambozen fruit beer. Ten or so wines are promised by the glass, along with what must be the country's finest list of classic bottled beers; this includes Freedom Pilsner (brewed locally in Fulham), Anchor Steam beer and Liberty Ale (from across the Atlantic), Coopers Sparkling Ale from Down Under, and the very best Belgium Trappist fruit beers. Bass Taverns. *Open 11-11 (Sun 12-10.30). Bar Food 12-3, 6-10. Beer Adnams Extra, Bass, M&B Highgate Mild, Harvey's Sussex Bitter, guest beer, seasonal speciality. Terrace, outdoor eating. Closed 24-27 Dec. Amex, MasterCard, VISA*

W8   Windsor Castle   A

Tel 0171-727 8491   Map 19 A4
114 Campden Hill Road Kensington W8 7AR

A charming Georgian pub built in 1828 when (the entrance on Campden Hill Road being at the same height as the top of St Paul's Cathedral) one could see Windsor Castle 20 miles away. The original panelling and built-in benches still remain and the three small bars have separate entrances. Traditional English cooking throughout the day; Sunday lunch roast rib of beef with Yorkshire pudding. A shaded and paved beer garden (one of London's busiest) at the rear is the main attraction in summer (and gets really packed), while a cosy country inn atmosphere prevails inside in winter. Both oysters (£5 for half a dozen) and champagne (£20 for Lanson Black Label) are sold at sensible prices. Not suitable for children inside. Bass. *Open 12-11 (Sun 12-10.30). Beer Bass, Adnams Extra, Hancock's HB, guest beer. Garden. Amex, MasterCard, VISA*

Many **B&B** establishments offer reduced rates for weekend and out-of-season bookings. Always ask about special deals for longer stays. Beware half-board terms in inns where we do not recommend the **FOOD.**

EC4 — Witness Box — FOOD

Tel 0171-353 6427
36 Tudor Street Temple EC4 0BH

Map 17 D4

Between the Embankment and Fleet Street, tucked away in the long basement of a modern office building. The decor is a mixture of traditional wood features, modern brick walls and painted murals of the Thames bank. Framed newspaper clippings of famous criminal events hang on the walls; there is even a special award for the best crime story of the year. Plenty of seating accommodates the busy crowd of regulars. The home-made cooking is only available at lunchtime and vanishes quite fast. The range covers sandwiches, salads, steak and kidney pie, lasagne and a few daily specials, possibly cheese, cauliflower and leek bake, lamb curry or braised lamb's liver and bacon. Proper home-made chips but the desserts don't get the kitchen's same attention. An equally traditional lunch menu is available (lunchtime only) in Chambers Wine Bar/restaurant at street level. 8-10 wines by the glass. Scottish Courage. *Open 11-11.* **Bar Food** *12-3 only.* **Beer** *Theakston Best, XB & Old Peculier, Courage Directors, Wadworth 6X. Pub closed Sat & Sun. Amex, Diners, MasterCard,* **VISA**

EC4 — Ye Olde Cheshire Cheese — A

Tel 0171-353 6170   Fax 0171-353 0845
Wine Office Court 145 Fleet Street EC4A 2BU

Map 17 D4

A pub has stood here since 1538 but all we see today is that which has been re-built since 1667 — all, that is, except the great cellar vaults which survived the fire and all else since. The old bar and upper-floor dining-rooms still retain their 17th-century chop house atmosphere, while new additions are more fashionably traditional. The Snug Bar, an extension in the front part of the building (entrance off Cheshire Court), is for those who enjoy bar billiards, darts and satellite television. What used to be the courtyard is now the Courtyard Bar, with its original pavement floor. The Cheshire Bar is a high-ceilinged rustic room that hosts hot and cold food counters. The Cellar Bar offers intimate corners, a pubby wine bar atmosphere and snacks. To complete the picture, three floors of atmospheric old dining-rooms offer 'traditional English fayre'. Our recommendation is to enjoy the atmosphere with a pint of Sam Smith's. *Open 11.30-11 (Sun 12-5 only).* **Beer** *Sam Smith's Old Brewery. Pub closed Sun eve. Amex, Diners, MasterCard,* **VISA**

EC1 — Ye Olde Mitre Tavern — A

Tel 0171-405 4751
1 Ely Court Ely Place EC1N 6SJ

Map 16 D3

Located behind St Ethelreda's church and converted from the Bishop's house, Ye Olde Mitre dates back to the 18th century and is run for Taylor Walker (Allied Domecq) by Don Sullivan. Access is between numbers 8 and 9 Hatton Garden or though a small passage in Ely Place. The Tavern's two small bars get extremely busy at lunchtime, bringing some life into the narrow Ely Court. Popular for their toasted sandwiches, Scotch eggs and pork pies (available all day) and other straightforward lunchtime snacks. The Bishops Room holds up to 30 for functions. *Open 11-11 Mon-Fri only.* **Beer** *Burton Ale, Friary Meux, Tetley Bitter. Pub closed Sat, Sun & Bank Holidays. No credit cards.*

ACCEPTED IN
HOTELS AND F
THAN MOST PE
EVER HAVE HO

VISA IS ACCEPTED FOR MORE TRANSACTION

MORE
ESTAURANTS
OPLE
DINNERS.

ORLDWIDE THAN ANY OTHER CARD.

KING LIFE EASIER THROUGHOUT ENGLAND

England

The addresses of establishments in the following former **Counties** now include their new Unitary Authorities:

Avon
North Somerset, Bath & North East Somerset

Cleveland
Redcar & Cleveland, Middlesbrough, Stockton-on-Tees, Hartlepool

Greater Manchester
Wigan, Bolton, Bury, Rochdale, Salford, Manchester, Trafford, Tameside, Oldham

Humberside
East Riding of Yorkshire, Kingston-upon-Hull, North Lincolnshire, North East Lincolnshire

Middlesex
Harrow, Hounslow, Hillingdon (also certain London Unitary Authorities like Brent and Ealing)

Tyne & Wear
Newcastle-upon-Tyne, North Tyneside, Gateshead, South Tyneside, Sunderland

West Midlands
Wolverhampton, Walsall, Dudley, Sandwell, Birmingham

South Yorkshire
Barnsley, Sheffield, Rotherham, Doncaster

West Yorkshire
Bradford, Leeds, Calderdale, Kirklees, Wakefield

All other counties remain the same

ABBOTSBURY   Ilchester Arms   B&B

Tel 01305 871243   Fax 01305 871225   Map 13 F3
Market Street Abbotsbury Dorset DT3 4JR
Zzz...

High on the list of places to visit in this most picturesque of Dorset villages, especially after a stroll round the narrow streets lined with mellow-stone cottages, or after exploring the famous Swannery, sub-tropical gardens, medieval tithe barn or the ancient St Catherine's Chapel, is the Ilchester Arms, a rambling, 16th-century coaching inn that dominates the heart of the village. Inside, a civilised and relaxed atmosphere prevails within the several heavily beamed, part-panelled and comfortably furnished rooms, complete with sofas in front of the inglenook and a wealth of interesting artefacts. Beyond the attractive and airy conservatory peaceful summer outdoor seating can be found on the sheltered patio and on the lawn which affords splendid views towards St Catherine's Chapel on top of the neighbouring hill. Delightful en suite bedrooms make this welcoming inn a most agreeable base from which to explore the area. All rooms are furnished to a high standard with darkwood reproduction furniture and decorated with quality wallpaper and matching fabrics – two rooms boasting canopied four-poster beds; one family room has a double and a sofa bed. Bathrooms are well equipped and other added comforts include TV, telephone and tea-making facilities. Premier Inn (Greenalls). *Open 11-11 (Sun 12-2, 7-10.30)*. *Beer Flowers Original, Bass, Wadworth 6X. Garden. Accommodation 10 bedrooms, all en suite, £48 (single £44). Children welcome overnight, cot available. Accommodation closed 24 & 25 Dec. MasterCard, VISA*

ABINGDON   Brewery Tap   A

Tel 01235 521655   Map 14a C3
40 Ock Street Abingdon Oxfordshire OX14 5AG

Real-ale enthusiasts in search of a first-class pint should locate Morland's distinctive brewery buildings in the town centre and visit this Grade II listed brick pub; originally it housed brewery offices and the head brewer's cottage, then it became store rooms before becoming a pub in 1993, perfectly positioned at the brewery gates. Here, in the comfortable and neatly refurbished bar areas, one can sample the complete range of Morland's cask conditioned ales – Old Speckled Hen, Tanner's Jack, Original, Independent IPA and seasonal bitters – all kept, as one would expect, in tip-top condition. *Open 11-11 (Sun 12-3, 7-10.30)*. *Beer Morland. No credit cards*.

ADDERBURY   Red Lion Inn   FOOD

Tel 01295 810269   Fax 01295 811906   Map 14a C1   B&B
The Green Adderbury Banbury Oxfordshire
♟

Overlooking the charming village green and set beside the A423 Oxford to Banbury road, this historic, mellow-stone coaching inn makes a handy overnight stop for M40 travellers (J11 is 4 miles away) and a comfortable base from which to explore the Cotswolds and the Heart of England. Beyond the atttractive, summer flower-decked facade lie several relaxing, interconnecting bars, one boasting a fine stone inglenook with winter log fire, another featuring some oak panelling, ceiling beams and cosy, soft sofas. Stylish decor and furnishings extend upstairs to the fifteen individually decorated en suite bedrooms, all of which sport Laura Ashley fabrics and wallpapers and a delightful mix of furniture, from antique French beds and wardrobes to rattan tables and chairs and painted pine. Direct-dial telephones, clock/radios, beverage-making facilities and TVs are standard throughout. Spotless bathrooms, some with jacuzzi baths, are well equipped and two unusual galleried bathrooms (reached via spiral staircases) feature freestanding baths. Front rooms, thankfully double-glazed to quell heavy early morning traffic noise, overlook the green. Home-cooked bar food is listed on regularly-changing blackboard menus and dishes range from filled baguettes, tagliatelle carbonara, vegetable crumble and minted lamb pie to chef's specials like lamb korma, chicken Basque and smoked salmon roulade. Restaurant à la carte choices (also served in the bar) may include Stilton and pork paté, lamb provençale and swordfish in herb butter, with bread-and-butter pudding and peach and raspberry crumble among the puddings. Private room seating 12 suitable for a dinner party or company board meeting; larger Brewhouse for functions. *Open 11-11 (Sun 11-3, 7-10.30). Bar Food 12-2.30, 7-10. Free House. Beer Hook Norton Best, Webster's Yorkshire Bitter, Ruddles County. Terrace, outdoor eating. Accommodation 14 bedrooms, all en suite, £65 (single £47.50). Children welcome overnight, additional bed (£10) & cot available. Amex, Diners, MasterCard,* **VISA**

ALBURY HEATH   King William !V   A

Tel & Fax 01483 202685   Map 15a E4
Little London Albury Heath Guildford Surrey GU5 9DB

A surprisingly old-fashioned pub in a popular walking area (children and dogs welcome); cottagey little rooms with flagstone floor, enormous inglenook fireplace in main bar (off which, up a few stairs, is a separate dining area), rustic furnishings and attractive odd bits of bric-a-brac. Loos are outside and equally old-fashioned, but the small front garden can be a delightful, dingly dell-style, away-from-it-all place for a quiet pint in good weather – worth driving or walking your way round the lanes to find. Children welcome. *Open 11-3, 5.30-11, (Sun 12-3, 7-10.30). Free House. Beer five regularly-changing real ales. Small front garden. No credit cards.*

ALCISTON   Rose Cottage   A

Tel 01323 870377   Map 11 B6
Alciston Polegate East Sussex BN27 6UW

Run by members of the Lewis family since 1960, this old-fashioned, wisteria-clad cottage pub nestles in the centre of a tiny hamlet on a dead-end lane near the base of the South Downs. Popular walkers' retreat and a venue for locals seeking a peaceful drink, either in the small front garden or in one of the rambling cosy rooms inside. Jasper, an African grey parrot, puts in regular lunchtime appearances before retiring upstairs in the afternoon to indulge in his predilection for watching war films. Each room is furnished with a good mix of sturdy tables and old, cushioned pews and adorned with a collection of harnesses, traps, farming memorabilia, stuffed birds or fishes in cases and other interesting bric-a-brac. Good relaxed atmosphere. Rear paddock with chickens, geese, ducks and a pond. *Open 11-3, 6.30-11 (Sun 12-3, 7-10.30). Free House. Beer Harveys Best, guest beer. Garden, outdoor eating, tables in garden. Closed all 25 & 26 Dec. Family room. No credit cards.*

ALDEBURGH   Ye Olde Cross Keys   A

Tel 01728 452637   Map 10 D3
Crabbe Street Aldeburgh Suffolk AP15 5BN

Simple, two-roomed old inn with the distinctive red and cream signage of Adnams. It's an ideal watering hole for breaking a stroll along the prom as there's an array of picnic tables outside on a long courtyard that leads from the rear of the pub almost up to the shingle beach. Choice of ten wines served by the glass. No children under 18 in bar areas. *Open 11-3, 5.30-11 (Sat 11-11, Sun 11-10.30 + all day during July & August). Beer Adnams. No credit cards.*

ALDERMINSTER   The Bell   FOOD

Tel 01789 450414   Fax 01789 450998   Map 14 C1
Alderminster Stratford-on-Avon Warwickshire CV37 8NX

Devoted to the enjoyment of some quite serious food, the Bell now defines itself as a "Bistro and bar". It has, nonetheless, a more than adequate public real ale bar and Keith and Vanessa Brewer produce meals of quality that is too good to ignore in a Guide devoted to good pub food. As a dining venue it falls somewhere between the two, with food ordered from monthly-changing handwritten menus, supplemented by daily blackboard specials in the bar and delivered with a fair amount of bustle in the bistro. The choice is extensive, from a carrot and orange soup, spinach mousse au gratin or water chestnuts with bacon and sweet and sour sauce to casserole of beef with kumquats, crispy topped lamb in cider, and cashew nut roast – there are regularly up to 17 main-course choices! In addition, a long list of fresh fish and seafood dishes (Salcombe crab and lobster, coquilles St Jacques, Dover sole, sea bass) changes daily and is obviously a major attraction. The kitchen's dedication to all fresh ingredients plays its part, and there's hardly a chip in sight. Keep on to the end of the road and you'll be rewarded with luscious puddings such as tipsy sherry trifle, coffee and almond malakoff or sticky toffee pudding. A special two-course lunch (perhaps mild chicken curry and rice plus apple crumble and custard, £5.95) is offered from Mon-Fri. Special events, from "Symphony Suppers" to a Hallowe'en Pie Party, play a regular part in the Bell's repertoire with complimentary year planners provided for diners to plan their next visit well ahead. Bookings advised for evenings. *Open 12-2.30 (till 2 Sun), 7-11.* **Bar Meals** *12-2, (till 1.45 Sun), 7-9.30 (till 10 Sat, 9 Sun). Free House.* **Beer** *Hook Norton Best, Flowers Original. Garden. Closed 25-27 Dec eves & all 1-2 Jan. MasterCard,* **VISA**

ALDWORTH	Bell Inn	A

Tel 01635 578272   Map 14a C3
Aldworth Reading Berkshire RG8 9SE

Standing in the heart of this unspoilt downland village and especially popular with walkers seeking refreshment along the Ridgeway Path, is the creeper-clad Bell, formerly a 14th-century manor hall that has been in the same family's hands for over 200 years. In keeping with its Grade I listed status the charmingly rustic interior has changed little over the centuries, with five real ales, excellent Arkell's 3B for instance, being dispensed from a glass-panelled hatch which serves instead of any bar counter. Drinkers stand around in the hall and beamed taproom with old benches and wood-burner, or squeeze themselves into one of the candle-lit brick alcoves which give the place so much character. Food is restricted simply to filled crusty rolls (salt beef, mature Cheddar cheese, home-cooked ham, Brixham crab) served up in wicker baskets and hearty soups made from home-grown vegetables (carrot, artichoke). In winter there may be hot sticky toffee pudding or chocolate sponge on the menu. Splendid summer garden filled with roses, and people on sunny Sundays. Worth a look nearby is the Norman village church famed for its massive stone effigies of the De La Beche family. *Open 11-3, 6-11 (Sun 12-3, 7-10.30). Closed all Mon except Bank Holidays & 25 Dec.* **Beer** *Morells Mild & Oxford, Arkell's 3B & Kingsdown Ale, West Berkshire Old Tiler. Garden. No credit cards.*

ALMONDSBURY	Bowl Inn	B&B

Tel 01454 612757   Fax 01454 619910   Map 13 F1
16 Church Road Lower Almondsbury Bristol South Gloucestershire BS12 4DT

Zzz...

Just off the A38 and only two minutes' drive from the M5 (Junction 16), turn down Sunday's Hill to St Mary's Church in Lower Almondsbury; right next to it stands the Bowl, which in 1146 was a row of monks' cottages. Today's stone structure dates from the 16th century, though the more recent bedroom conversions will wear well into the 21st! Uncovered wall niches, exposed roof timbers and original fireplaces all contribute to these rooms' unique charm, to which individual fabrics in bright colours and spotless fitted bathrooms have been added with flair and style. Beverage tray, colour TV, clock radio, trouser press and hairdryer comprise the comprehensive modern-day amenities. The single bar with its attendant two tiers of restaurant space is a buzzing, highly popular local venue with plenty of overspill to picnic tables by the roadside and an enclosed beer garden. *Open 11-3, 5-11 (Sun 12-3, 7-10.30).* **Beer** *Courage Best & Directors, John Smith's, Wadworth 6X, Smiles Best, guest beer. Patio, garden.* **Accommodation** *8 rooms, all en suite, £86.50, (from £39 at weekends), single £56.50, (from £25 at weekends), Children welcome overnight (under-12s £10), additional bed & cot (£6) available. No dogs. Accommodation closed 25 Dec. Amex, Diners, MasterCard,* **VISA**

| **ALPHINGTON** | **Double Locks** | **FOOD** |

Tel 01392 56947   Map 13 D2
Alphington Exeter Devon EX2 6CT

The Double Locks isn't easy to find but it's well worth the effort. First find the Marsh Barton Trading Estate and drive through it to the council incinerator – don't worry, the pub is some way yet – until you reach the plank canal bridge, which is made for vehicles, although it may not appear to be. Once across, turn right, and a single-track road will bring you to the red-brick Georgian Double Locks in a splendid canalside location within sight of the Cathedral. Equally popular with business people and students, this is a fine summer pub: there are swans on the canal next to the lock, a large garden shaded by huge pine trees, and a barbecue both lunchtime and evening in summer, weather permitting. Inside is very informal. Several rooms have black-and white-tiled floors, draw-leaf domestic dining-room tables and lots of posters advertising local events – not far removed from a student bar at University. Nine real ales are drawn straight from the cask and chess, draughts, Monopoly, Scrabble and bar billiards are all keenly played. A huge blackboard displays the day's offerings, featuring almost as many options for vegetarians as for carnivores. Start, perhaps, with mushroom and coriander soup, garlic mushrooms and Stilton on toast or a selection of garlic breads with Cheddar, Stilton or goat's cheese topping, followed perhaps by turkey and mushroom pie, lasagne, baked potatoes, lamb kebabs and late breakfasts. Families welcome. *Open 11-11 (Sun 12-10.30).* **Bar Food** *11-10.30 (Sun 12-10).* **Beer** *Smiles Brewery Bitter, Best & Exhibition, Adnams Broadside, Greene King Abbot Ale, Wadworth 6X, Everards Old Original, two guest ales. Riverside garden, outdoor play area, outdoor eating, summer barbecue. Family room. MasterCard,* ***VISA***

> We do not accept free meals or hospitality – our inspectors pay their own bills
> and never book in the name of Egon Ronay's Guides.

| **ALRESFORD** | **Globe on the Lake** | **FOOD** |

Tel 01962 732294   Fax 01962 766008   Map 15 D3
The Soke Alresford Hampshire SO24 9DB

A superbly sited pub located at the bottom of Broad Street and on the banks of a reed-fringed lake – Alresford pond – complete with swans and dabbling ducks. The delightful waterside garden is a splendid summer spot for alfresco imbibing. Inside, the characterful and recently redecorated main bar has sturdy tables and chairs, and a deep, comfortable sofa in front of the open log fire; local photographs and prints decorate the walls and several traditional pub board games can be found behind the bar. The adjacent cosy restaurant overlooks the lake and has linen-clothed tables, candles and fresh flowers, while the tiny, intimate no-smoking dining extension is ideal for a small dinner party. Chef-partner Terry McTurk's home-cooked, value-for-money bar snacks are listed on the ever-changing blackboard, which may include Stilton and walnut paté or smoked fish platter for starters, followed by salmon fishcakes, cod in batter, chicken grilled with courgettes and peppers, cheddar and onion flan, all accompanied by good, crisp vegetables. Ploughman's lunches and sandwiches are always available. Chocolate mousse, Belgian biscuit cake and sticky toffee pudding are typical puddings. Separate evening restaurant fare – carrot, honey and ginger soup, lamb fillet with red wine sauce, pork escalope with Parma ham and Emmental. A sign within reads "well-behaved children only". Park over the bridge on Broad Street. *Open 11-3. 6-11 (Sun 12-3, 7-10.30).* **Bar Food** *12-2, 6.30-9.30 (Sun 7-9.30).* **Beer** *Wadworth 6X, Marston's Pedigree, John Smith's, Courage Best. Garden, outdoor eating. Amex, MasterCard,* ***VISA***

| **ALSTONEFIELD** | **The George** | **A** |

Tel 01335 310205   Map 6 C3
Alstonefield Ashbourne Staffordshire DE6 2FX

The nearby Manifold Valley is a famous haunt for ramblers, and easy to get lost in. Drivers should follow the Deve valley road which connects Hulme End (B5054) with the A515. At the heart of this picturesque Derbyshire stone village, the Grandjean family warmly welcomes all comers, as long as muddy boots are left at the door.

Service is from a tiny triangular stone-built bar; seating in three rooms in front of cosy fires, at picnic tables in the rear stable yard (with family camping available in the next field) or in front of the pub by the village green. The George gets pretty hectic at peak times and the crush can be quite convivial. *Open 11-2.30, 6-11 (Sat 11-11, Sun 12-10.30). Beer Burtonwood Bitter, James Forshaw's Buccaneer, Top Hat, guest beer. Patio. Family room. Closed all 25 Dec. No credit cards.*

ALVEDISTON   Crown Inn   FOOD

Tel 01722 780335   Map 14 B3
Alvediston Salisbury Wiltshire SP5 5JY

Charming, 15th-century thatched inn nestling in a tiny hamlet within the peaceful and unspoilt Ebble valley between Salisbury and Shaftesbury. Despite being rebuilt and extended after a severe fire in 1989 the Crown maintains an old-world character in its relaxing and welcoming interior. Head-cracking low beams, two inglenook fireplaces (one with woodburner), walls adorned with hunting prints and a comfortable mix of furnishings, from old dining-room tables and church pews to modern pine characterise the carpeted interconnecting bars and adjacent dining-room. Good blackboard menus highlight the daily-prepared dishes available which often feature fresh fish from Poole, game in season from nearby estates and quality meat from local suppliers. Lunch choices may include steak and venison pie, wild boar ragout in cider, fresh cod in batter, Dorset lamb cutlets with orange and mint sauce, pan-fried halibut with white wine and dill, and seafood medley. Home-made soup (Stilton, apple and celery), filled baguettes, ploughman's and salads are readily available for those popping in for just a snack. Evening fare may offer red mullet with soy and ginger sauce, medallions of kangaroo with Madeira, and salmon with white wine and mushroom sauce alongside the regular and equally interesting printed menu. Standard list of puddings. Summer alfresco eating on the sheltered rear patio or bench-filled lawn. Overnight accommodation in cottagey, en suite bedrooms may come on line during 1997. 3 miles from the A30 at Ansty – well worth the detour! *Open 11.30-3, 6.30-11 (Sun 12-3, 7-10.30). Bar Food 12-2.30, 7-9.30 (till 10 Sat). Free House. Beer Courage Best & Directors, Wadworth 6X, Hampshire Ironside, guest beer. Garden, patio, outdoor eating, children's play area. MasterCard, VISA*

AMBERLEY   Black Horse   A

Tel 01453 872556   Map 14 B2
Amberley Gloucestershire GL5 5AD

Teetering on the very edge of the escarpment just below Minchinhampton Common, the pub's westerly aspect comes into its own on glorious summer evenings. Behind the bar itself is a picture window, and beyond it a prominent conservatory from which to soak in the panoramic views. Below are a tiered patio and garden, though parents should be mindful of a steep drop from the bottom wall to the meadow below. The upper garden has swings and picnic tables, and there's a separate games room with pool table and darts. A wide and regularly-changing range of real ales draws aficionados from far and wide. *Open 12-3, 6-11 (Sat 12-11, Sun 12-10.30). Free House. Beer Smiles, Hook Norton Best, Fuller's London Pride, Tetley, Archers Best, three guest beers. Garden. MasterCard, VISA*

AMPNEY CRUCIS   Crown of Crucis   B&B

Tel 01285 851806   Fax 01285 851735   Map 14a A2
Ampney Crucis Cirencester Gloucestershire GL7 5RS

 Zzz...

One of four Gloucestershire Ampneys, Crucis stands by the A417, 3 miles east of Cirencester. Established over 400 years, the refined, upmarket Crown has seen rapid growth in the last handful of years with the building of 25 hotel-style bedrooms, refurbishment of the oak-beamed bar and two-tiered restaurant and now a conservatory extension. Furnishings and decor in the bedrooms are uniform, as are up-to-date amenities and neat, fully-tiled bathrooms with over-bath showers. Fourteen ground-floor rooms are especially handy for those needing easy access; one room is specifically equipped for disabled guests; the clever courtyard lay-out affords most rooms a view over Ampney Brook, connected to the cricket ground opposite by a wooden footbridge. All-day room service shows that this is more inn than pub. Good selection of real ales and wines by the glass in the bar. *Open 11.30-10.45 (Sun 12-10.30).* **Beer** *Boddingtons, Ruddles County, Archers Village. Patio, stream-side garden.* **Accommodation** *25 bedrooms, all en suite, £74 (from £52 single). Children welcome overnight (£17.50 if sharing parents' room), additional bed & cot available. Accommodation closed 24-30 Dec. Amex, Diners, MasterCard,* **VISA**

ANDOVERSFORD   Kilkeney Inn   FOOD

Tel 01242 820341   Fax 01242 820133   Map 14 C1
Andoversford Cheltenham Gloucestershire GL54 4LN

Formerly a terrace of six cottages (dating from 1856), this attractive stone-built country pub-cum-brasserie is located beside the A436 Gloucester to Cirencester road on the edge of the village; it commands enviable views across a beautiful rolling Cotswold landscape from its front windows and well-maintained garden. Refurbished by John and Judy Fennel some six years ago, the spacious and airy open-plan bar sports neatly arranged tables and chairs, numerous watercolours, newspapers and magazines to browse and a good log fire and woodburner for chilly winter nights. A warm welcome awaits those popping in for just a drink, but most who venture through the door are in search of the imaginative choice of home-cooked food served in both the bar and in the fine conservatory dining-room (no-smoking). It is certainly the 'place to eat' in the area, the monthly-changing main menu and daily-typed list of chef's specials offering an interesting and varied choice of dishes to suit all tastes. From light lunch dishes like fisherman's pie, garlic brioche topped with tomato provençale and cheese or a smoked ham baguette to a warm tartlet of wild mushrooms starter and main courses like noisettes of lamb grilled with a herb crust and a minted pear sauce or pan-fried fillet of pork with garlic butter and a confit of fennel, onion and fresh lime, the preparation and presentation of dishes is commendable. For pudding, try the warm caramelised apple frangipane tart or the brandy and apricot bread-and-butter pudding and throughout the meal expect good service from cheerful and efficient staff. In the evenings the dining atmosphere is enhanced by candlelight and on Fridays fresh fish is a major feature, alongside the normal menu and specials. To complement the food there is a sound list of wines, as well as three real ales and a good selection of malt whiskies. Booking essential at weekends, especially for Sunday lunch. *Open 11.30-2.30 , 6.30-11 (Sun 12-2.30, 7-10.30). Closed Sun eve in winter, all 25 & 26 Dec.* **Bar Food** *12-2, 7-9.30 (till 9 Sun). Free House.* **Beer** *Ruddles Best, Hook Norton Best, Theakston Best. Garden, patio, outdoor eating. MasterCard,* **VISA**

ANSTY   Ansty Arms   B&B

Tel 01203 611817   Fax 01203 603115   Map 7 D4
Brinklow Road Ansty Coventry CV7 9JP

Pub with accommodation lodge, two-tier eating, large conservatory and children's "Jungle Bungle" indoor play barn on high ground overlooking (and within earshot of) both motorways – a good spot and highly accessible – once you know the way! Take B4065 to Ansty from M6 at Junction 2 where it connects with the M69, and then follow B4029 signs to Rolls Royce PLC. Premier Lodge (Greenalls). *Open 11-11 (till 10.30 Sun).* **Beer** *Tetley Best, guest beers. Garden.* **Accommodation** *28 bedrooms all en suite £41.50 midweek, £34.50 Fri-Sun. Children welcome overnight, additional bed & cot available. Disabled access & toilet. Amex, Diners, MasterCard,* **VISA**

APPLEBY-IN-WESTMORLAND   Royal Oak Inn   FOOD   B&B

Tel 017683 51463   Fax 017683 52300   Map 5 D3
Bongate Appleby-in-Westmorland Cumbria CA16 6UN

Parts of the original building here are documented as being over 750 years old, and as it was once a coaching inn on the Penrith to Scarborough route, the Royal Oak can boast an unbroken history as a hostelry back to the 17th century. Both the snug and the Taproom are pristine examples of the traditional English pub. Oak panelling and stone walls, smoky-black beams and open log fires make a perfect environment in which to enjoy a particularly well-kept pint of real ale of which at least half a dozen brands plus guests and Bongate Special Pale (brewed by Hesket Newmarket Brewery) are always on tap. Accompany your pint or glass of wine (from a good selection available by the glass) with a reliable bar meal. A varied main menu highlights Bongate lamb pudding with sweet leeks, Indian chicken with peppers, onion and tomato, Cumberland sausage with apple sauce and interesting vegetarian options – lentil, red pepper and mushroom lasagne or sesame seed topped vegan vegetables with chick peas and cumin. Daily specials enhance the list further, especially fresh fish such as roast sea bass on fennel with a tomato and onion salsa or tuna steak with lemon and rosemary. Blackboard options may also feature summer herb soup, twice-baked cheese and spinach soufflé and Goosnargh duck with green apple sauce. Separate sandwich and filled bap menu. Bedrooms are necessarily small but nonetheless homely with leaded windows and creaky floors and the two single rooms, although not en suite, have their own bathrooms across the corridor. A heavily-beamed attic is used as the family bedroom, and two rear rooms have doors opening directly on to the garden. There are also two stylish dining-rooms, one of them reserved for non-smokers, and a first-floor residents' lounge looking out over the Bongate towards Appleby Castle. *Open 11-3, 6-11 (Sun 12-3, 7-10.30).* **Bar Food** *12-2, 6.30-9.* **Beer** *Bongate Special Pale Ale, Yates Bitter, Theakston Best, Younger's Scotch, Black Sheep Bitter, up to five guest beers. Terrace. Family room.* **Accommodation** *9 bedrooms, 7 en suite, £59.50-£73 (single £28.50-£40.75). Children welcome overnight (under-10s stay free in parents' room), additional bed (£10) & cot (£5) available. Accommodation closed 24 & 25 Dec; pub closed all 25 Dec. Amex, Diners, MasterCard,* **VISA**

APPLEY   Globe Inn   FOOD

Tel 01823 672327   Map 13 E2
Appley Wellington Somerset TA21 0HJ

Rambling, 500-year-old pub tucked away among a myriad of narrow lanes in a peaceful hamlet amid rolling, unspoilt countryside. Despite its isolated location this rural retreat draws a good dining clientele from nearby Wellington and attracts famished travellers using the A38. Deep, coloured walls and a delightful mix of rustic furniture characterise the series of intimate rooms that radiate off a central stone-flagged corridor and hatchway bar, which dispenses an excellent pint of Cotleigh Tawny alongside a further West Country guest ale (Dartmoor Best or Exmoor Ale) and a good local farmhouse cider. The charming front room is adorned with pictures of magpies and enjoys relaxing views of the village street. Printed menu fare not only highlights traditional pub favourites (steaks, chili, garlic prawns and steak and kidney pie) but also lists more adventurous dishes like chicken breast stuffed with pine nuts, bacon, raisins amd apricots with Madeira sauce, a generously served home-made seafood pancake and a well-flavoured fish soup. Equally reliable are the limited daily specials such as fillet of sea perch with cream, white wine and chive sauce, and lamb chops with shallots and red wine. Popular Sunday roasts. All in all, a good locals' pub complete with skittle alley and traditional pub games. *Open 11-3, 6.30-11 (Sun 12-3, 7-10.30). Closed Mon lunch (except Bank Holidays).* **Bar Food** *12-2, 7-10 (till 9.30 Sun). Free House.* **Beer** *Cotleigh Tawny, guest beer. Garden, outdoor eating, children's play area. Family room. MasterCard,* **VISA**

ARDINGTON   Boars Head   FOOD

Tel 01235 833254   Map 14a B3
Church Street Ardington Wantage Oxfordshire OX12 8QA

Since arriving at the Boars Head, an attractive timbered pub set in a timeless estate village off the A417 between Wantage and Didcot, Duncan and Liz Basterfield have succeeded in tastefully refurbishing the homely interior as well as producing above-average pub food. Dating back some 400 years and enjoying a lovely spot beside the parish church, this welcoming village local comprises three interconnecting rooms: a relaxing 'public' bar area – ideal for those calling in for a drink – and two small dining-rooms, both furnished with old pine furniture and neatly laid-up for the eager diners that regularly fill the available seats in the evenings (booking essential).

Attractive fabrics, fresh flowers, evening candlelight and open log fires enhance the cosy dining ambience. The main attraction here is the short, daily-changing blackboard menu that hangs by the bar. Duncan Basterfield uses good fresh produce, including game from the estate, in creating interesting starters like pressed chicken terrine with pine nuts and pesto, roasted pepper and tomato soup and creamed chick peas with spicy sausages and balsamic vinegar, all of which are accompanied by a basket of home-baked bread and unsalted butter. Main-course options may include casserole of king scallops, stuffed quails with grapes and tarragon, peppered pork with apple and herb mustard or ostrich on foie gras butter with lentils. Round off a satisfying meal with home-made pistachio mousse with honey tuilles or millefeuille of roast bananas with butterscotch sauce. Limited lighter snacks include toasted filled bagels and ploughman's lunches. Good house wines and well-kept real ales. As business is booming and space is limited, the Basterfields are extending the pub in 1997, creating an extra dining area and function room (16 seats), as well as landscaping a rear patio. Children are made most welcome. *Open 11-2.30, 6-11 (11-11 May and August Bank Holidays), Sun 12-3, 7-10.30. Closed all Mon. **Bar Food** 12-2, 7-9.30 (no food Sun eve). Free House. **Beer** Morland Original, Fuller's London Pride, guest beers. Front patio, outdoor eating. MasterCard,* **VISA**

ARMATHWAITE — Duke's Head Hotel — B&B

Tel 01697 472226   Map 4 C3
Armathwaite Carlisle Cumbria CA4 9PB

Zzz...

A long-standing favourite in the area, the Lynches' pub stays firmly traditional, and retains an instant appeal for those with plenty of time to linger and reminisce. Its fishing connections are well documented in the Last Cast Lounge, from where it's only a few paces into a glorious garden with flower beds and beech trees disappearing down to the very banks of the River Eden below. The half-dozen bedrooms are traditionally furnished, with TVs and beverage facilities throughout; most popular are the three with en suite shower facilities, the remaining two each having a separate neatly-kept bathroom. *Open 11-3, 6-11 (Sun 12-3, 7-10.30). **Beer** Boddingtons, Castle Eden Ale. Riverside garden. **Accommodation** 5 bedrooms, 3 en suite, £47.50 (single £22.50). Children welcome overnight (under-12s 50% adult tariff). MasterCard,* **VISA**

ARNOLD — Burnt Stump — A

Tel 0115 963 1508   Map 7 D3
Burnt Stump Hill Arnold Nottingham Nottinghamshire NG5 8PA

It is the location, in 30 acres of country park on the fringe of Sherwood Forest, which makes the evocatively-named Burnt Stump such a popular spot. Four miles out of Nottingham, turn off the A60 Mansfield road a mile or so north of its junction with the A614. There's a wealth of open space for one or more of the family to exercise the dog, a cricket pitch below the terrace for others to watch Ravenshead cricket club at play, while children can act out their latest Robin Hood adventures in an extensive playground under the trees. In summertime there are bouncy castles and barbecues and a covered pop and crisps counter. Indoors, hungrier little outlaws have their own menu and non-alcoholic cocktail list, while at lunchtime the peckish in-laws are promised a 'Hot Hoagie' in less than nine minutes. *Open 11-11 (Sun 12-10.30). **Beer** Mansfield Riding Mild, Bitter & Old Baily. Garden, children's play area. Family room. Amex, MasterCard,* **VISA**

ASENBY — Crab & Lobster — FOOD

Tel 01845 577286   Fax 01845 577109   Map 5 E4
Asenby Thirsk North Yorkshire YO7 3QL

Splendid out-of-the-ordinary thatched pub located just off the A1. Very different in both concept and performance, the pub's popularity continues to grow. With an almost Bohemian interior of scatter rugs, jazz accompaniments (live every first Tuesday of the month) and liberally scattered junk in every nook and cranny, the *Crab & Lobster* is an unusual pub by any standards. A brasserie-type menu has a natural

affinity towards fish, and the bar leaves plenty of room by day for pub-goers happy with a pint of Theakston's and a toasted BLT sandwich. Light lunches might include tagliatelli of smoked haddock, tarragon and mushrooms or, more substantially, chargrilled lamb steak with rosemary, garlic and roasted peppers. By mid-evening, space is taken up with crudités and garlic sausage nibbles at the bar, where some congestion does occur in the wait for tables. Salmon and halibut in filo with spinach and shellfish sauce and smoked haddock fishcakes with a mustard sauce head the list of fish specialities with turbot with a chervil crust and tournedos of salmon, red wine and shallots further indications of the kitchen's vast and varied output. Non-fish eaters will not be disappointed with Thai beef pancakes and calf's liver with olive mash, caramelised onions and bacon. Restaurant tables can be reserved separately by those wanting a little more elbow room and willing to pay a little extra. In summer, Sunday jazz barbecues make use of the marquee that has now become a permanent fixture. North of England Regional Winner of our 1997 Seafood Pub of the Year award.
Open 11.30-3, 6.30-11 (Sun 12-3 only). Closed Sun eve. **Bar Food** *12-2.30, 6.30-9.30 (no food Sun eve). Free House.* **Beer** *Theakston Best & XB, Timothy Taylor Bitter & Landlord, Black Sheep Bitter, John Smith's. Garden, outdoor eating, summer barbecue. Amex, MasterCard,* ***VISA***

ASHBY ST LEDGERS   Olde Coach House Inn   FOOD

Tel 01788 890349   Fax 01788 891922   Map 15 D1   B&B
Ashby St Ledgers Rugby Warwickshire CV23 8UN

 ▼ ♇ Zzz... ☺

Despite its Warwickshire address, Ashby St Ledgers is just across the county border in Northants, 3 miles from the M1, J18; alternatively, take the single track road signed off the A361, 4 miles north of Daventry. At the centre of this once-feudal village (population now 70) is Brian and Philippa McCabes' admirable pub where, from outside, you'd least expect to find one. Behind its ivy-covered facade is the cavernous, hollowed-out interior of a row of former cottages. Stone chimney breasts and cast-iron ranges still point to a certain antiquity. The jokey printed menu encompasses chargrills, pasta dishes (seafood tagliatelle, lasagne) vegetarian options, chicken and fish dishes. Separate children's menu (puzzles, crayons, high-chairs, booster seats and baby-changing facilities are all provided). The warm welcome to families extends to special children's activities on summer Sundays. The Coachman's Fayre menu lists a short selection of more adventurous meals: spiced lamb kebab with onion and mint salad, strips of pork with a creamy leek and cider sauce and trout baked with olive oil, basil and tomato. There are half a dozen bedrooms, all en suite, with TVs and tea trays, pine bedsteads and floral drapes plus abundant peace and quiet. A multi-purpose children's adventure climbing frame is a popular attraction in the protected, walled garden, allowing parents to get a break; once tired out, the children will hopefully sleep soundly in the main family bedroom, which offers a double and two single beds plus en suite bathroom; two further rooms feature both double and sofa beds. With a happy mix of mid-week corporate customers, weekend function overnighters and those seeking out good pub food and exceptional real ales, the Olde Coach House Inn is a busy place. Winner of our Family Pub of the Year award in 1996. *Open 12-2.30, 6-11 (Sat 12-11, Sun 12-4, 7-10.30).* **Bar Food** *12-2, 6-9.30 (Sun 12-3, 7-9). Free House.* **Beer** *St Ledger Ale (Chiltern Brewery), Flowers Original, Boddingtons, Everards Old Original, guest beers. Garden, outdoor eating.* **Accommodation** *6 bedrooms, all en suite, £56 (four-poster £61, single £46). Children welcome overnight (under-5s stay free in parents' room), additional bed (£5) & cot supplied. Disabled WC. Amex, MasterCard,* ***VISA***

ASHFORD-IN-THE-WATER   Ashford Hotel   B&B

Tel 01629 812725   Fax 01629 814749   Map 6 C2
1 Church Street Ashford-in-the-Water Bakewell Derbyshire DE45 1QB

☺

The former Devonshire Arms stands at the head of this picturesque Derbyshire village, just off the A6 and a mere stone's throw from the historic stone Sheepwash Bridge. Much original oak is retained in the beamed bar where log fires burn in winter; residents have use of their own cosy lounge, which opens on to a rear courtyard and enclosed garden. Each of the seven bedrooms (two with four posters) have been carefully remodelled in appropriately country style with floral-patterned wallpapers and bed linen; all are well equipped with direct-dial phones, TVs, clock radios and trouser presses. *Open 11-11 (Sun 12-10.30). Free House.* **Beer** *Mansfield Cask Bitter & Riding Bitter, guest beers. Garden. Family room.* **Accommodation** *7 bedrooms, all en suite (three with bath), £75 (four-poster & family room £85, single £50). Children welcome overnight, additional bed & cot (£10) supplied. Amex, Diners, MasterCard,* **VISA**

ASHPRINGTON   Durant Arms   FOOD

Tel 01803 732240   Map 13 D3
Ashprington Totnes Devon TQ9 7UP

Cream-painted, 18th-century pub located in a peaceful village just outside Totnes and close to the river Dart. A flagged entrance hall leads into the main bar, with a bay window seat overlooking the village street, and into the spick-and-span dining-room with neatly laid-out darkwood tables and chairs and a few settles. Lunchtime fare consists of hearty home-cooked snacks listed on a daily-changing board and may include chicken and ham pie, leek, cheese and potato pie, prawn creole, seafood bake and ploughman's. More imaginative dishes, using fresh local produce, are featured on the evening blackboard which could offer mussels in white wine for starters, followed by a poussin and mixed herbs, pheasant with port and orange, whole Dover sole or medallions of pork with Stilton and mushroom sauce. Good home-made puddings – fresh fruit pavlova and treacle tart. For those wishing to linger in this beautiful area there are two upstairs bedrooms (one with en suite shower) available (£40 double, £20 single), as well as a self-contained cottage sleeping three in one bedroom plus a sofa bed – book well in advance); this accommodation has not yet been inspected. Afternoon teas. *Open 11.30-2.30, 6-11 (Sun 12-2.30, 7-10.30).* **Bar Food** *11.30-2, 6-9.45. Free House.* **Beer** *Flowers Original, Greenalls Royal Wessex Bitter, guest beer. Garden. Family room. MasterCard,* **VISA**

ASHPRINGTON   Waterman's Arms   FOOD

Tel & Fax 01803 732214   Map 13 D3   **B&B**
Bow Bridge Ashprington Totnes Devon TQ9 7EG

Zzz... ☺

Delightfully situated on the banks of the River Harbourne, at the top of Bow Creek, the Waterman's is a favourite summer venue for alfresco riverside imbibing with resident ducks and – if you are lucky – kingfishers to keep you company. Bow Bridge is recorded in the Domesday Book and the inn until recently was a smithy and prior to that a brewery and a prison during the Napoleonic Wars. Recently purchased by Discovery Inns, who intend to maintain the successful formula – home-cooked food and quality overnight accommodation – that makes this friendly inn so popular. 'Tardis'-like inside, a series of neatly-furnished rooms radiates away from the central servery, all filled with a mix of rustic furniture, old photographs, brass artefacts and other memorabilia. Home-cooked bar food caters for all tastes, from hearty snacks such as sandwiches, salads and platters to regular menu favourites – served in both the bar and candlelit restaurant – including fresh pasta dishes, steak and kidney pie, rack of Devon lamb and steaks. A daily-changing blackboard enhances the choice by offering the likes of huntsman's pie, whole gurnard with crab and ginger sauce and the very popular mixed seafood salad platter (crab, prawns and fresh salmon). Good-value table d'hote menu at £15. A separate pudding board may highlight home-made banoffi pie and crème brulée. Ten beautifully fitted-out bedrooms have floral, cottagey fabrics and co-ordinating friezes around the walls, attractive dark-stained modern furniture and spotlessly-kept bathrooms with shower cubicles and efficient, thermostatically-controlled showers. Added comforts include telephone, cabinet-housed TV and tea-making facilities. Front rooms overlook the river and surrounding valley sides while the five newest rooms, complete with en suite bathrooms, overlook the gardens; two family rooms have a double and a single bed plus room for a cot or further bed. *Open 11-3, 6-11 (Sun 12-3, 7-10.30).* **Bar Food** *12-2.30, 6.30-9.30 (Sun 7-9.30). Free House.* **Beer** *Dartmoor Best, Palmers IPA, Tetley Bitter, Bass. Riverside terrace, garden, outdoor eating. Family room.* **Accommodation** *15 bedrooms, all en suite, £54-£70 (family room £58-£88, single £32-£39 according to season). Children welcome overnight (under-3s free, 3-5s £5, 6-10s £10, 11-14s £15), additional bed & cot supplied. MasterCard,* **VISA**

ASKERSWELL   Spyway Inn   A

Tel 01308 485250   Map 13 F2
Askerswell Bridport Dorset DT2 9EP

Tucked down a winding country lane a mile off the busy A35 Dorchester to Bridport road, this gloriously situated pub is the perfect spot in which to escape traffic tensions. Unwind in the traditional Spyway Bar where scrubbed pine tables, old settles and a longcase clock create a timeless atmosphere. A further bar and dining area are pine-furnished and display an impressive assortment of farming memorabilia, brass artefacts and a collection of cups hanging from the beams. The garden is a delightful summer retreat, complete with shrubs, flowers, tiny stream and superb downland views. It is a popular tourist area; be early in summer. Around twenty wines are served by the glass; in addition, twenty-three George Gale country wines are on offer. *Open 11-2.30 (till 3 Sat), 6-11 (Sun 12-3, 7-10.30). Closed all Mon (except Bank Holidays). Free House.* **Beer** *Ruddles County, Ushers Best, Adnams Southwold. Garden, terrace, children's play area. Amex, Diners.*

ASKHAM   Punch Bowl Inn   FOOD

Tel & Fax 01931 712443   Map 4 C3
Askham Penrith Cumbria CA10 2PF

Four miles from Junction 40 of the M6, this low, stone-built 18th-century inn, opposite the longest village green in Cumbria, is at the heart of the Earl of Lonsdale's Lowther Estate. Despite the cramped and often crowded bar which serves the front lounge, it is spacious beyond, with a family room, a second bar and a cosy dining-room to the rear. A vast menu which claims international status serves throughout. Alongside the 'Punch Bowl Specials' (Coltermell chicken – stuffed with haggis – and Riggindale pot – venison in red wine pie) are Stilton fries with Cumberland sauce, barbecue spare ribs, Mesand meatloaf, and vegiatelle – almond-filled pasta parcels with mushroom sauce. Puddings include sticky banana pudding and apple and almond tart with pistachio ice cream. With plenty to please and amuse the youngsters, and the entire village green to play out on, the Punch Bowl's a popular family venue. *Open 11.30-3, 6-11 (12-3, 7-11 winter), Sun 12-3 6-10.30 (from 7 winter).* **Bar Food** *12-2, 6.30-9.(from 7 winter).* **Beer** *Whitbread Castle Eden, Boddingtons, Morland Old Speckled Hen, guest beer. Patio, outdoor eating. Family room. MasterCard,* **VISA**

ASKRIGG   King's Arms Hotel   FOOD

Tel 01969 650258   Fax 01969 650635   Map 5 D4   **B&B**
Market Place Askrigg Leyburn North Yorkshire DL8 3HQ

Zzz...

Liz and Ray Hopwood's characterful former coaching inn has an unbroken history dating back to 1760 when outbuildings, where the Back Parlour is now, housed John Pratt's racing stables. Turner is known to have stayed here while recording on canvas the tranquil Dales scenery of the early 1800s; today, the high-ceilinged main bar, complete with saddle hooks, oak settles and hunting prints, is universally recognised as The Drover's Arms as depicted on TV in James Herriot's All Creatures Great and Small. The smaller, low-beamed front bar retains a wig cupboard within its panelling; side snugs surround the green marble fireplace. The back bar is simply furnished and home to shove ha'penny and darts boards. Food outlets operate on two floors of this fascinating maze of interlocked cottages. A large blackboard menu complements the printed bar menu (sandwiches, patés and ploughman's lunches) and evolves with the seasons. Typical of the 20 or so offerings are Waldorf salad with Atlantic prawns, rack of Dales lamb, baked Kilnsey trout, supreme of duck forestière, steak and ale pie and home-made puddings (crepes normande with Calvados cream sauce). Upstairs, the elegant, panelled Clubroom Restaurant (30 seats, no children under 7, no smoking) serves fixed-price à la carte dinners and table d'hote lunches; the adjacent, 40-seater, no-smoking Silks Grill Room provides a balancing act between substantial Yorkshire breakfasts, simple steaks and fish, and sumptuous afternoon teas. All the eleven bedrooms retain original features that are in keeping with the inn's manor-house style,

the many oak beams and uneven floors complemented by antique furniture, one four-poster, half-tester and canopied brass beds, and quality colour-co-ordinated fabrics; two suites attract the highest tariff. No children under 5 in the bar after 8pm.
Open 11-3, 6.30-11 (Sun 11-2.30, 7-10.30). **Bar Food** *12-2, 7-9 (Sun 7-8.30).*
Free House. **Beer** *Younger's Best & No 3, Theakston Bitter, Dent Bitter.* **Accommodation** *10 bedrooms, all en suite, £75, £89 & £108 (single £50, £55 & £70). Children welcome overnight (under-16s free if sharing parents' room, own room 70% rate). Courtyard. Family room. Amex, MasterCard,* **VISA**

ASTON — Flower Pot — FOOD

Tel 01491 574721   Map 15a D3   **B&B**
Ferry Lane Aston Henley-on-Thames Oxfordshire RG9 3DG

Zzz...

Brick-built pub (1890) situated off the A423 down a narrow lane in Aston and adjacent to a bridlepath which links with the Thames Path 300 yards away, where a sign advertises the pub's presence. The Flower Pot is popular with walkers who fill the two rooms furnished with banquette seating and adorned with rowing gear or spill out into the large garden on sunny days which seats about 50. Landlady Pat Thatcher's food is simple and served in ample portions: home-made soup – carrot and ginger – ploughman's lunches, ham, egg and chips and blackboard specials like steak and kidney pie, grilled skate wing and roast pheasant. A traditional Sunday lunch is served in winter. Upstairs accommodation comprises three homely bedrooms (two with en suite showers), all with Edwardian furnishings, TVs and tea-makers. *Open 10.30-3, 6-11 (Sun 12-3, 7-10.30); open all day occasionally in summer, often at weekends.*
Bar Food *12-2, 6.30-9 (no food Sun eve).* **Beer** *Brakspear. Garden, outdoor eating.*
Accommodation *3 bedrooms, 2 en suite (showers), £49 (single £39). Children welcome overnight (under-10s stay free in parents' room), additional bed available. No dogs. MasterCard,* **VISA**

ASWARBY — Tally Ho Inn — FOOD

Tel 01529 455205   Map 7 E3   **B&B**
Aswarby Sleaford Lincolnshire NG34 8SA

Just south of Sleaford before the turning off the A15 to Aswarby stands this fine mellow stone estate inn, which dates back some 200 years. The pleasant bar boasts exposed stone and brickwork aplenty, country prints, old settles, pews, open log fire and additional woodburner for cold winter days. More especially a good atmosphere prevails for relaxing diners tucking into the reliable home-cooked fare that is listed on a bar menu card and the daily-changing blackboard menu. Satisfying choices may include chicken, apricot and brandy pie, rich venison stew, savoury stuffed halibut and lighter bites such as grilled goat's cheese and crispy bacon salad, and freshly-filled baguettes. For pudding, try the chocolate, coffee and walnut pudding or caramelised lemon tart. Good-value table d'hote Sunday lunch served in the attractive, pine-furnished restaurant. An adjacent stable block houses the six well-kept bedrooms, all of which have compact en suite facilities (only two have a bath). Rooms are spacious, simply furnished, soothingly decorated and provide plenty of hanging and writing space. TVs and tea-makers are standard extras. *Open 12-3, 6-11 (Sun 12-3, 7-10.30).* **Bar Food** *12-2.30, 6.30-10 (Sun 12-2.30, 7-10).* *Free House.* **Beer** *Batemans XB, Bass, guest beer. Garden, children's play area.* **Accommodation** *6 bedrooms, all en suite, £45 (single £30). Children welcome overnight. Accommodation closed 24-27 Dec; pub closed all 26 Dec & 1 Jan eve. MasterCard,* **VISA**

Many **B&B** establishments offer reduced rates for weekend and out-of-season bookings. Always ask about special deals for longer stays. Beware half-board terms in inns where we do not recommend the **FOOD**.

AUST   Boar's Head   A

Tel 01454 632278   Map 13 F1
Main Road Aust South Gloucestershire BS12 3AX

A hidden, out-of-the-way spot, yet just a stone's throw from the M4 traffic thundering towards the Severn Bridge. The Aust lane is now a dead end. Standing by the church, the Boar's Head is a favoured local watering hole. Candles, lacy cloths and a succession of alcoves and inglenooks imbue an 18th-century feel to it all at night, and in winter a huge log fire flickers. To the rear there's a pretty stone-walled garden with a wishing well and beyond it a popular caravan site. *Open 11-3, 6.30-11 (Sun 12-3, 7-10.30). Beer Courage Best, Flowers Original, three guest beers. Garden and patio. Amex, Diners, MasterCard,* **VISA**

AXBRIDGE   Lamb Inn   B&B

Tel 01934 732253   Map 13 F1
The Square Axbridge Somerset TA6 2AP

Rambling, ancient town pub, romantically set opposite King John's hunting lodge, now an interesting museum. Open-plan bar area with bric-a-brac, beams and settles, as well as more modern intrusions. Overnight accommodation comprises a delightful large double room with older-style, freestanding furniture, Laura Ashley fabrics and a good-sized bathroom, and two further more basic and homely bedrooms that include a spacious family room. Attractive rear patio. *Open 12-2.30 (from 11 Sat), 6.30-11 (Sun 12-3, 7-10.30), Free House. Beer Butcombe Bitter, Bass, Wadworth 6X, occasional guest beer. Garden, patio.* **Accommodation** *3 bedrooms, 2 en suite (one with bath), £40-£45 (single £18-£25). Children welcome overnight, additional bed (£10) available. Check-in bar hours only. MasterCard,* **VISA**

AXFORD   Red Lion Inn   FOOD

Tel 01672 520271   Map 14a A4   **B&B**
Axford Marlborough Wiltshire SN8 2HA

In a small hamlet three miles from Marlborough, this attractive 17th-century brick and flint inn offers clean and comfortable accommodation in a picturesque rural setting. Views across the lush Kennet Valley can be enjoyed from the modern, simply-furnished dining-room and bar and from the small grassy area with benches, adjacent to the car park. Beyond the standard bar menu of pub favourites, large blackboards in the restaurant list an impressive list of fish dishes and more elaborate meals which can be served anywhere in the pub or garden. For starters there might be smoked eel with horseradish sauce and pan-fried scallops in ginger and spring onions, while main-course options may include mixed seafood – crab claws, prawns, tiger tails, mussels – pan-fried in garlic, Dover Sole, sea bass, lobster, lamb cutlets with grain mustard and honey, and local game in season. Good list of wines with twelve available by the glass. Four compact and freshly decorated bedrooms are kept in very good order, each having TVs, beverage trays, hairdryers and newly fitted en suite facilities with shower units. Two of the bedrooms are located in Pear Tree Cottage, reached by a path through the garden, where guests have use of a kitchen, sitting room and sunny patio with scenic views. *Open 11-3, 6.30-11 (Sun 12-3, 7-10.30). Bar Food 11.30-2.30, 6.30-10.30 (Sun 12-2.30, 7-10). Free House. Beer Wadworth 6X, Hook Norton Bitter, guest beer. Garden, children's play area.* **Accommodation** *4 bedrooms, all with en suite shower, £45 (single £30). Children over 3 welcome overnight. MasterCard,* **VISA**

AYOT ST LAWRENCE   Brocket Arms   B&B

Tel 01438 820250   Fax 01438 820068   Map 15a F2
Ayot St Lawrence Hertfordshire AL6 9BT

Splendid medieval pub – an unspoilt 14th-century gem – set within an equally splendid village close to Shaw's Corner, where George Bernard Shaw lived for forty years (now National Trust-owned). Classic unadulterated three-roomed interior with a wealth of oak beams, an inglenook fireplace, a rustic mix of furniture and tasteful piped classical music. Those wishing to experience the historic charm further can stay upstairs in one of the four characterful bedrooms built into the timbered eaves. Furnished in traditional style – one with a four-poster bed – the rooms are simple and homely, and reputedly haunted by a monk from the local abbey. All share two adequate bathrooms. Those guests craving more modern creature comforts can book one of the three newer bedrooms housed in a converted old stable block across the courtyard. These are neatly carpeted and comfortably furnished in modern pine (one also boasts a four-poster bed), and (unlike main building rooms) have central heating. Two have rather compact shower rooms, the third a clean en suite bathroom, and all are equipped with tea-makers and clock radios. Pleasant walled garden for peaceful alfresco drinking and for enjoying a summer cream tea (3-6pm May-Oct). Families welcome. *Open 11-11 (Sun 12-10.30). Free House.* **Beer** *Greene King Abbot & IPA, Wadworth 6X, Theakston Best, Adnams Broadside, Ruddles Best, guest beer. Garden.* **Accommodation** *7 bedrooms, 3 en suite, £55-£70 (single £40). Children welcome overnight, additional bed (£10) & cot supplied. Amex, MasterCard,* **VISA**

BAGINTON | Old Mill Inn | B&B

Tel 01203 303588   Fax 01203 307070   Map 6 C4
Mill Hill Baginton Coventry CV8 2BS

A handy place to stay, close to the A45 (and A46) and five miles from the M6, yet tucked away peacefully in pine-studded grounds running down to the River Sowe. Public areas still retain many features of the 19th-century working mill and, outside, a riverside patio is linked by a bridge to the garden. A well-designed modern block houses the bedrooms which have pine furniture, Laura Ashley fabrics and views of the river and weeping willows. Ample car parking. *Open 11-3, 5-11 (Sun 12-3, 7-10.30).* **Beer** *John Smith's Bitter, Courage Directors, Theakston Best. Large garden, children's play area.* **Accommodation** *20 bedrooms, all en suite, £65 (single £60). Children welcome overnight, (under-2s stay free in parents' room), additional bed (£5) & cot available. No dogs. Amex, Diners, MasterCard,* **VISA**

BAINBRIDGE | Rose & Crown Hotel | B&B

Tel 01969 650225   Fax 01969 650735   Map 5 D4
Bainbridge Wensleydale North Yorkshire DL8 3EE

In the heart of the Wensleydale forest, Bainbridge is a village of mellow stone houses set around the triangular green by which the old stocks stand. At its head, the 15th-century Rose & Crown still houses the Forest Horn, blown nightly from Holy Rood to Shrovetide as a guide to travellers towards its welcoming safety. Original beamed ceilings, open fires and antique furnishings give the small flagstoned bar its great character, though the adjacent games room is rather more utilitarian and less appealing. Bedrooms are cosy though not overly large. Three boast four-poster beds to complement their cottage decor; all are equipped with TV, radio and hairdryers. Only four, however, have full bathrooms en suite, the remainder having WC and shower rooms only. *Open 11-11 (Sun 12-10.30). Free House.* **Beer** *Webster's Yorkshire Bitter, Younger's Scotch Bitter. Garden.* **Accommodation** *12 bedrooms, all en suite £60 (single £24-£28.50). Children welcome overnight (half-price), additional bed & cot (both £5) available. MasterCard,* **VISA**

BALDWIN'S GATE | Slater's | B&B

Tel 01782 680052   Fax 01782 680136   Map 6 B3
Marfield Gate Farm Baldwin's Gate Newcastle under Lyme Staffordshire ST5 5ED

Zzz... ☺

Five miles from Junction 16 on the M6, this skilful conversion of former outbuildings on a working farm (they still have a 100-head milking herd) has created a stylish accommodation pub with super facilities for youngsters. In addition to the family/function room there's a safe, enclosed rear garden full of play equipment and a pair of ducks and geese to talk to. Set around a cobbled courtyard behind the pub proper, three self-contained cottage suites contain just about everything for overnight or longer stays: en suite bathrooms with over-bath showers, fitted kitchenettes and breakfast area, plus extra beds and cots at no extra charge. Two further en suite bedrooms for overnight guests complete the picture. Breakfast in the dining-room if self-catering residents prefer. Music on Tuesday and Sunday evenings. *Open 11-3, 5.30-11 (Sun 12-10.30 summer). Free House.* **Beer** *Marston's Bitter & Pedigree, Boddingtons. Garden, children's play area. Family room.* **Accommodation** *5 bedrooms, all en suite, £47, (four-poster & family room £50). Children welcome overnight (stay free if sharing parents' room), additional bed & cot available. Amex, Diners, MasterCard,* **VISA**

BAMBURGH · Lord Crewe Arms · B&B

Tel 01668 214243   Fax 01668 214273   Map 5 D1
Front Street Bamburgh Northumberland NE69 7BL

Friendly old inn in the middle of Bamburgh, a town dominated by its massive castle. Public areas include two rustic-style bars and two unpretentious lounges. Upstairs, bedrooms offer modest comforts with TVs and beverage trays but no telephones; five rooms have en suite showers only. The one room that does not have en suite facilities is particularly good value for those wanting budget accommodation – £46, single £34. A suite features a four-poster and one room has a bed-settee in addition to the double bed. No children under 5 overnight. The bar is only open at lunchtime in winter. *Open 11.30-3, 6-11 (Sun 12-3, 6-10.30). Closed winter evenings. Free House.* **Beer** *Bass, Stones Bitter. Patio.* **Accommodation** *20 rooms, 19 en suite, £68 (single £46), reductions during October. Children over 5 welcome overnight. Accommodation closed Nov-end Mar. MasterCard,* **VISA**

BAMFORD · Yorkshire Bridge Inn · FOOD

Tel 01433 651361   Fax 01433 651812   Map 6 C2   **B&B**
Ashopton Road Bamford Derbyshire S30 2AB

🍷 **Zzz...** ☺

In the heart of the Derbyshire Peak District, this inn dates from 1826 and is named after an old packhorse bridge on the River Derwent. Views from the central bar take in the peak of Win Hill – a beautiful setting in which to enjoy some good, reliable cooking. Bar food is split between a lunchtime and an evening menu. Lunchers may choose from hot or cold sandwiches, ploughman's lunches, traditional hot dishes of the home-made steak and kidney pie variety, or from four vegetarian dishes (broccoli and cream cheese bake); fresh fish is listed on a blackboard on market days. In the evening similar fare is supplemented by chargrilled steaks and salmon and additional specials like roast lamb with mint gravy, chicken and mushroom pie and barbecue pork chops. Accommodation takes the form of an adjoining hotel converted from barns, now housing ten en suite bedrooms, all with satellite TVs, radios, telephones, and beverage-making facilities; for those wishing to escape the hurly-burly there is a peaceful lounge and a residents-only dining-room. Non-smokers have the pleasure of the conservatory and children are well catered for both on the menu (fish fingers, sausages or burgers) and outside where there is a slide and climbing frame. *Open 11-11 (Sun 12-10.30).* **Bar Food** *12-2, 6-9 (till 9.30 Sat), Sun 12-9. Free House.* **Beer** *Stones, John Smith's Magnet, Bass, Boddingtons. Garden, outdoor eating, children's play area. Family room.* **Accommodation** *10 bedrooms, all en suite, £49.50 (single £38). Children welcome overnight (under-4s stay free in parents' room, 5-12s £5), additional bed & cot available. No dogs. MasterCard,* **VISA**

> We only recommend food (Bar Food) in those establishments highlighted with the **FOOD** symbol.

BANBURY · Ye Olde Reine Deer Inn · FOOD

Tel 01295 264031   Map 14a B1
47 Parsons Street Banbury Oxfordshire OX16 8NB

With its inn sign hanging out over the middle of the road, this town-centre pub is the oldest building in Banbury (1570), where Oliver Cromwell once held court in the panelled Globe Room (now used for functions). Landlord John Milligan of the *Falkland Arms* at nearby Great Tew (see entry) has renovated the building and introduced a policy of 'over-21s only'. Food, served only at lunchtimes, offers traditional favourites like filled jacket potatoes, ploughman's lunches and 'doorstep' sandwiches, plus a few dishes of the day such as a home-made soup (mushroom, leek and potato), 'Cromwell' pies, salmon fishcakes, cod and prawn crumble and a vegetarian option (pasta napolitana). For pudding there may be sticky toffee sponge or apple pie. Luxuriant hanging baskets of flowers decorate the front of the building and there is a small courtyard bar for summer drinking. A dozen country wines are dispensed from Victorian glass barrels behind the bar. *Open 11-2.30, 5-11 (from 7 Sat). Closed all Sun & all 25 Dec.* **Bar Food** *11.30-2 only (no food Sun).* **Beer** *Hook Norton Best, guest beer. Courtyard, outdoor eating. MasterCard,* **VISA**

BANTHAM   Sloop Inn   B&B

Tel 01548 560489   Fax 01548 561940   Map 13 D3
Bantham Kingsbridge Devon TQ7 3AJ

Set in an attractive coastal hamlet just 300 yards from the sea and one of the finest sandy beaches along this part of the coast, the 16th-century Sloop is a most peaceful inn from which to explore the area. Associations with smuggling are deep for it was at one time owned by the notorious South Hams wrecker and smuggler John Whiddon. The atmospheric flagstoned interior has a strong nautical feel to it, with lots of sea-going memorabilia and the rear, plainly-furnished dining area is designed in the shape of a ship's cabin. In the main building there are five clean and neat en suite bedrooms, generally of a good size, with modern furniture, clock/radio, TV and beverage-making kits. There are also self-catering flats available to the rear of the inn. *Open 11-2.30, 6-11 (Sun 12-2.30, 7-10.30). Free House.* **Beer** *Bass, Ushers Best Bitter, Blackawton Bitter, guest beer. Patio. Family room.* **Accommodation** *5 bedrooms, all en suite, £56 (single £28). Children welcome overnight (under-6s free if sharing parents' room, 6-15s £14), additional bed & cot (£2) available. Check-in by arrangement. No credit cards.*

> We endeavour to be as up-to-date as possible but inevitably some changes to landlords, chefs and other key staff occur after the Guide has gone to press.

BARDWELL   Six Bells Country Inn   FOOD

Tel 01359 250820   Map 10 C2   B&B
The Green Bardwell Bury St Edmunds Suffolk IP31 1AW

Approached via a track (once the original coaching highway) off the village green, this rather plain, cream-painted 16th-century inn (Grade II listed) is surrounded by open countryside, views of which can be appreciated from both the warm and comfortable beamed bars and the converted stable-block bedrooms. Reliable home-cooked food listed on different lunch and dinner blackboard menus – served in both bar and restaurant – encompasses potted shrimps and warm tandoori chicken salad for starters, with main-course options like prawn and pesto pasta, seafood pithiviers and breast of Barbary duck with cranberry and port sauce. Fresh fish and shellfish feature strongly on Fridays – try their deep-fried cod with hand-cut chips at lunch or lobster in the evening. The interesting, 30-bin list of wines from Adnams includes eleven half bottles. Peaceful and homely overnight accommodation is in converted barn and stable buildings; the eight en suite bedrooms are furnished with modern pine and co-ordinating bedcovers and fabrics. All have clean, compact shower rooms, TVs, telephones and tea-makers and all are on the ground floor. In the past year a new conservatory extension to the restaurant has been built and serves as the venue for live classical music evenings. Children are well catered for, with a Wendy House in the much improved garden, high-chairs inside and a vanity unit for baby-changing in the Ladies. *Open 12-2.30, 7-11 (till 10.30 Sun & winter).* **Bar Food** *12-1.45, 7-9.15. Free House.* **Beer** *John Smith's Bitter, Adnams Southwold, guest beer. Garden, outdoor eating, children's play area.* **Accommodation** *8 bedrooms, all en suite shower, £55 (four-poster £60, single £40). Children welcome overnight, additional bed (£5) available. Closed all 25 & 26 Dec. MasterCard,* **VISA**

BARFORD ST MARTIN   Barford Inn   B&B

Tel 01722 742242   Map 14 C3
Barford St Martin Salisbury Wiltshire SP3 4AB

The Barford Inn is a useful place to know if travelling the A30 or if seeking good-value overnight accommodation close to Salisbury (5 miles). Situated at the junction of the A30 and B3089 in the village centre this old inn has been carefully extended and refurbished, its characterful bars featuring some panelled walls, cushioned wall bench seating and open log fires. Converted outbuildings house the four homely, en suite bedrooms with matching floral fabrics, dark pine furnishings and clean, yet basic, bathrooms. Standard extras include TVs and tea- and coffee-making facilities. A little more thought towards creature comforts would not go amiss. Badger Inns. *Open 11.30-3, 6-11 (11.30-11 May -Sept), Sun 12-3, 7-10.30. Beer Hall & Woodhouse. Garden. Disabled facilities. Accommodation 4 bedrooms, all en suite, £40 (single £28). Children welcome overnight. No dogs. MasterCard, VISA*

. BARLEY   Fox & Hounds   FOOD

Tel 01763 848459   Map 15 F1
High Street Barley Royston Hertfordshire SG8 8HU

Pleasingly traditional white-painted 15th-century village local, with rambling, low-ceilinged rooms, splendid open fires and a separate dining area and conservatory. A beer drinker's favourite – the Fox & Hounds has 10 handpumps in constant use. Diners have the choice of a short lunchtime only bar menu offering the usual popular snack meals and a longer main menu which operates throughout the pub at lunchtime and in the evenings (bar and restaurant): steak, Flame Thrower and Stilton pie, 16oz stuffed plaice, paella and a daily fish special – swordfish braised in tomatoes. Vegetarians are well catered for with their own extensive menu which may well feature cashew nut paella and vegetable korma. Ice creams and sundaes are a speciality (9 varieties are on offer), as well as puddings such as strawberry flan and paw-paw cheesecake. Traditional pub games are very popular with indoor and outdoor skittles, bar billiards, shove-ha'penny, darts and dominoes; there's also a boules pitch. The children's play area has a multi-purpose climbing frame with slide and swing; inside the pub there are baby-changing facilities and a children's menu is offered. *Open 12-2.30, 6-11 (Sun 12-3, 7-10.30). Bar Food 12-2, 6.30-10 (Sun 7.15-9.30). Free House. Beer home-brewed Nathaniel's Special (3.3%) & Flame Thrower (4.4%), Boddingtons, Adnams Southwold, six guest beers. Garden, outdoor eating, children's play area. Family room. Disabled WC. MasterCard, VISA*

BARNARD GATE   Boot Inn   FOOD

Tel 01865 881231   Fax 01865 358910   Map 14a B2
Barnard Gate Witney Oxfordshire OX8 6XE

About 5 miles from Oxford, just off the Oxford-Cheltenham A40, the popular Boot Inn is run by George Dailey. The secret of its success is happy, young staff offering good food at extremely competitive prices. The result is a very busy pub at almost all times, so you would be well advised to book a table. A well-built extension complements the bar with apricot walls covered with prints and stone-flagged floors and has enabled the Boot to offer a larger menu with special dishes of the day on a blackboard next to the large open log fire. A terrace complete with fountain offers more tables outside; it's illuminated at night, creating the festive feeling of being abroad. The menu might include terrine of pork, pigeon and quail with cranberry sauce, Brixham cod with a herb crust, tomato salsa and hollandaise, Thai chili chicken curry and two or three vegetarian dishes. Steaks are good and there is a selection of puddings (sticky toffee pudding, banoffi pie or crème brulée). Note the unique collection of 'celebrity' boots that adorn the pub walls, all donated by well-known figures like Gary Lineker, Ian Botham and Raymond Blanc. *Open 11-11 (Sun 12-10.30). Bar Food 12-2.30, 7-10 (Sun 12-3, 7-9.30). Free House. Beer Hook Norton, guest beer. Terrace, outdoor eating. Closed all 25 Dec. MasterCard, VISA*

BARNOLDBY-LE-BECK   Ship Inn   A

Tel 01472 822308   Map 7 E2
Main Road Barnoldby-le-Beck North East Lincolnshire DN37 OBG

17th-century village pub with a real fire, a separate restaurant and an award-winning garden. The landlord, Mr Gillis, is an avid supporter of Grimsby Town football team, who show an equal support for his ales. Smartly refurbished interior and a profusion of hanging baskets and tubs brings a seasonal splash of colour to the exterior. Six miles from the end of M180. Trent Taverns. *Open 11-3, 6.30-11 (Sun 12-3, 6.30-10.30).* **Beer** *Flowers Original, Theakston Best, Younger's No 3, Boddingtons, guest beer. Patio.* *MasterCard,* **VISA**

BARNSLEY   Village Pub   B&B

Tel 01285 740421   Map 14a A2
Barnsley Cirencester Gloucestershire GL7 5EF

Clearly once a row of roadside cottages next to the village school, the Village Pub is commendable for retaining both its unusual name and a cottage interior, quite in keeping with open fires, brass-hung beams and antique settles. The single bar gives on to carpeted lounges and dining-room on one side and to drinkers on the summer patio through a quaint service window. So close is the main road that access to the pub is now sensibly to the rear, as are the bedrooms (thus well insulated from any traffic noise). Accommodation, as one might expect, is modest yet comfortable, all but one having en suite WC/shower rooms, the remaining single enjoying the benefit of its own, consequentially private, bathroom. On the B4425 Cirencester to Bibury road. *Open 11-3, 6-11 (Sun 12-3, 6-10.30). Free House.* **Beer** *Wadworth 6X, King & Barnes Twelve Bore. Garden, patio.* **Accommodation** *5 bedrooms, all en suite, £45 (single £30). Children welcome overnight, (under-2s free, over-2s £5), additional bed available. Pub and accommodation closed all 25 Dec. Amex, MasterCard,* **VISA**

BARNSTON   Fox & Hounds   FOOD

Tel & Fax 0151 648 1323   Map 6 A2
Barnston Road Barnston Wirral L61 1BW

Lunchtime snacking pub by hazardous bends on the A551; Barnston post office is 100 metres away. Alongside sandwiches and filled potatoes, the likes of quiche and Coronation chicken are reliably fresh. Home-cooking rises to lasagne and garlic bread, Barnston smokie (fish pie), venison sausages and stuffed peppers – all listed on a short daily-changing blackboard menu. Choice of two roasts on Sundays. No chips, no music, no cigarette machine and no food any evening. *Open 11.30-3, 5.30-11 (Fri & Sat 11.30-11, Sun 12-10.30).* **Bar Food** *12-2 only. Free House.* **Beer** *Courage Directors, Webster's Yorkshire, Ruddles County & Best, Marston's Pedigree. Garden. No credit cards.*

BASSENTHWAITE LAKE   Pheasant Inn   B&B

Tel 017687 76234   Fax 017687 76002   Map 4 C3
Bassenthwaite Lake Cockermouth Cumbria CA13 9YE

Originally a farm, the Pheasant looks like the archetypal Victorian roadside inn (mercifully by-passed these days by the A66), as it was converted in 1826. Period appeal abounds in the three lounges (one non-smoking) and atmospheric bar, complete with open log fires, beams hung with brasses, old prints and antique firearms and tobacco-brown walls. Adequate, simply fitted bathrooms are the only obvious nod to modernity. No phones, TVs or dogs in the homely bedrooms – just the pervading Lakeland peace and quiet. The flower-filled garden is a splendid spot for afternoon tea. *Open 11.30-2.30 (Sat 11-3), 5.30-10.30 (till 11 Fri), Sun 12-2.30, 7-10.30 (till 10 winter).* **Beer** *Theakston Best, Bass, Morland Old Speckled Hen. Garden.* **Accommodation** *20 bedrooms, all en suite, from £72 (Sep/Oct £96-£100, single £58-£60 – winter reductions). Children welcome overnight, additional bed (£20) & cot (£5) available. No dogs. MasterCard,* **VISA**

BATCOMBE   Batcombe Inn   ★   FOOD

Tel 01749 850359   Fax 01749 850615   Map 13 F1
Batcombe Shepton Mallet Somerset BA4 6HE

   ☺

Tucked away down a web of country lanes in the very rural Batcombe Vale, Derek
and Claire Blezard's old honey-coloured stone coaching inn enjoys a peaceful position
away from the main village, next to the church. The long and low-ceilinged main bar
has exposed stripped beams and is warmly and tastefully decorated; terracotta sponged
walls with ivy leaf stencilling are hung with several old paintings, creating a relaxed
and homely atmosphere. A mix of individual chairs, deep window seats and darkwood
furniture fronts a huge stone inglenook with log fire. Adjoining the bar is a high-
ceilinged, no-smoking dining area in what used to be the old barn and toll-house.
Bar food is reliably good with blackboards listing daily-changing specials such as bream
with tomato and fresh basil, skate wing with capers and lemon butter, home-made
spring and crab rolls with chili sauce and good vegetarian dishes – basil roulade. The
printed menu is better than most, offering a range of hearty snacks, starters and main
dishes, from duck and sun-dried tomato salad and home-made salmon and watercress
fishcakes to lamb topped with mint stuffing and asparagus and baked in filo pastry.
Accompanying salads are enormous and imaginative and main-dish vegetables are
served separately and generously. Traditional Sunday lunch is always popular, as are
non-alcoholic drinks such as elderflower pressé and a tasty ginger brew. Bookings are
taken anywhere in the pub. A big welcome is made to families: children not only
have their own 'Kiddies Corner' menu with a choice of nine items but they also have
their own fully-equipped room complete with mini-trampoline, doll's house, drawing
board, books, toys (including a Nintendo games console) and a video recorder with a
good choice of films – enough to placate any child while relaxed parents enjoy their
meal. Children's facilities extend to the rear garden play area for fine-weather activity;
there is also a changing and feeding area in an ante-room to the Ladies. *Open 12-2.30,
7-11 (Sun 12-2.30, 7-10.30).* **Bar Food** *12-2, 7-10 (till 9.30 Sun). Free House.*
Beer *Butcombe Bitter, Wadworth 6X. Garden, patio, children's play area. Family room.
MasterCard,* **VISA**

BATHAMPTON   George Inn   FOOD

Tel & Fax 01225 425079   Map 13 F1
Mill Lane Bathampton Bath & North East Somerset BA2 6TR

☺

Hard by a stone-arched road bridge which crosses the Kennet and Avon canal (there's
even a door into the pub from the tow-path), this is truly a picturesque spot. The Hall
family have furnished it with hanging flower baskets every year for twenty years and
the summer crowds regularly overflow on to the patio and into the garden. Diners
order their food on pre-printed pads at a single bar and then wait at their chosen
table. As ever, daily specials are probably the best bet: minty lamb casserole, beef in
red wine and Stilton, Thai stir-fry and poached salmon bonne femme, with crunchy
chocolate fudge, perhaps, to follow. Children enjoy the creaky, spiral staircase which
leads them to a beamed family room at eye level with the canal. *Open 11-2.30, 6-11
(11-11 Sat & Bank Holidays, Sun 12-10.30).* **Bar Food** *12-2, 6.30-9.45 (Sat & Sun 12-
9.45).* **Beer** *Courage Best & Directors, Wadworth 6X. Garden, patio, outdoor eating. Family
room. No credit cards.*

BEACONSFIELD   Greyhound   FOOD

Tel 01494 673823   Map 15a E3
Windsor End Beaconsfield Buckinghamshire HP9 2JN

The unassuming Greyhound pub enjoys a relatively undisturbed position on a
tree-lined avenue, opposite the parish church at the peaceful 'Windsor End' of
Beaconsfield. Its plain exterior appearance belies the characterful interior, which dates
back to the 15th century and comprises three traditional, low-beamed bars with
simple furnishings, open fires and a welcoming atmosphere. No music or intrusive
games. Small rear dining-room with terracotta walls, cloth and candle-topped tables,

quality watercolours and a relaxing ambience. Reliable home-cooked bar food is listed on a printed menu – home-made burgers flavoured with garlic, basil and tomato, filled baguettes, chicken, leek and Stilton pie, bubble-and squeak with pork and leek sausages – and on twice-daily-changing blackboards, both available throughout the pub. Interesting specials may include warm salad of crispy duck and spring onion, gurnard marinated in fresh coriander and olive oil, salmon fishcakes with tomato sauce, lamb in garlic and rosemary with red wine glaze, vegetarian lasagne, and a choice of fresh pasta dishes. Accompanying vegetables are crisp and plated separately. Round off your meal with sticky toffee pudding. No children under 14 inside. *Open 11-3, 5.30-11 (Sun 12-3, 7-10.30). **Bar Food** 12-2.15, 7-10 (no food Sun eve). Free House. **Beer** Courage Best, Fuller's London Pride, Wadworth 6X, two guest beers. Garden, outdoor eating. Amex, MasterCard, **VISA***

BEAUWORTH   **Milbury's**   **A**

Tel 01962 771248   Fax 01962 771910   Map 15 D3
Beauworth nr Alresford Hampshire SO24 0PB

Set on a hill just to the south of the village, the site of some bronze age burial mounds or barrows, the pub's name is actually a corruption of Mill-Barrow, the name of the last remaining mound just 150 yards away. The South Downs Way passes by the front door of this old tile-hung pub. The main bar boasts old brickwork, a flagstone floor and rough hewn three-legged tables, but the most fascinating feature is an enormous treadmill, within which a poor donkey once walked to raise water from a 300-foot well. For the price of a donation to the Guide Dogs for the Blind, you are invited to drop an ice-cube down the well and count the nearly eight seconds it takes to splash in the water far below. Children are made positively welcome, with their own small section on the menu and a large safe garden to play in. There is also a skittle alley, which must be booked. *Open 11-3, 6-11 (Sat 11-11 summer), Sun 12-3, 7-10.30 (12-10.30 summer). Free House. **Beer** Milbury's (4.3%), Hampshire Brewery King Alfred & Pendragon, guest beers. Garden, outdoor eating, children's play area. Family room. Amex, MasterCard, **VISA***

> We only recommend food (Bar Food) in those establishments highlighted
> with the **FOOD** symbol.

BECKINGTON   **Woolpack Inn**   ★   **FOOD**

Tel 01373 831244   Fax 01373 831223   Map 14 B3   **B&B**
Beckington Bath Somerset BA3 6SP

Zzz...

A splendidly restored former coaching inn that benefits greatly from a new section of the A36 trunk road that now bypasses Beckington. In the easy-going atmosphere within diners are encouraged to consume simply what they'd like just how and where they'd like it, and there is plenty of choice on the one menu that is served throughout. The bar boasts a revealed original fireplace, recreated window shuttering in lieu of curtains and re-laid traditional flagstone flooring. Behind it, the Garden Room leads out on to a walled garden; this is the most popular dining area; the no-smoking Oak Room dining area seats a further twenty. Chef David Woolfall's menus are equally all-embracing with no obligation to order more than a starter-sized serving of, say, salad niçoise, duck liver paté with Cumberland sauce or baked goat's cheese on a ciabatta croute with pesto (although all the starter dishes are dual-priced as starter or main course). There's every temptation to indulge further, though: particularly good daily fish specials (roast turbot with olive oil dressing and ratatouille), pheasant and venison casserole with artichokes, saddle of lamb in filo with wild mushrooms and rosemary sauce, fillet of beef with tarragon and mustard and confit of duck with Oriental vegetables and sweet soy sauce. Prices are high, but so is the quality. Round off with walnut tart with honey and rum glaze and pistachio ice cream or a plate of interesting cheeses. Investment and attention to detail in the bedrooms are evident, with each room's individual design incorporating many original features supplemented by custom-built freestanding furniture and a comprehensive range of comforting amenities. The bathrooms are particularly well appointed, with plenty of bright light, generous supplies of towels and toiletries and particularly powerful over-bath showers. Three larger 'Executive' rooms (one with four-poster) attract the higher tariff and two have direct access to the residents' rear garden. Residents' lounge and conference facilities. No under-5s after 8pm or overnight. *Open 11-3, 6-11 (Sun 12-3, 7-10.30).* ***Bar Meals** 12-2, 7-10 (till 9 Sun).* ***Beer** Bass, Wadworth IPA & 6X, guest beer. Walled garden, terrace, outdoor eating.* ***Accommodation** 12 bedrooms, all en suite, £64.50-£84.50 (single from £54.50). Children over 5 welcome overnight, additional bed available for sharing with parents in larger, Executive rooms only. MasterCard, **VISA***

BECKLEY   Abingdon Arms   FOOD

Tel 01865 351311   Map 14a C2
High Street Beckley Oxfordshire OX3 9UU

A beautifully positioned, stone-built pub with inspiring views and a splendid garden and terrace for relaxing summer alfresco drinking. Within, the interior is plainly furnished with cloth-covered wall seats in the lounge and a separate public bar with a bar billiards table. Hugh and Mary Greatbatch have now been here for over 25 years and Mary's cooking is still a great attraction. Her excellent food mirrors the seasons, with a delicious summer salad menu featuring fresh crab with ginger dressing, Greek salad with taramasalata and smoked chicken with yoghurt and mint sauce. Warming soups, curries with basmati rice and other hot dishes (baked ham with mustard) appear in winter. Puddings like apple and almond tart and a mousse-like chocolate torte. In winter, regular special evenings are organised (on alternate Fridays) highlighting food from one particular country or region – booking is essential. Only children over 14 inside. Note late Sunday eve opening. *Open 11.30-2.30, 6.30-11 (Sun 12-2.30, 8-10.30).* ***Bar Food** 12.15-1.45, 7.15-9 (no food Sun eve). Free House.* ***Beer** Tetley, Wadworth 6X. Garden, outdoor eating. Closed all 25 Dec. No credit cards.*

BEDFORD   Embankment Hotel   B&B

Tel 01234 261332   Fax 01234 325085   Map 15 E1
Embankment Bedford Bedfordshire MK40 3PD

A small Tudor-style town-centre hotel sitting on the embankment of the River Ouse and providing comfortable accommodation that is popular with visiting businessmen. Twenty spacious upstairs bedrooms are furnished and decorated in uniform style with modern built-in furniture, good writing space and adequate en suite shower rooms; TVs, tea-makers, radios and trouser presses are standard throughout. Both the bar areas and lounge have been refurbished in the past year. *Open 11-2.30, 6-11 (Sat 11-11, Sun 12-10.30).* ***Beer** Bass.* ***Accommodation** 20 bedrooms, all en suite, £59.50 (single £49.50); weekend £49.95 (single £29.95). Children welcome overnight (under-2s stay free in parents' room), additional bed (£5) & cot supplied. Amex, Diners, MasterCard, **VISA***

BEENHAM VILLAGE   Six Bells   FOOD

Tel 01734 713368   Map 14a C4   B&B
Beenham Village Reading Berkshire RG7 5NX

Dating back some 200 years, this pub is a mixture of old and new. The bar is old, dimly lit, with mahogany counter and all the characteristics of an old village pub. To the rear they have added an extension which has a large room suitable for parties and wedding receptions. Reliable home-made food is on offer, such as chicken tikka, chili, chicken wrapped in bacon, cottage pie, fresh asparagus in season, and fruit pavlova or treacle and walnut tart to finish. A two-course roast meal is served on Sundays. Upstairs, there are four letting rooms, with tea/coffee-making facilities, radios and televisions. The bathrooms are adequate, the beds comfortable and all the rooms have lovely views over the neighbouring farmland. One single room has shower only. *Open 12-2.30, 6.15-11 (Sun 12-3, 7-10.30).* ***Bar Food** 12-2.30, 7-10 (Sun 12-3, 7-10). Free House.* ***Beer** Flowers Original, Marlow Rebellion, Brakspear Bitter, occasional guest beer. Garden, outdoor eating.* ***Accommodation** 4 bedrooms, all en suite, £49 (single £36). Children welcome overnight (rate depends on age), additional bed available. MasterCard, **VISA***

BEER — Anchor Inn — FOOD

Tel 01297 20386   Fax 01297 24474   Map 13 E2   **B&B**
Fore Street Beer Seaton Devon EX12 3ET

 Zzz... 😊

One of Britain's best-situated inns, the Anchor overlooks the stony beach whence the local crab boats set to sea in the early morning. Fish dominates the menu; dishes include not only local haddock and plaice, but also in the evenings fillet of pollock Cajun style, brill with banana and mango chutney and pan-fried tuna steak with fresh tomato and herb sauce. Meat-eaters will not be disappointed with roast guinea fowl with apple and calvados sauce or steak au poivre and vegetarians are also well catered for in the spacious and comfortably furnished bars. Ploughman's lunches and sandwiches are served lunchtimes only. Each of the eight recently upgraded bedrooms has private facilities (though not all are en suite and some have shower only); bright co-ordinated fabrics enliven them all, and some enjoy fine sea views. Entrance for residents is separate from the pub proper; there's a clubby TV lounge and the clifftop garden opposite is a spectacular location for an early evening drink. *Open 11-2.30, 5.30-11 (Mon-Fri 11-11 summer, Sat 11-11, Sun 12-10.30). Bar Food 12-2, 7-9.30. Free House. Beer Otter Ale, Wadworth 6X, guest beers. Garden, outdoor eating. Accommodation 8 bedrooms, all en suite, £59 (single £35). Children welcome overnight, (under-5s free if sharing parents' room), additional bed (£5) & cot supplied. No dogs. Accommodation closed all 25-26 Dec. MasterCard,* **VISA**

BEETHAM — Wheatsheaf — B&B

Tel 01539 562123   Map 4 C4
Beetham Kilnthorpe Cumbria LA7 7AL

Just off the A6, a mile or so North of the Lancashire border, Mrs Shaw's homely hostelry has been in the same ownership now for over 25 years. Unsurprisingly, her many returning guests are welcomed as members of the extended family. Behind a facade of black-and-white gables and leaded windows are three interlinked bars which are very much the focal point of village life, while for more retiring residents there's a comfortable TV lounge available upstairs. The bedrooms are neat and attractively decorated, if on the whole rather small. There are TVs and tea-makers, and spotlessly kept carpeted private bathrooms. The popular front rooms have views over the village and church grounds down towards the River Bela. *Open 11-3, 6-11 (Sun 12-3, 7-10.30). Free House. Beer Boddingtons, guest beer. Accommodation 6 bedrooms, all en suite, £40 (single £30). Children welcome overnight, additional bed (£10). Accommodation closed 24-26 Dec; pub closed 25 Dec eve. MasterCard,* **VISA**

BELFORD — Blue Bell Hotel — B&B

Tel 01668 213543   Fax 01668 213787   Map 5 D1
Market Square Belford Northumberland NE70 7NE

 Zzz... 😊

Creeper-clad, the Bell stands at the head of the village on a cobbled forecourt. In front are the old Market Place and stone cross (restored by English Heritage), and the Norman parish church stands on a hill behind. The pubbiest part is the Belford Tavern, licensed in old stables in the courtyard, where there's a games room, a children's menu and just one regularly-changing real ale on offer. The hotel's stone-flagged foyer leads to a stylish cocktail bar boasting a collection of miniature hand bells, and a restful residents' lounge. Bedrooms are a mix, from those in the annexe (with shower/WCs only) to superior and de luxe rooms with full bathrooms and lovely views of the Blue Bell's 2-acre "garden of 10,000 blooms". One ground-floor room is equipped for disabled guests. *Open 11-3, 6.30-11 (Sun 12-3, 7-10.30). Accommodation 17 bedrooms, all en suite, £74-£92 (single £35-£42). Children welcome overnight (under-12s stay free in parents' room, 12-16s £4) additional bed & cot available. Amex, MasterCard,* **VISA**

BELLINGDON   Bull   FOOD

Tel & Fax 01494 758163   Map 15a E2
Bellingdon Road Bellingdon Buckinghamshire HP5 2XU

Delightful little redbrick cottage on the north side of the village, enjoying a peaceful rural aspect as it's surrounded by fields. The attractive, low-beamed bar boasts a large inglenook, various display cases and every table is neatly laid out with place mats, for the Bull is now very much a dining pub. Bar food is reliable, with an interesting selection of dishes being listed on regularly-changing blackboard menus; there may be up to a dozen or so choices at each stage (including puddings). Choices may range from home-made soups and patés and roll-mop herrings with sour cream to pan-fried turbot with lime and lemon gravy, grilled salmon with dill, chargrilled lemon chicken supreme, and vegetable tikka masala with rice, sambals and popadom. Fish is the thing here and the chef even brings the dressed crab back from Cromer himself. Sandwiches are not served, but a 'cold board' of home-cooked gammon with new potatoes and salad, jumbo sausages and hot peppered mackerel are popular as snackier dishes. Home-made puddings may include Bramley apple pie and West Indian rum and treacle tart. *Open 12-3, 7-11 (Sun 12-3 only). Closed Sun eve.* **Bar Food** *12-3, 7-10 (no food Sun eve).* **Beer** *Ind Coope Burton Ale, Benskins Best, Marston's Pedigree. Garden, outdoor eating, summer barbecue. MasterCard,* **VISA**

BENENDEN   King William IV   FOOD

Tel 01580 240636   Map 11 C6
The Street Benenden Kent TN17 4DJ

16th-century tile-hung village inn, up-market in style, reflecting its well-heeled location. Fresh flowers on plain wooden tables, a log fire in the huge inglenook, exposed beams and a relaxing lived-in air. By contrast, a splendidly traditional public bar with bare boards, TV, games machine and time-honoured pub games. Short daily-changing selection of good home-made dishes with fresh accompanying vegetables and little sign of chips – unless asked for. Choices may include carrot and coriander soup, seafood mornay, leek and turkey flan and roast loin of pork for Sunday lunch. Bread-and-butter pudding may feature on the pudding board. *Open 11-3, 6-11 (from 5 Fri & Sat), Sun 12-3, 7-10.30.* **Bar Food** *12-2.30 (till 2 Sun), 7.30-10 (no food Sun eve).* **Beer** *Shepherd Neame Master Brew & Spitfire. Small side garden. No credit cards.*

BENTWORTH   Sun Inn   FOOD

Tel 01420 562338   Map 15a D4
Sun Hill Bentworth Alton Hampshire GU34 5JT

Hidden down a tiny lane on the village edge, this pretty flower-decked and unspoilt rural pub dates from the 17th century when it was a pair of cottages. Little has changed inside over the years, where brick and board floors are laid with a rustic mix of old and new pine tables, benches and settles, original beams are hung with various horse brasses, walls are adorned with prints and plates and tasteful cosmetic touches – quality magazines, fresh and dried flowers – enhance the overall unblemished atmosphere. Two large inglenook fireplaces with open log fires warm the two main interlinking bars. To provide more seating space, a third adjoining room was added in a similar style, maintaining the unique traditional character of the pub. As well as the Sun's charm, real ale and a good selection of home-cooked dishes (listed on a hand-written menu and a regularly-changing blackboard menu) are prime reasons for visiting. Reliable, uncomplicated dishes range from ploughman's lunches and watercress soup to salmon fishcakes with crab sauce, chicken, leek and ham pie and beef casserole with sun-dried tomatoes. To finish, try the Bakewell tart or treacle tart. Outside to the front and side, among the flower tubs and baskets, there are several wooden tables for alfresco sipping. No children under 10 inside after 8pm. *Open 12-2.30 (till 3 Sat), 6-11 (Sun 12-3, 7-10.30). Closed Sun eve Nov-Easter).* **Bar Food** *12-2, 7-9.30 (till 9 Sun). No food Sun eve Nov-Easter. Free House.* **Beer** *Sun Special (Hampshire Brewery), Wadworth 6X, Marston's Pedigree, Courage Best, Ruddles Best, Cheriton Brewhouse Pots Ale, Ringwood Best, guest beer. Terrace, outdoor eating. Family room. Closed 25 Dec. No credit cards.*

BERWICK   Cricketers   A

Tel 01323 870469   Map 11 B6
Berwick Polegate East Sussex BN26 6SP

Unspoilt, 500-year-old brick and flint creeper-clad cottage located just off the A27
Lewes to Polegate road and a handy watering-hole for walkers from the South Downs
Way. Inside, three charming rooms are delightfully unpretentious and traditional with
half-panelled walls, open fires and simply furnished with scrubbed tables and wall
benches on quarry-tiled floors. Popular locals' pub with a good chatty atmosphere and
decent Harveys ales tapped straight from the barrel in a rear room. Surrounded by a
magnificent cottage garden – foxgloves, roses and flower-borders – it is an idyllic
summer pub. No children inside. Since last year's guide a new landlord/chef has
introduced a promising list of daily specials, highlighting some interesting seafood
dishes (not yet inspected). *Open 11-3, 6-11 (Sun 12-3, 6.30-10.30).* **Beer** *Harveys
Best Bitter. Garden, outdoor eating. No credit cards.*

BICKLEY MOSS   Cholmondeley Arms   FOOD

Tel 01829 720300   Fax 01829 720123   Map 6 B3   **B&B**
Bickley Moss Malpas Cheshire SY14 8BT

Virtually opposite Cholmondeley Castle and gardens on the A49 and still part of the
Viscount's estate is this redbrick former schoolhouse replete with family heirlooms,
educational memorabilia, bell tower without and blackboards within. These last
provide interesting reading, the daily-changing list possibly featuring goat's cheese
soufflé with devilled tomato sauce, Mediterranean fish soup, and terrine of
sweetbreads with bacon and garlic among the starters, followed by chicken breast in
a mushroom, Dijon mustard and cream sauce, rabbit braised in red wine, monkfish
provençale or Kashmiri lamb curry. Finish, perhaps, with rhubarb and ginger crumble
or bread-and-butter pudding. Overnight accommodation is across the car park in what
must have been the head teacher's house. Four recently refurbished and two new self-
contained bedrooms (five doubles and a family room) are bright and cottagey with en
suite WC and shower rooms (one with bath); one of the two new bedrooms having
French doors leading out into the garden. All have telephones, television and clock
radios, tea trays and hairdryers. It's back to school in the morning to report in for
a slap-up breakfast. *Open 11-3, 7-11 (from 6.30 Sat), Sun 12-3, 7-10.30.*
Bar Food *12-2.15, 7-10 (from 6.30 Sat, till 9.30 Sun). Free House.* **Beer** *Boddingtons,
Flowers IPA & Original, guest beer. Garden, outdoor eating. children's play area. Family room.*
Accommodation *6 bedrooms, all en suite, £53.50 (family room £80, single £38.50).
Children welcome overnight (£7.50 if sharing parents' room), additional bed & cot available.
Check-in by arrangement. Closed 25 Dec. MasterCard,* **VISA**

BIDDENDEN   Three Chimneys   FOOD

Tel 01580 291472   Map 11 C5
Biddenden Ashford Kent TN27 8HA

The Three Chimneys has every natural advantage of being a classic country pub, its
original, small roomed layout and old-fashioned furnishings remain delightfully intact.
Old settles, low beams, wood panelled walls, flagstone floors, warming open fires,
evening candlelight, absence of music and electronic games – glorious. Then there's
the range of more than decent home-cooked bar food listed on the daily-changing
blackboard. A typical menu may feature seafood chowder, spinach and ham mousse
and Stilton and pear tartlet for starters, followed by smoked fish lasagne, Kentish lamb
pie, and rabbit in cream and mustard sauce. Basic bread and cheese – mature farmhouse cheddar or Stilton – comes with chunks of fresh granary bread and home-made
chutney or pickled onions. Daily choice of four puddings – gooseberry and almond
tart, nutty treacle tart, ginger pudding – served with fresh Jersey cream. Good ales
tapped direct from the casks behind the bar and a heady farm cider from Biddenden.
The Garden Room is suitable for families and the shrub-filled garden is lovely for
summer eating. Don't, incidentally, look for the three chimneys on the roof – the
name comes from the pub's location at the meeting of three lanes, or Trois Chemins –

1 mile west of Biddenden on the A262 – as it was called by French prisoners of war kept near here in another century. *Open 11-2.30, 6-11 (Sun 12-2.30, 7-10.30). Bar Food 12-2, 7-10. Free House. Beer Fremlins, Adnams Best, Brakspear Best, Marston's Pedigree, Morland Old Speckled Hen, Wadworth 6X, Harvey's Best (& Old Ale in winter). Garden, outdoor eating. Family room. Closed 25 & 26 Dec. No credit cards.*

BIRCH VALE	Sycamore Inn	B&B

Tel 01663 742715   Fax 01663 747382   Map 6 C2
Sycamore Road Birch Vale Hayfield Derbyshire DE55 6FG

☺

Surrounded by woods of sycamore and silver birch, this quietly located pub at the fringe of the village (turn off the A6015 at Station Road) is built precariously into the side of a steep hill. In ten acres of grounds, the paddock slopes steeply down to the River Sett (although you can't see it), while beyond the lower car park there are a barbecue terrace, dovecotes, mini-aviary and a children's Tarzan trail playground. There are bars at two levels, the lower with regular entertainment and a clubby atmosphere while that above is given over largely to eating in neatly partitioned dining areas which include non-smoking and family rooms. With one exception, bedrooms look out across the valley; they're neatly appointed with whitewood furniture and patchwork quilts; all have en suite facilities (four with baths), satellite TVs, radios, beverage trays and trouser presses. For those with other pressing business, the only telephone provided is on the upper landing. New chalet-style family B&B accommodation is being built in the grounds; two will come on line at the end of 1996. Children welcome indoors. *Open 11-11 (Sun 12-10.30). Beer John Smith's, Marston's Pedigree, Sycamore Bitter, guest beer. Garden. Accommodation 6 bedrooms, ll en suite, £45 (family room sleeping four, £55, single £29.50, weekend reductions). Children welcome overnight, additional bed (£10) & cot supplied. MasterCard, **VISA***

BIRCH VALE	Waltzing Weasel	FOOD

Tel & Fax 01663 743402   Map 6 C2   **B&B**
New Mills Road Birch Vale Hayfield Derbyshire SK12 5BT

🍷 Zzz...

Lynda and Michael Atkinson's stone-built roadside inn is set below Kinder Scout, the highest of the Derbyshire peaks. The pubby bar is decorated with antiques and sporting prints; roaring fires are cheerful in winter – a relaxing setting in which to enjoy chef George Benham's good bar food like soup, marinated anchovies or crayfish tails; more substantial dishes might include steak and kidney pie, seafood tart, grilled lemon sole or perhaps chicken curry. Save room for treacle tart or bread-and-butter pudding. The eight bedrooms are all tastefully decorated with quality reproduction antique furniture, pretty bedspreads and matching curtains; their modern en suite bathrooms have brass fittings. One bedroom has a fine half-tester bed; one single room has a shower (not bath); lovely views. An excellent breakfast is cooked to order in the morning – a perfect precursor to a brisk walk or a day's fishing in the beautiful local countryside. There is a more expensive à la carte restaurant but it is not specifically recommended here. *Open 12-3, 5.30-11 (Sun to 10.30). Bar Food 12-2, 7-9.30 (Sun till 9). Free House. Beer Marston's Best & Pedigree. Accommodation 8 bedrooms, all en suite, £78-£95 (+ one double at £65, single £45-£75); 25% reduction for 2+ nights. Children welcome overnight, additional bed supplied (£12). Garden. Amex, MasterCard, **VISA***

BIRCHOVER	Druid Inn	FOOD

Tel 01629 650302   Fax 01629 650599   Map 6 C2
Main Street Birchover Derbyshire DE4 2BL

Climb the long hill from the B5056 signposted Stanton Moor Stone Circle, and be sure not to miss a glimpse of Rowtor, high above the pub, where extraordinary fissures and passageways through the rock suggest very early occupation by man; hence the inn's unusual name. From portal to chimney pot, the pub's entirely ivy-covered, with a terrace in front, and to one side, a partly no-smoking restaurant area on two floors, connected by a tiled passageway. Very much a dining pub whose menu fills four blackboards, including a vegetarian selection (lentil, carrot and hazelnut rissoles). A starter might be New Zealand mussels in garlic cream sauce followed by a main course like salmon baked with sweet and hot spices or cod, prawn and mushroom bake, and perhaps finish with a Bakewell pudding for dessert, all partnered by an above-average range of good-value wines by glass or bottle. Booking advisable for weekends and evenings. Outside, the terrace overlooks fields. *Open 12-2.30 (till 3 Sat), 7-11 (Sun 12-3, 7-10.30).* **Bar Food** *12-2, 7-9 (till 9.30 Sat & 9 in winter). Free House.* **Beer** *Mansfield Bitter, Morland Old Speckled Hen, Adnams Bitter, Ashbourne Belt & Braces, guest beer. Patio/terrace. Amex, Diners, MasterCard,* **VISA**

BIRDLIP   Air Balloon   A

Tel & Fax 01452 862541   Map 14 B2
Crickley Hill Birdlip Gloucester Gloucestershire GL4 6JY

A prominent 17th-century inn adjacent to the A417/A436 junction, equidistant from Gloucester and Cheltenham, amusingly named to commemorate the exploits of a local balloonist. He took off from the top of nearby Crickley Hill on a maiden flight in 1802 and promptly vanished into thin air (or so the story goes). Today's tale is of a busy Whitbread Wayside Inn which packs in the families year-round. In winter there are large log fires; on summer days hill-top gardens set out with play equipment and a bouncy castle. There are also picnic tables on the sheltered rear patio under a permanent awning. *Open 11-11 (Sun 12-10.30).* **Beer** *Wadworth 6X, Flowers Original, Boddingtons, Whitbread Castle Eden Ale. MasterCard,* **VISA**

BLACKAWTON   Normandy Arms   B&B

Tel 01803 712316   Map 13 D3
Chapel Street Blackawton Dartmouth Devon TQ9 7BN

Homely, 15th-century village inn with a welcoming atmosphere. Rustic pub furniture and various displays and memorabilia on the Normandy Landings theme adorn the much-modernised bars. Upstairs, comfortable accommodation is provided in five delightfully cottagey bedrooms, all with modern pine furniture, matching fabrics and spotlessly clean en suite facilities with baths. TVs and beverage-making facilities are standard and hot-water bottles are thoughtfully provided for cooler nights. Front rooms enjoy good rural views. *Open 11-3, 6.30-11 (12-2, 7-11 winter), Sun 12-3, 7-10.30.* **Beer** *Blackawton Bitter, Bass, guest beers. Garden, outdoor eating.* **Accommodation** *5 bedrooms, all en suite, £48 (family room sleeping three £58, single £30). Children welcome overnight (under-2s stay free in parents' room), cot available (£5). Check-in by arrangement. Closed all 25 Dec. MasterCard,* **VISA**

BLACKBOYS   Blackboys Inn   FOOD

Tel 01825 890283   Map 11 B6
Blackboys Uckfield East Sussex TN22 5LG

Splendid black-weatherboarded pub dating from 1389 and enjoying an attractive position set back from the B2192 west of Heathfield, overlooking an iris- and lily-covered pond. The delightfully old-fashioned interior has a series of interconnecting rooms featuring various pieces of antique furniture, interesting bric-a-brac and sought-after alcove window seats with views over the pond. Separate traditional public bar with bare boards, wooden furnishings, old juke box and pub games. A reliable range of bar food is listed on an extensive blackboard menu above the bar and may include a large bowl of home-made vegetable soup, grilled sardines and baked crab mornay for starters. Main-course choices range from steak and kidney pie and braised oxtail to rack of lamb, fresh lobster and calf's liver sautéed in butter. For dessert try the bread-and-butter pudding, crème brulée or treacle tart and custard. Ploughman's lunches, filled jacket potatoes and salads for those wanting a lighter bite. Good alfresco seating beside the pond and the front green beneath the horse chestnut trees. *Open 11-3, 6-11 (Sun 12-3, 7-10.30).* **Bar Food** *12-2.30, 6.30-10 (Sun 7-10).* **Beer** *Harveys. Garden, terrace, outdoor eating, children's play area. Family room. MasterCard,* **VISA**

BLACKBROOK — The Plough — FOOD

Tel 01306 886603   Map 15a F4
Blackbrook Road Blackbrook Dorking Surrey RH5 4DS

Popular, isolated rural inn located on a country lane south of Dorking, parallel with the A24. Two spacious, comfortable and warmly welcoming bars (with pleasant views through large windows) boasting a vast collection of over 500 ties and numerous old saws and farm tools. Well-stocked bar offering the full complement of King and Barnes ales, as well as 14 wines and seven vintage ports served by the glass. Choose one to accompany a reliable pub meal, especially a dish listed on the regularly-changing blackboard menu such as a Stilton, onion and chestnut soup, beef, lime and coconut curry, spiced lamb hotpot with dumplings, and whole lemon sole with prawn, crab, cucumber and dill sauce. The printed menu is more routine, with regular pub favourites. Treacle tart and hot carrot pudding may feature on the pudding list. Sheltered rear garden with chalet-style children's play house. No children under 14 inside. *Open 11-2.30 (till 3 Sat), 6-11 (may close 10.30 in winter), Sun 12-3, 7-10.30.* **Bar Food** *12-2, 7-9.30 (no food Mon eve).* **Beer** *King & Barnes. Garden, children's play area. Closed 25, 26 Dec & 1 Jan. No credit cards.*

BLACKO — Moorcock Inn — FOOD

Tel 01282 614186   Map 6 B1
Gisburn Road Blacko Nelson Lancashire BB9 6NF

Standing on its own alongside the A682 north of Blacko, the whitewashed Moorcock Inn is situated in wonderful rolling countryside near Pendle Hill and the Forest of Bowland. Inside is unassuming and unpretentious. Two adjoining rooms and the adjacent dining-room have plain painted walls, simple prints, brass plates and a collection of china plates; stone fireplaces are topped with ornaments and brassware. All the tables are laid for dining and large picture windows offer lovely views over the surrounding landscape. Licensee Elizabeth Holt has built up an enviable reputation for good fresh food, and custom comes from far and wide, especially for Sunday lunch. The short printed bar menu, offering favourites like soup, sandwiches and lasagne, is backed up by a daily-changing blackboard of specials (now the mainstay), where dishes could include pork fillet in peach and brandy sauce, Dalesman pie, sweet and sour chicken, and haddock and smoked salmon mornay. Home-made, old-fashioned puddings to finish. The cooking is perfectly competent, prices realistic, portions generous and the service both friendly and quick. The Moorcock is a useful resting place after a bracing morning on the moors – the Pendle Walk almost passes the door – and in sunny weather the garden is lovely. Homely B&B in three upstairs bedrooms which are due to have en suite facilities in 1997. *Open 12-2.30, 6.30-11. (Sun 12-10.30).* **Bar Food** *12-2, 7-10 (Sun 12-10).* **Beer** *Thwaites. Garden. Closed 25 Dec. MasterCard,* **VISA**

BLAKESLEY — Bartholomew Arms — B&B

Tel 01327 860292   Fax 01327 860965   Map 15 D1
High Street Blakesley Northamptonshire NN12 8RE

Charming, welcoming 17th-century inn with a collection of model ships and nautical artefacts in the public bar, plus guns and cricket memorabilia in the lounge. Simple, well-kept bedrooms at very reasonable prices. Pleasant garden with summer house. Particularly good choice of malt whiskies. *Open 11-3, 6.30-11 (Sun 12-3, 7-10.30). Free House.* **Beer** *Marston's Pedigree, Tetley. Garden.* **Accommodation** *4 bedrooms, 1 en suite (shower), £30-£34 (single £16). Children welcome overnight (under-5s stay free in parents' room, 5-10s £5.50), additional bed & cot available. No credit cards.*

We only recommend food (Bar Food) in those establishments highlighted with the **FOOD** symbol.

BLANCHLAND Lord Crewe Arms FOOD

Tel 01434 675251   Fax 01434 675337   Map 5 D2   **B&B**
Blanchland Consett Durham DH8 9SP

Zzz...

Wild and remote, Blanchland lies some 3 miles below Derwent Water in a deep valley. Blanchland Abbey can trace its origins back to 1165 – despite dissolution in 1576 the layout of its surrounding village remains unchanged to this day. At its heart is one of England's finest inns, containing relics of the abbey lodge and kitchens and set in a cloister garden which is now an ancient monument. Lord Crewe purchased the entire estate in 1704 from one Tom Foster, a Jacobite adventurer; the ghost of his sister Dorothy is claimed still to be in residence. A sense of history pervades the building's remarkably modernised yet largely unchanged interior, no more so than in the Crypt bar. The meals served here are substantial: German pork sausage with sauerkraut and warm potato salad and wild boar and pheasant pie with salad do not constitute the average pub lunch. Evening options of baked salmon, minute steak or cheese-filled pasta are rather more traditional. Ploughman's and filled brown rolls are lunchtime alternatives, while Sunday lunch features a hot and cold buffet. A three-course Sunday lunch is also served in the stylish first-floor restaurant overlooking the garden. Bedrooms, needless to say, are splendidly individual; suitably traditional in the old house with stone mullion windows and restored fireplaces and mantels, yet up-to-date with accessories from colour TVs to bespoke toiletries and thoughtful extras from mending kits to complimentary sherry. Altogether more contemporary are the style and furnishings of rooms in the adjacent Angel Inn – once a Wesleyan Temperance House – a mere newcomer dating from the 1750s. *Open 11-3, 6-11 (Sun 12-3, 7-10.30).* **Bar Food** *12-2, 7-9. Free House.* **Beer** *Vaux Samson. Garden.* **Accommodation** *20 bedrooms all en suite from £105 (single from £75). Children welcome overnight (under-14s stay free if sharing parents' room). Amex, Diners, MasterCard,* **VISA**

BLANDFORD FORUM Crown Hotel B&B

Tel 01258 456626   Fax 01258 451084   Map 14 B4
Blandford Forum Dorset DT11 7AJ

This fine Georgian coaching house has a civilised, old-fashioned air and is busy in typical market-town style. Bars, lounges and reception area are more hotelly than pubby in atmosphere, all being heavily wood-panelled and furnished with comfortable deep leather chairs and settees, especially in the traditional lounges. Rambling corridors lead to 32 well-maintained bedrooms. Uniformly decorated in pale green, they all boast clean, fresh bathrooms, light modern furniture and are well equipped with satellite TV, telephones, radio alarms and beverage-making facilities. There is an attractive and secluded Victorian walled garden for residents' use and guests are welcome to fish – in season – on the banks of the River Stour, which flows through the hotel grounds. Badger Inns. *Open 10-2.30, 6-11 (Sun 7-10.30).* **Beer** *Hall & Woodhouse. Garden.* **Accommodation** *32 bedrooms, all en suite, £74 (4-poster £75, family room £90, single £58). Children welcome overnight (under-5s stay free in parents' room), additional bed (£10) & cot available. Accommodation closed 25-27 Dec. Amex, Diners, MasterCard,* **VISA**

BLEDINGTON Kings Head Inn ★ FOOD

Tel 01608 658365   Fax 01608 658902   Map 14a A1   **B&B**
The Green Bledington Kingham Oxfordshire OX7 6HD

   **Zzz...**

A more delightful spot would surely be hard to find: facing the village green with its brook and border-patrolling ducks, this is surely the quintessential Cotswold pub. Dating back to the 15th century, it stands on the Gloucester border with its easterly wall resident in Oxfordshire. Inside, the low-ceilinged bar is full of ancient settles and simple wooden furniture and there's a separate lounge and dining-room – all equally agreeable settings in which to enjoy the Royces' imaginative pub food. Lunchtime 'bar fayre' offers a wide range, from unusual sandwiches (vodka-soused red mullet with mayonnaise, cucumber and tarragon) to basil and mozzarella pancake, steak, mushroom and wine pie, a wide range of salads in summer (perhaps feta and olives or black pudding and walnuts), bowls of pasta with shredded beef and horseradish, and interesting weekly-changing specials like artichoke, asparagus and feta pithiviers on tomato coulis and salmon, scallop and prawn pie. These might be supplemented in winter by the likes of jugged hare, local rabbit and venison. An à la carte evening menu sees plenty of variety without undue elaboration among the deftly-sauced main courses; the ever-popular half honey-roasted duck may come with a green peppercorn sauce and apple purée. Sweets like toffee and walnut flan and rum flavoured bread pudding are genuinely home-made. A set-price 'Snippets menu' is a monthly-changing, three-course table d'hote with alternative choices at each stage – particularly good value for residents at £9.95. Excellent overnight accommodation in twelve superbly furnished en suite bedrooms. Meticulous attention has been paid to their detail; the three ground-floor rooms in the rear extension are an added bonus for less mobile guests. The older, cottagey bedrooms (no-smoking) over the pub should not suffer by comparison (though they may be less suitable for an early night) although the floorboards may be a little creaky. Their appointments nonetheless are top class, with direct-dial phones, TVs, clock radios and an array of extras. Residents here enjoy the use of a quiet smokers' lounge and a private patio. A changing mat and facilities are available on request in the Ladies. *Open 11-2.30, 6-11 (from 5.30 Sat), Sun 12-2.30, 7-10.30.* **Bar Meals** *12-2, 7-10 (from 6.30 Fri & Sat, till 9.30 Sun).* **Beer** *Hook Norton Best, Wadworth 6X, four guest beers. Garden, outdoor eating. Family room.* **Accommodation** *12 bedrooms, all en suite, £60-£75, (single £40). Children welcome overnight, (under-5s stay free if sharing parents' room, 5-15s £10), additional bed & cot supplied (both £5). No dogs. Closed 25 Dec.* MasterCard, **VISA**

BLEDLOW   Lions of Bledlow   A

Tel 01844 343345   Map 15a D2
Church End Bledlow Buckinghamshire HP27 9PE

Tracks lead up into the Chiltern beechwoods from this unspoilt, low white-painted 16th-century former coaching inn, making it an ideal walking base. Summer visitors can imbibe in the attractive rear garden or on the edge of the village green, where benches enjoy a pleasant rural outlook. In winter, the charming, heavily-beamed and unadorned interior comes into its own. Ancient tiled floors, a huge inglenook with open fire, oak stalls with rustic tables, various brasses and copper pots and a chatty atmosphere characterise the four seating areas of this cosy, traditional country pub. *Open 11-3 (till 4 Sat), 6-11 (Sun 12-4 & 7-10.30). Free House.* **Beer** *John Smith's, Wadworth 6X, Marlow Rebellion IPA, Marston's Pedigree, Ruddles County, guest beer. Garden. Family room.* Amex, Diners, MasterCard, **VISA**

> We only recommend food (Bar Food) in those establishments highlighted
> with the **FOOD** symbol.

BLEWBURY   Blewbury Inn   FOOD

Tel 01235 850496   Fax 01235 850691   Map 14a C3   **B&B**
London Road Blewbury Didcot Oxfordshire OX11 9PD

Modest but appealing, white-painted roadside dining pub whose two rooms (one is the no-smoking restaurant) feature pine boarding to dado height and wheelback chairs. It's run by a keen young couple: Martine looks after front-of-house while chef Paul works in the kitchen. A short yet always interesting menu serves both bar and restaurant with some four or five choices at each stage; there is usually an omelette at lunch but other than that there is no traditional snacky pub food offered. It's priced à la carte to encourage snacking but with a maximum price of £22.50 if all three courses are taken. Well-executed dishes such as duck confit with plum sauce, baked goat's cheese with toasted pine kernels, new season lamb with rosemary scented chickpeas, mushroom ravioli with roast shallots (there's always a vegetarian option), and skate wing with tomato and olive sauce demonstrate Paul's modern style. Equally good puds might include a white chocolate crème brulée. The lunch menu is slightly simpler and cheaper but is in a similar vein (smoked salmon and scrambled eggs, cheese omelette, sautéed pigeon breast with celeriac purée). A plated selection of cheeses (from a selection of around ten) is also offered. Three modest bedrooms (no phone, no remote-control for the TV and no dressing table/work space) are clean and well kept, each with its own en suite shower room. *Open 12-3, 6-11 (Sun 12-3 only). Closed Sun eve & all Mon.* **Bar Meals** *12-2, 7-9 (till 9.30 Fri & Sat) Free House.* **Beer** *Hook Norton Old Hooky, Brakspear Bitter, Adnams Southwold.* **Accommodation** *3 bedrooms, all en suite, £50 (single £32). Children welcome overnight (stay free if sharing parents' room) Check-in by arrangement. MasterCard,* **VISA**

BLICKLING   Buckinghamshire Arms Hotel   B&B

Tel 01263 732133   Map 10 C1
Blickling Aylsham Norfolk NR11 6NF

Zzz... ☺

Splendid Grade I listed 17th-century inn which stands deferentially at the gates of the even more magnificent Blickling Hall. Once the estate builders' house and later the servants' quarters to the fine National Trust property, it is an excellent place to stay with two of the three bedrooms having dramatic evening views across to the flood-lit hall. Attractively decorated, each room boasts original features, with 'real' four-posters and sturdy old stripped pine and dark oak furnishings making this a most characterful and peaceful bed and breakfast stop. One room has an en suite shower room, the others share a clean, good-sized bathroom with an old fashioned tub. Downstairs, the three charming and well-furnished bars have open fires and are typically National Trust in style of decor and taste. No children overnight. Recently acquired by Humble Inns who intend revamping the accommodation and improving the food – watch this space! *Open 11-3, 6-11 (11-11 school holidays), Sun 12-3, 7-10.30. Free House.* **Beer** *Adnams Bitter & Broadside, two guest beers. Garden.* **Accommodation** *3 bedrooms, one en suite (shower), £60 (single £45). MasterCard,* **VISA**

BLOCKLEY   Crown Inn & Hotel   FOOD

Tel 01386 700245   Fax 01386 700247   Map 14a A1   ■ **B&B**
High Street Blockley Moreton-in-Marsh Gloucestershire GL56 9EX

 Zzz...

At the heart of this most picturesque of Cotswold villages the Champion family's Crown is the jewel. Whilst retaining all the charm of a 16th-century coaching inn, it has been totally restored with loving care and considerable style. At street level the inn is fronted by a split-level bar decorated in muted tones and furnished with deep-cushioned sofas and leather club chairs. Here at any time, and at pavement tables in summertime, is a splendid spot to enjoy some simply executed yet consistently tasty bar snacks, which are supplemented daily by best-available produce from the fish markets. Honey-baked ham or beef with horseradish comes in 1½-round sandwiches or baguettes; winter may see a steak, Guinness and mushroom pie giving way in summer to salad of avocado and asparagus with yoghurt and mint dressing, seafood platter and cod in beer and chive batter. In season are pristine fresh oysters, mackerel fillets with mustard vinaigrette and baked trout with prawns and mushrooms. For a treat, leave room for a good dessert like apricot and frangipane tart or strawberry pavlova. Adjacent is the Crown's brasserie which extends the range of food choices. The Crown's smartly-refurbished bedrooms have en suite bath or shower rooms, TV, radio, hairdryer and beverage facilities. Exposed timberwork and original beams, the mellow stone walls and cast-iron bedroom fireplaces add to each room's individual appeal, while even more space is to be found in the splendid four-poster rooms and suites. A relaxing residents' library is away from the bar's bustle. *Open 11-11 (11-3, 6-11 in winter), Sun 12-3, 7-10.30.* **Bar Food** *12-2, 7-10. Free House.* **Beer** *Hook Norton Best, Donnington PA, Goff's Jouster, four guest beers. Outdoor eating.* **Accommodation** *21 bedrooms, all en suite, £84-£120 (single £60). Children welcome overnight (under-12s £10 if sharing parents' room). Amex, Diners, MasterCard,* **VISA**

We do not accept free meals or hospitality – our inspectors pay their own bills and **never** book in the name of Egon Ronay's Guides.

BLYFORD — Queen's Head — FOOD

Tel 01502 478404   Map 10 D2   **B&B**
Southwold Road Blyford Suffolk IP19 9JY

Resplendent in summer when the hanging baskets are on display, when the sun brightens the cream-painted fascia, throwing shadows over the splendid thatch; cars on the B1123 between the pub and the village church opposite are the only discordant note amid the harmony of such a bucolic setting. The full range of Adnams beers (including their seasonal ales), fine home cooking from landlord Tony Matthews and upmarket accommodation (not yet inspected) – two rooms, one suite with a four-poster bed and private lounge – are the other attractions. Low oak beams, a huge log fire and traditional furnishings (old lamps, teapots and brasses) create a delightful atmosphere in which to enjoy some of the freshest, crispest fish (line-caught, 'longshore' cod from Lowestoft) and chips that you'll ever encounter; look to the blackboard menu for up to 14 daily-changing dishes like wonderful home-made game soup, roast pheasant, steak and kidney pie, dressed crab and prawn salads, traditional roasts (there's always a choice on Sundays) – all 'real' pub food, expertly cooked and generously served. No-smoking dining-room. Wooden seats to the front of the pub take in the countryside views and picnic tables in the side garden allow parents to watch their children let off steam. Inside, two 'regulars' appear to enjoy the friendly welcome. *Open 10.30-3, 6.30-11 (Sun 12-3, 7-10.30). Bar Food 11.30-2, 6.30-9 (Sun 12-2.30, 7-9). Beer Adnams. Garden, outdoor eating. Accommodation 2 bedrooms: suite £50, double w/shower £40. Children welcome overnight, additional bed provided (£2 breakfast charge). Check-in Wed pm by arrangement. Closed 2 weeks Sept/Oct. No dogs. No credit cards.*

BOLDRE — Red Lion — A

Tel 01590 673177   Map 14 C4
Boldre Lymington Hampshire SO41 8NE

Dating mainly from around 1650 and also mentioned as an alehouse in the Domesday Book, this most attractive New Forest pub has been run by the Bicknell family for over 20 years. Outside, an old cart is strewn with flowers, and hanging baskets and troughs are a riot of colour in summer. Inside, a rambling series of four black-beamed rooms have their own country style, with real fires, a mix of old furnishings, hunting prints, farm tools, man-traps, tapestries and unusual collections of old bottles and chamber pots. Delightful secluded rear flower garden. No children under 14 allowed inside. *Open 11-3, 6-11 (Sun 12-3, 6-10.30). Beer Eldridge Pope. Garden, patio, children's play area. Closed 25 Dec. MasterCard, VISA*

BOLLINGTON — Church House Inn — FOOD

Tel 01625 574014   Fax 01625 576424   Map 6 B2   **B&B**
Church Street Bollington Cheshire SK10 5PY

This quiet corner of Cheshire's largest village is where the discerning drop in for carefully-prepared lunchtime snacks and evening meals. The long menu offers filled baked potatoes and sandwiches (lunchtime only) through to chicken à la crème and steak Diane. There's an upper dining-room for evening use and private parties; to the rear, an enclosed garden for summer drinking. Daily specials complete the picture: perhaps goujons of lemon sole, fillet steak with garlic, mushrooms and cream and guinea fowl with cranberries, with bilberry pie or bread-and-butter pudding to finish. All the bedrooms (three singles, one twin and one double) are furnished in pine and have en suite bathrooms, TVs and beverage-making facilities. *Open 12-2.30 (till 3 Sat), 5.30-11 (Sun 12-3, 7-10.30). Bar Food 12-2. 6.30-9.30 (Sun 7-9). Free House. Beer Theakston Best, Boddingtons, Jennings Bitter, Marston's Pedigree, Tetley Best. Garden. Family room. Accommodation 5 bedrooms, all en suite, £45 (family room £55, single £35; weekends: £37.50 double, £45 family, £27.50 single). No dogs. MasterCard, VISA*

BOLTER END   Peacock   FOOD

Tel 01494 881417   Map 15a D3
Lane End Bolter End Buckinghamshire HP14 3LU

Bolter End is a crossroads with a few houses and the pub is located opposite the
Common. The only bar is divided into three sections and one menu applies
throughout. Main-menu items include steak and kidney pie, chicken breast stir-fried
with lime and ginger and served with saffron rice, and fish curry; daily fresh fish such
as red snapper with Mediterranean vegetables; Aberdeen Angus steaks are also popular.
Home-made puddings are the traditional kind – fruit crumbles and almond, chocolate
and wild cherry tart. No children under 14 inside. *Open 11.45-2.30, 6-11 (Sun 12-3,
7-10.30).* **Bar Food** *12-2, 7-10 (no food Sun eve).* **Beer** *Ind Coope ABC Bitter, Tetley,
Wadworth 6X, guest beer. Garden, outdoor eating. Amex, Diners, MasterCard,* **VISA**

BONCHURCH   Bonchurch Inn   A

Tel 01983 852611   Map 15 D4
The Shute Bonchurch Isle of Wight PO38 1NU

Italians Ulisse and Aline Besozzi give an invigorating Continental flavour to
Bonchurch's village 'local', which has a good nautical atmosphere. There's a family
room, a small saloon bar and the public bar, complete with old-fashioned pub games,
is cut into the rocks of the Shute; a few tables are set in a cobbled, enclosed courtyard.
Overnight accommodation (not inspected) is provided in three modest bedrooms
(£34 double) and an extra bed or cot can be provided. From the main A3055 road
(the one that goes round the whole of the south of the Island, Ryde-Freshwater), take
the turning opposite the Leconfield Hotel down to Old Bonchurch. *Open 11-3 (till
3.30 summer), 6.30-11 (Sun 12-3, 7-10.30). Free House.* **Beer** *Courage Best & Directors,
Marston's Pedigree, Morland Old Speckled Hen. Courtyard. Family room. MasterCard,* **VISA**

BOOT   Burnmoor Inn   B&B

Tel 01946 723224   Fax 01946 723337   Map 4 C3
Boot Eskdale Cumbria CA19 1TG

An attractive old pebbledash inn, parts of which date back to 1578, nestling in a tiny
hamlet, only three minutes' walk from the Eskdale railway terminus. Across the Esk
by an old stone bridge are the restored Corn Mill and bridleways to Eel Tarn and
Wasdale Head. The Fosters have run a friendly and welcoming house here for a
decade or more with a popular Austrian slant to much of Heidi's cooking. Residents
enjoy the use of a neat, secluded dining and breakfast room – many come for the
abundant peace and quiet. The bedrooms, four with bath and two with shower en
suite (the remaining two sharing a toilet and bathroom) look out down the dale, or
back up the hills towards Scafell; unencumbered by TVs or telephones, they are neat
and simply furnished. *Open 11-2.45, 4.45-11 (Sun 12-2.45, 7-10.30). Free House.
Children's play area.* **Beer** *Jennings Bitter, Cumberland Ale & Snecklifter. Garden.*
Accommodation *8 bedrooms, all en suite, £54 (single £25). Children over 2 welcome
overnight, (under-5s free if sharing parents' room), additional bed available. Check-in during bar
hours. No dogs. MasterCard,* **VISA**

BOTTLESFORD   Seven Stars   FOOD

Tel 01672 851325   Fax 01672 851583   Map 14a A4
Bottlesford Woodborough Pewsey Wiltshire SH9 6LU

Set in a charming rural location, almost lost down narrow lanes deep in the Vale of
Pewsey with views across country to the White Horse, is the splendid thatched and
creeper-clad Seven Stars. Make for Woodborough from the A345 at Pewsey (past the
hospital), or from the mini-roundabout at North Newnton. Delightful rambling
interior of beams and black oak panelling and a central brick bar with quarry tile
flooring. There's plenty of room to enjoy some masterfully produced bar food from
the ever-enthusiastic, sometimes inspired Philippe Cheminade. Moules marinière,
confit of duck and pork fillet normande attest equally to his Gallic origins as to
a broad range of skills, which also extend to fine presentation of the more traditional

venison and mushroom pie, jugged hare and lamb moussaka. Daily fish deliveries in summer from Cornwall satisfy the popular seafood platters (encompassing both lobster and winkles) and unusual dishes like Merlin steak with garlic and tomato sauce and pan-fried blue shark; both sandwiches and ploughman's lunches are also available. Two self-contained rooms at either end of the building double up for evening dining à la carte. The pub also boasts splendid gardens and grounds; a nine-acre tranche of land borders a shallow stream which winds down to the River Kennet; there are picnic tables here and hampers can be organised by arrangement. *Open 11.30-3, 6-11 (Sun 12-3, 7-10.30). Closed Sun eve Oct-Easter.* **Bar Food** *12-2, 7-9.30 (no food Sun eve & all Mon Oct-Easter). Free House.* **Beer** *Bunces Pigswill, Wadworth 6X, two guest beers. Garden, outdoor eating. children's play area, Family room. MasterCard,* ***VISA***

BOUGHTON ALUPH   Flying Horse Inn   FOOD

Tel 01233 620914   Fax 01233 661010   Map 11 C5   **B&B**
Boughton Aluph Ashford Kent TN25 4HH

Handily placed for Le Shuttle travellers (6 miles away), this 15th-century vine- and wisteria-clad inn occupies a charming spot overlooking the village green/cricket pitch, just off the A251 north of Ashford. Plenty of alfresco seating; ideal for lazy summer evenings watching the cricket. Single, beamed front bar with open log fire and adorned with hopbines and a collection of old ties. Small neat rear dining-room where promising, daily-changing blackboard specials can be enjoyed. Beyond a straightforward snack menu choices may include liver and bacon casserole, poached pork chops cooked in cider, seafood tagliatelle, steak and kidney pie and a few fresh fish dishes, all accompanied by a selection of a least nine vegetables. Four neat and homely upstairs bedrooms have views across the green and surrounding countryside through unusual arched Gothic windows. Two have shower cubicles, all have washbasins and share two clean and spacious bathrooms. TVs and tea-makers are standard. No children under 14 inside or overnight. *Open Mon & Tue 11-3, 6-11, Wed-Sat 11-11 (11-3, 6-11 Mon-Fri winter), Sun 12-10.30.* **Bar Food** *12-2.15, 6.30-9.30 (from 7 Sun).* **Beer** *Wadworth 6X, Courage Best, Marston's Pedigree, Morland Old Speckled Hen, John Smith's, guest beer. Garden, outdoor eating.* **Accommodation** *4 bedrooms, 2 en suite (shower), £40 (single £25). Check-in by arrangement. Accommodation closed all 24 & 25 Dec, pub closed 25 Dec eve. Amex, MasterCard,* ***VISA***

BOWDEN HILL   Rising Sun   A

Tel 01249 730363   Map 14 B2
32 Bowden Hill Lacock Wiltshire SN15 2PP

It's the location and the friendly, chatty atmosphere that draw people to this tiny honey-coloured stone pub, set high on the hill above historic Lacock. The single rustic bar and adjoining room have a mix of old chairs, pine settles and kitchen tables laid out on flagstoned floors. A few old prints adorn the walls and in winter a good log fire warms the bar. The pub is belongs to Roger Catté, owner of Mole's Brewery, so expect the full range of Mole's ales, all kept in tip-top condition. On sunny, clear days space is at a premium on the two-level, flower tub- and bench-filled terrace, from where an unrivalled view of some 25 miles across the Avon Valley can be appreciated. On still summer evenings hot-air balloons can often be seen drifting across the sky. Children welcome. *Open 11-3, 6-11 (Sun 12-3, 7-10.30). Free House.* **Beer** *Mole's Ales: Tap Bitter, Best Bitter, Landlord's Choice & Brew 97, occasional guest beer. Garden, children's play area. Closed 25 Dec. No credit cards.*

We endeavour to be as up-to-date as possible but inevitably some changes to landlords, chefs and other key staff occur after the Guide has gone to press.

BOWLAND BRIDGE   Hare & Hounds   B&B

Tel 01539 568333   Map 4 C4
Bowland Bridge Grange-over-Sands Cumbria LA11 6NN

Zzz... ☺

Truly rural, good-looking old inn owned by ex-international soccer player Peter Thompson and his wife Debbie. The bar successfully blends ancient and modern, with its rough stone walls, discreet farming bric-a-brac and simple wooden furniture; open fires spread warmth in winter weather. The dramatically high-ceilinged dining-room is for residents only; the residents' lounge is rather more chintzy. Bedrooms are immaculately kept, beamy, floral, and on the small side. Delightful garden. *Open 11-11 (till 10.30 Sun). Free House.* **Beer** *Tetley. Garden, children's play area.* **Accommodation** *16 bedrooms, 13 en suite (showers), £48 (single £34). Children welcome overnight (under-2s stay free in parents' room, 3-5s £5, over-5s £10), additional bed & cot available. MasterCard,* **VISA**

We only recommend food (Bar Food) in those establishments highlighted with the **FOOD** symbol.

BOX   Bayly's   FOOD

Tel 01225 743622   Map 14 B2   **B&B**
High Street Box Corsham Wiltshire SN14 9NA

A busy and lively, solid-looking Bath stone inn, standing four-square on the A4 Bath to Chippenham road. It is named after the pub's first landlord in the early 1600s, Jacob Bayly, whose last will and testament hangs to this day behind the bar. Most noteworthy of its many period features is a magnificent open stone fireplace, and the circular pool table is quite a talking point. As we went to press the pub's opening hours were limited to evenings only Mon-Sat. The bar food menu was also greatly reduced. For peace and quiet, and for weary travellers, Bayly's offers three bedrooms, all with neat en suite WCs and showers, colour TV and beverage trays. *Open 7-11 (Sun 12-2.30, 7-10.30).* **Bar Food** *7-9. Free House.* **Beer** *Wadworth 6X, Bass, guest beer.* **Accommodation** *3 bedrooms, all en suite (shower), £48 (single £28-£30). Children welcome overnight (under-5s free if sharing parents' room, 5-10s £10), additional bed & cot available. Small dogs only. No credit cards.*

We do not accept free meals or hospitality – our inspectors pay their own bills and never book in the name of Egon Ronay's Guides.

BRADLEY GREEN   Malt Shovel Inn   B&B

Tel 01278 653432   Map 13 E1
Blackmoor Lane Bradley Green Cannington Somerset TA5 2NE

Located beside a tiny lane just outside Cannington, this rambling 300-year-old pub enjoys a peaceful rural position surrounded by open farmland. Traditional homely interior with settles and sturdy elm tables and chairs in the main bar and a cosy snug bar with quarry-tiled floor. Two upstairs bedrooms (one en suite) are clean and comfortable – one being a spacious family room – with modern furnishings, TVs, tea-makers and views across fields to the Quantock Hills, their proximity making this a useful base from which to explore. *Open 11.30-2.30 (till 3 Fri & Sat), 6.30-11 (from 7 winter), Sun 12-3, 7-10.30. Free House.* **Beer** *Butcombe Bitter, John Smith's Bitter, Morland Old Speckled Hen, guest beer. Garden. Family room.* **Accommodation** *2 bedrooms, 1 en suite (bath), £38 (family room sleeping four £46, sleeping three £39.50, single £21.50). Children welcome overnight (under-3s stay free in parents' room,). Closed 25 Dec. No credit cards.*

BRAMDEAN   Fox Inn   FOOD

Tel 01962 771363   Map 15 D3
Bramdean Alresford Hampshire SO24 0LP

Attractive and comfortably modernised 400-year-old white weatherboarded pub set
back from the main road (A272) in the village centre. Good lunchtime bar food is
simple with such dishes as steak and kidney pie, pan-fried lamb's liver with bacon, and
whole grilled plaice, as well as a range of sandwiches and ploughman's lunches. The
evening blackboard menu attracts a discerning clientele as the selection is more
imaginative and restauranty (with prices to match), offering excellent fillet steaks
accompanied by a choice of sauces, breast of guinea fowl Normandy and fresh fish
from Portsmouth (monkfish with tarragon and cream, grilled Dover sole), all
accompanied by dish of well-cooked vegetables; for dessert, home-made puddings like
pavlova, crème brulée and treacle tart are worth leaving room for. Popular Sunday
lunch. No children under 14 inside, but there's a large garden at the rear. *Open 10.30-
3, 6-11 (Sun 12-3, 7-10.30). **Bar Food** 12-2, 7-9. **Beer** Marston's. Garden, outdoor
eating, children's play area. Closed all 25 & 26 Dec. Amex, MasterCard,* **VISA**

BRANSCOMBE   Masons Arms   FOOD

Tel 01297 680300   Fax 01297 680500   Map 13 E2   **B&B**
Branscombe Seaton Devon EX12 3DJ

Picturesque Branscombe lies in a steep valley, deep in National Trust land and only a
ten-minute walk from the sea. Occupying most of the village centre is this delightful
14th-century, creeper-clad inn and its neighbouring terraces of cottages, which house
most of the comfortable bedrooms. Beyond the pretty front terrace is a most charming
bar with stone walls and floors, an assortment of old settles and a huge inglenook with
open fire, which not only warms the bar but also cooks the beef or lamb spit-roasts
that appear on the evening menu. Reliable bar food from the extensive regular menu
includes various sandwiches and ploughman's lunches (lunchtime only), New Orleans
stewed pork, salmon parcels, jambalaya and baked marinated rack of lamb. Daily
dishes are listed on a blackboard and features good fish (grilled lemon sole and plaice),
beautifully fresh crab caught off Branscombe beach that morning, as well as turkey and
ham pie, beef bourguignon and home-made chili. On Sundays there's also a roast for
lunch. Attractive and tastefully-decorated restaurant (dinner only) with an old-world
ambience. Exposed beams and the odd piece of antique furniture add to the charm of
attractive bedrooms in the inn and old cottages opposite the pub; TVs, phones and
clock/radios are standard throughout. Conference/function room. Two miles off
A3052, between Sidmouth and Colyford. *Open 11-3, 6-11 (Sat 11-11 winter, Mon-Sat
11-11 summer, Sun 12-10.30). **Bar Food** 12-2, 7-9.30. Free House. **Beer** Bass, Otter
Bitter, three guest beers. Terrace, outdoor eating. **Accommodation** 21 bedrooms, 19 en suite,
£74 (hotel), £54-£64 (cottages), £80 (The Linny), single from £22. Children welcome
overnight (2-10s £10), additional bed & cot available. Dogs welcome (£3 + food per night).
MasterCard,* **VISA**

BRASSINGTON   Ye Olde Gate   A

Tel 01629 540448   Map 6 C3
Well Street Brassington Derbyshire DE4 4HJ

Revered by generations of pub-goers for its resolute resistance to change, two tiny
rooms with a convivial atmosphere (accentuated by communal-sized tables) are hung
everywhere with pewter tankards, copper pans and Toby jugs; big log fires in winter.
They'll sell you a filled baguette – a 'hero' or a 'submarine' – to keep hunger at bay.
No under-10s indoors. Ramshackle ("rustic and in keeping with the pub's general
style" might be a kinder description, says the landlord) rear garden. *Open 12-2.30
(till 3 Sat), 6-11 (Sun 12-3, 7-10.30). Closed Mon lunch (except Bank Holidays).
Beer Marston's. Garden. No credit cards.*

BRAUNSTON	**Blue Ball Inn**	FOOD

Tel 01572 722135   Fax 01572 724167   Map 7 E4
6 Cedar Street Braunston Oakham Leicestershire LE15 8QS

The Blue Ball of its title represents previous obfuscation of the inn sign of the 'Globe' pub, which has stood in braunston since the early 1600s – surely one of the county's oldest pubs. Thatched and quaint with a well refurbished interior boasting a wealth of old beams and timbers, exposed inglenook fireplaces, a rustic mix of candle-topped tables and a civilised dining ambience. Although recently purchased by the Old English Pub Company, the Blue Ball continues to be run by the same French staff and, more importantly, the same chef. Throughout the bar areas a good snack menu (fishcake with chutneys, spare ribs with barbecue sauce, salads) is supplemented by a daily-changing blackboard proclaiming, perhaps, chicken liver parfait with orange and shallot confit, rack of lamb with wild rice, thyme and honey jus, poached monkfish with spinach and lobster sauce, and pork fillet served with tagliatelle and Dijon mustard sauce. Finish off with raspberry bavarois or dark chocolate mousse. At least ten wines served by the glass. *Open 11-3, 6-11, (Sun 12-10.30).* **Bar Food** *12-2 (till 3 Sun), 7-10 (till 9.30 Sun). Free House.* **Beer** *Bass, Marston's Pedigree, Greene King Abbot Ale, Ruddles County, Tetley, guest beer. Amex, MasterCard,* **VISA**

BRAUNSTON	**Old Plough**	FOOD

Tel 01572 722714   Fax 01572 770382   Map 7 E4
Church Street Braunston Leicestershire LE15 8QY

Well-regarded local innkeepers Amanda and Andrew Reid have brought a wealth of experience also to their tastefully modernised inn on the fringe of the village. Healthy eating options and vegetarian alternatives (cauliflower and chickpea curry) are well interspersed throughout an extensive menu encompassing 'famous Plough crusties' (large home-baked granary filled rolls) through pasta meals (seafood tagliatelle) and steaks to chef Nick Quinn's specials. Pork ribs with barbecue sauce, liver and bacon, sage chicken, and beef and mushroom pie might arrive with chef's potatoes of the day and crisp, fresh vegetables. There is a separate ice cream menu but better options might be lemon and cream cheese roulade and sticky toffee pudding. With light lunches on the terrace and candle-lit dining in the picturesque conservatory a sense of occasion is easily engendered. Children are allowed in the bar to eat at lunchtime only. *Open 11-3.30, 6-11 (Sun 12-3.30, 7-10.30).* **Bar Food** *12-2, 7-10 (till 9.30 Sun). Free House.* **Beer** *Theakston XB, Oakham JHB, Ten Fifty & Triple B, Ruddles Best, guest beer. Garden, outdoor eating. Family room. Amex, Diners, MasterCard,* **VISA**

BRAY-ON-THAMES	**The fish at Bray**	FOOD

Tel 01628 781111   Fax 01628 23571   Map 15a E3
Old Mill Lane Bray-on-Thames Berkshire SL6 2BP

Chef-proprietor Jean Thaxter moved to Berkshire's gastronomic epicentre last May, transforming the former Albion pub into the very model of a modern pub/restaurant, majoring on food and generally in things fishy (delivered direct from Newlyn in Cornwall). You might find baked green-lipped mussels with herbs and garlic, scallops with black pasta and a saffron sauce, roast saddle of hake with confit of onions and fennel, a smoked fish platter with grain mustard cream and 'red caviare' and even lobster. A few meat (brochette of pork, bacon and prunes with sauce dijonnaise, chargrilled spring lamb steak with redcurrant glaze and broad bean mash) and pasta (garganelle with porcini mushrooms and cream) dishes, salads (warm chicken, bacon and avocado) and good puds (sticky toffee pudding, chocoholic brandy pot, interesting home-made ice creams) complete the picture. Coffee is served in cafetières. One of the three open-plan rooms is a nicely airy, no-smoking conservatory, another a homely setting with parquet floor, dresser, fireplace and rug. A delightful, friendly pub/restaurant with real ales and picnic tables in the small garden. Well-behaved children welcome. *Open 11-3, 6-11 (Sun 12-3 only).* **Bar Food** *12-2.30, 7-9.30 (Sun 12-2.30 only). Free House.* **Beer** *Flowers IPA, Brakspear Bitter. garden, outdoor eating. Closed Sun eve & 25 Dec. MasterCard,* **VISA**

BRENDON — Stag Hunters Hotel — FOOD

Tel 01598 741222   Fax 01598 741352   Map 13 D1   **B&B**
Brendon Lynton Devon EX35 1PS

Nestling beside the East Lyn River deep in the Doone Valley, this friendly, family-run hotel makes a good base for guests wishing to explore Exmoor. Adequate overnight accommodation is in fifteen neatly-kept rooms (most with en suite facilities) kitted out with varying styles of furniture plus TVs and tea-makers. Comfortable residents' lounge. Homely, simply-furnished bars offer a short menu of home-cooked fare, such as steak and kidney pie and reliable snacks like ploughman's lunches and filled French sticks. Look to the blackboard for good specials, espcially game in season. Choices may range from grilled sardines and seafood filo roulade to rabbit cooked with apples and cider, home-made faggots with tagliatelle, and venison in red wine. Popular riverside garden. *Open 11-11 (11-3, 5-11 Nov-Easter), Sun 12-3, 7-10.30.*
Bar Food 12-9.30pm (12-2.30, 6-9.30 Nov-Easter). Free House. Beer St Austell Hicks Special, Staghunter Bitter, Wadworth 6X, guest beer. Riverside garden, outdoor eating.
Accommodation 15 bedrooms, 11 en suite, £58 (single £39). Children welcome overnight (stay free in parents' room), additional bed & cot available. Amex, Diners, MasterCard, VISA

BRERETON GREEN — Bears Head Hotel — FOOD

Tel 01477 535251   Fax 01477 535888   Map 6 B2   **B&B**
Brereton Green Sandbach Cheshire CW11 9RS

🍷

Fronted by the original half-timbered inn (which dates from 1615, if not earlier), this celebrated roadhouse alongside the A50 has expanded into a collection of buildings. Panels of wattle and daub, carefully preserved and displayed in the bar, are evidence of the building's longevity and, despite the many more recent extensions, its inglenook fireplaces and oak beams hung with horse brasses still have lots of old-fashioned charm. Today's pub, run by the Tarquini family for over 30 years, is divided into cosy alcoves by means of cleverly placed original timbers and panels, and is full of the fragrance of ubiquitous fresh flowers. Lunchtime and evening bar food is both stylish and substantial, ranging from open steak sandwiches to satisfying hot dishes like grilled fillet of plaice Caprice, home-made steak and kidney pie and lasagne; daily specialities typically feature medallions of lamb in black bean sauce, a traditional roast or cold poached salmon with salad. By night the restaurant evokes the stuff of dinner dates and anniversaries tinged with more than a hint of déjà-vu. Mammoth desserts arrive by trolley, the choice including home-made Italian ice cream. And so to bed, where practical considerations for the business traveller generally take precedence over romance, with formica-topped, dual-purpose dressing tables and work spaces, television, radio, dial-out phones, hot beverage facilities and trouser presses.
Open 12-3, 6-11 (Sun 12-3, 7-10.30). Bar Food 12-2, 6.30-10 (Sun 7-9.30). Free House. Beer Bass, Burtonwood Best, Courage Directors, guest beer. Patio/terrace, outdoor eating. summer barbecues. Accommodation 24 bedrooms, all en suite (4 with bath), £65.50 (suite £74, single £42; 20% tariff reduction at weekends). Children welcome overnight, additional bed (£10) available. No dogs. Amex, MasterCard, VISA

BRETFORTON — Fleece Inn — A

Tel 01386 831173   Map 14a A1
The Cross Bretforton Evesham Hereford & Worcester WR11 5JE

The stone, thatch and half-timbered Fleece has been owned by the National Trust since 1977, bequeathed by retiring landlady Lola Taplin on strict condition that the pub remained unaltered, and potato crisps weren't sold. It stands out today as a living, yet very lived-in, museum whose three interior rooms, the Brewhouse, the Dugout and the smoking-free Pewter Room (with unique pewter collection on an oak dresser), are now preserved for posterity. There's an array of antiquities and all the interior is original – grandfather clock, settles, rocking chair, inglenook fireplaces, beams, timbers, flagstone floors, cheese moulds et al. Children get a look in, except in the tiny bar, and are catered for superbly outside: there's a thatched heraldic barn, barbecue, extensive orchard garden and adventure playground. The wealth of hanging baskets and flower-filled stone tubs which adorn the central flagged and pebbled yard are an absolute picture in summer. It's always busy, so get there early at lunchtime to ensure a table. *Open 11-2.30, 6-11 (Sun 12-2.30, 7-10.30). Free House.* **Beer** *M&B Brew XI, Everards Beacon, Uley Old Spot & Pig's Ear, guest beers. Garden. No credit cards.*

BRIDPORT   Bull Hotel   B&B

Tel & Fax 01308 422878
34 East Street Bridport Dorset DT6 3LF   Map 13 F2

This white-painted 16th-century coaching inn stands in the historic town centre. A traditional relaxing interior includes a convivial bar and a comfortably furnished reception area and lounge. Across the pretty courtyard is a large function room and bar which attracts local bands and a good following at weekends. Rooms are light, clean and functional and decorated in soothing pastel shades and attractive fabrics; just over half have adequate en suite facilities. Modern cream-coloured units, TVs and beverage-making facilities are standard throughout. Snooker room. *Open 10-11 (Sun 12-2.30, 7-10.30).* **Beer** *Bass, Flowers Original & IPA, Teignworthy Reel. Courtyard.* **Accommodation** *22 bedrooms, 13 en suite, £39-£49 (single £24.50-£39). Children welcome overnight (under-5s stay free in parents' room, 5-16s £10), additional bed & cot available. Dogs (£5). Amex, Diners, MasterCard,* **VISA**

BRIDPORT   George Hotel   FOOD
Map 13 F2 **B&B**

Tel 01308 423187
4 South Street Bridport Dorset DT6 3NQ   Map 13 F2

Zzz...

A delightful eccentric air pervades throughout this handsome Georgian building located opposite the Town Hall, which opens its doors at 8.30am for Continental breakfast – excellent freshly-squeezed orange juice, coffee and croissants – served in the relaxing and informal main bar and tiny dining-room. Old-fashioned in style with Regency-style wallpaper, Victorian-style red painted bar and oil paintings on the walls, it is filled with soothing classical music during the day and often louder jazz and opera in the evenings. Reliable bar food is produced from the kitchen – on view – at one end of the bar. The regular menu lists excellent snacks like mushrooms on toast with garlic, Welsh rarebit with bacon, smoked haddock omelette, kidneys in Madeira and freshly-cut sandwiches. Daily specials feature fish fresh from West Bay – lemon sole stuffed with crab in a cream and vermouth sauce – and might also include soft herring roes on toast, home-made ham, chicken and mushroom pie and chargrilled steaks. Vegetables, salads and potatoes are charged separately. The full range of Palmers ales are dispensed on handpump – the brewery is only just down the road. Three modest bedrooms share a bathroom and toilet. *Open 8.30am-11pm (Sun 12-3, 7-10.30).* **Bar Food** *12-2.30, 7-9.30 (no food Sun lunch, Bank Holidays & winter eves by arrangement).* **Beer** *Palmers. Family room.* **Accommodation** *3 bedrooms, £37 (single £18.50). Children welcome overnight (under-6s stay free, in parents' room, 7-10s half-price), additional bed & cot available (charge). Accommodation closed Easter, Christmas & New Year Bank Holidays; pub closed all 25 Dec. MasterCard,* **VISA**

BRIGHTON   The Greys   FOOD

Tel 01273 680734
105 Southover Street Brighton East Sussex BN2 2UA   Map 11 B6

Climb from the Old Steine towards Kemp Town to find this gem of a dining pub with just one bar and half a dozen tables laid for lunchtime eating. Piped classical music (at lunchtimes) and enthusiasm abound. A short yet varied menu is provided by Belgian chef Jean-Paul Salpetier, and evolves daily, changing entirely every three weeks or so. Starters might include cassolette of queen scallops and tiger prawns 'Ardennes' style, Andalucian gazpacho soup and goat's cheese with tapenade croutons. Main courses are equally interesting: Thai spicy fishcakes with sweet chili dip, chicken with coconut and Thai red curry sauce, magret of duck with Belgian kriek beer and black cherries, and Iranian saffron risotto with mushrooms, sun-dried tomatoes and parmesan. Good desserts (mainly from the deep freeze) such as French lavender ice cream with honey and roasted pinenut sauce. Tuesday and Wednesday evenings are

Supper Club theme nights, providing a table d'hote menu – each month a different area of the world is featured – alongside the lunchtime carte. Visitors are entertained with live jazz, blues or Latin music Sunday lunchtimes and Monday evenings. A descriptive beer menu offers up to 13 Belgian beers, each served with their own glass. If Brewery-on-Sea's Spinnaker Buzz is the guest beer, try it – it's an unusual brew, made with honey. No children under 14. *Open 11-3, 5.30-11 (Sat 11-11, Sun 12-10.30). No food Sun lunch.* **Bar Food** *12-2, 7.30-9 (Tue & Wed only, bookings only). No food Sun lunch.* **Beer** *Flowers Original, Adnams Best, guest beers. Patio/terrace, outdoor eating. No credit cards.*

BRIGHTWELL BALDWIN   Lord Nelson   FOOD

Tel 01491 612497   Map 14a C3
Brightwell Baldwin Watlington Oxfordshire OX9 5NP

Already a couple of hundred years old when it was named after Admiral Nelson (the pub's name was changed to Lord Nelson when England's most famous sailor was elevated to the peerage). Later additions to the original stone buildings include 18th-century gable ends and a quaint verandah at the front, where it faces the parish church of this sleepy hamlet. Inside, it's immediately clear that this is a 'dining' pub; half is set up as a restaurant and raffia place mats on the remaining tables are ready to receive some of the good bar meals on offer here. Choices range from a traditional steak and kidney pie or ploughman's to spicy dishes like Thai curries, bobotie and fresh pasta with a spicy tomato sauce. The restaurant menu (also available in the bar) highlights more elaborate fare such as roast guinea fowl with lime and ginger, tiger prawns with coriander, chili and garlic, and salmon with prawns and asparagus. Home-made puddings may include tiramisu or coconut ice cream with hot chocolate sauce. There's a patio with tables for summer eating and a pretty garden overhung by a large weeping willow. Popular theme evening (seafood and chardonnay, game and claret) on the last Friday in the month. "Well-behaved" children welcome. *Open 12-3, 6.30-11 (Sun 12-3, 7-10.30).* **Bar Food** *12-2, 7-9.30 (till 9 Sun).* **Beer** *Ruddles Best Bitter, guest beer. Patio, outdoor eating. Amex, MasterCard,* **VISA**

BRIMFIELD   The Roebuck   ★   FOOD

Tel 01584 711230   Fax 01584 711654   Map 14 A1   **B&B**
Poppies Restaurant Brimfield Ludlow Shropshire SY8 4NE

Zzz...

Carole Evans's pub and restaurant has been a leading light since 1983. It's a very individual pub and worthy of an exceptional detour just to savour the superb hospitality on offer. It takes so much effort to run a quality establishment at this level that Carole's energy simply has to be admired. There is certainly no finer pub restaurant (recommended in our *1997 Hotels & Restaurants Guide*) round these parts than Poppies at the Roebuck. The public bar retains a pubby atmosphere, whereas the lounge bar – a characterful room with a 15th-century beamed ceiling and dark oak panels – could be the restaurant. It isn't – there's a separate dining-room which is a bright and cheery room with parquet floor and cane-back chairs in chintzy style, in keeping with the rest of the building. You can, however, book tables in the lounge bar, where Carole's food can be enjoyed at less than the restaurant prices. Her command of composition and subtle blends of colour and flavour are frankly bewildering. The long, exciting bar menu might encompass mushroom and herb risotto, coarse duck liver paté with melba toast, confit of duck on a bed of red cabbage with an orange sauce, monkfish with mustard dressing, whole lemon sole with limes and capers, and cider chicken pie. There's a comprehensive list of hot and cold desserts to follow: chocolate soufflé with a bitter chocolate sorbet, bread-and-butter pudding with apricot sauce, and steamed marmalade pudding with whisky-flavoured custard – leave room! Some twelve cheeses are listed on a tip-top cheese menu, from Longridge Fell (oak-smoked Lancashire cheese) to Shropshire Blue. Ploughman's lunches are served with home-made pickles; a selection of cheeses is served with home-made oat cakes and walnut and sultana bread. The excellent wine list has a large selection of half bottles. There are three lovely cottage bedrooms (two doubles with showers and a twin with full bathroom) in which to stay overnight.

Here, you'll find home-made biscuits, cake, cafetière coffee and quality teas – an example of the care you're likely to receive. A wonderful country breakfast, including Herefordshire apple juice, honey from the garden and Carole's home-made sausages, will set you up for the day and set the seal on a memorable stay. *Open 12-3, 7-11 (Sun 12-3, 7-10.30). Closed all Sun & Mon.* **Bar Food** *12-2, 7-10 (no food Sun & Mon) Free House.* **Beer** *Morland Old Speckled Hen, guest beer. Patio/terrace, outdoor eating.* **Accommodation** *3 bedrooms, all en suite, £60 (single £45). Children welcome overnight. Check-in by arrangement. Pub & accommodation closed 25 & 26 Dec. MasterCard,* **VISA**

BRINKWORTH   Three Crowns   FOOD

Tel 01666 510366   Fax 01666 510694   Map 14 C2
Brinkworth Chippenham Wiltshire SN15 5AF

Set back from the road, close to the village church and green, Anthony and Allyson Windle's old stone pub draws a discerning clientele from miles around, who seek out the unusual and often adventurous dishes that are listed on the comprehensive blackboard menu. Diners can sit in the main bar, furnished with a variety of old and new pine and featuring two remarkable tables created from huge 18th-century bellows, or they can relax in the light, airy and tastefully pine-furnished conservatory extension, which overlooks the tree- and shrub-bordered garden. Food is taken very seriously here, the selection of freshly-prepared dishes changing regularly, depending on the seasonal availability of produce. A giant blackboard proclaims the likes of baked black bream filled with leek, apricot, tomato and fresh basil stuffing, medallions of venison, Somerset wild boar, ostrich fillet, and quail filled with wild mushroom stuffing. All are elaborately described and accompanied by inventive sauces plus crisply-cooked vegetables. Those palates desiring plainer fare will not be disappointed: the menu also includes hearty pies, such as pork and venison and duck and leek plus a range of steaks, salads and a couple of imaginative vegetarian dishes. Lighter 'big' bites are offered at lunchtime, including a selection of filled double-decker rolls. Delicious home-made puddings. Children are welcome inside where they have there own menu, as well as high-chairs and changing facilities for toddlers *Open 10-2.30 (Sat 11-3), 6-11 (Sun 12-3, 7-10.30).* **Bar Food** *12-2, 6-9.30 (from 7 Sun).* **Beer** *Archers Village Bitter, Bass, Boddingtons, Wadworth 6X, guest beer. Garden, outdoor eating, children's play area. Amex, Diners, MasterCard,* **VISA**

BRISLEY   Bell   FOOD

Tel 01362 668686   Map 10 C1
The Green Brisley Norfolk NR20 5DW

Enjoying a magnificent, isolated position set back from B1145 and just 200 yards from the village centre, this attractive, 16th-century warm brick-built pub overlooks the largest piece of common land in Norfolk, some 200 acres. Within, there's a small, refurbished bar area with old beams, large brick fireplace and exposed brick walls, plus a separate, neatly laid-up dining-room. Emphasis on the extensive blackboard menus, especially the restaurant board, is on fresh fish (whole plaice, skate in black butter, haddock mornay) hand-selected in Lowestoft, as well as lobster and delicious Cromer crabs. Choose wisely from the bar food board and printed list for a value-for-money, home-cooked meal. Dishes range from good soups (broccoli and Stilton), smoked mackerel, and chili to steak and mushroom pie and gammon steak served with freshly-cut chips, but there is the option for potatoes and fresh vegetables. Puddings include home-made strawberry cheesecake and treacle tart. Sunny front patio, summer barbecue area and benches by the pond for fine weather alfresco eating. *Open 11-3, 6-11 (Sun 12-3, 7-10.30).* **Bar Food** *12-2.30, 6-9.30.* **Beer** *Boddingtons, Flowers IPA, John Smith's, Whitbread Best Bitter. Garden, outdoor eating area. MasterCard,* **VISA**

> We endeavour to be as up-to-date as possible but inevitably some changes to
> landlords, chefs and other key staff occur after the Guide
> has gone to press.

BRISTOL   Highbury Vaults   A

Tel 0117 973 3203   Map 13 F1
164 St Michael's Hill Kingsdown Bristol BS2 8DE

A serious contender for Bristol's busiest pub, close to the University and Infirmary, thus popular with students and nurses. The tiny front snug bar and rear bar as well as the walled patio at the back are all often crowded with young people who seem to enjoy the odd libation or two. No music or machines. *Open 12-11 (Sun 12-10.30).* **Beer** *Smiles Exhibition, Best & Brewery, Brains SA, three guest beers. Patio, summer barbecues. Closed all 25 & 26 Dec. No credit cards.*

BROAD CAMPDEN   Bakers Arms   FOOD

Tel 01386 840515   Map 14a A1
Broad Campden Chipping Campden Gloucestershire GL55 6UR

Mid-way by road between Chipping Campden and Blockley, the pub stands at a convenient junction for walkers following the Heart of England Way. Real ales, real fires and 'real food' are the promised order of the day. Of the first, seven may be on tap at any one time, with guest ales prominently displayed. Log fires burn when required at each end of the single bar; space can be limited here in poor weather. Real enough, the food is varied and invariably prepared to order with consequent delays: be sure to take a table number when ordering if sitting outside. Most ambitious are the daily specials: lamb and orange pie, salmon and broccoli tagliatelle and bacon and onion suet pudding. Reliable favourites feature on the main menu, namely chicken, ham and leek pie, moussaka and smoked haddock bake. Good vegetarian choice (aubergine pesto pasta). Family weekends (July), folk music nights, beer festivals and a hot-air balloon meeting are annual events. *Open 11.30-2.30, 6.30-11 (Sun 12-3, 7-10.30).* **Bar Food** *12-2, 6.30-9.30 (Sun 7-8.45). Free House.* **Beer** *Stanway Stanney Bitter, Donnington BB, Wickwar Brand Oak Bitter, up to four guest beers. Garden, outdoor eating, children's play area. Closed all 25 Dec & 26 Dec eve. No credit cards.*

BROAD CHALKE   Queen's Head Inn   B&B

Tel & Fax 01722 780344   Map 14 C3
Broad Chalke Salisbury Wiltshire SP5 5EN

This homely, stone-built village inn, located close to a meandering chalk stream in the Ebble valley, was once a bakehouse and stables before becoming an alehouse and outlasting the three other inns that once existed in the parish. The main Village Bar has stone walls, a beamed ceiling and a large inglenook, but the place to sit on fine days is in the sheltered rear courtyard, amid the honeysuckle and roses. With doors leading off the courtyard is the modern brick-built accommodation, which houses four light and spacious bedrooms, all of which offer en suite facilities (all with bath), beverage-making kits, remote-control TVs and direct-dial telephones. New owners plan to upgrade the bedrooms this year. Cream teas are served on summer afternoons (Jun-Aug 3-6) *Open 11.30-3, 6-11 (Sun 12-3, 7-10.30), all day Jun-Aug. Free House.* **Beer** *Wadworth 6X, Bass, Ringwood Best, guest beer. Courtyard. Family room.* **Accommodation** *4 bedrooms, all en suite, £45 (family room sleeping three £65, single £25). Children welcome overnight (under-3s stay free in parents' room, 4-14s £12.50), additional bed available. MasterCard, VISA*

BROADHEATH   Old Packet House   FOOD

Tel 0161 929 1331   Map 6 B2   **B&B**
Navigation Road Broadheath Altrincham Cheshire WA14 1ON

Hard by a canal bridge on the main A56, the distinctive Packet House stands dwarfed by newer development, its former purpose in life scarcely recalled by the old wharf behind it. Black and white outside, with its heavy leaded-light windows protected by ornamental wrought-iron, it's unexpectedly spacious within and lent a cottagey feel by open brick fireplaces, patterned curtains and button-back banquettes in the lounge and raised dining sections. Chalk-board menus offer lunchtime snacks like a daily soup (broccoli and Stilton), beef and vegetable curry, braised beef and onions, vegetable bake and full evening meals, extending the range with typically substantial portions for hearty eaters; main dishes such as deep-fried king cod in tartare sauce, a daily roast, rib-eye steak and rack of lamb exemplify the range. Service is informal, verging on the jovial, diners replenishing their real ales and (draught) house wines direct from the bar. Of the four bedrooms, one double has bath/WC en suite, the two singles and remaining twin sharing two spacious bathrooms. TVs, trouser presses, fitted mahogany furniture and bright brass taps are generally smart and modern. Delightful beer garden. *Open 11.30-11 (Sun 12-10.30).* **Bar Food** *12-2.30, 6.30-9.30 (Sun 12-8).* **Beer** *Boddingtons, Webster's Yorkshire Bitter, Wilson's Bitter. Patio, outdoor eating. Family room.* **Accommodation** *4 bedrooms, 1 en suite, £65 (single £45). Children welcome overnight (charge depends on age), additional bed & cot available. No dogs. Amex, Diners, MasterCard,* **VISA**

BROADHEMBURY   Drewe Arms   ★   FOOD

Tel & Fax 01404 841267   Map 13 E2
Broadhembury Devon EX14 0NF

Dating back to the 15th century, the small, thatched Drewe Arms has a charmingly rustic feel with dado-boarded walls, a pile of old magazines next to the inglenook fireplace (with real log fire), various rural artefacts and a warm, convivial atmosphere created by Nigel and Kerstin Burge. The blackboard bar menu majors on open sandwiches – marinated herring, Stilton and sirloin steak, gravad lax with dill and mustard sauce – plus good, fresh seafood delivered daily from Newlyn or Brixham (monkfish with whole grain mustard sauce, sea bream with herb butter, and tuna with pesto) and the likes of a smoked salmon and dill soup and mushroom, crab and cheddar bake. Diners are welcome to order just a main course (£15), or the complete three courses (£19) from the totally fish orientated dining-room menu and eat it in the bar or garden, as there are no rules on where you can eat. Hot lemon pudding, sticky toffee, chocolate and banana pudding and caramelized oranges may be listed on the short pudding menu. Everything is freshly cooked and served in generous portions. West Country Regional Winner of our 1997 Seafood Pub of the year award. *Open 11-2.30, 6-11 (Sun 12-2.30, 7-10.30).* **Bar Food** *12-2, 7-10 (no food Sun eve).* *Free House.* **Beer** *Otter Bitter, Bright, Ale & Head. Garden, outdoor eating. Family room. No credit cards.*

> We only recommend food (Bar Food) in those establishments highlighted
> with the **FOOD** symbol.

BROCKHAMPTON   Craven Arms   FOOD

Tel 01242 820410   Map 14 C1
Brockhampton Gloucestershire GL54 5XQ

A deservedly popular pub hidden down winding lanes deep in the rolling Gloucestershire countryside: Brockhampton is 2 miles north of the A436 Cheltenham to Gloucester road. Approached under a stone lych gate, the garden extends to an enclosed paddock with a children's play area which includes a small summer house containing games for soggier days. Revealed within the Craven Arms are stone-flagged floors and a warren of rooms given over primarily to eating. Real ales are well represented in the bar, where the less adventurous may order gammon, egg and chips or steak pie. Look to the the daily blackboard menu for good quality dishes like poached salmon with lemon and thyme, beef bourguignon and aubergine and mushroom bake with Stilton sauce. Round off a value-for-money meal with traditional home-made treacle tart or banana and peach crumble. Dining tables are predominantly pine, their evening adornment of fresh carnations and candles quite in keeping with the pub's relaxed environment. *Open 11-2.30, 6-11 (Sun 12-3.30, 7-10.30).* **Bar Food** *12-2 (from 12.30 Sun), 7-9.30. Free House.* **Beer** *Butcombe Bitter, Hook Norton, Best Wadworth 6X, Worthington Best, occasional guest beer. Garden, outdoor eating, children's play area. MasterCard,* **VISA**

BROCKTON   Feathers   ★   FOOD

Tel & Fax 01746 785202   Map 6 B4   **B&B**
Brockton Much Wenlock Shropshire TF13 6JR

An object lesson in good pub-keeping, Martin and Andrea Hayward's Shropshire inn of deceptively modest outward appearance is little short of a gem within. Located at a crossroads on the B4378 between Much Wenlock and Ludlow its gradual extension and improvement over the last six years has revealed yet more of the interior's inherent charm through the creation of a succession of interlinked dining areas on different levels (one non-smoking) whose theme is co-ordinated by their quarry-tile floors, exposed timbers and stonework and Andrea's imaginative interior designs. Ably assisted by chef Duncan Macintyre, their food is both substantial and seriously good without losing that special appeal of remaining essentially a pub, with a certain wine bar/bistro feel to it, worthy this year of a star. There are two separate blackboard menus from which to make a choice, though that is never easy; from one comes the 'regular' selection of Stilton and bacon salad and king garlic prawns, through flash-fried chicken and teriyaki duck to a peppered fillet steak at the top of the price range. From the specials board, meanwhile, starters may be grilled goat's cheese and tomato salad or lamb's kidneys in red wine and mushroom sauce followed by fillets of red bream, coconut chicken curry and baked filo parcels of Brie with apple, celery and walnuts. The board listing puddings is a little more mobile as seated customers are encouraged to become a little less so! Choose here from lemon soufflé, treacle, cherry and walnut tart, poached pear in chocolate sauce and cinnamon apple pancakes; the wide selection of wines by the glass also extends to one or two for the sweeter-toothed, while for the true trencherman both the Banks's bitter and Marston's Pedigree are cask-conditioned and kept in fine condition. Two en suite bedrooms came on stream in 1996, their colour co-ordinated decor in a somewhat bijou style suited to their size, and there are plans for a further extension of the overnight facilities through the coming year; Continental breakfasts are provided in the room for those wishing to make an early start, or for that matter a suitably tardy one. Well-behaved children are made properly welcome, including overnight by arrangement, though the space is limited: no dogs are allowed. Do note that the Feathers does not open at lunchtime from Monday to Friday, nor will you find a mere 'snack' at weekends; the pub is all the better for that! *Open 12-3 Sat & Sun only, 6.30-11 (Sun 7-10.30) Closed all Mon & Tue-Fri lunch. **Bar Food** 12-2 (Sat & Sun only), 6.30-9.30 (Sun 7-9). Free House. **Beer** Banks's Bitter, Marston's Pedigree. Patio, outdoor eating.* **Accommodation** *2 bedrooms, both en suite, £40. Check-in by arrangement. No credit cards.*

BROMHAM   Greyhound Inn   FOOD

Tel 01380 850241   Map 14 B3
Bromham Chippenham Wiltshire SN15 2HA

Located just three miles from Devizes Locks (longest set of locks in Europe) and dating back some 300 years the ever-popular Greyhound continues to thrive through the enthusiasm of hard-working owners George and Morag Todd. Two dining-rooms seating 18 and 50 respectively are the setting for some unusual pub food, the often ingenious menu featuring interesting Malaysian and Thai dishes – pork devils (tenderloin with garlic, cream and chili sauce). Changing blackboard menus may highlight curry Laksa, Tom Yam noodles, and crab, prawn and avocado bake at lunchtime, with evening specials like mixed grill, grilled grouper or red snapper, fresh Dover sole and chicken Dijon. On Sunday the roast lunch is available as just a main course. For pudding, try the home-made strawberry shortcake or damson soufflé. Tons of atmosphere, thanks largely to walls and ceilings festooned with bric-a-brac in both bars – over 500 advertising jugs in one! Parents can get extra plates for informal children's portions. *Open 11-2.30, 6.30-11 (Sun 12-3, 7-10.30). **Bar Food** 11-2, 7-10.30 (Sun 12-2, 7-10). Free House. **Beer** Wadworth IPA. Garden, outdoor eating.* MasterCard, **VISA**

BROOM — Broom Tavern — FOOD

Tel 01789 773656   Fax 01789 772983   Map 14 C1
High Street Broom Warwickshire B50 5HL

Pretty, timbered village pub dating back to the 16th century with virginia creeper clinging to the outside and lots of black beams and brass within. The bar menu (mostly home-made although some puds and soups are not) offers plenty of choice, from ploughman's lunches, sandwiches and starters like smoked salmon mousse and black pudding with hot mustard sauce to main-course dishes such as whole grilled plaice, chicken, gammon and mushroom pie, rack of lamb with rosemary, and various pasta dishes. Children are catered for with a special menu, high-chairs and, on summer weekends and during school holidays, a 'bouncy castle' out in the garden. *Open 11-3, 6-11 (Sun 12-3, 7-10.30).* **Bar Food** *12-2, 6.45-9.30 (Sat 6.30-10, Sun 7-9).*
Beer *Hook Norton Best Bitter, two guest beers. Garden, outdoor eating. Family room. Amex, MasterCard,* **VISA**

BROOM — Cock Inn — A

Tel 01767 314411   Map 15a F1
23 High Street Broom Bedfordshire SG18 9NA

Stretching back from the only street of a village with no middle, no shops and a postage stamp-sized post office in the postmistress's front room, the Cock is a conversion of three interlinked Victorian cottages, its three panelled sitting areas furnished with bench seats and varnished tables, and a games room complete with the locally popular chair-skittles table. Look inside the two front rooms and find a novel collection of metallised tobacco adverts and shelves of aged beer and medicine bottles. The bar, central to everything here, has remained unchanged for over a century, its cellar down four wooden steps, where the Greene King ale is drawn direct from the cask. *Open 12-4, 6-11 (Sun 12-4, 7-10.30).* **Beer** *Greene King. Garden, children's play area. Family room.* **VISA**

BUCKDEN — Buck Inn — FOOD B&B

Tel 01756 760228   Fax 01756 760227   Map 5 D4
Buckden North Yorkshire BD23 5JA

 Zzz...

Both the creeper-clad Georgian coaching inn and the village take their names from the fact that this was once the meeting place for local stag hunts; today it is tourists and walkers who are attracted to this fine old inn. The small bar with flagstone floor and old stone fireplace is in great contrast to the smart staff who offer swift, efficient service both in the extensive, carpeted bar-meal areas and in the pretty restaurant formed out of what was once the courtyard where local sheep auctions were held. The menu offers something for everybody from snacks like ploughman's lunches and open sandwiches to full meals with such dishes as Whitby haddock, beef goulash and salmon with béarnaise at lunch and evening specials from the blackboard which could include wild boar paté, medallions of pork with black pudding risotto and a grain mustard sauce, Whitby crab tartlet and braised shank of lamb in filo with tomato and coriander sauce. There are also vegetarian meals (terrine of provençale vegetables with tapénade crostini) and children's sections, and a long list of home-made puddings such as orange Cointreau tart and trio of Swiss chocolate terrine. No chips or sandwiches in the evening. Pretty bedrooms with matching floral duvets and curtains are furnished in pine and all have TV, direct-dial telephone and tea- and coffee-making kit (although there is also room service available throughout the day and evening). Bathrooms, like the bedrooms, are smart and well-kept, mostly just with showers but five have bathtubs. *Open 11-11 (till 10.30 Sun).* **Bar Food** *12-2, 6.30-9 (till 9.30 Sat). Free House.* **Beer** *Theakston Old Peculier, Best & XB, Black Sheep Bitter & Special, guest beer. Patio, outdoor eating. Family room.* **Accommodation** *14 bedrooms, all en suite, £68-£78 (single £34). Children welcome overnight (under-5s free, 5-10 half-price, 11-14 two-thirds adult rate if sharing parents' room), additional bed & cot (both £3) available. MasterCard,* **VISA**

BUCKLAND   Lamb Inn   FOOD

Tel 01367 810475   Map 14a B3   **B&B**
Buckland Faringdon Oxfordshire SN7 8QN

Zzz...

Civilised, 18th-century stone inn hidden away in the heart of a tranquil Oxfordshire village, yet only a minutes drive from the busy A420 Oxford to Swindon road. Apart from the charming position it is the Lamb's relaxing atmosphere and chef/landlord Paul Barnard's excellent home-cooking that draws discerning diners to this country haven. Since arriving here in 1992, Peta and Paul Barnard have gradually refurbished the building, creating a small uncluttered bar with tasteful furnishings, prints and specially-made lamb motif carpet and an attractively appointed dining-room, complete with crisp table linen, candles and fresh flowers. Listed on a blackboard and served throughout the pub (even a light lunchtime snack can be savoured in the restaurant) is a short and imaginative selection of freshly-prepared dishes that make the most of good raw ingredients. From decent snacks and starters like curried apple soup, warm spiced chicken, bacon and avocado salad, rabbit and guinea fowl terrine, pheasant mousse with wild mushroom sauce, and salmon and prawn kedgeree the choice extends to such main-course options as roast duckling with apple and Calvados, baked sea bass with a light Pernod sauce, chicken, almond and coconut curry or saddle of hare roasted on a bed of root vegetables. The sweet-toothed can tuck into apple, pear and mincemeat pudding, lemon and lime tart or chocolate and brandy mousse. Alternatively, finish off with a plate of farmhouse cheeses. Satisfying food is complemented by a well-chosen list of wines including interesting house wines, several half-bottles and around 12 by the glass. Useful overnight accommodation is offered in four en suite upstairs bedrooms, all of which are gradually being refurbished and upgraded as time allows. The best is the large double room with a pink-upholstered sofa littered with scatter cushions, a mix of pine and darkwood furniture and pretty co-ordinating fabrics. Others vary in size and standard, but all boast direct-dial phones, TVs, beverage-making facilities and clean, well-maintained bath/shower rooms. Peaceful rear garden and patio, ideal for summer sipping and Sunday evening barbecues. *Open 11-3, 5.30-11 (Sun 12-3, 7-11). Bar Food 12-2, 6.30-9.30 (Sun 12-2.30, 7-9). Free House. Beer Morland Original, Adnams Broadside. Garden, patio, outdoor eating, barbecue. Accommodation 4 bedrooms, all en suite, £35-£45 (single £35). Children welcome overnight, additional bed (£15) & cot (£10) available. Check-in bar hours only. No dogs. MasterCard, VISA*

BUCKLAND NEWTON   Gaggle of Geese   A

Tel 01300 345249   Map 13 F2
Buckland Newton Dorset DT2 7BS

Formerly the Royal Oak, The Gaggle of Geese is so named since a previous landlord bred geese as a hobby; the building dates back to 1834 when it started life as the village shop. Twice-yearly goose charity auctions still take place here. Located on the B3143, about halfway between Dorchester and Sherborne, this tranquil village pub has a civilised and attractive main bar and pretty garden complete with pond. Children are allowed in the skittle alley and dining-room. *Open 12-2.30, 6.30-11 (Sun 12-3, 7-10.30). Free House. Beer Hall & Woodhouse Badger Best, Bass, Wadworth 6X, Butcombe Bitter, two guest beers. Garden, children's play area. Family room. No credit cards.*

BUCKLER'S HARD   Master Builder's House Hotel   B&B

Tel 01590 616253   Fax 01590 616297   Map 15 D4
Buckler's Hard Beaulieu Hampshire SO42 7XB

The grassy areas in front of this updated and extended 18th-century hotel run right down to the banks of the Beaulieu River, where many famous ships were once built for Nelson's fleet. The Yachtsman's Bar is popular with yachtsmen and tourists alike, and residents have their own homely lounge with easy chairs, period furniture and a large inglenook fireplace. Creaky floorboards and old-world charm make the six bedrooms in the main house appealing (and quiet once the tourists have gone home); rooms in a purpose-built block are plainer but well equipped. *Open 11-3, 6-11 (11-11 in summer), Sun 12-3, 7-10.30 (12-10.30 summer). Beer Courage Best & Directors. Garden, terrace. Accommodation 23 bedrooms, all en suite, £60-£70 (four-poster £67-£77, single from £42). Children welcome overnight (under-14s stay free in parents' room), additional bed & cot supplied. Amex, Diners, MasterCard, VISA*

BURCOT   Chequers   FOOD

Tel 01865 407771   Map 14a C3
Abingdon Road Burcot Oxfordshire OX14 3DP

Originally a staging post for River Thames barges and their crews, until what is now the A415 was built outside. Charming, part 16th-century beamed and thatched building with unspoilt quarry-tiled bars, open fires and a choice of books for customers to read. A daily-changing blackboard menu is the same for the bar and dining-room. Cook Mary Weeks offers simple home-made fare (including bread) – chicken, sage and mushroom or seafood pies, tomato and aubergine crumble, lamb and courgette lasagne and (genuine old-fashioned suet) steak and kidney pudding – followed by melting meringues filled with peaches and cream and Mary's disaster cake! Sunday lunch is served on the first Sunday of every month. Piano music on Friday and Saturday nights. *Open 11-2.30, 6-11 (Sun 12-3, 7-10.30).* **Bar Food** *12-2, 6.30-9 (no food Sun eve). Free House.* **Beer** *Ruddles County, Ushers Best, Archer's Village Bitter. Garden, outdoor eating. MasterCard,* **VISA**

BURFORD   Inn For All Seasons   FOOD

Tel 01451 844324   Fax 01451 844375   Map 14a A2   **B&B**
The Barringtons Burford Oxfordshire OX18 4TN

Zzz...

Despite its Burford address, the inn's actually in Gloucestershire, alongside the A40 by the Barringtons turn. A regular clientele travel miles to enjoy the comforts of this small hotel whose interior has been meticulously restored to reflect 17th-century elegance. Leather wing chairs grace a flagstone bar adorned with rugby, motoring and flying memorabilia, much of the latter with local war-time connections. The nine bedrooms are models of comfort with TVs tea-makers, trouser presses and hairdryers. All rooms have simple, neatly kept en suite bathrooms and those in front are double-glazed against any intrusive noise from the busy road. The Inn is run by Matthew Sharp, whose menus might encompass ploughman's lunches, Wiltshire ham terrine, oxtail stew, beef Wellington and fresh Brixham fish (Dover sole with cucumber and prawn butter, roast monkfish with wild mushrooms and red wine sauce). For pudding try the terrine of white and dark chocolate mousse or the hot sticky toffee pudding. Only bread and ice cream are bought in, all other fare is prepared on the premises; the meat is supplied by good local butchers. *Open 11-2.30, 6-11, (Sun 12-3, 7-10.30).* **Bar Food** *11.30-2.30 (from 12 Sun), 6.30-9.30 (from 7 Sun). Free House.* **Beer** *Hall & Woodhouse Badger Best, Wadworth 6X, Wychwood Bitter. Garden.* **Accommodation** *10 bedrooms, all en suite, £77 (family room £110, single £42.50). Children over 10 welcome, (10-15s 50% of single tariff), additional bed available. Closed 25 & 26 Dec. Amex, MasterCard,* **VISA**

BURFORD   Lamb Inn   FOOD

Tel 01993 823155   Fax 01993 822228   Map 14a A2   **B&B**
Sheep Street Burford Oxfordshire OX18 4LR

It's difficult to exaggerate the mellow charm of the 14th-century Lamb Inn, tucked down a quiet side street off the High Street in this most attractive Cotswolds town. Public rooms range from a rustic bar at one end of the building to a chintzy lounge at the other with in between a combination of the two featuring rugs on the flagstone floor, a collection of brass ornaments over the fireplace, a display of china figurines on a window shelf, fresh flowers and antique furniture – all polished and buffed to please the most exacting housekeeper. Warmed within by log fires for most of the year; there is also a very pretty walled garden to take advantage of the ever-improving English summers. Bar lunches, served throughout the ground floor, run from various ploughman's lunches, filled baguettes, soup with granary bread (cream of celery and red pepper) and grilled sardines, warm salad of smoked duck, smoked haddock quiche, steak and ale pie and pan-fried escalope of salmon. Puddings may include rhubarb and apple charlotte and summer pudding. No bar snacks in the evening. Separate attractive restaurant offering a table d'hote menu and set Sunday lunch; recommended in our *1997 Hotels and Restaurants Guide.* What the bedrooms lack in extras, they make up for with cottagey appeal; all have antique furniture, pretty floral fabrics and many also have old beams and timbers in evidence. Remote-control TVs remind you it's the

20th century, but there are no telephones. One room features a four-poster bed.
Open 11-2.30, 6-11 (Sun 12-3, 7-10.30). **Bar Food** *12-2 (no food Sun). Free House.*
Beer *Wadworth IPA & 6X, Hook Norton Best. Garden, terrace. Family room.*
Accommodation *16 bedrooms, all en suite, £90 Sun-Thu (£100 Fri & Sat, single £57.50,*
£75 weekends). Children welcome overnight, additional bed (£20) & cot (£6) available.
Dogs £5. Closed 25 & 26 Dec. MasterCard, Visa.

BURHAM   Golden Eagle   FOOD

Tel 01634 668975   Map 11 B5
80 Church Street Burham Kent ME1 3SD

Rather plain-looking village local with a carpeted and simply furnished open-plan bar,
original beams adorned with mugs and jugs and striking views across the Medway
valley and the North Downs. Worthy of a visit for its unusual bar food, the changing
blackboard menu consisting of some 30-odd Malaysian dishes: perhaps pork in satay
sauce, beef and peppers in black bean sauce, crispy lemon chicken and a good range of
vegetarian dishes. In addition, at lunchtime you may find ploughman's lunches, jacket
potatoes, sandwiches and gammon steak. *Open 11-2.30, 6.15-11 (Sun 12-3, 7-10.30).*
Bar Food *12-2, 7-10. Free House.* **Beer** *Wadworth 6X, Marston's Pedigree, guest beer.*
Paved garden, outdoor eating. Closed all 25 & 26 Dec. MasterCard, VISA

We only recommend food (Bar Food) in those establishments highlighted
with the **FOOD** symbol.

BURITON   Five Bells   FOOD

Tel 01730 263584   Map 15 D3   **B&B**
Buriton High Street Petersfield Hampshire GU31 5RX

Zzz...

Dating back to the 16th century this well-refurbished brick and stone free house
nestles in an attractive village at the base of the South Downs, a couple of minutes off
the busy A3 (signposted heading south). Popular with South Downs Way walkers –
400 yards away – and a mixed local clientele, the pub offers a delightful rustic
ambience within the series of rambling bars. Warmed by four large open fires and
furnished with mainly sturdy pine on rug-strewn wood-block floors, it is a welcoming
place in which to relax. The extensive menu – listed on beams and boards – is
conveniently sectioned for ease of choice (spicy dishes, fish, vegetarian and so on) and
the food is reliably good. The fish board may feature whole Selsey crab, grilled red
snapper and swordfish in garlic butter, while the main-course board could offer
partridge stuffed with bacon, walnuts and Stilton, chicken breast in herbs and garlic,
steak and kidney pie, and more game dishes in winter. Good vegetarian choices (nut
roast with red wine and mushroom sauce) and hearty lunchtime snacks – filled jacket
potatoes, French sticks and ploughman's lunches to sustain hungry walkers. Interesting
home-made puddings. Sunday lunch includes a vegetarian option. Good sheltered
summer garden with vine-bearing trellis and fruit trees. Live monthly jazz and weekly
Wednesday folk or country and western. A recently converted barn offers self-catering
accommodation in two spacious and neatly furnished units. Generally let by the week
or weekend they are, however, available for overnight guests willing to prepare their
own breakfast in the well-equipped kitchen area. Excellent value and perfect for
South Downs explorers. If you stay overnight and see a small lady dressed in grey
peasant clothes, don't worry – she's been around for a long time! No under-14s in bar
areas. *Open 11-2.30 (till 3 Fri & Sat), 5.30-11, (Sun 12-3, 7-10.30).* **Bar Food** *12-2,*
7-10 (till 9.30 Sun). Free House. **Beer** *Ballard's Best Bitter, Adnams Bitter, Ringwood Old*
Thumper, Friary Meux Best Bitter, Tetley, Eldridge Pope Hardy Country Ale, guest beer.
Garden, outdoor eating. **Accommodation** *2 bedrooms, both en suite (shower), £35 (per room).*
Children welcome overnight (stay free), additional bed available. Amex, MasterCard, VISA

BURNHAM MARKET   **Hoste Arms**   ★   **FOOD**

Tel 01328 738257   Fax 01328 730103   Map 10 C1   **B&B**
The Green Burnham Market Norfolk PE31 8HD

◁▷ 🗋 ▼ ♟ Zzz... ☺

A handsome, pale yellow-painted 17th-century inn (now much extended to the rear) occupying a prime position overlooking the green and parish church of a most picturesque village. Paul Whittome's relentless enthusiasm for the property (and the business) over the past six years has transformed the Hoste into one of the most popular inns along the Norfolk coast. It goes from strength to strength, with a new block of six elegant, extremely comfortable bedrooms only recently added. Two carefully-renovated front bars feature dark wood panelling, open brick fireplaces with winter log fires, rustic wooden floors and cushioned bow window seats with village views. Of note are the original paintings by wildlife artist Bruce Pearson illustrating a series of rural walks from the inn, Lord Decies' shell collection displayed in cabinets, and a permanent exhibition of Stephen Heffer's Norfolk coastal photographs. Live traditional jazz and R&B are popular Friday and Monday night events in the comfortably furnished piano bar. Tip-top bar food draws on supplies of fresh local and seasonal produce from within a twenty mile radius and everything is prepared on the premises. Varied menu choices range from open sandwiches, local Burnham Norton oysters, smoked chicken salad with mango dressing and pan-fried black pudding on a salad of beetroot with hazelnut oil to risotto of smoked haddock with saffron and chives, millefeuille of monkfish and mangetout with langoustine butter sauce, grilled lamb's liver and bacon, and penne pasta with chargrilled vegetables. To finish, try the apple crumble, chocolate and hazelnut torte, a selection of three English cheeses or Prospero ice creams, made locally in Holt. Vegetarians might enjoy braised cos lettuce with vegetarian oyster sauce and toasted sesame seeds. Sunday roasts. Cooking in the dinner-only (7-9) restaurant (now recommended in our *1997 Hotels and Restaurants Guide*) moves up a gear with a short, daily-changing dinner menu that is imaginative and offers good value; look out for beef from Wroxham Broads, mussels from Brancaster Staithe or sea bass and sea trout from Scolt Head Island. The global list of well-priced wines has sensible prices, useful notes and a selection of half bottles; well-kept ales are drawn straight from the cask. Upstairs, beyond the small gallery/lounge, are the majority of the charming bedrooms, four of which now boast four-posters. The rooms are all individually decorated, some with freestanding pine, others with antique pieces, designer fabrics and fittings. Spotless en suite facilities and TV, radio, tea-maker, telephone and hairdryer are all provided. The six newest rooms offer superb comfort and one can really look forward to a good night's sleep after exploring the Norfolk's north-coast salt marshes and sand dunes. Top of the range of bedrooms is a huge room with custom-built four-poster and luxurious bathroom – a bargain in low season! First-rate breakfasts are served in the conservatory, which is also the venue for afternoon teas (free to residents). Year-round tariff reductions are offered for stays of two nights and over; the best deal is half price (Sun-Thu) from November to the end of March. Quite delightful garden with rustic benches and dry hop-filled conservatory. Winner of our 1996 Pub of the Year Award. *Open 11-11 (Sun 12-3, 6-10.30). Bar Food 12-2, 7-9. Free House. Beer Morland Old Speckled Hen, Greene King IPA & Abbot Ale, Woodforde's Wherry Bitter, guest beers. Garden, outside eating.* **Accommodation** *21 bedrooms, all en suite, £84-£108 (single £60). 2+ night rates: £60-£76 (weekends £66-84), £42-£54 Nov-Mar (exc. Christmas and New year). Children welcome overnight (under-2s free if sharing parents' room), additional bed & cot provided (£15).* Amex, MasterCard, **VISA**

We endeavour to be as up-to-date as possible but inevitably some changes to landlords, chefs and other key staff occur after the Guide has gone to press.

BURNHAM THORPE   Lord Nelson   A

Tel 01328 738241   Map 10 C1
Walsingham Road Burnham Thorpe Norfolk P31 8HN

Unspoilt rural cottage located in a sleepy village close to Burnham Market and named after England's most famous seafarer, who was born in the nearby rectory. A narrow, worn brick-floored corridor leads to two rooms; a timeless, old-fashioned bar on the left boasting some magnificent high-backed settles and a few sturdy tables and plain chairs on a re-tiled floor. Nelson memorabilia in the form of prints and paintings adorn the walls. There is no bar; excellent Greene King ales are drawn straight from the cask in the adjacent cellar room and brought to the table. Also available is a popular rum concoction called "Nelson's Blood", which is made to a secret recipe by the previous long-serving landlord who still resides near the pub. A further warmly decorated and simply furnished room is ideal for families. The adjacent barn has recently been renovated to provide more seating and the new toilets, including disabled facilities. Good-sized garden with bowling green, bat & ball, football net, basketball net, swing and slide for active youngsters to let off steam. *Open 11-3, 6-11 (Sun 12-3, 7-10.30), longer hours in summer.* **Beer** *Greene King. Garden. Family room, children's play area. No credit cards.*

BURNHAM-ON-CROUCH   Ye Olde White Harte Hotel   B&B

Tel & Fax 01621 782106   Map 11 C4
The Quay Burnham-on-Crouch Essex CM0 8AS

An old seaside inn where on sunny summer days you can take your drink to a lovely waterside terrace overlooking the busy yachting activity. Two characterful, wood-panelled bars have polished-oak furnishings, exposed beams, a good open fire and a nautical atmosphere; there's also a small, traditional residents' lounge. The best of the ninteen bedrooms (which vary in size and standard) are the eleven comfortable en suite rooms with smart, modern decor, good fabrics and simple furniture. Five clean, tiled bathrooms have bath and shower. Original beams and brick fireplaces, and splendid estuary views are notable features. Eight rooms are self-styled as "basic". *Open 11-11 (Sun 12-10.30). Free House.* **Beer** *Adnams, Tolly Cobbold Bitter, guest beer. Waterside terrace. Family room.* **Accommodation** *19 bedrooms, 11 en suite, £50.60/ £59.40 (single £19/£37.40). Children welcome overnight, additional bed (£6) & cot (£4.50) available. Amex, MasterCard,* **VISA**

BURPHAM   George & Dragon   FOOD

Tel 01903 883131   Map 11 A6
Burpham Arundel West Sussex BN18 9RR

Burpham is signposted off the A27 near Arundel. At the end of three miles of a winding, climbing lane, one is rewarded with some fine views of the Arun valley, with Arundel Castle in the distance, and the pretty George & Dragon with its good food and real ales. Once the haunt of smugglers, the inn dates back to the mid-18th century; it is now divided into two very different halves: the bar with its exposed timbers, rustic tables and country chairs, and the smart dining-room with crisp white napery and elegant Regency-style chairs. The printed bar food lunch and supper menu covers the standard items – home-made soup, gammon and pineapple, ploughman's lunches and granary sandwiches – while a daily-changing blackboard menu lists good fresh fish dishes (orange tilapia fillet with tarragon butter, whole black bream), duck and black cherry pie and pork with apricot and thyme sauce. Another blackboard lists a particularly good range of home-made puddingss, perhaps a bread-and-butter pudding and raspberry crème brulée. Separate restaurant serving fixed-price menus and Sunday lunch. The 100-year-old cricket club is next door (as is Mervyn Peake, author of *Gormenghast*, who is at rest in the village churchyard). Children over 10 are allowed in the bar to eat. No music or dogs allowed and "smoking is not encouraged". Grosvenor Inns. *Open 11-2.30, 6-11 (Sun 12-3, 7-10.30). Closed Sun eve Nov-Easter.* **Bar Food** *12-2, 7-9.45 (till 9 Sun).* **Beer** *Courage Directors, Arundel Best, four guest beers. Terrace, outdoor eating. Amex, MasterCard,* **VISA**

BURSLEDON   Jolly Sailor   A

Tel 01703 405557   Fax 01703 402050   Map 15 D4
Lands End Road Old Bursledon Hampshire SO31 8DN

Three miles from M27 Junction 8, the Jolly Sailor overlooks the busy yachting marina activity on the River Hamble. Parking is restricted outside the pub but there is free parking at Old Bursledon railway station, which is a couple of minutes' walk up the lane; there are then 40 steps down (and back up!) to the pub entrance. Built as a shipbuilder's house in 1700 and later a vicarage, it became a pub in the early 1900s. It has its own jetty and yachtsmen have used this harbourside pub as a retreat ever since the days of Lord Nelson. More recently, it was featured in BBC TV's *Howard's Way.* The large terrace is a lovely spot to watch the nautical world go by and within the unspoilt interior the nautical front bar also has good views from sought-after bay window seats; the flagstoned back bar is old and characterful. Splendid alfresco seating on the bench-filled front terrace and along the jetty jutting out over the river. Try one of the fifteen fruity country wines on offer from Gales of Horndean. Small, lawned garden area has a 100-year-old yew tree for shade. *Open 11-11 (Sun 12-10.30).* **Beer** *Hall & Woodhouse Badger Best and Tanglefoot, Wadworth 6X, three guest beers. Riverside garden. Closed all 25 Dec. Amex, Diners, MasterCard,* **VISA**

BURTON   Old House at Home   FOOD

Tel 01454 218227   Map 14 B2
Burton Chippenham Wiltshire SN14 7LT

A soft-stone building with a warm and welcoming timbered interior and log fires in winter, the Old House at Home is somewhat up-market for a village local, producing considerably more than the home cooking its name suggests. Daily-changing dishes may include avocado and prawns and kidneys turbigo for starters, followed by celery and parsley stuffed trout, chicken and mushroom lasagne, fruits de mer and veal cordon bleu. Fresh fish is now a strong feature and might include salmon, monkfish, fillet of plaice or red snapper. Granary sandwiches and ploughman's at lunchtime only. Music, food and wine from various countries are featured on a Monday theme evening once a month. Children allowed in bar to eat at lunchtime only. *Open 11.30-2.30, 7-11 (Sun 12-3, 7-10.30). Closed Tue lunch.* **Bar Food** *12-2 (except Tue), 7-10 (till 9.30 Sun). Free House.* **Beer** *Smiles, Bass, Wadworth 6X, Old Timer (winter). Garden, outdoor eating. Amex, MasterCard,* **VISA**

BURY ST EDMUNDS   The Nutshell   A

Tel 01284 764867   Map 10 C2
17 The Traverse Bury St Edmunds Suffolk IP33 1VJ

Blink and you will miss this unique miniature pub tucked away between a newsagents and a building society on a pedestrianised zone just off the main market square. It claims to be the smallest pub in Britain, a title that is difficult to dispute as the single bar – measuring barely a hundred square feet – is positively crowded if eight people are inside drinking. Despite its size there are plenty of curios to interest the eye, notably collections of 'smallest' items, bank notes from around the world, military memorabilia and, unbelievably, a mummified cat and mouse hanging from the ceiling. Good, well-kept Greene King ales, a welcoming chatty atmosphere and the signing of the visitors book is obligatory. *Open 11-11 Mon-Sat (closed Sun).* **Beer** *Greene King. No credit cards.*

Many **B&B** establishments offer reduced rates for weekend and out-of-season bookings. Always ask about special deals for longer stays. Beware half-board terms in inns where we do not recommend the **FOOD**.

BUTTERLEIGH   Butterleigh Inn   A

Tel 01884 855407   Map 13 E2
Butterleigh Tiverton Devon EX15 1PN

Unspoilt 400-year-old farming pub in glorious countryside, just three miles from Junction 28 of the M5 motorway. The main beamed bar is half lounge with a warming winter fire in an inglenook fireplace, half public end with simple wooden furnishings and old-fashioned pub games; a tiny snug takes just four intimate tables. Children are welcome indoors at lunchtime only. Black Hand cider (made on a local farm) is available in the summer. *Open 12-2.30 (till 3 Sat), 6-11 (from 5 Fri), Sun 12-3, 7-10.30. Free House. Beer Cotleigh Tawny, Barn Owl & Hobby, occasional guest beer. Garden. MasterCard,* **VISA**

BUTTERMERE   Bridge Hotel   B&B

Tel & Fax 017687 70252   Map 4 C3
Buttermere Cumbria CA13 9UZ

▌ Zzz...

Looking across the valley to Red Pike and High Stile between which cascades Sourmilk Gill's waterfall, this is an idyllic spot, beloved of generations of fell-walkers. There are distinctly contrasting sides to the business, however. The Walker's bar is kept suitably rustic for rucksack and dirty boot-clad fell walkers to relax in. A mere few paces distant, residents are treated to complimentary afternoon tea in the hotel lounge. Most of the bedrooms get a share of the majestic surrounding hills; the best of them have tiny wooden balconies teetering above the fast-rushing stream that bisects the property. Though general decor can be a little dark, all are enlivened by bright tiled bathrooms. No TVs or radios in the rooms, just P&Q. *Open 10.30am-11pm (till 10.30 Sun). Free House. Beer Theakston Old Peculier, Tetley Bitter & Imperial, Ind Coope Burton Ale. Patio.* **Accommodation** *22 bedrooms, 21 en suite, £77, (four-poster £89, single £38.50), six apartments in grounds available on weekly terms. Children welcome overnight (under-3s stay free if sharing parents' room, 6-11s £19.25), additional bed & cot (£5) available. MasterCard,* **VISA**

BYTHORN   White Hart   FOOD

Tel 01832 710226   Map 7 E4
Bythorn Huntingdon Cambridgeshire PE18 0QM

17th-century coaching inn nestling in a peaceful village just off the A14 Huntingdon to Kettering road. The rambling interior comprises four relaxing and varied inter-connecting rooms featuring plenty of exposed brick, beams and boards, quarry tiles and colourful rugs topped with an interesting rustic assortment of furniture, including an old Chesterfield. Huge open fireplaces with log fires for winter days and tables strewn with books and magazines beckon those who intend settling down for a relaxed stay. Food emphasis in this welcoming establishment is rooted in the airy restaurant extension, although a short blackboard bar menu (except Saturday evenings) lists good lighter bites (no sandwiches) – perhaps pigeon pie, spicy Thai fish soup toasted Brie with bacon and garlic, and ricotta pasta with spinach. However, those wishing to stay in front of the fire are welcome to choose from the more imaginative bistro fare. Starters range from mushrooms in garlic and gravadlax to chicken and tuna salad and farmhouse terrine, followed by chicken with Parma ham and asparagus, pork fillet en croute and sea bass with tomato and tarragon sauce. Puddings include praline parfait and chocolate pot. Four-course Sunday lunch. *Open 11-11 (Sun 12-3 only). Closed all day Mon and Sun eve. Bar Food 12-2, 7-10 (no bar food Sat eve). Free House. Beer Greene King IPA & Abbot Ale. Paved patio, outdoor eating. MasterCard,* **VISA**

We only recommend food (Bar Food) in those establishments highlighted with the **FOOD** symbol.

BYWORTH   Black Horse   FOOD

Tel 01798 342424   Map 11 A6
Byworth Petworth West Sussex GU28 0HO

Built on the site of a 15th-century friary in a sleepy village setting – just off the A283 Petworth to Pulborough road – the unusual three-storey Georgian façade of this friendly pub hides an ancient rustic interior. Beams, bare-boarded floors, scrubbed tables and padded wall seats characterise the three attractive interconnecting rooms and extraordinary upstairs Elizabethan dining-room. Bar food ranges from hearty snacks like ploughman's lunches, filled baguettes and baked potatoes to reliable, daily-changing blackboard specials such as pork chop in ginger and spring onion sauce and salmon with creamy asparagus sauce, as well as exotic fish dishes, home-made pasta meals and various pies and quiches. The favourite among the short list of puddings is the home-made treacle tart. Splendid summer alfresco imbibing on an old cobbled patio or among the flower borders and shrubs in the fine terraced garden with peaceful wooded valley views. *Open 11-3, 6-11 (Sun 12-3, 7-10.30).* **Bar Food** *11-1.45, 6-9.45 (Sun 12-2, 7-9.45). Free House.* **Beer** *Young's Bitter, Flowers Original, Hall & Woodhouse Badger Best, Fuller's London Pride. Garden, outdoor eating, barbecue. Family room. Closed 25 Dec eve. Amex, MasterCard,* **VISA**

CADEBY   Cadeby Inn   A

Tel 01709 864009   Map 7 D2
Main Street Cadeby Doncaster DN5 7SW

This atmospheric old inn was clearly once an elegant country farmhouse and stands today in a mature orchard garden full of flowering shrubs. There's plenty of space here for little ones to play safely, and the picnic tables are especially popular when there's a barbecue on. Original flagstones and fireplaces survive in the two bars whose counters are built in brick, while the walls are hung with horse collars, brasses and webbing. *Open 11.30-3, 5-11 (Sat 11-11, Sun 12-3, 7-10.30). Free House.* **Beer** *Tetley Best, Courage Directors, John Smith's Best & Magnet, Samuel Smith's Old Brewery, guest beer. Garden, children's play area. Family room. MasterCard,* **VISA**

CADNAM   White Hart   FOOD

Tel 01703 812277   Fax 01703 814632   Map 14 C4
Cadnam Lyndhurst Hampshire SO40 2NP

The Emberley family run this attractive and smartly-refurbished old coaching inn, located on the edge of the New Forest beside the A31 and convenient for Junction 1 of the M27. A big welcome awaits familes either in the extensive sheltered garden, complete with a paddock of animals, or in the spacious interior which boasts plenty of exposed brick, open fires and a comfortable mix of old and new furniture. Well worth stopping for is the reliable selection of bar food on offer here. As well as tried and tested dishes (freshly battered cod and chips, mixed grill, prawn open sandwich, noisettes of lamb with fresh herb jus) listed on the varied printed menu, blackboard specials improve the choice further with game in season (venison with spring onion, bacon and oyster mushrooms) and fresh fish dishes such as sea bass with home-made lobster sausages, brill with pistou salad, and tournedos of hake with pesto dressing. Theior substantial Cheddar cheese and bacon soup was judged a runner-up in the 1997 Ilchester Cheese Pub of the Year awards (see page 26). For pudding try the chocolate and banana strudel or the brioche butter pudding. Set three-course Sunday roast lunch, good selection of real ales and at least nine wines available by the glass. *Open 11-2.30, 6-11 (Sun 11-3, 7-10.30).* **Bar Food** *11.30-2, 6-9.30 (Sun 12-2, 7-9).* **Beer** *Morland Old Speckled Hen, Wadworth 6X, Courage Best, Flowers Original. Garden, outdoor eating. MasterCard,* **VISA**

Ilchester

CALVER   Chequers Inn   FOOD

Tel 01433 630231   Fax 01433 631072   Map 6 C2   **B&B**
Froggatt Edge Calver Derbyshire S30 1ZB

🐟 🛏 **Zzz** ...

Originally four stone-built 18th century cottages, the Grade II listed Chequers stands
alongside the B6054, a mile or so above Calver on the steep banks of Froggatt's Edge.
Behind the pub, a landscaped beer garden gives way to some ten acres of steep, wild
woodland. A daily-changing blackboard might offer warm salad of pan-fried salmon
with pepper dressing, spinach and seafood terrine with tomato vinaigrette, medallions
of pork topped with apple and cider purée, and baked monkfish with seafood sauce.
The regular 'Innkeeper's Fare' sees a wide choice of interesting bar food, from hearty
sandwiches (prawn and avocado) and potted crab to chicken casserole, braised kidneys
in red wine and lamb steak marinated with orange and rosemary. To follow, try the
lime tart with citrus custard or a chilled white chocolate flan. The six bedrooms are
furnished with pine bedsteads (one a four-poster) and pristine fabrics in muted tones.
With plenty of space for armchairs, satellite TV and cosy bathrooms (with strong
over-bath showers) these are truly comfortable rooms, with the promise of a restful
night. *Open 11-3, 5-11 (Sun 12-10.30). Free House.* **Bar Food** *12-2 2.30, 6-9.30 (Sun
12-10.30).* **Beer** *Wards. Garden, outdoor eating.* **Accommodation** *6 bedrooms, all en suite,
£53 (four-poster £64, single £42). Children welcome overnight (under-3s stay free in parents'
room), additional bed (£10) & cot available. MasterCard,* **VISA**

CAMBRIDGE   The Eagle   A

Tel & Fax 01223 505020   Map 15 F1
Bene't Street Cambridge Cambridgeshire CB2 3QN

🍺

Splendidly atmospheric city-centre pub situated close to the Corn Exchange and a
stone's throw from King's College. Hidden behind the plain Georgian stone facade are
five rooms of great architectural interest dating back to the 16th century. Sensitively
restored in recent years, each relaxing room has a distinct, individual charm, boasting
original features such as stripped pine panelling, mullioned windows, fine brick
fireplaces and two medieval paintings. Tastefully adorned with sturdy wooden
furnishing, William Morris fabrics and attractive prints, it is the haunt of students,
dons and businessmen alike. Of particular interest is the red-painted ceiling in the Air
Force Bar which preserves the hundreds of signatures of British and American airmen
which were burnt on by candles and lighters during the Second World War. Cobbled
and galleried courtyard with summer seating. *Open 11-11 (Sun 12-10.30).*
Beer *Greene King. Courtyard. Amex, Diners, MasterCard,* **VISA**

CAMBRIDGE   Free Press   FOOD

Tel 01223 68337   Map 15 F1
Prospect Row Cambridge Cambridgeshire CB1 1QU

Tiny, totally non-smoking and highly atmospheric rowing-mad pub tucked away
behind the police station, close to the city centre. Simply furnished, unspoilt interior,
the snug is also used as the dining area, and rowing photographs are everywhere. It
gets extremely busy; be early. Simple, hearty home-cooking is of the sort to defrost a
cold-numbed oarsman – try the home-made soup (curried parsnip, Stilton and onion),
followed by ragout of lamb, cod and courgette lasagne and beef and beer casserole. In
addition, there are usually hot and cold vegetarian dishes – nut roast, creamy leek
croustade and carrot and cumin bake. Finish off with apple and almond pie or date
and apricot slice. *Open 12-2.30 (till 3 Sat), 6-11 (Sun 12-3, 7-10.30).* **Bar Food** *12-2
(till 2.30 Sat & Sun), 6-8.30 (Sun 7-9).* **Beer** *Greene King. Garden, outdoor eating area.
Closed 25 Dec eve & all 26 Dec. No credit cards.*

We endeavour to be as up-to-date as possible but inevitably some changes to
landlords, chefs and other key staff occur after the Guide
has gone to press.

CAMBRIDGE — Tram Depot — A

Tel 01223 324553   Map 15 F1
Dover Street Cambridge Cambridgeshire CB1 1DY

Located half a mile east of the city centre, just off East Road, this lively and unusual pub occupies the brilliantly converted Cambridge Street Tramway Company stables. Designed in classic alehouse style with brick and flagstone floors topped with a rustic mix of old pine furniture, it has a good city atmosphere. Further seating in an upstairs gallery and out in the sheltered courtyard on warmer days. Piped classical music plays at lunchtime; jazz and blues in the evening. *Open 11.30-2.30, 5-11 (from 6 Sat), Sun 12-2.30, 7-10.30).* **Beer** *Everards Tiger & Old Original, Adnams Southwold, three guest beers. Courtyard. No credit cards.*

CANTERBURY — Falstaff Inn — B&B

Tel 01227 462138   Fax 01227 463525   Map 11 C5
8 St Dunstan's Street Canterbury Kent CT2 8AF

A centuries-old coaching inn by the outer walls of the city. Day rooms, including the good pubby bar, get character from original beams, leaded windows and polished oak tables. Bedrooms are neat and pretty and the majority use solid modern furniture that suits the feel of the place perfectly; two rooms feature a four-poster bed (small supplement to the regular tariff). Within easy walking distance of the town centre and historic cathedral, near the Westgate Tower. Good pubby bar. Country Club (Whitbread) Hotels. *Open 11-11 (Sun 12-10.30).* **Beer** *Flowers Original, Wadworth 6X, guest beer.* **Accommodation** *24 bedrooms, all en suite, £75 (single £68, room only – breakfast £7.50-£8.95). Children welcome overnight (under-16s stay free in parents' room), additional bed & cot available. Amex, Diners, MasterCard,* **VISA**

CAREY — Cottage of Content — B&B

Tel 01432 840242   Fax 01432 840208   Map 14 B1
Carey Hereford Hereford & Worcester HR2 6NG

Zzz...

Follow prominent signs to Hoarwithy from the A49 or B4399 to find the only river crossing on this hidden stretch of the Wye. Deep in the valley, this aptly-named pub stands at the heart of a tiny village, fronted by a patio and porch; across the lane is a small stream and parking over a rickety wooden bridge. Within are flagstone floors and timbered alcoves with hops hanging from the beams and a central open staircase leading off the bar seemingly into the roof space. There are just four, suitably cottagey, bedrooms with sloping floors under their heavy roof timbers; three have en suite bathrooms which are carpeted and neat, yet tiny. Oak furniture is on the sturdy side, while TVs and tea-makers appear almost incongruous in the setting. No children overnight. *Open 12-2.30, 7-11 (till 10.30 Sun). Closed Mon & Tue lunch in winter. Free House.* **Beer** *Hook Norton Best & Old Hooky, Ruddles Best & County. Garden.* **Accommodation** *4 bedrooms, 3 en suite, £48 (single £30). Check-in bar hours only. Pub and accommodation closed 25 Dec. Amex, MasterCard,* **VISA**

CARLTON IN COVERDALE — Foresters Arms — FOOD

Tel & Fax 01969 640272   Map 5 D4   **B&B**
Carlton in Coverdale Leyburn North Yorkshire DL8 4BB

Chef Barrie Higginbotham is the licensee at this privately-owned free house at the heart of Coverdale. Look for signs off the A684 at West Witton to reach this successful, upmarket dining pub. Indeed, the diversity of the blackboard menus suggests sufficient ambition to test any kitchen, yet the quality of ingredients and results are not seriously in doubt. From a simple soup and ham and eggs through to warm salad of black pudding with poached quail's eggs and smoked bacon and red mullet with sun-dried tomatoes and pesto, followed by chargrilled steaks, pot-roast guinea fowl with Madeira or rosettes of lamb with orange and ginger marmalade, a broad range of tastes can be pandered to. Best available produce from the fish markets is something of a speciality with good shellfish and, typically, fillet of sea bream with scorched scallops and garlic cream, and Dover sole with a mousseline of salmon and a chive and vermouth cream. No sandwiches, but a Foresters platter with paté or cheese is offered at lunch only. Hot baked hazelnut soufflé and tarte tatin with ginger ice cream, individually cooked to order, represent some classily turned-out puddings. The three en suite bedrooms (two with showers only) have bright cottagey decor and crisp white duvets (upgrading of rooms is planned for the coming year). In addition to TVs, radios, hairdryers and trouser presses, each room has its own plug for use of the communal pay phone. Ask for the rear twin for one of the finest bedroom views in the Dales. *Open 12-3, 6.30-11 (Sun 12-3, 7-10.30). Closed Mon lunch.* **Bar Food** *12-2, 7-9 (no food Sun eve & all Mon). Free House.* **Beer** *John Smith's, Theakston Best, Tetley, two guest beers. Outdoor eating.* **Accommodation** *3 bedrooms, all en suite, £55 (single £30). Children welcome overnight (under-10s free if sharing parents' room, 10-16s full rate), additional bed & cot (charge) available. Check-in by arrangement. Accommodation closed 25 Dec & proprietors' holiday. MasterCard,* **VISA**

CARTERWAY HEADS   Manor House Inn   FOOD

Tel 01207 255268   Map 5 D3   **B&B**
Carterway Heads Shotley Bridge Northumberland DH8 9LX

The former Bolbec Manor House, standing high on the A68 (close to its junction with the B6278) was once part of an estate which traces its history back to the Norman Conquest. Almost a millennium later the Bolbec name has been revived in a dining-room converted from 200-year-old stables after renovations by the Pelley family. A wide choice of 'distinctly different' pub food is served throughout the pub's four rooms and is proclaimed on massive chalk boards. For starters, perhaps creamy vegetable soup, pasta gratin with spinach, mushrooms and mozzarella or marinated juniper herrings. Wild salmon with puy lentils and baby spinach, rack of lamb with courgette and mushroom confit, cod fillet with leeks, saffron and wild mushrooms, and pork casserole with tomato and mustard are substantial main courses. Snackier items include French bread sandwiches, home-made paté and soup. There's a hand-picked selection of small grower's wines on show, racked for inspection. Four bedrooms are fitted out in pine and equipped with TVs, beverage trays and hairdryers. Planning restrictions, however, have left them all facing the main road; they share two bathrooms, both fully tiled and comprehensively equipped, and arguably enjoy the best view of any loos in the land. *Open 11-3, 6-11 (Sun 12-3, 7-10.30).* **Bar Food** *12-2.30, 7-9.30 (till 9 Sun). Free House.* **Beer** *Butterknowle Bitter, Big Lamp Bitter, two guest beers. Garden, outdoor eating. Family room.* **Accommodation** *4 bedrooms, £38.50 (family room £60, single £22). Children welcome overnight, (under-2s stay free in parents' room), additional bed (£10) & cot available. No dogs. Accommodation and pub closed all 25 Dec. Amex, MasterCard,* **VISA**

> We do not accept free meals or hospitality – our inspectors pay their own bills and never book in the name of Egon Ronay's Guides.

CARTHORPE   Fox & Hounds   FOOD

Tel 01845 567433   Map 5 E4
Carthorpe Bedale North Yorkshire DL8 2LG

The B6285, some 10 miles north of Ripon off the A1, leads to this sleepy Bedale village. If criticism there be of the former smithy which now houses the village pub, it must be of a lack of innate pubbiness which appears entirely due to Bernadette and Howard Fitzgerald's success in catering to a well-heeled clientele with some thoughtfully produced food. Served in both bar and restaurant of the L-shaped interior is a single menu of reliably home-cooked dishes updated daily; sandwiches and ploughman's lunches are also available to 'those who ask'. Strongly represented are the day's offerings from some careful shopping at the fish markets; queen scallops and prawn mornay, and fresh mussels in cheese sauce as curtain-raisers to poached halibut with mustard sauce and sea bass with tomato and onion. Pork fillet with onion and apple sauce and lamb cutlets with redcurrant gravy appease meat-eaters and home-made puddings – profiteroles with chocolate sauce or apple and cinnamon flan – to follow will assuage the heartiest appetites. It is a good bet that from their varied list more wines are sold than the single real ale, though never on a Monday when the pub closes entirely. Children are welcome to eat in the dining-room. *Open 12-2.30, 7-11 (Sun 12-2.30, 7-10.30). Closed all Mon & 1st week Jan. Bar Food 12-2, 7-10 (till 9.30 Sun). Free House. Beer John Smith's. MasterCard, VISA*

CARTMEL FELL   Masons Arms   ★   FOOD

Tel 01539 568486   Fax 01539 568780   Map 4 C4
Strawberry Bank Cartmel Fell Cumbria LA11 6NW

The well-loved Masons Arms is a classic if ever there was one. The setting is glorious, perched on the hillside at Strawberry Bank with Lakeland views in all directions, and the interior is equally inspiring – a series of quaint, unspoilt little farmhouse rooms. In the main bar are polished old flagstones, a big open fire, sagging ceiling beams, simple country furniture and well-chosen pictures. Several cottagey anterooms offer old pews, odd bits of furniture, a sideboard, an old stove, and a curious little cupboard set into the wall. Tiny thickset windows frame pretty valley views. Aside from excellent bar food, there's an array of drinks – including their own four home brews (named after local resident Arthur Ransome's books) and, in their comprehensive bottled beer list, well over 200 interesting international names. The main menu offers a pleasing variety of home-made dishes including half a dozen or so vegetarian choices. Simple country casseroles like Cumberland sausage and beef in red wine feature strongly alongside fisherman's pie, chicken and mushroom pie and fresh salads (ham, hummus, lentil and hazelnut paté) served with home-made chutney. Daily specials may highlight brazil, almond and cashew nut loaf, caramelised onions, cranberry and Brie strudel, Portuguese fish lasagne and home-made pea and ham soup. Puddings, mostly of the good old-fashioned sort, are also not to be missed (sticky toffee pudding, chocolate fudge cake). Simple, well-cooked food tastes outstandingly fine in such splendid surroundings; be early for a seat on the terrace in summer as the Masons Arms is one of the Lake District's most popular pubs. There's also a no-smoking dining-room upstairs. Children welcome. *Open 11-3, 6-11 (Fri & Sat 11.30-11, Sun 12-10.30). Bar Food 12-2, 6-8.45. Free House. Beer Own Brews: Amazon, Great Northern, Big Six, Damson; Thwaites Bitter, guest beers. Garden, outdoor eating. Amex, MasterCard, VISA*

CASTERTON   Pheasant Inn   FOOD

Tel & Fax 01524 271230   Map 4 C4   **B&B**
Casterton Kirkby Lonsdale Cumbria LA6 2RX

Melvin and May Mackie run this well-maintained, white pebbledash building at the heart of the village, enjoying some fine rear views over open country to the hills beyond. The Garden Room, a small summery lounge full of parlour plants, leads to the main bar, which is sectioned around a central servery; burgundy banquette seating, polished wood tables with fresh flowers and country pictures on the walls make for a pleasant, restful spot in which to enjoy some reliable bar food. Printed menu fare features sandwiches, omelettes, salad platters and chargrills, while interesting specials, notably fish, grace a changing blackboard menu. Choices may include Loch Fyne cockles provençale-style or pea and ham soup, followed by baked sea bass with fresh herbs, parrot fish grilled in lime butter, beef Wellington and crispy roast duck with port and Stilton, all accompanied by a dish of fresh vegetables. While by no means luxurious (some recently upgraded), the bedrooms are both comfortable and well kept, with colour television, direct-dial phones, radios, beverage trays and neat, compact, bathrooms. There's one four-poster bed for the romantically-inclined, and a twin-bedded ground-floor room suitable for the disabled; most bedrooms have lovely countryside views. *Open 11-3, 6-11 (till 10.30 Sun). Bar Food 12-2, 6.30-9 (till 9.30 Fri & Sat). Free House. Beer Theakston Best & XB, Charles Wells Bombardier, two guest beers. Garden, outdoor eating. Family room. Accommodation 10 rooms, all en suite, £64 (single £37.50). Children welcome overnight (rate depends on age), additional bed (£10) & cot available (£5). Diners, MasterCard, VISA*

CASTLE ASHBY Falcon Hotel FOOD

Tel 01604 696200   Fax 01604 696673   Map 15 E1   **B&B**
Castle Ashby Northamptonshire NN7 1LF

Zzz...

Just six miles from Northampton (and easily found off the A428 Bedford road), Jo and Neville Watson's charming roadside establishment strikes a happy balance between historic country inn and well-appointed modern cottage hotel. Its founding in 1594 is commemorated in the small, atmospheric Cellar Bar that is approached by way of an original flagstone stairway. Bar meals (including sandwiches and ploughman's at lunchtime only) are served here on mahogany-topped, beer-barrel tables. More upmarket daily offerings might include asparagus soup with home-made bread, baked stuffed aubergine, chicken with lemon and tarragon sauce and fillet of bream with tomato and herb butter. Lunch and dinner are also served in the rear dining extension that overlooks a delightful garden; fresh from it come the courgette flowers, artichokes and garden herbs which feature on seasonal menus. Pine furniture and tasteful fabrics imbue the main-house bedrooms with the country freshness their surroundings suggest; the bathrooms here are immaculately appointed – they even have telephones! No less countrified, and recently completely refurbished, are the cottage bedrooms a stone's throw away at the heart of the village, just two minutes' walk away from the magnificent grounds and gardens of Castle Ashby House; two further rooms are in a cottage on the other side of the car park. Home-made jams and jellies are a memorable feature of the Falcon's hearty country breakfasts. No cheques or credit cards taken for under £20. Substantial tariff reductions in summer for two-night weekend stays (except during Castle Ashby House special events). *Open 12-3, 7-11 (Sun 12-2.30, 7-10.30).* **Bar Food** *12-2.30, 7-9.30. Free House.* **Beer** *Worthington Best, Marston's Pedigree, Jennings Bitter, Adnams Extra. Garden, outdoor eating.* **Accommodation** *16 bedrooms, all en suite, £75 (single £62.50). Children welcome overnight (under-12s – 1 child only – stay free in parents' room), additional bed & cot available. Amex, MasterCard,* **VISA**

CASTLE CARY George Hotel FOOD

Tel 01963 350761   Fax 01963 350035   Map 13 F2   **B&B**
Market Place Castle Cary Somerset BA7 7AH

Stone from the original 13th-century castle was used to build this listed 15th-century, thatched coaching inn – one of the oldest pubs in the country. In part, it is even older – the elm beam over the inglenook fireplace in the front bar dates back a further 500 years and has been carbon dated to the 10th century. Each of the fifteen rooms is decorated in an individual, cottagey style using either pine or darkwood furniture. All rooms have TV, radio, telephone and tea or coffee-making facilities. The food has improved here since the arrival last year of Martin Barrett from the *Walnut Tree* at nearby West Camel. His varied and interesting bar menu, listed on a daily-changing blackboard, may highlight warm salad of crispy duck and stir-fried vegetables in a honey and oil dressing or carrot and ginger soup for starters, followed by lamb and mint sausages on a bed of chive mash and gravy, Somerset lamb casseroled in a herb-flavoured gravy or steak, kidney and mushroom pie. There is always a good pasta dish, a vegetarian option and a daily fresh fish choice (perhaps grilled sea bass) available. Separate restaurant menu. *Open 10.30-3, 6-11 (Sun 12-2.30, 7-10.30).* **Bar Food** *12-2, 7-9. Free House.* **Beer** *Butcombe Bitter, Bass. Patio/terrace.* **Accommodation** *15 bedrooms, all en suite, £70 & £85 (family room sleeping four £95, single £45). Children welcome overnight, additional bed (£12.50) & cot available. Amex, MasterCard,* **VISA**

We only recommend food (Bar Food) in those establishments highlighted with the **FOOD** symbol.

| CASTLE COMBE | Castle Inn | B&B |

Tel 01249 783030   Fax 01249 782315   Map 14 B2
Castle Combe Chippenham Wiltshire SN14 7HN

Zzz...

At the centre of one of England's prettiest villages, right by the ancient monument stone cross, this famous hostelry can trace its own origins back to the 12th century. Now in the Hatton Hotels' group, it is arguably one of England's smartest inns. Attention to detail in exposing and retaining the intricate old stonework and centuries-old beams has been commendable, and nowhere is this better evidenced than in the conservatory that opens on to a private, enclosed patio; as a location for breakfasts served in several international guises, it is perhaps unparallelled. Each of the bedrooms has been modelled in individual style to a very high standard. Two 'Executive' rooms have en suite whirlpool bathrooms and a third a Victorian-style slipper bath. Accessories which might elsewhere be thought of as luxuries are standard throughout, with remote-control TVs, radio-alarms with phones, trouser presses and hairdryers. Here, the truly cossetting extras are complimentary fruit and mineral waters, boiled sweets, towelling robes, rubber ducks and resident teddy bears. *Open 11-11, (Sun 12-10.30). Free House.* **Beer** *Ruddles County, Courage Best, guest beer.* **Accommodation** *7 bedrooms, all en suite, £85-£95 (single £65-£75). Children welcome overnight, additional bed (£20) & cot available. No dogs. Amex, Diners, MasterCard,* **VISA**

> We do not accept free meals or hospitality – our inspectors pay their own bills and never book in the name of Egon Ronay's Guides.

| CASTLE COMBE | White Hart | A |

Tel 01249 782295   Map 14 B2
Castle Combe Chippenham Wiltshire SN14 7HS

Down and across the village square from the central stone cross stands the historic, cream-painted White Hart. It's down another step into the main bar, all leaded lights, stone alcoves and flagstone floors, which echo times past, warmed by the thigh-high dog grate that can throw an uncomfortable height of heat in winter. Convivial at the best of times, it can also be a crush. Across the passage, a carpeted lounge and family room have rather more space and less frenetic activity. To the rear, a glass-covered conservatory with flagstone floor leads through into a rear, cobbled beer garden. Parking is very limited in central Castle Combe; be warned that it's some 300 yards' walk down from the public car park. *Open 11-2.30, 6-11 (11-11 summer), Sun 12-2.30, 6-10.30 (12-10.30 summer).* **Beer** *Wadworth 6X, guest beer. Garden. Family room. MasterCard,* **VISA**

| CASTLETON | Castle Hotel | B&B |

Tel 01433 620578   Fax 01433 621112   Map 6 C2
Castle Street Castleton Derbyshire S30 2WG

This pleasant old inn dating back in part to the 17th century features strongly for its accommodation. Comfortable bedrooms in the main house and stable-block annexe are all prettily decorated, with solid darkwood furnishings, including four-posters, and smartly tiled en suite facilities (three have whirlpool baths). Despite modernisation, the bars still offer plenty of old-world atmosphere – notably the Castle Bar with its flagstoned floors and low beamed ceilings. Bass Taverns. *Open 11-11 (Sun 12-10.30).* **Beer** *Stones, Worthington Best, Bass. Garden. Family room.* **Accommodation** *9 bedrooms, all en suite, £59-£95 (single £39.50, Fri & Sat £59). Children welcome overnight (under-12s £12 if sharing parents' room), additional bed & cot available. Check-in by arrangement. Small dogs only. Amex, Diners, MasterCard,* **VISA**

CAULDON   Yew Tree Inn   A

Tel 01538 308348   Map 6 C3
Cauldon Waterhouses Stoke-on-Trent Staffordshire ST10 3EJ

Alan East has acquired his vast collection of antiques and bric-a-brac over the last 35 years as landlord of this old-fashioned, stone-built pub. Persian rugs overlay original quarry-tiled floors and there are cast-iron copper-topped tables, a working pianola and giant Victorian music boxes which still operate for just 2p. Sleepy and undiscovered it is not, but worth a visit, nevertheless; go in the evening and hear the landlord performing on the pianola. Between A52 and A523, eight miles west of Ashbourne, five miles from Alton Towers. Children allowed in the 'Polyphon Room'. *Open 10-2.30 (till 3 Sat), 6-11 (Sun 12-3, 7-10.30). Free House. Beer Bass, Burton Bridge Bitter, M&B Dark Mild. Family room. No credit cards.*

CERNE ABBAS   New Inn   A

Tel 01300 341274   Map 13 F2
Cerne Abbas Dorchester Dorset DT2 7JF

'New' refers to 16th-century modernisation to an 11th-century structure – a redbrick arch and steep slate-stone roof – so no nasty architectural shocks here. It was originally used as a dormitory for the nearby Abbey, accommodating passing pilgrims, before becoming a coaching inn during the 16th century. There's a comfortably furnished bar adorned with farming memorabilia and where good Eldridge Pope ales and an excellent selection of up to 14 wines by the glass, chosen from the wide-ranging list of 50 bottles, can be enjoyed. At the end of the courtyard is a large, peaceful walled garden with rose-beds and benches. The picturesque village is well worth a visit, as is the Bronze Age fertility symbol – the Cerne Abbas Giant – carved on the hillside above the village. *Open 11-3, 6-11 (Sun 12-3, 7-10.30). Beer Eldridge Pope, guest beer. Garden. Amex, MasterCard,* **VISA**

CERNE ABBAS   Red Lion   FOOD

Tel 01300 341441   Map 13 F2
Cerne Abbas Long Street Dorchester Dorset DT2 7JF

Unassuming, ancient Grade II listed pub with an unusual Victorian facade, thanks to a late 19th-century fire. The single carpeted bar is simply furnished and boasts a splendid 16th-century fireplace, crackling with logs in winter. Bar food ranges from a printed menu offering the usual favourites to a more interesting blackboard selection of hearty home-cooked dishes, which are the main emphasis of the kitchen. A two-tiered pricing system offers small or larger portions of rabbit, pork and apple pie, fresh cod or haddock in ale batter, Portland crab salad, hare in port wine or fresh salmon lasagne. There is always a choice of two home-made soups such as cream of spinach or mushroom. Good desserts may include Dorset apple cake or treacle tart. In summer months the delightful, well-tended and sheltered south-facing garden is a real oasis away from the busy village street. Visitors wishing to stay in this charming village and explore the area further can make use of one of the four new en suite bedrooms (£47 double) that were due to come on line at the end of 1996. The ladies' loo is a real 5-star luxury specimen. *Open 11.30-11 (Sun 12-3, 7-10.30). Bar Food 11.30-2.30, 6.30-11 (Sun 12-2.30, 7-10). Free House. Beer Wadworth 6X & IPA, local guest beer. Garden, outdoor eating.* **VISA**

CHADLINGTON   Tite Inn   FOOD

Tel 01608 676475   Map 14a B1
Mill End Chadlington Oxfordshire OX7 3NY

This warm 16th-century Cotswold-stone pub is as pretty as a picture, complete with cottage roses clambering up the walls. Inside, the original rough stone walls remain, but otherwise it is almost too neat and tidy, with its modern carpeted floor and wheelback chairs. A table displaying newspapers and magazines is a nice touch, though, and there is also a garden room which features bunches of grapes hanging from a vine covering the roof. Michael Willis behind the bar looks after the real ales, while Susan looks after the kitchen. Hearty home-made soups, haddock smokey with salad, lambs kidneys braised in port, bobotie (spicy South African dish) and spinach and ricotta lasagne are amongst the offerings listed on the regularly-changing blackboard menu, and there are always several vegetarian dishes available. A traditional roast is served on Sundays. Popular puddings include fruit crumble, hot sticky toffee pudding and chocolate and rum mousse. Children are made genuinely welcome and small portions are no problem. *Open 12-3, 6.30-11 (Sun 12-3, 7-10.30).* *Closed Mon (except Bank Holidays).* **Bar Food** *12-2, 7-9 (no food Mon).* *Free House.* **Beer** *Archers Village, Wychwood The Dog's Bollocks, two guest beers. Garden, outdoor eating. No credit cards.*

CHALE   Clarendon Hotel & Wight Mouse Inn   FOOD

Tel & Fax 01983 730431　　　　　　　Map 15 D4　　**B&B**
Chale Isle of Wight PO38 2HA

🐕 Zzz... ☺

John and Jean Bradshaw's frenetic family hotel and pub is set well back from the A3055 overlooking Chale Bay and the Needles; an object lesson in good innkeeping it continues year-round to pull in the crowds from near and far, even providing for those from afar private transport, the Mousemobile, by arrangement. The pub's interior, full of ships' beams, antique artefacts and musical instruments includes a cluster of family rooms and play areas matched only by outdoor facilities which include adventure playground and barbecue terrace where there are Punch and Judy shows in summer and pony rides to be had on Syd the Welsh cob and Arthur the Shetland pony. For a kitchen producing hundreds of meals all day, every day, output is remarkably consistent; anything goes, from a child's egg and chips through local crab for grandma to Wiener Schnitzel with potato salad and fried egg and the giant Clarendon mixed grill for trenchermen. There's a free lucky bag given with every child's meal ordered, while to keep the grown-ups happy there are as many wines as there are weeks in a year, a different real ale for every day of the week and 365 different whiskies on sale, including "Famous Mouse", and 366 again next Leap Year – 2000 AD! Fully half the en suite bedrooms have three or more beds, and there are two self-contained family suites with sitting areas and two full-size bedrooms, one of them (for parents only!) containing a water-bed. Everything from early teas to mid-evening entertainment is designed to be as likeable as possible, as reflected by charges for children, inclusive of all meals, on a graduating scale from £14 weekly for 2-year-olds to £25 per day at age thirteen. *Open 11-midnight (Sun 12-10.30).* **Bar Food** *11.30-10 (Sun 12-9.30).* *Free House.* **Beer** *Marston's Pedigree, Wadworth 6X, Boddingtons, Whitbread Fuggles Imperial, Strong Country Bitter, Morland Old Speckled Hen, guest beer. Garden, outdoor eating, children's play area. 3 Family rooms.* **Accommodation** *13 bedrooms, 10 en suite (3 with bath), £66 (suite £89, single from £35, higher in season). Children welcome overnight (0-2 £3.50, 3-7 £8, 8-13 £25, 14-16 £33), additional bed & cot available. Dogs £3.50. MasterCard,* **VISA**

CHARING   Royal Oak Inn   B&B

Tel 01233 712612　Fax 01233 713355　　　Map 11 C5
High Street Charing Ashford Kent TN27 0HU

Homely inn located in the centre of an attractive medieval village at the base of the North Downs, just off the A20. Good pubby bar with bare boards and simple pine furniture and an upstairs function area in the old malting room. Neat, simply furnished accommodation in five en suite bedrooms, the best rooms being located in the new rear extension. Good, clean bathrooms or compact shower rooms and TVs and tea-making facilities for added comfort. Handy overnight stop for the ferry ports or the Chunnel. *Open 11-2.30, 6-11.* *Free House.* **Beer** *Bass, Fuller's London Pride, Shepherd Neame Master Brew, guest beer.* **Accommodation** *5 bedrooms, all en-suite, £45 (family room £50, single £35). No children under 6 overnight, additional bed supplied. No dogs. MasterCard,* **VISA**

CHARLBURY — Bell Hotel — B&B

Tel 01608 810278   Fax 01608 811447   Map 14a B2
Church Street Charlbury Oxfordshire OX7 3PP

Zzz...

Historic Charlbury with its 7th-century St Mary's Church was royally chartered to hold cattle markets in 1256: the last one was held behind the Bell some 700 years later. With its own datestone of 1700, the mellow stone inn is full of character. The small flagstoned bar and sun-lounge makes guests feel much at home and in fair weather the patio looking down a long, sloping garden is a picturesque spot. Access to bedrooms is by steep staircases and narrow passageways yet the rooms themselves are spacious and neatly appointed with matching fabrics and up-to-date accessories which include hairdryers, trouser presses and welcome clock-radios. The three smaller doubles have en suite WC/showers only and one single is not en suite, though its adjacent bathroom is private. Conference facilities in the converted stable block accommodate up to 55. *Open 10.30-11 (Sun 12-10.30). Free House.* **Beer** *Hook Norton Best, Wadworth 6X. Family room.* **Accommodation** *14 bedrooms, all en suite, £75 (single £50). Children welcome overnight (under-16s stay free in parents' room), additional bed & cot available. Amex, Diners, MasterCard,* ***VISA***

CHARLBURY — Bull Inn — ★ — FOOD

Tel 01608 810689   Map 14a B2   **B&B**
Charlbury Oxfordshire OX7 3RR

Having bought the 16th-century Bull Inn (a handsome stone pub overlooking the main street of this charming Cotswold country town) in the spring of 1995 when it was just another run-down 'local', Roy and Suzanne Flynn promptly closed it and spent the whole summer totally refurbishing and, in some areas, rebuilding the premises. The result has been well worth waiting for, as it is a real gem for atmosphere and good home-cooked food, as well as for promising overnight accommodation. Time, effort and money have been seriously invested by the highly personable Flynns to make the Bull a welcome newcomer to the Guide. The rather upmarket appearance of the spruced-up exterior is matched inside with a most relaxing and tastefully furnished lounge and dining-room, both adorned throughout with personal items collected over the years. Intending diners can sink with a drink into two large comfortable sofas and matching armchairs, all cosily arranged on the coir matting floor in front of the huge stone fireplace with open log fire, and savour the appealing surroundings. From warm, ragged-yellow walls, some exposed stone, a wealth of beams and stripped-pine furniture to old Persian rugs on modern flagstones in the dining-room area, a collection of blue and white china in a corner cupboard, numerous antiques and a fine dresser topped with a huge bowl of fresh fruit, pot pourri and dried flowers, there is much to catch and please the eye. The adjacent bar area and rear extension is equally welcoming, boasting wooden floors, wicker chairs around round tables and an array of old baskets hanging from the beams. Ex-rock band manager and restaurateur Roy Flynn is a natural 'front' person, keen to please all that come through the door and dividing his time from pulling pints of ale for the locals to chatting to and advising diners on menu choices in the lounge. Suzanne Flynn toils away behind the scenes in the kitchen to produce superior pub food, which is attracting a loyal dining clientele from miles around. Both the above-average printed menu and the imaginative lists of specials are served throughout the pub, with filled French baguettes available in the bar only at lunchtimes. Among the snacks/starters there may be fresh mushroom soup, houmus with hot pitta bread and black olives, and a warm salad of chicken livers and bacon with raspberry vinaigrette, with mouthwatering main-course options like a generous bowl of Mediterranean-style fish stew – crammed with chunks of fish and shellfish in a rich tomatoey sauce – baked sea bass with fennel and Pernod, Thai green chicken curry, breast of chicken stuffed with crab meat on a creamy saffron sauce, breast of duck with honey, lime and ginger, or fresh salmon fishcakes with hollandaise. Good vegetables or crisp salads with walnut-oil dressing. Daily vegetarian dishes may feature fresh tortellini with wild mushroom sauce and fresh parmesan. Sound puddings from sticky toffee pudding or apple, raspberry and walnut crumble to a rich, dark chocolate mousse with Cointreau and cream. Traditional Sunday lunch – booking advisable. Three smart and spotless upstairs bedrooms await investment and upgrading, when period pieces of furniture will replace the modern darkwood furnishings that characterise the rooms at present. All have TVs, tea-making equipment and clean en suite facilities (two with shower/WC only). Well-behaved children are welcome indoors if eating and only over-8s are allowed to stay overnight. Roy and Suzanne win our Pub Hosts of the Year Award for 1997. *Open 12-2.30, 6.30-11 (Sun 12-3 only). Closed Sun eve, except Bank Holidays).* **Bar Food** *12-2, 7-9 (till 9.30 Fri & Sat). No bar food Sun eve. Free House.* **Beer** *Greene King IPA & Abbot Ale, guest beer. Terrace, outdoor eating.* **Accommodation** *3 bedrooms, all en suite, £60 (single £50). No under-8s overnight. Check-in by arrangement. No dogs. MasterCard,* **VISA**

CHARLESTOWN — Pier House Hotel — B&B

Tel 01726 67955   Fax 01726 69246   Map 12 B3
Charlestown St Austell Cornwall PL25 3NJ

Nearly all the rooms at this 18th-century hotel have either far-reaching sea views or they overlook the attractive harbour of this charming and popular little port; the setting for many a television or film production. Bedrooms vary in size and style; some feature attractive modern darkwood pieces of furniture, others are rather plain, but all are neat and clean with pretty floral fabrics, TVs, radio/alarms, telephone and tea-making facilities; good shower/bathrooms. Four family rooms have both a double and a single bed. Public areas include a small pubby bar and a rear dining area, which is open during the day for snacks and cream teas. Disabled WC. *Open 11-2.30, 6-11 (11-11 & Sun 12-10.30 in summer). Free House.* **Beer** *Bass, Boddingtons.* **Accommodation** *25 bedrooms, all en suite (five with bath), £59-£62 (single £30/£37, family room £78). Children welcome overnight, additional bed & cot available. No dogs. MasterCard,* **VISA**

CHARLESTOWN — Rashleigh Arms — B&B

Tel 01726 73635   Map 12 B3
Charlestown St Austell Cornwall PL25 3NJ

Under the same ownership as the Pier House Hotel on the quay, this much-extended and refurbished Georgian inn has an attractive flower-bedecked facade and a vast open-plan interior. The main interest of this inn is the five neat and comfortable first-floor bedrooms that are ideal for visiting St Austell businessmen and popular with holidaymakers not requiring the formalities and facilities of a hotel. All have modern pine furniture, floral duvets and curtains, bedside lamps, TVs, tea-making facilities and are light and airy with clean, compact shower rooms. *Open 11-11 (Sun 12-10.30). Free House.* **Beer** *Wadworth 6X, Ruddles County, Bass, Tetley Bitter, guest beer. Garden. Family room.* **Accommodation** *5 bedrooms, all en suite (showers), £48 (single £24). Children welcome overnight. No dogs. MasterCard,* **VISA**

CHARLTON — Horse & Groom — FOOD

Tel 01666 823904   Fax 01666 823390   Map 14 C2   **B&B**
Charlton Malmesbury Wiltshire SH16 9DL

Zzz...

The solidly elegant Cotswold stone house fronted by a tree-sheltered lawn stands in its own paddock well back from the B4040. Its history as a coaching inn dating back to the 16th century is well documented by the framed prints and drawings which hang in the rustic main bar which retains an evocative air of exposed stonework, woodblock flooring and assorted country farmhouse-style pine chairs and tables. The adjacent lounge and dining areas (where bookings are taken) are rather more intimately conducive to the enjoyment of the good bar food. Groomburgers, lasagne, and ham, egg and chips should satisfy traditionalists, while adventurous eaters can be tempted by roast duck breast with a redcurrant and strawberry sauce, seafood provençale, Normandy pork – cooked in apple brandy sauce – and pan-fried beef medallions with tarragon butter. For a pub of apparently modest size and appointments, meanwhile, the three double bedrooms are a revelation: 32-channel satellite TV, hi-tech phones and complimentary fruit and mineral water are all provided. Gold-tapped, tiled bathrooms with towelling robes and his-and-hers toiletries provide hotel-style trappings.

The task of co-ordinating operations (and fulfilling such high expectations) is undertaken by the two young licensees, Nichola King and chef Philip Gilder, who approach the challenge with great relish and good humour. Children not encouraged overnight. *Open 12-2.30, 7-11 (from 6 Sat, till 10.30 Sun). Bar Food 12-2, 7-10 (till 9.30 Sun). Free House. Beer Archers Village, Wadworth 6X, guest beer. Garden, outdoor eating, children's play area. Family room. Accommodation 3 bedrooms, all en suite, £69.50 (single £55). Check-in by arrangement. MasterCard, VISA*

CHATTON   Percy Arms   B&B

Tel 01668 215244   Map 5 D1
Chatton Alnwick Northumberland WE66 5PS

☺

"A romantic retreat, situated in a favourite neighbourhood, several miles of free fishing water in the Till. Half an hour's walk from Chillingham Castle, Park and wild cattle. Well-aired beds. Good stabling". Posted prominently at the bar, the words of John Fitzgerald, proprietor at the turn of the century, ring equally true today. Stabling – for residents – is as good as ever with beds as well-aired: one wonders what the former landlord would have made of en suite WCs and showers, colour TVs and beverage trays, let alone the guests' private sauna and solarium. The sole village pub since 1874, today's black oak bar is many times bigger than that of yesteryear, with a children's games room to the rear and a tiny garden in front. *Open 11-3, 6-11 (Sun 12-3, 7-10.30). Free House. Beer Theakston XB, guest beer. Garden. Family room. Accommodation 7 bedrooms, 5 en suite (showers), £40 (family room £50, single £20). Children welcome overnight (under-3s free and 4-12s £10 if sharing parents' room), additional bed & cot available. Accommodation closed 25 Dec. MasterCard, VISA*

CHENIES   Red Lion   FOOD

Tel 01923 282722   Fax 01923 283797   Map 15a E2
Chenies Rickmansworth Hertfordshire WD3 6ED

Just up the lane from Chenies Manor, an unassuming, white-painted pub with a plain, simply-furnished main bar and a charming small dining area housed in the original 17th-century cottage to the rear with a tiled floor, old inglenook and rustic furniture. A varied selection of home-cooked bar food includes French bread sticks, wholemeal baps and jacket potatoes with unusual fillings, popular pies straight from the oven (venison with seed mustard and pepper crust), halibut steak with herb butter and liver and bacon casserole. A blackboard lists a few daily specials, including the home-made soup – cream of broccoli and almond – Thai-style noodles and chicken salad, and warm mozzarella and Mediterranean vegetable salad for vegetarians. Puddings range from home-made ice creams to rhubarb crumble. The pub is not suitable for children. *Open 11-2.30, 5.30-11 (Sun 12-3, 6.30-10.30). Bar Food 12-2, 7-10 (Sun 6.30-9.30). Beer Benskins Best Bitter, Wadworth 6X, Lion Pride (brewed by Rebellion Beer Company), guest beer. Amex, MasterCard, VISA*

CHERITON   Flower Pots Inn   FOOD   B&B

Tel 01962 771318   Map 15 D3
Cheriton Alresford Hampshire SO24 0QQ

Originally built as a farmhouse in the 1840s by the head gardener of nearby Avington House, this unassuming and homely brick village pub is a popular place in which to enjoy simple, honest bar food, good home-brewed ales and comfortable overnight accommodation. Two traditional bars are delightfully music- and electronic game-free, the rustic public bar being furnished with pine tables and benches and the cosy saloon bar having a relaxing sofa among other chairs. Both have open winter fires and an added feature is a 27ft glass-topped well. A separate room has some easy chairs, numerous books and a television to keep children amused. A short value-for-money menu offers honest home-cooked snacks and features a range of jacket potatoes with decent fillings (not Sat & Sun lunch), generously-filled baps, chili and hearty 'Pots' hotpots – liver and bacon, beef and ale stew or lamb and apricot, served with crusty bread. Puddings are not available. These quick, filling snacks can be washed down by a choice of three real ales of varying strengths, brewed on the premises in the Cheriton

Brewhouse. Also across the car park are five neat, pine-furnished bedrooms housed in a well-converted outbuilding. Downstairs rooms are compact, while the two attic rooms are light and airy with additional sofa beds; all have floral fabrics, TV, tea-makers, magazines and spotless, tiled shower rooms. *Open 12-2.30, 6-11 (Sun 12-3, 7-10.30).* **Bar Food** *12-2, 7-9 (no bar food Sun eve). Free House.* **Beer** *Cheriton Brewhouse Pots Ale, Best Bitter, Diggers Gold & occasional brews (Flower Power, Turkey's Revenge). Garden, outdoor eating.* **Accommodation** *5 bedrooms, all en suite (showers), £43.50 (single £26). Check-in bar hours only. No credit cards.*

CHERITON BISHOP — Old Thatch Inn — FOOD

Tel 01647 24204   Fax 01647 24584   Map 13 D2   **B&B**
Cheriton Bishop Exeter Devon EX6 6HJ

Attractive, white-painted and thatched roadside inn, located on the old A30 and a useful detour from the dual carriageway for comfortable overnight accommodation and above-average bar food. A central fireplace is lit in winter and warms the rambling, carpeted and plainly furnished main bar; the smaller side room – Travellers Nook – is unusually decorated with Ordnance Survey maps. Bar food relies on an extensive printed menu that features standard favourites alongside a few more imaginative dishes that are well described; results on the plate should not disappoint. Starters or snacks include freshly-prepared soups (tomato, onion and herb), peppered mushrooms and Greek salad, while main-course fare ranges from Thatcher's lamb – cooked in a tomato and garlic sauce – and Normandy pork steak with apple, cream and calvados to pork satay, jugged rabbit and chicken cordon bleu. Regular sweets include Creole bananas and pears in red wine. Homely, good-value accommodation is offered in three neat bedrooms with 'stag' furniture, TVs, tea-making kits, radio/alarms and clean en suite facilities. No children under 14 on the premises. *Open 12-2.40 (Sat from 11.30 summer), 6.30-11 (from 6 Fri & Sat, from 7 Mon-Thu winter), Sun 12-2.40, 6.30-10.30.* **Bar Food** *12-2.15 (till 2 Sun), 6.30-9.30 (from 6 Fri & Sat, till 9 Sun, from 7 Mon-Thu winter). Free House.* **Beer** *Wadworth 6X, Cotleigh Tawny Bitter, Hall & Woodhouse Tanglefoot.* **Accommodation** *3 bedrooms all en suite (baths), £45 (single £33.50). Check-in by arrangement. No dogs. Pub & accommodation closed 1st 2 weeks Nov.* MasterCard, *VISA*

CHESTER — Ye Olde King's Head — B&B

Tel 01244 324855   Fax 01244 315693   Map 6 A2
48/50 Lower Bridge Street Chester Cheshire CH1 1RS

A striking black and white timber-framed building just a stone's throw from the Roman walls and river, yet handy for high street shopping. Residents find evening refuge from popular all-day bars in a first-floor lounge bar and Hudson's restaurant. Second-floor bedrooms have recently been refurbished and house some remarkable features, the superb 16th-century roof trusses fortunately reinforced with forged steel pins. Dark hardwood fittings and co-ordinated fabrics stay in keeping, while comforts are plentiful with dial-out phones, TVs, tea trays and trouser presses: en suite bathrooms are necessarily small, but are neatly appointed. Premier Inn (Greenalls). *Open 12-11 (from 11 Sat, till 10.30 Sun).* **Beer** *Greenalls, guest beer. Family room.* **Accommodation** *8 bedrooms, all en suite, £51.40 (four-poster £59.90, single £41.50). Children welcome overnight (£5, under-5s free), additional bed & cot available. No dogs.* Amex, Diners, MasterCard, *VISA*

CHICKSGROVE — Compasses Inn — FOOD

Tel & Fax 01722 714318   Map 14 C3   **B&B**
Chicksgrove Tisbury Salisbury Wiltshire SP3 6NB

A timeless air pervades this attractive, 16th-century thatched inn, set on a peaceful lane, deep in rolling Wiltshire countryside. An old cobbled path leads to the entrance of the charmingly unspoilt bar, which has a low-beamed ceiling, partly flagstoned floor and an assortment of traditional furniture arranged in many secluded alcoves. Various farming tools and tackle from bygone days adorn the bare walls and a 100-year-old set of table skittles maintain the old-world atmosphere. Sarah Lethbridge produces a short, regularly-changing blackboard list of home-cooked dishes which may highlight cream of carrot and leek soup and avocado and crispy bacon salad for a starter or snack. More substantial offerings may include steak and Guinness pie, breast of chicken with stem ginger, medallions of pork with paprika and cream and chargrilled steak with garlic butter, all served with crisp vegetables. A separate board lists the lunchtime sandwiches and ploughman's platters. A small adjoining dining/ children's room leads out to a sheltered rear garden with rural views – ideal (as is the front brolly- and bench-filled lawn) for a peaceful summer alfresco pint. Reached via a covered outside staircase are three homely, simply furnished bedrooms, one tucked beneath the heavy thatch. Two have en suite shower rooms, the third having its own private facilities across the communal lounge, which has easy chairs, tea-making equipment, TV and bookcases. A peaceful, rural base from which to explore this beautiful area. *Open 11-3, 6.30-11 (Sun 12-3, 7-10.30). Closed Mon (except Bank Holidays, then closed following Tue).* **Bar Food** *12-2, 7-9 (till 9.30 Fri & Sat). Free House.* **Beer** *Tisbury Old Wardour, Bass, Wadworth 6X, Adnams Southwold. Garden, children's play area. Family room.* **Accommodation** *3 bedrooms, 2 en suite, £45 (single £25). Children welcome overnight (under-2s stay free in parents' room), additional bed (£10) available. Check-in by arrangement. No dogs. MasterCard,* **VISA**

CHIDDINGFOLD   Crown Inn   B&B

Tel 01428 682255   Fax 01428 685736   Map 11 A5
The Green Petworth Road Chiddingfold Surrey GU8 4TX
Zzz...

Originally a guest house for pilgrims and Cistercian monks, the creeper-clad, medieval timber-framed Crown (built around 1258) is still offering hospitality to travellers. The soft furnishings in the main bar area have recently been refurbished and one's eye is taken by the massive old beams and huge inglenook fireplace. A panelled restaurant, of slightly later date, boasts an ornate plaster ceiling and examples of the stained glass for which Chiddingfold was famous during the 13th and 17th centuries. Creaking stairs and corridors lead to the bedrooms, some full of character with antique furniture (three with four-poster beds), and others lighter and more modern in style. All have remote-control TV, direct-dial phone, beverage tray and trouser press. Badger Inns. *Open 11-11 (Sun 12-10.30).* **Beer** *Hall & Woodhouse Tanglefoot & Badger Best, Wadworth 6X, Charles Wells Eagle IPA. Garden, terrace, courtyard.* **Accommodation** *8 bedrooms, all en suite, from £57 (four-poster £78, suite £90, single £47). Children welcome overnight (under-4s stay free in parents' room), additional bed & cot available. Amex, Diners, MasterCard,* **VISA**

CHIDDINGSTONE   Castle Inn   A

Tel 01892 870247   Fax 01892 870808   Map 11 B5
Chiddingstone Edenbridge Kent TN8 7AH

Located at the end of a unique, unspoilt row of Tudor timbered houses opposite the parish church, this historic tile-hung building dates from 1420 and boasts leaded casement windows and projecting upper gables. Like the rest of the village street, the pub is owned by the National Trust and remains delightfully unchanged with two traditional, atmospheric bars. Classic public bar with chequered quarry-tiled floor, beams, an old brick fireplace and rustic wall benches. Extra comfort can be found in the beamed lounge bar and alfresco summer eating in the pretty rear garden and courtyard. Children are welcome in the lounge bar. Excellent wine list. *Open 11-3, 6-11 (Sat 11-11, Sun 12-10.30). Free House.* **Beer** *Harveys Sussex Bitter, Larkins Traditional, guest beer. Garden. Amex, Diners, MasterCard,* **VISA**

CHILGROVE   White Horse Inn   FOOD

Tel 01243 535219   Fax 01243 535301   Map 15 D3   B&B
Chilgrove Chichester West Sussex PO18 9HX
⟨◇ 🛏 🍷 Zzz...

Wisteria-clad pub and restaurant (recommended in our *1997 Hotels & Restaurants Guide*) in a glorious Sussex Downs setting. The bar is quite modest in appearance – red plastic banquettes and pink draylon chairs around simple wooden tables – and the only beer served comes from a small barrel sitting on the bar counter. The selection of wines is another matter, though, as landlord Barry Phillips (here for over 25 years) has created one of the best cellars in the country and from which around twenty wines (including champagne or a South African sparkler) are available by the glass at any one time. Bar meals, the responsibility of chef-partner Neil Rusbridger, are displayed on cards pinned up on a cork noticeboard. Typically the selection might include fresh lobster, asparagus pancake, lamb's liver and bacon, steak and kidney pie along with ploughman's lunches, sandwiches and salads. There are always a couple of vegetarian options (spinach and mushroom vol au vent) and possibly chocolate and chestnut mousse among the choice of puddings. In the evenings there is also a short, three-course supper menu at £12.50 including coffee. No children indoors but there's plenty of room outdoors in good weather. Overnight accommodation is available in the adjacent, superbly restored 16th-century cottage (Forge Cottage); five charming bedrooms (four doubles and one single: Tel 01243 535335) boast beams, original features – one has an old bread oven – and all have en suite bathrooms. Four are approached up steep stairs, while a further couple are at ground-floor level and have facilities for the disabled. No under-16s overnight. *Open 11-2.30, 6-11 (Sun 12-3 only). Closed Sun eve, all Mon, last week Oct & 3 weeks Feb.* **Bar Meals** *12-2, 6-10 (no food Sun eve & all Mon). Free House.* **Beer** *Ballard's Best. Garden, outdoor eating.* **Accommodation** *5 bedrooms, all en suite, £70 (single £35-£50). Diners, MasterCard,* **VISA**

CHILHAM — White Horse — A

Tel 01227 730355   Map 11 C5
The Square Chilham Kent CT4 8BY

Probably the most photographed pub in the county, this attractive, white-painted and part-timbered pub nestles within what is arguably the prettiest village square in Kent. Sited next to the church and surrounded by medieval timbered houses, the White Horse dates from 1422 and offers weary tourists a welcome retreat within the three comfortably-furnished, interconnecting rooms, which are warmed by good winter log fires – one in a massive inglenook. An intriguing history includes the discovery in 1956 of two skeletons, possibly soldiers killed at the Battle of Chilham during the Wat Tyler rebellion of 1380 and now buried in the churchyard next door. Walled garden and front benches with village square views. No children under 14 inside. Whitbread Wayside Inn. *Open 11-11 (Sun 12-10.30).* **Beer** *Fremlins Bitter, Flowers Original, Boddingtons, guest beer. Walled garden, outdoor eating area. MasterCard,* **VISA**

CHILHAM — Woolpack — B&B

Tel 01227 730208   Fax 01227 731053   Map 11 C5
The Street Chilham Kent CT4 8DL

Dating from 1420, this pretty salmon pink-painted inn lies within 100 yards of Chilham's charming square and castle. A historic place with a refurbished olde-worlde bar, an attractive dining-room and thirteen en suite bedrooms. A new landlord since last years guide has redecorated and upgraded most of bedrooms which vary in size and location, the sole main building bedroom and one of the three wool store rooms boasting fine four-poster beds. Good overnight accommodation for families, one of the decent-sized family rooms having access to a sheltered garden with seating. All have clean bath or shower rooms and TVs, tea-makers, telephones and clock-radios for added comfort. The suite has three separate rooms: a double, single and twin plus a bathroom; priced up to £110 for 6 adults. *Open 11-11 (Sun 12-3, 5-10.30).* **Beer** *Shepherd Neame. Garden, courtyard.* **Accommodation** *13 bedrooms, all en suite, £49.50 (family room with garden £65-£85, four-poster £65, suite from £85, single £38.50). Children welcome overnight, additional cot available. Amex, MasterCard,* **VISA**

We endeavour to be as up-to-date as possible but inevitably some changes to landlords, chefs and other key staff occur after the Guide has gone to press.

CHILLENDEN   Griffin's Head   FOOD

Tel 01304 840325   Map 11 C5
Chillenden nr Canterbury Kent CT3 1PS

An architectural gem of a building nestling in a tiny farming hamlet amid rolling open countryside south-east of Canterbury. Dating from 1286, the Griffin's Head is a fine black-and-white, half-timbered Wealden hall house that was originally built as a farmhouse to serve the local estate. Ale and cider were always brewed on the premises for the workers but it was only granted an ale licence in 1743 so that the rector could hold tithe suppers in the building. The present Tudor structure is built around the original wattle and daub walls, remains of which can be viewed in one of the three delightfully unspoilt rooms, which also feature flagstone floors, exposed brick walls and beams and a tasteful mix of furnishings, from old scrubbed pine tables and chairs to church pews. The full complement of cask-conditioned Shepherd Neame ales and a good list of wines, including interesting bin ends, a wine of the week and an impressive choice of champagnes, are served to accompany the reliable pub food. A varied and regularly-changing blackboard list of dishes highlights hearty snacks like ploughman's lunches, home-made soup (thick vegetable) and seafood mornay, alongside lamb's liver and bacon, Barnsley lamb chops, home-made lasagne, chicken breast stuffed with cream cheese, mushrooms and bacon and evening extra like good steaks and fresh fish dishes. Puddings may include lemon and almond Bakewell tart and apple and toffee crumble. Rambling roses and clematis fill the attractive garden, the setting for popular summer weekend barbecues. Children are not encouraged indoors. Chillenden's restored open trestle post mill built in 1868 is well worth closer inspection. *Open 11-11 (Sun 12-3, 7-10.30). Bar Food 12-2, 7-9.30 (no food Sun eve). Beer Shepherd Neame. Garden, patio, outdoor eating, barbecue. Amex, MasterCard, **VISA***

CHILLINGTON   Chillington Inn   FOOD

Tel 01548 580244   Map 13 D3   **B&B**
Chillington Kingsbridge Devon TQ7 2JS

The front door of this white-painted 16th-century inn opens directly on to the main road through the village, with no pavement in between, so take care when leaving after a convivial evening. Inside, the unpretentiously snug bar has some unusual carved oak wall benches and tables, a warming open fire and two blackboards listing the monthly-changing selection of bar food. The highlight of the menu is the splendid range of up to nine home-made soups (mushroom and hazelnut, broccoli and Stilton), which are a lunchtime favourite. Other good-value and hearty home-prepared snacks include French bread sandwiches, ploughman's lunches, curries, grilled sardines, spicy crab parcels and local scallops. For more substantial meals the small attractive restaurant, boasting a fine stone fireplace, provides a short hand-written menu listing interesting dishes like roast duck with cranberry and orange sauce, herb-crusted rack of lamb with damson sauce, good steaks from a local butcher and popular fresh fish (brill with tarragon and prawns, monkfish kebabs). Home-made puddings – bread-and-butter pudding and and sticky toffee pudding – come with thick clotted cream. Two charming bedrooms have matching wallpaper and fabrics and a clean, good-sized bathroom across the corridor. A stable-block conversion houses a family suite which is available (by prior arrangement) for daily B&B or weekly lets. No immediate off-street parking for residents, but you can park right outside on the road or 50 yards away. *Open 12-2 (till 3 Sat), 6-11 (Sun 12-3, 7-10.30). Bar Food 12-2 (till 2.30 Sat) & 7-10. Free House. Beer Bass, Palmers IPA, occasional guest beer. Small garden, outdoor eating. Accommodation 2 bedrooms, £39 (single £23.50). Children welcome overnight, additional bed (£10) and cot (£5) available, family suite by arrangement. Check-in by arrangement. Diners, MasterCard, **VISA***

> We only recommend food (Bar Food) in those establishments highlighted
> with the **FOOD** symbol.

CHIPPING CAMPDEN   Eight Bells Inn   FOOD

Tel 01386 840371   Fax 01386 841669   Map 14a A1   **B&B**
Church Street Chipping Campden Gloucestershire GL55 6JG

Originally built in the 14th century to house masons building the nearby church (and to store the bells), and over the years the pub is reputed to have played host to royalty and quite possibly William Shakespeare as well. A tiny, low Cotswold stone frontage hung with flower baskets reveals through its cobbled entranceway two cosy bars and an enclosed courtyard with abundant greenery. Paul and Patrick Dare offer a blackboard menu that deserves serious consideration and they provide slick service. Dishes to contemplate may include warm salad of scallops and bacon, poached salmon with tarragon mayonnaise, steak and kidney pie and king prawns with ginger and spring onion; to follow, fruit brulée or strawberry and Cointreau mousse. French-stick sandwiches and ploughman's lunches are offered at lunchtime only. The additional tap bar is now available as an additional dining area. A converted barn houses three double en suite bedrooms, each with TVs and tea trays. *Open 11-3, 6-11 (Sun 12-3, 7-10.30).* **Bar Food** *12-2.30, 6-9.30 (Sun 7-9). Free House.* **Beer** *Tetley Bitter, Burton Ale, Wadworth 6X, Greene King Abbot Ale. Garden, outdoor eating.* **Accommodation** *3 bedrooms, all en suite, £45. Children welcome overnight (under-2s stay free in parents' room, 2-10s £10), additional bed (£10) available. Check-in by arrangement. No credit cards.*

> We only recommend food (Bar Food) in those establishments highlighted
> with the **FOOD** symbol.

CHIPPING CAMPDEN   Noel Arms   B&B

Tel 01386 840317   Fax 01386 841136   Map 14a A1
High Street Chipping Campden Gloucestershire GL55 6AT

Zzz...

Centuries-old traditions of hospitality live on at the inn where Charles II is said to have rested after his defeat at the battle of Worcester in 1651. In terms of atmosphere, however, the Noel Arms, right at the centre of this old wool-traders' town, has somehow lost a little of its old-world charm following recent extensions to the building. The best and most authentic parts remain in the Dovers bar which opens direct on to the High Street through solid oaken doors. Lined in Cotswold stone and adorned with many genuine artefacts, the open double-sided fireplace and dog grate are of particular interest. From here, though, the pub opens out into the open-plan residents lounge and bright rear conservatory. Today's accommodation is a similar mixture of ancient and modern with the older bedrooms in the original building making up in character for what they lack in amenities, though by 17th-century standards the en suite bathrooms, colour TV and dial-out phones are pretty civilized. Disabled guests will greatly appreciate the bedrooms (one room is fully equipped for those with limited mobility) in the rear extension that have access direct from the car park. *Open 11-3, 6-11 (Fri & Sat 11-11, Sun 12-2.30, 7-10.30).* **Beer** *Hook Norton Best, Bass, guest beer.* **Accommodation** *26 rooms, all en suite, £85-£95 (single £60). Children welcome overnight (under-10s stay free in parents' room), additonal bed (£20) & cot available. Amex, Diners, MasterCard,* **VISA**

CHISLEHAMPTON   Coach & Horses   B&B

Tel 01865 890255   Fax 01865 891995   Map 14a C2
Chislehampton Oxford Oxfordshire OX9 7UX

Though pretty much modernised over the years, the Coach & Horses still keeps some traces of its 16th-century beginnings. The bedrooms offer smartly kept, good practical accommodation with TVs and direct-dial phones. Showers are the norm, but a couple have bathtubs. The inn stands on the B480 south of Oxford. *Open 11.30-3, 6-11 (Sun 11.30-3, 7-10.30). Free House.* **Beer** *Hook Norton Bitter, Flowers Original, Boddingtons. Garden.* **Accommodation** *9 bedrooms, all en suite, £50 (four-poster £55, single £45). Children welcome overnight (under-5s stay free in parents' room), additional bed (£5) & cot available. Amex, Diners, MasterCard,* **VISA**

CHORLEYWOOD — Sportsman Hotel — B&B

Tel 01923 285155   Fax 01923 285159   Map 15a E3
Station Approach Chorleywood Hertfordshire WD3 5NB

The Sportsman was built on a hillside across the road from the underground station and dates from the late 19th century. Popular with visiting businessmen during the week, the 18 bedrooms are a bit of a mix, but all are generally comfortable with modern darkwood furniture (some have modern pine) and brass light fittings; all are well equipped with TV, direct-dial telephones, radio-alarms, tea-making kits and trouser presses. En suite bath/shower rooms are fully tiled. Light attractive decor extends to the public areas and the Garden Bar with its airy, plant-filled conservatory overlooking the spacious garden, terrace and children's play area. The hotel has a children's certificate. *Open 11-11 (Sun 12-10.30).* **Beer** *no real ale. Garden, children's play area. Family room.* **Accommodation** *18 bedrooms, all en suite, £67.50 (single £57.50). Children welcome overnight, additional bed & cot (both £15) available. Amex, Diners, MasterCard,* **VISA**

CHURCH ENSTONE — Crown Inn — B&B

Tel 01608 677262   Map 14a B1
Mill Lane Church Enstone Oxfordshire OX7 4NN

Accommodation is a strong point at this 1760 Cotswold-stone, creeper-covered inn standing in a quiet village near the A34. Bedrooms – all kept in apple-pie order – have pretty fabrics and furnishings, very comfortable beds, TVs and tea-makers. Three rooms have en suite bathrooms. The welcoming stone-walled bar has an inglenook fireplace and serves well-kept real ale. *Open 12-3, 7-11 (till 10.30 Sun). Free House.* **Beer** *Boddingtons, Flowers Original, guest beer. Garden.* **Accommodation** *4 bedrooms, 3 en suite, £42/£45 (single £30/£32). Children over 12 welcome overnight. No credit cards.*

CLANFIELD — The Plough at Clanfield — B&B

Tel 01367 810222   Fax 01367 810596   Map 14a B2
Bourton Road Clanfield Oxfordshire OX18 2RB

Zzz...

Dating back to 1560, the Plough is picture-postcard pretty with its mellow Cotswold stone further softened by roses and wisteria climbing its walls. The bar, warmed by a real fire at night and at weekends, is crowded with wing armchairs under a beamed ceiling. More old beams are to be found in the six cosy bedrooms, two with four-posters, one with an old brass bedstead and one a full suite. The two on the top floor have shower only (but also share a separate spa bathroom); the others, which are non-smoking, all have their own spa bathtubs. *Open 11-11 (Sun 12-10.30).* **Beer** *Ansells Bitter, Eldridge Pope Hardy Country Ale, guest beer. Garden.* **Accommodation** *6 bedrooms, all en suite, £110-£125 (single £65). Children over 12 welcome overnight, additional bed (£15) & cot available. No dogs. Closed 20-28 Dec. Amex, Diners, MasterCard,* **VISA**

CLAVERING — Cricketers — FOOD

Tel 01799 550442   Fax 01799 550882   Map 10 B3   **B&B**
Clavering Saffron Walden Essex CB11 4QT

Comfortable 16th-century dining pub located 200 yards from the cricket green with a good local reputation for well-prepared home-made food. The main restaurant menu (also available in the bar) is changed every two months and is supplemented by chalk-board specials and regular theme nights – Tuesday highlights fish and Wednesday is 'Pudding Night' – steak and kidney, Yorkshire and sweet steamed puds – all, of course, home-made. Good starters/snacks to choose from may include home-cured gravad lax with dill and yoghurt, prawn and courgette provençale, coarse pork and chicken liver paté with Cumberland sauce, and filo parcels of duck with sweet and sour sauce, followed by rack of lamb with Madeira and rosemary sauce, chargrilled sirloin of beef with brandy and peppercorn sauce or fresh tuna steak with basil beurre blanc. Up to a dozen desserts are offered daily – try the treacle tart or lemon meringue pie. The restaurant offers a 3-course Sunday lunch with choice of 10 starters and main courses for £16.50. Well-appointed overnight accommodation is offered in the house next door, where six individually decorated en suite bedrooms are equipped to a high standard with added comforts like TVs, direct-dial phones, tea-makers, radio-alarms and a thoughtful extras like a decanter of sherry and a tray of petit fours on arrival. Ten minutes from Stansted Airport. *Open 12-2, 7-11 (Sun 12-3, 7-10.30).* **Bar Food** *12-2 (till 2.30 Sun), 7-10 (till 9.30 Sun). Free House.* **Beer** *Flowers IPA & Original, Wethered Bitter, Boddingtons. Terrace, outdoor eating. Family room.* **Accommodation** *6 bedrooms, all en suite £60 (single £50). Children welcome overnight, additional bed (£10) & cot available. No dogs.* Amex, MasterCard, **VISA**

CLEARWELL	**Wyndham Arms**	**FOOD**

Tel 01594 833666   Fax 01594 836450   Map 14 B2   **B&B**
Clearwell Coleford Gloucestershire GL16 8JT

♈ Zzz... ☺

The Stanford family, here since 1973, are the imperturbable hosts of the tranquil 600 year-old Wyndham Arms. Traditional hand-pulled real ales, 17 wines served by the glass and a notable malt whisky collection are indicators of the public bar's civilised style, to which the menu is entirely apposite. A lunch still favoured by many is the 18-dish hors d'oeuvre trolley, the daily special might be hot seafood platter or guinea fowl Montmorency, while main bar menu choices include Stilton stuffed pears with orange sauce and home-made soup (cream of asparagus). Accommodation is divided between original bedrooms in the evocative main building and a stone extension where room sizes, decor and comforts are altogether more modern. There's plenty of space for young children (cots, high-chairs and baby-listening are all readily available), and the less mobile appreciate use of 6 ground-floor bedrooms with easy ramps into the pub. Early evening turn-down and dawn shoe-cleaning patrol aren't found in every pub: along with a hearty breakfast, it's all part, here, of the Wyndham service. Secure car-parking. *Open 11-11 (Sun 12-10.30).* **Bar Food** *12-2, 7-9.30. Free House.* **Beer** *Flowers Best, Boddingtons, Bass. Garden, patio, outdoor eating.* **Accommodation** *17 bedrooms, all en suite, £65 (single £49.50). Children welcome overnight (stay free if sharing parents' room), additional bed & cot available.* Amex, Diners, MasterCard, **VISA**

CLEY-NEXT-THE-SEA	**George & Dragon**	**B&B**

Tel 01263 740652   Fax 01263 741275   Map 10 C1
High Street Cley-next-the-Sea Holt Norfolk NR25 7RN

☺

Standing head and shoulders above its neighbouring whitewashed cottage, this striking brick inn was rebuilt in 1897 in Edwardian style and enjoys an enviable position close to Cley's fine windmill overlooking an expanse of unspoilt salt marsh. For decades the inn has been a popular base for visiting naturalists, walkers and holidaymakers, and the good pubby bars have witnessed the forming of the Norfolk Naturalists Trust in 1926 and today daily bird observations are recorded in the "bird bible" – a large volume placed on a lectern in the main bar. Upstairs, most of the homely, simply furnished bedrooms, including the four-poster room, have far-reaching salt marsh views and six have clean, adequate en suite facilities. TVs and tea-makers are standard. The residents lounge is the internal hide, complete with scrape-facing window and a pair of binoculars. Good-sized garden across the lane with pétanque pitch. Being a well-visited coastal village, families are very welcome and well catered for if staying overnight. Good-sized family rooms, extra beds and cots, early evening meals from 6pm, and young diners have their own menu and use of a high-chair. However, children must be carefully supervised in the garden. Summer afternoon cream teas. *Open 11-2.30, 6.30-11 (from 6 Sat, 11-11 in high summer), Sun 12-3, 7-10.30. Free House.* **Beer** *Greene King IPA, Abbot Ale & Rayments Bitter. Garden.* **Accommodation** *8 bedrooms, 6 en suite, £40-£50 (four-poster £65, family room sleeping four £55-£75, single £30). Children welcome overnight (babies free), additional bed & cot available. Check-in by arrangement. Accommodation closed 25, 26 & 31 Dec. No credit cards.*

CLIFFE   Black Bull   FOOD

Tel 01634 220893   Fax 01634 221382   Map 11 B5
186 Church Street Cliffe Kent ME3 7QP

Late-Victorian pub on a historic tavern site with three homely bars and specialising in Far-Eastern cooking. Eating may be in one of these or in the non-smoking, 48-seat, 18th-century cellar restaurant which is usually booked only once in an evening, so there's no hurry to leave, especially as they have an extended licence to serve up to midnight. Soh Pek Berry prepares some unusual pub food such as spring rolls, *murtabak* (Malaysian bread stuffed with spicy beef) and satay for starters, followed by king prawn sambal, hokkien special pork, nasi goreng and kofta curry. Sandwiches, ploughman's lunches, salads and scampi and chips for those seeking 'ordinary' pub fare. Served in the restaurant only, alongside a varied carte, are set meals (two starters, four main dishes, rice and dessert) for two to four people. Look out for the excellent and very popular 'Ethnic Nights' (£5 per head – bookings only) on the first Wednesday in each month.
Open 12-3, 7-11 (Sun 12-3, 7-10.30). **Bar Food** *12-2, 7-9.30 (no food Sun & Mon eve).*
Free House. **Beer** *Courage Best & Directors, guest beer. MasterCard,* **VISA**

CLIFTON   Duke of Cumberland's Head   FOOD

Tel 01869 338534   Fax 01869 338643   Map 14a C1   **B&B**
Clifton Deddington Oxfordshire OX5 4PE

A comfortable thatched pub on the B4031 with old beams, inglenook fireplace and wheelback chairs. Sam Harrison in the kitchen produces a strictly French menu for the small restaurant and more varied blackboard menu for the bar. A typical selection might include smoked salmon mousse, Algerian lamb stew with apricot, shellfish paella and steak and stout pie. Good value, three-course menu of the month, served in both the bar and restaurant, offers such dishes as seafood pancakes mornay followed by tenderloin of pork calvados. Good puddings like honey and ginger cheesecake and raspberry and apple crumble. Upstairs, under the eves, three simple bedrooms have en suite shower rooms with WC, old pine furniture, TV and hot beverage kit but no telephones. *Open 12-3, 6.30-11 (till 10.30 Sun).* **Bar Food** *12-2, 7-9.30 (from 7.30 Sun) No food Sun eve Nov-Apr. Free House.* **Beer** *Hook Norton Best, Wadworth 6X, Hampshire King Alfred Bitter, Adnams Southwold. Garden, outdoor eating.*
Accommodation *3 bedrooms, all en suite (shower), £37.50 (single £27.50). Children welcome overnight (under-3s free if sharing parent's room). Check-in by arrangement.*
MasterCard, **VISA**

CLIFTON HAMPDEN   Plough Inn   FOOD

Tel 01865 407811   Fax 01865 407136   Map 14a C3   **B&B**
Clifton Hampden Abingdon Oxfordshire OX14 3EG

Zzz... ☺

A 16th-century thatched and timber-framed gem of a building, lovingly run by Turkish-born landlord Yuksel Bektas – always impeccably dressed, often in tail coat in the morning and dinner suit at night – and his family. Their tireless energy and enthusiasm over the past few years has created a delightful country pub that not only oozes charm and character but offers tasteful overnight accommodation in eight en suite bedrooms and good food. The cosy main bar and adjoining room feature low beams, deep red-painted walls and the open fires at each end of the bar give a welcoming feel immediately on entering. Two separate dining-rooms, one of which leads out into the well maintained garden. Characterful touches include Turkish coffee in the bar, pitta bread and toast with the particularly good breakfast and a fox's head resplendent with fez in the bar. The pub has an open-all-day policy, and food is served as long as the doors are open; the "no fried or frozen foods" policy is admirable. One can either eat informally in the bar rooms (or garden) or more formally in the restaurant up a few steps from the small bar. The former sees a menu of light dishes (warm smoked chicken salad with pesto sauce, steak and beer pie, smoked salmon sandwiches), while the latter extends to roast loin of lamb with shallot and mint sauce and oven-roasted duck with red wine and Grand Marnier sauce. Up a few stairs off the bar, tucked beneath the thatch, is a spacious bedroom, tastefully decorated with four-poster bed, deep pink walls, attractive floral rose fabrics and matching Oriental bedside lamps; a basket of fruit, satellite TV and video, mini-bar and a splendid private bathroom, complete with telephone, all add up to unusually good pub accommodation. Another spacious bedroom is up a few stairs at the other end of the building, while three further bedrooms, all as stylish as the original with quality fabrics and furnishings and superb bathrooms, occupy original, converted buildings just across the gravel yard. The newest bedrooms (with en suite showers) are to found above the recent dining-room extension. The Plough is one of a kind − no-smoking throughout, quality accommodation, good food and service, and Turkish hospitality (Mr Bektas will even drive you home if you've had a few too many, wash your car and shine your shoes overnight if you ask − nothing is too much trouble) − all in the heart of a pretty Oxfordshire village on the A415 Abingdon to Dorchester road. *Open 11am-11pm.* **Bar Food** *11am-11pm.* **Beer** *Webster's Yorkshire Bitter, Ruddles County, Courage Best. Garden, outdoor eating.* **Accommodation** *8 bedrooms, all en suite, £64.50-£75 (single £44.50-£55). Children welcome overnight (under-12s stay free in parents' room, 12-16s £10), additional bed & cot provided. No dogs (except guide dogs).* MasterCard, **VISA**

COCKWOOD — Anchor Inn — FOOD

Tel 01626 890203
Cockwood Dawlish Devon EX6 8RA

Map 13 E3

The small vine-covered verandah of this 400-year-old fisherman's cottage pub is a super spot in which to sit and watch the colourful fishing boats and wildlife in the tiny harbour across the lane and the Exe estuary beyond. Inside, although extended over the years, the rustic main bar remains unspoilt, with black panelling, low ceilings and lots of intimate little alcoves in the three snug areas, one of which has a welcoming coal fire. Local seafood, especially shellfish, is the main attraction here, especially the impressive range of sauces for scallops, mussels and oysters, which are delivered daily from local beds along the River Exe. Also worth investigating is the fresh fish board which often features exotic fish − parrot fish, yellow-tail snapper, baracuda − alongside halibut with lemon butter and herbs. Daily specials such as home-made soup, seafood grill and honey-roast lamb enhance the extensive main printed menu, which offers a fairly routine choice of pub favourites, but the choice of real ale is anything but mundane. Parking can be difficult, especially on busy summer days. *Open 11-11 (Sun 12-2.30, 7-10.30).* **Bar Food** *12-3, 6-10 (till 9.30 Sun).* **Beer** *Bass, Flowers Original, Eldridge Pope Royal Oak, Marston's Pedigree, Whitbread Fuggles Imperial & Pompey Royal, two guest beers. Terrace, outdoor eating.* MasterCard, **VISA**

COCKWOOD — Ship Inn — FOOD

Tel 01626 890373
Cockwood Dawlish Devon EX6 8PA

Map 13 E3

Originally an old victualler's house, dating from 1633, this welcoming, cream-painted inn overlooks the old harbour inlet and reedbeds. Carefully modernised inside but still retaining much of its traditional character, it is a popular place in which to appreciate a bar food menu that favours fresh fish. The daily blackboard selection may list tiger prawns with sweet and sour dip, fish pie, grilled halibut, home-made fish brochettes, haddock with mustard sauce and grilled black bream. Sandwiches and other light bites are also offered, while non fish-fanciers can tuck into Cajun chicken salad, beef and Guinness casserole, pan-fried lamb's kidneys with cream and calvados or a vegetarian selection. Eating outdoors is best enjoyed from the three-tiered gardens, which afford splendid open views across the Exe estuary to Exmouth. *Open 11-3, 5.30-11 (Sat 11-11), Sun 12-3, 7-10.30 (12-10.30 summer), all day every day in August.* **Bar Food** *12-2 (Sun to 2.30), 6.30-10 (from 6 summer, Mon-Fri winter 7-9, Sun 7-9.30). Family room.* **Beer** *Ushers Best, Founder's Ale & Four Seasons (seasonal ales), John Smith's. Garden, outdoor eating.* Amex, MasterCard, **VISA**

COLCHESTER   Rose & Crown Hotel   B&B

Tel 01206 866677   Fax 01206 866616   Map 10 C3
East Street Colchester Essex CO1 2TZ

Magnificent ancient black-and-white timbered inn that has stood on the corner of the old Ipswich and Harwich roads since the 15th century. Once an old posting house, it is now a well-appointed inn having been carefully extended and refurbished over the past few years. A pubby bar attracts a busy local trade and is full of character with open fires, heavy beams and antique, cushioned pews and settles. Old-world charm extends upstairs into the main-building bedrooms – three of which boast sturdy four-poster beds – with leaded windows, wall timbers and uneven floors. Newer extension bedrooms are uniform in size, decor and furnishings, all being very comfortable and well equipped with older-style darkwood furniture and quality co-ordinating fabrics. Fully-tiled bathrooms have overhead showers. Full complement of added comforts from remote-controlled TVs (with satellite channels) to trouser presses. *Open 12-2.30, 6-11 (Sun 12-3, 7-10.30). Free House. **Beer** Tetley Bitter. **Accommodation** 30 bedrooms, all en suite, £58-£119 (single £58). Children welcome overnight (under-12s stay free in parents' room), additional bed & cot available. No dogs. Closed 27-29 Dec. Amex, Diners, MasterCard, VISA*

COLEFORD   New Inn   FOOD

Tel 01363 84242   Fax 01363 85044   Map 13 D2   **B&B**
Coleford Devon EX17 5BZ

Pretty, 13th-century thatched cottage inn set beside the River Cole in an equally attractive village, deep in the heart of unspoilt Devon countryside. 'Captain', the chatty resident parrot, welcomes folk into the characterful rambling interior, with the charming ancient bar blending successfully with dining-room extension into the old barns: fitted red carpets, fresh white walls, heavy beams, simple wooden furniture and settles and a discreet variety of attractive brass and bric-a-brac. Bar food is reliable and home-cooked, relying on fresh local produce: Brixham fish (fillet of brill with cream, lemon and butter sauce), West Country cheeses, eggs and cream from a nearby farm. The comprehensive blackboard menu has an international flavour, featuring warm pigeon breast and smoked bacon salad with orange vinaigrette, tomato and basil soup and grilled goat's cheese with walnuts, with main-course options that include lamb Wellington, venison sausages with Cumberland sauce and salmon en croute with a green herb sauce. Local estate game appears regularly on the winter menu. Good home-made puddings. Overnight accommodation in five spacious, light and airy en suite bedrooms – including two newly completed de luxe rooms – all with floral fabrics and antique furniture plus TV and tea-making facilities as added comforts. There's a stream-side patio for quiet alfresco summer drinking. Small conference room. *Open 12-2.30, 6-11 (Sun 12-2.30, 7-10.30). **Bar Food** 12-2, 7-10 (till 9.30 Sun). Free House. **Beer** Otter Ale, Hall & Woodhouse Badger Best, Wadworth 6X, guest beer. Garden, outdoor eating. Family room. **Accommodation** 5 bedrooms, all en suite, £52.50-£60 (family room £70, single £38). Children welcome overnight, additional bed (£10) & cot (£5) available. No dogs. Amex, Diners, MasterCard, VISA*

COLLYWESTON   Cavalier Inn   B&B

Tel 01780 444288   Map 7 E4
Collyweston Stamford Lincolnshire DE9 3PQ

Previously the Slaters Arms, the pub changed its name when the slate mine closed and the work force moved away. The inn itself is a terrace of small 19th-century cottages, yet a glass window let into the bar floor reveals a much earlier stone spiral stairway to a tiny cellar. All the bedrooms are on the first floor and have been totally refurbished by the new landlord. They are equipped with TVs, beverage facilities (but no phones) and all have views of the church and across the valley. The new style of menus also look promising (not yet inspected). *Open 12-2.30, 6-11 (Sat 11-11, Sun 12-10.30). Free House. **Beer** Everards Tiger & Beacon, guest beer. Garden. **Accommodation** 5 bedrooms, all en suite, £40 (family room £45, single £35). Children welcome overnight, additional bed & cot available. Check-in by arrangement. No dogs. No credit cards.*

COLN ST ALDWYNS   New Inn   ★   FOOD

Tel 01285 750651   Fax 01285 750657   Map 14a A2   **B&B**
Coln St Aldwyns Cirencester Gloucestershire GL7 5AN

 Zzz...

Since Brian and Sandra-Anne Evans came to this sleepy Cotswolds village in 1992, they have transformed the New Inn into a delightfully romantic, creeper-covered inn. Behind its picture postcard frontage of flower baskets and ivy, interior conversion has created a succession of little rooms as adaptable to the demands of diners as are the menus to satisfy them. The Courtyard bar menu – ideal for lighter lunches in the long bar with its dried hops, bare Cotswolds stone walls, quarry-tiled floor and inglenook fire – offers a wide choice, from bacon, lettuce and tomato bap and ploughman's lunches (with a selection of four cheeses, chutney and pickles) to whisky and kipper paté, braised shoulder of lamb, mash and rosemary, salmon fishcakes with chive sauce, and rhubarb crumble with ginger anglaise for pudding. "Ask at the bar for children's meals." In the evening (and at Sunday lunchtimes) one can push the boat out and enjoy new chef Stephen Morey's fixed-price à la carte menu in the candlelit restaurant, perhaps commencing with French onion tart or salad of pan-fried duck livers, bacon and balsamic vinegar dressing, followed by peppered monkfish tail with sweet peppers and basil pesto, medallions of pork with prunes and armagnac, fillet of cod with tapénade and tomato pesto, or confit of belly pork with creamed potatoes, spring onions and sesame. Leave room for caramelised rice pudding with compote of plums and cardamom or poached pears with honey and ginger ice cream. The selection of British and French cheeses is also very good. Configuration of the bedrooms, utilising virtually every angle of the roof space, is for each resident to discover and all to wonder at – here a romantic four-poster room, there the sunken bath in a former stair-well – and epitomise the delights in store for those who come to stay; self-styled as "a private castle of comfort", it isn't far off! There are carefully-chosen floral prints on the walls and chintz drapes at the windows; direct-dial phones, remote-controlled TVs and tea- and coffee-making facilities are all provided. Tip-top food in both bar and restaurant, stylish overnight accommodation and warm hospitality. *Open 11.30-2.30, 5.30-11 (Sat 11.30-11, Sun 12-3, 7-10.30).* **Bar Food** *12-2 (till 2.30 Sun), 7-9.30. Restaurant L (Sun only) £14.50, D £22.50. Free House.* **Beer** *Hook Norton Best, Wadworth 6X, Morland Original, guest beer. Terrace, outdoor eating. Family room.* **Accommodation** *14 bedrooms, all en suite, £79 (suite/family room £95, single £55). Children welcome overnight (under-4s stay free in parents' room), additional bed (£18) & cot (£6) available. No dogs. Amex, Diners, MasterCard,* ***VISA***

COLSTON BASSETT   Martins Arms   FOOD

Tel 01949 81361   Map 7 D3
School Lane Colston Bassett Nottinghamshire NG12 3FD

Formerly the Squire's residence, set among horse chestnuts in an estate garden, the pub exudes quiet country-house charm (scatter cushions, window drapes, hunting prints) to which the bar itself seems almost an intrusion; however, you will find some top-notch Batemans XB and impeccable wines from Lay & Wheeler. Food is offered on different menus in both the antique-furnished dining-room complete with its own lounge and in the bar, which opens on to a lawn. Particularly good bar snacks cover the range from speciality sandwiches (tomato, mozzarella, mixed leaves, red onion and basil) to light appetisers like smoked salmon and scrambled egg with Welsh rarebit; main courses might be chargrilled spicy Toulouse sausages, rich game pie, marinated lamb steak or four vegetarian choices. Freshly-made desserts – Belgian chocolate tart, crème brulée – and a selection of six cheeses (including Colston Bassett Stilton, of course) to follow. Children under 14 are not permitted inside. Landlords Lynne Bryan and Salvatore Inguantas also run the *Crown Inn* at Old Dalby (see entry). *Open 12-3, 6-11 (Sun 12-3, 7-10.30).* **Bar Food** *12-2, 6-10 (no food Sun eve). Free House.* **Beer** *Marston's Best & Pedigree, Batemans XB & XXXB, Morland Old Speckled Hen, Greene King Abbot Ale, Timothy Taylor's Landlord, Garden, outdoor eating. No credit cards.*

COMBE HAY — Wheatsheaf — FOOD

Tel 01225 833504   Map 13 F1
Combe Hay Bath Somerset BA2 7EG

Tucked down twisting narrow lanes in a charming village south of Bath and perched on a hillside looking across a small valley, the 17th century Wheatsheaf is as pretty as a picture, its black and white facade smothered in flowers and pierced with the entrances to dovecotes, built into the walls and still inhabited. Well-spaced rustic tables and benches in the large, now terraced garden make the best of the views, an ideal spot for summer eating and drinking. Inside there are rough stone walls, massive solid wooden tables, and also a huge blackboard menu: food is important here. Typical dishes from the blackboard bar menu are game terrine, home-made soup, smoked salmon paté and rack of lamb with rosemary, honey and mint sauce, while the interesting à la carte dining-room menu (also served in the bar) may offer salmon marinated in brandy mustard and dill, sautéed fillet of pork with wild boar sausages, cream and Calvados, medley of seafood, and plaice with herbs and white wine. Home-made puddings include tiramisu, summer fruit pudding and chocolate and rum terrine. Real ales are drawn direct from the barrel. Children welcome. A recent conversion of an old stable block houses three cottagey en suite bedrooms (£50-£60), all furnished in old pine and each having TVs and phone/faxes – ideal for the business traveller (not yet inspected). *Open 11-2.30 (till 3 Sat), 6.30-11 (from 5.30 summer), Sun 12-3, 7-10.30.* **Bar Food** *12-2, 7-9.30.* **Beer** *Courage Best, Wadworth 6X. Garden, outdoor eating, barbecue. No credit cards.*

COMPTON — Coach & Horses — FOOD

Tel 01705 631228   Map 15 D3
The Square Compton nr Chichester West Sussex PO18 9NA

Located in the village square and beside the B2146 Chichester to Petersfield road, this white-painted 15th-century coaching inn caters for all desires within its homely Village Bar and separate beamed lounge and restaurant. Mellow pine characterises the lively locals' bar where one can enjoy a good hearty bar snack, such as home-made pies, avocado and spinach bake and grilled plaice, as well as soup, ploughman's platters and sandwiches, all of which are listed on a blackboard menu. Those seeking a more convivial dining atmosphere could venture next door into the charming lounge and adjacent restaurant, both boasting open log fires. A further board features more imaginative and pricier fare (monkfish with shellfish sauce, grilled sea bass with dill, duck breast with caramelised onions, wild boar with brandy, mushroom and cream sauce) to suit the surroundings. Puddings include a brandy snap basket with chestnut cream and brandy ice cream. A small secluded garden lies beyond the skittle alley. Children welcome anywhere. *Open 11-2.30, 6-11 (Sun 12-2.30, 7-10.30).* **Bar Food** *12-2, 6-9.30 (Sun 12-2.30, 7-9).* Free House. **Beer** *Fuller's ESB, Youngers IPA, four guest beers. Garden, outdoor eating. MasterCard,* **VISA**

CONGRESBURY — White Hart — FOOD

Tel 01934 833303   Map 13 F1
Wrington Road Congresbury North Somerset BS19 5AR

Combined quaint village pub and dining venue hidden down a long lane off the A370 (follow the Wrington Road). A conventional line in snacks and salads is supplemented by some more promising home-cooked fare: crab parcels, chicken korma, lasagne, chicken and mushroom pie and tuna pasta bake served with a choice of potatoes and vegetables or salad. An increasing attraction is Sunday lunch, especially with families, who have use of a neat conservatory looking across the large pub garden and away towards the Mendips; no children are allowed in the bars. With plastic bottles of pop from the bar youngsters can amuse themselves in full view on the play equipment. There's also an aviary by the terrace. *Open 11-2.30, 6-11 (Sun 12-3, 7-10.30).* **Bar Food** *12-2, 6-9.30 (from 7 Sun).* **Beer** *Hall & Woodhouse. Garden, patio, children's play area. Family room. MasterCard,* **VISA**

CONSTANTINE   Trengilly Wartha Inn   FOOD

Tel & Fax 01326 340332   Map 12 B4   **B&B**
Nancenoy Constantine Helston Cornwall TR11 5RP

 Zzz... ☺

One mile due south of Constantine down country lanes, the Inn sits in a beautiful wooded valley looking down towards Polpenwith Creek on the Helford River. The unpretentious main bar is happily unmodernised with games machines and pool table relegated to a separate room and another tapestry upholstered 'lounge' area where families are welcome; there's a small children's section on the menu too. For summer there are tables on the vine-covered patio and in the garden beyond. A further alfresco area is around a lake in the valley bottom. There is a long list of 'Trengilly Classics' (smoked chicken strudel, and cassoulet) on the bar food menu but the most interesting options appear on the blackboard. This features fresh fish from Newlyn like baked cod with chive cream sauce, monkfish in a piquant tomato sauce and Thai fish soup; in addition there might be rabbit pie, tagliatelle with avocado and smoked trout and homely puddings. Lighter bites include crab open sandwiches and ploughman's lunches. The separate restaurant offers a two- or three-course dinner. Good range of wines by the glass selected from a list of 160, regularly-changing real ales and three strong scrumpy ciders. Six cosy bedrooms are light and pretty with good, modern carpeted bathrooms and up-to-date conveniences such as remote-control TV and direct-dial telephones. Well maintained and comfortable accommodation. *Open 11-3 (till 2.30 winter), 6-11 (Sun 12-3, 7-10.30). Bar Food 12-2.15 (till 2 Sun), 6.30-9.30 (from 7.15 Sun). Free House. Beer Sharp's Cornish Coaster, Furgusons Dartmoor Best, St Austell HSD, two guest beers. Garden, outdoor eating. Family room. Accommodation 6 bedrooms, 5 en suite, £60 (single £40). Children welcome overnight, additional bed (£8) & cot (£2) provided in one larger room. Amex, Diners, MasterCard, VISA*

COOKHAM DEAN   Inn on the Green   FOOD

Tel 01628 482638   Fax 01628 487474   Map 15a E3
The Green Cookham Dean Marlow Berkshire SL6 9NZ

 ☺

Tucked away in one corner of the large village green, this interesting pub has four dining areas but only a small bar. Two small drinking rooms (with just seven tables) lead through to a Swiss chalet-style dining-room, off which the high-ceilinged Lamp Room restaurant and a small conservatory lead. The bar menu (and daily blackboard specials) might offer reliable snacks like home-made soup (white onion, vegetable), various open sandwiches, home-cured bresaola with balsamic vinegar and olives, grilled sardines and home-made burgers. From a more adventurous dining-room menu (also available in the bar) start with seafood sausage or Caesar salad and move on to venison with juniper, sea bass pan-fried in fennel and Pernod or corn-fed chicken with aubergine and pesto noodles. Finish off with strawberry and mascarpone tart or summer pudding. Outside, there's a large walled courtyard barbecue area (lit by wall lights and heated by tall gas burners, Apr-Oct) and an acre of paddock behind the car park. It's a wonderful summer pub for families with youngsters: the rear grassed area features picnic tables, a tree house, a chalet-style 'Nut House', double slide, climbing frame and rubber tyre swings. Overnight accommodation now comprises six cottagey pine-furnished bedrooms (£60 double, £40 single) – not yet inspected. *Open 12-3, 6-11 (Sun 12-3, 7-10.30). Bar Food 12-2, (till 2.30 Sun), 7-10. Free House. Beer Brakspear Bitter, Boddingtons, Fuller's London Pride, guest beer. Garden, terrace, outdoor eating, children's play area. Amex, MasterCard, VISA*

> We endeavour to be as up-to-date as possible but inevitably some changes to landlords, chefs and other key staff occur after the Guide has gone to press.

COOKHAM DEAN — Jolly Farmer — FOOD

Tel 01628 482905   Map 15a E3
Cookham Dean Marlow Berkshire SL6 9PD

☺

Homely and traditional village pub located opposite the parish church and close to the vast village green. Two simply furnished interconnecting bars with open fires, and a separate small and cosy dining-room in which to enjoy wholesome, home-cooked pub food. Blackboard choices may range from Stilton and cider soup and warm goat's cheese on beef tomato salad to ham, egg and chips, chicken and mushroom stroganoff, poached salmon in white wine and dill sauce, and calf's liver, bacon and onions. Sandwiches and ploughman's at lunchtime only. Apple pie and crème brulée are typical pudding options. Good summer garden with children's play area. Well-behaved children only inside. *Open 11.30-3, 5.30-11 (from 6 Sat), Sun 12-3, 7-10.30.*
Bar Food 12-2.30, 7.30-9.30, (no food Mon eve). Free House. **Beer** *Courage Best, two guest beers. Garden, outdoor eating, children's play area. Closed 25 & 26 Dec eve.* MasterCard, **VISA**

CORBRIDGE — Angel Inn — FOOD

Tel & Fax 01434 632119   Map 5 D2 — **B&B**
Main Street Corbridge Hexham Northumberland NE45 5LA

Zzz...

Saxon Corbridge, just off both the A68 and A69 trunk routes, stands above the 17th-century stone bridge across the Tyne where the former Head inn was once the town's posting inn. Its latest guardian angel, Mandy McIntosh Reid, has certainly dusted the place with a little of her own magic. The Angel today is smartly carpeted throughout (except in the locals' Tap Room) and an upmarket approach is reinforced by the food: here you will find reliable Northumbrian cooking of a style and value which has achieved regular local approval. Daily-changing bar/lounge menus encompass the likes of chicken and vegetable soup, Northumbrian lamb and leek dumplings, game and ale casserole, and stir-fried lemon chicken. In the foyer lounge, nonetheless, space is found for morning coffees, a lunchtime sandwich and afternoon teas. The five neatly refurbished bedrooms haven't been skimped over either. There are satellite TVs, roomy bathrooms with a certain feminine touch (cotton buds and bath foam) quality free-standing pine furniture and bold colour schemes. The three twins (families welcome) are roomier than the doubles: views are either from the front down to the river or to the rear overlooking a pretty walled garden. *Open 11-3, 5-11 (Sun 12-3, 7-10.30). Free House.* **Beer** *Theakston Best & XB, Younger's No 3, McEwan's 80/-, guest beer. Bar Food 12-2.15, 6-9.15 (Sun 7-9.15pm). Garden.* **Accommodation** *5 bedrooms, all en suite, £64 (single £42). Children welcome overnight, additional bed & cot available. Accommodation closed 25 Dec eve & 1 Jan eve.* Amex, Diners, MasterCard, **VISA**

CORFE CASTLE — The Fox — A

Tel 01929 480449   Map 14 D4
West Street Corfe Castle Dorset BH20 5HD

Unspoilt 16th-century inn, with a very snug little front bar and slightly less enchanting larger lounge. Recent renovations uncovered a doorway which has been turned into an alcove, a 13th-century fireplace and a well that is now lit and glass-covered. Its mature, pretty garden with views of the famous ruin make the Fox especially appealing in summer. Children under 14 are not allowed indoors. No intrusive music or games, just a pleasant chatty atmosphere. *Open 11-11 (11-2.30 (till 3 Sat), 6.30-11, winter) Sun 12-3, 7-10.30. Free House.* **Beer** *Gibbs Mew Bishop's Tipple, Wadworth 6X, Greene King Abbot Ale, Ind Coope Burton Ale, Eldridge Pope Royal Oak. Garden. Closed all 25 Dec. No credit cards.*

CORNWORTHY   Hunters Lodge Inn   FOOD

Tel 01803 732204   Map 13 D3
Cornworthy Totnes Devon TQ9 7ES

Unspoilt, simply-furnished country local with a low-ceilinged bar and a cosy dining-room with an old stone fireplace and attractive blue table linen. Vast blackboard menus hide some good home-cooked dishes among the deep-fried choices with chips and the bought-in puddings. The lunchtime-only board will offer home-made soups (chicken and herb), fresh lobster, salmon fishcakes, beer-battered plaice and a splendid steak and kidney pie served with huge portions of four crisp vegetables and a bowl of potatoes; sandwiches and ploughman's at lunch also. On the long menu (available in both bar and restaurant) more elaborate dishes might include steak au poivre, lamb steak in redcurrant wine, and fish specialities such as the special mixed grill (a mix of fish and meat), whole cracked crab, salmon Wellington and tandoori halibut. A three-course Sunday lunch is a popular event and it is advisable to book in the evenings and at weekends. No children under 14 in the restaurant (except Sun) but they are very welcome in the bar where there are games, toys and a high-chair available. Cider lovers should sample the 'Pig's Squeal'. *Open 11.30-3, 6.30-11 (Sun 12-3, 7-10.30).* **Bar Food** *12-2 (from 12.30 Sun), 7-9.30. Free House.* **Beer** *Blackawton 44, Ushers Best, guest beer. Garden, outdoor eating, No credit cards.*

CORSCOMBE   Fox Inn   ★   FOOD

Tel 01935 891330   Map 13 F2
Corscombe Dorset DT2 0NS

"Real Ale, Country Cooking. No Chips or Microwaves" it says on the postcard, showing Martyn Lee's pretty little thatched pub of stone and cob, built in 1620 and located down a web of narrow lanes deep in unspoilt Dorset countryside (the village is signposted off the A356 Crewkerne to Dorchester, then follow signs to the pub – it's not easy to find). All is equally appealing inside the two welcoming bars, one, with its hunting prints, old pine furniture and band of chatty locals, the other prettily furnished with blue gingham curtains, tablecloths, banquette seat covers – even the fabric covering the bar stools. A huge old stone fireplace boasts a real log fire in winter, while behind the bar real ale and farm cider is dispensed straight from the cask. Although still a locals' pub, complete with cricket team, discerning diners are travelling miles to this rural backwater to sample chef Will Longman's imaginative bar food. Quality produce from good local suppliers, including fresh fish from Bridport and game in season from local estates help create the interesting daily-changing blackboard menu. Choices may include chargrilled aubergine filled with ricotta and parmesan plus a rich tomato sauce or devilled crab meat to start, followed by salmon fishcakes with spicy sauce, fillet of turbot with mussel and saffron sauce, red mullet roasted with olive oil and tomato, Basque chicken with red peppers and white wine, and roast rack of Dorset lamb. Sunday usually sees a choice of roasts. Puddings range from chocolate roulade and sticky toffee pudding to an excellent cheeseboard featuring, among others, local Denhay Cheddar, Somerset goat's and Shropshire Blue. Alfresco eating across the lane by the brook or at the sturdy, long wooden table in the attractive conservatory; it seats 20 and is ideal for parties. By the Spring of 1997 the Fox will have four tastefully-furnished en suite bedrooms; three in a converted outbuilding to the rear and one in a charming attic room tucked beneath the thatch in the main building. *Open 12-3 (till 4 Sat), 7-11 (till 10.30 Sun).* **Bar Food** *12-2, 7-9. (till 9.30 Sat). Free House.* **Beer** *Smiles Best, Fuller's London Pride, Exmoor Ale, guest beer. Garden, outdoor eating. No credit cards.*

Many **B&B** establishments offer reduced rates for weekend and out-of-season bookings. Always ask about special deals for longer stays. Beware half-board terms in inns where we do not recommend the **FOOD**.

CORSHAM   Methuen Arms   B&B

Tel 01249 714867   Fax 01249 712004   Map 14 B2
2 High Street Corsham Wiltshire SN13 0HB

Housed around the remains of a 14th-century nunnery, and converted into a brewery
and coaching inn around 1608, there's abundant history here. Among notable features
in public areas are the 100ft Long Bar containing its own skittle alley, and outstanding
examples of stonemasonry through the ages to be found in the Winter's Court
restaurant. Practical rather than luxurious accommodation with bedrooms in the main
building featuring wicker decorated furniture and pastel colours. To the rear the
newer bedrooms, housed in a 16th-century annexe set around a courtyard facing the
serene garden, have a touch more elegance, enhanced in the honeymoon suites by
four-poster and half-tester beds. Five bathrooms have shower only and some a tub but
no shower. *Open 11-2.30, 6-11 (Sun 12-2.30, 7-10.30). Free House. **Beer** Bass, Tetley,
Gibbs Mew Salisbury Best. Garden. Family room. **Accommodation** 24 bedrooms, all en suite,
£50/£65 (family room £55, single £38, weekend reductions). Children welcome overnight
(under-10s free if sharing parents' room), additional bed available. Disabled WC. Diners,
MasterCard,* **VISA**

> We endeavour to be as up-to-date as possible but inevitably some changes to
> landlords, chefs and other key staff occur after the Guide
> has gone to press.

COVENTRY   William IV   FOOD

Tel 01203 686394   Map 6 C4
1059 Foleshill Road Coventry CV6 6ER

There's a sign to Bedworth (B4113) from the M6, Junction 3, and the pub is about
equidistant from this point and the city centre in Foleshill. What was arguably
Britain's first authentically Indian pub remains unusual as the Himalayan Balti cooking
favoured here is now much copied using convenience preparations. Perminder and
Jatinder Bains offer a range of "Pele's" curries that runs to one hundred or more
variations including Balti meat or chicken rogan josh, both meat and vegetarian thalis
and the speciality chicken saagwla. Eating here is quite an experience and shows up
the majority of British pub curries for the sham that they are. M&B mild is served on
electric pump. Bass Taverns. *Open 11-2.30 (till 3 Fri & Sat), 6-11 (from 5 Fri & Sat),
Sun 12-3, 7-10.30. **Bar Food** 12-2, 6-10 (till 10.30 Sat, from 7 Sun). Garden. Amex,
MasterCard,* **VISA**

COXWOLD   Fauconberg Arms   FOOD

Tel 01347 868214   Map 5 E4   B&B
Main Street Coxwold North Yorkshire YO6 4AD

☗ ☺

This is a charmingly civilised, if invariably busy place, with handsome old furnishings
and an open fire, located near Shandy Hall and Byland Abbey. Landlady Nicky Jaques
produces adventurous and varied bar food: chicken liver and ham terrine, leek and
smoked salmon mousse, Old Peculier steak and kidney pie; sandwiches and
ploughman's at lunchtime only. The restaurant offers a 3-course table d'hote menu at
Sunday lunch, and in the evenings one menu applies throughout the pub, offering
choices such as smoked chicken and bacon pancake with tomato salsa, medallions of
pork with a cream, cider and calvados sauce, and roast monkfish tail with aubergines
and tomatoes, with dark chocolate mousse among the pudding choices. At least eight
wines are available by the glass. Bedrooms have long been popular here too, and still
look like good value. The setting is delightful, in a peaceful, straggling village, and the
church across the road is worth a look; Lawrence Sterne is buried there. *Open 11-3,
6-11 (from 7 winter), Sun 12-3, 7-10.30. **Bar Food** 12-2, 7-9. (no food Mon eve). Free
House. **Beer** Tetley, Theakston Best, John Smith's. Patio, outdoor eating. **Accommodation** 4
bedrooms, one en suite (shower), £40 (single £24). Children welcome overnight, additional bed
(£10) available. Check-in by arrangement. MasterCard,* **VISA**

CRANBORNE   Fleur de Lys   B&B

Tel 01725 517282   Fax 01725 517631   Map 14 C4
5 Wimborne Street Cranborne Dorset BH21 5PP

Historical connections are many at this ivy-clad inn set in the heart of the village;
Thomas Hardy visited when writing *Tess of the D'Urbervilles* in 1891, Rupert Brooke
wrote a poem on the premises, and Hanging Judge Jeffreys also once stayed the night.
The pub itself is modernised and pleasant, with period features remaining. Good-sized
en suite bedrooms are clean and comfortable, and decorated in country style with
pretty floral fabrics and modern darkwood furniture. Equipped with central heating,
TVs and tea-makers, they make an ideal base from which to explore this unspoilt part
of Dorset, especially Cranborne Chase. *Open 10.30-3, 6-11 (Sun 12-3, 7-10.30).*
*Beer Hall & Woodhouse. Garden. Family room. **Accommodation** 8 bedrooms, all en suite*
(three with bath), £38-£55 (single £24-£35). Children welcome overnight (under-5s free
if sharing parents' room, 5-12s half-price), additional bed & cot available.
*Amex, MasterCard, **VISA***

CRANMORE   Strode Arms   FOOD

Tel 01749 880450   Fax 01749 880598   Map 13 F1
Cranmore Shepton Mallet Somerset BA4 4QT

Large, stone coaching inn with mullion windows, formerly a farmhouse, dating from
the 14th century and overlooking the village pond. Spacious bar areas are neatly laid-
out with comfortable country furnishings and warmed by open log fires and welcome
touches include daily newspapers to peruse. Both the bar and adjacent carpeted dining
area are adorned with memorabilia from the East Somerset Railway (otherwise known
as the Strawberry Line) which is 500 yards away. It is a popular destination for local
diners, who come to sample a reliable bar meal from either the varied printed menu
or the more interesting daily blackboard list of dishes. Choices range from scallop and
bacon salad, deep-fried Brie and home-made soup to chicken ham and leek pie,
salmon fishcakes and roast rack of lamb, all served with fresh vegetables or bubble and
squeak. Good home-made puddings include treacle tart and a delicious banana and
walnut slice. Vintage cars meet outside on the first Tuesday of the month. No
children under 14 in the bars; plenty of room outside in good weather, either on the
front terrace or in the sheltered beer garden to the rear. *Open 11.30-2.30, 6.30-11*
*(Sun 12-3, 7-10.30). Closed Sun eve Oct-Mar. **Bar Food** 12-2, 7-9.30 (till 10 Sat)*
*Free House. **Beer** Flowers IPA, Marston's Pedigree, Wadworth 6X, guest beer. Garden,*
*outdoor eating. MasterCard, **VISA***

CRASTER   Jolly Fisherman   A

Tel 01665 576461   Map 5 E1
Haven Hill Craster Alnwick Northumberland NE66 3TR

The village's only pub perches on a craggy hill above the quay, home of the local
lifeboatmen and a summer haunt for visiting landlubbers. Its best aspects are from a
raised lounge bar revealing massive seascapes through picture windows on two sides,
and from a lower garden and patio, a little above high water, with pathways down by
the harbour wall to the rocky shoreline. With boats in the harbour and the local
fishery opposite, crab soup, kipper paté and seafood sandwiches are their stock-in-
trade: crab, prawn and salmon. *Open 11-11 (11-3, 6-11 winter), Sun 12-10.30 (12-3,*
*7-10.30 winter). **Beer** Wards Thorne Best Bitter, Younger Scotch Bitter. Garden. Quayside.*
Family room. No credit cards.

Many **B&B** establishments offer reduced rates for weekend and
out-of-season bookings. Always ask about special deals for longer stays. Beware
half-board terms in inns where we do not recommend the **FOOD**.

CRAWLEY — Fox & Hounds — FOOD

Tel & Fax 01962 776285   Map 15 D3   **B&B**
Crawley Winchester Hampshire SO21 2PR

 Zzz...

A splendid redbrick pub built (like the rest of the picturesque village) at the turn of the century and converted to look much older than it is, with a fine overhanging timber facade and bow windows. The open-plan interior is comfortably furnished and lots of china plates decorate the walls of both bar and adjacent dining-room. The regularly-changing blackboard menu features game in season and good-value fresh fish such as whole lemon sole and salmon with lobster sauce. Other popular speciality dishes include home-made soups (lamb and vegetable broth) and pies – lamb, leek and rosemary – pork chop normande and mixed-bean casserole. Sandwiches and ploughman's at lunchtimes (except Sunday). Bread-and-butter pudding and Fox and Hounds 'bombe' (pancakes filled with ice cream and hot blackcurrants) complete a meal. Upstairs are three pristinely-kept, en suite bedrooms, all attractively decorated in pastel shades with tasteful co-ordinating fabrics and furnished with individual pieces of pine and antique furniture. Extra touches include two well-equipped, large bathrooms, good TVs, magazines and china crockery on each beverage tray. *Open 11.30-2.30, 6.30-11 (Sun 12-3, 7-10.30).* **Bar Food** *12-2, 7-9.30 (till 9 Sun). Free House.* **Beer** *Wadworth 6X, Gales BB. Garden, patio, outdoor eating.* **Accommodation** *3 bedrooms, all en suite, £60 (single £45). Children welcome overnight, additional bed (£12) available. MasterCard,* **VISA**

CRAY — White Lion Inn — A

Tel 01756 760262   Map 5 D4
Cray Buckden Skipton North Yorkshire BD23 5JB

Titular headquarters of the Wharfdale Head Gun Club, the Lion nestles in a deep valley on the road (B6160) between Wharfdale and Bishopsdale at the foot of Buckden Pike. For droves of fell walkers and families it's a sure shot in all weathers. Flagstoned within by a huge open range, the bar is a chummy place to dry off over a welcome pint of Moorhouse's (leaving muddy boots outside, please!). A sun-soaked front patio comes into its own in summer; parents can relax while across the road children in their dozens splash in and around the Beck, seemingly oblivious to the true purpose of its aged stepping stones. Children and well-behaved dogs are welcome indoors. *Open winter 11-3, 6-11 (Sat 11-11), Sun 12-3, 7-10.30, summer 11-11 (Sun 12-10.30). Free House.* **Beer** *Tetley Best, Moorhouse's Premier & Pendle Witches Brew, guest beer. Family room. Amex, Diners, MasterCard,* **VISA**

CRAZIES HILL — The Horns — A

Tel 01734 401416   Map 15a D3
Crazies Hill Wargrave Berkshire RG10 8LY

Recently renovated (but not too much) by Brakspear's brewery, the Horns started life in Tudor times as a hunting lodge to which a barn (now converted as part of the pub) was added some 200 years later. Very much the unspoilt country pub in style, it has no fruit machines and no piped music, just country furniture, traditional pub games – darts, shove ha'penny – and conversation. Disabled WC. New landlord, chef and style of menus since last year – not yet inspected. *Open 11-2.30, 5.30-11 (Sun 12-3, 7-10.30).* **Beer** *Brakspear. Garden. Closed 25 & 26 Dec. MasterCard,* **VISA**

CRESSWELL — Izaak Walton Inn — FOOD

Tel 01782 392265   Map 6 B3
Cresswell Stoke-on-Trent Staffordshire ST11 9RE

A good place to know in this area, despite being somewhat wedged between the busy A50 and the Stoke-Nottingham railway: turn off to the village from the old A522 at Draycott-in-the-Moors. Carpeted throughout with smartly varnished tables and chairs, yet very much a 'pub serving food', it is popular enough these days to render weekend booking virtually essential, although standards of cooking have been variable recently. Once tables are allocated, order at the bar from a lengthy, all-embracing menu supplemented by snacks and sandwiches at lunchtime (not Sunday) and chef's specials on a strategically placed blackboard: pork fillet with apricots and brandy, hake with herb crust and grilled sea bream with lemon butter, with home-made brandy basket with toffee ice cream among the puddings. No smoking in dining area. *Open 12-3, 6-11 (from 6.30 Sat), Sun 12-10.30.* **Bar Food** *12-2, 6-10 (from 6.30 Sat), Sun 12-10. Free House.* **Beer** *Marston's Best & Pedigree. Garden, outdoor eating. Closed all 25 & 26 Dec.* MasterCard, **VISA**

CROSCOMBE   Bull Terrier   B&B

Tel 01749 343658   Map 13 F1
Croscombe Wells Somerset BA5 3QJ

This lovely old pub was originally a priory where the abbots of Glastonbury used to live and was first licensed in 1612. Three bars: the Inglenook with red carpet, cushioned wall seats and original Jacobean beams, the Snug and the Common bar plus a family/dining-room. The attractive, elevated walled garden which backs on to the church (floodlit at night) overlooks the surrounding countryside. Simple overnight accommodation comprises three neat and homely upstairs bedrooms. Two sport compact en suite facilities (one with tub, one with shower only) while the third shares with the landlord's family. All have TVs, radio-alarms and tea- and coffee-making facilities. No children under 10 or dogs overnight. *Open 12-2.30, 7-11 (till 10.30 Sun). Closed all Mon Oct-Mar. Free House.* **Beer** *Butcombe Bitter, Greene King Abbot Ale, Brains Bitter, Hook Norton Best, Theakston XB. Garden. Family room.* **Accommodation** *3 bedrooms, 2 en suite, £46 (single £30). Children over 10 welcome overnight. Check-in by arrangement. No dogs.* MasterCard, **VISA**

CROSTHWAITE   Punch Bowl Inn   ★   FOOD

Tel 01539 568237   Fax 01539 568875   Map 4 C4   B&B
Crosthwaiter Kendal Cumbria LA8 8HR

Enjoying a peaceful position next to the parish church, the 16th-century Punch Bowl Inn is attracting a discerning dining clientele, keen on tucking into some above-average pub food and overnight guests looking to explore the picturesque Lyth Valley and the Lakes further afield. The homely interior, which incorporates an old converted barn, is clearly set up to welcome hungry visitors and at busy times all but a few tables are occupied by diners; food is clearly important here (and very good it is, too). Chef-landlord Steven Doherty's menu is full of tempting dishes like a deliciously light and flavoursome soufflé suissesse (an upside-down cheese soufflé), Cumbrian goat's cheese salad, leg of lamb steak provençale, fillet of sea bass with a ginger, spring onion and soy sauce, seared fillet of salmon with basil, tomato, anchovy and black olives, and breast of duck with green peppercorn sauce. Don't forget to leave room for such puds as Tunisian orange cake and hot vanilla and white chocolate sponge. At lunchtime there are also sandwiches; otherwise, it's the same menu lunch and evening (for snacks as well as full meals), except for Sunday lunch which is a two- or three-course fixed-price affair (£8.50/£10.50) that always includes a traditional roast among the options. Good-value list of wines with 10 available by the glass. There are three double rooms available, all with en suite bathrooms and modern pine furniture with four-poster beds. Irritatingly, however, there are no bedside lamps, and the light switches are not within reach of the beds. A truly splendid cooked breakfast includes free-range eggs, good bacon, black pudding, Cumberland sausage, fried mushrooms and tomatoes – all the highest quality – the perfect start to a day's walking. *Open 12-3 & 6-11 (till 10.30 Sun).* **Bar Food** *12-2 & 6-9. Free House.* **Beer** *Theakston Best Bitter, guest beers. Patio.* **Accommodation** *3 bedrooms, all en suite, £45 (single £30). Children welcome overnight. No dogs. Closed all 25 Dec.* MasterCard, **VISA**

We endeavour to be as up-to-date as possible but inevitably some changes to landlords, chefs and other key staff occur after the Guide has gone to press.

CROWBOROUGH   White Hart   FOOD

Tel 01892 652367   Fax 01892 662656   Map 11 B6
1 Chapel Green Crowborough East Sussex TN6 2LB

In July 1994 after several failed leases, including the Beefeater chain, the future of the run-down White Hart – a large mock-Tudor and suburban-looking pub located on top of Crowborough Hill – seemed very uncertain. Against all the odds in come Carl and Judith Martin, a confident and enterprising couple who, having done their homework, knew the exact potential of the property as a family-orientated pub. Within weeks this big 'white elephant' of a pub was transformed through the hard work and dedication of the Martin family and now, come rain or shine, the White Hart is foremost in local parents' minds when considering a family meal out. Whether parents arrive with babes-in-arms or hyperactive youngsters every conceivable facility has been thought of and provided to satisfy their needs or keep them amused. Inside, a series of well-refurbished inter-connecting rooms feature some exposed brick, pine furnishings, plenty of plants and bygones and, ideally placed between the bar and restaurant, a splendid indoor play area for inclement days. While mum and dad tuck into reliable and generously-served bar food, from filled jacket potatoes and ploughman's to home-made steak and ale pudding, lamb and mint pie, sausage casserole with mushrooms and red wine and large battered cod, accompanied by a pint of one of the eight real ales on handpump or a glass of good English wine, children can amuse themselves in the kitchen playhouse, watch a video on TV, play with multiplication tables and chalkboards or read one of many books available. For peckish children their are jars of baby food and an imaginative kids menu offering fishcakes, pizza, Speldhurst sausages and mash and a nourishing lunch box with sandwiches, crisps, apple and kit-kat. In addition, sugar-free drinks are listed on a board, several high-chairs/booster seats are readily available and a spotless and well-equipped baby-changing area is located in the disabled toilet. Sunny summer days attract hordes of children and the safe rear garden is paradise for all ages. Those with the energy can explore the well-equipped play area (due to be upgraded further in 1997), which features a bouncy castle, a wooden fort, a climbing rope ladder, a Wendy house full of toys, a sandpit with bucket and spade and, for the tots, a baby-swing suspended from a holly tree. However, the most popular feature by far is the Wibbly Wobbly Farmyard or mini-zoo that houses an ever-growing collection of animals, from Shallwe the pot-bellied pig and Cash 'n' Carry the pygmy goats to numerous rabbits, ducks, chickens and guinea-pigs. Children can access the pens and pet the animals at certain times and notices explain the animals and warn of the dangers of too much intrusion. And, if this is not enough family entertainment, Carl and Judith stage various fun events to mark Easter and Hallowe'en, as well as summer family barbecues and a special party with games and fireworks to celebrate each anniversary at the pub. Winner of our Family Pub of the Year 1997. *Open 11-11 (Sun 12-10.30). Bar Food   11-10 (from 12 Sun). Free House. **Beer** Morland Old Speckled Hen, Young's Special, Pot-bellied Bitter (brewed for pub), Flowers Original, Wadworth 6X, Fuller's London Pride, Greene King Abbot Ale, guest beers. Garden, outdoor eating, children's play area, mini-zoo. Disabled facilities. Amex, Diners, MasterCard, **VISA***

> We only recommend food (Bar Food) in those establishments highlighted with the **FOOD** symbol.

CULLOMPTON   Manor House Hotel   B&B

Tel 01884 32281   Fax 01884 38344   Map 13 E2
2/4 Fore Street Cullompton Devon EX15 1JL

Built as the town house for a rich wool merchant, this hotel-cum-inn dates in part to 1603, and fine old casement windows jut out from the freshly-painted black and white facade. Inside has an attractive mix of styles, the knotty pine bar Victorian in feel but with a distinct, pubby atmosphere. The appealing bedrooms are all individually decorated, with stylishly co-ordinated fabrics, nicely framed botanical prints, plenty of pieces of china and plates on the walls and good freestanding furniture in mahogany or an orangey pine finish. All the usual modern comforts: TV (with satellite), radio, telephone, tea/coffee-making facilities and a trouser press.

Carpeted bathrooms have good thermostatically-controlled showers over the baths, and nice touches like cotton wool, pot-pourri and decent toiletries. Most rooms are at the front of the building facing the main road (double-glazing helps to reduce the traffic noise) and one of the two quieter rooms to the rear has a pair of bunk beds for families. Excellent-value overnight accommodation. *Open 11-11 (Sun 12-10.30). Free House.* **Beer** *Boddingtons, Flowers IPA, Morland Old Speckled Hen. Patio/terrace. Family room.* **Accommodation** *10 bedrooms, all en suite, £53.50 (family room sleeping 4 £68.50, single £41.50). Children welcome overnight, additional bed (£7.50) & cot available. Amex, MasterCard,* **VISA**

| **CUMNOR** | **Bear & Ragged Staff** | ★ | **FOOD** |

Tel 01865 862329   Fax 01865 865366   Map 14a B2
Appleton Road Cumnor nr Oxford Oxfordshire OX2 9QH

Having settled in well at this busy pub south-west of Oxford, Bruce Buchan continues to impress diners by serving quality pub food in both the comfortable, flagstoned bar with its bare stone walls, beams and open fires and in the dining-room. The former might see good vegetarian options like spinach dumplings with tomato salsa and parsnip and leek crumble with walnut vinaigrette, five or so fishy dishes – Scottish mussels in wine and cream and salmon fishcakes with tomato coulis – plus dishes like chicken teriyaki, steak, kidney and Guinness pudding, various salads and a handful of interesting, very upmarket sandwiches (prawn, cucumber and mayonnaise, steak and onion baguette, toasted ciabatta and Welsh rarebit). The restaurant menu, served throughout the pub, is very much in a modern English mode with the likes of warm salad of Toulouse sausage, pigeon and crispy bacon, warmed Loch Fyne oysters with chive potatoes, and crispy duck and five-spice salad among the daily selection of around four starters; the main courses always feature particularly good fresh fish: chargrilled monkfish with roasted ratatouille, tranche of brill with gruyère rarebit, and fillet of Cornish sea bass with spinach 'subrics' and tomato fondue. Combine this superb fish selection with a choice of meat cuts such as roast saddle of hare with glazed shallots and its confit, medallions of local pork with Stilton and walnuts, and breast of duck with tomato and ginger chutney and you've got a very interesting menu that would not disgrace even the most modern of London restaurants. A selection of British farmhouse cheeses, chocolate quenelles with coffee-bean sauce and strawberry and pineapple gratin complete the culinary picture for the starry-eyed. Accompany your meal with a one of eight wines available by the glass, or select a bottle from the well-chosen list of wines. To find the ivy-clad pub, follow signs to Cumnor from the A420, continue along the one-way system into the village, then bear left into the High Street and Appleton Road is on the left. *Open 12-3, 5.30-11 (from 5 Fri, from 6 Sat), Sun 12-3 & 7-10.30.* **Bar Food** *12-2.15, 7-10.* **Beer** *Bass, Morrells Oxford Bitter, Varsity & Mild. Garden, outdoor eating, barbecue. Closed 3 days between Xmas and New Year. Amex, MasterCard,* **VISA**

| **CUMNOR** | **Vine Inn** | **FOOD** |

Tel 01865 862567   Fax 01865 200303   Map 14a B2
11 Abingdon Road Cumnor nr Oxford Oxfordshire OX2 9QN

Situated just off the A420 south-west of Oxford, this homely 18th-century village pub is leased by the proprietors of Whites Restaurant in Oxford, so it is understandable that the emphasis here is on producing above-average pub food. Beyond the vine-covered stone facade the original low-ceilinged and plainly furnished core has been extended to incorporate a more modern dining-room, but what it lacks in atmosphere it makes up through the choice and quality of the food on offer. An extensive and interesting blackboard menu should not disappoint, with starters available in small or large portions (priced accordingly) so as to satisfy hearty appetites. Choose from fresh crab soup, marinated duck salad and hoi sin sauce, mussels in white wine and garlic, or pigeon breast salad with onion marmalade for starters, followed by stir-fried spicy lamb, Thai beef curry, fillet of pork with sherry and green peppercorn sauce, good fresh fish (monkfish, halibut, turbot) with maybe basil and tomato or tarragon sauce and various grills like tandoori lamb kebab and spare ribs. A short list of puddings may highlight sticky toffee pudding and baked vanilla cheesecake. Good summer garden in which to enjoy a well-kept pint and a game of Aunt Sally, while children expend some energy on the play equipment. *Open 11-2.30, 6-11 (Sun 12-3, 7-10).* **Bar Food** *12.30-2.15, 6.30-9.15 (from 7 Sun).* **Beer** *Greene King Abbot Ale, Adnams Bitter, Tetley, Wadworth 6X, guest beer. Garden, outdoor eating, children's play area. Family room.* MasterCard, **VISA**

DALWOOD	**Tuckers Arms**	**FOOD**
Tel 01404 881342 Fax 01404 881802	Map 13 E2	**B&B**
Dalwood Axminster Devon EX13 7EG		

Picture-book-pretty, thatched pub in a delightful Axe Valley village, signposted off the A35 west of Axminster. Parts of the bar date back 700 years to when the building was a manor house; it later became an important coaching inn on the old London–Exeter road. The main low-ceilinged bar complete with inglenook, beams and rustic furnishings is the setting in which to sample some reliable bar food. Beyond the routine snack menu (with French-stick sandwiches and ploughman's lunches) an interesting daily-changing blackboard list favours fresh fish: seafood chowder, grilled herrings with orange and mustard glaze, hake with garlic, prawns and basil and sautéed monkfish with peppercorns, cream and brandy, as well as maybe hot Brie salad, rack of lamb or venison steak with wild mushrooms and red wine. A rear extension houses the five clean and functional bedrooms with floral curtains and matching bed covers. All have TVs, tea-makers and well-fitted, fully tiled en suite bathrooms with showers. In summer months the exterior is festooned with colourful flower tubs and baskets. *Open 11.30-3, 6.30-11 (Sun 12-3, 7-10.30).* **Bar Food** *12-2.30, 7-10 (till 9.30 Sun).* *Free House.* **Beer** *Wadworth 6X, Flowers Original, Otter Ale & Bright. Garden, outdoor eating. Family room.* **Accommodation** *5 bedrooms, all en suite (showers), £40 (family room sleeping three £55, single £25). Children welcome overnight. Check-in by arrangement. No dogs.* Amex, MasterCard, **VISA**

DAMERHAM	**Compasses Inn**	**FOOD**
Tel 01725 518231 Fax 01725 518880	Map 14 C3	**B&B**
Damerham Fordingbridge Hampshire SP6 3HQ		

Attractive 16th-century coaching inn located in the heart of the village with a splendid flower-filled garden next to the cricket green – ideal for watching an innings or two with a pint on sunny summer Sunday evenings. Spartan public bar with traditional games and a carpeted open-plan lounge bar with pine furniture, central woodburner, pretty wallpaper and a short blackboard menu listing reliable home-cooked specials. Choose from a daily soup (chicken and herb), sardines with Cajun spices, pork chops with garlic, coriander and lemon, or maybe red mullet with an orange and herb crust. Impressive ploughman's lunch list with a choice of over seven cheeses, served with home-made pickle, and good standard pub dishes (sandwiches, various curries, steak and mushroom pie, lasagne, steaks) featured on a printed menu. Overnight accommodation in six cottagey bedrooms (one family room); these are light and airy with small print wallpapers, co-ordinating fabrics, comfortable furnishings and tiled en suite facilities plus TVs and tea-makers. A warm welcome extends to children with the provision of a play area, menu and baby-changing facilities. *Open 11-2.30, 6-11 (Sat 11-11, Sun 12-3, 7-10.30).* **Bar Food** *12-2, 7-9.30 (Sun 12-2.30, 7-9).* *Free House.* **Beer** *Wadworth 6X, Flowers Original, Ringwood Best, Hampshire Brewery Compasses Ale, guest beer. Garden, Family room, children's play area.* **Accommodation** *6 bedrooms, all en suite (two with bath), £50 (four-poster £60, single £29.50). Children welcome overnight (under-2s free, 2-12s half-price if sharing parents' room).* MasterCard, **VISA**

We only recommend food (Bar Food) in those establishments highlighted with the **FOOD** symbol.

DANBY · Duke of Wellington · B&B

Tel 01287 660351   Map 5 E3
Danby Whitby North Yorkshire YO21 2LY

Just two miles from the A171 and approached across a windswept moor, the ivy-clad stone pub stands at the head of Danby village; Esk Dale's activity centre is just a half-mile walk away. Despite its somewhat ramshackle exterior, there's a warm welcome within from the Howat family. Nine comfortable bedrooms have pine furniture, appealing decor, colour TVs and tea-making equipment; all but one have their own en suite facilities, the remaining room having an adjoining private bathroom. There's a cosy, private residents' lounge for those wishing to escape with a good book, while in the bar an agreeable mixture of tourists, fell-walkers and locals soon strike up acquaintances over a pint or two of the Duke's well-kept real ales. *Open 11-3, 7-11 (Sun 12-3, 7-10.30). Free House. Beer John Smith's, Ruddles Best; Marston's Pedigree, Cameron Strong Arm. Terrace. Accommodation 9 bedrooms, 8 en suite, £44 (single £22). Children welcome overnight (under-5s stay free in parents' room, 5-10s half-price), additional bed & cot available. Amex, MasterCard, **VISA***

DARTINGTON · Cott Inn · FOOD · B&B

Tel 01803 863777   Fax 01803 866629   Map 13 D3
Dartington Totnes Devon TQ9 6HE

 Zzz...

A delightful 14th-century stone- and cob-built inn, continuously licensed since 1320, with a wonderful, 183ft thatched roof. Landlords David and Susan Grey keep both the bar and tiny restaurant neat, with lots of blackened beams, open fires, a mixture of antique and older pieces of furniture and plenty of gleaming brass bits and pieces. Lunch is an impressive hot and cold buffet affair offering home-made quiches, various meats, Dart salmon and an array of freshly-prepared salads. Evening fare is more imaginative with blackboards in the bar listing such dishes as medallions of lamb fillet with lavender and Cumberland sauce, venison with juniper and redcurrants, and tenderloin of pork with cream, mustard and prunes; vegetarian options. Interesting fresh fish dishes may include fillets of gurnard with hazelnut and blue cheese sauce, halibut with artichokes and basil, and fillet of cod with sweet ginger and lime salsa. Satisfying, home-made puddings may include lemon and lime posset, chocolate and strawberry roulade and the ever-popular Old English treacle tart. There's usually a choice of three roasts for Sunday lunch. Overnight accommodation comprises six compact bedrooms tucked beneath the heavy thatch. All are neat and tidy with modern pine furnishings, pretty floral fabrics; four have compact bathrooms with overhead showers. TVs, tea-makers and telephones are standard throughout. *Open 11-2.30, 5.30-11 (Sun 12-3, 7-10.30). Bar Food 12-2.15 (till 2.30 Sun), 6.30-9.30 (from 7 Sun). Free House. Beer Bass, Butcombe Bitter, Cott Bitter. Garden, outdoor eating. Accommodation 6 bedrooms, all en suite, £55 (single £45). Children over 5 welcome overnight, additional bed (£10) available. Pub & accommodation closed 25 Dec eve. Amex, MasterCard, **VISA***

DARTMOUTH · Cherub · FOOD

Tel 01803 832571   Map 13 D3
13 Higher Street Dartmouth Devon TQ6 9BB

This magnificent example of a medieval timbered house (Dartmouth's oldest building, dating from 1380) was at one time a wealthy wool merchant's house. Famous for its overhanging beamed facade and the unusual first-floor windows, it takes its name from the type of boat built on the Dart for the wool export trade. Inside, the busy table-crammed tiny bar is full of atmosphere with original oak timbers and inglenook fireplace, plus a narrow, twisting staircase leading up into the small restaurant. Bar food might include French onion soup, deep-fried tiger prawns in filo pastry, smoked whole prawns, grilled swordfish steak and poached salmon; sandwiches and ploughman's lunches are also available all day. Fresh fish dishes – sea bass with ginger and spring onions, pan-fried scallops with garlic butter and mange tout – are listed on the blackboard, as well as on the more elaborate evening restaurant menu, alongside duck breast with caramelised ginger and Cointreau sauce and chargrilled lamb steak with fine herbs. No children in the bar but children over four are allowed in the restaurant before 9pm. *Open 11-3, 6-11 (Sun 12-3, 7-10.30), July & Aug 11-11 (Sun 12-10.30)*. *Bar Food 12-2.30, 7-10. Free House*. *Beer Wadworth 6X, Morland Old Speckled Hen, Flowers Original, guest beer. MasterCard,* **VISA**

DARTMOUTH   Royal Castle Hotel   B&B

Tel 01803 833033   Fax 01803 835445   Map 13 D3
11 The Quay Dartmouth Devon TQ6 9PS

Zzz...

Commanding the best site overlooking the small harbour and the Dart estuary beyond, this handsome, established inn/hotel is a most welcoming and comfortable place to stay. Originally four Tudor houses built on either side of a narrow lane, which now forms the lofty and attractive hallway, it boasts some oil paintings, antique furniture and the magnificent Bell Board, full of room-call bells, each one pitched at a different note. Of the two bars, the Harbour Bar is distinctly pubby and lively throughout the day, whereas the more refined and spacious Galleon Bar is a popular coffee stop and sports a weaponry display. All the 25 bedrooms are beautifully decorated, each in its own individual style with quality wallpapers and matching fabrics. Some rooms have four-posters, others antique brass beds and most are furnished with tasteful pieces of furniture. Several more expensive rooms enjoy river views and are light and airy with huge bathrooms, two with jacuzzi baths, some with showers only. Added touches include tissues, cotton wool balls and Woods of Windsor toiletries. TVs, telephones and tea-makers are standard throughout. If up early, linger over a good breakfast at one of the three sought-after window seats, overlooking the harbour and river. Twelve wines by the glass. Private garage facilities available. *Open 11-11 (till 10.30 Sun). Free House*. *Beer Boddingtons, Flowers IPA, Courage Directors, Blackawton Bitter. Garden*. *Accommodation 25 bedrooms, all en suite, £79-£89 (river view £99-£119, single £44.50-£64.50, depending on season). Children welcome overnight (under-16s stay free in parents' room). MasterCard,* **VISA**

> We endeavour to be as up-to-date as possible but inevitably some changes to landlords, chefs and other key staff occur after the Guide has gone to press.

DEDDINGTON   Deddington Arms   FOOD

Tel 01869 338364   Fax 01869 337010   Map 14a C1   **B&B**
Horsefair Deddington Oxfordshire OX15 0SH

Formerly known as the Kings Arms, this attractive, 16th-century coaching inn overlooks the pretty village street and boasts a wealth of timbering, numerous nooks and crannies, open logs fires and popular window seats in its welcoming interior. Spick-and-span throughout following serious investment in the property, resulting in the complete refurbishment of the bars, a new air-conditioned dining-room and the addition of seven en suite bedrooms upstairs. Finishing touches to the rooms were being made at the time of inspection, but the presence of brass beds, a fine reproduction dark oak carved four-poster, smart decor with matching fabrics, tasteful prints and splendid en suite bathrooms, complete with power showers over tubs, gold coloured fittings and thick towels, suggests this is superior pub accommodation. All are equipped with direct-dial phones, satellite TVs and tea-making facilities. Guests staying overnight should find 'eating in' a pleasure as well, for the food on offer here is both interesting and imaginative. Regularly-changing specials with monthly themes (perhaps fish – pan-fried turbot with lime and green ginger, chargrilled marinated kingfish steak, dressed crab) supplement the main seasonally-changing menu, which lists 'beginnings' like ragout of caramelised onions and baby leeks, roast pigeon breasts, smoked haddock florentine and shellfish stew followed by braised monkfish with tomato, basil and cream, roulade of pork tenderloin with creamy tarragon sauce, turkey and ham pie or fillet steak Diane for 'middles'. The choice of home-made 'afters' may include dark chocolate and rum mousse with coffee bean sauce, lemon tart and passion fruit cheesecake with apricot and orange coulis. Good range of real ales, malt whiskies and seven wines are available by the glass. Look out for the popular monthly events such as Irish and Caribbean nights. *Open 11.45-2.45, 5.30-11 (Sat 11.45-11), Sun 12-10.30.* **Bar Food** *12-2.15, 6.30-10.30. Free House.* **Beer** *Tetley, Adnams Bitter, Wadworth 6X, two guest beers. Garden, outdoor eating.* **Accommodation** *7 bedrooms, all en suite, £62.50 (four-poster £75, single £52.50). Children welcome overnight (under-16s £10), additional bed & cot (both £10) available. Check-in bar hours only. Dogs by arrangement. Closed 25 Dec eve. MasterCard,* **VISA**

DEDHAM   Marlborough Head Hotel   FOOD

Tel 01206 323250   Map 10 C3   **B&B**
Mill Lane Dedham Essex CO7 6DH

Dedham is a charming village surrounded by picturesque Constable country, and the Marlborough Head, which occupies that most traditional of sites directly opposite the church, has been dispensing hospitality for over 550 years. Woodcarving is a speciality here, outside on the black and white timbered upper storey of the building, inside above a massive old fireplace in the entrance lobby. Several other rooms and bars, one featuring a heavily beamed ceiling, are furnished with good eating-height tables and the odd copper or brass ornament. Food orders are made at a leather-topped desk, quoting the number painted on a little stone on your table, from a long menu that runs the gamut from sandwiches (ham, cream cheese, walnut and onion) or a simple jacket potato to the likes of hunters hare casserole, beef and Stilton pie, halicot of lamb with barbecue sauce, Greek style moussaka and braised lambs hearts. Try to leave room for pudding, too, perhaps a chocolate and pecan nut brownie or treacle tart. Spacious bedrooms, two doubles and two singles, are modestly but pleasantly furnished with a variety of pieces from the antique-ish and old pine to more modern bedside tables. Each has a few old timbers and sloping floors, and candlewick bedspreads add a homely touch. All except one have compact, lino-floored en suite shower rooms with toilets; one of the doubles has a proper bathroom. *Open 10-11 (Sun 11-10.30).* **Bar Food** *12-2.30 (till 3 Sat & Sun), 7-9.30 (till 10 Sun). Morning coffee, afternoon and high teas also served.* **Beer** *Ind Coope Burton Ale, Greene King IPA. Garden, patio, outdoor eating. Family room.* **Accommodation** *4 bedrooms, all en suite, £51 (family room sleeping three £60, single £32.50). Children welcome overnight (£10). Accommodation closed 25 Dec. Amex, Diners, MasterCard,* **VISA**

DENT   Sun Inn   A

Tel 01539 625208   Map 5 D4
Main Street Dent Cumbria LA10 5QL

Right on the cobbled main street and looking out over the parish church towards the Dale's surrounding hills, the Sun is picture postcard pretty outside and postage stamp size within, a shining example of a sadly-dying breed of village local. Dent beers, brewed nearby since 1990, prove a big draw here, and the setting of original timbers, winter log fires and a gravelled beer garden "out back" are all conducive to its enjoyment. The three modest upstairs bedrooms, all of which share a bathroom, are due to be upgraded this year *Open 11-3, 6.45-11 (from 6 Fri, Sat & school holiday periods 11-11), Sun 12-10.30. Free House.* **Beer** *Dent Bitter, Kamikaze & T'Owd Tup stout. Gravelled beer garden. Family room. MasterCard,* **VISA**

Many **B&B** establishments offer reduced rates for weekend and out-of-season bookings. Always ask about special deals for longer stays. Beware half-board terms in inns where we do not recommend the **FOOD**.

DERBY   Abbey Inn   A

Tel 01332 558297   Map 6 C3
Darley Street Darley Abbey Derby Derbyshire DE22 1DX

Probably used for guest accommodation by the monks of the Abbey of St Mary of Darley in the 12th century, this medieval hall-house fell into gradual decay following the monasteries' dissolution in 1538. Fully 440 years elapsed before its restoration again saw the doors open for all to enjoy the Abbey's hospitality. High, exposed roof trusses and hammer beams are a feature of the upper bar whose leaded lights and church pew seating are quite in keeping. Approached by spiral stairs, the cavernous Under Croft Bar plays host to gregarious night-time activity, with folk evenings every other Sunday. The toilets here, though, remain appropriately primitive. *Open 11.30-2.30 (from 12 Sat), 6-11 (Sun 12-10.30). Beer Sam Smith's Old Brewery Bitter. Closed all 25 Dec. No credit cards.*

DERBY   Ye Olde Dolphin Inn   A

Tel 01332 349115   Map 6 C3
6/7 Queen Street Derby Derbyshire DE5 1NR

The oldest pub in Derby, dating from the 16th century, in a conveniently central spot in the city centre. No juke box or machines and real open fire. There are four rooms: snug, bar, lounge and the Offilers Bar which is devoted to the former brewery of that name with memorabilia adorning the walls. *Open 10.30-11 (Sun 12-10.30). Beer M&B Highgate Mild, Bass, Stones, Worthington, Marston's Pedigree, two guest beers. Patio. MasterCard, VISA*

DEVIZES   Bear Hotel   FOOD

Tel 01380 722444   Fax 01380 722450   Map 14 C3   **B&B**
Market Place Devizes Wiltshire SN10 1HS

This famous old town-centre coaching inn has been welcoming guests for over 400 years, including George III accompanied by Queen Charlotte and more recently Harold Macmillan when he was Prime Minister. It is still a comfortable place to visit and stay, for it retains that old-fashioned air within its beamed and panelled lounges and dining-rooms. The main bar, furnished with winged wall settles and plush chairs around a large open fire, opens early, as it is a popular coffee stop for shoppers. Later, at lunchtime, it fills again with people seeking out the popular bar snacks, such as home-made soup, a range of ploughman's lunches and freshly-cut sandwiches and ham, egg and chips. Evening bar snacks range from pub favourites to home-cooked specials like sautéed chicken Mexican style and lamb cutlets with a green peppercorn and mustard sauce. Buffet-style lunches – which can also be eaten in the bar – and weekend evening suppers are available in the traditional, oak-panelled Lawrence Room, while a more imaginative carte and table d'hote menu is served in the elegant Master Lambton Restaurant. Rambling staircases and a labyrinth of sloping corridors lead to the comfortable and spacious en suite bedrooms, all of which are equipped, furnished and maintained to a very high standard, as one would expect from a hotel of this standing. Several rooms have four-posters and residents have their own lounge with deep armchairs, sofas and open fires. *Open 11-3 (coffee from 9.30), 6-11 (Thu-Sat 11-11), Sun 11.30-3, 7-10.30. Bar Food 9.30-2.30 (till 2 Sun), 7-9.30 (till 10 Fri & Sat). Beer Wadworth 6X & IPA, guest beer. Patio, outdoor eating. Family room.* **Accommodation** *24 bedrooms, all en suite, £75 (four-poster £85, single £45). Children welcome overnight (under-5s stay free in parents' room), additional bed (£15) & cot available. Pub and accommodation closed all 25 & 26 Dec. MasterCard, VISA*

We only recommend food (Bar Food) in those establishments highlighted with the **FOOD** symbol.

| DIGGLE | **Diggle Hotel** | B&B |

Tel 01457 872741   Map 6 C2
Station House Diggle Oldham OL3 5JZ

If approaching from the north on the A670, you'll need to pass the turn-off to the village of Diggle and use the turning circle as left turns are prohibited. Once through the village, watch out for signs for the Diggle Hotel (by the school). The hotel itself, a dark stone building by the railway line, dates back to 1789, and is neat and unpretentious inside. The main room (and adjoining small room where children can sit) is full of polished brass and copperware, and the plain walls are decorated with a number of country pictures. Upstairs there are three neat, unfussy double bedrooms, two of them quite compact, the largest with views towards the village. Modern fitted furniture is used in all rooms, as are duvets with pretty floral covers, and washbasins. The shared and carpeted bathroom also has a separate shower unit. A homely residents' lounge has fawn upholstered seating, books and games. The Mitchell family are friendly and charming hosts, and their staff are equally pleasant. *Open 12-3, 5-11 (Sat 12-11), Sun 12-3, 5-10.30. Free House.* **Beer** *Timothy Taylor's Golden Best & Landlord, Boddingtons, Flowers Original, Oldhay Bitter. Garden. Family room.* **Accommodation** *3 bedrooms, sharing bathroom, £35 (single £25). Children welcome overnight (under-10s free if sharing parents' room), additional bed & cot available. No dogs. Amex, MasterCard,* **VISA**

| DODDISCOMBSLEIGH | **Nobody Inn** | FOOD |

Tel 01647 252394   Fax 01647 252978   Map 13 D3   B&B
Doddiscombsleigh Exeter Devon EX6 7PS

🛏 🍴 🍷 Zzz...

Difficult to find, but this delightful old village inn is worth the hazardous drive through narrow lanes off the A38 at Haldon Racecourse, 3 miles west of Exeter. According to legend, a previous owner closed and locked the door against the knocking of weary travellers, pretending that there was nobody in, and it has remained the 'Nobody Inn' ever since. The mood is set by a wealth of old beams, ancient settles and a motley collection of antique tables; horse brasses and copper pots and pans decorate the inglenook fireplace, and a real fire burns in winter. The varied and value-for-money bar menu might include sandwiches made with locally-baked malted wheatmeal bread, a home-made coarse duck liver paté with port and herbs and the special Nobody soup made with chicken stock, vegetables and fruit. More substantial dishes appear on the daily-changing blackboard such as lamb and lime in coriander sauce, venison casserole, pork with ginger, rhubarb, honey and pasta, and mixed bean and barley bake. But ensure you leave room for possibly the best collection of West Country cheeses to be found anywhere. Six different cheeses can be chosen from a selection of up to forty, including cow's, goat's and ewe's milk cheeses, many of them unpasteurised. Their own vegetable garden supplies all the herbs for the kitchen plus globe artichokes, among other vegetables. The globe-trotting wine list is impressive, featuring over 700 bins. Twenty wines are also offered by the glass and there are at least 250 whiskies from which to choose. Four of the modestly comfortably bedrooms are in the inn itself, two with en suite shower and toilet, plus tea-makers and a drinks tray bearing full bottles of brandy, gin and sherry – charged up by consumption at bar prices. For that extra peace and quiet visitors should book one of the three larger en suite rooms located in a small, early 17th-century manor house (Town Barton) about 150 yards away, next to the church. These are comfortably and traditionally furnished and a ready-to-serve Continental breakfast is provided in the fridge; alternatively, stroll up to the inn for a cooked breakfast. General upgrading of bedrooms is planned for 1997. No children under 14. B&B for horses 150yds down the road! *Open 12-2.30, 6-11 (from 7 winter), Sun 12-3, 7-10.30.* **Bar Food** *12-2, 7-10. Free House.* **Beer** *Bass, RCH PG Steam, Nobody's Bitter (brewed by Branscombe Vale Brewery), guest beer. Garden, outdoor eating.* **Accommodation** *7 bedrooms, 6 en suite (one with bath), £59 (single from £23). Children over 14 welcome overnight. Pub & accommodation closed 25 Dec eve. No dogs. Amex, MasterCard,* **VISA**

DONINGTON-ON-BAIN   Black Horse   B&B

Tel 01507 343640   Map 7 E2
Main Road Donington-on-Bain Lincolnshire LN11 9TJ

Zzz... ☺

Attractively set in a delightful Wolds village and on the Viking Way walk, this much extended and modernised inn is a popular destination locally and also with visitors seeking comfortable overnight accommodation. Inside, a rambling series of rooms radiate out from the original 18th-century core or snug back bar with its low ceiling (beware of the perilously low central beam) and brick fireplace with log fire. Separate dining area and lively public bar and games room. Light and spacious bedrooms are housed in the adjacent 'motel-style' block (wheelchair access) and feature modern pine furnishings, wicker chairs, pretty fabrics and extras like remote-controlled TV and tea-makers. Spotless, compact en suite facilities with efficient showers. The Black Horse is also a favourite with families as children are made very welcome in the mural room and adjacent dining-room, where they can order from their own menu and enjoy an early evening meal if staying overnight. Two high-chairs and a changing shelf in the Ladies may make life easier for parents. Summer days can be enjoyed in the safe rear garden where youngsters can let off steam on the swings, slide and climbing frame. *Open 11.30-2.30, 6.30-11 (Sun 12-2.30, 7-10.30). Free House.*
Beer Courage Directors, Ruddles Best Bitter, John Smith's Bitter, guest beers. Garden, children's play area. Family room. Accommodation 8 bedrooms, all en suite with showers, £40 (single £25). Children welcome overnight (under-3s stay free in parents' room), additional bed (£5-£10) & cot available. Check-in by arrangement. Accommodation closed 24 & 25 Dec. MasterCard, VISA

DORCHESTER   Kings Arms   B&B

Tel 01305 265353   Fax 01305 260269   Map 13 F2
30 High East Street Dorchester Dorset DT1 1HF

A substantial Georgian inn dominating the busy main street of this attractive county town, famous for its associations with the author Thomas Hardy, who resided in the nearby village of Lower Bockhampton. Locals fill the comfortable, low-ceilinged bar, while good-value overnight accommodation is proving popular among businessmen, families on the move (each room sleeps two adults and two children under 16) and tourists following the Hardy trail. Bedrooms are uniformly decorated in restful pastel colours and floral fabrics, with easy chairs and well-equipped bathrooms (all with bath/shower) enhancing a relaxing stay, although bow-fronted rooms overlooking the High Street could suffer from traffic noise. Tea-makers, satellite TV, trouser press, hairdryer and telephone are standard extras. Housed in an adjacent building are two unusual 'theme' rooms; the Tutankamun room and the Lawrence of Arabia room (£99 a night including champagne and breakfast). Residents' lounge. Premier Lodge (Greenalls). *Open 11-3, 6-11, (Fri & Sat 11-11), Sun 12-3, 7-10.30. Beer Wadworth 6X, Boddingtons, Flowers Original, Bass, Courage Directors, weekly guest beer.*
Accommodation 33 rooms, all en suite, £41.50 excluding breakfast (Fri-Sun £34.50) Children welcome overnight (under-12s stay free in share parents' room), additional cot available. No dogs. Amex, Diners, MasterCard, VISA

DORCHESTER-ON-THAMES   George Hotel   B&B

Tel 01865 340404   Fax 01865 341620   Map 14a C3
High Street Dorchester-on-Thames Oxfordshire OX10 7HH

With a history spanning more than 500 years, the George is one of the oldest inns in the land. Focal point of the public area is a fine beamed bar. Bedrooms in the main building have a solid, old-fashioned feel, some cosy and snug under oak beams, two with solid four-posters. Other rooms have less character but are still very adequate. Refurbishment of all the bedrooms was due to be completed at the end of 1996. *Open 11-11 (till 10.30 Sun). Free House. Beer Brakspear Bitter, guest beer. Garden. Family room. Accommodation 18 bedrooms, all en suite, £65-£75 (family room £85, single £52.50). Children welcome overnight, additional bed & cot (£10) available. Amex, Diners, MasterCard, VISA*

DORSTONE   Pandy Inn   FOOD

Tel & Fax 01981 550273   Map 9 D5
Dorstone Golden Valley Hereford & Worcester HR3 6AN

The Pandy (located off the B4348) is the oldest inn in Herefordshire. It was built in 1185 by Richard De Brito, a Norman knight, to house his workers while building Dorstone Church as atonement for his part in the murder of Thomas Becket. Vegetarians are well catered for with a variety of dishes to choose from including banana and wild mushroom curry and red dragon pie – aduki bean cottage pie. Extensive main menu dishes include chicken and vegetable terrine, vine leaves stuffed with lamb and mint with tzatzki, beef and tomato cobbler, seafood crumble and garlic chicken cooked with mustard seeds, garlic and yoghurt. An imaginative specials board may also offer rabbit and cabbage broth, supreme of goose with raisin sauce and red cabbage, jugged hare and red mullet with stir-fried vegetables and a honey and soy sauce. Finally, choose one of the dozen or so desserts (mostly home-made), which include locally-made sheep's milk ice cream in some unusual flavours. Sandwiches and ploughman's platters are offered at lunchtime only. Lawned garden with swing for children. *Open 12-3 (till 4 Sat & Sun), 7-11 (till 10.30 Sun). Closed all Mon & Tue Nov-Easter.* **Bar Food** *12-2.15, 7-9.30 (till 9.45 Fri-Sun). Free House.* **Beer** *Bass, Hereford Supreme, Everards Tiger. Garden, outdoor eating. No credit cards.*

> We only recommend food (Bar Food) in those establishments highlighted
> with the **FOOD** symbol.

DOWNHAM   Assheton Arms   FOOD

Tel 01200 441227   Map 6 B1
Downham Clitheroe Lancashire BB7 4BJ

The pub's unusual name commemorates the Assheton family, Earls of Clitheroe and landlords of the entire village since 1558. Standing at its head by the church and surrounded by picturesque stone cottages, the village local retains a cheerfully warm, traditional air. Single bar and sectioned rooms house an array of solid oak tables, wing-back settees and window seats. There's no mystery, either, attached to the food, ordered at a separate counter where the kitchen is in full view. Predictable starters run through chicken liver paté and devilled whitebait. Grills of plaice or steaks, steak and kidney pie and treacle sponge and custard follow familiar lines. The daily-changing specials board has a generally fishy emphasis with the likes of pan-fried monkfish with mixed peppercorns and a crab and brandy sauce and brochette of king scallops with bacon, mushrooms and peppers showing the kitchen at its best. Sandwiches and ploughman's platters are not available on Saturday evenings and Sunday lunchtimes. *Open 12-3, 7-11 (Sun 12-3, 7-10.30).* **Bar Food** *12-2 (till 2.30 Sun), 7-10.* **Beer** *Boddingtons, Whitbread Castle Eden Ale, Flowers Original. Patio, outdoor eating. Family room. Amex, MasterCard,* **VISA**

DRAKEHOLES   Griff Inn   FOOD

Tel 01777 817206   Map 7 D2   **B&B**
Drakeholes Bawtry Nottinghamshire DN10 5DF

Zzz...

Standing above the Chesterfield canal, where the A631 meets the B6045, and fronted by a large patio and canalside picnic tables, the Griff (once known as the White Swan) dates from the 18th century, but its interior echoes the grand style of an earlier age, with its marble-floored entrance foyer and bar, and intimate oak-panelled cocktail lounge. Grand eating is not, however, de rigueur, the extensive bar menu encompassing home-made steak pie, sandwiches, ploughman's platters, lasagne and a seafood platter. There is a carvery every day at lunchtime and from 6-8pm. The restaurant combines table d'hote and a Sunday lunch with an ambitious à la carte. The Griff is certainly useful to know for a quiet country stay in the Idle valley. Bedrooms are neatly appointed in pastel shades and varnished pine, which create a cottagey effect without frill or particular luxury and the absence of phones, (but not television) add to a peaceful nights stay. En suite bathrooms are spacious and airy with good, powerful showers for early morning invigoration prior to a substantial country breakfast. *Open 11.30-3, 6-11 (Sun 11.30-10.30). Closed Sun eve & all Mon Nov-Apr.* **Bar Food** *12-2.15, 6-9.30 (Sun 12-9.30). Free House.* **Beer** *Whitbread Castle Eden Ale, Boddingtons, Flowers IPA. Garden, outdoor eating.* **Accommodation** *3 bedrooms, all en suite, £50 (single £35). Children welcome overnight, additional bed (£7.50) & cot available. Check-in by arrangement. MasterCard,* **VISA**

DRAYTON — The Roebuck — FOOD

Tel 01295 730542   Map 14a B1   **B&B**
Drayton Banbury Oxfordshire OX15 6EN

Standing next to the A422 about a mile from Banbury is an attractive 16th-century stone pub which has built up a strong local following for its excellent food. The low-beamed bars with their rough, painted walls and solid wooden tables provide a cosily atmospheric setting for everything from sandwiches, ploughman's lunches, home-made soup and the 'Roebuck Special' (fresh cold ham off the bone) to Cajun chicken, tagliatelle niçoise and beef curry. There are two neat bedrooms with up-to-date furniture, one with exposed beams and a sloping ceiling. They share a functional shower room and are both equipped with remote-control TVs, tea-makers and magazines. *Open 11-2.30 (till 3 Sat), 6-11 (Sun 12-3, 7-10.30).* **Bar Food** *11.30-2.15, 6.30-9.30 (Sun 12-2.30, 7.15-9). Free House.* **Beer** *Hook Norton Best, Boddingtons, Fuller's London Pride, Young's Special, guest beer. Patio.* **Accommodation** *2 bedrooms (shared shower room), £36 (single £26). Children over 12 welcome overnight (12-14s £15). Accommodation closed Christmas. No dogs. MasterCard,* **VISA**

DRIFFIELD — Bell Hotel — B&B

Tel 01377 256661   Fax 01377 253228   Map 7 E1
Market Place Driffield East Riding of Yorkshire YO25 7AP

Period charm and modern amenities combine in a coaching inn that's more than 250 years old, but now very much a hotel. Conference and function facilities are in the restored Old Town Hall, and further conversion houses a leisure complex. Day rooms include the 18th-century wood-panelled Oak Room, the flagstoned Old Corn Exchange buffet/bar and a residents' lounge. Bedrooms boast antique furniture and up-to-date comforts; three are suitable for disabled guests. The 20 acres of gardens (800yds away from the hotel) provide both formal gardens and mixed wetland; deer have been introduced. *Open 11-2, 6-11 (Sun 12-3, 7-10.30). Free House.* **Beer** *four regularly-changing real ales. Garden, indoor swimming pool, spa bath, steam room, sauna, solarium, squash.* **Accommodation** *14 bedrooms, all en suite, £91 (single £62). Children over 12 welcome overnight. No dogs. Accommodation closed 24-30 Dec. Amex, Diners, MasterCard,* **VISA**

DRONFIELD — Old Sidings — FOOD

Tel 01246 410023   Map 6 C2
91 Chesterfield Road Dronfield Derbyshire S18 6XE

Tucked by a bridge on the main Sheffield railway line, there's nothing particularly pretty about the Old Sidings, although extensive refurbishments have spruced up the interior with the installation of wood panelling and even some railway paraphernalia. Vast menus signal the galley's intentions, with plenty of goods on which to stoke up, such as lamb casserole with Stilton dumplings, beef stroganoff, lemon chicken and pork and apricot casserole. Once aboard, the special Shunters menu and Buffet Car dining are just the ticket. Sunday lunch is popular (half price for children). Ten wines served by the glass. *Open 12-2.30, 5-11 (Fri & Sat 12-11), Sun 12-10.30.* **Bar Food** *12-2 (till 2.30 Fri & Sat), 5.30-8.30 (Sun 12-8.30). Free House.* **Beer** *Stones Bitter, Worthington Best, Highgate Dark, Hancock's HB, Bass. Patio. Diners, MasterCard,* **VISA**

| DUDDINGTON | Royal Oak Hotel | B&B |

Tel 01780 444267   Map 7 E4
Duddington Stamford Lincolnshire PE9 3QE

Zzz...

Popular, small family-run hotel set beside the A43 Stamford to Corby road at the end of this charming village. The bar is modern, but by no means without character, due in part to plush banquette seating, lots of greenery and well-lit prints of Victorian scenes. Comfortable overnight accommodation in six decent-sized rooms, attractively done out in pastel shades and floral wallpapers, have antique-style reproduction pieces, Victorian prints and good beds with brass bedsteads. TVs, phones and tea-makers are standard and the clean, carpeted shower rooms (one with bath) are fully tiled. Handy stopover point for weary travellers heading north or south. *Open 11-3, 7-11 (till 10.30 Sun). Free House.* **Beer** *Ruddles County. Garden.* **Accommodation** *6 bedrooms, all en suite (five with shower), £45 (single £28.50). Children welcome overnight, additional bed (£8) available. Check-in by arrangement. Closed all 25 Dec. Amex, MasterCard,* **VISA**

| DUMMER | The Queen | FOOD |

Tel 01256 397367   Fax 01256 397601   Map 14a C4
Down Street Dummer Basingstoke Hampshire RG22 2AD

Handy for M3 travellers, this attractive whitewashed inn is set in an equally pretty and up-market village, less than a mile from Junction 7. The neat, low-ceilinged and softly-lit bar area is open-plan in style, with several brick and wall partitions creating cosy alcoves and a small, intimate dining area. A printed bar menu highlights some good favourites (fish and chips, pasta carbonara, steak and kidney pie, curries, gigantic sandwiches), while the daily-changing blackboard may list shark steak with anchovy butter, half shoulder of lamb with thyme and red wine, or spicy vegetable chili. Separate restaurant menu and a good-value 4-course lunch is the attraction on Sundays. The rear sun-trap terrace and lawn with benches is ideal for summer eating. No under-14s in bar areas. New landlords. *Open 11-3, 5.30-11 (Sun 12-3, 7-10.30).* **Bar Food** *12-2.30, 6.45-10 (Sun 12-2.15, 7-9.30).* **Beer** *Courage Best & Directors, Marston's Pedigree, guest beer. Garden, outdoor eating. Amex, MasterCard,* **VISA**

| DUNSTAN | Cottage Inn | B&B |

Tel 01665 576658   Map 5 D1
Dunstan Alnwick Northumberland WE66 3SZ

Purchased as a row of derelict cottages by Lawrence & Shirley Jobling in 1975, reconstruction into quite a modest guest house preceeded their finally opening the Cottage Inn as a pub in 1988. Central to the entire conversion, and fully visible in the bar, is the three-foot thick orchard wall of Craster Tower, which stands on the fringe of the pub's 8-acre wooded garden. In front, facing Dunstan's only street, are several self-contained apartments (available for weekly lets) while to the rear the wing of ground-floor bedrooms faces a garden of pine and poplar, with dovecote and abundant wildlife. Fully equipped with baths and showers, all are kitted out with TVs, room phones and coffee-making equipment. In between are the clubby bar, games room and a wealth of memorabilia in the Harry Hotspur Room. Both children and wheelchair users are particularly well-catered for. Hearty breakfasts are served in the bright, flower-filled conservatory. *Open 11-3, 6-11 (Sun 12-3, 7-10.30). Free House.* **Beer** *Ruddles Best, Theakston Best. Garden. Family room.* **Accommodation** *10 rooms, all en suite, £57 (single £35). Children welcome overnight (under-2s stay free in parents' room, 3-12s £8.50), additional bed & cot available No dogs. MasterCard,* **VISA**

We endeavour to be as up-to-date as possible but inevitably some changes to
landlords, chefs and other key staff occur after the Guide
has gone to press.

DUNWICH   Ship Inn   FOOD

Tel 01728 648219   Fax 01728 648675   Map 10 D2   **B&B**
St James Street Dunwich Suffolk IP17 3DT

Well-loved old smugglers' inn overlooking the salt marshes and sea in a peaceful
coastal hamlet – 2½ miles off B1125 at Westleton – and popular with walkers and
birdwatchers from the nearby RSPB Minsmere reserve. The delightful unspoilt public
bar offers nautical bric-a-brac, a wood-burning stove in a huge brick fireplace, flagged
floors and simple wooden furnishings. There's also a plain carpeted dining-room and a
conservatory room for families. The welcoming and enthusiastic owners – Stephen
and Ann Marshlain – have been at the helm here for over 11 years now and offer
good, simple food; the restaurant menu applies throughout the pub in the evenings;
bar meals at lunchtime only. For lunch, choose home-made soup, leek and potato pie
or prawn ploughman's from the galley chilled servery and in the evenings maybe hot
garlicky prawns, the locally renowned Dunwich fish'n'chips (always available) or
lemon chicken from the printed menu. Finish off with home-made desserts such as
boozy bread-and-butter pudding, apple crumble and apple and cider flan. Beyond the
bars a fine Victorian staircase leads to three, simple cottagey bedrooms, (all now with
en suite shower), which are light and clean with pretty fabrics, period features and
splendid views from leaded pane windows. Summer imbibing on a sheltered paved
yard (resplendent in summer with hanging baskets and flowering tubs) and in the very
secure garden surrounded by a hedge. *Open 11-3 (Sat 11.30-3.30), 6-11 (Sun 12-
3.30, 7-10.30).* **Bar Meals** *12-2, 7.30-9.15 (till 9 Sun). Free House.* **Beer** *Adnams
Southwold & Broadside, Greene King Abbot Ale. Garden, outdoor eating. Family room.*
Accommodation *3 bedrooms, all en suite (shower), £55 (single £30). Children welcome
overnight (under-2s stay free in parents' room), additional bed (£12.50) & cot supplied.
Check-in during bar hours. Accommodation closed 24-26 Dec; pub closed 25 Dec eve.
MasterCard,* ***VISA***

DUXFORD   John Barleycorn   FOOD

Tel 01223 832699   Map 10 B3
Moorfield Road Duxford Cambridge CB2 4PP

Tucked at the far end of the village, a mile from the A1301, this well-kept, 17th-
century thatched pub is resplendent with hanging baskets, tubs and borders in high
summer. Delightful, single low-beamed and softly-lit bar with a rustic mix of country
furniture, large brick fireplace and neatly decorated with plates, horse harnesses and
tasteful prints. A comfortable, relaxing and uncluttered bar and an ideal venue in
which to enjoy a hearty home-cooked meal from a varied list of dishes. Good
favourites – ploughman's lunches, salads, chili and grills – plus substantial choices like
jugged hare, venison, mushroom and vegetable pie and honey roast chicken.
Interesting open sandwiches – smoked salmon and cream cheese with dill pickle.
Summer alfresco eating on the rear patio with additional seating in the converted
barn. No under-14s in the bar. *Open 12-2.30, 6.30-11 (Sun 12-2.30, 7-10.30).*
Bar Food *12.15-2, 6.45-10 (from 7 Sun).* **Beer** *Greene King. Garden, outdoor eating.
Closed all 25 Dec & 1 Jan. No credit cards.*

EASINGTON   Mole & Chicken   FOOD

Tel & Fax 01844 208387   Map 15a D2
Easington Aylesbury Buckinghamshire HP18 9EY

Between Junction 7 of the M40 and Aylesbury; take the B4011 from Thame past
Long Crendon (2 miles), following the Chilton road outside the village and turn left
at the top of Carters Lane (opposite the Chandos Arms), then straight on for half
a mile. This pretty pub boasts truly magnificent views of the Oxfordshire/Bucking-
hamshire countryside. Inside, the rag-washed walls are hung with hunting prints and
candle lighting; a low, beamed ceiling and hand-painted floor in the Tuscany style are
complemented by two roaring log fires. There's seating for 60 people at oak and pine
tables, and half a ton of French oak on bricks forms the attractive bar. Good, home-
cooked food such as chicken breast satay with garlic bread and spicy peanut dip, pasta
with pesto sauce, interesting warm salads (duck and bacon with plum and red wine

sauce), half shoulder of lamb with honey, garlic and rosemary glaze, chicken methi sahib, chargrilled pork steaks with Dijon and gruyère sauce, and good fresh fish specials (baby brill with garlic and herbs, seared salmon with lime and oatmeal crust, monkfish poached in white wine) – an eclectic selection if ever there was one. Hot and cold desserts are home-made. Extensive selection of wines by the glass. *Open 11-3, 6-12 (Sun 12-10.30). **Bar Food** 12-2, 7-10 (Sun 12-9.30). Free House. **Beer** Hook Norton Bitter, Morland Original & Old Speckled Hen. Garden, outdoor eating. Amex, MasterCard,* **VISA**

EAST CHALDON   Sailors Return   FOOD

Tel 01305 853847   Map 14 B4
East Chaldon Dorchester Dorset DT2 8DN

Well extended 18th-century cottage enjoying an isolated rural position overlooking the peaceful village and beyond to the Purbeck Hills. Charming and welcoming interior comprising a comfortable dining area, a larger bar area, complete with barn-type roof, old timbers, ropes, floats and lobster pots and, in the original cottage, two delightful low-ceilinged interconnecting rooms with old flagstones and scrubbed pine tables. Also sited here is the large blackboard menu listing the wide range of good-value bar food. Typical home-made dishes may include lamb and apricot casserole, shoulder of lamb with garlic, honey and rosemary sauce, pigeon bourguignon and several vegetarian options like vegetable and Stilton pie and cauliflower and broccoli bake. The daily fresh seafood selection often features whole grilled plaice, sardines in garlic butter, mussel stroganoff and seafood thermidor. Steaks ranging from 8oz to 24oz are very popular here. Alfresco diners are spoilt for choice with a front bench-filled terrace with uninterrupted views and a sheltered rear garden to choose from. *Open 11-2.30, 6.30-11 (from 6 Fri & Sat), Sun 12-3, 7-10.30. **Bar Food** 12-2 (till 2.30 Sun), 7-9 (till 9.30 Fri & Sat). Free House. **Beer** Wadworth 6X, Whitbread Strong Country Bitter, guest beer. Garden, terrace, outdoor eating. Family room. MasterCard,* **VISA**

EAST DEREHAM   Kings Head Hotel   B&B

Tel 01362 693842   Fax 01362 693776   Map 10 C1
Norwich Road East Dereham Norfolk NR19 1AD

Modest 17th-century coaching inn located near the town centre. A cosy red-carpeted bar, busy with locals, looks out past the patio to an attractive, lawned family garden set with tables and chairs. Bedrooms have tasteful, darkwood furniture and pretty fabrics, five of which are located in the light and airy converted stable block; the remainder are in the main building. All offer TV, clock-radio, direct-dial telephones and tea-making kits and fifteen have neat en suite facilities. Two large rooms are ideal for families. A grass tennis court is available for residents and locals (booking required). *Open 11-11 (Sun 12-10.30). Free House. **Beer** John Smith's, Woodfordes Wherry, Marston's Pedigree, Websters Yorkshire Bitter, guest beer. Garden. **Accommodation** 17 bedrooms, 15 en suite, £40-£50 (single £40). Children welcome overnight (under-3s stay free in parents' room, 3-16s half-price), additional bed & cot available. No dogs. Amex, Diners, MasterCard,* **VISA**

EAST GARSTON   Queens Arms Hotel   B&B

Tel 01488 648757   Fax 01488 648642   Map 14a B4
Newbury Road East Garston Newbury Berkshire RG16 7ET

Set in the heart of horse-country and frequented by an assortment of stable lads, well known jockeys and prominent trainers, this modernised and extended rural inn is a good base from which to explore the scenic Lambourn valley, or for those keen race goers attending the Newbury meeting. It is also a convenient stopover for M4 travellers, with J14 only 3½ miles distant. Bedrooms are clean and comfortable with simple limed fitted furniture, modern co-ordinating fabrics and an attractive pastel decor. Well-fitted, tiled bathrooms or compact shower rooms (one single room has a bathroom opposite). All boast TVs, telephones, trouser presses and tea-makers for added comfort. Relaxing, wood-panelled bar and adjoining restaurant. *Open 12-11 (Sun 12-10.30). No real ales. Garden, children's play area. **Accommodation** 13 bedrooms, all en suite (four with bath), £47.50 (single £35). Children welcome overnight (under-3s stay free in parents' room), additional bed available. No dogs. Amex, MasterCard,* **VISA**

EAST HADDON — Red Lion Hotel — FOOD

Tel 01604 770223   Fax 01604 770767   Map 15 D1   **B&B**
East Haddon Northamptonshire NN6 8BU

Thatch-roofed little hotel built of golden stone in a country location seven miles from
Junction 18 of the M1. Pleasant, relaxing lounge bar with a mix of furnishings, china
and pewter, smaller, plainer public bar. Recommended for its cottagey, well-kept
bedrooms (two twins, two doubles and a single; all en suite with shower plus two
bathrooms available to share); TVs, phones and beverage facilities are all provided.
Sunday lunch (£15.95) offers a good choice, as does the long, hand-written list of bar
food: mushroom and chicken terrine, Loch Fyne kippers with scrambled egg, cod,
haddock and broccoli pie, steak and kidney pie, grilled lamb cutlets, cheese and
mushroom roulade and freshly-cut sandwiches – "everything is home-made except
the mayonnaise". Leave plenty of room for homely puddings like Bakewell tart, apple
and raspberry crumble and lemon syllabub. No dogs in rooms, but kennels are
provided. *Open 11-2.30, 6-11 (Sun 12-2.30, 7-10.30).* **Bar Food** *12.15-2, 7-9.30 (no
bar food Sun eve).* **Beer** *Charles Wells Eagle & Bombardier, Marston's Pedigree, Adnams
Broadside, Morland Old Speckled Hen, guest beer. Garden.* **Accommodation** *5 bedrooms, all
en suite, £65 (single £55). Children welcome overnight (under-4s stay free in parent's room,
5-12s half-price), additional bed & cot available. Check-in by arrangement. No dogs. Amex,
Diners, MasterCard,* **VISA**

EAST ILSLEY — The Swan — B&B

Tel 01635 281238   Fax 01635 281791   Map 14a C3
East Ilsley Newbury Berkshire RG16 0LF

A well-run, friendly family pub at the heart of an attractive Berkshire village: turn
off the A34 just 3 miles north of the M4, Junction 13. The Swan is operated by
Morlands, the brewers from nearby West Ilsley, and by the bar is posted a record of
their landlords, unbroken since 1865. The pub, however, was a coaching inn in the
early 1700s and despite today's open-plan interior many original features remain
within its many rooms and alcoves, alongside collections of brewery artefacts,
cartoons, local photographs and miniature bottles which have been accumulated over
the years. Residents overnight enjoy the best of the old building's charm in carefully
modernised en suite bedrooms, all neatly equipped with beverage trays, colour TVs
and direct-dial phones – two are non-smoking. In summer, the trellised rear patio is a
picturesque spot where parents can sit while the children let off steam in the adjacent
garden. *Open 11-2.30, 6-11 (Sun 12-3, 7-10.30).* **Beer** *Morland, guest beer. Patio,
garden, children's play area. Family room.* **Accommodation** *10 rooms, all en suite (three with
bath), £47 (family room £60, single £34). Children welcome overnight. Check-in by
arrangement. Amex, MasterCard,* **VISA**

EAST MEON — Ye Olde George Inn — FOOD

Tel 01730 823481   Fax 01730 823759   Map 15 D3   **B&B**
East Meon Hampshire GU32 1NH

Nestling beside the River Meon in the centre of this picturesque village is the 15th-
century Olde George Inn which has been welcoming customers for over 300 years.
Originally two cottages it boasts four inglenooks, a wealth of heavy beams, bare brick
walls and an assortment of sturdy scrubbed tables in its rambling bar and attractive
adjacent restaurant. The unusual horseshoe-shaped bar dispenses well-conditioned ales
and a selection of country wines, while the kitchen produces an interesting range of
home-cooked bar food. A reliable selection of bar meals are listed on an extensive
menu board in the bar and choices range from hearty home-made soups (carrot and
coriander), filled baguettes and jacket potatoes (Brie and cranberries) to ham, egg and
chips and chicken, bacon and tarragon pie with fresh vegetables. The printed à la carte
restaurant menu (also served in the bar) offers crabcakes with tomato and basil coulis,
lamb steak with rosemary and redcurrant sauce and fillet steak. Finish off with home-
made rhubarb fool or blackberry and almond tart. Cream teas are served all week in

summer and at weekends in winter. Upstairs, six simply-furnished, good-sized rooms are clean, light and airy with the usual comforts of TV, tea-making kits and standard en suite facilities. Children welcome. New chef and menus were being introduced, and bedroom upgrading was underway, as we went to press. *Open 11-11 (Sun 12-3, 7-10.30). Bar Food 12-2.30, 7-10. Free House. Beer Greene King IPA & Abbot Ale, Bass, Fuller's London Pride, Worldham Old Dray, guest beer. Patio, outdoor eating. Accommodation 6 bedrooms, all en suite, £50-£60, (single from £25). Children welcome overnight (under-5s free in parents' room, 5-12s half-price), additional bed available. No dogs. Amex, MasterCard, VISA*

EAST WITTON	Blue Lion	FOOD

Tel 01969 624273   Fax 01969 624189   Map 5 D4   **B&B**
East Witton Leyburn North Yorkshire DL8 4SN

 ☕ ⚑ Zzz...

At the gateway to Coverdale and Wensleydale, East Witton stands on the A6108 just a mile from the Cover Bridge. The rather stern-looking, stone-built Blue Lion, originally a coaching inn in the 19th century, has been sympathetically restored to former glories, yet retaining its truly evocative mood. The single bar faces a huge stone fireplace where a log fire burns year-round. Here the blackboards offer freshly prepared dishes using quality local produce such as Mediterranean tart with smoked chicken topped with a parmesan tapénade crust and sliced smoked haunch and rilettes of wild boar with toasted brioche and tomato chutney, following with main-course dishes like smoked haddock, mackerel and mussel fishcake, jugged hare with parsnip mash, braised lamb shank with root vegetables and horseradish dumplings, and cassoulet of chicken with tomato, ham and haricot beans topped with pesto. Tarte tatin and bread-and-butter pudding may appear on the pudding list. Sandwiches and ploughman's platters may be available at lunchtime, but, in general, this is serious, upmarket pub dining. For residents, the dining-room at night is candle-lit and intimate. Bedrooms (including three newly-created rooms) are all individually furnished, with a mixture of period furniture and state-of-the-art additions such as remote-control TVs. En suite bathrooms are more than adequate, while comfort and commensurate privacy are ensured by the lack of any telephones. *Open 11-11 (Sun 12-10.30). Bar Food 12-2.15 (till 2 Sun), 7-9.30. Free House. Beer Theakston Best & Black Bull, Black Sheep Bitter & Riggwelter. Garden, outdoor eating. Accommodation 12 bedrooms, all en suite, £70 (family room sleeping three £80, single £39.50). Children welcome overnight (under-5s free), additional bed (£5) & cot available. MasterCard, VISA*

EAST WOODLANDS	Horse & Groom	FOOD

Tel 01373 462802   Map 14 B3
East Woodlands Frome Somerset BA11 5LY

Peacefully positioned beside a narrow rural lane on the edge of the Longleat Estate, this attractive, white-painted 17th-century pub remains delightfully rustic, comprising two simple bars, notably the unspoilt slate-floored public bar with its huge inglenook, log fire and collection of stripped-pine tables, chairs and old pews. The attraction here, apart from the atmosphere and three excellent ales drawn straight from the cask, is the range of interesting bar food on offer, the popularity of which has led to the addition of a side conservatory dining-room to cater for the increased trade. A daily-changing blackboard lists the varied and value-for-money choice of bar meals, from generously-filled baguettes, hearty ploughman's and home-made game soup to Sri Lankan-style prawns, liver and bacon, pigeon breast with bacon and game sauce, stir-fried chicken and mixed vegetables with black bean sauce and cod and crab gratinée. Vegetarian bakes (ratatouille and hazelnut) and pasta dishes (asparagus and pesto) are served in large or small sizes and good fresh vegetables accompany main meals. Evening fare steps up a gear with the likes of medallions of venison with blueberry and cassis sauce or fresh cod wrapped in salmon with a coriander and cream sauce. Neat front garden with pollarded lime trees and pleasing rural views. Well worth tracking down after a tiring day out exploring Longleat House and Estate. Children welcome in the small lounge bar. *Open 11.30-2.30 (from 12 Mon, till 3 Sat), 6.30-11 (Sun 12-3, 7-10.30). Closed 2 weeks Sep. Bar Food 12-2, 6.30-9 (till 9.30 Fri & Sat). No food Sun eve & all Mon. Free House. Beer Butcombe Bitter, Wadworth 6X, Batemans XB, guest beer. Garden, outdoor eating. MasterCard, VISA*

EASTGATE   Ratcatchers Inn   FOOD

Tel 01603 871430   Map 10 C1
Eastgate Cawston Norfolk NR10 4HA

A pleasantly old-fashioned free house, dating from 1861, standing in a rural spot just off the B1149 one mile south of Cawston. A warm and friendly atmosphere pervades the neatly furnished bar and restaurant areas which are both laid up for diners, for food is very much the thing here. The appeal is the extensive range of home-cooked meals listed in a veritable tome of a menu, a 14-page epic of jokily-named dishes. Nevertheless, additional imaginative daily specials and a packed pub – it is advisable to book – instills confidence in the enthusiastic kitchen. Use of fresh local produce is clearly evident – fish from Lowestoft, shellfish direct from the North Norfolk coast, produce from local smokehouses and naturally-aged cuts of meat from a nearby butcher. The 'home-made' policy extends to freshly-baked bread, herb oils, chutneys, stocks and pickled samphire plus the use of fresh herbs from the garden. Fish comes in a variety of forms (duo of salmon and cod wrapped in bacon on baby spinach, brill with sun-dried tomato and saffron sauce, tempura of scallops with a beurre blanc sauce) and dipping into the menu might reveal fowl and funghi pie served with either a short-crust or puff-pastry top, Jaffri's madras curry, Shylock's tagliatelle carbonara, salads, doorstep sandwiches, at least 15 vegetarian, vegan or diabetic options, plus grills named after film stars. Having digested the main menu selection, look to the specials board for even more tantalising dishes such as fresh oysters, melon and squid cocktail and venison with a wild mushroom and port wine sauce. Home-made puddings have Dickensian titles like Mr Micawber's cake (Belgian chocolate cheesecake). Separate cheese menu listing twelve varieties, six of them British. An interesting list of wines has at least a dozen available by the glass. Plans are to build some bedrooms. East of England Regional Winner of our 1997 Seafood Pub of the Year award. *Open 11.45-2.30, 5.45-11 (Sun 12-3, 7-10.30).* **Bar Food** *11.45-2, 6-10 (Sun 12-2, 7-10). Free House.* **Beer** *Hancock's Best Bitter, Bass, Adnams Extra. Garden, outdoor eating. Closed all 26 Dec. No credit cards.*

EASTLING   Carpenter's Arms   FOOD   B&B

Tel 01795 890234   Fax 01795 890654   Map 11 C5
The Street Eastling Faversham Kent ME13 0AZ

Character redbrick 14th-century pub tucked away in a North Downs village with a charming interior. Two inglenook fireplaces – one in the bar and another in the cosy, brick-floored restaurant – warm the homely interior, while the short and simple bar menu highlights a hearty home-made soup (broccoli and Stilton), chicken and mushroom pie with vegetables, and a few standard snacks such as burgers and countryman's lunch (ploughman's with ½lb spicy Kent sausage). Popular for fish'n'chips on Fridays. Next door in a typically Kentish white clapperboard house, reached via its own old brick path, are three peaceful bedrooms, two of them rather on the small side with shower cabinets and toilets en suite. The best room is much more spacious with a full en suite bathroom. All have TVs and radio alarms. Children over 7 are welcome in the restaurant only – no under-14s in the bar. *Open 11-4, 6-11 (Sun 12-4, 7-10.30), all day in summer.* **Bar Food** *12-2.30 (till 1.30 Sun), 6.30-10 (no food Sun eve).* **Beer** *Shepherd Neame. Garden, outdoor eating area, summer barbecue.* **Accommodation** *3 bedrooms, all en suite, £45 (single £35). Children over 10 welcome overnight (no extra bed supplied). No dogs. Amex, MasterCard, VISA*

EBBESBOURNE WAKE   Horseshoes Inn   FOOD   B&B

Tel 01722 780474   Map 14 B3
Ebbesbourne Wake Salisbury Wiltshire SP5 5JF

The Ebble valley and more especially the village of Ebbesbourne Wake seem to have escaped the hustle and bustle of modern day life, as it nestles among the folds in the Downs, close to the infant River Ebble. This peaceful unspoilt rural charm is reflected in the village inn that has been run "as a proper country pub" by the Bath family for over 20 years. Its 17th-century brick facade is adorned with climbing roses and honeysuckle, while inside the traditional layout of two bars around a central servery still survives. The main bar is festooned with an array of old farming implements and country bygones and a mix of simple furniture fronts the open log fire. Well-kept real ales are served straight from the cask and both local farm cider and free-range eggs are also sold across the bar. Bar food is good value and homely, the best choice being the freshly-prepared dishes that are chalked up on the blackboard menu, featuring liver and bacon casserole, beef in ale, duck with gooseberry sauce, and home-made game pie. Fresh fish to order. The standard printed menu highlights the range of sandwiches, ploughman's lunches and other hot dishes. The set 3-course Sunday lunch at £9.25 is superb value for money, extremely popular and served throughout (booking necessary). The flower- and shrub-filled garden is perfect for summer alfresco eating and safe for children, who also have access to view the four goats in the pets area. Those wanting to explore this tranquil area further can stay overnight in one of the two modest bedrooms at either end of the inn; both are decorated in a cottagey style with pretty fabrics and wallpaper and have TVs, tea-making kits and their own private facilities. A peaceful night's sleep is guaranteed. *Open 12-3, 6.30-11, (Sun 12-3, 7-10.30).* *Bar Food 12-2, 7-9 (till 9.30 Sat). No food Sun & Mon eve. Free House.* *Beer Adnams Broadside, Wadworth 6X, Ringwood Best, guest beer. Garden, outdoor eating, pet area.* *Accommodation 2 bedrooms, both en suite (one with bath), £40 (single £25). Children welcome overnight, (under-2s stay free in parents' room, 3-12s by arrangement), additional bed & cot available. No credit cards.*

ECCLESHALL   St George Hotel   B&B

Tel 01785 850300   Fax 01785 861452   Map 6 B3
Castle Street Eccleshall Staffordshire ST21 6DF

A carefully restored 250-year-old coaching inn which enjoys a central crossroad position in Eccleshall. The oak-beamed bar, which is open all day, has an opaque glass 'smoke room' panel and red brick inglenook, and there is also a relaxing little lounge. Cottage-style bedrooms, many with open fires, exposed beams with vaulted ceilings and canopied or four-poster beds, are thoughtfully equipped and all have private facilities. A recently-opened micro brewery provides the hotel with their own Slater's Ales: bitter (3.6%), original (4%), Hi-duck (4.1%) and premium (4.4%). *Open 11-11 (Sun 12-10.30). Free House.* *Beer Slater's Ales, two guest beers.* *Accommodation 10 bedrooms, all en suite, £70, (single £49), weekend reductions (£25 per person Fri-Sun). Children welcome overnight (under-8s stay free in parents' room), additional bed & cot available. Amex, Diners, MasterCard, VISA*

EDBURTON   Tottington Manor   FOOD

Tel 01903 815757   Fax 01903 879331   Map 11 B6   **B&B**
Edburton Henfield West Sussex BN5 9JL

🛏️ Zzz...

Positioned at the base of the South Downs and enjoying delightful views from its splendid summer garden, restaurant and bedrooms, this 17th-century Grade II listed inn-cum-hotel is an attractive destination for those seeking peace and quiet and some good food. Light meals/snacks (sandwiches, ploughman's lunches, pasta dishes) are only available at lunchtime in the simple pubby bar, the emphasis here being on the more elaborate fare served in the dining-room at both lunchtime and evenings. Choices range from warm salmon and crab sausages, home-made pie (steak and Guinness) and cider baked ham to lamb steak with port wine, rosemary and redcurrants, and good fish specials like pan-fried sea bass, Dover sole or oven-roasted halibut with shallots and garlic. Residents can take advantage of the 3-course table d'hote menu that includes a half bottle of wine. Traditional Sunday roast is served in the Downs Room. Bedrooms are pretty, with soothing colours and good sturdy furniture. All are neat and tidy with added touches like magazines, biscuits, mineral water and a box of tissues in each room. No children under 5 allowed in the bar or restaurant. Conference room. *Open 11-3, 6-11 (Sun 12-3 only). Closed Sun eves.* *Bar Food 12-2.15, 7-9 (no snacks eves). Free House.* *Beer Fuller's London Pride, guest beer. Garden, outdoor eating. Family room.* *Accommodation 6 bedrooms, all en suite (three with baths), £62.50-£70 (single £45). Children welcome overnight (under-3s stay free in parents' room, 4-12s £10), additional bed & cot available. Closed all 26-28 Dec. Amex, Diners, MasterCard, VISA*

EGLOSHAYLE   Earl of St Vincent   A

Tel 01208 814807   Map 12 B3
Egloshayle Wadebridge Cornwall PL27 6HT

Originally built as a boarding house for the masons who constructed the church and named after one of Nelson's admirals, the Earl is a most extraordinary pub hidden away in the old part of a rambling village. Lovingly rescued from being a run-down local, it is now a splendid, welcoming hostelry filled to the brim with Edward Connolly's personal antique collection. The relaxing atmospheric bar has heavy beams, some wood panelling, an open fire fronted by two comfortable armchairs, various sturdy tables and chairs, old paintings and prints and, most noticeable of all, an amazing collection of antique clocks – from grandfather clocks to unusual ball-bearing clocks – that fill every available surface. Unbelievably, all are in perfect working order and 'time' is called by a cacophony of chimes, bongs and cuckoos. A tiny intimate snug bar resounds with ticking clocks. Those with time on their hands can while away an hour or two in the award-winning garden, ablaze with flowers in summer. *Open 11-3, 6.30-11 (Sun 12-3, 7-10.30).* **Beer** *St Austell. Garden. MasterCard,* **VISA**

ELKESLEY   Robin Hood Inn   FOOD

Tel 01777 838259   Map 7 D2
High Street Elkesley Nottinghamshire DN22 8AJ

 ☺

Modest Whitbread pub run by Alan Draper, an enthusiastic landlord/chef who prepares a interesting selection of bar meals which are served in the comfortable lounge and tiny dining-room. One menu is offered throughout and this might offer salad niçoise, mussels baked with tomato, garlic, basil and cheese, and home-made soup to start, following with baked sea bream Portuguese style, monkfish wrapped in bacon, smoked haddock chowder, cassoulet of duck and sausage, as well as regular favourites like steaks, curries and grilled gammon steak. Baguette sandwiches and ploughman's platters are served at both lunch and dinner. Finish off with baked bananas with caramel sauce or chocolate truffle cake. Note: only light snacks are served on Monday evenings. *Open 12-3, 7-11 (Sat 12-11), Sun 12-3, 7-10.30.* **Bar Food** *12-2, 7-9.30 (till 10 Sat, till 9 Sun).* **Beer** *Whitbread Castle Eden Ale, Boddingtons, guest beer. Garden, outdoor eating, children's play area. MasterCard,* **VISA**

ELLERBY   Ellerby Hotel   FOOD

Tel 01947 840342   Fax 01947 841221   Map 5 E3   **B&B**
Ellerby nr Saltburn-by-Sea Redcar & Cleveland TS13 5LP

Zzz... ☺

David & Janet Alderson have transformed a run-down village pub into a country inn. The much-extended main bar and attendant dining-room provide plenty of space in which to enjoy a wide range of substantial fare, of which a large proportion is changed daily and posted on prominent blackboards. From starters encompassing home-made soup and lamb samosa with curry dip, progress to steak pie, chargrills and interesting specials like medallions of beef, fillet of pork wrapped in smoked gammon with a sweet pepper sauce, and rabbit, hare and grouse pie. Freshly-cut sandwiches and ploughman's lunches are also available. Monthly Chinese banquets have proved highly popular. Nine bedrooms are furnished to a commendably high standard with varnished pine furniture and bright floral drapes; all have TVs, dial-out phones, trouser presses and hairdryers. Bathrooms are fully tiled and carpeted, with large baths and separate shower stalls (two have shower only). Refurbishment to all bedrooms was underway as we went to press. *Open 12-3, 6.30-11 (till 10.30 Sun).* **Bar Food** *12-2, 6.30-10 (till 9.30 Sun). Free House.* **Beer** *John Smith's Bitter & Magnet, Courage Directors. Garden, outdoor eating.* **Accommodation** *9 bedrooms, all en suite, £54 (single £32). Children welcome overnight (under-5s stay free in parent's room, 6-13s £11, over-14s £16), additional bed & cot available. Accommodation and pub closed all 25 Dec. MasterCard,* **VISA**

ELLISFIELD   The Fox   A

Tel 01256 381210   Map 14a C4
Green Lane Ellisfield Basingstoke Hampshire RG25 2QW

Four miles from the M3, Junction 6, tucked down a leafy lane in unspoilt countryside,
this homely village pub is a popular lunchtime venue for business people from
Basingstoke. Its appeal (apart from its location) is the excellent selection of up to
seven well-kept real ales, which are dispensed by handpump in two comfortable bars
featuring exposed brick walls, light-oak wood panelling, open log fires and a convivial
atmosphere. Delightful flower-filled summer garden. New landlords intend
introducing more home-cooked specials and generally improving standards.
*Open 11.30-2.30 (till 3 Sat), 6.30-11 (Sun 12-3, 7-10.30). Free House. **Beer** Gales
HSB, Marston's Pedigree, Wadworth 6X, Hall & Woodhouse Tanglefoot, Theakston Old
Peculier, Hampshire Brewery King Alfred's Bitter. Garden. MasterCard,* **VISA**

ELSENHAM   The Crown   FOOD

Tel 01279 812827   Map 10 B3
High Street Elsenham Bishop's Stortford Hertfordshire CM22 6DG

Once a row of three 300-year-old character cottages, this attractive, flower-decked
and well-cared-for village inn has a traditional carpeted and low-ceilinged interior
complete with brasses, beams, open fires and a relaxing atmosphere. Separate lively
public bar offering a variety of games. Bar food relies primarily on an extensive and
varied printed menu featuring good pub favourites – lasagne, stuffed pancakes and
fisherman's pie – as well as interesting home-cooked dishes like hot smoked haddock
pots, turkey and mushroom pie, chicken in red wine and mushroom sauce, pork fillet
with apples and calvados, and fresh fish dishes like monkfish with watercress and
cream, and seafood mixed grill. To accompany them, there are well-cooked vegetables
or choose a selection of fresh salads from the self-service salad bar. Large granary baps,
freshly-made Crownburgers served with home-made whisky relish, and ploughman's
platters are served at lunchtime only. Home-made puddings include the tireless
landlady Barbara Good's unusual ice creams such as stem ginger, marmalade and gin
and toffee fudge – up to 14 at any one time; rhubarb crumble with proper custard,
summer pudding, fresh fruit trifle. Barbara also hand-makes the pub's chips and crisps
every day! South-facing front patio with benches and a beer garden to the rear (with
children's play area). Children welcome in the pub to eat. *Open 11-2.30, 6-11,
(Sun 12-2.30, 7-10.30). **Bar Food** 12-2, 7.30-9.30 (no food Sun). **Beer** Crouch Vale
Bitter, Marston's Pedigree, Benskins Bitter, Nethergate Bitter, guest beer. Garden, children's
play area. Amex, Diners, MasterCard,* **VISA**

ELSLACK   Tempest Arms   B&B

Tel 01282 842450 Fax 01282 843331   Map 6 B1
Elslack Skipton North Yorkshire BD23 3AY

Zzz... ☺

Just off the A56 near its junction with the A59 and only three miles from Skipton, the
pub nestles in a verdant hollow with its own stream winding picturesquely round the
garden. To the rear of the pub proper, and with its own secure entrance, a purpose-
built block houses well-appointed bedrooms that are fully equipped for the '90s with
TVs, telephones and plenty of well-lit workspace for the business guest. En suite
bathrooms are a little small, but being fully tiled with strong over-bath showers they
are more than adequate. Two rooms have three beds. Double-glazed and well back
from the road, accommodation here promises less Tempest than Midsummer Night's
Dream. *Open 11-11 (Sun 12-10.30). **Beer** Jennings Bitter, Cumberland Ale, Mild &
Cocker Hoop, two guest beers. Garden. **Accommodation** 10 bedrooms, all en suite, £54
(family room sleeping three/four £66, single £47). Children welcome overnight (under-5s
stay free in parents' room), additional bed (£12) & cot available. No dogs. Amex, Diners,
MasterCard,* **VISA**

ELSTEAD   Woolpack   FOOD

Tel 01252 703106   Map 15a E4
The Green Elstead Surrey GU8 6HD

Originally built as a wool-bale store in the 18th century, the attractive tile-hung Woolpack is now comfortably countrified and adorned with various artefacts relating to its previous use: bobbins and spindles of yarn, a lamb's fleece and a partly woven rug. Today folk flock here to enjoy the famously-generous portions of home-cooked dishes chosen from a long blackboard menu which might encompass duck casseroled in sherry, gammon with honey, mustard and caper cream sauce, pork steak with apples and cider, and good fresh seafood like dressed crab salad, mussels, and swordfish in apricot wine and mint sauce. No sandwiches, but ploughman's platters are popular. Genuinely home-made puddings might include fruit pavlovas, raspberry and hazelnut roulade and crème brulée. Arrive early on Sundays, especially if intending to tuck into a decent roast, as it gets very busy. Children can have smaller portions at smaller prices, or opt for baked beans and tinned spaghetti on toast. A family room has nursery rhyme murals and bunches of flowers hung up to dry from the ceiling; there's also a slide, swing and climbing frame in the pretty garden. *Open 11-2.30, 6-11 (Sun 12-3, 7-10.30).* **Bar Food** *12-2, 7-9.45 (Sun 7.30-9).* **Beer** *Green King IPA, Young's Bitter, Ansells Bitter, guest beers. Garden, outdoor eating, children's play area. Family room. Diners, MasterCard, VISA*

ELSTED   Three Horseshoes   A

Tel 01730 825746   Map 15 D3
Elsted Midhurst West Sussex GU29 0JX

Bowed walls, terracotta-tiled floors, gnarled beams, mellow stained plasterwork and a good open fire in the vast inglenook all create an atmosphere of genuinely unspoilt charm in this popular 16th-century inn, originally built as a drovers ale house. Evening candlelight enhances the romantic old-world atmosphere. Enjoy some excellent real ales, dispensed straight from the cask, in the well-tended garden, complete with rustic tables and benches and lovely views over the South Downs – a splendid spot to unwind on lazy summers days. *Open 11-2.30, 6-11 (Sun 12-3, 7-10.30). Closed Sun eve Oct-Easter. Free House.* **Beer** *Ballard's Best Bitter, Cheriton Brewhouse Pots Ale, Ringwood Best & Fortyniner, guest beers. Garden. MasterCard, VISA*

ELSTED MARSH   Elsted Inn   FOOD

Tel 01730 813662   Map 15 D3
Elsted Marsh Midhurst West Sussex GU29 0JT

Unprepossessing Victorian roadside pub built to serve the railway in the steam age (when there was a station here), but later left stranded by Dr Beeching's 'axe' in the 1960s. This explains the old railway photographs that adorn the thankfully unmodernised and unpretentious bars, in what is very much a local community pub, free of background music and electronic games but with plenty of traditional pub pastimes like shove ha'penny, darts, cards, dominoes and even conversation. There are two small bars with lots of original wood in evidence, original shutters and open fires. A small dining-room, candle-lit in the evening, boasts an old pine dresser and colourful cloths on a few dining tables surrounded by a motley collection of old chairs. Tweazle Jones and her partner Barry Horton produce varied menus with dishes that are always home-made and based on good local produce – hand-made bread from the National Trust bakery at Slindon and free-range eggs, ducks and chicken from a nearby farm, to name but a few suppliers. Local specialities listed on the daily-changing blackboards may include Ron Puttock's hand-made sausages, Sussex bacon pudding, downland rabbit in mustard, Sussex cassoulet, and boiled mutton in caper sauce. Choices extend to home-made soups (creamy onion), mussels baked with garlic and cheese, salmon fishcakes, and vegetarian bean korma, alongside good snacks like hand-cut sandwiches, ploughman's lunches and filled baked potatoes. The sweet-toothed can indulge in a gooey treacle tart, dark chocolate mousse or home-made banana and chocolate ice cream. Winter Wednesday nights are popular curry nights. Booking essential at weekends. Children can have half portions at half price, and there's a wooden playhouse in the shady garden to keep them amused, plus pétanque for the adults. The rear coach house is due to be converted into four en suite letting rooms. *Open 11-3, 5.30-11(from 6 Sat), Sun 12-3, 6-10.30. Bar Food 12-2.30, 7-9.30 (till 10 Fri & Sat, till 9 Sun). Free House. Beer Ballard's Best, Trotton, Nyewood, Gold & Wassail, Fuller's London Pride, guest beers. Garden, outdoor eating, boules. Family room. MasterCard, VISA*

ELTERWATER   Britannia Inn   B&B

Tel 01539 437210   Fax 01539 437311   Map 4 C3
Elterwater Ambleside Cumbria LA22 9HP

 Zzz...

Next to the tiny village green dominated by a magnificent maple tree, fronted by its own colourful window boxes, the black-and-white-painted Britannia is a summer picture. Ever-popular with the walkers who throng to the Langdale valley are the garden chairs and slate-topped tables on the pub's front terrace, as both front and rear bars are tiny. Residents have their own chintzy lounge with oak beams, antiques and an open log fire. Within the pub, six of the bedrooms have entirely adequate en suite facilities while a seventh has its own private bathroom across the corridor. All have individually controlled central heating, colour TVs, telephones, hairdryers and beverage-making facilities. Alternative accommodation across the green at Maple Tree Corner is especially handy for family use and generously priced at a lower rate, which nevertheless includes a hearty Lakeland breakfast served back at the inn. *Open 11-11 (Sun 12-10.30). Free House. Beer Jennings Bitter & Cumberland Ale, Boddingtons, two guest beers. Terrace. Family room. Accommodation 13 bedrooms, 7 en suite (showers), £60 (single £23-£48). Children welcome overnight (under-3s £4, 3-6s 50%, 7-12s 66% adult tariff), additional bed & cot available. Accommodation closed 24-26 Dec, pub closed all 25 Dec. Amex, Diners, MasterCard, VISA*

EMERY DOWN   New Forest Inn   FOOD B&B

Tel & Fax 01703 282329   Map 14 C4
Emery Down Lyndhurst Hampshire SO43 7DY

Prettily set in woodland, the building of the inn was the result of the first successful establishment of squatters' rights on Crown land in the early 18th-century. The original caravan that used to sell ale forms part of the front lounge porchway. Much extended since, it has a big, modern open-plan bar with effective country touches and real fires. The reliable bar food available here aims to please all tastes, and the regular printed menu features old favourites and chips, as well as some interesting home-cooked dishes. A daily-changing specials board enhances the choice further with possibly rabbit in peaches and cream, rack of lamb with Cumberland sauce and sautéed pork in green peppercorn and cream sauce. Home-made puddings like sticky toffee pudding and cheesecake round off the meal. Recently redecorated bedrooms are clean, comfortable and homely, three having en suite facilities (two with bath), the fourth having its own private, but not en suite, bathroom. The three-level rear garden is a super summer spot for alfresco imbibing. Whitbread Wayside Inn. *Open 11-11 (Sun 12-10.30). Bar Food 12-9.30 (till 9 Sun). Beer Flowers Original, Strong Country Bitter, Greene King Abbot Ale, Boddingtons, Garden, outdoor eating, summer barbecue. Accommodation 4 bedrooms, 3 en suite, £50 (single £25). Children welcome overnight (under-5s stay free in parents' room), additional bed (£10) available. MasterCard, VISA*

> We endeavour to be as up-to-date as possible but inevitably some changes to landlords, chefs and other key staff occur after the Guide has gone to press.

EMPINGHAM   White Horse   FOOD

Tel 01780 460221   Fax 01780 460521   Map 7 E3   **B&B**
2 Main Street Empingham Oakham Leicestershire LE15 8PR

Zzz... ☺

A stone's throw from serene Rutland Water, Roger Bourne's civilised pub (including a newly-refurbished bar area) is the centre of village life, a meeting-place for walkers and birdwatchers and convenient for access from the A1 at Stamford and the market town of Oakham. In attempting to be all things to most callers its day stretches from morning coffee and croissants through lunches and cream teas to late evening suppers. Central to the three eating areas, which include a family room, is the food counter displaying cold meats and home-made sweets backed by a blackboard of daily dishes offering the likes of beef chasseur, Rutland chicken, sweet and sour prawns, and cod mornay, plus baked ham, self-served salads, junior pizzas and filled baguettes (lunch only). The best bedrooms are in the stables, kitted out in varnished pine and each with its own well-appointed bathroom. In the main building, rooms are bright and neat though more modest, with shared bathing facilities. One room has a four-poster. *Open 11-11 (till 10.30 Sun). **Bar Food** 12-2.15, 6.30-9.45 (till 10 Sat, till 9.30 Sun). **Beer** John Smith's, Courage Directors, Ruddles Best, guest beer. Garden, outdoor eating. Family room. **Accommodation** 14 rooms, 9 en suite, £55 (four-poster £60, family room sleeping three £55-£65, single £32). Children welcome overnight (under-2s stay free in parents' room), extra bed & cot available. Disabled WC. Amex, Diners, MasterCard, **VISA***

ESKDALE GREEN   Bower House Inn   FOOD

Tel 01946 723244   Fax 01946 723308   Map 4 C3   **B&B**
Eskdale Green Holmbrook Cumbria CA19 1TD

Zzz... ☺

The Connors' informal, friendly inn is a delightful place to stay for peace and quiet in the beautiful Eskdale valley, as the growing numbers of returning guests will vouch for. Comfortable bedrooms are divided between the main house, where they are abundant in character, the converted stables and garden cottages, subtly extended and thoughtfully equipped to meet modern-day demands. In the clubby bar, incidently the Headquarters of the Eskdale cricket team who play in the adjacent field, there is a warming winter fire and country furnishings, and opens on to an enchanting, enclosed garden of pine and shrub, with a tiny wooden bridge traversing the village stream. For the best choice of home-cooked food look to the specials board for such dishes as wild boar cooked in cider, guinea fowl with cranberry sauce, nut roast with tomato sauce and puddings like lemon mousse and sticky toffee pudding. A fixed-price dinner menu is the preferred choice of residents. A warm welcome extends to families; there are three large rooms suitable for family occupation and children can play safely in the garden. After a restful night, it's traditional to tuck into a hearty Lakeland breakfast. *Open 11-11 (Sun 12-3, 6.30-10.30). **Bar Food** 12-2, 6.30-9.30. Free House. **Beer** Theakston Best, Hartleys XB, Courage Directors, Younger Scotch Bitter, guest beer. Riverside garden, outdoor eating, children's play area. **Accommodation** 24 rooms, all en suite, £60 (family room £72, single £47). Children welcome overnight (under-5s £6, 5-12s £10 in parents' room), additional bed & cot available. No dogs. Amex, MasterCard, **VISA***

ETTINGTON   Houndshill   B&B

Tel 01789 740267   Map 14 C1
Banbury Road Ettington Stratford-on-Avon Warwickshire CV37 7NS

A friendly, family-operated roadhouse which includes children's play areas and a licensed campsite in its extensive grounds. The clean, tidy decor of the lounge bar and adjoining dining-room is repeated in the pine-clad bedrooms and compact bathrooms with over-bath showers. Up-to-date direct-dial phones and remote-control TVs ensure a degree of comfort commensurate with the price range. Very useful to know, as it's beside the A422 Banbury road, four miles south of Stratford. *Open 12-3, 6-11 (from 7 Sat), Sun 12-3, 7-10.30. Free House. **Beer** Theakston Best, & XB. Garden, children's play area. Family room. **Accommodation** 8 bedrooms, all en suite, £45 (family rooms sleeping up to four £60, single £28). Children welcome overnight, additional bed (from £10) & cot (£5) available. Pub and accommodation closed all 25 & 26 Dec. MasterCard, **VISA***

EWEN | Wild Duck Inn | B&B

Tel & Fax 01285 770310   Map 14 C2
Drakes Island Ewen Cirencester Gloucestershire GL7 6BY

❦ Zzz...

Convenient for the Cotswolds and the nearby Water Park, Tina and Brian Mussell's tumbledown country seat has a long tradition of hospitality at its informal best. An interior of coral-coloured walls hung with ubiquitous portraits, hop-laden oak beams and candlelit pine tables in front of blazing log fires in winter sets a much-copied scenario at which the Wild Duck excels, while in summer the enclosed courtyard garden adds a further hidden delight. In the oldest part of the building the two four-poster bedrooms are much the most appealing: by contrast those in the garden wing are surprisingly modern with thoroughly up-to-date accessories such as direct-dial phones, radios, TVs, trouser presses and hair-dryers. *Open 11-11 (Sun 12-10.30). Free House. Beer Younger's Duck Pond, Theakston Best & Old Peculier, Wadworth 6X, guest beers. Garden. Accommodation 10 bedrooms, all en suite, £79.50 (four-poster £80/£90, single £49.50). Children welcome overnight, additional bed (£10) available. Amex, MasterCard, VISA*

EWHURST GREEN | White Dog Inn | B&B

Tel & Fax 01580 830264   Map 11 C6
Ewhurst Green Bodiam East Sussex TN32 5TD

Enjoying a lovely village setting near the parish church, with fine views over the Rother Valley to Bodiam Castle, this much-extended tile-hung pub dates back to the 15th century. Original features remain in the attractive beamed bar, which boasts a huge inglenook fireplace and a polished brick floor. Upstairs, three functional and good-sized bedrooms make the most of the pretty country views. All are individually decorated in a neat and simple style and feature TVs, tea-making equipment and clean en suite facilities. Residents have use of the heated swimming pool in the pleasant rear garden. *Open 12-3 (till 3.30 Sat) 6.30-11 (Sun 12-3.30, 7-10.30). Closed Mon lunch. Free House. Beer Harveys Best, Fuller's London Pride, guest beer. Garden, patio. Accommodation 3 bedrooms, all en suite, £40 (single £30). No children under 12 overnight. Check-in by arrangement. Dogs by arrangement. MasterCard, VISA*

EXFORD | Crown Hotel | FOOD

Tel 01643 831554   Fax 01643 831665   Map 13 D1   **B&B**
Exford Somerset TA24 7PP

🍴 Zzz...

Long a favourite among the huntin', shootin' and fishin' set, the 17th-century Crown stands by the green in a lovely village and offers country pursuit followers a touch of luxury in the heart of Exmoor. Seventeen, very comfortable en suite bedrooms have been tastefully furnished with quality pieces and equipped with TVs, telephones and hairdryers; room service is provided for refreshments. Lots of traditional charm in the lounge and rustic pubby bar, in which some above-average bar food, prepared by a talented new chef, can be enjoyed. Good snacks include filled rolls and sandwiches, ploughman's lunches and salads. The daily blackboard selection might include courgette and potato soup, rabbit sausage and salmon fishcakes with soy sauce dressing, with main-course options including fresh fish and shellfish from Brixham (fillet of cod deep-fried with a herb crust with tomato and basil sauce, fresh lobster salad), braised lamb with a cassoulet of white beans and smokey bacon, and chargrilled rib-eye steak. To finish, try the sticky toffee pudding with clotted cream or mixed fruit crumble. Separate restaurant menu. Stabling available for those wishing to bring their own horses. *Open 11-3 (from 12 Sun), 6-11. Bar Food 12-2, 6.30-9.30. Free House. Beer Brakspear Bitter, Flowers Original & IPA. Garden, outdoor eating. Family room. Accommodation 17 bedrooms, all en suite, £76-£90 (single £40-£55). Children welcome overnight (under-10s stay free in parents' room, 10-15s 50% adult tariff), additional bed (£17) & cot supplied. Amex, MasterCard, VISA*

EXLADE STREET   Highwayman   FOOD

Tel 01491 682020   Fax 01491 682229   Map 14a C3   **B&B**
Exlade Street Checkendon Berkshire RG8 0UA

Tucked away off the A4074 Reading to Wallingford road in a secluded hamlet on the edge of the wooded Chiltern Hills is the Highwayman, an atmospheric old inn that dates from 1625 and provides a splendid destination for a decent meal or a peaceful night; there's a wealth of Chiltern walks and the Thames Valley to explore nearby. The historic core of the inn has been added to over the years, resulting in three tastefully-furnished interconnecting bars and a modern conservatory dining-room, which in turn leads out to a rear courtyard and terraced garden. The space is much-needed as the pub positively bustles with an eager dining clientele, all the tables being neatly laid-up with candles and check cotton napkins (linen in the evenings). Scatter cushions on comfortable wall benches, exposed brick walls, open logs fires and walls adorned with paintings and china add to the cosy dining atmosphere. Home-cooked food highlights an above-average printed menu and a regularly-changing specials board, the latter offering such dishes as smoked salmon and crab parcel, grilled fillet of red mullet in anchovy sauce and fresh asparagus for starters, followed by crispy lemon chicken and several fish choices – sesame monkfish, whole peppered tilapia and gourmet seafood platter. From the varied main menu one can sample good steaks, rack of lamb, salmon fishcakes and a decent steak, Guinness and mushroom pie with a baked-on puff-pastry lid and a generous dish of crisp vegetables. Sandwiches, ploughman's lunches and filled baguettes are available lunchtimes only. Finish off with summer pudding, toffee apple tart or chocolate marquise. Well-kept real ales, freshly-squeezed orange juice and good wines from a well-stocked bar. A relaxing overnight stay can be enjoyed in one of the four attractively decorated bedrooms located to the rear of the inn across a patio. All are kitted out with modern pine furnishings, Laura Ashley fabrics and spotless modern shower rooms, with added comforts like remote-controlled TV, telephone, hairdryer and tea-making equipment. One room has its own terrace with tables and chairs – ideal on summer evenings. Children are welcome in the dining-room if eating but are not encouraged overnight. *Open 11-3, 6-11 (Sun 12-10.30).* **Bar Food** *12-2.30, 6-10.30 (Sun 12-10). Free House.* **Beer** *Brakspear Bitter, Fuller's London Pride, Gibbs Mew Bishops Tipple, two guest beers. Garden, patio, outdoor eating. Accommodation 4 bedrooms, all en suite (shower), £65 (single £50). Check-in by arrangement. No dogs. MasterCard,* **VISA**

EYAM   Miner's Arms   FOOD

Tel 01433 630853   Map 6 C2   **B&B**
Water Lane Eyam Derbyshire S30 1RG

Conveniently located just off the main square behind a butcher's shop (drive gently up Water Lane to locate the rear car park) is Nick and Ruth Cook's historic village inn. Built in 1630 it is reputedly haunted by two girls who perished in a fire on the site of the inn and by victims of Eyam's plague in 1665/6 who were buried in the adjacent croft. A balanced selection of bar lunches might include smoked chicken and avocado salad, crispy roast duck, braised beef in stout, Cumberland sausages in onion gravy, and salmon and brocolli quiche; to follow, Bakewell tart and fresh fruit pavlova. More imaginative fare appears on the evening à la carte, offering such dishes as warm salad of chicken livers with Madeira sauce, minted lamb kebabs, grilled halibut with chive butter and tenderloin of pork with Stilton and cider sauce; this is careful cooking, neatly presented, with service supervised by the caring Nick Cook. The seven bedrooms extend through into the adjoining cottages; they are clean and bright with adequate en suite facilities (one single has WC/shower only). Welcoming touches include mineral water and a selection of books; more practical are remote-control TVs, clock radios and a hot beverage tray. *Open 12-3, 7-11 (Sun 12-3 only). Closed Sun eve and Mon lunch.* **Bar Food** *12-2 (except Sun – restaurant only till 1.30). Free House.* **Beer** *Tetley Bitter, Stones Bitter. Patio, outdoor eating (lunchtime only).* **Accommodation** *7 bedrooms, all en suite (two with bath), £50 (family room £55, single £25). Children over 10 welcome overnight, additional bed available. Accommodation closed 1st 2 weeks Jan. MasterCard,* **VISA**

EYNSHAM · Newlands Inn · FOOD

Tel 01865 881486   Fax 01865 883672   Map 14a B2
Newland Street Eynsham Witney Oxfordshire OX8 1LD

🐟 🍷 ☺

A lost corner of the 16th century hides just off the A40 – devoid of street lamps at night the setting can be magical – in the form of the mellow Cotswold stone-built Newlands Inn. Period features – flagstone floors, heavy oak beams, exposed stone walls, roaring log fires – create the draw in winter, especially in the candle-lit dining-room (where bookings are taken); on summer evenings the rear patio with its canvas awning is a pleasant spot for a snack and occasionally there will be a barbecue in progress. Landlord/chef Nick Godden charcoal grills excellent steaks and offers a good blackboard menu of daily dishes which may highlight tomato and basil soup, salmon kebabs, Cajun catfish, beef bourguignon, smoked haddock and tomato gratin, and home-made puddings like apple and sultana crumble and chocolate mousse. No food on winter evenings. Children welcome. *Open 11-2.30, 5.30-11, (Sun 12-3, 7-10.30). Closed Sun eve in winter.* **Bar Food** *12-2, 7-9.30 (no food Sun eve or late Oct-late Mar eves).* **Beer** *Greene King IPA, Ansells Bitter, guest beer. Garden, patio, outdoor eating, summer barbecues.* MasterCard, *VISA*

FACCOMBE · Jack Russell Inn · FOOD B&B

Tel 01264 737315   Map 14a B4
Faccombe Andover Hampshire SP11 0DS

🐟 Zzz... ☺

Narrow, winding lanes off the A343 north of Hurstbourne Tarrant lead to this tiny, off-the-beaten-track estate hamlet nestling in rolling North Hampshire countryside. Located opposite the pond in the centre of the village is the creeper-clad redbrick Jack Russell Inn, the present building dating from just 1983 after the previous structure fell down while being renovated. Inside, the simply-furnished bar and attractively light and airy conservatory extension are popular, especially in the evening, with diners. A bi-monthly-changing menu, supplemented by daily specials, lists a varied selection of bar food such as warming home-made soups (carrot, honey and ginger) served with freshly-baked bread, warm salad of smoked haddock mousse, crab fishcakes with lemon and chili butter, whole grilled plaice and steak and kidney pie. Game from the estate is a regular feature – perhaps pan-fried wood pigeon on a bed of cabbage and bacon with game sauce or roast venison with blackcurrant and peppercorn sauce. For fresh fish, come on a Thursday; for Mexican cooking, book a table for Friday evening. Three simple bedrooms, just one with en suite bathroom (the other two rooms share a bath) offer good, clean accommodation with TVs, but no telephones. Peaceful, totally secure rear garden with a children's play area. *Open 12-3, 6-11 (Sun 12-3, 7-10.30).* **Bar Food** *12-2, 6-9.30 (Sun 12-2, 7-9). Free House.* **Beer** *Hampshire Brewery Ironside, Theakston Best, guest beer. Garden, outdoor eating, children's play area.* **Accommodation** *3 bedrooms, 1 en suite, £50 (single £30). Children welcome overnight (under-5s stay free if sharing parents' room). Check-in by arrangement.* Amex, MasterCard, *VISA*

FARNHAM · Museum Hotel · FOOD B&B

Tel 01725 516261   Map 14 C3
Farnham Blandford Forum Dorset DT11 8DE

🐟 🍷

The Museum Hotel owes its name and its present existence to General Pitt Rivers who took over a Gypsy School nearby and housed one of his Museums in it, the most famous of which still exists in Oxford. The present 'curator' (and chef) is John Barnes. The main bar – Coopers Bar – dates from Cromwellian times and occupies the original long and low cottage. It boasts a large inglenook fireplace, light oak and pine tables, tasteful green fabrics, local paintings and soothing classical music – a civilised dining atmosphere. A small, intimate dining-room is in an airy conservatory extension. In complete contrast, the Woodlands Bar attached to the far side of the building, is simply furnished and houses an assortment of pub games. Bar food ranges from steak, kidney and oyster pudding, chicken curry and a choice of grills to regularly-changing specials – lentil and smoked chicken soup, medallions of monkfish Newburg, pheasant with Drambuie and pink grapefruit sauce and lamb and spinach curry – which enhance proceedings at both lunchtime and in the evening. Sandwiches and ploughman's platters are also available. Stable block accommodation comprises four modest, compact bedrooms with modern pine, matching fabrics and spacious, en suite bathrooms. Sun-trap patio and sheltered walled garden. *Open 11-3, 6-11 (Sun 12-3, 7-10.30). **Bar Food** 12-2, 7-9.30. Free House. **Beer** Wadworth 6X, two guest beers. Garden, patio, outdoor eating. **Accommodation** 4 bedrooms, all en suite, £50 (four-poster £65, single £35). Check-in by arrangement. No dogs. Accommodation and pub closed 25 Dec. MasterCard,* **VISA**

FAVERSHAM   Albion Tavern   FOOD

Tel 01795 591411   Map 11 C5
Front Brents Faversham Creek Faversham Kent ME37 1DH

Having succesfully cooked at two other popular food pubs in Kent over the last few years, chef Patick Coevoet has at last taken charge of his own pub, a tenancy at this charming, white-weatherboarded building which overlooks Faversham Creek, a stones' throw from the owning brewery – Shepherd Neame. A gem of a place it is too: the small character bar has a distinct nautical atmosphere with oars, a hammock, old photographs of boats and other artefacts decorating the ceiling and deep green walls. Old pine dining-room tables topped with candles are neatly laid out on sea-grass matting, while dried flowers, stencilled hessian curtaining and picture windows overlooking the creek add to its charm. A small rear conservatory, covered with a vibrant vine, leads out to a pretty, flower-filled garden. As space is limited it is essential to book a table, as Patrick's imaginative cooking is proving very popular locally. Beyond a board listing the range of snacks (ploughman's, filled baguettes) and starters like fish soup, a light and creamy Roquefort and nut terrine or mussels, tomato and garlic cassoulette with Emmental cheese topping, the weekly-changing specials board may highlight interesting main dishes such as baked poussin with piri-piri dressing, rabbit casserole with redcurrant and horseradish, chicken and ham pie with shortcrust pastry, lamb rump with light mustard and cream sauce and a good choice of fresh fish from Whitstable – grilled mackerel with ginger and rhubarb sauce or baked parcel of halibut with julienne of vegetables. A filo parcel of chick peas, fennel, leek, apricot, mushroom and tomato should please vegetarian diners. Those with room left can tuck into steamed date and apple pudding or chocolate truffle torte for pudding. As one would expect, the Shepherd Neame ales – Master Brew, Spitfire, Bishop's Finger – are in tip-top condition. *Open 11-3, 6.30-11 (from 6 Fri & Sat), Sun 12-3, 6-10.30. **Bar Food** 12-2, 7-9.30 (from 6 Sun, till 10 Fri & Sat). **Beer** Shepherd Neame. Garden, patio, outdoor eating, barbecue. Family room (summer only). Amex, Diners, MasterCard,* **VISA**

FENSTANTON   King William IV   FOOD

Tel 01480 462467   Map 15 F1
High Street Fenstanton Cambridgeshire PE18 9JF

Look out for the old clock tower as this attractive white-painted inn is next door. Once three separate cottages, it is very much the hub of village life with a lively bar area and a comfortably furnished dining area, including a rear, plant-festooned Garden Room. Food is reliable with home-cooked dishes appearing on the bi-monthly-changing printed menu and the constantly varying blackboard list. Choose, perhaps, from sandwiches, ploughman's platters (these at lunch and Sun evening only) or stuffed mushrooms, fresh grilled sardines and home-made soup to start, followed by a traditional steak and kidney pudding, fillet of pork or fricassee of monkfish with lemon and ginger. Good, separately-plated vegetables. Vegetarians will always find two options on the board. Popular Sunday roast and a selection of six puddings, notably hot chocolate sponge and treacle and walnut pie. Capability Brown is buried in the village churchyard. *Open 11-3.30, 6-11 (Sun 12-3, 7-10.30). **Bar Food** 11-2.15, 7-10 (Sun 12-2.15, 7-9). **Beer** Greene King. Amex, MasterCard,* **VISA**

FERNHURST   Red Lion   FOOD

Tel 01428 653304   Map 11 A6
The Green Fernhurst West Sussex GU27 3HY

A cosy little pub on the corner of the village green, just off the A286 Haslemere to Midhurst Road. The emphasis is firmly on bistro-style dining with two tiny, no-smoking dining-rooms off each side of the two-roomed open-plan bar; a counter runs along the back of both bar rooms, one of which has a roaring modern fire, horse brasses and copper post horns to complete the country air. Small blackboards offer a choice of twenty or so dishes, from shell-on garlic prawns, home-made soup, paté and garlic-stuffed mushrooms topped with melted Brie to Sussex pie (sausage meat, leeks and mushrooms), salmon with asparagus and cream cheese en croute, game pie, grilled sardines, fresh mackerel, Armenian lamb with rice pilaf, braised pheasant with winter vegetables, smoked haddock with spinach and a good range of home-made puddings (tiramisu, a particularly light sticky toffee pudding, walnut and caramel torte). Cooking can be inconsistent (undercooked pastry and an underseasoned and rather bland-tasting, if generous, selection of vegetables) but the intentions are good. Ciabatta sandwiches, jacket potatoes and ploughman's are always available for those who wish to hedge their bets. The loos have been improved and the Gents now features some saucy 40s' prints. Children are welcome away from the main bar area. *Open 11-3, 5-11 (Sun 12-3, 7-10.30).* ***Bar Food*** *12-2.30, 5.30-10.30. Free House.* ***Beer*** *Wadworth 6X, King & Barnes Sussex, Adnams Southwold Bitter, guest beer. Garden. Amex, MasterCard,* ***VISA***

FINGEST   Chequers Inn   A

Tel 01491 638335   Map 15a D3
Fingest Henley-on-Thames Buckinghamshire RG9 6QD

Charming 15th-century brick-and-flint pub located opposite a unique Norman church in a tiny hamlet set deep in the Chiltern Hills. Unspoilt and traditionally furnished interior – free from intrusive music and electronic games – boasting ceiling beams, an 18th-century settle, open fires and tastefully adorned with prints, horsebrasses, decorative plates, and a few guns and pistols. Sunny lounge area with French windows opening out on to a delightful sun-trap garden with colourful flower borders and rural views. Good walking country. Fingest is signposted off B480 Marlow to Stokenchurch road. *Open 11-3, 6-11 (Sun 12-3, 7-10.30).* ***Beer*** *Brakspear. Garden. Family room. Amex, Diners, MasterCard,* ***VISA***

FIR TREE   Duke of York   FOOD

Tel 01388 762848   Map 5 D3   **B&B**
Fir Tree Crook Durham DL15 8DG

From whitewashed stone pub to extended and comfortable roadside inn (standing by the A68 one mile from Crook town), the grand old Duke – in landlord Roy Suggett's family for several generations now – continues to march along. Mr Suggett provides more-than-adequate ale and refreshment for a perceptibly discerning market. Blackboards offer chicken Marengo, beef stroganoff, lamb in hot pepper, pork in ginger, and gammon with sherry and peaches, with, perhaps, chicken liver paté with brandy to start and Belgian apple flan or sherry trifle to follow. Alongside are snacks like home-made soup, open sandwiches, hot beef in a bun, ploughman's platters and grilled steaks from an all-encompassing menu. Separate restaurant menu. Four en suite bedrooms are individually decorated in a "luxurious but olde-worlde" style; they are named after Co Durham castles and furnished with stained solid pine furniture, remote-controlled TVs, direct-dial telephones and beverage facilities. Ten further bedrooms are planned along with a residents' lounge and conference facilities. Incidentally, all the bar fittings, tables and light fittings are by 'Mouseman' Thompson (look out for his carved trademark) and date from 1967. Children are made very welcome. *Open 11-11 (12-3, 7-10.30).* ***Bar Food*** *12-2.30, 6-10 (Sun 12-2.30, 7-10). Free House.* ***Beer*** *Bass, guest beer. Garden, outdoor eating.* ***Accommodation*** *4 bedrooms, all en suite (two with bath), £59 (single £48). Children over 10 welcome overnight, additional bed (£12) available. No dogs. MasterCard,* ***VISA***

FIRLE — Ram Inn — FOOD

Tel 01273 858222   Map 11 B6   **B&B**
Firle West Firle Lewes East Sussex BN8 6NS

🍺 🍴 Zzz...

The road runs out once it eventually reaches Firle village at the foot of the Downs. It's a quiet backwater now, but this (almost unbelievably) was once a main stage-coach route and the Ram an important staging post. Built of brick and flint and partly tile-hung, the inn displays a fascinating mixture of periods. The Georgian part was once the local courthouse. Other parts are older, and the kitchen dates back nearly 500 years. The main bar is a simple, unpretentious affair with a motley collection of tables and chairs and old photos. A no-smoking snug bar is similarly modest. A daily-changing blackboard menu lists the selection of home-made food which makes use of good local produce. Choose from an excellent range of ploughman's lunches – choice of five Sussex farm cheeses – a deep, hearty bowl of leek and mushroom soup, baked seafood soufflé, Sussex pork pie, chicken curry, and leek and Stilton filo. Puddings include banana and toffee pie and baked pear and fresh ginger sponge. Vegetarians are well catered for. Simple bedrooms are bright and fresh, with a variety of antique furniture. The largest and best en suite room enjoys downland views and features a shower cabinet and en suite toilet; the other three rooms share a rather basic shower room. The fourth bedroom is up two flights of stairs in the attic, with a very high elevation and views over the garden; it shares facilities and does not have a hand basin. All rooms have tea and coffee-making kits but, as a matter of policy, no televisions or radios. Splendid flint-walled garden for peaceful summer drinking. *Open 11.30-3, 7-11 (Sun 12-3, 7-10.30). Bar Food 12-2, 7-9. Free House. Beer Harveys Sussex Bitter, Otter Bitter & Honiton Bitter, two guest beers. Garden, outdoor eating. Family room.* **Accommodation** *4 bedrooms, 1 en suite (shower), £50-£60 (single £35). No children under 14 overnight. Check-in by arrangement. Accommodation closed 25 & 26 Dec; pub closed 25 Dec eve. MasterCard, VISA*

FITTLEWORTH — The Swan — B&B

Tel 01798 865429   Fax 01798 865546   Map 11 A6
Lower Street Fittleworth Pulborough West Sussex RH20 1EN

☺

One can luxuriate in the peaceful beauty of the lovely award-winning garden of flowers and herbs of this 14th-century tile-hung inn, and see where the River Arun meets the Rother by taking a peaceful river walk. Inside, fresh flowers adorn the hallway and reception and the dark panelled picture lounge boasts a fine collection of early 19th-century paintings embedded in the upper panels. Spotless Laura Ashley-style bedrooms are comfortable and well appointed – TVs, tea-makers, trouser presses, telephones, hairdryers – and feature modern pine furniture, although two rooms have fine mahogany four-poster beds. Good en suite facilities, with three of the bedrooms sharing two smart bathrooms. A warm welcome awaits families; children can eat with parents anywhere in the bar, choose from their own menu or request smaller portions of adult dishes and eat at any time of the day. A wooden climbing frame in the safe garden will keep the more active offspring amused on fine days. Whitbread Wayside Inn. *Open 11-11 (Sun 12-10.30). Beer King & Barnes Sussex, Boddingtons, Wadworth 6X, Flowers Original, Gales HSB. Garden, children's play area. Accommodation 10 bedrooms, 7 en suite, £40-£50 (single £25.50). Children welcome overnight (stay free in parents' room), additional bed & cot available. No dogs. Amex, Diners, MasterCard, VISA*

FLETCHING — Griffin Inn — FOOD

Tel 01825 722890   Fax 01825 722810   Map 11 B6   **B&B**
Fletching East Sussex TN22 3NS

🐷 🍸 Zzz... ☺

Simon de Montfort's army camped outside Fletching church prior to the Battle of Lewes in 1256. These days visitors with a more peaceful intent are made more than welcome at the 16th-century Griffin Inn, which is at the heart of Saxon Fletching's picturesque main street, and is everything a village local should be. The main bar has old beams and wainscot walls, a copper-hooded brick fireplace and a motley collection of old pews and wheelback chairs; the public bar provides a pool table and fruit machine for the amusement of the local youth and there's a pretty restaurant. Good home-made food is a major attraction, with a varied blackboard menu available in the bar and a short, more imaginative daily-changing à la carte menu on offer in the restaurant (more extensive Fri and Sat evenings) – all draw on local, mostly organic, suppliers. An eclectic choice in the bar might range from celery, leek and Stilton soup, potted shrimps with hot ciabatta and local asparagus to Thai-spiced salmon fishcakes for starters, followed by main-course options like fish pie, lamb shank braised in Moroccan spices on couscous, steak and ale pie, roast Mediterranean vegetable flan or fresh cod and home-made chips. There are also chargrills, homely puddings (tarte tatin, summer pudding, white chocolate and Baileys mousse) and generous ploughman's platters. Excellent wine list with at least eight available by the glass. There are four charming, bedrooms, three with four-poster beds purpose-built to counteract the sloping floors and to ensure a level night's rest. All have en suite power showers (one with bath and shower), tea- and coffee-making kits and TVs. The substantial breakfast is worth getting up for. In summer, the rear garden offers outstanding views across rolling Sussex countryside and delicious weekend barbecues. *Open 12-3, 6-11 (till 10.30 Sun, maybe 12-11 Sat in summer – if fine).* **Bar Food** *12-2.30, 7-9.30. Free House.* **Beer** *Harveys Sussex Bitter, Hall & Woodhouse Tanglefoot, Fuller's London Pride, Hog's Back Traditional English Ale. Garden, patio, outdoor eating, summer weekend barbecue.* **Accommodation** *4 bedrooms, all en suite, £55-£65 (weekends £75, single £40). Children welcome overnight (stay free on sofa bed in parents' room). Check-in by arrangement. Pub & accommodation closed all 25 Dec. No dogs. Amex, MasterCard,* **VISA**

FONTHILL GIFFORD   Beckford Arms   B&B

Tel 01747 870385   Fax 01747 851496   Map 14 B3
Fonthill Gifford Tisbury Salisbury Wiltshire SP3 6PX

Peacefully situated on a minor road (follow signposts to Fonthill Bishop from the A303), opposite Fonthill Estate and adjoining its vineyard, this 18th-century stone-built inn is a good base from which to explore the estate footpaths and the unspoilt scenery of the Nadder Valley. The modernised, yet attractive lounge bar with open fire and the airy Garden Room lead out on to a sun-trap patio and a delightful raised, flower- and shrub-filled garden – ideal for summer alfresco imbibing. The seven compact and comfortable bedrooms are upstairs and two of them feature four-poster beds. All rooms are spacious, neat, clean and refreshingly decorated with matching floral wallpaper and fabrics; they are also well equipped with TV, clock-radio, tea-making kit, hairdryer and good toiletries. Most are fully en suite, although the three single rooms (shower/hand-basin) share two separate WCs. *Open 11-3, 6-11 (Sun 12-3, 7-10.30). Free House.* **Beer** *Courage Best, Wadworth 6X, John Smith's Bitter, guest beer. Garden, outdoor eating. Family room.* **Accommodation** *8 bedrooms, all en suite, £49.50 (four-poster £54.50, single £29.50). Children welcome overnight (under-5s stay free in parents' room, 5-16s £9.50) additional bed & cot available. Small dogs only. Amex, MasterCard,* **VISA**

FORD   Dinton Hermit   FOOD

Tel 01296 748379   Map 15a D2
Ford Aylesbury Buckinghamshire HP17 8XH

In an isolated hamlet and set back from the lane, this 15th-century stone cottage pub is named after John Briggs, clerk to one of the judges who condemned Charles I to death. Two small and homely bars are well maintained, each having part exposed stone walls, brick fireplaces and a mix of rustic furniture. Popular locally, both bars fill quickly with customers seeking out the hearty, home-cooked food – lasagne, kidneys in cognac sauce, steak and mushroom pie, vegetetable curry and decent sandwiches and salads. Additional dishes like pork fillet in pineapple, peppers and sweetcorn sauce, and chicken florentine appear on the evening menu. Large, pretty garden with rural views – ideal for sunny days. *Open 11-2.30, 6-11 (Sun 12-2, 7-10.30). Closed Mon lunch, 2 weeks Jan & 2 weeks July.* **Bar Food** *12-2 & 7-9.30 (no food Sun or Mon).* **Beer** *Ind Coope ABC Bitter, Adnams Southwold, Wadworth 6X. Garden, outdoor eating, children's play area. No credit cards.*

FORD — Plough Inn — FOOD

Tel 01386 584215   Map 14a A1   **B&B**
Temple Gutting Ford Gloucestershire GL54 5RU

A gregarious pub in something of an agrarian setting on a bend in the B4077. There's an old well in the walled garden and a mixture of abandoned filling station and farmyard behind. The simply furnished bars recall the pub's past days as a farmhouse with flagstone floors, pine tables and high-backed settles, and diners move easily through to a neatly-laid dining-room which is cosily candle-lit at night. Food starts at breakfast (served from 9-11.30), with the best of the lunch and dinner choices (prepared by a new chef since lasts year's guide) prominently displayed on blackboards. Choices may range from home-made leek and potato soup and pheasant paté for starters to tagliatelle with smoked haddock and prawns, steak, mushroom and Guinness casserole, rabbit casseroled in red wine and ginger, fish pie, and knuckle of lamb cooked with garlic and herbs as substantial main courses; freshly-cut sandwiches are served at lunch only, ploughman's platters available all day. In increasing numbers regulars are leaving room for the generously-portioned, home-made, steamed orange and treacle sponge and chocolate tart. Four simple bedrooms: three in a converted courtyard barn with en suite showers, and one within the main pub building with en suite bathroom; all have remote-controlled TVs and hot beverage facilities. *Open 9am-11pm (Sun 12-3 & 7-10.30). Bar Food 12-2.30, 6.30-9.30 (till 10 Fri & Sat, till 9 Sun). Beer Donnington BB & SBA. Garden, outdoor eating, children's play area. Accommodation 4 bedrooms, all en suite, £40 & £50 (family room sleeping three £65, single £35). Children welcome overnight (under-3s stay free in parents' room), additional bed (£15) & cot available. No dogs. Pub & accommodation closed 25 Dec. MasterCard, VISA*

FORD — White Hart — FOOD

Tel 01249 782213   Fax 01249 783075   Map 14 B2   **B&B**
Ford Chippenham Wiltshire SN14 8RP

Idyllically situated beside a babbling trout stream in the Wyvern Valley, this rambling, mellow-stone, 16th-century coaching inn offers both character and charm in its low-ceilinged bar and in the adjacent dining areas. The inn is well run by its owners, Chris and Jenny Phillips, who cater for all requirements, providing good ale, consistently reliable food and a high standard of accommodation. Subsequently the White Hart is a very popular and busy inn. The cosy, unspoilt half-panelled bar throngs with drinkers, many of whom are attracted by the continually varying selection of up to ten real ales that are drawn from the cellar. Discerning diners, seeking out imaginative and well-cooked food head next door into one of the two attractive dining areas where antiques, various rugs, an array of furniture and numerous paintings help create a convivial atmosphere. Choosing from a sensibly-short, weekly-changing menu – created by a new chef since our last edition but with the same modern, imaginative style – one might start with chicken and Stilton terrine with apple and sultana chutney or home-made vegetable soup, following with a good choice of meat dishes (perhaps breast of duck with caramelised apples and orange brandy sauce), a fish dish (whole grilled lemon sole with lemon butter) and two vegetarian options (onion tart topped with grilled goat's cheese and brie with roasted peppers and watercress sauce). Lighter snacks like macaroni cheese, ploughman's platters and a range of sandwiches are available at lunchtimes only. The final ingredient to this successful inn is the comfortable en suite accommodation, most of the rooms being located across the lane in the converted stables. All are attractively decorated and furnished (some with four-posters) and equipped with TV, beverage tray, radio, telephone and trouser press. Residents have use of an outdoor swimming pool (heated in summer). Five miles from Junction 17 of the M4. *Open 11-3, 5-11. Bar Food 12-2, 7-10. Free House. Beer Smiles Best, Wadworth 6X, Hall & Woodhouse Tanglefoot, Boddingtons, Bass, Marston's Pedigree & Owd Roger, Fuller's London Pride, Black Sheep Bitter, regular guest beers. Patio, outdoor eating. Accommodation 11 bedrooms, all en suite, £65 (single £45). Children welcome overnight, (under-2s free), additional bed (£10) & cot available. Amex, Diners, MasterCard, VISA*

FORDCOMBE — Chafford Arms — FOOD

Tel 01892 740267   Map 11 B5
Fordcombe Tunbridge Wells Kent TN3 0SA

Festooned with colourful, overflowing hanging baskets, this imposing rather than beautiful tile-hung village pub is a great summer attraction, especially for its splendid (if somewhat wild) summer garden with secluded benches and tables, and for delicious crabs (perhaps dressed with prawns) and Dover soles delivered fresh from Hastings. These are the highlight of a longish home-cooked menu which changes weekly and offers more usual pub food – chicken Napoleon, gammon steak, steak and chips and fresh trout. Service is particularly friendly and good-humoured and there is a sense of dedication and commitment in the cooking, even when the pub is exceptionally busy. *Open 11-3, 6-11 (Sun 12-4, 7-10.30).* **Bar Food** *12.30-2 (till 2.30 Sun), 7.30-9.45 (no food Sun eve).* **Beer** *Fremlins, Whitbread Castle Eden Ale, Larkins Bitter. Garden, outdoor eating. MasterCard,* **VISA**

FOREST ROW — Brambletye Hotel — B&B

Tel 01342 824144   Fax 01342 824833   Map 11 B6
Forest Row East Sussex RH18 5EZ

Well refurbished hotel located beside the busy A22 in the village centre and close to the Ashdown Forest. The attractive building houses a good locals bar, Black Peter's, dispensing real ales, and comfortable overnight accommodation in twenty-five en suite bedrooms. Most rooms occupy a rear extension that surrounds a pleasant courtyard, and all are neatly furnished in modern style with light oak furniture and good fabrics. Main-building rooms have more charm and character, but all have TVs, telephones and tea-makers for added comfort. *Open 11-11 (Sun 11.30-10.30). Free House.* **Beer** *Harveys Best Better, Courage Directors. Paved courtyard. Family room.* **Accommodation** *25 bedrooms, all en suite, £55-£65 (family room sleeping four £75, single £45). Children welcome overnight, additional bed & cot (£5) available. Amex, MasterCard,* **VISA**

FORTY GREEN — Royal Standard of England — A

Tel 01494 673382   Fax 01494 523332   Map 15a E3
Forty Green Beaconsfield Buckinghamshire HP9 1XT

Granted its title and coat-of-arms in 1651 by Charles II who sheltered here after the Battle of Worcester, this splendid pub is one of our oldest free houses with a history dating back over 900 years. Tremendous interior with many of the magnificent oak beams having nautical origins, including the massive carved transom from an Elizabethan ship, which now forms part of the entrance hall. Amid a superb array of collectors' items and artefacts this is a truly atmospheric setting for a drink. Hamlet signposted off the B474 north of Beaconsfield. *Open 11-3, 5.30-11 (Sun 12-3, 7-10.30). Free House.* **Beer** *Marston's Pedigree & Owd Roger, Morland Old Speckled Hen, Brakspear Bitter, guest beers. Garden. Family room. MasterCard,* **VISA**

FOTHERINGHAY — Falcon Inn — FOOD

Tel 01832 226254   Map 7 E4
Fotheringhay Oundle Northamptonshire PE8 5HZ

By night, the imposing, illuminated church serves as a golden beacon, visible for miles. Standing almost beside it in the main street of this historic village, the Falcon is in many respects the perfect village pub – busy, with a lively friendly crowd and charming staff. Their reputation for offering good value food for lunch and dinner has spread far and wide, so booking is advisable to avoid disappointment. Prices are marginally cheaper at lunchtime though the choice remains the same – changing daily. Some dishes such as wild boar in orange and nutmeg sauce and lamb steak with redcurrant sauce can run out – they only make a batch of 8 or so for each sitting, helping to ensure the freshness of their produce. The menu encompasses everything from a ploughman's lunch or supper, quail's eggs with smoked salmon and watercress and leek mousse to bobotie and pan-fried trout with almonds. The food is generally simple and unfussy, reflecting the delightful informality of this inn. *Open 10-3, 6-11 (Sun 12-3, 7-10.30). Closed Mon Jan-Mar.* **Bar Food** *12.15-2, 6.45-9.30 (Sun 7-9), Free House.* **Beer** *Adnams Southwold, Elgood's Cambridge, Ruddles County, Nethergate IPA, Bass, Greene King IPA. Garden, outdoor eating. MasterCard,* **VISA**

FOWEY — King of Prussia — B&B

Tel 01726 832450
Quayside Fowey Cornwall PL23 1AT

Map 12 C3

Zzz...

Pride of place on the tiny quay goes to this most unusual three-storey pink-washed building, which overlooks the perpetually busy quayside and river estuary and across to Pont Pill creek, a sheltered inlet filled with sailing craft. It was built by and named after the notorious smuggler John Carter, who operated from Prussia Cove. A clergyman by day and smuggler by night, his ill-gotten gains built the pub and his dual role in life is reflected in the unusual double-sided inn sign. Beyond the lively main bar, complete with juke box and a young crowd, are six delightful en suite bedrooms, all of which have splendid river views. Neatly refurbished with co-ordinating colours, fabrics and friezes and furnished with modern pine, they are fresh, clean and very comfortable. Facilities include satellite TV and tea-makers, plus in summer months your own colourful window-box of flowers which spill into the room. Bathrooms are compact, well fitted-out and spotless. Breakfast is taken in the tiny pine-furnished restaurant. *Open 11-11 (Sun 12-10.30).* **Beer** *St Austell.* **Accommodation** *6 bedrooms, all en suite, £46 (family room sleeping three £57, single £23). Children welcome overnight, cot available. MasterCard,* **VISA**

FOWEY — Ship Inn — B&B

Tel 01726 833751
Fowey Cornwall PL23 1AZ

Map 12 C3

Tucked away among the narrow streets and only 200 yards from the quay, the Ship dates from the 16th-century and is one of the oldest buildings in an attractive little fishing town. Local fishermen congregate in the main bar, which has exposed stone walls and various nautical items. Of the six bedrooms, the most popular is the one located in what remains of the original building, which boasts an ornamental ceiling, fine panelled walls and a carved chimney-piece with the date 1570. Remaining rooms are modern in style and simply furnished with new pine. One room has en suite facilities (and both double and single beds), the others wash basins in the room and all share two spacious and fully-tiled bathrooms; one further room (not en suite) also sleeps three. Large residents' lounge. *Open 11-11 (Mon-Thu in winter 11-2, 5.30-11), Sun 12-10.30.* **Beer** *St Austell.* **Accommodation** *6 bedrooms, 1 en suite, £37-£41 (single £18.50). Children welcome overnight (under-3s stay free in parents' room, 3-14 50% adult tariff), additional bed & cot (£3.50) available. MasterCard,* **VISA**

FOWLMERE — Chequers Inn — FOOD

Tel 01763 208369   Fax 01763 208944
High Street Fowlmere Cambridgeshire SG8 7SR

Map 15 F1

When Samuel Pepys spent a night here in 1659, the inn was already a popular travellers' rest. Its period charm largely survives and it still goes into many diaries as a good place for refreshment. Beyond the most appealing white-painted facade a civilised, up-market ambience pervades the comfortably furnished and carpeted split-level bar area, the conservatory extension and the adjacent galleried restaurant. The convivial atmosphere is an ideal one in which to enjoy some good, reliable bar food. Choices are listed on a daily-changing blackboard menu and may feature creamed broccoli and almond soup and chicken liver paté – both served with excellent warm French bread – hot-smoked fish platter, poached pollack with mild cream curried sauce and stir-fry vegetables, Thai-style chicken and venison steak with red wine sauce. Accompanying vegetables are crisp and salads imaginative. Vegetarian offerings include aubergine filled with mushrooms and sun-dried tomatoes. Good Irish cheeses served with walnut bread and a good global wine list, with at least seven wines served by the glass. Plans are to introduce one menu serving both bar and restaurant. *Open 12-2.30, 6-11 (Sun 12-2.30,, 7-10.30).* **Bar Food** *12-2 (till 2.30 Sun), 7-10 (till 9.30 Sun). Free House.* **Beer** *Adnams Southwold & Broadside. Garden, outdoor eating. Closed all 25 Dec. Amex, Diners, MasterCard,* **VISA**

FOWNHOPE — Green Man — B&B

Tel 01432 860243   Fax 01432 860207   Map 14 B1
Fownhope Hereford & Worcester HR1 4PE

Zzz... ☺

A fine old black-and-white, half-timbered inn at the heart of the village and less than a 10-minute walk from the banks of the River Wye. The 'Naked Boy' as it was once called, dates back possibly to the year of Henry VII's accession in 1485. Its historical associations continue through the Civil War to the 18th and 19th centuries when the Green Man became a petty sessional court and coaching inn on the Hereford to Gloucester route (now called the B4224). There is still plenty of timber and stonework extant in the succession of interconnecting rooms which surround the central bar servery. Residents perhaps get the pick in a comfortable lounge with armchairs set around an open log fire, and choice of dining areas including one for non-smokers. Accommodation is of a varying, though commendably high standard, divided between the inn and some smaller annexe rooms, with pride of place going to the old four-posters and former 'Judge's Room', well equipped for family use, which overlooks an enclosed rear courtyard. Here there is also the Stable Room, ideal for residents who prefer to be on the ground floor. Appointments, which run from TV and telephones to tea-trays, hairdryers and trouser presses, are standard throughout. *Open 11-3, 6-11 (Sun 12-3, 7-10.30). Free House.* **Beer** *Samuel Smith Old Brewery Bitter, Marston's Pedigree, Hook Norton Best, Courage Best. Garden, children's play area. Family room.* **Accommodation** *20 bedrooms, all en suite, £49-£51 (single £31-£32). Children welcome overnight (under-12s £2.50, 12-15s £7.50 in parents' room), additional bed & cot available. Dogs (£2.50). Amex, Diners, MasterCard,* **VISA**

FRAMPTON MANSELL — Crown Hotel — B&B

Tel 01285 760601   Fax 01285 760681   Map 14 B2
Frampton Mansell Stroud Gloucestershire GL6 8JB

Zzz...

Of 16th-century origin, the Crown stands at the heart of the village just off the A419 and just within the Cotswold district; its extensive acreage of ground falls steeply away through mature woods and orchard to the Thames/Severn canal far below. While the bar areas are typically quaint, the pub opens out into larger rear extensions. The largest of these houses a dozen spacious bedrooms uniformly fitted out with mahogany furniture, gold-tapped avocado bathrooms and close carpeting. The four ground-floor rooms, with direct access from the car park, are especially convenient for the less mobile, while it's the abundant peace and quiet amid restful panoramic views which proves to be one of the pub's greatest assets. Recently acquired by Discovery Inns, who plan to introduce new menus and completely refurbish the premises. *Open 11-2.30, 6-11 (all day July-Sep), Sun 12-3, 7-10.30. Free House.* **Beer** *Morland Old Speckled Hen, Flowers Original, Wadworth 6X. Garden.* **Accommodation** *12 bedrooms, all en suite, £45 (family room sleeping up to four £55, single £25). Children welcome overnight (under-2s stay free in parents' room, 3-14s £15), additional bed & cot available. MasterCard,* **VISA**

We do not accept free meals or hospitality – our inspectors pay their own bills and **never** book in the name of Egon Ronay's Guides.

FREELAND   Shepherds Hall Inn   B&B

Tel 01993 881256   Map 14a B2
Witney Road Freeland Oxfordshire OX8 8HQ

Once known as the 'Shepherds All' and originally a 13th-century shelter for shepherds and drovers, the green-shuttered inn today offers plain and practical accommodation. The exterior of the pub is resplendent with colourful flower boxes in summer and there's a dovecote in the car park. Within the pub, the bar is filled with antique furniture, copper and brass and wheelback chairs, and a collection of plates adorns the walls. Five bedrooms (three of which are in an annexe) are clean, comfortable and modern in style, and include TVs, radios, telephones and tea-making facilities. The annexe rooms have neat, tiled shower rooms, and the pub rooms have private bathrooms. The patio and lawned garden with flowerbeds is safe for children, who also have their own purpose-built play area. On the A4095 halfway between Woodstock and Witney. *Open 10.30-2.30, 6-11 (Sun 12-3, 7-10.30). Free House.* **Beer** *Wadworth 6X, Flowers IPA. Garden, children's play area. Family room.* **Accommodation** *5 bedrooms, all en suite (two with bath), £40 (single £25). Children welcome overnight, additional bed & cot (both £5) available. MasterCard,* **VISA**

FRILFORD HEATH   Dog House Hotel   B&B

Tel 01865 390830   Fax 01865 390860   Map 14a C3
Frilford Heath Marcham Abingdon Oxfordshire OX13 6QJ

 Zzz... ☺

As we went to press a major bedroom refurbishment programme was nearing completion at this handsome inn owned by local Abingdon brewers, Morland. Its tile-hung and light stone exterior belies the modernity within that makes it a comfortable midweek resting place for businessmen. Warmth comes from both the sun that streams into the breakfast room (buffet breakfasts only) and the stone fireplace to one end of the spacious lounge bar where Morland's ales, eleven wines by the glass and improving bar snacks are served. At weekends there is a substantial tariff reduction but the otherwise tranquil atmosphere (and setting) may be completely transformed by wedding parties in summer. Bedrooms are comfortable, with bright bathrooms, satellite TV and cottagey, antiqued pine furniture; top of the range is a four-poster room and a couple of family rooms sleeping three (plus room for a cot). Large, lawned garden with a few old picnic tables, a pétanque piste, swings and a climbing frame. Take the turning east off A338 (between A415 and A420) near the golf club – ten minutes' drive or so from Oxford. *Open 11-11 (Sun 12-3, 7-10.30). Beer Morland. Garden, children's play area. Accommodation 19 bedrooms, all en suite, £79 (four-poster £88, single £69, Fri & Sat double £48, family rooms £63). Children welcome overnight, cot (£5) available. Amex, Diners, MasterCard,* **VISA**

FRILSHAM   Pot Kiln   A

Tel 01635 201366   Map 14a C4
Frilsham Hermitage Berkshire RG16 0XX

A remote country pub on the Yattendon to Bucklebury lane, delightful in summer in the pretty sheltered garden with its soothing outlook across open fields to woodland. The name derives from this being the site of old brick kilns (abandoned after the war) and the building is, appropriately, of attractive redbrick construction. Also adopting a name linked to the history of the site is a fine ale (Brick Kiln Bitter) brewed in the new micro-brewery – West Berkshire Brewery – located in outbuildings to the rear. Inside is distinctively old-fashioned, with three simply-furnished bars leading off a small lobby bar. Bare boards, sturdy wooden tables, cushioned wall bench seating and warming open fires characterise the good, relaxing atmosphere, with a successful mix of chatty locals and passing ramblers filling the unspoilt bars. Impromptu folk music some Sunday evenings. Well-behaved children who don't leave an "appalling mess" are welcome indoors. *Open 12-2.30, 6.30-11 (Sun 12-3, 7-10.30). Free House.* **Beer** *Arkell's Best, Morland Original & Old Speckled Hen, Brick Kiln Bitter. Garden. Family room. No credit cards.*

FULKING   Shepherd & Dog   FOOD

Tel 01273 857382   Map 11·B6
Fulking Henfield West Sussex BN5 9LU

In a truly glorious setting nestling at the base of the South Downs in a picturesque village, this 14th-century pub is named after the shepherds who farmed the surrounding downs and once served the travelling shepherds on their way to nearby Findon fair. It boasts inglenook fireplaces, polished oak tables, a low beamed ceiling and is decorated with numerous old artefacts, including a collection of shepherds crooks. The reliable selection of bar meals on offer may include carrot and coriander soup, smoked salmon paté and tiger prawns among the choice of starters, with main-course options like whole lemon sole, fillet of lamb with mint and mushroom sauce, scrumpy chicken and old favourites – lasagne and steak and stout pie. Lighter lunchtime snacks include a range of ploughman's lunches, granary sandwiches and salads. The list of home-made puddings may highlight lemon crunch and treacle and nut tart. Idyllic terraced summer garden with stream and play area. No children under 14 inside. *Open 11-3, 6-11 (Sat 11-11, Sun 12-10.30). **Bar Food** 12-2.15, 7-9.30 (Sun 12-9.30). Free House. **Beer** Harveys Best Bitter, Flowers Original, Boddingtons, guest beers. Garden, outdoor eating. Amex, MasterCard,* **VISA**

FULLERS MOOR   Copper Mine   FOOD

Tel 01829 782293   Map 6 A3
Nantwich Road Fullers Moor Broxton Cheshire CH3 9JH

Geoff and Linda Aldridge's carpeted and pine-clad dining pub is interestingly adorned with mining memorabilia inside, while outside there's a spacious summer garden and barbecue. Wholemeal sandwiches, open or closed, speciality batches with hot fillings and baked jacket potatoes (perhaps topped with creamy blue cheese, coleslaw and peppers or prawns in seafood sauce) are always on offer on the snack menu. More substantially, look for the daily specials like Tunisian 'bric' with tomato sauce (tuna, spinach and egg in filo pastry), pork with raisins and orange sauce, mahi-mahi (white Hawaiian fish) with prawn and lemon dressing, and veal and pepper medley. A variety of steaks and sauces is also offered in the evening, as is a selection of five or so vegetarian dishes (mushroom and cashew nut risotto). Sunday lunches see a choice of roasts alongside five or so further hot selections; children's favourites (or a small portion of the roast) come with a free 'goody' bag. 'Traditional puddings, tempting desserts and luxury ice creams' complete the picture. *Open 12-3, 7-11 (Sun 12-3, 7-10.30). **Bar Food** 12-3, 7-10. **Beer** Burtonwood, Bass. Garden, outdoor eating. Patio. Amex, Diners, MasterCard,* **VISA**

FYFIELD   White Hart   A

Tel 01865 390585   Fax 01865 390671   Map 14a B2
Main Road Fyfield Abingdon Oxfordshire OX13 5LN

John and Sherry Howard's 500-year-old former chantry house (abolished in 1548) has been a pub since 1580 when St John's College in Oxford, large local landowners, leased it to tenants but reserved the right to 'occupy it if driven from Oxford in pestilence' – so far this has not been invoked! At some time in its history the large hall was divided into two floors, but in 1963 this was removed, thereby restoring the main hall's original proportions and exposing the 15th-century arch-braced roof to view. There's still a splendid 30-foot-high minstrel's gallery overlooking the main bar and the interior features original oak beams and flagstone floors. The very large, rambling lawned garden includes a children's play area. Just off the A420, seven miles from Abingdon and eight miles from Oxford. *Open 11-3, 6-11 (Sun 12-3, 7-10.30). Free House. **Beer** Boddingtons, Hook Norton Best, Wadworth 6X, Theakston Old Peculier, two guest beers. Garden, children's play area. Family rooms. Closed all 25 & 26 Dec. Amex, MasterCard,* **VISA**

We do not accept free meals or hospitality – our inspectors pay their own bills and never book in the name of Egon Ronay's Guides.

GEDNEY DYKE   The Chequers   FOOD

Tel & Fax 01406 362666   Map 7 F3
Main Street Gedney Dyke Lincolnshire PE12 0AJ

Gedney Dyke lies off the A17, 3 miles east of Holbeach, isolated amid vast open fenland. One can find this unassuming white-painted pub in the heart of the village, but you will not be alone for this humble establishment attracts diners from miles around, as well as having a loyal local clientele. The homely carpeted bar has a chatty atmosphere, an open fire and is simply furnished, a trend which continues into the adjacent, unfussy dining area. Space is at a premium, especially during busy times. The 'just-a-bite' bar menu offers open sandwiches (Cumbrian air-dried ham with seasonal dressed salad), mushroom crostini, home-made soup and ploughman's lunches. Most, however, order from the more imaginative restaurant menu and daily-changing specials board – also available in the bar – which features some interesting dishes, for example, bang-bang chicken (smoked chicken with satay-style sauce), wood pigeon served with pickled red cabbage and Cumberland sauce, and steak Diane. Fresh fish (cod fillet with roast garlic and vegetable purée, monkfish with herb crust and tomato and chilli salsa) is delivered from Grimsby. A separate pudding board may highlight sticky toffee pudding and peach and brandy trifle. Well-chosen global list of wines from Adnams at sensible prices. *Open 12-2.30, 7-11 (Sun 12-3, 7-10.30).* **Bar Food** *12-2, 7-9 (till 9.30 Fri & Sat, till 8.30 Sun). No food Sun eve Jan-Mar. Free House.* **Beer** *Adnams Best, Bateman XXXB, Greene King Abbot Ale, Bass, Morland Old Speckled Hen. Garden, outside eating. Family room. Closed all 25 Dec. Amex, Diners, MasterCard,* **VISA**

GLEMSFORD   Black Lion   FOOD

Tel 01787 280684   Fax 01787 280817   Map 10 C3
Lion Road Glemsford Suffolk CO10 7RF

On entering the Lion, it turns out to have a treasure of a Tudor interior complete with half-timbered walls and rehabilitated timbers, quarry-tiled floors, country prints, leather armchairs and bay-window seats, all of which is at once both uncluttered and charming. Licensee Anne Curran concentrates on producing good home cooking: Suffolk hotpot, chili, speciality pizzas, traditional Indian curries, fisherman's pie and pork steaks in cider and apple sauce are good examples on the straightforward menu and specials board that serve both bar and dining-room. Their fruit pies and toffee apple tart are also home-made. A three-course traditional Sunday lunch is also offered. *Open 11-3, 6-11 (Sun 12-3, 7-10.30).* **Bar Food** *12-2.30, 6-9.30 (from 7 Sun).* **Beer** *Greene King. Garden, outdoor eating, summer barbecues, children's play area. Family room. No credit cards.*

> We do not accept free meals or hospitality – our inspectors pay their own bills
> and never book in the name of Egon Ronay's Guides.

GLOOSTON   Old Barn   FOOD   B&B

Tel 01858 545215   Map 7 D4
Main Street Glooston Leicestershire LE16 7ST

On the route of the Old Roman road called the Gartree, the Old Barn stands at the centre of a tiny hamlet and just across the road from a picture postcard row of stone terraced cottages; the pub's 16th-century frontage of tiny leaded windows framed by flowering boxes and hanging baskets also makes a summer picture. Within, a small upper bar leads down into the larger cellar bar where a log fire burns in winter; bookings are taken in the upper, no-smoking restaurant part only. Monthly-changing menus, supplemented by regular pub favourites, may list fish terrine wrapped in salmon and marinated in white wine with a lemon vinaigrette, roast breast of duck with a honey, olive and cumin sauce, and medallions of pork topped with a horseradish crust and served with a Provençal sauce. The handful of puddings are all home-made: perhaps banoffi pie, chocolate mousse, summer pudding or a plate of cheese. Fixed-price, three-course Sunday lunches offer exceptional value. The bedrooms – two doubles and a twin, are well fitted out, with duvets, trouser press and hairdryer, small televisions and bedside radio. Owing to lack of space, the modular fitted shower rooms are a cramped, if practical, solution. Hosts Charles and Claire Edmondson-Jones and chef/partner Stewart Sturge offer good food, good service and genuine friendliness; the Old Barn is simply one of those pubs to which people keep going back. *Open 12-2.30, 7-11. Closed Mon-Fri lunch & Sun eve.* **Bar Food** *12-1.45 (Sat snacks only, Sun blackboard and fixed-price lunch), 7-9.30. Free House.* **Beer** *Theakston Best, Greene King Abbot Ale, two guest beers. Garden, outdoor eating.* **Accommodation** *3 bedrooms, all en suite (shower), £49.50 (single £37.50). Children welcome overnight (under-10s stay free in parents' room), additional bed and cot available. Check-in bar hours only. Accommodation closed Sun eve. Amex, MasterCard,* **VISA**

GOATHLAND	**Mallyan Spout Hotel**	FOOD

Tel 01947 896486   Fax 01947 896327   Map 5 F3   **B&B**
Goathland Whitby North Yorkshire YO22 5AN

⌖ ⌂ Zzz... ☺

Goathland village is tucked into a fold in the moors two miles off the A159 and some 9 miles from Whitby. The unusual name of Peter and Judith Heslop's inn derives from the waterfall which cascades down the wooded valley just yards from the pub garden; hugging the valley's contours runs the North Yorkshire Moors Railway. Lunchtime in the Spout Bar can be a busy occasion with customers regularly overflowing into the Hunt Bar and hotel lounge next door. Hearty and ever-popular dishes are the lamb and barley broth, casserole of oxtail and butterbeans in red wine, Whitby codling and chips, and pot-roast knuckle of lamb with flageolet beans. Sandwiches and ploughman's lunches are also available. Puddings to follow may include rhubarb crumble and baked banana with caramel sauce. Evenings see the hotel restaurant move up a gear, with bar food restricted to the Spout public bar only. Bedrooms, indubitably upmarket in a purely pubby context, are housed to the rear and the side of the Jacobean-style, ivy-covered hotel; of the four small and cottagey rooms in the coach house, two are on the ground floor for those with mobility problems. Four large bedrooms (no dogs or children in these) have splendid views of the valley – two rooms have balconies; some rooms have half-tester or Laura Ashley coronet-draped beds. En suite bathrooms are generally on the small side, except in the four newest rooms. Negotiate, if you can, a larger room if arriving with a family; no reduction for children's meals in the restaurant at dinner (when children under 10 are not welcome); high-tea served from 6-7pm. *Open 11-11 (Sun 12-10.30).* **Bar Food** *12-2, 6.30-9 (from 7 Sun). Free House.* **Beer** *Malton Best Bitter. Garden, patio, outdoor eating.* **Accommodation** *24 bedrooms, all en suite, £75/£80 (family room £90 single). Children welcome overnight, additional bed (£10) & cot (£5) available. Closed all 25 Dec. Amex, MasterCard,* **VISA**

GODSTOW	**Trout Inn**	A

Tel 01865 54485   Map 14a C2
195 Godstow Road Lower Wolvercote Oxford Oxfordshire OX2 8PN

This famous medieval pub situated on the River Thames at Godstow on the outskirts of Wolvercote still attracts thousands of visitors every year. In summer, the cobbled terrace beside the fast-running river with its weir makes a restful place for a quiet pint while watching the peacocks wandering round the terrace and catching a glimpse of the chub in the clear water. The bridge across to the private island is now sadly falling apart but it is still possible to see across to the island with its famous stone lion, and on to the now-ruined Godstow Nunnery where the fair Rosamund (Henry II's mistress) was imprisoned. Inside the pub you'll find flagstone floors, beamed ceilings and bare floorboards, with welcoming open fires in winter. Be warned, the Trout can get very busy in the summer. *Open 11-11 (Sun 12-10.30).* **Beer** *Bass, Hancock's HB, guest beer. Riverside garden. Family room. Amex, Diners, MasterCard,* **VISA**

> We endeavour to be as up-to-date as possible but inevitably some changes to
> landlords, chefs and other key staff occur after the Guide
> has gone to press.

GOOSNARGH — Bushells Arms — FOOD

Tel & Fax 01772 865235   Map 6 B1
Church Lane Goosnargh Preston Lancashire PR3 2BH

Just 4 miles from Junction 32 of the M6, this modernised Georgian building offers a splendid alternative to the expensive plastic food of the motorway service areas. To reach the pub, follow the A6 North and turn on to the B5269; once in the village, take the left turn opposite the post office, and you'll find the Bushells Arms about a quarter of a mile along on the right. It's run by the experienced David and Glynis Best, who have written a book on the business side of pub catering, using much of their own experience. Certainly the food at the Bushells is first-rate; cooking is in the hands of Glynis, who produces a long, wide and cosmopolitan selection of specials, blackboard-listed behind the food counter, as well as those on the distinguished printed menu – steak and kidney pie, fish pie, chicken Olympus. A truly international menu may include Syrian potato omelette, Thai-style lemon chicken, Mediterranean bean pot casserole, kleftiko, Madras vegetable curry and lamb's liver and onions. Main courses can be ordered with O'Brien potatoes, a delicious mix of diced potato with cream, peppers, spices, garlic and parmesan cheese. For pudding, try the Westmorland tart or rhubarb and strawberry crumble. No sandwiches, but ploughman's platters are available all day. Accompany your meal with a bottle of wine from the carefully-chosen list of wines which features excellent tasting notes. The interior of the pub itself is cleverly divided into a number of alcoves by using effective wooden screens and exposed sandstone columns and walls. To the rear is a well-maintained garden with white plastic patio furniture, useful in summer when the pub can get extremely busy. Staff are noticeably welcoming and friendly. *Open 12-3, 6-11 (till 10.30 Sun). Occasional bar closures on Mon. Bar Food 12-2.30, 7-9.30. Beer Tetley Bitter, Boddingtons. Garden, outdoor eating. Closed all 25 Dec. No credit cards.*

GOSFIELD — Green Man — FOOD

Tel 01787 472746   Map 10 C3
The Street Gosfield Essex CO9 1TP

A rust-brick roadside pub on the A1017, 2 miles off the A131. The bar and eating areas are more or less one and the same, presided over by two tropical fish tanks. The day's dishes are displayed on the blackboard: mostly English – perhaps tomato soup, beef casserole with dumplings, salmon cutlet, or liver and bacon, all accompanied by two vegetables and a choice of potatoes. Lighter snacks, including Welsh rarebit, soft roes on toast with bacon, and sandwiches are also available. The centrepiece, however, is the cold lunchtime buffet, laden with home-cooked ham on the bone, roast turkey, pork, beef and lamb joints, a whole salmon and a colourful selection of salads. Equally inviting are the delights on the sweet trolley, a rarity in pubs, with temptations such as Paris-Brest, apricot and ginger charlotte, profiteroles, chocolate gateau, pear tart – most certainly none of your bought-in puds here! Landlord John Arnold keeps an eye on diners, making sure their needs are satisfied. *Open 11-3, 6.30-11 (Sun 12-3, 7-10.30). Bar Food 12-2, 6.30-9.30 (no food Sun eve). Beer Greene King. Garden, outdoor eating.* Amex, MasterCard, **VISA**

GOUDHURST — Star & Eagle — B&B

Tel 01580 211512   Fax 01580 211416   Map 11 B5
High Street Goudhurst Kent TN17 1AL

Behind the splendid timbered and gabled facade vintage charm and modern comfort blend harmoniously in a fine 14th-century hostelry owned by Whitbread. Period appeal survives in exposed beams, vaulted stonework and old brick fireplaces in the public rooms, while creaking floors and odd angles are the order of the day in the bedrooms. These vary in size and shape and the majority are furnished in pine, though the four-poster room has some antiques. The inn is less than two miles from the A21. *Open 11-11 (Sun 12-10.30). Beer Flowers Original, Fremlins. Garden. Family room, children's playroom. **Accommodation** 11 bedrooms, 9 en suite, £48 Sun-Thur, £53 Fri & Sat (four-poster £60-£70 Fri & Sat, single £35-£40). Children welcome overnight (under-5s stay free in parents' room, 3-16s £15), additional bed & cot available.* Amex, MasterCard, **VISA**

GRANGE MOOR   Kaye Arms   FOOD

Tel 01924 848385   Map 6 C1
29 Wakefield Road Grange Moor West Yorkshire WF4 4BG

🐟 ☺ ☿

The Kaye Arms, under the guidance of the enthusiastic and hard working Coldwell
family, continues to thrive, attracting a loyal dining clientele from miles around.
Arrive early for the table of your choice (there are no reservations) and lunch at
leisure from a legion of choices. Top sellers include the cheese soufflé with Waldorf
salad and smoked chicken; sandwiches like marinated chicken or smoked salmon and
cream cheese are always popular, as are ploughman's platters – all served with home-
made bread (36 loaves are now baked daily to keep up with demand). More
substantial lunch and evening fare brings into play the likes of swordfish with salsa
verde, marinated tuna steak with Caesar salad, first-class chargrilled steaks and
vegetarain options like flat mushrooms stuffed with goat's cheese, walnuts and leeks.
For pudding try the home-made sticky toffee pudding or the crème brulée. To the
uninitiated (and the brewery, perhaps), the complaint might be that this is no pub, as
crisps and real ales are totally overlooked; yet the choice of twelve carefully-chosen
wines by the glass remain, in this context, a better complement. A policy of three
pounds added to the cost price of any bottle (rather than a triple multiplication of it)
provides plenty of choice and value at a price which the average pub-goer should
appreciate. No children in the evenings. *Open 11.30-3, 7-11 (Sat 6.30-11). Closed
Mon lunch.* **Bar Food** *12-2 (except Mon), 7.30-9.30 (Sat from 6.30, Wed-Sat till 10).
No real ales. MasterCard,* **VISA**

GRAYSWOOD   Wheatsheaf Inn   ★   FOOD
                                       Map 11 A6   B&B

Tel 01428 644440
Grayswood Haslemere Surrey GU27 2DE

🐟 ☐ ☺

Victorian village inn, located beside the busy A286 near the parish church, cricket
pitch and green (where there's a children's playground), run by Rex and Janet
Colman. There's a neat and comfortable bar area with older-style furniture, quality
prints and fabrics, with the adjacent spacious L-shaped restaurant sporting artistic
plants, marble-topped tables, a terracotta-tiled floor and cushioned rattan chairs,
creating a relaxing 'Italian-style' ambience. Quality of cooking and food presentation
matches the stylish surroundings, with both the regularly-changing lunch and dinner
menus listing imaginative pub fare; one menu is served throughout. Typical dishes
might include Parma ham and melon, cod in home-made beer batter, warm salad of
mushrooms, garlic and chicken, and freshly-prepared soups – parsnip and ginger – as
well as lighter snacks like sandwiches, a mixed-cheese ploughman's and ham, egg and
bubble and squeak. Specials might encompass rack of lamb with chargrilled vegetables
and rosemary jus, fishcakes with lemon butter, fillet of cod with herb crust and fresh
tomato sauce and rib-eye steak. Round off the meal with a home-made pudding:
perhaps lemon cheesecake with strawberry coulis or summer pudding. Short, global
list of keenly-priced wines. Seven comfortable, en suite bedrooms are housed in a rear
brick extension. Uniformly modern in decor and furnishings, they have clean, marble-
floored bathrooms, as well as TVs, telephones and tea-makers for added comfort.
Children welcome. *Open 11-3, 6-11 (Sun 12-3, 7-10.30).* **Bar Food** *12-2, 6.30-10.
Free House.* **Beer** *Ballard's Best & Wassail, Wadworth 6X, Wheatsheaf Bitter, Hall &
Woodhouse Badger Best, occasional guest beer. Garden, outdoor eating.* **Accommodation** *7
bedrooms, all en suite, £60 (single £45). Children welcome overnight (under-5s stay free in
parents' room), additional bed (£5) & cot available. Check-in by arrangement. No dogs.
Amex, MasterCard,* **VISA**

We endeavour to be as up-to-date as possible but inevitably some changes to
landlords, chefs and other key staff occur after the Guide
has gone to press.

GREAT CHESTERFORD   Plough   A

Tel 01799 530283   Map 10 B3
High Street Great Chesterford Essex CB10 1PL

☺

Delightful 18th-century village pub with a traditional, unspoilt and well-cared-for
interior, despite the addition of a more modern rear extension which houses the bar.
Original cottagey bars feature exposed standing timbers and ceiling beams, two
warming winter fires in inglenooks and neatly arranged tables. The airy extension
leads out on to an attractive patio and lawn for summer alfresco drinking. Children
can enjoy the large adventure playground with its aerial runway, wooden climbing
frames and swings. *Open 11-3, 6-11 (Sun 12-4, 7-10.30).* **Beer** *Greene King. Garden,
children's play area. Family room. MasterCard,* **VISA**

GREAT MISSENDEN   The George   B&B

Tel 01494 862084   Fax 01494 865622   Map 15a E2
94 High Street Great Missenden Buckinghamshire HP16 0BG

A Grade II listed ancient monument, the George still has its 15th-century timbers
intact; there are a dozen foot-thick beams on the bar parlour ceiling alone. There are
two intimate rooms for the main bar and a wood-burning fire, while a further room
is also warmed by a fire. Six smart and spacious en suite bedrooms are individually
decorated and have TV, radio, hairdryer, trouser press, telephone and tea/coffee-
making facilities; four have en suite bathrooms, the other two just a shower. A grass
and shingle patio/garden at the back is safe for children. *Open 11-11 (Sun 12-3.30,
7-10.30).* **Beer** *Wadworth 6X, Adnams Southwold, Bass. Patio, garden, children's play area.*
Accommodation *6 bedrooms, all en suite, £49.95 (four-poster £76 – room only prices,
breakfast £3.25-£7.50). Children welcome overnight. Closed 25 & 26 Dec lunch. Amex,
Diners, MasterCard,* **VISA**

GREAT RISSINGTON   The Lamb   FOOD

Tel 01451 820388   Fax 01451 820724   Map 14a A2   B&B
Great Rissington Cheltenham Gloucestershire GL54 2LP

Zzz...

Enjoying views over the village and rolling Cotswold countryside, this mellow stone-
built pub dates back some 300 years to when it was a farmhouse. Well extended over
the years by the Cleverly family, the interior comprises two civilised and comfortable
bars, both decorated with plates, pictures and collections of old cigarette tins; above
one of the fireplaces is a propeller from a wartime bomber which crashed in the
garden. Home-cooked bar food is listed on a blackboard and ranges from French
onion soup and chicken liver paté for a snack or starter to steak pie, liver and bacon,
lamb curry and whole lemon sole. A separate menu operates in the neat rear
restaurant. Tranquil overnight accommodation is offered in fourteen charming
bedrooms. All are individually decorated with pretty fabrics and wall coverings,
antique furnishings and two sport carved four-poster beds. Maintained to a good
standard with good en suite facilities (five with showers rather than baths), they make
a virtue out of not having television or radios in most of the rooms, but addicts will
find a television (and log fire) in the cosy residents' lounge as well as in the six top-of-
the-range suites. Two new spacious suites 'Millie's House' and 'Jemmima's House' are
located at the bottom of the garden on the site of the indoor swimming pool. The
peaceful summer hillside garden makes the most of the views, as do some of the
bedrooms. *Open 11.30-2.30, 6.30-11 (Sun 12-2.30, 7-10.30).* **Bar Food** *12-1.45, 7-9
(till 9.30 Fri & Sat). Free House.* **Beer** *Morland Old Speckled Hen, guest beer. Garden,
outdoor eating.* **Accommodation** *14 bedrooms, all en suite, £52 (four-poster £60, suite £65-
£75, single from £30). Children welcome overnight (under-2s free if sharing parents' room),
additional bed (£10) & cot available (£3.50). Dogs £1.50. Pub and accommodation closed
25 & 26 Dec. Amex, MasterCard,* **VISA**

Many **B&B** establishments offer reduced rates for weekend and
out-of-season bookings. Always ask about special deals for longer stays. Beware
half-board terms in inns where we do not recommend the **FOOD.**

GREAT RYBURGH	Boar Inn	B&B

Tel 01328 829212   Map 10 C1
Great Ryburgh Fakenham Norfolk NR21 0DX

Zzz...

If you are looking for peaceful and quiet accommodation within handy reach of the
Norfolk coastline, the Boar Inn, a white-washed pub nestling near the River Wensum
in a sleepy village, is the place to go. On chilly nights a log fire crackles in the huge
inglenook fireplace of the low-beamed bar and there are more beams upstairs in the
cottagey bedrooms. By early 1997, the three homely bedrooms with shared facilities
will have been upgraded and extended, creating five fully en suite rooms, including
one family room. *Open 11-2.30, 6.30-11 (Sun 12-3, 7-10.30). Free House.*
Beer Greene King IPA, Wensum Bitter, Adnams Bitter, guest beer. Garden. *Accommodation*
5 bedrooms all en suite, £45 (single £25). Children welcome overnight (under-4s free, 4-10s
£5, over-10s £8 in family room), cot available. MasterCard, VISA

GREAT TEW	Falkland Arms	FOOD

Tel 01608 683653   Fax 01608 683656   Map 14a B1   **B&B**
Great Tew Oxfordshire OX7 4DB

Great Tew has the inestimable advantage of being a bit out of the way and not on the
main tourist trail. It must be one of the prettiest of Cotswold villages. Despite the
ambition implied by its name, it's actually rather a small place, with barely a score of
mostly thatched cottages, a small general store and, naturally, in its rightful place
opposite the church, the village inn. Dating back to the 16th century, the creeper-clad
Falkland Arms must be close to everybody's ideal country pub, with high-backed
settles, a flagstone floor and a prized collection of hundreds of jugs and mugs hanging
from the old beams. 60 malt whiskies, 20 country wines and nine well-kept ales are
available, as are snuff and even clay pipes ready-filled with tobacco. Food is served at
lunchtimes only from a short, but varied, blackboard menu that changes daily but
always includes a vegetarian dish (spinach and tomato quiche), along with a
ploughman's and filled baps. Everything is home-made, from Stilton and cauliflower
soup and lasagne to chicken and ham pie and lamb steak with mushroom gravy. Four
cottagey bedrooms, two with four-poster beds and two with old iron bedsteads, are
furnished with antiques and decorated with pretty co-ordinating fabrics and wall
coverings. The largest, under the eaves, has a pitched ceiling, exposed timbers and
its own en suite bathroom. Others have showers and, all but one, their own toilets.
Televisions and tea/coffee facilities are standard, and you can help yourself to fresh
milk from the kitchen. A pretty garden shaded by a large hornbeam tree, complete
with dovecote, is the perfect spot for summer alfresco drinking. Well-behaved
children are welcome indoors. *Open 11.30-2.30, 6-11 (Sun 12-2, 7-10.30). Closed*
Mon lunch (except Bank Holidays). Bar Food 12-2 (except Sun & Mon). Free House.
Beer Donnington Best, Hook Norton Best, Wadworth 6X, Hall & Woodhouse Tanglefoot,
five guest beers. Garden, outdoor eating, children's play area. Accommodation 4 bedrooms,
3 en suite (one with bath), £50 (single £30). Children welcome overnight (under-5s free if
staying in parents' room). Check-in by arrangement. No dogs. No credit cards.

GREAT YELDHAM	White Hart	★ FOOD

Tel 01787 237250   Fax 01787 238044   Map 10 C3
Poole Street Great Yeldham Halstead Essex CO9 4HJ

On the northern outskirts of the village alongside the main road (A604, between
Halstead and Haverhill), this substantial black-and-white timbered inn dates from 1505.
Chef-patron Roger Jones, previously at the *Pheasant* in Keyston (qv), opened up here as
part of the Huntsbridge Group in 1995. Oak beams, pillars, and polished, candle-lit
tables create a comfortable, smart and very traditional ambience in the restaurant where
you'll find an exciting and varied menu that's modern and innovative but also has its
classical elements. Mediterranean and Oriental influences feature strongly on this main
menu, which is available throughout the building (as is a lighter snack menu with
ploughman's, pasta, Greek salad and Lincolnshire sausages with mash and gravy), and

one may choose very informal service in the bar and garden or more formal presentation in the no-smoking restaurant. Typically, one might find dishes like ravioli of Mediterranean vegetables and gorgonzola with a tomato and chili relish and rocket salad, hot Thai soup with chicken, coconut milk, ginger, coriander, lemon grass and noodles, roast monkfish with black tagliatelle, mangetout and sun-dried tomato chutney, and a very generous chargrilled sirloin steak with field mushrooms, roasted onions, roasted plum tomatoes and really splendid, chunky chips. Desserts are unmissable: try the bourbon whisky and maple syrup (or honey and cardamom) ice cream with pistachio shortbread, hot chocolate tart with crème fraiche or raspberry brulée with an almond tuile; interesting dessert wines tempt on the bottom of the pudding menu. The main wine list is yet another fabulous volume prepared by John Hoskins (who runs the Huntsbridge Group). Quite simply, you'll see none better – you might find longer lists, but in terms of quality, this is the real business with diverse, very fairly-priced wines from around the world, each carefully described. Lots are also available by the glass, offering fantastic value. Drink well and enjoy! Service couldn't be more charming and obliging. No smoking. *Open 12-3, 6-11.* **Bar Meals** *12-2, 6-10. Free House.* **Beer** *Adnams Bitter, two guest beers. Closed 25 Dec eve, all 26 Dec & 1 Jan. Amex, Diners, MasterCard,* **VISA**

GRETA BRIDGE — Morritt Arms Hotel — B&B

Tel 01833 627232   Fax 01833 627392   Map 5 D3
Greta Bridge Rokeby Barnard Castle Co Durham DL12 9SE

Former 17th-century inn located just off the A66 4 miles from Barnard Castle, offering traditional charm and hospitality. In the past two years, owners Peter Phillips and Barbara-Anne Johnson have worked hard recreating the warmth and style of days gone by. The atmosphere of the public rooms is characterised by polished block floors laid with Chinese carpets and the deeply-comfortable, loose-covered armchairs arranged in small groups in the cosy lounge with its open log fire. The main Dickens Bar, named after Charles Dickens who stayed here in 1839 while researching Nicholas Nickleby, has a mural painted in 1946 by John Gilroy, who took well-known local figures and created a Dickensian theme around them; the Sir Walter Scott Bar has more of a 'local' atmosphere. The bedrooms are simple and homely, some boasting four-poster and brass beds and each have a trouser press, hairdryer, mineral water and remote-controlled TV. Attractive gardens. *Open 11-11 (Sun 12-10.30). Free House.* **Beer** *Tetley Cask, Theakston Best. Garden, croquet, bowls, children's play area.* **Accommodation** *17 bedrooms, all en suite, £70-£95 (single £45-£55). Children welcome overnight (under-16s stay free in parents' room), additional bed & cot available. Amex, Diners, MasterCard,* **VISA**

GRETNA — Gretna Chase Hotel — B&B

Tel 01461 337517   Fax 01461 337766   Map 4 C2
Gretna Carlisle Cumbria DG16 5JB

Patrons of the first marriage house over the Scottish border used the nearby Gretna Chase for stabling their horses. That function has long since ceased, but today's honeymooners can install themselves in a splendid four-poster suite. All rooms (with TVs and direct-dial phones) feature quality furniture and fabrics, and most overlook the award-winning garden of 2 ½ acres. There is a spacious Victorian reception hall, plenty of bar space and a little lounge. Impending upgrading of bedrooms will see all having en suite facilities. *Open 11-3, 6-11 (Sat 11-11, Sun 12-3, 6-10.30).* **Beer** *Theakston Best. Garden.* **Accommodation** *8 bedrooms, 6 en suite, £60 (four-poster £80, single from £38). Children welcome overnight (under-3s stay free in parents' room, 4-12s, £5), additional bed & cot available. Amex, MasterCard,* **VISA**

GRETTON — Royal Oak — FOOD

Tel 01242 602477   Fax 01242 602387   Map 14 C1
Gretton Winchombe Gloucestershire GL54 5EP

Extensive gardens and playing areas (including a tennis court for rent) and regular summer visits by the steam train from Winchombe all contribute to the irresistible summer attractions of the Royal Oak. Low hop-hung beams adorned with pewter mugs and chamber pots and open log fires, whose glow is reflected in polished flagstones, make it equally appealing in winter. Add to this a good range of real ales and a vast blackboard menu and you have unravelled the secrets of this Cotswold pub's popular success. Mussels grilled with Stilton, chicken liver paté and garlic mushrooms can be either snacks or starters. Main courses run from Gloucester sausages with Cumberland sauce and ham, cheese and mushroom pasta bake to lamb cutlets with mint sauce. Twice-weekly fish deliveries may yield halibut with yoghurt and Cajun spices, alongside the usual trout and mackerel dishes. No sandwiches, but ploughman's platters are served all day. Finish off, perhaps, with chocolate fudge cake or caramelised Granny's apple. Children welcome. *Open 11-3, 6-11 (Sun 12-3, 7-10.30).* **Bar Food** *12-2, 7-9.30. Free House.* **Beer** *Smiles Best, John Smith's, Wadworth 6X, Ruddles County, Morland Old Speckled Hen, Marston's Pedigree. Garden, outdoor eating. Closed all 25 & 26 Dec. Amex, MasterCard,* **VISA**

GRINDLEFORD — Maynard Arms Hotel — FOOD

Tel 01433 630321   Fax 01433 630445   Map 6 C2   **B&B**
Main Road Grindleford Derbyshire S30 1HP

 Zzz... ☺

A solid-stone roadside inn located in the Peak National Park, on a hillside outside the village. There's a spacious and attractive public bar, and the Longshaw cocktail bar exudes a stylish and comfortable ambience for the enjoyment of some simply conceived and reliably produced bar food. Regular dishes include almond chicken, seafood linguine and original Yorkshire puddings filled with beef stew or Cumberland sausage. More adventurous choices may include swordfish steak with lemon butter, braised steak with a rich red wine sauce and half rack of ribs with barbecue sauce. All comers are invited also to leave room for the traditional Bakewell pudding served hot with cream. As befits an old coaching inn, the grand style, large, airy bedrooms overlook the Derwent Valley through elegant stone mullion windows. Suitably up-to-date accessories include direct-dial phones, remote-control TVs and trouser presses. Residents' lounge and conference/function facilities. *Open 11-3, 6-11, (Sun 12-10.30).* **Bar Food** *12-2, 6-9.30 (Sun 12-9.30). Free House.* **Beer** *Flowers Original, Morland Old Speckled Hen, Boddingtons. Garden, outdoor eating. Family room.* **Accommodation** *11 bedrooms, all en suite, £65-£75 (weekend £85-£95, single £49-£55, weekend £60). Children welcome overnight, additional bed (£15) & cot available. Amex, MasterCard,* **VISA**

GUITING POWER — Ye Olde Inne — A

Tel 01451 850392   Map 14a A1
Winchcombe Road Guiting Power Stow-on-the-Wold Gloucestershire GL54 5UX

The far end of the single lane running through this picturesque Cotswold village goes by the unlikely name of Th'Ollow Bottom. Here the Olde Inne nestles – a low, listed, 17th-century stone pub and a little hollowed out itself inside. Best of the three tiny rooms is the flagstone-floored dining-room with its sandblasted ceiling timbers and exposed inglenook. New owners took over as we went to press. *Open 11.30-2.30, 6-11 (from 5.30 Fri), Sun 12-3, 7-10.30. Free House.* **Beer** *Hook Norton Best, Bass, guest beer. Garden, patio, outdoor eating. MasterCard,* **VISA**

GUNWALLOE — Halzephron Inn   ★ — FOOD

Tel 01326 240406   Map 12 A4   **B&B**
Gunwalloe Helston Cornwall TR12 7QB

Zzz...

Situated four miles south of Helston on the west coast of the Lizard peninsula, the 500-year-old Halzephron Inn commands an enviable position perched high up above Gunwalloe Fishing Cove, with spectacular views across Mount's Bay to Penzance and the Land's End peninsula (in fine weather). Its rugged stone exterior feels the full force of 2,000 miles of wild Atlantic weather, but inside there is a genuine warm welcome from amiable hosts Angela and Harry Davy Thomas. The two spick-and-span, low-ceilinged inter-connecting bars have been simply, yet tastefully refurbished and feature warming winter fires, general fishing memorabilia and original watercolours of Cornish scenes. The intimate 'Captain's Table' cottage dining-room has a head-cracking low ceiling, stone walls and a cosy atmosphere, plus a charming sea view.

Both lunch and evening printed menus offer a varied selection of dishes to please all tastes, from pub favourites to good steaks and home-cooked fare. However, the real emphasis is on the twice daily-changing blackboard menu which lists more imaginative fare using the best of local ingredients, notably fresh fish. Here everything is home-made, from mushroom and watercress soup, scallops with white wine and herb sauce, monkfish kebabs, fish pie, hot baked savoury crab, spicy garlic chicken, lamb's livers in orange sauce, and pork with praprika and sherry. Vegetarians will not be disappointed with cheese and herb soufflé or tomato and courgette bake. Puddings like treacle sponge pudding and pecan and maple syrup tart. High standards extend upstairs to the two delightful bedrooms which have been kitted out with flair; they enjoy rolling country views. Notable features include old stripped-pine furniture, Laura Ashley fabrics and wallpapers, colourful cushioned director's chairs, hand-made quilts, original watercolours and nice added touches like fresh fruit, biscuits, mineral water and various books and magazines. No children under 14 overnight. Restless children will be kept amused in the family room, complete with blackboard, toys and games (and a children's menu) and created from an outside stone and slate store. An excellent base from which to explore this unspoilt corner of Cornwall. *Open 11-3, 6.30-11 (Sun 12-3, 7-10.30)*. **Bar Food** *12-2, 7-9.30 (till 9 Sun)*. *Free House.* **Beer** *Fergusons Dartmoor Best Bitter, Sharp's Own & Doombar. Garden, outdoor eating. Family room.* **Accommodation** *2 bedrooms, both en suite (one with bath), £50 (single £35). Check-in by arrangement. Accommodation closed 24 & 25 Dec, pub closed all 25 Dec. MasterCard,* **VISA**

HAILEY	Bird in Hand	FOOD

Tel 01993 868321   Fax 01993 868702   Map 14a B2   **B&B**
Whiteoak Green Hailey Witney Oxfordshire OX8 5XP

A delightful 'residential country inn' in a rural setting, one mile north of Hailey on B4022. The neat, low-walled roadside garden gives an indication of the standards aimed for inside and the large car park shows its popularity as a dining pub. Inside, four stone-walled bar rooms include one with a long bar, sofa, pews and old tables, plus another with an inglenook where a wood fire burns during winter; the rooms are candle-lit at night. Ivan Reid's menu offers a long list of dishes that might include smoked goose breast with pickled red cabbage and pear, smoked salmon fishcake with home-made pesto, three or so pasta dishes (linguine with queen scallops, salmon and prawns in a wine and dill sauce), rack of lamb with aubergines and tomato in a redcurrant sauce, and confit of duck with potato rösti and pulses. These are supplemented by a blackboard of daily fresh fish (roast shark steak with pimentos and sweet chili sauce, grilled octopus and fennel with tomato salsa, turban of salmon and sole with scallops and chives) and other specials like globe artichoke with smoked salmon and scrambled egg, and roast lamb hock with garlic, rosemary and honey. The snack card offers the likes of ploughman's lunches, sandwiches, scampi, home-cooked cold ham and children's favourites. Sixteen spacious and comfortable, cottagey rooms are in a U-shaped, two-storey building with wooden balconies overlooking a central grassed courtyard. Two ground-floor twin rooms for the disabled; two large, family rooms have a double and a single bed plus a sofa bed and room for a cot. Pine furnishings, thoughtful touches and good housekeeping bring all rooms up to an above-average pub standard. Room-only prices are quoted, but the prices we quote here include cooked breakfasts (as for all the entries in this Guide). *Open 11-11 (Sun 12-3, 7-10.30)*. **Bar Food** *12-1.45, 7-9.30 (till 9.15 Sun)*. *Free House.* **Beer** *Boddingtons, Marston's Pedigree, Wadworth 6X. Patio, outdoor eating.* **Accommodation** *16 bedrooms, all en suite, £53.95 Sun-Thu, £65 Fri & Sat (single £46.95, £53 Fri & Sat). Children welcome overnight (under-3s stay free in parents' room, over-3s £15), additional bed & cot available. Check-in by arrangement on Sun afternoon. Closed all 25 & 26 Dec. MasterCard,* **VISA**

We only recommend food (Bar Food) in those establishments highlighted with the **FOOD** symbol.

HALLATON — Bewicke Arms — FOOD

Tel 01858 555217   Map 7 D4
1 Eastgate Hallaton Leicestershire LE16 8UB

☺

400-year-old thatched country inn standing above the Welland Valley in the heart
of fine Leicestershire countryside. Hallaton itself is locally renowned for the parish
church's Norman tower, the conical butter cross on the village green – right across the
road from the pub – and the tiny village museum which offers a unique insight into its
rural past. The pub is a cracking good local and a predictable printed menu lists the
usual steaks and grills, ploughman's lunches and sandwiches – look to the specials board
for more adventurous options. Starters typically include a 'help yourself' crock of
home-made soup (carrot and tomato) and deep-fried Brie, while top-sellers among the
main courses include beef goulash, orange chicken, and salmon with lemon and dill
butter. Vegetarians get a good look in, too, with aubergine and chick pea moussaka,
and there's a fair choice of home-made puddings of the banoffi pie and treacle sponge
and custard genre. The pub is consistently busy and the Bottom Room, stone clad with
a bow window, Austrian blinds and an effective library theme, opens when demand
dictates. At weekends it's almost certain to be full, so better book. Children welcome.
Open 12-2.30 (till 3 Sun), 7-11. **Bar Food** *12-2, 7-9.45. Free House.* **Beer** *Marston's
Pedigree, Ruddles Best & County, Bass. Garden, patio, outdoor eating. MasterCard,* **VISA**

HALTWHISTLE — Milecastle Inn — FOOD

Tel 01434 320682 & 321372   Map 5 D2
Military Road Haltwhistle Northumberland NE49 9NN

A mere 500 yards from the 42nd milecastle of Hadrian's Wall, the Paynes' neatly-kept
inn stands on the B6318, 1½ miles out of town. Probably once a small farm with
attendant drover's cottages, it would seem to have a long history of hospitality.
Today's cosy, stone-lined interior is hung with a vast collection of brass ornaments and
artefacts. The bar nonetheless runs to no more than a half dozen tables. Daily menus
are thus kept sensibly short with an emphasis on hearty pies (wild boar and duckling)
and specials like venison and redcurrant casserole and chicken breast with port and
basil sauce. A straightforward printed menu lists the usual pub fare, including
sandwiches and ploughman's (lunchtime only). There's a front patio and a large, safe
garden for leisurely enjoyment of the good real ales. Walkers in muddy boots (and
children under 5) are not allowed in the bar. *Open 12-2.30, 6.30-11 (till 10.30 Sun).
Closed Sun eve in winter.* **Bar Food** *12-2, 6.30-9. Free House.* **Beer** *Tetley, Richardson
Four Seasons, Ind Coope Burton Ale, guest beers. Garden, outdoor eating. Amex, Diners,
MasterCard,* **VISA**

HAMSTEAD MARSHALL — White Hart Inn — FOOD / B&B

Tel 01488 658201   Fax 01488 657192   Map 14a B4
Hamstead Marshall Newbury Berkshire RG20 0HW

The splendid herbaceous borders around the neat lawn at the front of this 16th-
century inn are very English, and the pride and joy of Dorothy Aromando, but inside
the Latin influence of husband Nicola predominates in the White Hart's Italian menu.
A few old beams, mingling with some newer ones, give clues to the age of the
building, but the decor is basically simple: red plush in the bar, red cloths on the tables
of the restaurant leading off it. The same hand-written menu serves for both bar and
restaurant. Nicola makes his own pasta and consequently there's a selection of pasta
dishes alongside meat dishes. The menu also offers mushrooms stuffed with pine nuts
and herbs and topped with goat's cheese and garlic oil, Dover sole poached in white
wine and served with prawns and cream, and pancetta wrapped scallops grilled with
lemon butter. Amongst the home-made puddings, the crème caramel is outstanding,
freshly cooked and with the topping caramelised to just the right degree; tiramisu and
cassata might also appear alongside sticky toffee pudding. An old barn to the rear of
the pub has been converted into six uncluttered bedrooms with pine furniture and
good cotton bedding. All have neat en suite bathrooms with showers over their

bathtubs. Get one of the two large rooms under the eaves, if you can, which have sloping ceilings and exposed timbers, as well as an extra bed for family use. The two single rooms are very compact. Good, freshly-cooked breakfasts set you up for the day ahead. *Open 11.45-3.30, 6-11. Closed Sunday.* **Bar Food** *12-2.30, 6.30-9.30 (till 10 Fri & Sat). Free House.* **Beer** *Wadworth 6X, guest beer. Garden, outdoor eating.* **Accommodation** *6 bedrooms, all en suite, £65 (family room sleeping three £65, single £45). Children welcome overnight, additional bed available. Check-in by arrangement. No dogs.* MasterCard, **VISA**

HARBERTON   Church House Inn   A

Tel 01803 863707   Map 13 D3
Church House Inn Harberton Totnes Devon TQ9 7SF

Tucked away by the church in a sleepy village amid steep narrow lanes off the A381 Totnes to Kingsbridge road, this fine building was originally a chantry house for monks, one of whom is said to be still lurking on the premises, and the Church House didn't pass out of clerical hands until 1950. The carefully removed plaster of centuries has revealed ancient fluted oak beams, a magnificent medieval oak screen, a Tudor window frame and 13th-century glass. The open-plan bar area was once the great chamber, and is now furnished with old pews and settles. The owners plan to offer accommodation in four bedrooms (sharing facilities) by late 1996. *Open 12-2.30, 6-11 (Sun 12-3, 7-10.30). Free House.* **Beer** *Bass, Courage Best, guest beers. Family room.* MasterCard, **VISA**

HARE HATCH   Queen Victoria   FOOD

Tel 01734 402477   Map 15a D3
Blakes Lane Hare Hatch Berkshire RG10 9TA

This convivial, low-ceilinged 17th-century two-roomed local can be found just off the A4 and is a popular refreshment spot between Reading and Maidenhead. Simply furnished interior which still has some of the original straw and dung walling, a collection of miniature jugs hanging from the ceiling rafters, a real fire and a fruit machine. Blackboards list a reliable selection of bar meals along with the usual favourites. Choices may include garlic mushrooms with black olive toast, spicy Thai kebab with rice and main dishes like pork escalope with grain mustard sauce, lamb and orange casserole and diced lemon chicken and rice. Colourful alfresco patio seating amid overflowing flower baskets and tubs. Children welcome. *Open 11-3, 5.30-11 (Sun 12-3, 7-10.30).* **Bar Food** *11.45-2.45, 6.30-10.45 (Sun 12-2.45, 7-10.15).* **Beer** *Brakspear, guest beer. Patio, outdoor eating. No credit cards.*

HAREWOOD   Harewood Arms   B&B

Tel 0113 288 6566 Fax 0113 288 6064   Map 6 C1
Harrogate Road Harewood Leeds LS17 9LH

Zzz...

A fashionable address opposite the gates of Harewood House and convenient location on the A61 halfway between Leeds and Harrogate ensure particular mention for this elegant inn. Formerly a coaching house, with a history dating back to 1815, it has been meticulously restored by Sam Smith, the brewers of Tadcaster. Though fully carpeted and rather studiously appointed, the three lounge bars retain an essentially pubby feel and are much frequented by a business, golfing and race-going fraternity. Traditional oak bed frames and freestanding furniture have been used as a unifying theme in individually designed bedrooms, the majority of which are in the former coachhouse wing overlooking the terrace, formal rose garden and rolling Yorkshire countryside. Four are conveniently located on the ground floor. A full range of room accessories – from remote-control TVs and trouser presses to bidets and over-bath showers – is impressive, a factor reflected in their rather higher-than-average room prices. *Open 11-11 (Sun 12-10.30).* **Beer** *Sam Smith's Old Brewery Bitter. Garden, terrace. Family room.* **Accommodation** *24 rooms, all en suite, £78 (reduced weekend tariff, single £50). Children welcome overnight, additional bed (£12) & cot (£8) available. Amex, Diners, MasterCard, **VISA***

HASCOMBE | White Horse | FOOD

Tel 01483 208258   Fax 01483 208200   Map 11 A5
Hascombe Godalming Surrey GU8 4JA

Grade II listed, 16th-century pub nestling in a beautiful corner of Surrey close to
Winkworth Arboretum (NT). Charming and immaculate interior comprising a
rambling series of unspoilt, beamed rooms, all tastefully decorated with Laura Ashley
wallpapers and kitted out with attractive pine in cosy alcoves, decent prints and open
fires. Neat restaurant area with linen-clothed tables and separate hop and farming
memorabilia-adorned public bar. Reliable bar food choices are chalked up on a daily-
changing blackboard and may include home-made green lentil soup, salmon
fishcakes, chargrilled steaks and puddings like blackcurrant and apple crumble and
carrot cake. Also on offer are imaginative door-step sandwiches (smoked salmon) and
a selection of ploughman's. Colourful summer terrace and pretty, extensive garden,
ideal for fine weather imbibing. *Open 11-3, 5.30-11 (Sat 11-11 summer, 12-3, 6-11
winter), Sun 12-3, 7-10.30 (12-10.30 summer).* **Bar Food** *12-2.20 (till 2.30 Sat & Sun),
7-10 (till 9.30 Sun).* **Beer** *Wadworth 6X, King & Barnes Sussex, Hall & Woodhouse
Badger Best. Garden, outdoor eating. Family room. Amex, MasterCard,* **VISA**

HASELBURY PLUCKNETT | Haselbury Inn | FOOD

Tel & Fax 01460 72488   Map 13 F2
Haselbury Plucknett Crewkerne Somerset TA18 7RJ

Spacious dining establishment located just off the A30 and run (in his own way!) by
James Pooley and wife Kathy. Comprehensive menus are on show for both the
Country Bar and Stables restaurant, candle-lit by night and set with lacy cloths and
fresh flowers. Specials boards supplement the bar offerings: chicken tikka masala, beef
steak kebabs, whole bacon hock. Fish, flesh and fowl all appear in voluminous guises
on the Continental influenced restaurant menu, while Sunday sees a roast lunch and
barbecue selections are offered nightly. While there is a clear reliance on the fryers,
vegetables at least are fresh and plentiful. Up to 25 gooey, creamy desserts with apple
strudel, treacle tart and fruit pavlovas being ever-popular. To end, there are plenty of
liqueur coffees and particularly good espresso. *Open 12-3, 7-11 (Sun 12-3, 7-10.30).
Closed Mon.* **Bar Food** *12-2, 7-10 (not Mon). Free House.* **Beer** *Hickelbury, Butcombe
Bitter, Wadworth 6X, Charles Wells Bombardier, Teignworthy Beachcomber, Smiles Best,
Eldridge Pope Potters Pride, Otter Bitter, Boddingtons. Garden, children's play area. Amex,
MasterCard,* **VISA**

HASTINGWOOD COMMON | Rainbow & Dove | A

Tel 01279 415419   Map 11 B4
Hastingwood Common Essex CM17 9JX

Charming old rose-covered pub dating from the 16th-century, its name a reference to
Noah's Ark (and it gets almost as crowded inside). Despite its close proximity to the
busy M11 (a quarter of a mile from J7), the garden is a popular attraction on summer
days. Escape the incessant traffic noise inside, within the three characterful and cosy,
low-beamed rooms with open fires, rustic furnishings and collections of horse brasses
and a few golf clubs. Children welcome. *Open 11.30-3, 5.30-11 (Sun 12-4, 7-10.30).*
Beer *Ansells Best & Mild (winter), Flowers Original, Bass, Friary Meux Bitter. Garden.
Amex, MasterCard,* **VISA**

Many **B&B** establishments offer reduced rates for weekend and
out-of-season bookings. Always ask about special deals for longer stays. Beware
half-board terms in inns where we do not recommend the **FOOD**.

HATHERLEIGH — George Hotel — B&B

Tel 01837 810454   Fax 01837 810901   Map 13 D2
Market Street Hatherleigh Okehampton Devon EX20 3JN

🍺 **Zzz...** ☺

Dating from 1450, this ancient cob-and-thatch town-centre inn was once a rest house and sanctuary for the monks of Tavistock. In later years it became a brewery, tavern, a law court and a coaching inn before developing into what is now a most comfortable and historic small hotel. Off the central cobbled courtyard in the converted brewhouse and coachman's loft is the main bar and family area extension, while the original inn's bar oozes charm and antiquity with old beams, an oak-panelled wall, an enormous fireplace and an assortment of cushioned seats and sofas. It is now largely confined to residents or waiting diners, as the attractive restaurant is next door. The Farmers Bar across the courtyard is like a small bistro and locals' bar and opens on Thu-Sat nights only. Sloping floors and low 'head-cracking' doorways lead to eleven individually furnished bedrooms with pretty chintz fabrics, pieces of old or antique furniture and generally good clean en-suite facilities. Three rooms have elegant four-poster beds. TVs, telephones and tea-making facilities are the added comforts and residents also have the use of a charming lounge and the outdoor swimming pool. Eight/ten wines available by the glass. New owners took over just as we went to press. *Open 11-3.30, 6-11 (Sun 12-3, 7-10.30). Free House.* **Beer** *Bass, Boddingtons, two guest beers.* **Accommodation** *11 bedrooms, 9 en suite, £69.50, four-poster £82, single £48-£55. Children welcome overnight, additional bed (£6) & cot supplied. Amex, MasterCard,* **VISA**

HATHERLEIGH — Tally Ho — B&B

Tel 01837 810306   Fax 01837 811079   Map 13 D2
14 Market Street Hatherleigh Okehampton Devon EX20 3JN

🍺

The exterior appearance of this market town-centre building belies the true age of this 15th-century inn, which boasts a charmingly rustic bar with a heavily beamed ceiling, sturdy old furnishings, two stone fireplaces, both with warming woodburners and various plates and attractive paintings decorate the walls. Owners Jason and Megan Tidy, who have continued the tradition of brewing on site the excellent range of real ales for the pub since taking over, plan to extend the dining-room and carry out further alterations in the coming year. Superior overnight accommodation is provided in three well-designed and comfortable bedrooms; all furnished with old pine and decorated with attractive fabrics and quality prints, with added comforts including TV, clock/radios and fresh and clean bathrooms with expensive sanitary ware. Children welcome. *Open 11-2.30, 6-11, (Sun 12-2.30, 7-10.30). Free House.* **Beer** *Own brews: Potboiler's Brew, Tarka's Tipple, Nutters, Thurgia, Jollop (winter), Master Jacks Mild (summer). Garden, aviary.* **Accommodation** *3 bedrooms, all en suite (one with bath), £60 (single £30). Check-in by arrangement. No dogs. Amex, MasterCard,* **VISA**

HATHERSAGE — Hathersage Inn — B&B

Tel 01433 650259   Fax 01433 651199   Map 6 C2
Hathersage Derbyshire S30 1BB

Ivy-clad, stone-built 18th-century inn standing by Hathersage's steep main street in the heart of the Peak District National Park; pub to the front where the Cricketers' Bar (bar snacks available at lunch and dinner) is full of local memorabilia and quietly residential to the rear with a lounge bar and cosy dining-room. Bedrooms are neatly kept, with plenty of extras from TV and radio-alarm to drinks tray and fresh fruit. There are six Executive rooms, two four-posters and a honeymoon suite. Children are not encouraged. *Open 11-3, 6-11 (Sun 12-10.30 – possibly closed Sun afternoons in winter). Free House.* **Beer** *John Smith's, Webster's Yorkshire Bitter, Courage Directors.* **Accommodation** *15 bedrooms, all en suite, £64.50 (four-poster & Executives £74.50, single £49.50-£54.50). Amex, Diners, MasterCard,* **VISA**

THE HAVEN | Blue Ship | A

Tel 01403 822709   Map 11 A6
The Haven Billingshurst West Sussex RH14 9BS

Hidden in the depths of the Sussex countryside along a tiny lane off the A29 north of Billingshurst, this splendid rural gem is well worth tracking down. An unassuming Victorian brick and tile-hung exterior – festooned with a rampant climbing clematis – hides a charming 15th-century core, characterised by the classic main bar, which features a worn redbrick floor, low heavy beams, a large inglenook and scrubbed pine tables and sturdy wooden benches. Well-kept King & Barnes ales tapped straight from the cask are dispensed via a small hatch servery. A flagstoned passageway leads to two further rooms added in later years, a games room full of traditional pub games – no music or electronic machines here – and access to the peaceful cottage garden, a delight on warm summer days. *Open 11-3, 6-11 (Sun 12-3,7-10.30). Beer King & Barnes Sussex Bitter, Broadwood & seasonal ales. Garden, lawn, patio. Family room. No credit cards.*

HAWKSHEAD | Drunken Duck Inn | FOOD

Tel 01539 436347   Fax 01539 436781   Map 4 C3   **B&B**
Barngates Hawkshead Ambleside Cumbria LA22 0NG

 Zzz...

Take the Tarn Hows turning at Outgate off the B5286 to find the Drunken Duck, formerly the Barngate Inn, standing high in the hills with spectacular views across distant Lake Windermere to its backdrop of craggy hills. There's a healthy range of well-kept real ales to accompany an impressive array of bar meals. A hard-working kitchen produces volumes of vegetarian fare from courgette, mushroom and mozzarella bake to Middle Eastern aubergine casserole. In addition to voluminous rolls and ploughman's at lunchtimes comes chicken, orange and butterbean casserole, lamb, spinach and apricot casserole or venison steak in Mexican marinade. Treacle tart and jam roly poly are traditionally filling walkers' puds. Overnight guests are housed in stylish, individually designed bedrooms, some in stripped pine others with carefully chosen antique pieces. Fabrics feature soft restful shades, while the well-lit bathrooms have good over-bath showers, good towelling and quality toiletries. TVs, telephones and tea trays are all provided. *Open 11.30-3, 6-11 (Sun 12-3, 6-10.30).* **Bar Food** *12-2, 6.30-9. Free House.* **Beer** *Yates Bitter & Drunken Duck Ale, Mitchell's Lancaster Bomber, Jennings Bitter, Theakston Old Peculier, Boddingtons. Garden, outdoor eating. Family room.* **Accommodation** *10 bedrooms, all en suite, £69/£79 (single £43.75). Children welcome overnight, additional bed & cot (both £12) available. Pub & accommodation closed 25 Dec. Amex, MasterCard,* **VISA**

> We only recommend food (Bar Food) in those establishments highlighted
> with the **FOOD** symbol.

HAWKSHEAD | Queen's Head Hotel | FOOD

Tel 01539 436271   Fax 01539 436722   Map 4 C3   **B&B**
Hawkshead Cumbria LA22 0NS

The Queen's Head here is that of Elizabeth I; at the heart of this traffic-free village the black and white painted 16th-century frontage hides a cavernous pub within, full of period character and camaraderie. Food from the wide-ranging menu can be enjoyed anywhere in the panelled bar areas and adjacent dining-room, although at busy times it's certainly advble to find a free table first! Begin with seafood risotto or Queen's club salad (black pudding and shredded duck), then, for main course, try the Westmorland pie, braised rabbit with apple and gooseberry sauce, smoked chicken and tarragon with pasta, or choose from the weekly-changing fish board (fresh fish and chips, poached halibut with vermouth, lobster and prawn salad). Lunchtime only snack menu offering sandwiches, ploughman's and filled jacket potatoes. Residents and others wishing to eat in the dining-room at night or for Sunday lunch (served all day) are advised to book in advance. Ten bedrooms within the pub have low beams, modest furnishings and compact en suite bathrooms; two have old-fashioned four-posters and there are a couple of family rooms sleeping three. The balance of the accommodation is in two adjacent cottages which are only yards away. *Open 11-11 (Sun 12-10.30)*. *Bar Food* 12-2.30, 6.15-9.30 (Sun 12-9.30). *Beer Hartleys XB, Robinson's Bitter & Frederic's Bitter. Family room*. *Accommodation* 13 bedrooms, 11 en suite, £59.50 (four-poster £70, single £35). *Children welcome overnight (under-10s £12.50, 10-16s £17.50), additional bed & cot available. Diners, MasterCard, VISA*

HAWORTH   Old White Lion Hotel   B&B

Tel 01535 642313   Fax 01535 646222   Map 6 C1
Main Street Haworth Bradford BD22 8DU

This Brontë village hotel goes back three hundred years. Formerly a coaching inn, part of the old building was a meeting room for masonics. Fourteen well-refurbished and individually decorated bedrooms have en suite bathrooms and are equipped with televisions, radio/alarms, telephones and tea/coffee-making facilities. Three single rooms have en suite showers and two family rooms sleep three and four. Guests can relax in the oak-panelled residents' lounge. The restaurant was created from three weaver's cottages. *Open 11-3, 6-11 (Sun 12-3, 7-10.30)*. *Free House*. *Beer Webster's Yorkshire, Wilson's Original, guest beer. Accommodation* 14 bedrooms, all en suite, £50-£60 (single from £38.50). *Children welcome overnight, additional bed & cot (both £11) available. No dogs (except guide dogs). Amex, Diners, MasterCard, VISA*

HAY-ON-WYE   Old Black Lion   FOOD

Tel 01497 820841   Map 9 D5   B&B
26 Lion Street Hay-on-Wye Hereford & Worcester HR3 5AD

Zzz...

Owners John and Joan Collins run this ever-popular 17th-century coaching inn situated close to what was once the Lion Gate, one of the entrances to the old walled town. On the extensive main bar menu dishes range from ploughman's lunches (try the Continental with salami, soft cheese and garlic sausage) to home-made venison burger, chicken and ham pie and vegetarian options (nut roast with leek, watercress and mustard sauce). The daily specials board might extend the range further to include prawn and bacon chowder, beef Wellington, loin of pork with caramelised apples and oranges, or ragout of wild boar with cranberries and marsala, finishing with chilled lemon tart with iced lime parfait, or apple and calvados pie. A separate bar menu is devoted solely to steaks, sauced or plain. In the evening the equally imaginative Cromwell restaurant menu is available throughout the dining areas. Bedrooms within the main building, of 17th-century origins, render the Black Lion justifiably famous. Refurbishment has generally enhanced the building's character and comforts of high degree that include direct-dial phones, TVs, radios, beverage trays and bright duvets (traditional bedding provided on request). Rooms in the annexe are more modern, though no less comfortable; all rooms (with the exception of one single with a private bathroom) have entirely acceptable en suite facilities. Families particularly enjoy the Cromwell Room with its gallery and two additional beds. Speciality breakfasts include a salmon fisherman's version with smoked eel and aquavit plus one for romantics: scrambled egg with caviar and a quarter bottle of champagne (for two). The whole pub is candle-lit at night and there's no smoking in the restaurant. Not suitable for children under 5 (over-8s in the restaurant only). *Open 11.30-11 (Sun 11.30-10.30)*. *Bar Food* 11.30-2.30, 7-9.30 (Sun 12-2.45, 7-9). *Free House*. *Beer Flowers Original, Fuller's London Pride, Wye Valley Hereford Bitter. Small patio, outdoor eating. Accommodation* 10 bedrooms, 9 en suite, £45.90 (family room sleeping 4 £67.90, single from £19.95). *Children over 5 welcome overnight (5-12s £10, over-12s £14 if sharing parents' room). Amex, MasterCard, VISA*

HAYDON BRIDGE   General Havelock Inn   FOOD

Tel 01434 684376   Map 5 D2
Ratcliffe Road Haydon Bridge Northumberland NE47 6ER

The dark green exterior of the General Havelock certainly helps it stand out from neighbouring cottages. It was named after Sunderland-born General Henry Havelock, who relieved the Indian town of Lucknow in the late 1880s. In the front bar area there are wrought-iron-legged tables, stripped wood and padded benches, and some brilliant wildlife photographs taken by a local photographer. The pub's main draw, though, is its dining-room in the converted stables to the rear, a high-ceilinged room with exposed beams and natural stone walls, The cooking is in the accomplished hands of self-taught chef Angela Clyde, who prides herself on using only fresh local produce. The short lunchtime menu includes soup (tomato and basil) or hot Shields smokie (smoked cod with cheese and white wine) amongst the starters, followed by a daily roast, a fish dish (whole plaice, fresh mussels) and a couple of salads. Sandwiches and ploughman's platters are available at lunchtime only. In the evenings a set price (£19.50) four-course menu has a more upmarket feel. Cooking is of a high standard (pork Dijon, chicken provençal, peppered fillet steak) and the puddings are also first-class: lemon tart and poached pear with butterscotch sauce are typical. Service is friendly and casual but efficient. To the rear of the dining-room is a paved patio which runs down to a lawn and the River Tyne. Weekends (including a popular Sunday lunch) can be very busy, so booking is advised. *Open Wed-Sat 11.30-2.30, 7-11, (Sun 12-2, 8-10.30). Closed all Mon and all Tue, first 2 weeks Sep & 2 weeks Jan.* **Bar Food** *12-2.30 (no bar food eves – restaurant only). Free House.* **Beer** *Tetley. Riverside garden, outdoor eating. No credit cards.*

> We endeavour to be as up-to-date as possible but inevitably some changes to landlords, chefs and other key staff occur after the Guide has gone to press.

HAYTOR VALE   Rock Inn   FOOD   B&B

Tel 01364 661305   Fax 01364 661242   Map 13 D3
Haytor Vale Newton Abbot Devon TQ13 9XP

Zzz...

Dating back 200 years, this sturdy pub stands in a tiny Dartmoor village below Haytor, the best known of the Dartmoor tors. A characterful, traditional interior has sturdy old furnishings, plenty of antique tables, settles, prints, a grandfather clock and various pieces of china over the two fireplaces. Both the main bar and the attractive adjoining rooms are popular settings in which to appreciate the reliably good bar food, with a particularly strong list of light meals (ploughman's lunches, sandwiches, filled jacket potatoes), good hearty snacks, and the promise of fresh vegetables. After a day on the moor healthy appetites can be satisfied with shank of lamb in minted gravy, steak and kidney pie, good steaks and fresh fish from Brixham – chargrilled sea bass served with a sherry sauce. To finish there may be toffee apple crumble pie and lemon crème brulée; Sunday roast is popular and there are six good West Country cheeses on the board. The ten bedrooms have recently been upgraded and are attractively decorated. Four de luxe rooms and the Georgian four-poster room are individually fitted out with quality fabrics, easy chairs and some period pieces of furniture, with prices to match. All rooms are spacious and well appointed, with TVs, tea-making kits, mini-bars, radios and telephones. Eight have clean en suite facilities, the remaining two sharing a bathroom. Children over 5 are welcome in the pub and overnight. Sheltered courtyard to the side and lawned area across the lane. *Open 11-11 (Sun 12-3, 7-10.30). Bar Food 11-2.15, 7-9.30. Free House.* **Beer** *Eldridge Pope Hardy Ale & Royal Oak, Dartmoor Bitter, Bass, Garden, Family room.* **Accommodation** *10 bedrooms, 8 en suite, £71 (four-poster £91, single £26.95-£50). Children welcome overnight (5-14s £10), additional bed available. Amex, MasterCard,* **VISA**

HEATH — King's Arms — A

Tel 01924 377527   Map 6 C1
Heath Common Heath Wakefield WF1 5SL

Built in the early 1700s and converted to pub use in 1841, the King's Arms has been operated by Clark's Brewery of nearby Wakefield since 1989 and enjoys a splendid position by the green in 100 acres of common grassland. Genuinely unaltered and commendably unspoilt. Gas mantles still burn in the three tiny flagstone bars which are lined with unique carved oak panelling. Don't expect miracles from the bar food; rather, just soak in the unique atmosphere. Clark's Festival Ale is the added bonus for beer drinkers. A conservatory is suitable for families and has access to the garden. *Open 11.30-3, 5.30-11 (Sun 12-3, 7-10.30). **Beer** Clark's Traditional Bitter & Festival Ale, Tetley Traditional, Timothy Taylor's Landlord. Garden. Family room.* MasterCard, **VISA**

HEATHTON — Old Gate — A

Tel 01746 710431   Map 6 B4
Heathton Claverley Shropshire WV5 7EB

A much-extended 17th-century inn down country lanes some five miles from Bridgnorth on the Staffordshire border. There's plenty to amuse antiquarians in the parlour: hanging from the beams are decorative Toby and water jugs, from the walls and lintels framed watercolours, old prints and brass flat irons. The Old Stable snug contains more suitable seating for families when the weather precludes use of the garden's picnic tables and play area. Eight miles from Junction 2 of the M5 and near Halfpenny Green Airport. *Open 12-2.30, 6.30-11 (Sun 12-3, 6.30-10.30). **Beer** Tetley Bitter, Holts (HP&D) Entire & Enville Ale, guest beer. Garden, children's play area. Family room.* Amex, Diners, MasterCard, **VISA**

HELFORD — Shipwrights Arms — A

Tel 01326 231235   Map 12 B4
Helford Helston Cornwall TR12 6JX

Stunningly located on the banks of the Helford estuary, its approach road is so narrow that in summer months it's restricted to pedestrian use only. The picturesque walk through the village is well worth it for this pretty thatched pub has a magical terraced garden, complete with colourful flowers, palms and picnic benches on the water's edge. The interior is quite special too, staunchly traditional, with rustic simple furnishings, plenty of nautical bits and pieces and lots of yachting types swapping unlikely stories. The pub and terraces can get extremely busy in the summer. *Open 11-2.30, 6-11 (Sun 12-2.30, 7-10.30). **Beer** Whitbread Castle Eden Ale, Flowers, IPA. Garden, riverside terrace.* MasterCard, **VISA**

HELMSLEY — Feathers — B&B

Tel 01439 770275   Fax 01439 771101   Map 5 E4
Market Place Helmsley North Yorkshire YO6 5BH

'Elmslac', a Saxon village on the river Rye settled in 600 AD was listed in Domesday, and as Helmsley, renowned for its Norman castle, had a well-documented history throughout the Middle Ages. Feathers was once a merchant's house with the highest rent in town, later it was split into two cottages and is now re-unified by the friendly Feather family. There are, of course, two entrances, two bars – with a unifying theme of the local 'Mouse Man' furniture – two dining-rooms and two stair-wells. Two floors of bedrooms provide accommodation that is more practical than luxurious; TVs and tea trays are provided, alarm clocks and hairdryers available on request. Family rooms (sleeping up to 4) with en suite bathrooms offer good value, with under-12s accommodated free (meals charged as taken). Several smaller rooms have en suite WC/shower rooms only, and the three remaining unconverted singles share adequate facilities. *Open 11-11 (Sun 12-10.30). Free House. **Beer** John Smith's, Theakston Best & Old Peculier, guest beer. Garden. Family room. **Accommodation** 17 bedrooms, 13 en suite, £60 (single £35). Children welcome overnight (under-12s stay free in parents' room), additional bed & cot available. Accommodation closed 24 Dec-2 Jan.* Amex, Diners, MasterCard, **VISA**

HENTON · Peacock Hotel · B&B

Tel 01844 353519   Fax 01844 353891   Map 15a D2
Henton Chinnor Oxfordshire OX9 4AH

Zzz...

This very pretty 600-year-old thatched, black and white timbered inn is in a sleepy village just off the B4009. The bar is comfortable and immaculately kept. There are now twenty smart and well equipped bedrooms in total, seventeen of them being located in a rear extension. Residents have use of the outdoor heated swimming pool. *Open 12-2.30, 6-11 (Sun 12-2.30, 7-10.30). Free House.* **Beer** *Brakspear. Patio.* ***Accommodation*** *20 bedrooms, all en suite, £62-£75 (single £52-£65), weekend tariff reductions. Children welcome overnight (rate depends on age), additional bed available. Amex, Diners, MasterCard,* **VISA**

HERMITAGE · Sussex Brewery · A

Tel 01243 371533   Fax 01243 379684   Map 15 D4
36 Main Road Hermitage Emsworth West Sussex PO10 8AU

A fresh carpet of sawdust is laid daily at this Grade II listed pub, and open fires are continually alight from October to Easter. No food recommendation here, but the remarkable selection of 48 different types of sausage (usually served with mash, beans, fried onions and gravy) on the bar menu, and the excellent range of real ales deserve a mention. There's no jukebox or fruit machine, not even a cigarette machine. *Open 11-11 (Sun 12-10.30). Free House.* **Beer** *Wadworth 6X, Hall & Woodhouse Badger Best & Tanglefoot, Burts Nipper & Vectis Venim, Charles Wells Eagle & Bombardier, guest beers. Garden. Amex, MasterCard,* **VISA**

HESKET NEWMARKET · Old Crown · A

Tel 016974 78288   Map 4 C3
Hesket Newmarket Caldbeck Cumbria CA7 8JG

Opened by Chris Bonnington by telex from Katmandu in 1988, the Old Crown's on-site brewhouse produces seven unusually-named beers, for example the award-winning 'Doris's 90th Birthday Ale'. Brewery tours take place on Tue, Wed and Thu evenings, followed by supper in the tiny dining-room (where there are now monthly curry suppers and tapas evenings every other Wednesday). Enjoy a splendid summer pint in the newly landscaped garden. *Open 11-3, 5.30-11 (Sun 12-3, 7-10.30). Closed Mon-Thu lunch in winter & Mon lunch other times (except summer & Bank Holidays). Free House.* **Beer** *own brewery: Great Cockup Porter, Skiddaw Special, Doris's 90th, Blencathra Bitter, Old Carrock Strong Ale, Catbells. Garden. No credit cards.*

HETTON · Angel Inn · ★ · FOOD

Tel 01756 730263   Fax 01756 730363   Map 6 C1
Hetton Skipton North Yorkshire BD23 6LT

Deservedly popular for its tip-top bar food, the Angel promotes a brasserie image with its smart attendants in ankle-length aprons. A dozen or more wines deserving of appreciation by the glass and tall bottles of chili dressing at every table help temper the traditionally pubby feel. Yet the country pub does remain in its central bar and progressive dining-rooms – from no-smoking snug to smart restaurant; the food has a modern British accent with many Mediterranean overtones. The superb bar menu might see tagliatelle with aubergines, courgettes and pesto sauce, Italian crostini, carpaccio of beef fillet with red pepper, chili and tomato ice cream, Oriental brochette of pork, confit of duck, and chargrilled rump steak caponata alongside a selection of daily fresh fish specials (perhaps chargrilled tuna with spinach and tomato fondue drizzled with pesto or sea bass on a bed of oyster mushrooms) – this is serious food, but the prices are still surprisingly reasonable. The menu proclaims: "We are not a fast food outlet! There are many specialists in this field. We cook everything with great care. When we are busy this will cause delay, even though our kitchen is working flat

out. We hope that any wait will be worthwhile." It certainly is – dishes score highly
for flavour, presentation and value. Ever-popular sticky toffee pudding with caramel
sauce, warm melting chocolate torte, tiramisu, and tia maria capuccino brulée are
among the enticements for the sweet-toothed. Printed placemats in the bar areas
invite customers to sample their fixed-price dinners (£23.95), but little further
inducement appears to be needed as reservations at night for the restaurant
(recommended in our *1997 Hotels & Restaurants Guide*) remain a virtual necessity;
here you will find superior touches like a choice of four home-baked breads. Three-
course Sunday lunches (£17.95) offer both an interesting choice and excellent value,
given the quality. Over two dozen malt whiskies at the bar and, usually, an interesting
trio of pudding wines by the glass (perhaps a Hungarian Tokaji Aszu 5 Puttonyos,
a South African Zonnebloem late-harvest or a riesling from Washington State).
Customers are requested to respect local residents' considerations when parking.
*Open 12-2.30, 6-11 (Sun 12-3, 6-10.30). Bar Food 12-2, 7-10 (from 6 in winter).
Restaurant Meals Mon-Sat 7-9.30, Sun 12-2 only (closed Mon-Sat lunch & Sun dinner).
Free House. Beer Black Sheep Best & Special, guest beer. Patio, outdoor eating.
Closed one week in Jan. MasterCard, VISA*

| HEXHAM | Dipton Mill Inn | FOOD |

Tel 01434 606577   Map 5 D2
Dipton Mill Road Hexham Northumberland NE46 1YA

Less than a 10-minute drive out of town (follow Whitley Chapel signs off the B6531
past Hexham Racecourse), Geoff and Janet Brooker's inn nestles by the stone road
bridge in a deep hollow. Within its tiny interior there's a single warm and intimate bar
with welcoming, open fires. If everything within is on a small scale, the daily lunch
menus are no less accidental in concept. Home cooking of manageable proportions is
limited on the blackboard to soup (carrot and celery), three or four daily hot dishes
like fish pie, bacon chop in cider, and chicken, bacon and mushroom pie with fresh
vegetables, commendable nursery puddings (perhaps syrup sponge and custard or
Eyemouth tart) and locally-produced ice creams. In addition to sandwiches there are
seven cheeses for ploughman's lunches, and vegetarians can tuck into a cheese and
broccoli flan. Sheer size restricts children from the bar; there's a tiny rear games room
for when it's cold or wet; the fine-weather benefit is a spacious, walled garden
complete with its own wooden bridge over the old mill stream – a splendid spot.
*Open 12-2.30, 6-11 (Sun 12-4.30, 7-10.30). Bar Food 12-2.30, 6.30-8.30 (from 7
Sun). Free House. Beer Hexhamshire Shire Bitter, Devil's Water & Whapweasel, Theakston
Best, guest beers. Garden, outdoor eating. Family room. Closed all 25 Dec. No credit cards.*

| HIGH RODING | Black Lion | A |

Tel 01371 872847   Map 11 B4
High Roding Great Dunmow Essex CM6 1NT

Attractive black-and-white timbered Tudor roadside pub in a charming Essex village,
full of character buildings. Landlord Osvaldo Ricci has made it his home for the past
24 years and the spick-and-span, intimate bar is full of old beams, standing timbers, a
rustic collection of wooden furniture and a brick-built bar counter. Cosy atmosphere
enhanced by piped light opera and classical music, and fresh flowers on each table.
Small, separate dining-room. *Open 11-3, 6-11 (Sun 12-3, 7-10.30). Beer Ridleys.
Garden, children's play area. MasterCard, VISA*

| HIGHCLERE | Yew Tree | FOOD |
| | | B&B |

Tel 01635 253360   **Fax 01635 255035**   Map 14a C4
Andover Road Hollington Cross Highclere Berkshire RG15 9SE

Former 16th-century coaching inn situated just south of the village on the A343 and
self-styled by owner Jenny Wratten as a 'restaurant with rooms'. Full of charm and
character with huge logs smouldering in the inglenook fireplace while old scrubbed
pine tables and the odd sofa sit beneath ancient beams. Several interconnecting rooms
comprise the main dining area but the same menu is served throughout. Seasonally-
changing choices (plus dishes of the day) might include hot chicken Caesar salad, duck

liver paté with a delicious spicy onion marmalade, Stilton and celery soup, salmon fishcakes with parsley sauce, beef and stout cobbler, smoked salmon and watercress pasta and daily fish dishes. Finish, perhaps, with steamed ginger pudding and custard, Emma's chocolate cheesecake or farmhouse cheeses served with apple, celery, water biscuits and their own walnut bread. Ten wines are offered by the glass, including a champagne. Six cottagey bedrooms offer overnight accommodation with direct-dial telephones, remote-control TVs, beverage trays and little extras like books and magazines; all have en suite bathrooms, half with shower and WC only. No under-14s in bar area. *Open 11-3, 5.30-11 (Sun 12-3, 7-10.30). **Bar Food** 12-2.30, 6.30-10 (Sun 12.30-3, 7-9.30). Free House. **Beer** Fuller's London Pride, Wadworth 6X, Hampshire King Alfred Bitter. Garden, patio, outdoor eating. **Accommodation** 6 bedrooms, all en suite, £60 (single £45). Children welcome overnight (under-5s stay free in parents' room). Amex, MasterCard,* **VISA**

HIGHER BURWARDSLEY   Pheasant Inn   FOOD

Tel 01829 770434   Fax 01829 771097   Map 6 A3   **B&B**
Higher Burwardsley Tattenhall Cheshire CH3 9PF

 Zzz... ☺

The Pheasant is best located by following signs to the candle factory from the A534. It is tucked into the hillside amongst the Peckforton hills, and on arrival, it's plain to see that the place was once a farm, and the more surprising, therefore, to find that there has been a pub here since the 17th century. The oldest part, a half-timbered sandstone farmhouse, is the venue for the bar, which claims to house the largest log fire in Cheshire. Adjacent is the Highland Room which in turn leads to an imposing conservatory that looks over a tiered patio and, beyond this, right across the Cheshire plain towards North Wales. Bar snacks encompass a broad range from hot avocado with seafood and lasagne to fresh fish (a speciality) and cold platters (ploughman's, salads). A selection of ten sandwiches is listed and children are offered the usual list of favourites. Daily specials extend the kitchen's repertoire to the likes of baked monkfish wrapped in bacon with a cream sauce and noisettes of lamb with provençale onions. Sunday lunch is always popular as it's such good value and as space is limited it is advble to book at all times. The old barn has been skilfully converted into eight very comfortable bedrooms, including two suites, equipped with televisions, clock-radios, hairdryers, mini-bars and roomy bathrooms. Stonework interiors are eye-catching, and nights tranquil. Two further bedrooms, housed in the pub proper, boast original beams and brighter bathrooms, as well as memorable views. It is an ideal spot for keen walkers, as the inn stands midway along the Sandstone Trail. Credit cards taken for amounts of £20 and over only. *Open 12-3, 7-11 (Sun 12-3, 7-10.30). **Bar Food** 12-2.30, 7-9.30. Free House. **Beer** Bass, guest beer. Garden, outdoor eating, children's play area. Family room. **Accommodation** 10 bedrooms, all en suite, £70 & £80 (single £40-£45). Children welcome overnight (under-10s stay free in parents' room, over-10s £10), additional bed & cot available. Amex, Diners, MasterCard,* **VISA**

HIMLEY   Crooked House   A

Tel 01384 238583   Map 6 B4
Coppice Mill Himley Dudley DY3 4DA

☺

This is not a particularly attractive setting; turning off B4176 between Womborne and Dudley, the long lane runs down through woods past urban forest, landfill and quarry. Yet the sight at the lane's end is simply extraordinary. Once the Glynne Arms, the 250-year-old building was a victim of subsidence in Victorian times and teeters alarmingly from right to left. One bar door opens out at an oblique angle and instills an uneasy feeling of collapsing through it – and this is on the way in! Meanwhile, in the upper bar, (for a charitable donation) customers can watch a ball-bearing apparently roll upwards along the dado. Despite some recent levelling of the floor, many's the customer who appears all at sea with his legs. A more recent extension houses a family-friendly conservatory overlooking a small adventure playground. Saturday barbecues. No children under 14 in the bars. *Open 11-11 (Sun 12-10.30) Apr-end Aug, 11.30-2.30, 6.30-11 (Sun 12-3, 7-10.30) Sep-Mar, **Beer** Banks's Mild & Bitter, Marston's Pedigree, guest beer. Patio, children's play area. No credit cards.*

HINDON   Lamb at Hindon   FOOD

Tel 01747 820573   Fax 01747 820605   Map 14 B3   **B&B**
Hindon Salisbury Wiltshire SP3 6DP

Wisteria clings to one corner of this mellow 17th-century coaching inn. At its height,
300 post horses were kept here to supply the great number of coaches going to and
from London and the West Country. Prime Minister William Pitt was apparently most
put out to find no fresh horses available when he stopped off in 1786. Inside, the long
bar is divided into several areas and is furnished with some sturdy period tables, chairs
and settles, and a splendid old stone fireplace with log fire creates a warm, homely
atmosphere, especially on cold winter nights. The blackboard bar menu is sensibly not
over-long, but still manages to offer a reasonable choice – fresh mussels, grilled hake
with capers and garlic, game casserole, lamb and mint casserole and, for pudding,
lemon tart with raspberry coulis and orange and nectarine brulée. Granary sandwiches,
ploughman's platters and salads are always available. The emphasis is fishy on
Wednesday and Fridays, and in winter there's also plenty of game from the estate
of the local landowner who bought the inn a few years ago. No-smoking restaurant.
Upstairs, there are thirteen en suite bedrooms, which are furnished and decorated to
varying styles and standards. *Open 11-11, (Sun 12-10.30).* **Bar Food** *12-2, 7-10.*
Free House. **Beer** *Wadworth 6X, Hook Norton Best, Ashvine Bitter, Ringwood. Best, guest
beer. Garden, outdoor eating.* **Accommodation** *13 bedrooms, all en suite, £55 (four-poster
£65, single £38). Children welcome overnight (under-3s stay free in parents' room), additional
bed & cot (both £10) available. Amex, MasterCard,* **VISA**

HOLNE   Church House Inn   B&B

Tel 01364 631208   Map 13 D3
Holne Ashburton Devon TQ13 7SJ

Situated in an attractive Dartmoor village on the southern flanks of the moor, this
welcoming inn was built in 1329 as either a dwelling house for the workers on the
church, or as a resting place for visiting clergy and worshippers in the church. It is still
a popular meeting place for locals, Dartmoor ramblers and car tourers alike. Pleasantly
rustic bars, furnished with a huge carved settle and an assortment of simple tables and
chairs are appealing. The six modest upstair bedrooms enjoy superb rural views and
are due to be upgraded in the coming year. All are neat and comfortable and simply
furnished, with four rooms having small clean bathrooms with showers; two rooms
share a bathroom. Added comforts of TV and tea-making kits are standard and
residents have the use of a cosy, antique-filled lounge. No under-14s in the bar areas.
Open 11.30-3, 6.30-11 (from 7 Mon-Thur Nov-Mar), Sun 12-3, 7-10.30. Free House.
Beer *Dartmoor Best Bitter & Legend, Wadworth 6X, Palmers IPA, guest beer. Patio.*
Accommodation *6 bedrooms, 4 en suite, £39-£50 (single £25-£27.50). Children welcome
overnight (under-2s stay free in parents' room, 3-14s £10), additional bed (£5) available.
MasterCard,* **VISA**

HOLT   Old Ham Tree   FOOD

Tel 01225 782581   Map 14 B3   **B&B**
Holt Trowbridge Wiltshire BA14 6PY

Two miles north of Trowbridge, a cleanly modernised, beamed and pleasant 18th-
century inn near the village green. Reliably good, simple food in the form of chicken
and mushroom pie, beef stir-fry, monkfish braised with shallots, mushroom and red
wine and loin of pork with apricot sauce. Sandwiches, filled baguettes, ploughman's
platters and vegetarian options (spinach and ricotta lasagne) are also offered. Puddings
are homely (and home-made): apple and peach pie and orange, cointreau and peach
cheesecake. Bedrooms are centrally-heated, clean and airy, white-painted with
matching furniture, pretty floral fabrics, and share a modern bathroom. Residents'
television lounge above the bar. *Open 11.15-3, 6.30-11 (Sun 12-3, 7-10.30).*
Bar Food *11.30-2.30, 6.30-10 (Sun from 7). Free House.* **Beer** *Wadworth 6X, Marston's
Pedigree, Robinson's Best. Garden, outdoor eating.* **Accommodation** *4 bedrooms, £32 (single
£22.50). Children welcome overnight (stay free in parents' room), additional bed available.
Dogs welcome by arrangement. Amex, Diners, MasterCard,* **VISA**

HOLYWELL | Old Ferry Boat | B&B

Tel 01480 463227   Fax 01480 494885   Map 10 B2
Holywell St Ives Cambridgeshire PE17 3TG

A thousand years of history are behind this delightful thatched and wisteria-draped riverside inn, originally a monastic ferry house. Situated by the River Great Ouse where there is ample mooring, the Old Ferry boat has a particularly charming panelled alcove off the main bar, and good views from the sun terrace. It is haunted by Juliet, a young victim of unrequited love, so don't go on March 17th unless you want to join the ghost hunters! The seven neatly refurbished bedrooms are individually decorated with quality wallpapers and fabrics, but vary in size and standard of facilities. Two boast space for old pine four-posters and good-sized bathrooms, others are compact (to say the least) with beds against the wall and tiny shower rooms. Despite these drawbacks, two have delightful views over the river and a serene rural scene. A pets corner, complete with goats and a pot-bellied pig should keep youngsters amused. *Open 11-3, 6-11 (Sun 12-10.30). Free House.* **Beer** *Bass, Worthington Best, Charrington IPA, Webster's Yorkshire Bitter, guest beers. Garden, terrace. Family room.* **Accommodation** *7 bedrooms, all en suite £54.50-£73 (single £44.50-£54.50). Children welcome overnight (stay free in parents' room). Check-in by arrangement. No dogs. MasterCard,* **VISA**

HOLYWELL GREEN | Rock Inn Hotel | B&B

Tel 01422 379721   Fax 01422 379110   Map 6 C1
Holywell Green Halifax Calderdale HX4 9BS

In a quiet village just a couple of minutes' drive from Junction 24 of the M62 (ask directions when booking), this inn began life as a row of 17th-century stone cottages. Considerably extended and revamped over the years by landlord Robert Vinson to incorporate function rooms (they specialise in weddings) as well as the bedrooms. The bar is most comfortable in modern, designer-Victorian style with red leather chesterfields, frilly glass lampshades and a new conservatory extension. Bedrooms are not large but manage to squeeze in everything from trouser press and hairdryer to satellite TV, beverage kit and drinks tray with a couple of beers and miniature spirits. All rooms are very similar, with dark-stained pine ceilings, rich Victorian colour schemes and compact bathrooms that all have showers over unusually deep, round tubs. Also unusual are the three 'four-posters' that do not actually have posts but mirrored canopies fixed to the ceiling. One room has a couple of bunk beds for children and another family room sleeps three. A notably friendly place. *Open 11.30-11 (Sun 12-10.30). Free House.* **Beer** *Theakston Best, Tetley, Scottish & Newcastle No. 3, Black Sheep, guest beer. Terrace. Family room.* **Accommodation** *18 bedrooms (3 with four-posters), all en suite, £72-£82 (family room £74, single £64-£74, weekend reductions). Children welcome overnight (under-10s stay free in parents' room, 11-16s 50%), cot available. Amex, Diners, MasterCard,* **VISA**

HOPE | Poacher's Arms | B&B

Tel 01433 620380   Map 6 C2
Castelton Road Hope Derybshire S30 2RD

Gladys Bushell's much-extended roadside pub (on the A625) is as popular as ever with walkers, cyclists and visitors to the Peak's National Park. With eating and seating areas which include a family room, rear conservatory, new patio and two dining-rooms there's just one central bar servery to cope with the crush. Amid the modern beamed decor there's a limited degree of elegance and comfort; there are wider seats, button-backed banquettes and copper-topped bar tables. En suite bedrooms are spacious, sporting a mixture of floral papers, curtains and bedspreads. Freestanding pine or mahogany furniture, remote control TV, clock radio, phone, hairdryer and hot drinks tray all combine to fulfil the basic requirements of a comfortable and restful stay. *Open 12-3, 6-11.* **Beer** *Courage Directors, John Smith's, Marston's Pedigree. Patio.* **Accommodation** *6 bedrooms, all en suite, £52 (single £39). Children welcome overnight (under-5s stay free in parents' room), additional bed & cot available. Amex, MasterCard,* **VISA**

HOPTON WAFERS   Crown Inn   FOOD

Tel 01299 270372   Fax 01299 271127   Map 6 B4   **B&B**
Hopton Wafers Cleobury Mortimer Shropshire DY14 0NB

Zzz..

The creeper-clad Crown in the Norman hamlet of Hopton Wafers is set in its own
garden which slopes down to one of the many streams (crossed here by the A4117)
that flow down to the Teme valley. Bounded on three sides by terraces of tables with
their colourful summer parasols, it's a splendid spot for alfresco eating. Inside, the
Rent Room, where once local villagers came to pay their rents, houses an
atmospheric and intimate bar. Promising menus from a keen new chef have a strong
fish emphasis (crab bisque, Irish mussels with cream and white wine, roast monkfish
with grilled red peppers and tomatoes), as well as dishes like pan-fried lamb steak with
sherry and rosemary jus and spinach, Stilton and roast almond pancake. Home-made
puddings might include almond crunch and pan-fried strawberries flamed in Pernod.
The decor and character of the bedrooms are commendable. Unsuspecting
overnighters are in for a treat of exposed rafters, sloping corridors and creaky
floorboards – with which the automatic trouser press and bathroom telephone
extensions seem faintly at odds. Three bedrooms are family rooms, there's one high-
chair and the garden is large, with trees, stream and pond. *Open 12-3, 6-11.*
Bar Food 12-2.30, 6.30-9.30. Free House. **Beer** *Greene King Abbot Ale, Boddingtons,
Marston's Pedigree, guest beer. Riverside garden, outdoor eating.* **Accommodation** *8 bedrooms,
all en suite, £69 (single £42). Children welcome overnight, additional bed (£20) & cot (£5)
available. MasterCard,* **VISA**

HORAM   Gun Inn   FOOD

Tel 01825 872361   Map 11 B6
Gun Hill Horam Heathfield East Sussex TN21 0JU

Extended 16th-century tiled and timbered pub, resplendent in summer with colourful
hanging baskets, enjoying a peaceful rural location just off the A22 north-west of
Hailsham. Neat open-plan interior with a series of comfortably furnished alcove
seating areas, several open fires and an old kitchen Aga. Head for the blackboard
menu for the daily-changing selection of home-cooked dishes, which supplements a
standard printed menu of pub favourites. Good reliable choices may include decent
pies – Sussex fidget, rabbit and lamb, apricot and rosemary – shank of pork, salmon
parcels, and Sussex smokie in white wine and mustard sauce. Fresh fish – whole plaice
and lemon sole – comes from Newhaven. Keen to cater for all tastes there is the
choice of fresh vegetables, chips, jacket potatoes or a selection of fresh, imaginative
salads from the regularly replenished salad bar. For a home-made pudding try the
treacle tart or apple crumble. Cream teas are available each afternoon between April
and October. Overnight accommodation comprises three homely, simply furnished
bedrooms with TVs, tea-makers and rural views. One has en suite facilities, the others
share a clean bathroom and two toilets. Continental breakfasts are served in the room.
Open summer 11-11, (Mon-Fri 11-3, 6-11 in winter), Sun 12-10.30. **Bar Food** *Apr-Oct
12-10, (12-2, 6-10 in winter), Free House.* **Beer** *Larkins Chiddingstone, Harveys Sussex
Bitter, Flowers original, guest beer. Garden, outside eating, children's play area. Family room.
Closed all 25 & 26 Dec. MasterCard,* **VISA**

HORNDON   Elephant's Nest   FOOD

Tel 01822 810273   Map 12 C3
Horndon Mary Tavy Tavistock Horndon Devon PL19 9NQ

Isolated 16th-century inn located on the flanks of Dartmoor and reached via narrow,
high-hedged lanes from the A386 Tavistock to Okehampton road at Mary Tavy
(signposted). Named after a portly landlord with a bushy beard it is a character pub
for wild winter weather with its window seats, rustic furnishings, old rugs, flagstones,
heavy beams and open fires. The large garden has open views across the moor and
picnic tables for summer days; rabbits, ducks, goats, geese and chickens in pens should
keep the children interested. It is a busy dining pub with an extensive blackboard

menu listing popular pub favourites as well as a range of home-cooked daily dishes – perhaps local game pie, lamb and lentil hotpot, seafood ragout and steak and kidney pie. 'Pete's Puds' include chocolate and brandy crunch cake and treacle and walnut tart. *Open 11.30-2.30, 6.30-11 (Sun 12-2.30, 7-10.30).* **Bar Food** *11.30-2 (from 12 Sun), 6.30-10 (till 9.30 Sun). Free House.* **Beer** *St Austell's HSD, Palmers IPA, Boddingtons, guest beers. Garden, outdoor eating. Family room. No credit cards.*

HORNDON-ON-THE-HILL   Bell Inn & Hill House   ★   FOOD

Tel 01375 673154   Fax 01375 361611   Map 11 B4   **B&B**
High Road Horndon-on-the-Hill Essex SS17 8LD

Located in the village centre a few doors from one another, John and Christine Vereker's 500-year-old Bell Inn offers a blackboard menu and a friendly rustic, pubby ambience including beams, unpolished wood tables and flagstone floors; Hill House next door has more formal dining in a pretty pastel-coloured room. A hot cross bun is nailed to a ceiling beam at the Bell every Good Friday, and the collection of shrunken, fossilised old buns is now pretty spectacular. The Bell menu features both simple and more unusual dishes: perhaps spinach, garlic and potato soup and venison carpaccio with balsamic vinegar for starters, followed by fillet of beef with haggis and port wine sauce, cod with Parma ham and mushrooms, and confit of duck with red cabbage and apple. A 'taffy' (affectionately named after a Welsh regular who liked his ploughman's with hot bread) is a ploughman's platter with a choice of ham or cheese and good, locally-baked bread; further traditional fare like steak and kidney pie and chili are also available as bar snacks. The Bell Restaurant, to the rear of the bar, is a relaxed, informal setting. In Hill House the restaurant is more formal and a fixed-price menu does away with the simpler, more pubby items. Chef Sean Kelly's cooking is imaginative, skilfully executed and produces very enjoyable results on the plate; a dish of seafood sausage with cream and leek sauce, and his personal favourite, lamb cutlets stuffed with haggis and baked in pastry. Orange sponge pudding with marmalade sauce and hot mango tart may be among the bar menu desserts. Above and also to the rear of Hill House are pretty, cottagey en suite bedrooms, each thoughtfully equipped and neatly maintained; four rooms are upstairs in the Bell. A sporty, friendly community pub, free from music, gaming machines and pool tables. Booking essential in the restaurants (both of which are recommended in our *1997 Hotels & Restaurants Guide*). Large courtyard with seating in summer. *Open 11-2.30 (till 3 Sat), 6-11 (Sun 12-3, 7-10.30).* **Bar Food** *12-2, 6.30-10 (from 7.15 Sun). Free House.* **Beer** *Bass, Hancock's HB, Fuller's London Pride, guest beers. Courtyard, outdoor eating.* **Accommodation** *14 rooms, all en suite, £62/£72. (family room £75). Children welcome overnight, additional bed (£10) & cot available. Amex, MasterCard,* **VISA**

HORNINGSEA   Plough & Fleece   FOOD

Tel 01223 860795   Map 10 B3
High Street Horningsea Cambridgeshire CB5 9JG

A Grade II listed building, built in the Dutch style so popular in the East Anglia of the late 18th century when Dutch engineers came to advise on the draining of the Fenlands. The generally very busy Plough & Fleece owes its great popularity to old-fashioned regional cooking, which is often given a modern interpretation. Come here for homely, comforting hot-pots, cottage pie and hot cockles with garlic butter, as well as more contemporary treatments of dinner-partyish food, like roast breast of duck with hot and spicy sauce, or beef Wellington with Madeira sauce. Puddings are suitably gorgeous and cream-laden; the Northamptonshire chocolate pudding in particular has an informal international fan club but there at least seven others to choose from. Sandwiches and ploughman's platters are offered at lunchtime, when there's a busy business trade. All this means the pub can get crowded but the dining-room extension provides a welcome haven for non-smokers. In addition to the traditional roast on the reduced Sunday menu, Romany rabbit proves equally as popular. The atmosphere is homely and traditional in feel, especially so in the unspoilt public bar, with its ancient settles, tiled floor, elm tables and custard-coloured walls. The lounge is comfortable rather than characterful and invariably packed with bar meal diners. Arrive early at lunchtime to beat the scrum. Children (minimum age 5) allowed in dining-room only. *Open 11.30-2.30, 7-11 (Sun 12-2, 7-10.30).* **Bar Food** *12-2 (till 1.30 Sun), 7-9.30 (no food Sun & Mon eve).* **Beer** *Greene King. Garden, outdoor eating. Closed 25 & 26 Dec eve. Amex, MasterCard,* **VISA**

HORRINGER   Beehive   FOOD

Tel 01284 735260   Map 10 C3
The Street Horringer Suffolk IP29 5SD

Genuine home-made food is served throughout the bar areas here, and tables can be booked: the ratio of reservations to casual droppers-in is usually about 50/50. A printed menu is much more imaginative than most, and a specials board with delicious fresh fish (sea bass, whole Dover sole) makes the choice even more difficult. The fish may be cooked simply – grilled with butter and wine. Other choices are scallops sautéed with mushrooms and white wine, pork and spinach sausages with white onion and cream confit, scrambled eggs with wild mushrooms and horseradish, and hot spicy ratatouille with cheesey garlic bread. Where better than to enjoy a plate of Suffolk ham carved from the bone and served with pickles and a salad bowl? End your meal with a selection from their home-made puddings – perhaps Beehive tart (sponge, butter and raisins) or treacle tart – or with a hot chocolate and whipped cream. Rambling, traditionally furnished little rooms radiate off a central servery, warmed by a wood-burning stove. The terrace has five or so tables and there are picnic tables on the lawn. As we went to press, landlords Gary and Diane Kingshott were also refurbishing *The Queen's Head* in Kirtling, Cambridgeshire. *Open 11.30-2.30, 7-11 (Sun 12-2, 7-10.30).* **Bar Food** *12-2, 7-9.30 (no food Sun eve).* **Beer** *Greene King. Garden, outdoor eating. Family room. MasterCard,* **VISA**

HORSEBRIDGE   Royal Inn   A

Tel 01822 870214   Map 12 C3
Horsebridge Tavistock Devon PL19 8PJ

Two excellent reasons for a detour to this informal and relaxing 15th-century pub, once a nunnery: to look at the ancient Tamar Bridge and to sample their own home-brewed ales (of which it is reported that no-one has been able to drink more than five pints!) Last year's guide stated a third reason for tracking down this isolated pub, namely the food on offer. However, the previous landlords have retired and new owners, David and Catherine Johnson, have taken over, but the menu looks interesting and features home-cooked fare. Future plans include accommodation and twice-yearly beer festivals. No children under 8 inside. *Open 12-2.30, 6-11. Free House.* **Beer** *Sharp's Own Cornish, Bass, plus own home brews: Heller, Horsebridge Best, Tamar, Right Royal. Patio, outdoor eating. Family room. No credit cards.*

> We endeavour to be as up-to-date as possible but inevitably some changes to
> landlords, chefs and other key staff occur after the Guide
> has gone to press.

HORTON-IN-RIBBLESDALE   Crown Hotel   FOOD

Tel 01729 860209   Fax 01729 860444   Map 5 D4   B&B
Horton-in-Ribblesdale Settle North Yorkshire BD24 0HF

Sandwiched between two road bridges on the B6479 where Bransgyll runs into the Ribble, the Crown is centrally located amid the Three Peaks at the heart of the Ribble Valley. At the pub, three generations now come into play. Landlady Norma Hargreaves moved here over 30 years ago with her parents; now, daughter Helen is in charge of the kitchen. She makes home-made pies and puddings, plus an extended range that might include pheasant and port pie, lamb and apricot pie, seafood pancake and Stilton and spinach quiche. Freshly-baked 'crusties' (small baguettes, lunchtime only) and ploughman's lunches are also offered. In terms of accommodation, to term the bedrooms modest is not to decry them, as an absence of TVs and phones remains intentional. Internal dimensions of this unaltered 17th-century inn dictate, though, against much modernisation and there are but two rooms with en suite bathrooms and a further five with added shower stalls. However, plans are afoot to add more en suite facilities. Two adjacent cottages offer self-contained private accommodation for larger parties. Being an altogether family-run affair there's also a special promise that "parents with children are welcome here to do exactly what other normal people like to do". *Open 11-11 (possibly closed earlier mid-week eves in winter), Sun 12-10.30.* **Bar Food** *12-2, 6-9.30.* **Beer** *Theakston XB & Old Peculier. Garden, outdoor play area.* **Accommodation** *9 bedrooms, 2 en suite, £34-£42 midweek, £39-£48 Fri, Sat & Bank Holidays (single from £17). Children welcome overnight (0-12s 75% adult tariff), addtional bed & cot available. No credit cards.*

HOUGHTON CONQUEST   Knife & Cleaver   B&B

Tel 01234 740387   Fax 01234 740900   Map 15a E1
Houghton Conquest Ampthill Bedfordshire MK45 3LA

Three miles from Ampthill and equidistant from Junctions 12 and 13 of the M10, opposite the medieval parish church in a sleepy village, the Knife & Cleaver is more an inn than a pub. The accommodation is especially pleasing, in spacious brick-built garden rooms standing alongside a mature orchard. In addition to TVs, telephones, radio-alarm clocks and beverage facilities, the mini-fridge in each room is thoughtfully stored each day with fresh milk. The less mobile are especially well catered for, with wide, paved bedroom access and ramps into the pub proper where there's a Jacobean oak-panelled bar and a Victorian-style conservatory restaurant behind. *Open 12-2.30, 6.30-11 (Sun 12-2.30 only). Closed Sun eve & Bank Holiday eve). Free House.* **Beer** *Batemans XB, Adnams Extra. Garden. Family room.* **Accommodation** *9 bedrooms, all en suite, £59/£69, (family room sleeping three £74, single £45). Children welcome overnight (under-12s stay free in parents' room), additional bed available. Accommodation Sun eve by arrangement. Amex, Diners, MasterCard,* **VISA**

HOVINGHAM   Worsley Arms Hotel   B&B

Tel 01653 628234   Fax 01653 628130   Map 5 E4
Hovingham North Yorkshire YO6 4LA
Zzz...

Built in 1841 as an adjunct to the unsuccessful development of Hovingham as a spa, the inn, described as "late-Georgian" in style, overlooks the green of this most unspoilt of North Riding villages. The Cricketers Bar, appropriately named as it's the headquarters of the local team, is hung with a unique photographic collection of the county's greatest in action, many of whom played at the Hovingham Hall ground. It's generally lively here, with some good Double Chance from the nearby Malton brewery and bistro-style bar food (soup, terrines, fishcakes, warm salads). The inn itself has a more refined feel in its elegant lounges with deep armchairs and abundant reading matter. Sunday lunches and table d'hote dinners are served in the sedate dining-room, heavy with fine 18th-century portraits. Spacious bedrooms echo the Georgian feel with large windows and sumptuous drapes and co-ordinated fabrics. Bathrooms with large bathsheets and abundant toiletries are best described as traditional. Having been in the hands of the Worsley family since it was built, this fine inn now has new owners. *Open 12-2.30, 6-11 (Sun 12-3, 7-10.30). Free House.* **Beer** *Malton Double Chance, John Smith's. Garden, outdoor eating, patio. Tennis, squash. Family room.* **Accommodation** *19 rooms, all en suite, £75 (single £55). Children welcome overnight, additional bed (£10) & cot available. Amex, Diners, MasterCard,* **VISA**

HOXNE   The Swan   FOOD

Tel 01379 668275   Fax 01379 668168   Map 10 C2
Low Street Hoxne Suffolk IP21 5AS

A Grade II listed 15th-century inn built by the Bishop of Norwich as the guest quarters to his now defunct summer palace. It's been a hostelry since at least 1619 and the interior, which features high ceilings and fluted oak joists, is suitably evocative of centuries gone by. Some good bar food includes sandwiches and omelettes (fillings to order), mixed cheese ploughman's and lamb cutlets on the main menu; Roquefort and cashew nut tart, duck, bacon and walnut salad, rabbit in cream and saffron, and peppers stuffed with tuna, olives, anchovies and tomato might feature as daily specials, along with bread-and-butter pudding and orange mousse for sweet. Only a cold buffet at summer Sunday lunchtime; three-course Sunday lunch menu in winter. No bar meals on Saturday evenings (only restaurant). Outside, there's a large, tree-bordered garden where you can play croquet. The village is pronounced Hoxon (in case you want to feel like a local). *Open 12-2.30 (till 3 Sat), 5.30-11, (Sun 12-3, 7-10.30).* **Bar Food** *12-2, 7-9 (no food Sat eve & all Sun). Free House.* **Beer** *Adnams Bitter, Old & Tally Ho (winter), Greene King Abbot Ale. Garden, outdoor eating. Closed all 25 Dec.* *MasterCard,* **VISA**

HURTMORE   The Squirrel   A

Tel 01483 860223   Fax 01483 860592   Map 15a E4
Hurtmore Godalming Surrey GU7 2RN

A convenient stopping point on the London-Portsmouth A3 road (which runs by rather unobtrusively behind the hedge at the top of the garden), just south of Guildford. Having made several immediate changes on moving in, landlord Jordi Vazquez has continued to improve The Squirrel. As well as having a comfortable, open-plan interior, an airy conservatory/brasserie, a gently terraced garden – complete with picnic tables, swings, slide and wooden play house – and a covered verandah (an ideal spot for a drink on a sunny day), the thirteen small, pine-furnished rooms, located in cottages across the car park, have been completely refurbished (£49.50-£55 single, £65 double). Children are made most welcome. *Open 11-3, 5.30-11 (Sun 12-10.30). Free House.* **Beer** *Ruddles County, Youngers Best, guest beer. Garden, terrace, children's play area. Amex, Diners, MasterCard,* **VISA**

> We do not accept free meals or hospitality – our inspectors pay their own bills and never book in the name of Egon Ronay's Guides.

IBSTONE   The Fox   B&B

Tel 01491 638289   Fax 01491 638873   Map 15a D3
Ibstone High Wycombe Buckinghamshire HP14 3GG

Zzz...

Much modernised and extended 300-year-old inn located on the Chiltern ridgeway opposite Ibstone Common, and close to acres of beechwood rambles. With the M40 (Junction 5) only a mile away, this rural inn is a handy overnight stop for travellers, for the nine en suite rooms are comfortable and well equipped. All rooms feature co-ordinating fabrics, modern pine furniture, clean fully tiled shower rooms and a full complement of added comforts – tea-makers, TVs, direct-dial telephones, clock-radios, trouser presses and hairdryers. Rear rooms have soothing views across fields and woodland. The oldest part of the building houses the relaxing, comfortably modernised lounge bar with wood-burner, and the simply furnished Country Bar with adjacent games/family room. Delightful sunny front terrace and well-tended garden. *Open 11-3, 6-11 (Sun 12-3, 7-10.30).* **Beer** *Brakspear Bitter, Fuller's London Pride, Marlow Rebellion IPA, Flowers Original, guest beer. Garden. Family room.* **Accommodation** *9 bedrooms, all en suite (shower), £58-£76 (single from £44). Children welcome overnight, additional bed (£10) available. Amex, Diners, MasterCard,* **VISA**

ICKLINGHAM   Red Lion   FOOD

Tel 01638 717802   Fax 01638 515702   Map 10 C2
High Street Icklingham Suffolk IP28 6PS

Fine 16th-century village inn set back from the A1101 with a neat front lawn and raised rear terrace overlooking fields. Sympathetically restored and well refurbished two-bar interior featuring low 'smoke' brown ceilings with heavy, black-painted beams, an exposed brick fireplace and an assortment of antique and sturdy furniture arranged on rug-strewn wooden floors. Relaxing ambience enhanced by piped classical music, various newspapers and magazines to read and evening candlelight. A reliable range of interesting home-cooked bar food is offered. Blackboard lists may mixed hors d'oeuvre, warm mixed sausage salad and Huntsman's grill (venison steak, liver and sausage and wild boar bacon). Fresh fish from Lowestoft may include poached ling in cheese and ale sauce, skate in prawn and salmon butter, and grilled sardines in garlic butter, and top 15 varieties on Thusday evenings. Good accompanying vegetables – definitely no chips! Granary sandwiches and ploughman's platters are available all day. Round the meal off with chocolate roulade, Eve's pudding or treacle tart. Well-kept Greene King ales and a good range of wines, including country fruit wines. Children welcome. The licensees also run the *Pykkerell Inn* at Ixworth (see entry). *Open 12-3, 6-11, (Sun 12-3, 7-10.30).* **Bar Food** *12-2.30, 6-10 (Sun 7-9).* **Beer** *Greene King. Garden, outdoor eating. MasterCard,* **VISA**

IGHTHAM COMMON   Harrow Inn   ★   FOOD

Tel 01732 885912   Map 11 B5
Common Road Ightham Common Borough Green Kent TN15 9ER

Coloured lights around the door offer a welcome at this unusual Virginia creeper-hung stone inn on a country lane full of pretty grand houses. In the small front bar a couple of stuffed birds in glass cases and old motor racing photos are mounted above dado pine panelling, and there's a pair of old leather armchairs and a pool table in the room next door; the whole effect wobbles on the very fine line between characterful and seedy, but boxes of board games and newspapers laid out on a side table are a nice touch, and the landlord and his friendly staff soon dispel any doubts. Gerard Costelloe has an impressive catering background, and the cooking is excellent. Well-balanced soups (carrot and coriander) arrive in large tureens, from which one helps oneself, along with a whole freshly baked rye loaf on its own bread board. There are always a couple of pasta dishes, at least one of them vegetarian, as well as the likes of chicken and pepper pie, lamb casserole with rosemary, skate with fennel and ginger, and leek and pork sausages. It's worth saving a little space for dessert, like bread-and-butter pudding or a classic summer pudding, properly made, its bread thoroughly soaked in the juice of soft fruits. The bars are not really suitable for children but they are welcome (particularly for Sunday lunch) in the cottagey restaurant, its conservatory extension complete with grape vine. The menu here tends to be somewhat more adventurous – grilled sea bass on a bed of fettuccine with ratatouille or venison Wellington. Given the rather tacky walls, the sloping flagstone floors and the very smoky and poorly-ventilated atmosphere in the bar, this is not the sort of place one expects to find such good food, served by friendly staff and sold at equally friendly prices – unusual and eccentric, yes, but worthy in its own special way. *Open 12-3, 6.30-11 (till 10.30 Sun).* **Bar Food** *12-2, 7-9.30. Free House.* **Beer** *Fuller's London Pride, Greene King Abbot Ale, Webster's Yorkshire Bitter. Garden, outdoor eating, summer barbecues. Amex, MasterCard,* **VISA**

ILMINGTON   Howard Arms   FOOD   B&B

Tel & Fax 01608 682226   Map 14a A1
Lower Green Ilmington Shipston-on-Stour Warwickshire CV36 4LT

Zzz...

For its location by the village green and setting in a mature orchard garden, the yellow-stone Howard Arms falls into the 'irresistible' category, a picture by day, romantically lit at night. Centuries-old connections with one of England's most illustrious families adds a touch of history to draw the crowds to its flagstoned bar and open-plan restaurant. Menus change daily, a single blackboard offering the same choices throughout, and all food orders are taken at the bar. Sandwiches and ploughman's platters, using freshly-baked crusty rolls, are offered at lunchtimes (not Sun). More substantially, seasonal asparagus is a popular starter or there's a home-made chicken liver parfait, perhaps; followed fishily with crispy cod in beer batter or supreme of salmon with dill cream; for meatier choices the likes of lamb's liver and smoked bacon, noisettes of venison with prunes and brandy and spicy chicken balti with naan bread and, to follow, summer pudding and rhubarb and banana crumble. Bookings are taken in the restaurant where the service is more formal; a traditional Sunday lunch is also offered here. Just two bedrooms are let, a large twin with quite enough space for a family to stay, and the king-sized double for the more romantically inclined; en suite facilities include both bath and shower, and there are no phones to impinge on the peace. *Open 11-2.30, 6-11 (Sun 12-3, 7-10.30).* **Bar Food** *12-2, 7-9 (till 9.30 Fri & Sat). No food Sun eve Oct-Mar. Free House.* **Beer** *Marston's Pedigree, Everards Tiger, two guest beers. Garden, outdoor eating. Family room.* **Accommodation** *2 bedrooms, both en suite, £50 (single £30). Children welcome overnight, additional bed & cot available (£5). Check-in by arrangement. No dogs. Amex, MasterCard,* **VISA**

IVY HATCH　　　The Plough　　　★　　　FOOD

Tel & Fax 01732 810268　　　　　　Map 11 B5
Coach Road Ivy Hatch Kent TN15 0NL

Quite apart from its outstandingly good cooking, the Plough is the kind of pub just about everyone would love to have as their local. A large mid 18th-century roadside inn dominating this little hamlet, it's just enough off the beaten track, although well signposted. Within, it's peaceful and genuinely unspoilt, with dark pitch mahogany in the light of a crackling log fire, and candlelight by night. By way of contrast, the conservatory dining extension is light and fresh, with its soft pink linens, cane furniture and decorative greenery. The chef-manager, Daniel Humbert, offers one menu throughout the pub and he continues to produce excellent food: choose seafood terrine of salmon, mussels and prawns with a lobster dressing, or smoked chicken salad with raspberry viniagrette, then perhaps pan-fried pork fillet with grain mustard and white wine sauce, roast duck with Cointreau and orange, cassoulet Toulousain (pork and garlic sausages with flageolet beans) or salmon fillet hollandaise. Finish with a classic, tangy tarte au citron, a delicate crème brulée, bread-and-butter pudding, sticky toffee pudding or strawberry tuile – all show a lightness of touch and substantial skill. Fixed-priced three-course menus include Le Menu Touristique (Apr-Sep), Le Menu Regional (Oct-Mar) and look out for the various speciality evenings; Bastille Day, July 14, is celebrated in suitably Gallic style – book well in advance – tables can be booked throughout (including the conservatory). Good list of wines, including some classic Bordeaux bottles. Air-conditioned. Children welcome.
Open 12-3 (till 3.30 Sun), 6-11. Closed Sun eve Nov-Mar & Bank Holiday Mon eve).
Bar Food *12-2, 7-10 (till 9.30 Sun). Free House.* **Beer** *Adnams Southwold & Broadside, Larkins Bitter, guest beer. Garden, patio, outdoor eating. MasterCard,* **VISA**

IXWORTH　　　Pykkerell Inn　　　FOOD

Tel 01359 230398　　　　　　Map 10 C2
High Street Ixworth Suffolk IP31 2HH

Don't be fooled by the unassuming brick exterior for it belies the true age of this rambling old coaching inn. Its medieval 15th-century charm has been carefully revealed throughout the series of rooms which ooze antiquity and atmosphere. Stripped ancient panelling, heavily carved beams, bare-boarded floors strewn with colourful Persian rugs, a library and a delightful mix of antique tables and chairs characterise this most civilised place. Added welcome touches include brass candle-holders on tables, soothing classical music and newspapers to browse. Food matches the ambience and decor in quality and style, with imaginative home-cooked dishes – using fresh local ingredients – in both bar and à la carte restaurant drawing a generally upmarket clientele from far and wide. Various blackboards list the day's fare, notably fresh fish from Lowestoft such as supreme of hake with white wine and cream and sole Veronique. Further choices range from green-lipped mussels, peppered pork chops with cheese and cider sauce, guinea fowl with mushrooms and Madeira sauce, rack of lamb with blueberry and mint, and vegetarian dishes like vegetable pasta bake, all served with crisp fresh vegetables. More adventurous restaurant fare can also be ordered in the bar. Leave room for an excellent pudding like banana crumble and chocolate and Bailey's mousse. Good range of wines, including over 15 country fruit wines. Rear courtyard seating for warmer days overlooks a fine timber-framed Elizabethan barn. Licensees also run the *Red Lion* at Icklingham (see entry).
Open 12-2.30, 6-11, **Bar Food** *12-2.30, 6-10.* **Beer** *Greene King. Courtyard seating, outdoor eating. Family room. MasterCard,* **VISA**

Many **B&B** establishments offer reduced rates for weekend and out-of-season bookings. Always ask about special deals for longer stays. Beware half-board terms in inns where we do not recommend the **FOOD**.

KEGWORTH   Cap & Stocking   FOOD

Tel 01509 674814   Map 7 D3
20 Borough Street Kegworth Leicestershire DE74 2FF

Far from being either Leicestershire's oldest or most fashionable pub, today's high-flying 'Cap' is as evocative as its name, remarkable not least for its pétanque piste in the old walled garden and the ancient tradition of Bass-served-in-the-jug. Two unpretentious front rooms; the 'tap' room boasting etched glass and cases of stuffed birds and fish.. The kitchen crew produces customer-inspired dishes from meat and provisions bought in daily. As well as filled cob rolls, ploughman's platters and pizzas, the clamour is for ever-spicier curries such as Sri Lankan chicken, wider vegetarian options – alu Chule (green lentil curry) – and even more custard with the popular puddings like hot treacle sponge. Parking very limited. Convenient for M1 J24. *Open 11.30-3, 6-11 (Sun 12-3, 7-10.30). Bar Food 12-2.30, 6.30-9 (from 7 Sun). Beer Bass, M&B Mild, Hancock's HB, two guest beers. Garden, outdoor eating, pétanque. Family room. No credit cards.*

KELSTON   Old Crown   A

Tel 01225 423032   Map 13 F1
Bath Road Kelston Bath & North East Somerset BA1 9AQ

Standing alongside the old coaching route from Bristol to Bath (now the A431), with its car park across the busy road, the Old Crown is a gem of a place which has the carefully cultivated air of being by-passed by time. By day and by night flickering candles along the bar and mantleshelves, constantly highlighting strings of hops above the bar, are reflected in the glass of the pub's collection of framed prints and montages. The front rooms have shining, uneven flagstone floors, polished tables and carved oak settles. Real-ale buffs though, can enthuse over the authentic bank of four unaltered 1930s' beer engines which still dispense some fine Bass, Butcombe and regular guest brews. No children under 14 inside; however, there are picnic tables at the back, prettily laid-out in a mature orchard. *Open 11.30-2.30, 5-11 (Sun 12-3, 7-10.30). Free House. Beer Bass, Butcombe, Wadworth 6X, Smiles Best. Garden. Closed 25 Dec eve & all 26 Dec. MasterCard, VISA*

KEMPSEY   Walter de Cantelupe Inn   FOOD

Tel 01905 820572   Map 14 B1
Kempsey Worcester Hereford & Worcester WR5 3NA

In a modest former cider house on the A38 one and a half miles south of Worcester's city boundary, Martin Lloyd Morris has been plying his trade since late 1991. He provides a welcoming atmosphere, well-kept real ales and purposefully fresh food selections kept sensibly simple; the menu changes with the seasons. Beside a lunch menu offering the likes of doorstep sandwiches, hot filled baguettes, lamb curry made with authentic spices, seafood pot and a ploughman's lunch with local Ansty's Double Worcester cheese, there are daily lunch blackboard specials (chicken with Dijon mustard). As evenings draw a hungrier crowd, the range then might run to warm spring lamb and rocket salad, chicken liver paté, pork tenderloin stuffed with apricots and mushrooms, aubergine, courgette and sweet pepper risotto, and daily fresh fish dishes like fresh lemon sole and tilapia. For pudding try hot apple and cinnamon crumble, locally-made ice creams or a selection of British farmhouse cheeses. Book ahead or arrive early to avoid disappointment, as dishes are limited by the supply of fresh produce. Children under 10 welcome inside until 8.30, if eating with parents. *Open 11.30-2.30, 5.30-11 (12-2, 6-11 in winter), Sun 12-3, 7-10.30. Closed Mon lunch (except Bank Holidays). Bar Food 12-2.30 (till 3 Sun), 6-10 (from 6.30 Sat). No bar food Sun eve. Free House. Beer Timothy Taylor's Landlord, Marston's Best, Wadworth 6X (winter) guest beer. Patio, outdoor eating. MasterCard, VISA*

KEYSOE   Chequers Inn   A

Tel 01234 708678   Map 15 E1
Pertenhall Road Keysoe Bedfordshire MK44 2HR

Dating back to 1520, the Chequers' one bar is divided into two by an unusual pillared fireplace; log fires in cold weather. The separate lounge opens on to a large, lawned garden complete with a Wendy House, playtree and swing. *Open 11.30-2.30, 6.30-11 (Sun 12-3, 7-10.30). Closed all Tue. Free House.* **Beer** *Hook Norton Best Bitter, guest beer. Garden, children's play area. MasterCard,* **VISA**

KEYSTON   Pheasant Inn   ★   FOOD

Tel 01832 710241   Fax 01832 710340   Map 7 E4
Village Loop Road Keyston Bythorn Cambridgeshire PE18 0RE

Nestling in a sleepy village off the busy A14 between Huntingdon and Kettering, this old white-painted thatched inn is a mecca for the food lovers of this part of the country. The cosy interior with its candlelit, polished heavy oak tables and walls hung with old hunting prints is the setting for chef/patron Martin Lee's very well prepared food. Whether you eat in the informal bar lounge with its roaring winter log fire or in the smarter, more formal 'Red Room', the menu's the same with no restrictions as to how much or how little you eat. The latter is a no-smoking room. The menu of mouthwatering dishes offers the likes of a double-baked goat's cheese soufflé served amid a generous pile of leaves and apple and walnut salad, seared queen scallops with a courgette chutney, or chicken, mushroom and basil sausage with braised lentils to begin. Follow with wild boar sausages with mashed potato and an onion and Dijon mustard sauce, confit of duck leg, or baked fillet of cod with a herb crust, leeks and red wine sauce. Wonderful chips are a possible accompaniment. As wel as Neal's Yard unpasteurised cheeses there are stunning desserts like dark chocolate tart with Jersey double cream or apple tart to round off a very splendid meal. Superb wine list. Young staff provide willing service with a smile. Booking essential for dinner. *Open 11-3, 6-11 (Sun 12-10.30).* **Bar Food** *12-2, 6-10 (from 7 Sun). Free House.* **Beer** *Adnams Best, three guest beers. Garden, outdoor eating. Family room. Closed 25 & 26 Dec lunch. Amex, Diners, MasterCard,* **VISA**

KILVE   Hood Arms   B&B

Tel 01278 741210   Fax 01278 741477   Map 13 E1
Kilve Bridgwater Somerset TA5 1EA

Zzz...

Pristine, summer flower bedecked 17th-century village coaching inn nestling at the front of the Quantock Hills, a mile from the sea. Modernised, comfortable interior with collection of copper and brass and a wood-burning stove in the neat, carpeted main bar. New owners have refurbished the lounge bar, filling it with fresh flowers and introducing some home-cooked food (not yet inspected) and good local ales. Improvements extend to redecoration of the bedrooms; all have en suite baths, TV, beverage facilities, trouser press and hairdryer; two rooms at the rear are the quietest and overlook the pleasant garden. *Open 11-2.30, 6-11 (Sun 12-2.30, 7-10.30). Free House.* **Beer** *Exmoor Ale, Cotleigh Tawny, Flowers Original. Garden.* **Accommodation** *5 bedrooms, all en suite, £48-£65 (single £35-£38). Children welcome overnight (under-12s stay free in parents' room, 12-16s £10). Check-in by arrangement. MasterCard,* **VISA**

Many **B&B** establishments offer reduced rates for weekend and
out-of-season bookings. Always ask about special deals for longer stays. Beware
half-board terms in inns where we do not recommend the **FOOD**.

KING'S LYNN   Tudor Rose   B&B

Tel 01553 762824   Fax 01553 764894   Map 10 B1
St Nicholas Street off Tuesday Market Place King's Lynn Norfolk PE30 1LR

Located just off the main Market Place, this medieval timber-framed merchant's house was built around 1500 with a brick townhouse extension added in the 1640s. Beyond the medieval oak studded door lies a good panelled pubby bar, a charming 15th-century beamed restaurant and twelve neat and tidy bedrooms, some of which have views of St Nicholas's Chapel. Ten rooms have clean en suite facilities and added comforts – TV, clock-radio, tea-makers, telephones and hairdryers – are standard throughout. Upgrading and refurbishment of all the modest bedrooms should be complete by the end of 1996. *Open 11-11 (Sun 12-3, 7-10.30). Free House.* **Beer** *Boddingtons, Bass, Woodforde's Wherry, guest beer. Garden.* **Accommodation** *13 bedrooms, 10 en suite (two with private bath not en suite), £50 (single £30). Children welcome overnight (under-2s free), additional bed (£5) & cot supplied. Amex, Diners, MasterCard,* **VISA**

KINGSAND   Halfway House Inn   FOOD

Tel 01752 822279   Map 12 C3   **B&B**
Kingsand Torpoint Cornwall PL10 1NA

 ☺

Attractive pink-washed inn tucked among the narrow lanes and houses of this quaint fishing village, and only a few yards from the seafront. Comfortably refurbished by David and Sarah Riggs it has become a popular place in which to dine and more recently to stay. Relaxing, carpeted and stone walled bar furnished with a mix of old pine and small copper-topped tables and warmed by a good woodburning stove. A routine bar menu (sandwiches, granary rolls, ploughman's platters, jacket potatoes, all-day breakfast) is enhanced by an imaginative blackboard selection of dishes that are served in both the bar and the small cosy restaurant. As one might expect, it is very fish orientated. Start, perhaps, with delicious crab puffs in a pool of pesto sauce, a selection of smoked fish, or marinated red peppers, followed by stuffed red mullet wrapped in vine leaves, pan-fried scallops with Puy lentil sauce, or jugged rabbit and pork tenderloin stuffed with apricots. chocolate brandy biscuit cake may feature on the pudding board. Co-ordinating Laura Ashley fabrics, wall friezes and wallpapers grace the well kitted out, fresh and clean en suite bedrooms which are furnished with modern pine pieces, cane chairs, and attractive prints with a seashore theme adorn the walls. Each window has its own colourful and overflowing box of flowers in the summer. A family bedroom has bunk beds. Value-for-money overnight accommodation. *Open 12-4, 6-11 (from 7 in winter), Sun 12-3, 7-10.30.* **Bar Food** *12-2.30 (till 3 Sat & Sun), 6.30-9.30 (from 7 in winter). Free House.* **Beer** *Bass, Boddingtons, Flowers Original, Wadworth 6X, guest beer (summer). Family room.* **Accommodation** *5 bedrooms, all en suite (shower), £40 (family room £60, single £20). Children welcome overnight (under-3s free, 3-12s half-price), additional bed & cot available. Amex, Diners, MasterCard,* **VISA**

> We do not accept free meals or hospitality – our inspectors pay their own bills and never book in the name of Egon Ronay's Guides.

KINGSCOTE   Hunters Hall   B&B

Tel 01453 860393   Fax 01453 860707   Map 14 B2
Kingscote Tetbury Gloucestershire GL8 8XZ

☺ ♉

Five miles from Tetbury on the A4135 Hunters Hall is an ideal spot for a family day out. It sports a lovely tree-lined garden with extensive play areas and assault course, while on wet days parents and little ones use the gallery room, almost hidden above the pub's interlinked beamed and flagstoned bars. Standing separately, a Cotswold stone block of recent construction houses the bedrooms, residents' lounge and a conference facility. With roomy en suite bathrooms, remote-control TV and dial-out phone, neither space nor comfort is stinted: two ground-floor rooms incorporate facilities for the disabled, and a large suite has two double bedrooms. Good selection of wines by the glass. New management (Old English Pub Company), head chef and menus since last year's guide. *Open 11-11 (Sun 12-10.30). Free House.* **Beer** *Bass, Hook Norton Best, Marston's Pedigree, Uley Old Spot. Garden, barbecue, children's play area. Family room.* **Accommodation** *12 bedrooms, all en suite, £60 (four-poster £70, family room for three £70, for four £85, single £45). Children welcome overnight (under 4s stay free in parents' room, 5-14s £10), additional bed & cot available. Amex, Diners, MasterCard,* **VISA**

KINGSDON	**Kingsdon Inn**	FOOD

Tel 01935 840543   Map 13 F2
Kingsdon Somerton Somerset TA11 7LG

Weary A303 travellers should take note of this pretty little thatched cottage (located in the village centre only a few minutes' drive from Podimore Island), as it is the ideal spot to relax over a good home-cooked lunch or supper. A picture-postcard exterior is complete with flower-edged front path leading to the front door, either side of which are picnic benches for peaceful summer drinking and enjoying the pastoral views. The interior is equally charming, especially the older front section of the bar with its low ceiling beams, huge stone inglenook (not used) and splendid fruit garland over the bessamer beam. There's a warm and welcoming atmosphere throughout the three distinct areas, all of which are tastefully decorated (pale apricot ragged walls with friezes), furnished with scrubbed pine and old stripped tables and chairs, and warmed by a blazing log fire on cooler days. Separate short lunch and evening blackboards feature a reliable mix of pub favourites at lunchtime, from filled jacket potatoes and ploughman's platters to steak and kidney pie, celery and Stilton quiche, tagliatelle with ham, cream and mushrooms and lamb's liver and bacon. More imaginative evening fare may include mussels with white wine and shallots, game liver paté, medallions of pork with apricots and almonds, monkfish in Pernod, wild rabbit with Dijon mustard sauce and roast duck with 'local' scrumpy sauce. Raspberry and almond tart and chocolate and brandy roulade are typical puddings. All-in-all, a good village local – they can field rugby, golf and cricket teams as well as offer traditional pub games. *Open 11-3, 6-11 (Sun 12-3, 7-10.30).* **Bar Food** *12-2, 7-10. Free House.* **Beer** *Fuller's London Pride, Smiles Best, Oakhill Best, guest beers. Garden, outdoor eating. No credit cards.*

KINGSKERSWELL	**Barn Owl Inn**	FOOD
		B&B

Tel 01803 872130   Fax 01803 875279   Map 13 D3
Kingkerswell Newton Abbot Devon TQ12 5AN

Zzz...

Look out for a sign on the A380 to the Barn Owl Inn, which offers decent food, good bedrooms and a friendly welcome. Lovingly restored by the Warners, the original 16th-century farmhouse has a neat if unremarkable exterior which makes its characterful interior even more of a surprise. Old beams, rough stone walls and flagstoned floors have been uncovered, and real log fires warm each of the three bars in winter. One room features an inglenook fireplace, another an ancient black-leaded range, while in the largest bar (now more intimate), oak panelling and an ornate plasterwork ceiling are rather grander than might be expected of a modest farmhouse. A printed bar menu offers a standard choice of pub meals, from cold platters and filled jacket potatoes to steaks. Home-cooked daily specials listed on the blackboard improve matters significantly with such dishes as darne of salmon with horseradish crust, medley of seafood, Oriental pork stir-fry, monkfish kebabs, and beef Wellington with Madeira sauce, all accompanied by a decent selection of fresh vegetables. Remember to bring your appetite; portions are generous. Six bedrooms within the original farmhouse combine considerable charm with conveniences like television and direct-dial telephones. Extensive sound-proofing effectively eliminates any noise from the bars below. Rooms are cottagey in style with black beams, white plaster walls, dark-stained pine furniture locally made in solid country style and their own individual floral fabrics. Bowls of fruit, fresh flowers and mineral water add the final homely touch to the pristinely kept rooms. No children under 14 are permitted in either bars or bedrooms, but they are welcome in the small walled garden. *Open 11.30-2.30, 6.30-11 (Sun 12-2.30, 7-10.30).* **Bar Food** *11.30-2 (from 12 Sun), 6.30-10 (from 7 Sun). Free House.* **Beer** *Fergusons Dartmoor Best, Ind Coope Burton Ale, Marston's Pedigree. Garden, outdoor eating.* **Accommodation** *6 bedrooms, all en suite, £60-£75 (single £47.50). No dogs. Pub & accommodation closed 25-27 Dec. Amex, Diners, MasterCard,* **VISA**

KINGSTEIGNTON   Old Rydon Inn   ★   FOOD

Tel 01626 54626   Fax 01626 56980   Map 13 D3
Old Rydon Road Kingsteignton Newton Abbot Devon TQ12 3QG

Hermann Hruby (pronounced Ruby) continues to maintain his high standards in producing some of the best pub food in the South West, and in that respect little has changed since the Hrubys bought the Old Rydon in 1978 except for the building of a splendid, and large, heated conservatory, leafy with vines, jasmine, bougainvillaea and other plants. It's a Grade II listed former farmhouse, converted in the 1960s with an original old cider loft forming an attractive part of the bar, previously the farm stables. Underneath the plank and beam ceiling adorned with pewter mugs is a raised log fire; the whitewashed stone walls are hung with antlers and horns. Tables here are drinking style, too small and cramped for relaxed dining, and many of the seats are converted barrels. The place to dine is in the comfortable conservatory, or on warm sunny days at a table on the patio or in the sheltered walled garden – an ideal summer venue for lunch. Separate from the bar, a relaxing diners' lounge leads through to the charming little restaurant, in the oldest part of the building. Most visitors come for the delicious and interesting food (including sandwiches and ploughman's platters) which, in the bar, is listed on twice daily-changing blackboards and might include seafood pancake in shellfish sauce, goujons of Brixham fish with a spicy coating and lime mayonnaise, strips of pollock with lemon, honey and ginger with stir-fried vegetables, grilled lamb neck fillet with rosemary scented rice and red pepper sauce, venison or hare pie, various pasta specials (chargrilled vegetables with tapénade), and vegetarian options like large local flat mushrooms with tomato, red pepper and basil sauce. Excellent puddings range from spiced banana cake to home-made lemon layer pudding. Service is polite and very efficient. No children under 8 in the pub after 8pm. The pub is awkward to locate as it now hides within a modern housing estate, but it is best approached along Longford Lane off the A381, then take Rydon Road which lies on your left. *Open 11-2.30, 6-11 (Sun 12-3, 7-10.30).* **Bar Food** *12-2, 7-9.30. Free House.* **Beer** *Wadworth 6X, Bass, guest beer. Garden, outdoor eating. Family room. Amex, Diners, MasterCard,* **VISA**

KINGSTON   The Juggs   FOOD

Tel 01273 472523   Fax 01273 476150   Map 11 B6
The Street Kingston Lewes East Sussex BN7 3NT

☺

Just off the A27, a short distance from Brighton, you will find this picturesque little 15th-century inn made from two tiny cottages. The name 'Juggs' originates from the leather jugs the women used to carry on their heads to collect fish from the market. The main bar is particularly characterful with its low ceilings, rough black timbers, rustic benches and yellowing walls; there's also a small no-smoking dining area (same menu in both, bookings taken) and a rear no-smiking family room. Daily specials like mushroom, spinach and garlic lasagne or tuna, sweetcorn and spring onion quiche are prominently displayed. The home-made steak and kidney puddings have a reputation for being enormous and good value, the Sussex bangers are made by a local butcher and served with proper chips, and puddings, all home-made, are considered a speciality: perhaps apple strudel lemon cheesecake or redberry crème brulé. Open sandwiches, ploughman's platters, home-made soups and salads are also offered, as well as a Sunday lunch buffet (limited hot food). Large outdoor seating area on a bricked terrace and underneath a pergola. In addition to the pub's wooden climbing frame there's a new playground on the other side of the car park. Head up the lane past the church and you'll find yourself right at the bottom of the Downs. *Open 11-2.30, 6-10.45 (till 11 Fri & Sat, 11-11 July & Aug), Sun 12-3, 7-10.30,* **Bar Food** *12-2, 6-9.30 (from 7 Sun) Free House.* **Beer** *Harveys Best, King & Barnes Festive, guest beer. Garden, outdoor eating, children's play area. Family room. Closed all 26 Dec. MasterCard,* **VISA**

KINTBURY   Dundas Arms   FOOD

Tel 01488 658263   Fax 01488 658568   Map 14a B4   **B&B**
53 Station Road Kintbury Newbury Berkshire RG15 0UT

Reached via Halfway, past the Kintbury turnoff from the Hungerford-bound A4, this well-loved, reliable old-fashioned waterside inn, by the Kennet and Avon canal, has been run by the Dalzell-Pipers since the 1960s. The civilised bar has a striking display of blue patterned plates entirely covering one wall. The riverside patio is very popular on summer lunchtimes. The comfortable dining-room with canal views is the stage for owner David's cooking. Fresh local ingredients are prepared with skill, confidence and a notable lack of fuss. These talents show up well in dishes like paté-stuffed quail with peppered red jelly and grilled red mullet with a lively citrus sauce which appear on the 3-course lunch menu; ploughman's lunches and further light dishes (potted duck with sweet red pepper relish, crab au gratin, steak and kidney pie, Cajun spiced chicken with stir-fry vegetables and children's meals) appear on a short lunchtime bar menu. Dinner is à la carte: perhaps fried scallops with tomato and coriander, red mullet with saffron onions, roast monkfish with passion fruit glaze, knuckle of lamb with rosemary and garlic, and seared salmon with couscous and courgette cream. The Dalzell-Pipers are particularly proud of their outstanding wine list which features genuinely cheap prices for some classy wines. Food is also served in the small 'Cocktail' bar. Pleasant bedrooms are in a converted livery and stable block, with French windows opening on to a quiet private terrace, where garden furniture is provided for each room. Also recommended in our *1997 Hotels & Restaurants Guide*. *Open 11-2.30, 6-11 (Sun 12-2.30, 7-10.30). Bar Food   12-2, 7-9 (no food all Sun & Mon eve). Beer Morland Original & Old Speckled Hen, Charles Wells Bombardier, guest beer. Canalside patio/terrace, outdoor eating. Accommodation 5 bedrooms, all en suite, £65 (single £55). Children welcome overnight, additional bed (£5) available. Check-in by arrangement. Amex, MasterCard,* **VISA**

KIRKBY LONSDALE   Snooty Fox Tavern   FOOD

Tel 01524 271308   Fax 01524 272642   Map 4 C4   **B&B**
Main Street Kirkby Lonsdale Cumbria LA6 2AH

Completely refurbished former Jacobean coaching inn near the town square. Inside, the various bars and eating areas sport all sorts of interesting bits and pieces from a collection of period clothing to numerous stuffed animals and birds in glass cases. Chef-manager Gordon Cartwright, who runs things with wife Joanna, operates a long menu with a wide range of around 40 dishes, from smoked salmon and dill mousse, home-made soup (with apricot and walnut bread) and Cumberland sausage with an onion and mignonette sauce and mashed potato to leek and Brie tart with tomato sauce, honey roast lamb with Madeira and caramelised onions, sweet and sour pork and chargrilled medallions of Angus fillet with chips; not forgetting jacket potatoes, salads, spotted dick and much else besides. Everything is home-made and enjoyable and bookings are suggested for Sunday lunches. There is a small walled beer garden to the rear across a cobbled courtyard. Children are made welcome with small portions and high-chairs. Well-refurbished bedrooms, of which there are now nine (and all no-smoking), boast a variety of furniture (sometimes antique) and pretty duvet covers with co-ordinating curtains. Many have characterful exposed timbers and all are en suite; just one has a bath, the others fully-tiled shower rooms. No telephones in the bedrooms. Breakfasts show that Gordon Cartwright's experience in the kitchens at Sharrow Bay in Ullswater has paid dividends: choose from pan-fried apple rings, sautéed mushrooms, hash browns and Berry black pudding to go with the more usual egg, smoked bacon, local pork sausage, roasted tomato and fried bread – all served on elegant Villeroy & Boch plates. *Open 11-11 (Sun 12-10.30). Bar Food 12-2.30, 6.30-10 (Sun 7-9.30). Free House. Beer Hartleys XB, Theakston Best, Timothy Taylor's Landlord. Garden, outdoor eating. Accommodation 9 rooms, all en suite (one with bath), £49.50-£52.50 (single £29). Children welcome overnight, additional beds (£10) & cot (£5) available. Accommodation closed all 25 Dec, 31 Dec & 1 Jan. Amex, Diners, MasterCard,* **VISA**

KIRKBYMOORSIDE — George & Dragon Hotel — FOOD

Tel & Fax 01751 433334   Map 5 E4   **B&B**
Market Place Kirkbymoorside North Yorkshire YO6 6AA

🐟 ♍ Zzz...

Agreeably fulfilling its dual role of town-centre hostelry and quiet country inn, Stephen and Frances Colling's George and Dragon stands imposingly by the cobbled square of picturesque Kirkbymoorside. There's a single bar in front, with sporting prints and paraphernalia, where bar food is listed on large blackboards and every available beam above the servery. Choices here start with seafood hotpot and broccoli and Stilton soup, progressing to minted lamb casserole, fillet of pork with prunes and cider sauce, and fresh fish from Whitby (monkfish in vermouth sauce) and local game from the moors (venison in red wine), with voluminous puddings (chocolate fruit and nut slice) to follow. Ever-popular, however, remain the steak and mushroom pie with Guinness and two-course Sunday roast. Sandwiches and ploughman's platters at lunchtimes only. Housed in two detached rear buildings, one a former brewhouse, the spacious bedrooms overlook an enclosed wall garden. Artistic interior designs greatly enhance their individual appeal and all feature remote-control TVs, dial-out phones and hairdryers; bathrooms have smart over-bath showers and complimentary toiletries. Residents enjoy exclusive use of the garden lounge. *Open 11-3, 6-11 (Sun 12-3, 7-10.30).* **Bar Food** *12-2.15, 6.30-9.15. Free House.* **Beer** *John Smith's, Timothy Taylor's Landlord, Black Sheep Bitter. Garden, patio, outdoor eating.* **Accommodation** *19 bedrooms, all en suite, £73-£83 (single £49). Children welcome overnight (under 16s stay free in parents' room), additional bed & cot available. MasterCard,* **VISA**

KNAPP — Rising Sun — FOOD

Tel 01823 490436   Map 13 E2
Knapp North Curry Taunton Somerset TA3 6BG

🐟 ♍

Directions here are hard to give and just as hard to follow. Meander down the lanes from the hamlet of Ham (six miles west of Junction 25 on the M5), right on the lip of the Somerset levels, and then keep a lookout for the arrows. Built as a Longhouse in 1480 and 'rediscovered' since the arrival of Tony Atkinson in 1989, the Rising Sun attracts its fill of worshippers of fine, fresh fish these days, and diners should mark out their spot especially early at weekends. Separated by a lounge bar with deep sofas in front of a cast-iron stove, two cottage dining areas are now given over to some serious eating with top billing given to fresh fish from Brixham and elsewhere – Tony self-styles the Rising Sun as a 'restaurant with a bar', although there are no table cloths and the service is not formal. Chef Wendy Repton's prodigious output from the kitchen might include chunky bouillabaisse or crab fishcakes to start, following with John Dory with sun-dried tomatoes, anchovies and capers, brill topped with salmon mousse and cucumber with a white wine sauce, and crevettes pan-fried with cajun spices; so popular are the megrims (Torbay sole), lobsters and langoustines that availability cannot be promised to later arrivals. Meat eaters may prefer a steak or chicken with mushroom and garlic sauce. More traditional, pubby lunchtime snacks (open sandwiches, ploughman's platters, ham, egg and chips) are also available; in the evening the place steps up a gear and the snackier items are not served. Half portions for children, popular Sunday lunch with roast rib of beef, Yorkshire pudding and hot fishy bits on the bar and flowery summer patios are all added draws. *Open 11.30-2.30, 6.30-11 (Sun 12-3, 7-10.30).* **Bar Food** *12-2, 7-9.30. (no food Sun eve Oct-Apr). Free House.* **Beer** *Boddingtons, Bass, Exmoor Ale. Patio. Family Room. MasterCard,* **VISA**

We endeavour to be as up-to-date as possible but inevitably some changes to
landlords, chefs and other key staff occur after the Guide
has gone to press.

KNIGHTWICK — Talbot Hotel — FOOD

Tel 01886 821235   Fax 01886 821060   Map 14 B1   **B&B**
Knightwick Worcester Hereford & Worcester WR6 5PH

On the banks of the River Teme, on which it has fishing rights, the Talbot stands by
a disused road bridge and conveniently back from the new crossing on the busy A44.
Dating in parts from the 14th Century, it retains an evocative interior of oak beams
and blackened brick, the bar's finest feature being the back-to-back open fire and cast-
iron, wood-burning stove which share a central chimney. There's a whizz in the
kitchen, producing commendably varied home-cooking on a daily menu that services
both bar and dining-room. For a snack, try the crab and mushroom tart, four cheese
tagliatelle or fresh scallop beignets, while diners may satiate themselves on a three-
course meal of pigeon breast salad, venison Wellington or pan-fried wild salmon with
a sorrel and cream sauce with, to follow, Normandy apple flan or sticky date and
toffee pudding. Fish (mackerel with confit of spring onions, ginger and garlic) is
becoming increasingly popular. The bedrooms' up-to-date amenities include colour
TVs, tea trays and dial-out telephones with little other obeisance to ostentation or
modernity. Furnishings and decor are generally modest and comfortable in a cottagey
style – best employed in the newer bedroom extension. Above the bars, three
bedrooms are larger and more characterful but share their bathing and toilet facilities.
Open 11-11 (Sun 12-10.30). **Bar Food** *12-2, 6.30-9.30 (Sun 7-9). Free House.*
Beer *Bass, Worthington Best, Hobson's Bitter. Patio/terrace, outdoor eating. Family room.*
Accommodation *10 bedrooms, 7 en suite, £56.50 (family room £52-£66.50, single £24-
£31). Children welcome overnight (charged according to age), additional bed (£10) & cot
available. MasterCard,* **VISA**

KNOWL HILL — Bird in Hand — B&B

Tel 01628 826622   Fax 01628 826748   Map 15a D3
Bath Road Knowl Hill Twyford Berkshire RG10 9UP

Zzz...

Set well back from the A4, the inn that exists today bears little resemblance to the
hostelry bestowed with a Royal Charter by King George III in the late 1700s. Today's
extensions to the lounge bar and patio, with umbilical connections to a 15-bedroom
wing have incorporated much of the old stonework on the inside. In places it's a
seamless join, elsewhere the stitch lines are visible. Leather armchairs, wood panelling
and a huge canopied open fireplace are the major features of the sturdy oak lounge.
The bedrooms are centred round a brick courtyard facing a secluded and mature
garden. Though light on decor, with blush walls and lined fitted units, the bedrooms
are fully equipped for today's executive market (and priced accordingly, although rates
are reduced at weekends). Trouser presses and hairdryers are added to the usual
accoutrements of direct-dial phones and remote-control TVs. Bright bathrooms are
three-quarter tiled with strong over-bath showers. Double-glazing throughout keeps
noise from the busy road fully at bay. Disabled WC. *Open 11-3, 5.45-11 (Sun 12-3,
7-10.30). Free House.* **Beer** *Fuller's London Pride, Brakspear Bitter, Flowers Original.
Garden.* **Accommodation** *15 bedrooms, all en suite, £90 (weekend double/twin £70, single
£67-£70, weekend £55). Children welcome overnight (family room sleeping four £100),
additional bed & cot available. Accommodation closed 1 week Christmas. Amex, Diners,
MasterCard,* **VISA**

KNOWSTONE — Masons Arms — FOOD

Tel 01398 341231 & 341582   Map 13 D2
Knowstone South Molton Devon EX36 4RY

Thatched, 13th-century inn tucked away in a tranquil hamlet in the foothills of
Exmoor (just off A361 between Tiverton and South Molton), in the sort of spot
where dogs fall asleep in the middle of the road. Grade II listed with a charming
unspoilt interior characterised by heavy black beams, sturdy old furniture, huge
inglenook with roaring winter log fire and a delightful chatty atmosphere. Super spot
to while away an hour or two with a pint and play a traditional pub game. Those

tempted to linger for something to eat will find that the home-cooked food complements the surroundings: rustic, hearty and value-for-money. Light snacks or starters include freshly-made soups (curried parsnip), excellent patés such as cheese and walnut – and salads. More substantial, daily-changing specials might range from Devon cider cassoulet, fish pie, roast cod with lentils, pasta with smoked salmon and cream to leg of Exmoor lamb with rosemary and garlic; good curries – Thursday night is 'curry night' – and chip-shop style cod and chips with mushy peas. Puddings like home-made pear and strawberry crunch and chocolate terrine, plus West Country cheeses. To accompany the food there is a good list of wines and real ales dispensed straight from the cask. Peaceful rear patio and garden with rolling rural views towards Exmoor. Gradual upgrading of the homely accommodation continues and all bedrooms should be en suite in 1997 (not recently inspected). *Open 11-3, 6-11 (12-2.30, 7-11 winter), Sun 12-3.30, 7-10.30.* **Bar Food** *12-2, 7-9.30 (till 9 Sun & in winter). Free House.* **Beer** *Cotleigh Tawny Ale, Hall & Woodhouse Badger Best. Garden, outdoor eating. Family room. Closed 25 & 26 Dec eve. No credit cards.*

LACOCK — George Inn — FOOD

Tel 01249 730263
4 West Street Lacock Chippenham Wiltshire SN15 2LH

Map 14 B2

The virtual epitome of the traditional village pub. The George could scarcely be in a more ideal spot than the National Trust village of Lacock. Starting life in 1361 as the Black Boy with its own brewery in farm buildings to the rear, its many modernisations have preserved and re-utilised many of the original timbers. Central to the bar is a unique mounted dog-wheel built into the open fireplace and used for spit-roasting in the 16th-century (the dog was not roasted, but trained to rotate the wheel). Today's pub lives well alongside such idiosyncrasy with its close-packed tables on odd levels set beneath a wealth of old pictures at many an odd angle. From a menu of firm favourites, traditional steak and kidney pie is always popular alongside wild boar steak with sweet and sour sauce, fisherman's pie, chicken stew and dumplings and a vegetable balti curry. "You can have anything from a bowl of chips to a Dover sole", says the landlord. For pudding, try the banana and toffee crunch or the triple chocolate cheesecake. The large garden stretches out on both sides of the rear car park; beyond it is a safe play area for youngsters, close by an old stocks to restrain the most troublesome. True to its long-standing identity as a family concern, the licensees' family not only provides overnight farmhouse accommodation nearby but also lays on complimentary transport to and from the pub. Enquiries should be addressed to the pub. *Open 10-3, 5-11 (10-11 Sat summer), Sun 12-10.30.* **Bar Food** *12-2, 6-10.* **Beer** *Wadworth. Garden, outdoor eating, children's play area. MasterCard,* **VISA**

LAMARSH — Red Lion — A

Tel 01787 227918
Lamarsh Essex CO8 5EP

Map 10 C3

Enjoying a peaceful location overlooking the gently-rolling landscape bordering the River Stour valley, this charming little tiled Essex pub dates from the 14th century. It's a wonderful place to frequent on a sunny summer's evening when the perfectly-positioned front benches make the most of the view. Beams abound in the comfortable modernised interior with its rather ecclesiastical, carved and inscribed bar counter, restored pews, attractive walls murals of Suffolk scenes and welcoming winter log fire. The 16th-century barn holds a games room and is popular with locals. *Open 11-3, 6-11 (Sat 11-11, Sun 12-3, 7-10.30). Free House.* **Beer** *Greene King IPA, Fuller's London Pride, Wadworth 6X. Garden, children's play area. Family room. MasterCard,* **VISA**

LANGDALE — Three Shires Inn — B&B

Tel 01539 437215 Map 4 C3
Little Langdale Ambleside Cumbria LA22 9NZ

Zzz...

Little Langdale stands at a point in the Cumbrian mountains where the former three shires of Cumberland, Westmorland and Lancashire once came together. Built in 1872 entirely in Lakeland slate, the inn sustained those crossing the nearby Wrynose and Hardknott passes to and from the coast. Still a travellers' haven today, the Three Shires is notable for its tranquillity amid restful scenery whose only early morning intrusions are the birds and nearby brook. The slate bar and streamside patio are nonetheless very popular with walkers throughout the day. Residents enjoy use of their own lounge and flower-laden verandah from which to soak up the views and relax. Bedrooms are bright and spotless with generally floral-patterned decor. Though four of the rooms are on the small side, and only three are family-size, their perennial popularity is due in no small measure to an absence of TVs (they are now in some rooms) and telephones: as ever was, solitude here is king. Families are well catered for; there's a terraced garden to one side of the pub through which a stream runs, and the restaurant and snug bar are designated non-smoking. *Open Feb-end Oct 11-11 (Nov-Jan 12-3, 7-10.30), Sun 12-10.30. Free House. Beer Webster's Yorkshire, Ruddles County, guest beers. Garden. Family room. **Accommodation** 10 rooms, all en suite, £54-£70 (single £37-£45). Children welcome overnight (under 6s stay free in parents' room), additional bed & cot available. Accommodation closed Mon-Thu Dec & Jan. No dogs. No credit cards.*

LANGLEY — Brewery Inn — A

Tel 0121 544 6467 Map 6 C4
91 Station Road Langley Birmingham B69 4LW

Turn off the M5 at Junction 2 and head directly into the industrial estate (originally named Junction 2 Industrial Estate); just less than a mile later, Station Road bears left past Albright and Wilson. Though it can't be seen now, there's a Thomas Telford bridge over the canal, known here as "The Crow", which is the highest navigable waterway in Europe. By the bridge, brewers Holt, Plant and Deakin's pub is a modern, yet authentic restoration of the Telford era; the Victorian 'snob windows' which separate the lounge bar servery from the 'public' may be one of only two sets left in existence. A larger window, picture-size, allows tipplers a view of the brew house where Holt's ever-popular beers are brewed. Legions of real ale afficionados accompany it with a 'Dibble Donker' – a doorstop sandwich with three layers of thick, crusty locally-baked bread filled with cheese, onion and black pudding! Landlord Tony Stanton feels, he says, more like a curator than a publican, as there's such a wealth of history here and many gallons of pure enjoyment – in fact, it's a barrel of laughs. Classical music or big band jazz plays. *Open 11.30-2.30, 6-11 (from 7 Sat), Sun 12-2.30, 7-10.30. Beer Holts Bitter, Entire & Mild. No credit cards.*

LANGLEY MARSH — Three Horseshoes — FOOD

Tel 01984 623763 Map 12 E2
Langley Marsh Wiveliscombe Somerset TA4 2UL

Handsome 300-year-old red sandstone village inn with a homely old fashioned interior that is full of curiosities, from collections of banknotes and beermats to model aeroplanes and pictures of vintage cars – the landlord's spare-time passion. Lively 'locals' front room with traditional games and a comfortable back bar with piano, stone fireplace, a rustic mix of sturdy furniture and perhaps piped jazz music. Further attractions are the numerous real ales and Perry's farmhouse cider – all tapped straight from the cask – and the reliably delicious food which is all home-cooked. You will not find chips or fried food on the constantly-changing hand-written menu (nor on the children's menu), just hearty, freshly-prepared dishes with interesting vegetarian options and vegetables from the pub garden. Choices may include lamb casserole with fresh mint and garlic, steak, kidney and ale pie, pork curry, steaks cooked to order and spiced black bean stew. Filling snacks include warming soups (thick vegetable, lentil and bacon), filled rolls and jacket potatoes; pizzas – in two sizes, normal and enormous – are something of a speciality and cooked in the aga. If there's room, finish with mincemeat, apple and brandy pancakes or raspberry and almond cream. Alfresco seating on the verandah or in the garden for warmer days. No under-14s in the bar, only in the family games room. *Open 12-2.30, 7-11 (till 10.30 Sun).* **Bar Food** *12-2 7-9.30. Free House.* **Beer** *Ringwood Best Bitter, Young's Bitter, Dartmoor Best, Morland Old Speckled Hen, Palmers IPA, guest beers. Garden, outdoor eating, children's play area. No credit cards.*

LANGSTONE   Royal Oak   A

Tel 01705 483125   Map 15 D4
19 Langstone High Street Langstone Havant Hampshire PO9 1RY

Historic 16th-century pub with stunning views over Chichester Harbour. Right on the water's edge, the water reaches the front door when the tide's exceptionally high! Originally a row of cottages used in conjunction with the adjacent old mill, they later traded under a 'tidal licence' before the bridge to Hayling Island was built, allowing travellers a drink while waiting for the ebb tide. An individual rustic charm characterises the unspoilt interior. The neatly kept bars boast flagstone and polished pine floors, exposed beams, open fires and old wooden furnishings; a cosy haven on wild winter days. Warmer sunny days can be enjoyed with a drink on the front benches or in the secluded rear garden, which is a safe refuge for families and where a pet's corner runs the gamut from budgies to goats and a pot-bellied pig. No under-14s in bar areas. Whitbread Wayside Inn. *Open 11-11 (Sun 12-10.30).* **Beer** *Flowers Original, Boddingtons, Marston's Pedigree, guest beer. Garden, outdoor eating beside water's edge. MasterCard,* **VISA**

We do not accept free meals or hospitality – our inspectors pay their own bills and **never** book in the name of Egon Ronay's Guides.

LAVENHAM   Angel Inn   FOOD

Tel 01787 247388   Fax 01787 248344   Map 10 C3   **B&B**
Market Place Lavenham Suffolk CO10 9QZ

First licensed in 1420, the Angel looks on to the market place of one of the best preserved medieval towns in England. Inside, the bar has been opened up without losing any of its original charm, with half set up for eating and the other half well supplied with board games, playing cards and shelves of books. There are quiz and bridge nights and on Friday evenings Roy Whitworth (one of the partners) entertains with classical music at the piano. Leek and lentil soup, mushroom roulade, honey-roast pork fillet, rabbit braised with bacon and prunes and steak and kidney pie are typical offerings from the daily-changing evening menu; lunchtime brings similar dishes (at slightly lower prices) plus some more snacky items like ploughman's and cauliflower cheese. Good puddings include bread-and-butter pudding and lemon tart. Bedrooms are all en suite (five with shower, three with bath) and full of character with old beams, sloping floors and traditional freestanding furniture. All have TV, direct-dial phone and tea- and coffee-making kit. Children are made welcome with a couple of high-chairs, various toys, free cots and "put-u-up" beds; ask for small menu portions. For summer there are tables in a secluded garden plus benches and brollies overlooking the market place. *Open 11-11 (Sun 12-10.30).* **Bar Food** *12-2.15, 6.45-9.15. Free House.* **Beer** *Nethergate Bitter, Adnams Southwold, Mauldons White Adder, guest beer. Garden, patio, outdoor eating.* **Accommodation** *8 bedrooms, all en suite, £50-£60 (Sat half board only £90-£100, family room sleeping three £60-£70, single £37.50). Children welcome overnight (babies in cot free), additional bed (£10) & cot available. Closed all 25 & 26 Dec. Amex, MasterCard,* **VISA**

LEDBURY — Feathers Hotel — FOOD

Tel 01531 635266   Fax 01531 632001   Map 14 B1   **B&B**
High Street Ledbury Hereford & Worcester HR8 1DS

Right in the town centre, a classic timber-framed former coaching inn and corn exchange dating from 1564 with oddly-shaped, en suite, double-glazed bedrooms (including one with a lovely four-poster), original Elizabethan wall paintings, uneven, creaky floors and drunken staircases. Remote-control TV, direct-dial phones, bedside tea-tray and hairdryers are standard throughout. Lunchtime bar snacks in the hop-bedecked Fuggles bar may include spinach and ricotta tartlet and stir-fried sesame prawns with mangetout and garlic for starters, followed by chargrilled steaks, home-made hamburgers, salmon and fennel seed cakes and seafood and spinach lasagne. The simpler offerings are the best bet (more involved dishes like duck breast with five spice, garlic and sweet soy are less successful and offered at restaurant prices). For dessert you might find warm fig tartlet with almond cream and apricot and brandy syllabub. Annual real ale and cider festival on August Bank Holiday, music weekly on Wednesday and small rear patio available in good weather. Four miles from the M50 Junction 2. *Open 11-11. **Bar Food** 12-2 (till 2.30 Sat), 7-9.30 (till 10 Sat & Sun). **Beer** Bass, Worthington Best, two guest beers. Patio. **Accommodation** 11 bedrooms, all en suite, £65-£95 (family room £92-£100, single £49.50-£65). Children welcome overnight, additional bed & cot available. Amex, Diners, MasterCard, **VISA***

LEDBURY — Ye Olde Talbot Hotel — B&B

Tel 01531 632963   Fax 01531 633796   Map 14 B1
New Street Ledbury Hereford & Worcester HR8 2DX

The historic Talbot is a Grade II listed building and dates back to 1596; it was the scene of a well-documented skirmish between the Cavaliers and Roundheads in 1745. The classic Oak Room panelling is complete to this day with the bullet holes to prove it; here also there are magnificent Jacobean carvings and overmantel. Past a vast carved oak door guests have their own use of a tiny first-floor lounge in a bow-fronted cantilever room which overhangs the street above the front door. Bedrooms, complete with exposed beams and creaking, uneven floors, are much in character. Three only have room for en suite WC/shower rooms, the remainder sharing loos and a bathroom: all offer TV, beverage tray and clock radio. Two beamed, copper-hung bars, warmed by open winter fires, are intimate and convivial, and there's also a rear courtyard for summer drinking and occasional barbecues. The barn at the end of the courtyard is due to be converted in summer 1997 to provide more accommodation. *Open 11.30-3, 5-11 (Sun 12-3, 7-10.30). Free House. **Beer** Bass, Hancock's HB, Marston's Bitter. Courtyard. **Accommodation** 7 bedrooms, 3 en suite, £34.50 (single £29.50 – room only prices, breakfast £3.75-£5.75). Children welcome overnight (under-12s stay free in parents' room), additional bed & cot available. Amex, MasterCard, **VISA***

LEDSHAM — Chequers Inn — A

Tel 01977 683135   Map 7 D1
Claypit Lane Ledsham South Milford Leeds LS25 5LP

Deep in the Don valley at the heart of a hidden village stands the old ivy-covered Chequers, a popular, thriving local, complete with a low, roadside, bow-fronted window that lends the pub an almost Dickensian air. The entrance to the bar and first-floor restaurant is round to the rear, and the servery has its back to the village street. Tiered above a pebbled walkway are the colourful flower-filled patios which form the beer garden, so well frequented in summer. *Open 11-3, 5.30-11, (Sat 11-11). Closed Sun. **Beer** Younger's Scotch, No 3 & Best, Theakston Best, John Smith's. Patio. Family Room. MasterCard, **VISA***

We only recommend food (Bar Food) in those establishments highlighted
with the **FOOD** symbol.

LEEDS   Whitelocks   A

Tel 0113 245 3950   Map 6 C1
Turks Head Yard Briggate Leeds LS1 6HB

Lauded by the poet laureate, John Betjeman, as "the very heart of Leeds", this was the city's first-ever Luncheon Bar. Owned for nigh on a century up to 1944 by the Whitelock family (who were builders and piano tuners), it's virtually unchanged since its last facelift (it coincided with the arrival in Leeds of electricity). The bar top is copper and the sandwich servery marble; the whole bar is fronted by hand-finished ceramic tiles. The well-heeled may lunch in a panelled rear dining-room while the more down-to-earth may encroach on the many park benches which stretch the length of Turks Head Yard. Today's Luncheon Bar offers little beyond sandwiches, a pie or two and the famed Yorkshire puddings served with mince and onion gravy. Over a decent pint of Younger's ale customers hark back to the pre-war prices (Pie 2d; Cheese and Biscuits 1d) etched on the old servery mirrors – evocative reminders of the Whitelock's heyday. No children indoors. No adjacent parking. Look for the pub sign high above Briggate (a pedestrianised shopping street opposite Debenham's); the entrance to the yard is now a tunnel and can be easily missed. *Open 11-11 (Sun 12-10.30).* **Beer** *Younger's IPA, Scotch Bitter, 80/- & No 3, Theakston Best & XB. Terrace. Amex, Diners, MasterCard,* **VISA**

LEICESTER   Welford Place   FOOD

Tel 0116 247 0758 Fax 0116 247 1843   Map 7 D4
9 Welford Place Leicester Leicestershire LE1 6ZH

Follow signs for the Phoenix Arts Centre (whose car park is almost directly opposite) to find this striking Victorian building, a former Victorian gentlemen's club adjoining the Leicester magistrates' courts. Welford Place, built in 1876 and restored in 1991 still retains an aura of grandeur. Michael and Valerie Hope (who also run the *Wig & Mitre* in Lincoln) have created a spacious bar and restaurant, self-styled as a "Restaurant Pub of Rare Quality" (and they're not far off). The former is a striking semi-circular room with high windows overlooking Welford Place itself and furnished with leather armchairs and glass-topped tables, while the latter, a quietly civilised room has two great chandeliers suspended from its lofty ceiling. The menus operate throughout the day all year and any item is available at any time, but the restaurant is reserved for full meals. There is a set menu (£10.50) as well as the à la carte, both in a style of cooking that is modern while retaining traditional elements. Typical starters might include Mediterranean fish soup, creamed salt cod with grilled polenta, and baked cheese soufflé. Main dishes could be breast of duck with oranges, confit of salmon with marinated courgettes on a tomato coulis, baked guinea fowl wrapped in Parma ham and filo pastry, and fillet of sea bass with spinach and saffron butter sauce. Try the cappuccino mousse, the warm treacle tart or the interesting selection of cheeses, generally with a mix of British and French, for pudding. On-street parking during the evenings and on Sundays. *Open 11-11 (breakfast 8am-12), drinks with meals only on Sun (to 10.30).* **Bar Food** *all day (to 10.30 Sun), breakfast and snack menu served 8-12 & 3-6. Free House.* **Beer** *Ruddles Best & County. Amex, Diners, MasterCard,* **VISA**

LENHAM   Dog & Bear Hotel   B&B

Tel 01622 858219   Fax 01622 859415   Map 11 C5
The Square Lenham Maidstone Kent ME17 2PG

This attractive coaching inn dates from 1602 and overlooks the pretty village square. Splendid oak beams combine with up-to-date decor and comfortable seating in the bar, and there is a welcoming little foyer-lounge. Centrally-heated bedrooms with darkwood furniture and bright contemporary fabrics all have direct-dial telephones, TVs, tea-making facilities and neatly-kept, en suite bathrooms. Main building rooms have more charm and character, with the rooms beyond the rear courtyard offering more space. 10 minutes from Leeds Castle. Invicta Country Inns (Shepherd Neame). *Open 11-11 (Sun 12-10.30).* **Beer** *Shepherd Neame. Garden, paved courtyard.* **Accommodation** *24 bedrooms, all en suite, £49.50 (family room sleeping four £65, four-poster £55, single £38.50). Children welcome overnight (first child free, second £15.50), additional bed & cot available. Amex, MasterCard,* **VISA**

LEOMINSTER — Royal Oak Hotel — B&B

Tel 01568 612610   Fax 01568 612710   Map 14 A1
South Street Leominster Hereford & Worcester HR6 8JA

☺

Modest accommodation in an early-18th-century coaching house on the corner of
Etnam Street and South Street. Historic relics of its earlier glories are to be found in
the Regency Room, complete with chandeliers and minstrel's gallery, and the brick-
lined cellar bar which is a cosy spot in the evenings. The main Oak Bar boasts two
enormous log fires and serves good real ales. Bedrooms come in a mixture of sizes and
styles with one or two smallish singles, six spacious family rooms and a fine four-
poster suite. All have carpeted bathrooms, while room comforts run through TV and
intercom (for baby listening and wake-up calls) to tea and coffee makers and electric
blankets. *Open 10-2.30, 6-10.30 (till 11 Fri & Sat), Sun 12-2.30, 7-10.30. Free House.*
Beer Wood's Special, Brains Bitter. Small patio. Family room. **Accommodation** *18 bedrooms,
all en suite, £45 (four-poster £55, single £31.50). Children welcome overnight (stay free in
family rooms), additional bed & cot available. Dogs £2. Amex, Diners, MasterCard,* **VISA**

LEY HILL — The Swan — A

Tel 01494 783075   Map 15a E2
Ley Hill nr Chesham Buckinghamshire HP5 1UT

☺

The Swan is bedecked with planted tubs and hanging baskets in summer and is well
positioned – opposite a golf tee, village cricket ground and open common land – for
its patrons to walk off any excesses of hospitality! Within, it's cosy in winter and the
rather quaint, low-ceilinged main bar is a warren of old, beamed rooms that ramble
round to an airy, no-smoking family room extension with a hop-bedecked ceiling.
French windows lead out on to the rear garden with picnic tables and a large area in
which children may play on swinging tyres and climbing ropes. It is a popular dining
pub but the home cooking is a bit of a hit or miss affair: a traditional Sunday lunch of
roast pork was poor, but home-made Stilton and walnut paté, steak and mushroom
pie and children's options all showed some promise. Simpler, lunchtime-only
sandwiches are probably the best bet. They go to the trouble of having a 'this loo was
inspected by ...' sign, but why don't they fill it in for three days? Company policy
versus landlord's attitude? *Open 11-2.30, 5.30-11 (Sat 11-11, Sun 12-10.30).*
*Beer Ansells Dark Mild, Benskins, Burton, Tetley. Garden, children's play area. Family room.
Amex, MasterCard,* **VISA**

LIFTON — Arundell Arms — FOOD — B&B

Tel 01566 784666   Fax 01566 784494   Map 12 C2
Lifton Devon PL16 0AA

🍺 🍷

Set in a valley of five rivers, close to the uplands of Dartmoor, Anne Voss-Bark's
upmarket, creeper-clad old Devon inn is a favourite destination for those who enjoy
the country pursuits of shooting, riding, walking, birdwatching and in particular
fishing – the River Tamar flows past the bottom of the garden and the inn has 20
miles of fishing rights along its length. A truly civilised air pervades throughout its
smart interior, from the elegant lounge with deep comfortable sofas and armchairs,
antique furnishings, tasteful fabrics and hunting prints, to the refined hotel-like bar
where good-quality bar snacks are served. The short printed menu may feature a soup
with home-baked bread or a salad of avocado, leeks, French beans and tomato with
basil dressing to start, followed by interesting salads (perhaps smoked salmon with
cucumber pickle) and light, imaginative hot dishes such as salmon fishcakes, spiced
venison burgers, mignon of beef fillet and a warm salad of smoked duck breast.
Various sandwiches (egg and anchovy, croque monsieur) and a ploughman's platter
with three mixed local cheeses, salad, pickle and home-made bread are also available,
as is the daily dessert choice. The attached and independently-run Courthouse Bar
is a very pubby locals' bar serving real ale and basic bar snacks. Expensive decor and
furnishings extend upstairs to the 29 bedrooms, although some have plainer wall-fitted
units, road-facing rooms are double-glazed to quell traffic noise. Bathrooms are well

appointed with good toiletries and, as one can expect at this level, all the usual comforts grace each room. The hotel and handsome restaurant are also recommended in our *1997 Hotels & Restaurants Guide*. *Open 11-2.30, 6-11.* **Bar Food** *12-2.30, 6-9.30. Free House.* **Beer** *up to four real ales in the Courthouse Bar. Garden, outdoor eating.* **Accommodation** *29 bedrooms, all en suite, £78-£97 (single £39-£61). Children welcome overnight (under-16s stay free in parents' room), additional bed & cot available. Accommodation closed 3 days Christmas. Amex, Diners, MasterCard,* **VISA**

LINCOLN   **Wig & Mitre**   **FOOD**

Tel 01522 535190   Fax 01522 532402   Map 7 E2
29 Steep Hill Lincoln Lincolnshire LN2 1LU

The Hope family's trendy city-centre pub is not the historic ale-house it purports to be, but is nonetheless a classic. Its really rather ordinary exterior, a glass shop front under a flower-laden cast-iron balcony, stands between the Lincoln Vintner and Chantilly's bridal shop; Lincoln cathedral is just a stone's throw away across cobbled streets where once the Roman *via principalis* ran, and its echoing hourly chimes are almost deafening. The pub's interior – which also has a rear access from Drury Lane – is meticulously restored with genuine Tudor timbers, between which sections of 13th-century daub and wattle walls are still visible. Connected by three staircases, there's a warren of rooms in which to eat, two bars and a tiny rear patio, as well as a table from which you can pick up the day's papers for a browse. The menu encourages all comers to eat as little or as much as they'd like at any time throughout the premises, thus encompassing every taste and pleasing all pockets, and the catering is ambitious: breakfast starts at 8am with the papers and food is served through to 11pm. There are two daily-changing menus, one taking over from the other at around 5.30pm. More serious offerings might include cod and leek chowder, confit of chicken with cabbage, smoked bacon and thyme, a daily fresh fish dish (red mullet with black pasta and saffron butter sauce) and roast loin of pork with a tartlet of onion marmalade. Separate snack menus list smoked salmon with scrambled eggs, toasted crumpets, Lincolnshire plum bread, warm breast of chicken with mayonnaise and lettuce sandwiches and good cheeses (both French and British). Puddings may include almond and banana loaf with toffee sauce. Good choice of wines by the glass. *Open 11-11 (Sun 12-10.30).* **Bar Food** *8am-11 (snack menu 8am-12 & 3-6). Free House.* **Beer** *Sam Smith's Old Brewery Bitter. Patio/terrace, outdoor eating. Closed 25 Dec. Amex, Diners, MasterCard,* **VISA**

LINTON   **Fountaine Inn**   **FOOD**

Tel 01756 752210   Map 6 C1
Linton Skipton North Yorkshire BD23 JHJ

An idyllic village green complete with stone bridge over a little stream is the setting for this charming mid-17th century inn. Several interconnecting rooms (one for non-smokers) feature old beams and built-in settles. A new chef has taken charge in the kitchen and is producing some interesting daily specials. Follow celery, apple and calvados soup or mousseline of salmon and oyster mushrooms with medallions of monkfish with a grain mustard sauce, Ayrshire pork with a cider and apple sauce, braised shank of lamb in red wine served with lentils and root vegetables, or wild mushroom stroganoff. A short printed menu highlights popular dishes like Whitby haddock, Cumberland grill and various open sandwich platters. For the sweet-toothed there are some good home-made puds, while for those with more savoury tastes there's the local Wensleydale cheese which comes either blue, smoked or in the traditional white style. The village green is well used in summer although the publican is not allowed to put out any tables or chairs. *Open 12-2.30, 7-10.30 (till 11 Sat). Closed Sun eve & all Mon in winter.* **Bar Food** *12-2, 7-9. Free House.* **Beer** *Black Sheep Best Bitter, Theakston Best & XB. No credit cards.*

> We only recommend food (Bar Food) in those establishments highlighted with the **FOOD** symbol.

LINWOOD — High Corner Inn — B&B

Tel 01425 473973   Fax 01425 480015   Map 14 C4
Linwood Ringwood Hampshire BH24 3QY

Much extended and modernised, early 18th-century inn set in seven acres of the New Forest and located along a quarter-mile gravel track off the narrow lane linking Lyndhurst and the A338 near Ringwood. A quiet hideaway in winter, mobbed in high summer, it is a popular retreat for families with numerous bar-free rooms, a Lego/Duplo room, an outdoor adventure playground and miles of Forest walks. Overnight accommodation comprises eight well-equipped bedrooms offering teletext TV, telephone, trouser press, hairdryer, tea-makers and en suite facilities. *Open 11-2.30, 7-10.30 winter, (11-3, 6-11 summer), Sat 11-4, 6-11 winter, (11-11 summer), Sun 12-4, 7-10.30 (12-10.30 summer).* **Beer** *Wadworth 6X, Hampshire King Alfred Bitter. Garden, outdoor play area. Family room (three rooms), indoor play room. Squash court, DIY stabling.* **Accommodation** *8 bedrooms, all en suite, £69 (single £47), Children welcome overnight (under-3s free), additional bed (£4) & cot available. Check-in by arrangement. Amex, Diners, MasterCard,* **VISA**

LITTLE BRAXTED — Green Man — FOOD

Tel 01621 891659   Map 11 C4
Kelvedon Road Little Braxted Essex CM8 3LB

Tucked away in a long, straggling little hamlet signposted off B1389 near the A12 Witham bypass. Keep going down the lane past St Nicholas's church, back into open countryside, past a couple of farms, take a right branch of the road and eventually you'll come to the Green Man. This unspoilt little brick-and-tiled pub has a comfortable lounge decorated with a large collection of horse brasses, a traditional, tiled public bar off which is a games room and a tree-shaded garden to the rear – ideal for summer drinking . Good, wholesome home-cooked and value-for-money food attracts a loyal clientele to this secluded country destination. A printed snack (filled baguettes and jacket potatoes – "robust" is an understatement, portions are generous) menu is supplemented by a sensibly-short, daily-changing blackboard list of dishes that might encompass home-made soup (apple and coriander), lasagne, liver and bacon casserole, sweet and sour pork, and sweet chili chicken wings. Vegetarian options may include mushroom stroganoff and stuffed aubergines. Finish off with Bakewell tart, chocolate cheesecake or strawberry pavlova. No children under 14 in the bar. *Open 11.30-3, 6-11 (Sun 12-3, 7-10.30).* **Bar Food** *12-2.15, 7-9.15 (Sun 12-2, 7-9). No food Sun eve in winter.* **Beer** *Ridleys. Garden, outdoor eating. No credit cards.*

LITTLE CANFIELD — Lion & Lamb — A

Tel 01279 870257   Map 10 B3
Little Canfield Great Dunmow Essex CM6 1SR

On the A120 Colchester to Puckeridge road, three miles from Junction 8 of the M11 (3 miles west of Great Dunmow), this large family-dining pub is 200 years old in parts with more modern extensions. Open brickwork, exposed pine and artefacts inside while the fenced garden is ideal for children (bouncy castle on long weekends and an old boat has been turned into a play area). Children may eat in the restaurant and choose from their own menu. *Open 11-2.30, 6-11 (Sun 12-3, 7-10.30).* **Beer** *Ridleys. Garden, children's play area, disabled WC. MasterCard,* **VISA**

LITTLE COMPTON — Red Lion Inn — FOOD / B&B

Tel 01608 674397   Fax 01608 674521   Map 14a B1
Little Compton Moreton-in-Marsh Gloucestershire GL56 0RT

David and Sarah Smith run their charming 16th-century village inn with warmth and pride, offering good plain cooking to match the simple surroundings of exposed stone walls, beams and sturdy wooden furnishings. Follow home-made chicken liver paté or smoked salmon and prawn creole with seafood pie, tagliatelle niçoise, home-made lasagne or chargrilled rump steak cut from the joint to your own specification. Ploughman's platters and filled granary rolls make lighter bites and there are puddings like toffee and pecan cheesecake and treacle sponge. Upstairs, the three bedrooms overlook the attractive garden and share a spacious carpeted bathroom, and each has its own washbasin and tea-making facilities. Two rooms feature original beams and two have open stone walls. No smoking in the bedrooms. *Open 11-2.45, 6-11 (Sun 12-3, 7-10.30).* **Bar Food** *12-2, 7-9 (till 9.45 Sat, till 8.45 Sun).* **Beer** *Donnington BB and SBA. Garden, outdoor eating.* **Accommodation** *3 bedrooms, share bathroom, £36 (single £24). Children over 8 welcome overnight, Check-in during bar hours. No dogs. MasterCard,* **VISA**

LITTLE COWARNE   Three Horseshoes   FOOD

Tel 01885 400276   Map 14 B1   **B&B**
Little Cowarne Bromyard Hereford & Worcester HR7 4RQ

Zzz... ☺

Though not immediately obvious, one can still make out the remains of a tiny two-roomed pub that once stood on this site: the newest brick is an uneven match with the old and dormers have been added to the frontage. The Shoes' interior is now a spacious dining pub, with considerable thought given equally to the needs of children and the elderly or disabled. The success of Norman and Janet Whittall in attracting both in equal measure is to be commended. Kitchen production is also prodigious from light bar snacks of red pepper and tomato soup and cider soused herrings through to a carvery Sunday lunch. Seasonally-changing main courses offer near endless variety, pheasant in Arabian spices, fresh haddock in crab sauce, fillet of pork with spiced plum sauce, and hot spicy chicken with rice. The sauté potatoes are particularly good and a local baker makes crusty bloomers and granary loaves for the sandwiches and ploughman's platters (perhaps served with home-made pickled pears, spiced damsons or apple and ginger chutney). Home-made desserts may feature damson soufflé, toffee and banana cheesecake and gooseberry crumble, and the home-made ice creams are outstanding: rhubarb and elderflower or loganberry, and one made with damsons – fresh from trees in the paddock, naturally. A pair of quiet country bedrooms (one double, one a twin) are done in an appropriate country style with a lovely rural aspect. Free from intrusive telephones, they're otherwise bang up-to-date with colour TVs, clock radios, tea-making facilities and small but effective WC/shower rooms. *Open 11-3, 6.30-11 (Sun 12-3, 7-10.30). Possibly open all day during summer.* **Bar Food** *12-2.30 (till 2 Sun), 6.30-10 (Sun 7-9.30).* **Beer** *Webster's Yorkshire, John Smith's, Ruddles County. Garden/patio, outdoor eating, barbecue.* **Accommodation** *2 bedrooms, both en suite, £35 (single £17.50). Children welcome overnight (under-5s stay free in parents' room, 5-11s half-price), additional bed available. Check-in by arrangement. Closed 25 Dec. MasterCard,* **VISA**

LITTLE HAMPDEN   Rising Sun   FOOD

Tel & Fax 01494 488393   Map 15a E2
Little Hampden Great Missenden Buckinghamshire HP16 9PS

♟

Nestling among beech trees at the end of a sleepy village lane, this smart brick-built pub has become a popular dining venue in this peaceful part of the Chilterns. A central bar serves three neat and simply-furnished interconnecting rooms, warmed by an open fire and a woodburner during the winter. A short inventive selection of dishes (rather than the standard range of pub fare) is listed on both the printed menu and on the daily-changing blackboards. For starters or a light snack one might, typically, choose from grilled sardines with lemon and herbs, mixed Italian seafood, hot croissant filled with gruyère and ham, and pan-fried curried prawns. Varied main courses may feature nasi goreng, chargrilled rump steak, sweet and sour barbecue chicken and fillet of lamb with rosemary and honey sauce, all served with fresh vegetables. The Woodman's lunch is a particularly good value and hearty lunch – soup, roll, paté, Stilton, Cheddar, Brie, pickles and salad. Orange and lemon cheesecake and chocolate rum pie might be found among the eight or so listed on the pudding board. Walkers are welcomed, but their muddy boots aren't in the bar. Well behaved children only indoors. *Open 11.30-2.30, 6.30-11 (Sun 12-3 only). Closed Sun eve & all Mon (except Bank Holiday lunch).* **Bar Food** *12.30-2 (from 12 Sun), 7-9 (not Sun). Free House.* **Beer** *Marston's Pedigree, Brakspear Bitter, Adnams Southwold, Morland Old Speckled Hen. Garden, outdoor eating. MasterCard,* **VISA**

LITTLE LONGSTONE   **Packhorse Inn**   A

Tel 01629 640471   Map 6 C2
Little Longstone Bakewell Derbyshire DE45 1NN

18th-century village cottage tavern in the Peak District National Park, full of old-fashioned charm. Real fires and no music inside; outside, there's a steep little garden with a fish pond, rabbits and goats. Popular with walkers doing the Monsal Trail which runs between Bakewell and Millers Dale. *Open 11-3, 5-11 (from 6 Sat), Sun 12-3, 7-10.30.* **Beer** *Marston's Pedigree & Best Bitter. Garden. Family room. No credit cards.*

LITTLE ODELL   **Mad Dog**   A

Tel 01234 720221   Map 15 E1
212 High Street Little Odell Bedfordshire MK43 7AR

A one-bar-only thatched pub close to the Harrold-Odell country park. Real fire (and a ghost) in the inglenook, no music, and a roundabout for the children in the garden. The name comes from a supposed cure for the bite of mad dogs which 18th-century landlords took in payment of a debt. Children welcome indoors. *Open 11-2.30, 6-11 (Sun 12-3, 7-10.30).* **Beer** *Greene King IPA, Abbot Ale, guest beer. Garden, children's play area. MasterCard,* **VISA**

LITTLEBURY   **Queen's Head**   FOOD

Tel 01799 522251   Fax 01799 513522   Map 10 B3   **B&B**
Littlebury Saffron Walden Essex CB11 4TD

Occupying a corner site in the village centre, this attractive yellow-painted inn dates from the early 15th-century and welcomes visitors into its carefully refurbished bar and dining-room, which preserve low beamed ceilings, some standing timbers, a rustic red-and-black tiled floor and two cosy snug areas. Reliable home-cooked food is a popular attraction here, the short daily-changing blackboard menu featuring an imaginative choice of dishes that draw on fresh herbs, vegetables and fruit grown in their extensive kitchen garden, as well as vegetables and fish hand-chosen from London markets by the landlord. A typical menu may list crab, apple and bacon broth, warm samphire with tarragon butter, and grilled sardines with fresh rosemary among the starters, followed by fresh seafood specialities – chargrilled cod fillet with warm vierge dressing, whole baked crab with ginger, pan-fried halibut with basil and cream – plus chargrilled pork with fresh apricots, gammon topped with cheese and onion and interesting vegetarian dishes like chargrilled peppers with tomato, basil and garlic coulis. Extra evening dishes generally include game options like roast pheasant brigerade. Puddings range from gooseberry pie and fresh summer fruits to chocolate ginger cake. Accommodation comprises six uniformly decorated and furnished bedrooms (including two family rooms) with clean, tiled en suite bathrooms. All – except the quiet rear room – face the main road and with no secondary glazing they could well be noisy. TVs, telephones, clock/radios and tea-makers are standard. Continental breakfasts only (the price below, along with all the B&B prices in this guide, includes cooked breakfast – £6). Sheltered walled garden with play equipment geared for younger children, also indoor games and colouring books for inclement days. *Open 12-11 (Sun 12-10.30).* **Bar Food** *12-2, 7-9 (no food Sun eve). Free House.* **Beer** *Benskins Best, Tetley, Timothy Taylor's Landlord, Bass, four guest beers. Garden, outdoor eating, children's play area.* **Accommodation** *6 bedrooms, all en suite, £55.95 (single £35.95). Children welcome overnight, additional bed & cot (both £5) available. No dogs. Closed 25 & 26 Dec. Diners, MasterCard,* **VISA**

We endeavour to be as up-to-date as possible but inevitably some changes to landlords, chefs and other key staff occur after the Guide has gone to press.

LITTON   Red Lion Inn   A

Tel 01298 871458   Map 6 C2
Litton Tideswell Derbyshire SK17 8QH

The Hodgson family have run their pub in their inimitable way since the 1950s. The less the Red Lion changes all these years on the more special it becomes as there are so very few left like it. One secret is to find the pub open and pop in for a "Boddy" or a pint, for instance, of a guest beer from a firkin racked up on top of the bar. Yet to eat here remains an evening, or weekend lunch, to be planned well in advance, especially in view of the Red Lion's restricted opening hours (which we list below), and its total resistance to change (which, hopefully, will continue). *Open 12-2 Sat & Sun only, 7-11 Tue to Sat. Closed all Mon, Tue-Fri lunch, Sun eve & two weeks end Sep. Free House.* **Beer** *Boddingtons, guest beer. MasterCard,* **VISA**

LIVERPOOL   Philharmonic Dining Rooms   A

Tel 0151 709 1163   Map 6 A2
36 Hope Street Liverpool L1 9BX

An extraordinary cathedral of Victorian confidence and excess. Built in 1896 as a gentlemen's club, this Grade A listed building has glorious tiling, carving, panelling and etched glass. The woodwork was handcrafted by the shipbuilders at the time. It's a social museum piece but with modern intrusions like a juke box and fruit machine. Remarkable Victorian toilets (ornate with marble and tiles – the throne room)! Not a pub for children! *Open 11.30-11, (Sun 12-3, 7-10.30).* **Beer** *Jennings Bitter, Ind Coope Burton Ale, Walker Best Bitter, Tetley Bitter & Imperial. No credit cards.*

LLANFAIR WATERDINE   Red Lion Inn   B&B

Tel 01547 528214   Map 9 D4
Llanfair Waterdine Knighton Shropshire LD7 1TU

New owners – Chris and Judy Stevenson – have recently taken over this 16th-century low stone, whitewashed pub which nestles in a tiny hamlet just off the B4355 beside the River Teme. With just a few cottages, the Post Office and the parish church (opposite) for company, the inn enjoys a truly peaceful spot with valley views and an attractive garden with picnic tables from where the ground slopes away, sharply, down to the river. Within, there's a stone-flagged village bar, a red-carpeted lounge bar with a huge inglenook fireplace and a conservatory dining area to the rear. At present, two of the three small but neatly kept bedrooms have washbasins and share bathroom facilities, the third has an en suite bathroom, however, the intention is to upgrade the bedrooms during 1997. The menu lists traditional home-cooked pub fare alongside Italian influenced dishes and looks promising (not yet inspected). *Open 12-2 (till 3 Sun), 7-11. Closed Tue lunch. Free House.* **Beer** *Tetley, Marston's Pedigree, Hereford Wye Valley Bitter. Garden. Family room.* **Accommodation** *3 bedrooms, 1 en suite, £35-£40 (single £25). Children over 5 welcome overnight (half-price). Check-in by arrangement. No dogs. No credit cards.*

LLANYMYNECH   Bradford Arms   FOOD

Tel 01691 830582   Map 8 D3
Llanymynech Oswestry Shropshire SY22 6EJ

Village pub (the building is in England, but entry is via Wales through the front door!) with above-average food in its spotless, comfortably traditional bar. It's an old coaching inn that's been Victorianised. The monthly-changing bar menu ranges from grilled herb and cashew nut stuffed chicken, spinach and feta cheese filo parcels to baked crab with fresh coriander and cream, venison in rosemary and red wine sauce, tandoori chicken masala and pork loin with apricot and brandy sauce. A blackboard might proclaim daily specials like fillet of sea bass poached in dry vermouth. The à la carte restaurant menu (evenings only) may offer sautéed guinea fowl with a red wine and black pepper sauce or fillet steak Dijonaise. Very good puddings – rum and walnut gateau, blueberry and almond pie or apple strudel. 12 tip-top "real" British cheeses are helpfully described on the menu and served with good, crusty bread (or biscuits), celery and apple. The 80-strong wine list offers a good spread. *Open 12-2.30, 7-11 (till 10.30 Sun).* **Bar Food** *12-2, 7-10 (till 9.30 Sun). Free House.* **Beer** *one monthly-changing real ale. Patio, outdoor eating. Closed Mon (except Bank Holidays) & second week Jan. No credit cards.*

LODERS · Loders Arms · FOOD

Tel 01308 422431   Map 13 F2
Loders Bridport Dorset DT6 3SA

When Roger and Helen Flint took over this unassuming stone pub it was just another struggling village local trying to survive on little custom. Nowadays, their honest home-cooking is imaginative, good value for money and very popular, so it is advisable to book at both lunch and dinner in the tiny, 24-seat dining-room. Those popping in for just a bar snack will not be disappointed with the short choice of hearty, hot dishes that are generally available such as spiced mixed bean and chickpea casserole, home-made soups (potato, bacon and fennel), spaghetti putanesca and lasagne plus generously-filled French baguettes. More imaginative fare can be appreciated in the simply-furnished dining-room, where a short yet varied list of interesting dishes is chalked up on a blackboard. To start, there may be baked Camembert with onion confit in filo pastry, avocado salad with spicy bacon and red pepper vinaigrette, followed by a choice of at least eight well-presented main courses, for example smoked haddock fillet with dill mayonnaise, sea bass salsa verde and roast rack of lamb studded with garlic. As well as new potatoes, each dish is accompanied by four or five crisply-cooked vegetables. Round off your meal with steamed lemon and ginger sponge or walnut and praline cheesecake. Summer diners can wait for their table in the small rear garden which enjoys rural hillside views. *Open 11.30-3, 6-11 (Sun 12-10.30)*. **Bar Food** *12.30-2, 7.30-9 (no food Sun eve in winter)*. **Beer** *Palmers IPA, Bridport Bitter, Tally Ho (winter) & 200 (summer). Garden, outdoor eating.* MasterCard, **VISA**

LODSWORTH · Halfway Bridge · FOOD

Tel 01798 861281   Map 11 A6
Lodsworth Petworth West Sussex GU28 9BP

On the A272 midway between Petworth and Midhurst, the mellow, red-brick Halfway Bridge was originally built as a coaching inn in 1740. Today, efficiently run by the friendly Hawkins family, it's still catering to travellers with real ales and real food from an extensive blackboard menu that may range from home-made chicken and vegetable broth, warm salad of chicken livers and filo wrapped prawns to red snapper with olives and tomatoes, lambs kidneys in Dijon mustard and fromage frais and confit of duck with honeyed cabbage. Large open sandwiches are served with salad and sauté potatoes at lunchtimes only. If you're really hungry go for the half roast shoulder of English lamb served with fresh vegetables. Those with room for a pudding could try the gooseberry and honey crumble or the banana toffee pie. The same menu operates in both the neat country-style dining-room and throughout the series of cosy, tastefully furnished interconnecting rooms that form the bar. Real fires (one room features an old kitchen range) offer a warm welcome in winter; for the summer there are tables out on the lawn and on the sheltered rear patio. For a celebration, try a bottle of the local Gospel Green *méthode champenoise* cider. No children under 10 inside *Open 11-3, 6-11 (Sun 12-3, 7-10.30). Closed Sun eve in winter.* **Bar Food** *12-2 (till 2.30 Sat & Sun), 7-10. Free House.* **Beer** *Gale's HSB, Cheriton Brewhouse Pots Ale, Fuller's London Pride, guest beer. Garden, patio, outdoor eating.* MasterCard, **VISA**

LONG CRENDON · The Angel Inn ★ · FOOD

Tel 01844 208268   Fax 01844 238569   Map 15a D2   **B&B**
Bicester Road Long Crendon Buckinghamshire HP18 9EE

Restaurant or pub? The distinction becomes rather blurred here, and really doesn't matter anyway – the fact is that the food here is indisputably good. Whether having just a bowl of soup or a full meal one can eat either in the bar area with its old sofas and wooden settles or in one of the several eating rooms – one showing some of the original wattle and daub construction, another a Lloyd Loom-furnished conservatory – with soft floral cloths on the tables. The same menu appears on blackboards above the bar and on typed sheets if eating 'restaurant-style' – with everything from freshly-baked baguette sandwiches, pasta dishes like salmon, spring onion and cream, gravadlax, cucumber and sweet mild mustard dressing, steak frites and ploughman's to platter of beef carpaccio and parma ham with chili oil and parmesan, chicken breast stuffed with Stilton and wrapped in bacon, and brochette of lamb and beef with chargrilled vegetables and a piquant sauce. With deliveries direct from Billingsgate, Scotland and Cornwall three times a week it's worth checking out the day's fish dishes (rightly considered their speciality) too: perhaps Mediterranean fish soup, baked cod with tomato fondu and spinach, whole roasted bream with deep-fried vegetables, and steamed halibut with spring onions and lime cream. The Angel is the overall winner of our 1997 Seafood Pub of the Year Award. Of the three appealing, en suite bedrooms two are particularly characterful with old black beams. Furniture varies from old pine to some more modern pieces and all rooms have TV, direct-dial phones and tea/coffee-making facilities. *Open 12-2.30, 6.30-10 (Sun 12-3 only). Closed Sun eve & all Sun in summer May-Aug.* **Bar Food** *12-2.30, 6.30-10 (no food Sun eve). Free House.* **Beer** *Brakspear Bitter, Flowers IPA.* **Accommodation** *3 bedrooms, all en suite, £50 (single £35). Children welcome overnight. Check-in during bar hours only. No dogs. MasterCard,* **VISA**

LONG MELFORD   Bull Hotel   B&B

Tel 01787 378494   Fax 01787 880307   Map 10 C3
Hall Street Long Melford Sudbury Suffolk CO10 9JG

Situated in the heart of this attractive old wool town, a magnificent half-timbered inn, originally built for a rich wool merchant in 1450. It became an inn over a century later and boasts a wealth of impressively carved and moulded oak beams throughout its elegantly refurbished interior. Beyond the entrance hall are two relaxing and tastefully-furnished lounges with huge inglenooks and a separate pubby bar serving real ale. Weary travellers will find that the civilised ambience and high standards extend upstairs to the comfortable and well-appointed bedrooms; added extras include TVs, clock-radios and telephones. Ten bedrooms are designated non-smoking and three are suitable for families. Splendid courtyard with wrought-iron furniture beneath the old weavers gallery. Room service from 7.30am to 11pm. A Forte hotel. *Open 11-11 (Sun 12-10.30).* **Beer** *Greene King IPA, Nethergate Old Growler, Bass, Worthington Best.* **Accommodation** *25 bedrooms, all en suite, £85 & £95 (superior & family rooms), mini suite £100, suite £110 (single £65): room-only prices (cooked breakfast £8.50 per person). Children welcome overnight (under-16s free if sharing parents' room), additional bed & cot available. Amex, Diners, MasterCard,* **VISA**

LONGFRAMLINGTON   Granby Inn   FOOD

Tel 01665 570228   Fax 01665 570736   Map 5 D2   B&B
Longframlington Northumberland NE65 8DP

On the A697, cosy, attractively modernised little 18th-century inn with colourful window boxes and a busy dining business. Food is served in the restaurant as well as the bar-and-lounge. For the latter, food is ordered at the bar and from then on, tables are waitress served. The menu is extensive (from egg mayonnaise to seafood platter and plaice and chips to beef stroganoff) and helpings are very generous, served on enormous oval plates; vegetarian options like wheat and walnut casserole are also offered. Sandwiches and ploughman's platters are always available. Good puddings might include sticky toffee pudding and fresh fruit cheesecake. Main-building bedrooms are small, neat and modern. Three garden chalets (mobile homes) incorporate a small sitting area, fridge and bathroom, and standards of housekeeping are reliably high everywhere. Children over 8 allowed (if eating) in lounge at lunchtime. *Open 11-3, 6-11 (Sun 12-3, 7-10.30).* **Bar Food** *11-2 (from 12 Sun), 6-9.30 (from 7 Sun). Free House.* **Beer** *Worthington Best Bitter. Garden, patio, outdoor eating.* **Accommodation** *5 bedrooms, all en suite, £52 (chalet £42) single £29.50 (chalet £26). Children over 8 welcome overnight in chalets (sleep three). No dogs. Closed all 25 Dec. MasterCard,* **VISA**

LONGSTOCK   Peat Spade   FOOD

Tel 01264 810612   Map 14 C3
Longstock Stockbridge Hampshire SO20 6DR

Unusual paned windows overlook the peaceful village lane and idyllic heavily
thatched cottages at this striking, red-brick and gabled Victorian pub that nestles in
the heart of the Test Valley, only 100 yards from the famous trout stream. Until
recently the Peat Spade was more restaurant than pub, the atmosphere far from being
conducive for the locals' to enjoy a pint at the bar. However, since the arrival of
Sarah Hinman and Bernie Startup the villagers are happy as they have their 'local'
back, yet it is still a place worth travelling to for some good pub food which is served
throughout the uncluttered and neatly-furnished bar and adjacent eating areas. A
sensibly short blackboard menu offers a reliable selection of home-cooked meals, from
'small eats' – basil and garlic tagliatelle with smoked salmon and cream, Szechuan pork
with noodles, steak frites – and starters like creamed watercress soup, home-made
pork paté and marinated Orkney herrings, to substantial main courses, for example,
rack of lamb with rosemary and garlic, medallions of pork fillet with redcurrant coulis,
and roasted peppers with baked goat's cheese and balsamic dressing. Well-kept
Eldridge Pope ales, a regularly-changing local brew or a choice of seven wines by the
glass to accompany your meal. Small rear garden for warm weather drinking – ideal
after a summer evening stroll to see Hampshire's finest chalk stream. Children
welcome. *Open 11.30-2.30 (till 3 Fri-Sun), 6-10.30 (till 11 Fri & Sat). Closed Sun eve,
all Mon (except Bank Holidays) & 25-26 Dec.* **Bar Food** *12-2, 7-9.30 (no food Sun &
Mon).* **Beer** *Eldridge Pope Popes Ale & Thomas Hardy Country Ale, guest beer.
Garden, outdoor eating. No credit cards.*

LOSTWITHIEL   Royal Oak   FOOD

Tel 01208 872552   Map 12 C3   **B&B**
Duke Street Lostwithiel Cornwall PL22 1AH

Popular, 13th-century inn just off the main road in the original capital of Cornwall
and supposedly linked to nearby Restormel Castle by a smuggling or escape tunnel.
Catering for all tastes, the lively, slate flagstoned public bar (complete with juke box,
modern and traditional games) attracts a good local following. In contrast, the
comfortably furnished and carpeted lounge bar has tables with red and white checked
cloths and is very much geared to a dining clientele. Close inspection of a fairly
standard printed menu and of the additional blackboard selection of meals will reveal
some good home-cooked dishes, such as fish pie, Mrs Hine's 'famous' cow pie,
sautéed chicken in red wine and an authentic curry choice. Chips may arrive with the
lasagne, but most main courses have the option of a full salad or a selection of four
well-cooked vegetables. Plainer pub fare (no sandwiches or ploughman's platters in
the evening) – Angus beef steaks, grilled trout and salads – is unlikely to disappoint in
either quality or presentation. For dessert try the home-made apple pie topped with
fresh clotted cream. Those wishing to explore the area will find one of the upstairs
bedrooms a most comfortable base. Spacious, well-decorated and furnished with a mix
of period and pine furniture, they all have TV, radio/alarms, and beverage-making
facilities, with two of the rooms boasting clean, en suite bathrooms. Children
welcome. *Open 11-11 (Sun 12-10.30).* **Bar Food** *12-2, 6.30-9.30. Free House.*
Beer *St Austell Trelawney Pride, Bass, Fuller's London Pride, Marston's Pedigree, Sharp's
Own, two guest beers. Terrace, outdoor eating. Family room.* **Accommodation** *6 bedrooms,
4 en suite, £48.74-£53.75 (single from £27.50). Children welcome overnight (under-4s free,
5-12s half-price). Closed 25 Dec. Amex, Diners, MasterCard,* **VISA**

LOUTH   Masons Arms   B&B

Tel 01507 609525   Map 7 F2
Cornmarket Louth Lincolnshire LN11 9PY

Useful to know in an area not highly blessed with accommodation pubs is the
Masons, a former posting inn dating from the 18th century. Right in the centre of the
Cornmarket, this welcoming and friendly inn is run by resident proprietors Mike and
Margaret Harrison, who offer five bedrooms complete with well-equipped, en suite
facilities. Five further bedrooms share two bathrooms (one a restored Victorian
bathroom) and an extra WC. Bars are open all day, with fastidiously-tended real ales
on handpump and six wines available by the glass. Children welcome indoors; baby-
changing facilities in Ladies. *Open 11-11 (Sun and Bank Holidays 12-3, 7-10.30),
Free House.* **Beer** *Bateman's Dark Mild, XB, XXXB & Salem Porter, Marston's Pedigree,
Bass, guest beer.* **Accommodation** *10 bedrooms, 5 en suite (3 with bath), £49.50 (single
£20). Children welcome overnight, additional bed & cot (both £5) available. No dogs.
Accommodation closed 24-26 Dec; pub closed 25 Dec eve. MasterCard,* **VISA**

LOW CATTON   Gold Cup Inn   A

Tel 01759 371354   Map 7 D1
Low Catton East Riding of Yorkshire YO4 1EA

☺

Five miles east of York, south of Stamford Bridge on the A166; can also be
approached from east of Kexby, off A1078. Modernised but pleasant, relaxing and
unpretentious pub run by Ray and Pat Hales; there are two welcoming bars, real fires
and high-backed wooden pews in the rambling three-room lounge in contrast to a
noisier back games room. The beer garden/paddock at the rear of the building
features ponies, goats and geese to delight children and has access to the river bank.
Children welcome. *Open 12-2.30, 6-11 (Sat 12-11, Sun 12-10.30). Closed Mon lunch
(except Bank Holidays). Free House.* **Beer** *Tetley, John Smith's. Garden, children's play area.
No credit cards.*

LOW NEWTON BY THE SEA   The Ship   A

Tel 01665 576262   Map 5 D1
Low Newton by the Sea Alnwick Northumberland NE66 3EL

The 'village green' is just a grassy area enclosed on three sides by fishermen's cottages,
one of which is the pub, and on the fourth side by the beach itself. As with so many
coastal villages, public parking is restricted to an area just away from the beach, leaving
you a short walk to the sand, green or pub – indeed popular with holidaymakers and
locals alike. The Ship is quite charming, largely as a result of the Hoppers, who run
it in a very friendly fashion. Outside, there are picnic tables on the grass, while inside
it has the air of somewhere from the early part of the century – creels hang over the
bar to remind you of the seaside location. *Open Easter-end Oct 11-11 (Sun 12-10.30),
Nov-Easter 11-3, 7-11 (Sat 11-11, Sun 12-10.30). Free House.* **Beer** *Ruddles Bitter,
guest beer. Garden. No credit cards.*

LOWER ASHTON   Manor Inn   FOOD

Tel 01647 252304   Map 13 D3
Lower Ashton Christow Devon EX6 7QL

Small, traditional Teign Valley local with garden in front overlooking fields and valley.
The welcome is friendly within the two homely and simply furnished bars which are
warmed in winter by open fires. Good, unfussy, honest and home-cooked food
prepared by landlady Clare Mann using fresh ingredients (not a chip in sight here!)
sees such hearty dishes as beef and red wine casserole, hunters chicken, lamb goulash,
chili pork topped with cheese and vegetarian choices – vegetable and nut curry – on
the daily specials board. Fish from Brixham is becoming increasingly important and a
daily fish board might offer smoked fish bake, grilled lemon sole and seafood pasta
mornay. Sandwiches are made using locally-baked malted loaves and jacket potatoes

and ploughman's platters are always available. Real-ale lovers have four brews to choose from plus regularly changing guest beers (over 750 different ales have been offered since 1981); 30 ales at the annual beer festival in September. *Open 12-2.30, 6-11 (from 7 Sat), Sun 12-2.30, 7-10.30. Closed Mon except Bank Holidays.* **Bar Food** *12-1.30, 7-9.30 (till 9 Sun). Free House.* **Beer** *Wadworth 6X, Theakston XB, Shepherd Neame Spitfire, Teignworthy Reel Ale, guest beer. Garden, outdoor eating. No credit cards.*

LOWER BEEDING   Jeremy's at The Crabtree ★   FOOD

Tel 01403 891257   Fax 01403 891606   Map 11 B6
Brighton Road Lower Beeding West Sussex RH13 6PT

The cream-painted, Georgian fronted Crabtree public house stands immediately alongside the A281 just south of Lower Beeding and dates back to 1579 when it was a haunt for smugglers. Mentioned briefly in Hilaire Belloc's *The Four Men*, the pub is now tied to King and Barnes and in the very capable hands of talented chef/landlord Jeremy Ashpool. The bar is very simply furnished with just a few round tables and stools and dispenses a good range of King and Barnes ales, including their new range of seasonal draughts. One has to book to ensure a table in one of the restaurant's two rooms; either in the no-smoking dining-room or in the characterful Smugglers, an ancient beamed room at the rear with an inglenook. In the evening the emphasis is very much on a more upmarket, three-course à la carte (but fixed-price) menu and there's a special two-course lunch, as well as a good-value, set three-course menu midweek; the latter might feature grilled tuna with a garlic, lemon and dill mayonnaise and sautéed fennel followed by leg of lamb baked in tomato, chili, peppers and coriander, and end with chocolate truffle cake with mango mousse. There is also a daily-changing, short à la carte lunch menu with dishes such as salad of roasted Mediterranean vegetables with shaven parmesan, pan-fried duck livers with sweet onion compote and walnut oil, and marinated herrings; more substantial dishes might be chicken in Thai spices with chili and coconut cream, rabbit and mushroom pie, and feta, leek and apple strudel with walnuts and fresh basil. Delicious puddings to finish include a rhubarb upside-down sponge. Otherwise, there are simple sandwiches (prawn, smoked salmon) and ploughman's with cheddar, Stilton, Tornegus or Shropshire blue for lunch only. *Open 11-3, 5.30-11 (Sun 12-3, 7-10.30).* **Bar Food** *12.30-2 (reduced bar menu Sun or fixed-price roast lunch menu), 7.30-9.30 (no eve bar menu, Monday gourmet nights, Tue-Thu set menu & 3-course, fixed-price à la carte). No food Sun eve.* **Beer** *King & Barnes. Garden, outdoor eating. Amex, MasterCard,* **VISA**

> We only recommend food (Bar Food) in those establishments highlighted
> with the **FOOD** symbol.

LOWER FROYLE   Prince of Wales   FOOD

Tel 01420 23102   Map 15a D4
Lower Froyle Hampshire GU34 4LJ

A rather modern and ordinary looking Edwardian-style village pub, built in the 1930s after the original thatched pub had burnt down. The modest open-plan bar and dining-room is often busy with a dining clientele seeking out the reliably good home-cooked food. A regularly-changing blackboard menu highlights the old favourites – lamb's liver and bacon, lasagne – seasonal salads (Caesar, smoked duck, chargrilled chicken) and a few imaginative choices such as pork fillet with crème fraiche and mushrooms and a fresh fish list (mainly Thu-Sun) which may include baby turbot and scallop ragout, king scallops with bacon, cream and Cointreau sauce or hake baked with lemon, garlic and onion; lobster and crab are also very popular. In the evenings, a separate printed menu accompanies the blackboard and features beef Wellington. A traditional 3-course Sunday lunch is good value. *Open 11-2.30, 6-11 (Sun 12-3, 7-10.30).* **Bar Food** *12-2, 7-9.30 (no food Sun eve). Free House.* **Beer** *Fuller's ESB & London Pride, Timothy Taylor's Landlord, Brakspear Special, guest beer. Garden, outdoor eating. MasterCard,* **VISA**

LOWER ODDINGTON   The Fox   ★   FOOD

Tel 01451 870888   Fax 01451 870666   Map 14a A1
Lower Oddington Stow-on-the-Wold Gloucestershire GL56 0UR

Among the pretty mellow-stone buildings in this charming Cotswold hamlet is the Fox, an elegant and civilised eating establishment that attracts discerning diners from far and wide for its relaxing dining atmosphere and quality cooking – no bookings are taken, so arrive early as the place fills up rapidly. Behind the yellow stone facade lies a first-class interior that has been fitted out with style and flair. Its balance between country brasserie/bistro and country pub has been carefully thought-out, in a succession of simply-furnished rooms with graduated colour schemes – from fresh, summery lemon through magnolia to the rag-washed bar with 'designer nicotine overtones'. In addition to the warm and welcoming decor there are comfortable old pine tables on polished slate floors, fresh flowers, classical music and soft, evening candlelight to enhance the convivial atmosphere. Food asserts its prominence in imaginative and colourful dishes that exhibit an equal attention to both flavour and balance. Choose from the regularly-changing hand-written menu and begin pehaps with pea and mint soup, deep-fried Brie with redcurrant jelly or a delicious asparagus and cheese tart, following with rack of lamb and onion sauce, salmon fishcakes with parsley sauce, pasta with sun-dried tomatoes, mushrooms and pine kernels or smoked haddock fish pie. There are also daily dishes like fresh lobster and spinach mousse with anchovy mayonnaise, peppered steaks, a Sunday sirloin roast (served rare) and simpler snacks like French bread sandwiches (hot sausage and Meaux mustard). Among the desserts, the warm walnut tart, rich chocolate mousse and sticky toffee pudding are all home-made, too. Diners are spoilt for choice by the impressively-stocked bar: from fresh orange juice and three real ales to nine excellent wines served by the glass (from an interesting global list) and numerous malt whiskies. Outside is half an acre of walled garden. *Open 12-3, 6.30-11 (Sun 12-3, 7-10.30). Bar Food 12-2, 7-10 (Sun to 9.30). Free House. Beer Hook Norton, Marston's Pedigree, guest beer. Garden, terrace, outdoor eating. MasterCard, **VISA**.*

LOWER PEOVER   Bells of Peover   A

Tel 01565 722269   Map 6 B2
The Cobbles Lower Peover Knutsford Cheshire WA16 9PZ

Recommended primarily for its atmosphere (although it's a popular local dining pub): originally a home for monks, a lovely, creeper-covered old pub by the church, at the end of a cobbled lane off the B5081. Toby jugs of all sizes and styles make amusing company in the snug, where the bar counter is to be found; the barless main room has a collection of copper and brass and decorative blue plates. No children under 14 in the bar area. *Open 11.30-3, 5.30-11 (from 6 Sat), Sun 12-3, 7-10.30. Beer Greenalls. Patio/terrace. MasterCard, **VISA***

LOWER WIELD   Yew Tree Inn   FOOD

Tel 01256 389224   Map 14a C4
Lower Wield Alresford Hampshire SO24 9RX

Isolated beside a narrow country lane off the B3046 Alresford-Basingstoke road, the Yew Tree acquires its name from the 300-year-old tree by which it stands. The local cricket pitch lies opposite and the sport is taken very seriously in these parts, the main, simply furnished, bar being particularly busy on summer Sundays. At other times, this welcoming rural retreat is a popular dining venue; the tables in the cosy, beamed restaurant are neatly laid with place mats, fresh flowers, linen napkins and are candlelit in the evenings. The attraction here is the reliable range of home-cooked food, from decent bar snacks like warm crusty baguettes filled with rare roast beef and horseradish, baked potatoes (tuna topped with anchovies and olives), oak smoked salmon with fresh lime, and Cornish crab salad to a blackboard menu listing more inventive and ambitious dishes. To start, there may be toasted brioche filled with lightly scrambled egg and seasoned with fresh truffle, or hot vichyssoise soup, followed by lamb shank braised in red wine with root vegetables and whole lemon sole finished with capers, tomato and olive oil, all served with a separate dish of fresh crunchy vegetables. To finish, try the bread-and-butter pudding or lemon delice. The simpler bar snacks are not available Friday or Saturday evenings. Traditional Sunday lunch features a choice of three roasts; children are charged half price. Large peaceful garden with rural outlook. *Open 12-3, 6-11 (Sun 12-3, 7-10.30). Closed Sun eve winter & Mon eve. Bar Food 12-2, 7-9.30 (Tue-Sat only). Free House. Beer Cheriton Brewhouse Pots Ale & Diggers Gold. Garden, patio, children's play area. MasterCard, VISA*

LOWESWATER   Kirkstile Inn   B&B

Tel 01900 85219   Map 4 C3
Loweswater Cockermouth Cumbria CA13 0RV

Stretching as far as the eye can see, the woods, fells and lakes are as much a draw today as they must have been in the inn's infancy some 400 years ago. The beck below meanders under a stone bridge, oak trees fringing its banks with mighty Melbreak towering above. The pub's interior retains the warm cosiness of interlinked rooms with an enclosed verandah, a TV lounge reserved for residents and the Little Barn housing a games room for wet days. Consistent with Lakeland tradition, lunches and afternoon teas are kept rather basic, with residents returning for table d'hote dinner (reservations only, although our recommendation here is for B&B only). The oldest, and smallest bedrooms in the original cottage share bathroom and toilets, while those in the extension have more space and en suite facilities. All have background heating, quilts and beverage facilities; communal laundry and drying rooms are readily available for the droves of walkers who return nightly to make Kirkstile their home. *Open 11-11 (Sun 12-10.30). Free House. Beer Jennings Bitter & Cockerhoop. Garden. Family room. Accommodation 10 bedrooms, 8 en suite, £45-£55 (family room from £55, single £35-£45). Children welcome overnight (under-2s stay free in parents' room, 3-11s £10), additional bed (£10) & cot (£5) available. MasterCard, VISA*

LOWSONFORD   Fleur De Lys   A

Tel & Fax 01564 782431   Map 14 C1
Lowsonford Henley-in-Arden Warwickshire B95 5HJ

A long, low Whitbread pub dating from the 17th century, with crooked chimneys and wrinkly roof whose canalside position and outdoor tuck shop deservedly attract a family clientele. A score or more picnic tables spread out along the bank, from where parents can watch the longboats while the under-12s master the climbing frames. Galleried family dining room and atmospheric bars with low-beamed ceilings, oak furniture and stone floors. *Open 11-11 (Sun 12-10.30). Beer Flowers Original, Wadworth 6X, Morland Old Speckled Hen. Garden, children's play area. Family room. MasterCard, VISA*

LUDGVAN   White Hart   A

Tel 01736 740574   Map 12 A4
Ludgvan Penzance Cornwall TR20 8EY

Dating from the 14th century and possibly older than the adjacent church, this stone village local is well worth a trip inland, away from the busy coast. The atmospheric interior has been carefully created in old-fashioned style and is a most welcoming and relaxing place in which to enjoy a drink, free from modern-day intrusions of piped music and games machines. Ochre coloured walls, low beams, a rug-strewn wooden floor and a motley assortment of rustic tables and chairs characterise the main bar, and various jugs, mugs, books, prints and bric-a-brac fill every nook and cranny around the room. An adjacent small dimly-lit room (families welcome here) boasts an old black kitchen range and two intimate boxed seating areas, one ideal for two people, the other for a small private gathering. Real ale is tapped straight from the cask and if visiting on a Monday evening you may find the local male voice choir in full song. *Open 11-2.30, 6-11 (Sun 12-3, 7-10.30). Beer Flowers IPA, Marston's Pedigree, guest beer (summer). Garden. No credit cards.*

| LUDLOW | **Church Inn** | B&B |

Tel 01584 872174   Map 6 A4
Church Street Buttercross Ludlow Shropshire SY8 1AW

One of the oldest sites in Ludlow, going back at least seven centuries, the former
'Wine Taverne by the Cross' stands wedged between the old Buttercross and St
Laurence's church. A compact and convivial all-day bar opens on to pedestrian
Church Street; regularly-changing guest ales, landlord Stuart Copland's particular pride
and joy, are a feature here. Above, the bedrooms offer practical comforts, pastel-
coloured duvets, remote-control TVs and beverage facilites. All are en suite, though
four have shower/WC only, and there's one spacious family suite sleeping three.
Parking may appear difficult but ask about on-street parking around the corner.
Children welcome. *Open 11-11 (Sun 12-10.30). Free House.* **Beer** *Ruddles County,
Webster's Yorkshire, Courage Directors, guest beers. Family room.* **Accommodation** *9
bedrooms, all en suite (4 with shower), £45 (family room £55, single £28). Children
welcome overnight, additional bed (£5) & cot available. No dogs (except guide dogs).
MasterCard,* **VISA**

| LUDLOW | **Unicorn Inn** | FOOD |

Tel 01584 873555   Map 6 A4   B&B
Lower Corve Street Ludlow Shropshire SY8 1DU

🍴 Zzz... ☺

At the end of a row of 17th-century farmers' cottages stands this tiny half-timbered
pub backing on to the river Corve, which flows into the Teme at Ludlow. Though
dating from 1635, unbelievably only a few years ago it housed a disco; today, under
the impeccable guidance of Alan and Elisabeth Ditchburn, it's a jewel of a pub. The
bar is all linenfold panels and original timbers in front of a vast stone-lined fire grate.
Through to the rear, dining tables are neatly laid and cosily candle-lit at night.
An eat-anywhere policy is sensibly applied to the main meals, chalked up daily on
strategically-hung boards. Typically, dishes might include a home-made soup (broccoli
and Stilton), grilled sardines with fresh tomato salsa, steak and kidney pie, black
pudding with cider and mustard sauce and three daily fish dishes (perhaps red snapper
with orange and ginger coulis); to follow, try strawberry fool, double chocolate
pudding with truffle sauce or Dorset apple cake. For those of lesser appetite are bar
snacks of open sandwiches, jacket potatoes and an English cheese platter. Additionally,
a comprehensive vegetarian menu, regularly amended, offers the likes of white nut
roast and garlic mushroom pancake. Not only is the food good, but the welcome is
genuine and the service informal and friendly. Bedrooms are limited by space – and
listed building constraints – from undergoing unsuitable alterations. Exposed roof
trusses are certainly original and the creaking floors wholly in character. There are
TVs available for those who can't endure the abundant peace and quiet. One
bedroom only has a full en suite bathroom – and it's tiny; two more have
showers/WC only, while the remaining two bedrooms share adequate adjacent
facilities. *Open 12-2.30 (till 3 Sat), 6-11 (Sun 12-3, 7-10.30).* **Bar Food** *12-2.15 (till
2.30 Sat & Sun), 6-9.15 (till 9.30 Sat), Sun 7-9. Free House.* **Beer** *Bass, Worthington.
Riverside terrace, outdoor eating.* **Accommodation** *5 bedrooms, 3 en suite, £40 (family room
£50, single £20). Children welcome overnight (under-12s stay free in parents' room),
additional bed & cot available. Check-in by arrangement. Amex, MasterCard,* **VISA**

Many **B&B** establishments offer reduced rates for weekend and
out-of-season bookings. Always ask about special deals for longer stays. Beware
half-board terms in inns where we do not recommend the **FOOD**.

LURGASHALL   Noah's Ark   A

Tel 01428 707346   Map 11 A6
Lurgashall Petworth West Sussex GU28 9ET

450-year-old pub in a classic village green setting by the church and overlooking the
cricket pitch; longer Sunday opening hours could at last assuage the afternoon thirsts
of the cricketers and allow them to celebrate successes or drown their sorrows.
Perhaps best in summer when the tile-hung frontage is bedecked with flowers in
hanging baskets and tables are set outside on the front grassed area; cosy in winter.
*Open 11.30-2.30 (till 3 summer), 6-11 (Sun 12-3, 7-10.30). Beer Greene King IPA,
Abbot Ale & Rayments Special Bitter. Family room. Garden. MasterCard,* **VISA**

LUXBOROUGH   Royal Oak   FOOD

Tel 01984 640319   Map 13 E1   **B&B**
Luxborough Dunster Somerset TA23 0SH

Nestling by a stream at the bottom of a steep-sided valley, deep in Exmoor's Brendon
Hills, the thatched Royal Oak is a truly rural 14th-century inn. New owners, Kevan
and Rose Draper, intend maintaining the rustic atmosphere that makes this place so
popular, the unspoilt interior being devoid of piped music, fruit machines and posh
fixtures and fittings. The several rooms have flagstoned or cobbled floors, low beams,
old kitchen tables and hardly a pair of matching chairs. Besides uncontrived charm,
another good reason for a visit here is the splendid choice of well-kept real ales tapped
straight from the cask. Imminent plans include opening a micro-brewery behind the
pub. An extensive, all-day menu ranges widely, from sandwiches and jacket potatoes
to home-made soups partnered by great wedges of crusty bread, and substantial main
dishes like beef and beamish pie, vegetable and Stilton pie and lamb curry. Game
features in season – perhaps rabbit, pigeon, pheasant or partridge. Steaks, venison
casserole, poached chicken breast with dill and cream sauce and fresh fish dishes
(monkfish with green peppercorn sauce, salmon and sole filo parcels) appear for the
additional evening menu. It's still very much a locals' pub: Tuesday night is quiz
night, and every Friday a folk club takes over the back room, which has a pool table
(in winter only). Since arriving, the Drapers have upgraded the three existing simple
bedrooms, one now having en suite facilities, the others sharing an improved
bathroom. By the end of 1996 a further four en suite bedrooms will be on line
making the Royal Oak a handy Exmoor base. However, their enthusiasm in the
property is not matched by their service towards the customer, as this does not always
appear to be what it was under the previous owners. *Open 11-2.30, 6-11 (Sun 12-3,
7-10.30). Bar Food 11.30-2, 7-10 (Sun 12-2, 7-9.30). Free House. Beer Flowers IPA,
Cotleigh Tawny, Exmoor Gold, up to four guest beers. Garden, outdoor eating.*
Accommodation *3 bedrooms, 1 en suite, £45 (single £20). Children welcome overnight
(under-5s stay free in parents' room), additional bed (10) available. No credit cards.*

LYDDINGTON   Old White Hart   FOOD

Tel 01572 821703   Fax 01572 821965   Map 7 E4
51 Main Street Lyddington Uppingham Leicestershire LE15 9LF

Truly a traditional local, standing by the village green with its honey-coloured
cottages and backdrop of the picturesque Welland valley. Gatherings of the pétanque
club are a regular feature of summer evenings when the flower-filled beer garden is at
its best. Menus throughout the bars and restaurant are firmly British and equally
traditional. For lunch there's hot buttered crab, and Wensleydale cheese roll (cream
cheese, summer herbs and walnuts). More elaborate evening fare adds 'Oxford John'
(lamb cutlets with minted redcurrant gravy) and 'Earl Sefton's salmon' (poached
Scottish salmon with sherry and asparagus). There's plenty of choice for vegetarians on
request and home-made desserts like strawberry profiteroles and chocolate mousse
with brandy cream. *Open 12-3, 6.30-11 (till 10.30 Sun). Bar Food 12-2, 7-10.
Free House. Beer Greene King IPA & Abbot Ale, Marston's Pedigree. Garden,
outdoor eating. Ten flood-lit pétanque areas. MasterCard,* **VISA**

LYDFORD   Castle Inn   FOOD

Tel 01822 820242   Fax 01822 820454   Map 12 C3   **B&B**
Lydford Okehampton Devon EX20 4BH

Just a stone's throw from open moors, the pink-washed, wisteria-entangled Castle is certainly a pretty little pub, but it's not until you go inside that you realise how old it is. Much is 12th-century, with various later additions, and it just oozes atmosphere, with its slate floor and low sagging ceilings turned a deep amber colour by time and smoke. The place is literally crammed with bits and pieces collected by landlords over the years, including several marvellous old high-backed settles (some with little roofs), dozens of decorative plates and a fine collection of Hogarth prints (not a fruit machine or juke box in sight). Seven of only 31 remaining Lydford pennies minted by Ethelred the Unready in the 10th century are on display, the rest being held by the British Museum. The Castle's reputation for good food and a friendly welcome is safe in the hands of owners Mo and Clive Walker. Mo controls proceedings in the kitchen, producing an eclectic range of dishes listed on a daily-changing blackboard in the bar. Favourites are the Oriental-style dishes – chicken and coconut soup, Thai green curry of duck with basmati rice – and well-cooked traditional dishes like salmon and cod plait with champagne and lemon thyme sauce, Provençal chicken, steak and kidney pie and roasted red pepper roulade, all served with fresh vegetables. At lunchtime (when there are no sandwiches, but there is a very good Devon cheese platter), this menu applies throughout the inn, but at night it's limited to the smaller bar and snug, when the main bar becomes a restaurant (bookings taken) offering a fixed-price three-course menu (with supplements). Look out for the special Asian curry nights during the winter. Bookings are also taken for dining on the covered patio outside, where five tables are a lovely spot for summer alfresco eating. Six of the modestly comfortable bedrooms are en suite while the other two share a perfectly acceptable bathroom; antique furniture features in all rooms, the Castle Room sporting a four-poster bed. By January 1997 a new extension will house two further en suite bedrooms and a residents' lounge (open Easter). Just a short walk away is the picturesque Lydford Gorge (NT) and its woodland walks. *Open 11.30-3, 6-11 (Sun 12-3, 7-10.30). Bar Food 12-2.30, 6.30-9.30 (Sun 7-9). Free House. Beer Blackawton Bitter, Wadworth 6X, Fuller's London Pride, two guest beers. Garden, patio, outdoor eating. Family room. Accommodation 8 bedrooms, 6 en suite, £44-£55 (four-poster £59, family room £71, single £28.75-£38.75). Children welcome overnight (under-5s stay free in parents' room, 6-11s £6), additional bed (from £5) & cot (£5) available. Pub & accommodation closed 25 Dec. Amex, Diners, MasterCard, VISA*

LYDGATE   White Hart   ★   FOOD

Tel 01457 872566   Fax 01457 875190   Map 6 C2
51 Stockport Road Lydgate Oldham Lancashire OL4 4JJ

Local boy Charles Brierley had his first beer at this typical blackened-stone, 200-year-old Lancashire pub. He must have liked it (the pub, that is, as well as the beer), because – moving on a few years – he returned and bought it. It was then in an almost derelict state, but a year of refurbishment has turned the White Hart into a smart and comfortable hostelry. A couple of areas are reserved for drinkers but the rest is set up for eating from a Brasserie menu that ranges well beyond the usual pub fare: salad of warm, home-smoked trout with horseradish, terrine of chicken breast with sautéed livers wrapped in brioche, maize-fed chicken with truffle pasta, lamb's liver with smoked bacon and spring onion potato, and fillet of hake with creamed potatoes and red wine jus. There are also steaks, a roast ham sandwich (with home-made chutney) and afters like chocolate mousse with fresh fruits, hot banana muffin with chocolate mousse and a selection of British farmhouse cheeses. The quality and sophistication of the food is down to head chef John Rudden (formerly at *The Angel,* Hetton – our 1995 Pub of the Year) whose kitchen also serves a separate, first-floor restaurant. At Sunday lunchtimes there is a set, two- or three-course lunch, with roast sirloin of beef offered in addition to the regular menu. Various gourmet dinners arranged throughout the year. The bar wines, with about eight served by the glass, are just a sample from the main restaurant list that is available on request. Plans for the coming year include the addition of twelve letting bedrooms – watch this space! The village of Lydgate is located about three miles north-east of Oldham on the A669 – neither the village nor the road number are marked on most road maps; head for Grasscroft and you'll be on the right track! *Open 12-3 & 5-11 (Sat 11-11, Sun 12-10.30). Closed Mon lunch (except Bank Holidays).* **Bar Food** *12-2.30, 6-9.30 (till 8.30 Sat). Free House.* **Beer** *JW Lees, Coach House Innkeepers Special Reserve, Boddingtons, Webster's Green Label Best, guest beers. Garden, outdoor eating. MasterCard,* **VISA**

LYMPSHAM	Batch Country House Hotel	B&B

Tel 01934 750371   Fax 01934 750501   Map 13 E1
Lympsham Weston-super-Mare Somerset BS24 0EX

Mr and Mrs Brown's hotel, with its 50-acre grounds, stands in open farmland through which the River Axe flows. Origins of the former farmhouse are evident in the beams which adorn the bar and residents' lounges, while the neat, practical bedrooms enjoy views of either the Mendip or Quantock hills. The adjoining Somerset Suite is a popular venue for functions up to 85. Lympsham is about 3 miles from Junction 22 of the M5. *Garden, coarse fishing.* **Accommodation** *8 bedrooms, all en suite, £58-£64 (single £37). Children welcome overnight (under-1s free, 1-7s 25%, 8-14s 50% adult tariff), additional bed & cot available. No dogs. Closed 1 week Christmas. Amex, Diners, MasterCard,* **VISA**

LYNMOUTH	Rising Sun Hotel	B&B

Tel 01598 753223   Fax 01598 753480   Map 13 D1
Harbourside Lynmouth Devon EX35 6EQ

Zzz...

Hugo Jeune has spent a great deal of money in lovingly restoring his 14th-century thatched pub and adjacent cottages which climb steeply up the slope from the Lynmouth breakwater. The bedrooms (four recently completely refurbished) boast individual decor, stylish fabrics, pine furniture, colour TV, direct-dial phones and spotless bathrooms; the top cottage, where the poet Shelley spent his honeymoon in 1812, has been decked out for modern newly-weds, complete with four-poster bed, sitting room and a private garden. Romance is in the air; Shelley wrote of his stay: 'the climate is so mild that myrtles of immense size twine up our cottage and roses bloom in the open air in winter'. There's another literary connection: R.D. Blackmore wrote part of *Lorna Doone* here. The inn owns a stretch of river for salmon fishing. *Open 11-3, 6-11 (Sun 12-3, 7-10.30). Free House.* **Beer** *Exmoor Ale, Ruddles Best, Webster's Yorkshire Bitter, Courage Best. Garden.* **Accommodation** *16 bedrooms, all en suite, £79-£99 (cottage £118, single from £45). Children over 5 welcome overnight (5-12s half price if sharing parents' room), additional bed (£10) & cot (£5) available. No dogs. Amex, Diners, MasterCard,* **VISA**

MACCLESFIELD	Sutton Hall	FOOD
		B&B

Tel 01260 253211   Fax 01260 252538   Map 6 B2
Bullocks Lane Sutton Macclesfield Cheshire SK11 0HE

Zzz...

Central to the building, a wood- and stone-built 16th-century mansion in use as a nunnery until just 30 years ago, is the pub itself, which has a stunning interior. The black oak beams, gnarled and knotted, that frame the bar are certainly of much older origin than the rest of the structure (there having been a manor house on this site since 1093), and a unique atmosphere is created by the combination of oak panelling, exposed stonework, leaded windows and two large log-burning fireplaces, one of them guarded by a medieval knight in armour. The traditional bar menu features starters or snacks like home-made soup (orange and parsnip), feta and olive salad, smoked haddock mornay, taco shells filled with chili, and the usual sandwiches and ploughman's lunches, while main-course options include steak and kidney pie, Chinese-flavoured lamb cutlets or roast duck with orange and Cointreau sauce. The adjacent restaurant, kitted out in flock wallpaper with polished yew tables, takes itself a little more seriously. Bedroom conversion has seen the installation of bathrooms throughout, plus modern-day amenities like remote-control televisions, direct-dial phones, trouser presses and hairdryers. The antique flavour, however, is well preserved in lace-covered four-poster beds and deep leather easy chairs, although (a penalty of antiquity) there's a distinct shortage of natural daylight through their leaded Gothic windows, further dimmed by heavily overhanging eaves. Genuine warm welcome from owners Robert and Phyllida Bradshaw and their friendly staff. *Open 11-11 (Sun 12-4, 7-10.30). Bar Food 12-2.30 (till 2 Sun), 7-10. Free House. Beer Bass, Stones, Marston's, guest beer. Large garden, outdoor eating. Family room (weekend lunch). Accommodation 10 bedrooms, all en suite, £85 (single £42.50). Children welcome overnight (rates negotiable), cot (£5) available. Check-in by arrangement. Dogs (£5). Amex, MasterCard, VISA*

MADINGLEY   Three Horseshoes   ★   FOOD

Tel 01954 210221 Fax 01954 212043   Map 15 F1
High Street Madingley Cambridgeshire CB3 8AB

Built in the early 1900s, this neat white-painted, thatched pub with tables outside and a pretty garden is all about eating. Young chef/manager Richard Stokes's modern Mediterranean style of cooking is reflected on the imaginative and comprehensive three-weekly-changing menu, which is available throughout the relaxed bar and slightly more formal restaurant (also recommended in our *1997 Hotels & Restaurants Guide*). Begin with fennel, tomato and pepper ragout with king prawns in basil and olive sauce, confit of duck with rösti potato, foie gras and a watercress, orange and red onion salad or grilled and marinated salmon and leek terrine with cucumber, herbs and caviar. Main-course options may feature roast turbot with ginger, lime, steamed greens and coriander potatoes, chargrilled leg of lamb with roast red onions and salsa verde, and whole roast wood pigeon with rösti potato, braised lettuce and peas with bacon and mint; all demonstrate how far this is from standard pub fare. Puddings are more familiar – warm chocolate tart, bread-and-butter pudding, figs baked in port, cumin and cinnamon – and there are some splendid unpasteurised British cheeses from Neal's Yard Dairy. About 20 wines by the glass (if one includes the dessert wines and a couple of vintage ports) chosen from a commendable list of good-value wines. *Open 11.30-2.30, 6-11 (Sun 12-2.30, 7-10.30). Bar Food 12-2, 6.30-10 (Sun 7-9.30). Free House. Beer Adnams Southwold, two guest beers. Garden, outdoor eating. Amex, Diners, MasterCard, VISA*

MAIDENSGROVE   Five Horseshoes   FOOD

Tel 01491 641282 Fax 01491 641086   Map 15a D3
Maidensgrove Stonor Henley-on-Thames Oxfordshire RG9 6EY

Well established as an eating house, this old brick pub stands alongside the lane which winds past Russell's Water, off the B481. Paper money from around the world frames the bar where food is ordered, and there's little enough available, for two, for less than a crisp bill or two. From a comprehensive list, are the likes of a warm salad of chicken and coriander, cassoulet, fillet of fresh baracuda with Cajun spices and black butter, and breast of duck with caramelised orange sauce, as well as ploughman's lunches and filled baked potatoes. Daily dishes are nonetheless prominent, with main courses like deep-fried Nile perch in a lightly curried crisp batter or lemon peppered king prawns sautéed in garlic. Follow with home-made ice creams, crème brulée or nutty treacle pie. Barbecues in fine weather (Thursday evening, Sunday lunch and evening) feature steaks and lamb, chicken and seafood kebabs and there's patio seating under a swaying octagonal awning. Hidden away to the pub's rear, the Café Shoes attempts a little more adventure with main courses in much the same price range. Individual tables, or a whole room for 20, are bookable in advance. No children under 8 permitted in the bar. *Open 11.30-2.30, 6-11 (Sun 12-3, 7-10.30). Bar Food 12-2, 7-10 (till 9 Sun). Beer Brakspear, guest beers. Barbecue patio, garden, outdoor eating. Family room. MasterCard, VISA*

We only recommend food (Bar Food) in those establishments highlighted with the **FOOD** symbol.

MANCHESTER   Lass O'Gowrie   A

Tel & Fax 0161 273 6932   Map 6 B2
36 Charles Street Chorlton-cum-Medlock Manchester M1 7DB

A short walk from the city centre, right by the BBC, Lass O'Gowrie is a must as much for Manchester's students of architecture as for enthusiasts of real ale and micro-brewing. The building's facade is fully tiled in brightly-glazed browns and greens, quite literally shining as a credit to the city's clean air. Inside, the cavernous neo-Victorian recreation (somewhat gentrified for today's consumers) comes complete with gas mantles, sanded floorboards and mock-antique signboards. Above the bar are lined up some fine examples of the ancient art of cooperage, while the lining of the pub's upper walls and ceiling consists entirely of stretched hopsacks whose former contents have doubtless featured in many a brew. Central to the main bar is a glassed-in canopy through which the curious can gaze down into the cellar to see the vats. Lighter LOG 35 and maltier LOG 42 – the names indicative of their respective strengths – are the home brews hand-pulled up to the single servery and dispensed in staggering quantities. To temper a heavy lunchtime session cut sandwiches and the likes of bacon baps are on offer at very reasonable prices. No under-14s inside. Whitbread. *Open 11.30-11 (Sun 12-10.30).* **Beer** *LOG 35 & LOG 42, Castle Eden Ale, guest beers. No credit cards.*

MANCHESTER   Mark Addy   FOOD

Tel 0161 832 4080   Map 6 B2
Stanley Street Salford Manchester M3 5EJ

Head for New Bailey Street where the old Albert Bridge crosses the River Irwell into Salford; on the Manchester bank opposite is the Pump House People's History Museum. Once a jetty and waiting room for the river ferry, this is an imaginative and truly different pub that takes its name from the only civilian to be presented the Royal Albert Medal (VC) by Queen Victoria. Born on the banks of the Irwell, Mark Addy received this award for rescuing fifty drowning passengers from the river. Behind a waterside courtyard the single bar still sports the old flagstone floor and sandstone, barrel-vaulted brick ceiling encased behind full-length picture windows. Such is the range of cheeses on offer that it's best to visit in a sizeable party. Platefuls of tangy white Cheshire, Windsor Red and Sage Derby constitute a colourful display and are accompanied by baskets of freshly-baked granary bread. Shopping is meticulous: the blue Stilton comes only from Long Clawson Dairy in Melton Mowbray and the full-blooded Cricketer from Cricket Malherbie farm in Somerset. As there are also several Belgian patés (including vegetarian varieties) to add to the feast it's unsurprising – though undeniably generous – that take-away bags are also provided. Children welcome. *Open 11.30-11 (Sun 12-10.30).* **Bar Food** *11.30-10 (Sun 12-10). Free House.* **Beer** *Boddingtons, Marston's Best, guest beer. Terrace, outdoor eating. Closed 25 & 26 Dec. No credit cards.*

MANCHESTER   New Ellesmere   B&B

Tel 0161 728 2791   Fax 0161 794 8222   Map 6 B2
East Lancs Road Swinton Manchester M27 3AA

Very handy (and decently-priced) accommodation – especially for families – midway between the city centre and M62 (Junction 14) on the East Lancashire Road. 'Per room' prices apply, including weekend discounts, with all the ground-floor doubles including fold-out sofa beds. While remaining furniture and fittings are a mite utilitarian, up-to-date amenities include free satellite TV and radio channels, direct-dial phones, hairdryers and trouser presses. Full en suite facilities include heated towel rails and over-bath showers. Children welcomed, with high-chairs, changing facilities, indoor play area, garden and play area all provided. Premier Lodge (Greenalls). *Open 11.30-11 (Sun 12-10.30).* **Beer** *Greenalls Original, Tetley, Boddingtons, guest beer. Garden. Family room.* **Accommodation** *27 bedrooms, all en suite, £41.50 (per room, weekends £34.50), breakfast extra. Children welcome overnight, additional bed & cot available. No dogs. Amex, Diners, MasterCard,* **VISA**

MARKET OVERTON   Black Bull   FOOD

Tel 01572 767677   Map 7 E3
Market Overton Leicestershire LE15 7PW

Having bought a semi-derelict, part-thatched ale-house in 1986, John and Valerie Owen have single-mindedly created a relaxed local pub with good-value dining. The bar's agreeable interior of red banquettes, polished tables, poker-back chairs and background popular music (there are speakers everywhere, even in the loos!) creates a chatty, relaxed atmosphere in which to engage in banter and enjoy the beer. Across a central area of original flagstone floor is the dining-room, converted from a garage, which offers the likes of beef stir-fry with Cantonese sauce, calf's liver with caramelised onions and port, chicken korma, various grills (fillet Rossini) and fresh fish dishes – 16oz lemon sole or sea bream with prawn and lemon sauce. Sandwiches available lunchtime only. Upstairs, one en suite double and a twin bedroom (not inspected) are equipped with televisions. *Open 12-2.30, 6-11 (Sun 12-3, 7-10.30).* **Bar Food** *12-2, 6.30-10 (from 7 Sun).* **Beer** *Ruddles Best, Theakston Best & XB, Oakham Grainstore, guest beer. Patio, outdoor eating. MasterCard,* **VISA**

> We do not accept free meals or hospitality – our inspectors pay their own bills and **never** book in the name of Egon Ronay's Guides.

MARSH BENHAM   Water Rat   FOOD

Tel 01635 582017   Map 14a B4
Marsh Benham Newbury Berkshire RG16 8LY

Kenneth Grahame's immortal *Wind in the Willows* was reputedly inspired by the countryside around here, and the book is also behind the name and decor of this attractive brick-and-thatch pub, which nestles in a tiny hamlet off the A4 and a short stroll from the Kennet and Avon Canal. The interior has been opened up into two rug-floored areas; one with exposed brick walls (a more formal restaurant area), while the other has walls covered with murals of riverside scenes featuring the characters of the book. Chef David Errington draws on produce from good local suppliers, including game from nearby estates, to prepare the Mediterranean-style dishes that feature on both the monthly-changing menu and daily specials board – good fresh fish dishes – and one served throughout the pub. Typical dishes may include chilled avocado soup with chili and coriander, summer vegetable and herb risotto and Caesar salad for starters, followed by pork fillet with carrot and basil butter, olive pasta and roast peppers, grilled chicken breast marinaded in chili and lime with guacamole and haricot bean purée, roast monkfish basquaise or black bream grilled with African spices, all served with vegetables or mixed leaf and herb salad. For pudding, try the bitter chocolate and bourbon truffle cake, zabaglione or sticky toffee pudding. Swift, efficient service from friendly, well-dressed staff. Essentially a dining pub – booking advble – free from intrusive games and music, but casual drinkers at the bar are made most welcome. Extensive garden and terrace area filled with upmarket picnic benches that are ideal for summer alfresco eating. *Open 12-3, 6-11 (from 7 Sun).* **Bar Food** *12-2.30. 6-10 (from 7 Sun). Free House.* **Beer** *Wadworth 6X, Brakspear Best, Archers Village. Garden, outdoor eating, children's play area. Amex, MasterCard,* **VISA**

MARSH GIBBON   The Greyhound   FOOD

Tel & Fax 01869 277365   Map 14a C1
Marsh Gibbon Bicester Buckinghamshire OH6 0HA

A listed, traditional old pub with 17th-century brickwork without and an unusually modern food offering within. Thai snacks (satay, wun tuns, spring rolls, spare ribs) and main courses – sweet and sour prawns, salmon in black bean sauce, 'weeping tiger' (steak stir-fried in garlic, coriander and pepper with a spicy hot sauce) – are served to diners at sewing-machine tables in the beamed main bar with its bare stone walls. A £10 minimum food charge applies in the restaurant where there is an extensive à la carte and £16 set menus for four or more people. Picnic tables are set on the attractive front garden; to the rear is another garden, this time with trees and a swing and climbing frame for children. A friendly society of bell-ringers (and up to 1000 friends!) has met here for around 200 years on the nearest Saturday to May 29th. The Greyhound is south-east of Marsh Gibbon, best approached via Blackthorn on the Bicester-Aylesbury A41. *Open 12-11 (till 10.30 Sun). Bar Food 12-3.30, 6.30-10 (from 7 Sun). Free House. Beer Fuller's London Pride, Greene King Abbot, Hook Norton Best, McEwan's Export. Garden, children's play area. Amex, Diners, MasterCard, VISA*

MARSHSIDE   Gate Inn   FOOD

Tel 01227 860498   Map 11 C5
Boyden Gate Marshside Canterbury Kent CT3 4EB

Delightfully set beside a lane in a tiny hamlet – 2 miles from A28 Canterbury to Margate road at Upstreet – and surrounded by farmland and marshes, this unpretentious rural retreat prides itself on still being "a talkers' pub", in tandem with a thriving bar meal trade. Two welcoming and rustic interconnecting rooms have quarry-tiled floors, a central brick fireplace with winter log fire and a selection of sturdy pine tables, chairs and old pews. Fresh, local produce is used to produce homely, honest English fare (like a spicy mushroom hotpot), and perhaps a home-made cheesey salad gateburger with mild chili relish, pasta with pesto and bacon with garlic bread, black pudding ploughman's or a steak and mushroom hot torpedo. Well-kept Shepherd Neame ales are dispensed direct from the barrel and free-range eggs and local vegetables are also sold over the bar. Splendid summer garden with cottage flowers, stream and duck pond with resident ducks and geese – a constant amusement to children. Quiz night is Thursday night. *Open 11-2.30 (till 3 Sat), 6-11 (Sun 12-3, 6-10.30). Bar Food 11.45-2, 6-9.30 (Sun 12-2.30, 7-9). Beer Shepherd Neame. Garden, outdoor eating area, summer barbecue. Family room. No credit cards.*

MAYFIELD   Rose & Crown Inn   FOOD

Tel 01435 872200   Fax 01435 873809   Map 11 B6   **B&B**
Fletching Street Mayfield East Sussex TN20 6TE

Zzz...

Delightful 16th-century pub in a historic village, alongside what was the original London-Brighton road, now a quiet village lane. Unspoilt bars, particularly the two small front ones, have ochre walls, beams, inglenook fireplace, two log fires, and an atmosphere in which shove ha'penny and cribbage are still keenly played. A short snacky bar menu – fish pie, moules, gammon, egg and chips, ploughman's (lunch only) – is supplemented by the comprehensive and seasonally-changing carte (not always available at lunch or Sun eve) which features reliable home-cooked dishes and applies both in the bar and cosy restaurant where there's an extensive global wine list, of which nine are available by the glass. Start, perhaps, with beef carpaccio with parmesan, salad of asparagus, smoked chicken and quail's eggs, or tiger prawns in filo with ginger, moving on to chicken and lobster sausages, crispy duck on mixed leaves with cassis dressing, sautéed John Dory with ginger and chives, and sea bass and salmon with champagne sauce, followed by one of the home-made puddings, perhaps nougat praline with red fruit coulis or poached pears with ice cream and caramel sauce. Upstairs are three quaint, beamed bedrooms, each with antique pine furniture – one with a fine brass bed – and a comfortable easy chair; they are equipped with beverage-making facilities, TVs clock/radios, hairdryers and trouser presses. Spotless en suite bathrooms, all with bath and shower. Breakfast is charged extra. Landscaped front terrace with village views. *Open 11-3, 6-11 (Sat 11-11, Sun 12-3, 7-10.30).*
Bar Food 12-2.30, 6.30-9.30 (till 10 Fri & Sat), Sun 7-9.30. Free House.
Beer Harveys Sussex Bitter, Flowers IPA & Original, Ind Coope Burton Ale, Bass, guest beer. Garden, paved terrace, outdoor eating. Accommodation 3 bedrooms, all en suite, from £48 (single £38 – not Fri & Sat), breakfast £13.90 for 2 extra. Children welcome overnight, additional bed (£10) available. Check-in bar hours only. Small dogs only. MasterCard, VISA

MELKSHAM — King's Arms Hotel — B&B

Tel 01225 707272   Fax 01225 702085   Map 14 B3
Market Place Melksham Wiltshire SW12 6EX

Across from Melksham's Market Place, the Bath-stone former coaching inn with its cobbled forecourt and abundant flower displays is the old town's summer centrepiece. Residents here are well catered for with a quiet, cosy lounge leading through to an intimate dining-room. By contrast, the lounge bar is functional and less private. Bedrooms vary between a period, beamed style and the bright and more spacious, arched doubles probably favoured by those with work to do. Ten bedrooms have en suite facilities (one with shower only), while three smaller singles share two barely adequate public bathrooms, a fact reflected in their lower tariff. *Open 11-2.30, 5-11 (Sat 11-3, 5.30-11, Sun 12-3, 7-10.30).* ***Beer*** *Wadworth, guest beer.* ***Accommodation*** *13 bedrooms, 10 en suite, £49 (single £30-£45). Children welcome overnight (under-16s stay free in parents' room), additional bed & cot available. Amex, Diners, MasterCard,* **VISA**

MELLOR — Devonshire Arms — FOOD

Tel 0161 427 2563   Map 6 C2
Longhurst Lane Mellor Stockport SK6 5PP

A regular Devonshire drinker claims to have lived in Derbyshire, Cheshire and Greater Manchester without ever having moved house, so close is the pub to this area's ever-changing boundaries. When Brian and Joan Harrison moved in here, on to the menu came tiger prawns in filo pastry, mussel chowder and Kung-Po chicken with sherry sauce, thus extending the boundaries of good pub food and drawing eager diners from all four counties. Authentic curries, however, remain Brian's abiding passion, with fresh spices and nan regularly ferried in from cosmopolitan Stockport. Kabalic chicken, carbonade of beef, Raseda Jingha with prawns, ginger and yoghurt, buttered chicken masala and 'malaida unday' (the last word in curried eggs) are a representative sample. While the full menu is currently served only at lunchtime, the rear lounge, opening on to the rear patio and recently extended garden, is available for evening 'entertaining', supplemented by jazz on Thursday nights. *Open 11.30-3, 5.30-11 (Sun 12-3, 7-10.30).* ***Bar Food*** *12-2.30, evening meals Mon only 7-9.30.* ***Beer*** *Robinson's Best, Hatter's Mild & occasionally Frederic's. Garden, outdoor eating. Closed 25 Dec eve. No credit cards.*

MELLOR — Millstone Hotel — FOOD B&B

Tel 01254 813333   Fax 01254 812628   Map 6 B1
Church Lane Mellor Blackburn Lancashire BB2 7JR

 Zzz... ☺

Daniel Thwaites, the Blackburn brewers, operate the Shire Inns chain; its original flagship, the Millstone remains true to its roots and is closest to the brewery. Pub first and foremost, it has a thriving local trade and is consistently busy for their Miller's bar food which offers the likes of fish soup, chicken liver paté and oak smoked Lune salmon as starters; main courses might extend the choice to cod in beer batter, lamb balti, steak, kidney and mushroom pie, Scottish mussels or spicy Cumberland sausage and Bury black pudding with onion gravy and apple chutney. By comparison, the à la carte restaurant and en suite bedrooms are decidedly 'hotel' and priced accordingly. At the time of going to press a new chef had just been appointed (Adrian Sedden), who intends improving the quality of the food and maintaining the style of cooking. Smart bedrooms (ten non-smoking) come in both standard and executive grades (including three suites), with satellite TV, direct-dial telephones, trouser presses and hairdryers throughout. Executive rooms receive rather more space, towelling bathrobes and top-drawer toiletries in the en suite bathrooms. Of great benefit to the less active is the wing of five ground-floor bedrooms (there is no lift) which are also appreciated by parents of very little ones. Six new bedrooms, boasting similar high standards of decor and comfort, are located in the adjacent, recently-acquired property. *Open 11-11 (Sun 12-10.30).* ***Bar Food*** *12-2, 7-8.45.* ***Beer*** *Thwaites Mild, Bitter & seasonal beer. Patio.* ***Accommodation*** *24 bedrooms, all en suite, £92-£112 (single £73-£90), weekends £58 (single £49). Children welcome overnight (under-14s free if staying in parents' room), additional bed & cot available. Amex, Diners, MasterCard,* **VISA**

MELLS   Talbot Inn   FOOD

Tel 01373 812254   Map 13 F1
Mells Frome Somerset BA11 3PN

At the heart of this timeless feudal village with its splendid church, magnificent manor house and unspoilt stone cottages is the Talbot Inn, a rambling, 15th-century coaching inn with an attractive cobbled courtyard and a series of friendly bars. Terracotta-painted stone walls, old ceiling beams, country prints and a stone fireplace with winter log fire feature in the comfortable lounge, while the separate public bar sports a rustic wooden floor and a loyal band of locals. The adjacent 'Oxford Bar', named after Lord Oxford who lives in the manor next door, is a relaxing room with its high, green ceiling, candle-topped pine tables and shuttered windows. Reliable home-cooked food ranges from ratatouille flan, tagliatelle with smoked salmon and prawns, and blackboard specials like carrot and orange soup, lamb and potato stew, and spicy chili beef at lunchtime plus lamb and apricot pie, pork with apple and cider sauce, and chargrilled steaks on the evening à la carte menu. A short selection of more imaginative evening specials highlight local game (pheasant braised in red wine, casserole of wild boar with port and herbs) and fresh fish (Oriental mackerel, poached whiting with herb and tomato cream sauce). Popular events include an Irish music weekend in September and, over the Easter weekend, the English Civil War Society re-enact a battle in the village. Functional overnight accommodation is available in seven en suite bedrooms (not specifically recommended). *Open 12-3, 6-11 (Sun 12-3, 7-10.30). Bar Food 12-2, 7-9.30. Free House. Beer Butcombe Bitter, Bass, guest beer. Garden, outdoor eating. Family room. MasterCard,* **VISA**

MELMERBY   Shepherds Inn   FOOD

Tel 01768 881217   Map 4 C3
Melmerby Penrith Cumbria CA10 1HF

Martin and Christine Baucutt have built up a fine reputation here. At the heart of their operation is Christine's cooking which draws on fresh local produce, and it's no exaggeration that regulars cross and re-cross the Pennines simply to sample the variety on offer. Ever popular dishes like chicken Leoni, Cumberland sausage hotpot, venison and Roquefort crumble and steak and kidney feature alongside new daily menus, which may offer beetroot and potato soup with home-made roll or Stilton and walnut pasta bake for starters, followed by lamb and apricot lattice pie, grilled red snapper with Cajun sauce, carrot and nut loaf or freshly battered pollock with chips and peas. Those popping in for just a quick snack may find a chicken balti pancake or an open smoked salmon sandwich on the menu. Up to a dozen sweets displayed on the counter come with lashings of 'Jersey' cream, while cheese enthusiasts can choose from some fifteen or more on offer, including interesting North Country varieties. A sensible, no-nonsense attitude towards the young enables grown-up meals as they'd like. No fish fingers here, but chips possible and scrambled egg, even, on request; high-chairs, too. A twenty-one bin wine list can be supplemented by 'tastings' from Martin's private cellar; less exotically, English country fruit wines are available by the glass and there is a selection of at least 50 malt whiskies. *Open 11-3, 6-11 (Sun 12-3, 7.10.30). Bar Food 11-2.30 (from 12 Sun), 6-9.45 (from 7 Sun). Free House. Beer Jennings Cumberland Ale & Sneck Lifter, three guest beers. Cobbled patio, outdoor eating, barbecue. Closed 25 Dec. Amex, Diners, MasterCard,* **VISA**

MELTHAM   Will's O'Nat's   FOOD

Tel 01484 850078   Map 6 C2
Blackmoorfoot Road Meltham Huddersfield Kirklees HD7 3PS

The unusual name – meaning 'William's (place), son of Nathaniel' – might also be topographically described as 'Reservoir's (side) O'Meltham'. Avoiding the village alto-gether, it's easiest to find off the A62 just south of Slaithwaite, passing Blackmoorfoot reservoir, from where the pub's in full view. By the same simple terms, the Schofields' food might be described as populist, yet it's evidently fathered from a long-standing pedigree. Regular instances of top-selling specials running out is, as ever, indicative of a dedicated kitchen, and the constantly-updated blackboards demonstrate a downright determination to feed all comers. A plethora of sandwiches runs from steak and onion and jumbo hot dog to smoked salmon and black pudding and bacon; snacks and salads galore include hot and spicy bean casserole, ham and mushroom tagliatelle and deep-fried black pudding with apple fritters. Some plentiful home cooking produces the likes of chicken, ham and mushroom pie, wild boar sausage with onion sauce and braised steak with onions. In addition, there's daily fresh fish, home-made puddings (summer fruit gateau, chocolate and orange tart) and a good range of English cheeses, notably some interesting Northern cheeses – Cannon Lodge oak-smoked Lancashire. The majority of diners choose the upper eating area, away from the central bar servery, where views are of the moorland and surrounding hills. They're well served by friendly, hard-working youngsters who wear their tabards proudly and make light at peak periods of inevitable delays. *Open 11.30-3 (till 3.30 Sat), 6-11 (from 6.30 Sat), Sun 12-3, 7-10.30. Bar Food 11.30-2, 6-10 (from 6.30 Sat), Sun 12-2, 7-10. Beer Tetley Bitter & Mild, Old Mill Bitter. Patio, outdoor eating. Amex, MasterCard, VISA*

METAL BRIDGE	Metal Bridge Inn	B&B

Tel & Fax 01228 74206   Map 4 C2
Floriston Metal Bridge Cumbria CA6 4HG

Pretty bed and breakfasting hostelry (formerly a fisherman's house), with old beamed bars decorated with nets and rods, enjoying a picturesque hamlet setting on the Esk estuary. The five refurbished bedrooms, four of which are en suite, are agreeably rustic with pine furniture and nice views, and all have TVs; one is a single with a separate (but private) bathroom. No smoking in the conservatory. *Open 11-3, 5.30-11 (Sun 12-3, 7-10.30). Beer Scottish & Newcastle Scotch, McEwan's Export, Theakston Best, Younger's Scotch. Riverside garden. Family room. Accommodation 5 bedrooms, 4 en suite, £45 (family room £50, single £25/35 – room only rates, breakfast £5). Children welcome overnight (stay free if sharing parents' room), additional bed & cot available. Amex, Diners, MasterCard, VISA*

MICHELDEVER	Dever Arms	FOOD

Tel 01962 774339   Map 15 D3
Winchester Road Micheldever Hampshire SO21 3DG

Enthusiastic owners Michael and Violet Penny run this well-maintained pub set in the heart of a charming, thatched and timbered village. Three neatly furnished and carpeted interconnecting rooms sport a village local atmosphere, with a sensibly-placed bar billiards table and darts board at one end. For diners, there's a comfortable eating area close to the inglenook fireplace plus a smart little adjacent dining-room. Popularity stems from the interesting selection of freshly-prepared bar meals. A printed 'hearty snack' menu – home-made salmon and watercress fishcake with sorrel sauce, steamed mussels, sandwiches, ploughman's lunches – is supplemented by daily-changing blackboard menus, displayed around the fireplace, which may include mushrooms and smoked bacon in white wine and garlic or gratin of rigatoni pasta with roasted peppers. Main courses range from spicy lamb and apricots, Oriental beef stir-fry and beef and mushroom pie to medallions of pork with a green peppercorn sauce and poached salmon steak with white wine and dill. Sunday roast lunches. A well-stocked bar boasts a good range of locally-brewed real ales, all of which can be sampled on summer days on the quiet patio to the rear of the pub. *Open 11.30-3, 6-11 (Sun 12-3, 7-10.30). Bar Food 12-2, 7-9.45 (no food Sun eve). Free House. Beer Hop Back Summer Lightning, Ringwood Best, Cheriton Brewhouse Pots Ale, guest beers. Garden, outdoor eating area. Family room. Amex, MasterCard, VISA*

> We endeavour to be as up-to-date as possible but inevitably some changes to landlords, chefs and other key staff occur after the Guide has gone to press.

MICKLEHAM — King William IV — FOOD

Tel 01372 372590   Map 15a F4
Byttom Hill Mickleham Surrey RH5 6EL

It's not particularly easy to find this old alehouse originally built for Lord
Beaverbrook's estate staff; parts of the pub date back to 1790. Up a track above the
Frascati restaurant (before the sign to Mickleham) on the main A24 heading south,
north of Dorking; park at the foot of the hill and it's a short walk up to the pub.
Since the pub is on a steep slope it's rather rambly but the terraced garden is lovely,
with splendid views across Norbury Park and the Mole Valley, arbours, rambling roses
and terracotta planters as a centrepiece; and there's even a serving hatch to the garden
– handy for walkers with muddy boots. On a typical blackboard menu you might find
a particularly good selection of vegetarian dishes (perhaps up to six), ploughman's
lunches, filled jacket potatoes, Thai green curry, spinach, nut and mozzarella bake,
steak and kidney pie, and Barnsley chop with honey and mint. Sandwiches are not
served at weekends and Bank Holidays, and there's not a chip in sight. Homely puds
may include marmalade and apricot pudding or hot butterscotch banana. Sunday roast
lunches. No children under 14 in main bar area. Only suitable for families in summer.
Open 11-3, 6-11, (Sun 12-3, 7-10.30). **Bar Food** *12-2, 7-9.45 (no food Mon evening).*
Free House. **Beer** *Adnams Best, Hall & Woodhouse Badger Best, Hogs Back Traditional
English Ale, guest beer. Garden, outdoor eating, barbecues. MasterCard,* **VISA**

> We do not accept free meals or hospitality – our inspectors pay their own bills
> and **never** book in the name of Egon Ronay's Guides.

MIDDLEHAM — Black Swan — B&B

Tel 01969 622221   Map 5 D4
Market Place Middleham North Yorkshire DL8 4NP

The stones that built this town-centre inn came from Middleham Castle at the time
when Cromwell was punishing it for being on the Royalist side in the Civil War.
Today Middleham is a rather more peaceful and quite pretty little market town – the
smallest in Yorkshire apparently. The comfortable bar comes complete with old beams
and cushioned high-backed settles but it is the bedroom accommodation that we
recommend here. The four rooms at the front are the most characterful (and the
largest), with exposed ceiling beams; however, all are equally prettily decorated in co-
ordinating floral fabrics and wall coverings and most have French-style, sometimes
fitted, furniture. All have neat, carpeted bathrooms (the small single has shower and
WC only) with showers over tubs; all rooms have TV, direct-dial phones and tea- and
coffee-making kits. The resident ghosts are reputedly quite friendly. *Open 11.30-3.30
(from 12 Sun), 6-11 (from 6.30 Sun), Sat 11-11 & Sun 12-10.30 summer. Free House.*
Beer *John Smith's, Theakston Best, Mild, XB & Old Peculier, guest beer. Garden.*
Accommodation *7 bedrooms, all en suite, £44/59 (single £25). Children welcome overnight,
additional bed & cot available (£5). Check-in by arrangement. Accommodation closed 24, 25
& 26 Dec. MasterCard,* **VISA**

MIDDLETON — Ye Olde Boar's Head — A

Tel 0161 643 3520   Map 6 B2
Long Street Middleton Oldham M24 3UE

Established as a hostelry in 1632 and first licensed in 1753, this striking, timbered set
of buildings is Elizabethan in appearance but arguably has even earlier origins; some
remarkable remains of its original construction were unearthed and carefully preserved
during restoration work by JW Lees's brewery in 1989. A small snug commemorates
Middleton's favourite 19th-century son, the poet and radical Samuel Bamford.
Elsewhere within a splendid building still divided by original timbers and oak
partitions, the Fisherman's and Sessions room (the latter now given over to TV
and darts) are careful recreations of former times. *Open 11.30-3, 5-11 (from 7 Sat),
Fri 11-11, Sun 12-10.30.* **Beer** *Lees. Patio. Family room. No credit cards.*

MIDDLETON STONEY   Jersey Arms   B&B

Tel 01869 343234   Fax 01869 343565   Map 14a C1
Middleton Stoney Bicester Oxfordshire OX6 8SE

Zzz...

Small, family-owned and -managed, 17th-century Cotswold-stone inn, now a hotel and restaurant. Alongside the B430 (between Junctions 9 & 10 of the M40), it is well placed for Woodstock, Blenheim Palace and Oxford (even Silverstone race circuit). Day rooms include a low-ceilinged bar warmed by an open fire and a relaxing lounge with half panelling and comfortable seating. Cottagey bedrooms are divided between the main house (where wooden beams and creaking floors abound) and the courtyard where they are a little more up to date; the Langtry Suite has a four-poster bed and sitting room. Rooms are equipped with colour teletext TVs, direct-dial telephones, hairdryers and en suite bathrooms (bath and shower). Room service 7.30am-10.30pm. *Open 11-3, 6-11. Free House.* **Beer** *Courage Best, Theakston Best. Garden.* ***Accommodation*** *16 bedrooms, all en suite, £79.50/£89/£120 (single £65/£75/£85). Children welcome overnight (under-15s stay free in parents' room), additional bed (£15) & cot available. No dogs. Amex, Diners, MasterCard,* **VISA**

MIDDLETON-IN-TEESDALE   Teesdale Hotel   FOOD

Tel 01833 640264   Fax 01833 640651   Map 5 D3   B&B
Market Place Middleton-in-Teeside Barnard Castle Co Durham DL12 029

At the centre of this stone-built village deep in the High Pennines the Streit family have been practising their own brand of hospitality for nearly twenty years. Over the years the dayrooms have been carefully modernised throughout, tastefully furnished and immaculately kept. Audrey and her daughter handle the kitchen in a style which brings new respectability to the term "home cooking" while in the front-of-house former chef Dieter, in his own words, "helps to take the strain". Commendably varied bar menus (including an entire vegetarian section) run from vegetable samosas with mint chutney for a snack through to stir-fried beef and chicken in tomato and mushroom sauce. A tapas-style menu – yellow pea and smoked sausage casserole, smoked duck breast and redcurrant jelly – is served all day in the Rally Bar, which leads out on to a large summer terrace. Individually-decorated and comfortable bedrooms are for the most part full of colour and natural light, those on the first floor having neatly-kept en suite bathrooms. At the top level, three fully-tiled en suite shower rooms have been carefully incorporated and the newly refurbished family room should have en suite facilities in the coming year. In keeping with their own philosophy the Streits have resisted the provision of so-called "hospitality trays" (and room phones, too) in favour of a cheerily delivered early morning tea tray. Children over 3 welcome in bar area. *Open 11-11 (till 10.30 Sun).* **Bar Food** *12-2, 6-9.30 (till 11 Sat, tapas menu 11-10.30). Free House.* **Beer** *Tetley, Ind Coope Burton Ale, Butterknowle High Force Bitter. Terrace, outdoor eating.* ***Accommodation*** *10 all en suite £50 (single from £38.50). Children welcome overnight (under-1s stay free in parents' room, 8-14s £8), additional bed & cot available. Mastercard,* **VISA**.

MIDHURST   Angel Hotel   ★   FOOD

Tel 01730 812421   Fax 01730 815928   Map 11 A6   B&B
North Street Midhurst West Sussex GU29 9DN

Zzz...

Once a coaching inn dating back to the 16th century, the Angel is virtually plumb in the town centre. The plain white-painted Georgian facade gives no real indication of the warmth and welcome waiting within. Public rooms are largely centred around the two bars and restaurants with a relatively quiet residents' open lounge area at the front. Furnishings throughout are a mixture of well-maintained polished antiques, deep relaxing armchairs and settees with paintings and prints on the walls – the usual traditional trappings that befit a well-cared-for establishment such as this. Bedrooms, all on upper floors, are of a good size and comfortably appointed, offering all expected extras. Bathrooms are up-to-date and kept in good order, with all, except one, having showers over tubs. Four rear rooms, including newer suites, overlook the ruins of

Cowdray Castle in the distance. Diners have a choice of two eating places: the brasserie area, adjacent to the bar, is rustic in style and less informal in character, while the dining-room (Cowdray Room), in contrast, is spacious and classically elegant with large, well-spaced tables, Here one can enjoy a good-value table d'hote lunch or investigate the imaginative à la carte menu. Chef Andrew Stevenson, working in conjunction with owner Peter Crawford-Rolt, produces dishes as diverse as Normandy onion and cider soup, smoked haddock fishcake with rocket salad and salsa cruda, and stew of borlotti beans, confit of rabbit, smoked sausage and aïoli (Brasserie), to fillet of Cornish brill and scallops with saffron noodles and ginger and lime sauce, and rack of lamb with couscous, apricot timbale and Madeira sauce, served in the dining-room. The fish is particularly good here, the style of cooking is eclectic and the execution of the dishes first-rate. Victorian walled garden. Children welcome. *Open 10.30-3, 6-10.30 (till 11 Sat), Sun 12-3, 6-10.30.* **Bar Food** *12-2.30, 6-9.30 (till 10 Sat). Free House.* **Beer** *Gale's, guest beer. Garden.* **Accommodation** *25 bedrooms, all en suite, £80-140 (single from £75). Children welcome overnight, additional bed (£20) & cot available. No dogs. Amex, Diners, MasterCard,* **VISA**

MIDHURST	**Spread Eagle Hotel**	**FOOD**

Tel 01730 816911   Fax 01730 815668   Map 11 A6   **B&B**
South Street Midhurst West Sussex GU29 9NH

Former coaching inn close to the town centre, now a smart and civilised hotel occupying an appealing collection of 15th- and 17th-century buildings that ooze historic charm and atmosphere. Despite being an upmarket hotel, the splendid lounge bar is a most welcoming and relaxing place in which to unwind after travelling the A272 or exploring the town. Heavy oak beams set in low ceilings, comfortable settees and armchairs neatly laid out on the rug-strewn oak floor, some in front of the huge inglenook fireplace, fresh flowers and leaded windows set the scene in which to enjoy good lunchtime snacks. The short menu may list roasted red pepper and tomato soup, smoked haddock-topped Welsh rarebit, lentil paté with toasted brioche, mushroom and herb tart, steamed salmon salad and a hot dish of the day (stir-fried chicken, lasagne). Puddings might include pear and chocolate tart and elderflower mousse. Bedrooms are individually decorated and furnished with a mixture of reproduction and antique pieces and most, including the four-poster rooms, boast old exposed timbers and wood panelling. Secluded courtyard and afternoon teas. *Open 11-2, 6-11.* **Bar Food** *12-2 only (no bar food Sun lunch).* **Beer** *Fuller's London Pride. Courtyard, outdoor eating.* **Accommodation** *41 bedrooms, all en suite, £95 (four-poster from £130, single £75). Children welcome overnight, additional bed (£19.50) & cot (£7.50) available. Amex, Diners, MasterCard,* **VISA**

> We endeavour to be as up-to-date as possible but inevitably some changes to landlords, chefs and other key staff occur after the Guide has gone to press.

MILL GREEN	**Viper**	**A**

Tel 01277 352010   Map 11 B4
Mill Green Ingatestone Essex CM4 0PS

Surrounded by woodland and common land a few miles north of Ingatestone and the A12, the Viper is a popular, idyllically set little country pub (formerly two cottages), best enjoyed after a wander through the surrounding countryside. The charm of the environment is enhanced by a peaceful, large garden full of shrubs and flowers and the traditional, simply-furnished interior of the two small bars. A further draw is the choice of well-kept real ales. Simple snacks available lunchtime only. No children inside. *Open 11-2.30 (Sat 3), 6-11 (Sun 12-3, 7-10.30). Free House.* **Beer** *three regularly-changing real ales. Garden. No credit cards.*

MILTON   Jolly Brewers   A

Tel 01223 860585
Map 10 B3

5 Fen Road Milton Cambridgeshire CB4 6AD

Painted cream and dark green, with a picket fence around the front garden, and with its roses and hanging baskets, from a distance the Jolly Brewers resembles a cottage. Located 1½ miles from the A45, in the old part of the village, it's appealingly unpretentious, with low-beamed ceilings, pine and darkwood tables, and jugs of fresh flowers in the two bars. The back garden has a slide and a swing. Children allowed in the bar to eat at weekend lunchtimes. The pub is said to "host a ghost". *Open 11.30-2.30, 6-11 (Sat 12-3, 7-11, Sun 12-3, 7-10.30).* **Beer** *Flowers IPA. Garden, children's play area. No credit cards.*

MILTON ABBAS   Hambro Arms   FOOD

Tel 01258 880233
Map 14 B4   **B&B**

Milton Abbas Blandford Forum Dorset DT11 0BP

Crowning the top of this idyllic 'showpiece' village street lined with uniform thatched cottages and lawns is the attractive, long thatch of the 18th-century Hambro Arms. Most days, especially in summer, the attractively-furnished lounge and dining-room of this friendly inn are busy with people seeking refreshment after a visit to Milton Abbey or after climbing the long village street. Inside the lounge bar there is a comfortable collection of tables and chairs and two open fireplaces, one with woodburner, while the separate, livelier and rather spartan public bar houses a juke box and pool table. The choice of food runs from standard snacks to more substantial dishes such as their speciality pies – perhaps steak and mushroom or beef and oyster – a range of steaks and a selection of four vegetarian meals. More elaborate dishes are featured on the daily-changing blackboard, which regularly lists fresh fish from Weymouth (whole lemon sole, sea bream with tomato and basil) and well-sauced meat dishes like medallions of venison with red wine and wild mushrooms. Four-course Sunday lunch carvery. Upstairs, overlooking the village street, are two pretty, individually-decorated en suite bedrooms. Floral, chintzy fabrics abound with matching curtains and bedcovers and as well as the usual comforts of TVs, clock-radios and tea-makers there are thoughtful extras like a stocked mini-fridge, fresh flowers, pot pourri and biscuits. A further ten en suite rooms are available in a village house a few miles away. No children in accommodation or pub. *Open 11-3, 6-11 (Sun 12-3, 7-10.30).* **Bar Food** *12-2, 7-9.30 (till 8.30 Sun).* **Beer** *Flowers Original, Boddingtons. Patio, outdoor eating area.* **Accommodation** *2 bedrooms, both en suite, £50 (single £30). Check-in by arrangement. No dogs. MasterCard,* **VISA**

MITHIAN   Miners Arms   FOOD

Tel 01872 552375
Map 12 B3

Mithian St Agnes Cornwall TR5 0QU

Ancient inn located in a picturesque village and only a mile or so from the bustling beaches of the north coast. Built in 1577, the inn is delightfully unspoilt and typically Cornish in character for it retains its traditional layout, featuring low ceilings, wonky walls, woodblock floors and an open fire in the main bar. A cosy lounge displays a genuine Elizabethan ceiling frieze, half wood-panelled walls and shelves full of books, bottles and interesting ornaments. Also of note is the fascinating wall painting of Elizabeth I and the penance cupboard which at one time had a beautifully carved mahogany seat. The cellar bar is ideal for families and leads out into the sheltered garden. Bar food choices are limited to a short printed menu and a few daily specials, but what is on offer is good and mostly home-made. Local crab is used in preparing the crab bake which is served with walnut and dill bread, and soups (broccoli and Stilton) are freshly prepared. Main-course dishes include fish pie, Italian pasta bake, steak and kidney pie and, possibly, fresh grilled sea bass on the specials board. Attractive front cobbled terrace with picnic benches. *Open 12-3, 6-11 (Sun 12-3, 7-10.30).* **Bar Food** *12-3, 7-9.30.* **Beer** *Marston's Pedigree, Bass. Garden, patio, outdoor eating area. Family room. No credit cards.*

MOLESWORTH   Cross Keys   B&B

Tel 01832 710283   Fax 01832 710098   Map 7 E4
Molesworth Huntingdon Cambridgeshire PE18 0QF

Skittles, darts and pool are all enjoyed by the locals at this unpretentious, 200-year-old pub which has a relaxed and friendly atmosphere. The bedrooms are warm, quiet and comfortable and all offer en suite bathrooms (bath and shower), TVs, direct-dial phones and tea-makers. Breakfast is extra (£2.50–£3.50). Active youngsters will be kept amused in the adventure playground in the garden. *Open 11-11 (Sun 12-10.30). Free House. Beer Bateman's XB, guest beer. Garden, children's play area. **Accommodation** 10 bedrooms, all en suite, £37 (single £27). Children welcome overnight (under-5s stay free in parents' room, over-5s price depends on age), additional bed (£5) & cot available. Amex, MasterCard, VISA*

MONKSILVER   Notley Arms   ★   FOOD

Tel 01984 656217   Map 13 E2
Monksilver Taunton Somerset TA4 4JB

Sarah and Alistair Cade run their white-painted roadside village pub with inimitable flair and have built up a formidably good reputation. The interior is charmingly simple: an L-shaped bar with plain wooden furniture, black and white timbered walls, candles at night, and twin wood-burning stoves; a small but bright and cheery family room leads off, and there's a stream at the bottom of the trim, cottagey garden. The big attraction here, though, is the bar food, which roughly divides into three categories – the traditional, the Eastern or exotic, and the vegetarian – all given equal thought, using the finest fresh ingredients and cooked with sure-handed skill. Old favourites and four or five daily hot specials are chalked up on the blackboard: start with an excellent home-made soup, like a well-balanced, tasty tomato and fresh plum or carrot and caraway soup (served with French-flour bread). For a light but satisfying lunch, choose one of the delicious pitta bread sandwiches with garlic butter, tender meats and good crispy salad. Chinese red roast pork features well-marinated cubes of meat in a soy, five spice and hoi sin sauce, with stir-fried pimento and courgette. The fresh salmon and spinach strudel, old-fashioned lamb casserole with onion dumplings, home-made fresh pasta dishes, bacon, leek and cider suet pudding and spicy courgette kofta are equally fine, as are puddings, with light pastry and good local cream. Try the lemon and cottage cheese cheesecake, apricot bread-and-butter pudding or treacle tart, or a locally-made ice cream. A few more restaurant dishes like steaks and trout are added to the evening menu. Despite the crowds at peak times, all runs effortlessly smoothly and with good humour. *Open 11.30-2.30, 6.30-11 (Sun 12-2.30, 7-10.30). Closed 2 weeks end Jan-early Feb. Bar Food 12-2 (till 1.45 Sun), 7-9.30 (till 9 Sun). Free House. Beer Exmoor Ale, Morland Old Speckled Hen, Ushers Best, Wadworth 6X. Riverside garden, outdoor eating. Family room. No credit cards.*

MONTACUTE   King's Arms Inn   FOOD

Tel 01935 822513   Fax 01935 826549   Map 13 F2   **B&B**
Montacute Somerset TA15 6UU

 Zzz...

Former 16th-century hamstone coaching inn in a very picturesque and unspoilt village at the base of Ham Hill. Today's comfortable little inn, in the enthusiastic hands of Karen and Johnathan Arthur, has a relaxing lounge (Windsor Room) with deep sofas and the popular Pickwick Bar. The latter features a log fire in winter, real ales and has a much sought-after window seat with village views. Both the bar and adjacent comfortable seating area fill up quickly at lunchtimes with Montacute House (NT) visitors in search a good bar meal. Beyond the lunchtime help-yourself buffet (except Sun – set roast lunch) there is varied range of dishes that are listed on a seasonally-changing menu: hot and sour prawns with fresh yoghurt, tomato, mozzarella and basil salad with pink grapefruit dressing, turkey and apricot pie and pan-fried chicken breast stuffed with crab meat with red pepper sauce. Blackboard specials highlight fresh fish – grilled plaice with shellfish sauce. Separate restaurant serving an à la carte menu. Characterful and comfortable accommodation is in thirteen recently upgraded en suite (bath and shower) bedrooms, especially in the well-appointed executive rooms which have dark mahogany furnishings and attractive fabrics; one room boasts an elegant four-poster. Follow a peaceful night with a walk on the National Trust's wooded St Michael's Hill behind the hotel. *Open 11.30-2.30, 6-11 (Sun 12-2.30, 7-10.30).* **Bar Food** *12-2, 7-9.30. Free House.* **Beer** *Bass, Hall & Woodhouse Tanglefoot. Garden.* **Accommodation** *13 bedrooms, all en suite, £69-£75 (four-poster £85, single £53-£59). Children welcome overnight, additional bed & cot (both £8) available. No dogs. Accommodation closed 25 Dec-8 Jan. Amex, MasterCard,* **VISA**

MORETON-IN-MARSH   Redesdale Arms   B&B

Tel 01608 650308   Fax 01608 651843   Map 14a A1
High Street Moreton-in-Marsh Gloucestershire GL56 0AW

Flagstone floors, some old pine panelling and exposed stonework and a real log fire in winter give character to the bars at this brewery-owned former coaching inn on the main street of town. There's also a small rattan-furnished conservatory to the rear. Bedrooms offer all the usual amenities plus carpeted, en suite bathrooms, all with shower over the tub. Greenalls' Premier Lodge. *Open 11-11 (Sun 12-10.30).* **Beer** *Bass, Boddingtons, Tetley, guest beer. Garden. Family Room.* **Accommodation** *17 bedrooms, all en suite, £41.50 (room only, breakfast £3.65-£4.95 extra). Children welcome overnight (under-10s stay free in parents' room), additional bed & cot available. Amex, Diners, MasterCard,* **VISA**

MORETONHAMPSTEAD   White Hart Hotel   B&B

Tel 01647 440406   Fax 01647 440565   Map 13 D2
The Square Moretonhampstead Devon TQ13 8NF

A fine, traditional 400-year-old inn, formerly a Georgian posting house, set in the heart of a village on the edge of Dartmoor. The oak-beamed bar, where an open fire adds its cheery glow, houses all sorts of copper and brass bric-a-brac, and there is a comfortable lounge. TVs, radios, trouser presses and phones are provided in the spotless bedrooms, which are comfortably furnished in old-fashioned style; all of the rooms have private facilities that include power showers. The hotel makes a splendid base from which to explore the area; activities include a round of golf on any one of 15 golf courses within 30 miles, plus fishing on the Teign and marvellous walks in Dartmoor National Park. Conference facilities and afternoon cream teas. *Open 11-11 (Sun 12-10.30). Free House.* **Beer** *Boddingtons, Bass, Butcombe Bitter. Family room.* **Accommodation** *20 bedrooms, all en suite, £65 (single £43). Children welcome overnight, additional bed available. Garden. Amex, Diners, MasterCard,* **VISA**

MORWENSTOW   Bush Inn   A

Tel 01288 331242   Map 12 C2
Morwenstow Bude Cornwall EX23 9SR

Set in an isolated cliff-top hamlet close to bracing coastal path walks, the simple, traditional and very unspoilt Bush makes an ideal resting place. Once a monastic resting house on the pilgrim route between Spain and Wales, it is reputed to be one of the oldest pubs in Britain with parts dating back to 950 when it was a hermit's cell. Further evidence of its antiquity is the Celtic piscina carved from serpentine stone and set into one wall of the bar. Flagged floors, ancient built-in settles, old stone fireplaces and rustic furnishings characterise the charming interior that is thankfully devoid of intrusive games and music. No children indoors. No dogs. Signposted off A39 at Crimp. *Open 12-3, 7-11 (Sun 12-3, 7-10.30). Closed Mon Oct-Mar (except Bank Holidays). Free House.* **Beer** *St Austell HSD & Duchy Bitter. Garden. No credit cards.*

MOTCOMBE   Coppleridge Inn   FOOD

Tel 01747 851980   Fax 01747 851858   Map 14 B3   **B&B**
Motcombe Shaftesbury Dorset SP7 9HW

 Zzz... ☺

The Coppleridge Inn is a splendid example of how to convert an 18th-century farmhouse and its adjoining farm buildings into a successful all-round inn. Set in 15 acres of meadow, woodland and gardens it enjoys a lofty position with far-reaching views across the Blackmore Vale. The old farmhouse forms the nucleus of the operation, comprising a welcoming bar with stripped pine tables, attractive prints and a small gallery with seating. There's a comfortable lounge with flagstoned floor and inglenook fireplace and a delightful light and airy restaurant with open country views. Diners can choose from three menus – bar, bistro and restaurant – which are served throughout the inn. Dishes range from creamy garlic soup, smoked trout terrine, French lamb casserole and venison in wild mushroom sauce in the bar to fillet of sea bass with pernod and prawn sauce and pork fillet with tarragon and mushroom sauce on the restaurant menu. Puddings include chocolate St Emilion and ginger syllabub. Home-made pizzas are a speciality on Tuesday and Friday nights. Across the lawned courtyard are ten well-appointed, en suite bedrooms, all superbly incorporated into the single-storey old barns. Tasteful, attractive fabrics, pine furniture, mini-bar, TV, telephone, radio, sparkling clean bathrooms (one with shower only) with bidet and rural views characterise these comfortable rooms. Also part of the complex are two tennis courts, a cricket pitch, a hair salon and a magnificent barn that has been converted into a conference and function room. *Open 11-11 (Sun 12-10.30).* *Bar Food 12-2.30, 6-9.30 (from 7 Sun). Free House. Beer Butcombe Bitter, Hook Norton Best, guest beer. Garden, outdoor eating, children's play area. Family room. Accommodation 10 bedrooms, all en suite, £70 (single £40). Children welcome overnight (under-5s stay free in parents' room, 6-14s £10), additional bed (£10) & cot (£5) available. Amex, Diners, MasterCard, VISA*

MOULSOE — Carrington Arms — FOOD

Tel 01908 218050   Fax 01908 217850   Map 15a E1   **B&B**
Cranfield Road Moulsoe Newport Pagnell Buckinghamshire MK16 0HB

Lovely old Grade II listed building with leaded windows, run by Edwin and Trudy Cheeseman, who have created an informal dining pub (no bookings except for business lunches), where their 'cooking in view' concept is definitely the main attraction: plain or marinated Aberdeen Angus steaks and fresh seafood – perhaps sea bass, tilapia, salmon, parrot fish, red mullet, halibut and tiger prawns – are all invitingly laid out for you to make your choice; live lobsters and duck breasts marinated in gin and chili might also be on offer. Both fish and meat are sold by the ounce, so you can choose your cut and portion size as well as style of cooking, which is either flame-grilling, steaming or smoking (hot-smoked salmon is worth waiting for). Jacket potatoes or gooey, garlicky potatoes and a small salad are the only accompaniments, although an excellent dish of wild mushrooms cooked with bacon and garlic can be shared between diners. The oyster bar – Edwin will tempt you with just one oyster if you've never sampled them – is a most unusual pub attraction, admirably complemented by a selection of chilled vodkas (try a shot of Absolut pepper vodka with your bivalves!). The latest offering is Beluga caviar served with either hot blinis, chopped shallots or sour cream. Carrington's Old Peculier beef pie, Thai red beef, hot Scotch kipper fillet roll with orange chutney, and ploughman's lunches complete the savoury picture, with the likes of apple and apricot crumble and tangy lemon tart to finish. Family dining is actively encouraged here and children generally enjoy seeing the food on display and choosing their meal; just a few ounces of fish or meat will readily be cut for smaller appetites. To the rear of building is a block of seven small bedrooms decorated in straightforward, cottage style with pine fittings and en suite bathrooms. The bedrooms lead directly out on to the orchard-like back garden – possibly bad news on busy summer evenings but a boon for parents who can sit in a deck chair outside their bedroom door with a pint in hand while the offspring head off to the Land of Nod inside. The fact that this is no ordinary pub is exemplified by the interesting New World house wines and the tiny Gents, where a carpet graces the floor and where both stencilling and Thelwell prints adorn the walls. Now *this* is what we call a welcome motorway break: really good, proper food and budget-priced, modest accommodation in a quiet, straggling village setting, just one mile from Junction 14 of M1 via A509. Newcomer of the Year in our 1996 guide. *Open 11-2.30, 6-11 (Sun 12-3, 7-10.30). Bar Food 12-2, 6-10 (Sun 12-2.30, 7-9.30). Free House. Beer Charles Wells Eagle IPA & Bombardier, Boddingtons, guest beer. Garden. Accommodation 7 rooms, all en suite, £45.50 (single £42, Continental breakfast in room only). Children welcome overnight (stay free in parents' room), additional bed available. Check-in bar hours only. No dogs. Amex, Diners, MasterCard, VISA*

MOULTON   Black Bull Inn   FOOD

Tel 01325 377289 Fax 01325 377422   Map 5 E3
Moulton Richmond North Yorkshire DL10 6QJ

A mile south of Scotch Corner, this usually very busy retreat from the A1 is as popular as ever for its bar food. The lunchtime meals venue is the characterful, relaxing bar, warmed by a roaring fire in winter. Light meals include smoked salmon paté, spicy skewered lamb with saffron pilau and fresh pasta carbonara. The attractive Conservatory (complete with huge grapevine) and one of the original Pullman carriages, vintage 1932, from the Brighton Belle and the adjacent Seafood Bar open for the evening trade, when the pub becomes a fish and seafood restaurant proper, serving shellfish from the west coast of Scotland and seafood from the east coast of England. The Black Bull pub and restaurant's reputation, nurtured by the Pagendam family for over 30 years, extends far beyond North Yorkshire and is also recommended in our *1997 Hotels & Restaurants Guide*. Not suitable for children under 7. *Open 12-2.30, 6-10.30 (till 11 Fri & Sat), Sun 12-3. Closed Sun eve & 24-27 Dec.* **Bar Food** *12-2 (no food Sun). Free House.* **Beer** *Theakston Best, Tetley. Patio/terrace, outdoor eating. Amex, MasterCard,* **VISA**

> We endeavour to be as up-to-date as possible but inevitably some changes to landlords, chefs and other key staff occur after the Guide has gone to press.

MOUSEHOLE   Ship Inn   B&B

Tel 01736 731234   Map 12 A4
Mousehole Penzance Cornwall TR19 6QX

Delightfully unassuming little fishing pub, set by the harbour in this beautiful coastal village of pretty fisherman's cottages and attractive narrow alleyways. The plain stone facade shields a most characterful interior, which retains much of its original rustic charm with heavy black beams and panelling, granite floors, built-in wooden wall benches and, as one might expect, a nautical theme pervades the bars. Busy harbour scenes and the panorama over Mount's Bay can be appreciated by residents from two of the three recently refurbished bedrooms. Now furnished in old pine, all have en suite shower rooms, TV, hairdryer and tea-making facilities. A small sun-trap terrace overlooks the village rooftops. *Open 10.30-11 (Sun 12-10.30).* **Beer** *St Austell. Terrace, outdoor eating. Family room.* **Accommodation** *3 bedrooms, all en suite, £30-£40 (single £25). Children welcome overnight (under-15s stay free in parents' room), additional bed available. No credit cards.*

MUCH WENLOCK   Talbot Inn   FOOD

Tel 01952 7277077 Fax 01952 728436   Map 6 B4   B&B
High Street Much Wenlock Shropshire TF13 6AA

 Zzz...

Highly experienced themselves in pub catering, Sean and Cheryl Brennan retained all three kitchen "girls" (total joint service just 39 years!) when they took over here in July 1995. There's healthy competition amongst them all to come up with the best daily specials which are the pick of a varied menu running from smoked salmon sandwiches to sirloin steaks and a regular Sunday roast. Tomato and basil soup and smoked haddock and cheese smokey, followed by pork and apricot pie and fresh fish collected by Sean from Birmingham market typify the blackboard's bill of fare. But leave room for pudding: the apple and blackberry pie, lemon roulade and traditional bread and butter pudding are just like mother used to make. The modern pine-furnished bedrooms are across a courtyard, well away from the body of the pub and with convenient rear access for motorists through the public car park at the back. Decor may be on the plain side but their upkeep is spotless, all having fairly compact en suite bathrooms, colour TVs and hot drink trays; they're phone-free and smoking is actively discouraged. There is, however, a small smoking lounge reserved for residents next to a bright breakfast room, complete with its own self-contained service kitchen, which contributes to an unhurried start to the day. *Open 10.30-3, 6-11 (Sun 12-3, 6.30-10.30).* **Bar Food** *12-2, 7-9.30 (till 8.30 Sun). Free House.* **Beer** *John Smith's, Courage Directors, Ruddles Best, guest beers. Courtyard, outdoor eating.* **Accommodation** *6 bedrooms, all en suite, £80 (single £40). Children welcome overnight (under-4s stay free in parents' room), additional bed & cot available. No dogs.* *MasterCard,* **VISA**

MUCH WENLOCK	Wenlock Edge Inn	FOOD

Tel 01746 785403   Fax 01746 785285   Map 6 B4   **B&B**
Hilltop Much Wenlock Shropshire TF3 6DJ

Zzz...

The somewhat austere look of this stone roadside pub on the B4371 belies the warmth of welcome you'll find inside. To find it, follow the road a good four miles up the edge from Much Wenlock and into the National Trust Park; from the large car park opposite is a pathway to the spectacular observation point at Ippikins Rock. Home to the Waring family for over eleven years now, its reputation as one of the area's friendliest hostelries is well deserved – and that's not as tall a story as some of those told at the monthly 'story-telling-Monday' gatherings. The menu, like the landlord, is on the chatty side with winter's popular 'wedgie pie' (beef and South Shropshire venison), 'oink and apple' (pork and apple pie) or beef and vegetable pie giving way to such summery delights as baked salmon salad, salmon and dill flan, smoked ham and chicken flan and marinated Orkney herring with dill. Stephen Waring plays host from the bar, breaking the ice between diners who are virtually rubbing shoulders at closely-packed tables and insistently urging follow-up portions of Bakewell tart, apple and gooseberry crumble or home-made ice cream. Demand for overnight accommodation is constant from talkers and walkers, conservationists and conversationalists who, when the babble dies down, are assured of a quiet night's sleep. All three bedrooms are smart and comfortable, with pine furniture and plenty of thick winter bedding; they have en suite WCs and pressure showers supplied from the pub's own spring. Detached from the pub proper, the cottage room is the most spacious, with a convenient hallway to house walkers' boots and canine companions. A hearty breakfast here is de rigueur. Children welcome indoors if eating. *Open 11.30-2.30, 6.30-11 (Sun 12-2.30, 7-10.30). Closed Mon lunch (except Bank Holidays).* **Bar Food** *12-2, 7-9 (no food Mon). Free House.* **Beer** *Hobsons Best & Town Crier, Ruddles Best. Garden, outdoor eating.* **Accommodation** *4 bedrooms, all en suite, £60-£65 Fri & Sat (single £45). No children under 8 overnight. Dogs (£5) in cottage only. Amex, MasterCard,* **VISA**

MYLOR BRIDGE	Pandora Inn	FOOD

Tel & Fax 01326 372678   Map 12 B3
Restronguet Creek Mylor Bridge Falmouth Cornwall TR11 5ST

Yachtsmen are welcome to moor their craft at the end of the 140ft pontoon that extends out into the creek from this superbly sited and most attractive thatched 13th-century building – one of Cornwall's best-known inns. Although a boat is by far the easiest way to approach this creek-side inn, it lies at the end of a series of narrow lanes off the A39 (from which it is signposted) and it is advble to arrive early as the car park soon fills to capacity on fine days. Named after the naval ship sent to Tahiti to capture the mutineers of Captain Bligh's Bounty, the Pandora retains its unspoilt traditional layout and boasts low wooden ceilings, wall panelling, flagged floors, a good winter log fire, a black-painted kitchen range and many maritime mementoes. It is not only the pub's position, patio and pontoon that attract folk here; the range of bar food is unlikely to disappoint. Good fresh seafood and local fish is the main emphasis, with dishes like Restronguet fish pie, local crab salad and Mediterranean fish stew. Puddings include home-made treacle tart and locally-made ice creams. Very popular are the hearty sandwiches, in particular the Pandora Club and chocolate spread (with chips!) for chocoholic children! Daily specials might be chicken and apricot pie, deep-fried lemon sole, beef, mushroom and Guinness pie, or vegetable couscous. The Andrew Miller restaurant upstairs serves more imaginative dishes, especially fish, and enjoys peaceful river views. During the summer Cornish cream teas are served every afternoon in the bar or on sunny days out on the pontoon. Over a dozen wines served by the glass. *Open 11-11 (Sun 12-10.30) summer & Sat & Sun in winter, 12-3, 6.30-11 Mon-Fri in winter.* **Bar Food** *12-2.30 (till 2 in winter), 6.30-10 (till 9.30 Sun & Mon-Thu in winter).* **Beer** *St Austell, Bass. Creekside terrace, pontoon, outdoor eating. Family room. Amex, MasterCard,* **VISA**

NAYLAND   White Hart   ★   FOOD

Tel 01206 263382   Fax 01206 263638   Map 10 C3
High Street Nayland nr Colchester Suffolk CO6 4JF

A rustic 15th-century inn has been transformed by a partnership of Michel Roux (Waterside Inn, Bray) and chef/patron Mark Prescott – who has worked for both the Roux brothers for many years – into a dining pub par excellence. Good, 'traditional English farmhouse food' – albeit with a modern angle – is the order of the day. The monthly-changing lunch menu offers fancy 'sandwiches' (ploughman's, grilled vegetables with feta, aïoli and houmus or steak with red onions and a fried egg – not on Sundays) or a choice of four dishes at each stage with a fixed price for 1-3 courses. Start, perhaps with mussels, gravad lax with cucumber pickle or chicken liver parfait with apricot and walnut chutney, followed by a warm, creamy leek tart, omelette of your choice, confit of duck leg with honey and rosemary or fillet of salmon with white wine and sorrel sauce; finish off a fine meal with a daily tart, steamed golden syrup sponge with custard or nougat glace with raspberry sauce. Dinner is à la carte only, with the addition of grills (Scotch sirloin, lamb cutlets or lobster) and seven or so daily-changing blackboard specials. Children are offered their own menu that includes ravioli in tomato sauce and the usual favourites with chips, vegetables or salad. A decent wine list of over fifty bottles offers a good range from around the world with helpful tasting notes and fair prices. Good bread, Italian-style coffee and spot-on service make dining here a very enjoyable experience – more 'pubby' in summer than in winter. A snackier patio menu (encompassing olives, corn chips, oysters and lobster – remember the Roux connection!) is available when the weather's fine and when the 48-seat alfresco seating area is opened. Upstairs is a private dining-room for 48. *Open 12-3, 6-11 (Sun from 6.30).* **Bar Food** *12-2 (Sat & Sun till 2.30), 6.30-9 (Fri & Sat till 9.30, Sun till 8.30). Set L £9.50/£13.50/£16.* **Beer** *Greene King IPA, guest beer. Closed Mon (except Bank Holidays), 26 Dec & 1 Jan. Amex, Diners, MasterCard,* **VISA**

NEEDINGWORTH   Pike & Eel   B&B

Tel 01480 463336   Fax 01480 465467   Map 10 B2
Needingworth St Ives Cambridgeshire PE17 3YW

Located at the end of a long and narrow country lane right on the banks of the River Great Ouse, adjacent to a marina, the Pike and Eel dates back to the 17th century. The present owner, John Stafferton, has been here over 20 years and in that time has gradually upgraded and enlarged the property. The whole place has a very homely, traditional atmosphere with polished, beaten copper tables in the huge, oak-beamed bar. Next door is a much smaller, quieter residents' lounge where there's a warming coal fire in the open fireplace in winter. Upstairs, there's a further residents' lounge. They are all decorated in an attractive and pretty style, some with old-fashioned pieces of furniture, all well co-ordinated. TVs and tea and coffee facilities are provided. Carpeted bathrooms are neat, modern and of a good size. Plans for Spring 1997 include converting four chalets in the garden to B&B accommodation. *Open 11-11 (Sun 12-10.30). Free House.* **Beer** *Bass, Greene King IPA, Ruddles County, occasional guest beer. Riverside garden. Family room.* **Accommodation** *6 bedrooms, all en suite £55 (single £40). Children free under 2 years, additional bed (£15) & cot available. Amex, MasterCard,* **VISA**

> We only recommend food (Bar Food) in those establishments highlighted
> with the **FOOD** symbol.

NETTLEBED — White Hart — FOOD

Tel 01491 641245   Fax 01491 641423   Map 15a D3   **B&B**
Nettlebed Oxfordshire RG9 5OD

The Worsdells have revived this 16th-century coaching inn on the A423. The red-brick exterior belies its age but once inside, old timbers, low beams and the creaking floor boards of the bedrooms tell of its history. In more recent times, the White Hart was the unofficial 'Mess' for nearby RAF Benson, with Douglas Bader a frequent visitor; scenes from the film of his wartime exploits, *Reach for the Sky*, were filmed here. Today, food is a major attraction with a seasonally-changing menu listing favourites like lamb wrapped in spinach and bacon with a grain mustard sauce, and a lunchtime snack menu offering filled baguettes, chili and ploughman's lunches. A blackboard highlights daily specials like cottage pie, chicken Madras, home-made lasagne and poached Scottish salmon. Separate, more sophisticated restaurant menu, and afternoon teas include home-made scones and fruit cake. Six characterful bedrooms offer good cotton bedding, feather pillows and carpeted en suite bath/shower rooms with large, soft bath-sheets. All rooms have remote-controlled TV and direct-dial phones plus extras like fresh fruit and a welcoming glass of sherry. Five of the six rooms face the road so some traffic noise is unavoidable despite the secondary glazing. A neat garden and patio to the rear make a good spot for summer drinking and eating. Children welcome. *Open 11-11 (Sun 12-10.30).* **Bar Food** *12-2.30, 2.30-6 (afternoon tea), 6-10 (Sun 12-3, 7-9.30).* **Beer** *Brakspear. Garden, outdoor eating. Family room.* **Accommodation** *6 bedrooms, all en suite, £69.50 (four-poster £79.50, single £49.50). Children welcome overnight, additional bed available. MasterCard,* **VISA**

NETTLECOMBE — Marquis of Lorne — FOOD

Tel 01308 485236   Fax 01308 485666   Map 13 F2   **B&B**
Nettlecombe Bridport Dorset DT6 3SY

Modernised and extended 16th-century inn set in an isolated rural position at the base of Eggardon Hill and run by friendly and welcoming landlords Ian and Anne Barrett. Comfortably refurbished bar areas, named after local hills, have access to the extensive and well-maintained garden (with a much improved children's play area) and enjoy beautiful valley views across Powerstock village. Reliable, unpretentious home-cooked pub food can be found on the regularly-changing blackboard menu that serves the whole pub. Wintertime favourites include hearty casseroles – beef in port and orange, pork in mustard and ale – giant filled Yorkshire puddings (steak and kidney), while summer salads accompany fresh crab, smoked fish platter and spinach and walnut lasagne. Other notable dishes include freshly-battered cod and chips, local plaice with lime butter and grilled fresh brill. Good soups (curried parsnip), crisp vegetables and home-made puddings (sticky toffee pudding, treacle tart). Overnight accommodation in six comfortable, light and airy bedrooms, all of which have spotless shower rooms. Most have smart, modern pine furnishings, while others are kitted out, at present, with more functional furniture; all have remote-controlled TVs, telephones, hairdryers and beverage-making facilities. Most enjoy splendid views across unspoilt Dorset countryside. Best reached from the A3066 north of Bridport (5 miles), by following signs for West Milton and Powerstock along narrow country lanes. *Open 11-2.30, 6-11 (from 6.30 winter), Sun 12-3, 7-10.30.* **Bar Food** *12-2, 7-9.30.* **Beer** *Palmers. Garden, outdoor eating, children's play area. Family room.* **Accommodation** *6 bedrooms, all en suite, £55 (single £35). Children over 10 welcome overnight, additional bed (£10) available. No dogs. Accommodation closed 24 &25 Dec; pub closed 25 Dec eve. MasterCard,* **VISA**

NEW YORK — Shiremoor House Farm — A

Tel 0191-257 6302   Fax 0190-257 8602   Map 5 E2
Middle Engine Lane New York Newcastle-on-Tyne North Tyneside NE29 8D2

The Fitzgerald group discovered and restored this former set of derelict farmhouse buildings to which they felt they could attract a discerning clientele of pub-goers. Shiremoor remains unique, its circular gin-gang (a kind of horse-powered threshing machine) forming the back drop to a bar from which radiates a succession of eating areas, carefully broken up by upturned barrels, easy chairs and an assortment of

Britannia and scrubbed pine tables. Outdoors are picnic tables on the patios, a wooden pill-box seat for the hardy on windy days, and plenty of safe space, albeit without play equipment, for roaming about in. *Open 11-11 (Sun 12-10.30). Free House.* **Beer** *Theakston Best & Old Peculier, Stones Best, Timothy Taylor's Landlord, Mordue Radgie Gadgie, various guest beers. Terrace. Family Room. Amex, MasterCard,* **VISA**

NEWCASTLE-ON-TYNE   Cooperage   A

Tel 0191 232 8286
Map 5 E2
32 The Close Quayside Newcastle-on-Tyne NE1 3RF

Arguably the oldest pub in town, the timber-framed former brewery teeters roadside by the "Long Stairs" on Newcastle's famed waterfront, where a succession of high-and lower-level bridges criss-cross the Tyne. For real ale buffs a single bar merits attention, resting on halved wooden kilderkins and bedecked with pewter and pottery mugs. Up to seven beers and two draught ciders are on tap at any one time. 5 miles from A194. *Open 11-11 (Sun 12-10.30). Free House.* **Beer** *Tetley Best, Burton Ale, Marston's Owd Roger, Hadrian Gladiator, weekly-changing guest beers. Closed 25 Dec. Amex, MasterCard,* **VISA**

NEWNHAM   George Inn   FOOD

Tel 01795 890237
Map 11 C5
Newnham Faversham Kent ME9 0LL

Fine rugs on polished wood floors, exposed beams, open fires, evening candlelight, tasteful prints, pretty flowers and a piano are a sample of the civilised ingredients at this lovingly cared for 16th-century tile-hung village pub. The food is always imaginative and varied, and takes over the whole interior at mealtimes, as there's no separate dining or restaurant area. All needs are satisfied with the regular menu listing popular lunchtime favourites from ploughman's lunches and sandwiches to interesting salads, decent pies – steak and kidney – and pasta dishes. More substantial choices include a range of steaks and chicken supreme. Beyond this is a short, hand-written list of weekly-changing specials. Inventive dishes using game according to season, and fresh local produce may include smoked halibut timbale filled with smoked trout or local asparagus hollandaise to start, followed rabbit pudding, pheasant normande and chicken breast stuffed with prawn mousseline with a cream sauce. Good accompanying vegetables. Unusual vegetarian choices may include roast parsnips in coconut and ginger paste or stir-fried broccoli served with mushroom dahl. For pudding try an old-fashioned suet pudding or chocolate roulade. Large, peaceful garden backing on to sheep pastures. Children welcome. *Open 10.30-3, 6-11 (Sun 12-3, 7-10.30). Bar Food 12-2 (till 1.45 Sun), 7-10 (no bar food Sun eve & all Mon).* **Beer** *Shepherd Neame. Garden, outdoor eating. No credit cards.*

NEWTON   Queen's Head   FOOD

Tel 01223 870436
Map 15 F1
Newton nr Cambridge Cambridgeshire CB2 5PG

For over thirty years now the Short family have owned and operated their tiny "fossilised" village pub which to this day resists change. Simple home-made soup served in earthenware mugs and sandwiches (good roast beef and smoked salmon) cut and filled to order in the tiny bar servery have achieved near cult status over the years, while the bitter, served direct from the cask, is a flat yet flavourful beer. Village tradition, preserved by skittles table and a dilapidated dart board, is echoed by pine settles, rickety chairs and old school benches. *Open 11.30-2.30, 6-11 (Sun 12-2.30, 7-10.30). Bar Food 11.45-2.15, 6.30-9.30 (Sun 12-2.30, 7-9.30). Free House.* **Beer** *Adnams Best, Broadside, Extra & Old Ale (winter). Outdoor eating. Family room. Closed all 25 Dec. No credit cards.*

We do not accept free meals or hospitality – our inspectors pay their own bills and never book in the name of Egon Ronay's Guides.

NEWTON　　　　Red Lion　　　　FOOD

Tel 01529 497256　　　　Map 7 E3
Newton Sleaford Lincolnshire NG34 0EE

In a quiet hamlet tucked away off the A52, this is a civilised, neatly-kept pub with shaded rear garden and play area. Popular unchanging formula is the cold carvery/buffet of fish and carefully-cooked cold meats, from home-cooked ham and ox tongue to home-made pork pie and fresh sardines in ratatouille. Price depends on size of plate and the number of meats chosen; help yourself from a dozen or more accompanying salads. Popular hot roast carvery every Saturday evening and Sunday lunchtime, with home-cooked hot dishes, such as turkey, ham and cheese pie and chicken curry featuring on the menu during the winter months. Choose from ever-changing array of home-made desserts – Bakewell tart, treacle tart and fresh fruit pavlova. Children's prices and eating areas; informal, easy-going atmosphere. *Open 11.30-3, 6-11 (from 7 Mon), Sun 11.30-3, 7-10.30.* **Bar Food** *12-2, 7-10 (till 9 Sun). Free House.* **Beer** *Bass, Bateman's XXXB. Garden, outdoor eating, children's play area. Family room. Closed 25 Dec No credit cards.*

> We endeavour to be as up-to-date as possible but inevitably some changes to landlords, chefs and other key staff occur after the Guide has gone to press.

NEWTON ON THE MOOR　　Cook & Barker Inn　　FOOD

Tel & Fax 01665 575234　　　Map 5 D2　　**B&B**
Newton on the Moor Felton Morpeth Northumberland

Lynn & Phil Farmer's stone pub with a burgeoning reputation for food stands just off (and literally overlooking) the A1, 10 miles north of Morpeth. From its elevated position superb views of the Northumbrian coast are an added attraction for those who come to stay. Those who do not book for lunch had best come early, as ordering at the bar and finding an agreeable spot in the maze of rooms can create a log-jam. Nevertheless the kitchen copes manfully, working to a menu of gargantuan proportions that includes sandwiches and filled pitta breads (pork stir-fry with ginger) and is supplemented by the daily labour of blackboard specials. Adventurous flavourings are the kitchen's hallmark: terrine of sole and salmon, casserole of seafood thermidor, lamb's liver and bacon and chicken tikka supreme. Barring a small selection on the blackboard in the snug, meals at night go up a gear in price and complexity; all of which is classy enough to suggest that an overnight stay could be special. With its spa bath and romantic setting, the best of four bedrooms certainly will not disappoint, and the rest aren't far behind with their en suite baths and showers, TVs, beverage trays and trouser presses. Young chef (22) David Barella, who gained the Cook & Barker its entry in this guide, is now cooking at the Farmers' new premises – *The Tankerville Arms*, Eglingham (not yet inspected). *Open 11-3, 6-11 (Sun 12-3, 6-10.30).* **Bar Food** *12-2, 6-8. Free House.* **Beer** *Theakston Best, Morland Old Speckled Hen, Boddingtons, guest beer. Garden, outdoor eating. Family room.* **Accommodation** *4 bedrooms, all en suite £65 (single £30). Children welcome overnight (under-12s stay free in parents' room). additional bed & cot available. No dogs.* Amex, MasterCard, **VISA**

NEWTON ST CYRES　　Crown & Sceptre　　FOOD

Tel 01392 851278　　　　Map 13 D2
Newton St Cyres Exeter Devon EX5 5DA

Alongside the A377 about two miles from Exeter, this simple roadside pub has in the past few years enjoyed a good local reputation for its food due to the presence of capable landlords Graham and Carolyn Wilson. The blackboard scripted menu lists generously-filled sandwiches like a Crown special – ham and cheese – as well as more substantial home-cooked dishes such as chicken, ham and leek pie and pork fillet with green peppercorn sauce or fresh fish from Brixham (perhaps cod in garlic butter).

Puddings might include pecan and toffee cheesecake with clotted cream. Roast Sunday lunch. Recent interior improvements have included combining and refurbishing the lounge and public bars, resulting in a more spacious dining area. Children's facilities extend to a baby-changing area in the Ladies and various toys and colouring books, while in the garden (over a footbridge across a fenced-off, safe stream) there is a tree house, swings, slides and climbing frame. *Open 11.30-2.30, 6-11 (Sun 12-2.30, 7-10.30). Bar Food 12-2, 7-9.30. Beer Bass, Boddingtons, guest beer. Garden, riverside patio, outdoor eating, children's play area. Family room. No credit cards.*

NORTH DALTON   Star Inn   B&B

Tel 01377 217688   Map 7 E1
Warter Road North Dalton East Riding of Yorkshire YO25 9UX

The Georgian Star sits right next to the village pond where the coach horses were watered at a stopping-off point on the old Minster Way. Inside, it has largely been remodelled in recent years with rough white plaster walls and exposed brick features in the cosy, welcoming bar and the creation of seven smart, comfortable bedrooms. All are of a good standard but vary a little; a couple have pine-boarded ceilings, one a splendid old brass bedstead; all have good solid wood furniture, neat, fully-tiled bathrooms – one with shower and WC only – direct-dial phone, remote-control TV and tea/coffee-making kit. Children not encouraged overnight. *Open 11.30-2.30, 6-11 (Sun 12-3, 7-10.30). Free House. Beer John Smith's, two guest beers. Garden. Family room. Accommodation 7 bedrooms, all en suite, £39.50 (single £29.50). No dogs (except Guide Dogs). MasterCard, VISA*

NORTH NEWNTON   Woodbridge Inn   ★   FOOD
B&B

Tel & Fax 01980 630266   Map 14a A4
North Newnton Pewsey Wiltshire SN9 6JZ

Akin to a 20th-century staging post, with a warm welcome to every weary traveller extended all day, every day by landlords Lou and Terri Vertessy. As well as the abundant enthusiasm that has contributed so much to the rejuvenation of this pub, their commitment and imagination has brought to these parts some truly unusual pub food. Terry's worldwide experience in the kitchen leans towards the American Deep South for her fish Creole; Mexican food has become a hot favourite, represented by sizzling beef fajitas and spicy chicken chimichangas; from the Far East comes kung po ji ding (hot and aromatic chicken stir-fry with cashew nuts). European offerings include seared salmon with fresh basil sauce, roasted marinated red peppers, and rump steak with béarnaise. Simpler bar food – sandwiches, steak and ale pie, woody vegetable pie, American-style burgers, Mexican burritos – are served all day, with the more serious restaurant fare available throughout the pub between 12-2.30 & 6-10 (from 7 Sun). Prospective weekend diners are advised to book; a self-contained back room is available for parties up to ten. The Vertessys have converted three neat and tidy bedrooms for guests' use, all with cottagey wallpapers and fabrics, freestanding darkwood or pine furniture and fresh flowers. One has en suite facilities, the others share an acceptable bathroom. Situated by the A345 bridge over the Avon, one and a half miles north of Upavon, it has a huge, colourful riverside meadow garden, part of which is fenced off to create an eating area where children can also play. Four pétanque pistes; trout fishing can be organised on the River Avon. No under-10s after 8pm and no dogs indoors. *Open 11-11 (Sun 12-10.30). Bar Food 11-10.30 (Sun 12-10, except 12-3, 7-10.30 Oct-Apr). Beer Wadworth, guest beer. Garden, outdoor eating, barbecue, children's play area. Accommodation 3 bedrooms, 1 en suite, £37.50 (single from £27). Children welcome overnight (under-5s stay free in parents' room), additional bed (£10) & cot available. Accommodation closed 24 & 25 Dec. No dogs. Amex, Diners, MasterCard, VISA*

We only recommend food (Bar Food) in those establishments highlighted with the **FOOD** symbol.

NORTH WOOTTON   Crossways Inn   B&B

Tel 01749 890237   Fax 01749 890476   Map 13 F1
North Wootton Shepton Mallet Somerset BA4 4EU

Enjoying a peaceful setting amidst lovely unspoilt countryside, the comfortably modernised Crossways Inn overlooks Glastonbury Tor across the historic Vale of Avalon. Well-kept bedrooms are pleasantly decorated with floral fabrics and all have good thick carpets and duvets as well as hairdryers, trouser presses, TVs and tea-makers. Compact, modern en suite (most with showers) facilities throughout. There is a small lounge for residents' use and families are made very welcome, but there's no garden. *Open 11-3, 6-11 (Sun 12-3, 7-10.30). Free House.* **Beer** *Wadworth 6X, Bass, guest beer. Patio.* **Accommodation** *17 bedrooms, all en suite, £38 (single £28). Children welcome overnight (under-4s stay free in parents' room). MasterCard,* **VISA**

NORTH WOOTTON   Three Elms   B&B

Tel 01935 812881   Map 13 F2
North Wootton Sherborne Dorset DT9 5JW

Simple, old-fashioned local set beside the A3030 between Sherborne and Bishop's Caundle, and whose L-shaped bar was extended several years ago, creating a country coffee shop feel in one area and more pubby in the other. The focal point is landlord Howard Manning's collection of over 1000 die-cast model cars, gathered over the years. Added attractions include the range of nine real ales (local breweries are favoured) and the far-reaching views towards Bulbarrow Hill from the neat, lawned rear garden, complete with small play area. Three neat and tidy, cottagey bedrooms sport pretty wallpapers and fabrics, older-style pine furniture (including a four-poster bed) and numerous books and ornaments. All share an attractive bathroom, but, with the thoughtful addition of bathrobes behind each door, a midnight trip will not be an embarrassing exercise. "All well-behaved children welcome." *Open 11-2.30, 6.30-11 (from 6 Fri & Sat), Sun 12-3, 7-10.30. Free House.* **Beer** *Fuller's London Pride, Boddingtons, Butcombe, Shepherd Neame Spitfire, Smiles, four guest beers. Garden, children's play area.* **Accommodation** *3 bedrooms, not en suite, £35 (family room sleeping three £45, single £20). Children welcome overnight (under-4s stay free in parents' room, 4-12s £5). Check-in by arrangement. Closed 25 & 26 Dec. Mastercard,* **VISA**

> We do not accept free meals or hospitality – our inspectors pay their own bills and never book in the name of Egon Ronay's Guides.

NORTHLEACH   Wheatsheaf Hotel   FOOD
                                                          B&B

Tel 01451 860244   Fax 01451 861037   Map 14a A2
West End Northleach Gloucestershire GL54 3E2

Zzz...

Quietly situated in the celebrated Wood Town (just off the A429) is the Langs' people-friendly period coaching inn. Being family-run, it's family-orientated as well, with plenty of minor diversions for the young-at-heart in the bar while meals are ordered from a daily-changing, all-embracing menu. Sandwiches, salads, cheese ploughman's lunches, a handful of vegetarian options, hot croissant with smoked chicken and cream sauce, fresh cod in a light beer batter, baked Bibury trout with parsley and butter sauce show the style. As a base for walkers and Cotswold explorers, the Wheatsheaf offers bedrooms all individually furnished to a high standard; two have king-size beds, and while four of the en suite bathrooms have WC/showers only, all the rooms have TV, beverage trays and dial-out phones. *Open 12-3, 6-11 (till 10.30 Mon-Thu), Sun 12-3, 7-10.30.* **Bar Food** *12-2, 6-8.30 (till 9 Fri & Sat), Sun 12-2, 7-8.30. Free House.* **Beer** *Marston's Best & Pedigree. Garden, outdoor eating.* **Accommodation** *10 bedrooms, all en suite, £55-£69 (single £39 midweek only). Children over 7 welcome overnight. No dogs. MasterCard,* **VISA**

NORTON   Hundred House Hotel   FOOD

Tel & Fax 01952 730353   Map 6 B4   **B&B**
Bridgnorth Road Norton Shifnal Shrophire TF11 9EE

In the old 'hundred' of Brimstree, alongside what is today the busy A442, there's an unbroken history of there being a hostelry at Norton since the 14th century. The thatched barn which separates the car park from the road was once the local court and remains of the old stocks and whipping post are still to be found there. The main, creeper-clad redbrick inn, of Georgian origin, stands in its own mature orchard and garden in which all-comers are invited to wander at their leisure, and from which come the hand-dried flowers which hang from virtually every beam within the pub. All this is indicative of the personality Hundred House gains from the inimitable input of Henry and Sylvia Phillips and family (here since 1986). There's a particularly warm and intimate feel in the muted tones of the mellow-brick, tiled floors, stained-glass windows, colourful patchwork leather upholstery and festooned beams of the bar and dining areas, a setting to which the food has little trouble doing justice. Gateaux of Mediterranean vegetables topped with goat's cheese, coriander-cured salmon and rich fish soup typify the range of culinary skills and sources, while main courses may encompass steak and kidney pie, confit of Hereford duck with onion marmalade and red wine sauce, roast lamb with polenta, ratatouille and basil jus, and charlotte of roast carrot and coriander mousse with tomato coulis and baked shallots. Finish off a memorable meal with, perhaps, glazed apple tart or a white and dark chocolate marquise from the usually excellent desserts – the "ultimate dessert" brings a selection all on one dish with fresh fruit and home-made ice cream. Daily specials supplement both bar and à la carte menus. Those seeking a lighter snack can order a ploughman's platter at lunchtime or in the evening. Both names and colour schemes in the enchanting bedrooms return to the garden for their inspiration, incorporating pastel shades, brass bedsteads with patchwork covers, cane rocking chairs and even padded swing seats suspended invitingly from the rafters. From fresh flowers and pot-pourri to cotton buds and heart-shaped pin cushions, virtually every conceivable extra is contrived to make guests feel fully at home in cosy and cossetting surroundings; two superior rooms are very large. Well-equipped en suite facilities, all with bath, most with overhead showers. Throughout the day and evening there is room service of drinks and light snacks. *Open 11-3, 6-11 (Sun 12-3, 7-10.30).* **Bar Food** *12-2.30, 6.15-10 (7-9 Sun). Free House. **Beer** Phillips Heritage & Ailrics Old Ale, Buchanan Original, Whitbread Castle Eden Ale, Holts Entire. Garden, outdoor eating.* **Accommodation** *10 bedrooms, all en suite, £79-£90 (family room £90, single £59-£79). Children welcome overnight (free if sharing parents' room), additional bed & cot available.* Amex, MasterCard, **VISA**

NORTON ST PHILIP   George Inn   FOOD

Tel & Fax 01373 834224   Map 13 F1
Norton St Philip Bath Somerset BA3 6LH

Certainly one of the oldest licensed premises in the land, the George has been around since before liquor licenses were introduced! A Carthusian guest house since its first building in the 13th century, it has retained its present architectural features for over 700 years now. Surviving to this day are the massive Gothic doorway, sloping cobbled courtyard and unique timbered galleries. On 12th June 1668 Samuel Pepys and party dined here, while in June 1685 the Duke of Monmouth occupied the whole village for a week prior to his defeat at Sedgemoor. In this unique atmosphere, wonderfully steeped in history, landlords Andrew and Juliette Grubb have created a popular destination in which to sample good home-cooked meals listed on the reliable and varied bar menus. Dishes extend from good pub favourites, including filled baguettes (smoked trout yoghurt and cucumber – lunch only) and ploughman's lunches, to blackboard specials, for example, king prawns in garlic, leg of lamb casserole with juniper and orange, turkey breast filled with mozzarella and smoked ham, and whole fresh plaice, with main courses accompanied by a huge dish of fresh, crisp vegetables. Puddings include home-made lemon meringue and light and dark chocolate terrine with raspberry coulis. *Open 11-3, 5.30-11 (Sun 12-3, 7-10.30).* **Bar Food** *12-2.30, 6.30-10 (Sun 7-9.30). **Beer** Bass, Wadworth 6X, Henry's IPA. Courtyard, outdoor eating. Family room. MasterCard, **VISA**

NORWICH   Adam & Eve   A

Tel 01603 667423   Map 10 C1
Bishopsgate Norwich Norfolk NR3 2RZ

Historic old tavern – the oldest in the city – located along Palace Street close to the cathedral. Part 13th-century, it was built as a brewhouse to serve bread and ale to the workmen who built the cathedral, and later extended in the 14th and 15th centuries, with the addition of the Dutch gables which give this popular ale house a most unusual appearance. Reputedly haunted by the ghost of Lord Sheffield who was hacked to death here in 1549, the two bars and tiny snug feature ancient carved benches and high-backed settles built into part-panelled walls and old tiled floors. The lower bar is thought to be over 700 years old. Good summer drinking patio and a handy pay and display car park next door. *Open 11-11 (Sun 12-10.30).* **Beer** *Morland Old Speckled Hen, Ruddles County, Wadworth 6X, John Smith's Bitter, Adnams Southwold, guest beer. Patio, outdoor eating area. Family room. No credit cards.*

NOSTERFIELD   Freemasons Arms   FOOD

Tel 01677 470548   Map 5 E4
Nosterfield Bedale North Yorkshire DL8 2QP

The low, white-painted row of cottages and barn sparkles within, adorned in front of blazing log fires with a mish-mash of pub-associated artefacts from pewter pots to miners' lamps and horse-tack. To this was added a warmth of welcome and a confidence which suggests these young publicans know that they are going places. The food on offer here is very popular – booking advble – its success based not on trying to be a restaurant but nevertheless serving good food from fresh ingredients of a quality that would not go amiss in one. Alongside wild mushroom soup and smoked salmon for starters diners will find chargrilled lamb with herbs, half-roast Norfolk duckling with port wine sauce and fresh Grimsby haddock with home-made beer batter. Herbs from the pub garden contribute to the freshly-made soups and all the desserts and gateaux (crème caramel, chocolate fudge cake) are home-made. A hand-picked list of wines is that, too, of an enthusiast, while both Theakston's and the irresistible Black Sheep Bitter are kept in fine condition in the rebuilt beer cellar. *Open 12-2, 6-11, (Sun 12-2, 7-10.30). Closed all Mon. Free House.* **Bar Food** *12-2, 7-9 (no food Mon). Free House.* **Beer** *Theakston Best, Tetley, Black Sheep Bitter, guest beer. Amex, MasterCard,* ***VISA***

NOTTINGHAM   Lincolnshire Poacher   A

Tel 0115 941 1584   Map 7 D3
161-163 Mansfield Road Nottingham Nottinghamshire NG1 3FR

A true pub-goer's 'paraphernalia pub' is perhaps the best way to describe the former Old Gray Nag's Head, now leased by the Tynemill Group from brewers Bateman's. A large obituary to the hundreds (they say) of independents swallowed up by one major brewer is displayed above the bar, whilst an eminently more sensible arrangement with their current landlords enables a wide range of popular and little-known guest ales always to be on offer. Yet anyone out for a tasting needn't stop there, as nigh on six dozen whiskies and single malts (as well farmhouse scrumpy ciders and a range of Continental bottled beers) are an open invitation to the connoisseur. *Open 11-11 (Sun 12-10.30).* **Beer** *Bateman's Dark Mild, XB, Salem Porter, XXXB & Victory Ale, Bass, Marston's Pedigree, three guest beers. Patio. No credit cards.*

We only recommend food (Bar Food) in those establishments highlighted
with the **FOOD** symbol.

NOTTINGHAM · Ye Olde Trip to Jerusalem · A

Tel 0115 947 3171   Fax 0115 950 1185   Map 7 D3
Brewhouse Yard Castle Road Nottingham Nottinghamshire NG1 6AD

Built into the caves at the foot of Nottingham Castle's wall and formerly its brewhouse, Ye Olde Trip to Jerusalem (known as the Pilgrim in the 18th century) has been a pub for 800 years – "the oldest inn in England", a habitual resting place for crusading knights on their way to outwit the heathen overseas. The present building is mainly 17th-century; the unique rock-face walls are most apparent in the spooky upstairs bar, which is opened only when the pub is busy. Downstairs has panelled walls, built-in cushioned settles, and exposed-rock alcoves; visitors' banknotes and coins litter the beams. In fine weather there are patios to the side and back, and extra seating in the cobbled yard opposite; souvenirs are available at the bar. No under-18s in the bar. Closure for a major 3-month refurbishment was due to commence in September 1996. *Open 11-11 (Sun 12-10.30).* **Beer** *Hardys & Hansons Kimberley Best Bitter, Classic & Best Mild, Marston's Pedigree. Patio/terrace. Amex, MasterCard,* **VISA**

NUNNEY · George at Nunney · B&B

Tel 01373 836458   Fax 01373 836565   Map 13 F1
11 Church Street Nunney Somerset BA11 4LW

White-painted, street-fronting coaching inn, its sign stretched right over the road, opposite a brook and the 13th-century castle ruin in the centre of this picturesque village. Rambling much modernised open-plan interior with winter log fire. Bedrooms of various shapes are modestly furnished, apart from the comfortable four-poster room. Some overlook the pretty walled garden, some the castle; all have private bath or shower, telephones, satellite TV, tea-makers and trouser presses. *Open 12-3, 6-11 (from 6.30 winter), Sun 12-3, 7-10.30. Free House.* **Beer** *Bass, Wadworth 6X, guest beer. Garden. Family room.* **Accommodation** *9 bedrooms, all en suite, £58 (single £42). Children welcome overnight, additional bed (£10) & cot (£5) available. No dogs. MasterCard,* **VISA**

NUNNINGTON · Royal Oak · FOOD

Tel 01439 748271   Map 5 E4
Nunnington York North Yorkshire YO6 5US

A laid-back and friendly local with a food bias at the heart of the village, just up from a footbridge over the River Rye and hence a short walk from the National Trust's Nunnington Hall. Stone jugs and assorted farm implements hang from the beams while behind Tony's one-man bar are suspended the blackboards of best-bet specials which emanate from Bo Simpson's highly productive kitchen. Reliable choices range from home-made vegetable soup, Stilton paté with toast, good salads and ploughman's lunches to chicken breast in orange and tarragon, steak and kidney casserole, salmon and prawn tagliatelle and pork fillet in barbecue sauce. For pudding try the rhubarb crumble, lemon mousse or tiramisu. A quiet dining-room extension is available for reserved tables (and families), though the same menus hold good throughout. Light classical favourites provide a popular and relaxing background to the general hubbub of appreciative diners. No children under 8 in the bar. *Open 11.45-2.30, 6.30-11 (Sun 12-3, 7-10.30). Closed Mon.* **Bar Food** *12-1.45, 6.30-9 (from 7 Sun). Free House.* **Beer** *Tetley, Theakston Old Peculier, guest beer. MasterCard,* **VISA**

NUNTON · Radnor Arms · FOOD

Tel 01722 329722   Map 14 C3
Nunton Salisbury Wiltshire SP5 4HS

This welcoming ivy-clad village pub dates from the 17th century and part of it once served as the village stores and post office. Locals come now for the well-kept ale and for the honest home-cooked selection of meals that are served in its low-ceilinged and simply-furnished main bar and neat, opened-out dining areas. Traditional lunchtime favourites, including ploughman's and sandwiches (also available in the evenings), can be found on the printed menu, while the changing blackboard menu advertises the

lunch specials and evening choices. Look out for marinated venison steak, duck breast with orange and Amaretto, chicken breast stuffed with asparagus, and fresh fish dishes like cod and haddock grill, fresh scallops bonne femme and skate with capers and cream. For pudding try the sticky toffee pudding or the apricot and Amaretto cheesecake. The large rear garden has fine rural views, plenty of picnic benches and much to amuse energetic children. *Open 11-3, 6-11 (Sun 12-3, 7-10.30).*
Bar Food 12-2, 7-9.30 (no food Sun eve). Beer Hall & Woodhouse Tanglefoot & Badger Best. Garden, outdoor eating, children's play area, disabled WC. Family room. No credit cards.

NUTHURST	Black Horse	A

Tel 01403 891272   Map 11 A6
Nuthurst Street Nuthurst Horsham West Sussex RH13 6LH

Occupying an attractive row of 17th-century brick cottages, this charming pub was, unbelievably, a coaching inn on the old Brighton to Horsham road, now a quiet backwater off the A281 southeast of Horsham. Beyond the raised front terrace, hanging baskets and stripped pine doors lies a classic main bar featuring an old flagstoned floor, a huge inglenook with winter log fire, heavy beams and rustic pine furnishings. Character extends into the wooden floored snug bar and beamed dining-room with horse brasses, hunting prints and old photographs of local characters and village scenes. Good alfresco seating on the peaceful front terrace and in the sheltered rear garden complete with stream, shrubs and trees. Interesting local walks. *Open 11-3, 6-11 (Sat 11-11 summer), Sun 12-3, 7-10.30 (11-10.30 summer). Free House.*
Beer Eldridge Pope Hardy Country, Adnams Southwold, King & Barnes Sussex, Wadworth 6X, guest beers. Woodland garden, front terrace. Family room. MasterCard, VISA

ODDINGTON	Horse & Groom Inn	FOOD

Tel 01451 830584   Map 14a A1   **B&B**
Upper Oddington Moreton-in-Marsh Gloucestershire GL56 OXH

🍴 ☺ Zzz...

A typically picturesque Cotswold inn set back from the lane in an equally appealing village close to Stow-on-the-Wold. New owners since last year's Guide have gradually set about upgrading the interior, complete with flagstones, ceiling beams, stone walls, country furnishings and log fire, as well as introducing an extensive menu that is available in both the bar and adjacent dining-room. Dominating the vast blackboard in the bar is an impressive choice of seafood dishes such as dressed Cromer crab, Scottish oysters, chargrilled tuna marinaded in soy, Cornish crab cakes with tomato coulis and garlic mayonnaise, whole lemon sole and fresh halibut poached with chive hollandaise. Carnivores are not forgotten as there is space on the menu for terrine of wild boar and juniper berries, Cajun chicken, beef Wellington, pork tenderloin with Dijon mustard sauce and various chargrilled meats. Lighter bites include sandwiches, filled baguettes and ploughman's lunches. Homely bedrooms are rather on the small side, yet are neatly kept, unencumbered by intrusive phones and due to be refurbished in the coming year. Of the four rooms in the eaves above the bar, one has a full bathroom, while the others have 'cubby-hole' shower-rooms. Two bright bedrooms, with WC/showers, are in former stables across the yard. Good sloping summer garden with ornamental pond and children's play area. *Open 11-2.30, 6-11 (Sun 12-3, 7-10.30).*
Bar Food 12-2 (till 2.30 Sun), 6.30-9.30 (till 10 Fri & Sat, from 7 Sun). Free House.
Beer Hook Norton, Wadworth 6X, Wychwood. Garden, children's play area. Family room.
Accommodation 7 bedrooms, all en suite (one with bath), £60/£70 (single £37.50). Children welcome overnight, additional bed (£10) & cot (£5) provided. Check-in by arrangement. MasterCard, VISA

ODELL	Bell	FOOD

Tel 01234 720254   Map 15 E1
Horsefair Lane Odell Bedfordshire MK43 7AG

There's great virtue in being content with serving the very simplest of pub food when the circumstances demand it, and at the tiny Bell Inn they've got it just about right. From the front, it's a mellow-stone, thatched house, and the original two front rooms, connected by a single bar servery, can still be clearly seen. Round the back, a brick extension has brought a succession of little rooms at varying levels, their low tables and stools adding to the almost miniature feel of the place. Doreen Scott's stock-in-trade, in circumstances where the pub never appears less than full, is her single-dish flans of bacon, vegetables or pissaladière and pizza, and omelettes which come with salad or chips or both, and appear designed to be eaten with fork only, in a confined space – which they are. Otherwise, there are cold platters, toasties and sandwiches (with commendable hand-sliced bread) and ploughman's lunches, plus the likes of steak, kidney and Guinness pie and seafood pasta. Added to these is a section honestly labelled "deep-fried" for lovers of scampi and other such things, and a routine dessert list with boozy chocolate mousse, rhubarb fool and yokel pie. It gets extremely busy, overflowing on summer days on to the sunny patio and into the garden under trees down on the banks of the Great Ouse. *Open 11-3 6-11 (11-11 in summer), Sun 12-3, 7-10.30*. **Bar Food** *12-2, 7-9 (no food Sun eve in winter)*. **Beer** *Greene King. Riverside garden, outdoor eating. Family room. No credit cards.*

ODIHAM — George Hotel — B&B

Tel 01256 702081   Fax 01256 704213   Map 15a D4
High Street Odiham nr Basingstoke Hampshire RG29 1LP

First granted a licence in 1540, the privately-owned George is one mile from M3 (J5). Main-house bedrooms (including two four-posters) have creaking floors and low beams, while rooms in the converted coach house and former barn are modern behind original exteriors. Accessories throughout are thoroughly modern, and all rooms have private bath/shower facilities. Farming artefacts decorate the flagstoned bar, while the residents' lounge features exposed stonework. *Open 11-11 (Sun 12-3, 7-10.30)*. *Free House*. **Beer** *Courage Best & Directors, Wadworth 6X. Garden*. **Accommodation** *18 bedrooms, all en suite, £75/£90, (single £65) weekend reductions. Children welcome overnight (under-3s stay free in parents' room, 4-14s £15), additional bed & cot available. Amex, Diners, MasterCard,* **VISA**

OLD AMERSHAM — King's Arms — A

Tel 01494 726333   Fax 01494 433480   Map 15a E3
30 High Street Old Amersham Buckinghamshire HP7 0DJ

The jetty gables of the ancient black-and-white timbered King's Arms overlook the broad high street of this attractive old market town. Dating back to the 15th century it is one of the oldest pubs in England and a mellow atmosphere fills the main bar that retains much of its original character. A wealth of beams, standing timbers, tiny alcoves, two huge inglenook fireplaces and an assortment of settles and old furniture make it a fascinating pub to visit. There is a flower-filled courtyard and a sheltered lawn with seating. *Open 11-11 (Sun 12-10.30)*. *Free House*. **Beer** *Tetley, Benskins Bitter, Ind Coope Burton Ale, Rebellion IPA, guest beer. Garden, children's play area. Family room. No credit cards.*

OLD DALBY — Crown Inn — FOOD

Tel 01664 823134   Map 7 D3
Debdale Hill Old Dalby Melton Mowbray Leicestershire LE14 3LF

Tucked away down a lane in the village centre, this 300-year-old converted farmhouse is today the home of some enjoyable, often ambitious cooking. Cosy, antique-furnished bars are the setting for the sampling of such home-made dishes as potted chicken livers, grilled smoked salmon sausage with tagliatelle and herb cream sauce, followed by loin of lamb with basil, rosemary and red wine jus or blackened Cajun salmon on sweet potato and coconut stew, all of which may appear on the quarterly-changing menus. Puddings include baked Austrian strawberry cheesecake and treacle tart, while local Colston Bassett Stilton features amongst a good choice of cheeses. Simpler snacks like sandwiches and speciality baguettes (chicken and compote of mango) are available at both lunchtime and evening. Eat in either the restaurant or in the bar where there is a constantly-changing selection of draught bitters (up to 14) always available. A large, pleasant and secluded garden provides a haven for children and offers a terraced area for outdoor eating from which guests can watch regular games of pétanque organised by local enthusiasts. *Open 12-3, 6-11 (Sun 12-3, 7.10.30)*. **Bar Food** *12-2, 6-10 (no food Sun eve)*. *Free House*. **Beer** *up to 14 guest beers: Adnams, Marston's Pedigree, Hardys & Hansons Kimberley Bitter, Timothy Taylor Landlord, Black Sheep Bitter, Greene King Abbot Ale, Bateman's XB & XXXB. Garden, outdoor eating. Family room. No credit cards.*

OLD HEATHFIELD   Star Inn   FOOD

Tel & Fax 01435 863570   Map 11 B6
Old Heathfield Heathfield East Sussex TN21 9AH

Not the easiest pub to find, but head for the village church and the Star is right next door. Built as an inn for pilgrims in the 14th century with a rough, honey-stone facade, it has gained a few creepers over the centuries and the atmospheric interior has mellowed nicely with its low-beamed ceiling, rustic tables and chairs and huge inglenook fireplace surrounded by varnished copper and brass ornaments – all very cosy and welcoming in winter. The major attraction in summer is the peaceful, award-winning garden that abounds with colourful flowers and unusual picnic benches and affords impressive views across the High Weald. Popular bar food focuses on fresh fish from Billingsgate or direct from boats in Hastings and Pevensey. Specialities on the board include large cock crabs (for two people), lobster, prawn bisque, sea bass, smoked halibut, fresh marinated anchovies and mussels in saffron, white wine, garlic and cream. A hearty bouillabaise is a favourite winter dish. Those who may wish to forego the fish may be tempted by venison sausages in´red wine, mustard and juniper berries, pheasant casserole, gammon knuckle with onion sauce and butter beans or a mammoth ploughman's lunch – portions are generally not for the faint-hearted. The pudding board usually lists home-made banoffi pie and traditional bread-and-butter pudding, if you have room. The impressive church with its fine Early English tower is worth further exploration. *Open 11.30-3, 5.30-11 (Sun 12-4, 7-11). Bar Food 12-2.30, 7-9.30 (till 9 Sun). Free House. Beer Harveys Sussex, Fuller's London Pride, guest beer. Garden, outdoor eating. MasterCard,* **VISA**

OLDBURY-ON-SEVERN   Anchor Inn   FOOD

Tel 01454 413331   Map 13 F1
Church Road Oldbury-on-Severn South Gloucestershire BS12 1QA

The hamlet of Oldbury lies deep in the flatlands of the Severn estuary two miles west of Thornbury and just half a mile from the water's edge. Michael Dowdeswell's old pub has a flower-decked stone frontage, a brick-lined pine-furnished rear dining-room and extensive streamside garden where a game of boules in the orchard is known locally as "Petanchors". Chef Alex de la Torres continues to produce some reliable food, his extensive bar food menu, typed up each day and served throughout the pub, relies on fresh local produce and regular favourites include grilled Gloucestershire 'snorkers' sausages, an Oldbury 'Flat 'At' filled with roast beef and onion gravy, and sticky toffee pudding. Severn salmon baked with white wine, or cold with salad, leads the more substantial main meals alongside game and beef pie, lamb in garlic, and chargrilled sirloin steak, all served with vegetables and dauphinois potatoes, as this is a chip-free zone! Good choice of ploughman's lunches, filled rolls and salads. At least 75 whiskies, some of the cheapest ales for miles around (Bass and Theakston Old Peculier drawn from the cask) and plenty of wines, including ten served by the glass. Book for the dining-room. Disabled WC. *Open 11.30-2.30 (till 3 Sat), 6.30-11 (from 6 Sat), Sun 12-3.30, 7-10.30. Bar Food 11.30-2 (from 12 Sun), 6.30-9.30 (from 7 Sun). Free House. Beer Bass, Butcombe, Black Sheep Bitter, Worthington Best, Theakston Best & Old Peculier. Garden, outdoor eating. Closed 25 Dec. MasterCard,* **VISA**

OMBERSLEY   King's Arms   FOOD

Tel 01905 620315   Fax 01905 620145   Map 14 B1
Ombersley Droitwich Hereford & Worcester WR9 0EW

This wonderful, crooked-looking, black-and-white timbered inn sports thick, blackened oak beams hung with agricultural implements, gleaming brasses and polished copper pans that reflect the huge open fires in winter within its charterful bars. The Charles II and Devonshire lounges are predominantly designated for eating, with prompt service to your chosen table. From a single menu, the choice is wide, though more tried and trusted than bristling with novelty: home-made fish soup, ploughman's lunches and sandwiches (lunch only, except Sunday), garlic mussels, grilled sea bass, chicken and vegetable pie and Hungarian goulash; vegetarian options

– pasta with coriander pesto – and a reasonable line of home-made puddings such as sticky fig pudding and fruit crumble and custard. Owing to its popularity, the pub is unsuitable for children under 8, and 8-16s are admitted for full meals only until 8.30. There is, however, a sheltered rear patio to accommodate the unsuspecting and the hardy. Just off the A449 between Worcester and Kidderminster. *Open 11-2.45, 5.30-11 (Sun 12-10.30).* **Bar Food** *12.15-2.15, 6-10. (Sun 12-10). Free House.* **Beer** *Bass, Wadworth 6X, Worthington Best, M & B Brew XI. Terrace, outdoor eating. Closed 25 & 26 Dec. Amex, MasterCard,* **VISA**

ONECOTE   Jervis Arms   FOOD

Tel 01538 304206   Fax 01538 304514   Map 6 C3
Onecote Leek Staffordshire ST13 7RU

 ☺

On B5053 (off A523) and positioned just at the edge of the Peak National Park, the pub stands on one bank of the Hamps river – park on the opposite bank and cross a footbridge into the garden. While the picnic tables, play area and ducks are super, parents should be mindful of the littlest ones by this fast-flowing stream. Vegetarian and children's meals both feature prominently on the printed menu (curried nut, fruit and vegetable pie; egg, chips and beans) alongside pretty standard pub grub. A little more adventure emanates from the blackboard: beef Madras, seafood tagliatelle and ocean pie. Adjacent to the pub is holiday accommodation in a converted barn. Baby-changing facilities in the Ladies. *Open 12-2.30 (till 3 Sat), 7-11 (from 6 Sat), Sun 12-10.30.* **Bar Food** *12-2, 7-10 (from 6 Sat), Sun 12-10. Free House.* **Beer** *Theakston XB, Mild & Old Peculier, Bass, Marston's Pedigree, Ruddles County, Worthington Best. Riverside garden, children's play area. Family rooms. Closed 25 & 26 Dec. No credit cards.*

OSMOTHERLEY   Three Tuns   FOOD

Tel & Fax 01609 883301   Map 5 E3   **B&B**
Osmotherley Northallerton North Yorkshire DL6 3BN

The Three Tuns is often referred to as "the Fish Pub", as it offers a diverse selection of fresh market fish and seafood: langoustines, moules or king scallops; grilled sea bass, Dover sole and, perhaps, turbot with prawn and cheese topping, all served with fresh vegetables and a personal bread board. Behind the single, oak-framed bar a quietly elegant dining-room is the popular place to enjoy the likes of non-aquatic alternatives such as Barbary duck with Madeira sauce and beef Wellington. Customers in the bar needn't be the poorer cousins: fresh sardines, pork with apricot and sage, and roast half shoulder of lamb can be enjoyed as a snack and the equally popular doorstep sandwiches (home-cooked ham, smoked salmon) are knife-and-fork affairs. Home-made puddings range from brandy and orange pudding and sticky toffee pudding to strawberry and whisky trifle. Service here may, however, be suspended as the dining-room fills up: booking essential at weekends. Upstairs under the eaves are three stylish, if compact, bedrooms; with en suite facilities (two with showers only), teletext TVs, dial-out phones, hairdryers, shoe-cleaning kits and stylish towelling bathrobes they have gained overnight popularity with a discerning business clientele. Children not encouraged overnight. *Open 11-45-3, 6.45-11 (Sun 12-3, 7-10.30).* **Bar Food** *12-2.30, 7-9.30 (Sun 12-2.30 only). No food Sun eve. Free House.* **Beer** *Theakston Best, XB & Old Peculier, Younger's Scotch & No 3. Garden, outdoor eating.* **Accommodation** *3 bedrooms, all en suite, £60 (single £47.50). No dogs. MasterCard,* **VISA**

OVER HADDON   Lathkil Hotel   FOOD

Tel 01629 812501   Map 6 C2   **B&B**
Over Haddon Bakewell Derbyshire DE45 1JE

The Lathkil scores with its unparalleled views of the Peak National Park and spectacular Lathkil Dale several hundred feet below. Signposted from the B5055 White Peak scenic route, just two miles from Bakewell, it's been a pub since 1813 or earlier and extensions in the 1930s created a Victorian-style bar whose use of miniature-sized tables and chairs gives an illusion of space; there's also a post-war dining-room extension with huge picture windows for making the most of the view. Lunch is served buffet-style from a hot and cold counter to the rear, with standard bar food including soup, paté, filled cob rolls, steak and kidney pie and vegetarian lasagne. Dinner à la carte (for residents only on Sunday evening) produces Stilton stuffed eggs, mushrooms in red wine, baked trout in white wine and basil, mustard grilled pork fillet and nut roast. Puddings are home-made and frequently change at peak times, Bakewell pudding and treacle tart giving way to walnut flan and Italian trifle. Four bedrooms with en suite bathrooms (one a single with shower only) may be limited in space but are comprehensive in facilities: all have TV, clock radio and a personal bar and fridge. The best two, at the front, look across the dale to Youlgrave and the original village of Nether Haddon, now part of the Haddon estate. *Open 11.30-3, 6.30-11 (Sun 12-3, 7-10.30). Bar Food 12-2, 7-9 (restaurant only Fri & Sat eve in winter, Sun eve all year residents only). Free House. Beer Wards Best, Thorne Best & Mild. Patio, outdoor eating. Family room (lunchtimes only). Accommodation 4 bedrooms, all en suite, £70 (single £35). Children welcome overnight (under-2s stay free in parents' room). Accommodation closed 24 & 25 Dec; pub closed 25 Dec. MasterCard, VISA*

OVER PEOVER · The Dog · FOOD · B&B

Tel & Fax 01625 861421   Map 6 B2

Well Bank Lane Over Peover Knutsford Cheshire WA16 8UP

Frances and Jim Cunningham promote The Dog as a pub serving food, and so popular has it proved that these days table reservations are the norm. A well-tried formula invites choice of snacks – extensive sandwich and ploughman's lunch menu – starters and main courses from the daily-updated blackboard that offers a range of soups (perhaps carrot and coriander), Welsh rarebit with bacon, and home-roasted spare ribs ahead of an equally wide range of main courses. Substantial dishes with vegetables and choice of potatoes are all well priced; venison casserole, ham shank with parsley sauce, roast duck with plum sauce and grilled plaice exemplify the range. Home-made desserts are selected from a groaning sideboard and cold cabinet replete with fruit pies, bread-and-butter pudding, pavlovas and gateaux. The Dog's identity as village local is retained in the Tap Room, while there's plenty of space for casual drinking on the front patio or in a rear garden, where a more limited snack service operates. In terms of its food, the pub could write North-Western appetites into folklore, the term 'volume' being applicable equally to the portions as to the numbers who tuck into them. The individually-decorated bedrooms are equally popular, their cottage appeal enhanced by the practical addition of spacious, carpeted bath/shower rooms, TVs, trouser presses and beverage trays – they attract a clientele quite capable of providing their own telephones! Plans are to add three further en suite bedrooms in the near future. *Open 11-3, 5.30-11 (Sun 12-3, 7-10.30). Bar Food 12-2 (bookings essential Sun), 6.30-9. Free House. Beer Greenalls Original, Boddingtons, guest beer. Garden, outdoor eating. Accommodation 3 bedrooms, all en suite, £62.50 (single £45). Children welcome overnight (charge depends on age). MasterCard, VISA*

OVER STRATTON · Royal Oak · A

Tel 01460 240906   Map 13 F2

Over Stratton South Petherton Somerset TA13 5LQ

This row of three 400-year-old thatched cottages merges with its neighbours in the main street of the village and, but for the pub sign, it would be easy to miss altogether; at the South Petherton roundabout (A303) take the old Ilminster town-centre road. Cottage atmosphere is still the secret of an interior with a real sense of style. Original features like old beams, hamstone and flag floors (as well as a couple of stone pillars that look to have been there for ever but were actually salvaged from the cellars of a nearby house a few years ago) blend successfully with dark rag-rolled walls, scrubbed wooden tables, a polished granite bar counter and extensive displays of dried flowers, hops and strings of garlic. In the safe rear garden there are swings, a junior assault course and trampolines to keep the kids amused. *Open 11-3, 6-11 (11-11 Mon-Sat in Aug), Sun 12-3, 7-10.30. Beer Hall & Woodhouse Tanglefoot, Badger Best & Stratton Ale (brewed for pub). Garden, children's play area. MasterCard, VISA*

Stilton, leek and mushroom croustade can be preceded by avocado and smoked turkey salad with bacon or followed by the likes of lemon citrus tart or French chocolate flan. Ploughman's platters and sandwiches are always available for those calling in for a light snack. *Open 11-3, 6-11 (Sun 12-3 7-10.30).* **Bar Food** *12-2 (till 1.45 Sun), 7-9.30 (till 8.30 Sun). Free House.* **Beer** *Ruddles County & Best, Wood's Wonderful, guest beer. Patio/terrace, outdoor eating. Family room. No credit cards.*

PENELEWEY   Punch Bowl & Ladle   A

Tel 01872 862237   Map 12 B3
Penelewey Feock Cornwall

The idyllic exterior of rose-covered walls, heavy thatched porches and roof belie the true size of this much-extended, 15th-century cottage, set sideways on to the road. Tacked on to the back is a vast dining area, but the main interest here is the warren of unspoilt rooms housed in the original cottage. Once used as a courthouse and a meet for Customs and Excise men, the charming series of interconnecting, low-beamed rooms have a relaxing ambience in which to enjoy a pint and read some of the tourist literature and daily papers provided. There is much to catch the eye, from collections of rural bygones, plates, books, photographs and old tins to an array of rustic pine tables, sofas, easy chairs and some antique pieces of furniture. A handy stop for Trelissick Gardens (NT) and the King Harry Ferry across the River Fal. *Open 11-11 (Sun 12-10.30).* **Beer** *Flowers Original, Bass, Courage Directors. Patio. MasterCard,* **VISA**

PENISTONE   Cubley Hall   FOOD

Tel 01226 766086   Fax 01226 766361   Map 6 C2
Mortimer Road Penistone Barnsley S30 6AW

The interior of this unusual conversion from Edwardian country house to what is almost a 'stately pub' is resplendent with oak panelling, mosaic floors and ornate ceilings. It echoes a bit when empty but hums along busily when full and, with sizeable parties accommodated in the conservatory, there can be a scrum for tables to eat at. Food ranges from ploughman's platters, baguettes and hot-filled pittas (Danish smoked bacon) through to the steak and grill meals, but the daily specials enhance the choice: beef and vegetable pie, fresh jumbo cod and chips, home-made pasta with seafood, chargrilled leg of lamb steak with Provençal vegetables and a choice of fresh fish dishes are better indicators of a capable kitchen which also produces more imaginative fare for the adjacent restaurant and carvery. The well-tended gardens and grounds with play areas (even with the occasional bouncy castle) and drinking patios are a major draw for families through the summer. No smoking in the 'Green Room'. Recent refurbishment and the addition of a rear extension has created twelve en suite bedrooms, seven in the elegant main house (not inspected), and a new conservatory leading out to the extensive gardens. *Open 11-11 (Sun 12-10.30).* **Bar Food** *12-10 (till 9 Sun). Free House.* **Beer** *Tetley Bitter & Imperial, guest beers. Large garden and patio, outdoor eating, children's play area. Family room. Amex, Diners, MasterCard,* **VISA**

> Many **B&B** establishments offer reduced rates for weekend and out-of-season bookings. Always ask about special deals for longer stays. Beware half-board terms in inns where we do not recommend the **FOOD**.

PENN STREET   Hit or Miss   FOOD

Tel 01494 713109   Fax 01494 718010   Map 15a E3
Penn Street Amersham Buckinghamshire HP7 0PX

200-year-old brick-built village pub with an attractive wisteria-clad facade and located opposite its own cricket pitch. Unpretentious and comfortably modernised interior with two neat yet simply furnished bars, an open fire, a separate restaurant and a relaxing music, and game-free atmosphere. Extensive menus listed on four blackboards should suit all tastes, with standard favourites plus a selection of reliable, home-cooked dishes and daily fresh fish specials. Typical bar fare encompasses ploughman's platters, home-made soup (broccoli and Stilton), Cajun chicken, Florida sole platter, whole plaice and Hungarian goulash. The restaurant à la carte menu can be ordered in the bar and offers more imaginative fare — medallions of venison with blackcurrant and port sauce, and marinated monkfish on a bed of Oriental leaves. Roast Sunday lunch is a popular affair. Under the same ownership as *The Dove* (see entry) in Hammersmith, London W6. *Open 11-3, 5.30-11 (11-11 in summer), Sun 12-3, 7-10.30 (12-10.30 in summer). Bar Food 11-2.30 (from 12 Sun), 6-10 (from 7 Sun). Free House. Beer Brakspear Bitter, Fuller's London Pride & Chiswick Bitter, Hook Norton Old Hooky. Garden, outdoor eating. Amex, MasterCard, **VISA***

PERRANUTHNOE   Victoria Inn   A

Tel 01736 710309
Perranuthnoe Penzance Cornwall TR20 9NP

Map 12 A4

New enthusiastic landlords have taken over this pretty pink-washed village inn, originally built to accommodate the masons who extended the church in the 12th century, and officially described as a safe house for the clergy. With the sea and a safe beach just down the road the comfortable, typically Cornish stone-walled bar, adorned with various seafaring and fishing memorabilia, and the sheltered sun-trap rear terrace fill up early with visitors. A warm welcome is offered to families, who make use of the spacious games room. The two homely en suite bedrooms (recommeded last year as a convenient stopover for walkers and for those catching the early morning ferry from Penzance to the Scilly Isles) are due to be upgraded in the coming year. *Open 11.30-3, 6.30-11 (Sun 12-3, 7-10.30). Beer Ushers. Garden. MasterCard, **VISA***

> We only recommend food (Bar Food) in those establishments highlighted
> with the **FOOD** symbol.

PETWORTH   Welldiggers Arms   FOOD

Tel 01798 342287
Pulborough Road Petworth West Sussex GU28 0GH

Map 11 A6

Once occupied by welldiggers as its name suggests, this 300-year-old roadside cottage can be located along the A283 Pulborough road, 2 miles east of Petworth. Two low-ceilinged bars furnished with a rustic collection of sturdy oak tables and benches are generally bustling with diners as this is very much a dining-orientated pub. Popular with enthusiasts of racing (Goodwood), shooting and polo (Cowdray Park), it is a useful rendezvous or stopping-off point in which to enjoy some reliable bar food. Excellent seafood – fish soup, grilled prawns in garlic butter, fresh mussels, whole sea bass, fresh lobster, whole Dover sole, seafood platter – and properly hung steaks, especially T-bones. Alternatives on the blackboard menu may include home-made paté, calf's liver and onion, braised oxtail, courgette and cheese bake and local game (poacher's pot, roast pheasant or partridge) in season. For pudding, try the home-made lemon pie or banana fritters. Sunday roasts feature a choice of lamb and prime English beef. Alfresco eating on the rear patio with views towards the South Downs and a summer house for children to play in. *Open 11-3, 6-11 (Sun 12-3 only). Closed Sun eve. Bar Food 12-2, 6-10. Free House. Beer Young's Best Bitter & Special, Ballards Best. Garden, outdoor eating. Family room. Amex, Diners, MasterCard, **VISA***

PHILLEIGH   Roseland Inn   FOOD

Tel 01872 580254   Fax 01872 580951
Philleigh Cornwall TR2 5NB

Map 12 B3

17th-century cob-built Cornish treasure peacefully positioned beside the parish church in an out-of-the-way village, two miles from the King Harry Ferry that crosses the River Fal. The front terrace is delightfully floral with colourful climbing roses, while indoors there are old-fashioned seats, lovely old settles, worn slate floors, fresh flowers, low beams and a welcoming fire. Spotlessly kept and run with enthusiastic panache by Graham and Jacqui Hill, the Roseland is a popular rural destination for reliable pub food. The menu and blackboard specials cover a range from decent sandwiches and ploughman's platters, salad niçoise and smoked fish platter to navarin of lamb, crab Newburg and bean and potato goulash. Evening extras may include Oriental monkfish and seafood 'extravaganza' (24hrs' notice); the fish is delivered daily from a local trawler. The garden is closed off from the road and has a rocking horse and slides for children. *Open 11.30-3, 6-11 (from 6.30 in winter), Sun 12-3, 7-10.30.* **Bar Food** *12-2.15, 7-9.* **Beer** *Marston's Pedigree, Greenalls Bitter, Bass. Garden. No credit cards.*

PICKERING	White Swan	FOOD

Tel & Fax 01751 472288   Map 5 E4   B&B
The Market Place Pickering North Yorkshire YO18 7AA

⊳○ ❐ ♇ Zzz...

After twelve years at the helm of this charming town centre inn, Dierdre Buchanan has stepped back to allow son Victor and his wife Marion to control the day-to-day running of this highly popular establishment. For the regulars and the casual drinker there's the traditional pubbiness of the oak-panelled bar and snug which overlook Pickering's sloping main street. Residents both new and oft-returning enjoy privileged use of a quietly elegant lounge and a warm welcome from the Buchanan family which helps make them feel well at home. Quality bar food ranges from sound pub favourites (ploughman's, sandwiches – lunch only) to competently-cooked specials like braised lamb shank with root vegetables, venison sausage casserole, half a lobster (summer) and a good fish board selection – whole lemon sole, baked smoked haddock Welsh rarebit. Separate vegetarian menu which may highlight chargrilled vegetables with couscous on a bed of tomatoes and basil. Desserts are generous and nicely presented (bread-and-butter pudding with crème anglaise or rich dark chocolate terrine) or there's a Yorkshire cheeseboard available. At least seven wines are available by the glass. Presently, the twelve comfortable and well-equipped en suite (bath and shower) bedrooms feature quality pine furniture or personally selected antique pieces, rich floral borders and matching duvet covers. All are due to be completely refurbished at the end of 1996. *Open 11-3.30, 6-11 (Mon 11-11), Sun 12-3, 7-10.30.* **Bar Food** *12-2.30, 6.15-9.30. Free House.* **Beer** *Theakston Best, Black Sheep Bitter. Garden, outdoor eating area.* **Accommodation** *12 bedrooms, all en suite, £76 (single £55). Children welcome overnight, additional bed (£15) & cot available. Amex, MasterCard,* **VISA**

PICKHILL	Nag's Head	FOOD

Tel 01845 567391   Fax 01845 567212   Map 5 E4   B&B
Pickhill Thirsk North Yorkshire YO7 4JG

⊳○ Zzz... ▮ ♇

Ever-youthful and enthusiastic publicans Raymond and Edward Boynton will shortly celebrate their Jubilee at the pub which has become synonymous with Yorkshire hospitality at its best. Immaculately-kept real ales, monthly wine selections (offered also by the glass from a good global list) and an array of 40-odd malt whiskies are the domain of one brother, against which his sibling's kitchen output measures up admirably. Menu boards here do not so much proclaim daily specials as spell out the kitchen's entire repertoire. For starters, go perhaps for wild boar terrine with chutney or grilled fresh sardines with pesto. For a bar snack, try large cod and chips or mushroom risotto cake with tomato and basil sauce or a choice of sandwiches and ploughman's platters. Main meals extend to roast saddle of hare with wild berry and mushroom sauce and king scallops on spinach and watercress sauce, plus traditional puddings such as sticky toffee pudding and apple and honey crumble to follow. Similar fare, plus a few select extras and a good-value fixed-price lunch menu are served in the restaurant. As a place to stay, the Nag's Head is similarly above reproach. Accommodation, including eight recently-refurbished bedrooms, is divided between the pub and next-door house standing in a neatly tended garden, and a self-contained cottage which can be let in its entirety. Remote-control TV, dial-out phone and beverage tray are standard appointments in the rooms, the majority of which have plenty of desk space, as well as neat, well appointed bathrooms, four with WC/shower only. Yorkshire breakfast in the morning could prove irresistible. Well-behaved children welcome in the bar areas. *Open 11-11 (Sun 12-10.30).* **Bar Food** *12-2, 6-10 (till 9.30 Sun). Free House.* **Beer** *Hambleton Bitter, Goldfield & Stud, Theakston Best, XB & Old Peculier. Garden, outdoor eating, barbecue.* **Accommodation** *15 bedrooms, all en suite, £48 (single £34). Children welcome overnight (under 5s stay free in parents' room), additional bed (£10) & cot available. Amex, MasterCard,* **VISA**

PICKLESCOTT   Bottle & Glass Inn   FOOD

Tel 01694 751345   Map 6 A4   **B&B**
Picklescott Church Stretton Shropshire SY6 6NR

Zzz...

Follow well-signed lanes from the A49 at Dorrington, or the scenic route over Long
Mynd from the Strettons to happen on this epitome of locals. Rear extensions to the
original two-roomed stone-built pub have been sympathetically handled, the dining
area leading to a barbecue terrace and rear garden. Food throughout stays with the
safe options: home-baked ham, grills of steak and fish supplemented by daily specials
(tomato and carrot soup, cod in lemon and parsley, chicken with garlic and herbs,
sweet and sour pork) and lunchtime salads, sandwiches and savoury-filled baked
potatoes. Sunday carvery with eight fresh vegetables; booking essential. Families are
very welcome; there are picnic tables on a sun-trap front patio and safe playing by the
village stream opposite. Comfortable, character bedrooms have been expertly created
in the roof space with brass bedsteads, co-ordinated fabrics and gold-tapped bathrooms
with over-bath showers. The temptation of telephones has been resisted in favour
of TVs, tea trays and trouser presses. *Open 11-3, 7-11 (Sun 12-3, 7-10.30).*
Bar Food 12-2, 7-10. Free House. **Beer** *Bass, Worthington Best. Garden, patio, barbecue.*
*Accommodation 3 bedrooms, all en suite, £50 (single £25). Children welcome overnight,
additional bed (£10) available. Check-in by arrangement. No dogs. No credit cards.*

PIDDLEHINTON   Thimble Inn   A

Tel 01300 348270   Map 13 F2
Piddlehinton Dorchester Dorset DT2 7TD

The Thimble is no longer thimble-sized nor is it the quaint, creeper-clad village local
that we once knew. The traditional two-bar layout has disappeared and a splendid
thatched extension has been built. This curves along the tiny River Piddle with small
bridges linking it to the attractive, summer flower-filled garden, which enjoys rolling
country views. Internally, it is very smart with tasteful decor, good prints and subdued
lighting; the open-plan bars are furnished with an assortment of pub tables and chairs.
A feature of the bar is the 27ft glass-topped well. Children welcome indoors.
Open 12-2.30, 7-11 (till 10.30 Sun). Free House. **Beer** *Ringwood Old Thumper, Eldridge
Pope Hardy Country Ale, Hall & Woodhouse Badger Best. Garden. Disabled facilities.
No credit cards.*

PIMPERNE   Anvil Hotel   B&B

Tel 01258 453431   Fax 01258 480182   Map 14 B4
Pimperne Blandford Forum Dorset

Set back from the busy A345 Salisbury to Blandford road, this pretty, thatched cottage
dates from 1535. Low ceilings, thick walls, old black beams and an inglenook fireplace
characterise the tile-floored restaurant, while more modern plush wall-bench seating
features in the neat and relaxing lounge bar and in the Forge Bar extension. Up a
narrow, steep staircase and tucked beneath the thatch are ten clean and comfortable
bedrooms. All are attractively decorated and furnished with modern telephones and
tea-making facilities. Compact en suite facilities, all with bath and shower, are
spotlessly clean. Delightful, flower-filled front garden with a shady spot beneath a
huge weeping willow tree. *Open 12-2.30, 6.15-11 (Sun 12-3, 7-10.30). Free House.*
Beer *Wadworth 6X, Bass. Garden. Accommodation 10 bedrooms, all en suite, £70 &
£110 (family room £80, single £45). Children welcome overnight, additional bed (£7.50)
& cot (£5) available. Amex, Diners, MasterCard,* **VISA**

PIN MILL   Butt & Oyster   A

Tel 01473 780764   Map 10 C3
Pin Mill Chelmondiston Ipswich Suffolk 1RP 1JW

Classic riverside pub set in a tiny hamlet off the B1456 at Chelmondiston, south-west
of Ipswich. Dating from the 17th century, this old bargeman's retreat is still frequented
by sailors and fishermen and on busy summer days it is chock full of tourists, all
enjoying the simple charm of its old settles, tiled floors and fine views across
Buttermans Bay, part of the River Orwell. Nautical artefacts and photographs adorn

the wood-panelled walls of the main bar and the 'smoke room' features a collection of model ships. Both bars are free of intrusive music and electronic games. Be early for the sought-after waterside window seats, or one of the sturdy benches adjacent to the slipway; it's an ideal spot to watch the setting sun on fine summer evenings. Traditional winter pub games are popular when the crowds have gone home. *Open 11-3, 7-11 (11-11 summer), Sun 12-3, 7-10.30 (12-10.30 summer).* **Beer** *Tolly Cobbold Original, Bitter, Mild, Shooter & IPA. Garden, outdoor eating. No credit cards.*

PITTON   Silver Plough   FOOD

Tel 01722 712266   Map 14 C3
Pitton Salisbury Wiltshire SP5 1DZ

The Silver Plough was a farmhouse until after the Second World War. Everything about the attractive, long building is neat and well kept: the lawns at the front, full of white plastic tables and chairs for summer drinking, and the tastefully-furnished main bar with its dust-free jugs, bottles and curios hanging from the ceiling timbers. Sturdy antique oak settles, various tables and quality paintings and prints characterise this bar and the snug bar with its neighbouring skittle alley – both popular with locals. It's very much a dining pub, offering a good range of home-cooked bar meals using fresh local produce from reliable local suppliers, including Pitton's smokery. Menu choices include an above-average bar snack menu – unusual cheese ploughman's lunches, various pasta dishes, French-style casserole – and blackboard specials like salmon on samphire with tomato and anchovy sauce or chargrilled tuna with chili salsa. Further inventive dishes such as smoked duck breast with red onion and sweet pepper marmalade and pan-fried red snapper with grilled aubergine and tomato and pepper salsa highlight the restaurant à la carte (also served in the bar), which, like the bar menu, changes every six weeks. The global wine list is strong on New Zealand wines (with no less than ten offered by the glass) and a raft of country wines. *Open 11-3, 6-11 (Sun 12-3, 7-10.30).* **Bar Food** *12-3, 7-10 (till 9 Sun). Free House.* **Beer** *John Smith's, Courage Directors, Eldridge Pope Hardy Ale, Wadworth 6X. Garden, outdoor eating. Amex, Diners, MasterCard,* **VISA**

PLUCKLEY   Dering Arms   FOOD

Tel 01233 840371   Fax 01233 840498   Map 11 C5
Pluckley Ashford Kent TN27 0RR

Located a mile from the village beside Pluckley Station, this impressive manorial building was once the Dering Estate hunting lodge and boasts curving Dutch gables, rounded triple lancet 'Dering' windows, and a rather spooky grandeur. Splendid interior to match, with high ceilings, wood or stone floors, a tall, exposed brick fireplace, stripped-pine doors, various sturdy wooden tables, long Victorian benches and some old leather easy chairs. A relaxing atmosphere is created in which to enjoy the good bar food listed on two short blackboard menus. Favourite snacks – sandwiches and ploughman's platters with home-made chutney – can be found on one; a range of interesting home-cooked dishes on the other. A typical choice may include potted crab, mussels in cider and cream sauce, pheasant casseroled in red wine and rack of lamb with a herb crust. Fresh fish from Hythe dominates the imaginative, daily-changing restaurant menu (also available in the bar), for example monkfish in a creamy bacon and orange sauce or fresh tuna baked with saffron onions. Good local Goacher's ales and a Biddenden farm cider are favoured here; wine drinkers can choose from an interesting list of 82 wines. Regular gourmet evenings, summer barbecues and live jazz or classical music in the sheltered garden. 1997 South of England Regional Winner of our Seafood Pub of the Year award. *Open 11-3, 6-11 (Sun 12-3, 7-10.30).* **Bar Food** *12-2 & 7-9.30 (till 10 Fri & Sat). No food Sun eve. Free House.* **Beer** *Goacher's Maidstone Ale, Dering Ale, Dark Mild & Dark Ale. Garden, outdoor eating. Family room. Closed 26 & 27 Dec. Amex, MasterCard,* **VISA**

We endeavour to be as up-to-date as possible but inevitably some changes to landlords, chefs and other key staff occur after the Guide has gone to press.

PLUSH   Brace of Pheasants   FOOD

Tel 01300 348357   Map 13 F2
Plush Dorchester Dorset DT2 7RQ

Originally two cottages and a forge, dating from the 16th century, this attractive
collection of thatched, brick and flint buildings became an inn in the mid-1930s and
must surely be one of the prettiest in Dorset. The location is idyllic, nestling in a
peaceful rural hamlet, surrounded by rolling downland. A brace of glass–encased
stuffed pheasants hangs above the main cottage door that leads into the charmingly
unspoilt bar, complete with a huge inglenook (used for seating), a further log fire and
an assortment of traditional furniture. The attraction here, other than its setting, is
the bar food. Separate blackboards for both lunch and evening fare list the weekly-
changing specials that supplement an extensive printed menu selection. Lunch features
the usual ploughman's platters and salads, plus a range of lighter bites, including queen
scallops and bacon salad, crab savoury and soft herring roes. Substantial home-cooked
lunch dishes may include lamb and rosemary pie, smoked haddock mornay, lasagne,
venison sausages and grilled lemon sole. Evening fare is more adventurous. Puddings,
listed on a board, range from mango cheesecake to apple and plum crumble. There is
a delightful garden with mature trees and shrubs. No under-14s in bar areas. *Open 12-
2.30, 7-11 (Sun 12-3, 7-10.30).* **Bar Food** *12-1.45, 7-9.45 (till 9.30 Sun). Free House.*
Beer *Smiles Best, Flowers Original, Fuller's London Pride. Garden, outdoor eating, children's
play area. Family room. Closed 25 Dec eve. MasterCard,* **VISA**

PLYMOUTH   The China House   A

Tel 01752 260930   Map 12 C3
Marrowbone Slip Sutton Harbour Plymouth Devon PL4 0DW

The China House has had many uses since being built as a quayside warehouse in the
mid-1600s: King's bakehouse, hospital for seamen, porcelain factory (from which
period it takes its name) and prison, amongst other uses. Now cleverly rebuilt inside
to reflect its warehouse days with great bulks of timber, cast-iron pillars and sets of
mock cargo, it makes a most unusual hostelry. There is a no-smoking area and a
narrow verandah jutting out over the water of Sutton Harbour. Regular jazz and
blues nights. *Open 11-11 (till 1am Thu-Sat), Sun 12-10.30.* **Beer** *Ind Coope Burton
Ale, Tetley, Dartmoor Best, guest beer. Terrace. Amex, MasterCard,* **VISA**

POLKERRIS   Rashleigh Inn   A

Tel 01726 813991   Map 12 B3
Polkerris Fowey Cornwall PL24 2TL

Literally on the beach in a tiny isolated cove and known locally as the 'Inn on the
Beach', the Rashleigh is well worth seeking out for its magnificent setting. Once the
old lifeboat station, until becoming a pub in 1924, it is a popular refreshment spot for
coast path walkers and for families using the beach in the summer. Summer alfresco
drinking is unrivalled in this area, for the table-filled terrace is a splendid place from
which to watch the sun set across St Austell Bay. On cooler days the sea views can
still be admired from the warmth of the main bar, especially from the bay-window
seats. Parents enjoying a drink (possibly a well kept pint of St Austell Hicks Special
tapped from wooden casks) on the terrace can keep an eagle eye on their children
playing on the beach. No under-14s inside unless eating. *Open 11-3, 5.30-11 (Sun 12-
3, 6-10.30). Free House.* **Beer** *St Austell HSD, Ind Coope Burton Ale, Bass, Bolsters Best,
two guest beers. Terrace. MasterCard,* **VISA**

PORT GAVERNE   Port Gaverne Hotel   B&B

Tel 01208 880244   Fax 01208 880151   Map 12 B3
Port Gaverne Port Isaac Cornwall PL29 3SQ

Zzz...

Set in a sheltered cove 50 yards from the beach is this charming 17th-century inn, run
by Midge Ross for the last 27 years. The ship-shape, character pubby bar has a polished
slate floor and the tiny snug bar features a collection of china, old local photographs,

a genuine ship's table and carved chest, and an interesting diorama of the port years ago. Upstairs, along the warren of corridors lined with attractive paintings and watercolours lie nineteen cheerful, individually decorated bedrooms which boast pretty fabrics and wallpapers and attractive en suite bathrooms. Antique furniture grace the older rooms in the main building, but all have thoughtful homely touches like pieces of china and ornaments, plus tissues, TV, hairdryer and telephone for added comfort. Fresh, clean and comfortable accommodation, the best room affording a magnificent sea view. Self-catering cottages are also available. Children welcome in the Green Door bar opposite (open all day in summer) and in the small 'Cabin' bar in winter. *Open 11-2.30, 6-11 (Sun 12-3, 7-10.30), summer 11-11 (Sun 12-10.30). Free House. Beer Sharp's Doombar Bitter, Flowers IPA, Bass. Garden. Accommodation 19 bedrooms, all en suite, £94 (single £47). Children welcome overnight (under-3s stay free in parents' room, 3-12s half price), additional bed & cot available. Hotel closed early Jan-mid Feb.* Amex, Diners, MasterCard, **VISA**

PORTHLEVEN — Harbour Inn — B&B

Tel 01326 573876 Map 12 A4
Porthleven Helston Cornwall TR13 9JB

Situated in an unspoilt fishing village, this old fisherman's pub enjoys good views across the colourful collection of fishing boats and dinghies that fill the picturesque little harbour twenty yards away. Inside, there is a comfortable lounge area and a much larger and livelier public bar area, while upstairs accommodation is offered in ten en suite bedrooms, six of which have harbour views. Cottagey in style with pretty floral fabrics, wallpaper and matching duvet covers, they are neatly furnished with modern pine and six have large, adequately-equipped bathrooms with good overhead showers. Added comforts include TV, telephone, hairdryer and beverage-making facilities. *Open 11-11, (Sun 12-10.30). Beer St Austell. Family room. Accommodation 10 bedrooms, 8 en suite, £38-£56 (family room £80, single £31), additional cot (£8) available.* No dogs. Amex, MasterCard, **VISA**

PORTHLEVEN — Ship — A

Tel 01326 572841 Map 12 A4
Porthleven Helston Cornwall TR13 9JS

Set in the cliffside and perched on the harbour wall, this old fisherman's pub enjoys a magnificent position looking out across the quaint working harbour and out to sea. The view is best appreciated in summer from the series of terraced lawns that rise up the cliff behind the pub. On wild winter days, climb the flight of stone steps and savour the view from the warmth of a window seat in the nautical bric-a-brac adorned bar, complete with good log fires and a good range of real ales, as the landlord, Colin Oakden, has recently bought the premises. The family room – the 'Smithy' – adjoins the garden, while the ground-floor cellar bar is used only in the summer. The tiny harbour is attractively lit by fairy lights at night. *Open 11.30-3, 7-11 (11.30-11 July-Sept), Sun 12-3, 7-10.30. Free House. Beer Sharp's Coaster & Doombar, Fuller's London Pride, Greene King Abbot Ale, guest beer. Family room.* No credit cards.

POWERSTOCK — Three Horseshoes Inn — FOOD

Tel 01308 485328 Fax 01308 485577 Map 13 F2 **B&B**
Powerstock Bridport Dorset DT6 3TF

'The Shoes' (as it is affectionately known locally) is a Victorian stone inn set in a sleepy village amid narrow, winding lanes and best reached from the A3066 north of Bridport. Rebuilt in 1906 after a devastating fire, but solidly old-fashioned in style with simple country furnishings in both the bustling bar and in the two pine-panelled dining-rooms. People come from miles around to this reliable old favourite for the chef/licensee Pat Ferguson's food; it's not cheap, certainly, but it is fresh and delicious, specialising in fish from local boats, Dorset lamb and seasonal game. The extensive, daily-changing blackboard list of home-cooked dishes serves both bar and restaurant. Begin, perhaps, with terrine of pork and game with chutney, cheese soufflé, mussels steamed in white wine onion and garlic, and grilled sardines with garlic butter; fish fanciers can then continue with monkfish provençale, local lobster, sea bass served on a bed of spinach with garlic sauce or fresh local crabs steamed with ginger, garlic and chili. Meat and game dishes like garlic-studded roast rack of Dorset lamb with rosemary-scented jus and marinated duck breast are all served with well-cooked vegetables. Lighter bites include interesting fresh pasta dishes, salads and freshly-baked baguettes. Traditional puddings include rhubarb crumble and fresh fruit parfait. Must book for busy Sunday lunches (£12.50). Good Palmers ales and a choice of twenty wines by the glass. Delightful terraced garden and rear patio with village and valley views for summer eating. Four simple, centrally-heated bedrooms with traditional older-style furniture, TV and tea-maker provide homely overnight accommodation. Two are spacious and comfortable with clean, en suite bathrooms, the others are rather too compact and share a bathroom. *Open 11-3, 6-11 (Sun 12-3, 7-10.30).* **Bar Food** *12-2, 7-10 (till 9 Sun).* **Beer** *Palmers BB & IPA. Garden, patio, outdoor eating, children's play area.* **Accommodation** *4 bedrooms, 2 en suite, £60 (single £40). Children welcome overnight, additional bed & cot available. Check-in by arrangement. Amex, MasterCard,* **VISA**

Many **B&B** establishments offer reduced rates for weekend and out-of-season bookings. Always ask about special deals for longer stays. Beware half-board terms in inns where we do not recommend the **FOOD.**

PRIORS DEAN   White Horse   A

Tel 01420 588387   Map 15 D3
Priors Dean Petersfield Hampshire GU32 1DA

Also called the *Pub with No Name*; there is no sign. Fiendish to get to: leave Petersfield on the A272 Winchester-bound, turn right towards Steep, then after about 5 miles, take the East Tisted road at the crossroads, then immediate right down the second gravel track. It's worth the effort, for this is a quite wonderful 17th-century farmhouse pub of utterly simple charm. Genuinely unspoilt by modernity, it boasts two splendid bars, each with open log fires, a motley collection of old tables and chairs, a wealth of memorabilia, from old clocks to farm implements, and a rich, warm patina on the walls only associated with age. First World War poet Edward Thomas wrote his first published work, *Up in the Wind*, about the pub; it's 750 feet up on the top of the Downs, with peaceful views on every side. There are 21 country wines and up to ten real ales on handpump. Long-serving landlord Jack Eddleston has recently retired and the new tenants have introduced a short, promising list of home-cooked bar meals. *Open 11-2.30 (till 3 Sat), 6-11 (Sun 12-3, 7-10.30).* **Beer** *Ballard's Best Bitter, No Name Best & Strong, Ringwood Fortyniner, Gale's BB, IPA & HSB, Bass, Theakston Old Peculier, guest beer. Garden, outdoor eating, children's play area. MasterCard,* **VISA**

RAMSBURY   Bell at Ramsbury   FOOD

Tel 01672 520230   Map 14a A4
The Market Square Ramsbury Marlborough Wiltshire SN8 2PE

The Bell's stock-in-trade remains the provision of good-quality, carefully-prepared bar food at affordable prices. Sensibly short and to the point, both the printed and daily-changing blackboard menus give equal billing to ploughman's platters and sandwiches (lunch only), home-made soups and patés, and single-course snacks such as seafood fettuccine, beef and ale pie, pork stroganoff, Sussex smokey pie and chicken and cashew nut curry, while fresh fish (monkfish, bream, lemon sole) and steaks, sauced or plain, are accompanied by plainly-cooked fresh vegetables; Sunday roast. To follow are plenty of traditional nursery puddings from Spotted Dick to rhubarb crumble and home-made ices and sorbets. No-smoking area. *Open 12-2.30, 6.30-11 (Sun 12-3, 7-10.30).* **Bar Food** *12-2 (till 2.30 Sat and Sun), 7-9 (till 9.30 Sat). No food Sun eve in winter. Free House.* **Beer** *Wadworth 6X & Henry's IPA, Hook Norton Best, two guest beers. Garden, outdoor eating. Family room. Amex, MasterCard,* **VISA**

RAMSHOLT — Ramsholt Arms — FOOD

Tel & Fax 01394 411229   Map 10 D3   **B&B**
Dock Road Ramsholt nr Woodbridge Suffolk IP12 3AB

In a glorious tidal estuary setting, with a large terrace overlooking the river Deben and (most surprisingly) a sandy beach and grassy area between – surely the most beautiful pub location in Suffolk. Birdlife on the shoreline, the rattle of stays on the masts of boats moored in the river, general leisure boating activity and views of fields and marshes beyond give the Ramsholt Arms a lovely atmosphere. The pub's open-plan interior is now modernised with one room (overlooking the water) assigned to diners and a long, curving bar that leads round to a more snug area where interesting details are posted about a Lancaster bomber that ditched in the water during the Second World War. The fortnightly-changing blackboard menu is kept sensibly short, offering the likes of sautéed scallops, Irish oysters, a plate of charcuterie, first-rate fish and chips, locally-caught lobster and crab, game in season and a weekend roast; definitely leave room for a superb, rich chocolate mousse served in a tall wine glass. Upstairs are four delightful, airy bedrooms (all of which were given a new lease of life when the new landlords took over last year) that directly overlook the river; they share two bathrooms. Friendly staff. Good local walks along the riverbank. Winner of our Pub Newcomer of the Year Award 1997. Ramsholt may not be marked on all maps but it is signposted off B1083 from Woodbridge. *Open 11-3, 6-11 (Sun 12-4, 6-10.30).* **Bar Food** *12-2.30, 7-9 (Sat & Sun till 9.30).* **Beer** Adnams. **Accommodation** *4 bedrooms, 2 en suite, £55 (single £30). Children welcome overnight, extra bed (£10) & cot available. Check-in by arrangement. Closed 25 Dec.* MasterCard, **VISA**

RAVENSTONEDALE — Black Swan Inn — B&B

Tel 01539 623204   Fax 01539 623604   Map 5 D3
Ravenstonedale Kirkby Stephen Cumbria CA17 4NG

Zzz...

A ten-minute drive from J38 of M6 via A685 brings you into this peaceful village nestling on the edge of the Howgill fells, where, at its heart, is The Black Swan, a quiet little turn-of-the-century Lakeland stone hotel run since 1988 by Gordon and Norma Stuart. One of the stone-walled bar rooms is very much a locals' bar, while the other has a refined pub air with highly-polished, copper-topped tables and interesting guest beers. Three spacious, ground-floor bedrooms have particularly good disabled facilities (and ramp access into the bars), while the rest – "above stairs" – are comfortably furnished in traditional style with floral decor. Residents have use of a homely sitting room, with books and open fire, on the first floor. A new extension incorporating the adjacent former police house will be completed for 1997. Across the road is a delightful, sheltered garden with a small footbridge across the local beck. The local tennis court is available to residents and lake fishing is within a two-mile walk; their own river fishing requires the use of a car to reach it. *Open 12-3, 6-11 (Sun 12-3, 7-10.30), Mon-Sat all day in summer. Free House.* **Beer** Theakston Best, Younger's Scotch, Jennings Cumberland, three guest beers. Garden, lake and river fishing, tennis. **Accommodation** *16 bedrooms, all en suite, £70-£80 (single £45). Children welcome overnight, additional bed (£10) & cot available.* Amex, Diners, MasterCard, **VISA**

RAVENSTONEDALE — Fat Lamb — B&B

Tel 01539 623242   Fax 01539 623285   Map 5 D3
Crossbank Ravenstonedale Kirkby Stephen Cumbria CA17 4LL

Dramatic panoramic views soak in every changing mood of the surrounding fells and moorland at this remote but popular walking and touring base on the A683. Originally built in the 17th century as a farmhouse, Paul and Helen Bonsall's inn offers a warmth inside that contrasts vividly with its rather bleak open-countryside setting. The small, cosy main bar room leads through to a lounge that overlooks a rear patio and lawned garden edged by large ash trees; at the bottom of the lower field is a wetland nature reserve. Several bedrooms are conveniently on the ground floor, in former outhouses, with wheelchair access; all have neat, if compact, bathrooms and tea-making facilities but no TVs. Rooms in the original building have the best views; four family rooms sleep up to four. Nine miles from M6 J37 via Sedbergh, or take the A685 to Ravenstonedale (turn right at Newbiggin-on-Lune) from J38 and continue down the narrow, dry-stone-walled country lanes for two miles until the junction with A683. *Open 11-3, 6-11 (Sun 12-3, 6-11), also for coffees and teas.* **Beer** *Mitchell's Bitter. Patio, garden, children's sand pit. Family room.* **Accommodation** *12 bedrooms, all en suite, £56 (single £32). Children welcome overnight (under-6s stay free in parents' room, 6-12s £6), additional bed & cot provided. No credit cards.*

REDMILE   Peacock Inn   FOOD

Tel 01949 842554   Fax 01949 843746   Map 7 D3
Church Corner Redmile Nottinghamshire NG13 0GA

Turn off the A52 at the signs to Belvoir Castle to find Redmile deep in the flatlands. Its pub, the Peacock, was rescued from dereliction some seven years ago. The interior is a tribute to the skills of landlord Colin Crawford whose restoration of its old fireplaces and former ships' timbers is commendable, as is his work in enclosing the rear flagstoned patio to create a sky-lit Garden Room replete with wrought-iron tables and fanciful murals. Frank Garbez supervises a busy kitchen: from the interesting, daily-changing blackboard, crab mousse, pan-fried scallops and leeks, and salmon sautéed with mangetout with saffron sauce could precede such main courses as pan-fried red snapper on stir-fry vegetables and sun-dried tomato sauce or tuna loin on beef tomatoes and shallot compote with chive dressing, with crème brulée or profiteroles to follow. A la carte dishes – perhaps ragout of salmon, cod and prawn in langoustine bisque and loin of lamb with shiitake mushrooms and a rosemary and courgette crust – come in less-than-authentic French translations. Fixed-price menus (£12.95-£14.95) are also offered. A lighter snack menu features, among others, fresh pasta dishes, spicy mussels, spare ribs and filled baguettes. The atmosphere, however, remains one of the Crawfords' village local, for they were brought up here: their 'locals' in turn have much to be grateful for. Booking advble for both bar and restaurant. With such a regular and varied selection of fish, the Peacock Inn wins our 1997 Midlands/Heart of England region Seafood Pub of the Year award. *Open 11-11 (Sun 12-10.30).* **Bar Food** *12-2 (till 3 Sun & Bank Holidays), 6.30-10 (from 7 Sun). Free House.* **Beer** *Theakston Best, Timothy Taylor Landlord, Bass, Marston's Pedigree, guest beer. Garden, outdoor eating. Family room. Diners, MasterCard,* **VISA**

REETH   Buck Hotel   B&B

Tel 01748 884210   Fax 01748 884802   Map 5 D3
Reeth Richmond North Yorkshire DL11 6SW

☺

An imposing building standing at the head of this prettiest of Dales villages; the fascinating Swaledale Folk Museum is a short walk away across the green. The Buck scores highly with families for its separate games room, safe back garden, children's menus and choices of family accommodation. All ten bedrooms have TVs, tea trays and en suite facilities (two with shower only); the best have fabulous views of the surrounding hills. Afternoon teas. *Open 11-2, 6-11 (till 1am Fri, 11am-1am Sat except 11-3, 6-11 in winter), Sun 12-2, 7-10.30.* **Beer** *Theakston Best & XB, John Smith's, Black Sheep Bitter. Garden. Family room.* **Accommodation** *10 bedrooms, all en suite £49 (family room £55-£60, single £25). Children welcome overnight (under-12s stay free in parents' room), additional bed & cot available. MasterCard,* **VISA**

REMENHAM   Little Angel   FOOD

Tel 01491 574165   Fax 01491 411879   Map 15a D3
Remenham Henley-on-Thames Oxfordshire RG9 2LS

♀

Just over the bridge from Henley-on-Thames, on the Berkshire side of the river, the 17th-century Little Angel in Remenham (not to be confused with The Angel public house on the Henley side of the bridge) is very much an eating pub. Order from either the bar/brasserie menu or the restaurant list of dishes and relax in the pubby bar with its dark red ceilings, or continue through to the rear dining-rooms and conservatory restaurant with crisply-clothed tables. Alternatively, eat outside in the recently-landscaped garden and on summer weekends you get the added attraction of being able to watch the local cricketers, whose pitch is right next door. Dishes from the bar menu include grilled sardines, chicken, ham and leek pie and casserole of lamb with apricots and mint, while restaurant menu choices range from salmon and dill mousse and pheasant terrine to chargrilled medallions of beef with Madeira sauce. Sandwiches and ploughman's platters are served in the bar area. Accompany your meal with one of ten wines served by the glass. Smart young uniformed men and women provide efficient service. *Open 11-3, 6-11 (Sun 12-3, 7-10.30).* **Bar Food** *12-2.30, 7-10.* **Beer** *Brakspear Bitter & Special, two guest beers. Terrace, summer barbecue, outdoor eating. Amex, Diners, MasterCard,* **VISA**

RENNINGTON | Masons Arms | B&B

Tel 01665 577275   Fax 01665 577894   Map 5 D1
Rennington Alnwick Northumberland WE66 3RX

Zzz...

Just one and a half miles from the A1, the "Stamford Cot" (as it's known locally) stands in open country well back from the Northumbrian coastal resorts. There's a genuinely warm welcome here from Frank and Dee Sloan to their skilfully converted single-room bar, with open fires at each end, and cosy dining-room. Guests should be aware, however, that the pub does get very busy with quite an up-market crowd, so that some participation in the convivial atmosphere thus engendered is practically de rigueur. Main-house accommodation comprises one large suite with a double and single room, plus a lounge and en suite bathroom. Four smart and fully-equipped en suite (bath only) bedrooms are housed in former stables to the rear of the inn. A hearty Northumbrian breakfast is guaranteed, firmly setting up guests for a day's exploring. No children under 14 overnight or in the bar. No infants in the dining-room in the evening. *Open 12-2 6.30-11 (Sun 12-2.30, 7-10.30). Free House.* **Beer** *Courage Directors, Ruddles Best, Whitbread Castle Eden Ale. Patio. Family room.* **Accommodation** *5 bedrooms, all en suite, £47-£50 (single £38.50). MasterCard,* **VISA**

REYDON | The Cricketers | B&B

Tel 01502 723603   Fax 01502 722194   Map 10 D2
Wangford Road Reydon nr Southwold Suffolk IP18 6PZ

One mile from the centre of Southwold, the accommodation at The Cricketers is seemingly in a time-warp. However, this is its charm – only a few of the furnishings have been updated in recent years, but all is kept in good order by managers Teresa and Kevin Ellis, who have been managing this Adnams hotel since 1989. The B&B-style accommodation is sensibly priced (for the area) and particularly convenient for the coast, with two family bedrooms sleeping up to 4. The Back Bar remains a 'local', while the front bar is smartly decorated with warm yellow walls, cricketing memorabilia, pine tables and wicker chairs – a pleasant place for a drink. Generously-served, undyed, locally-smoked haddock and kippers for breakfast, but dishes on the blackboard bar menu don't always turn out as good as they sound. Also a pity is the fact that an Adnams house can only serve a couple of house wines by the glass; still, the beer's good (but it doesn't have far to travel!). *Open 11-2.30, 6-11 (Sat 10.30-3, 6-11, Sun 12-3, 6-10.30).* **Beer** *Adnams. Garden.* **Accommodation** *9 bedrooms, 8 en suite (1 with private facilities), £49 (family room £69, single £33). Children welcome overnight, additional bed (£6) & cot provided. No dogs. MasterCard,* **VISA**

RICKLING GREEN | Cricketers Arms | B&B

Tel 01799 543210   Fax 01799 543512   Map 10 B3
Rickling Green Saffron Walden Essex CB11 3YE

☺

Victorian redbrick-built pub enjoying a peaceful position overlooking the village green and cricket pitch. Inside there is a homely bar and lounge, a comfortable dining-room and a small and cosy side room which has access to the delightful front terrace – a popular spot in which to relax and watch an innings or two. People needing an overnight stop close to Stansted airport (ten minutes' drive away) will find the five comfortable bedrooms, housed in a modern rear extension, most convenient and acceptable. All are uniformly equipped with reproduction darkwood furniture, decent fabrics and have clean, tiled en suite shower rooms. Added comforts include TVs, radio alarms, telephones, trouser presses, hairdryers and tea-makers. Two family rooms with additional beds. *Open 12-3, 6-11 (Sun 12-3, 7-10.30). Free House.* **Beer** *Flowers IPA, guest beers. Patio. Family room.* **Accommodation** *7 bedrooms, all en suite, from £60 (single £50), family room £70 (sleeps 3-5). Children welcome overnight (1st child under 16 free in parents' room, each additional child £5), additional bed & cot available. Amex, Diners, MasterCard,* **VISA**

RINGLESTONE   Ringlestone Inn   FOOD

Tel 01622 859900   Fax 01622 859966   Map 11 C5
Ringlestone Harrietsham Wormshill Kent ME17 1NX

Splendidly atmospheric 16th-century inn, remotely tucked away beside the Pilgrim's Way on top of the North Downs between Harrietsham and Wormshill. An ale house since 1615, its three charming inter-connecting bars boast brick-and-flint walls and floors, low-beamed ceilings, a huge inglenook with winter woodburner and a good assortment of rustic furniture, including carved settles and a magnificent 17th-century oak dresser with the inscription 'A Ryght Joyouse and welcome greetynge to ye all' etched into it. This still rings true today with visitors attracted by the range of ales drawn straight from the cask, local scrumpy ciders, the selection of 28 strong country wines served by the glass and the reliable bar food on offer. Lunchtime fare is help-yourself buffet-style with a choice of casseroles, curries and pies, or a range of salads, ploughman's platters and sandwiches. Arrive early for the best of the food and to avoid the queues that form around the cramped servery! Evening fare is more formal within the candle-lit bars and adjacent dining-room, with the home-made pies – turkey, bacon and walnut, rabbit and gooseberry, lamb and apricot – being the highlight of the printed menu. Puddings include rich chocolate, plum and elderberry trifle. Delightfully peaceful summer patio and garden. Cream teas 3-6pm in summer. Children welcome. *Open 12-3, 6-11 (from 6.30 in winter, except Sat), Sun 12-3, 7-10.30.* **Bar Food** *12-2, 7-9.30. Free House.* **Beer** *Harveys Sussex, Tetley, Shepherd Neame Spitfire, Fuller's London Pride, Theakston Best & Old Peculier, Young's Bitter, regular guest beers. Garden, outdoor eating. Closed 25 Dec. Amex, Diners, MasterCard,* **VISA**

RIPLEY   Boar's Head Hotel   FOOD   B&B

Tel 01423 771888   Fax 01423 771509   Map 6 C1
Ripley Harrogate North Yorkshire HG53 3AY

Zzz..

Dating back to 1830 when the Lord of the Manor rebuilt the village next to his castle (open to the public during the summer), this former coaching inn in the cobbled village square was refurbished by the present Lord (Sir Thomas Ingilby) some five years ago and turned into a hotel. Oil paintings and furniture from the castle help to create the country-house feel in tranquil drawing and morning rooms and the individually decorated bedrooms (five non-smoking), which favour plain walls and stylish matching fabrics. Antique furniture features in rooms in the main building and in the larger rooms in another house across the cobbled square, while those in the former stable block are furnished with white-painted wicker pieces. As well as a warm red decorated dining-room serving various set menus, there is a pubby bar/bistro offering good snacks (which we specifically recommend here): mushroom stroganoff, venison sausages and mash, fresh pasta dishes, daily fish specials (red snapper, tilapia), sandwiches and ploughman's (lunch only), and puddings like chocolate torte and fresh fruit terrine. Accompany your meal with a bottle of wine from the excellent and kindly-priced list. Tea is served from 4 to 5pm in the two lounges – home-made sponges, fruit cakes, scones and sandwiches. Residents have complimentary access to Ripley Castle Estate. *Open 11-3, 6-11 (summer 11-11), Sun 11-3, 7-10.30 (summer 11-10.30).* **Bar Food** *12-2.30, 6.30-10 (Sun 7-9.30). Free House.* **Beer** *Theakston Best & Old Peculier, three guest beers. Courtyard, garden, outdoor eating, tennis, coarse fishing.* **Accommodation** *25 rooms, all en suite, £90/£105 (single £75/£95). Children welcome overnight (under-3s free, 3-12s £20 if sharing parents' room), additional bed & cot available. Garden, tennis, coarse fishing. Amex, Diners, MasterCard,* **VISA**

RIPPONDEN   Old Bridge Inn   A

Tel 01422 822595   Fax 01422 824810   Map 6 C1
Priest Lane Ripponden Sowerby Bridge Calderdale HX6 4DF

Ancient pub (dating back to 1313) with medieval character, enormously thick stone walls and some nice old furniture in its three connecting bars. Probably originally a 14th-century monastic guest house. The modern world intrudes little into the finished interior which has remained delightfully unspoilt for the past 33 years, since Ian Hargreaves-Beaumont arrived here. No machines, music or pool table, and pump clips are only tolerated for guest beers. There isn't even an inn sign. Children not allowed indoors. No garden, but tables and chairs are set on the cobbled frontage. *Open 12-3, 5.30-11 (Sat 12-11, Sun 12-10.30). Free House. Beer Black Sheep Special, Timothy Taylor's Best & Golden Best, Ryburn Bitter, guest beer. MasterCard,* **VISA**

ROCHDALE   Egerton Arms   A

Tel 01706 46183   Fax 01706 715343   Map 6 B1
Ashworthy Road Bamford Rochdale Lancashire OL11 5UP

☺

Positioned high on the moor above Rochdale, and known locally as the Chapel House as it stands next to St James's chapel, this 500-year-old inn is reputedly haunted by a friendly ghost called Margaret, who was killed on the chapel steps during the Reformation. Turn onto the Ashworth road off the Bury and Heywood Road (A680) by the Ashworth reservoir. Family dining forms an integral part of the set-up. *Open 12-3, 6-11 (till 10.30 Sun). Free House. Beer Ruddles Best & County, Webster's Yorkshire, guest beer. Patio. Closed 26 Dec. MasterCard,* **VISA**

ROCKBEARE   Jack in the Green   ★   FOOD

Tel 01404 822240   Map 13 E2
Rockbeare Exeter Devon EX5 2EE

A few years ago even the most weary of A30 travellers would not have given this roadside inn a second glance. Nowadays, rather than accelerating away, the brake should be applied, ready for the turning into the car park of what has become a most welcoming refreshment stop. Enthusiastic owners Paul Parnell and Charles Manktelow (and credit must also go to chef Matthew Mason, ex-*Gidleigh Park* hotel) run this white-painted roadside pub, one of the best eating establishments along this popular route to and from Devon. The smart exterior is bedecked with attractive flower tubs and baskets, while inside the open-plan bar and dining areas have neatly arranged darkwood furniture, church pews a carved oak dresser and an open fire warms the main, recently extended dining area. Choosing from the excellent-value set (but regularly-changing) menu, an imaginative and well-presented meal may begin with chicken and fresh asparagus terrine or tomato, orange and coriander soup, followed by roast guinea fowl with garlic, lentils and smoked bacon and sea bass with stir-fried vegetables, soy and ginger. Those travellers popping in for a quick, lighter bite will not be disappointed by the interesting range of generously-served bar meals. Blackboards list the choice, including a whole menu board of eleven ploughman's platters alone, while other daily chalked-up menus may offer spicy pork and prawn jambalaya, quail pasties with redcurrant sauce and salmon and dill fishcakes with lemon mayonnaise. Delicious desserts like cappuccino chocolate mousse and caramelised lemon and banana tart. Good-value set Sunday lunch. A carefully-chosen selection of over 80 wines includes wines of the month, a range of half-bottles and a menu of twelve wines served by the glass. Alfresco imbibers wishing to escape the traffic noise can relax in the sheltered rear courtyard or retreat to the splendid orchard garden and its open rural views. Well-behaved children welcome; those with larger appetites in the evening!. Disabled WC. Five miles from Junction 29 of the M5. *Open 11-2.30 (till 3 Fri & Sat), 6-11 (from 5.30 Fri), Sun 12-3, 7-10.30. Bar Food 12-2 (till 2.30 Fri, Sat & Sun), 6.30-9.30 (till 10 Fri & Sat, from 7 Sun). Free House. Beer Bass, three regularly-changing South West guest ales. Patio, garden, outdoor eating. Closed all 25, 26 & 27 Dec. MasterCard,* **VISA**

ROCKBOURNE   Rose & Thistle   FOOD

Tel 01725 518236   Map 14 C3
Rockbourne Fordingbridge Hampshire SP6 3NL

Originally two 17th-century thatched cottages, this delightful, long and low whitewashed pub enjoys a most tranquil location within one of Hampshire's most picturesque and affluent downland villages. Country-style fabrics, dried flowers and magazines are tasteful touches in the charming, beamed bars which boast a collection of polished-oak tables, carved settles and benches and two huge fireplaces with winter log fires. Quality pub food, served in the civilised, music-free lounge/dining area, is light and simple at lunchtimes, including a daily home-made soup, tagliatelle carbonara, rabbit casserole, chicken and mushroom pie and ploughman's platters. Evening fare is more elaborate: a monthly-changing menu and a daily specials board that might feature smoked duck breast and nut salad and king prawns to start, followed by quail en croute with an apricot and brandy sauce or pan-fried sea bass with peppers, celery and lemon butter. Mainly home-made puddings such as sticky toffee pudding and chocolate roulade. Traditional roast and many other options at Sunday lunchtime (booking advised). Children allowed only in the 30-seater dining-room. *Open 11-3, 6-11 (Sun 12-3, 7-10.30).* **Bar Food** *12-2.30, 7-9.30 (no food Sun eve in winter). Free House.* **Beer** *Courage Best, Marston's Pedigree, Wadworth 6X, guest beer. Garden, outdoor eating. MasterCard,* **VISA**

ROKE   Home Sweet Home Inn   FOOD

Tel 01491 838249   Map 14a C3
Roke Benson Oxfordshire OX9 6JD

A row of low, stone white-painted former cottages (just off the B4009) well befits its homely title and image as a gentrified country pub. The pretty, walled garden in front has picnic tables and a pantiled wishing well. Popular lunchtime snacks are most notable for their number, with a vast selection of 30 sandwiches offered – from crab and cucumber to smoked salmon and cream cheese club-style – and 40 more variations on salad and baked-potato themes. Cooked lunches selected from the blackboards may well include calves liver and bacon with mushroom and onion sauce, salmon fishcakes with parsley sauce, steak and kidney pudding, garlic and herb chicken breast and a separate vegetarian menu (mushroom and cashew nut stroganoff, spicy vegetable curry). A more extended menu selection in the evening, served in either the bar or a prettily-appointed dining-room, engages further flights of fancy based around grilled steaks and exotic fish dishes. Children welcome. *Open 11-3, 5.30-11 (Sun 12-3, 7-10.30).* **Bar Food** *12-2, 5.30-9.30 (till 10 Fri & Sat, from 7 Sun). Free House.* **Beer** *Brakspear Bitter, Eldridge Pope Royal Oak. Garden. MasterCard,* **VISA**

ROMALDKIRK   Rose & Crown   ★   FOOD

Tel 01833 650213   Fax 01833 650828   Map 5 D3   B&B
Romaldkirk Barnard Castle Co Durham DL12 9EB

 Zzz...

Built in 1733 as a coaching inn, the stone-built Rose and Crown nestles beside the church and green in an unspoilt Teesdale village. Since arriving here in 1989, Christopher and Alison Davy's welcoming inn has gone from strength to strength; Christopher's consistent cooking attracting a discerning dining clientele, with his restaurant now firmly established as an entry in our *1997 Hotels and Restaurants Guide*. Both at lunchtime and in the evenings meals served in the elegant lounge bar and Crown Room are not, however, overlooked to any degree. Traditional favourites, from steak, kidney, mushroom and Old Peculier pie to fresh pasta baked with Cotherstone cheese in fresh tomato sauce are always cooked with flair; colourful presentation, with coleslaw and marinated mushrooms, turns a humble brown bread bap into a memorable repast: roast ham with mustard and lettuce constitutes a typical filling. Best value of all, though, are the daily lunch specials which are rightly used as the showcase for a kitchen which is never slow to experiment and always actively evolving new dishes. Parfait of goose livers with port and orange sauce is a fine starter to salmon and chive fishcakes, sautéed wood pigeon with juniper and onion confit or rabbit with grain mustard sauce. Exemplary puds, typified by hot apple and calvados tart and stem ginger ice cream with rhubarb compote, and perfectly-selected local cheeses (Cotherstone, Blue Wensleydale) make for a difficult choice of 'afters'. Creaking floorboards, beams, stripped stone walls, well-chosen antique furniture and contemporary fabrics feature in the en suite bedrooms (all, except one, having bath and showers) and duvets can be swapped for sheets and blankets. Front rooms enjoy lovely views over the village green. Five further rooms (three recently completely refurbished), across the courtyard, are more uniform in size and design. *Open 11-30-3, 5.30-11 (Sun 12-3, 7-10.30). Bar Food 12-1.30, 6.30-9.30 (7-9 Sun). Free House. Beer Theakston Best & Old Peculier, Marston's Pedigree, Morland Old Speckled Hen. Accommodation 12 bedrooms, all en suite, £78 (single £56). Children welcome overnight (under-3s free if sharing), additional bed (£12) available. Accommodation closed 25 & 26 Dec. MasterCard, VISA*

ROOKLEY — Chequers Inn — FOOD

Tel 01983 840314
Niton Road Rookley Isle of Wight PO38 3NZ

Map 15 D4

☺

Sue and Richard Holmes are the houseproud owners of this family-friendly pub just a mile off the A3020 at Rookley (take the road signed to Niton). Nestling in a shallow dell looking out over the rolling downlands, the pub makes a feature of its garden with lots of picnic tables from which parents can watch over their little ones enjoying the playhouse, toboggan run and bouncy castle; pony rides, too, in fine weather. Just outside the family room there's a ball pool and soft-shape gym, while inside are high-chairs, bibs and colouring sets in abundance, a purpose-built Lego table and, close by, a well-kept nappy-changing facility. Children's menus are a little more varied than most, with potato skins or prawn cocktail followed by 4oz steak with mushrooms and tomato for youngsters and loads of things such as bacon, onions, more mushrooms and hot chili sauce to pile on top of their burgers. There are voluminous bar snacks, grills, fish specials and à la carte main courses to keep the adults amused; beef stroganoff, casseroled game pie and salmon with puff pastry arrive with plentiful fresh vegetables. Those not travelling en famille need not despair as they have use of a youngster-free lounge bar in which to enjoy the views in relative peace, with one of five real ales to accompany their meal, or a choice from a modestly-priced wine list. *Open 11-11 (Sun 12-10.30). Bar Food 12-10 (till 9.30 Sun). Free House. Beer John Smith's Bitter, Courage Best & Directors, Fuller's London Pride, Morland Old Speckled Hen. Garden, outdoor eating, children's play areas. Family room. MasterCard, VISA*

ROSEDALE ABBEY — Milburn Arms — FOOD

Tel & Fax 01751 417312
Rosedale Abbey Pickering North Yorkshire YO18 8RA

Map 5 E3   **B&B**

◇ 🍽 🍺 🛏 Zzz...

Tranquil surroundings in the beautiful North Yorkshire moors are the big attraction of Terry and Joan Bentley's delightful country hotel which has parts dating back to the 1700s. It is very much the village pub; its spacious low beamed bar has a good pubby atmosphere, complete with games, hand-pulled ales and warming winter log fire. But it's the extensive range of bar meals that is the big attraction; goat's cheese with red onion marmalade, smoked salmon with dill mayonnaise, breast of chicken with mushrooms and tarragon, rib of pork with apples and cider, supreme of salmon with herb butter, mulled fruit brulée and banana bread-and-butter pudding demonstrate the range. Choose from seven wines available by the glass. Bedrooms are individually decorated in a variety of styles – rich reds and blues, pale pink and yellow, pastel seersucker fabric – and furnished with a mixture of pine, freestanding darkwood and hotel unit-style furniture. All have good bathrooms (with showers over tubs) plus TV, direct-dial phone and beverage kit. A good spot in summer is the peaceful garden, opposite the village green, with tables set out under a splendid 150-year-old cedar tree. *Open 12-3, 6-30-11 (Sun 12-3, 7-10.30). Bar Food 12-2, 7-9.30. Free House. Beer Bass, Stones, Black Sheep Bitter, Special & Riggwelter, guest beer. Garden, outdoor eating. Accommodation 11 bedrooms, all en suite, £68-£74 (single £41.50-£44.50). Children welcome overnight (under-5s £6.50, 5-12s £10, over-12s £15 if sharing parents' room) additional bed & cot available. Dogs welcome in ground-floor annexe rooms only. Accommodation closed 25 & 26 Dec. Diners, MasterCard, VISA*

ROSEDALE ABBEY   White Horse Farm Hotel   FOOD

Tel 01751 417239   Fax 01751 417781   Map 5 E3   **B&B**
Rosedale Abbey Pickering North Yorkshire YO18 8SE

Zzz...

The White Horse was a farm when Rosedale Abbey was a thriving mining village with a population ten times greater than it is now. As was then the practice, one end of the farmhouse was turned into a 'taps room' for the miners and its transformation into today's hotel had begun. The bar is full of interest with a couple of rough-hewn tree trunks acting as poles holding up the ceiling beams, stuffed birds, a fish in a glass case, horse harness and much more besides decorating the walls, some of which are of rough, exposed stone. Yorkshire fare features strongly on the bar menu: Yorkshire pudding with roast beef and onion gravy, Ryedale mushrooms stuffed with cream cheese, Barnsley lamb chop with honey glaze along with pork and apple casserole and breast of chicken wrapped in bacon with cider sauce. There are also various sandwiches, ploughman's platters and a short list of puds. New chef since last year's Guide. Bedrooms, including two de luxe rooms with separate sitting areas, are prettily decorated with matching floral bedcovers (no duvets here), curtains and dado band around the woodchip walls. Even the en suite bathrooms, half with showers and half with tubs, co-ordinate with their respective bedrooms. All rooms have TV and tea- and coffee-making equipment and some have wonderful views across Rosedale. No children in the bar areas after 8.30pm. Take the A170 out of Pickering going north; after approximately three miles turn right – follow signs to Rosedale for seven miles and the pub is clearly signposted from the village. *Open 12-2.30, 6.30-11 (Sat 12-11, Sun 12-3, 6.30-10.30). Bar Food 12-2 (till 2.30 Sat & Sun) 6.30-9.30 (till 9 Sun). Free House. Beer Tetley Traditional, Theakston Best & XB, guest beers. Garden, outdoor eating. Family room. Accommodation 15 bedrooms, all en suite, £68-£80 (single £35) – winter reductions. Children welcome overnight (under-5s £5, 5-14s half price if sharing parents' room). additional bed & cot available. Accommodation closed 24 & 25 Dec. Amex, Diners, MasterCard, VISA*

ROWDE   George & Dragon   ★   FOOD

Tel 01380 723053   Fax 01380 724738   Map 14 B3
High Street Rowde Wiltshire SN10 2PN

Inspired, inventive and realistically-priced cooking emanates from the kitchen of Tim and Helen Withers' village pub leased from Wadworth's brewery. A single bar has half a dozen Britannia tables and there are two dozen assorted bentwood chairs in the dining-room set at plain, unclothed tables. Everywhere are blackboards proclaiming what's on offer, the emphasis firmly being on fresh fish from Cornwall. Dishes run from imaginative ploughman's platters, mussel and oyster soup or home-cured salt beef and sweet pimento chutney to well-presented main-course dishes such as wild rabbit risotto, grilled rib of beef and garlic butter, cheese soufflé baked with parmesan and cream and excellent fish choices such as halibut with crab sauce, wild Irish sea trout with hollandaise, and red mullet with cucumber and mustard. A set lunch menu offers alternatives only at each course. Puddings may feature blackcurrant meringue pie and plum and armagnac tart. Out of 60 names on the wine list a commendable 13 are available by the glass and the pub's 'English-only' policy is extended to the mineral water and cheeses, of which Stilton, Allerdale, Sharpham and Cotherstone are a typical selection. Booking is always advised, at least one week in advance for tables at weekends; further seating is available in the walled garden during good weather. *Open 12-3, 7-11. Closed all Sun & Mon, 25, 26 Dec & 1 Jan. Bar Food 12-2, 7-10 Tue-Sat only. Beer Wadworth 6X & IPA. Garden, outdoor eating. MasterCard, VISA*

Many **B&B** establishments offer reduced rates for weekend and out-of-season bookings. Always ask about special deals for longer stays. Beware half-board terms in inns where we do not recommend the **FOOD**.

RUDGE · Full Moon · B&B

Tel 01373 830936   Fax 01373 831366   Map 14 B3
Rudge Frome Somerset BA11 2QF

Conveniently located two miles from the A36 at its junction with the A361 (and equally close to the Woodland Park) is the sleepy hamlet of Rudge. It has a white-painted village inn of 16th-century origins whose interior has been meticulously restored; there's a wealth of interior stonework, old fireplaces and uneven flagstone floors in a succession of intimate nooks and alcoves; the focal point is a friendly locals' bar. All manner of local history and memorabilia provides the starting point for a tall story or two. An extension which threatens to dwarf the original has its ground floor given over to a function room. Above are the five en suite bedrooms (four with shower only), purpose-built and a little cottagey in style. All are neatly equipped with TV, direct-dial phone, radio-alarm and tea- and coffee-making facility; there's one decent-sized family room. To the pub's rear the walled garden is neatly kept and has some swings; from here, as from the bedrooms, there are lovely rural views down to Broker's Wood. *Open 12-3, 6-11 (Sun 12-10.30). Free House.* **Beer** *Bass, Wadworth 6X, Butcombe Bitter. Garden, children's play area. Family room.* **Accommodation** *5 bedrooms, all en suite, £45 (family room £60, single £35). Children welcome overnight (under-5s stay free in parents' room), additional bed (£10) & cot available. Amex, MasterCard,* **VISA**

RUNNING WATERS · Three Horseshoes Inn · B&B

Tel & Fax 01913 720286   Map 5 E3
Sherburn House Running Waters Durham Co Durham DH1 2SR

With fine views over open country and north-west towards Durham (4 miles), the 'Shoes' stands by the busy A181, fronted by old ploughshares and farming implements; the Running Waters of its location reflects olden times when water was carried from its underground stream by the monks of nearby Sherburn House. While none of the recently refurbished bedrooms are particularly spacious, they all have en suite facilities (two with shower-trays only), TV, tea-maker and radio-alarm, and are decorated in a bright, cottagey style. There's a small residents' lounge area and a fenced-in rear garden; front double-glazing ensures that the morning traffic will not become intrusive. *Open 11.30-2.30, 6.30-11 (Sun 12-3, 7-10.30). Free House.* **Beer** *Ruddles Best, Marston's Pedigree, guest beer. Garden.* **Accommodation** *6 bedrooms, all en suite £46 (single £35). Children welcome overnight (under-6s stay free in parents' room), additional bed & cot available. Diners, MasterCard,* **VISA**

RUSPER · Star Inn · A

Tel 01293 871264   Map 11 A5
High Street Rusper West Sussex RH12 4RA

4 miles west of Crawley, close to the A24 and just south of the Sussex/Surrey border, the Star is close (but not particularly convenient for) Gatwick Airport. A heavily-beamed, traditional old coaching inn dating back to 1460. The menu stays sensibly short and game dishes feature in season. Landlord Derek Welton has been running the Star in his own inimitable style for 13 years. Whitbread Wayside Inns. *Open 11-11 (Sun 12-10.30).* **Beer** *Fremlins, Brakspear Bitter, Marston's Pedigree, Morland Old Speckled Hen. Garden. Family room, MasterCard,* **VISA**

SADDLEWORTH · Green Ash Hotel · B&B

Tel 01457 871035   Fax 01457 871414   Map 6 C2
Denshaw Road Delph Saddleworth Oldham OL3 5TS

Zzz...

Just over a decade ago, one man saw this burned-out Co-Op warehouse and barn as an unrivalled investment opportunity; today, Terry Ogden's civilised country inn is the realisation of that dream. Rebuilt and extended entirely in handsome Derbyshire stone, it stands proud on the A640 above Delph village enfolded by the woody moors. Each of the bedrooms enjoys a share of the view; they possess in common a high degree of comfort and practical up-to-date accoutrements with satellite TV, radio alarms, hairdryers, tea-making facilities, direct-dial phones and trouser presses. Included in executive standard rooms are mini-bars; all bathrooms are bright, fully-tiled and have over-bath showers. This is decidedly more inn than pub; there's Tetley bitter on handpump to enjoy in the bar or on the scenic, sun-trapped patio. Small well-trained" dogs in rooms only. No under10s in the bar Mon-Sat evenings Nearest motorway Junctions: 21 & 22 of M6=2. *Open 11-3, 5-11 (Sun 12-10.30). Free House.* **Beer** *Tetley, guest beer. Garden.* **Accommodation** *15 bedrooms, all en suite, £52/62= weekends room only £39.50 (single £39.50 = weekends room only £20). Children welcome overnight (under=2s stay free in parents' room, 3-9s £5), additional bed & cot available.* Amex, MasterCard, **VISA**

SAFFRON WALDEN   Eight Bells   FOOD

Tel 01799 522790   Map 10 B3
18 Bridge Street Saffron Walden Essex CB10 1BU

A solidly traditional pub whose bar is partitioned by ancient wall timbers into two smaller rooms, complete with old furniture and exposed timbers and brick. The old barn restaurant has been extended to include a central gallery and the walls are hung with tapestries and flags. The bar and restaurant menus offer reliably good food: ploughman's lunches, home-made soup (broccoli and Stilton), salmon with white wine and mushroom sauce, whole plaice or lemon sole, prawn thermidor, half guinea fowl with ham, mushrooms and red wine, and chicken stuffed with prawns and a saffron sauce; chocolate and brandy pot or raspberry and walnut pavlova for pudding. *Open 11-3, 6-11 (Sun 12-10.30).* **Bar Food** *12-2.30, 6.00-9.30 (till 10 Sat), Sun 12-9.30. Free House.* **Beer** *Adnams Southwold, Ind Coope Burton Ale, Friary Meux, Tetley, guest beer. Garden, outdoor eating. Family room.* Amex, MasterCard **VISA**

SAFFRON WALDEN   Saffron Hotel   FOOD   B&B

Tel 01799 522676   Fax 01799 513979   Map 10 B3
High Street Saffron Walden Essex CB10 1AY

Formerly a coaching inn with origins in the 16th century, the Saffron Hotel is more hotel than pub today but the green plush bar still welcomes all and offers real ale and bar snacks. The printed bar menu includes steak and kidney pie, gammon steak and pineapple, baked cod fillet and tagliatelle provençale, as well as baguettes and baked potatoes with different fillings. The blackboard menu changes daily – leek and potato soup, pan-fried lamb's liver and bacon, chargrilled lamb cutlet with mint gravy. Bedrooms come in all shapes and sizes, some with head-threatening beams. The best and largest have been refurbished with stylish fabrics and smart new veneered furniture, the worst are cramped singles that share a shower room. All have direct-dial telephone, beverage-making facilities and TV. Children welcome. *Open 11-2.30, 6-11 (summer 11-11), Sun 12-3, 7-10.30.* **Bar Food** *12-2, 7-9 (till 9.30 Fri & Sat). Free House.* **Beer** *Flowers IPA, Adnams Southwold, Marston's Pedigree, Greene King IPA. Terrace, outdoor eating.* **Accommodation** *17 bedrooms, all en suite, £65 (four-poster £85, single £45/£50). Children welcome overnight (0-3s stay free in parents' room), additional bed (£10) & cot available.* Amex, Diners, MasterCard, **VISA**

> We only recommend food (Bar Food) in those establishments highlighted
> with the **FOOD** symbol.

ST AGNES   Driftwood Spars Hotel   B&B

Tel & Fax 01872 552428   Map 12 B3
Trevaunance Cove St Agnes Cornwall TR5 0RT

Constructed in the 17th century of huge ship's timbers and spars (hence the name), with stone and slate, the hotel – once a marine chandlery and tin miners trading post – is located just 100 yards from one of Cornwall's best beaches, making it an ideal family destination for a holiday. Accommodation comprises nine neat and tidy en suite rooms – one family room with bunk beds – featuring attractive co-ordinating fabrics, and a mix of furnishings that ranges from comfortable new pine to modern-style white furniture. Rooms are well equipped with direct-dial phones, TVs, hairdryers and tea-makers and two afford peaceful sea views. Guests are treated to the sound of waves on the beach and live music on Fridays and Saturdays. *Open 11-11 (Sun 12-10.30). Free House. Beer St Austell HSD, Sharp's Doom Bar, Tetley, Ind Coope Burton Ale, Bass, guest beer. Garden, patio. Family room. Accommodation 9 bedrooms, all en suite, £54-£58 (single £38-£40). Children welcome overnight (under-4s stay free, 4-13s half price if sharing parents' room), cot available. Dogs (£1.50). Accommodation closed 25 Dec. Amex, Diners, MasterCard, VISA*

ST ALBANS   Rose & Crown   A

Tel 01727 851903   Map 15a F2
St Michael's Street St Albans Hertfordshire AL3 4SG

This is a pleasingly simple, woody and traditional 300-year-old pub located in the upmarket St Michael's 'village' suburb of the town, close to Verulamium Park and the Roman Museum. Classic public bar with heavy beams, huge fireplace, sturdy furnishings and a chatty atmosphere free from intrusive music and games. Simple, unadorned and comfortable lounge bar and flower-decked side patio for fine weather imbibing. Renowned locally for its imaginative and unusual range of American-style 'gourmet' sandwiches available at lunchtimes. Live folk and blues music on Mondays, barbershop singing and quiz nights. Children welcome. *Open 11.30-3, 5.30-11 (from 6 Sat), Sun 12-3, 7-10.30. Beer Adnams Southwold, Tetley, Wadworth 6X, Greenalls Original, guest beer. Garden. No credit cards.*

ST AUSTELL   White Hart   B&B

Tel 01726 72100   Fax 01726 74705   Map 12 B3
Church Street St Austell Cornwall PL25 4AT

Attractive and comfortable accommodation is offered in this three-storey town-centre hotel, dating from the 16th century and located opposite the church. All the well-looked-after bedrooms have smart darkwood furniture, quality floral fabrics, pink and plum decor and the usual comforts of satellite TV, telephones, tea-making facilities and hairdryers. Modern carpeted bathrooms (two with shower only) are spacious, fully-tiled and clean. Public areas include the well-furnished Admirals Bar and the more pubby Captains Bar, complete with pool tables, darts and other games. Decent prints decorate the walls throughout the inn. Afternoon cream teas are served. Note: nearby parking is difficult. *Open 11-11 (Sun 12-3, 7-10.30). Beer St Austell. Accommodation 18 bedrooms, all en suite, £63 (single £40). Children welcome overnight (under-12s stay free in parents' room), additional bed & cot available. Closed 25 & 26 Dec Amex, Diners, MasterCard, VISA*

ST BRIAVELS   George Inn   B&B

Tel 01594 530228   Fax 01594 530260   Map 14 B2
High Street St Briavels Lydney Gloucestershire GL15 6SP

A moody old part-medieval pub whose sombre stonework and blackened beams yet create intimate nooks and crannies warmed by real log fires in winter, with one of the bars featuring a fascinating 10th-century Celtic coffin lid. In full view of the ruined medieval St Briavels castle, rooks and royalty joust on an inlaid patio chessboard. Modest yet comfortable accommodation provided in four en suite bedrooms (two with WC/showers only) is housed under the eaves with an outlook either up the village street or down over the castle, which like the inn is reputed to be haunted. Choice of 25 malt whiskies at the bar. No under-5s in bar areas. *Open 11-3, 6.30-11 (Sun 12-2.30, 7-10.30). Free House. Beer Wadworth 6X, Marston's Pedigree, Wye Valley Hereford Pale Ale, guest beer. Patio, Family room. Accommodation 4 bedrooms, all en suite, £40-£50 (single £25). Children welcome overnight (under 5s stay free in parents' room), additional bed (£20). Check-in bar hours only. No credit cards.*

ST KEW   St Kew Inn   A

Tel 01208 841259   Map 12 B3
St Kew Wadebridge Cornwall PL30 3HB

Well off the beaten track, amid tiny lanes in a small hamlet in a splendid wooded
valley, the 16th-century St Kew Inn is a peaceful spot in which to savour a relaxing
summer drink in the large attractive garden, which looks towards the parish church.
Inside, the atmospheric main bar has a slate floor laid with high-backed settles and
Windsor chairs; a popular window seat overlooks the cobbled courtyard, resplendent
with summer flower tubs and baskets. A fine black-painted kitchen range burns logs
and warms this bar in winter, old meat hooks hang from the ceiling and generally
a good chatty atmosphere prevails. There is a further stone-walled bar and a small
dining-room. Local ales are served in the traditional way, straight from the barrel.
Open 11-2.30, 6-11 (Sun 12-2.30, 7-10.30). **Beer** *St Austell. Streamside garden,*
Family room. MasterCard, **VISA**

ST MARGARET'S-AT-CLIFFE   Cliffe Tavern   FOOD

Tel & Fax 01304 852400   Map 11 D5
High Street St Margaret's-at-Cliffe Dover Kent CT15 6AT

Long a favourite for its particular charm, the Cliffe Tavern is a series of attractive
17th-century Kentish clapboard buildings with a pretty-walled rose garden, located
opposite the Norman church in the heart of the village. Since taking over in 1994
Malcom and Lucie Walker have undertaken the long and painstaking task of
upgrading the property. Progress was curbed in 1995 when a fire and flood threatened
their existence, but work on the tall, three-storey main building is well underway and
houses the friendly public bar, the comfortable lounge bar and adjacent 'romantic'
dining-room. The latter are tastefully decorated in pastel greens with colour-washed
beams and brickwork, relaxing sofas, leather armchairs, fresh and silk flowers and, in a
intimate dining area, a candelabra hangs above a long, candle-topped table (ideal for
larger 'house' parties) and white material swags the window. Lucie is in charge of the
kitchen and her good home-cooked food complements the surroundings, with short
menus listing the day's dishes. Chalked up on the lunchtime board may be local
lobster and prawn salad, Toulouse sausages with red onion jam and mash, penne
carbonara, salad niçoise, grilled fresh sardines, home-made fish soup, beef curry and
'big' baguettes (melted Brie and tomato or ham and mustard). More imaginative
dishes grace the evening menu, typically kipper paté with brioche to start, followed
by chargrilled rib-eye steak with mushroom and shallot sauce, Italian chicken with
spinach, mozzarella, cream and tarragon or roast duck with citrus sauce; all are served
with commendable vegetables. Delicious puddings range from French lemon tart
and summer pudding to chocolate rum slice. Malcolm controls proceedings behind
the bar where he offers five well-kept real ales and a good list of wines; he escapes
on Wednesday evenings to entertain customers with his exceptional jazz band.
Accommodation is provided in twelve simply-furnished, en suite bedrooms, but the
on-going revamp by the enthusiastic landlords should see much-needed upgrading
and refurbishing completed in the coming year. *Open 11-3, 6-11 (Sun 12-4, 7-10.30).*
Bar Food *12-2.30, 7-9.30 (till 10 Fri & Sat). Bar snacks only Mon & Tue Nov-Apr.*
Beer *Shepherd Neame Master Brew, Spitfire & Bishops' Finger, Adnams Extra, guest beer.*
Garden, outdoor eating. Amex, Diners, MasterCard, **VISA**

ST MAWES   Rising Sun   B&B

Tel 01326 270233   Map 12 B4
The Square St Mawes Cornwall TR2 5DJ
Zzz...

Occupying a splendid position overlooking the quaint harbour and its 19th-century
quay, this popular and lively blue- and white-painted hotel/inn underwent total
refurbishment during the winter of 1995/96. The busy 'locals' bar has a good pubby
atmosphere and is a favourite among the gig rowers. More refined is the attractive
front conservatory which houses the lounge bar and has access to the harbour-view
terrace that attracts the crowds when the sun shines. Upstairs, smaller bedrooms have
been amalgamated and all now have smart, wicker-featured furniture and stylish

colour schemes. Bathrooms have been given something of a traditional Cornish feel with white-painted, boarded walls except where tiled around the bathtubs, all of which have showers above. Front rooms enjoy peaceful harbour and headland vistas. At the time of inspection finishing touches were being given to the public areas and a new brasserie (Anthony's), complete with new kitchen brigade, about to be opened. *Open 11-11 (Sun 12-10.30), winter 11-2.30, 6-11, Sun 12-3, 7-10.30.* **Beer** *St Austell. Terrace.* **Accommodation** *9 bedrooms, all en suite, £89 (single £45-£55). Children welcome overnight (under-10s stay free in parents' room), additional bed & cot available. Amex, MasterCard,* **VISA**

St Mawgan — Falcon Inn — A

Tel 01637 860225   Map 12 B3
St Mawgan Newquay Cornwall TR8 4EP

In the heart of the holiday land where good unspoilt traditional pubs are an endangered breed, the Falcon survives and is a haven for the discerning pub-goer. Nestling in a most attractive village, deep in the Vale of Lanherne and a stone's throw from its tiny stream, this 16th-century wisteria-clad inn is a popular summer destination with those escaping the bucket-and-spade brigade on the beach. Inside, the main bar is neatly arranged and decorated with pine farmhouse tables and chairs, trellis wallpaper and decent prints and is thankfully music and game-free. The adjacent dining-room has a rug-strewn flagged floor, a pine dresser and French windows leading out into the bench-filled cobbled courtyard. Beyond a rose-covered arch there is a splendid terraced garden, ideal for enjoying some summer refreshment. *Open 11-3, 6-11 (Sun 12-3, 7-10.30).* **Beer** *St Austell. Garden, children's play area. Family room. Diners, MasterCard,* **VISA**

St Neots — Chequers Inn — FOOD

Tel 01480 472116   Map 15 E1
St Mary's Street Eynesbury St Neots Cambridgeshire PE19 2TA

A lovely old English country pub, where you can sit in the main bar with its roaring winter fires and highly-polished dark furniture or at tables with green tablecloths for bar food, or in the dining area for more substantial meals. The changing blackboard bar menu offers home-cooking by landlord David Taylor: hearty ploughman's, liver and bacon, chicken and mushroom pie, fricasee of chicken, home-made quiche and vegetarian choices like pasta and courgette provençale. Puddings include chocolate orange mousse cake, crème brulée and fresh raspberry pavlova. Set family Sunday lunch £13. Children are welcome indoors and are kept amused on sunny days in the outdoor play area in the fenced-off garden. *Open 10.30-3, 7-11 (Sun 12-2, 7-10.30).* **Bar Food** *12-2, 7-9.45 (till 9 Sun). Free House.* **Beer** *Boddingtons, Bass. Garden, outdoor eating, children's play area. Amex, Diners, MasterCard,* **VISA**

St Neots — Eaton Oak — B&B

Tel 01480 219555   Fax 01480 407520   Map 15 E1
Crosshall Road Eaton Ford St Neots Cambridgeshire PE19 4AG

The Eaton Oak is located at the junction of the A1 and A45 but the bedrooms are happily undisturbed by traffic – you can expect a comfortable overnight stay. The rooms in the motel extension are large and warm, with fitted units, colour TVs, tea-makers, direct-dial telephones and well-fitted bath/shower rooms. In the main building (once a farmhouse) the bar has been extended along with the restaurant and a conservatory added which leads on to the garden. Families are well looked after (even a free kiddies menu) and an outdoor play area is provided. Disabled WC. *Open 11-11 (Sat 11-2.30, 6-11, Sun 12-10.30).* **Beer** *Charles Wells, guest beer. Garden, children's play area. Family room.* **Accommodation** *9 bedrooms, all en suite, £50 (single £40). Children welcome overnight, additional bed (£12) available. Amex, MasterCard,* **VISA**

SALISBURY   Haunch of Venison   A

Tel 01722 322024   Map 14 C3
1-5 Minster Street Salisbury Wiltshire SP1 1TB

Antiquity and charm ooze from this ancient and tiny city-centre pub, which dates
from 1320 when it was built as a church house for nearby St Thomas's Church. Three
rooms, usually busy with tourists, radiate from the minuscule pewter-topped bar and
are affectionately known as the 'horsebox', a tiny snug off the entrance lobby; the
'House of Commons', which features a chequered stone floor and plenty of wooden
panels, beams and carved oak benches; and the upper room or 'House of Lords',
boasting a 600-year-old fireplace with a small side window displaying a mummified
hand holding a pack of 18th-century playing cards, which were discovered here in
1903. Surprisingly, there are over 100 malt whiskies crammed behind the bar! Well-
behaved children welcome. *Open 11-11 (Sun 12-3, 7-10.30).* **Beer** *Courage Best &
Directors. Amex, Diners, MasterCard,* **VISA**

SALISBURY   King's Arms Hotel   B&B

Tel 01722 327629   Fax 01722 414246   Map 14 C3
7a-11 St John's Street Salisbury Wiltshire SP1 2SB

The half-timbered, wattle and daub facade of this historic city inn, located opposite the
Cathedral Close, dates from the early 1600s, while the main core of the inn was built at
least ninety years before the first foundations were laid for the magnificent cathedral.
Oak panelling and beams abound in the log fire-warmed bars and in the clean and
comfortable en suite bedrooms, two of which have four-posters, and reached by a
winding staircase plus a series of sloping-floored corridors. The converted stable across
the courtyard houses three bedrooms decorated in a light, modern style. A high
standard of comfort is guaranteed with all rooms having TVs, telephones, tea-making
kits, hairdryers and trouser presses. Residents' lounge. *Open 11-3, 6-11 (Sun 12-10.30).
Free House.* **Beer** *Flowers Original, Boddingtons, guest beer. Courtyard.* **Accommodation** *15
bedrooms, all en suite, £58-£88 (family room £98, single £45-£55). Children welcome
overnight (under-2s stay free in parents' room, 3-12s £12), additional bed & cot available.
Amex, Diners, MasterCard,* **VISA**

SATWELL   Lamb Inn   A

Tel 01491 628482   Fax 01491 628900   Map 15a D3
Satwell Shepherds Green Henley-on-Thames Oxfordshire RG9 4QZ
⚲ ☺

An untypically tiny Thames Valley inn, tucked away off the B841, two miles south of
Nettlebed. Beneath a weird agglomeration of unevenly pitched roofs, it contains only
two small rooms within; floors are quarry tile and the tables are assorted. Every nook
and cranny seems taken up with collectables: old beer bottles (glass and earthenware)
dating back to the last century; an old dog grate, butter churn and mangle. There's
extra room to spread out in the garden, while very little ones can frolic on a swing or
a slide. Minimum of six wines by the glass. *Open 12-11 (Sat 12-3, 6-11, Sun 12-3,
7-10.30).* **Beer** *Brakspear. Garden, children's play area. Family room. No credit cards.*

SAUNDERTON   Rose & Crown Inn   B&B

Tel 01844 345299   Fax 01844 343140   Map 15a D2
Wycombe Road Saunderton Princes Risborough Buckinghamshire HP27 9NP

Located beside the A4010, this large pub dates back to 1840 and has a spacious,
neatly-furnished bar and lounge area. Business-orientated accommodation comprises
modest, functional bedrooms with built-in units and compact en suite facilities (seven
with showers only), while the two superior bedrooms are particularly well furnished
and decorated. TVs, tea-makers, telephones and radio-alarms are standard and double-
glazing helps to reduce traffic noise on road-facing rooms. All rooms, however, enjoy
pleasing views over the Chiltern Hills. Attractive sun-trap terrace reached through
French doors leading off the no-smoking Beechwood Restaurant. *Open 11-2.30, 6-11
(Sun 12-2.30, 7-10.30). Free House.* **Beer** *Brakspear Bitter, Morrells Varsity, Morland
Original. Garden. Family room.* **Accommodation** *17 bedrooms, 14 en suite £68.95-£72.95
(single £39.95-£62.95). Children over 8 welcome overnight, additional bed & cot
(both £5) available. Pub and accommodation closed 1 week Christmas. No dogs. Amex,
Diners, MasterCard,* **VISA**

SAWLEY Sawley Arms FOOD

Tel 01765 620642 Map 6 C1
Sawley Fountains Abbey Ripon North Yorkshire HG4 3EQ

A fine old-fashioned dining pub whose immaculate upkeep and enduring popularity are a tribute to the devotion of June Hawes, who has been in control here for some 27 years. The garden, her pride and joy, is a recent Britain in Bloom winner, while the pub inside is flower-filled and homely. In a succession of alcoves and tiny rooms (two being non-smoking), legions of regulars find their chosen spots and order at the bar from a varied menu amply supplemented by truly tempting daily specials. Pride is taken equally in June's range of freshly-cut sandwiches, delicious soups, which on any one day might be celery, apple and tomato or leek and apricot; pancakes, another popular item, may be filled with salmon and herbs, with home-made apple pie for dessert. The range of food is further extended by night when one end of the pub becomes rather more restaurant and choices will include Stilton, port and celery paté, chicken breast with mushroom sauce and halibut fillet with prawn sauce. Capable, friendly service in a warm atmosphere. No children under 9 indoors. *Open 11.30-3, 6.30-10.30 (Sun 12-3, 7-10.30). Bar Food 11.30-2, 6.30-9 (no food Mon eve in winter, except Bank Holidays). Free House. Beer Theakston Best, Younger's Scotch. Garden, outdoor eating. MasterCard, VISA*

SAXTON Plough Inn ★ FOOD

Tel 01937 557242 Map 7 D1
Headwell Lane Saxton Tadcaster North Yorkshire lS24 9PB

Once a farmhouse, this white-stone Victorian building in the main street of the village is officially a pub, although now more of a restaurant. However, you can still have just a drink in the carpeted bar with its pew seating, armchairs and sewing-machine tables. At lunchtime only one can enjoy chef/landlord Simon Treanor's bar snacks, either one of the lunchtime specials (Cajun-spiced chicken with spicy red pepper chutney, breast of pigeon with wild mushroom sauce), a sandwich (cheese and home-made pickle), ploughman's lunch or something from the restaurant's blackboard menu. The latter might include starters like dressed crab salad, confit of duck with balsamic dressing and chorizo sausage with spicy red cabbage, and main dishes such as fillet of lamb with ratatouille and port wine jus or roast corn-fed chicken with pesto-flavoured noodles and home-dried tomatoes. Good puds like chocolate marquise and date tartlet with mango coulis. About half-a-dozen wines are available by the glass. In summer there a few tables out on the roadside lawn. Children welcome. Between Tadcaster and Sherburn in Elmet off A162, not far from A1 (via B1217). *Open 12-3, 6-11. (Sun 12-3 only). Closed Sun eve, all Mon & 10 days Jan. Bar Meals 12-2, Restaurant 12-2, 6.30-10 (no food Sun or Mon). Free House. Beer Theakston's Best Bitter, guest beers. Garden, outdoor eating. MasterCard, VISA*

SCALES White Horse FOOD

Tel 01768 779241 Map 4 C3
Scales Threlkeld Cumbria CA12 4SY

Set back from the A66 between Keswick and Penrith and 1000 feet above sea level, the whitewashed White Horse is surrounded by stunning Cumbrian countryside and is within easy reach of splendid walking country. Immaculately kept, the interior has uneven whitewashed walls, a low beamed ceiling, a slate fireplace and well-polished copper pans and lots of plants add to the rustic atmosphere. Cumbrian-born owners Bruce and Pauline Jackson continue to maintain the pub's reputation for honest home-cooking using fresh local ingredients, with produce supplied by a trout-farming uncle from Borrowdale, a farming brother, local butchers and game from a nearby estate. Lunchtime choices are listed on a blackboard menu and may feature Wabberthwaite sausage with mustards or home-made pickles, ploughman's platters with a choice of Northern cheeses and a hearty home-made soup. Evenings bring candlelight and a more restauranty menu. Dishes on the printed list – Borrowdale trout with capers and parsley butter and roast duck with celery, apple and walnut stuffing – are supplemented by daily specials like salmon with spring onion, garlic, lemon grass, ginger and prawns or chicken stuffed with Cumbrian ham and mozzarella with a basil and tomato sauce. For dessert try the sticky toffee pudding or Eve's pudding (apple sponge). *Open 12-2.30, 6.30-11 (till 10.30 Sun). Closed Mon Nov-Easter.* **Bar Food** *12-1.45, 6.45-9.* **Beer** *Jennings Best, Hesket Newmarket Blencathra, guest beer. Patio, outdoor eating. Family room. MasterCard,* **VISA**

SCOLE	Scole Inn	B&B

Tel 01379 740481　　Fax 01379 740762　　　　　Map 10 C2
Ipswich Road Scole Diss Scole Norfolk IP22 4DR

Built in 1655 by a wool merchant, this grand-looking redbrick inn is Grade I listed for its architectural interest. Splendid brick gables front and rear show a Dutch influence. Bedrooms in the Georgian stable block are more modern than those in the main building, which are full of character, many having carved oak doors, old timbers and fireplaces plus four-poster or half-tester beds. All bedrooms have well-equipped bath/shower rooms. The beamed, pubby bar is also full of atmosphere with a vast brick fireplace, dark oak furniture and an 'old English Inn' ambience. Undergoing extensive renovation by new owners, The Old English Pub Company. *Open 11-11 (Sun 12-10.30).* **Beer** *Adnams Southwold & Broadside, two guest beers. Garden.* **Accommodation** *23 bedrooms, all en suite, £66-£76 (family room £81, single £52). Children welcome overnight (under-5s stay free in parents' room, 6-15s half-price), additional bed (£7.50) & cot available. Amex, Diners, MasterCard,* **VISA**

SEAHOUSES	Olde Ship	FOOD
		B&B

Tel 01665 720200　　Fax 01665 721383　　　　　Map 5 D1
9 Main Street Seahouses Northumberland NE68 7RD

❚ **Zzz...**

Perched above the small harbour with splendid sea views out to the Farne Islands, the Olde Ship began life as a farmhouse in 1745 and was first licensed in 1812. It has been in present licensees Alan and Jean Glen's family since 1910. Behind the grey stone exterior there lies a real treasure trove of nautical paraphernalia collected over the years. The saloon bar is full of objects hanging from ceiling, walls and bar; a ship's figurehead, oars, diving helmet, brass lamps, ship's wheel, baskets, model boats, pictures, barrels, fishing gear and more besides. The smaller cabin bar has panelling, royal blue upholstered seating and even more collectibles; both welcoming bars are popular in the evenings with locals and fishermen who mix well with visitors. Bar food is generously priced and ranges from crab soup and sandwiches to spicy lamb stew, seafood lasagne and liver and onions, followed by old-fashioned English desserts (plum sponge, sherry trifle). Upstairs, the nautical theme continues, with a fine collection of large model boats in one of the first-floor hallways. The bedrooms, including three in outside annexes, are clean, neat and unfussy, with plain painted walls and cottagey bedspreads; furniture varies from modern fitted units to more traditional freestanding pieces; two rooms have four-poster beds. Direct-dial telephone, television (with satellite) and mineral water are standard, and every room is en suite, though half have shower only, and some are on the small side. An on-going programme of refurbishment has seen several bedrooms upgraded in the past year. The pub also has its own lawn and summerhouse overlooking the harbour and enjoying fabulous views. No under-16s in bar areas. *Open 11-3, 6-11 (Sun 12-3, 7-10.30).* **Bar Food** *12-2, 7-8.30. Free House.* **Beer** *Theakston Best & XB, Marston's Pedigree, Morland Old Speckled Hen, Boddingtons, Ruddles Best, guest beers. Garden, putting, outdoor play area.* **Accommodation** *16 bedrooms, all en suite, £70 (single £35), winter reductions. Children over 10 welcome overnight. Check-in after 2pm. No dogs. Accommodation closed mid Nov-mid Feb. MasterCard,* **VISA**

> Many **B&B** establishments offer reduced rates for weekend and out-of-season bookings. Always ask about special deals for longer stays. Beware half-board terms in inns where we do not recommend the **FOOD**.

SEAVIEW — Seaview Hotel — FOOD

Tel 01983 612711   Fax 01983 613729   Map 15 D4   **B&B**
High Street Seaview Isle of Wight PO34 5EX

A small early Victorian hotel, charmingly and efficiently run by Nicholas and Nicola
Hayward; the hotel's two pubby bars are at the very heart of this small seaside town's
life and the bar meals are always popular. Just yards from the seafront with its pebble
beach and pretty assortment of sailing dinghies bobbing in the Solent, the hotel has
enormous charm, starting with the small front patio complete with flagpole, and the
little rear courtyard which heaves in season with youngsters. Both bars have a nautical
theme, one with small round tables and a myriad of photos of old ships on the walls,
the other more rustic in style with bare floorboards, dado pine panelling and, more
unusually, part of an old ship's mast. Try a pint of the particularly good Goddard's,
brewed on the Island. The bar menu is served both inside and outside on the terrace:
hot crab ramekin (a speciality), chicken liver and wild mushroom paté, seafood
quiche, and chicken with salad, garlic mayonnaise and chips. Traditional Sunday lunch
served (ring to check availability). Pretty bedrooms – blues and yellows are the
favoured colours – are most appealing, with lots of pictures, books and objets d'art.
The best, and largest, rooms feature antique furniture; others have simple white-
painted built-in units, and most en suite facilities feature baths and power showers.
Two of the rooms have small patios (unfortunately overlooking the small rear car
park), while the three smallest rooms now boast south-facing balconies. On the top
floor there's also a family suite, its two bedrooms separated by a sitting-room. The
cosy lounge on the first floor is non-smoking. Serious investment during winter
1995/96 saw four of the bedrooms completely refurbished and the addition of
a new air-conditioned, modern dining-room. Recommended in our *1997 Hotels &
Restaurants Guide.* Open 11-3, 6-11 (Sun 12-3, 7-10.30). **Bar Food** 12-2.30, 7-9.30.
Free House. **Beer** *Flowers IPA, Goddard's Special, guest beer. Patio/terrace, outdoor eating.
Family room.* **Accommodation** *16 bedrooms, all en suite, from £60-£95 (single from £40-
£80). Children welcome overnight (in own room half-price – high season exceptions),
additional bed (£12.50) & cot (£2.50) available. Amex, Diners, MasterCard,* **VISA**

SEDGEFIELD — Dun Cow Inn — B&B

Tel 01740 620894   Fax 01740 620895   Map 5 E3
43 Front Street Sedgefield Stockton-on-Tees Cleveland TS21 3AT

Zzz...

A splendid old inn – in this village of near a dozen pubs – which received Civic Trust
awards for its bedroom conversions in 1974. Roof beams and black and white timber-
framed walls have been exposed and restored, skilfully set off by the tapestry-weave
fabrics used for the bed-heads, counterpanes and curtains. There are no en suite
bathrooms, though the three which are shared (including one fully tiled with a
modern pulse shower) do enter into the spirit with splendidly evocative, yet up-to-
date, bathroom fittings. Teletext TVs, fresh fruit and bedside boiled sweets greet the
overnight visitor – breakfast orders placed the night before are cheerfully served at
guests' chosen hour next morning. Hopefully, three of the bedrooms will be en suite
by the end of 1996. Open 11-3, 6-11 (Sun 12-3, 7-10.30). *Free House.* **Beer** *Theakston
Best & XB, Newcastle Exhibition, McEwan's Scotch, several weekly-changing guest beers.*
Accommodation *6 bedrooms, not en suite £45 (single £36.50). Children welcome overnight
(under-10s stay free in parents' room), additional bed & cot available. Amex, Diners,
MasterCard,* **VISA**

SELLACK — Loughpool Inn — FOOD

Tel & Fax 01989 730236   Map 14 B1
Sellack Ross-on-Wye Hereford & Worcester HR9 6LX

A popular dining pub and an equally pleasant spot for summer drinking around picnic
tables under the weeping willows. The generally unspoilt interior features flagstones,
log fires and two dining-rooms whose cloths and candles create a rather more sedate
dining ambience. An extensive menu enhanced by daily specials offers a good choice

of reliable dishes. Regular favourites include smoked fish roulade, Greek-style goat casserole, beef and orange carbonade, chicken korma and interesting vegetarian dishes like lentil moussaka and barley and ale strudel. For pudding try the chocolate rum pot or Dutch apple pie. *Open 11-30-2.30, 6.30-11 (Sun 12-2.30, 7-10.30). Bar Food 12-2 (till 2.30 Sat), 7-9.30 (till 9 Sun). Free House. Beer Bass, Wye Valley Hereford Supreme, John Smith's. Garden, outdoor eating. Family room. Closed 25 Dec. MasterCard, VISA*

SELLING — White Lion — FOOD

Tel 01227 752211 Map 11 C5
The Street Selling Faversham Kent ME13 9RQ

Surrounded by tubs of flowers, this charming 300-year-old village pub is decorated inside in traditional Kentish-style with swags of hops. Half set up for eating and half for drinking there are wheelback chairs, an inglenook fireplace, dressers loaded with plates and tureens and lots of fresh flowers and plants. The extensive menu always includes a traditional beef suet pudding and steak and kidney pie plus steaks, freshly-cut sandwiches and ploughman's lunches (three cheeses with apple) along with the likes of lasagne, pork fillet with grain mustard and cream sauce, Mexican chicken burritos and beef curry. For those with particularly spicy tastes Monday night is curry night, accompanied by live jazz. Fish specials (red mullet in Pernod and cream) appear on the chalk board every Friday night. Good selection of puddings (home-made lemon meringue pie, brandy and apricot roulade). Afternoon teas served at weekends. *Open 11-3, 6.30-11 (11-11 Sat), Sun 11-10.30. Bar Food 12-2.15, 7-9.15 (Sat 12-9.30, Sun 12-9.15). Beer Shepherd Neame. Garden, outdoor eating. Family room. MasterCard, VISA*

> We endeavour to be as up-to-date as possible but inevitably some changes to
> landlords, chefs and other key staff occur after the Guide
> has gone to press.

SEMINGTON — Lamb on the Strand — FOOD

Tel 01380 870263 Map 14 B3
99 The Strand Semington Trowbridge Wiltshire BA14 6LL

A carefully refurbished old ivy-clad farmhouse, set beside the A361 between Devizes and Trowbridge and run in civilised-style by the hard-working Flaherty family. Original features and fireplaces have been revealed and a tasteful collection of old darkwood furniture, farmhouse high-back chairs, a carved oak corner cupboard, quality fabrics and prints have created a relaxed and upmarket air in both the neat bar and small intimate dining-room. The latter, painted dark green and candle-lit, is particularly popular in the evenings and the soothing tones of light classical music enhance the overall atmosphere of this charming country pub. Quality bar food is the main emphasis at the Lamb, the daily-changing blackboard menu offering a pleasing variety of home-made dishes, all of which make use of fresh local produce. Start with confit de canard, fresh squid or smoked chicken with mango cream, followed by well-presented main-course dishes such as medallions of beef with red wine, pork tenderloin with Stilton sauce and spicy chicken. Fresh fish – lemon sole, monkfish provençale – and good vegetarian dishes (carrot and nut roast, quorn with cheese and mushroom sauce) feature on the menu. To round off a meal, inviting puddings may include bread pudding in whisky sauce and raspberry marshmallow meringue. A competitively-priced wine list includes at least eight house wines served by the glass. To the side of the pub is a delightful garden with shrubs, trees and wrought-iron tables and chairs, from which there are fine views over open countryside. The whole pub is completely no-smoking. *Open 12-2.30, 6.45-10.30 (till 11 Sat), Sun 12-3 only. Closed Sun eve. Bar Food 12-2 (till 1.45 Sat), 7-9 (no food Sun eve). Free House. Beer Eldridge Pope Hardy Country Ale & Dorchester Bitter. Garden, outdoor eating. MasterCard, VISA*

SEMLEY   Benett Arms   FOOD

Tel 01747 830221   Fax 01747 830159   Map 14 B3
Semley Shaftesbury Dorset SP7 9AS

This unusually tall, white-painted building enjoys an enviable rural location on the
edge of the village, opposite the green and overlooking the isolated church. Inside, a
warm welcome is ensured in the rustic, split-level and simply furnished bar, which is
warmed in winter by an open fire. The printed bar menu covers the standard items –
various sandwiches, ploughman's platters, steak and kidney pie, lasagne and Wiltshire
ham, egg and chips – while a daily-changing blackboard menu displays the more
interesting and unusual dishes that are on offer. Fresh fish from Poole features well
and may include hake, grilled lemon sole and red mullet with Normandy butter. The
unusual comes in the form of chorizo served with sauerkraut, and game features well
in season, notably pheasant casserole and jugged hare. Home-made puddings usually
include apple crumble and chocolate mousse with rum. On Sunday a good-value table
d'hote lunch is served. An above-average selection (about 10) of worldwide house
wines is served, by both bottle and glass. *Open 11-2.30, 6-11 (Sun 12-3, 7-10.30).*
*Bar Food 12-2, 7-9.30. Beer Gibbs Mew. Garden, outdoor eating, children's play area.
Family room. Closed 25 & 26 Dec. Amex, Diners, MasterCard, **VISA***

SENNEN COVE   Old Success Inn   B&B

Tel 01736 871232   Fax 01736 871457   Map 12 A4
Sennen Cove Penzance Cornwall TR19 7DG
Zzz...

Located off the A30, next to the huge expanse of Whitesands Bay and only a mile
north of Land's End, this 17th-century inn has been well refurbished to provide
accommodation in twelve comfortable bedrooms that have impressive sea views.
Especially popular are the rooms that capture the famous sunset sinking into the sea,
the most attractive being the spacious honeymoon suite with its four-poster bed. All
rooms have pretty floral curtains and print wallpaper, solid modern pine furnishings
and good clean en suite facilities. Added comforts include satellite TV and tea-makers
and residents have use of a stylish lounge complete with picture window and sea view.
The pubby 'Charlies Bar' is modern and open-plan in layout with a mix of pub
furniture, stools and high-backed benches and various local seafaring photographs
of bygone days decorate the walls. Children welcome. *Open 11-11 (Sun 12-10.30).
Free House. Beer Bass, St Austell Trelawney's Ale, Sharp's Doom Bar, guest beer. Terrace,
Accommodation 12 bedrooms, 10 en suite, £32-£73 (single from £19). Children welcome
overnight (under-2s stay free in parents' room, 2-15s half-price), additional bed & cot available.
MasterCard, **VISA***

SEVENOAKS   Royal Oak   FOOD   B&B

Tel 01732 451109   Fax 01732 740187   Map 11 B5
High Street Sevenoaks Kent TN13 1HY

A former coaching inn in the heart of town with abundant atmosphere and character.
Rich, bold colours perfectly complement the fabric of the building and traditional or
antique furniture is used in the bedrooms, which are decorated in individual, often
striking style and all boast neat, bright bathrooms. Among the day rooms are a cosy
pub-like bar/bistro with candle-topped scrubbed pine tables, comfortable, well-
upholstered seats and an informal menu listing the likes of stuffed pittas, filled
baguettes, steaks and winter hotpots. There is also a beautifully furnished drawing
room, a conservatory and a charming restaurant comprising several rooms that are
partially panelled and cleverly lit, creating a relaxing atmosphere. Here, both the à la
carte and the good-value set lunch and dinner menus offer something for everyone.
New chef since our last visit. Creeper-clad patio for summer alfresco eating. Brook
Hotels. *Open 11-3, 6-11 (Sun 12-3, 7-10.30). Bar Food 12-2.30, 7-10 (Sun till 9.30).
Patio, outdoor eating, tennis. Free House. Beer Ruddles Best, Courage Directors, Morland Old
Speckled Hen. Accommodation 37 rooms, all en suite, £89 (single £75). Children welcome
overnight (under-10s stay free in parents' room), additional bed (£15) & cot (£10) available.
Amex, Diners, MasterCard, **VISA***

SHALDON — Ness House Hotel — B&B

Tel 01626 873480   Fax 01626 873486   Map 13 D3
Marine Drive Shaldon Devon TQ14 0HP

Originally built as a summer residence by Lord Clifford in 1810, the Regency looking Ness House Hotel is set in 22 acres of parkland and overlooks the Teign estuary and across to the town of Teignmouth. The twelve rooms (1 bridal suite, five apartments, 2 family suites, 3 doubles and 1 single) all have en suite facilities and are equipped with modern facilities. There is a spacious open-plan bar with a no-smoking area and, at the back, a small, simple lounge. Room service is available. *Open 11-11 (Sun 12-10.30). Free House.* **Beer** *Eldridge Pope Royal Oak, Palmers IPA, Tetley, Fergusons Dartmoor Legend, guest beer. Garden.* **Accommodation** *14 bedrooms, all en suite, £65-£80 (family room £95, single from £39). Children welcome overnight (under-14s stay free in parents' room), additional bed (£15) & cot available. No dogs. Amex, MasterCard,* **VISA**

SHAMLEY GREEN — Red Lion Inn — FOOD

Tel 01483 892202   Fax 01483 894055   Map 15a E4   **B&B**
Shamley Green Surrey GU5 0UB

Listed, 300-year-old building overlooking the village green and cricket pitch, with a smart and well-cared-for interior boasting three open fireplaces, a pleasant mix of modern pine and antique furnishings, tasteful prints and fresh flowers and candles on tables. Reliably good, homely food listed on the blackboard in the bar – ham, egg and chips, steak and mushroom pie, lasagne, seafood crepes, chicken curry – with printed restaurant menu fare (also served in the bar) offering more substantial main courses such as lamb cutlets with redcurrant sauce, breast of chicken with cream and tarragon, fresh lemon sole and steak with mushroom sauce. Popular puddings include summer pudding and hot chocolate fudge cake. Those popping in for just a snack will find filled baguettes, ploughman's lunches and jacket potatoes among the lighter-bite options. Fresh, chintzy, antique-furnished bedrooms upstairs – one has a four-poster – all with en suite facilities (three with shower only). *Open 11-11, (Sun 12-5, 7-10.30).* **Bar Food** *12-3, 6.30-10 (Sun 7-9.30)* **Beer** *Flowers Original, Ansells Bitter, Tetley Imperial. Garden, outdoor eating.* **Accommodation** *4 bedrooms, all en suite, £45 (single £40). Children welcome overnight (family room from £50), additional bed & cot available. No dogs. Amex, Diners, MasterCard,* **VISA**

SHARDLOW — Old Crown — FOOD

Tel 01332 792392   Map 7 D3
Cavendish Bridge Shardlow Derbyshire DE72 2HL

Signed just of the A6, Cavendish Bridge was the old road crossing of the Trent into Derbyshire, now mercifully a dead end, where the old bridge collapsed, some thirty feet above the river. The Old Crown, rescued from a possibly similar fate, positively bustles within stone walls hung with old tobacco and brewery posters and beams hung at every conceivable point with pottery water jugs. A high turnover of real ales draws the locals and high-piled plates of food almost everyone else. Landlord Peter Morton-Harrison operates his own inimitable food-ordering system on his note pad (cometh the man, cometh the menu) while the best food bets on the specials board are equally idiosyncratic. Alongside upside-down fish pie fish pie laced with brandy and wine, and rib steak with pepper sauce, the board may offer Normandy pork, Mediterranean chicken and lamb with cheese and mint. Vegetarian are catered for and those popping in for just a snack can tuck into a hot-filled baguette or ploughman's platter. The balance of a conservative menu places volume, perhaps, above variety, though no one seems to care that much. Good ale and a genial atmosphere more than paper over any cracks. *Open 11-3, 5-11 (Sun 12-4, 7-10.30).* **Bar Food** *12-2 (till 3 Sun). Free House.* **Beer** *Marston's Pedigree, Bass, four guest beers. Garden, outdoor eating. No credit cards.*

SHAVE CROSS — Shave Cross Inn — A

Tel 01308 868358   Map 13 F2
Marshwood Vale Bridport Dorset DT6 6HW

Once a busy resting place for pilgrims on their way to Whitchurch Canonicorum, as well as monastic visitors, who frequently had their tonsures trimmed while staying, hence the name. Delightfully situated off-the-beaten track in the beautiful Marshwood Vale, 5 miles from Bridport, this charming 14th-century thatched cob-and-flint inn has a stone floor, inglenook fireplace, beamed ceiling, rustic furnishings, and a delightful flower-filled suntrap garden. Through the skittle alley, there's a children's play area. Local scrumpy cider. *Open 12-3 (till 2.30 in winter), 7-11 (till 10.30 Sun). Closed Mon except Bank Holidays. Free House.* **Beer** *Bass, Eldridge Pope Royal Oak, Hall & Woodhouse Badger Best. Garden, children's play area. Family room. No credit cards*

SHELF — Duke of York — B&B

Tel 01422 202056   **Fax 01422 206618**   Map 6 C1
West Street Stone Chair Shelf Halifax Calderdale HX3 7LN

The 17th-century former coaching inn, right by the A644, is pub in front and flooring factory to the rear. Local foundries have contributed over the years to the collection of brassware and blow-torches which adorn the interior, alongside the whisky jugs, chamber pots and jam pans which hang from its blackened oak beams. Bedrooms, meanwhile, attract a mid-week business clientele in an area not over-blessed with comparable competition. In addition to five en suite bedrooms in the pub, there are seven self-contained rooms in a row of weavers' cottages across the road. These retain the old stone walls and fireplaces, and on the ground floor, it's plain to see that the bathrooms (with shower/WC only) were once the kitchens. *Open 11-11 (Sun 12-10.30). Free House.* **Beer** *Boddingtons, Whitbread Castle Eden Ale, Timothy Taylor's Best & Landlord, Flowers Original, two guest beers. Patio.* **Accommodation** *12 bedrooms, all en suite (six with shower only), £50 (family £60, single £35), weekend reductions. Children welcome overnight. No dogs. Amex, Diners, MasterCard,* **VISA**

SHELLEY — Three Acres Inn — ★ FOOD

Tel 01484 602606   **Fax 01484 608411**   Map 6 C1   B&B
Roydhouse Shelley Huddersfield Kirklees HD8 8LR

Set high in the Pennines above Huddersfield, the Emley Moor television mast (red-lit at night) provides a useful landmark for finding the unassuming, greystone Three Acres, which is on the Emley road, off B6116 at Shelley village. Central to the inn is a long bar counter framed in darkwood panelling beneath solid oak beams, lent further character at night by candle-lit tables and lively accompaniment from the grand piano. With over 27 years' consistent performance at the top level, Neil Truelove and Brian Orme still attract the crowds for bar food which is commendable for its unswerving quality and simplicity. Among the comprehensive range of unusually good sandwiches (available lunch and evening) one will find toasted hot smoked ham with grain mustard and gruyère cheese and toasted ciabatta with roasted tomatoes, aubergines, basil, mozzarella and spinach salad – most are a meal in themselves. For a full meal, main courses ranging from cassoulet of duck with haricot beans and garlic bread, and chicken breast with prosciutto, herb ricotta farci, polenta and tomato jus vie for prominence alongside roasts of the day, shortcrust-topped steak, kidney and mushroom pie and Whitby haddock (served with chips and traditional mushy peas). To follow are the justifiably memorable desserts such as lemon tart with hot cherries, ginger and marmalade sponge with lemon grass custard and chocolate tart with caramel sauce. At either end of the bar are two more formal dining-rooms offering an evening à la carte and traditional 3-course Sunday lunch. Booking here is essential. The quality, however, of this dedicated team's food is beyond question, and anyone looking for such adventurous flavours – and not a little conviviality of atmosphere – will surely not be disappointed. The Three Acres bridges the gap between small hotel and country inn with a choice of quality accommodation. Bedrooms in the main building are spacious and airy, and furnished in traditional-style natural pine with colour co-ordinated fabrics. Much similar decor has been used in the newer annexe, housed in much older stone cottages across the lane, where the rooms are that good bit smaller and single rooms are equipped with WC and showers only; those businessman with work to do may find these a little cramped. Three rooms are large enough for families and one pair connect. All are nonetheless immaculately kept and equipped with TVs, direct-dial phones, trouser presses and plenty of toiletries. *Open 12-3, 7-11 (till 10.30 Sun). Closed Sat lunch.* **Bar Food** *12-2, 7-9.45 (no food Sat lunch). Free House.* **Beer** *Mansfield Cask, Riding Bitter, Dark Mild & Old Baily, Timothy Taylor's Landlord, guest beer. Garden, outdoor eating.* **Accommodation** *20 bedrooms, all en suite, £57.50 (single £47.50), weekend reductions. Children welcome overnight (stay free if sharing parents' room), additional bed & cot available. No dogs.* Amex, MasterCard, **VISA**

SHENINGTON   Bell Inn   FOOD

Tel 01295 670274   Map 14a B1
Shenington Banbury Oxfordshire OX15 6NQ

Just five miles west of Banbury (turn off the A422) Shenington is a comfortable, sleepy village boasting a celebrated Norman church. By the three-acre green, the Bell is very much at the heart of village life. Don't miss the locals' bar down one side of the pub if you're in search of a fine pint of Hook Norton – the originating brewery is only six miles away. To the front, the two dining-rooms with attendant log fires are cosy and intimate. Jennifer Dixon is the genius behind a regularly-evolving range of seasonal food, as well as preparing freshly-cut sandwiches and popular ploughman's platters. A typical starter would be deep-fried Brie or kipper paté, followed by duck with port and black cherries, pork in watercress sauce, salmon with cucumber sauce or spinach and ricotta lasagne. Super puddings follow the lines of gooseberry crumble, srawberry pavlova and sticky toffee pudding. *Open 12-4, 6.30-11 (Sun 12-4, 7-10.30).* **Bar Food** *12-3 (till 4 Sun), 6.30-9.30. Free House.* **Beer** *Boddingtons, Hook Norton Best. Garden, outdoor eating.* MasterCard, **VISA**

SHEPPERTON   Anchor Hotel   B&B

Tel 01932 221618   Fax 01932 252235   Map 15a F4
Church Square Shepperton Middlesex TW17 9JZ

A favourite haunt of Charles Dickens, the historic Anchor has dominated Shepperton's tiny square for over 400 years. Despite serious fire damage some years ago, the Disraeli Room retains original linenfold oak panelling, and the evocative Anchor Bar has been meticulously restored. Bedrooms, of which only seven are doubles and all but one have shower/WCs only, all offer TVs, tea-makers and direct dial telephones. The best front doubles overlook the tiny square where once illegal prizefighters stood toe to toe; when the Bow Street runners were spied approaching, they would escape across the Thames to open country. Gradual upgrading of the bedrooms will take place in the coming year. *Open 11-2.30, 5.30-11 (Sun 12-3, 7-10.30). Free House.* **Beer** *Morland Original & Old Speckled Hen, guest beer. Patio.* **Accommodation** *29 bedrooms, all en suite, £79.50 (family room £85, single £59.50), weekend reductions. Children welcome overnight, additional bed & cot available. No dogs.* Amex, Diners, MasterCard, **VISA**

We only recommend food (Bar Food) in those establishments highlighted with the **FOOD** symbol.

SHEPPERTON   King's Head   A

Tel 01932 221910   Map 15a F4
Church Square Shepperton Middlesex TW17 9JY

Across the square from the Anchor, the name of Nell Gwynne is most commonly associated with the King's Head. Although the two front bars have recently been made one, the traditional feel of its interior remains unchanged; floors are flagstoned, connecting doorways and alcoves are tiny and in winter log fires burn in an impressive inglenook. To the rear, a summer gazebo and enclosed patio are conducive to sociable drinking, though just as many may meander down from the square, glasses in hand, to take in a view of the river. *Open 11-11 (Sun 12-10.30). Free House.* **Beer** *Courage Best & Directors, Ruddles Best, Theakston Best. Courtyard. Family room.* MasterCard, **VISA**

SHEPPERTON — Warren Lodge — B&B

Tel 01932 242972   Fax 01932 253883   Map 15a F4
Church Square Shepperton Middlesex TW17 9JZ

Arguably the least pubby of Shepperton's hostelries, it nonetheless enjoys the choicest location. Riverside terrace and garden are shaded by a handsome old walnut tree, and there's comfortable seating both in the spacious beamed bar and panelled reception lounge. Most bedrooms, both in the main 18th-century house and two wings of later additions, share serene river views: all have TVs, tea-makers and hairdryers. On-going refurbishment will result in baths replacing most of the remaining en suite shower facilities. *Open 12-3, 6-11 (Sun 12-3, 7-10.30). No real ales. Garden.* **Accommodation** *48 bedrooms, all en suite, £88 (single £72.50), weekends reductions. Children welcome overnight (under-16s stay free if sharing parents' room), additional bed & cot available. No dogs. Amex, Diners, MasterCard,* **VISA**

We endeavour to be as up-to-date as possible but inevitably some changes to
landlords, chefs and other key staff occur after the Guide
has gone to press.

SHEPTON MONTAGUE — Montague Inn — ★   FOOD

Tel & Fax 01749 813213   Map 13 F2   **B&B**
Shepton Montague Somerset BA9 8JW

Zzz...

Having spent several years scouring the country in search of their ideal pub, David and Valerie Haskey finally bought the neglected and run-down Montague Inn in April 1995, a basic 'local' pub nestling in a peaceful Somerset village midway between Bruton and Castle Cary. With three public schools and Wincanton Racecourse close by (and the A303 only a short drive away), it was the perfect location, in their minds, in which to establish a discerning country inn. After a year of careful restoration and building – including the addition of three stylish, en suite bedrooms, plus the addition of talented chef, Rozanne Maclean, to the family team – the result is commendable and business is thriving. Behind the smart cream and green painted facade, adorned with overflowing hanging baskets, lies an equally tasteful and spotlessly maintained interior. David Haskey's interior-design talents are evident in the decor of the comfortable bar – attractive green and apricot paintwork and fabrics, Oriental rug-strewn floor, wall benches with scatter cushions, old dark-pine furniture – and in the two small adjacent dining-rooms, one boasting deep terracotta-painted walls, the other a huge inglenook fireplace. White china, candle-topped tables and various personal items enhance the relaxing charm of these rooms. Attention to detail extends to the imaginative, French-influenced cooking of Rozanne Maclean. She uses only quality fresh produce in preparing her short, regularly-changing list of simple, well-executed and full-flavoured dishes that grace the hand-written light lunch (duck terrine with cognac sauce, pan-fried cod on a bed of caramelised onions, mussels, flash-grilled prosciutto with tossed green salad) and informal supper menus. Evening specials like smoked haddock soup (served with warm bread), confit of duck with crisp potato galette, monkfish with fennel crust and pastis sauce, and red mullet served on marinated aubergine with a honey vinegar sauce supplement main menu choices such as fresh tomato mousse, thyme-roasted rack of lamb with garlic cream and a rustic cassoulet of smoked goose breast, fillet of lamb and Toulouse sausage. Good accompanying vegetables and attentive service from the Haskeys. Puddings may include warm lemon tart with a confit of kumquats, chocolate terrine with Cointreau crème anglaise or armagnac mousse on a raspberry coulis. Well-kept real ales, especially the splendid local Moor Brewery Withycutter, are dispensed straight from the cask behind the bar and there is a good-value list of wines to complement the menu; ask for the current cellar list to peruse the bin end selection of interesting classic wines. Style and a great deal of thought have been given to the three delightful bedrooms tucked away at the rear of the building. Co-ordinating colours and fabrics (pastel shades of peach and apricot to pale green and cream), small sofas with cushions, stencilled hand-made pine beds, neat en suite shower rooms, TVs, tea-makers and added extras like bathrobes, fresh fruit and mineral water characterise the level of comfort in this excellent-value overnight accommodation. One bedroom enjoys pleasing views across open farmland, as does the rear flower-filled gravelled terrace, complete with shrubs in tubs, a rustic arbor and picnic benches. No under-14s inside. *Open 12-2 (till 3 Sat), 5.30-11 (Sun 12-3, 7-10.30). Closed Mon lunch & every lunchtime mid-Oct to Easter.* **Bar Food** *12-2, 7-9 (no food Sun or Mon lunch). Free House.* **Beer** *Moor Brewery Withycutter, Butcombe Bitter, Greene King IPA, Marston's Pedigree, guest beers. Garden, outdoor eating.* **Accommodation** *3 bedrooms, all en suite (shower), £40 (single £25). No children under 14 overnight. Check-in by arrangement. No dogs. Accommodation closed 24 Dec-5 Jan. MasterCard,* **VISA**

SHERFIELD ENGLISH   Hatchet Inn   FOOD

Tel 01794 322487   Map 14 C3
Sherfield English Romsey Hampshire SO51 6FP

Set back from the main road, this homely 17th-century pub is a popular stopping-off point for A27 travellers between Salisbury and Romsey. Refreshment is provided in two simply furnished and carpeted bars, the larger lounge/dining-room housing the blackboard menu which lists the good value bar snacks and the weekly-changing choice of more substantial main meals. Light meals include steak and kidney pie, lasagne, filled jacket potatoes and a range of ploughman's platters, sandwiches and salads. More substantial main courses feature up to six fresh fish dishes – scallops with garlic and bacon, whole lemon sole, stir-fried monkfish with vegetables and soy – as well as pork fillet with Stilton and port, chargrilled breast of duck au poivre and a good choice of vegetarian pasta dishes (gnocchi with tomato and tarragon). Sunday is a busy day here: the traditional roast draws a full house, booking essential. *Open 12-3.30, 6-11 (Sun 12-3, 7-10.30).* **Bar Food** *12-2, 7-9.30. Free House.* **Beer** *Fuller's London Pride, Wadworth 6X, Bass. Garden, outdoor eating. Family room. MasterCard,* **VISA**

SHERSTON   Rattlebone Inn   A

Tel & Fax 01666 840871   Map 14 B2
Church Street Sherston Wiltshire SN16 0LR

Only 6 miles from the M4 this busy old Cotswold-stone pub still has its original stone roof intact, and lots more exposed stone, oak beams and open fires inside. Boules competitions in the fenced garden. Choice of over 80 malt whiskies. *Open 11.30-3, 5.30-11 (Sat and Bank Holidays 11-11, Sun 12-10.30). Free House.* **Beer** *Smiles Best, Bass, Wadworth 6X, Archer's Village Bitter, guest beers. Garden. Family room. Amex, Diners, MasterCard,* **VISA**

SHIFNAL   Oddfellows   FOOD   B&B

Tel 01952 461517   Fax 01952 463855   Map 6 B4
Market Place Shifnal Telford Shropshire TF11 9AH

What was once the Star Hotel close to the railway station is now part-pub, part-brasserie in a novel ground-floor conversion which utilises wood-block flooring and a pine-clad bar canopy to balance the trendy installation of assorted pine and cast-iron tables, sofas, banquettes and pews which form the tiered quartet of eating areas. An assorted age group seems as at home with a mixture of 1960s' and 70s' pop classics as they are with menu concepts as diverse as grilled sardines with garlic and pesto mash, venison sausages with coarse-grain mustard sauce and lamb rogan josh with mango chutney. Some of the better fare appears towards the top of this wide price range: roast pheasant with cream and redcurrant jelly, grilled halibut with champagne and pink peppercorns and marinated lamb steak with honey and rosemary butter. Accompany your meal with one of the 20 wines served by the glass, including champagne. There is still overnight accommodation available in four pine-furnished en suite (showers only) bedrooms above; but it appears to be on a rather random basis with Continental breakfast obtainable from a communal kitchen. The best we can suggest is that one phones ahead for clarification. Live jazz on Sundays. *Open 12-3, 6-11 (Sun 12-3, 7-10.30).* **Bar Food** *12-3, 6.30-10 (from 7 Sun). Free House.* **Beer** *Boddingtons, Timothy Taylor's Landlord, guest beers. Patio.* **Accommodation** *4 bedrooms, all en suite, £50 (single £25). No children overnight. Check-in by arrangement. Amex, MasterCard,* **VISA**

SHIPBOURNE   Chaser Inn   B&B

Tel 01732 820360   Fax 01732 810941   Map 11 B5
Shipbourne Tonbridge Kent TN11 9PE

Set back from the A227 midway between Tonbridge and Sevenoaks , this striking, Colonial-style building with its impressive porticoed front (bedecked with immaculate hanging baskets in summer) stands beside the parish church and enjoys pleasing views over the village green. Built in the 1880s for nearby Fairlawne House, its name is a reminder of the late Peter Cazalet, the Queen Mother's trainer, whose National Hunt racing stables were located on Fairlawne Estate. Old hunting pictures hangs in the welcoming and old pine-furnished bars, one of which leads on to the front verandah and an attractive paved courtyard to the rear. Well-converted stables surround the courtyard and house most of the inn's fifteen neat and tidy bedrooms. Ideal for the business traveller (M25, M20 and M26 are only minutes away), tourists and hikers walking the Greensand Way, which it passes the front door, each room has modern, light-oak furniture, floral fabrics and friezes and clean en suite facilities (nine with shower/WC only). Added extras include TVs, direct-dial telephones, radios, hairdryers and beverage-making kits. The inn also features a splendid vaulted restaurant, a flower-filled summer garden, well kept real ales and promising menus. *Open 11-3, 6-11 (Sun 12-3, 7-10.30). Free House.* **Beer** *Harveys Best, Shepherd Neame Master Brew. Garden, courtyard. Family room. Accommodation 15 bedrooms, all en suite, £60 (single £45). Children welcome overnight. Amex, MasterCard,* **VISA**

SHIPTON-UNDER-WYCHWOOD   Lamb Inn   FOOD

Tel 01993 830465   Fax 01993 832025   Map 14a B2   **B&B**
High Street Shipton-under-Wychwood Oxfordshire OX7 6DQ

Tucked away down a quiet side road, the Lamb is a typical 17th-century Cotswold building, complete with honey-coloured stone walls and stone tiled roof, and its neat little patio with parasol-shaded tables makes an ideal spot in summer. Inside, all is equally immaculate, the beamed bar boasting a polished woodblock floor and mostly antique furniture. At lunchtimes, the cold buffet displayed in the bar offers cold cuts like salmon, Cornish lobster, crab, ham and beef for salads, a vegetarian tart, hot dishes of the day (calf's liver, braised oxtail) and just a roast on Sundays. In the evening an extensive blackboard menu offers the choice of a full three-course meal or perhaps just a light snack. Main dishes like ham in cider, rack of lamb with rosemary and garlic, crispy roast duck or several fresh fish choices (plaice, lobster thermidor, baked sea bass with lime and fennel) come in generous portions with good simply-cooked fresh vegetables; as a bonus, someone in the kitchen has the cool, light hand needed to produce a melt-in-the-mouth pastry for the home-made fruit pies. For more formal dining there is a cosy, low-beamed restaurant offering an à la carte dinner menu. At least twelve wines available by the glass, including champagne (£4). The Lamb's five bedrooms (two with four-posters) are all as neat as a new pin, with spotless modern bathrooms, all with bath and shower. Three of the rooms boast some old beams and these help lend a little extra character. Televisions, radio-alarms, direct-dial phones and tea and coffee making kit are standard, with mineral water, fresh coffee, home-made biscuits and bowls of fruit as welcoming extras. Good hearty cooked breakfasts are worth getting up for. The Lamb was recently bought by the Old English Pub Company who, we are assured, intend keeping it as it is and that includes chef Robin Bancroft. *Open 11-3, 6-11 (Sun 12-3, 7-10.30).* **Bar Food** *12-2, 7-10. Free House.* **Beer** *Hook Norton Best, Wadworth 6X, Wychwood Fiddlers Elbow. Patio/terrace, outdoor eating.* **Accommodation** *5 bedrooms, all en suite, £75 (single £58). Children welcome overnight (under-3s stay free in parents' room), additional bed (£15) available. Amex, MasterCard,* **VISA**

Many **B&B** establishments offer reduced rates for weekend and out-of-season bookings. Always ask about special deals for longer stays. Beware half-board terms in inns where we do not recommend the **FOOD**.

SHIPTON-UNDER-WYCHWOOD   Shaven Crown Hotel   FOOD

Tel & Fax 01993 830330   Map 14a B2   **B&B**
High Street Shipton-under-Wychwood Oxfordshire OX7 6BA

Originally a 14th-century hospice to Bruern Abbey, this is a charming medieval
building constructed around a delightful courtyard garden (complete with goldfish
pond), where you can eat in good weather. In addition to lunch and dinner, visitors
are offered breakfast, morning coffee and afternoon tea. Choices on the Buttery Bar's
blackboard menu include smoked haddock mousse, bobotie, venison sausages brasied
in red wine, chicken and mushroom pie and plaice and chips. Vegetarian specials may
include walnut and mushroom pancake. Delicious desserts feature treacle tart, bread-
and-butter pudding and home-made ice-creams. A 2/3-course Sunday lunch is served
in the no-smoking restaurant where a more elaborate table d'hote dinner menu
operates in the evenings. Charming service. The newly-refurbished bedrooms vary in
size, some smaller than one might expect for the price. En suite facilities include three
with showers only. *Open 12-2.30, 7-11 (till 10.30 Sun).* **Bar Food** *12-2, 7-9.30 (till 9
Sun).* Free House. **Beer** *Hook Norton Best, guest beers. Courtyard, outdoor eating.*
Accommodation *9 bedrooms, 8 en suite, from £66/£82 (family room sleeping five £112,
single from £33). Children welcome overnight (under-2s free), additional bed (£5) & cot (£5)
available. No dogs. Closed 25 Dec eve. MasterCard,* **VISA**

SHOBDON   **Bateman Arms**   FOOD

Tel 01568 708374   Map 14 A1
Shobdon Leominster Hereford & Worcester HR6 9LX

Black and white timbered former farmhouse standing on the B4362 at the heart of the
village and enthusiastically run by the Williams family. The neatly refurbished bar and
carpeted dining area offers a conducive atmosphere in which to enjoy some reliable
pub food. Young Gary Williams looks after the bar and the business of eating while
Tracy keeps a watchful eye on the kitchen. Her blackboard menu features favourites
like sandwiches and ploughman's platters, grills, plus vegetarian selections (leek and
potato crumble), all supplemented by some varied and imaginative daily specials. Fish
terrine, grilled goat's cheese with damson relish, half shoulder of lamb with orange
glaze, local pheasant casserole and medallions of pork fillet with Dijon mustard sauce
are indicative of the choices. Up to four daily choices on the fresh fish board, the top
seller being "Elegant fish and chips": cod in beer batter with chips served up in pages
of the Financial Times and, perhaps, luxury fish crumble or grilled sea bream with
lime butter. A daily pudding board may highlight chocolate and raspberry roulade
and orange and ginger sponge. No-smoking dining area. *Open 12-2, 7-11 (Sun 12-3,
7-10.30).* **Bar Food** *12-2, 7-10 (till 9.30 Sun).* Free House. **Beer** *Bass, Woods Parish.
Garden, outdoor eating. MasterCard,* **VISA**

SHROTON   **Cricketers**   FOOD

Tel 01258 860421   Fax 01258 861800   Map 14 B4
Shroton Blandford Forum Dorset DT11 8QD

Homely village local, situated opposite the village green and close to the unique
sloping cricket pitch, which is superbly sited beneath Hambledon Hill. Thirsty
cricketers (this pub is their HQ), walkers refreshing themselves along the Wessex Way
and local drinkers fill the simply-furnished bar that includes, to one side, a pool table
and various cricketing memorabilia. Diners complete the cross-section of people that
frequent this humble establishment. They seek out the honest, home-cooked food,
especially the often unusual fresh fish and seafood selection – sea bass with lime and
ginger sauce, squid casseroled in red wine, garlic and tomato, whole Dover sole – that
are on the menus here. A no-frills bar snack menu, which includes filled baguettes, is
supplemented by freshly-prepared daily blackboard specials such as chicken curry, roast
partridge with port and juniper berries and steak and Guinness pie. Well-maintained
and sheltered rear garden with flower beds and a trellis of climbing roses is ideal for
outdoor eating. It is worth noting that Shroton is still referred to as Iwerne Courtney
on some maps. Children welcome *Open 11.30 3, 7-11 (from 6.30 Jun-Aug), Sun 12-3,
7-10.30.* **Bar Food** *12-2, 7-9.45 (till 9.15 Sun).* Free House. **Beer** *Flowers Original, Bass,
Smiles Best, guest beers. Garden, outdoor eating. MasterCard,* **VISA**

SIBFORD GOWER   Wykham Arms   A

Tel 01295 780351   Map 14a B1
Sibford Gower Banbury Oxfordshire OX15 5RX

Yellow stone, mature thatch and a blaze of flowers and hanging baskets are picture-postcard material here in summer at this attractive 17th-century village pub. In winter the interior is warmed by real fires and the tiny dining-room with low beams and exposed stone walls takes on an altogether more cosy air. The renovated bars are fully carpeted and quite sedate, their best feature being an old stone well, now glass-covered to form an unusual bay-window table. Well-kept Hook Norton Best and local micro-brewery Merivales Edgecutter. Children are made very welcome and there are swings under the trees and a play area in a pretty back garden. New owners are sprucing the Wykham up and intoducing home-cooked fresh food (not yet inspected) *Open 12-3, 6.30-11 (Sun 12-10.30). Free House. **Beer** Hook Norton Best, Wadworth 6X, Bass, Fuller's London Pride, Merrivales Edgecutter. Garden. Patio. MasterCard, **VISA***

SKIDBY   Half Moon Inn   FOOD

Tel 01482 843403   Map 7 E1
16 Main Street Skidby East Riding of Yorkshire HU16 5TG

Chips with everything is not the stuff of the Half Moon; its speciality is home-made Yorkshire puddings – eight different combinations including lamb chops or curry! They are almost big enough to obscure the waitress. The half-acre garden has its own 'Sproggies Bar' for children, together with the only huge, suspended spiral climbing frame in the country. The welcome to children of all ages extends to the provision of baby-changing facilities in the Ladies. The pub itself is not without idiosyncrasies, having four little bars and wooden pillar supports. Alongside snacks like ploughman's lunches and sandwiches are home-made pies, soups, chilis, curries and burgers. *Open 11-11 (Sun 12-10.30). **Bar Food** 12-9.30. **Beer** John Smith's, Marston's Pedigree. Garden, outdoor eating, children's play area. MasterCard, **VISA***

SKIRMETT   Old Crown   FOOD

Tel 01491 638435   Map 15a D3
Skirmett Henley-on-Thames Oxfordshire RG9 6TD

Set by the village lane overlooking open fields, this charming, 350-year-old pub has an unspoilt and restful atmosphere that pervades throughout its two cottagey rooms and adjacent old-fashioned tap room. Beams, quarry-tiled and flagstone floors, an inglenook fireplace and an assortment of rustic sturdy furniture characterise the traditional interior. There is no music, no games machines and no counter; the well-conditioned Brakspear ales are dispensed straight from the cask in the old still-room beyond the tiny serving hatch. Bar food is reliable and home-cooked and although the varied menu rarely changes – except for seasonal variations – the tried and tested formula is a successful if not a cheap one. To start, perhaps a freshly-prepared soup (watercress), deep-fried Camembert or smoked fish terrine, followed by well-presented main courses: lasagne, chicken breast with cream cheese and asparagus, grilled sea bass and half roast duck with port and orange, all served with good vegetables. Additions to the menu may include fresh salads, crab and scallops in summer and local game in winter. To finish, there may be sticky toffee pudding or raspberry pavlova. Those popping in for just a snack will find ploughman's platters (lunch only) and a range of filled jacket potatoes. Splendid secret summer garden with benched areas surrounded by mature shrubs, willows and flower-beds. No children under 10 either inside or out in the mature cottage garden; no draught lager, either, for that matter. 5 miles north of Henley. *Open 11-2.30, 6-11 (Sun 12-2.30, 7-10.30) Closed all Mon (except Bank Holiday lunch) & possibly Sun eve Nov-Feb. **Bar Food** 12-2, 7-9 (till 8.30 Sun), possibly closed for food Sun eve Nov-Feb. **Beer** Brakspear. Garden. No credit cards.*

SMALLBURGH   The Crown   FOOD

Tel 01692 536314   Map 10 D1   **B&B**
Smallburgh Norwich NR12 9AD

Thatched, beamed 15th-century village inn set beside the busy A149 Great Yarmouth
to Cromer road with a peaceful, well-tended rear beer garden, complete with flower
borders and picnic benches. Homely, simply-furnished bar areas with barrel furniture,
a large open fire and blackboard menus listing reliable, home-cooked daily specials.
Choices may include pigeon pie, chicken in tarragon, whole gammon hock with
parsley sauce and cod fillet baked with fresh coriander, all served with fresh vegetables.
Routine printed bar menu listing various sandwiches and ploughman's platters. Sunday
roasts. Upstairs in the roof space are two clean and tidy bedrooms with attractive
fabrics, sturdy furniture, dormer windows in the sloping roof and recently installed en
suite bathrooms. TVs, radios and tea-makers are standard. No children under 14 in
the bar, over-7s only in the restaurant. *Open 12-3, 5.30-11 (Sat 12-4, 7-11, Sun 12-4
only). Closed Sun eve.* **Bar Food** *12-2, 6-9 (Sat 7-9.30). No food Sun eve.* **Beer** *Greene
King Abbot Ale, Boddingtons, Tetley, Flowers IPA, guest beer. Garden, outdoor eating.*
Accommodation *2 bedrooms, both en suite £40 (single £25). Children over 7 welcome
overnight (7-12s £15), additional bed available. Check-in by arrangement. No dogs.
Accommodation closed Christmas & New Year. MasterCard,* **VISA**

> We do not accept free meals or hospitality – our inspectors pay their own bills
> and never book in the name of Egon Ronay's Guides.

SMARDEN   The Bell   FOOD

Tel 01233 770283   Map 11 C5
Bell Lane Smarden Kent TN26 8PW

Tiled and rose-covered medieval Kentish inn in peaceful countryside (take the road
between the church and Chequers pub, then left at the junction). Rambling and rustic
interior full of character with low, hop-festooned oak beams, inglenook fireplaces and
a motley mix of old wooden furnishings in three flagstoned bars that are candelit in
the evenings. Adjacent games/family room with pool table. Bar food is reliable,
especially the hearty range of home-made daily specials such as chicken in tarragon,
beef in beer casserole and pork with Dijon mustard sauce. Ploughman's platters and
sandwiches available lunch and evening. Well-stocked bar dispensing eight real ales
on handpump, the heady Biddenden scrumpy cider and eight wines by the glass.
No under-14s in the Cellar Bar or Monk's Bar. Good summer garden. *Open 11.30-
2.30 (till 3 Sat), 6-11 (Sun 12-3, 6.30-10.30).* **Bar Food** *12-2 (till 2.30 Sun), 6.30-10
(till 10.30 Fri & Sat). Free House.* **Beer** *Fremlins, Flowers Original, Fuller's London Pride,
Shepherd Neame Master Brew, Goacher's Best, Ringwood Old Thumper, guest beers. Garden,
outdoor eating. Family room. Closed 25 Dec. Amex, MasterCard,* **VISA**

SMARDEN   Chequers Inn   FOOD

Tel 01233 770217   Fax 01233 770623   Map 11 C5   **B&B**
1 The Street Smarden Kent TN27 8QA

14th-century weatherboarded pub located close to the church in the heart of this most
attractive village. Charming Chequers Bar with light oak woodblock floor, sturdy
wooden tables and chairs and an exposed brick fireplace. Separate, neatly furnished
lounge bar and dining area with open fire. No intrusive games or music. Decent bar
food listed on a regularly-changing menu runs from the simplest snack – sandwiches,
ploughman's platters – to more restaurant-style dishes that might include venison paté,
lamb cutlets with rosemary and redcurrant and up to five fresh fish dishes such as
seafood casserole, whole Dover sole and baked trout with fresh herbs. Separate dish
of good, well-cooked fresh vegetables. Five homely and cottagey bedrooms upstairs
feature exposed beams and wall timbers, simple decor with Laura Ashley fabrics and

a few older pieces of darkwood furniture. Three boast en suite facilities, the remaining two share a spacious and clean bathroom. Good choice for breakfast. *Open 10-3, 6-11 (Sun 12-3, 7-10.30). Bar Food 12-2.30, 6.30-9.30 (from 7 Sun). Free House. Beer Bass, Ruddles County, Young's Special, Morland Old Speckled Hen, guest beer. Garden, outdoor eating. Accommodation 5 bedrooms, 3 en suite, £48 (single £20). Children welcome overnight (under-10s stay free in parents' room), additional bed (£5) & cot available. Accommodation closed 24 & 25 Dec, pub closed 25 Dec. MasterCard, VISA*

SMARTS HILL   Bottle House Inn   FOOD

Tel 01892 870306   Fax 01892 871094   Map 11 B5
Smarts Hill Penshurst Kent TN11 8ET

Well-modernised 15th-century pub remotely situated on a country lane 2 miles south-west of Penshurst off the B2188. Low beams, a good inglenook fireplace and sturdy pub furniture characterise the friendly and welcoming bar and attractive dining-room. The varied bar menu is the main attraction here and it can get very busy early on with eager diners. Beyond a fairly standard selection of starters or lighter meals, including ploughman's platters, an extensive, daily-changing main-course menu hides some interesting and reliable dishes such as turkey and mushroom pie, chargrilled lamb fillet with rosemary gravy, salmon with dill and mustard, and red mullet with prawn and tarragon hollandaise. Vegetarian options may include stuffed aubergines topped with courgettes and cheese. Portions are generous and accompanying vegetables well cooked. Peaceful front lawn and patio with country views. *Open 11-3, 6-11 (Sun 12-3, 7-10.30). Bar Food 12-2, 7-10. Free House. Beer Larkins Bitter, Harveys Sussex, Ind Coope Burton Ale, guest beer. Garden, patio, outdoor eating. MasterCard, VISA*

SNAPE   Golden Key   FOOD

Tel 01728 688510   Map 10 D3   **B&B**
Priory Road Snape Suffolk IP17 1SQ

Zzz...

A delightful and tasteful 15th-century, cottage-style pub close to Snape Maltings concert hall, with a colourful summer hanging-basket-festooned facade and alfresco front patio. Inside, the main bar has a quarry-tiled old-fashioned public end and a carpeted lounge end, with neatly-arranged scrubbed pine tables and some fine old settles fronting one of the two open fires (blazing away, even in June!). The blackboard menu holds few surprises, but the food is carefully prepared and home-cooked. Choose from sound favourites such as home-made samosas with a yoghurt and mint dip and a decent soup – mixed bean – followed by a rather stodgy sausage, egg and onion pie, excellent honey-roast ham, smoked haddock quiche, whole lemon sole, sea bass, crab salad, brill, fresh lobster and a steak selection. There are freshly-filled rolls (no sandwiches), ploughman's platters, roast beef on Sundays and several wines are served by the glass. Puddings are popular, including the home-made chocolate brandy cake and hot lemon cake. Upstairs, tucked away under the eaves, are two fine new bedrooms (another is promised for next year), both of which are well insulated from the sounds of the bar and dining-room extension down below. They are unusually spacious and well-furbished for pub accommodation, with big beds, wing armchairs, sofa bed, good-sized teletext TV and modern bathrooms with bidet, shower over bath and darkwood fittings; a few little colourful and practical touches (perhaps a full-length mirror, tissues and better toiletries) would make this a truly cossetting place to stay after a special night out at the Maltings. No children under 14 in bar areas. *Open 11-3, 6-11 (Sun 12-3, 7-10.30). Bar Food 12-2.30, 6-9.30 (7-9.30 Sun). Beer Adnams, guest beers. Accommodation 2 bedrooms, both en suite, £55. Children welcome overnight, under-2s free, additional bed supplied (£15). Check-in by arrangement. Patio, outdoor eating. No credit cards.*

SNETTISHAM · Rose & Crown · FOOD

Tel 01485 541382 Fax 01485 543172   Map 10 B1   **B&B**
Old Church Road Snettisham King's Lynn Norfolk PE31 7LX

Tucked away just off the main road that runs through the village centre, Anthony and Jeanette Goodrich's splendid, white-painted 14th-century inn was originally built to house the craftsmen who built the beautiful local church just up the road. Beyond the attractive flower-decked facade lie a warren of three bars linked by a narrow, twisting corridor, off which are much-improved (and now rather smart) loos. Heavy oak beams, uneven red-tiled floors, inglenook fireplaces and comfortable settles characterise the two small front bar rooms; to one side of the front entrance is a small dining-room where breakfast is also served. Best bets on the food front are the blackboard menus: look for home-made soup, good pork and herb sausages, crab salad, pork stir-fry, supreme of chicken with wild mushrooms, and homely puds. A varied selection of five real ales usually includes two changing guest ales (try a pint of Wolf), plus there are good wines from Adnams, all available by the glass (but not all whites are served cool enough). To the rear is another bar, which leads through to a modern, poorly-ventilated extension that houses a third drinks servery area and (up a few steps or with direct access from the car park) a large, high-ceilinged dining-room with its own grill area (everything-with-chips and help-yourself salad). The pub can become very crowded when busy and the big rear extension helps cater for the families that flock here in season. After feasting on the under-12s' menu youngsters can escape into the safe, walled garden and clamber around the large play area that boasts a slide, play house, two wooden forts, monkey bars and a connecting walkway, all under a pretty willow tree. Less active children may find the guinea pig cage at one end of the lawned garden more entertaining. There is a mother's baby-changing unit in the Grill Room's Ladies and high-chairs are provided. Regular live music (mainly jazz). Upstairs, via a very steep, short staircase, are three airy, prettily decorated bedrooms (all with TV and tea-maker) – en suite, delightful and comfortable. Beware of the head-cracking low doorways! A tiny cottage 30 yards down the road is also available for B&B – fine for young families (as long as they don't mind poor TV reception). Plans are afoot to add further bedrooms above the rear extension.
Open 11-11, Sun 12-10.30. Free House. **Beer** *Bass, Adnams Bitter, Greene King Abbot Ale, two guest beers.* **Bar Food** *12-2.30, 6-9.30. Garden, outdoor eating, children's play area.* **Accommodation** *3 rooms, all en suite, £55 (single £35). Children welcome overnight, additional bed & cot available (£10). Closed 25 Dec. No dogs. MasterCard,* **VISA**

SOMERBY · Old Brewery Inn · A

Tel 01664 454866   Map 7 D3
High Street Somerby Leicestershire LE14 2PZ

Those to whom the quaffing of fine ale is akin to the staff of life will rejoice at the life the Old Brewery Inn has restored to the quiet village of Somerby. Once closed and derelict, it now houses landlord and brewer Barrie's commendable Parish brewery whose products already have a burgeoning reputation. In the bar, by the 40-foot well samples of Parish Special (£1.30 per pint), Somerby Premium and Poachers Ale hold more than their own alongside ever-changing guest brews – 16 hand pumps in total. For those in bolder mood, Baz's Bonce Blower, at 10% ABV, is probably the country's strongest ale. Food ranging from beefburgers to steaks ensures that there are plenty of foundations to lay under a sampling session. Increasingly popular are the brewery tours – £1.50 for a tour, £6 tour and buffet or, for twelve or more, £18 inclusive of food and all you can drink. For those who may find the experience totally overwhelming, there's bedroom accommodation (not en suite, £25) in the old stables where three twin rooms share the necessary ablutions. *Open 11.30-3, 6-11 (Sun 12-10.30). Free House.* **Beer** *Parish Special Bitter, Somerby Premium, Parish Farm Gold, Mild, Porter, Poachers Ale, Baz's Bonce Blower, Wild John, guest beers. Garden, outdoor eating, occasional barbecue. Children's play area. MasterCard,* **VISA**

SONNING — The Bull — A

Tel 01734 693901   Fax 01734 691057   Map 15a D4
High Street Sonning Berkshire RG4 0UP

Quintessential 16th-century English traditional pub, originally the guest house for pilgrims visiting the medieval chapel of St Andrews opposite, its ancient black and white exterior covered with plants and flowers. You can sit outside and admire them and the view across the peaceful parish churchyard opposite – while in its two linked rooms there are sturdy old beams, gleaming brass, quarry tiles, and an inglenook fireplace, alive with logs in winter, ablaze with flowers in summer. In the past year both the bar areas and the once-dated bedrooms have been completely revamped, the latter now boasting en suite facilities and one four-poster bed (£55 double, £45 single – not yet inspected). The inn attracted the attention of Jerome K Jerome who mentioned it in his novel *Three Men in a Boat*. Unusually, the brewery leases this fine village pub from the church who own the building. Children welcome. *Open 11-3, 5.30-11 (from 6 Sat), Sun 12-3, 7-10.30.* **Beer** *Gale's, guest beer. Patio/terrace. Amex, MasterCard,* **VISA**

SOUTH HARTING — Ship Inn — FOOD

Tel 01730 825302   Map 15 D3
South Harting West Sussex GU31 5PZ

Adorned in summer with colourful flower baskets this white-painted mid-17th-century inn enjoys a pleasant central position in this attractive Sussex village. Homely interior comprising a rustic public bar, complete with dart board and other games, and a separate comfortable lounge bar furnished with a mixture of varnished tables, banquettes and wheelback chairs with hunting prints on the walls. This main bar is largely given over to eating, with an extensive menu of mostly home-made dishes and a short daily specials board. Fresh seafood is a speciality and fish starters feature strongly on the menu – dressed Selsey crab, scallops à la bretonne or potted shrimps whilst the comprehensive list of main dishes offers plenty of variety: fish pie, seafood lasagne, chicken balti, game pie, rack of lamb with rosemary and salmon en croute. For pudding try the banana and meringue roulade or a traditional treacle tart. It's usually wise to book for meals but, at lunchtime and all afternoon, snacks are also offered, like sandwiches and crusty bread platters (Stilton and pickles). Diverse, carefully-chosen wine list. Children under 14 years are not allowed inside, but in fine weather are welcome in the small garden, which boasts an aviary with cockatiel and quail amongst other birds. *Open 11-11 (11-3, 5.30-11 Mon-Thu in winter), Sun 12-3, 7-10.30.* **Bar Food** *12-2.30, 7-9.30 (snacks all day, till 9 Sun). No food Sun eve Oct-Mar. Free House.* **Beer** *Palmers IPA, Ballards Bitter, Ringwood Best, guest beers. Garden, outdoor eating. Amex, Diners, MasterCard,* **VISA**

SOUTH HARTING — White Hart — FOOD

Tel 01730 825355   Map 15 D3
High Street South Harting West Sussex GU31 5QB

Pleasant village pub with three beamed bars, wooden tables, polished wood floors, log fires and a decent choice of good, fresh food. Known for their traditional country recipes, the licensees display their menu on a blackboard where specials appear daily – seafood mornay, spicy Mexican chicken and steak and kidney pie are typical choices. Separate simple bar snack menu includes sandwiches, salads and ploughman's platters. On Thursday, Friday and Saturday evenings the restaurant, formerly an old scullery, with flagstone floors and open inglenook fireplace, serves an à la carte menu. Vegetarians may wish to try the broccoli and cream cheese bake or vegetarian lasagne. Desserts may include pear and ginger gateau and various fruit pies. In fine weather, families may wish to venture into the beautiful garden overlooking the South Downs where children can safely play around the pond and waterfall. *Open 11-3, 6-11 (Sun 12-3, 7-10.30).* **Bar Food** *11-2 (from 12 Sun), 7-10 (no food Mon eve). Free House.* **Beer** *Ind Coope Burton Ale, Friary Meux Best, Tetley, guest beer. Garden, outdoor eating, children's play area. Family room (with toy box). No credit cards.*

SOUTH LEIGH   Mason Arms   FOOD

Tel 01993 702485   Map 14a B2
South Leigh Witney Oxfordshire OX8 6XN

To any unsuspecting traveller arriving at the Masons Arms, a delightful 15th-century thatched inn slumbering in a sleepy Oxfordshire village just off the A40 near Witney, one would think that they had found a typical, quintessentially English country pub. But all is not what it seems! A prominent sign on the wall informs you that this is 'Gerry Stonhill's Individual Masons Arms', then another on the door warns you that dogs, children and mobile phones are definately not welcome in his establishment. 'Character' (in more ways than one) is the word that immediately springs to mind. Flagstone floors strewn with old rugs, two huge inglenook fireplaces with blazing winter log fires, dark hessian-covered walls adorned with quality prints, paintings and objets d'art, dark oak antique tables topped with candles and various wine bottles and old cigar boxes scattered on shelves succeed in creating a Dickensian feeling of well-being throughout the bar and three rambling dining-rooms. In truth, the atmosphere is that of a civilised Gentleman's Club and closer inspection reveals that Mr Stonhill's very 'individual', some would say eccentric, character is etched all over the pub. Cosy clubbiness extends to a predominantly whisky- and cognac-stocked bar (tip-top Burton Ale is drawn from the barrel in the cellar), a very select French-only list of wines and the fact that this is very much a 'smoking' establishment, with no non-smoking areas anywhere and quality Cuban cigars being offered at the end of a meal. Different it certainly is, but the welcome, atmosphere and quality of the food make it difficult to ignore. Dishes on both the regular menu and the interesting specials board feature prime fresh produce, notably excellent Angus steaks and the largest Dover or lemon soles and sea bass on the market, the latter brought to the table for you to admire before cooking. Starters range from basil and tomato soup, mussels in vermouth and cream and Mr Baxter's potted shrimps to a plate of wild smoked salmon. Main courses, served with real hand-cut chips and decent vegetables, may include beef bourguignon, lamb and plum casserole, half a roast duck with Grand Marnier sauce and fresh salmon steaks. Round off with a traditional pudding (apple pie) or a plate of cheese. Finally, note the club-like tradition of adding a cover charge (£1 per head), the acceptance of only 'cash, American Express or cheques' as payment and the splendid bill paper, complete with 1d stamp. *Open 12-2.30, 6-11 (Sun 12-3 only). Closed Sun eve & all Mon.* **Bar Food** *12.30-2.30, 7.30-10.30 (Sun 1-3 only). Free House.* **Beer** *Ind Coope Burton Ale. Garden. Amex.*

> We do not accept free meals or hospitality – our inspectors pay their own bills and never book in the name of Egon Ronay's Guides.

SOUTH POOL   Millbrook Inn   FOOD

Tel 01548 531581   Map 13 D3
South Pool Kingsbridge Devon TQ7 2RW

Opening hours at this white-painted, 400-year-old pub vary somewhat according to the state of the tide in the creek that extends into the heart of the pretty village, bringing a number of the Millbrook's customers by boat. Inside, it is small and cosy with tapestry cushions on the wheelback chairs and ceiling beams decorated with old clay pipes, horse brasses, old bank notes and hundreds of visiting cards. To the rear, a tiny terrace overlooks a small stream which is home to a family of ducks. Home-cooked fare appears on the twice daily-changing blackboard menu; lunchtime favourites range from poached salmon or fresh crab sandwiches and savoury croissants to fisherman's pie and cheesy leek and potato bake, with evening extras like paella, halibut au poivre, smoked chicken, beef in ale casserole and fresh pasta dishes (smoked salmon, cream and dill). Home-made puds such as sticky toffee pudding and banoffi pie provide a sweet conclusion. *Open 11-2.30, 5.30-11 (winter from 6.30), Sun 12-3, 7-10.30.* **Bar Food** *12-2, 6.30-9.30 (Sun 7-9). Free House.* **Beer** *Bass, Ruddles Best, Wadworth 6X, guest beer. Covered forecourt & streamside terrace, outdoor eating. Family room. No credit cards.*

SOUTH STOKE   Perch & Pike   FOOD

Tel 01491 872415   Map 14a C3
South Stoke Streatley-on-Thames Oxfordshire RG8 0JS

Tucked away in the peaceful Thames Valley village of South Stoke, two miles north of Goring (and just a short stroll away from the river) is the charming Perch & Pike, a small brick-and-flint Brakspear pub that has been carefully refurbished and rejuvenated since Michael and Jill Robinson arrived here in 1993. Inside, two spick-and-span and delightfully furnished rooms, complete with low-beamed ceilings, red-tiled and brick floors, tasteful dark oak furniture (much of it antique), open fires, attractive china and a fine grandfather clock offer a civilised ambience in which to enjoy Jill Robinson's good home-cooking. Booking is essential for both lunch and dinner as the limited number of neatly-laid tables (28 covers) fill quickly with a well-heeled and discerning dining clientele. The attraction is the imaginative hand-written menu, which changes every two weeks, and the short list of daily blackboard specials. Start, perhaps, with tomato and basil soup, gravadlax with home-made dill sauce or mussels in white wine, garlic and cream, followed by rosti crab cakes with fresh mango and coriander salsa, chargrilled chicken marinaded with honey and ginger, mushroom and garlic tart with olives, parmesan and a tomato and basil coulis or fresh fish of the day – perhaps roast sand sole with lemon and herb butter – all well presented and served with crisp vegetables. For a snack, try the three-storey BLT, one of the good sandwiches or a ploughman's lunch. Finish off with banana cheesecake, treacle tart or bread-and-butter pudding. Good cafetière coffee. Of the list of 28 or so well-chosen and keenly-priced wines, around 15 are served by the glass, including a champagne (£5.50). Flower-filled window boxes and tubs give a splash of colour to the gravelled entrance with its adjacent picnic benches for fine weather drinking. No under-14s in the bar area. *Open 12-2.30, 6-11 (Sun 12-3, 7-10.30).* **Bar Food** *12-2, 7-9.30 (no food Sun eve).* **Beer** *Brakspear. Garden. Closed 25 Dec. MasterCard,* **VISA**

SOUTH ZEAL   Oxenham Arms   B&B

Tel 01837 840244   **Fax 01837 840791**   Map 13 D2
South Zeal Devon EX20 2JT

Just off the A30, 17 miles west of Exeter this ancient, romantically fronted, creeper-covered inn is in the centre of rural South Zeal. Built in the late 12th century by lay monks and first licensed in 1477, it remains genuinely unspoilt inside too, with worn flag floors, vast open fires, original beams, rough plaster walls, spooky passageways, solidly traditional drinking areas, and a relaxing clubbish lounge. Isolated garden overlooking Dartmoor at the back. Nice, old-fashioned bedrooms (one with four-poster) offer discreet modern comforts; delightful place to stay. *Open 11-2.30, 6-11 (Sun 12-2.30, 7-10.30).* Free House. **Beer** *Furgusons Dartmoor Best, Princetown Jail Ale. Garden. Family room.* **Accommodation** *8 bedrooms, 7 en suite, £60 (single £45). Children welcome overnight, additional and bed (£5.50) & cot (£3) available. Amex, Diners, MasterCard,* **VISA**

SOUTHWOLD   The Crown   ★   FOOD   B&B

Tel 01502 722275   **Fax 01502 727263**   Map 10 D2
High Street Southwold Suffolk IP18 6DP

Zzz...

Next-door brewers, Adnams, take the credit for the stylish restoration of Southwold's central Georgian inn. While not without fault in attempting to be most things to all comers, the Crown is to be applauded for its success in bringing straightforward food, prime-condition beers and excellent wines to the average spender. The nautically themed rear bar is complete with binnacle and navigation lamps; the bar's curved and glassed-in rear panel gives the entirely fitting impression of being the flagship's bridge. To the front, facing the High Street, the Parlour serves as lounge and coffee shop; the front bar and attendant restaurant, decked out with green-grained panelling and Georgian-style brass lamps, has a refined air, yet is totally without pretension or stuffiness. New head chef Gary Marsland offers a daily-changing bar menu highlighting excellent local fish such as steamed fillet of cod with asparagus, kumquat and dill cream, grilled whole herrings on mixed leaves with a lime and leek syrup, and

Thai-style shell and seafish chowder. Other options range from cream of onion soup and escalope of pork with Stilton and walnut glaze to venison sausage and black pudding casserole. Most meals are served in both starter and main-course sizes at good-value prices. Finish off with date and almond cheesecake, iced rhubarb parfait with stem ginger or a selection of Neal's Yard cheeses. In addition to the fine wine list chosen by Simon Loftus there's a splendid supplementary, monthly-changing list of 18 or so wines, available by both glass and bottle. The non-smoking restaurant has interesting fixed-price menus. Traditional roast beef and Yorkshire pudding is served in the restaurant on Sundays. Bedrooms are well equipped, with antique or decent reproduction pieces and bright fabrics and furnishings: all have private bathrooms though three are not strictly en suite (the bathroom is across a corridor); one family room has a double and two single beds. Pleasant staff offer a warm welcome and good but informal service. A light breakfast is served promptly in the bedroom along with the morning paper. *Open 10.30-3, 6-11 (from 7 Oct-Apr), Sun 12-3, 7-10.30.* ***Bar Food*** *12.15-1.45, 7.15-9.45.* ***Beer*** *Adnams. Patio, outdoor eating.* ***Accommodation*** *12 bedrooms, 9 en suite, £72 (family room £87, single £41). Children welcome overnight, additional bed (£10) & cot (£5) available. Check-in from 2pm onwards. No dogs. Pub & accommodation closed 1 week Jan. Amex, Diners, MasterCard,* **VISA**

SOWERBY BRIDGE   The Hobbit   B&B

Tel 01422 832202   Fax 01422 835381   Map 6 C1
Hob Lane Sowerby Bridge Calderdale HX6 3QL

Standing on the very lip of the moor (follow directions, below, carefully), the Hobbit enjoys panoramic views over the Pennines and Sowerby Bridge far below. A relaxed and welcoming place, it's a haven for families, with Bilbo's bistro open all day, every day: youngsters receive a fun pad on arrival. Connecting bedrooms are available for families, with special weekend rates, while a thoughtful array of accessories appeals equally to the mid-week business traveller. Satellite TVs, for instance, include a video channel and fresh milk is conveniently kept in a corridor fridge. A cottage annexe across the road contains a pair of splendidly-furnished executive bedrooms which also benefit from the finest views down the valley. No-smoking areas in bistro and restaurant. Watch out for the many and varied theme nights, notably the murder and mystery evenings, and special children's events. Take the A58 to Sowerby Bridge by the Railway Viaduct, turn onto Station Road, then right at the police station, left at the T-Junction, continue up the hill and then right at the crossroads. *Open 12-11 (up to 2am with meals), Sun 12-10. Free House.* ***Beer*** *Theakston Best, Ruddles Best, guest beer. Garden, two patios.* ***Accommodation*** *22 bedrooms, all en suite (14 with shower only), £63-£73 (single £42/£49), weekend reductions. Children welcome overnight (under-6s stay free in parents' room, 6-12s £11), cot available. No dogs. Amex, Diners, MasterCard,* **VISA**

SPARKFORD   Sparkford Inn   A

Tel 01963 440218   Fax 01963 440358   Map 13 F2
Sparkford Yeovil Somerset BA22 7JH

Families driving west along the A303 with restless children should take note of this former 15th-century coaching inn, which is situated a minute's drive away in the centre of Sparkford village, 6 miles west of Wincanton. Youngsters can expend some energy in the well equipped and safe outdoor play area or, especially when the weather is inclement, amuse themselves in the supervised 'Snakes and Ladders' indoor play room (open weekends and school holiday lunchtimes). Here they will find a 25ft bouncy castle, punch bag and balls, trampoline and large soft play area with see-saws, animal shapes and slide. Facilities for children extend to their own menu, high-chairs and a baby-changing shelf in the Ladies. With children happily entertained, parents can relax with a drink in the beamed and comfortably furnished bars that retain many original features. Menus, especially the blackboard specials, looked promising on a recent visit; upstairs, there are three homely and simply furnished en suite bedrooms (£32 double). Owners Nigel and Suzanne Tucker also run the *Star Inn* at Stanton St John, Oxfordshire (see entry). *Open 11-2.30 (till 3 Sat), 6.30-11 (Sun 12-3, 7-10.30). Free House.* ***Beer*** *Bass, Wadworth 6X, Worthington Best, Fuller's London Pride, guest beer. Garden, children's play area. Family room. Amex, MasterCard,* **VISA**

SPARSHOLT   The Plough   FOOD

Tel 01962 776353   Map 15 D3
Sparsholt Winchester Hampshire SO21 2NW

A delightful flower- and shrub-filled garden complete with children's playhouses, wooden garden chalet, chickens and donkeys is a popular summer feature at this much-extended 200-year-old cottage, located on the edge of the village. The smartly refurbished bar area, incorporating the original cottage front rooms, feature pine tables, a dresser and comfortable cushioned chairs, with plenty of attractive prints brightening up the walls and an open fireplace for cooler days. New tenants have settled in well and have maintained the high standard of cooking that earned the Plough our recommendation for food under the previous landlords. Two sensibly short blackboards list the varied range of decent pub food on offer, from hearty, home-cooked snacks served with fresh crusty bread (broccoli and almond soup, cauliflower cheese, salmon tagliatelle, bourride of fish, moules marinière) to steak, ale and mushroom pie with vegetables and more imaginative, sauced dishes such as rack of lamb with wild mushrooms and brandy cream, and shark steak with mixed peppercorn sauce. A handwritten menu on the bar lists 'doorstep' sandwiches (salmon and cucumber, beef and horseradish, fresh crab) that require a knife and fork to eat. Short list of home-made puddings. Well-kept Wadworth ales and at least eight wines are served by the glass. *Open 11-3, 6.30-11 (Sun 12-3, 7-10.30).* **Bar Food** *12-2, 7-9 (Fri & Sat to 9.30).* **Beer** *Wadworth 6X & Henry's IPA, guest beer. Garden, children's play area. No credit cards.*

SPREYTON   Tom Cobley Tavern   B&B

Tel 01647 231314   Map 13 D2
Spreyton Devon EX17 5AL

This peaceful white-washed village local draws plenty of visitors in the summer months due to its name and associations with 'Widecombe Fair'. It was in 1802 that Tom Cobley and all left the village for Widecombe and his cottage still stands opposite the pub. The unspoilt main bar has an open fire, cushioned settles and dispenses some good Devon ale straight from the cask. Those on the historical trail can be accommodated in one of the four homely and comfortably furnished bedrooms which have attractive fabrics and bedcovers. None are en suite, but the adjacent bathroom facilities are spotlessly clean. Summer alfresco drinking can be enjoyed on the pretty flower-bedecked gravel terrace or in the rear garden with its far-reaching views. *Open 12-2, 6-11 (Sun 12-3, 7-10.30). Closed Mon lunch. Free House.* **Beer** *Cotleigh Tawny, Butcombe Bitter, guest beer. Garden. Family room.* **Accommodation** *4 bedrooms, not en suite, £36 (single £18). Children welcome overnight (under 6 months stay free, under-5s £6, 6-12s £12 in parents' room), additional cot available (£6). Check-in by arrangement. No credit cards.*

SPRINGTHORPE   New Inn   FOOD

Tel 01427 838254   Map 7 E2
16 Hill Road Springthorpe Lincolnshire DN21 5PY

Created from a row of brick cottages over 100 years ago, this homely off-the-beaten-track village local enjoys a peaceful position close to the parish church and overlooking the small green. An unpretentious and welcoming atmosphere awaits visitors in the comfortable carpeted lounge and in the separate, spartan locals bar. Along the corridor is a neat and cottagey dining-room, which bustles with set Sunday lunch diners (bookings only). A short and simple printed bar menu features mainly standard dishes, but standing out from the rest are the landlady's traditional home-cooked specials such as a hearty soup – cheese and broccoli – served with warm rolls, beef stew and dumplings, chicken with mushroom and tarragon sauce, crispy Chinese pork or smoked haddock and cheesey cod bake. *Open 12-2, 7-11 (till 10.30 Sun). Closed Mon eve.* **Bar Food** *12-2, 7-10. Free House.* **Beer** *Bateman XXXB, Marston's Pedigree, guest beer. MasterCard,* **VISA**

STALISFIELD GREEN   Plough   FOOD

Tel 01795 890256
Stalisfield Green Ashford Kent ME13 0HY

Map 11 C5

Splendid, 15th-century Kentish hall house nestling by the green in an unspoilt hamlet high up on the North Downs north of Charing; it enjoys far-reaching views across the Swale estuary and the Isle of Sheppey. Two well-maintained and welcoming beamed bars are furnished with a comfortable mix of old and new pine and warmed by two open log fires. There's a cosy dining-room and an attractive, light and airy garden room with access to a peaceful patio and side garden with rustic tables and benches. French proprietor/chef Joel Gross offers a weekly-changing blackboard menu that has a distinct Gallic flavour (even the menu is written in French). Begin, perhaps, with hot oysters and cream of langoustine, French onion soup or home-made paté, then progress to monkfish with balsamic vinegar, seafood platter (24hrs' notice), fresh lobster, swordfish or reliable meat dishes like tournedos of beef with Madeira and wild mushrooms, confit de canard and baby chicken with sauce diable. Chocolate tart and apple crepes with cassis sorbet may appear on the pudding list. Ploughman's lunches and sandwiches are always available for those desiring a lighter snack. Good real ales and an interesting choice of wines, including a short, value-for-money list of bin ends. 2% charge for using credit cards. No children indoors. *Open 12-3, 7-11 (Sun 12-3 only). Closed Sun eve & all Mon.* **Bar Food** *12-1.45, 7-9.15.* **Beer** *Harveys Best, Adnams Extra, Shepherd Neame Master Brew. Garden, outdoor eating.* MasterCard, **VISA**

STAMFORD   George of Stamford   FOOD

Tel 01780 755171   Fax 01780 757070
71 St Martins Stamford Lincolnshire PE9 2LB

Map 7 E3   B&B

Arguably the finest and grandest of England's old coaching inns, the George is a fully modernised hotel (recommended in our *1997 Hotels & Restaurants Guide*) that retains some wonderful period atmosphere. It's believed that there's been a hostelry of sorts here since the Norman period, originally as a stopping place for pilgrims on their way to the Holy Land, and a crypt under what is now the cocktail bar is certainly medieval, while much of the present building, which dates from 1597, remains in the veritable warren of rooms that make up the public areas. Facing the High Street, the oak-panelled London Suite and York Bar were once waiting rooms for the "twenty up and twenty down" stages which passed this way, but for the modern pub-goer this bar is probably the least attractive, being solidly masculine in its appearance. The Garden Lounge, however, which is exotically bedecked in orchids, palms and orange trees, provides a fine setting for informal eating throughout the day (7am-11pm): dishes range from open sandwiches and pasta meals to sizzling beef with ginger and mushrooms and noisettes of lamb with green peppercorn and brandy sauce. Lunch includes a fine cold buffet, with which, incidentally, up to 13 wines are offered by the glass. Next door, and by far the most picturesque spot, is the enclosed courtyard. Surrounded by the ivy-covered hotel buildings, hung with vast flowering baskets and illuminated by old street lamps, it makes an ideal venue for morning coffee and afternoon tea, as well as barbecues on mid-summer evenings. Restaurant dining, in an elegant, chandeliered hall sporting silver urns, duck presses, and domed carving wagons (daily roast joints) and serving trolleys (smoked salmon, cheese, desserts) still in daily use, runs along traditional (and comparatively pricey) lines with adventurous touches; gentlemen are 'respectfully' requested to wear a jacket and tie. The super wine list is keenly priced, expertly compiled and simple to use. Accommodation at the George is strictly hotel, which is fine if you're prepared to pay. A liveried porter shows you to the room and there's a full, cosseting night service. The comfort of plushly-draped bedrooms, close-carpeted through to the bathrooms fitted out with bespoke toiletries, generous towels and rather wonky telephone showers is all wonderfully 'British'. A morning tray of tea (with folded daily paper – no, it's not ironed!) appears at the appointed time, and a traditional English breakfast is served down in the Garden Lounge. *Open 11-11 (Sun 12-10.30).* **Bar Food** *12-11 (till 10.30 Sun).* *Free House.* **Beer** *Adnams Broadside, Ruddles Best. Cobbled courtyard, outdoor eating, beautician, hair salon. Family room.* **Accommodation** *47 bedrooms, all en suite (3 single rooms with shower only), £105-£160 (single £78/£88). Children welcome overnight, additional bed (£20) & cot available.* Amex, Diners, MasterCard, **VISA**

STANFORD DINGLEY   Old Boot   FOOD

Tel 01734 744292   Map 14a C4
Stanford Dingley Reading Berkshire RG7 6LS

White-painted brick building with black woodwork and hanging baskets of flowers, located in an attractive village. Its simple and homely interior comprises one large bar with a mix of darkwood and pine furnishings, country prints and a large inglenook with a log fire in winter. Several blackboards list the extensive and varied selection of food available in both bar and the adjacent dining-room. Choices range from good pub favourites (beef and Brakspear pie, lasagne and luxury sandwiches – roast beef with horseradish – served with coleslaw, salad and crisps) to interesting vegetarian options like wild mushroom and broccoli tart or more ambitious specials such as crispy duck with honey and almond sauce, salmon and crab wrapped in a vine leaf with lime and ginger, chicken stuffed with spinach and Stilton, and various steaks, all accompanied by five fresh vegetables. Separate fresh fish board (steamed sea bass with spinach and coriander) on weekdays, with a limited menu on Sunday (traditional roast lunch) and Mondays. Four well-kept real ales are offered and there's a delightful rear summer garden with a wishing-well and dovecote. *Open 11-3, 6-11 (Sun 12-3, 7-10.30).* **Bar Food** *12-2, 6-10 (Sun from 7).* Free House. **Beer** *Brakspear Special, three guest beers. Garden, outdoor eating. MasterCard,* **VISA**

STANFORD DINGLEY   Bull Country Inn   FOOD

Tel 01734 744409   Map 14a C4
Stanford Dingley Reading Berkshire RG7 6LS

The pretty redbrick Bull has its origins genuinely in the 15th century and its sturdy oak pillars mid-bar are certainly load-bearing. They divide the beamed lounge bar into two intimate areas which are primarily made over to eating, and their refined air is augmented by light classical background music. With only half a dozen or so tables to service, and a tiny kitchen from which to work, menus are kept sensibly short while the service shines by being so friendly and obliging. For a snack there are filled baked potatoes and ploughman's platters; home-cooked daily specials are typified by lamb and rosemary casserole, tandoori chicken and sun-dried and roasted tomato risotto. Main menu dishes include carrot and orange soup, avocado mousse with prawns followed by drunken fish pie and sirloin steak; those in the know will go for the excellent 'pommes Dauphinoise'. Children are allowed in the saloon bar up to 8.30pm (except Saturday evenings). Six miles from Junction 12 of the M4 – follow the A4 west to the second roundabout, turn right on the A340 towards Pangbourne, take the first left to Bradfield, then left again after which you will find Stanford Dingley signposted on the right. *Open 12-3, 7-11 (till 10.30 Sun). Closed Mon lunch (except Bank Holidays).* **Bar Food** *12-2.30, 7.30-10. Free House.* **Beer** *Bass, Archers Village, Brakspear Bitter, West Berks Brewery Good Old Boy. Garden, outdoor eating. Family room. No credit cards.*

STANNERSBURN   Pheasant Inn   FOOD

Tel & Fax 01434 240382   Map 5 D2   **B&B**
Stannersburn Falstone Kielder Water Northumberland NE48 1DD

Zzz...

Just a mile from Kielder Water in the Northumberland National Park stands the four centuries old farmhouse which now houses the Pheasant. The Kershaw family's conversion of the former Crown Inn has been painstaking and purposeful. The carpeted Lounge Bar is in muted tones and in the warm mellow pine dining-room traditional pub food is served from a kitchen reliably run by Irene and son Robin. Always available are the likes of ploughman's platters and sandwiches (lunch only), lasagne, haddock fillets and steak and kidney pie: daily specials encompass Indonesian style rice with prawns, mussels, salmon and monkfish, and seafood provençale with tagliatelle. Follow with banoffi pie or raspberry crumble. There are no chips here; rather, the kitchen's reputation rests firmly on freshly-cooked vegetables and roast prime sirloin for a commendable Sunday lunch. The Barn and Hemmel house ten comfortable bedrooms; furnishings are colourful and TV, hairdryers and beverage trays the standard fittings. Fully en suite, the family room and three larger twins have full-size bathtubs with showers; remaining doubles have WC and showers only. All are smartly tiled and brightly lit. All bedrooms and the dining-room are non-smoking areas. *Open 11-3, 6-11 (12-2, 7-10.30 Dec-Mar), Sun 12-3, 7-10.30. Closed Mon Dec-Mar.* **Bar Food** *12-2.30 (till 2 Sun), 7-9. Free House.* **Beer** *Tetley, Ind Coope Burton Ale, Theakston Best & XB. Garden, outdoor eating.* **Accommodation** *8 bedrooms, all en suite, £54 (family room £76, single £30). Children welcome overnight (under-4s stay free in parents' room, 4-6s £10), additional bed (£8) available. Check-in by arrangement. Closed all 25 & 26 Dec. MasterCard,* **VISA**

STANTON ST JOHN	**Star Inn**	FOOD

Tel & Fax 01865 351277   Map 14a C2
Stanton St John Oxford Oxfordshire OX9 1EX

☺

A former 18th-century butcher's shop and abattoir (now owned by Wadworth) with lots of period feel in two bars on two levels, both low-beamed, one brick-floored, the other carpeted and furniture-crammed. Families can eat in a separate no-smoking room. Beyond a straightforward printed menu listing ploughman's, sandwiches, grills and children's dishes, daily specials may feature pork and cider casserole, game pie and sea trout and turbot pie, with banana and ginger cheesecake or treacle and walnut tart to finish. A separate vegetarian menu offers a choice of six dishes. £1 charge for paying by credit card. Landlords the Tuckers also own the *Sparkford Inn* in Somerset (see entry). *Open 11-2.30, 6.30-11 (Sun 12-3, 7-10.30).* **Bar Food** *12-2, 7-10 (till 9.30 Sun).* **Beer** *Wadworth Henry's IPA, 6X, Old Timer (in winter) & Farmer's Glory, Hall & Woodhouse Tanglefoot, guest beer. Garden, outdoor eating, children's play area. Family room. Closed 25 Dec. Amex, MasterCard,* **VISA**

STANTON ST JOHN	**The Talkhouse**	FOOD
		B&B

Tel 01865 351648   Fax 01865 351085   Map 14a C2
Wheatley Road Stanton St John Oxford Oxfordshire OX33 1EX

🗺 🍴 🍷

Set beside the B4027 four miles north-east of Oxford, this well-converted and extended 17th-century inn is landord Johnny Chick's latest venture, having successfully established the Mole and Chicken (see entry) at nearby Easington. Beyond the stone and partly-thatched exterior lies an interesting open-plan bar with low beams, an attractive tiled floor and a huge stone fireplace with welcoming log fire, which leads through to the adjacent and tasteful barn conversion with its high-pitched roof, exposed rafters, stone walls and motley mix of dining-room and farmhouse kitchen tables topped with candles. A further room and tiny 'snug' bar are equally attractive with ragged walls, beams and open fires and, generally, the interior exudes a warm Gothic-style ambience. A reliable selection of modern pub dishes is listed on a printed menu and enhanced by daily specials, the choice ranging from cream of cauliflower soup, salad of roast peppers, pine nuts and cheese, and duck liver paté with armagnac and orange for starters to chargrills, chicken Madras curry, pan-fried calf's liver with bacon and sage, ham and chicken pie, and shoulder of lamb with honey, rosemary and garlic for main course. Puddings may include Italian trifle and bread-and-butter pudding. A good, global list of wines includes eight available by the glass. An attractive courtyard to the rear of the pub, complete with fountain and director's chairs, is lined on one side by four neat, compact and pleasantly furnished bedrooms. Each has a TV, direct-dial phone, tea-making equipment and en suite bathroom with a shower over the tub. *Open 11-3, 6-11 (Sat 11-11, Sun 12-10.30).* **Bar Food** *12-3, 6-10 (Sat & Sun 12-10). Free House.* **Beer** *Morland Tanner's Jack, Original & Old Speckled Hen, Hook Norton Best, guest beer. Courtyard, outdoor eating, disabled facilities. Family room.* **Accommodation** *4 bedrooms, all en suite, £59 (single £45.50). Children over 5 welcome overnight. No dogs. Amex, Diners, MasterCard,* **VISA**

STANTON WICK · Carpenters Arms · FOOD

Tel 01761 490202 Fax 01761 490763 Map 13 F1 **B&B**
Stanton Wick Pensford nr Bristol Bath & North East Somerset BS18 4BX

The Carpenters Arms is all one would expect of a country inn, complete with roses clambering up the walls and tubs of colourful flowers. It was converted from a row of 17th-century miners' cottages in the tiny hamlet of Stanton Wick, which overlooks the Chew valley. Inside, there are low oak beams, natural stone walls and warming log fires; at one end of the building is a restaurant for formal eating, at the other, the less formal Coopers Parlour. The printed menu here includes grills, home-made soup – French onion soup – filled baguettes, lamb cutlets with rosemary jus, salmon fishcakes and a good choice of vegetarian dishes (wild mushroom and asparagus quiche). There are also daily specials on the short blackboard menu, for example chicken liver parfait, chicken in cream and grain mustard sauce and rack of lamb with redcurrant and apple jelly. The restaurant menu has a more elaborate choice of dishes on an à la carte menu. Traditional sweets include summer fruit brandy basket and tiramisu, and the speciality ice creams are home-made. Good Sunday lunch menus. There are some six wines available by the glass from a good realistically-priced wine list and a handful of real ales to wash down the food. Immaculate bedrooms are appropriately cottagey in style, with pine furniture and pretty co-ordinating fabrics and wall coverings. Modern conveniences are included and there are smart, modern carpeted bathrooms. No children under 12 in bar areas. *Open 11-11 (Sun 11.30-10.30). **Bar Food** 12-2.15, 7-10. Free House. **Beer** Bass, Butcombe Bitter, Wadworth 6X, Boddingtons, guest beer. Terrace, outdoor eating.* **Accommodation** *12 bedrooms, all en suite, £65.50 (single £48). Children over 12 welcome overnight, additional bed (£10) available. No dogs. Amex, Diners, MasterCard,* **VISA**

STAPLE FITZPAINE · Greyhound Inn · FOOD

Tel 01823 480227 Fax 01823 480773 Map 13 E2
Staple Fitzpaine Taunton Somerset TA3 5SP

Built as a hunting lodge by the local lord of the manor in 1640, the much extended creeper-clad Greyhound nestles in rolling landscape close to the Blackdown Hills. The rinterior comprises a series of rambling, connecting rooms, some with flagstone floors, some with old timbers or natural stone walls and stools made out of old barrels. The gravelled terrace garden has a play area with a splendid rustic climbing frame and slide and the welcome to youngsters extends indoors to their own menu, baby-changing facilities in the Ladies and an annual 'fun day'. The bar menu encompasses chargrills with a choice of sauces, baked jacket potatoes, ploughman's platters, sandwiches, Mexican tacos, home-made burgers, devilled whitebait, deep-fried Brie and vegetarian options (vegetable lasagne); a more exciting, daily-changing à la carte menu (home-made carrot and coriander soup, grilled sea bass with mushroom and white wine sauce, peppered pork, summer pudding, strawberry cheesecake) is also available in the bars. Live jazz and blues on Thursdays, a comedian performs once a month on a Saturday and an annual beer festival featuring 20 real ales. Four en suite letting bedrooms should be completed in late 1996. *Open 12-3, 5-11 (from 6 Sat), Sun 12-4, 7-10.30. **Bar Food** 12-2 (till 2.30 Sat), 7-10 (till 9.30 Sun). Free House. **Beer** Exmoor Ale, Flowers Original, Cotleigh Tawny, Bass, guest beer. Terrace, outdoor eating, summer barbecue, children's play area. Family room. MasterCard,* **VISA**

STARBOTTON · Fox & Hounds · FOOD

Tel 01756 760269 Fax 01756 760862 Map 5 D4 **B&B**
Starbotton North Yorkshire BD23 5HY

A typical 400-year-old stone-built, white-painted Yorkshire pub the inside of which is quite unspoilt, with flagstone floors, a few plates on the wall for decoration and a motley collection of jugs, pots and mugs hanging from the ceiling beams, plus a real fire in the stone fireplace in winter. In summer there are a few tables outside. An ever-changing blackboard menu offers the likes of steak and mushroom pie, chicken and coriander burger, carrot and orange soup and parsnip, chestnut and tomato crumble. At lunchtimes there is also a ploughman's lunch (three cheeses) that comes with an apple and home-baked granary bread, and crusty French stick sandwiches.

Extra evening dishes may include baked salmon steak with creamy white wine and dill sauce. Puddings range from double chocolate crunch to whisky marmalade bread-and-butter pudding. Two single, charming bedrooms with en suite shower rooms offer comfortable overnight accommodation with TV and tea and coffee-making kit. *Open 11.30-3, 6.30-11 (Sun 12-3, 7-10.30). Closed Mon eve (all day Mon Oct-Mar) & Jan-mid Feb. Bar Food 12-2, 7-9 (no bar food Mon). Free House. Beer Theakston Best, Old Peculier & XB, Black Sheep, guest beers. Terrace, outdoor eating. Accommodation 2 bedrooms, both en suite, £50 (single £30). Children welcome overnight (under-16s half price if sharing parents' room). Accommodation closed mid Dec-mid Feb. MasterCard, VISA*

STAVERTON — Sea Trout Inn — FOOD

Tel 01803 762274 Fax 01803 762506 — Map 13 D3 — **B&B**
Staverton Totnes Devon TQ9 6PA

A warm welcome heralds a pleasant stay at the Sea Trout, a country inn that is a particular favourite of fishermen. The fishing theme runs through the pub, some specimens mounted in showcases, others depicted in paintings or on plates. There's a conservatory leading from the restaurant to the patio-style garden complete with pond and fountain. Bedrooms are decorated in cottagey style and have TVs, telephones, tea-makers and en suite facilities (three with shower only). The extensive bar menu features local produce, notably fresh fish, and additional blackboard specials are offered. *Open 11-3, 6-11 (Sun 12-3, 6.30-10.30). Free House. Beer Fergusons Dartmoor Best, Wadworth 6X, Bass, guest beer. Garden. Accommodation 10 bedrooms, all en suite, £60-£68 (single £39.50) winter reductions. Children welcome overnight (£8.75 if sharing parents' room), additional bed & cot available. Accommodation closed 24-26 Dec, pub closed 25 &26 Dec eve. Amex, MasterCard, VISA*

STEDHAM — Hamilton Arms — FOOD

Tel 01730 812555 Fax 01730 817459 — Map 11 A6
School Lane Stedham Midhurst West Sussex GU20 0NZ

Suhail Hussain's and Mudita Karnasuta's little piece of the Orient is hardly what one expects to find in a quiet Sussex village. As they say: "with so little magic left in the world you owe it to yourself to visit us" – be it advertising hyperbole or a genuinely warm invitation, the Hamilton Arms is out of the ordinary and worth dropping by. Bar food encompasses toasted sandwiches and the usual pub favourites (lasagne, fish and chips, steak and kidney pie and so on) but there is a choice of Thai dishes – from 'mixed titbits' to one-dish noodle and rice dishes, red and green curries and roast duck with light sesame sauce and pickled ginger – alongside the real ale (and Singha Thai beer). Waitresses in national costume serve in the Nava Thai Restaurant, adjacent to the bar, where a long list of unpronounceable (but helpfully translated) dishes entices diners further. Special menus on Valentine's Day and Thai New Year in early April. 10% of the net profits of the pub are put towards the Mudita Trust which supports abused, distressed and underprivileged children in Thailand; proceeds from an annual Eastern Cultural Fete held on the village green opposite the pub every Spring Bank Holiday also benefit the Trust. Children welcome. *Open 11-3, 6-11, (Sun 12-3, 7-10.30, from 6 in summer). Closed Mon (except Bank Holiday lunch). Bar Food 12-2.30, 6-10.30 (Sun 12-2.30, 7-9.30). No food Mon. Beer Ballards Best, Courage Directors, Fuller's London Pride, guest beer. Patio, barbecue, children's play area. MasterCard, VISA*

STEEP — Harrow Inn — FOOD

Tel 01730 262685 — Map 15 D3
Steep Petersfield Hampshire GU32 2DA

The 400- to 500-year-old Harrow is a modest little pub tucked down a sleepy country lane that dwindles into a footpath by a little stream. The tenancy has been in the same family since 1929 and in 1992 landlord Edward McCutcheon finally managed to buy the inn from the brewery and keeps it very much as it must have been in the last century (earlier, even). Two small rooms have boarded walls, an old brick inglenook fireplace, scrubbed wooden tables and a hatch-like bar, behind which barrels of beer sit on racks, with bundles of drying flowers hanging above. There's a small cottage garden to one side, and some old sloping rustic benches and tables out at the front. The food is limited to a few wholesome snacks, generously-filled sandwiches, a split-pea and ham soup full of fresh vegetables, served with great chunks of bread; a few salads and ploughman's platters of beef, cheese or home-cooked ham; home-made Scotch eggs and, perhaps, home-made quiche or lasagne. For pudding there may be treacle tart and lemon crunch. Apart from the beers, there's a good selection of fruit wines. The Petersfield Bypass on the A3 has drastically changed the road layout round these parts, so here we go: heading south or north on the A3, take the A272 turning to Midhurst & Petersfield, follow exit road to roundabout, take first left on to A272 Midhurst road (old A3); at bottom of hill (about 350yds) take first turning on the left (opposite the garage); follow this road to Sheet church (about 350yds), take the road on the left opposite the church signposted Steep ½ mile – this will take you via the level crossing and the bridge over the A3 to the Harrow Inn. Directions courtesy of the landlord, who will be waiting to serve you a well-deserved ale or two! *Open 11-2.30 (till 3 Sat), 6-11 (Sun 12-3, 7-10.30).* **Bar Food** *12-2, 6.30-9.30 (Sun 12-2, 7.30-9). Free House.* **Beer** *Flowers Original, Boddingtons, Whitbread Strong Country Bitter, Marston's Pedigree. Garden, outdoor eating. No credit cards.*

STEEPLE ASTON   Red Lion   FOOD

Tel 01869 340225
South Street Steeple Aston Oxfordshire OX6 3RY

Map 14a C1

Colin and Margaret Mead run this pretty 330-year-old village pub, just off the main Oxford-Banbury A4260. A small flower-filled terrace leads into a comfortable beamed bar to the left and a small dining-room to the right. Very well kept beer, a multitude of malt whiskies and an extensive wine list all complement Margaret's cooking. Quality lunchtime snacks include stockpot soup, fresh crab and smoked salmon, home-made hot-pots (broad bean and pork or game) in winter, rare roast beef sandwiches and ploughman's lunches made with British cheeses are specialities in the bar, while a more creative and imaginative small menu (3-course meal with coffee is priced according to main dish) is offered in the dining-room at night, making use of fresh fish (brill hollandaise, monkfish), game in season, good steaks and local produce. Home-made puddings include Craigellachie cream (Scottish syllabub made with syrup of marmalade and malt whisky) and crème brulée. *Open 11-3, 6-11 (Sun 12-3, 7-10.30).* **Bar Food** *12-2 (no food Sun). Restaurant 7.30-9.15 (except Sun & Mon). Free House.* **Beer** *Hook Norton Best, two guest beers. Garden, outdoor eating. Amex, MasterCard,* **VISA**

STIFFKEY   Red Lion   FOOD

Tel & Fax 01328 830552
44 Wells Road Stiffkey Wells-next-the-Sea Norfolk NR23 1AJ

Map 10 C1

Nestling in the Stiffkey valley amid rolling Norfolk countryside, this peaceful village once boasted three pubs, but all became victims of the Watney revolution in the 1960s. After 28 years as a private house the Red Lion, a fine 16th-century white-painted brick and flint cottage on the main coast road, was resurrected in 1990 as a free house and has been thriving ever since, attracting a loyal local clientele. Inside, three charming rooms have bare board or quarry-tiled floors, three warming logs fires – one in a splendid inglenook – and a simple rustic mix of wooden settles, pews and scrubbed tables. Apart from the ambience, it is the good home-cooked food, which focuses on fresh local produce, that draws people here. A blackboard menu lists the daily-changing choice of dishes which may include Cromer crab, Stiffkey mussels marinière, Thai spring rolls and soft herring roes on toast for starters, followed by fish pie, game pie, pan-fried rump steak, wild mushroom and broccoli lasagne and grilled fresh fish from King's Lynn. Lunchtime snacks include ploughman's lunches, filled French sticks and bread and cheese. For pudding try the deep-pan apple pie, summer pudding or treacle and nut tart. Good range of East Anglian beers and a short list of Adnams wines (several served by the glass in summer). After a day on the beach or strolling the Peddars Way this is a good stop for families, who have use of a large and airy rear conservatory with access to the terraced garden. *Open 12-3, 7-11 (from 6 Bank Holidays & school holidays), Sun 12-3, 7-10.30.* **Bar Food** *12-2, 7-9. Free House.* **Beer** *Greene King Abbot Ale & IPA, Woodforde's Wherry, Nelson's Revenge & Great Eastern Ale, guest beer. Garden, outdoor eating. Family room. MasterCard,* **VISA**

STILTON   Bell Inn   FOOD

Tel 01733 241066   Fax 01733 245173   Map 7 E4   **B&B**
Great North Road Stilton Peterborough Cambridgeshire PE7 3RA

Reputedly the oldest coaching inn on the Great North Road, the Bell boasts a
Roman well in its courtyard and an impressive 15th-century stone frontage. Discreetly
concealed from the road are two wings of en suite bedrooms whose 20th-century
trappings include telephones, satellite television and whirlpool baths, while tokens
of the past are confined to the odd four-poster bed. This is a pity, as the rest of the
building is simply splendid. The village bar retains its stone-flagged floor and cosy
alcoves huddled round the great log fire; this is where the original Stilton cheese was
sold to travellers in the 1720s. Today it's served on its own with plum bread, or in a
celery soup, or in a lamb casserole with Stilton dumplings. For the less single-minded,
there's steak, ale and mushroom pie or coriander lamb, followed by home-made
traditional desserts like sticky toffee pudding and crème brulée. More serious food on
a weekly-changing table d'hote and set four-course dinner ($£22.50$) menus is on offer
in the galleried restaurant, where linen-covered tables are widely spaced in two
sections under gnarled oak beams and a vaulted ceiling with original exposed rafters.
Recommended in our *1997 Hotels and Restaurants Guide*. Open 12-2.30, 6-11 (Sun
12-3, 7-10.30). *Bar Food* 12-2, 6.30-9.30 (Sun 7-9). Free House. *Beer* Marston's
Pedigree, Ruddles Best, Tetley, guest beer. Garden, terrace, outdoor eating. **Accommodation**
19 bedrooms, all en suite, £74-£94 (single £59-£64). Children welcome overnight (under-3s
stay free if sharing parents' room), additional bed (£5-£10) & cot available. No dogs.
Closed 1 week Christmas. Amex, MasterCard, **VISA**

STOCKLAND   Kings Arms Inn   FOOD

Tel 01404 881361   Fax 01404 881732   Map 13 E2   **B&B**
Stockland Honiton Devon EX14 9BS

Well signposted from the Chard-Honiton stretch of the A30 this cream-faced thatched
village pub dates from the 16th century, became a coaching inn in the early 18th
century and is now Grade II listed. Although this rambling building has been
considerably renovated and extended in recent years it retains a marvellously unspoilt
interior, especially in the beamed Cotley Bar dining area. Divided by a medieval
oak screen, it has a vast inglenook and good sturdy furnishings. The daily-changing
blackboard menu is popular with local diners, listing starters like smoked
mackerel paté and prawns in garlic, followed by monkfish marseillaise, lamb
medallions and beef stroganoff. Booking is advble at all times. A separate snack menu
is available at lunchtimes only and features a selection of sandwiches, ploughman's,
salads and hot dishes like braised pork in ale. As well as local ales there is a good
choice of German bottled beers, a tremendous range of Island malt whiskies and an
interesting wine list, with at least eight offered by the glass. Live music on Sunday
evenings. Three neat and comfortable bedrooms are traditionally furnished and offer
TV, phones, beverage-making facilities and clean, older-style bathrooms.
No children under 12 in the dining-room. *Open* 12-3, 6.30-11 (Sun 12-3,
7-10.30). *Bar Food* 12-1.45, 6.30-9 (from 7 Sun). No food Sun lunch (except Whit &
Aug Bank Holidays & Mother's Day). Free House. *Beer* Exmoor Ale, John Smith's, Otter
Ale, Ruddles County. Garden, outdoor eating, barbecue. **Accommodation** 3 bedrooms, all en
suite, £40 (single £20). Children welcome overnight (under-3s stay free in parents' room),
additional bed (£10) available. Accommodation closed 1 week Christmas, pub closed 25 Dec.
MasterCard, **VISA**

Many **B&B** establishments offer reduced rates for weekend and
out-of-season bookings. Always ask about special deals for longer stays. Beware
half-board terms in inns where we do not recommend the **FOOD**.

STOCKPORT   Red Bull   FOOD

Tel 0161 480 2087   Map 6 B2
14 Middle Hillgate Stockport Cheshire SK3 4YL

Modest little pub with good, unpretentious home-cooking – pea and bacon soup, large open sandwiches, gammon and egg, and fish and chips. You might also find a daily curry, lasagne, a good cheeseboard, a couple of vegetarian options, plaice fillets or chicken Kiev. Homely puddings like treacle sponge and custard, apple and blackberry pancake roll or chocolate fudge cake. Children welcome at lunchtime only. *Open 11.30-3, 5-11, (Fri 11.30-11, Sat 12-11, Sun 12-3, 7-10.30). Bar Food 12-2.45 Mon-Fri only. Beer Robinson's Best & Hatters Mild. No credit cards.*

STOKE ST GREGORY   Rose & Crown   FOOD

Tel 01823 490296   Fax 01823 490996   Map 13 E2
Woodhill Stoke St Gregory Somerset TA3 6EW

17th-century cottage pub tucked away in a tiny, basket-making hamlet on the Somerset Levels. Beyond a flower-filled summer patio the interior has a homely furnished bar and dining-room with lots of nooks and crannies, horse brasses and a 60ft well. Extensive and wideranging menus continue to attract diners to this out-of-the-way spot. Snacky items include good home-made granary sandwiches, ploughman's lunches, salads and various omelettes, while main-menu choices run the gamut of steaks and grills and their famous scrumpy chicken to plenty of fish such as seafood platter, whole grilled plaice and stuffed sole bonne femme. Popular puddings include crème caramel, home-made apple pie and chocolate mousse cake. Three-course traditional roast lunch on Sundays. Children welcome. *Open 11-2.30, 6.30-11 (Sun 12-3, 7-10.30). Bar Food 12.30-2, 7-10. Free House. Beer Exmoor Ale, Eldridge Pope Royal Oak, Butcombe Bitter, guest beer. Terrace, outdoor eating. Access, VISA*

We only recommend food (Bar Food) in those establishments highlighted
with the **FOOD** symbol.

STOKE-BY-NAYLAND   Angel Inn   ★   FOOD

Tel 01206 263245   Fax 01206 263373   Map 10 C3   **B&B**
Stoke-by-Nayland Colchester Suffolk CO6 4SA

Soft lamplight glows invitingly in the window of this solid, beautifully restored 16th-century inn which can be found beside the B1068 in the village centre. Careful renovation and conversion by owners Peter Smith and Richard Wright have revealed the true charm of this fine building. Inside, the delightful bar divides into two; a comfortable lounge area with exposed carved beams, log-burning stove, wooden furnishings, and a real relaxing sitting room with deep sofas, wing chairs and a grandfather clock. Tasteful touches like fresh flowers and candles on tables, quality prints and paintings, a few antique pieces and a warming dark green and cream decor enhance the overall ambience. The Angel fills early with discerning diners seeking out the imaginative, twice daily-changing blackboard menus which feature predominantly fresh fish – delivered daily from Billingsgate – as well as well-sauced meat dishes, including local game, and unusual vegetarian choices. A typical meal may start with mushroom and pistachio paté or home-made fishcakes with remoulade sauce, followed by brochette of scallops wrapped in bacon, roast ballotine of duck with cassis sauce or steamed fillets of salmon and halibut with dill sauce, with German-style bread pudding and dark chocolate granache gateau to finish. Traditional Sunday lunch. Well-priced selection of global wines. The same menu applies in the charming Well Room restaurant – once the old brewhouse – with its high-vaulted ceiling, 52-ft well and green linen covered tablecloths. Tables can be booked here (£1.50 cover charge). Reached via a small gallery above this room are five decent-sized, individually decorated bedrooms, all with stylish, co-ordinating wallpaper and fabrics, comfortable easy chairs and spotlessly clean en suite facilities (all with bath and shower). A further room is housed in an annexe across the rear courtyard. No children in the bar, no under-8s overnight. Wheelchair access. *Open 11-2.30, 6-11 (Sun 12-3, 7-10.30).* **Bar Food** *12-2, 6.30-9 (from 7 Sun). Free House.* **Beer** *Greene King Abbot Ale & IPA, Adnams Southwold, guest beer. Patio, outdoor eating.* **Accommodation** *6 bedrooms, all en suite £59 (single £45) Children over 8 welcome overnight, (additional bed £12) available. No dogs. Pub & accommodation closed 26 & 27 Dec. Amex, Diners, MasterCard,* **VISA**

STOKENHAM   Tradesman's Arms   FOOD

Tel 01548 580313   Map 13 D3
Stokenham Kingsbridge Devon

Tucked in the heart of a picturesque old village, this 14th-century cottage takes its name from the tradesmen who once used the coastal bridle path between Kingsbridge and Dartmouth, using the inn as their first night's lodging. With so many pubs catering for the hundreds of visitors that crowd this area in the summer, it is refreshing to find this small, refined village local doing just the opposite, even refusing to let young children inside (older minors in dining-room only) Inside, you will find few tradesmen in the quaint, beamed and simply-furnished main bar, which has an upmarket ambience with tasteful classical music, 'Harrods' bar towels and a clientele to match. More rustic than smart, the bar enjoys fine views from the three small windows across the valley to the church. The adjacent dining-room has a collection of modern settles and light oak tables topped with red and green gingham tablecloths, candles and dried flowers. The draw here, other than the genuinely warm welcome, is the honest home-cooked food. There are no frills and pretence to the short printed menu on each table which features main dishes like chicken with tarragon cream, rack of lamb with red wine and redcurrant, fresh pasta with herb and tomato sauce and a selection of freshly-prepared patés served with warm toast and salad. A separate lunch menu highlights the range of sandwiches and ploughman's platters on offer and a small blackboard lists a few dishes of the day, notably a fresh fish (delivered daily from Plymouth) option such as Dart River salmon, halibut steak, fresh lobster or crab, and cod and chips. Rather than a roast on Sundays, authentic Indian curries make up the menu and are extremely popular – booking advisable. *Open 12-3, 6-11 (Sun 12-3, 7-10.30). Closed Sun-Thu evenings Jan-Mar.* **Bar Food** *12-2.30, 6-9.30 (from 7 Sun). Free House.* **Beer** *Bass, Adnams Southwold, Hook Norton Best, Brakspear Bitter, guest beer. Garden, outdoor eating. No credit cards.*

STONY STRATFORD   Cock Hotel   B&B

Tel 01908 567733   Map 15a D1
High Street Stony Stratford Milton Keynes Bucks MK11 1AH

In the heart of town, this former coaching inn dates from 1300 and was rebuilt after a fire in 1742. 'Ride a cock horse to Banbury Cross' – the horse was apparently from the Cock Hotel stables and with its neighbour the Bull gave rise to the phrase 'Cock and Bull story'. Continued investment in the building has seen the comfortable pubby bar and adjacent lounge refurbished with modern wallpaper and deep sofas, the addition of a permanent function marquee to the sheltered walled garden and the gradual upgrading of the 28 en suite bedrooms. All are well furnished, the superior rooms (housed in a converted ballroom) having lightwood furniture and clean bath/shower rooms, some with bidet. Residents' lounge. Handy for racing at Silverstone, but supplements may apply during busy periods. *Open 11-3, 5.30-11 (Sun 12-3, 7-10.30). Free House.* **Beer** *Theakston Best & XB, Jennings Best, Fuller's London Pride, Greene King IPA, Morland Old Speckled Hen, guest beer. Walled garden.* **Accommodation** *31 bedrooms, all en suite, £67-£77.50 (single £57.50), weekend reductions. Children welcome overnight (under-4s stay free in parents' room), additional bed & cot (both £10). Amex, Diners, MasterCard,* **VISA**

We do not accept free meals or hospitality – our inspectors pay their own bills
and never book in the name of Egon Ronay's Guides.

STOURTON — Spread Eagle Inn — B&B

Tel 01747 840587   Fax 01747 841552   Map 14 B3
Stourhead Stourton Warminster Wiltshire BA12 6QE

Zzz... ☺

Fine 18th-century brick inn owned by the National Trust and peacefully located within a neat complex of buildings – tea room and National Trust shop – close to the tiny parish church and Stourhead House with its magnificent landscaped gardens, enchanting lakes and woodland walks. As one would expect, the interior of the inn has been tastefully refurbished, the bars sporting sturdy wooden furnishings, good prints and paintings and warming open fires. High standards extend to the five charming, recently refurbished en suite bedrooms which retain architectural details, including Georgian and Regency fireplaces, and boast quality co-ordinating fabrics, antique and older-style furniture, easy chairs and various ornaments, clocks and pieces of china adding a homely touch. Each room has a TV, telephone, beverage-making kit and spotless bathroom with both a bath and overhead shower. The inn can get busy in the summer months with Stourhead visitors, but out-of-season this is an idyllic rural retreat. *Open 11-11, (Sun 12-10.30). Free House.* **Beer** *Ash Vine, Stourhead 50, Eldridge Pope Hardy Ale & Pope's Traditional. Courtyard. Family room.* **Accommodation** *5 bedrooms, all en suite, £69 (single £45). Children welcome overnight, additional bed (£12.50) & cot available (£5). No dogs. Amex, Diners, MasterCard,* **VISA**

STOW BARDOLPH — Hare Arms — FOOD

Tel 01366 382229   Fax 01366 385522   Map 10 B2
Stow Bardolph Downham Market Norfolk PE34 3HT

A picturesque country pub in a delightful Norfolk village nine miles south of King's Lynn off the A10. Inside is pleasantly refurbished and immaculately run by David and Tricia McManus (who are celebrating their twentieth year here), with a cosy bar, elegant restaurant, popular no-smoking conservatory extension (also the family room) and an intriguing coach house in the garden for children. The pub gets its name, not from the animal, but from a prominent local family, still found in these parts. Good bar food ranges from a fairly routine printed menu listing sandwiches (lunch only), home-made curries, lasagne and grills alongside standard favourites with chips; daily-changing blackboard specials include home-made soup (Stilton and celery), excellent pies – steak and kidney or pigeon – or more imaginative dishes like sea bream with red pepper sauce, lamb steak with redcurrant and rosemary sauce and stir-fried chicken and Chinese vegetables with sweet and sour sauce. Puddings include pecan pie and fruit meringues. A bi-monthly changing table d'hote dinner menu is offered in the restaurant as well as a seasonally-changing à la carte choice. *Open 11-2.30, 6-11 (Sun 12-2.30, 7-10.30).* **Bar Food** *12-2, 7-10.* **Beer** *Greene King. Garden, outdoor eating. Family room. Closed 25 & 26 Dec. MasterCard,* **VISA**

STRATFIELD TURGIS — Wellington Arms — FOOD / B&B

Tel 01256 882214   Fax 01256 882934   Map 15a D4
Stratfield Turgis Basingstoke Hampshire RG27 0AS

 🗋 **Zzz...**

Hard by the A33, a charming old inn with a handsome white Georgian facade and a mix of the old and the new inside. The cosy, pubby L-shaped bar features a polished flagstone floor, a characterful mish-mash of wooden tables and chairs laid for bar snacks; it leads directly round into a friendly drawing room in country-house style with open fire, sunken-cushioned sofas, gilt-framed oil portraits and French windows which open on to a small lawned area where bench picnic tables are set. Light meals and snacks include sandwiches and ploughman's platters, tomato and sweet pepper quiche, mussels in white wine and garlic, stir-fry chicken and tagliatelle carbonara and daily blackboard specials (perhaps grilled supreme of coley and whole baked plaice) complete the picture. Fifteen bedrooms in the original building include two 'luxury doubles' (one a suite with a heavily-carved four-poster and spa bath); 20 further rooms are in a two-storey modern extension to the rear, uniformly decorated with Laura Ashley pastel blues and yellows plus modern light oak furniture suites; hotel room facilities like a comfortable armchair, remote-controlled TV, powerful showers and tea/coffee making facilities are standard. A couple of modern suites serve as both small meeting rooms and family rooms with pull-down additional beds. Next door to the Duke of Wellington's estate (Stratfield Saye House, where river fishing can be arranged) and close to Wellington Country Park (ideal for family outings). Badger Inns. *Open 11-11 (Sun 12-10.30).* **Bar Food** *12-2.30, 6-10 (Sun 7-9.30).* **Beer** *Hall & Woodhouse. Garden, outdoor eating.* **Accommodation** *35 bedrooms, all en suite, £70/£85/£95/£110 (single £60/£75), weekend £50/£75 (single £40), family room £120. Children welcome overnight, additional bed & cot (both £10) available. Amex, Diners, MasterCard,* **VISA**

STRATFORD-ON-AVON   Dirty Duck   A

Tel 01789 297312   Map 14 C1
Waterside Stratford-on-Avon Warwickshire CV35 6BA

This "theatre of the gastronomic arts" once went by the name of the "Black Swan", the traditional "Mucky Duck" of English pub folklore. Today's crowds are drawn more in hope of meeting a theatre type than a gastronome, the panelled and wood-block Theatre Bar containing a gallery of autographed photographs of RSC stars down the years which will keep many a theatre-goer long a-guessing. Standing above and back from the Waterside with its crazy-paved patio, it's the closest pub to the Royal Shakespeare theatre, with one of the town's most peaceful river views framed by massive horse chestnut trees. Just 50 yards down the road the hand-operated chain-link ferry (20p) conveys foot passengers back across the Avon to the playgrounds, amenities and long-term car parks. *Open 11-11 (Sun 12-10.30).* **Beer** *Flowers IPA & Original, Boddingtons. Patio/terrace. Amex, Diners, MasterCard,* **VISA**

STRETTON   Ram Jam Inn   FOOD

Tel 01780 410776   Fax 01780 410361   Map 7 E3   B&B
Great North Road Stretton nr Oakham Leicestershire LE15 7QX
♟ ☺

Hard by a service station nine miles north of Stamford on the northbound lane of the A1 (southbound drivers take the B668 exit to Oakham and follow signs), the Ram Jam Inn, named after a special brew produced in its early days, makes a very welcome break. Public rooms are primarily devoted to informal eating areas. All-day snacks and meals are available in the three interconecting dining-rooms, one of which is set up as a restaurant; the two other informal rooms overlook the orchard; outdoor eating with 20 seats on a terrace. One menu is served throughout, with granary baps and open sandwiches for quick snacks. Typical dishes include an ever-popular chargrilled chopped steak burger piled high with deep-fried shaved vegetables, half a pint of shell-on prawns, home-made gravad lax, daily-changing soup, fish and pasta dishes, Rutland sausages with onion marmalade and mash, a quartet of marinated herrings with sour cream and crusty fresh bread, and good desserts like lemon tart or chocolate mousse terrine with black cherry coulis and praline ice cream. A roast is added to the menu for Sunday lunchtimes. New 'instant lunch' menu (£6.25/£7.95), served 12-2, offers particularly good value. Good children's options and pleasantly informal service; high-chairs and changing facilities provided. All the bedrooms overlook the garden and orchard and are individually and tastefully decorated with limed-pine furniture; they are surprisingly quiet, considering the proximity to the road. To one side of the entrance is an air-conditioned conference room seating up to 30. If only every roadside inn was as good as this! *Open 7am-10pm.* **Meals** *7am-10pm.* **Beer** *Ruddles Best & County, Tetley – all under pressure.* **Accommodation** *7 bedrooms, all en suite, £60 (family room sleeping 4 £68, single £50). Children welcome overnight, cot provided (£10, free in family room). Garden, terrace, outdoor eating. Closed 25 Dec. Amex, Diners, MasterCard,* **VISA**

STRINESDALE   Roebuck Inn   FOOD

Tel & Fax 0161 624 7819   Map 6 B2
Brighton Road Strinesdale Stockport OL4 3RB
🐟 ☺

A family welcome from Sue, Mark, Mary and Peter, and a prodigious choice from the menu await those who venture up the moor to the Howarth and Walters families' imposing hillside pub; the pub's not easy to find on a map – it's about a mile off the A672, taking Turfpitt Lane south of Denshaw. While the little ones can choose from fish fingers, beefburgers or sausages, a monthly-changing specials board can help buck the otherwise chips-and-peas mentality. Go, perhaps, for pot-roast leg of lamb with red wine, chicken tikka masala or poached halibut with mushroom sauce. Sandwiches and ploughman's platters are readily available lunch and evening for those in need of a lighter bite. Value-for-money mid-week 3- and 4-course set menus. From bookable tables by the picture windows views down the moor's edge end in an urban skyline; in the foreground a paved yard beckons animal-loving youngsters whose parents don't mind them getting mucky. *Open 12-3, 6-11 (Sun 12-10.30).* **Bar Food** *12-2.30, 6-10 (Sun 12-10). Free House.* **Beer** *Oldham Bitter, Boddingtons. Garden, outdoor eating, children's play area. Amex, MasterCard,* **VISA**

STROUD   Old Nelson   B&B

Tel 01453 765821   Fax 01453 765964   Map 14 B2
Stratford Lodge Stratford Road Stroud Gloucestershire GL5 4AF

From the M5 Junction 13 follow the Superstore signs when coming into Stroud on the A419 to find this pub where a block of bedrooms was added a few years ago. All the rooms, except for two specially adapted disabled bedrooms, have en suite baths and showers. Family rooms with sofa beds offer good value with inexpensive breakfasts. There's a spacious non-smoking conservatory and safe garden, but no play area. Premier Lodge (Greenalls). *Open 11-11 (Sun 12-10.30).* **Beer** *Tetley Best, guest beer. Garden. Family rooms.* **Accommodation** *32 bedrooms, all en suite, £41.50 (weekends £34.50 – room only rates). Children welcome overnight (stay free in parents' room), additional bed & cot available. No dogs. Amex, Diners, MasterCard,* **VISA**

Many **B&B** establishments offer reduced rates for weekend and out-of-season bookings. Always ask about special deals for longer stays. Beware half-board terms in inns where we do not recommend the **FOOD.**

STURMINSTER NEWTON   Swan Inn   B&B

Tel 01258 472208   Fax 01258 473767   Map 14 B4
Market Place Sturminster Newton Dorset DT10 1AR

Pride of place in the market place of this busy little town goes to the Swan, a fine, brick 18th-century coaching inn that offers a warm welcome to both locals and visitors alike in its comfortably furnished open-plan main bar with brick fireplace and open fire, and in the adjacent attractively decorated dining-room. Tasteful fabrics and furnishings extend upstairs to the five individually styled en suite bedrooms. one of which has a four-poster bed. Relaxing pastel shades of colour, quality wallpaper, co-ordinating fabrics, decent prints and good modern pine furniture ensure a comfortable stay. Added comforts include remote-control TVs, clock-radios, telephones and tea-making equipment. Rather compact bathrooms have both baths and overhead showers. All bedrooms overlook the bustling market place and housekeeping is of a high standard. Badger Inns. *Open 10.30-2.30, 6.30-11 (Sun 12-3, 7-10.30).* **Beer** *Hall & Woodhouse Badger Best. Garden.* **Accommodation** *5 bedrooms, all en suite, £52.50 (single £39). Children over 12 welcome overnight. Amex, MasterCard,* **VISA**

SULGRAVE   Star Inn   FOOD

Tel 01295 760389   Map 14a C1   **B&B**
Manor Road Sulgrave Oxfordshire OX17 2SA

Zzz...

A cosy, creeper-clad village pub, created out of a 300-year-old former farmhouse, where Andy Willerton provides the bonhomie and partner Caroline Shoebridge the home cooking. Blackboard menus provide something for most tastes and appetites from double-decker sandwiches (perhaps oak-smoked ham or Norwegian prawn) and leek and potato soup via smoked goose breast with port and cranberry jelly to watercress and feta tart, authentic curries and lamb meatballs in spicy tomato sauce. At Sunday lunchtimes the menu includes a traditional roast. For afters, try lemon fudgecake, toffee crunch cheesecake or pecan pie. Ploughman's platters and sandwiches are not available weekend evenings. A small patio and lawn to the rear of the car park provides for summer eating and drinking. Four spotless bedrooms (one mini-suite), all with en suite shower rooms, feature old timbers and modern comforts like remote-control TV and tea and coffee kits but no telephone. *Open 11-2.30, 6-11 (Sun 12-3, 7-10.30)*. *Bar Food 12-2, 6.30-9.30 (Sun 12-2, 7-9)*. *Beer Hook Norton Best & Old Hooky, guest beer. Garden, patio, outdoor eating*. *Accommodation 4 bedrooms, all en suite, £50 (single £25). Children over 14 welcome overnight (half-price), additional bed available. Check-in by arrangement. No dogs. Pub and accommodation closed 25 Dec. No credit cards*.

SUTTON   White Horse Inn   B&B

Tel 01798 869221   Fax 01798 869291   Map 11 A6
Sutton Pulborough West Sussex RH20 1PS

In a sleepy village tucked beneath the South Downs and amid a maze of narrow lanes – signposted off the A285 Petworth to Chichester road – the 250-year-old White Horse offers peaceful overnight accommodation in six en suite bedrooms. All rooms are well fitted out with dark mahogany furniture, pale floral fabrics and spotlessly clean tiled bathrooms (one with shower only). Added comforts include TVs, beverage-making facilities, telephones and hairdryers, with mineral water, a basket of fruit and magazines being welcoming touches. Reached via its own path across the rear garden, the phone-free Gardener's Cottage room is ideal for those seeking isolation, although a handy brolly by the door will encourage a trip to the bar on rainy nights. Good standard of housekeeping. If follows that public areas are smart and well looked after with attractive prints, carpets and fabrics, fresh flowers and traditional darkwood furniture. No under-14s in bar areas. *Open 11-3, 6-11 (Sun 12-3, 7-10.30)*. *Free House*. *Beer Bateman's XB, Young's Bitter & Special, Courage Best, Arundel Best Bitter. Garden*. *Accommodation 6 bedrooms, all en suite, £58 (single £48). Children welcome overnight, additional bed (£10) & cot available. No dogs. Amex, Diners, MasterCard,* **VISA**

SUTTON COURTENAY   The Fish   ★   FOOD

Tel 01235 848242   Fax 01235 848014   Map 14a C3
4 Appleford Road Sutton Courtenay Abingdon Oxfordshire OX14 4NQ

Since taking over The Fish, an unassuming, late 19th-century brick-built village pub, in August 1995 Mike and Jenny Gaffney have maintained the high standards that earned the pub our star for outstanding food in previous editions of this Guide. During the summer of 1996 the combined efforts of the Gaffney's enthusiasm and serious investment by the brewery (Morland) has led to a larger kitchen and dining-room (now 60 covers rather than 34), improvements to the patio and garden and the addition of accommodation, all of which should help in coping with the demand for space at this discerning dining establishment. Table mats, linen napkins, quality cutlery and candles grace polished-mahogany tables in the Victorian-style restaurant, which is decorated in warm greens and terracottas; French doors lead out to a patio and garden – a splendid spot for summer alfresco dining. A chatty atmosphere fills the newly-refurbished bar area where local drinkers mingle with intending diners, who can enjoy a pre-prandial drink and deep bowls of herby olives on the bar while perusing the various menus on offer. Restaurant diners can choose from a short, weekly-changing à la carte or a set 3-course menu (£12.95 lunch, £17.95 dinner), all of which rely on quality produce from good, reliable suppliers. The focus of chef Paul Keeble's innovative cooking is imaginative fish dishes with excellent fresh fish being delivered direct from Brixham and Penzance. Begin a memorable meal with chargrilled dived Cornish scallops with elderflower and fennel marmalade, creamy fish soup with croutons and red pepper rouille or stir-fried lamb's sweetbreads with black beans, chili and Chinese leaves; then move on to exciting main dishes like chargrilled tuna with pan-fried samphire and Japanese horseradish, fillet of cod with crab and mozzarella rarebit, chorizo oil and beetroot fritters, or roast English lamb with thyme, roasted tomatoes and olive tapnade. To round off your meal, try the selection (7-8) of unusual farmhouse cheeses, or the chocolate tart with sharp lime ice cream or orange and semolina brulée with local cherries. Hand-made truffles appear with the good, strong cafetière coffee. In the bar, the 'lighter options' blackboard menu lists some of the restaurant dishes, which are available in starter or main-course portions (priced accordingly), as well as interesting snacks like Angus beef steak on mixed leaves in ciabatta, trio of sausages with parsley mash and onion gravy, or Welsh rarebit on French bread. However, on Friday and Saturday evenings the bar area becomes an extension of the restaurant with the carte and set menu being served throughout – booking essential! To complement your meal there is a decent list of wines (eight available by the glass) and Morland's Original on hamdpump. Overnight accommodation (£45 double, £35 single) in three upstairs bedrooms (one with en suite shower/WC) were due to come on line in October (not yet inspected). No under-14s in bar area. *Open 12-3, 6-11 (Sun 12-3, 7-10.30).* **Meals** *12-2, 7-9 (restaurant only Fri & Sat eve, bar food only Sun eve, last week Dec & first week Jan, except New Years Eve).* **Beer** *Morland. Garden, patio, outdoor eating. Closed 25 Dec. Amex, Diners, MasterCard,* **VISA**

SUTTON GAULT	Anchor Inn	FOOD

Tel 01353 778537   Fax 01353 776180   Map 10 B2   **B&B**
Bury Lane Sutton Gault Sutton Ely Cambridgeshire CB6 2BD

Deep in Fen country, just off the A142 at Sutton village, the Anchor is protected from the 'hundred foot drain' (built by the Dutch in 1650 to drain the Fens and now called the New Bedford River) by a veritable rampart of earthworks. Descend, then pass a new riverside patio into the low, brick-built pub. Beer jugs hang from hooks in the low-beamed bar, racked Burton Ale is served direct from cask and landlord Robin Moore's preference for classical music seems entirely apposite to the setting. A long menu which relies heavily on fresh produce indicates careful shopping. The daily-changing menu starts with home-made soup – cream of leek and fresh tarragon – and chicken liver, hazelnut and brandy paté and progresses to savoury seafood crumble, fillet of pike with whisky, cream and thyme, and pork steak stuffed with pistachio nuts, ginger, garlic and raisins with coconut gravy. Home-made puddings are served with clotted cream and might include chocolate and almond torte or orange mousse gateau. A medley of unusual British cheeses with warm bread is another option. Lighter lunchtime snacks, plus a good value 3-course lunch for those with an appetite. Those with children or particularly favouring the non-smoking Inglenook Room are well advised to book; it's virtually essential at weekends. In addition to the beer and a 100-plus wine list from Lay and Wheeler (seven available by the glass), other beverage choices include freshly-squeezed orange juice and cups of cappuccino, chocolate or speciality teas. Two en suite upstairs bedrooms consist of a comfortable suite and a spacious twin-bedded rooms. Both are well equipped with TV, direct-dial phones, radio-alarms and tea-making kits, and enjoy views across the river. *Open 12-2.30, 7-11 (from 6.30 Sat), Sun 12-3, 7-10.30.* **Bar Food** *12-2, 7-9 (Sat 6.30-9.30). Free House.* **Beer** *Greene King IPA, Ind Coope Burton Ale, Adnams Southwold. Garden, outdoor eating. Family room.* **Accommodation** *2 bedrooms, both en suite, £57.50 & £77.50 (single £45). Children over 5 welcome overnight. Check-in by arrangement. No dogs. Closed 25 & 26 Dec. Amex, MasterCard,* **VISA**

SWANTON MORLEY	Darby's	FOOD

Tel & Fax 01362 637647   Map 10 C1   **B&B**
Swanton Morley Dereham Norfolk NR20 4JT

Zzz... ☺

A "family" free house converted from two brick cottages in 1986 by the licensee – John Carrick – a local farmer, after the local mega-brewery closed the village's last traditional pub. A rustic ambience has been created in the main bar with beams, exposed brick walls and open brick fireplace with log fire. Both here and in the neatly laid-out dining area visitors can enjoy reliable, home-cooked meals, as well as filled baguettes and ploughman's platters. Main menu choices include popular favourite plus garlic and Stilton mushrooms, venison and turkey pie and vegetable bake. Daily blackboard specials may feature Brancaster mussels with white wine and cream, beef and vegetable casserole and tagliatelle carbonara. Puddings may include blackberry and apple crumble and chocolate cheesecake. Sunday roasts are a popular attraction. Younger diners have their own menu (Peter Rabbit – small ham salad) which is served in the dining area or in the small children's room, complete with

a box of toys for impatient toddlers. Those seeking overnight accommodation will be surprised when directed 3/4 mile along the narrow lane to Park Farm, a fine farmhouse peacefully located in open countryside. Six fresh, airy and spotless en suite bedrooms (four with showers only) are housed in a splendid cattleyard conversion offering exposed ceiling timbers, freestanding pine furnishings, TVs, clock-radios and beverage-making facilities. One room is geared to accept wheelchair visitors. Overflow accommodation in the farmhouse is more modest; four bedrooms, including two character attic rooms share two bathrooms. Guests wishing to venture to the pub have use of a free taxi service and sleeping children will be well looked after if parents want a night out. The welcome attributed to visiting children extends beyond the menu, children's room and toy box into the garden, where an enclosed play area on a soft wood-chip floor boasts a climbing net and frame. Down on the farm there is a connecting family room, provision of a further bed and cot (£2), high-chair at breakfast, a kitchen area for mums to prepare food and numerous animals to keep youngsters amused. 3- to 13-year olds are charged £1 per year old per night.
*Open 11-2.30, 6-11 (Sat 11-11, Sun 12-3, 7-10.30). **Bar Food** 12-2, 7-9.45 (Sat 12-9.45, Sun 12-2.30, 7-9.30). Free House. **Beer** Adnams Southwold, Mild & Broadside, Woodforde's Wherry, Hall & Woodhouse Tanglefoot, four guest ales. Garden, outside eating, children's play area. Family room. **Accommodation** 9 bedrooms, 5 en suite £40 (family room £60, single £20-£24). Children welcome overnight. MasterCard, VISA*

SWAVESEY   Trinity Foot   FOOD

Tel 01954 230315   Map 15 F1
Huntingdon Road Swavesey Cambridgeshire CB4 5PD

Although parts of the building date back to 1870, this fairly modern pub next to the A604, is named after Trinity College's hunt (Colonel Whitbread was Master of the Trinity Beagles), or rather more specifically, its horse-less followers. The fish shop on the corner (which is also owned by the pub) supplies the superb fish for the many dishes on the menu – from oysters to baked salmon, grilled Dover sole, fresh lobster and monkfish in Pernod and cream. A more standard menu of pub favourites offers omelettes, ploughman's platters, grills to fillet steak, sandwiches, salads and a small selection of sweets – banana split, apple and blackberry sponge. Airy conservatory.
*Open 11-2.30, 6-11 (Sun 12-3 only). Closed Sun eve. **Bar Food** 12-2 (till 1.30 Sun), 6-9.30 (till 10 Fri & Sat). **Beer** Flowers Original, Boddingtons. Patio, outdoor eating. Amex, MasterCard, VISA*

TALKIN VILLAGE   Blacksmiths Arms   FOOD

Tel 01697 73452   Map 4 C2   **B&B**
Talkin Village Brampton Cumbria CA8 1LE

At the heart of this immaculately kept village just 9 miles from Carlisle and only 6 from the M6 at Junction 43, the revitalised Blacksmiths Arms is the pub all and sundry are talkin' about. The Bagshaws, Pat and Tom, run it very much as a family concern with quiet good humour and nothing appears too much trouble for them. Pat's kitchen tries not to overextend itself while offering a wide range of fare from the 'Hot and Simple' steak and kidney pie, leg of lamb chop and fresh haddock in her own beer batter through to some more adventurous daily specials such as chicken provençale, beef teriyaki and crispy garlic and herb prawns. Sandwiches and ploughman's lunches are also offered at both lunchtime and in the evening. Simplicity has also remained the key to careful conversion of the bedrooms, all of which now boast full en suite facilities. Decor follows a country theme without being overly cottagey, furniture and fittings are of durable quality and colour TVs and tea- and coffee-making kits ensure an entirely adequate degree of guests' comfort. *Open 11-3, 6-11 (till 10.30 Sun). **Bar Food** 12-2, 7-9. **Beer** Boddingtons, Theakston Best, guest beer. Garden, outdoor eating. **Accommodation** 5 bedrooms, all en suite, £38 (single £25). Children welcome overnight (under-10s stay free in parents' room), additional bed & cot available. No dogs. Amex, MasterCard, VISA*

We only recommend food (Bar Food) in those establishments highlighted with the **FOOD** symbol.

TANGLEY	Fox Inn	FOOD

Tel 01264 730276

Map 14a B4 **B&B**

Tangley Andover Hampshire SP11 0RU

🐟 ♈ **Zzz...**

Well worth the diversion off the A343 north of Andover, the Fox is a remote white-painted brick and flint cottage pub with a welcoming atmosphere in its tiny, rustic bars and homely restaurant. Reliably good food from the landlady cook (Gwen Troke), her daily-changing blackboard menus listing value-for-money lunchtime snacks – lamb, bacon and red wine casserole, Normandy pork, chicken and mushroom pie and sweet and sour bean pot. More imaginative evening restaurant fare (also available in the bar) may include rack of lamb, duck with orange and Grand Marnier sauce and grilled salmon with dill mayonnaise. Home-made ice cream, sticky toffee pudding and fruit pavlova are some of the puddings. The landlord, John Troke, has a comprehensive wine list, eight of which are available by the glass. Accommodation comprises one spacious and comfortable twin-bedded room, which is furnished in modern pine and has a spotless en suite shower room. TV, tea-maker, mini-fridge and help-yourself Continental breakfast with muffins, bread, jam, honey, marmalade, cheese, ham and fruit. *Open 11-3, 6-11 (Sun 12-3, 7-10.30).* **Bar Food** *12-2 (till 3 Sun), 6.30-10 (from 7 Sun). Free House.* **Beer** *Bass, Eldridge Pope Royal Oak, Courage Best.* **Accommodation** *1 bedroom with shower, £40. Children welcome overnight (free), additional bed & cot available. Dogs by arrangement. Closed 25 & 26 Dec eve. No credit cards.*

TARPORLEY	Rising Sun	FOOD

Tel 01829 732423

Map 6 B2

High Street Tarporley Cheshire CW6 0DX

High-street pub satisfying both diners and drinkers; very popular in the area and with the local cricketers. Forty-plus item bar food blackboard runs the gamut of choices from steak bordelaise down to spaghetti bolognaise; sandwiches and ploughman's at lunchtime only. Evening grills are supplemented by duck with cherries, beef stroganoff and veal cordon bleu. Bookings taken for Sunday lunches. One little bar is available for just drinking. No under-18s in bar areas. *Open 11.30-3, 5.30-11 (Sun 12-3, 7-10.30).* **Bar Food** *12-2, 5.30-9.30.* **Beer** *Robinsons Best Bitter & Mild. No credit cards.*

TARPORLEY	Swan Hotel	B&B

Tel 01829 733838   Fax 01829 732932

Map 6 B2

50 High Street Tarporley Cheshire CW6 0AG

Formerly a coaching-house of reknown, the Swan was destroyed by fire in 1735 and rebuilt with its unusual Georgian frontage around 1769. Within, however, the flagstoned kitchen bar containing heraldic insignia of the Fettered White Swan, dates back to 1565. Stylish modern designs and patterned, matching fabrics lend the main building bedrooms a distinctly classy feel, to which the TV, tea tray and trouser press add suitably up-to-date comfort. En suite bathrooms offer heated towel rails, smart towels and toiletries. The newest six bedrooms are housed in a well-converted coach house. 50 malt whiskies and an inpressive range of bottled beers from around the world. Bar snacks are no longer offered; a brasserie menu has taken their place. *Open 11-3, 6-11 (Sat 11-11, Sun 12-3, 7-10.30).* **Beer** *Weetwood Ale, Ruddles Best, M&B Highgate Saddlers, guest beers. Garden.* **Accommodation** *20 bedrooms, all en suite, £62.50 (single £48.50). Children welcome overnight (under-5s stay free in parents' room), additional bed (£10) available. Amex, MasterCard,* **VISA**

We do not accept free meals or hospitality – our inspectors pay their own bills and **never** book in the name of Egon Ronay's Guides.

TARRANT MONKTON   Langton Arms   FOOD

Tel 01258 830225 Fax 01258 830053   Map 14 B4   **B&B**
Tarrant Monkton Blandford Forum Dorset DT11 8RX

🍴 ☕ Zzz... ☺

Thatched, rose- and creeper-clad, this mellow 17th-century brick pub, picturesquely
situated opposite the parish church, is surely everybody's idea of a traditional village
inn. A splendid 'local' atmosphere pervades the beamed bars where drinkers can
sample well-kept small brewery beers and diners can tuck into reliable home-cooked
bar meals. Favourite dishes – cod and chips, chicken curry, lasagne and filled baguettes
– are listed on a printed menu, while daily specials such as chicken and leek pie,
Somerset Brie and bacon filo, Langton marinated chicken, mixed fish kedgeree, carrot
cake and treacle tart are highlighted on two boards. Evenings bring speciality themes
for different nights of the week – fish 'n' chips on Monday, steaks on Thursdays. Extra
evening dishes and a Sunday lunch menu are served in the adjacent Langton's Bistro.
In general, food prices are exceptionally keen. Summer barbecues are a regular and
popular feature. At least 12 wines are offered by the glass from a short list supplied by
Christopher Piper wine merchants. Three single-storey blocks built around the rear
courtyard house six spacious and well-maintained en suite bedrooms, all with bath and
shower, furnished in pine and sporting pretty duvets and curtains. TV, tea-maker,
telephone and hairdryer are standard extras. A warm welcome awaits children, who
not only have their own room filled with toys but also a separate menu, food bar and
excellent play areas, including a bouncy castle, in the spacious and safe rear garden.
Open 11.30-2.30, 6-11 (Sat 11-11, Sun 12-3, 7-10.30). **Bar Food** *11.30-2.30, 6-10
(Sun 12-2.45, 7-10). Free House.* **Beer** *Smiles Best, Wadworth 6X, four guest beers.
Garden, outdoor eating, children's play area.* **Accommodation** *6 bedrooms, all en suite,
£54 (single £35). Children welcome overnight, additional bed (£5) & cot available.
MasterCard,* **VISA**

TATENHILL   Horseshoe Inn   A

Tel 01283 564913 Fax 01283 511314   Map 6 C3
Main Street Tatenhill Burton-on-Trent Staffordshire DE13 9SD

☺

A splendid summer spot just two miles from the A38 Burton-on-Trent by-pass, in the
village once owned by Lady Godiva. So busy does it get that the staff run their little
socks off, though generally the fun stops about there as, more restaurant-style than pub,
there's waitress service to all interior tables. The garden, though, is pretty special in the
summer months with loads of play equipment, the brand-new play area featuring,
among other activities, slides, animals and Postman Pat. Children's menu lunchtimes
only and regular barbecue events. Long hours on Bank Holiday weekends; long games
of dominoes or cards to while away the winter evenings. *Open 11-3, 5.30-11 (Bank
Holiday Mon 11-11, Sat 11.30-11, Sun 12-10.30).* **Beer** *Marston's Pedigree & Head
Brewer's Choice, Owd Roger in winter. Garden, outdoor eating. Family room. Amex,
MasterCard,* **VISA**

TESTCOMBE   Mayfly   A

Tel 01264 860283   Map 14 C3
Testcombe Chilbolton Stockbridge Hampshire SO20 6AZ

Idyllically situated right on the banks of the swiftly flowing River Test, this beamed
old farmhouse (dated 1808) has a traditional bar, a bright conservatory and a splendid
riverside terrace. Unrivalled tranquil river scenes, complete with ducks and swans,
make the Mayfly a popular drinking spot, but on fine sunny days the whole place can
be unbearably crowded, so arrive early to appreciate its superb position. The buffet
food operation tries hard to cater for the volume of people. Be prepared to queue for
the food and then be patient for a seat at peak times, especially in the summer. On the
A3057 Stockbridge–Andover road. Children welcome. Whitbread Wayside Inns.
Open 11-11 (Sun 12-10.30). **Beer** *Flowers Original, Boddingtons, Pompey Royal, two guest
beers. Riverside garden. MasterCard,* **VISA**

TETBURY   Gumstool Inn   FOOD

Tel 01666 890391   Fax 01666 890394   Map 14 B2
Calcot Manor Tetbury Gloucestershire GL8 8YJ

A successful addition to Calcot Manor country house hotel with its own driveway and car park. Designed as a traditional pub, complete with an open fireplace and old flagstone floor, it has the diner very much in mind. With the kitchen sharing the hotel's brigade it is to be expected that the Gumstool menu shows interest and imagination. A new chef is offering such dishes as baked cheese soufflé, roasted confit of pork with mash, soya, ginger and spring oinion, lamb and lemon, coriander and cumin casserole, and seared cod with pesto mash and tomato sauce, alongside quality snacks like smoked ham baguette and various ploughman's lunches; daily blackboard specials add further interest. Children are allowed in the bar to eat and are offered their own menu; six high-chairs provided. A south-facing terrace provides additional tables in fine weather. Booking is essential for weekend eating. *Open 11.30-3, 6-11 (Sun 12-3, 7-10.30).* **Bar Food** *12-2, 7-9.30.* **Beer** *Bass, Duckers (house beer), Wadworth 6X, guest beer. Garden, outdoor eating, children's play area. Amex, Diners, MasterCard,* **VISA**

THAME   Abingdon Arms   FOOD

Tel 01844 260116   Fax 01844 260338   Map 15a D2
21 Cornmarket Thame Oxfordshire OX9 2BL

Known locally as 'The Abo', this 18th-century, former coaching inn offers a fairly modest face to the main street of town but inside several rooms have been opened up to create a long bar with rug-strewn, bare board floors, some exposed brickwork, magazines and newspapers to read and a lively, friendly atmosphere. To the rear, an old barn, is used for functions in the evening and offers an additional lunch menu in summer; beyond this a beer garden comes with rustic tables (some with rustic baby seats attached), slide, swing and climbing frame. Features of the menu are hugely thick 'doorstep' sandwiches and bowls of home-made tagliatelle with various toppings. Other items range from ploughman's platters and burgers to steak and kidney pudding, bangers and mash, Exeter stew with parsley dumplings and an all-day breakfast. All main menu items are available in children's portions at half price. Disabled WC. *Open 11-11 (Sun 12-10.30).* **Bar Food** *12-2.30, 6-9 (till 8.30 Fri, Sat & Sun). Free House.* **Beer** *Hook Norton Best, Boddingtons, Marston's Pedigree, Wychert Ale, guest beers. Garden, outdoor eating, children's play area. Closed 25 Dec. MasterCard,* **VISA**

THAXTED   Farmhouse Inn   B&B

Tel 01371 830864   Fax 01371 831196   Map 10 B3
Monk Street Thaxted Essex CM6 2NR

Surrounded by open fields and farmland, 1 mile south of the village off the B184, this former 16th-century farmhouse has been much extended and modernised in recent years and provides overnight accommodation in eleven rooms with en suite bath and shower. Located around a courtyard, bedrooms are standard and functional with built-in furniture, TVs, telephones, tea- and coffee-making facilities and adequate bathrooms. Ideal for a peaceful, rural stopover en route to a flight out of Stansted Airport, only 8 miles away. *Open 11-3, 6-11 (Sat 11-11, Sun 12-3, 7-10.30). Free House.* **Beer** *Wadworth 6X, Greene King IPA, Adnams Southwold. Garden, children's play area.* **Accommodation** *11 bedrooms, all en suite £42.50 (single £32.50). Children welcome overnight, additional bed & cot (both £5) available. No dogs. Amex, MasterCard,* **VISA**

We do not accept free meals or hospitality – our inspectors pay their own bills and never book in the name of Egon Ronay's Guides.

THELBRIDGE   Thelbridge Cross Inn   B&B

Tel 01884 860316   Fax 01884 860316   Map 13 D2
Thelbridge Witheridge Devon EX17 4SQ

Two miles west of Witheridge on the B3042 this attractive, white-painted inn is isolated high up in a very rural part of Devon with views across to Dartmoor. The much modernised interior is carpeted and open-plan in layout with some comfortable settees, a couple of log fires and is delightfully free of live music, juke box or pool table. The bar offers some good local cider, country wines and some sixty whiskies including twenty malts. The adjacent barns have been well converted to provide a comfortable block of seven bedrooms and a large self-catering apartment. Bedrooms are rather compact with pretty matching fabrics and modern units, but room is found for a telephone, TV, tea-maker and a small fully-tiled private shower room in each. An occasional attraction is the original 'Lorna Doone' stagecoach which brings extra Sunday lunch trade. *Open 11.30-3 (from 12 Sun), 6.30-11. Free House.* **Beer** *Bass, Butcombe Bitter, Wadworth 6X (summer). Garden, children's play area. Family room.* **Accommodation** *8 bedrooms, all en suite, £60 (family room sleeping four £70, single £35). Children welcome overnight (under-10s stay free in parents' room, 10-14s 75% adult tariff), additional bed & cot available. No dogs. Amex, Diners, MasterCard,* **VISA**

THOMPSON   Chequers Inn   A

Tel 01953 483360   Map 10 C2
Griston Road Thompson Thetford Norfolk IP24 1PX

Well off the beaten track, this splendid, long and low, thatched 14th-century inn is worth finding – 1 mile off the A1075 Watton to Thetford road along a tiny lane on the edge of the village – for its peaceful location and unspoilt charm. Beneath the steep-raked thatch of this ancient ale house, once a row of several cottages, lies a series of low-ceilinged inter-connecting rooms served by a long bar. Wonky wall timbers, low doorways, open log fires, a rustic mix of old furniture and collections of farming implements, brass and copper characterise the well-maintained and atmospheric interior. Good rear garden with rural views and children's play area. Handy for excellent local woodland walks. *Open 11-3, 6-11 (Sun 12-3, 7-10.30). Free House.* **Beer** *Adnams Southwold, Bass, Tetley, Fuller's London Pride, guest beers. Family room. Diners, MasterCard,* **VISA**

THORNTON   Ring O'Bells   FOOD

Tel 01274 832296   Fax 01274 831707   Map 6 C1
Hilltop Road Thornton Bradford BD13 3QL

Up on a windy, woody moor just 3 miles from Bradford, the Ring O'Bells is firmly established as one of the area's top dining venues. Over the last four years the combined talents of Clive and Ann Preston at the helm and daughter Michelle Bone part of the team in the kitchen have gained quite a reputation for their food. Behind some jokey names on the menu there are substantial Yorkshire offerings: for 'Neptune's Kingdom' read home-made fishcakes with fresh dill, white wine and cream, while the 'chicken Florentino' produces chicken stuffed with spinach with a Madeira and mushroom sauce. The daily blackboards, however, eschew such flippancy and much of what is produced is seriously done. Ragout of French wild mushrooms with bacon, black pudding and mustard, and smoked salmon terrine with cucumber marinade typify the starters. The day's fish special might be pan-fried pollock with herb crust and an orange and basil sauce; no less popular is a daily game dish: perhaps supreme of guinea fowl with ginger and coriander jus. Similarly inventive sweets include French lattice apple and cinnamon tart. Early-evening (5.30-7) table d'hote menus, served in the bar, offer good value. Nonetheless, Ring O'Bells remains essentially a pub, with well-spaced tables set away from the bar and a restaurant area (booking advised, no smoking) providing the same food and waitress service with just a little more comfort. *Open 11.30-3.30, 5.30-11 (Sun 12-3, 7-10.30).* **Bar Food** *12-2, 5.30-9 (from 7 Sat & Sun).* **Beer** *Webster's Yorkshire, Theakston XB, guest beer. Closed 25 Dec. MasterCard,* **VISA**

THRESHFIELD   Old Hall Inn   FOOD

Tel 01756 752441   Map 6 C1
Threshfield Skipton North Yorkshire BD23 5HB

A lovely stone-built Dales inn, based on a Tudor hall from which its name comes, the Taylors' pub gains further character from its idiosyncratic individuality. An eccentric mix of flagstone floors, classical music and chamber pots suspended from the ceiling is accentuated by the 'Brat Board' at ankle height by the fireplace: chicken nuggets and chips followed by two scoops of multi-flavoured ice creams seem fairly brat-proof. One daily-changing blackboard menu offers up to 15 starters and main courses; perhaps Dales sausage with onion gravy, tortellini with tomato sauce, crepe Alfredo (chicken, spinach and garlic), Wensleydale ploughman's and wild boar and pheasant pie with a Cumberland sauce, with fresh market seafood specials. More elaborate evening dishes might include pan-fried venison with garlic mash and caramelised onions, medallions of monkfish with bacon, mushrooms and garlic and pan-fried chicken breast with mozzarella and Madeira and mushroom sauce. Finish off with lemon tart or pecan and maple cheesecake. A perennially hectic place; ordering and paying at the bar can be a little chaotic, though for a little peace and quiet the garden is a delightful alternative. *Open 11.30-3, 6-11 (Sun 12-3, 6-10.30). Closed Mon lunch.* **Bar Food** *12-2, 6.15-9.30 (no food all day Mon & Sun eve in winter). Free House.* **Beer** *Timothy Taylor's Best & Landlord, Theakston Best, guest beers. Garden, outdoor eating. Family rooms. No credit cards.*

> We do not accept free meals or hospitality – our inspectors pay their own bills and **never** book in the name of Egon Ronay's Guides**.**

THURSLEY   Three Horseshoes   A

Tel 01252 703268   Map 15a E4
Dye House Road Thursley nr Godalming Surrey GU8 6QD

One minute off the A3 between Milford and Hindhead, a characterful, 300-year-old beamed local with Thursley Common and the Devil's Punchbowl nearby. 1½-acre garden. No juke box or games machines. Children only welcome if over 5 and eating at lunchtime – it's too small a pub! B&B is offered in a one-bedroom cottage in the pub grounds (£30 double). *Open 12-3 (from 11 Sat), 6-11 (Sun 12-3, 7-10.30). Free House.* **Beer** *Gale's Butser Brew Bitter & HSB. Garden. MasterCard,* **VISA**

TICHBORNE   Tichborne Arms   FOOD

Tel 01962 733760   Map 15 D3
Tichborne Alresford Hampshire SO24 0NA

Heavy thatch predominates throughout this idyllic hamlet nestling in the peaceful Itchen Valley; it cloaks the local pub, a popular and attractive destination for both lunch and supper. Over the years, a series of fires have destroyed the pub here, but the present structure, built in 1940, survives and is very much the hub of village life, being the venue for the village carol service, harvest supper and the polling station – a good turn out is generally guaranteed! At other times, locals and visitors alike are attracted here to sample the range of real ales dispensed straight from the cask and to taste the reliable, home-cooked food that is served in both the small comfortable panelled bar and in the larger and livelier 'locals' bar. Home-made soup (tomato and basil), generously-filled jacket potatoes and salads are supplemented by a good range of home-made daily specials such as bacon, leek and cheese quiche, beef cobbler, local pink trout with lemon mayonnaise, and beef curry, with home-made fudge and walnut flan and lemon sponge to finish. The well-tended and sheltered rear garden is a perfect spot for warm-weather imbibing. No children under 14 allowed inside the pub. Six miles from M3 Junction 9. *Open 11.30-2.30, 6-11 (Sun 12-3, 7-10.30).* **Bar Food** *12-1.45, 6.30-9.45 (Sun 7-9.30). Free House.* **Beer** *Wadworth 6X, Flowers IPA, Fuggles IPA, guest beer. Garden, outdoor eating. No credit cards.*

TIDESWELL   George   B&B

Tel 01298 871382   Fax 01298 872408   Map 6 C2
Commercial Road Tideswell Derbyshire SK17 8NU

Market town coaching inn dating from 1730. Small snug, traditional locals' noisy tap room, dining lounge and dining-room proper. Shaded courtyard garden with goldfish pond, creeping vines and flowers. Beautiful parish church known as 'Cathedral of the Peak' next door. The four-poster and double rooms have en suite shower rooms, the other two have their own basins and share one bathroom and toilet. Live music every Friday evening. *Open 11-3, 7-11 (Sun 12-3, 7-10.30).* **Beer** *Hardys & Hansons. Courtyard. Family room.* **Accommodation** *4 bedrooms, 2 en suite (shower), £50-£60 (single £25). Children welcome overnight (under-5s stay free in parents' room, 5-12s 40% adult tariff)), Check-in bar hours only. Amex, MasterCard,* **VISA**

TILLINGHAM   Cap & Feathers   A

Tel 01621 779212   Map 11 C4
8 South Street Tillingham nr Southminster Essex CM0 7TH

Crouch Vale Brewery's only tied house – a delightfully unspoilt, classic white-painted, weather-boarded Essex village inn dating from 1427. A timeless, old-fashioned atmosphere remains within the warm and woody low-ceilinged interior with its eclectic mix of traditional furnishings, board floors and a real open fire. Several distinct areas ramble about, including a small rear carpeted area with woodburner and dresser, and a section housing time-honoured pub games (table skittles and an ancient bar billiards table that still operates on shillings); no music, one-armed bandits or quiz machines here! Home-cooked blackboard specials feature locally-smoked fish and meats. Modest bed and breakfast accommodation, the three rooms sharing a shower room. *Open 11.30-3, 6-11 (Sun 12-3, 7-10.30).* **Beer** *Crouch Vale Ales, guest beer. Garden. Family room. No credit cards.*

TILLINGTON   Horseguards Inn   FOOD

Tel 01798 342332   Map 11 A6   **B&B**
Tillington Petworth West Sussex GU28 9AF

Zzz...

Charming 300-year-old inn peacefully positioned opposite the parish church just off the A272 Petworth to Midhurst road. Raised up from the village lane it was originally three cottages and enjoys good views towards the South Downs. Inside, a rambling series of relaxing and tastefully refurbished rooms feature exposed stripped beams, original pine panelling, open fires, various antique and pine furnishings and collections of hunting prints, brass blow lamps and polo mallets. Beyond the small bar area each table is neatly laid with fresh flowers and candles, as this is very much a dining pub attracting an upmarket clientele from miles around for the imaginative, twice-daily-changing menu. Lunchtime fare includes snacks like sandwiches and ploughman's lunches, and courgette and Cheddar mousse. In the evenings the atmosphere remains informal, but the cooking moves up a gear with maybe smoked duck breast with ginger and citrus dressing or carrot and coriander soup for starters. Main-course options range from well-presented supreme of salmon and monkfish medallions with white wine sauce and baked brill with garlic butter to roast partridge with mushroom sauce and venison with blueberry sauce, all served with a dish of decent fresh vegetables. Good home-made puddings. The global list of wines continues to develop and there's a selection of fine wines – including dessert wines and vintage port – highlighted on a blackboard. Sunday roast. Large, secluded rear garden and front terrace for fine-weather alfresco imbibing. Overnight accommodation comprises two attractive and cottagey bedrooms upstairs and a further comfortable room in a converted outbuilding. All have TVs, tea- and coffee-making kits and clean, en suite facilities. Children not encouraged overnight. *Open 11-3, 6-11 (Sun 12-3, 7-10.30).* **Bar Food** *12-2, 7-10. Free House.* **Beer** *Hall & Woodhouse Badger Best, King & Barnes Sussex Bitter. Garden, outdoor eating.* **Accommodation** *3 bedrooms, all en suite, £55 (Jul-Sept £57.50). Check-in by arrangement. No dogs. MasterCard,* **VISA**

TITCHFIELD   Fishermans Rest   A

Tel 01329 842848   Map 15 D4
Mill Lane Titchfield Fareham Titchfield Hampshire PO15 5RA

Mill Lane is a turning north off A27, 3 miles west of Fareham (take J9 off M27). An attractive brick country inn, ideally located opposite the entrance to the impressive ruins of Titchfield Abbey and on the banks of the idly flowing River Meon. Inside, the well-refurbished series of rambling rooms feature flagstones, exposed brick walls and an interesting variety of fishing paraphernalia adorns the walls. Good spot to relax as the bars are devoid of intrusive electronic games and background music. Large waterside garden for sunny summer days. Whitbread Wayside Inns. *Open 11-11 (Sun 12-10.30).* **Beer** *Wadworth 6X, Flowers Original, Boddingtons Bitter & Mild, Gale's HSB, guest beer. Garden. MasterCard,* **VISA**

TIVETSHALL ST MARY   Old Ram   B&B

Tel 01379 676794   Fax 01379 608399   Map 10 C2
Ipswich Road Tivetshall St Mary Norfolk NR15 2DE

Zzz... ☺

Conveniently situated beside the A140 between Norwich and Ipswich, this old 17th-century inn positively bustles with people all day with travellers and locals seeking refreshment within the rambling and carefully refurbished series of rooms. Road-weary visitors in need of overnight accommodation will not be disappointed with the five "luxury" en suite bedrooms built into the eaves with sloping roofs and exposed timbers. Tastefully decorated with Laura Ashley wallpaper and co-ordinating fabrics and kitted out with quality modern lightwood, each boasts satellite TV, direct-dial telephone, tea-maker, trouser press and hairdryer. Two are mini-suites with comfortable easy chairs and all gain top marks for their spotless bathrooms with gleaming tiles, fluffy towels and robust, powerful showers over tubs. Room prices are also quoted without breakfast. Staff are particularly friendly and efficient. No under-7s after 8pn. Disabled WC and baby-changing facilities. *Open 7.30-11 (till 10.30 Sun). Free House.* **Beer** *Ruddles County, Adnams Southwold, Boddingtons, Ram Bitter (brewed by Woodforde's). Garden.* **Accommodation** *5 bedrooms, all en suite £55-£61.90 (single £37.50-£42.50). Children welcome overnight (under-2s stay free in parents' room, 2-10s £10). Check-in after noon. No dogs. Closed 25 & 26 Dec. MasterCard,* **VISA**

TOOT HILL   Green Man   FOOD

Tel 01992 522255   Map 11 B4
Toot Hill Ongar Essex CM5 9SD

Early 19th-century coaching inn located in a tiny hamlet amid a web of lanes between Ongar and Epping, and efficiently run by the Roads family for the past 28 years. Unpretentious exterior enhanced each summer by a magnificent, award-winning floral display in its sheltered courtyard. Equally simple interior with a pleasant carpeted bar with open fire and an adjoining comfortably furnished dining area. Popular locally for home-cooked bar food set out on a blackboard: choices might range from light lunchtime snacks (no sandwiches, but ploughman's platters offered) to a short, daily-changing evening selection of dishes such as fresh crab mornay, salmon in ginger and raisin parcel, grilled red snapper with roasted peppers, Cajun chicken, rabbit casserole with herb dumplings and steak and kidney pie. Among the list of home-made puddings there may be blueberry and apple crumble or summer pudding with orange and brandy. The Longbow restaurant is across the courtyard, but it's the bar food that we specifically recommend. Good range of real ales and a list of over 100 wines that includes 20 half bottles and numerous champagnes. No children under 10 inside. *Open 11-3, 6-11 (Sun 12-3, 7-10.30).* **Bar Food** *12-2, 7-9.30).* **Beer** *Crouch Vale Bitter, two guest beers. Garden, outdoor eating. Closed 25 Dec. MasterCard,* **VISA**

We endeavour to be as up-to-date as possible but inevitably some changes to landlords, chefs and other key staff occur after the Guide has gone to press.

TOPCLIFFE · Angel Inn · B&B

Tel 01845 577237   Fax 01845 578000   Map 5 E4
Long Street Topcliffe Thirsk North Yorkshire YO7 3RW

At the junction of the A167 and A168, the pre-Norman village of Topcliffe is convenient for, and equidistant from, both the A19 and A1 (3 miles). The 17th-century Angel, once a coaching inn, has been sympathetically remodelled and extended by its present owners. Three bar areas, games room, residents' lounge and a large garden complete with rockery and ornamental fish pond allow a multiplicity of choices for guests' relaxation. The purpose-built wing of bedrooms (above a self-contained function suite) is tastefully furnished in varnished pine, and facilities in all rooms include satellite TVs and mini-bars as well as dial-out phones, hairdryers and trouser presses. Residents have their own entrance, allowing them free access and security 24 hours per day, and effective double-glazing ensures a completely restful night. *Open 11-11 (Sun 12-10.30). Free House.* **Beer** *John Smith's, Theakston Best. Garden. Family room.* **Accommodation** *15 bedrooms, all en suite, £50 (family room £60-£70, single £35-£40). Children welcome overnight (additional cot available). No dogs.* MasterCard, **VISA**

TORCROSS · Start Bay Inn · FOOD

Tel 01548 580553   Fax 01548 580513   Map 13 D3
Torcross Kingsbridge Devon TQ7 2TQ

Arguably the 'best pub fish and chips in Devon' can be found at this 14th-century thatched inn, which is superbly situated between the beach at Slapton Sands and the freshwater lagoon and nature reserve of Slapton Ley. Landlord Paul Stubbs is a keen diver and fisherman and his catch of fresh seafood contributes to the vast amount of fresh fish that is delivered daily to this extremely popular seaside inn. The modest bar and dining areas are simply furnished with a mix of tables and chairs and various old photographs of the storm-ravaged pub adorn the walls. Every available seat is taken soon after opening, especially in the summer. Fish and chip connoisseurs come eager to sample the delicious battered cod, haddock and plaice, available in three sizes, the jumbo size served on a huge plate accompanied by good, plump chips. Blackboards outside inform you that only polyunsaturated oils are used for frying. Also on the menu are daily fish specials such as whole lemon sole, monkfish tails, skate wings and scallops in garlic butter or batter. The freshest of crab is cooked and dressed on the premises and used in their platters and sandwiches. The rest of the menu lists standard pub fare that will not disappoint meat eaters; vegetarians might now be offered the likes of spinach and mushroom lasagne or mushroom balti. Although the service is fast and efficient, be prepared to wait a little while as the fish is cooked to order. *Open 11.30-2.30, 6-11 (Sun 12-2.30, 7-10.30), end July-Sept 11.30-11, (Sun 12-10.30).* **Bar Food** *11.30-2 & 6-9 (till 10 Fri & Sat), Sun 12-2, 7-9.* **Beer** *Flowers IPA & Original, Bass. Beachside patio, outdoor eating. Family room. No credit cards.*

TORMARTON · Compass Inn · B&B

Tel 01454 218242   Fax 01454 218741   Map 13 F1
Tormarton Badminton South Gloucestershire GL9 1JB

Creeper-clad in summer, the oldest part of the inn dates back to the late 17th century and the not entirely unspoilt bars boast some old timbers and exposed stonework. The Orangery, a sort of glass-roofed courtyard, is a good spot in summer and has new garden-type furniture this year. Most of the generally good-sized bedrooms are in a newer wing. Darkwood fitted furniture is the norm with wing armchairs and the usual amenities – beverage tray, trouser press (some with iron and ironing board attached), hairdryer etc. Most of the well-kept bathrooms have tubs (just two have shower only), many with shower above. There are also several meeting rooms. Less than half a mile from M4 Junction 18. Secure car parking for overnight residents. *Open 11-11 (Sun 12-10.30). Free House.* **Beer** *Bass, Smiles Best, Archers Village. Garden, terrace. Family room.* **Accommodation** *28 bedrooms, all en suite, £79.95-£99.50 (single £59.95). Children welcome overnight (under-14s stay free in parents' room – breakfast charge), additional bed & cot (£3) available. Dogs by arrangement. Accommodation closed 24-26 Dec, pub closed 26 Dec eve.* Amex, Diners, MasterCard, **VISA**

TREGADILLET — Eliot Arms (Square & Compass)   A

Tel 01566 772051   Fax 01566 773010   Map 12 C3
Tregadillet Launceston Cornwall PL15 7EU

The pretty, creeper-covered Eliot Arms was built in the 14th century as a coaching inn. Once inside, it's like being in the 'Old Curiosity Shop', as every inch of wall space is littered with a host of memorabilia. Pride of place goes to the splendid collection of over 70 clocks, including six grandfather clocks, as well as paintings, plates, books, ornaments and a collection of 400 snuff boxes. Unspoilt layout with lots of rambling little rooms with rug-strewn slate floors and nice old furniture freely and successfully mixing with modern seating. Overnight accommodation is offered in two bedrooms (not en suite). Sheltered garden. *Open 11-2.30 (till 3 Sat), 6-11 (Sun 12-2.30, 7-10.30). Family room. Free House.* **Beer** *Marston's Pedigree, Flowers Original, Wadworth 6X, Morland Old Speckled Hen. Garden, children's play area. Family room. Closed 25 Dec. No credit cards.*

TRENT — Rose & Crown   FOOD

Tel 01935 850776   Map 13 F2
Trent Sherborne Dorset DT9 4SL

Nestling in sleepy village deep in rural Dorset, Charles & Nancy Marion-Crawford's thatched pub is refreshingly unpretentious within with its rug-strewn stone floors, roaring winter log fires and simple furnishings. No pub games, fruit machines or music to disturb the peace, but children's play things can be found in the garden, which enjoys open country views. The emphasis is on good, fresh food, making excellent use of local garden vegetables, game (in winter) and beef. A sensibly-short, weekly-changing blackboard menu is served throughout the pub and the attractive and airy 40-seat conservatory makes a pleasant dining-room. Interesting main courses may include herb-crusted mignons of beef with wild mushroom sauce, home-made crab cakes with roasted pepper mayonnaise and hot and sour pork medallions on a bed of Singapore noodles, with chocolate and banana roulade or a decent West Country cheeseboard to finish. Good fresh fish highlight the board in summer (herb-crusted fillet of hake with a fruit sabayon, whole West Bay plaice with lemon and prawn butter). Sandwiches and ploughman's platters are available lunchtime and evening. Vegetarians can sample vegetable biriyani with naan bread and pickles or tagliatelle with mixed vegetables and Cajun spices. Families are well catered for – it's an ideal venue for a family outing on a summer's evening. *Open 12-2.30, 7-11 (Sun 12-3, 7-10.30). Closed Sun eve winter & all 25 Dec.* **Bar Food** *12-1.45, 7-9 (till 9.30 Fri & Sat). Free House.* **Beer** *Shepherd Neame Spitfire, Butcombe Bitter, two guest beers. Garden, outdoor eating, children's play area. Family room (no smoking).* Amex, MasterCard, **VISA**

TROUTBECK — Mortal Man Hotel   FOOD

Tel 01539 433193   Fax 01539 431261   Map 4 C3   **B&B**
Troutbeck Windermere Cumbria LA23 1PL

Zzz...

A hotchpotch of antique seating, gleaming copper-topped tables, beams, horse brasses, pewter tankards, hunting horns and views of a gentle green valley through the windows give the Mortal Man plenty of rustic charm. It's a bright, well-kept inn of 17th-century origins, with an established reputation for hospitality. One of the bars is kept mainly for residents, but it provides an overspill when the public bar is full. There is a plentiful supply of food on offer such as home-made soup – cream of vegetable – home-cooked ham, lovely fresh summer salads, Cumberland sausage and plaice goujons, which highlight the lunchtime-only menu. Evening fare ranges from Sally Birkett's hotpot (pork in cider) and beef in ale pie to rack of lamb with rosemary and fillet steak. Finish with a selection from the sweet trolley (summer pudding, chocolate fudge cake), a choice of cheeses with celery and biscuits or a savoury of grilled lamb's liver with paprika on toast. The restaurant offers a set five-course dinner. Roast Aberdeen Angus beef for Sunday roast lunch. The bedrooms are clean and comfortable, with attractive, homely decor in co-ordinated colours and well-cared-for furniture. A sunny lounge overlooks the Troutbeck Valley. All have smart, clean, en suite bathrooms, TVs and entrancing views. Housekeeping is excellent. Half-board terms only. *Open 12-2.30, 5.30-11 (Sun 12-2.30, 7-10.30). Closed mid Nov-mid Feb.* **Bar Food** *12-1.45, 6.30-9 (from 7 Sun). No food Mon eve. Free House.* **Beer** *Theakston Best, Younger's Scotch Bitter. Garden.* **Accommodation** *12 bedrooms, all en suite, £100-£114 half-board terms (reduced tariff out of season, single £57). Children over 5 welcome overnight (5-12s half-price). No credit cards.*

TRUSHAM	Cridford Inn	FOOD

Tel 01626 853694   Map 13 D3   **B&B**
Trusham Newton Abbot Devon TQ13 0NR

 Zzz...

Hidden in the Teign Valley between Exeter and Dartmoor, the thatched Cridford Inn is the oldest domestic dwelling in Devon dating from 1081 and features a mosaic datestone discovered in the original Saxon floor in what is now the dining-room, and in the bar one can see the earliest example of a domestic window in Britain. The charming interior displays original huge beams, stone fireplaces and floors; the low-ceilinged lounge/dining-room has relaxing easy chairs and sofas, tasteful pictures and five mahogany tables topped with fresh flowers, gleaming cutlery and glassware, while rustic stone floors characterise the two interconnecting bars with woodburner, and pew and settles in cosy partitioned seating areas. David Hesmondhalgh produces a varied range of good home-cooked dishes that use fresh local produce and are listed on a regularly-changing à la carte menu that is served throughout the pub. Among the choice of starters there may be salad of warm asparagus with hollandaise or chicken liver paté, with main-course options like steak and kidney pie, chicken in red wine, bacon and mushroom sauce, steak béarnaise and fresh fish, delivered daily from Brixham – pan-fried lemon sole with parsley, dressed crab, battered cod with chips. Home-made puddings range from summer pudding and brandy snap basket with summer fruit to banoffee pie with caramel sauce. Short list of wines with helpful tasting notes from Christopher Piper wine merchants; nineteen wines are available by the glass. Four characterful, upstairs bedrooms are individually decorated to a high standard with pretty, co-ordinating cottagey fabrics in floral designs – all are comfortably furnished. Well-equipped, en suite bathrooms. Homely touches include fresh flowers, pot pourri, tissues, china tea service and magazines to read. No children overnight. *Open 11.30-2.30, 6-11 (Sun 12-2.30, 7-10.30).* **Bar Food** *12-2, 6.30-9 (from 7 Sun). Free House.* **Beer** *Trusham Ale, Bass, Adnams Broadside, Smiles Best, Exmoor Ale, guest beer. Terrace, outdoor eating. Family room.* **Accommodation** *4 rooms, all en suite, £60 (single £40). No dogs. Closed 25 Dec. MasterCard,* **VISA**

TUNBRIDGE WELLS	Sankeys Cellar Wine Bar	FOOD

Tel 01892 511422   Map 11 B5
39 Mount Ephraim Tunbridge Wells Kent TN4 8AA

Reached via a flight of steps from the street, this informal cellar wine bar/bistro has a pubby atmosphere with its York stone paved floor, gas lighting, rustic pine tables, kitchen chairs, church pews, antique mirrors and pub bric a brac. Go for enjoyable seafood dishes, or just for a relaxing glass of wine or pint of real ale, especially sitting out on the very Continental, sun-drenched patio in summer. Excellent daily-changing bar meals range from fishy dishes like clam chowder, potted shrimps, fresh cod and chips and seafood paella to aubergine parmigiana, duck cassoulet, Moroccan chicken and imaginatively-filled baguettes. Puddings may include French apple tart and bread-and-butter pudding. Restaurant fare (steamed fillet of bass with stir-fried vegetables, Cornish cock crab served hot with chili black bean sauce) normally available in the four neatly-laid upstairs rooms can also be ordered in the cellar bar. Interesting list of wines with at least 10 available by the glass. Live music on Sunday evenings (but no food). No under-14s in the bar. *Open 11-11, (Sat 11-3, Sun 7-10.30 only). Closed Sun lunch.* **Bar Food** *12-3 (till 2 Sat), 7-10 (till 9 Sat). No bar food Sun eve, restaurant closed Sat lunch & all Sun). Free House.* **Beer** *one changing real ale. Terrace, outdoor eating. Closed 25 & 26 Dec. Amex, Diners, MasterCard,* **VISA**

TURVEY — Three Cranes — B&B

Tel 01234 881305   Map 15 E1
High Street Loop Turvey Bedfordshire MK43 8EP

Enjoying a peaceful village setting adjacent to the parish church and close to an interesting abbey, this predominantly Victorian stone inn offers comfortable and good-value overnight accommodation in five cottagey bedrooms: attractive and welcoming, with modern pine furnishings, tasteful wallpaper and contrasting fabrics and clean en suite facilities; TV, radio and tea-making kits are standard. Downstairs there is a neatly-furnished and well-decorated, open-plan bar which displays plenty of plants, decent framed prints, plates and other pieces of china. The front of the building is a real picture in summer with hanging baskets, flower borders and virginia creeper, while to the rear is a safe, sheltered garden. Children are made very welcome. *Open 11-3, 6-11 (Sun 12-3, 7-10.30). Free House.* **Beer** *Fuller's London Pride & ESB, Bass, Smiles Best, Black Sheep Bitter, guest beer. Garden, children's play area.* **Accommodation** *5 bedrooms, all en suite (shower), £40 (single £30). Children over 6 welcome overnight, additional bed (£15) available. Check-in by arrangement. No dogs. Closed 25 Dec. MasterCard,* **VISA**

TURVILLE — Bull & Butcher — FOOD

Tel 01491 638283   Map 15a D3
Turville Henley-on-Thames Oxfordshire RG9 6QU

Back in the early 1600s some workmen on the local church went on strike for want of refreshments, prompting an enterprising cottager to turn his home into one; thus the Bull & Butcher was born. Inside the attractive black-and-white timbered building are two unspoilt, low-ceilinged bars with cushioned wall benches and settles, open fires, a collection of horse brasses and a welcoming atmosphere. A daily-changing blackboard generally lists a choice of patés – Stilton and walnut – popular dishes like venison and mushroom pie, lemon chicken, macaroni cheese and hot and spicy cod, as well as rack of lamb, whole grilled tilapia and dressed crab. Home-made soup and ploughman's lunches are also offered. Good puddings include chocolate and cherry roulade and Nancy's treacle tart (prepared by the 84-year-old lady who lives across the lane). Winter Sunday roasts. Excellent local walks, quaint village and an impressive white windmill (featured in the film *Chitty Chitty Bang Bang*) on the hill opposite. *Open 11-3, 6-11 (Sun 12-3, 7-10.30).* **Bar Food** *12-2 (till 3 Sat & Sun), 7-9.45.* **Beer** *Brakspear. Garden, outdoor eating. MasterCard,* **VISA**

TUSHINGHAM — Blue Bell Inn — A

Tel 01948 662172   Map 6 B3
Bell O' Th' Hill Tushingham Whitchurch Cheshire SY13 4QS

🍺 ☺

'Bell O' Th' Hill' is the sign to look for by a new stretch of the A41, four miles north of Whitchurch. Standing in extensive grounds on a bend in the old road is this remarkable building of 17th-century origins with a black and white, timbered frame, massive oak doors and a wealth of original timbers, oak panelling and memorabilia within. There's a single bar, the pub's focal point, where the ales are real and the welcome's a mite unusual. Landlord Patrick Gage hails from California, while his wife Lydia is from Moscow. This somehow matches the mild eccentricity of an establishment which lists amongst its claims to fame the presence of a ghost duck and the more physical presence of a Great Dane and a miniature poodle. Wooden benches in front for an alfresco drink look suitably ancient, while 'paddock' rather than garden would describe the safe outdoor area allocated to youngsters who are particularly welcome to play with the Gage children (and the dogs). *Open 12-3, 6-11 (Sun 12-3, 7-10.30). Free House.* **Beer** *Hanby Drawwell, Treacleminer & Black Magic Mild, occasional guest beer. Garden. Family room. No credit cards.*

TUTBURY   Ye Olde Dog & Partridge Inn   B&B

Tel 01283 813030   Fax 01283 813178   Map 6 C3
High Street Tutbury Burton-on-Trent Staffordshire DE13 9LS

Zzz...

With parts dating back to the 15th-century, this resplendent half-timbered inn on the high street is as popular today as it was in the 18th century when it was extended to accommodate passengers on the busy Liverpool to London coaching route. Successive extensions and improvements over the centuries can be traced within. Tapestries adorn the main bar with its thatched servery, and residents enjoy use of a restful timber-framed lounge well away from the busy self-service Carvery restaurant. The oldest accommodation, with creaking floors and oak panelling, are the three rooms in the original buildings, while the adjacent Georgian house, built around an impressive central spiral staircase contains the bulk of the recently refurbished bedrooms which are more routinely up-to-date. Accoutrements which run to satellite TV, mini-bars and forceful over-bath pulse showers are all decidedly up-market for a pub, and tend to be priced accordingly, though the weekend rates are something of a bargain.
Open 11-2.30, 6-11 (Sun 12-2.30, 7-10.30). Free House. **Beer** *Marston's Pedigree, guest beer. Garden, terrace.* **Accommodation** *17 bedrooms, all en suite, £72.50-£78 (weekend £49.50, four-poster £78, single £55-£62.50). Children welcome overnight, additional bed & cot available. Accommodation closed 25, 26 Dec & 1 Jan. Amex, MasterCard,* **VISA**

ULCOMBE   Pepper Box Inn   FOOD

Tel & Fax 01622 842558   Map 11 C5
Fairbourne Heath Ulcombe Maidstone Kent ME17 1LP

The Pepper Box is a cottagey pub with low eaves and white-painted stone walls, surrounded by fields of corn and affording views across the expanse of the Kentish Weald. Dating back to the 15th-century, it was once the haunt of smugglers and takes its name (apparently unique) from their favourite weapon, the Pepper Box pistol. A three-piece suite takes pride of place in front of an inglenook fireplace in the beamed bar and old pewter mugs hang above the bar counter along with decorative hopbines. Part of the bar has recently been knocked through, exposing beams and stone walls to create a no-smoking dining area. A Shepherd Neame-owned house, the tenancy of which has been in the same family since 1958, with Sarah and Geoff Pemble currently providing the hospitable welcome. Highlights of interesting, regularly-changing blackboard menus include Brie wedges with redcurrant coulis, pan-fried lamb's liver with apple and sage, chili chicken with basil and coconut cream sauce and poached trout with lime butter sauce. The pudding list may feature tiramisu or pecan and maple syrup tart. Good-value roast plus ploughman's platters, sandwiches, a fish and a vegetarian dish replace the regular menu for lunch on Sunday. There's a short list of wines, and the Shepherd Neame ales are drawn direct from the barrels behind the bar. No children inside, but they are welcome in the large, pretty garden. *Open 11-3, 6.30-11 (Sun 12-3, 7-10.30).* **Bar Food** *12-2 & 6.30-9.45 (no food Sun eve).* **Beer** *Shepherd Neame. Garden, outdoor eating area. Closed 25 Dec eve. MasterCard,* **VISA**

ULVERSTON   Bay Horse Inn   ★   FOOD   B&B

Tel 01229 583972   Fax 01229 580502   Map 4 C4
Canal Foot Ulverston Cumbria LA12 9EL

Zzz...

1½ miles from Ulverston (from the A590, follow the signs for Canal Foot and continue driving through the Glaxo factory), an old pub in a lovely location on the shore of the Leven Estuary. Sympathetically converted, with an intimate conservatory restaurant that makes the most of the picturesque views over the water. The bar retains a pubby character with its old beams and gleaming brassware and one can enjoy a drink or snack at one of the few tables set out by an old stone breakwater. Chef Robert Lyons gives full rein to his wide-ranging repertoire; he worked with John Tovey at nearby *Miller Howe* for 18 years and the influence is still evident in dishes like smoked goose breast and avocado pear with Cumberland sauce, tomato, apple and celery soup, spinach and mushroom roulade with Marsala and coriander cream, and parcels of air-dried ham filled with an egg and watercress mousse. Snacks are not overlooked, as starters can be ordered with a baked potato as a more substantial dish, and filled home-made baps are also offered. Lunch in the restaurant offers a limited choice of two dishes (fennel and red pepper soup, pork cutlet with apple and Calvados, tipsy trifle) at each of the four courses (£15.75) plus a few more desserts. In the evening, both an à la carte and a grill menu with well-hung Aberdeen Angus steaks are offered; the carte might start with avocado pear filled with cheese and herb paté, following with medallions of veal fillet pan-fried with chestnuts, mushrooms, cream and Marsala; finally, apple and strawberry pie or a cheese platter with home-made biscuits and soda bread – serious stuff. Two excellent wine lists, notably an outstanding and keenly-priced New World list (50+). Bedrooms are generally not large, but six of the seven enjoy splendid views across the estuary from picture windows that open on to a balcony. All have the same pale yellow walls, matching bed covers and curtains in a variety of attractive fabrics and the usual amenities of direct-dial phone, remote-control TV, hairdryers and the like. Beds are turned down in the evening. Smart bathrooms, all with showers over the tub, come with quality toiletries and little extras like DIY dry-cleaning kit and a jar of soap flakes. Half-board terms only, with good reductions for two- or three-night weekend stays. "Children under 12 are not catered for." Recommended in our *1997 Hotels & Restaurants Guide. Open 11-11 (Sun 12-10.30). Bar Food 12-2 (except Mon). Restaurant Meals 12-1.30 (except Sun & Mon), 7.30 for 8. Free House. Beer Mitchell's Original & Lancaster Bomber, guest beer. Riverside terrace, outdoor eating. Accommodation 7 rooms, all en suite, £130-£160 +10% service (half-board only, single £80 +10% service). No children under 12 overnight. MasterCard,* **VISA**

UPPER BENEFIELD — Wheatsheaf Hotel — FOOD

Tel 01832 205254   Fax 01832 205245   Map 7 E4   **B&B**
Upper Benefield Oundle Northamptonshire PE8 5AN

Situated beside the A427 Corby to Oundle road, this stone inn was originally built as a farmhouse in 1659 and subsequently became a coaching inn with the addition of stables to the rear. These have been neatly converted to house eight functional en suite bedrooms, featuring modern pine furnishings, built-in wardrobes and good writing space for visiting businessmen. TVs, tea-makers, telephones and radios are standard throughout. Food on offer here ranges from a new cosmopolitan menu (pizzas, Cajun steak, club sandwiches, German potato soup, steak and kidney pie) served in the Garden Bistro to an à la carte menu in the small restaurant. Specials may include Dover sole with fennel butter sauce, John Dory or ostrich steaks! Children's facilities include high-chairs, board games and toys and a swing in the garden. *Open 11-11 (Sun 12-3, 7-10.30). Bar Food 12-2, 6-10 (Sun 7-9). Free House. Beer Courage Directors, guest beer. Garden, outdoor eating. Accommodation 9 bedrooms, all en suite, £55-£65 (single £45); weekend reductions (£48/£38). Children welcome overnight (under-2s free), additional bed (£15) & cot (£10) available. Dogs by arrangement. Amex, Diners, MasterCard,* **VISA**

UPPER SHERINGHAM — Red Lion — FOOD

Tel & Fax 01263 825408   Map 10 C1
Holt Road Upper Sheringham Norfolk NR26 8AD

Converted from three rather plain, 300-year-old brick and flint cottages, this homely village inn is popular locally for its above-average home-cooked food. Two friendly bars are filled with a rustic mix of sturdy pine furniture on quarry-tiled and bare boarded floors, and are delightfully music- and game-free. The smaller snug bar is also a no-smoking room. Reliable bar food is listed on a twice-daily-changing blackboard menu. Begin with home-made soup – mushroom and celery – served with a basket of fresh bread or fresh Morston mussels; follow that with pork with cider and thyme, lemon sole baked in herb butter with crab sauce or treacle-cured bacon steaks with honey and mustard sauce, all accompanied by crisp, fresh vegetables. Puddings include summer pudding and bread-and-butter pudding steeped in whisky (Scotsman's Delight). Fresh Sheringham crab is always on the board and special meals include 3-course Wednesday evening suppers in winter (Wednesday barbecues in summer), seafood night on Thursdays, and on Saturdays their mustard-glazed ham lunch attracts folk from miles around. Sunday lunchtimes see a choice of traditional roasts, probably rib of beef and leg of pork. No sandwiches (or chips, for that matter), but ploughman's lunches are offered. Choice of over 60 malt whiskies. *Open 11.30-3 (from 10.30 Sat), 6-11 (from 6.30 in winter), Sun 12-3, 7-10.30.* **Bar Food** *12-2, 6.30-9 (from 7 Sun). No food Sun eve in winter. Free House.* **Beer** *Woodforde's Wherry Bitter, Greene King IPA, guest beer. Garden, outdoor eating. Closed 25 Dec eve. No credit cards.*

Upton   French Horn   FOOD

Tel 01636 812394
Map 7 D3
Main Street Upton Southwell Nottinghamshire NG23 5SY

Plenty of good things are to be found within the Carters' almost self-effacing local. A single bar where the majority of tables are pre-laid for diners, dispenses the range of Wards ales, bottled beers and ciders from around the globe and a fair choice of wines by the glass. Behind the bar hangs the polished French horn, albeit little blown, and they don't make a great song and dance about their competently-cooked bar food either. Fresh fish predominates on the blackboard, the daily choices including, perhaps, swordfish in Cajun spices, monkfish with cucumber and caper beurre blanc and haddock in beer batter. Meaty alternatives are along the lines of chicken stuffed with Brie on a sweet pepper sauce or pan-fried venison steak, whilst a separate vegetarian menu offers the likes of home-made Stilton, blue cheese and mushroom lasagne. Good snacks, including steak pie, sandwiches and ploughman's platters served all day. Upstairs, in a rear, pantiled former barn, the restaurant opens on Sunday for a three-course lunch (also available in the bar); in the evenings, when the accent is on steaks, grills and game, booking is advised. Children welcome indoors if eating. *Open 11-11, (Sun 12-10.30).* **Bar Food** *12-10 (till 9 Sun, light snacks 3-6).* **Beer** *Wards Thorne Best Bitter & Waggledance Honey Beer, guest beer. Garden, outdoor eating. Closed 25 Dec eve. No credit cards.*

Upton Bishop   Moody Cow   FOOD

Tel 01989 780470   Fax 01989 780568
Map 14 B1
Upton Bishop Ross-on-Wye Hereford & Worcester HR9 7TT

South Herefordshire pub-goers will remember this one (just off the M50 from Junction 3 or 4) as the Lord Wellington. Extension of the old stone building to incorporate a formerly derelict barn has produced an entirely different animal. Creature comforts have certainly been improved in an ambience enhanced by wall-to-wall carpeting and candle-lit tables. Menus cover a full range from bangers with bubble and squeak to Chateaubriand with béarnaise. This is not all cow pie: interspersed in the menu are their unusual soups, feta filo parcels, chicken liver parfait and fresh mussels with tomato and garlic among the starters or snacks and main courses from cod 'n' chips or steak and kidney pie to chargrilled steaks or noisettes of lamb with redcurrant and mint sauce and sautéed lamb's liver with onion and red wine gravy. Sandwiches and ploughman's platters are served all day. The atmosphere of a chummy village local lives on and 10p from the sale of every pint of the cleverly-named Raging Bull (a "dark, bitter" bitter brewed on the premises) goes towards the Upton 2000 fund for a new village hall – so why not sink a pint and help contribute towards their sinking-fund? There's also a food take-away service, live jazz on Thursday nights and quarterly cookery demonstrations; mood swings which are indicative surely of a conscious effort to do more than just fill the old Lord's boots. No under-14s in bar areas. *Open 12-2.30, 6.30-11 (Sun 12-2.30, 7-10.30).* **Bar Food** *12-2, 6.30-9.30. (no food Sun eve & all Mon except Bank Holiday weekends). Free House.* **Beer** *Herefordshire Wye Valley Best, Boddingtons, West Country Pale Ale, Raging Bull (own brew-summer only), Flowers Original. Garden, outdoor eating, barbecue. Amex, Diners, MasterCard,* **VISA**

We endeavour to be as up-to-date as possible but inevitably some changes to landlords, chefs and other key staff occur after the Guide has gone to press.

| VENTNOR | Spyglass Inn | FOOD |

Tel & Fax 01983 855338   Map 15 D4   **B&B**
The Esplanade Ventnor Isle of Wight PO38 1JX

After totally rebuilding the distinctively pink-painted Spyglass Inn, Stephanie and Neil Gibbs (both native Islanders) reopened it in 1988. Wandering around the several interconnecting rooms, which include two reserved for non-smokers and several where children are welcome, it is difficult to believe that the pub is not hundreds of years old. The bar counter is built of old pews and the whole place is full of old seafaring prints and photographs, as well as numerous nautical antiques ranging from a brass binnacle and ship's wheel to old oars and model ships in glass cases. The setting could not be better, at one end of the seafront with a front terraced area stretching right to the edge of the sea wall. In winter, the waves break right over the wall and more than one customer has been known to get a soaking by mistiming their exit from the pub. Inside, you might try ham and mushroom tagliatelle, chicken and ham pie, chili or pork spare ribs, but the thing to look out for is the local seafood: crab served out of its shell in generous bowlfuls with salad, and locally-caught lobsters. In winter, there are home-made soups from a blackboard menu, and on Saturday nights a candle-lit dinner, for which booking is advisable, complete with pianist. There is live music nightly (not Mon in winter) from a small group who might play country, folk or jazz. Three neat little flatlets with upholstered rattan furniture and a sea-facing balcony offer accommodation for up to four adults and two children; DIY breakfasts in the kitchenettes. A public car park is just 50 yards away, but check your brakes before venturing down here – the road to the seafront has hairpin bends and a gradient of 1 in 4. 'Children, well-behaved dogs and muddy boots welcome.'
*Open 10.30-11 (closed 3-7 Sept–May), Sun 12-10.30. **Bar Food** 12-2.15, 7-9.30 (summer school holidays 12-9.30, till 9 Sun). Free House. **Beer** Hall & Woodhouse Badger Best & Tanglefoot, Wadworth 6X, guest beers. Patio/terrace, outdoor eating. Family room.*
Accommodation** 3 en-suite flatlets, sleeps 4, from £40. Children welcome overnight (under-8s stay free). Closed 25 Dec eve. MasterCard, **VISA

| WADDESDON | Five Arrows Hotel | FOOD |

Tel 01296 651727   Fax 01296 658596   Map 15a D2   **B&B**
High Street Waddesdon Buckinghamshire HP18 0JE

Zzz...

A delightful Victorian confection built by the Rothschilds to house the architects and artisans working in nearby Waddesdon Manor (NT) – itself worth a visit. The name comes from the family crest with its arrows representing the five sons sent out by the dynasty's founder to set up banking houses in the financial capitals of Europe. Restored in 1993 from top to toe and often bedecked with flowers (there's a fine garden to the rear) the hotel/inn is in the capable hands of Robert Selbie and chef Julian Alexander-Worster. One enters straight into the bar, from which open several rooms with antique tables, colourful upholstered chairs plus the odd settee and armchair; pictures from Lord Rothschild's own collection grace the walls along with numerous photos of old Waddesdon – charmingly un-pub-like. A short, modern blackboard menu might offer smoked marinaded venison with an orange confit and rich mushroom soup to start, followed by Cajun blackened salmon with a rémoulade sauce or baked cod with a herb crust, with home-made puddings like treacle tart and chocolate liqueur terrine for dessert. The good wine list majors on the various Rothschild wine interests that extend to Portugal and Chile as well as the famous Chateau Lafite. Six good-sized bedrooms are individually decorated with matching en suite bathrooms (two with shower and WC only) and boast extra large beds (with pure Egyptian cotton sheets) and antique Victorian washstands along with modern comforts: remote-control TV, direct-dial phones and tea/coffee-making facilities. No smoking in the bedrooms. *Open 11.30-3 & 6-11, (Sun 12-3 & 7-10.30). **Bar Food** 12-2.30 (till 2 Sun), 7-9.30 (till 9 Sun). Free House. **Beer** Fuller's London Pride & ESB, Chiltern Brewery Beechwood Bitter, Theakston Old Peculier. Garden, outdoor eating.*
Accommodation** 6 bedrooms, all en suite, £65 (single £50). Children welcome overnight (stay free in parents' room), additional bed available. No dogs. MasterCard, **VISA

WALL   Hadrian Hotel   B&B

Tel 01434 681232   Map 5 D2
Wall Hexham Northumberland NE46 4EE

A handsome Jacobean-style 16th century house standing in its own attractive gardens by the A6079, about a mile from Hadrian's Wall and only three from nearby Hexham. The best feature for residents is the welcoming, if small, foyer lounge with deep sofas set around the open fire. Unopposed in this tiny village, the bar is a convivial place for meeting the locals. Four bedrooms boast full en suite facilities (three with bath). In the remainder are wash-hand basins and free-standing plastic shower cubicles whose practicality, like the water pressure, is limited. Colour TVs and beverage trays are standard. Plans to upgrade the rooms during 1997. *Open 12-3, 6-11 (Sun 12-3, 7-10.30). Beer Vaux Sampson, Wards Thorne. Garden. Family room. **Accommodation** 6 bedrooms, 4 en suite, £49 (single £30-£42). Children welcome overnight (under-3s stay free in parents' room), additional bed (£10) available. Check-in by arrangement. No dogs.* MasterCard, **VISA**

WALLISWOOD   Scarlett Arms   A

Tel 01306 627243   Map 11 A5
Walliswood Surrey RH5 5RD

Originally a pair of 17th-century labourers' cottages, this attractive white-painted and red-tiled roofed village pub preserves a splendid unspoilt interior. Four small rambling rooms have low ceilings, sturdy wooden furnishings on either carpeted or flagstoned floors, various country prints and old photos, and a good open fire to sit in front of on cold winter days. Relaxing chatty atmosphere and the full complement of well-kept King & Barnes real ales. Benches and brollies fill the front lawn for peaceful summer alfresco drinking. No children under 14 indoors. *Open 11-2.30, 5.30-11 (Sun 12-3, 7-10.30). Beer King & Barnes Festive, Broadwood, Sussex & Mild plus Old Ale in winter. Garden. No credit cards.*

WANSFORD-IN-ENGLAND   The Haycock   ★   FOOD

Tel 01780 782223   Fax 01780 783031   Map 7 E4   **B&B**
Wansford-in-England Peterborough Cambridgeshire PE8 6JA

◁▷ 🛏 ☂ Zzz...

A lovely 17th-century honey-coloured stone coaching inn located next to the junction of A1 and A47 and set in 6 acres of grounds that include lovely gardens stretching along the banks of the river Nene and the village cricket pitch. It has been much extended in sympathetic style, the most recent additions being a large conference/ballroom (a lovely setting for functions with its soaring oak beams, enormous fireplace and private garden, catering for up to 200) and the stone-walled Orchard Room with all-day bar and coffee-shop menu (7am-11pm, with a fine lunchtime buffet). Other day rooms include a pubby bar and two traditional lounges. Bedrooms in the older parts of the building are full of character, but all have been decorated with great style and flair using high-quality fabrics and furnishings; one ground-floor twin room has a wide door and handrails for disabled guests. Bathrooms are equally luxurious. The variety of food on offer in both bar (excellent bar snacks – fish and chips, spicy ribs of pork, smoked chicken salad, linguine with prawns and olive oil, open mushrooms with cream cheese and garlic, Montgomery Cheddar or Colston Bassett Stilton, home-baked cheesecake, tiramisu), Orchard Room (one room is non-smoking) and restaurant caters for all tastes and pockets; an outdoor barbecue takes place daily in summer, with seating for 100 in a courtyard. Candelabras and highly-polished silver add to the mellow, traditional atmosphere of the twin dining-rooms. The restaurant menu is pretty traditional, too, with a daily roast sirloin of prime English beef always featuring on the silver trolley. Outstanding, carefully compiled and sensibly-priced list of wines with helpful notes; twelve available by the glass. Arcadian Hotels; hotel, inn and pub all rolled into one. Recommended in our *1997 Hotels & Restaurants Guide. Open 7am-10pm. **Bar Food** 12-10.30. Beer Ruddles Best & County, Bass, Batemans XB, John Smith's, guest beer. Garden, croquet, fishing, pétanque, helipad. **Accommodation** 50 bedrooms, all en suite, from £99-£125 (four-poster from £140, suite from £175, single £78-£90). Children welcome overnight (under-5s stay free in parents' room, 5-14s half price), additional bed & cot available. Amex, Diners,* MasterCard, **VISA**

WARDLOW   Bull's Head   FOOD

Tel 01298 871431   Map 6 C2
Wardlow Tideswell Derbyshire SK17 8RP

A friendly village local with a dining emphasis, only three miles from Ashford-in-the-Water: the B6465 passes scenic Monsal Head on the way. A straightforward printed bar menu is enhanced by illuminated blackboard specials; options may include home-made leek and onion soup, chicken and ham pie, seafood mornay and stuffed trout. Plenty of homely desserts like fruit crumbles and treacle sponge or maybe choose Hartington blue Stilton. Sandwiches at lunchtime only. Family dining in the Loose Box; picnic tables in a small but scenic garden. *Open 11.30-3, 6.30-11.30 (Sun 12-3, 7-10.30). Closed Tue & Thu lunch.* **Bar Food** *12-2 (except Mon, Tue & Thu), 6.30-9.30 (Sun 7-9). Free House.* **Beer** *Wards Bitter. Garden, outdoor eating. Family room. No credit cards.*

WARENFORD   Warenford Lodge   ★   FOOD

Tel 01668 213453   Map 5 D1
Warenford Belford Northumberland NE70 7HY

There's a wonderfully eclectic range of good bar food on offer at the rather un-pubby Warenford Lodge, a solid stone building on the village loop road off the A1; there's no sign outside so you'll have to look hard for it. Inside, it's a handsome old place, with exposed thickset stone and a modern air which blends well with the atmosphere of an old-fashioned private house. There are little mullion windows, polished light pine tables and cushioned benches in the split-level bar, a big stone fireplace in the lower part, and a woodburning stove (no longer used) in the upper area, which has armchairs and sofas just made for relaxing; the bar area is probably more attractive an area in which to eat than the restaurant. Menus change here twice-yearly, in spring and autumn, reflecting seasonal produce, especially fish, but a random selection of favourites might well feature local kipper with fresh tomato sauce, lobster cooked with prawns and squid in a lime hollandaise, Warenford pigeon pot and stincotto (Italian shank of pork roasted with wine and herbs). Not all puddings are home-made, but those that are, such as a fruit terrine, are wonderful. The menu is clever, well presented and most unusual – a shining star in the firmament of pubs! The unifying factor behind it all, exotic or homely, is the instinctive, hearty cooking of the landlady, Marion Matthewman, at work in the kitchen while Ray tends to the bar. Her dish of 'Rabbit Victoriana' (see awards pages) was judged a runner-up in the 1997 Ilchester Cheese Pub of the Year awards. Owing to the popularity of the Warenford you need to book for weekend evenings (or any time in summer). No under-14s in bar areas (dining-room only) *Open Sat & Sun 12-2, Tue-Sat 7-11 (Sun 7-10.30). Closed all Mon & Tue-Fri lunch.* **Bar Food** *12-1.30 (Sat & Sun only), 7-9.30 (Tue-Sun). No real ales. Diners, MasterCard,* **VISA**

WARHAM ALL SAINTS   Three Horseshoes   FOOD   B&B

Tel 01328 710547   Map 10 C1
Warham All Saints Wells-next-the-Sea Norfolk NR23 1NL

Warham is a sleepy rural backwater situated only a mile or so from the North Norfolk coast. At its heart, close to the church, lies the Three Horseshoes, a timeless gem of a village local, comprising a row of 18th-century brick and flint cottages and the Old Post Office which closed 15 years ago. Owned by nearby Holkham Hall until 1960, it is a rare survivor, remaining delightfully unchanged internally since the 1930s. An old-fashioned ambience pervades the three unspoilt rooms with numerous gas-lights, nicotine yellow walls, scrubbed deal tables, plain wooden chairs and red leatherette railway waiting room-style benches, a 1930s' one-arm bandit and a pianola which performs occasionally. A good choice of home-cooked food is served, especially traditional Norfolk dishes using fresh local produce, including fish and game. Local ladies prepare the meals that appear on the interesting main menu – potted herrings, coarse paté of livers and local game, and Norfolk tavern pudding (beef, beer and vegetables with a suet lid) – and the hearty dishes on the daily specials board, for example rabbit and vegetable broth, mushroom and nut pie, skate wing in mussel sauce and cranberry pigeon. Fresh vegetables are the order of the day; definitely no chips. Sandwiches are served all day, and smaller appetites may enjoy a 'ploughboy's' lunch! For dessert, try the peppermint and chocolate sponge or summer fruit pie. Well-conditioned ales are drawn straight from the cask and home-made lemonade and orangeade is served in the summer. Four homely bedrooms in the adjacent Old Post Office accommodate overnight guests. Simply furnished with old darkwood furniture – some antique pieces – washbasins and latch-doors, they share a clean bathroom (one has an en suite shower). Added touches include a box of tissues, cotton wool, a range of teas and a dressing-gown. Residents have use of a sitting-room with TV and easy chairs. No under-14s overnight. *Open 11.30-3, 6-11 (from 6.30 in winter), Sun 12-3, 6.30-10.30.* **Bar Food** *12-2, 7-9 (from 6 Fri & Sat). Free House.* **Beer** *Greene King Abbot Ale & IPA, Woodforde's Wherry Bitter & Mardlers Mild, guest beers. Garden, outdoor eating. Family room.* **Accommodation** *4 bedrooms, 1 en suite £44 (single £18). Accommodation & kitchen closed 25 & 26 Dec. No credit cards.*

WARNHAM   Greets Inn   A

Tel 01403 265047   Map 11 A6
Friday Street Warnham West Sussex RH12 3QY

Tucked along Friday Street on the western edge of the village – off the A24 north of Horsham – this attractive, tile-hung and timbered old farmhouse dates from 1320. Preserved inside is the original layout of a series of charming rooms radiating out from a central bar which boasts a stone floor, a vast inglenook with log fire, a fine high-backed settle and sturdy tables. Part-stripped pine and oak furnishings and gleaming copper and brass artefacts characterise the unspoilt rooms and traditional locals' bar. Good alfresco seating in the sheltered rear garden among the roses, flower beds and apple trees. *Open 11-2.30, 6-11 (Sun 12-3, 7-10.30).* **Beer** *Flowers Original, Whitbread (Morrells) Strong Country Bitter, Fuller's London Pride. Garden, outdoor eating. Amex, Diners, MasterCard,* **VISA**

WARREN STREET   The Harrow   FOOD

Tel 01622 858727   Map 11 C5   **B&B**
Hubbards Hill Warren Street Lenham Maidstone Kent ME17 2ED

Once a resting place for Canterbury pilgrims, now a converted and refurbished downland inn not far from the A20 above Lenham (signposted) and the M20. Comfortable open-plan lounge, much used for dining and warmed in winter by a good log fire. Separate, neatly laid-up conservatory restaurant (with a separate menu), but it's the bar food that we recommend, to be enjoyed overlooking the sun-trap courtyard and garden with waterfall and pool – access for residents and restaurant diners only. Standard range of bar snacks supplemented by decent home-made specials such as pan-fried pork with pepper and mustard sauce, chargrilled salmon steak with prawn and dill butter, seafood platter and roast half-shoulder of lamb with sherry. Sandwiches and ploughman's platters served all day. Good bed and breakfast, too, the fifteen spacious bedrooms, including five family rooms, being kitted out with neat darkwood furniture, clean bathrooms and added comforts (TV, beverage facilities, direct-dial phones). *Open 11.30-2.30, 7-10.30 (Sat 6.30-11), Sun 12-3, 7-10.30.* **Bar Food** *12-2, 7-9.30. Free House.* **Beer** *Shepherd Neame Master Brew, guest beers. Water garden, patio, outdoor eating.* **Accommodation** *15 bedrooms, all en suite, £49.50 (single £39.50). Children welcome overnight (under-14s £5 if sharing parents' room), additional bed (£5) & cot (£5) available. No dogs. Closed 25 & 26 Dec. Amex, MasterCard,* **VISA**

WASDALE HEAD   Wasdale Head Inn   B&B

Tel 019467 26229   Fax 019467 26334   Map 4 C3
Wasdale Head Gosforth Cumbria CA20 1EX

▌ Zzz...

At the head of Wasdale, in a setting of romantic grandeur, with steep fells by way of backdrop, this is a famous, traditional mountain pub popular with walkers and climbers. Ritson's Bar, named after its first landlord (the world's biggest liar), has high ceilings, a polished slate floor, wood panelling, and cushioned old settles. There's a residents' bar, a relaxing lounge, and the nine en suite bedrooms are comfortable and unfussy, with telephones and beverage trays provided. 9 self-catering cottages right next to the pub are available from £233 to £600 per week. Under new management. *Open 11-11 (11-3, 5.30-11 in winter), Sun 12-10.30. Closed mid Nov-24 Dec.* **Beer** *Jennings Bitter & Cumberland Ale, Yates Bitter, Theakston Best & Old Peculier, guest beer. Riverside garden. Family room.* **Accommodation** *9 bedrooms, all en suite, £58 (family room £87, single £29-£34). Children welcome overnight, additional bed & cot available. Dogs £3. Accommodation closed mid Nov-28 Dec. MasterCard,* **VISA**

WASS   Wombwell Arms   ★   FOOD

Tel 01347 868280   Map 5 E4   **B&B**
Wass North Yorkshire YO6 4BE

🏠 ⏍ **Zzz...**

This whitewashed village inn dates from the 18th century and sits in the shadow of the Hambleton hills, just a couple of miles from the A170, east of Thirsk. The interior consists of four connecting rooms with stylish fabrics and furnishings. The first room to the left of the entrance has lightwood floorboards, stripped pine tables and chairs, and half-panelling. This room is especially good for families. The bar and its adjoining dining area have a mix of flagstone and red-tiled flooring, some exposed stone walls, more panelling and original beams. Some walls have attractive Laura Ashley wallpapers, while farmhouse kitchen-style tables are covered with colourful cloths. The final room is similarly appointed. Throughout the pub, there are splendid fresh and dried flower displays, watercolours of chickens, foxes and other country subjects, magazines and books. A huge blackboard displays the day's choice of interesting bar food. Rather bistro in style, this is the preserve of Lynda Evans, who is a more than competent cook. Only fresh, mostly local produce is used, and the choice is extensive and varied: perhaps king prawns in garlic butter, lamb's liver with mushrooms and onion gravy, venison sausages with red cabbage and salmon fishcakes at lunch, with pork fillet with mushroom and Dijon mustard sauce and pot-roasted lamb shank with shallots and garlic among the evening fare. There are interesting fish dishes (grilled tuna with lime and fennel butter, hake with pepperonata) and good vegetarian dishes, too: cashew curry with cucumber raita, aubergine with parmesan and mozzarella cheese. Wholemeal sandwiches and ploughman's platters at lunchtime only. Desserts are well up to standard, with lemon posset and caramelised rice pudding. Booking recommended for weekends. The bedrooms are equally impressive, kitted out in colourful Laura Ashley wallpapers, with matching curtains and duvet covers, and stripped pine furniture. They're impeccably kept and offer a selection of magazines as well as televisions and radio alarms. To immaculate housekeeping is added a sense of fun: plastic ducks are provided. Alan Evans looks after the bar and is an extremely jovial host. A quite exceptional country pub, well worth a detour. *Open 12-2.30-7-11 (Sun 12-3, 7-10.30). Closed Sun eve & all Mon Oct-Apr & 10 days Jan.* **Bar Food** *12-2, 7-9 (till 9.30 Sat). No food Sun eve or all day Mon Oct-Apr. Free House.* **Beer** *Timothy Taylor Landlord, Black Sheep Bitter, guest beer. Family room.* **Accommodation** *2 bedrooms, both en suite, £49 (single £24.50). Children over 8 welcome overnight (8-10s free if sharing parents' room), additional bed available. Check-in by arrangement. No dogs. MasterCard,* **VISA**

WATERLEY BOTTOM   New Inn   B&B

Tel 01453 543659   Map 13 F1
Waterley Bottom North Nibley Dursley Gloucestershire GL11 6EF

🚩 **Zzz...**

Ruby Sainty's friendly, idiosyncratic pub takes some driving to down the country lanes from North Nibley on the B4060, yet cyclists and walkers find it unerringly from their maps. The setting is serene, the garden a blaze of colour shaded by beech, silver birch and horse chestnut; for the youngsters, swings, see-saw and a terrestrial tree house are a safe distance away. Overnight guests are assured the tranquillity of this hidden valley quite undisturbed. The two bedrooms have TVs and hot-beverage kits (but no phones) and share a single bathroom; breakfast is worth getting up for; book well in advance. No children overnight or under-14s in bar areas. *Open 12-2.30, 7-11 (Sun 12-3, 7-10.30). Free House.* **Beer** *Cotleigh WB (house brew) & Tawny, Smiles Best, Theakston Old Peculier, Greene King Abbot Ale, guest beer. Garden, outdoor play area.* **Accommodation** *2 bedrooms, £35 (single £20). Check-in bar hours only. No dogs. Accommodation closed 1 week Christmas; pub closed 25 Dec eve. No credit cards.*

WATH-IN-NIDDERDALE   Sportsman's Arms   FOOD

Tel 01423 711306   Fax 01423 712524   Map 6 C1   **B&B**
Wath-in-Nidderdale Pateley Bridge Harrogate North Yorkshire HG3 5PP

Zzz...

Nestling in a wooded valley just 2 miles from Pateley Bridge, the Sportsman's is
prominently signed across a tiny stone hump-backed bridge over the Nidd. A carpeted
lounge bar with its own side entrance suggests at once that this is no ordinary pub.
As one would expect from an inn whose restaurant is recommended in our *1997
Hotels & Restaurants Guide* the food, too, has an identity all its own, the emphasis
being on fresh local produce, notably fish from Whitby. Chicken liver terrine with
apple chutney, and king scallops with garlic and gruyère can be starters or just a snack;
Scarborough woof with mustard and a garlic crust or chicken stuffed with duxelles in
a garlic sauce are decidedly main meals. Further dishes might be monkfish provençale,
steamed haddock with tomato and basil sauce, and grilled lobster with garlic.
Sandwiches and ploughman's platters are served all day. Alongside ever-present sticky
toffee pudding with fresh cream the pudding menu may list chocolate roulade and
raspbery brulée. Stripped pine doors are the unifying theme of the single corridor of
bedrooms, which are of modest size and appointment; returning guests appreciate
rather the total peace and quiet and an absence of room telephones (however, there
are TVs in the rooms). While all are equipped with wash basins, only two have en
suite facilities; two WCs and two separate bathrooms are shared by the rest. A long,
leisurely and very large breakfast is served at 9am. *Open 12-3-6.30-11.* **Bar Food** *12-
2.30, 7-9.30. Free House.* **Beer** *Theakston Best. Garden, outdoor eating.* **Accommodation** *7
bedrooms, 2 en suite (shower), £60 (single £35). Children welcome overnight (under-5s stay
free in parents' room, 5-10s £10), additional bed (£10) & cot (£5) available. Dogs by
arrangement. Pub & accommodation closed 25 Dec. MasterCard,* **VISA**

WATLINGTON   Chequers   A

Tel 01491 612874   Map 15a D3
Love Lane Watlington Oxfordshire OX9 5RA

A useful stop, less than two and a half miles from Junction 6 of the M40. It's a
characterful, rambling old pub with a lovely summer garden and conservatory
(children are now allowed in here). Unprepossessing exterior, cosy interior with an
eclectic mix of paraphernalia – from dried flowers to an unusual collection of bottles
and paintings. *Open 11.30-2.30, 6-11 (Sun 12-3, 7-10.30).* **Beer** *Brakspear. Garden.
MasterCard,* **VISA**

WATTON-AT-STONE   George & Dragon   FOOD

Tel 01920 830285   Map 15 F1
High Street Watton-at-Stone Hertfordshire SG14 3TA

The George & Dragon is popular with a wide range of customers, from OAPs to
business men and women, and its well-balanced bar menu attracts a fair number of
locals. On any one day, the specials board could highlight Mediterranean tart, beef
stroganoff and pork casserole with cream and tarragon, with the regular menu offering
Corsican fish soup, rack of lamb with rosemary, and bobotie. Fish is delivered daily
and prices never exceed £10 – perhaps whole lemon sole and fresh scallops poached
in white wine. In addition, a traditional roast lunch is served on Sundays. Sandwiches
and ploughman's served all day. Desserts such as summer pudding, sticky toffee
pudding and apricot and apple crumble. Inside the homely bars there are exposed
beams, open fireplaces, yellow stained walls hung with a mixture of framed oil and
watercolour paintings and welcome touches like fresh flowers and the day's
newspapers. Furnishings are a mixture of blue upholstered bench seating and simple
wood chairs around oak tables topped with candles. This is a difficult pub to miss, as
it dominates the centre of the village, and is of pink-painted pebbledash. Children are
welcome in the dining-room only. *Open 11-2.30, 6-11 (Sat 11-11, Sun 12-3, 7-
10.30).* **Bar Food** *12-2, 7-10 (no food Sun eve).* **Beer** *Greene King. Garden, patio/terrace,
outdoor eating. Closed 25 & 26 Dec. Amex, Diners, MasterCard,* **VISA**

WELL   Chequers   FOOD

Tel 01256 862605 Fax 01256 862133   Map 15a D4
Well Odiham Hampshire RG25 1TL

Deep in the heart of the Hampshire countryside, this 17th-century pub provides a retreat from the modern world and an opportunity to enjoy the old-world charm. A flourishing vine covers the enclosed patio outside, and inside, the homely rustic bar features low wooden ceilings, panelled walls, bare floorboards, plenty of beams and a mix of old scrubbed tables, chairs and church pews. The regularly-changing selection of bar food is chalked up on a blackboard in the bar and the good-value choice of light dishes ranges from deep-fried Brie and seafood lasagne to scrambled egg and smoked salmon, and chargrilled lamb steak with herb butter. Sandwiches and ploughman's platters are served all day. Puddings may include pear charlotte and crème brulée. Adjacent pine-panelled restaurant where a short à la carte French-influenced menu is served on Thu, Fri & Sat evenings only. A peaceful drink or meal can be savoured in the attractive rear garden, which affords rural views across fields. Five miles from the M3 Junction 5. *Open 11-3, 5.30-11 (Sun 12-3, 7-10.30).* **Bar Food** *12-2.30, 7-10 (till 9.30 Sun). Free House.* **Beer** *Boddingtons, Flowers Original, guest beer. Garden, patio, outdoor eating. MasterCard,* **VISA**

WELLS-NEXT-THE-SEA   Crown Hotel   FOOD   B&B

Tel 01328 710209 Fax 01328 711432   Map 10 C1
The Buttlands Wells-next-the-Sea Norfolk NR23 1EX

Standing at the foot of a tree-lined green, the Buttlands, is the Crown, a modest black-and-white painted hotel offering homely accommodation and reliable bar food. Inside, the bar progresses on three levels from front to back, where a family-friendly conservatory of high-backed settles opens on to the rear patio and stableyard. Within, there's an open log fire and it's rather dark – mind the steps! An extensive bar menu features single-course meals of pasta dishes and omelettes that come in generous portions, alongside grills ranging from a rump 'steakwich' through to herby home-made burgers and a full mixed grill. Plenty of salads, sandwiches, ploughman's platters, and sausage/burger/fish finger combinations for the children, and daily blackboard specials like pea and ham soup, seafood hotpot, pork steak with plum sauce and apricot brulée complete the picture. Booking is essential for Sunday lunch in the adjacent restaurant. Bedrooms are simply but adequately furnished and even the smallest offers a view of the charming old town, across the Lion Yard where the London mail coach once pulled in, and over pantiled roofs to the sturdy Norman church below. *Open 11-2.30, 6-11 (Sun 12-2.30, 7-10.30).* **Bar Meals** *12-2, 6-9 (till 9.30 in summer). Free House.* **Beer** *Adnams, Marston's Pedigree, Bass. Terrace, outdoor eating. Accommodation 15 bedrooms, 10 en suite, £58-£64 (family room £100, single £35-£45). Children welcome overnight (under-2s stay free in parents' room, 2-12s £10), additional bed & cot available (£3). Amex, Diners, MasterCard,* **VISA**

WEOBLEY   Ye Olde Salutation Inn   FOOD   B&B

Tel 01544 318443 Fax 01544 318216   Map 14 A1
Market Pitch Weobley Hereford & Worcester HR4 8SJ

🛏 🍷 **Zzz...**

Chris and Frances Anthony run this wonderfully evocative former 14th-century ale and cider house. It commands the view down picturesque Broad Street to Weobley parish church, and is both the village local and a bespoke country inn. Frances supervises a hard-working kitchen which daily produces both traditional and imaginatively different bar meals: diners may feast on the likes of warm seafood salad, home-baked ham with mustard and parsley sauce, spinach and Stilton roulade and roast leg of lamb with honey and rosemary sauce. Vegetarian specials might be lentil and apricot terrine or pasta and blue-cheese bake. For a lighter lunchtime-only meal try a ploughman's or hot filled roll (cheese, bacon and mushroom or steak) made with bread baked freshly on the premises. Popular desserts like lemon tart with raspberry coulis or sticky toffee pudding. The non-smoking Oak Room restaurant serves an à la carte menu and a highly popular 3-course Sunday lunch (booking essential), but our specific recommendation is for bar food. Victorian furniture, cast-iron bedsteads and brass-topped bathroom fittings set the tone in the bedrooms. The three larger rooms (one with a four-poster) have en suite WC/shower rooms, while the fourth boasts a Victorian-style bathroom en suite. To follow the most restful of nights, a splendid country breakfast is served in the recently added conservatory. Due to the building's age, guests are requested not to smoke in their rooms, though smoking is permitted in the residents' lounge. An adjacent self-contained cottage with lounge, kitchen/diner, bathroom and two double bedrooms accommodates up to 5 people in the first timber-framed building to be put up in Weobley since the 17th century. A fitness room has exercise machines – perhaps rather incongruous given the surroundings. Pub rooms are not suitable for children under 14 (except babes in arms) but the cottage is fine for families. *Open 11-3, 7-11 (Sat 11-11, Sun 12-10.30).* **Bar Food** *12-2, 7-9.30 (till 9 Sun). Free House.* **Beer** *Hook Norton Best, guest beers. Garden, patio, outdoor eating.* **Accommodation** *4 bedrooms, all en suite, £58-£62.50 (cottage £63 + £15 per child, single £34). Children over 14 years welcome overnight (babies by prior arrangement). Closed 25 Dec. Amex, Diners, MasterCard,* **VISA**

WEST BEXINGTON   Manor Hotel   FOOD

Tel 01308 897616   Fax 01308 897035   Map 13 F2   **B&B**
Beach Road West Bexington Bridport Dorset DT2 9DF

Richard and Jayne Childs' old manor house is just a short walk from Chesil Bank and has a stone-walled cellar bar, leafy conservatory and residents' lounge. Reliable bar food encompasses good fish dishes (perhaps fish soup, whole plaice, Dover Sole), lobster thermidor, oysters, rabbit in mustard, venison in red wine and juniper, and Thai chicken curry. Hearty snacks are available in the form of sandwiches, ploughman's platters, lasagne and steak and kidney pie. Good choice at Sunday lunchtimes and at least 20 wines by the glass to chose from. For pudding, try the chocolate roulade or summer pudding. Books, magazines and dried flower arrangements add a homely, welcoming touch to simply furnished but well-equipped bedrooms that come complete with tea and coffee kits, TVs, direct-dial phones, sherry, elderflower water and goodnight chocolates. A couple of larger, family bedrooms will sleep up to four (two additional beds are supplied). *Open 11-11 (Sun 12-10.30).* **Bar Food** *12-2, 6.30-10 (from 7 Sun). Free House.* **Beer** *Furgusons Dartmoor Bitter, Wadworth 6X, Manor Bitter. Garden, outdoor eating, children's play area. Family room.* **Accommodation** *13 bedrooms, all en suite, £78-£84 (single £45-£49). Children welcome overnight, additional bed (£7.50) & cot (£4) available. No dogs. Accommodation closed 25 Dec. Amex, Diners, MasterCard,* **VISA**

WEST BROMWICH   Manor House   A

Tel 0121 588 2035   Fax 0121 588 8033   Map 6 C4
Hall Green Road Stonecross West Bromwich Sandwell B71 2EA

Five minutes' drive from the M6 motorway, a 13th-century, moated manor house run as a pub by Banks's, the Wolverhampton brewery. It's surrounded by well-tended lawns, so it can be a useful spot to break a motorway drive on a sunny day; inside, the main hall has a steeply-pitched roof, kitsch medieval theming, piped music and formulaic food (almost all dishes served with great mounds of chip-shop chips). Nevertheless, it is an interesting, atmospheric oasis for a flagon of ale. Directions from M6 J9: take A461 towards Wednesbury, then first left into Woden Road East; at T-junction turn left into Crankhall Lane; continue some way up to roundabout, pub is just by right turning into Hall Green Road. *Open 12-2.30 (till 3 Sat), 6-11 (from 5.30 Sat), Sun 12-10.30.* **Beer** *Banks's. Garden. Family room. MasterCard,* **VISA**

WEST CAMEL   Walnut Tree   FOOD

Tel & Fax 01935 851292   Map 13 F2   **B&B**
West Camel Sparkford/Yeovil Somerset BA22 7QW

Zzz...

Smartly modernised and extended 100-year-old village inn located half a mile off the A303 between Sparkford and Ilchester, and named after the magnificent walnut tree that stands in the pretty, shrub-filled garden. Pristinely-kept carpeted bar and lounge featuring lots of plush chairs and benches, some comfortable easy chairs and sofas and attractive silk flower arrangements. Good relaxing ambience in which to enjoy reliable, above-average bar food; on busy evenings every table can be booked, leaving little space for those just popping in for a drink! Fresh local produce is used in compiling the value-for-money, twice-daily-changing blackboard menu which may list seafood tagliatelle, beef stroganoff, salmon fishcakes with tomato and basil sauce and fresh fish from Poole – perhaps red sea bream with mushrooms and mustard sauce or pollock with tomato, onion, garlic and white wine. Excellent accompanying vegetable selection – definitely a chip-free zone! A ploughman's lunch is also offered. Puddings might include sticky toffee pudding and white and dark chocolate mousse with Tia Maria. Good-value overnight accommodation in seven individually decorated bedrooms. The spacious and little-used restaurant has recently been converted into three splendid bedrooms (one featuring a four-poster), each boasting rich co-ordinating fabrics, well-appointed en suite bathrooms and their own private patio, complete with tables and chairs. Equally tasteful refurbishment extends upstairs to the four original en suite bedrooms (one with shower only). TV, direct-dial phone, radio, hairdryer and trouser press are standard throughout. An ideal refuge for weary A303 travellers looking for a comfortable and peaceful night's rest. No children in the pub or overnight. *Open 11-2.30, 5.30-11 (Sun 12-2.30, 7-10.30).* **Bar Food** *12-2, 7-9.30 (till 9 Sun). Free House.* **Beer** *Butcombe Bitter, Bass. Garden, outdoor eating.* **Accommodation** *7 bedrooms, all en suite, £49.50-£55 (four-poster £80, single £39.50-£45). No dogs. Amex, MasterCard,* **VISA**

WEST HUNTSPILL   Crossways Inn   B&B

Tel 01278 783756   Map 13 E1
West Huntspill Highbridge Somerset TA9 3RA

Popular proprietor-run 17th-century inn located beside the A38 and a handy overnight stop for travellers using the M5 (3 miles from Junctions 22 and 23). Simple old-fashioned interior comprising a series of inter-connecting low-ceilinged rooms, featuring exposed beams, winter log fires, a mix of sturdy furniture and a welcoming atmosphere. Clean and comfortable accommodation in three neat, modern pine-furnished upstairs bedrooms. Two boast compact en suite facilities, the third's bathroom is private but not en suite, and all have TVs and beverage-making kits for added comfort. Picnic tables among the fruit trees in the rear garden. *Open 12-3, 5.30-11 (Sun 12-3, 7-10.30). Free House.* **Beer** *Flowers IPA & Original, Eldridge Pope Royal Oak, guest beers. Garden. Family room.* **Accommodation** *3 bedrooms, 2 en suite (one with bath), £34 (single £24). Children welcome overnight (stay free in parents' room), additional bed & cot available. Check-in by arrangement. Closed 25 Dec. MasterCard,* **VISA**

WEST ILSLEY   Harrow Inn   ★   FOOD

Tel & Fax 01635 281260   Map 14a C3
West Ilsley Newbury Berkshire RG16 0AR

A mile from the Ridgeway footpath on the edge of the Berkshire Downs, in a lovely village green setting, complete with lazy ducks on the pond, there are many good reasons to visit the ever-popular Harrow Inn. Within, antique furniture and several country settles create a smartly rustic but simple and old-fashioned atmosphere. There's plenty of space in which to relax and enjoy an excellent pint of Morland (who founded their brewery in this village in 1711, but are now based in Abingdon) and some tip-top food from Heather Humphreys – the consistency of approach and cooking is admirable. The menu changes monthly and is supplemented by a daily-changing specials board (wild rabbit pie, beef and Guinness casserole, fillet of haddock with aubergines and fresh tomato sauce) – a variety wide enough to suit all tastes and pockets. Soups, salads, bread and puddings are reliably good, the home-made puddings (orange chocolate mousse, lemon cheesecake and plum and almond tart with unpasteurised local Peasemore cream from a Guernsey herd) especially, and a fine selection of constantly varying British cheeses puts the seal on a splendid bill of fare. Portions are generous and vegetarians are thoughtfully catered for (perhaps mushroom and Stilton tart with walnut and herb crumble topping); granary rolls, sandwiches and ploughman's platters are also offered all day. All in all, a properly pubby combination of the imaginative and homely, which keeps people coming back. You can even take home one of their particularly good pies. Regular 'pie nights' (last Tuesday and Thursday in the month). A good garden for children has playthings and animals (ducks, geese, goat, chickens). Disabled WC. *Open 11-3, 6-11 (Sun 12-4, 7-10.30).* **Bar Food** *12-2.15, 6-9.15 (Sun 7-9). No food Sun eve in winter.* **Beer** *Morland. Garden, outdoor eating, children's play area. Amex, MasterCard,* **VISA**

WEST WITTON — Wensleydale Heifer — FOOD

Tel 01969 622322   Fax 01969 624183   Map 5 D4   **B&B**
West Witton Wensleydale North Yorkshire DL8 4LS

The signs of good breeding which abound at John and Anne Sharp's well-tamed heifer are manifest. At the heart of every good pub is the bar – here it holds no more than four tables and attracts a healthy mixture of residents and locals and dispenses a hearty pint of Theakston's. To one side, a snug room and chintz foyer/lounge are available for sitting out, while to the other the bistro daily pushes out the fatted calf with quite serious intent. Typical starters include mushroom and Stilton bake and smoked salmon paté, followed by fish pasties with tarragon sauce, chicken basque and casseroled Yorkshire lamb with Stilton dumplings. Sandwiches are served in the bar at lunchtimes only along with a Yorkshire Cheese lunch of three varieties of Wensleydale (of course). Accommodation comprises traditionally-furnished and comfortable en suite bedrooms not only in the pub itself but also in the Old Reading Room, standing in its own garden over the road. All rooms have radio, TV and beverage trays with telephones providing a baby listening facility. *Open 10.30-11.* **Bar Food** *12-2, 6-9.30. Free House.* **Beer** *John Smith's, Theakston Best & Old Peculier, guest beer. Garden, outdoor eating. Family room.* **Accommodation** *15 bedrooms, all en suite £70-£80 (family room sleeping four £90, single £49). Children welcome overnight, addtional bed (£15) & cot (£6) available. Dogs (£3). Amex, Diners, MasterCard,* **VISA**

WEST WYCOMBE — George & Dragon — FOOD

Tel 01494 464414   Fax 01494 462432   Map 15a D3
High Street West Wycombe Buckinghamshire HP14 3AB

Imposing Tudor coaching inn set in a National Trust village beside the A40. Beyond the fine cobbled archway entrance (one of several surviving original features) lies an appealing period bar with large oak beams, settles and Windsor chairs by a roaring fire. Friendly staff offer a promising bar food menu ranging from smoked haddock and spinach mornay, home-made soup and various ploughman's to ham, leek and cider pie, beef Wellington and fillet steak. Follow with a rich, gooey treacle tart or fresh fruit crumble. Up the haunted staircase are eight recently-refurbished bedrooms (£58 double). Peaceful rear garden with a play area for children. *Open 11-2.30, 5.30-11 (Sat 11-11, Sun 12-10.30).* **Bar Food** *12-2 (till 2.30 Sun), 6-9.30 (till 9 Sun).* **Beer** *Courage Best, guest beers. Garden, outdoor eating, children's play area. Family room. Amex, Diners, MasterCard,* **VISA**

WESTON — Otter Inn — FOOD

Tel & Fax 01404 42594   Map 13 E2
Weston Honiton Devon EX14 0NZ

Situated 400 yards off the busy A30 and beside the River Otter, this much-extended 14th-century cottage is a popular refreshment stop en route to and from the West Country, and a particular favourite with families. The original old cottage interior is delightfully unspoilt, with a vast inglenook fronted by comfortable armchairs and old tables. Plenty of prints, books and various bric-a-brac make this a cosy and relaxing spot in which to sit. The main bar extension is very much in keeping, with heavy beams, a real assortment of old sturdy tables and chairs, an unusual chamber pot collection hanging from the beams and the added touch of fresh flowers on each table. Beyond some double doors is a skittle alley and games room. A hand-scripted bar menu highlights many of the usual snacks such as sandwiches, salads, ploughman's lunches, filled jacket potatoes and steaks; main-course specialities include smoked fish platter, steak and kidney pie, chicken Gloria, home-made pasta stuffed with cheese with a garlic, basil and wine sauce, and locally-made sausages with mash. Lunchtime salad buffet as well as daily dishes chalked up on boards offering more variety and greater interest, such as baked sea bass, duck with fresh cherry and orange sauce, lamb and fillet steak platter with spinach and Stilton sauce and a vegetarian dish of the day (asparagus and nut mousse). Winter spit-roasts over the open fire on Thursday evenings. Children who have been cooped up in the car for long periods will relish their own 'ducklings' menu ("ask for crayons and paper to keep you happy") and the space in the splendid riverside garden, which offers youngsters the chance to paddle in a very safe shallow section of the river; they may also be entertained by the resident rabbits, guinea pigs, ducks and chickens. Babes in arms are extremely well catered for, with free baby food offered and changing facilities provided in the Ladies. *Open 11-3, 6-11, (Sun 12-3, 7-10.30).* **Bar Food** *12-2, 7-10 (till 9.30 Sun). Free House.* **Beer** *Eldridge Pope Hardy Country, Bass, Boddingtons, Worthingtons, guest beer. Garden, outdoor eating, summer barbecue, indoor and outdoor play area. Family room. MasterCard,* **VISA**

WESTON-ON-THE-GREEN   The Chequers   FOOD

Tel 01869 350319   Fax 01869 350024   Map 14a C2
Weston-on-the-Green Bicester Oxfordshire OX6 8QH

Thai food-lovers will find this attractive 18th-century thatched pub a delight, as will famished M40 and A34 travellers, for it lies just off Junction 9, north of Oxford – a most useful refreshment stop. The draw here is the authentic Thai cuisine that dominates the food selection available, although there is a rather standard choice of English 'pub' dishes (various steaks, deep-fried dishes and pies) to satisfy less exotic tastes. Popularity has resulted in recent extensions to the comfortably-furnished main bar and carvery (traditional Sunday lunch) area, creating a further cosy dining-room and a landscaped rear garden, complete with animals and aviary, for summer alfresco eating. Adventurous palates can tuck into tom yam goong (hot and spicy prawn soup), Thai fishcakes or pee gai yad sai (deep-fried stuffed chicken wings with sweet and sour sauce) for starters, followed by various noodle (Thai-style pork with chili sauce, ground peanuts, bean sprouts and egg) and stir-fried rice (chicken with red curry paste and bamboo shoots) dishes, or possibly a curry (beef with green curry paste, coconut milk, Thai herbs and sweet basil). Separate menu of Thai 'specialities' and a good choice for vegetarians. Children welcome.*Open 11.30-3, 6-11 (Sun 12-3, 7-10.30).* **Bar Food** *12-2.30, 6.30-10 (Sun 12-2, 7.15-10).* **Beer** *Fuller's. Garden, outdoor eating, barbecue. Amex, Diners, MasterCard,* **VISA**

WHITELEAF   Red Lion   B&B

Tel 01844 344476   Map 15a D2
Upper Icknield Way Whiteleaf Princes Risborough Buckinghamshire HP27 0LL

Cream and red-painted 17th-century village pub, set back from the lane in a quiet, attractive village. Inside, the two homely and cosy interconnecting rooms and adjacent dining-room are neatly arranged with a pleasant mix of polished pine and antique settles, a good log fire and various brasses, sporting prints and dried flower arrangements. Reached via stairs behind the bar are four simply-furnished bedrooms with modern dark-patterned fabrics, TV and tea makers and compact en suite facilities (only one with bath). Front-facing rooms enjoy good rural views. *Open 11.30-3, 5.30-11 (Sat 11-11, Sun 12-10.30). Free House.* **Beer** *Hook Norton Best, Morland Original, Brakspear, guest beer. Garden.* **Accommodation** *4 bedrooms, all en suite (one with bath), £39.50 (single £29.50). Children over 3 welcome overnight (under-10s stay free in parents' room), addtional bed avaialable. Check-in by arrangement. No credit cards.*

We endeavour to be as up-to-date as possible but inevitably some changes to landlords, chefs and other key staff occur after the Guide has gone to press.

WHITEWELL — Inn at Whitewell ★ FOOD

Tel 01200 448222   Fax 01200 448298   Map 6 B1   **B&B**
Whitewell Forest of Bowland Clitheroe Lancashire BB7 3AT

 Zzz...

Our 1997 Pub of the Year Award winner is set amid the wild beauty of North
Lancashire, well away from the hurly burly, standing next to the village church; it
overlooks the River Hodder (on which the inn has eight miles of fishing rights) at the
head of the Trough of Bowland, one of the least-known areas of outstanding natural
beauty in the country. Back in the 14th century, the inn was home to the keeper of
the King's deer, and the Queen still owns the building as part of the Duchy of
Lancaster. Inside, it's wonderfully relaxed, laid-back, even mildly eccentric, with a
haphazard arrangement of furnishings and bric-a-brac. In the main bar there are
wooden tables, old settles, roundback chairs, a stone fireplace, log fire in cold weather,
and heavy ceiling beams. An entrance hall has colourful rugs, more settles, even a
piano, and a selection of magazines, papers and books for some serious loitering.
A wide variety of pictures, dotted about the building, comes from the Inn's own art
gallery; there's also a small wine merchant business. Head chef Breda Murphy was
enticed over from the *Ballymaloe* cookery school in Ireland. Her food is served in both
the bar and restaurant, which overlooks the river; the interesting bar meal selection
offers the likes of a daily home-made soup (onion and thyme), chicken liver paté,
seafood pancake, fishcakes, leek, potato and mushroom gratin, Cumberland bangers
with champ (Irish mashed potatoes with spring onions), salads, substantial sandwiches,
cheeses from London's Neal's Yard Dairy and home-made puddings (chocolate
mousse, lemon meringue pie). The bar supper menu is similar but varies slightly,
perhaps offering goujons of fresh fish, chicken breast stuffed with banana and mango
and specials like plaice stuffed with salmon mousse. Good Arabica coffee is served in
a cafetière and ground coffee is also packed for taking home – typical of the kind of
thought that goes into Richard Bowman's running of the inn. A good wine list
completes the picture. There are eleven bedrooms, all furbished with antique
furniture, peat fires and Victorian baths. Unusual extras include video recorders and
superb stereo systems, as well as books, magazines, and a set of binoculars; the best and
largest rooms overlook the river and the country beyond (and attract the higher tariff).
Everything is usually immaculately clean. On sunny days the attractive rear lawn –
furnished with simple benches – is an ideal spot to relax and soak in the view.
Children are made most welcome. All-in-all, the Inn at Whitewell comes up trumps
in everything it sets out to do – satisfaction for overnight guests is almost guaranteed,
and it's not often that we say that! *Open 11-3, 6-11 (Sun 12-3, 7-10.30). Bar Food
12-2, 7.30-9.30. Free House. Beer Marston's Pedigree, Boddingtons. Riverside garden,
outdoor eating. **Accommodation** 11 bedrooms, all en suite, £69/£78 (suite £98, single
£49.50-£79). Children welcome overnight (under-12s £12, over-12s £15), additional
bed & cot available. Amex, Diners, MasterCard, **VISA***

WHITMORE — Mainwaring Arms — A

Tel 01782 680851   Fax 01782 680224   Map 6 B3
Whitmore Newcastle-under-Lyme Staffordshire ST5 5HR

Close to the site of the Manor of Whitmore, which was listed in the Domesday Book,
the same families, Mainwarings and Whitmores, have run a hostelry here since time
immemorial. Today's version, in cream-painted brick and creeper-clad with an ivy-
covered porch, plays host to a wide cross-section of locals in congenial surroundings.
Timber cross-beams frame the single mahogany bar and access to three large yet cosy
rooms, each with its own log fire in winter. For summer evening entertainment,
tiered patios to the rear are the setting for regular barbecues. Sundry sandwiches and
the likes of deep-fried fish at lunchtimes only. Three miles from Junction 15 of the
M6. *Open 12-3, 5.30-11 (Fri & Sat 12-11, Sun 12-10.30). Free House. Beer Bass,
Boddingtons Bitter & Gold, Marston's Pedigree. Patio. Family room. No credit cards.*

We endeavour to be as up-to-date as possible but inevitably some changes to
landlords, chefs and other key staff occur after the Guide
has gone to press.

WHITNEY-ON-WYE — Rhydspence Inn — FOOD

Tel 01497 831262 Map 9 D4 **B&B**
Whitney-on-Wye Hay-on-Wye Hereford & Worcester HR3 6EU

🛏 **Zzz...** ☺

Set in the heart of Kilvert country, on the A438 about a mile out of Whitney-on-Wye, this is a well-loved, reliably entertaining inn with a delightful timbered interior, two attractive bars with real fires, old furniture and beams aplenty. Nice touches include magazines and newspapers, creating an atmosphere in keeping with the old library chairs. The charming dining-room and restaurant overlook the garden. Five comfortable bedrooms have beams, sloping floors, plus an armchair at the least; some rooms are more romantic; one has a four-poster; all have TVs and hot beverage facilities but no phones. Bar food suggestions include seafood pie, lasagne, beef curry, sizzling Cajun chicken and vegetable stir-fry. Separate restaurant menu (not recommended here) including popular Sunday lunches. Summer lunchers can enjoy the view over the Wye Valley from the terraced garden. *Open 11-2.30, 7-11 (Sun 12-2.30, 7-10.30).* **Bar Food** *11-2 (from 12 Sun), 7-9.30.* **Beer** *Bass, Robinson Best, guest beer. Garden, outdoor eating. Family room.* **Accommodation** *7 bedrooms, all en suite, £55-£65 according to season (4-poster £75, single £27.50-£32.50,). Children welcome overnight (under-2s stay free in parents' room), additional bed & cot (£12) available. No dogs. Amex, MasterCard,* **VISA**

We do not accept free meals or hospitality – our inspectors pay their own bills and never book in the name of Egon Ronay's Guides.

WHITWELL — Noel Arms — B&B

Tel 01780 460334 Fax 01780 460531 Map 7 E3
Main Street Whitwell Rutland Water Leicestershire LE15 8BW

A pub very much of two halves, the thatched original building with a tiny village bar standing sideways on to the road (A606). Hidden behind is landlord Sam Healey's labour of love, a stone extension, tucked into the hillside, containing lounge bar, dining-rooms (all newly refurbished), and, above, the recently upgraded wing of dormer-windowed bedrooms. Neatly appointed and individually decorated, all enjoy the benefit of colour TV, radios, phones, beverage trays and, for four rooms, new en suite facilities. Barely a long cast from the banks of Rutland Water, the bar's a base for fishing stories late into the night, and the hearty fisherman's breakfast makes a fine start the following morning. Conference facility. *Open 10-11 (Sun 12-10.30). Free House.* **Beer** *Marston's Bitter & Pedigree, guest beer. Patio, outdoor eating, children's play area. Family Room.* **Accommodation** *8 bedrooms, all en suite, £55 (family room £65, single £45). Children welcome overnight (under-12s stay free in parents' room), additional bed & cot available. No dogs. MasterCard,* **VISA**

WIDECOMBE-IN-THE-MOOR — Rugglestone Inn — FOOD

Tel 01364 621327 Fax 01364 621224 Map 13 D3
Widecombe-in-the-Moor Devon TQ13 7TF

Unspoilt gem of a rural pub set beside moorland within walking distance of the picturesque village. Named after the Ruggle Stone, a huge mass of granite nearby, this rustic stone inn comprises two tiny rooms, one a delightful, old-fashioned parlour with beams, open fire and simple furnishings; both are devoid of modern-day intrusions. Excellent Butcombe Bitter and Flowers IPA are tapped straight from the cask and served with one of the hearty, home-made 'one-pot' meals – chicken pie, steak and kidney pie, cauliflower cheese, cottage pie – that make a satisfying meal. Ploughman's platters are served all day. Puddings include blackcurrant pie and treacle and walnut tart with clotted cream. All the food is cooked and delivered daily by two local girls who have a shop in the village. Across the babbling brook to the front of the pub lies a lawn with benches and peaceful moorland views. No children under 14 inside. *Open 11.30-2.30, 6-11 (from 7 in winter), Sat 11.30-3 5-11, Sun 12-3, 6-10.30.* **Bar Food** *12.15-2.15, 6.30-9 (from 7 in winter), Sat & Sun 12.15, 6-9). Free House.* **Beer** *Butcombe Bitter, Flowers IPA. Garden, outdoor eating. No credit cards.*

WIGGLESWORTH · Plough Inn   FOOD

Tel 01729 840243   Map 6 B1   **B&B**
Wigglesworth Skipton North Yorkshire BD23 4RJ

☺

For over sixteen years now the Goodall family have operated, enlarged and improved their 18th-century country inn which was once the farm buildings and ale house of a vast Dales estate. The busy food operation features the output of a wood-burning pit barbecue whose contents can be hot- or cold-smoked over hickory, mesquite or oak chippings. Around the resultant rack of ribs, hickory chicken and smoked halibut steak is a menu full of Yankeeisms, from potato skins with sour cream and corn on the cob 'thro' Caesar salad with smoked chicken to 'steak and prawn combo'. More traditionally, there are still bistro-style bar snacks served in the original village bar and evening meals in a bright conservatory restaurant. Accommodation offered is either Standard (over the original pub) or Superior in a carefull-conceived extension which blends in immaculately with the original timbered black-and-white frontage. Within are all the trappings of modern-day comfort from TV and radio to direct-dial phones and tea and coffee trays: all the rooms are of a decent size with well-kept en suite bathrooms and effective double glazing. While the front rooms look across a village street where practically nothing happens from day to day, those to the rear soak in the ever-changing moods of the twin Dales peaks of Ingleborough and Pen–Y–Ghent. *Open 11.30-3, 7-11 (Sun 12-3, 7-10.30).* **Bar Food** *12-2, 7-9.30. Free House.* **Beer** *Tetley Best, Boddingtons. Garden, outdoor eating. Family room.* **Accommodation** *12 bedrooms, all en suite £55 (single £32.45). Children welcome overnight (under-2s stay free, 2-12s £5 in parents' room), additional bed & cot available. No dogs. Amex, Diners, MasterCard,* **VISA**

WINCHCOMBE   Old White Lion   B&B

Tel & Fax 01242 603300   Map 14 C1
37 North Street Winchcombe Gloucestershire GL5H 5PS

A reminder that good things come in very small packages, the hitherto unsung, 400-year-old Old White Lion is a rare find. Only the tiny enamelled inn sign and black oak door distinguish it from the other listed buildings in North Street. With a cosy front room, tiny rear parlour easy chairs and varnished tables, the whole place has a relaxed and homely air. Six small bedrooms, restored with great care and good taste, also have a special feeling of closeness to antiquity with many of their original features unaffected by careful and unobtrusive addition of the requisite televisions and clock radios, though phones have not been added. While five rooms (including just one single) have en suite WCs and showers only, there's a roomier 4-poster bedroom with both a rubber bath and separate shower en suite. New owners plan to upgrade bedrooms and add a new family room sleeping four. *Open 11-11 (Sun 12-3, 7-10.30). Free House.* **Beer** *Marston's Pedigree, Timothy Taylor's Landlord, guest beer. Garden. Family room.* **Accommodation** *6 bedrooms, all en suite, £52.50-£67.50 (single £32.50). Children welcome overnight (under-5s stay free in parents' room, 6-15s £12.50), additional bed available. MasterCard,* **VISA**

WINCHESTER   Wykeham Arms   ★   FOOD

Tel 01962 853834   Fax 01962 854411   Map 15 D3   **B&B**
75 Kingsgate Street Winchester Hampshire SO23 9PE

🏠 🍸

Tucked away in the narrow back streets of Winchester, immediately south of the Cathedral Close (by Kingsgate on the junction between Canon Street and Kingsgate Street), Graeme and Anne Jameson's mellow, redbrick, 250-year-old 'Wyk' is one of the finest hostelries in the land. The main bar has old-fashioned schoolroom desks with integral seats, some authentically carved with the initials of inattentive pupils from years gone by. Collections of hats, mugs and fascinating old prints and cartoons adorn the bar and no less than five other interconnecting rooms, all set up for eating, with a special dining area for non-smokers. The old pine, candle-lit dining tables each have a brass money slot to collect donations for the upkeep of the cathedral. 'The Wyk' is by no means a secret and booking for food is essential. Lunchtime favourites – 'Wyk' cottage pie, mixed cheese platter with ciabatta and open steak sandwich – are enhanced by daily blackboard choices such as roasted vegetable terrine, duck confit with rocket salad and beef and Guinness casserole. Begin a memorable evening meal with Mediterranean fish terrine or spinach, apple and Stilton strudel, then choose from an imaginative list of main courses – roast rack of lamb with rich port wine and roasted garlic sauce and honey-roast duck breast with apricot and almond stuffing and Madeira sauce, all served with fresh vegetables. Finish off with a mouth-watering dessert like lemon cream tart and upside-down apricot and cinnamon sponge. The Sunday menu comprises various cold platters (game pie, ham, sausage plait, beef, ploughman's) that are served with salad and a cottage loaf. Eighteen names on the well-chosen wine list, complete with Graeme's personal and informative notes, are also available by the glass, and for summer eating and drinking there is a neat, walled garden. Individually decorated bedrooms have stylish matching bedcovers and curtains and mostly honeyed-pine furniture. All have mini-bars, hot-beverage facilities, TV and telephone, plus homely extras like fresh flowers, books, magazines and pot-pourri. Modern en suite bathrooms, all with showers over tubs, boast quality Woods of Windsor toiletries. First-rate cooked breakfasts, with freshly-squeezed orange juice, are served in a charming period breakfast room on the first floor. No children under 14 overnight or in the pub. Three non-smoking rooms. *Open 11-11 (Sun 12-10.30).* **Bar Food** *12-2.30 (sandwiches served till 6), 6.30-9 (Sun 2.30-9).* **Beer** *Eldridge Pope. Garden, outdoor eating.* **Accommodation** *7 bedrooms, all en suite, £77.50 (single £67.50). Children over 14 welcome overnight (£10 in parents' room). Accommodation closed 25 Dec. Amex, MasterCard,* **VISA**

WINDLESHAM	Brickmakers Arms	FOOD

Tel 01276 472267   Fax 01276 451014   Map 15a E4
Chertsey Road Windlesham Surrey GU20 6HT

An unassuming roadside pub on B386 Bagshot-Sunningdale road, a couple of minutes from M3 J3. The majority of the interior is given over to a restaurant dining area (with a no-smoking part) that runs the length of one side of the pub; food is taken seriously here – not only by landlord Gerry Price but also by chef Christine Sheppard in the kitchen – and it shows; if the restaurant is very busy (booking is recommended) then bar food service may take longer than usual. The flagstoned bar area itself has only half a dozen or so tables; here you'll find serious 'brickies big bites' – generously-filled (but at a price) ciabatta sandwiches (sliced Brie with tomato and chives, hot Cajun chicken with roasted red peppers) served with salad – and a short menu of interesting dishes – perhaps fishy home-made soup, oven-baked Brie, black pudding with grain mustard sauce, salmon fish cakes with parsley sauce, steak and kidney pie, and tagliatelle with seafood sauce. Seafood is a major feature and always features among the daily specials – moules marinière, ultra-fresh cod with sautéed new potatoes or scallops with fennel. Tip-top, creamy smoked haddock kedgeree served with a soft-poached egg, a choice of rolls and unsalted butter is worth making a special visit for! A two-course, fixed-price (£9.95) menu is also offered at lunchtime: soup or chicken liver paté followed by sausages and mash or meatballs in a rich tomato sauce with tagliatelle. The restaurant menus cry out to be taken more seriously – à la carte dishes like avocado and pear with a light ginger butter sauce, and calf's liver with caramelised orange and Cointreau jus sit happily alongside a £17.50, three-course table d'hote (Sunday lunch £15). A selection of up to eight British and French cheeses is usually on display. The garden is packed to the brim with picnic tables and four tables are on a small, enclosed patio off the restaurant. Chobham Common is nearby for those who might need to walk off sticky toffee pudding, ever-popular crème brulée, treacle tartlet or any excessive indulgence in the interesting wine list (ask for Gerry's bin-end list); around eight wines are served by the glass, including house champagne at £4. The walls in the bar feature framed restaurant bills from the locals' excesses and photos of other exuberant pastimes. 'Mini-adults' (ie those children over 5 who can sit at table) are welcome only in the restaurant. 5 minutes from the 10th hole of Sunningdale Golf Club! *Open 11.30-3, 5-11 (Sun 12-4, 6-10.30).* **Bar Food** *12-2.30, 6-10 (Sun 12-3, 6-9). No food 26 Dec.* **Beer** *Fuller's London Pride, Courage Best, guest beer. Garden, outdoor eating, boules pitch. Closed 25 Dec, 1 Jan eve. Amex, Diners, MasterCard,* **VISA**

WINEHAM　　Royal Oak　　A

Tel 01444 881252　　Map 11 B6
Wineham Haywards Heath West Sussex BN5 9AY

Part-tiled, black-and-white timbered cottage dating back to the 14th century and located on a country lane between the A272 and B2116 near Henfield. It is a classic ale house, a true rural survivor that has been serving the locals for over 200 years and is delightfully traditional and unspoilt in every way. Head-cracking low beams, huge inglenook with warming winter fire, part wooden and part stone flagged floor topped with sturdy wooden furnishing characterise the charming bar and tiny rear room. Old corkscrews, pottery jugs and mugs, old photographs and other old artefacts adorn the walls. Ale is drawn straight from the cask in a rear room and in keeping with ale house tradition food is limited to good freshly-made sandwiches and a thick soup served on cold winter days. Extensive summer gardens and adjacent children's/function room with TV and books. *Open 11-2.30, 5.30-11 (from 6 Sat), Sun 12-2.30, 7-10.30.* **Beer** *Whitbread Pompey Royal, Flowers Original, Harveys Sussex, guest beer. Garden, outside eating. Family room. No credit cards.*

WINFORTON　　Sun Inn　　★　　FOOD

Tel 01544 327677　　Map 9 D4　　**B&B**
Winforton Hereford & Worcester HR3 6EA

Just three miles inside England on the A438 Wye Valley Road, the Sun is hospitably run by Wendy and Brian Hibbard. Wendy's seemingly endless stream of inventiveness produces something different and exciting whenever we visit, whatever the season. Her winter regular, the hearty stockpot soup and summer's latest addition, a chilled almond and garlic version, are a typical case in point; winter's speciality venison and chestnut pie is likely to be replaced, perhaps, by roasted red mullet fillets with asparagus and leek mousse as the warmer weather approaches. A crab and ginger tarlet is served with hollandaise and a sweet pepper sauce enhances a vegetable and wholemeal pasta gateau – among several interesting dishes for vegetarians. Wendy's inexhaustible repertoire of imaginative dishes may also highlight half-shoulder of lamb with cider, leek and lentil gravy, maize-fed guinea fowl with wild mushrooms and splendid seafood options like warm fish terrine (crab, prawn and halibut), River Exe mussels with coriander, leek and ginger, crab and mango tart and grilled Tavy salmon with laverbread sauce. Carefully cooked and neatly-presented dishes of vegetables (perhaps lightly-honeyed carrots and caraway-seeded cabbage) might be the embellishments – rather than mere accompaniments – which serve to point up the star quality of her cooking. Incidentally, Wendy never uses salt in her cooking. Puddings, conceived both to amuse and satisfy, are equally stellar: walnut cheesecake with gooseberry sauce, 'heaven on a plate' – the ultimate chocolate torte – clearly illustrate the point. Overnight accommodation is offered in three en suite bedrooms; they share a private entrance and unfussy decor of commendable quality, their accoutrements including TV, radio, beverage tray and hairdryer; a pay phone is located in the hall. Children welcome in the bar to eat but not overnight. The recently-constructed 18-hole crazy golf course should keep families amused. *Open 11-3, 6.30-11 (Sun 12-3, 7-10.30). Closed all Tue Nov-May and Tue eve Jun-Oct)* **Bar Food** *12-2, 7-9.30 (till 9 Sun). Free House.* **Beer** *Woods Parish, Jennings Cumberland Bitter, Morland Old Speckled Hen. Garden, outdoor eating.* **Accommodation** *3 bedrooms, all en suite, £46 (single £30). No dogs. No credit cards*

WINGFIELD　　De La Pole Arms　　FOOD

Tel 01379 384545
Wingfield Diss Suffolk IP21 5RA

Lost down country lanes close to the Norfolk border and lovingly restored after being closed and left in a derelict state for three years, the 16th-century De La Pole Arms (named after William de la Pole, First Duke of Suffolk, whose family owned and lived in the fine Old College opposite) is once again open to those who find their way to its door. Excellent real ales, including wheat and fruit beers, from the landlord's new brewery – St Peter's Brewery in nearby Bungay – and quality home-cooked food, notably fresh fish and seafood, are enticing discerning pub-goers back down the tortuous lanes for a decent meal in civilised surroundings. Two charming bars and the adjacent restaurant boast rug-strewn quarry-tiled floors, open fires, antique tables and chairs and a wealth of exposed timbers while, outside, upmarket garden furniture adorns the side terrace that overlooks the historic parish church. From a select and good-value seasonally-changing bar menu and a list of daily blackboard specials, one might start with moules marinière, tagliatelle with spinach and almond pesto, steaming bowls of langoustines or mixed seafood, or cream of pear and Stilton soup, followed by local cod and hand-cut chips, grilled whole lobster with herb butter, casseroled rabbit with mushrooms and red wines, or rich beef stew with parsley dumplings, with most of the main courses accompanied by fresh, crisp vegetables. Restaurant dishes (baked crab, avocado and Stilton soufflé, salmon with coriander, lime and ginger wrapped in filo with a herb sauce) are also served in the bar. Finish off with home-made steamed chocolate sponge and custard or lemon posset. For a light snack try the scrambled egg and smoked salmon or a Brie and sun-dried tomato filled baguette (lunch only). Well-behaved children welcome. Having enjoyed a summer weekend lunch why not visit the Old College with its 3-acres of walled gardens, medieval Great Hall and changing exhibitions. Hamlet signposted off the B1118 south-east of Diss. *Open 11-3, 6-11 (Sun 12-3, 7-10.30).* **Bar Food** *12-2, 7-9.30.* **Beer** *St Peter's Brewery Best, Mild, Extra, Wheat Beer, Fruit Beer & Strong. Terrace, outdoor eating.* *MasterCard,* **VISA**

WINKTON   Fisherman's Haunt Hotel   B&B

Tel 01202 484071   Fax 01202 478883   Map 14 C4
Salisbury Road Winkton Christchurch Dorset BH23 7AS

The river Avon is just across the road from this well-kept, wisteria-clad hotel, which stands on the B3347 Christchurch-Ringwood road about 2 miles from Bournemouth (Hurn) Airport. Stuffed fish and an old well with running spring water are unusual features of the characterful beamed bars, and there is an airy conservatory. The good bedrooms, which are in the main 17th-century building, extended coach house and nearby cottage, blend pretty fabrics with a mixture of modern and traditional furnishings. All offer TVs, telephones and tea-makers and two rooms also boast four-poster bedS. Now under the ownership of Gales' Horndean Inns. *Open 10.30-2.30, 6-11 (Sat 10.30-11, Sun 12-10.30).* **Beer** *Gales BBB & HSB, Bass, guest beer. Garden.* **Accommodation** *19 bedrooms, 16 en suite, £59-£63 (single £36.50). Children welcome overnight (under-11s stay free in parents' room). MasterCard,* **VISA**

WINSFORD   Royal Oak Inn   FOOD

Tel 01643 851455   Fax 01643 851009   Map 13 D2   B&B
Winsford Exmoor National Park Somerset TA24 7JE

Zzz...

Located in a sleepy, picture-postcard pretty Exmoor village, this lovely old thatched inn, dating from the 12th century, has recently been rebuilt to its former pristine condition following a serious fire that destroyed much of the main building. The inn has fishing rights to a mile of the River Winn that runs through the village. Home-made favourites like seafood pancake, chicken and leek pie, steak and kidney pudding and various grills feature on the straightforward bar menu alongside freshly-cut sandwiches and ploughman's lunches. Eight bedrooms in the main building (some nestling under newly re-thatched eves) have been immaculately restored and decorated in charming floral fabrics. All are well appointed with en suite bathrooms and new high-tech telephones along with the usual amenities. Five further bedrooms in a modern annexe and the family cottage formed out of an old cowshed were undamaged by the fire. *Open 11.30-2.30, 6-11 (Sun 12-3, 6-10.30).* **Bar Food** *12-2 & 6-9.30 (from 7 Sun).* **Beer** *Flowers Original & IPA, Marston's Pedigree, Whitbread Castle Eden Ale, Greene King Abbot Ale, guest beer. Patio, outdoor eating.* **Accommodation** *14 bedrooms, all en suite, £90-£95 (single £75-£80). Children welcome overnight in cottage (£15), additional bed & cot available. Amex, Diners, MasterCard,* **VISA**

WINSLOW   Bell Hotel   B&B

Tel 01296 714091   Fax 01296 714805   Map 15a D1
Market Square Winslow Buckinghamshire MK18 3AB

Handsome Georgian coaching inn that proudly overlooks the market square in this pleasant small town. Good pubby bar with heavy beams and inglenook fireplace, and comfortable lounge areas with oak and leather furniture, easy chairs, attractive prints and plates. At present there are seventeen bedrooms, two designed for the disabled, all spacious with floral fabrics, reproduction darkwood furniture – one with a four-poster – clean, tiled bathrooms and added extras like TVs, telephones, tea-makers, hairdryers and trouser presses. A further twenty two bedrooms are currently being built. *Open 10am-11pm (Sun 12-10.30).* **Beer** *Greene King. Courtyard.* **Accommodation** *17 bedrooms, all en suite, £44.50-£49.50 (family room sleeping three £49.50, single £39.50-£47). Children welcome overnight, additional bed (£5) & cot available. Amex, MasterCard,* **VISA**

WINTERTON-ON-SEA   Fisherman's Return   FOOD

Tel 01493 393305   Map 10 D1   **B&B**
The Lane Winterton-on-Sea Norfolk NR29 4BN

Small it maybe, but this prettily-kept row of former fishermen's cottages is an ideal hang-out for locals and visitors alike, be they fishermen or not. Built in traditional brick and flint, the buildings are probably 16th-century, and unaltered over the last quarter century or more. The cheery public bar, complete with warming wood-burner, is lined in varnished tongue-and-groove panelling and hung with sepia photographs and prints of Lowestoft harbour, the Norfolk Broads and the pub itself. A smaller and possibly older lounge, low-ceilinged, with a copper-hooded fireplace and oak mantel, is carpeted these days and ideal for a quick, if cramped, snack. Families will more likely head to the 'Tinho', a timbered rear extension with pool table and games machines which leads mercifully quickly to a lovely enclosed garden with a pets' corner and an adventure playground. The printed menu offers standard pub fare, but look to the blackboard for interesting daily specials like spicy aubergine soup, salmon and mussel lasagne, baked lamb in gooseberry sauce, and plum and apple crumble. Toasted sandwiches and ploughman's platters are served all day. A tiny flint-lined spiral staircase leads up under the eaves to three cosy bedrooms, which share the house television (propped up on a seaman's trunk) and two bathrooms (one with shower only). The largest room, a family room, also has a sitting area with its own television. Modest comforts, maybe, but entirely adequate for a brief stay, a stone's throw from the beach and long walks over the dunes. Visitors are made truly welcome by John and Kate Findlay, and seen on their way with the heartiest of seafarer's breakfasts. *Open 11-2.30, 6-11 (from 7 in winter), Sat 11-11, Sun 12-3, 6.30-10.30.* **Bar Food** *12-2, 6-9.30 (from 6.30 Sun, from 7 in winter). Free House.* **Beer** *John Smith's, Adnams Best, Wolf Bitter, guest beers. Garden, outdoor eating, children's play area. Family room.* **Accommodation** *3 bedrooms, £45 (single £30). Children welcome overnight (babies free if in own cot), additional bed (£5) available. Check-in by arrangement. No credit cards.*

WITHYPOOL   Royal Oak Inn   FOOD

Tel 01643 831506   Fax 01643 831659   Map 13 D1   **B&B**
Withypool Somerset TA24 7QP

 Zzz...

A stylish, friendly and thoroughly laid-back country inn, well-beloved of hunting and shooting parties in season. The Royal Oak was a favoured haunt in the 1860s of 'Lorna Doone's' author, R.D. Blackmore. Despite modern-day bedroom comforts, little enough appears changed today: hunting trophies adorn the Resident's Bar, while the Rod Room Bar is dedicated more to angling memorabilia. An all-encompassing bar menu with everything from sandwiches to grilled steaks is supplemented by a daily-changing blackboard menu of home-cooked specials. Choices range from red pepper, olive and Camembert tart and pink trout salad to monkfish kebab and meatballs in tomato sauce. Fresh apricot pie and tiramisu may appear on the list of puddings. Table d'hote and à la carte dinner menus in the adjacent restaurant. The comfortable bedrooms have a comprehensive range of facilities: TV, radio, direct-dial phone, hot beverage-making facilities and hairdryer. A couple of the bathrooms have shower/WC only. By night, the peace and quiet are total. Withypool is just off the B3223 from Dulverton. *Open 11-3, 6-11 (Sun 12-3, 7-10.30).* **Bar Food** *12-2, 6.30-9.30 (from 7 Sun). Free House.* **Beer** *Flowers IPA, Marston's Pedigree. Patio, outdoor eating.* **Accommodation** *8 bedrooms, 7 en suite, £76-£80 (single £38). Children over 8 welcome overnight (half-price), additional bed (£15) available. Accommodation closed 24-26 Dec. Amex, Diners, MasterCard,* **VISA**

WOLTERTON   Saracens Head   FOOD

Tel 01263 768909   Map 10 C1   **B&B**
Wolterton Erpingham Norfolk NR11 7LX

🛏️ **Zzz..**

To locate this isolated and very individual rural inn follow signs for Erpingham off the A140 Aylsham to Cromer road, then pass through Calthorpe before bearing left on to a narrow lane, signposted Wolterton; your efforts will be well rewarded. Only 250 yards from the main gates to Wolterton Hall, this most unusual red-brick inn was built in 1806 by Lord Walpole as a coaching inn for the main house and was modelled on a Tuscan farmhouse. Inside, the ambience is decidedly civilised and upmarket – no piped music or intrusive games – with high ceilings, soothing terracotta painted walls with friezes, stylish patterned clothed tables, open log fires and an eclectic mix of furniture. Scatter cushions, magazines, newspapers and evening candlelight enhance the relaxed atmosphere. Landlord/chef Robert Dawson-Smith produces an interesting, short selection of dishes that are listed on a blackboard menu that changes twice daily. No chips, scampi or sandwiches (bread and cheese is available at lunchtime, though) are served here, so expect pub fare that is well above average and book a table! Imaginative choices may begin with baked eggs and smoked salmon with cream, mackerel soused with cider and apple and gamey paté maison with salad (all make ideal snacks), followed by sautéed monkfish with fresh mango and turmeric, salmis of rabbit and ham with mustard sauce, and whole plaice with pesto butter, all accompanied with a dish of well-cooked vegetables. Finish with a traditional pudding such as treacle tart or banana fritters with maple syrup. Popular events are the roast Sunday lunch, the special Sunday 2-course supper, a weekday 'two choice' lunch and the monthly 'feast' nights – French, seafood and Old English, for example. Short list of well-chosen wines. Individual charm extends to the top floor of the inn into the four attractive en suite bedrooms, each furnished with freestanding pine – one with brass bed – wicker chairs and quality fabrics. TV, hairdryer, and beverage-making facilities are standard, but fresh milk and earthenware jars of tea and coffee are a welcome touch, as are the excellent breakfasts. Sheltered courtyard garden and delightful walled garden for sunny days. No under-5s in bar areas. *Open 11-2.30, 6-11 (Sun 12-2.30, 7-10.30).* **Bar Food** *12.30-2.15, 7-9.30 (till 9 Sun). Free House.* **Beer** *Adnams Southwold, guest beer. Garden, courtyard, outdoor eating.* **Accommodation** *4 bedrooms, all en suite £50 (family room sleeping three £60, single £40). Children welcome overnight, additional bed (£10) & cot available. Check-in by arrangement. Amex, MasterCard.* **VISA**

WOOBURN COMMON   Chequers Inn   FOOD

Tel 01628 529575   Fax 01628 850124   Map 15a E3   **B&B**
Wooburn Common Beaconsfield Buckinghamshire HP10 0JQ

🛏️🍷

The charming 17th-century Chequers Inn lies midway between the M4 and M40, perched on the rolling Chiltern Hills and has been carefully and lovingly developed over the years by Peter Roehrig. Find him chatting to the locals in the convivial beamed bar, where you'll find simple but stylish snacks. Choose from home-made beef burger, open smoked salmon and avocado sandwich, Thai-style chicken with wild rice, and lamb steak with honey and grain mustard sauce. There is a separate restaurant but our specific recommendation here is for bar food. The pine-furnished, cottagey bedrooms, many enjoying open country views, all have en suite facilities and are equipped with TVs (plus Sky), telephones, clock-radios, trouser presses, tea/coffee making facilities. One room has a four-poster. Conference facilities. *Open 11-11 (Sun 11-10.30).* **Bar Food** *12-2.30, 6-9.30 (from 7 Sun). Free House.* **Beer** *Fuller's London Pride, Marston's Pedigree, Wadworth 6X, Wexford Bitter. Garden, outdoor eating.* **Accommodation** *17 bedrooms, all en suite, £82.50-£95 (single £77.50), weekend reductions. Children welcome overnight. No dogs. Amex, MasterCard,* **VISA**

Alchester

WOODBASTWICK   Fur & Feather   A

Tel 01603 720003   Map 10 D1
Woodbastwick Norwich Norfolk NR13 6HQ

Nestling within an unspoilt estate village on the edge of the Norfolk Broads, this
picturesque thatched brick building was converted from two farm cottages into
a pub only a few years ago. Owned by Woodforde's brewery, who established their
brewhouse in the farm buildings behind some eight years ago, the Fur and Feather
serves as the 'Brewery Tap' dispensing their full range of award-winning cask ales.
Tip-top Wherry Best Bitter (the 1996 Champion Beer of Britain), Nelson's Revenge,
Great Eastern, Baldric, the 1992 champion beer Norfolk Nog and the deceptively
strong Headcracker (ABV 7%) can all be enjoyed in the traditionally refurbished bars
or on the peaceful front lawn on fine weather days. *Open 11-3 (from 12 in winter), 6-
11 (Sun 12-3, 7-10.30). **Beer** Woodforde's. Garden. Family room. No credit cards.*

WOODCHESTER   Ram Inn   A

Tel 01453 873329   Map 14 B2
South Woodchester Stroud Gloucestershire GL5 5EL

One of Gloucestershire's more way-out pubs both in clientele and location –
a splendid spot above the A46 (follow signs uphill to South Woodchester). Visitors
are rewarded with fine views back down the valley and across to Minchinhampton
Common. Niceties are kept to a minimun with picnic tables on a tarmac patio,
assorted pine tables and bentwood chairs in the L-shaped bar and plain floorboards
surrounding the single stone-built box counter. Two log fires are a great draw in
winter. The Ram's pride and joy, however, is its selection of real ales – (any nine
are on tap at any one time) – running through the alphabet from Archers and
Boddingtons to Uley Old Spot. *Open 11-3, 5.30-11, (Fri & Sat 11-11, Sun 12-10.30).
Free House. **Beer** Uley Old Spot, Archers Best, Boddingtons, Buchanan's Best, John Smith's,
Bass, guest beers. Garden. MasterCard, **VISA***

WOODCHESTER   Woodchester Inn   ★   FOOD

Tel 01435 872735   Map 14 B2
Church Road North Woodchester Stroud Gloucestershire GL5 5PQ

Eamonn Webster and his partners have a winning formula on their hands at their
recently re-opened pub premises just off the A46 east of Stroud. It's all neatly
explained on the bistro menu whose concept is for diners to choose as little or as
much as their hunger dictates and order accordingly either starter or main-course
portions of some two dozen dishes. Firm favourites are the Cromer crab and plum
tomato salad, tagliatelle with smoked salmon and cream, and spicy beef stir-fry, served
mild, hot or very hot according to taste. Smoked trout terrine, crispy duck and bacon
salad and baked goat's cheese with tapénade, following the same formula, are equally
toothsome alternatives. Strictly main course dishes also come from the char-grill, with
salmon, tuna and Dover sole offered alongside duck breast, rack of lamb and four cuts
of steaks. To follow, the choices include sticky toffee pudding and raspberry brulée,
apple and fudge tart with Calvados cream and peppered pineapple with home-made
ice cream. This is indeed prodigious output from Eamonns' pocket-sized kitchen,
from where the food emerges via a central bar servery to five open-plan interlinked
rooms, their bare boards and scrubbed pine tables engendering a naturally lively and
informal atmosphere. To all this will be added a conservatory and patio for spring
1997: indications are that you should book early! *Open 12-3, 7-11 (till 10.30 Sun).
Closed Mon Jan-Mar. **Bar Food** 12-2.30, 7-10. **Beer** Worthington Best, Hancocks HB,
Bass. Garden, patio, outdoor eating. Family room. Amex, Diners, MasterCard, **VISA***

WOODNEWTON   White Swan   FOOD

Tel 01780 470381
Main Street Woodnewton Northamptonshire PE8 5EB

Map 7 E4

When the White Swan was closed and bought by a developer in 1988 the villagers thought they had lost their pub, but after a campaign which involved residents lobbying council planning meetings, the White Swan was saved and reopened, after extensive renovations, in 1990. Simple, single oblong room, one end focusing on the bar and a wood-burning stove, with the other end neatly set up as a dining-room. A single blackboard menu serves both bar and dining area, offering such dishes as steak and kidney pudding, fresh plaice, swordfish, monkfish and crab, as well as steaks, vegetarian options (nut log) and puddings like summer pudding, tiramisu and chocolate cups. *Open 12-3, 7-11 (till 10.30 Sun)*. **Bar Food** *12-2, 7-10. Free House.* **Beer** *Fuller's London Pride, Oakham JHB, Hall and Woodhouse Tanglefoot, guest beer. Garden, outdoor eating. MasterCard,* **VISA**

WOODSTOCK   Feathers Hotel   FOOD   B&B

Tel 01993 812291   Fax 01993 813158
Market Street Woodstock Oxfordshire OX7 1SX

Map 14a B2

Zzz...

Eight miles north of Oxford, within walking distance of Blenheim Palace. Situated in the heart of a historic village, behind a 17th-century Cotswold-stone frontage, the Feathers hotel offers a comfortable range of superior accommodation with bedrooms differing in price by size (suites are particularly attractive). All have elaborately draped curtains and a useful range of extras that includes mineral water, chocolates, fresh flowers, magazines and tea on arrival. Some rooms have draped awnings over the beds, while the best have four-posters. Bathrooms are luxuriously fitted in marble throughout, with bathrobes and an abundance of toiletries provided. The upstairs drawing room with a library and open fire is the most inviting of the day rooms and a cosy bar has flagstone flooring and an open fireplace. During warm weather the courtyard garden is a delightful spot for light meals (which are also served in the bar). A quiet, sophisticated air pervades the dining-room, where à la carte and fixed-price menus provide a choice of interesting options. Recommended in our *1997 Hotels & Restaurants Guide.* Lighter eating in the Whinchat Bar – from asparagus soup or chicken liver parfait with brioche and sweet onion marmalade to confit of duck with braised red cabbage, fishcake with sweet and sour chili sauce, chargrilled chicken burger with tartare mayonnaise and ginger pudding. Afternoon tea is served from 3.30-5.30. Service is courteous and efficient. Children welcome. *Open 11-3, 5.30-11, (Sun 12-3, 7-10.30).* **Bar Food** *12.30-2.15, 7.30-9.15 (no bar food Sat or Sun eve).* **Beer** *Wadworth 6X. Courtyard garden.* **Accommodation** *16 rooms, 15 en suite, £99-£150 (suites £185-£225, single from £78), breakfast charged separately. Children welcome overnight, additional bed & cot (both £20) available. Dogs (£5) by arrangement. Amex, Diners, MasterCard,* **VISA**

WOOLHOPE   Butcher's Arms   FOOD   B&B

Tel 01432 860281
Woolhope Hereford & Worcester HR1 4RF

Map 14 B1

Zzz...

The infectious enthusiasm of the Power family and a commendable reliance on local produce bring customers from far and wide to their 14th-century pub which is not easily found down the narrow country lanes. A black-and-white timber frontage, copiously hung with flower baskets, and the neat, colourful brookside garden and patio induce an anticipation more than adequately fulfilled by the food. Good, reliable main bar menu highlighting the ever-popular Woolhope pie (wild rabbit and cider) and hearty sandwiches with a choice of 15 different fillings (ham with celery and apple mint mayonnaise). Blackboard dishes enhance the selection further: Glastonbury lamb, salmon in dill and lemon sauce, beef and Beamish pie, pork and apricot curry and butter bean and mushroom au gratin being typical examples of the daily cooked dishes. Plenty of home-made puddings (perhaps ginger and coffee meringue cake, banana split or summer pudding). The three bedrooms are small and cosy with tea-makers, TVs and telephones: decor is in an appropriate cottage style, and they share a bathroom. There's abundant peace and quiet in this hidden valley, and a substantial breakfast, come the morning. *Open 11.30-2.30, 7-11 (from 6.30 Fri & Sat & in summer), Sun 12-3, 7-10.30. **Bar Food** 12-2 (till 2.15 Sat & Sun), 7-10. Free House.* **Beer** *Hook Norton Best & Old Hookey, two guest beers. Garden, outdoor eating. Family room.* **Accommodation** *3 bedrooms (not en suite) £39 (single £25). Children welcome overnight (over-10s £15). Check-in by arrangement. No dogs. Accommodation closed 24 Dec. No credit cards.*

WOOLLEY MOOR   White Horse   FOOD

Tel 01246 590319   Map 6 C3
White Horse Lane Woolley Moor Derbyshire DE5 6FG

☺ ▼

Bill and Jill Taylor are the landlords of the smart, friendly and very popular White Horse. Approached from the A61 at Stretton, Woolley Moor is a tiny hilltop hamlet above the river Amber at the point where it flows into Ogston reservoir. The large paddock and garden have a sandpit, swings, and small adventure playground to help keep the youngsters happy and there's both a boules pitch and a football pitch. There are at least two dozen trestle tables outside; bag one for a summer lunch, but remember the number before going inside to order. Within, there's restaurant seating for around 60 people, and it fills up quickly, so booking is recommended. On the printed menu, dishes such as steak and kidney pie, creamy chicken pie and seafood quiche are offered alongside filled jacket potatoes, ploughman's and sandwiches. Gooey desserts could include chocolate and brandy mousse and butterscotch and walnut fudge cake. Blackboard specials may feature venison sausage bake, pork chop with orange and cranberry sauce and wild mushroom ragout. It's substantial stuff, nicely cooked and presented and, above all, tasty. The Smoke Room still remains the village local, with is quarry-tiled floor, red leather banquettes, Britannia tables and prominent dartboard; Monday night dominoes are played in a seriously competitive spirit. This is where a good drop of ale comes in. In addition to draught Bass, a healthy rotation of guest beers is publicised well in advance, a good proportion of them from independent breweries. Piped music, when playing, is of the classical kind. This is a smart and impressive pub, professionally managed, and it runs like clockwork. No under-14s in the bar areas. *Open 11.30-2.30, 6-11 (Sat 11.30-3.30, 6-11, Sun 12-3.30, 5-10.30). **Bar Food** 11.30-2 (till 2.15 Sat), 6.30-9 (Sat 6-9.15, Sun 12-2.15, 5.30-8.30). Free House.* **Beer** *Bass, Jennings Dark Mild, three guest beers. Garden, outdoor eating, children's play area. No credit cards.*

> We do not accept free meals or hospitality – our inspectors pay their own bills and never book in the name of Egon Ronay's Guides.

WOOTTON RIVERS   Royal Oak   FOOD

Tel 01672 810322   Fax 01672 811267   Map 14a A4   B&B
Wootton Rivers Marlborough Wiltshire SN8 4NQ

Situated only 100 yards from the Kennet and Avon Canal in one of Wiltshire's most picturesque villages, this 16th-century, black-and-white timbered, thatched pub offers visitors an old-world charm in its low heavily beamed and comfortably furnished bars and dining room. A good atmosphere prevails in which to enjoy well-kept ale – Wadworth 6X drawn from the wood – and a wide choice of bar food. The comprehensive printed menu features standard snacks and favourites, including a good range of steaks, while the photocopied handwritten menu advertises the freshly-prepared daily specials. Begin with fresh crab cocktail, herrings in dill sauce or chicory, spinach and bacon salad followed by a hearty steak and Guinness pie, Armenian lamb, green Thai chicken curry, oven-baked lemon sole or home-made lasagne. Local game features on the menu in winter and popular vegetarian choices may include Stilton and vegetable bake. Puddings range from orange sorbet with Grand Marnier and fresh fruit meringues to orange and brandy pudding. Six fresh, clean and comfortable bedrooms – four with en-suite or private facilities – are located in a large modern house to the rear of the pub. Guests have the use of communal tea- and coffee-making facilities in the TV lounge and for early risers their own breakfasts, the ingredients of which are supplied, with the washing-up being attended to later. Breakfast can also be taken in the pub. *Open 11-3 (coffee from 10.30), 6-11, (Sun 12-10.30).* **Bar Food** *12-2.30, 7-9.30 (till 9 Sun). Free House.* **Beer** *Brakspear Bitter, Wadworth 6X, Boddingtons, Ushers seasonal beer. Patio, outdoor eating. Family room.* **Accommodation** *6 bedrooms, 4 en suite showers, £40 (single £27.50). Children welcome overnight, (under-2s stay free in parents' room, 2-5s £5, 5-10s £10), additional bed available. Amex, MasterCard,* **VISA**

WOOTTON WAWEN   Bull's Head   FOOD

Tel 01564 792511   Map 14 C1
Stratford Road Wootton Wawen Warwickshire B95 6BD

A smart, black-and-white timber-framed 16th-century pub just a mile or so from the picturesque village of Henley-in-Arden (A3400) with rug-strewn flagstone floors, old pine furnishings and low, gnarled oak beams. Determined emphasis on fresh fish attracts an ever-increasing clientele, the iced seafood platter proving a tempting indulgence on a hot summer's evening. Notable equally for size and variety, hearty portions of monkfish tails marinated in balsamic vinegar, tomatoes and fresh herbs, seafood tartlet and salmon fishcakes tempt diners choosing from the daily-updated blackboards. The less fishy, meanwhile, may plump for braised beef and vegetables or chargrilled chicken with chili butter. Puddings may include warm pear and cinnamon flan and crème brulée. Sandwiches at lunchtime only. A fair and generously-priced selection of wines by the glass is supplemented by good-value bin-end bottles. *Open 12-3.30, 6-11 (Sun 12-3.30, 7-10.30).* **Bar Food** *12-3, 7-10.30 (till 10 Sun). Free House.* **Beer** *Marston's Best & Pedigree, Morland Old Speckled Hen, Wadworth 6X. Fuller's London Pride, Adnams Bitter. Garden, terrace, outdoor eating. Closed 25 Dec. MasterCard,* **VISA**

WORTH   St Crispin Inn   B&B

Tel 01304 612081   Fax 01304 614838   Map 11 D5
The Street Worth Sandwich Kent CT14 0DF

Zzz...

Peacefully located along the village street just off the A258 south of Sandwich, this attractive and pleasantly refurbished local has a single, characterful bar, which is full of heavy timbers, brick walls, a big log fire and a collection of rustic pine tables and chairs. Interesting range of six real ales tapped straight from the cask behind the bar. Spacious rear terrace with an all-weather retractable awning and an excellent summer garden with benches among the flower borders and trees. Three charming upstairs bedrooms – one with a fine half-tester bed – have stripped pine doors, a good mix of older/antique style furniture and clean en suite facilities with showers over tubs. Three further, larger rooms are housed in a converted outbuilding and feature modern built-in furniture and compact bathrooms. All have satellite TV and tea-makers. The pub is a handy base for golfers playing the Royal links courses at the end of the lane. *Open 11-2.30, 6-11 (Sun 12-4.30, 7-10.30). Free House.* **Beer** *Shepherd Neame Master Brew, Gale's HSB, Marston's Pedigree, Boddingtons Mild, two guest beers. Rear garden and courtyard.* **Accommodation** *6 bedrooms, all en suite, £50 (single £35). Children welcome overnight, additional bed available (£5). Check-in bar hours only. Closed 24 Dec eve. Amex, MasterCard,* **VISA**.

We endeavour to be as up-to-date as possible but inevitably some changes to
landlords, chefs and other key staff occur after the Guide
has gone to press.

WYE   New Flying Horse Inn   FOOD

Tel 01233 812297   Map 11 C5   **B&B**
Upper Bridge Street Wye Kent TN25 5AN

Zzz...

With a 400-year-old history, this well maintained village centre inn is characterised by low ceilings, black beams, open brickwork and a large open fireplace. The spick and span main bar has gleaming, copper-topped tables and simple chairs while the neat lounge bar boasts some comfortable armchairs and access to the splendid sun-trap patio and extensive lawned garden. Reliable bar food is listed on a changing chalk board; dishes may include watercress soup, avocado and smoked chicken, spicy roast poussin and halibut with tomato and rosemary. For pudding, try the pear and almond flan or the double chocolate mousse. Ploughman's and sandwiches are available at lunchtime only. Evening restaurant menu. Six main-building bedrooms – including one four-poster and one spacious family room – have been smartly refurbished with attractive pastel colours, quality fabrics and some decent individual pieces of furniture. Good bathrooms with showers over tubs. In addition, there are four uniform, en suite rooms in a converted stable block. Invicta Country Inns. *Open 11-3, 6-11 (Sun 12-3, 7-10.30)* **Bar Food** *12-2.15, 6.30-9.15.* **Beer** *Shepherd Neame. Garden, patio, outdoor eating, summer barbecue. Family room.* **Accommodation** *9 bedrooms, all en suite, £47.50 (single £37.50). Children welcome overnight (under-5s stay free in parents' room).* MasterCard, **VISA**

WYKEHAM   Downe Arms Hotel   B&B

Tel 01723 862471   Fax 01723 864329   Map 5 F4
Wykeham Scarborough North Yorkshire YO13 9QB

An imposing stone building at the roadside (A170) just five miles from Scarborough, the hotel has remained part of the Downe family estates since its conversion into a coaching inn some 120 years ago. A century later the Orangery, designed by Sir Martin Beckett on an 18th century theme, was added to provide extensive function facilities. The rather less-than-pubby bar and lounge nonetheless remain suitably comfortable and intimate for the resident guest, and there's a spacious garden and patio for family use in summertime. En suite facilities were added to the bedrooms just eight years ago, although the listed nature of the original structure limited several to WC and shower rooms only. All are kept, however, in apple-pie order with bright matching fabrics adding a welcome splash of colour. Direct-dial telephones, trouser presses, TVs and hospitality trays are standard throughout *Open 11-3, 6.30-11 (Sun 12-3, 7-10.30). Free House.* **Beer** *Tetley Best, Theakston Best. Garden.* **Accommodation** *10 bedrooms, all en suite, £50 (single £25). Children welcome overnight (under-5s stay free, 5-15s £10 if sharing parents' room), additional bed & cot available.* MasterCard, **VISA**

WYRE PIDDLE   Anchor Inn   FOOD

Tel 01386 552799   Map 14 C1
Main Street Wyre Piddle Pershore Hereford & Worcester WR10 2JB

 ☺

Standing low and white-painted at the roadside, bedecked with fairy lights and flower baskets, the Anchor reveals its wealth of talents on further investigation. This is one of the region's premier summer pubs with its grassy terraces and rolling lawn graduating down to the Avon river bank where holidaymakers may moor their narrowboats. Views across the river take in the verdant Vale of Evesham whence come the asparagus and strawberries that enrich the summer menus. Seasonal printed menus – garlic mushrooms, steak and kidney pie, salads and scampi – are supplemented by blackboard specials such as artichoke and crab bake, chicken livers with mushroom and Burgundy sauce, grilled sardines and duck breast with apple and calvados. Round off your meal with apple and raspberry pie or a chocolate choux bun. No sandwiches, but open baps and ploughman's platters are available all day. An elevated dining-room has possibly the best view (although it's the food in the bar that we specifically recommend here). Family Sunday lunch. Watch out for the theme nights, live music and ten real fruit wines. *Open 11-2.30 (till 3 Sat), 6-11 (Sun 12-3, 7-10.30).* **Bar Food** *12-2.15 (till 2.30 Sat & Sun), 7-9.15 (till 9.30 Sat, 9 Sun).* **Beer** *Marston's Pedigree, Flowers IPA, Boddingtons, two guest beers. Garden. Closed 25 Dec eve & all 26 Dec.* Amex, MasterCard, **VISA**

WYTHAM   White Hart   A

Tel 01865 244372   Map 14a C2
Wytham Oxfordshire OX2 8QA

This famous old creeper-clad pub in the centre of the pretty village of Wytham has
a part-panelled bar with a flagstone floor, open fire and high back settles. Outside is
a very pretty courtyard garden, popular for barbecues in the summer beyond which
extra seating has been provided by converting the loose boxes in the old stables into
booths. *Open 11-11,(11-2.30, 6-11 winter), Sun 12-10.30 (12-3, 7-10.30 winter).*
Beer Aylesbury ABC Bitter, Tetley, Ind Coope Buton Ale, guest beer. Garden. Amex,
MasterCard, **VISA**

YATTENDON   Royal Oak   FOOD

Tel 01635 201325   Fax 01635 201926   Map 14a C4   **B&B**
The Square Yattendon Newbury Berkshire RG16 0UF

⬥ Zzz...

Formed out of a row of 16th-century cottages facing the village square, the wisteria-
clad Royal Oak has a long, celebrated history: Oliver Cromwell dined here on the
eve of the battle of Newbury in 1664. Two entrances lead separately to the residents'
lounge and to the three interconnecting rooms, including the single bar, whose
assorted pine and mahogany tables are laid up for the reserved eating. Good bar food
ranges from gratin of Arbroath smokies with smoked salmon and cucumber or smoked
chicken salad for starters to mussel, saffron and fennel stew, honey-glazed hock of ham
with a casserole of lentil, and home-made steak and kidney pudding among the list of
main courses. A blackboard lists the soup – cream of cauliflower – and fish dish of the
day, such as oven-baked monkfish with cracked black pepper and chive velouté.
Finish with rhubarb and ginger brulée, bread-and-butter pudding or home-made ice
cream. Smart new en suite bathrooms are the result of remodelling of the five
bedrooms to a high standard throughout; the pick of these, converted from the two
small singles, is now a stylishly furnished mini-suite. From the bar, French windows
lead to an enclosed rear garden with picnic tables and a vine-laden trellis, the perfect
spot for a summer drink. Regal Hotels. *Open 11-3, 6-11 (Sun 12-2.30, 7-10.30).*
Bar Food 12-2 (till 2.30 Fri & Sat), 7-9.30 (till 10 Fri & Sat), Sun 12-2.30, 7.30-9.30.
Beer Banks's Bitter, Camerons Strongarm, guest beer. Garden, outdoor eating.
Accommodation 5 rooms, all en suite, £99-£114 (single £89.50). Children welcome
overnight (under-14s stay free in parents' room), additional bed & cot available. Amex,
Diners, MasterCard, **VISA**

YEALAND CONYERS   New Inn   FOOD

Tel 01524 732938   Fax 01524 734502   Map 4 C4
40 Yealand Rd Yealand Conyers Carnforth Lancashire LA5 9SJ

Signed off the A6 north of Carnforth, and just a mile or two short of the Cumbrian
border, the village attracts its fair share of visitors both to Leighton Hall and the
nearby Leighton Moss Nature Reserve. An added attraction, conveniently located
between the two, is Ian and Annette Dutton's ivy-clad listed pub. Cumbrian foodies
connect the Dutton name with the *Miller Howe Café* in Windermere and this by
association with John Tovey, whose protegés pepper the Lake District. Here the
village's only pub bar is quite gentrified, with carpeting and marble-topped tables,
regularly doubling as the overflow to a 40-seat dining area, daily filled to capacity.
Food-wise, the legacy, if not the hand of Tovey remains; the ubiquitous side salad
bowls are forcefully flavoured not only with orange, fresh pineapple and grapes but
also dried banana and candied walnuts beneath a cream cheese dressing and mustardy
vinaigrette. Snacks (served all day at weekends) include home-made soup (perhaps
broccoli, cheese and onion), filled baps, jacket potatoes, Cumberland sausage with
apple sauce and date chutney, quiche and snacks that include the 'Miller Howe cheese
and herb paté'. Look to the blackboard for main courses which may include whole
quail stuffed with bacon, hazelnuts and apricots, beef in beer and fresh home-made
pasta with asparagus and cheese sauce. Puddings include lemon soufflé and white
chocolate rum creams. *Open 11-3, 5.30-11 (Sat & school holidays 11-11), Sun 11-
10.30.* **Bar Food** *11.30-2.30, 5.30-9.30 (Sat and Sun 11.30-9.30).* **Beer** *Robinson's*
Best, Hartleys XB, Hatters Mild, Bitter, Frederic's & Old Tom. Garden, outdoor eating.
MasterCard, **VISA**

ACCEPTED IN
HOTELS AND
THAN MOST P
EVER HAVE HO

VISA IS ACCEPTED FOR MORE TRANSACTIO

MORE
STAURANTS
OPLE
DINNERS.

ORLDWIDE THAN ANY OTHER CARD.

KING LIFE EASIER THROUGHOUT SCOTLAND

Scotland

The addresses of establishments in the following former
Counties now include their new Unitary Authorities:

Borders
Scottish Borders
Central
Stirling, Falkirk
Fife
Fife, Clackmannanshire
Grampian
Aberdeen City, Aberdeenshire, Moray
Lothian
East Lothian, City of Edinburgh, Midlothian,
West Lothian
Strathclyde
Argyll & Bute, East Ayrshire, West Dunbartonshire,
East Dunbartonshire, City of Glasgow, Inverclyde,
East Renfrewshire, North Ayrshire, (inc Isle of Arran),
North Lanarkshire, Renfrewshire, South Ayrshire,
South Lanarkshire
Tayside
Angus, Dundee City, Perth & Kinross

Dumfries & Galloway, Highland (+ Orkney, Shetland
& Western Isles) remain essentially the same

ABERDEEN   Prince of Wales   FOOD

Tel 01224 640597   Map 3 D4
7 St. Nicholas Lane Aberdeen City AB1 1HF

By a modern shopping centre (St. Nicholas), in the heart of the city, the Prince of Wales dates back to the middle of the last century and still has a very Victorian feel with bare-board floor, old flagstones, panelled walls, some booth seating and the longest bar counter in town. Straightforward cooking is available at lunchtimes only from a self-service counter, with dishes such as chicken and ham or steak pies, fried haddock and beef olives. Substitute these with salads, jacket potatoes or a soup for smaller appetites, throw in a pile of filled baps (made and served over the bar until they run out) – and it's a winning combination. *Open 11am-11.45pm. (Sun 12.30-11.30pm) Bar Food 11.30-2. (Sat till 4, Sun 12.30-2.30). Free House. **Beer** Bass, Caledonian 80/- Ale, Theakston Old Peculier, Orkney Dark Island, guest beers. No credit cards.*

ALMONDBANK   Almondbank Inn   FOOD

Tel. 01738 583242   Map 3 C5
Main Street Almondbank Perth & Kinross PH1 3NJ

Just off the A85 to the west of Perth, on the village main street, the whitewashed Almondbank enjoys fine views over the River Almond from its small well-kept rear garden. It's a bustling place with juke box and a pool table, yet despite the jokey familiarity of the Birdcage Bistro menu, food is taken pretty seriously. All the beef used is Aberdeen Angus from the licensee's own family butcher, and even the scampi is fresh and crumbed on the premises. The menu itself is long, running from first courses like crispy potato skins and prawns Indienne to main courses such as Chicken George, fresh local haddock and a whole list of Aberdeen Angus steaks with a variety of sauces. All come with fresh vegetables as well as some first-rate home-made chips; puddings are largely ice cream based and there's good cappuccino and espresso coffee. On Friday and Saturday evenings, a slightly different menu is heavy on steaks and chicken . The uniformed staff are friendly and approachable. *Open 11-2, 5-11 (Fri & Sat 11-11.45, Sun 12.30-11). Bar Food 12-2.15 (Sun from 12.30), 5-8.30 (Fri & Sat 6.30-10). Free House. **Beer** Broughton Greenmantle 80/-. Closed 25 & 26 Dec, 1 & 2 Jan. Riverside garden, outdoor eating.* MasterCard, **VISA**

> We do not accept free meals or hospitality – our inspectors pay their own bills and never book in the name of Egon Ronay's Guides.

ANSTRUTHER   Dreel Tavern   A

Tel 01333 310727   Map 3 D5
16 High Street Anstruther Fife KY10 3DL

Attractive, traditional three-storey 16th-century stone pub with a garden overlooking Dreel Burn. Real fires. *Open 11-midnight. At least two guest ales are always on tap and the pub holds an annual beer festival. Free House. **Beer** Caledonia 80/- Ale, Alloa Archibald, Arrol's 80/-, Orkney Dark Island, guest beers. Garden. No credit cards.*

APPLECROSS   Applecross Inn   FOOD

Tel 01520 744262   Map 2 A3   B&B
Shore Street Applecross Highland IV54 8LR

This most unpretentious of pubs has a superb setting looking out across Raasay to the Isle of Skye beyond, and is run by expatriate Yorkshire folk Berni and Judith Fish, with Berni looking after the bar while Judith makes good use of excellent seafood in the kitchen. From the blackboard menu the things to go for are the queen scallops cooked in wine and cream with mushrooms, squat lobster cocktail, dressed crab salad perhaps, or a half-pint of shell-on-prawn tails with dip. There are steak and chicken main courses, too, and a variety of snacks from speciality home-made soup and garlic mushrooms to venison- and veggie-burgers. Homely puds like rhubarb crumble and raspberry cranachan and a good cheeseboard follow. Five modest bedrooms are clean and cosy and share a shower room, a pine bathroom and memorable sea views. A peat fire warms the small lounge that is also used by the owners, and the large garden is right on the shore. No smoking in the bedrooms. Fifty malt whiskies on offer. *Open 11am-12pm (Sat till 11.30, Sun from 12.30), closed 2.30-5 Tue-Fri, Sun eve and Mon lunch in winter.* **Bar Food** *12-9.* **Beer** *McEwan's 80/-, Theakston's. Seashore garden.* **Accommodation** *5 bedrooms (none en suite), £45 (single £22.50). Children welcome overnight (under-5s stay free in parents' room, 5-14s £10). Accommodation closed 25 Dec and 1 Jan. MasterCard,* **VISA**

ARDENTINNY	Ardentinny Hotel	FOOD

Tel 01369 810209   Fax 01369 810241   Map 3 B5   **B&B**
Ardentinny Loch Long nr Dunoon Argyll & Bute PA23 8TR

Zzz... ☺

On the very edge of Loch Long, within the Argyll Forest park (where there are 50 miles of traffic-free walks), with views over the Loch to the moody 2,000ft Creachan Mor, plus an interesting, rambling garden – these are the hotel's main attraction. Hearty bar food is served in both pubby Viking and Harry Lauder bars and the Buttery; Clyde yachtsmen, who can tie up at the hotel's own jetty or free moorings, are regular visitors. A good choice of food might include salmon and broccoli fishcakes with dill mustard sauce as a snack or main meal and Musselburgh pie (big, chunky pieces of steak braised with ale and mussels). Smoked haddock rarebit, cod fillet and mash with piquant spinach sauce, and haggis with Drambuie en croute are other regular favourites, and Sunday brunch is a popular affair. The best bedrooms (all up a narrow, winding staircase) are designated 'Fyne' and attract a considerable supplement for their fine views, larger bathroom and remote-controlled television; accommodation is generally modest but comfortable, neat and bright; some rooms have showers only and others are large enough for families (further supplements are payable). A few steps lead directly down from the hotel to the pebbly shoreline; ask the way to the nearby sandy beach with its lovely rhododendron-lined setting. The hotel can arrange boat trips for pleasure or fishing, and mountain bikes can also be hired. *Bar open 11-11 (often later on Fri & Sat eve).* **Bar Food** *12-2.30, 6-9.30 (Sat 12-3.30, 6-9.30, Sun noon-9). Children's menu, children allowed in bar to eat. No real ale. Lochside garden, outdoor eating.* **Accommodation** *11 bedrooms, all en suite, £86 (single from £45), reductions Mar-mid May & Oct. Children welcome overnight, additional beds (£10) & cots supplied (£3); dogs £3. Hotel closed 1 Nov-15 Mar. Amex, Diners, MasterCard,* **VISA**

ARDFERN	Galley of Lorne Inn	FOOD

Tel 01852 500284   Map 3 B5   **B&B**
Ardfern by Lochgilphead Argyll & Bute PA31 8QN

Just off A816, north of Lochgilphead and just south of Arduaine on B8002, David and Susan Garland's inn is as close to a traditional pub as you'll find round these beautiful parts of Argyll; inside, there's a cosy, down-to-earth bar, an airy L-shaped dining-room with picture windows and straightforward bedroom accommodation (seven rooms, all now en suite). Typical offerings in the restaurant might include corn on the cob with lashings of melted butter, haggis, grilled wild salmon and breast of pheasant, all with decent accompanying vegetables. Passionfruit and peach sorbets, good bar snacks and charming service complete the dining picture. Summer days see the large garden coming into its own with its views over the quiet yacht moorings at the top of Loch Craignish and the surrounding hills. Home-made shortbread is offered with coffee between 9.30 and midday, after which McEwan's or a wee dram might be a more appropriate tipple. *Open 11-2.30, 5-11 (11-12 Fri & Sat, 12-12 Sun in summer); hours may vary in winter.* **Bar Food** *12-2, 6.30-9 (6.30-8 only in winter). Restaurant meals evenings only (booking required).* **Accommodation** *7 bedrooms, all en suite, £65/£70 (single £37.50). Garden. No real ale. No credit cards.*

We do not accept free meals or hospitality – our inspectors pay their own bills and never book in the name of Egon Ronay's Guides.

ARDUAINE   Loch Melfort Hotel, Chartroom Bar   FOOD

Tel 01852 200233   Fax 01852 299214   Map 3 B5
Arduaine by Oban Argyle & Bute PA34 4XG

Self-styled as "the finest location on the West Coast", Loch Melfort Hotel is indeed in a glorious setting, with a vast panorama of water and mountains unfolding past the field that sweeps down from the hotel to the water's edge. All the public rooms have picture windows to make the most of the wonderful views down the Sound of Jura. The user-friendly Chartroom, enlarged and smartened up this year, is not a pub at all but a glorious setting in which to enjoy some good bar food and a pint, and the picnic tables outside the bar are much in demand when the sum comes out. The snack menu encompasses both filled baguettes and steaks; blackboard specials offer a daily home-made soup, the ever-popular local langoustines and include as main dishes such tempting treats as seafood ravioli and 'wee haggis parcels' served with creamed leeks. There are home-made puds to follow. Yachtsmen can tie up at the hotel's own moorings, row in and walk up to the hotel through the front field (there are even showers provided for non-residents). Lawned gardens lead across to the Scottish National Trust's Arduaine Gardens, well worth a visit to see the rhododendrons, azaleas and magnolias in full bloom. *Open 10-11.* **Bar Food** *served till 9pm. No real ale. Garden, moorings. Closed Jan 5-Feb 25. Amex, MasterCard,* **VISA**

ARDVASAR   Ardvasar Hotel   B&B

Tel 01471 844223   Map 3 A4
Ardvasar Sleat Isle of Skye Highland IV45 8RS

Bill and Gretta Fowler's handsome, white-stone coaching inn dates back to the 18th century, and is a mile from the Armadale ferry (from Mallaig), in the wooded Sleat peninsula (often referred to as the Wild Garden of Skye); not far from the shore, it looks out across the Sound of Sleat to the mountains beyond. Improvement to the heating system now allows them to open in winter (except on Mondays) and, to aid this process, there are a cockle-warming two dozen malt whiskies available at the bar! The bar stays open all day in the summer months, with picnic tables in front at which to sit and take in the wonderful views. **Beer** *Scottish Cask Master, Morland Old Speckled Hen & regularly-changing guest beer. Patio/terrace.* **Accommodation** *10 rooms, all en suite, £70. Accommodation closed all Nov, 10 days Christmas. MasterCard,* **VISA**

BEAULY   Lovat Arms   B&B

Tel 01463 782313   Fax 01463 782862   Map 2 B3
High Street Beauly Highland IV4 7BS

The red-stone hotel in the centre of town is owned by the Fraser family whose clan tartan is much used in the good-quality soft furnishings of the public areas. These include a banquette-seated lounge bar and conservatory adjoining an entrance hall/reception that, with its real log fire and deep armchairs, also doubles up very well as a lounge. A different tartan features in each of the 22 bedrooms, of which the best, often with elaborate bedhead drapes or canopies, are on the first floor, but the three bedrooms above a noisy public bar are best avoided if you plan an early night. *Open 11-11 (Fri till 1, Sat till 11.45, Sun from 12.30). Free House.* **Beer** *regularly-changing guest beer.* **Accommodation** *22 rooms, all en suite, £60 (single £35). MasterCard,* **VISA**

BURRELTON   Burrelton Park Hotel   FOOD

Tel 01828 670206   Fax 01828 670676   Map 3 C5   **B&B**
High Street Burrelton by Cooper Perth & Kinross PH13 9NX

Nine miles north of Perth on the A94 this is a long, low roadside inn in typical Scottish vernacular style. It is as neat outside in its brown and cream livery as it is well-kept within. On completion of extensive renovations to the public areas (due as we went to press), the increased capacity of the lounge and bar has given rise to an all-new, all-day menu encompassing choices from haddock and chips to sirloin steak baguettes, with added vegetarian options and a section for children. While the restaurant retains its à la carte format, a daily menu-of-the-moment bridges the gap with fresh seafood dishes being a house speciality. Six spotless, low-ceilinged bedrooms have TV but no phones, and good en suite bathrooms, each with a thermostatically-controlled shower over the tub. Efficient double-glazing effectively cuts out the traffic noise. Note that credit cards are not accepted for bills of less than £20. New owners. *Open 11-11 (Fri & Sat till 12).* **Bar Food** *12-10.30 (Restaurant 6.30-10). Free House.* **Beer** *Theakston's, guest beer. Family room.* **Accommodation** *6 bedrooms, all en suite, £45 (single £30). Children welcome overnight, additional bed & cot available. Pub closed 1 Jan. MasterCard,* **VISA**

BUSTA	Busta House Hotel	FOOD

Tel 01806 522506   Fax 01806 522588   Map 2 D1   **B&B**
Busta Brae Shetland Islands ZE2 9QN

This 16th century former laird's home overlooking the sea is a tremendously civilised hotel in a wild place, simply furnished in Scottish rural style with four acres of walled garden and a private harbour too. Open to non-residents for good home-cooked bar lunches and suppers recent specials have included crabmeat, mushroom and coriander tagliatelle; turkey, spring onion and cranberry quiche and nut roast with spicy tomato sauce, followed by whisky and marmalade trifle and home-made orange and Cointreau ice cream. Raven Ale from 'nearby' Orkney and 136 malt whiskies on offer guarantee a loyal drinking fraternity. P&O ferries sail to the Shetland Islands from Aberdeen and holidays of the fly/sail and drive kind are readily arranged. *Open 12-2.30 (Sun from 12.30), 6-11 (Sun from 6.30).* **Bar Food** *12-2.30 (Sun from 12.30),6.30-9.30 (6.30-9 winter, except Fri & Sat).* **Beer** *Orkney Raven Ale. Garden, outdoor eating.* **Accommodation** *20 bedrooms, all en suite, £84 (single £63). Children welcome overnight (if sharing parents' room £10), additional bed and cot available. Bar and accommodation closed 22 Dec-3 Jan. Amex, Diners, MasterCard,* **VISA**.

CANONBIE	Riverside Inn	FOOD

Tel 013873 71512   Map 4 C2   **B&B**
Off A7 Canonbie Dumfries & Galloway DG14 OUX

This pristine white-painted Georgian country inn is in a quiet spot overlooking the River Esk, just over the Scottish border, some twelve miles from the top of the M6. Within, it's authentically rural rather than rustic in style, neat, clean and simple with a definite and individual charm. The carpeted bar has simple country chairs, some cushioned, some not, around sewing machine tables, and a stone fireplace and bar front; a few discreet decorations line the plain cream walls, framed fishing flies, the odd old cider jar, but there are otherwise few frills. The dining-room is similar, but with proper eating-height tables and chairs, and the small, cosy residents' lounge, which has the air of a private-house sitting-room, has a chintzy three-piece suite and a few other chairs arranged around a log-effect fire. Bar food takes particular care with first-rate fresh ingredients – local fish (some of it from the river only yards away), local suppliers, an increasing use of organic and farm produce, vegetables from their own garden, and a fine range of unpasteurised British cheeses. Hosts here since 1974, Robert and Susan Phillips share the cooking duties, producing as starters light, well-flavoured terrines and patés and intriguing soups (carrot and sage, for instance). Always strong on fresh fish, main courses offer skate wings with capers and black butter alongside proper fish and chips, baked free-range chicken Basque-style and vegetarian Homity Pie. Follow with deep lemon tart, spiced bread pudding or rhubarb and ginger fool. Bread comes from the renowned Village Bakery at Melmerby. There's also a daily-changing 5-course table d'hote restaurant menu (recommended in our *1997 Guide to·Hotels and Restaurants*). Bedrooms are the prettiest feature of the the inn, two of them with draped bedheads, another with a four-poster bed, and all individually styled with good-quality fabrics and thoughtful little extras, electric blankets among them. Bathrooms are spotless, with decent toiletries. Satisfying, hearty breakfasts. **Bar Food** *12-2 (except Sun), 7-9. Free House.* **Beer** *Yates, guest beers. Garden, outdoor eating, children's play area.* **Accommodation** *7 bedrooms, all en suite, £75 (single £55). Children welcome overnight (cot-age free if sharing parents' room). Pub and accommodation closed 2 weeks Feb & 2 weeks Nov, 26 Dec & 1/2 Jan. MasterCard,* **VISA**

CARBOST · Old Inn · B&B

Tel & Fax 01478 640205   Map 2 A3
Carbost Isle of Skye Highland IV47 8SR

On the shores of Loch Harport, and near the Talisker distillery, a charming chatty
little island cottage, popular as a walkers' base. Accommodation is offered in six
rooms, all en suite, although all but one have shower only. One family room has
a connecting bunk room for children, and all have colour TV but no phones.
Open 11-2.30 (Sun from 12.30), 5-12 (Sat to 11.30, Sun 6.30-11) and all day in summer.
No real ales. Family Room. Lochside patio/terrace, children's play area. **Accommodation** *6*
rooms £47, (single £23.50). Children welcome overnight (under-4s stay free in parents' room,
5-9s£7.50, 10-15s £12.50). MasterCard, **VISA**

CASTLECARY · Castlecary House Hotel · B&B

Tel 01324 840233   Fax 01324 841608   Map 3 C5
Castlecary Village by Cumbernauld North Lanarkshire G68 OHD

The original private house has been extended to incorporate a large lively bar with
fruit machines, a large selection of draught beers and a more peaceful, partitioned-off
'snug' with plush seating. Good modern bedrooms are mostly in a couple of 'cottage'
blocks set motel-style around the car park; comfortable beds have crisp cotton sheets
and feather pillows and all rooms have direct-dial phones, remote-control TV,
beverage tray, trouser press and fully-tiled bathroom (about half with tub and half with
shower). Four single rooms in the main building share a shower room and come at a
considerably reduced rate. Two flats have a double and a twin room each (£66 plus
£10 per extra adult). Four more rooms have recently been converted from an old
outbuilding. *Bar open 11-11 (Fri/Sat till 11.30, Sun 12.30-11). Free House.*
Beer *Belhaven, Bass, Caledonian Deuchars IPA, three guest beers.* **Accommodation** *48*
bedrooms, 44 en suite, £45 (Club £55, single £15). Children welcome overnight
(0-12 yrs free if sharing parents' room), additional bed (£10) & cot available. Diners,
MasterCard, **VISA**

CLACHAN SEIL · Tigh-an-Truish Inn · FOOD · B&B

Tel 01852 300242   Map 3 B5
Clachan Seil Seil by Oban Argyll & Bute PA34 4QZ

Miranda Brunner's fiercely traditional 18th century inn – right by the single-span
'Bridge over the Atlantic' at the top of Seil Sound – is not signposted from A816, so
check your map to find the turning on to B844 (towards Easdale, and on to the Isle
of Luing). Delightfully unchanged (and rather basic) within, there's a limited winter
menu (perhaps only soup and sandwiches, (lunchtime only), but in high-season bar
food with a strong fish bias takes centre stage, with locally smoked salmon, home-
made fish pie and squat lobster curry, followed by such home-made sweets as
chocolate biscuit cake and sticky toffee pudding. Bed and breakfast is available in two
good-sized bedrooms, one with bath, the other shower only, with breakfast very
much a self-service affair. The wonderful bridge is well worth a detour, particularly
when the delightful, rare purple flowers on it are in bloom (around the end of May
or early June). Incidentally, the name means 'house of the trousers' in Gaelic and
refers back to the 1745 Rebellion when soldiers were banned from wearing kilts on
duty. *Open 11-11 (Sun from 12.30), closed 2.30-5 in winter.* **Bar Food** *12-2.15, 6-8.30.*
Free House. **Beer** *McEwan's 80/-, guest ale. Garden, outdoor eating. Family Room.*
Accommodation *2 bedrooms, both en suite, £40 (single £25). Children welcome overnight,*
additional bed (£5). Accommodation closed Dec & Jan. No credit cards.

CLACHAN SEIL · Willowburn Hotel · FOOD · B&B

Tel 01852 300276   Map 3 B5
Clachan Seil Isle of Seil by Oban Argyll & Bute PA34 3TJ

Zzz...

A little further down the road from the 'Bridge over the Atlantic' (which dates
back to 1792) is this bungalow-style hotel with a pubby bar and lovely garden in
a picturesque setting with lawned gardens leading down to the shore of Seil Sound.
Willowburn is neither really a pub nor and inn but a small 60s-built hotel; there is,

however, a bar with pine ceiling, wood–burning stove and bar counter built of local slate (plus picture windows overlooking the water). Good bar snacks feature local seafood like squat lobsters with lemon mayonnaise dip and half-a-pint of prawns, along with smoky fish and leek pie, caramelised onion, mushroom and pepper flan, home-baked ham, Aberdeen Angus steaks and home-made puds such as chocolate fudge pudding and wholemeal cinnamon and apple crumble. A few tables outside on the lawn are popular when the weather allows. Both the comfortable residents' lounge and dining-room enjoy fine views across the sound, as do all but one of the neat, well-kept bedrooms with TV, tea-making kit and modern en-suite bathrooms (four with shower and WC only). *Open 12.30-2.30, 6-11.* **Bar Food** *12.30-2, 6-8.30. No real ale. Garden, outdoor eating.* **Accommodation** *6 bedrooms, all en suite, half-board terms only £88 (single £44). Hotel closed Nov-Easter (open for New Year). MasterCard,* **VISA**

CRAIL	Golf Hotel	B&B

Tel 01333 450206   Fax 01333 450795   Map 3 D5
4 High Street Crail Fife KY10 3TB

Reputed to be one of the oldest licensed inn in Scotland (dating from the 14th century), the neat old black and white inn in the centre of town has a choice of bars, one modestly comfortable in red plush, the other more characterful with exposed stone walls and beamed ceiling. Upstairs, five immaculate bedrooms have pretty duvets with matching curtains, pine furniture and neat en suite shower rooms with WC. All have remote-control TV and tea/coffee making facilities but no phones. A further TV with satellite channels is to be found in the comfortable and appealing residents' lounge. *Open 11-12 (Sun 12-12). No real ales.* **Accommodation** *5 bedrooms, all en suite, £48 (single £28). MasterCard,* **VISA**

CROMARTY	Royal Hotel	B&B

Tel & Fax 01381 600217   Map 2 C3
Marine Terrace Cromarty Highland IV11 8YN

Formed out of a row of 18th-century coastguards' cottages facing the Cromarty Firth, the black-and-white painted 'Royal' is a hotel of considerable charm. Except in the warmest of weather a real fire burns in the homely lounge off which a Lloyd-Loom-furnished sun lounge looks across the road to the water beyond. The lounge bar features armchairs along with banquettes, or you can challenge the locals to a game of pool or darts in the Public Bar. Immaculate, individually decorated bedrooms. each with a sea view, have traditional furniture and crisp pure cotton bedding. Twenty miles from Inverness but only ten yards from the beach and sea! *Bar open 11-12 (Fri till 1am). No real ale. Garden, childrens' play area. Family room.* **Accommodation** *10 bedrooms, 8 en suite, £55 (single £32). Amex, MasterCard,* **VISA**

DUNDEE	Mercantile Bar	A

Tel 01382 225500   Map 3 C5
100 Commercial Street Dundee City DD1 2AJ

🍺

Gerry Morrison's large reconstructed Victorian bar in an old converted haberdashery warehouse has over 500 photos and prints with a trading or drinking theme adorning the walls and over 200 malt whiskies and 30 draught beers on offer. A city-centre pub for city-centre people, the long opening hours and ever-modest prices help retain the Inn's popularity. *Open 11-11 (Thur-Sat till midnight, Sun 7-11 only). Free House.* **Beer** *McEwan's 80/-, Maclay's 80/-, Burton Ale, Belhaven St. Andrew's Ale. Pub closed Sun lunch, 25 Dec & 1 Jan. MasterCard,* **VISA**

Many **B&B** establishments offer reduced rates for weekend and out-of-season bookings. Always ask about special deals for longer stays. Beware half-board terms in inns where we do not recommend the **FOOD**.

DYSART   Old Rectory Inn   FOOD

Tel 01592 651211   Map 3 C5
West Quality Street Dysart Fife KY1 2TE

Just a few hundred yards off the main road from Kirkcaldy to Leven, in the pretty village of Dysart, is the imposing single-storey Rectory Inn, resplendent on its corner site perched above the fishing harbour, and with a delightful walled garden. Interior furnishings are a mixture of old solid wood tables and chairs and more modern upholstered bench seating at tables pre-set with mats and fresh flowers. An extensive menu is supplemented by daily specials listed on a blackboard in the main bar; at lunchtimes perhaps a Bloody Mary soup, seafood risotto and lasagne verdi, supplemented at night by some first-class fresh fish – three-fish mousse, salmon supreme with citrus sauce and king prawns Thermidor. Vegetarians are not left out; a choice of six dishes includes chunky vegetable curry and mushroom Stroganoff. Favourite bar sweets include chocolate cheesecake and sticky toffee pudding, and unlimited real coffee with cream comes as a real bonus. A whole Stilton is renewed each week and at least seven wines are served by the glass. *Open 12-3, 6.30-11.* *Bar Food 12-2 (Sun to 2.30). 6.30-9.30. Children over 8 allowed in the bar to eat. Free House. Beer McEwan's 80/-. Garden, outdoor eating. Pub closed Sun night & all Mon, 1 week mid-Jan, 2 weeks mid-Oct. Amex, MasterCard, VISA*

> We do not accept free meals or hospitality – our inspectors pay their own bills and **never** book in the name of Egon Ronay's Guides.

EDINBURGH   Doric Tavern Wine Bar & Bistro   FOOD

Tel 0131-225 1084   Map 3 C6
15-16 Market Street City of Edinburgh EH1 1DE

As suggested by its title, this is a multi-faceted operation with its spartan public bar, trendy students' venue at the back, a bistro-style eating area and upstairs wine bar. Food is available all day from a variety of menus which include daily fixed-price lunches and dinners and an à la carte. Simplest choices in the bar are burgers, kebabs and chili; from the Doric menu dishes of tagliatelle or penne with hazelnut and coriander pesto, artichoke and leek fricassee, fresh mussels with garlic and mint, steamed halibut with almonds and rib-eye steak with pepper sauce appeal to all tastes and pockets. Healthy eating, organic foods and the bare minimum of refined and factory products are promoted throughout. There's tremendous atmosphere in the evenings, with deep reds and blues and candlelight; a dozen wines are available by the small or large glass and eight real ales are on offer. *Open noon-1am (Fri & Sat from 10, Sun from 12.30). Bar Food 12-6.30 (Bistro till 10.30). Beer Caledonian Deuchar's IPA, McEwan's 80/-, Bass, Courage Directors, guest ales. Pub closed 25 & 26 Dec, 1 & 2 Jan. Amex, MasterCard, VISA*

EDINBURGH   Fishers   FOOD

Tel 0131-554 5666   Map 3 C6
1 The Shore Leith City of Edinburgh EH6 6QW

Fishers is an outstanding seafood speciality bar which serves full meals all day, noon till 10.30pm. It's located in a renovated corner building at the end of The Shore, at the foot of what looks like an ancient bell-tower or lighthouse. The bar area, in which you can also eat, groups high stools around higher-still tables; up a short flight of steps the main eating area features light-wood panelling with night-sky blue tables and chairs, windows half of frosted glass, half giving a view of the harbour and beyond, and all presided over from a great height by a bejewelled mermaid figure. The pricing structure and the variety of food on offer are admirably suited to most appetites and pockets, whether for serious eating or quick snacking. In addition to the photocopied/hand-written menu, a blackboard of daily specials offers a host of starters and main courses which should appeal to more than fish fans alone. Tomato and basil soup and game terrine provide alternative starters to the ubiquitous sardines, smokies and calamari, and there's the odd meat alternative (lamb's liver with onion gravy, say) to the turbot with pesto, prawns and capers, and sea trout with a strawberry and basil sauce that are star turns on the daily specials board. The Fishers' dedication to the very best seafood makes it a worthy 1997 Scotland Regional Winner of our Seafood Pub of the Year award. Salads are fresh and in plenty; choose your dressing from a piquant selection of different vinaigrettes (eg onion, hazelnut or raspberry) thoughtfully provided on each table. If any room remains, there are simple home-made fruit flans, pies and crumbles. Altogether excellent quality and value-for-money; booking essential. *Open 11am-1am. **Bar Food** 12-10.30. Free House. **Beer** regularly changing guest beers. Riverside, outdoor eating. Family room. Pub closed 25 Dec & 1 Jan. MasterCard, **VISA***

EDINBURGH   Tattler   FOOD

Tel 0131-5549999   Fax 0131 2265936   Map 3 C6
23 Commercial Street Leith City of Edinburgh EH6 6JA

To step into Tattler is to step several decades back into the subdued splendour of Scottish Victoriana – fringed table lamps, some of smoked glass, a bird cage in the window, a chaise longue by the bar and most charming of all, attentive and old-fashioned courtesy from the bar staff. The bar is popular itself – a gentlemanly local for unhurried chat – but most come to eat. Music is speakeasy 1920s, with live piano some evenings. The walls are adorned with humorous antique prints, and an intricately-carved dark wood fireplace with inset tiles completes the picture. Diners may choose to use the lounge, parlour, snug, restaurant or bar – it's one menu throughout and portions are generous. Blackboard specials changed daily start with crayfish bisque and deep-fried brie croquettes and follow with dishes like roast monkfish with vegetable ribbons, seared duck with pear and parsnip tatin and leek, mushroom and horseradish pie, with apple and ginger crumble, buttercream gateau and huge scoops of ice cream for dessert. This is truly first-class value for money; an opportunity to splurge without overspending epitomised by the full cooked breakfast served on Sunday from 11.30am. *Open 11-11 (Fri/Sat till 1am). **Bar Food** 12-2.30, 6-10 (Sat 12-11, Sun 11-10). Free House. **Beer** Tetley Bitter, Burton Ale, Arrols 80/-, guest beer. Family Room. Amex, Diners, MasterCard, **VISA***

EDINBURGH   Waterfront Wine Bar   FOOD

Tel 0131-554 7427   Map 3 C6
1c Dock Place Leith City of Edinburgh EH6 6LU

The Waterfront's plain, redbrick exterior gives little indication of what lies within – this is one of Edinburgh's favourite food and drink spots. There are about 30 wines served by the glass and over 150 on the wine list as well as unusual bottled beers. Through the first doorway is a low-ceilinged room lit by low lamps, with nautical maps and wine-crate panels doubling as wallpaper. Further back the conservatory is attractively overhung by a growing vine, and looks out over the water; beyond this a narrow pontoon seats a few summer tipplers. There are no fixed or printed menus, and the dishes of the day are listed on a blackboard. Start with chargrilled sardines with summer herbs or tongue timbale in Cumberland jelly; to follow, braised chicken legs stuffed with woodland mushrooms and kippered salmon fillet with lemon sauce typify the alternatives. A very reasonable set-price menu along the same lines might include duck liver terrine followed by venison haggis with neeps and olive oil mash. Book well in advance for a weekend evening, especially in the conservatory. *Open 12-11 (Fri & Sat till 12, Sun from 12.30). **Bar Food** 12-2.30 (Sat & Sun 12-3), 6-9.30 (Fri & Sat till 10). Children over 5 allowed in to eat. Free House. **Beer** Caledonian 80/- Ale & Deuchars IPA. Riverside pontoon, outdoor eating. Pub closed 25 & 26 Dec. MasterCard, **VISA***

> We endeavour to be as up-to-date as possible but inevitably some changes to landlords, chefs and other key staff occur after the Guide has gone to press.

ELIE   Ship Inn   FOOD

Tel 01333 330246   Map 3 C5
The Toft Elie Fife KY9 1DT

Part of a terrace of old cottages down by the harbour, the Ship has been a hostelry since 1838. The original bar still has wooden benches around the dark-painted, boarded walls, beamed ceiling and a back room with booth seating. There are two restaurant rooms with old dining tables, sturdy kitchen chairs and, on the first floor, a small balcony with coin-operated binoculars for scanning the harbour. The single menu, available throughout, features traditional home-made dishes such as garlic mushrooms and sweet herring salad to start, and seafood crepes, spicy fried chicken and steaks with haggis whisky sauce for main course. There are some fairly standard desserts, blackboard specials, Sunday roast and a children's menu. Cakes and biscuits are served with tea and coffee throughout the day. In July and August, tables on the sea wall opposite the Ship are served by an open-air barbecue. When the tide is out a vast expanse of sand is revealed where the Ship's own cricket team plays regular Sunday fixtures. *Open 11am–midnight (Fri & Sat till 1), Sun 12.30-11. **Bar Food** 12-2.30 (Sun 12.30-3), 6-9.30 (Sun till 9). Free House. **Beer** Belhaven 80/- Ale, Boddingtons, Theakston Best. Family Room. Pub closed 25 Dec. MasterCard,* **VISA**

FOCHABERS   Gordon Arms   B&B

Tel o1343 820508   Fax 01343 820300   Map 2 C3
High Street Fochabers Moray IV32 7DH

Antlers decorate the exterior of this former coaching inn standing alongside the A96 and a short walk away from the River Spey, while the public bar sports a variety of fishing bric-a-brac, including stuffed prize catches. Simple overnight accommodation is provided by 13 well-equipped bedrooms with Tvs, tea-makers, hair dryers and direct dialled telephones; these include both older rooms with large carpeted bathrooms and a number of smaller but quieter ones in the extension. *Open 11-11 (Fri & Sat till 12.30, Sun from 12). Free House. **Beer** Theakston's, guest beer. Garden. Family room. **Accommodation** 13 bedrooms, all en suite, £65 (single £45). Children welcome overnight (from £10), cot available. Amex, MasterCard,* **VISA**

GARVE   Inchbae Lodge   FOOD   B&B

Tel 01997 455269   Fax 01997 455207   Map 2 B3
Inchbae by Garve Ross-shire Highland IV23 2PH

Zzz... ☺

A few miles north of Garve on the A835 by the Blackwater river (on which the hotel has a mile of fishing rights), Inchbae is a former private hunting lodge with a very pubby bar that is popular with locals. The bar menu which can cope with most appetites, ranges from a good soup with home-baked bread and a large platter of West Coast mussels to Brie and broccoli filo bake, breaded pink trout with flaked almonds, champion haggis with neeps and tatties and scottish steaks with a choice of sauces. There's always a selection of home-made puds and children get their own special menu. Bedrooms, half in the original lodge and half in an adjacent red cedar chalet, have no TVs, radios or telephones to disturb the peace, and all but four have shower and WC only. Those in the main building are prettiest, with plum and pale green colour scheme, pine and country antique furniture; three rooms have an extra bed or more for family use; smokers are restricted to the chalet rooms. Two lounges, warmed by real fires in winter, are filled with a motley collection of sofas and easy chairs. Children are welcome, and a high-tea of children's favourites is served at 5pm in the bar before the grown-ups' dinner. The 30-seat, no-smoking dining-room (dinner only, 7.30-8.30pm) is also recommended in our *1997 Hotels & Restaurants Guide. Open 11-2.30, 5-10.30 (Sun 12.30-2.30, 6.30-10.30. **Bar Food** 12-2, 5-8.30, (Sun 12.30-2, 6.30-8.30). No real ales. **Accommodation** 12 rooms, all en suite, £64 (single £37). Children welcome overnight (under-18s stay free in parents' room). Garden, children's play area. Pub & Accommodation closed 25-30 Dec. MasterCard,* **VISA**

GIFFORD	**Tweeddale Arms**	FOOD

Tel 01620 810240   Fax 01620 810488   Map 3 D6   **B&B**
High Street Gifford East Lothian EH41 4QU

Probably the oldest building in the village, the black-and-white Tweedale Arms stands alongside a peaceful village green. The comfortable, mellow lounge features some old oil paintings while the bar has tapestry-style upholstery and baskets of dried flowers hanging from the old beams. The bar menu offers a good selection of carefully cooked dishes ranging from pickled herrings and crab with avocado among a dozen starters and main dishes such as Aberdeen Angus steaks, tagliatelle with mushroom stroganoff, curried lamb and smoked haddock with broccoli and cheese sauce. Good clean bedrooms have either light or darkwood freestanding furniture and modern en suite bathrooms; all have TV, direct-dial phone, trouser press and a tea/coffee making kit. Family-run in friendly fashion, the inn also has three family rooms. *Open 11-11 (Fri & Sat till 12).* **Bar Food** *12-2, 7-9. Free House.* **Beer** *Burton Ale, Morland Old Speckled Hen, Greenmantle, two guest beers. Garden, children's play area. Family room.* **Accommodation** *17 bedrooms, all en suite, £65 (single £47.50). Children welcome overnight (under-12s stay free in parents' room), additional bed & cot available.* MasterCard, **VISA**

GLASGOW	**Babbity Bowster**	FOOD

Tel 0141-522 5055   Fax 0141-552 7744   Map 3 B6
16/16 Blackfriars Street City of Glasgow G1 1PE

A renovated Robert Adam town house in the city's business district is the setting for the splendidly informal and convivial Babbity Bowster (named after a dance), which is not exactly a pub, rather a light and stylish ground floor cafe-bar, with a restaurant and hotel attached. There's an outdoor patio with a covered awning that is pulled back when the weather permits and in summer the barbecue dishes out spicy lamb burgers and brochettes such as chicken or swordfish in great numbers. Within, the daily specials encompass potato and leek soup, spicy chicken stovies, bean hot-pot, beef stroganoff and fresh fish from the markets; then round things off nicely with home-made granny-apple pie. On the first floor, the Schottische Restaurant (also named after a dance) provides lunch, light meals and supper. *Meals from 8am, bar open 11-12 (Sun from 12.30).* **Bar Food** *12-11. Free House.* **Beer** *Maclay's 70/-, 80/-, Kane's Amber Ale & Oat Malt Stout, guest beer. Patio/terrace, outdoor eating. Amex, MasterCard,* **VISA**

GLASGOW	**Upstairs at the Ubiquitous Chip**	FOOD

Tel 0141-334 5007   Map 3 B6
26 Ashton Lane Glasgow City of Glasgow G12 8SJ

The busy bar above this famous Glasgow restaurant near to the university remains famous, trendy and Bohemian. Eating here is largely a vehicle for some serious people-watching and supping from the fine wine list, but it's impressive bar food of a resolutely simple kind. Try vegetarian haggis with neeps and tatties either as a starter or main course; alternatively begin with a squid and mussel salad with tarragon vinaigrette and follow with chicken casserole or baked vegetable falafel with yoghurt and cucumber dressing. Some novel salads include fennel à la greque and good local cheeses include Mull of Kintyre truckle cheddar and Inverlochy goat's cheese. On Sundays, breakfast is served from 12.30pm. Furstenburg, the heady and delicious unpasteurised German lager served here, is to be treated with respect. *Open 11-11 (Fri & Sat till 12, Sun from 12.30).* **Bar Food** *12-11 (Sun from 12.30).* **Beer** *Caledonian 80/- Ale, Deuchar's IPA. Closed Dec 25 & Jan 1. Amex, Diners,* **VISA**

> We only recommend food (Bar Food) in those establishments highlighted with the **FOOD** symbol.

388   Scotland

GLENDEVON — Tormaukin Hotel — FOOD

Tel 01259 781252   Fax 01259 781526   Map 3 C5   B&B
Glendevon by Dollar Perth & Kinross FK14 7JY

Just south of Gleneagles on the A823, and surrounded by glorious hill country, this
ruggedly handsome old white-painted inn is in a remarkably peaceful spot. The warm
and welcoming interior consists of several interlinked rooms, all with lots of exposed
stone, rough whitewashed walls and ceiling beams. Old settles, upholstered stools and
roundback chairs surround heavy iron-legged tables, and a splendid open fire makes
the Tormaukin an ideal retreat from the chill Scottish winter. Food's a major
attraction, to the extent that the bar menu makes a plea for patience at busy times;
this printed list is supplemented by a daily specials board featuring fresh fish such as
langoustines with garlic dip and chargrilled Cajun spiced red fish. More predictably
the lunch and supper menu offers a tureen of fish broth, braised loin of pork, chicken
stir-fry and a lentil and vegetable curry. A roast is available on Sundays, Scottish
cheese is featured on the board and all the puddings, such as gooseberry pie and
banoffee cheesecake are home-made. Bedrooms are extremely comfortable and
appropriately styled in keeping with the inn's age; original features include yet more
exposed stone and a generous sprinkling of beams. Floral fabrics match with pretty
wallcoverings, furniture is pine and free-standing; nice local toiletries and plenty of
towels compensate for slightly cramped bathroom sizes. Four of the rooms in a
converted stable block are more contemporary in style, and all the bedrooms are
named after whiskies (a subtle inducement no doubt to a night-cap in the bar!).
Service is admirably efficient and friendly. *Open 11-11, Sun from 12. Bar Food 12-1,
5.30-9.30 (Sun 12-9.30). Free House. Beer Burton Ale, Harviestoun Original 80/-, two
guest beers. Patio, outdoor eating. Accommodation 10 bedrooms, all en suite (8 with baths,
2 with showers), £72 (single £50). Children welcome overnight (rate depends on age),
additional bed & cot available. Hotel closed 2nd & 3rd weeks Jan. No dogs. Amex, Diners,
MasterCard, VISA*

GLENELG — Glenelg Inn — FOOD

Tel & Fax 01599 522273   Map 3 B4   B&B
Glenelg by Kyle of Lochalsh Highland IV40 8JR

 Zzz...

With a fine location on the shore of Glenelg Bay, Christopher Main's sympathetically
refurbished inn combines a rustic bar with civilised restaurant and, created out of the
old stable block, six spacious bedrooms which have been individually decorated and
furnished with antiques. The bar menu, for residents only on Sunday, offers dishes as
varied as venison liver pate, local seafood pie, hill-bred lamb cutlets and sticky toffee
pudding, with the addition of soups, sandwiches and pastries at lunchtime only. In the
non-smoking restaurant, the fixed-price dinner menu (served from 7.30 to 9pm) is
recommended in our *1997 Hotels & Restaurants Guide*. After dinner, residents repair to
the "Morning Room" where the atmosphere lends itself to conviviality; Victorian
paintings and photos. a green leather Chesterfield, stag's head and various antiques and
objects d'art make a comfortable setting. A large walled and fenced in garden
overlooks the sea and is safe for children. *Open 12-2.30, 5-11. Bar Food (no food Nov-
Mar) 12-2.30, 7-9. Garden. No real ales. Accommodation 6 bedrooms, all en suite, £80.
Children welcome overnight (under-3s stay free in parents' room), additional bed & cot
available. No dogs. Check-in by arrangement. Pub closed Sun & lunchtimes Nov-Mar,
Accommodation closed Nov-Mar. No credit cards.*

GLENFARG — Bein Inn — FOOD

Tel 01577 830211   Map 3 C5   B&B
Glenfarg Perth & Kinross PH2 9PY

Standing by the river in the glorious Glen of Farg, this former drovers' inn is five
minutes' drive from junction 9 of the M90, by the A912 south of Perth. Inside there
are old, well-worn wing chairs aplenty and a grandfather clock in one corner, while in
the bar the walls are cluttered with clan coat of arms plaques, a large map of Scotland,
rugby cartoons, golf prints and a few pieces of horse tack. On the food side there's

a daily table d'hote and a seafood and shellfish à la carte menu, while in the bar main courses such as steak and ale pie, chicken suédoise and pizza marinara are pretty run-of-the-mill. In addition a new chargrill steakhouse and tapas bar has been opened downstairs. Good overnight accommodation is provided in 13 bedrooms, 11 of them housed in an extension, the upper floors of which connect with the main building via a corridor. Ground floor rooms are the largest, upper rooms pretty compact. All are furnished in unpretentious fashion with fitted units, matching curtains and duvets, with fully-tiled bathrooms with showers over the bath. The remaining two rooms are in the main house, neither of them en suite, but sharing a well-maintained bathroom. The area is thick with golf courses, hence the Bein is popular with golfers. *Open 11-11 (Sun from 12.30). Bar Food 12-2, 5-9. Free House. Beer Belhaven, Sandy Hunter's Traditional Ale. Family Room. Accommodation 13 bedrooms, 11 en suite, £56 (single £38). Children welcome overnight (under-2s stay free), additional bed and cot available. MasterCard, VISA*

GREENLAW — Castle Inn — B&B

Tel 01361 810217   Fax 01361 810500   Map 3 D6
Greenlaw Scottish Borders TD10 6UR

The handsome Georgian Castle Inn is the sort of place you could take a variety of people to and feel confident that they would find something to their taste. The Mirror Room, where drinking and dining take place, has a large mirror above a marble fireplace transforming what would otherwise be a hall into a splendid room, with a comfortable sitting area by the fireplace and elegant Georgian windows through which there's a view to well-kept gardens. Family facilities are excellent, with high-chairs, baby foods, a children's menu served throughout the day, books in the library and cheerful, tolerant staff. Of the bedrooms, including two with plenty of family accommodation, only two have en suite bathrooms, the other four sharing two baths and a shower room. *Open 11-11 (Fri & Sat till 11.30, Sun from 12). Free House. Beer Caledonian 80/- Ale, guest beer. Garden. Family Room. Accommodation 6 bedrooms, 2 en suite, £50 (single £27.50). Children welcome overnight (free in parents' room, family room £60), additional bed and cot available. Amex, Diners, MasterCard, VISA*

INNERLEITHEN — Traquair Arms — FOOD

Tel 01896 830229   Fax 01896 830260   Map 4 F3   B&B
Traquair Road Innerleithen Scottish Borders EH44 6PD

Five minutes' walk from the River Tweed, the Traquair Arms is a handsome stone building on the road leading to St. Mary's Loch; incidentally, it's a delightful journey across country roads to one of the most picturesque parts of the Borders. A well-stocked bar features the Traquair's own Bear Ale on tap with a teddy bear-clad pump. The choice of dining areas including the garden, weather permitting, and a wide choice of freshly prepared meals served all day, is typical of the Traquair Arms' admirable flexibility, which also runs to breakfast for non-residents, morning coffee, afternoon tea and high tea. A variety of omelettes and salads is served in the bar and hot dishes include Finnan Savoury (smoked haddock in cheese, onion and cream sauce), Traquair steak pie (cooked in home-brewed ale), and at least three vegetarian dishes. One benefit of dining in the bar is that the glass doors lead off into the garden, which is enclosed and safe for youngsters to let off steam. Service is genuine and informal, the atmosphere convivial and children are positively welcomed. The smart, well-kept bedrooms (three are singles) have en suite facilities, colour TVs and phones; particularly recommended is the handsome Scottish breakfast complete with superb kippers. Traquair House next door is well worth a visit – it's a romantic old house with pretty grounds and contains an old brewhouse; the front gates of Traquair are firmly shut and will remain so until a Stuart returns to the throne of Scotland. *Open 11-12. Bar Food 12-9. Free House. Beer Traquair Bear Ale, Broughton Greenmantle Ale, occasional guest beers. Garden, outdoor eating. Accommodation 10 bedrooms, all en suite, £64 (single £42). Children welcome overnight (0-5s free, 6-12s 50% adult rate in parents' room), additional bed & cot available. Pub closed 2 days Christmas. Amex, MasterCard, VISA*

KENMORE   Kenmore Hotel   B&B

Tel 01887 830205   Fax 01887 830262   Map 3 C5
Kenmore by Aberfeldy Perth & Kinross PH15 2NU

Zzz...

The Kenmore, dating from 1572, claims to be Scotland's oldest inn and stands in a
lovely Perthshire village at the east end of Loch Tay on the A827. The Poet's Parlour
bar, devoted to Burns, is cosy with its green tartan seats; Archie's Bar is simpler, with
glorious views of the river. Bedrooms, 14 in a Victorian gatehouse opposite, vary
considerably in decor and furnishings with everything from melamine to antiques.
Guests have concessionary use of the swimming pool and leisure facilities at the
nearby Kenmore Club; Kenmore itself attracts both golf enthusiasts and fishermen;
they have 3 miles of private beats on the River Tay. *Open 11-11. Riverside garden.*
Family room. No real ales. **Accommodation** *39 bedrooms, all en suite, £97 (single £60).*
Children welcome overnight. Amex, MasterCard, **VISA**

KILBERRY   Kilberry Inn   ★   FOOD

Tel & Fax 01880 770223   Map 3 A6   **B&B**
Kilberry by Tarbert Argyll & Bute PA29 6YD

Zzz... 🍴

An invigorating 16 mile drive down a winding, single-track road with superb views
will bring you to this single storey white cottage located half a mile from the glorious
coastline. John and Kath Leadbeater, English chef-proprietors, are vigorously
interested in good food and justifiably proud of their achievements here, in an out of
the way spot where the vegetables come via van and taxi, and fresh fish is strangely
hard to get. It's very much a dining pub, though locals and others are equally
welcome to drop in for a drink; the building was originally a crofting house, and the
snugly comfortable little bar, with a peat fire at one end, a wood-burning stove at the
other, still has and unpretentious rural style. Leading off at the left, the brighter,
plainer dining and family room has good sized pine dining tables. The daily
blackboard-listed short menu (perhaps only four or five main courses at lunchtime) is
cheerfully annotated. Typical dishes might include fresh tomatoes stuffed with "locally
caught haggis", a hearty country sausage pie with fresh salad or a fish pie of local
salmon; at night a few fancier dishes are also added, perhaps chunks of rump steak
cooked in Theakston's Old Peculier Ale or prime pork fillet cooked in cider with
apples. Kath has a famously light hand and the pastry is superb; she also makes the
bread as well as a selection of over 25 pickles, jams and chutneys on sale at the bar.
Whatever you do, make sure you leave room for one of Kath's delicious fruit pies,
which are laid out on the counter as soon as they come out of the oven. Equally
scrumptious are the bread-and-butter pudding, fresh lemon cream, grapefruit
cheesecake and chocolate fudge. Accommodation is offered in two smart en suite
bedrooms (one double, one twin (£55 double, £34.50 single), no smoking, breakfast
served 8-9am, no food Sundays apart from breakfast. Note that the pub never opens
on Sundays. *Open 11-2.30, 5-11. Bar Food 12.15-2, 6.30-9. No real ales. Family room*
(no smoking). Inn closed Sun. **Accommodation** *closed mid Oct-Easter. MasterCard,* **VISA**

> We do not accept free meals or hospitality – our inspectors pay their own bills
> and **never** book in the name of Egon Ronay's Guides.

KILMAHOG   Lade Inn   FOOD

Tel 01877 330152   Fax 01877 331039   Map 3 B5
Kilmahog by Callander Perth & Kinross FK17 8HD

Standing 200 yards back from the River Teith, the stone-built Lade Inn is part of the
surrounding Leny Estate owned by the Roebuck family. One bar to the left of the
entrance hall has panelling, pine tables and chairs; there's another bar to the right. The
walls are mainly exposed stone and beams; floors are carpeted throughout, while prints
and whisky boxes adorn the walls; the whole effect is clean, fresh and spacious. The
food operation now has a restaurant à la carte and the "Wayside Feast" bar menu,

supplemented by fresh West Coast fish regularly featured on the specials board. A daily selection of fresh vegetables accompanies main courses such as shoulder of Highland lamb, Scottish seafood vol-au-vent and local venison sausages in onion gravy. Several menu items come in small portions for children, with home-made fish fingers also held in reserve; high-chairs are available. The non-smoking dining area leads out into the garden; sandwiches available at lunchtime only. *Open 11-11 (Sun from 12.30), closed 3-5.30 in winter. Bar Food 12-2.30 (Sun from 12.30), 5.30-9.15. Free House. Beer Greenmantle, Morland Old Speckled Hen and guest ales. Garden, outdoor eating. Family Room. MasterCard, VISA*

KINCARDINE O'NEIL   Gordon Arms Hotel   FOOD

Tel 013398 84236   Map 3 D4   **B&B**
North Deeside Road Kincardine O'Neil Aberdeenshire AB34 5AA

An early 19th century coaching inn of sombre grey stone, the Gordon Arms stands alongside the busy A93, almost opposite the derelict 13th century village church. The main bar area is spacious and sparsely furnished; a large rough stone fireplace is decorated with old cider jars, and the walls above hung with a couple of fishing rods (this is a rich fishing area); there's a piano, splendid antique sideboard and a warm informal atmosphere. Bar menus which at lunchtime include daily roasts of beef and chicken in large or small portions, filled jacket potatoes and burgers extend in the evening to encompass pork cutlets, beef steak pie and 'vegetarian chilli con carne'(!). They also do a very popular Scottish high tea, in which toast and tea, scones and cakes are included in the price of a main course; the bread, too, is baked on the premises. The seven bedrooms are comfortable and unfussy. Care has been taken to keep decor and furnishings in keeping with the building's age, and all are of useful size, with extra beds for family use in three of them. Four of the en suite rooms have rather compact shower rooms, and two have slightly larger bath/shower. *Open 11.30-11 (Thu-Sun till 12). Bar Food 12-2, 5-9. Free House. Beer Courage, guest beer. Accommodation 7 bedrooms, 6 en suite, £45 (single £30). Children welcome over night (under-5s stay free in parents' room), additional bed (from £5) & cot available. Accommodation closed 25/26 Dec & Jan 1. Amex, MasterCard, VISA*

KIPPEN   Cross Keys   FOOD

Tel 01786 870293   Map 3 C5   **B&B**
Main Street Kippen Stirling FK8 3DN

☺

A simple welcoming Scottish pub with rooms, set in a pleasant rural village not far from Stirling. The locals' public bar is large and basic, a smaller, long and narrow lounge is where most of the food is served, and an adjoining family room has high-chairs primed and ready for use. Bar food, chosen from a standard printed menu, enhanced by daily specials, includes the ever-popular "humble haddie" pancakes (as a starter or main course) and the likes of sweetcorn fritters with chilli dip, Kashmiri chicken Korma, poached salmon with lime and ginger sauce and a home-made Clootie Dumpling to finish. Most of the produce is from local suppliers and Kippen's bakery supplies the bread. The best bedrooms under the eaves have sloping ceilings and fine views, with the usual tea and coffee kits, wash handbasins and good quality towels. Breakfasts served on linen-laid tables in the restaurant are hearty, traditional fry-ups (but not too greasy) and service is pleasant and helpful. There's a beer garden, with a children's play area, at the rear with access from both the public and lounge bars. *Open 12-2.30 (Sun from 12.30), 5.30-11 (Fri & Sat till 12). Bar Food 12-2 (Sun from 12.30), 5.30-9.30. Free House. Beer Broughton Greenmantle Ale, Younger's No. 3. Garden, play area, outdoor eating. Family room. Accommodation 3 bedrooms (2 twins, 1 single), sharing a bathroom, £39 (single £19.50). Children welcome overnight (under-5s stay free in parents' room). Pub closed 1 Jan. MasterCard, VISA*

We endeavour to be as up-to-date as possible but inevitably some changes to
landlords, chefs and other key staff occur after the Guide
has gone to press.

KIRKCALDY   Hoffmans   ★   FOOD

Tel 01592 204584   Map 3 C5
435 High Street Kirkcaldy Fife KY1 2SG

Situated to the east of the town centre (don't be fooled by the High Street address),
this is an unlikely-looking venue for a pub serving imaginative food, but first
impressions can deceive. Converted by owners Paul and Vince Hoffman with subtly
toned wall-coverings, brown-upholstered bench seating, polished tables, a large central
ceiling fan, angled mirrors and fake greenery, it's smart and sophisticated within, and
so popular that booking is advised for lunch as well as dinner. Local suppliers are listed
at the front of the menu which is handwritten and changes daily; often it's not even
decided on until just before opening-time, when suppliers and fishmongers have been
visited and produce assessed. Fish is a particular interest of Vince's, from traditional
deep-fried haddock to seafood and mushroom ragout; alongside such dishes as pan-
fried liver and bacon and Chinese-style pork with noodles, the under-£5 lunchtime
price remains remarkable value. In the evening the room is partitioned, half the space
reserved for drinkers, the other run as an à la carte bistro, where tables are laid,
candles lit and waitresses serve. Dishes are slightly more elaborate but no less value
for money; spicy vegetable filo parcels, fresh halibut glazed with chili and lime and
Dundee Bonnet – home-made by Vince's wife, Jan. Capable service is also genuinely
friendly thanks to the Hoffman teamwork. It's not a drinkers' pub and children are
encouraged – the idea being to "try to wean them into using pubs for the right
reasons". High-chairs and "portions of proper food" are available. *Open 11am-
midnight.* **Bar Food** *12-2, 7-10. Free House.* **Beer** *McEwan's 80/-, guest beer.
Pub closed all Sun. No credit cards.*

KIRKCUDBRIGHT   Selkirk Arms Hotel   FOOD

Tel 01557 330402   Fax 01557 331639   Map 4 B3   **B&B**
Old High Street Kirkcudbright Dumfries & Galloway DG6 4JG

The Selkirk Grace: "Some hae meat and canna eat; and some would eat that want it;
but we hae meat and we can eat; and sae the Lord be thankit", was reputedly written
here by Robert Burns in 1794. Today he'd find a new lounge-bar/bistro, part of the
ambitious extensions made by owners John and Susan Morris which have included an
additional bar and restaurant. The largely unchanged menu still features favourites like
smoked trout and melon salad, haggis, neeps and tatties, salmon steak with lemon
butter and grilled lamb cutlets with fresh mint sauce. Baked potatoes and open
sandwiches are included at lunchtime, and both table d'hote and à la carte menus in
the restaurant. Small children have their own menu available in the lounge bar until
8pm. The majority of the well-kept bedrooms have light oak fitted furniture; all have
TVs, direct-dial phones, hairdryers, beverage trays and modern bathrooms. There's
also a particularly attractive, sheltered garden with tables for summer eating. *Open 11-
12 (Sun from 12).* **Bar Food** *12-2, 6-930.* **Beer** *Bass, Tennents White Thistle and guest
beers. Garden, outdoor eating.* **Accommodation** *16 bedrooms, all en suite, £70 (single from
£47). Children welcome overnight (under-5s stay free in parents' room), additional bed & cot
available. Amex, Diners, MasterCard,* **VISA**

> We do not accept free meals or hospitality – our inspectors pay their own bills
> and **never** book in the name of Egon Ronay's Guides.

KIRKTON OF GLANISLA   Glenisla Hotel   FOOD

Tel & Fax 01575 582223   Map 3 C4
Kirkton of Glenisla nr Alyth Angus PH11 8PH

Simon and Lyndy Blake extend a traditional warm welcome to their 300-year-old
coaching inn set high up in Glenisla, one of the "Angus Glens", and dating back to
the days before the Jacobite rebellion; even in summer, on chilly days a real fire
smoulders in the bar. At lunchtime the daily-changing menu offers favourites like

haddock and chips, ploughman's platters, Aberdeen Angus steaks, macaroni cheese and Cumberland sausage. King Orkney scallops are an ever-popular starter at dinner, with main courses such as Glenisla venison and apricot casserole, grilled Esk salmon and mushroom and artichoke crepes, and sticky toffee pudding to follow. Afternoons bring cream teas – scones from the oven with home-made jam, and children's high tea at 5.30. *Open 11-2.30, 6-11 (Sat 11-11, Sun 12-10.30).* **Bar Food** *12.30-2.30, 6.30-8.45 (Sat till 9, Sun till 8).* **Beer** *Theakston's Best, McEwan's 80/-, Boddingtons. Garden, outdoor eating. Family room. The hotel has 6 en suite bedrooms (Double £65, single £32.50) and under-2s are accommodated free. Pub closed 25 & 26 Dec.* MasterCard, **VISA**

KYLESKU   Kylesku Hotel   FOOD

Tel 01971 502231   Fax 01971 502313   Map 2 B2   **B&B**
Kylesku Highland IV27 4HW

 Zzz...

Bypassed by the new bridge over Loch Glencoul in the early 80s, the modest Kulesku Hotel enjoys a glorious location down by the old ferry slipway where boats land the local seafood that forms the backbone of the blackboard menu: mussels baked in garlic, scallops, grilled salmon, fresh Lochinver haddock, langoustines grilled in their shells and served with a spicy mayonnaise dip and locally smoked salmon. Other items include home-made terrines and omelettes; chef/patron Marcel Klein adds a nightly table d'hote with similarly seafood bias. The hotel does boat trips to the Eas Coul Aulin, Britain's highest waterfall. One extra comfortable bedroom has recently been added and all are now en suite; accommodation is normally not available from end Oct-mid March. *Open 10-11.* **Bar Food** *11.30-9.30 (full meals 12-2.30, 6.30-9.30). No real ales. Garden, outdoor eating, barbecues. Family room.* **Accommodation** *8 bedrooms, all en suite, £55 (single £30). Children welcome overnight (under-5s stay free in parents' room).* MasterCard, **VISA**

LOCH ECK   Coylet Inn   FOOD

Tel & Fax 01369 840426   Map 3 B5   **B&B**
Loch Eck nr Kilmun Argyll & Bute PA23 8SG

Owner Richard Addis has been here 25 years now, and thankfully little has changed in that time least of all the really special setting – just the west coast road to Dunoon, shrouded in trees, separates the pretty white building from the glorious beauty of Loch Eck and the hills beyond. Not another house can be seen in any direction; be early for a window seat in the bar or dining-room. Inside the public bar is handsome and cosy, the hall is an attractively simple little dining bar, where families (even tiny babies) are welcome, and in the dining-room proper are half a dozen tables (one large group size, in the prize window spot), wheelback chairs and a piano. The food is a mix of standard bar menu stuff, sandwiches (even in the evening) and ploughman's platters to vast, well-cooked platefuls of haddock and chips, or sizzling steaks; but it's worth choosing from the specials board – a twice-daily changing short blackboard list. It might typically feature home-made liver pate and Scotch broth, local game in season, steak and kidney pie, salmon fishcakes, grilled local salmon or trout at lunchtime. In the evening, the board may feature mushrooms au gratin, venison collops in port and red wine sauce and langoustine risotto of tender, fresh Loch Eck langoustines in garlic, cream wine and herb sauce. Vegetables are also exceptional – crisp mangetout, perfect new potatoes and tender carrots all included in the main-course price. Puddings (all home-made) come in hefty portions; chocolate roulade, pineapple cheesecake or a real apple pie are typical of the choice. Upstairs are three tiny bedrooms which offer simple comfort; all have sash windows with views over the Loch and pretty cottagey print paper and fabrics. The twin is a bit bigger than the two doubles, while the shared bathroom, a very attractive, immaculately clean, carpeted and pine-panelled room, is bigger than any of them. Breakfasts are ungreasy and commendably accommodating of personal preference, and the service is genuine and friendly from both the resident owners and their few, able staff. Lochside garden. *Open 11-2.30 (Sun from 12.30), 5-11 (Fri & Sat till 12, Sun from 6.30).* **Bar Food** *12-2, (Sun from 12.30), 5.30-9.30 (Sun 7-9). Free House.* **Beer** *Younger's No.3, McEwan's 80/-, Caledonian Deuchar's IPA. Garden, outdoor eating. Family room.* **Accommodation** *3 bedrooms, sharing facilities, £35 (single £17.50). Children welcome overnight. Check-in by arrangement. No dogs.* MasterCard, **VISA**

MARKINCH — Town House Hotel — FOOD

Tel 01592 758459   Fax 01592 741 238   Map 3 C5   **B&B**
High Street Markinch Fife KY7 6DQ

Framed music hall song-sheets and old photographs of the locals and the locality grace
the watered silk-effect walls of the plush bar/lounge at this town centre inn which is
very much designed for eating. Favourites such as smoked haggis with whisky cream,
salmon and cauliflower crumble and gammon steak pizzaiola vie for prominence
alongside an Indian Balti curry and tagliatelle carbonara on lunch and supper menus
of somewhat confused identity. The supper seafood specialities may be the better bet;
mussel, prawn and leek stew, seafood au gratin and Finnan haddie topped with a
poached egg show reliable soundness in their execution. At weekends high teas start at
4pm with plenty for youngsters and waitress service. Four bright, well-kept bedrooms
offer TV and tea/coffee making facilities plus little extras like cotton wool balls; three
have en suite bathrooms, the other a private shower room with WC. *Open 12-2.30,
6-11 (Sat & Sun from 4). Bar Food 12-2, 6-9, (Sat & Sun from 4). No real ales.*
Accommodation *4 bedrooms, 3 en suite, £50 (single £25). Children welcome overnight
(under-5s free). Check-in by arrangement. Pub closed 1-7 Jan. Amex, Diners, MasterCard,*
VISA

MELROSE — Burts Hotel — FOOD

Tel 01896 822285   Fax 01896 822870   Map 4 C1   **B&B**
Market Square Melrose Scottish Borders TD6 9PN

Located 200 yards from the River Tweed is the imposing 18th century inn at the
heart of town, run by the Hendersons since 1970. Bar food shows an appetising
balance of the comfortingly traditional and modern aspirational. On the weekly lunch
menu might be pan-fried liver with lime, orange and grapefruit fillets or vegetable
patties in a tikka and taco crumb with cucumber yoghurt, while at supper-time there
are always char-grilled steaks, fried haddock fillets and home-baked sugar ham. Good
Scottish produce is featured on two table d'hote menus in the restaurant, and Sunday
lunch is always a roast. The bedrooms are light, contemporary and in pristine order;
five have just shower/WC. Over 40 malt whiskies, eight wines by the glass.
Bar Food *12-2, 6-9.30. Free House.* ***Beer*** *Belhaven 80/- Ale, Courage Directors, guest beer.
Garden, outdoor eating.* ***Accommodation*** *21 bedrooms, all en suite, £78 (single £45).
Children welcome overnight (under-6s stay free in parents' room). Pub closed 25 & 26 Dec.
Amex, Diners, MasterCard,* ***VISA***

MOFFAT — Black Bull — B&B

Tel 01683 220206   Fax 01683 220483   Map 4 C2
Churchgate Moffat Dumfries & Galloway DG10 8EG

Though much-modernised these days, this 16th century street-side local was
a favourite haunt of Robert Burns who is duly commemorated by a newly-unveiled
replica of his hand-etched window of c1790. Of the eight bedrooms, four look onto
the courtyard and four onto the churchyard opposite; each has a different colour
scheme and is fully equipped with TV, telephone and tea/coffee making facilities.
The family room, children's menu, beer garden and nearby duck pond make this a
popular summer haunt for holidaymakers. *Open 11-11 (Fri & Sat till 12, Sun 12.30-
11).* ***Beer*** *Theakston Best, McEwan's 80/-, two weekly-changing guest beers, Garden. Family
room.* ***Accommodation*** *8 bedrooms, 6 en suite, from £45 (single £29, family room £60).
Children welcome overnight (under-14s stay free in parents' room), additional bed & cot
available. No dogs. MasterCard,* ***VISA***

We endeavour to be as up-to-date as possible but inevitably some changes to
landlords, chefs and other key staff occur after the Guide
has gone to press.

MONYMUSK	**Grant Arms Hotel**	FOOD

Tel 01467 651226   Fax 01467 651494   Map 3 D4   **B&B**
The Square Monymusk nr Inverurie Aberdeenshire AB51 7HJ

With 6,000 acres of rough and driven shooting and 10 miles of salmon and trout fishing on the river Don, this is very much a sporting inn as the decor of the panelled bar – antlers, stag's head, stuffed birds and odd fishing rods – confirms. A typically solid, unspectacular 18th-century Scottish inn on the village green, the bedrooms are clean and bright if not luxurious. All have radio alarms, telephones and tea/coffee making facilities but no televisions (there is one in the residents' lounge). The bar menu offers something for most tastes – fresh oysters, lobster bisque, noisettes of spring lamb with rosemary and Arran mustard, chargrilled rainbow trout and a choice of steaks. *Open 11-2.30, 5-11, (Sat 11-11.30, Sun 12-11.30). Bar Food 12-2 (Sun from 12.30), 6.30-8.45 (Fri & Sat till 9.45, Sun from 6). Free House. Beer Scottish & Newcastle 80/-, two guest beers. Garden, outdoor eating, children's play area. Family room. Accommodation 16 bedrooms, 8 en suite, £62 (single £43). Children welcome overnight (0-2s stay free). Amex, MasterCard, VISA*

NETHERLEY	**Lairhillock Inn**	FOOD

Tel 01569 730001   Fax 01569 731175   Map 3 D4
Netherley Stonehaven Aberdeenshire AB3 2QS

Standing alone surrounded by fields, the Lairhillock is easily spotted from the B979; the closest major village is Peterculter, some four miles to the north and Netherley's a mile to the south. Formerly a farmhouse, the original building is 17th century and the interior is full of old rustic atmosphere. The public bar, in the oldest part, is by far the most characterful room, with its exposed stone, panelling, open fire, old settles and bench seating, every kind of horse tack, polished brasses and numerous other bits and pieces. The menu, changing daily, can be pretty polyglot with items such as gambas creole, crispinelli de spinato and crepes fruits de mer offered as starters, and as main courses chicken écossais or pork viennoise as alternatives to the venison escalopes, mixed grills and Aberdeen Angus steaks. The hugely popular sticky toffee pudding and Clootie Dumpling form the foundations of the dessert menu, with daily variations displayed on a blackboard. Across from the main building, in the old stables, is the evening restaurant which also serves traditional roasts on a Sunday. A conservatory with panoramic views, furnished with Lloyd Loom tables and chairs, provides an ideal room for families to eat in, with friendly, informal service. *Open 11-2.30, 5-11, (Fri & Sat till 12). Bar Food 12-2, 6-9.30 (Fri & Sat till 10). Free House. Beer Courage Directors, Thwaites Craftsman, McEwan's 80/-, Boddingtons, Flowers, guest beers. Patio & terrace, outdoor eating. Amex, Diners, MasterCard, VISA*

NEW ABBEY	**Criffel Inn**	B&B

Tel 01387 850305   Map 4 B2
The Square New Abbey Dumfries & Galloway DG2 8BX

Jim and Ann McAlister now run the Criffel; it's a solid Victorian place where things don't change much from year to year, and the basic philosophy remains unaltered. Upstairs, the residents' lounge has a domestic feel, and bedrooms with wood-effect melamine fitted furniture go in for a medley of floral patterns; only three currently have en suite showers but are being updated. Two bedrooms are of family size and there's one well-kept shared bathroom. *Open 12-2.30, 5.30-11 (Fri & Sat till 12). No real ales. Accommodation 5 bedrooms, 3 en suite, £44 (single £19). Children welcome overnight (under-3s stay free in parents' room, 6-12s half price), additional bed & cot available. MasterCard, VISA*

NEWTON STEWART — Creebridge House Hotel — FOOD

Tel 01671 402121   Fax 01671 403258   Map 4 A2   **B&B**
Minnigaff Newton Stewart Dumfries & Galloway DG8 6NP.

✎♡ ☺ Zzz...

Formerly home to the Earls of Galloway, the 18th century, stone-built Creebridge
House is set in very pretty gardens. It's more hotel than inn, but the bar with low
ceilings, reclaimed pitch pine timber furniture, old oak beams and horse brasses has
a comfortable country feel about it. There's a good range of bar meals from a snacky
lunchtime-only menu (including sandwiches and filled croissants) to some accomplished fish specials such as paupiettes of salmon and halibut with a crayfish sauce,
equally substantial Galloway venison, fillet of beef with mushroom sauce and "posh
fish and chips" (local haddock fillet in real ale batter) served in newspaper on your
plate. Bedrooms which include four family suites are all very well-kept and equipped
with TVs, telephones, hairdryers and tea/coffee making kits, and good modern en
suite bathrooms, all with shower over the tub. *Open 12-2.30, 6-11 (Fri, Sat & Sun
till 11.30). Bar Food 12-2 (Sun from 12.30), 6-9 (Sat till 10, Sun from 7). Free House.
Beer Tetley Burton Ale, Orkney Dark Island, guest beer. Garden, outdoor eating. Family
room. Accommodation 20 bedrooms, all en suite, £75 (single £40). Children welcome
overnight (under-12s free if sharing parents' room), additional bed & cot available.
Accommodation closed 24-26 Dec. Amex, MasterCard, VISA*

PORT APPIN — The Pierhouse — FOOD

Tel 01631 730302   Fax 01631 730521   Map 3 B5   **B&B**
Port Appin Pier nr Appin Argyll & Bute PA38 4DE

✎♡ Zzz...

Turn off A828 and head down to the end of the road where you'll find the distinctive
twin round-fronted buildings of the low, white Pierhouse; its setting is delightfully
tranquil and picturesque right on the water's edge of Loch Linnhe, where the little
Lismore passenger ferry docks. The terrace, the picture-windowed main bar room
(open all day) and small residents' sitting-room make the most of the evolving weather
scene that plays out over the towering Morvern Hills beyond the Isle of Lismore. In
the four, small, unpretentious dining areas, (one is no smoking) the best few tables
are at the picture windows, although those by the warming fire are an attraction in
winter; bright, interesting artwork – from George Devlin and Robin McGregor –
adorns the whitewashed walls. Callum Macleod provides energetic service-with-a-
smile and a sense of humour, taking obvious pride in his mother Sheila's particularly
good cooking. Seafood dishes may be served with cheese and wine, lemon and butter
sauces, but when it's so fresh (dark blue Mull lobsters, oysters and giant crabs are kept
in submerged creels off the pier) and the quality so good it seems appropriate to let
the natural ingredients' flavours speak for themselves. Go then for the Loch Etive
mussels in garlic butter, Lismore oysters from the shell (or grilled with mornay sauce)
and cracked crab claws with home-made mayonnaise, and any number of aquatic and
crustaceous combinations with equal confidence. Half a dozen Aberdeen Angus beef,
venison and chicken dishes complete the main-course picture. Those puddings that
are home-made, such as bread-and-butter pudding made with French bread or
a light, bitter chocolate roulade, are the ones to choose. Fine bar snacks are served at
lunchtime only. If it's really quiet in winter you may need to tell them you're coming.
Eleven smart, pine-furnished bedrooms are in a sympathetically designed two-storey
building to one side of the former ferry house; the front bedrooms have glorious loch
and island views, and a large family room has a double and a single bed (plus room for
a cot) together with good hanging and shelf space. Owners Alan and Sheila McLeod
and family are most hospitable and serve up a generous breakfast, too! Advance
arrangements can be made to see nearby Castle Stalker by boat and the basking seals
in the bay; yacht moorings are available for diners and overnight guests. Disabled
facilities. *Open 11-11. Meals 12-3, 6.30-9.30. Accommodation 11 bedroom all
en suite, £70 (family room £80). Children welcome overnight, additional cot provided.
Bicycle & boat hire, moorings. Accommodation closed 25 Dec. No dogs. MasterCard, VISA*

PORTPATRICK   Crown Hotel   FOOD

Tel 01776 810261   Fax 01776 810551   Map 4 A2   **B&B**
North Crescent Portpatrick Stranraer Dumfries & Galloway DG9 8SX

 ☺

Right down by the harbour, the blue-and-white painted Crown is a bustling, friendly place with a real fire burning even in summer on chilly days and a lively mixture of locals and visiting yachtspeople. Restaurant and bar share the same menu (except for basket meals and sandwiches available in the bar only) and the thing to go for is the seafood. Chef Robert Campbell knows that the lobster and crabs are fresh because he's out in his boat at 6am every morning to collect them; much of the other fish is bought direct from the Fleetwood trawlers that call in at Portpatrick to unload their catches. There are herring aplenty, trout, crab and lobster for a summer salad, and main dishes ranging from cod and chips to "surf with turf", a Crown speciality; for meat-eaters beef hot-pot and savoury pancakes supplement a range of steaks. Smart, appealing bedrooms have loose rugs over polished parquet floors, a variety of good freestanding furniture and attractive floral fabrics, along with pristine bathrooms and the standard modern necessities of direct-dial phone and TV; there is one family suite. *Open 11-11.30.* **Bar Food** *12-2 (Sat & Sun till 2.30), 6-10. Free House.* **Beer** *S&N 70/- & 80/-, Theakston's. Garden, outdoor eating.* **Accommodation** *12 bedrooms, all en suite, £70 (Single £35). Children welcome overnight (under-4s stay free in parents' room, 4-10s £10), additional bed & cot available. MasterCard,* **VISA**

RATHO   Bridge Inn   FOOD

Tel 0131-333 1320   Fax 0131-333 3480   Map 3 C6
27 Baird Road Ratho City of Edinburgh EH28 8RA

☺

Staring life as a farmhouse, and only becoming a hostelry when the Union Canal was built alongside, the Bridge Inn fell into decline along with the canal and was almost derelict when taken over by the irrepressible Ronnie Rusack 25 years ago. Not content with just reviving the Inn, Ronnie has been instrumental in making some seven miles of canal navigable again and runs two restaurant barges (one with a marriage licence!) and numerous pleasure craft including one for the disabled run by a charity Ronnie himself founded. Inside, the original Inn features boarded walls and a collection of the many old bottles found when clearing the canal; a family-orientated extension (the 'Pop Inn') features wheelback chairs and views over the water. The latter's informal menu delivers home-made broth and burgers, roasts and grills throughout the day and decent, locally made puds. From the à la carte menu served lunch and evening in the bar, steaks are a particularly good bet, with Scottish meat cooked in full view on an open grill and a good choice of sauces for the more adventurous. Children have their own special menu of favourites (with the likes of fish fingers, chicken drumsticks and fruit jelly and ice cream), as do the over-60s (with the "Golden Years" menu) should they wish it. There's an adult-powered carousel on the patio, a "pirate boat" play area in the grounds, proper baby-changing and nursing facilities (that come complete with complimentary nappies and baby powder) and plenty of high-chairs and booster seats. There is hardly room to list everything that goes on here but don't miss the "Pumpathon" of classic fire engines that gathers here annually on the first weekend in May. *Open noon-11 (Fri & Sat 11am-12pm, Sun 12.30-11).* **Bar Food** *12-8 (Sun from 12.30). Free House.* **Beer** *Belhaven 80/- Ale, guest beers. Garden, outdoor eating, children's play area. Amex, Diners, MasterCard,* **VISA**

We endeavour to be as up-to-date as possible but inevitably some changes to landlords, chefs and other key staff occur after the Guide has gone to press.

ST BOSWELLS — Buccleuch Arms Hotel — FOOD

Tel 01835 822243 Fax 01835 823963   Map 4 C1   **B&B**
The Green St Boswells Scottish Borders TD6 0EW

Alongside the main A68, this substantial red stone inn dates back to the 1700s when it stood on one of the main coaching routes between Scotland and England. The spacious wood-panelled bar has a nicely varied menu available throughout the day: home-made chicken liver paté, fillet of haddock and various home-made puds. Residents and others can take afternoon tea in an elegantly proportioned lounge or the enclosed rear garden. Bedrooms are in good order, with traditional darkwood furniture and colourfully matching duvet covers and curtains. All have satellite TV, telephone and tea/coffee-making facilities, the best (and quietest) rooms overlooking the garden; all but two have decent en suite bathrooms. Friendly staff create a pleasant atmosphere and help to make children especially welcome. *Open 11-11 (Sun from 12).* ***Bar Food** 12-2, 6-9 (Fri & Sat till 10). Free House. **Beer** Broughton Greenmantle Ale. Garden, outdoor eating. Family room. **Accommodation** 19 bedrooms, 17 en suite, £75 (single £42). Children welcome overnight (under-14s stay free in parents' room).* MasterCard, **VISA**

ST. MARY'S LOCH — Tibbie Shiels Inn — FOOD

Tel 01759 42231   Map 4 C1
St. Mary's Loch Scottish Borders TD7 5NE

The Inn itself is a lovely whitewashed cottage with later additions in the glorious Yarrow valley; Tibbie Shiels was the first licensee from 1803 to 1878 and her famously unforgettable name lives on still. It can be recommended for three main things: first, the atmospheric bar, busy with friendly locals and fishing and sailing types, second the quality of the meat dishes (Scottish lamb and Aberdeen Angus beef), and third the situation of the Inn itself on the shores of St. Mary's Loch. The large dining-room overlooks the loch and surrounding hills in this utterly remote and enchanting place. Dishes include chicken liver with port and brandy paté, poached salmon and poacher's venison(!) with seasonal apple and blackberry pie and year-round the Christmassy Cloutie Dumpling to follow. The Tibbie is an excellent place to stop after a sojourn of the Southern Upland Way, with high tea served from 4-6pm and a miniature menu for the minors. Five en suite rooms are available for bed and breakfast (£46). *Open 11-11 (Fri & Sat till midnight, Sun from 12.30).* ***Bar Food** 12.30-2.30, 6.30-8.30. Free House. **Beer** Belhaven 80/- Ale, Broughton Greenmantle Ale. Patio & terrace, outdoor eating. Family room. Pub closed Mon & Tue Nov-Mar.* MasterCard, **VISA**

SHERIFFMUIR — Sheriffmuir Inn — FOOD

Tel 01786 823285 Fax 01786 823969   Map 3 C5
Sheriffmuir Dunblane Clackmannanshire FK15 0LN

Built just 6 months before the battle of Sheriffmuir was fought almost literally on its doorstep between the Jacobites and the Hanoverians, the Inn has a wild and lovely location high up in the Ochil Hills, yet it's easy to reach and well-signposted from the main A9. Inside, all is neat and comfortable with and open fire and equally warm welcome from Roger Lee. Opt for the home-made items on brother Peter's daily specials board – Greek lamb casserole, chicken satay and trout with lemon butter sauce. There are always home-made soups, steak and Guinness pie, and chips with haddock for those of more catholic persuasion, with children's portions and vegetarian options always readily available. *Open 11.30-2.30, 5.30-11 (Sat 11.30-11 & Sun 12-11).* ***Bar Food** 11.30-2.30, 5.30-9 (Sat & Sun 11.30-9). Free House. **Beer** Marston's Pedigree, Tetley Burton Ale, Arrols 80/- , guest beer. Garden, outdoor eating, children's play area. Family room.* MasterCard, **VISA**

We do not accept free meals or hospitality – our inspectors pay their own bills
and **never** book in the name of Egon Ronay's Guides.

STONEHAVEN — Marine Hotel — FOOD

Tel 01569 762155   Fax 01569 766691   Map 3 D4   **B&B**
9 The Shorehead Stonehaven Aberdeenshire AB3 2JY

Down by the harbour, the Marine is very pubby with a regularly-changing selection of real ales and the same menu is served in the lounge/bar as in the more family-oriented, first-floor dining-room with its blue nautical decor and waitress service. It carries standard pub fare such as golden fried haddock steaks and salads but it's the exotic blackboard that people come back for: Cajun-blackened halibut, chicken Indienne, Thai curries, baltis and a range of Tex-Mex derivations. Equally popular in summer is the fresh fish and seafood, much of it landed just across from the pub. Six modest but clean bedrooms (the two largest are family rooms with cots available) all have harbour views and are furnished with fitted white melamine units and matching duvets and curtains; they have shower cabinets in the rooms but share two loos. All have phones, televisions and beverage kits. *Open 11-11.45 (Sun from 12).* *Bar Food 5-9.30 (in winter till 9). Children welcome overnight (under-3s stay free in parents' room, 3-12s £5). Free House. Beer Dunnottar Ale (the house brew), Bass, Timothy Taylor Landlord and guest beers. Family room. Accommodation 6 bedrooms £35 (single £25).* MasterCard, **VISA**

STRATHBLANE — Kirkhouse Inn — B&B

Tel 01360 770621   Fax 01360 770896   Map 3 B5
Glasgow Road Strathblane Stirlingshire G63 9AA

Zzz...

At the foot of Campsie Fell on the A81 just south of town this is decidedly more hotel than pub. Choose between the cocktail bar with its plush banquette seating or the large public bar which, despite the usual paraphernalia of amusements, is nonetheless quite civilised. Bedrooms are done out in a variety of pleasant colour schemes and either light or darkwood units; hotel-style en suite facilities run to remote-control TVs, trousers presses and 24 hour room service. Staff are notably friendly. *Bar open 11-11 (Fri & Sat till midnight, Sun from 12.30). Free House. Beer Maclay's 80/-. Garden, beauty salon. Accommodation 15 rooms, all en suite, £65 (single £45). Children welcome overnight (under-12s free if sharing parents' room), additional bed & cot available.* Amex, Diners, Mastercard, **VISA**

SWINTON — Wheatsheaf Hotel — FOOD

Tel & Fax 01890 860257   Map 3 D6   **B&B**
Main Street Swinton Berwickshire Scottish Borders TD11 3JJ

The Wheatsheaf, dominating this simple Scots farming hamlet six miles north of Coldstream, overlooks the plain little village green and has very limited parking; at busy periods the main street is full up with cars. This is very much a dining pub with a very well-regarded restaurant, the Four Seasons, and it's wise to book even for bar meals. The emphasis is on fresh produce with a menu reproduced on one blackboard, daily specials listed on another and lots of seafood. Scallops on a saffron-scented salad followed by whole sea bass with fennel and prawns typify the style; alternatives might include quail in Thai dressing, egg Florentine, pork and apricot stroganoff and courgette and aubergine provençale. Freshly baked wheaten rolls are presented as a matter of course, and butter comes in a slab on a saucer; salads are imaginative and fresh. There are four tidy bedrooms fitted with TVs; one has an en suite bathroom, and two more have showers. *Bar Food 12-2, 6-9.30 (Sun 12.30-2.15, 6.30-8.30). Free House. Beer Broughton Greenmantle Ale, guest beer. Garden, outdoor eating, children's play area. Accommodation 4 bedrooms, 3 en suite, £64 (single £42). Children welcome overnight (under-5s stay free in parents' room, 5-10s £7), additional bed & cot available. Pub closed all day Mon, Sun night in winter, two weeks Feb and last week Oct.* MasterCard, **VISA**

TALLADALE — Loch Maree Hotel — B&B

Tel 01445 760288   Fax 01445 760241   Map 2 B3
Talladale by Achnasheen Wester Ross Highland IV22 2HL

Zzz...

Mid-way between Gairloch and Kinlochewe on the main A832 stands the ultimate fishing hotel, beautifully situated on the banks of Loch Maree and much loved in former times by Queen Victoria herself. Recently though, things have changed dramatically from the time-warp of Victorian cosiness, and the latest additions and improvements have brought the bedrooms bang up to date. Best of all are those with a Loch view which attract a modest supplement. The hotel owns eight boats (complete with mandatory ghillies) for sea trout and salmon fishing on the loch. *Bar open 11-11. Garden, fishing, boating. No real ales.* **Accommodation** *30 bedrooms, all en suite, £75. Children welcome overnight, additional bed & cot available.* MasterCard, **VISA**

TAYVALLICH — Tayvallich Inn — FOOD

Tel 01546 870282   Map 3 A5
Tayvallich by Lochgilphead Argyll & Bute PA31 8PR

This simple, white-painted dining pub is in a marvellously pretty location at the centre of a scattered village stretching round a natural harbour at the top of Loch Sween. Sit outside, on the front terrace, at one of the five parasolled picnic tables, and enjoy the view of a dozen little boats, and low wooded hills fringing the lochside; the word Tayvallich means "the house in the pass". Inside the bar is tile-floored with raffia-back chairs and little wood tables, the dining-room similar, but spacious and relaxing, with a woodburning stove, attractive dresser, and bentwood chairs around scrubbed pine dining tables. The freshest local seafood is so local that oysters come from just yards away in Loch Sween itself, and 'hand-dived' scallops from the Sound of Jura just round the coast. Their seafood platter must surely be among the very best in the whole of the British Isles, well worth the long, seemingly endless descent down the one-track, bluebell-lined road (B8025) from Crinan. There are plenty of non-fish alternatives and half-portions in abundance for the kids; puddings such as chocolate nut slab and banoffi pie are all made by tireless landlady Patricia Grafton. The whole atmosphere is very informal and relaxed; holidaymakers turn up in shorts and babies are commendably tolerantly treated, with clip-on chairs and specially rustled-up toddler food and chips. *Open 11-2.30, 5-11 (Fri & Sat till 1am, Sun till 12, and all day July & August).* **Bar Food** *12-2, 6-8 (restaurant meals till 9, weekends only in winter). Free House.* **Beer** *Tetley. Patio/grassy foreshore, outdoor eating. Inn closed all Mon Nov-Easter.* MasterCard, **VISA**

TURRIFF — Towie Tavern — FOOD

Tel 01888 511201   Fax 01651 872464   Map 2 D3
Auchterless nr Turriff Aberdeenshire AB53 8EP

A favourite for its satisfying, wholesome food, this is a roadside pebbledash pub on the A497, some four miles south of Turriff and a short distance from the National Trust's 13th century Fyvie Castle. Seafood is featured at the Towie and the menu changes monthly, with daily blackboard specials; the 'Fisherman's choice' offers whatever is available that day with first-class goujons of lemon sole, coquilles of scallops and monkfish Mornay, and smoked chicken and Waldorf salad for the less fishy-minded. Spinach and vegetable crepes and home-made sticky toffee pudding complete the altogether rosy picture. Facilities for children include an outdoor play area. *Open 11-2.30, 6-12 (Sat 11-12, Sun 12-11).* **Bar Food** *12-2, 6-9.30 (Sun till 9). Free House.* **Beer** *Theakston's, guest beer. Terrace, outdoor eating.* MasterCard, **VISA**

We do not accept free meals or hospitality – our inspectors pay their own bills and never book in the name of Egon Ronay's Guides.

TWEEDSMUIR — Crook Inn — B&B

Tel 01899 880272 Fax 01899 880294   Map 4 C1
Tweedsmuir nr Biggar Peeblesshire Scottish Borders ML12 6QN

This famous old drovers' inn stands on the A710 Moffat to Edinburgh road in glorious Tweed valley countryside with a strange but winning amalgam of old stone-flagged farmers' bar and 1930s' ocean liner-style lounges. Burns wrote Willie Wastle's Wife in what is now the bar, and locally-born John Buchan set many of his novels in the area. Neat bedrooms are simple in their appointments, with no TVs or telephones to interrupt splendid solitude. A craft centre (glass-making a speciality) has recently been created from the old stable block, enforcing the Crook's claim to be Scotland's oldest licensed inn. New owners as we went to press. *Open 11-12 (Sun 11-11). Free House.* **Beer** *Broughton Greenmantle Ale. Garden. Family room.* **Accommodation** *8 rooms, all en suite, £52 (single £36). Children welcome overnight, under-12s stay free in parents' room), additional bed & cot available. Amex, Diners, MasterCard,* **VISA**

ULLAPOOL — Argyll Hotel — B&B

Tel 01854 612422   Map 2 B2
Argyll Street Ullapool Wester Ross Highland IV26 2UB

A well-kept, white-painted inn one street back from the harbourside, the Argyll has a comfortable main bar with ruffled curtains, velour banquettes, wheelback chairs and 60-plus malt whiskies to choose from. Locals gather in the characterful public bar, the only one in Ullapool and virtually unchanged in 50 years. Bedrooms offer modest comfort with pretty wallpaper, simple modern units, TV and beverage kits; six are en suite (three with tubs and three with showers), the others sharing two good bathrooms. A note behind the doors states that breakfast is served from 8 to 9am and checking out by 10am, but in practice things are a bit more flexible. Families are welcome, with two rooms having an extra bed and room for a cot. *Open 11-11.30 (Sun from 12.30). Free House.* **Beer** *Tennent's 80/-, Bass, guest beers.* **Accommodation** *8 bedrooms, 6 en suite, £59 (single £25). Children welcome overnight, (under-5s stay free in parents' room), additional bed & cot available. Pub closed 1 Jan. No dogs. MasterCard,* **VISA**

> We do not accept free meals or hospitality – our inspectors pay their own bills
> and never book in the name of Egon Ronay's Guides.

ULLAPOOL — Ceilidh Place — FOOD / B&B

Tel 01854 612103 Fax 01854 612886   Map 2 B2
West Argyle Street Ullapool Wester Ross Highland IV26 2TY

This row of whitewashed cottages does not really have the atmosphere of a pub or an inn and is impossible to classify, being a glorious mixture of arts centre, hotel, coffee shop and restaurant. In the coffee shop by day there's counter service of a range of home-made goodies like soup, filled rolls and baked potatoes, nut roast, haddock and chips, chicken and ham pie, Bakewell tart, scones and carrot cake. From early evening there's table service and a printed menu from which you can have just a single dish or a more formal meal in the conservatory area with its white-clothed tables. Peppered mackerel fillets, Loch Broom mussels and Arbroath smokies are typically fishy dishes, with local venison, lemon chicken and prize-winning haggis for carnivores and half a dozen vegetarian alternatives. Thirteen spotless bedroom (three not en suite) are simply but appealingly appointed, some with dark-stained fitted units, some with the odd antique and most with beamed ceilings; all the bathrooms have tubs with hand-held shower attachments. The first-floor residents' lounge with large windows on two sides is quite delightful; a separate Club House offers budget accommodation with bunk beds and communal showers, and live entertainment in the summer months. Their other establishment called John Maclean's General Merchants, on Shore Street down by the harbour, is a delicatessen, bakery and general store with a first-floor coffee shop run on much the same lines. *Open 11-11 (Sun from 12.30). Food 10-9.30. Free House.* **Beer** *McEwan's 80/-, Orkney Dark Island, Belhaven Light. Outdoor eating.* **Accommodation** *13 bedrooms, 10 en suite, £110 (single £55). Children welcome overnight, additional bed (from £6) & cot available free. Amex, Diners, MasterCard,* **VISA**

ULLAPOOL   Ferry Boat Inn   FOOD

Tel & Fax 01854 612366   Map 2 B2   **B&B**
Shore Street Ullapool Wester Ross Highland IV26 2UL

Right on the quayside, the Ferry Boat is formed out of a couple of 18th-century former crofters' cottages; the atmosphere is cosy and friendly and helped along on most Thursday evenings (more often in summer) by local folk musicians who gather here for impromptu performances. The bar food menu offers sound home-cooked fare: vegetable broth, ploughman's platters, local haddock with chips and peas, beef casserole, meat loaf and sandwiches (at lunchtime only). Puds like lemon meringue pie, coffee and ginger mousse and apple and raisin cake are particularly noteworthy. When the small restaurant is busy there is no 'bar food' in the evenings, but one can just have a main course from the short set menu. En suite bedrooms (three with shower and WC only), come in a variety of pleasant colour schemes with simple darkwood fitted units. Three at the front have splendid views, but some of the others have virtually none; consequently (perhaps!) a small TV lounge is provided for residents. Beer lovers should note that there is a constantly-changing selection of two cask-conditioned real ales that can come from as far afield as Penzance and the Orkneys. *Open 11-11 (Sun from 12.30).* **Bar Food** *12-2.30, 6.30-9. Free House.* **Beer** *Belhaven, McEwan's, two guest beers.* **Accommodation** *9 rooms, all en suite, £54, (single £28). Children welcome overnight, additional bed & cot available. Pub closed 1 Jan. Diners, MasterCard,* **VISA**

> We endeavour to be as up-to-date as possible but inevitably some changes to landlords, chefs and other key staff occur after the Guide has gone to press.

WEEM   Ailean Chraggan Hotel   FOOD

Tel 01887 820346   Fax 01887 820327   Map 3 C4   **B&B**
Weem by Aberfeldy Perth & Kinross PH15 2LD

Beautifully set against a steep woodland backdrop and with two acres of gardens overlooking the Tay this is a delightful little cottage inn. For over thirty years now Alastair Gillespie and family have produced simple, well-cooked meals highlighted by superb local seafood; try the Loch Etive mussels, served in huge steaming portions with garlic bread, or the Sound of Jura prawn platter. Bedrooms are equally commendable: spacious and light with nice pieces of old furniture, armchairs and, in two rooms, small dressing areas. All are equipped with TVs, hairdryers and tea/coffee making facilities. Ask for one of the front bedrooms, which have inspiring views looking south across the river. Patio and lawned garden. *Open 11-11.* **Bar Food** *12-2, 6.30-9 (Sat till 9.30). No real ales. Garden, outdoor eating, children's play area.* **Accommodation** *3 bedrooms, all en suite, £56 (single £28). Children welcome overnight (half price), additional bed & cot available. Closed 1 & 2 Jan, 25 & 26 Dec. MasterCard,* **VISA**

ACCEPTED IN
HOTELS AND
THAN MOST P
EVER HAVE HO

VISA IS ACCEPTED FOR MORE TRANSACTIO

MORE
STAURANTS
OPLE
DINNERS.

ORLDWIDE THAN ANY OTHER CARD.

MAKING LIFE EASIER THROUGHOUT WALES

Wales

The addresses of establishments in the following former **Counties** now include their new Unitary Authorities:

Clwyd
Conwy, Denbighshire, Flintshire, Wrexham

Dyfed
Ceredigion, Carmarthenshire, Pembrokeshire

Gwent
Monmouthshire, Torfaen, Newport, Caerphilly, Blaenau Gwent

Gwynedd
the new Gwynedd, Isle of Anglesey

Mid Glamorgan
Bridgend, Rhondda Cynon Taff, Merthyr Tydfil

South Glamorgan
Vale of Glamorgan, Cardiff

West Glamorgan
Swansea, Neath & Port Talbot

Powys remains the same

ABERDOVEY — Penhelig Arms Hotel — FOOD

Tel 01654 767215   Fax 01654 767690   Map 8 C3   **B&B**
Aberdovey Gwynedd LL35 0LT

 Zzz...

Built in the early 1700s as Y Dafarn Fach (The Little Inn) and for generations an integral part of the village's history. The black-and-white painted inn stands right on the main road (A493) with unrivalled views across the Dyfi estuary to Ynyslas. In front, now the tiny car park and sun terrace, was a shipbuilder's yard at the turn of the century, while behind, the Towyn to Machynlleth train rumbles out of a tunnel to the request stop at Penhelig Halt. For such a narrow site the Penhelig Arms utilises every square inch of available space and packs in a wealth of charm under the ever-present guidance of proprietors Robert and Sally Hughes. Its popularity at lunchtime ensures a regular overflow from bar to dining-room. Menus are updated daily, offering the likes of freshly-cut sandwiches, leek, bacon and broccoli soup, lamb curry and steak and mushroom pie; plus creamy fish and prawn pie, monkfish and salmon with hollandaise, treacle tart and chocolate roulade. Quality and price move up a gear at dinner. Sunday lunchtime sees a reduced bar menu as the fixed-price menu (£11.50) is always popular. In addition to real ales there's a range of house wines from an enthusiast's cellar; champagne at £3 a glass isn't offered everywhere! Care and attention to detail has gone into ensuring residents' every comfort in a relaxed atmosphere that contrives to make one feel immediately at home. What the smaller bedrooms lack in space they make up for in appealing interior design, careful addition of up-to-date comforts (TV, telephone to hairdryers and quality toiletries) and immaculately-kept en suite bathrooms. All but one have a share of the view, one of the finest of any hotel in Wales, and three superior rooms have a little extra space with easy chairs and super little front-facing balconies. It goes almost without saying that a splendid Welsh breakfast will set you up for the day's touring, sightseeing or just lazing around which lies ahead. *Open 11-3, 6-11 (Sun 12-3, 7-10.30). Bar Food 12-2, 7-9. Free House. Beer Tetley Bitter, Burton, guest beer. Garden, outdoor eating. Accommodation 10 bedrooms, all en suite, £68-£78 (single £39). Children welcome overnight (free if sharing parents' room), additional bed & cot available. Closed 25 & 26 Dec. MasterCard, VISA*

ABERGAVENNY — Llanwenarth Arms Hotel — FOOD

Tel 01873 810550   Fax 01873 811880   Map 9 D5   **B&B**
Brecon Road Abergavenny Monmouthshire NP8 1EP

A refined roadside inn (on the A40) between Abergavenny and Crickhowell, standing on an escarpment above the Usk valley. Chef/landlord D'Arcy McGregor's creative cooking leaves little to chance, his bar menus making full use of the best local produce available. The seasonally-changed main menu is served throughout the two bars, family conservatory dining area and splendid summer terrace set some 70 feet above the river with views across to Sugar Loaf Mountain. Smoked trout salad, fresh pasta, poached salmon, king prawns in a Chinese-style sauce, goujons of hake, chicken wrapped in Parma ham, steaks and pan-fried venison with a port and redcurrant sauce give the style; home-made puds range from profiteroles to waffles and bread-and-butter pudding (served with brown-bread ice cream for the indulgent). Cauliflower and ham soup, smoked salmon and fresh asparagus, baked sea bass with spring onions and ginger might feature as daily specials. Residents enjoy the use of their own lounge, and a Victorian-style conservatory furnished with comfortable cane furniture. Bedrooms, approached by way of a sheltered courtyard, are attractively furnished and immaculately kept, each one enjoying its fair share of the view. TVs, telephones, trouser presses, tea/coffee making facilities and hairdryers are all standard; bathrooms also have over-bath showers and ample supplies of toiletries. Salmon and trout fishing for residents. *Open 11-3, 6-11 (Sun 12-2, 7-10.30). Bar Food 12-2 (till 1.30 Sun), 7-10 (Sun 7-8.15). Free House. Beer Bass, Ruddles County. Patio, outdoor eating. Family room. Accommodation 18 bedrooms, all en suite, £59 (single £39). Children welcome overnight (under-16s half-price), additional bed & cot available (£5). No dogs. Amex, Diners, MasterCard, VISA*

ABERGORLECH — Black Lion — FOOD

Tel 01558 685271 Map 9 B5
Abergorlech nr Carmarthen Carmarthenshire SA32 7SN

At the heart of one of Wales's best-kept villages, the white-painted Black Lion stands between a tiny stone chapel and the Cothi River bridge; private fishing beats are nearby. The single bar with flagstone floors and high settles leads to a flat-roofed dining extension. On the main menu, pink trout, fillet steaks, boeuf bourguignon and generous salads satisfy the heartiest appetites, while blackboard daily specials might feature lasagne, butterfly king prawns or vegetable lasagne. Opposite the pub, a scenic riverside garden with picnic tables features regular summer barbecues. Children welcome. *Open 11.30-3.30, 7-11 (from 6.30 in summer), Sun 12-3, 7-10.30.* **Bar Food** *12-2, 7-9 (snacks only Mon lunch, no food Mon Eve, except Bank Holidays). Free House. **Beer** Worthington, guest beer. Riverside garden, outdoor eating. Amex, MasterCard,* **VISA**

AFON-WEN — Pwll Gwyn Hotel — FOOD

Tel 01352 720227 Map 8 C2
Afon-wen nr Mold Flintshire CH7 5UB

Formerly a 17th-century coaching inn of some renown with an unusual remodelled Victorian frontage (on the A541), Pwll Gwyn's fortunes are being revived today by enthusiastic and energetic tenants Andrew and Karen Davies. Andrew provides the brains (and the brawn) behind an intelligently run kitchen whose output is much dictated by his shopping from Liverpool's markets. Best bets for the bar food, therefore, come from the daily blackboard: avocado, chicken and curry mayonnaise, liver and smoked bacon with gravy and potato cake or fillet of cod with lemon pepper coating. Desserts, too, are impressive: cappuccino cake and toffee crunch cheesecake feature on a long list of home-made delights. More substantial cooking with a classical base comes in the form of weekly-changing specials available in the two separate dining-rooms (one for non-smokers); special event evenings (Italian, Chinese, Indian). *Open 12-3, 7-11, Sun 12-3, 5-10.30 (from 7 in winter).* **Bar Food** *12-2.30, 7-9.30. **Beer** Greenalls. Garden, outdoor eating. Family room. MasterCard,* **VISA**

BABELL — Black Lion Inn — FOOD

Tel 01352 720239 Map 8 D1
Babell nr Holywell Flintshire CH8 8PZ

Eating in the patio dining-room here offers not only impressive views of the Clwydian range without but also tempting value on the menu and blackboard within. For starters, grilled smoked mackerel or baked avocado with seafood mornay and, to follow, the likes of kidneys Turbigo, black pudding with grain mustard sauce and hake with prawn and white wine sauce. Nightly, except Sunday and Monday, in the Liszt Room, a four-course dinner is more formally silver-served and priced according to choice of main course. A classical French-biased wine list includes some carefully selected 'Landlord's Delights'. *Open Tue-Fri 12-2, Tue-Sat 7-11. Closed all Mon, Sat lunch & all Sun (except Easter Sun & Mother's Day).* **Bar Food** *12-2 (except Sat, Sun & Mon), 7.30-10.30 (except Sun & Mon). Free House. **Beer** Boddingtons. Garden. Family room. Amex, MasterCard,* **VISA**

We do not accept free meals or hospitality – our inspectors pay their own bills and never book in the name of Egon Ronay's Guides.

BEAUMARIS   Liverpool Arms Hotel   FOOD

Tel 01248 810362   Fax 01248 811135   Map 8 B1   **B&B**
Castle Street Beaumaris Isle of Anglesey LL58 8BA

A handsome Georgian-fronted inn with a maritime history recalling the days when there was a busy shipping trade between Beaumaris and Liverpool. At its heart the Admiral's Tavern contains a wealth of memorabilia and relics which include timbers both from Nelson's Victory and the 1830s' HMS Conway which was wrecked in the Menai Strait in 1953. A Quarterdeck and non-smoking Port Room are ideally set aside for sampling from Colleen Evans's daily-changing fare. There is no printed menu, instead a blackboard offers home-made pies and casseroles alongside, perhaps, popular lunchtime platters like Coronation chicken and assorted smoked fish; evening specials can range from sausage and apple slice and rack of lamb with red wine and garlic to kangaroo and alligator steaks! Round off your meal with a selection of local Welsh cheeses. The White Star Line replicated signs to 'First Class Accommodation', approached by a fine listed oak-panelled staircase, are no exaggeration. Bedrooms are boldly decorated and bathrooms smartly tiled; tea trays, TVs, hairdryers, shoe-cleaning kits and dial-out telephones are all provided. Honeymooners might enjoy the four-poster suite, and youngsters can double up in the bunk beds of one of the two family rooms. Lower tariff in winter. *Open 11-11 (Sun 12-10.30). Bar Food 12-2.15, 6-9.15. Free House. Beer Tetley Best, Bass, guest beer. Family room. Accommodation 10 bedrooms, all en suite, from £50 (four-poster £65, family room from £70, single £30). MasterCard, VISA*

BEAUMARIS   Ye Olde Bull's Head Inn   FOOD

Tel 01248 810329   Fax 01248 811294   Map 8 B1   **B&B**
Castle Street Beaumaris Isle of Anglesey LL58 8AP

Zzz...

A stone's throw from Beaumaris Castle, the Grade II listed Bull dates back to 1472, though it was largely rebuilt in 1617. Within its cavernous bars is a valuable array of antique weaponry, an ancient brass water clock and the town's old ducking stool. With its family home to the rear, this makes an ideal spot for lunch. Daily menus offer the best local produce splendidly scaled down for pubby enjoyment: alongside a split pea and vegetable broth and chicken terrine with coriander seed and orange may be braised ham shank with rosemary and root vegetables or roast chicken with tandoori spices. A grilled hamburger comes with rosemary and onion gravy, amply garnished sandwiches include beef and horseradish; sweets may be rich lemon tart and banana and rum parfait. Dinner menus take over from bar food in the evenings. The smartly-refurbished bedrooms are named after characters from the novels of Charles Dickens, a frequent visitor to the inn. Each room is individually decorated and contains its own special features: exposed rafters and beams, oddly-shaped doors and ingeniously-fitted bathrooms, all remain sympathetic to the Bull's unbroken history, while the phones, TVs and bedside radios satisfy today's requirements. Rooms in the converted stables all feature antique beds and furniture; the best (Mr Pickwick) has a four-poster. The 'Artful Dodger' twin room is not en suite and is let to parents with children (£15 each) who are old enough to sleep in their own room. *Open 11-11, (Sun 12-10.30). Bar Food 12-2.30 only (not Sun). Free House. Beer Bass, Worthington Best, guest beer. Accommodation 15 bedrooms, all en suite, £75/£77 (four-poster £89/£90, single from £45). Children welcome overnight, additional bed (£15) & cot available (£5). No dogs. Accommodation closed 25 & 26 Dec; pub closed 25 Dec eve. Amex, MasterCard, VISA*

BERRIEW   Lion Hotel   FOOD

Tel 01686 640452   Fax 01686 640604   Map 8 D3   **B&B**
Berriew nr Welshpool Powys SY21 8PQ
Zzz...

The Thomas family's smart little hotel stands adjacaent to the parish church at the heart of this prettily-kept village full of magpie-style architecture and half-timbered cottages. Within, head for the lounge bar and bistro to enjoy Lance Thomas's reliable food in an olde worlde setting of exposed beams and wattle-and-daub wall panels. Wild mushroom soup, smoked bacon and chicken pasta shells with cheese sauce, followed by carbonnade of beef and grilled cod in herb butter are typical of the daily selections on the blackboard. Regular alternative choices run from curry of the day and assorted grills to such speciality dishes as filo-wrapped king prawns with lemon and dill dip and Welsh lamb fillet with cranberry, mushrooms and cassis sauce. Ingeniously added by their present owners, the seven bedrooms nestle literally in the roof space with much of the original timber and panelwork neatly exposed. Stylish, cottagey decor predominates throughout, the smartest being in a two-roomed family suite and the romantic four-poster room. Bathrooms throughout are entirely adequate, though space is at a premium. No children under 14 in bar areas. *Open* 11.30-3, 5.30-11 (Sat from 7, Sun 12-3, 7-10.30). *Bar Food* 12-2, 7-9.30 (Sun to 9). *Free House. Beer* Worthington Best, Bass, guest beer. Patio. Family room. *Accommodation 7 bedrooms, all en suite, £80 (four-poster £90, single £50, family triple room £95). Children welcome overnight, cot provided. Amex, Diners, MasterCard, VISA*

BETTWS NEWYDD   Black Bear   FOOD

Tel & Fax 01873 880701   Map 9 D5
Bettws Newydd Usk Monmouthshire WP5 1JN

As proclaimed by a smart black canopy above the new entrance to his premises 'Food by Molyneux' is the biggest draw here, and very good it is too. Chef/proprietor Stephen Molyneux has continued steadily to improve the Black Bear since he bought it in somewhat dilapidated condition two years ago, and the interior is now much more conducive to the enjoyment of his punchy, highly individualistic food. The Bear Boards, as it were, proclaim a particular preference for fish in dishes like grey mullet baked with white wine and tarragon and salmon fillet in orange and whisky butter; alternatives might be chicken supreme in Stilton cream sauce and sirloin steak 'as you like it'. Starters and light snacks encompass chicken and spinach terrine, smoked duck with garlic mayonnaise and white fish goujons with tartare sauce, while some more substantial fare listed on the walkers' board includes fresh cod and chips and an open steak and onion baguette, ideal to accompany good real ales such as Shepherd Neame Spitfire and Fuller's London Pride, drawn these days direct from the cask. *Open 11-3, 6-11.30 (Sun 12-10.30). Bar Food 12-3, 7-10. (no food Sun eve). Free House. Beer Bass, two guest beers. Garden, outdoor eating. MasterCard, VISA*

> We endeavour to be as up-to-date as possible but inevitably some changes to landlords, chefs and other key staff occur after the Guide has gone to press.

BETWS-YN-RHOS   Ffarm Hotel   FOOD

Tel 01492 680287   Map 8 C1
Betws-yn-Rhos nr Abergele Conwy LL22 8AR

Eating is the main event at the Lomax family's discreet venue, hiding behind an impressive crenellated stone facade. The 18th-century granite manor house set in two acres of garden has been comfortably modernised and guests can choose to eat in either the bar, hall or library (suitable for families). The daily-changing blackboard menu offers specials such as rack of Welsh lamb in a redcurrant sauce, salmon with lemon and fresh tarragon, roast duckling with honey and ginger sauce, smoked haddock mornay, fennel and walnut bake followed by locally-made ice creams or cherry and coconut pudding. Very young children are not encouraged. Advisable to phone in advance to check opening times. *Open Sun 12-3 Easter to Sep only, 7-11 Tue-Sat (daily Easter to Sep). Bar Food 7-9.30 only. Free House. Beer Tetley Traditional. Garden, outdoor eating. Closed lunch all week & all Mon (except in summer). MasterCard, VISA*

BODFARI   Dinorben Arms   FOOD

Tel 01745 710309   Fax 01745 710580   Map 8 C2
Bodfari nr Denbigh Denbighshire LL16 4DA

The 17th-century Dinorben Arms is off the A541 (taking the B5429 and sign to Tremeirchion). David Rowlands has injected a new lease of life to this well-known old pub with much refurbishment undertaken and a variety of menus on offer. The emphasis is still very much on home-cooking and the standard is unlikely to change as long as Irene and Mary are in the kitchen (they've been there for 34 years between them!). Lunchtimes concentrate on the self-served smörgåsbord and in the evenings both cold starters and sweets are mostly served buffet-style in the Well Bar. The 'Chicken Rough', originally presented to be eaten with fingers, lives on since being introduced in 1961; the Farmhouse Buffet (Wed/Thu) and Carverboard (Fri/Sat) are more recent and very popular evening additions. Special dishes nightly may include rack of Welsh lamb or grilled halibut, however there are plenty more snacky items, children's and vegetarian choices (perhaps aubergine moussaka). Families are well catered for in their own room and on the smart, flower-decked, tiered patios, and at the top of the extensive hillside gardens is a children's adventure play area; changing unit in Ladies. For dedicated drinkers there are four real ales, eight wines by the glass, 25 cognacs and over 120 whiskies. *Open 12-3.30, 6-11 (Sun 12-10.30)*. **Bar Food** *12-3, 6-10.30 (Sun 12-10.30)*. *Free House*. **Beer** *John Smith's, Webster's Yorkshire Bitter, Ruddles County, guest beer*. *Garden, outdoor eating, children's play area. Family room. MasterCard,* **VISA**

BONTDDU   Halfway House   FOOD

Tel 01341 430635   Map 8 C3
Bontddu Dolgellau Gwynedd LL40 2UE

A striking, timbered magpie frontage dates this old hostelry (by the A496) as 17th-century; just behind the pub the old Clogau mine is renowned for producing gold for the Royal wedding rings. Smartened up by its new owners, the pub retains the old flagstone steps to an impressive hallway; within, all is newly carpeted, with the former living quarters opened out and incorporated into a cosy lounge bar. Two roadside dining areas with a grassed picnic terrace are adjacent. Home-cooked food mostly hits the mark; a blackboard menu might offer rainbow trout with aniseed butter cream or plaice fillets with a lime and ginger butter as daily specials. Soup 'n' steak or steak 'n' sweet specials feature alongside a comprehensive main menu that includes options for vegetarians and youngsters. Roast Sunday lunches, occasional theme nights and a halfway hospitable welcome from Tony and his wife Fred are all positive notes. *Open 12-3, 6-11 (from 7 in winter, Sun 12-2.30, 7-10.30)*. **Bar Food** *12-2, 6.30-9 (Sun from 7pm)*. *Free House*. **Beer** *Marston's Best & Pedigree. Family room. Garden, outdoor eating. MasterCard,* **VISA**

BURTON GREEN   Golden Grove Inn   A

Tel 01244 570445   Map 8 D2
Llyndir Lane Burton Green Rossett Wrexham LL12 0AS

Best found by turning off the B5445 at Rossett, by the signs to Llyndyr Hall; at the end of a lane seemingly leading nowhere stands a group of black and white timber-framed buildings which comprise the pub and its many outhouses. Within is a treasure trove of antiquity with some splendid 14th-century oak beams and magical old inglenooks and fireplaces. A modern extension housing a carvery dining-room leads to drinking patios and a large, safe garden replete with swings and wooden play equipment, justifiably popular in the summer months; regular barbecues. Live jazz Thursday and weekend evenings. *Open 12-3, 6-11, (Sat 12-11, Sun 12-4, 7-10.30)*. **Beer** *Marston's. Garden, children's play area. MasterCard,* **VISA**

CARDIGAN · Black Lion Hotel · B&B

Tel 01239 612532   Map 9 B4
High Street Cardigan Ceredigion SA43 1HJ

The Black Lion claims to be the oldest coaching inn in Wales, having established itself in 1105 as a 'one-room grog shop'. Much enlarged (but originally medieval) town-centre inn with a characterful beamed interior, complete with linenfold panelling in one of the bars. Pine-furnished bedrooms, and a comfortable upstairs television lounge, as well as a quaint little writing room. Bedrooms are equipped with tea/coffee-making facilities, TV and telephone. A family suite sleeps up to five; one double room also has a single bed and there's a connecting twin room – both share a bathroom. *Open 11-11 (from 10 for coffee), Sun 12-10.30. Free House.* **Beer** *Worthington Best, Hancock's HB.* **Accommodation** *14 bedrooms, all en suite, £40 (family suite price according to age, single £30). Children welcome overnight (under 10s stay free in parents' room), additional bed & cot available. No dogs. MasterCard,* **VISA**

CHEPSTOW · Castle View Hotel · FOOD

Tel 01291 620349   Fax 01291 627397   Map 9 D6   **B&B**
16 Bridge Street Chepstow Monmouthshire NP6 5EZ

Four miles from the M4 Junction 22, this 300-year-old house was constructed mostly using stone from Chepstow Castle which commands the huge riverbank opposite. Ivy-covered and genuinely welcoming, it's immaculately kept by Martin and Vicky Cardale. The original stone walls and timbers enhance the setting for a snack. Through both light and 'bigger bites', the bar menu encompasses omelettes and steak sandwiches, vegetable crêpes and hazelnut and mushroom fettuccine, with turkey, ham and sweetcorn or steak, kidney and Tetley pie as carnivorous alternatives. In the dining-room, an evening table d'hote is supplemented by a short à la carte on which the local Wye salmon is a regular feature. Up-to-date bedrooms with mahogany furniture and en suite bathrooms (one with shower only); radio and TV (with use of videos), mini-bars, direct-dial phones and beverage trays are standard throughout. The cottage suite (sleeping up to four) incorporates a quiet residents' lounge; overlooking the garden – a restful spot – are two spacious family rooms sleeping up to 4. *Open 12-2.30, 6-11 (Sun 12-2.30, 7-10.30).* **Bar Food** *12-2.30, 6.30-9.30 (no food Sun eve). Free House.* **Beer** *Tetley, guest beer. Garden, outdoor eating.* **Accommodation** *13 bedrooms, all en suite, £49.50-£57.50 (single £37.50). Children welcome overnight (under-12s stay free in parents' room, 12-16s half-price) additional bed & cot available. Amex, MasterCard,* **VISA**

We endeavour to be as up-to-date as possible but inevitably some changes to landlords, chefs and other key staff occur after the Guide has gone to press.

CLYTHA · Clytha Arms · FOOD

Tel & Fax 01873 840206   Map 9 D5   **B&B**
Clytha nr Abergavenny Monmouthshire NP7 9BW

Andrew and Beverley Canning's converted dower house successfully bridges the gap between local pub and residential inn. Their informal approach and innate sense of fun (check the mural cartoons in both loos) contribute greatly to the Clytha's burgeoning success. In the bar a varied range of real ales is the perfect accompaniment to super-value snacks such as salmon burger with tarragon mayonnaise, faggots and peas with beer and onion gravy, and leek and laverbread rissoles. Beyond a comfortable lounge bar with sofas is the no-smoking dining-room, an appropriate setting for some more classy cooking with rather more than a nod to Andrew's own Welsh roots. Bacon, laverbread and cockles, scallops with leeks and Caerphilly and chicken supreme with Carmarthen ham and parmesan all make the best use of locally-available produce. There are good home-made puds and interesting Welsh cheeses to follow. The Clytha Arms is the 1997 Wales Regional Winner of our Seafood Pub of the Year award. No bar snacks Sat or Sun (only restaurant menu). The three en suite bedrooms are decorated in individual styles; plum and cream roses in the Victorian twin room, a blue and yellow standard double and the rather special four-poster room, thoughtfully furnished and, for all but the truly unromantic, well worth a modest supplement. *Open 11.30-3 (not Mon), 6-11 (Sat 11.30-11, Sun 12-3.30, 7-10.30). Bar Food 12.30-2.15 (Tue-Fri only), 7.30-9.30 (Mon-Fri). Restaurant 12.30-2.15 (Sun till 2.30), 7.30-9.30 (not Sun). Free House. Beer Hook Norton Best, Brains Bitter, Bass, three guest beers. Accommodation 3 bedrooms, all en suite, £45 (4-poster £65, single £40). Children welcome overnight (under-5s stay free in parents' room), additional bed & cot supplied. Garden, outdoor eating, children's play area. Family room. Accommodation & restaurant closed Sun eve, all pub closed Mon lunchtime. MasterCard, VISA*

CREIGIAU	Caesar's Arms	FOOD

Tel 01222 890486 Fax 01222 892176   Map 9 C6
Cardiff Road Creigiau Cardiff CF4 8NN

A mostly-dining country pub in a dip of the road just outside the village (8 miles from the centre of Cardiff and 3 miles from the M4 J33) is the capable hands of Champers' restaurant owners, Benigno Martinez, Mark Sharples and Earl Smikle (also the chef). The well-tried formula of chargrilled steaks and a wide choice of fresh fish, cooked in full view, with accompanying self-served salads, garlic bread and chip shop-style chips works equally well here. Whole seabass baked in rock salt and spicy Bajan fishcakes are considered specialities, and dishes with mussels, cockles, laverbread and trout make good use of local ingredients. Typical daily specials might include Provençal fish soup, Dover sole with prawn and mushroom sauce or venison with port and redcurrant. The regular menu also encompasses game terrine with Cumberland sauce, asparagus hollandaise, dressed crab, chicken fillets Barbados, sticky toffee pudding and raspberry pavlova. The airy conservatory has double-glazed walls which dissassemble in summer to provide alfresco dining. Popular Sunday lunch destination. Excellent wine list, with several available by the glass. Only well-behaved children are welcome. *Open 12-3, 6-11 (Sun 12-6 only). Bar Food 12-2.30 (till 3.30 Sun), 7-10.30 (not Sun eve). Beer Hancock's HB. Garden. Closed Sun eve & all 25 Dec. Amex, Diners, MasterCard, VISA*

CRICKHOWELL	Bear Hotel	FOOD
		B&B

Tel 01873 810408   Fax 01873 811696   Map 9 D5
Brecon Road (A40) Crickhowell Powys NP8 1BW

Zzz...

One of the original coaching inns on the London to Aberystwyth route, the Bear today bristles with personality and honest endeavour. Front bars, a hive of activity, are resplendent with oak panelling, ornamental sideboards and welcoming log fires. Refurbishment of three of the inn's oldest bedrooms has revealed open stone fireplaces which date it back to 1432. Further top-grade bedroom accommodation is housed in a modern Tudor-style courtyard extension, and in a garden cottage containing two bedrooms and a suite with its own spa bath. A furter extension houses five new bedrooms, all of which are well appointed and boast jacuzzi baths Four-poster beds and antique furniture abound throughout. Reliable bar food encompasses gratin of cockles, mussels and laverbread, local hot smoked salmon and goat's cheese with honey and pine kernel dressing for starters, followed by baked mackerel with sage and lemon sauce, salmon fishcakes and Welsh lamb cutlets. Round off a meal with rich Belgian chocolate mousse cake or spiced fruit compote. Plenty of standards (paté, filled pancakes and pork pie) in small portions for little people; aubergine, tomato and parmesan charlotte for vegetarians. *Open 11-3, 6-11 (Sun 12-3, 7-10.300. Bar Food 12-2, 6-10 (Sun 7.30-9.30). Free House. Beer Bass, Ruddles Best & County, Webster's Yorkshire Bitter. Garden, outdoor eating. Family room. Accommodation 34 bedrooms, all en suite, £56-£90 (single £42-£70). Children welcome overnight (under-5s £5, 5-14s £10), additional bed & cot available. Amex, MasterCard, VISA*

CRICKHOWELL   Nantyffin Cider Mill   FOOD

Tel & Fax 01873 810775   Map 9 D5
Brecon Road Crickhowell Powys NP8 1SG

At the junction of A479 with A40, just over a mile west of Crickhowell, a pink-painted former cider mill (the original cider press is preserved in the dining-room) standing on the Tretower estates bordering the north-west bank of the Usk. Bar snacks and light meals are served in an intimate, carpeted lounge bar, and in summer in the length of a riverside garden. Snacks vary from summer lunchtime-only ploughman's lunch and open sandwiches (Loch Fyne smoked salmon, peppered sliced beef) to one-pot meals like braised oxtail, moussaka and home-made steak and kidney pie. More substantial offerings, served in the dining-room, might be lamb shank with olives, saffron and red peppers served on braised noodles or home-made venison sausages with bubble and squeak. Interesting vegetarian options: Indian-spiced yellow lentil fritter stir-fried with lemon grass, spinach, ginger and bean sprouts. Daily fresh fish and seafood features on the blackboard (scallops in a mango salsa, sea bream on warm niçoise salad), alongside Thai-style chicken, black pudding on leek and mushroom risotto and game in season. There's also a good selection of calorific desserts and Welsh cheeses. Fixed-price Sunday lunch menu. *Open 12-3, 6-11 (Sun 12-3, 7-10.30).* **Bar Food** *12-2.30, 6.30-10 (Sun 7-9.30). Free House.* **Beer** *two regularly-changing guest beers. Garden, outdoor eating. Closed all Mon, first 2 weeks Jan & 1 week Nov. Amex, MasterCard,* **VISA**

> We only recommend food (Bar Food) in those establishments highlighted with the **FOOD** symbol.

DINAS MAWDDWY   Dolbrodmaeth Inn   B&B

Tel 01650 531333   Fax 01650 531339   Map 8 C3
Dinas Mawddwy nr Machynlleth Powys SY20 9LP

Zzz...

A former farmhouse tucked off the A470 with gardens sloping down to the River Dovey, this is a little gem. Engineer Graham Williams, once with the BBC, and wife Jean, a former cookery teacher, run this rebuilt inn (almost destroyed by fire in 1982), which now houses two cosy bars and an airy dining lounge. From the latter there are picturesque views of grounds that include a paddock, river walk and private fishing. The eight bedrooms are floored with carpet tiles and sport bright home-spun curtains and duvets, designed and made by an artistic daughter and direct-dial telephones. Though small, the bathrooms are brightly tiled with over-bath showers and multifarious energy-conscious features – even the beer cooling system boasts hot water output. Families are welcome: two rooms interconnect as a suite and one room boasts a double and single bed (plus room for a cot); children's games (and badminton) can be played on the large lawn. *Open 11-11 (Sun 12-10.30). Free House.* **Beer** *Tetley Bitter, Burton Ale. Garden, outdoor eating,* **Accommodation** *8 bedrooms, all en suite, £52 (family room £84, single £38.50). Children welcome overnight, (under-10s free if stay in parents' room), additional bed and cot available. Dogs by arrangement. Closed 2 weeks Feb. Amex, Diners, MasterCard,* **VISA**

EAST ABERTHAW   Blue Anchor   FOOD

Tel 01446 750329   Fax 01446 750077   Map 9 C6
East Aberthaw nr Barry Vale of Glamorgan CF6 9DD

The old village of Aberthaw is hidden away between the Vale of Glamorgan and the sea. Long before a vast power station came along to spoil the view there was talk here of smuggling and the creeper-covered Blue Anchor is said to have played its full part in the trade in contraband. The pub's warren of tiny rooms had more than its share of hidey-holes and stone staircases now leading nowhere, giving the whole pub a wonderfully evocative feel. These days you'll not get robbed for the price of a pint (with six or seven real ales from which to choose) and, in the bar, meals scarcely cost a King's ransom. A daily-changing blackboard may list traditional Welsh rarebit, liver and bacon casserole, hake and chips, grilled lemon sole stuffed with prawns and spring onions fish pie or lamb stew with herb dumplings; sandwiches, jacket potatoes and children's favourites complete the bar food menu. In the evenings the board may also list steamed slices of monkfish with a crab and grain mustard sauce and pan-fried garlic and herb rump steak. Only restaurant meals Saturday evening and Sunday lunchtime. *Open 11-11 (Sun 12-10.30).* **Bar Food** *12-2, 6-8 (no bar food Sat eve & all Sun). Free House.* **Beer** *Crown Buckley Buckley's Best, Marston's Pedigree, Wadworth 6X, Boddingtons, Flowers IPA, Theakston Old Peculier, guest beer. Garden, outdoor eating. Family room.* MasterCard, **VISA**

ERBISTOCK — Boat Inn — FOOD

Tel 01978 780143   Map 8 D2
Erbistock nr Ruabon Wrexham LL13 0DL

A dead end lane past the Victorian church leads to the Boat, in an unrivalled position on the banks of the River Dee; there was once a ferry crossing here. Essentially pubby with its cosy flagstoned bar and open fires, it's a fine spot year round for a casual drink, but their is also a fairly serious attitude to food. At lunchtimes ploughman's, sandwiches and Dee salmon are a big draw (plain sliced or crispbreads available on request). On a daily bar menu, carrot and chive soup, Cumberland sausage with onion gravy, steak and ale pie and Barnsley lamb chop are typical choices. Table d'hote menus in the dining-rooms with seasonal alternatives à la carte. Accommodation is offered in a self-contained flat (not inspected). Summer afternoon teas (June–August). No under-14s in bar. *Open 12-3 (11.30-3.30 summer), 6.30-11, (from 7 summer) Sun 12-4 (12-10.30 summer). Closed Sun eve Sep-Apr.* **Bar Food** *12-2, 7-9. Free House.* **Beer** *Plassey, Cains Formidable Ale, guest beer. Riverside garden, outdoor eating. Family room.* MasterCard, **VISA**

FELINDRE FARCHOG — Salutation Inn — B&B

Tel 01239 820564   Map 9 B5
A487 Felindre Farchog nr Crymych Pembrokeshire SA41 3UY

☺

Felindre, a dot on the map where the A487 road bridge crosses the Nyfer, *is* the Salutation. Well-tended lawns slope down to the river, and there are gardens and terraces for a peaceful drink. The single-storey bedroom wing is neat and well-appointed. Bright duvets set the tone, with satellite TV, radio alarms, tea-makers and hairdryers providing up-to-date refinements. Three family rooms have bunk beds, and cots are also provided free of charge. Bar snacks and restaurant. *Open 12-2, 5.30-11, Sun 12-3, 7-10.30. Free House.* **Beer** *Burton Ale. Riverside garden, outdoor eating. Family room.* **Accommodation** *9 bedrooms, all en suite, £48 (family room £58, single £30). Children welcome overnight, (under-2s stay free in parents' room, 2-14s £5) additional bed & cot available. Check-in by arrangement.* MasterCard, **VISA**

GLANWYDDEN — Queen's Head — FOOD

Tel 01492 546570   Fax 01492 546487   Map 8 C1
Llandudno Junction Glanwydden Conwy LL31 9JP

One mile from Rhos-on-Sea and three miles from Llandudno, this one-time wheelwright's cottage – now the Queen's Head village pub – is particularly popular for a lunch stop-off. Hidden down a maze of country lanes, Glanwydden is best found by following the Llanrhos road from Penrhyn Bay (B5115). Motivator of the Queen's Head's admirable food operation is chef/landlord Robert Cureton, who sets great store by careful shopping for his daily-updated menus. Start, perhaps, with a home-made soup like mushroom with red wine and hazelnuts or smoked breast of goose with kiwi fruit. Main courses might feature a trio of vegetarian options, 'lighter meals' (quiche, Arbroath smokie, cheese-topped Conwy mussels), good fresh seafood (local sautéed king scallops and smoked bacon), grilled local lamb cutlets with a raspberry and amaretto sauce, venison casserole, and salads. The cold seafood platter is a house speciality and can be enjoyed either as a starter shared by two or as a main course. Finish with a selection from the particularly good nursery puddings displayed on the

Welsh dresser – perhaps cherry Bakewell tart or sticky toffee pudding. Hand-pulled beers are suitably well kept and the wine list is above average, compiled in association with Rodney Densem Wines of Nantwich; the house champagne is £17.95! Parties of six or more may only book for the early evenings or Sunday lunch. *Open 11-3, 6-11, (Sun 12-3, 7-10.30).* **Bar Food** *12-2.15, 6-9.* **Beer** *Tetley, Burton, Benskins Best, guest beer. Terrace, outdoor eating. Closed all 25 Dec.* MasterCard, **VISA**

HANMER	**Hanmer Arms**	**B&B**

Tel 01948 830532   Fax 01948 830740   Map 6 A3
Hanmer nr Whitchurch Wrexham SY13 3DE

☺

Standing in the shadow of St Chad's church at the heart of a quiet hamlet now mercifully by-passed by the A539. The mellow brick Hanmer Arms is certainly of 16th-century origin, with a history closely linked to the old communities of the Shropshire Lake District. In a newly hollowed-out interior of this self-styled 'village hotel' are contained two bars, reception lounge and restaurant, with further dining and function rooms on the upper level. The strong point here lies in the apartment-style bedrooms laid out in the reconstructed barn and outhouses which stand around a central cobbled courtyard full of old farming artefacts. Decorated in country style with full en suite bathrooms, they are well equipped with phones, radio alarms and satellite TV. The most spacious have plenty of room to accommodate families overnight, while for the businessman there's also plenty of work space. Boardroom and conferences for up to 90 delegates. Five-acre woodland trail. *Open 11.30-11 (Sun 12-3, 6-10.30). Free House.* **Beer** *Tetley Traditional, Burton Ale. Garden.* **Accommodation** *26 bedrooms, all en suite, from £48 (suites £58, single from £38). Children welcome overnight (under-9s stay free in parents' room, 9-16s £8), additional bed & cot supplied.* Amex, Diners, MasterCard, **VISA**

HAY-ON-WYE	**Kilverts**	**FOOD**
		B&B

Tel 01497 821042   Fax 01497 821580   Map 9 D5
Bull Ring Hay-on-Wye Powys HR3 5AG

 ☺ Zzz...

An inimitable collection of hats and Victorian Spy cartoons imbue the bar of Colin Thomson's hotel/pub/bar with great character; the atmosphere is also enhanced nightly by the playing of an upright piano and live jazz on alternate Thursdays. Food is a further attraction, with the likes of seafood pie and home-made spicy beefburger alongside daily specials ranging from chicken livers with Marsala sauce (plus sandwiches and ploughman's platters at lunchtime) to spinach and mushroom roulade; fresh fish (baked cod gratin with lemon and tarragon sauce, grilled lemon sole) is best from Thursdays to Sundays; other dishes might include roast poussin with chestnut stuffing and beef lasagne. Home-made desserts like crème brulée and summer pudding. Residents' accommodation is both comfortable and stylish with brass bedsteads, smoked-glass tables and attractive floral bed linen. In addition to tea trays, direct-dial phones, TVs and radios, accoutrements include hairdryers and trouser presses. Bathrooms are a little utilitarian, nonetheless incorporating powerful showers and copious amounts of hot water. A marquee is erected for functions in summer – it's also a venue for Hay Jazz at the end of July. *Open 11-11 (till 11.30 Bank Holidays), Sun 12-10.30.* **Bar Food** *12-2, 7-9.30. Free House.* **Beer** *Boddingtons, Whitbread Castle Eden Ale, Bass. Patio, garden, outdoor eating.* **Accommodation** *11 bedrooms, all en suite (6 with shower only), £48-£60 (single £24). Children welcome overnight (under-6s stay free in parents' room, 6-12s £6), additional bed & cot available. Accommodation closed 24 Dec, pub & accommodation closed 25 Dec.* Amex, MasterCard, **VISA**

> Many **B&B** establishments offer reduced rates for weekend and out-of-season bookings. Always ask about special deals for longer stays. Beware half-board terms in inns where we do not recommend the **FOOD**.

LANDSHIPPING — Stanley Arms — FOOD

Tel 01834 891227
Landshipping nr Narberth Pembrokeshire SA67 8BE

Map 9 A5

One must cultivate a certain desire to come to the Stanley Arms: it's five miles by road from Canaston Bridge (on the A40), a lengthy walk through the Minwear Forest and 200 yards from the moorings at Landshipping Cove, high up the Cleddau estuary. It is therefore a true pub-lovers' pub with a good mix of locals, yachtsmen, walkers and caravanners. Those with a serious taste for real ale will enjoy a splendid pint, while hearty appetites will be satisfied by Trish Fursse's home-cooking. Alongside pints of shell-on prawns and fresh fish (when available) the menu may list cheesy celery soup, Welsh chicken cobbler, pork and sage casserole and authentic Indian dishes like lamb rogan josh. Live music on summer Friday and Saturday nights. *Open 12-3, 6-11 (Sun 12-3, 7-10.30). **Bar Food** 12-2, 7-9.30 (till 9 Sun). Free House. **Beer** Worthington Best, Bass, guest beer. Garden, outdoor eating. No credit cards.*

LLANARMON DYFFRYN CEIRIOG — West Arms Hotel — FOOD

Tel 01691 600665   Fax 01691 600622   Map 8 D2   **B&B**
Llanarmon Dyffryn Ceiriog nr Llangollen Wrexham LL20 7LD

Zzz... ☺

In a picturesque hamlet at the head of the Ceiriog valley, this 16th-century former farmhouse stands to the front of well-manicured gardens which run down to the river bridge. Black and white painted outside and bedecked with creeper and summer flowers, it's a haven of cosy comfort within, the tone set by open log fires, flagstone floors, blackened beams and rustic furniture. Tucked round the back, the Wayfarers' Bar serves a modest selection of well-prepared snacks in chintzy surroundings with an adjacent family lounge and patio. Following soup and tuna and mixed bean salad, local Ceiriog trout heads a list of main meals which might include steak, kidney and mushroom pie, chicken kebabs with spicy sauce and various daily specials featuring fresh fish and local game in season. Jam roly-poly and bread-and-butter pudding are typical of the traditional puddings. Bedrooms retain the period comfort afforded by handsome antique furnishings alongside modern fitted bathrooms: homely extras include pot pourri and quality toiletries. Five rooms are reserved for non-smokers and the two suites have plenty of space for family use (sleeping up to 5). Room service 8am-11pm. Disabled facilities. *Open 11-11 (Sun 12-10.30). **Bar Food** 12-2.30, 7-9.30. Free House. **Beer** Boddingtons. Garden, outdoor eating. **Accommodation** 13 bedrooms, all en suite, £100-£110 (single £55). Children welcome overnight, additional bed (£25) & cot (£6.50) are available. Hotel closed 2 weeks Jan/Feb. Amex, Diners, MasterCard, **VISA***

LLANDDAROG — Butcher's Arms — FOOD

Tel 01267 275330
Llanddarog nr Carmarthen Ceredigion SA32 8NS

Map 9 B5

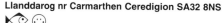

Well into a second decade at the Butcher's, self-taught butcher, proprietor and accomplished chef David James still runs his kitchen with unbridled enthusiasm. There have been changes aplenty over the years, of which the by-passing of Llanddarog by the A40 is not the least significant; hidden up a side road by the church, the Butcher's Arms is now a serene spot. As fads have come and gone, however, the kitchen here has remained constant and the food consistent. Familiar lunch dishes include avocado and bacon salad, cheese, ham and potato pie and seasonal tagliatelle with prawns and asparagus. Home-made pies – chicken and leek and seafood – are as popular today as a decade ago. In the evenings, generously-priced specials which supplement the menu are even more substantial. Fresh fish may be plaice fillets stuffed with asparagus and prawns with a white wine sauce. There may be Welsh lamb with mint and cider sauce, pork fillet with garlic and mushroom sauce and perhaps King Henry's feast, a single beef rib roast. Mavis James looks after the bookings (advised at weekends) and ordering with the same care that she applies to polishing the ubiquitous brass and miners' lamps, tending a roaring winter fire or arranging the floral displays which fill the fireplace in the tiny main bar in summer. Recent conversion of the old beer cellar and bottle store has created a further bar which, in turn, leads out to the rear garden. The Butcher's remains a village local, with a robust pint of Felinfoel a firm favourite among the loyal band of Welsh-speaking regulars. *Open 11-3 (not Sun), 5.30-11 (from 6.30 Sun).* **Bar Food** *11-2.30 (not Sun), 6-9.45 (Sat 5.30-9.45, Sun 7-9.30). Free House.* **Beer** *Felinfoel Bitter, Dark & Double Dragon, guest beers. Front patio, garden, outdoor eating. Closed Sun lunch. MasterCard,* **VISA**

LLANDOVERY — King's Head Inn — B&B

Tel 01550 720393
Map 9 C5
Market Square Llandovery Carmarthenshire SA20 0AB

Medieval stonework and timbers are still in evidence throughout the bars of this black-painted town-centre building. Charles I's insignia, incorporated in the Inn's sign, commemorates the later construction of the upper storeys. Here the bedrooms have been sympathetically added and are kept reasonably up-to-date with neat bathrooms, tea-makers and radio-alarms. There is also a first-floor residents' TV lounge. A flagstoned rear entrance in Stone Street leads into the Old Bank (which once it was) where light meals and bar snacks are served. *Open 12-2.30, 5.30-11, (Sun 12-3, 7-10.30). Free House.* **Beer** *Hancock's HB.* **Accommodation** *4 bedrooms, all en suite, £44 (single £26). Children by arrangement (free if sharing parents' room). No credit cards.*

LLANFIHANGEL CRUCORNEY — Skirrid Inn — A

Tel 01873 890258
Map 9 D5
Llanfihangel Crucorney Monmouthshire NP7 8DH

With some justification, the bloody Skirrid claims to be the oldest pub in Wales. It is recorded that one John Crowther was hanged here for sheep stealing in 1116; that the legendary Owain Glyndwr marshalled his troops in this yard before his march upon Pontrilas; and that rope marks on the old oak beams are from sentences handed down by the hanging Judge Jeffries following the papist plot of 1679. Today's high-ceilinged bar retains original Welsh slate, some Tudor oak settles and a collection of beaten copper pans and salvers echoing the inn's long and colourful history. Children are welcomed in the dining-room and garden only; hitching posts for horses in the yard. 4½ miles north of Abergavenny, signposted off the A465 Hereford road. *Open 11-3, 6-11, (Sat 11-11, Sun 12-3, 7-10.30).* **Beer** *Ushers. Garden. No credit cards.*

LLANFIHANGEL-NANT-MELAN — Red Lion Inn — FOOD
Tel 01544 350220
Map 9 D4 B&B
Llanfihangel-nant-Melan nr New Radnor Powys LD8 2TN

➤ 🍴 Zzz... 😊

A popular stopping point on the A44 between the Midlands and Aberystwyth, the Johns family's pub continues to please a regular discerning clientele. Not least among its virtues is chef Gareth's unstinting attention to fresh 'real food' – he produces pub food that is decidedly above-average. His fried cod with chips and mushy peas and traditional bangers with mash and gravy as popular at lunchtimes as the more accomplished dishes like peppered duck breast and monkfish Caribbean-style on the more involved evening menu. A home-made soup like cream of leek and nutmeg is made daily and their own paté is always popular. Family roast lunch on Sundays, home-made homely puddings (ginger sponge with lemon sauce, banana slice) and a commendable board of British cheeses (seven varieties, perhaps including Welsh Cheddar, Sage Derby and locally-produced farmhouse cheeses) provide further proof that the kitchen here is in good hands. Three spacious chalet bedrooms without TV or telephones offer abundant peace and quiet, well back from the road, with lightweight candy-striped duvets in summer and 'hotties' provided for winter nights. Bathrooms, with shower/WC only, are best described as practical, if a little spartan. Two family rooms sleep three. Conservatory and separate, no-smoking dining-room. *Open 11.30-2.30, 6.30-10.30 (till 11 Fri & Sat), Sun 12-3, 7-10.30. Closed Tue Nov-Apr & 1 week Nov.* **Bar Food** *12-2, 6.30-9 (till 9.30 Sat, from 7 Sun). Free House.* **Beer** *Hook Norton Bitter. Garden, outdoor eating. Family room.* **Accommodation** *3 bedrooms, all en suite, £32 (family room £40, single £17.50). Children welcome overnight (under-5s stay free in parents' room), additional bed (£10) supplied. MasterCard,* **VISA**

LLANFRYNACH — White Swan — FOOD

Tel 01874 665276   Map 9 C5
Llanfrynach nr Brecon Powys LD3 7BZ

Polished flagstones, open log fire in a vast inglenook, exposed oak beams and cattle byres separating the tables lend the White Swan a general air of antiquity, to which piped classical music adds a surprising footnote. There's plenty of space inside and an attractive rear patio of stone-topped tables under a straggling trellis. Food sticks to well-tried standards, but quantities are generous – French onion soup, ratatouille au gratin, lasagne, fisherman's pie, beef and mushroom pie, Welsh lamb chops and ploughman's. Puddings include chocolate cream mousse and apple crumble. Llanfrynach is a sleepy village just off the A40 three miles from Brecon. Children welcome. *Open 12-2.30, 7-11 (till 10.30 Sun). Closed all Mon except Bank Holidays & 3 weeks Jan.* **Bar Food** *12-2, 7-9.45 (till 9 Sun). Free House.* **Beer** *Brains Bitter, Flowers IPA. Garden, outdoor eating. Family room. No credit cards.*

LLANGATTOCK — Vine Tree Inn — FOOD

Tel 01873 810514   Map 9 D5
The Legar Llangattock nr Crickhowell Powys NP8 1HG

A picturesque row of low, pink-painted cottages just across a meadow from the River Usk, fronted by roadside picnic tables and a fine magnolia. Opposite, the stone packhorse bridge marks the old river crossing into Crickhowell. Exposed original stonework divides Stuart and Cynthia Lennox's pub into a succession of cosy alcoves, devoted almost entirely to eating. A blackboard menu runs the gamut of safe choices (stockpot soup, mackerel paté, lasagne and steaks) interspersed with a few more adventurous selections (smoked venison with cranberry sauce, pork stuffed with apricots in a tangy orange sauce), all generously served. Try, perhaps, lemon sole au gratin, monkfish with Pernod and white wine sauce, salmon in filo with a leek and cream sauce, or the speciality 'Chicken Cymru' with a white wine sauce with mushrooms and tomato. Popular Sunday roasts and half-a-dozen vegetarian dishes (nut roast with tomato and basil sauce) to choose from. Families are decidedly welcome and small portions readily available: booking though, is well advised. *Open 12-2.30, 6-11, (Sun 12-2.30, 7-10.30).* **Bar Food** *12-2.30, 6-10 (from 7 Sun). Free House.* **Beer** *Fremlins, Boddingtons, Wadworth 6X. MasterCard,* **VISA**

LLANGOLLEN — Britannia Inn — B&B

Tel 01978 860144   Map 8 D2
Horseshoe Pass Llangollen Denbighshire LL20 8DW

Zzz...

Cut back into the hillside by the A542 below the spectacular Horseshoe Pass, the inn stands in two acres of beautiful gardens, complete with trout pools, two miles above the town: directly below are the ruins of Crucis Abbey. Quite possibly this site started out in the 11th century as a hostel for the abbey and the monks' ale house, waters from the adjacent stream being used for the brew. Today's ales are a little more sophisticated, as is the accommodation, though some original and some later, 15th-century, features can still be seen. Bedrooms are cottage-style with lacy cotton bedspreads and have half-tester or four-poster beds. All rooms are on the small side with compact en suite facilities (two with WC and showers only), colour TVs and coffee-making kits. There are no telephones in the rooms: guests may simply wake to the dawn chorus and enjoy the memorable valley views. *Open 12-3 (from 11 Sat), 6-11 (Sat 11-11 summer), Sun 12-3, 7-10.30 (12-10.30 summer). Closed Mon eve in winter. Free House.* **Beer** *Theakston Best & Old Peculier, guest beers. Garden.* **Accommodation** *7 bedrooms, all en suite, £50 (family room sleeping three £55, single £35). Children welcome overnight (under-1s free) additional bed (£5) available. Accommodation closed 25 Dec. Amex, Diners, MasterCard,* **VISA**

We do not accept free meals or hospitality – our inspectors pay their own bills and never book in the name of Egon Ronay's Guides.

LLANGORSE · Red Lion · B&B

Tel 01874 658238   Fax 01874 658595   Map 9 D5
Llangorse nr Brecon Powys LD3 7TY

Just a mile from Llangorse Lake, at the heart of the village by St. Paulinus Church, stands the Rosiers' welcoming local. Picnic tables in front by the village stream make it a picturesque spot. Riding, fishing and water-skiing (mid-week only), all available locally, draw many regulars to the Red Lion. Accommodation in neat pastel-shade bedrooms with attractive duvets is practical rather than luxurious, though TV, radio-alarms and tea-makers ensure an acceptable level of comfort. Five have well-kept bathrooms en suite, the remainder (with showers and washbasins only) share a couple of adjacent toilets. Built into the hillside, all rooms have level access to a rear garden reserved for residents. Good selection of twenty malt whiskies. *Open 11.30-3, 6.30-11, (Sun 12-3, 7-10.30). Closed Mon-Fri lunch Nov-Feb. Free House.* **Beer** *Flowers Original, Boddingtons, guest beer. Streamside terrace/patio, outdoor eating.* **Accommodation** *10 bedrooms, 5 en suite, £40-£50 (family room £50, single £25-£30). Children welcome overnight (under-12s stay free in parents' room), additional bed & cot available. No dogs. No credit cards.*

LLANGRANNOG · Ship Inn · FOOD

Tel 01239 654423   Map 9 B4
Llangrannog Ceredigion SA44 6SL

Just 50 yards from the beach, the white-painted Ship Inn is located down a narrow winding road (watch out for a very steep hairpin bend) in a delightful little seaside village. It's run by two couples, the Boxes and the Browns: Lynne and De are responsible for the bar menu which, in addition to standard items like steak and kidney pie, steaks (well hung by the local butcher), ploughman's, jacket potatoes and sandwiches, roams far and wide with pizza, and from the blackboard 'Specials' menu, moussaka, mixed bean goulash and lamb rogan josh. Local seafood features strongly in summer with dressed crab, Dover sole, baked local herring, skate, or, given 24hrs' notice, a special seafood platter that includes lobster, scallops, cockles, mussels, whelks, crab and prawns. Guests can eat in one of the two bars or outside under colourful awnings that keep the showers at bay while you watch the world go by. *Open 12-11, (Sun 12-10.30).* **Bar Food** *12-3, 6-10 (from 7 Sun in winter). Free House.* **Beer** *Courage Directors, Ruddles County, Webster's Yorkshire Bitter. Outdoor eating. Family room. MasterCard,* **VISA**.

LLANGYNWYD · Olde House Inn · A

Tel 01656 733310   Fax 01656 737337   Map 9 C6
Llangynwyd nr Maesteg Bridgend CF34 9SB

At the heart of Llangynwyd's original village off the A4063, the Olde House is notable for its antiquity (dating back to 1147), its massive thatched roof, metre-thick Welsh stone walls and ubiquitous memorabilia. Modern-day amenities include a spacious conservatory dining-room, vast graded patios with a barbecue pit and a children's adventure playground complete with an old tractor. Drinkers may appreciate the selection of around 70 malt whiskies. Children welcome inside. *Open 11-11, (Sun 12-10.30). Free House.* **Beer** *Flowers IPA & Original, Brains Bitter, Morland Old Speckled Hen, guest beer. Garden, children's play area. MasterCard,* **VISA**

> We endeavour to be as up-to-date as possible but inevitably some changes to
> landlords, chefs and other key staff occur after the Guide
> has gone to press.

LLANNEFYDD   Hawk & Buckle   B&B

Tel 01745 540249   Fax 01745 540316   Map 8 C1
Llannefydd nr Denbigh Denbighshire LL16 5ED

Zzz...

Stone-built in the 17th century, tiny Llannefydd stands high up in the Denbigh hills.
Steady improvements here have produced an inn of high quality, run and personally
supervised by Bob and Barbara Pearson. Residents enjoy use of their own lounge bar
and may mull over their morning papers without fear of noisy intrusion. En suite
bedrooms with TVs, direct-dial telephones and fully-equipped bathrooms are
decorated in co-ordinating fabrics and mostly pastel shades; guests may choose
between duvets or traditional bedding. The best rooms, one of them with a pine four-
poster, are on the upper floor from where guests enjoy the finest views down to Cefn
Meiriadog and the North Wales coast. *Open 12-2, 7-11 (till 10.30 Sun).Closed Mon,
Tue, Thu & Fri lunch Oct-Apr & all 25 Dec. No real ales.* **Accommodation** *10 bedrooms,
all en suite, £50 (four-poster £60, single £38). No children under 10 overnight. Check-in
by arrangement. No dogs. Amex, MasterCard,* **VISA**

LLANTRISANT   Greyhound Inn   B&B

Tel 01291 672505   Fax 01291 673255   Map 9 D6
Llantrisant nr Usk Monmouthshire NP5 1LE

Just 2½ miles from Usk, the Greyhound occupies a hillside, with fine views of the
Lowes River valley which flows to the sea at Newport some 9 miles downstream.
The low stone 17th-century farm house is much extended now with split-level bar
and succession of drinking and eating rooms stepped into the hill. Conversion of the
former barn has produced a dozen en suite bedrooms with blackened roof trusses and
decorated in a cottage style becoming both the building's nature and its rural location.
Up-to-the-minute equipment includes remote-control TV and direct-dial phones;
two larger family rooms have an extra bed; all have both bath and showers. French
windows in the best, ground-floor rooms open on to private patios in a garden setting
with lily pond and ornamented fountain. There is no direct access from the nearby
A449 dual carriageway, so be sure to obtain exact directions on booking. Hundreds of
trees have been planted and all rooms are double-glazed to prevent any intrusive road
noise. *Open 11-3, 6-11, (Sun 12-3, 7-10.30). Free House.* **Beer** *Wadworth 6X, Flowers
Original, Marston's Pedigree, Boddingtons, Morland Old Speckled Hen, guest beer. Garden,
patio. Family room.* **Accommodation** *10 bedrooms, all en suite, £55-£60 (single £40-
£47). Children welcome overnight (under-5s stay free in parents' room), additional bed (£5)
& cot available. No dogs. Accommodation closed 24 & 25 Dec. MasterCard,* **VISA**

LLANYRE   Bell Country Inn   B&B

Tel 01597 823959   Fax 01597 825899   Map 9 C4
Llanyre Llandrindod Wells Powys LD1 6DY

Standing in hills above Llandrindod Wells, just two miles away, Llanyre is handily
placed for visitors to mid-Wales with the Elan and upper Wye valleys nearby and
multifarious outdoor activity within handy reach. Built originally for drovers headed
with their flocks to 'foreign parts' (Gloucester and Hereford), the Bell provided clean
straw and stabling throughout the 17th and 18th centuries. Today's version offers
high-quality accommodation in recent extensions. Standard equipment includes
satellite TV, radio alarms and telephones as well as beverage trays, trouser presses and
hairdryers. Bedrooms are brightly decorated in pastel shades with generously-sized
duvets and bathrooms sport smart white porcelain fitments with powerful over-bath
showers. Two larger rooms are suitable for family use (under-10s stay free and a cot
is available), one of these on the ground floor is quite suitable for disabled guests.
Open 12-3, 6.30-11 (Sun 12-3, 7-10.30), Free House. **Beer** *Worthington Best, Hancocks
HB, Theakston XB, guest beer. Small garden. Family room.* **Accommodation** *9 bedrooms,
all en suite, £60 (single £35/£37.50). Children welcome overnight (under-10s stay free
in parents' room), additional bed & cot available. Amex, Diners, MasterCard,* **VISA**

LLOWES	**Radnor Arms**	**FOOD**

Tel 01497 847460   Map 9 D5
Llowes Powys HR3 5JA

Landlord of the Radnor Arms for over ten years, Brian Gorringe offers culinary refinement in this 1000-year-old drinking house. The old stone building with a stone roof is overlooked by the Black Mountains on one side, the Beacons on another and the Beggins on the third. With only a dozen tables and no more than 40-60 seats, it's surprising to encounter six blackboards listing an extensive range of starters, snacks, main dishes and puddings from which to choose! The Radnor Arms divides by means of heavy oak panels into the bar area proper, popular by day, and a more spacious, lofty-beamed garden side for more leisurely evening enjoyment, and for which you ought to book. Either way, there's good beer on handpump plus a few unusual bottled beers and a modest selection of house wines. The menu on the blackboards might include cod and chips, French onion soup, lamb in redcurrant sauce, marinated venison with pickled walnuts, prawns Cantonese-style, haddock mornay or monkfish and prawn kebabs with tomato concassée sauce. Sandwiches, filled rolls and ploughman's platters are served all day. Puddings include toffee crunch cheesecake and apple and blackberry pie. *Open 11-2.30, 6.30-11 (not Mon), Sun 12-3 only.* **Bar Food** *11-2.30, 6.30-11 (except Sun eve and Mon). Free House.* **Beer** *Felinfoel Traditional. Garden, outdoor eating. Closed Sun eve & all Mon (except bank holidays).* *MasterCard,* **VISA**

LLWYNDAFYDD	**Crown Inn**	**FOOD**

Tel & Fax 01545 560396   Map 9 B4
Llwyndafydd nr New Quay Ceredigion SA44 6FH

A handsome, white-painted 18th-century inn at the head of the hidden romantic valley of Cwm. This highly popular spot with families in summer has a large patio and play area for the children (who are offered regular favourites on their own menu). In addition to a standard range of adult bar food (the evening restaurant menu is pricier) there are well-made curries and daily specials on a board like local fish (baked cod in cheese and prawn sauce, pan-fried local plaice, Teifi sewin and salmon), wild rabbit casserole, chicken pie and braised pigeon breast with tomato and mushrooms. Home-made pizzas, from children's-size to family-size, are made to order. Ice cream features on the dessert choice alongside home-made gateau and lemon soufflé. Popular for Sunday lunch (half price for children). *Open 12-3, 6-11 (till 10.30 Sun).* **Bar Food** *12-2, 6-9.30 (Sun 12-3, 6-9). Free House.* **Beer** *Flowers IPA & Original, guest beers. Garden, outdoor eating area, tiered patios. Family room. Closed Sun eve Oct-Easter (except Christmas period). MasterCard,* **VISA**

LLYSWEN	**Griffin Inn**	★	**FOOD**

Tel 01874 754241   Fax 01874 754592   Map 9 D5   **B&B**
Llyswen Brecon Powys LD3 0UR

  Zzz... ☺

Mythically speaking, the griffin is a creature of vast proportions, half lion, half dragon, its whole being considerably less awesome than its constituent parts. No such problems exist for Richard and Di Stockton, for their Griffin is nothing short of splendid in all departments and conspicuously well run. That locally-caught salmon and brook trout feature so regularly on the menu is scarcely surprising as the Griffin employs its own ghillie, and fishing stories abound in the bar, which is the centre of village life. It's hung with framed displays of fishing flies and maps of the upper and lower reaches of the Wye valley, and dominated by a splendid inglenook fire. In the adjacent lounge, low tables, high-backed Windsor chairs and window seats make a comfortable setting in which to sample their 'Tiffin' menu (dishes for two people served Monday to Friday evenings); this might offer sweet and sour pork with rice or lentil, pepper and pasta gratin followed by a long choice of home-made sweets (apple strudel, banana and caramel flan) and Welsh cheeses. Evening meals provide a wider choice of more substantial fare, either in the no-smoking restaurant or the bars, as space allows. Here you might order Cornish mussels in white wine and garlic, ragout of wild rabbit, pan-fried breast of wood pigeon with bubble and squeak in wine jus or chicken chasseur. Tip-top Sunday lunch is only served in the dining-room (no bar food) and booking is suggested at least a week ahead. The ten recently-refurbished, en suite bedrooms revert to the fishing theme. They are cottagey in style, wonderfully tranquil, and though there are telephones, television is considered superfluous. Two rooms are in an annexe across the road. A family suite has its own lounge, shares a bathroom and sleeps four. The splendid residents' lounge on the upper floor of the inn's oldest part is dramatically set under original rafters dating, it is thought, back to its origins as a 15th-century sporting inn. There is no garden but children may eat in the bar and small portions are served; two high-chairs provided. *Open 12-3, 7-11, (Sun 12-3, 7-10.30).* **Bar Food** *12-2 (no bar food Sun), 7-9 (Sun cold supper for residents only); Sun lunch at 1pm in dining-room only. Free House.* **Beer** *Boddingtons, Flowers IPA, guest beers. Outdoor eating.* **Accommodation** *8 bedrooms all en suite, £60 (family room £90, single £34.50). Children welcome overnight (under-10s stay free in parents' room), additional bed & cot available. Accommodation closed 25 & 26 Dec. Amex, Diners, MasterCard,* **VISA**

LYDART   Gockett Inn   FOOD

Tel 01600 860486   Map 9 D5
Lydart nr Monmouth Monmouthshire NP5 4AD

This former staging post on the St David's to London route stands atop an escarpment (now the B4293) three miles outside Monmouth. Central to the Inn's modern attractions are Hazel Short's daily selected menus, wherein brevity is made a virtue by careful buying of top-quality foodstuffs, and by her innovative approach to traditional recipes. Home-made soups are thick, flavourful and popular, along with the likes of prawns with fresh raspberry vinaigrette, paté maison with Cumberland sauce, tagliatelle with smokey bacon, leek and black pudding tart. Though all are officially starters, a light lunch of two of them is equally acceptable, except on Sundays, when bookings should be made for the fixed-price lunch. Alongside the hefty pies other main courses are equally substantial: poussin with mild fresh fruit curry sauce, fillet of beef en croute filled with Stilton cheese and Madeira sauce, plus a choice of fresh fish dishes. The pudding list which follows is simple but commendable in scope, mostly home-made offerings like treacle tart with home-made custard and bread-and-butter pudding. Leather banquettes, silk flowers and gathered drapes lend a bright, cottagey feel to the original dining-room which is hung with horse brasses and copper bed-warmers. The extended bar leads to an enclosed rear patio, and a neat garden for alfresco eating in fine weather. Disabled WC. *Open 11-11, (Sun 12-10.30).* **Bar Food** *12-2, 7-10 (7-9 Sun). Free House.* **Beer** *Bass, guest beers. Garden, outdoor eating. MasterCard,* **VISA**

MARFORD   Trevor Arms   B&B

Tel 01244 570436   Fax 01244 571244   Map 8 D2
Marford Wrexham LL12 8TA

Quaint 17th-century architecture is a feature of Marford's original buildings, which all incorporate a cross to ward off evil spirits. The Trevor Arms, built later as a coaching inn, echoes these features and also plays its full part in village life centred on a very busy locals' bar which occupies the pub's oldest part. The original and somewhat modest bedrooms are also housed here. Though not lacking in modern appointments such as TV, radio and direct-dial phones most offer only shower/WC en suite bathrooms. Six rooms, including one with a four-poster and a family room sleeping up to three, have en suite baths. Large garden, covered barbeque patio and children's play area. *Open 11-11.30 (Sun 12-10.30).* **Beer** *Thomas Greenalls Original, Greenalls Draught, Tetley Bitter, guest beers. Garden, barbecue, children's play area. Family room.* **Accommodation** *20 bedrooms, all en suite, £41-£47 (single £28), cooked breakfast £3.50 pp extra. Children welcome overnight (under-5s stay free in parents' room, 5-14s £10)), additional bed & cot available. MasterCard,* **VISA**

MENAI BRIDGE   Anglesey Arms   B&B

Tel 01248 712305   Fax 01248 712076   Map 8 B2
Menai Bridge Isle of Anglesey LL59 5EA

Just a mile from the Britannia rail and road bridge (A5), this brewery-owned former coaching inn stands right next to the older and more famous Thomas Telford suspension bridge that links Anglesey with the mainland. From the spacious bars, one a no-smoking family area, sliding glass doors open on to a hilltop terrace and enclosed, mature garden which share super views of the handsome old bridge and the swirling Menai Straits (long known as one of Britain's most trecherous waterways) below. Following its own recent re-fit everything is shipshape in the decently-sized bedrooms, all of which are now equipped with a full range of up-to-date accessories that includes colour TVs and alarm clock-radios. With the exception of two single rooms and one double with shower rooms only, all have en suite bathrooms; two family suites have bunk beds. *Open 11-11 (Sun 12-10.30). Beer JW Lees.* **Accommodation** *16 bedrooms, all en suite, £50 (single £32). Children welcome overnight, additional bed (£10 per child in bunk) & cot provided. Garden, children's play area.* MasterCard, **VISA**

NEVERN   Trewern Arms Hotel   B&B

Tel 01239 820395   Map 9 A5
Nevern nr Newport Pembrokeshire SA42 0NB

Zzz... ☺

This hidden hamlet in a valley on the B4582 is a world all on its own with historic pilgrims' church and Celtic cross, nurseries, cheese dairy and cake shop. Across the stone bridge over the Nyfer (or Nevern), the Trewern Arms is creeper-clad with sparkling fairy lights, exuding a magical air. Bedrooms, carefully added to the original 18th-century stone building, are furnished in cane and pine with floral curtains and matching duvets. The bathrooms are all en suite (7 with shower/WCs only); TVs and tea-makers are standard. There are three spacious family rooms (one sleeping up to four). A foyer lounge upstairs has plenty of literature for walkers and fishermen, and the lounge bar below sports comfortable armchairs and sofas. Children are welcome until 9pm. *Open 11-3, 6-11, (Sun 12-3, 7-10.30). Free House. Beer Whitbread Castle Eden Ale, Flowers Original, guest beers. Garden, children's play area.* **Accommodation** *9 bedrooms, all en suite, £45 double (family room sleeping three £55, single £30). Children welcome overnight, additional bed available. Check-in by arrangement. No dogs.* MasterCard, **VISA**

NEW INN   Tate's at Tafarn Newydd   FOOD

Tel 01437 532542   Map 9 B5
New Inn nr Rosebush Pembrokeshire SA66 7RA

Tafarn Newydd (literally translated as New Inn) stands conveniently at the crossroads of the B4313 and B4329 just outside the village of Rosebush. Once burned-down by a previous landlord, it is now the home of Tate's, whose name proprietor Diana Richards has brought with her from her former business in Goodwick. Welsh slate and quarry-tiled floors, newly-pointed walls, open log fires and candles by night imbue the interior with an immediately welcoming feel. The mish-mash of kitchen tables, chairs and settles, clocks, warming pans and dried flowers is delightfully individual, and there's even a miniature five-octave piano in the bar. Chalked up on large blackboards, the bar menu offers a selection of snacks and light meals such as Stilton and walnut paté, garlic mushrooms with cheese and a laverbread, bacon and cockle gratin. Main courses might be crab quiche, Thai pork curry, oxtail with olives and lamb's kidneys with sherry and wild garlic, with home-made meringues, plum crumble and baked rice pudding to follow. Two or three courses from a restricted choice are offered at a fixed price (£6.50/£8.50) at lunchtime, with further extension into a Bistro menu (£13.50 with house wine) and à la carte (main courses from £10) at night in the Brasserie. The handwritten menus and wine lists – one marked 'for enthusiasts', the other containing some 40 bottles at £12 or less – and rustic tables in an enclosed rear garden are equally indicative of the Tafarn's studied informality. All-day opening and afternoon teas, served from 3-5pm Whitsun-September, are further proof, if any were needed, of the dedication of Diana and her youthful team. 'Purveyors of frozen foods are shown the door.' *Open 11-11 (Sun 12-10.30), but check mid-week in winter. Bar Food 12-2.30, 6-9.30. Free House.* **Beer** *Buckley's Best & Reverend James, two guest beers. Family room. Garden. MasterCard,* **VISA**

NOTTAGE   Rose & Crown   B&B

Tel 01656 784850   Fax 01656 772345   Map 9 C6
Nottage Heol-y-Capel nr Porthcawl Bridgend CF36 5ST

Just a mile from Royal Porthcawl Golf Club and the town's West Bay stands this white-painted row of stone-built former cottages at the heart of a tiny hamlet. In an area short of good pub accommodation, its friendly, refurbished village bar and neat cottage bedrooms are justly popular. Pastel-shaded decor with fitted-pine furniture, practical bathrooms and room comforts including phone, TV and trouser press promise a restful and comfortable stay. Scottish & Newcastle. *Open 11.30-11, (Sun 12-3, 7-10.30).* **Beer** *John Smith's, Ruddles County & Best, Webster's Yorkshire Bitter, Theakston Best. Garden, children's play area.* **Accommodation** *8 bedrooms, all en suite, £34.95, breakfast £2.95-£5.50pp extra. Children welcome overnight (under-2s stay free in parents' room, 2-11s £2.95), additional bed & cot available. Guide dogs only. Amex, MasterCard, Diners,* **VISA**

> We only recommend food (Bar Food) in those establishments highlighted
> with the **FOOD** symbol.

OLD RADNOR   Harp Inn   FOOD

Tel & Fax 01544 350655   Map 9 D4   B&B
Old Radnor Presteigne Powys LO8 2RH

Zzz...

It's worth the drive scarcely a mile uphill from the A44 just to soak in the views of the Radnor Forest and surrounding hills from the common ground which separates the Harp from Old Radnor's Norman church. Flagstone floors, abundant old beams and a wonderful mish-mash of antique furniture and bric-a-brac epitomise the character of the three interlinked rooms which form the bar and dining areas. The Copes' kitchen adopts a homely approach and Dee makes a virtue of simplicity. Lunchtime snacks range from home-made soup to ploughman's platters, sandwiches garnished with crisps and salad and baked potatoes; daily specials might include salade niçoise or home-potted salmon. For dinner (booking advised) one might commence with deep-fried Brie, following with a daily special of scallops with lemon grass and chive sauce or more regular giant Yorkshire pudding filled with steak and kidney. Four spotless bedrooms, cosy and quiet without phones, share a brace of bathrooms in a higgledy-piddledy upper floor whose creaking, uneven floors and wood-pegged roof trusses are further evidence of the Harp's antiquity (reputedly 15th-century). *Open 11.30-11 (Sun 12-3, 7-10.30).* **Bar Food** *12-2, 7-9 (Fri, Sat & Sun 12-2.30, 7-9.30). No food Mon. Free House.* **Beer** *Wood's Special, Hanby Drawwell, guest beer in summer. Garden, outdoor eating, summer barbecue at weekends.* **Accommodation** *4 bedrooms, share 2 bathrooms, £40 (single £25). Children welcome overnight, additional bed (£10) & cot available. No credit cards.*

PANT MAWR   Glansevern Arms Hotel   B&B

Tel 01686 440240   Map 9 C4
Pant Mawr nr Llangurig Powys SY18 6SY

The art of "old-fashioned innkeeping" is still alive and well at the Glansevern Arms, which has been owned and run by Mr Edwards and family since 1966. On the A44, four miles west of Llangurig towards Aberystwyth (19 miles away), the inn commands a magnificent position amid the Plynlimon range, overlooking the upper reaches of the River Wye. An intimate bar and lounge soak in the glorious hill scenery by day and glow with warmth from log fires at night. Residents equally enjoy the peace and quiet afforded by bedrooms with private sitting areas, uninterrupted by any phones, where the views should provide a greater attraction than television. Also recommended in our *1997 Hotels & Restaurants Guide*. 'Old-fashioned' may often be used in a derogatory sense to describe such an operation, but here it seems entirely apposite. The hotel has one mile of fishing rights on the river. *Open 11-2, 6.30-11, (Sun 12-3, 7-10.30).* **Beer** *Bass*. **Accommodation** *7 rooms, all en suite, £60 (single £35). Children welcome overnight (under-12s half-price), additional bed available. Closed 20-30 Dec. No credit cards.*

PEMBROKE FERRY	**Ferry Inn**	**FOOD**

Tel 01646 682947
Map 9 A5

Pembroke Ferry nr Pembroke Dock Pembrokeshire SA72 6UD

Fresh fish and seafoods rightly predominate at the Ferry, which stands by ripping tidal waters right under the Cleddau Bridge – turn off the A477 by the tolls. Local oysters and crab share the daily blackboard with the likes of popular halibut with hollandaise, fish, prawn and mushroom crumble and whole Dover sole. For those of less fishy persuasion are the home-made curries and beefburgers, lamb kebabs, pork schnitzel with mushroom sauce and vegetable pancake roll. As there is only one small bar, children are welcome inside only at lunchtime (if well behaved) or they can roam the riverside patio and rocks when weather and tide permit. Sunday lunch carvery (and bar snacks). *Open 11.30-2.45, 6.30-11, (Sun 12-2.45, 7-10.30).* **Bar Food** *12-2 (carvery lunch Sun till 1.30), 7-10 (till 9.30 Sun). Free House.* **Beer** *Bass, Hancock's HB. Waterside patio/terrace, outdoor eating. MasterCard,* **VISA**

PENALLT	**Boat Inn**	**A**

Tel 01600 712615
Map 14 A2

Long Lane Penallt nr Monmouth Monmouthshire NP5 4AJ

Despite its Monmouthshire address, this Wye valley pub is commonly known as 'The Boat at Redbrook'; a signpost will direct you to park by the football field on the A466 Monmouth to Chepstow road and cross by a footbridge adjoining the disused railway line. In the pub garden, log tables teeter on the hillside which is by-passed on two sides by streams that cascade into the River Wye. Beer aficionados, attracted in part by Tuesday's folk/rock and Thursday's jazz/Blues nights, are offered a fine selection of beers direct from the cask. *Open 11-3, 6-11 (Sat 11-11), Sun 12-4, 6.30-10.30. Free House.* **Beer** *Hook Norton Best, Hall and Woodhouse Badger Best, Fuller's London Pride, Theakston XB & Old Peculier, Shepherd Neame Spitfire, Greene King Abbot Ale, three to four changing guest beers. Riverside garden, children's play area. Family room. Closed 25 Dec eve. No credit cards.*

> We do not accept free meals or hospitality – our inspectors pay their own bills and **never** book in the name of Egon Ronay's Guides.

PENMAENPOOL	**George III Hotel**	**B&B**

Tel 01341 422525   Fax 01341 423565
Map 8 C3

Penmaenpool nr Dolgellau Gwynedd LL40 1YD

Zzz... ☺

Squeezed in between the A493 (which is at roof level) and the head of the Mawddach Estuary, the 17th-century George III Hotel is run by five members of the Cartwright family. It enjoys magnificent views – shared by all but two of the bedrooms – across the water to wooded hills beyond. The unpretentious Dresser Bar – so named because the bar counter is made out of the bottom half of an old Welsh dresser – is a place where wooden tables are polished, brass ornaments gleam and a welcoming fire burns in the grate. The refurbished Cellar Bar (actually at ground level) is open only in the summer when there are also tables outside, on what was a railway line, next to the water. Residents have their own cosy lounge with beamed ceiling and inglenook fireplace. The bedrooms, half of which are in the adjacent, former Victorian railway station, have traditional freestanding furniture and pretty floral fabrics – William

Morris in the old station rooms – plus smart modern bathrooms. All have direct-dial phones, TV, trouser press and beverage kit. Families should head for the Cellar Bar; the children's menu offers popular favourites; baby-changing facilities are provided. Free fishing permits for residents and mountain bike hire. Disabled WC. *Open 11-11, (Sun 12.30-3, 7-10.30). Free House.* **Beer** *Ruddles Best, John Smith's, Cambrian Premium, guest beer. Garden, patio. Family room.* **Accommodation** *11 bedrooms, all en suite, £70-£88 (single £45). Children welcome overnight, additional bed (under-12s £12.50) & cot supplied. MasterCard,* **VISA**

PENMARK — Six Bells Inn — FOOD

Tel 01446 710229   Fax 01446 710671   Map 9 C6
Penmark nr Barry Vale of Glamorgan CF62 3BP

Don Hall's unspectacular pub, his home since 1978, underwent its most spectacular change in two centuries with the addition two years ago of completely new dining facilities in the once-derelict outbuildings. Proximity to Cardiff Airport (turn off the B4265 opposite BA's maintenance hangar) and a new-found dedication to good food have quickly reaped rewards. Traditional pub lunches include a daily roast, mushroom, tomato and herb pasta, and home-made pork and leek sausages with mash and onion gravy. Best choices for the most adventurous lie among fish dishes such as baked cod with garlic butter, grilled plaice with creamy mushrooms or a flaked salmon and French bean salad. Starters include avocado with crispy bacon and deep-fried Brie; finish with poached pear with cinnamon or glazed lemon tart. There's friendly waitress service to the well-spaced tables in the air-conditioned, split-level dining-room where chef Dave Richards' menus take on a more serious slant at night, with studious cooking and more serious prices. No children under 14 in bar areas. *Open 11.30-11 (Sun 12-10.30). Bar Food 12-2.30 only (Sun till 3). Free House.* **Beer** *Hancock's HB, Worthington Best. Patio. Amex, MasterCard,* **VISA**

PENYBONT — Severn Arms Hotel — B&B

Tel 01597 851224   Fax 01597 851693   Map 9 C4
Penybont nr Llandrindod Wells Powys LD1 5UA

A white-painted former coaching inn by the junction of the A488 and A44, at the heart of the Ithon Valley. Loved by JB Priestley for its creaky floors, old oak beams and sloping ceiling, it has some of the best family rooms around, tucked under the eaves of the pub's top storey, with pastoral views down the garden to a wooden bridge over the river. Caring management by Geoff and Tessa Lloyd has extended over twelve years and the bedrooms are both immaculately kept and well equipped; all en suite, most have trouser presses and all have TV, radio, direct-dial phones, hairdryers and tea-making facilities. From the flagstoned entrance there's access to the village bar festooned with local football trophies, a more sedate lounge bar and extensive dining-room. Residents enjoy use of their own quiet TV lounge on the first floor. *Open 11-2.30, 6-11, (Sun 12-3, 7-10.30). Free House.* **Beer** *Tetley, Worthington Best, Bass, John Smiths. Garden. Family room.* **Accommodation** *10 bedrooms, all en suite, £50 (single £28). Children welcome overnight (under-5s 33%, 5-12s 50% adult tariff), additional bed (£5) and cot (£2) available. Accommodation closed one week Christmas-New Year. Amex, Diners, MasterCard,* **VISA**

PISGAH — Halfway Inn — A

Tel 01970 880631   Map 9 C4
Devil's Bridge Road Pisgah nr Aberystwyth Ceredigion SY23 4NE

650 feet up, overlooking the Rheidol Valley below, Sally Roger's marvellous country pub is in a lovely setting with magnificent views. It's well known as a beer-lovers' favourite, with its choice of up to four real ales. Never modernised or extended, this 250-year-old Inn retains a traditional feel – candle-lit in the evenings and log fire in winter. Families use the Stone Room bar (walls made of stone). The grassy upper car park offers free overnight pitching for campers and pony-trekkers can leave their mounts in a paddock. *Open 11.30-2.30, 6.30-11 (may be open all day in summer), Sun 12-3, 7-10.30. Free House.* **Beer** *Felinfoel Double Dragon, Flowers Original, guest beers. Garden. Family room. No credit cards.*

RAGLAN — Beaufort Arms Hotel — B&B

Tel & Fax 01291 690412   Map 9 D5
High Street Raglan Monmouthshire NP5 2DY

Recent alterations uncovered remains of the original Tudor timberwork which are now preserved in the unusual and characterful Country Bar. Rumour has it that there still remains a secret underground passage from here to nearby Raglan Castle. Residents have use of their own lounge and bedrooms are kitted out with white wood furniture, floral fabrics, radios, telephones, TVs and beverage trays. Conference facilities. *Open 11.30-11, (Sun 12-3, 7-10.30. Free House.* **Beer** *Courage Directors & Best, Brains Bitter guest beer. Garden.* **Accommodation** *15 bedrooms, all en suite, £45 (family room sleeping four £55, single £35). Children welcome overnight, additional bed available. Dogs by arrangement. Amex, MasterCard,* **VISA**

RED WHARF BAY — Ship Inn — FOOD

Tel 01248 852568   Fax 01248 853568   Map 8 B1
Red Wharf Bay nr Benllech Isle of Anglesey LL75 4RJ

Landlord Andrew Kenneally has now been at the low, white-painted Ship for 26 years. The inn is fronted by hanging baskets and stands right on the bay shore. Quarry-tiled floors plus genuine exposed beams and stonework make for an interesting interior where the ship's wheels and chiming clocks, Tom Browne cartoons and Toby Jug collection give it great character. With food as the main draw, there's a steady stream of early arrivals and local regulars to sample from a selection of bar food which is sensibly varied daily between cold and hot choices and never overly long. Typical dishes might include deep-fried cockles, moussaka, vegetable chili, duck in orange sauce, braised beef in Guinness and baked half-shoulder of lamb with redcurrant and rosemary sauce; finish with dark and white chocolate gateau or pecan pie. The Cellar Room is no-smoking. There's a separate children's menu served in a smaller rear family room or out in the shoreside garden. A no-smoking restaurant opens upstairs for diners at weekends. *Open 12-3.30, 7-11 (11-11 summer), Sun 12-3, 7-10.30 (12-10.30 on summer).* **Bar Food** *12-2.30, 6-9.30 (from 7 in winter), Sun 12-2, 7-9. Free House.* **Beer** *Friary Meux, Tetley Bitter, Ind Coope Burton Ale, guest beers. Garden, front patio, outdoor eating area. Family room. MasterCard,* **VISA**

ST GEORGE — Kinmel Arms — FOOD

Tel 01745 832207   Map 8 C1
St George Abergele Conwy LL22 9BP

Just off the A55 expressway a mile east of Abergele, new partners Chris Buckley, Gary Edwards and Dermott McGee have chosen an ideal spot for their new venture in premises which were boarded up only two years ago; and what a good start the Kinmel Arms has made. There's a definite buzz to the bars in which reliably-cooked bar food can be ordered from a frequently-amended blackboard menu: haricot bean soup, tagliatelle with ham, cheese and cream sauce and smoked mackerel salad are typical starters while main courses encompass gamekeeper's pie, navarin of lamb, lasagne and vegetable curry with rice (all at under £5), and fancier specials might include grilled whole lemon sole and sirloin steak with leek and grain mustard sauce. Home-made sweets and Welsh cheeses that follow are of a similar high standard, and the service from a smart and youthful team has just the right degree of sharpness to go with it. In a new 40-seat dining-room to the rear, both food quality and prices step up a gear, with booking already essential most evening sessions and for Sunday lunch; a patio conservatory was due for completion as we went to press in an attempt to alleviate the congestion. Chris Buckley salutes and shepherds his flock with admirable skill, reeling off as he does so a list of such dinner delights as black pudding salad with apple dressing, ragout of lobster and monkfish, and warm lemon tart with raspberry coulis and sauce anglaise; all of which goes to suggest that the kitchen here is well set for greater things as the business grows. *Open 12-3, 7-11.* **Bar Food** *12-2, 7-9.30. Free House.* **Beer** *Marston's Best & Pedigree, guest beers. Garden, outdoor eating. MasterCard,* **VISA**

SHIRENEWTON   Carpenters Arms   FOOD

Tel 01291 641231   Map 9 D6
Shirenewton nr Chepstow Monmouthshire NP6 6BU

On the B4235 Usk road, 4 miles from Chepstow (turn by the race course) the Carpenters is a row of roadside cottages which once housed the local smithy and carpenter's shop, now quite literally hollowed out into a succession of seven interconnecting rooms served from a single bar. The choice of real ales is a serious draw and a plethora of baguettes and baked potatoes the regular lunchtime accompaniments. Amid a regularly-changing blackboard menu relying in large part on convenience items there's still room to seek out a quality sirloin steak and home-made steak and mushroom pie; daily specials might extend the range to include rabbit casserole, beef stroganoff and home-made quiche. There is no garden here but well-behaved children are welcome within. *Open 11-2.30, 6.15-11, (Sun 12-3, 7-10.30). Bar Food 12-2, 7-9.30 (till 10 Fri & Sat). No food Sun eve in winter. Free House. Beer Fuller's London Pride, Flowers IPA, Wadworth 6X, Boddingtons, Marston's Pedigree & Owd Rodger, Timothy Taylors Landlord, guest beer. Patio, outdoor eating. Family room. No credit cards.*

SHIRENEWTON   Tredegar Arms   FOOD   B&B

Tel 01291 641274   Map 9 D6
Shirenewton nr Chepstow Monmouthshire NP6 6RQ

Zzz...

Dominating the crossroads at the heart of this small hillside village of stone cottages (signed both from A48 and B4285 some five miles from Chepstow), the Tredegar Arms is in the sure hands of experienced locals Rob and Val Edwards. Facing a servery ingeniously cut back under a central staircase, the lounge bar is the focal point for food which shows a refreshing balance between conventional and empirical fare. Traditional main courses such as liver, bacon and onions and grilled trout with roasted almonds are listed alongside decidedly different specials, such as 14oz cod in Pernod and fennel sauce, a honeyed lamb ragout with mint, a 'cock-a-roosting fricassee' in parsley and lemon sauce, 'Bully Hole Bottom Pepperpot' and a fiery 'Welsh Dragon pie', actually made with lamb. Lemon meringue pie and bread-and-butter pudding are popular home-made puddings. Upstairs are two letting bedrooms, each with its own WC and shower room en suite. Equipped with colour TVs and tea- and coffee-making equipment, they are unfussily furnished and spotlessly kept and enjoy super views down the valley to the distant Severn estuary. A truly restful night is followed by gargantuan country breakfasts. *Open 12-3, 6-11 (12-11 summer), Sun 12-4, 7-10.30 (12-10.30 summer). Bar Food 12-2, 7-9.30. Free House. Beer Hook Norton Best, Hancock's HB, Bass, two guest beers. Accommodation 2 bedrooms, both en suite (showers), £40 (single £25). Check-in by arrangement. No dogs. No credit cards.*

> We endeavour to be as up-to-date as possible but inevitably some changes to landlords, chefs and other key staff occur after the Guide has gone to press.

TRECASTLE   Castle Coaching Inn   B&B

Tel 01874 636354   Fax 01874 636457   Map 9 C5
Brecon Road Trecastle Brecon Powys LO3 84H

☺

A famous inn on the old coaching route through the Brecons. The opened-out bar and dining areas make good use of natural daylight and retain sufficient of the pub's original features such as the flagstone floors and vast open fireplace to preserve the Castle's unique character. All the bedrooms are en suite, with smartly-tiled bathrooms and up-to-date amenities that include direct-dial phones, TVs, radio alarm clocks and hairdryers. There are two good-sized family rooms, one with bunk beds. To the pub's

rear there's a safe, enclosed garden in which to enjoy panoramic views down the
Gwyddor valley. Children are made very welcome; baby-changing facilities in the
Ladies. *Open 11-3, 6-11 (11-11 Easter-Sep), Sun 11-3, 7-10.30 (12-10.30 Easter-Sep).*
Closed Mon Jan-Mar. Free House. **Beer** *Courage Directors, Marston's Pedigree, guest beer.*
Garden. Family room. **Accommodation** *10 bedrooms, all en suite, £40-£45 (single £35).*
Children welcome overnight (under-10s stay free in parents' room, 10-16s £5), additional bed &
cot available. Check-in bar hours only. No dogs. MasterCard, **VISA**

TRELLECH — Village Green — FOOD

Tel 01600 860119   Map 9 D5   **B&B**
Trellech nr Monmouth Monmouthshire NP5 4PA

Bob and Jane Evans's 450-year-old village local combines bistro-style food with the
more traditional concept of pub-with-restaurant. Thus we find here a combination of
all three with an à la carte restaurant (recommended in our *1997 Hotels and Restaurants
Guide*) and a brace of pubby bars that offer traditional pub snacks like ploughman's
platters, sandwiches and baked potatoes. Between the two bars a stone-walled bistro,
festooned with dried flowers hanging from its rafters, offers an inviting menu: home-
made soup, smoked halibut with pickled samphire, bresaola with walnut oil and
toasted pine kernels, spicy lamb sausage with mango sauce and breaded king prawns
with lime mayonnaise – and these are just starters! Main courses are displayed on
daily-changing blackboards and might include Tuscan fish stew, ostrich sausages,
Indonesian pork and duck breast with winberries. It's back to the menu for sweets
such as sticky coffee and ginger pudding, pecan and caramel tart, apple and shortbread
pie and baked banana calypso with toffee ice cream. This is all inventive stuff and well
worth a detour. Alongside the pub two small bedroom suites with kitchenettes are let
on a bed-and-breakfast or self-catering basis. There is room for a small family
(children accommodated free) and TV is provided, but no phones; the en suite
facilities have WC and showers only. *Open 11-2.30, 6.30-12 (not Sun & Mon),
Sun 12-3 only.* **Bar Food** *12-2, 7-9.45 (not Sun & Mon eve).* **Beer** *Bass, Worthington
Best.* **Accommodation** *2 bedrooms, both en suite, from £45 (single £35). Children welcome
overnight (under-8s free in parents' room), additional bed available. Check-in by arrangement.
No dogs. Closed Sun eve, all Mon (except Bank Holiday Mon eves) & 1 week Jan.
MasterCard,* **VISA**

TREMEIRCHION — Salusbury Arms — FOOD

Tel 01745 710262   Map 8 C1
Tremeirchion St Asaph Conwy LL17 0HN

A former estate coaching house with origins dating back to the 14th-century. The
Grade II listed pub takes its name from Tremeirchion's ancestral owners. Jim and
Heulwen O'Boyle have carefully restored the building which is spick-and-span
within, with a cosy feel to its interlinked village bar, lounges and dining-room. Jim's
regularly-changing real ales are a serious attraction, as is Heulwen's bubbling welcome.
The Salusbury Grill, home-made steak and ale pie (or chicken and mushroom) are
regular favourites and there's usually a range of specials like Lancashire hotpot in
Yorkshire pudding, steamed mussels and garlic bread and fresh cod in batter, alongside
regular bar snacks like sandwiches, baked potatoes, vegetarian burgers, scampi and
breaded plaice; brunch fry-ups are also offered at lunchtime. A cheery welcome for
children (who'll find a lovely garden to play in), a burgeoning trade in family Sunday
lunches (booking advised), and a Welsh songstress entertaining on weekend evenings
completes the picture. *Open 11-11 (Sun 12-3, 7-10.30).* **Bar Food** *12-2.30, 7-9.30,
(no food Sun eve). Free House.* **Beer** *Boddingtons, Morland Old Speckled Hen, Flowers
Original guest beers. Garden, outdoor eating, Family room. No credit cards.*

We do not accept free meals or hospitality – our inspectors pay their own bills
and never book in the name of Egon Ronay's Guides.

TYN-Y-GROES   *Groes Inn*   FOOD

Tel & Fax 01492 650545   Map 8 C2
Tyn-y-Groes Conwy LL32 8TN

Claiming to be the first licensed house in Wales, 'Taverne-y-Groes' (by the cross)
boasts a history unbroken since 1573 and is now family-run by Tony and Dawn
Humphreys and their son Justin. The present building (from which are splendid views
of the Conwy estuary) contains much 16th- and 17th-century interior timberwork in a
succession of low-ceilinged rooms that have been extended these days to include a
formal dining-room and no-smoking conservatory that leads to the large rear garden.
Daily blackboards proclaim the most promising bar food: Indian haddock, rabbit
casserole, local mussels and home-made rissoles. with the likes of sticky toffee pudding
to follow. Bookings may be made for a three-course lunch, and there's à la carte dining
nightly. Well-behaved children are welcome in the conservatory and garden. 16 en
suite bedrooms boasting spectacular Snowdonia views were due to be completed in
October 1996. *Open 12-3, 6.30-11.30 (12-2.30, 7-11.30 in winter), Closed Sun eve in
winter. Sun 12-4, 6.30-11.* **Bar Food** *12-2, 6.30-9 (Sun 12-2.15, 6.30-9). Free House.*
Beer *Tetley, Ind Coope Burton Ale. Garden, outdoor eating. Family room. MasterCard,* **VISA**

USK   *Three Salmons Hotel*   B&B

Tel 01291 672133   Fax 01291 673979   Map 9 D5
Usk Monmouthshire NP5 1BQ

Zzz...

For long an inn of renown, the Three Salmons once hosted a civic luncheon to mark
the opening of the nearby Chain bridge over the Usk, in 1812. Much of the original
listed building has undergone a massive restoration. The single bar and public areas at
street level are immaculate and there's a friendly sense of purpose amongst the staff.
A separate bar and function room are on the first floor. In the main building little
expense has been spared in upgrading the bedrooms to modern-day requirements:
nestling under high-pitched eaves and roof timbers they are individual in character
and furnished to a high standard with direct-dial telephones, TVs and smart en suite
bathrooms in gleaming, gold-tapped, white porcelain. An annexe across the street was
once the 'Livery and Bait Stables'; outside, the Ostler's Bell still hangs. *Open 11-11
(Sun 12-3, 7-10.30). Free House.* **Beer** *Whitbread Best, Flowers Original.* **Accommodation**
*24 rooms, all en suite, from £65 (four-poster £80, single from £49.50). Children welcome
overnight, additional bed & cot available (£10). No dogs. Amex, MasterCard,* **VISA**

WHITEBROOK   *Crown at Whitebrook*   FOOD

Tel 01600 860254   Fax 01600 860607   Map 14 A2   B&B
Whitebrook nr Monmouth Monmouthshire NP5 4TX

Zzz... 🛏

It is a long mile up tracks and down lanes from the A466 at the Bigswear bridge to
Roger and Sandra Bates's 'auberge', hidden away in the wooded Wye valley. Self-
styled as a restaurant with rooms, its rather unprepossessing exterior and brown
window shutters lend it a Continental air. Within, there is homely overnight comfort,
culinary expertise from Sandra, front-of-house hospitality from Roger, low beams and
lovely views over the pretty garden. A light lunch menu (Welsh venison sausage rolls
with gratin potatoes, wild mushroom ravioli, smoked haddock fishcake, sticky toffee
pudding) is offered, but the three-course lunch menu – served in the cottagey,
beamed dining-room – is such good value (with four or five choices at each course)
that it should not be missed: a recent menu offered salad of home-cured salmon with
mustard and lime dressing, traditional Alsace tart of cheese, onions and smoked bacon
and venison and juniper terrine to start; included in the main-course choice was pan-
fried fillet of cod with grilled vegetables, tapénade and fresh tomato sauce and chicken
breast baked with garlic and thyme with a tarragon cream sauce; to finish, chocolate
and Grand Marnier truffle cake with hazelnut sauce and apple and mango strudel.
Very pleasant, family service. Dinner is rather more formal, revealing the true depth
of the quality in the cooking; booking is absolutely essential. Good Welsh cheeses.
Lightly whispering trees are likely to be the only intrusion to a thoroughly restful

night here. The individually decorated bedrooms (six of which were completely refurbished last year) are bright and comfortable, with up-to-date accoutrements including direct-dial phones, tea-makers, TVs and clock radios; spotless bathrooms are neatly carpeted. 'Manor Room' rate, with four-poster and whirlpool bath, is £82. Hearty Welsh breakfasts. Don't come looking for real ales, instead sample the dozen or more malt whiskies, the copious choice of cognacs or delve into the long wine list with plenty of half bottles and helpful notes. Not a pub, but such a lovely, inn-like place in which to stay and eat that we make it a special case for entry in this Guide; also recommended in our *1997 Hotels & Restaurants Guide*. **Meals** *12-2, 7-9. Garden, outdoor eating.* **Accommodation** *12 bedrooms, all en suite, £70-£82 (half-board £120, single £50/£77). Children welcome overnight (under-12s stay free in parents' room), additional bed & cot available. Closed Sun eve & Mon lunch to non-residents, 2 weeks Jan, 25 & 26 Dec. Amex, Diners, MasterCard,* **VISA**

We endeavour to be as up-to-date as possible but inevitably some changes to
landlords, chefs and other key staff occur after the Guide
has gone to press.

ACCEPTED IN MORE HOTELS AND RESTAURANTS THAN MOST PEOPLE EVER HAVE HOT DINNERS.

VISA IS ACCEPTED FOR MORE TRANSACTIONS
WORLDWIDE THAN ANY OTHER CARD.

MAKING LIFE EASIER

Channel Islands & Isle of Man

Alderney

ST ANNE	Georgian House	★	FOOD
Tel & Fax 01481 822471		Map 13 F4	**B&B**
Victoria Street St Anne Alderney			

🐟 🗋 **Zzz...**

There are numerous nice touches which make the Georgian House stand out; one
is a courtesy car between the house and the harbour (book it when you make your
reservation); another is the Garden Beyond, the peaceful, fragrant garden area
complete with open air bar and grill, designed to take full advantage of the kind
climate in summer, and a third is the friendly welcome from owners Elizabeth and
Stephen Hope. Food here is of the highest standard and locally-caught fish and
crustaceans feature strongly. The lunch menu is kept simple with the likes of
wonderful moules à la crème, whole fresh Alderney crab (price depends on weight),
and fish cakes with prawn and parsley sauce. In addition, the chalkboard announces
daily specials like home-made leek and potato soup, bargain Herm oysters, fresh sea
bass with thyme, hot salt beef with dumplings and pasta bolognese. The dinner menu
is more elaborate, with a platter of fruits de mer (24hrs' notice recommended in
winter) and 12oz sirloin flambéed in brandy typical of the offerings. Home-made
desserts are a must – summer pudding in the form of a layered terrine is made with
local berries and the raspberry flan with fruit from the owners' garden. Special 3-
course Sunday lunch menu. Bedroom accommodation with colour TV, direct-dial
telephones and en suite bathrooms is offered in a suite with its own sitting-room and
balcony (highly suitable for family use) plus two single rooms; ask about package deals
including air fares. *Open 10.30-3, 6.30-12. Bar Food 12-2.30, 7.30-9.30. Children
allowed in bar to eat, children's menu. Free House. Beer Ringwood Best & Fortyniner,
Guernsey Summer/Winter Ale. Garden, outdoor eating. **Accommodation** 1 suite (£55 –
family of 4 £70), 2 singles (£27.50), all en suite. Accommodation closed Christmas &
New Year. Pub closed Tue evenings. Amex, Diners, MasterCard, VISA*

Guernsey

LE BOURG	Deerhound Inn Hotel		FOOD
Tel 01481 38585 Fax 01481 39443		Map 13 E4	**B&B**
Le Bourg Forest Road Forest Guernsey GY8 0AN			

🐟 🗋 ☺

Per and Karon Bonthelius run this converted old Guernsey farmhouse situated above
Petit Bot valley and beach, off the main road and not far from the airport. The
welcome is warm and their approach is very much 'hands on', with Swedish chef
Mats assisting Karon in the kitchen. The bar food menu is nonetheless full of local
delights, particularly in the daily 'Fish Specials' such as the grilled turbot with garlic
and lime butter, scallops Thermidor and sole bretonne we recently found on offer.
A choice of dual-priced (starter/main) pasta dishes, large or double-decker sandwiches
and firm favourites like beef stroganoff and chicken curry supplement the summer
salads and usual favourites for 'the little people'. The bedrooms are generally modest
(as is their price) and only four have en suite bathrooms; one is a family room with
bunk beds. The TV lounge doubles as a children's playroom when needed; they've
just built an outdoor swimming pool and there are swings, a see-saw and a slide in the
garden. Baby-listening devices are provided and baby-sitting can be arranged. *Open
10.30-11.45, (Sun 12-2, 6-9.30 with meals only). Bar Food 12-1.45, 7-9.30.
Free House. Beer Tetley, Theakston Best, Ringwood, guest beers. Garden, outdoor eating,
children's play area. **Accommodation** 10 bedrooms, 4 with en suite showers, £30-£40
according to season (single £15-£20). Children welcome overnight (under-3s stay free in
parents' room, 3-12s half-price), additional bed & cot available. Amex, MasterCard, VISA*

CASTEL   Hotel Hougue du Pommier   B&B

Tel 01481 56531   Fax 01481 56260   Map 13 E4
Castel Guernsey GY5 7FQ

Zzz... ☺

A lovely inn dating back to 1712, 'Hougue du Pommier' means 'apple-tree hill'
and the apples from the ten acres of orchards surrounding this fine old Guernsey
farmhouse were once used to make local cider. The Tudor Bar exudes a traditional
atmosphere, with beams and an inglenook fireplace. By the solar-heated swimming
pool is a sunny Tea Garden in a secluded spot surrounded by trees where bar meals
are served all day; nearby are a sauna, sunbed room and a games room wih ping-pong
table and video games. There's also a 10-hole pitch-and-putt golf course and a
putting green, and the sandy beaches of Grandes Rocques and Cobo are just ten
minutes' walk away. Quiet bedrooms with a good range of family accommodation
overlook the particularly well-kept hotel gardens; all have remote-control TVs,
telephones and beverage trays. Children's High Tea served from 5.30pm.
Bar open 11-2, 6-11.30, Sun 12-3.30, 6-11.30 (Sunday open to diners and residents only).
Beer *Guernsey Brewery. Garden.* ***Accommodation*** *43 bedrooms, all en suite, £52-£78*
according to season (4-poster £72-£98, single £26-£50). Children welcome overnight (0-5
yrs stay free, 5-12 yrs 50% of tariff), additional bed & cot available. No dogs. Amex, Diners,
MasterCard, ***VISA***

KINGS MILLS   Fleur du Jardin Hotel   FOOD

Tel 01481 57996   Fax 01481 56834   Map 13 E4   B&B
Kings Mills nr Castel Guernsey GY5 7JT

🕭 🍸 **Zzz...**

Named after a prize-winning herd of Guernsey cattle kept here when it was a
working farm, this 16th-century inn is in the centre of Kings Mills village, close to
Vazon Bay, and has a tastefully traditional country feel. Several low-ceilinged, beamed
dining-rooms interconnect, creating a quiet atmosphere. The cooking is the highlight
here with an extensive menu on which the daily specials – strong on fish and game –
are probably the best bet: typically, grilled bream Provençal-style, medallions of
monkfish in crushed black pepper, and braised rabbit in Pommery mustard sauce.
Also, there are commendable vegetarian choices such as three bean chilli on a bed of
brown rice, and a popular four-course family Sunday lunch served in both the bar
and restaurant; eight or nine wines are available by the glass. The bedrooms are
attractive and amenities include remote-control TVs, telephones and tea/coffee-
making facilities; some rooms have trouser presses and small refrigerators. There's a
beautiful view of the surrounding countryside from the heated outdoor swimming
pool set in two acres of gardens and grounds, with plenty of free parking. *Open 11-
2.30, 5-11.45 (Sun 12-2, 7-9.30 with food only).* ***Bar Food*** *12-2, 6-9.30 (Sun from 7).*
Children allowed in bar to eat, children's menu. Free House. ***Beer*** *Guernsey Brewery*
Sunbeam & Summer/Winter Ale. Garden, outdoor eating, children's play area.
Accommodation *17 bedrooms, all en suite, from £55 to £75 according to season.*
Children over 4 welcome overnight (under-12s stay at 50% adult rate if sharing parents' room,
high-tea included), additional bed & cot available. No dogs. Amex, MasterCard, ***VISA***

PLEINMONT   Imperial Hotel   B&B

Tel 01481 64044   Fax 01481 66139   Map 13 E4
Pleinmont Torteval Guernsey GY8 0PS

☺

This attractive small hotel ideally located at the south end of sandy Rocquaine Bay,
and overlooking the harbour at Portelet is personably run by Patrick and Dianna
Lindley. Lounge bar, restaurant (restored to its all-wood design of 100 years ago) and
most of the bedrooms benefit from a beautiful view of the bay; sea view rooms attract
a supplement (up to £2.50 per person per day). Four rooms have attractive balconies
with patio furniture; all have clean and bright accommodation with tea-coffee
facilities, colour TV and direct-dial telephone. A self-catering apartment is also
available. Children are welcome overnight; there's an all-day patio cafe and High Tea
is served at 6pm. The hotel leads on to 20 miles of cliff walks, and is just a short walk

from the beach. *Open 10.30-11.45 (Mon-Wed to 11 in winter, Sun 11-3). Beer Randalls. Safe garden, outdoor eating.* **Accommodation** *17 bedrooms, all en suite, £45-£63 according to season (single £20-£42), £30-£45 room only; special Spring/Autumn tariffs include free car hire. Children welcome overnight, extra bed & cot provided (under-2s stay free). Lounge bar closed Sun eve Nov-Mar. Accommodation closed Dec-Feb. MasterCard,* **VISA**

St Peters	Longfrie Inn	B&B

Tel 01481 63107   Map 13 E4
Rue de Longfrie St Peters Guernsey GY7 9RX

Arguably Guernsey's most popular family pub is situated in its own grounds in a rural setting outside the village. Formerly a 16th-century farmhouse, it now contains an indoor 'fun factory' (supervised indoor bedlam might be a more apposite description) for children under 10, a large beer garden with swings and extensive playing area, ample car parking, and standard pub fare with a positively ghoulish selection for the little devils! Baby-changing facilities, high-chairs and helpful staff complete the family-friendly atmosphere; adults without children may find it all too much before 8.30pm. Under the same ownership as *Fleur du Jardin* (see entry under Kings Mills). Overnight accommodation is now available in five en suite double bedrooms with facilities for families (rates on application), and exclusive use of a private residents' lounge. *Open 11.30-2.30, 5.30-11.30 (Sun 12-2.30, 6.30-11.30 with food only). Beer Guernsey Brewery Sunbeam & Summer/Winter Ale. Garden, children's play area.* **Accommodation** *5 bedrooms, all en suite, £38-£52. Children welcome overnight (under-4s stay free). Amex, Diners, MasterCard,* **VISA**

St Peter Port	Ship & Crown	A

Tel 01481 721368   Map 13 E4
Pier Steps St Peter Port Guernsey GY1 2NB

The usually-buzzing yachting-types' place opposite the marina is St Peter Port's most traditional pub, with lots of maritime pictures and memorabilia in both the simply-furnished, busy main bar and a quieter drinking area at the back. These buildings housed the Germans' naval HQ during the World War II occupation of Guernsey. Thanks to the island's newly-liberated licensing laws, children are now welcome in the bar all day, but Sunday licensing still requires all pub patrons to purchase a bar meal. *Open 10am-11.45pm, (Sun 12-3.30, 6-11). Beer Guernsey Sunbeam, guest beers. No credit cards.*

We endeavour to be as up-to-date as possible but inevitably some changes to landlords, chefs and other key staff occur after the Guide has gone to press.

Herm

Herm Island	Ship Inn	FOOD

Tel 01481 722159   Fax 01481 710066   Map 13 E4
Herm Island via Guernsey GY1 3HR

Just 20 minutes by ferry from St Peter Port in Guernsey, safe, clean and pollution-free, with no cars, no crowds and no stress; how many hotels can boast an island as their garden? The harbourside White House Hotel offers comfortable accommodation (recommended in our *1997 Hotels & Restaurants Guide*: 38 rooms, half-board terms only, from £110) for those who want to escape the hurly-burly of mainland life. Under the same ownership as the hotel is the Ship Inn – a small, carpeted bar area with roaring log fire, connected to the first-floor Captain's coffee shop, a carvery-style restaurant. 'To pipe you aboard' are the likes of crab cocktail or bargain Herm oysters; continue with 'the daily catch' (perhaps fresh plaice or, for a real treat, lobster Thermidor), one of an extensive selection of baguettes or the usual 'midshipman's main courses including a daily roast and steaks. Children are very welcome and offered their own young sea dogs' menu (king-size sausage, fish fingers, chicken or vegetarian sweetcorn nuggets). Morning coffee with pastries, afternoon teas and Sunday lunch in the restaurant complete the picture. The sun-drenched patio is an ideal place to sample one of their splendid ice cream sundaes made with the highest buttermilk-content ice cream in the world. No dogs within the pub, but welcome on the island on a lead. *Open 9am-10.45pm (Sun 12-3.30).* **Bar Food** *9am-9.30pm, Sun 9-2.30. Patio, outdoor eating. Pub closed Sun eve & Oct-end Mar. MasterCard,* **VISA**

Jersey

GOREY	Dolphin Hotel	B&B

Tel 01534 853370   Fax 01534 855343   Map 13 F4
Gorey Pier Gorey Jersey JE3 6EW

On Jersey's east coast, the Dolphin is right on Gorey Pier beneath medieval Mont Orgueil castle and not far from the wide Grouville Bay which offers safe bathing and beach sports. Fish nets and boating accessories adorn the public Fisherman's Bar & Grill. Adequate bedrooms are equipped with remote-control TVs, telephones, radios, trouser presses, hairdryers and beverage trays; most contain shower rooms but only two have en suite baths. Best rooms are on the top floor overlooking the pier, and have sufficient room for additional children's beds. *Bar open 9.30am-11.30pm. No cask-conditioned ales.* **Accommodation** *17 bedrooms, all en suite, from £36-£64 according to season (single £18-£32). Children welcome overnight (under-3s stay free in parents' room, 3-12s 50% of tariff), extra bed & cot supplied. MasterCard,* **VISA**

ST AUBIN	Old Court House Inn	FOOD
		B&B

Tel 01534 46433   Fax 01534 45103   Map 13 F4
St Aubin The Bulwarks Jersey JE3 8AB

A family-run hotel/restaurant/inn with a popular alfresco eating trade and a long history dating back to 1450. The original 'Courthouse' at the rear of the building was largely restored in 1611, while the front portion of the property was a wealthy merchant's house with enormous cellars which (from the 17th century) stored privateers' plunder alongside legitimate cargo. The front terrace and new conservatory overlook the harbour, as popular a place to sample the bar food by day as is the rear courtyard at night. The menu runs from baked potato skins with cheese and bacon to ploughman's lunches, although seafood is the real attraction, with speciality 'fruits de mer' cocktail and fisherman's platters for two (with or without a whole lobster), good-value oysters, and 'daily deliveries of fresh local fish'. Children have their own short menu or scaled-down adult portions, charged accordingly. The beamed cellar bars are always popular and the upstairs bar has recently been turned into the Mizzen Restaurant (still recognisable by *Bergerac* fans as the *Royal Barge* pub). Charming bedrooms, the best with harbour views, are furnished with old pine; the two-bedroomed penthouse suite offers a large bathroom, a pleasant lounge with a beautiful view of the harbour and a private sun terrace with garden furniture. *Open 11-11, Sun 11-1 (to 3.30 if eating), 4.30-11.30.* **Bar Food** *12.30-2.30, 7.30-9.30 (Sun 12.30-3.30, no bar food Sun eve). Free House.* **Beer** *Marston's Pedigree, Theakston Best, Flowers, up to 5 guest beers. Family room.* **Accommodation** *9 bedrooms, all en suite, £60-£80 according to season, single £30-£60; suite £90-£195 sleeping up to 4. Children under 6 free, over-6s half-price if sharing parents' room, additional bed provided. Accommodation closed 25 Dec. Amex, Diners, MasterCard,* **VISA**

ST BRELADE — Old Smugglers Inn — FOOD

Tel 01534 41510 Map 13 F4
Ouaisné Bay St Brelade Jersey

Two 13th-century fishermen's cottages were rebuilt from their ruins in 1721 by local fishermen and remained as such until the early 1900s when they were enlarged and developed into the Finisterre hotel retaining most of the original granitework, beams and fireplaces. After the German occupation the property underwent further changes and the Old Smugglers Inn emerged. Today a succession of small dining-rooms (including a 50-seater family room with a non-smoking area) serve food from an extensive menu supplemented by daily market fish such as Jersey plaice, crab and lobster. Hot grilled crab claws with piri-piri sauce are a popular starter, followed by salad selections, the 'Burger Box' and traditional goodies from chicken and leek pie to fillet steak with garlic mushrooms. Separately, the chidren's menu provides puzzles and crayoning in case of a wait for Pirate Pete's fish fingers or Captain Hook's scampi. No children under 14 in the bar; baby-changing facilities available. Folk nights on Sunday. *Open 11-11.* **Bar Food** *12-2, 6-8.45 (no food Sunday eve in winter). Free House.* **Beer** *Bass, two guest beers. Terrace. Family room. Amex, MasterCard,* **VISA**

ST HELIER — Tipsy Toad Town House — A

Tel 01534 615000 Fax 01534 615003 Map 13 F4
57-59 New Street St Helier Jersey JE2 3RB

A sister pub to the *Star & Tipsy Toad* (see entry below) and converted from a large warehouse, the sprawling interior here includes a micro-brewery overlooked by a gallery (available for private hire) and conference facilities for up to 230 people in the Toad Hall function suites. Busy, bustling and attracting a youngish crowd, the open-plan bar areas are the venue for regular real ale festivals, and other good facilities include an in-house ale shop, baby-changing unit and disabled loo. There's no food on Monday evenings, nor on Sundays except in winter. *Open 11-11, Sun (11-1, 4.30-11). Free House.* **Beer** *Tipsy Toad, Jimmy's Bitter & Horny Toad home-brews; Crazy Diamond, Cyril's Bitter and independent guest ales. Amex, Mastercard,* **VISA**

ST LAWRENCE — British Union Hotel — FOOD

Tel 01534 861070 Map 13 F4
Main Road St Lawrence Jersey JE3 1NL

Owned by Guernsey's Ann Street Brewery, this pleasant pub with a good atmosphere and warm welcome stands across the road from St Lawrence Parish Church. A central bar divides two lounges, with an additional family/games room to the rear. Well-prepared daily specials will often include Jersey plaice alongside steak and ale pie and vegetarian options; there are the usual chicken, fishy and piggy dishes on the laminated menu as well as lots for the 'little angels' and ice cream, gateau and apple pie for dessert. *Open 10am-11.pm, (Sun 11-1, 4.30-11.30)* **Bar Food** *12-2, 6-8.30 (no food Sundays). Family room, children's menu.* **Beer** *Guernsey Sunbeam. Patio, outdoor eating. No credit cards.*

ST OUEN — Lobster Pot, Coach House — FOOD

Tel 01534 482888 Fax 01534 481574 Map 13 F4
L'Etacq St Ouen Jersey JE3 2FB

Housed in a modern hotel converted from an old granite farmhouse, the pubby bar in what was once the cow byre plays a contrasting role to the busy restaurant (recommended in our *1997 Hotels & Restaurants Guide*, especially for its first-class local seafood). A large open-air paved terrace is the main attraction at this very scenic spot overlooking sandy St Ouen's Bay. When we last visited a good mix of lunchtime bar food ranged from baked potatoes and omelettes to various steaks and fishy salads such as crab and lobster; some of the seafood is landed just 200 yards away, so it's as fresh and as local as you can get! As we went to press both the hotel and restaurant were due to close for a complete refurbishment over the winter months, so a new look Lobster Pot is eagerly awaited for the spring of 1997. It would be advisable to contact the hotel direct for further information on accommodation tariffs and opening hours. *No dogs allowed. Amex, Diners, MasterCard,* **VISA**

ST PETER'S VILLAGE   Star & Tipsy Toad Brewery   A

Tel 01534 485556   Fax 01534 485559   Map 13 F4
St Peter's Village Jersey JE3 7AA

Right on the A12, in St Peter's Village, the Star was Jersey's first brew pub back in 1992. The parlour, snug and conservatory all provide a view of early stages of the brewing process through a wall of windows, and guided tours and tastings are conducted daily. Indoor and outdoor play areas keep the 'Little Toadies' amused, while the family room with its children's menu (prices include ice cream!) and baby-changing facilities make this a perfect pub for families: no food, though, on Sundays or Monday nights in winter. A sister pub to St Helier's *Tipsy Toad Town House*, it has new proprietors since mid-1996 in Steve and Vicky Beer, and we're promised few changes – but how long before they start brewing Beers' Beers? There is live music Friday to Sunday nights and the Tipsy Toad folk festival is held annually during the 3rd week of September. *Open 10am-11pm, Sun 11-1, 4.30-11. Free House.* **Beer** *Tipsy Toad, Jimmy's Bitter and Horny Toad home-brews, Crazy Diamond, Cyril's Bitter and independent guest ales. Beer garden, children's play area. Disabled facilities. Family room, indoor play area. Amex, MasterCard,* **VISA**

Sark

SARK   Dixcart Hotel & Bar   FOOD

Tel 01481 832015   Fax 01481 832164   Map 13 E4   **B&B**
Sark via Guernsey GY9 0SD

Surrounded by 50 acres of gardens with private access to the Dixcart Bay beach, Sark's longest-established hotel (recommended in our *1997 Hotels & Restaurants Guide*) was originally a 16th-century longhouse. A charming public bar and barbecue terrace adjacent and under the same ownership has oak wall-panelling and solid pine furniture; paintings by local artists on the walls add to the warm, informal atmosphere. Bar snacks come from the kitchen of the main restaurant (also recommended) and include home-made pub favourites (assorted fish, chicken and mushroom and steak and kidney pies), local plaice and seafood, sandwiches and baked potatoes as well as a list of daily dishes such as liver and onions, crispy vegetable stir-fry and pan-fried Sark scallops when available. Children have their own no-smoking 'Snug' with toys and TV plus familiar 'children's choices' on the menu. *Open 11-11.45 (Sun from 12, to 10 in winter).* **Bar Food** *12-2.30, 6.30-9. Public bar closed winter evenings (& no bar food). Garden, outdoor eating. Family room.* **Accommodation** *15 bedrooms (all with shower only), from £50-£70 according to season. Children welcome overnight (0-4 50%, 5-9 60%, 10-14 75% of tariff). MasterCard,* **VISA**

Isle of Man

Tel 01624 842216 Fax 01624 843359   Map 4 A4
The Quayside Peel Isle of Man IM5 1AT

Slap bang on the harbour front, picnic tables abound in summer outside this bustling
pub with its large, bright and recently-enlarged bars. Friendly proprietors Robert and
Jean McAleer can always be found busily serving up fresh fish and seafood obtained
from the nearby fish yards. Home-made kipper and smoked salmon paté, salmon and
broccoli pie, 'queenies' served on the shell in a mornay sauce, and salmon and
mushroom supreme might all feature on the menu or among the blackboard specials,
with pride of place going nonetheless to their memorable Manx seafood platter.
Other offerings range from open sandwiches to curries and steak and kidney pie, with
several fruit tarts or home-made gateaux to follow. Junior diners are offered smaller
portions. A full selection of Irish spirits – from Bushmills to Dry Cork Gin – and at
least 10 wines by the glass supplement the four real ales on offer. As we went to
press, completion of four en suite bedrooms was scheduled for April 1997, to
coincide with the opening of a major new heritage centre opposite. *Pub open 10am-
11pm (Fri & Sat to midnight, Sun 12-3, 7-10.30). Free House.* **Bar Food** *11-10.45 (Sun
12-2, 7-10). Children's menu.* **Beer** *Okells Bitter & Mild, Tetley Bitter, Coachouse Bitter,
guest beer. Outdoor eating on the quayside. Children welcome in bar 12-2.30 only if eating.
Pub closed 25 Dec. MasterCard,* **VISA**

Northern Ireland

The addresses of establishments in the following former **Counties** now include their new Counties/Unitary Authorities:

Co Antrim
Antrim, Ballymena, Ballymoney, Belfast City, Carrickfergus, Larne, Moyle, Newtonabbey
Co Armagh
Armagh, Craigavon, Newry & Mourne (part)
Co Down
Ards, Banbridge, Castlereagh, Down, Lisburn, Newry & Mourne (part), North Down
Co Fermanagh
Fermanagh
Co Londonderry
Coleraine, Derry City, Limavady, Magherafelt
Co Tyrone

AGHADOWEY   Brown Trout Golf & Country Inn   FOOD

Tel 01265 868209 Fax 01265 868878   Map 20 C1   **B&B**
209 Agivey Road Aghadowey Coleraine BT51 4AD

Although golf is the major attraction (both the 9-hole course on the premises – green fees £4 Mon-Fri, £6 Sat, Sun & BH – and the nearby Portrush Golf Club), non-golfers will also warm to the relaxed atmosphere and friendly staff at Bill O'Hara's big-hearted country inn. Comfortable public areas have a convivial bar as the focal point, and bedrooms are all on the ground floor, arranged around a garden courtyard. Spacious and pleasantly decorated, with two (small) double beds, TV, phone and hospitality tray, all rooms are en suite with bath and separate shower. Although they may fall down on details such as placing of lights and the quality of towels and bedding, the overall level of comfort is more than adequate and there is plenty of room for golfing paraphernalia. One room is suitable for disabled guests. Other leisure facilities include a mini-gym, a putting green, fishing in the grounds and riding stables half a mile away. Up a steep staircase (with chair lift for the less able), the 42-seat restaurant commands a pleasant view of a magnificent tree and the garden end of the golf course. Good home cooking of fresh foods characterises meals that are not over-ambitious and all the better for it. There's an early high-tea (5-7pm) followed by an à la carte dinner menu (7-10, Sun to 9) offering favourites such as chicken liver paté with Cumberland sauce and fresh scampi. Weekly specials such as tender fillet of pork with a white wine sauce and desserts like Jamaican bananas baked with rum ensure variety. Also open for Sunday lunch (£9). In the bar, straightforward hot and cold sandwiches are complemented by home-made lasagne and burgers, steak, scampi, grilled butterflied trout, a golfer's fry-up and children's favourites. The Brown Trout is not that easy to find: it's in the townland of Aghadowey on the A54, 7 miles north of Kilrea and 5 miles south of Coleraine; ask for directions when booking. *Open 11-11.30 (Sun 12-10). Bar Food 12-10.30 (Sun till 9.30). Accommodation 17 bedrooms, all en suite, £80 (single £60). Children welcome overnight (under-6s free if sharing with parents, 6-16s £16). Garden, outdoor eating, children's play area. Family room. Amex, Diners, MasterCard, VISA*

BALLYCASTLE   House of McDonnell   A

Tel 01265 762975   Map 20 D1
71 Castle Street Ballycastle Moyle BT64 6AS

Unusually, even for a characterful old pub, McDonnell's is a listed building and as such no changes are allowed inside or out. Not that change is much on the cards anyway, as it has been in the family since the 18th century and is clearly much loved – as visitors soon discover from the landlady Eileen O'Neill. She enjoys nothing better than sharing the history of the long, narrow, mahogany-countered bar which was once a traditional grocery-bar. Alas, no food is now offered, but The Open Door, a good traditional Northern Ireland bakery across the road, has hot snacks and a wide range of fresh sandwiches to order. Inside the pub is a fine collection of original etched mirrors. Traditional Irish music on Friday nights (and Wednesday during the summer) and folk music on Saturday nights throughout the year. "In every sense, a real, traditional Irish pub." *Open 11.30-11 (Sun 12.30-2.30 & 7-10 – but 7-11 only Oct-Easter except Bank Holidays). No credit cards.*

We do not accept free meals or hospitality – our inspectors pay their own bills
and never book in the name of Egon Ronay's Guides.

BALLYMONEY   The Old Bank House   FOOD

Tel 01265 663924   Map 20 C1
9 Church Street Ballymoney BT53 6HS

Joey and Margaret Erwin have enjoyed only the briefest of 'retirement' since leaving *Blackheath House & MacDuff's Restaurant* (which were recommended in our *1997 Hotels & Restaurants Guide*) in Garvagh near Coleraine. Their new enterprise is a former Victorian bank, an impressive building in the centre of Ballymoney town with an extraordinary interior that they have changed as little as possible, retaining original details like the magnificent mouldings in the soaring banking hall. The food operation – bar food menus under Margaret's personal supervision, with help from some of their old staff – was just getting into full swing as went to press – and Joey had set up a wine shop on the same premises. *Open 11.30-11 (not Sun).* **Bar Food** *12-3, 5.30-7.30.* **Beer** *Bass – under pressure. Closed Sun & 25, 26 Dec. MasterCard,* **VISA**

BELFAST   Crown Liquor Salon   A

Tel 01232 325368   Map 20 D2
44 Great Victoria Street Belfast BT2 7BA

Belfast's most famous and best-preserved bar, High Victorian and wonderful in its exuberant opulence. 'Gaslight glints on painted windows, vivid in amber and carmine, on gilded glass and on highly-patterned tiles which abound everywhere. It reflects from shining brass, from ornate mirrors, and glows against the burnished ceiling embossed with entwining curves. Richly-carved wood, a granite-topped bar, bright panels of plasterwork – and a floor laid in a myriad of mosaics completes the picture of relentless decoration' – we couldn't put it better as it truly is an architectural fantasy. The building belongs to the National Trust and is run by Bass Taverns. Every visitor to Belfast should experience the joy of a pint in one of the delightful 'snugs' – if snugs could talk there would be many a tale to tell from these clandestine retreats! Upstairs, The Britannic Lounge, with an Edwardian feel, is fitted out with original timbers from the *SS Britannic,* sister ship to the *Titanic. Open 11.30-11.30, Sun 12.30-2.30 & 7-10.* **Beer** *Bass. MasterCard,* **VISA**

BELFAST   Kelly's Cellars   A

Tel 01232 324835   Map 20 D2
30/32 Bank Street Belfast BT1 1HL

A protected building, this characterful bar boasts the oldest cellars in Ireland, dating back to 1720. Friday and Saturday nights alternate a folk group with a blues or rock band (if the folk is on Friday one week it will be on Saturday the next). Some times there is also live traditional Irish music. *Open 11.30-11 (till 1am Thur-Sat). Closed Sun & some Bank Holidays. MasterCard,* **VISA**

CARNLOUGH   Londonderry Arms Hotel   FOOD

Tel 01574 885255   Fax 01574 885263   Map 20 D1   **B&B**
20 Harbour Road Carnlough Glens of Antrim Larne BT44 0EU

Attractive old inn situated close to the pretty little harbour and enjoying good views over Carnlough Bay towards the Antrim Mountains beyond. Owned by the O'Neill family for 25 years, they have gradually extended and upgraded the building and it makes a useful overnight stop or refreshment stop on the famous scenic coastal route. Well known locally for 'good plain food', with a satisfying range of bar snacks (home-made vegetable soup with wheaten bread, open prawn sandwiches, paté with Cumberland sauce, chef's home-made pie) served in both the pubby bar and hotel lounge. Seventeen spacious and comfortable new bedrooms have just been completed (total now is 35), each furnished and decorated to a modern, superior standard with co-ordinating fabrics, king-size beds, attractive wall coverings and well-appointed en suite bathrooms with power showers over the tubs. Original bedrooms, most due for a revamp, feature individual pieces of furniture (many of them antique) and a more traditional style of decor; top rooms enjoy views across the bay. *Open 11.30-11 (Sun 12-10.30).* **Bar Food** *12-3 only. Garden, disabled facilities.* **Accommodation** *35 bedrooms, all en suite, £70 (single £45). Children welcome overnight (under-3s stay free, 3-12s £15 in parents' room). Amex, Diners, MasterCard,* **VISA**

COLERAINE   The Salmon Leap   FOOD

Tel 01265 52992   Fax 01265 43390   Map 20 C1
53 Castleroe Road Coleraine BT51 3RL

Stylish riverside premises, hands-on management by owner Brian McGinnis, a characterful front bar, lively modern food from head chef Eamon Cosgrove's kitchen, and friendly, interested staff make a winning combination at The Salmon Leap. Functions and special music events such as jazz brunches are a regular part of the scene here and the 'Bailiff's Watch' bar has a late licence to 1am Mon-Sat. On the food side, the 'Poacher's Hide' bistro provides smart, informal meals, typically in fashionable, flavoursome dishes such as chargrilled ginger chicken (soaked in ginger, lemon, thyme and soy sauce, chargrilled and served with a garlic mayonnaise) or marinated beef kebabs (diced steak, threaded with onion and peppers, chargrilled and served with a tangy Szechuan sauce dip), both served with garlic potatoes or chunky chips in their skins. The layout and decor has been thoughtfully achieved, producing an unusual establishment that works well on a number of levels. A Sunday lunch carvery is offered in The Lennox Suite. The Still Water restaurant is open for dinner only from 6.30-9.30 Tue-Sat (but it is the bar food that we specifically reccommend here). *Open 11.30-11 (Sun 11.30-3, 7-10).* **Meals** *12-10.30 (Sun Carvery 12.30-3, 3.30-9.30). Closed 25 Dec. Amex, Diners, MasterCard,* **VISA**

CRAWFORDSBURN	Old Inn	B&B

Tel 01247 853255   Fax 01247 852775   Map 20 D2
15 Main Street Crawfordsburn North Down BT19 1JH

Located off the main Belfast to Bangor road, this 17th-century inn is in a pretty village setting and is supposed to be the oldest in continuous use in all Ireland. Its location is conveniently close to Belfast and its City Airport. Oak beams, antiques and gas lighting emphasise the natural character of the building, an attractive venue for business people (conference facilities for 150, banqueting for 90) and private guests alike. Individually decorated bedrooms vary in size and style, most have antiques, some four-posters and a few have private sitting rooms; all are non-smoking. Romantics and newly-weds should head for the honeymoon cottage (£135). Free private car parking for overnight guests. No dogs. *Open 11.30-11.30 (Sun 12-3, 7-10).* **Accommodation** *33 rooms, £70-£85 (Fri-Sun £65, single £45). Garden. Closed 24-26 Dec. Amex, Diners, MasterCard,* **VISA**

CUSHENDALL	P J McCollam	A

No Telephone   Map 20 D1
23 Mill Street Cushendall Moyle BT4 0RR

Currently run by Joe and Sheila Blaney (Joe is the nephew of Joe McCollam), McCollam's has been in the family for 300 years. It's a magical place with a tiny front bar complete with a patchwork of photographs of local characters, many of them sheep farmers (and great fiddle players) who come down from the glens at weekends. The range in the old family kitchen behind the bar is lit on cold evenings and a converted 'cottage' barn across the yard makes a perfect setting for the famous traditional music sessions. Hospitable and full of character. *Open 4-11 in summer (August 12.30-11, winter: Mon-Thu 8-11 & Fri, Sat 4-11). Closed Sunday lunchtime. No credit cards.*

DUNDRUM	Buck's Head Inn	FOOD

Tel 01396 751868   Fax 01396 751898   Map 20 D2
77 Main Street Dundrum nr Newcastle Down BT33 0LU

Situated on the main Belfast-Newcastle road, this attractive, welcoming family-run pub offers fairly traditional bar food from a blackboard menu which changes daily. The decor is traditional in a comfortably understated way, creating a warm, relaxed atmosphere. The restaurant is in a conservatory extension at the back of the pub, looking out on to a walled garden where tables are set up in summer. Light, bright and pleasantly furnished with cane chairs and well-appointed tables, the bar offers a blackboard menu that always features lasagne, home-made burgers, Dundrum mussels and oysters; in addition, you might find bang bang chicken, deep-fried Brie, pepper-crusted salmon, poached plaice with salmon mousse or lamb shank with champ. Three-course Sunday lunch. *Open 11.30-10.30 (Sun 12-2.30, 5.30-10).* **Bar Food** *12.30-2.30, high tea 5.30-7, 7-9.30 (Sun to 8.30, all day Jun-Aug). Garden, outdoor eating. Closed 25 Dec. Amex, MasterCard,* **VISA**

ENNISKILLEN   Blakes of the Hollow   A

Tel 01365 322143   Map 20 C2
6 Church Street Enniskillen Fermanagh BT74 7JE

The Blake family have reigned supreme over this wonderfully characterful pub in the centre of Enniskillen since 1929 (Donal himself has been here since 1953). It presents a double image, with its gleaming black and red shop-front brightening up an otherwise ordinary street and, from the riverside through-road, an immaculate (if, for first-time visitors, somewhat mysterious) alleyway and stairs straight up into a bar that has remained unchanged since 1875. Owners and regulars alike are rightly proud of their haven and delight in introducing visitors to it, through photographs and the story of the robin behind the bar. Pints of Guinness are the thing here (with a shamrock on top if you like) but, although food is not the reason for coming, they do home-made soup and a fresh, fatly-packed sandwich all the same (Mon-Fri 12.30-2.30 only). No children. *Open 11.30-11 (Sun 7-10). Closed lunch Sun. No credit cards.*

HILLSBOROUGH   The Hillside Bar   ★   FOOD

Tel 01846 682765   Fax 01846 682557   Map 20 D2
21 Main Street Hillsborough Lisburn BT26 6AE

A delightful, well-run establishment, The Hillside '1777' is easily found in the centre of this pretty little town – and very well worth finding it is, too. The atmosphere is warm and cosy in both the main bar, where a real fire burns all year, and a smaller one to the side. Throughout, the atmosphere is gently rustic – dark green paint and soft country browns and greys in natural materials – and comfortably set up for eating. The new Refectory Bar and a separate kitchen for bar food have alleviated much of the pressure on the bar food system that has recently arisen. Now, the bar menu is served throughout the day (with only a short break after lunch before cream teas are served in the afternoon) by charming young staff. Typical fare from the bar menu might tempura fo cod with roast pepper pesto, open ciabatta sandwiches, smoked haddock and leek tart with crispy bacon and herb aïoli, deep-dish lasagne plus daily specials like confit of duck with plum sauce or salmon escalope with puff pastry and a lemon sauce; home-baked fruit pie, tangy lemon meringue and Hillside banoffee among the puddings; in the evening, flame-grilled home-made burgers and steaks extend the range. The whole operation is overseen by Diane Shields and her family and a new chef, Albert Neilly, had just taken over as we went to press. His new restaurant menus promise good things: wild mushroom and rosemary soup finished with a light sabayon and poppy seeds, goujons of pan-fried salmon marinated in dill and yoghurt with sautéed spinach, wild rice and a tarragon and white wine sauce, and petit tarte tatin with a Grand Marnier crème anglaise – tempting stuff! Bar manager Randall Brennan offers Northern Ireland's best range of real ales: try the new White Water ale, brewed in nearby Kilkeel, one of Hilden's ales (also brewed locally) or seek out the Old Hen herself; you can even get a pint of Guinness at either cool room temperature or chilled, and the wine list offers around 12 wines by the glass. Outside seating on the recently-extended (and cobbled) beer garden. New disabled loo (access for bar food only). Our Ireland Pub of the Year in 1995. *Open 11.30-11 (Sun 12.30-2.30, 7.30-10.30).* **Bar Food** *12-2.30, 3.30-8. Restaurant 7-9.30 (not Sun eve). Beer White Water, Hilden, Morland Old Speckled Hen, Cains Traditional. Closed Good Friday & 25 Dec.* **Beer** *garden. Amex, Diners, MasterCard,* **VISA**

We endeavour to be as up-to-date as possible but inevitably some changes to landlords, chefs and other key staff occur after the Guide
has gone to press.

HILLSBOROUGH   The Plough Inn   FOOD

Tel 01846 682985 Fax 01846 682472   Map 20 D2
The Square Hillsborough Lisburn BT26 6AG

Former coaching inn, dating back to the 18th century, overlooking the Market Court House and the Secretary of State for Ireland's residence at the top of the main street in this historic small town, located just off the A1, 9 miles south of Belfast. Since purchasing the establishment in 1990, the hard-working Patterson family, especially the enthusiastic young head chef Derek Patterson, have created one of the most popular dining pubs in the area, if not Northern Ireland, famous for its seafood restaurant, warm hospitality and for hosting the Hillsborough Oyster Festival in September, when 3,000 oysters are consumed!. In fact, the Plough is to be commended for successfully running three distinct food operations each day, which, as a result, attracts a varied clientele, from a good lunchtime business trade to discerning evening diners. Derek Paterson's style of cooking on an assortment of menus has been influenced by his travels worldwide, with classical French blending with traditional Irish, ethnic and Oriental styles. Home-cooked 'pub' meals (open prawn sandwich, chicken, mushroom and bacon pie, Malaysian beef curry, summer salads, fresh fish of the day) are served in the comfortable front bar, complete with open fire, beams, memorabilia-adorned walls and well-kept Theakston Bitter, at lunchtime only. Served at the same time (and in the early evening 5-7pm) in the upstairs wine bar and bistro, is a more select range of dishes aimed at the business market. Here, Thai seafood kebab, pan-blackened cod fillet with chargrilled vegtables, and rib-eye steak can be accompanied by one of at least twenty wines available by the glass, or a bottle from the interesting list of wines with good tasting notes. After 7pm both the wine bar and main bar fill up with a young drinking clientele, while the kitchen shifts up a gear in preparation for the serious diners who eagerly await their table in the 'evening-only' rear restaurant – booking essential. Housed in the old stables with the atmosphere of a Scottish Baronial undercroft, this is where Derek Patterson excels in preparing the excellent choice of seafood dishes (Galway oysters Thai-style, fresh lobster, roast ray wing with crushed peppercorns, Donegal mussel and saffron scented soup, Cajun-spiced shark steak, pan-blackened Glenarm salmon with mushrooms and ginger soya) listed on the short, hand-written and daily-changing menu. Meat-eaters should not be disappointed with calf's liver, onion compote and lime jus, Oriental duck breast and deep-fried noodles, or a prime Angus sirloin steak. Well-executed dishes are carefully presented and service is efficient from young, keen staff. The Pattersons also find time to organise seasonal gourmet evenings, summer barbecues and a beer festival (October). No children in the pub. Winner of our Northern Ireland Regional Award for our 1997 Seafood Pub of the Year. *Open 11.30-11.30 (Sun 12-3, 7-10.30).* **Meals:** *Bar 12-2.15 only (from 12.30 Sun) Wine Bar/Bistro Tue-Sat 12-2.15, 5-7 Restaurant Tue-Sat 6-9 only. Wine Bar/Bistro & Restaurant closed Sun & Mon. Free House.* **Beer** *Theakston Best Bitter, guest beer. Garden, outdoor eating, barbecue. Amex, Diners, MasterCard,* **VISA**

We endeavour to be as up-to-date as possible but inevitably some changes to
landlords, chefs and other key staff occur after the Guide
has gone to press.

IRVINESTOWN   The Hollander   FOOD

Tel 01365 621231   Map 20 C2
5 Main Street Townhill Irvinestown nr Eniskillen Fermanagh BT94 1GJ

The Holland family – Jim and Margaret plus their son Stephen – run a tidy ship at this long-established town-centre eatery. Jim, the manager, is usually to be found in the bar (which has a fascinating array of aeronautical memorabilia spanning two World Wars) while Margaret and head chef Stephen look after the food side. Both family and formula work well together, producing a unique combination of food, drink and hospitality that draws locals and visitors alike, whether for popular bar food dishes like freshly-made burgers or seafood bakes with a special 'home-made' touch. House specialities are always on the evening menus but can be produced by arrangement at lunchtime for a group of four or more – all it takes is a phone call and the à la carte menu will be produced. Try the popular stuffed duck, a whole fresh duck, de-boned and stuffed, or the salmon en croute (shaped by Stephen to look like a fish). Hard-working and hospitable, Jim will even run boating visitors back to the local marina after dinner. Separate no-smoking room. Toilet facilities for the disabled. *Open 12-2, 5.30-11 (Sun 6.30-9.30).* **Bar Food** *12-2, 5.30-7. Restaurant 5.30-9.30 (Sun 6.30-9). Closed L Sun, all Mon & Tue (except July & August), 24-26 Dec. Amex, MasterCard,* **VISA**

KESH	Lusty Beg Island	FOOD

Tel 01365 632032   Fax 01365 632033   Map 20 C2   B&B
Kesh Fermanagh BT93 8AD

Bought by the Cadden family four years ago, Lusty Beg Island has been imaginatively developed to create a self-contained facility satisfying a number of different markets. As soon as guests enter the isolated phone box to call the little ferry that will spirit them across to the island they know this is going to be something different. The ferry (which is free) might just take two (very small) cars but it is mostly intended for foot passengers and their luggage, as self-catering cottages are the most obvious attraction on the island. But wait, is this a friendly inn we spy? – Indeed it is and very nice, too, serving good bar snacks (home-baked bread, wild Irish smoked salmon, garlic mussels, pizzas and baked potatoes). As we were going to press Lusty Beg was entering its penultimate stage of development (the final one is a swimming pool and leisure centre, to be ready in time for the 1997 season), with a bed & breakfast operation in village-style little houses and banqueting/conference facilities coming on stream in addition to the established self-catering chalets. Two rooms for the disabled. Ned's Cottage, a thatched tea room, is open for snacks in the summer only from 9am-7pm. *Bar open 10-11.30.* **Bar Food** *12-9. Restaurant 6.30-9.30. Garden, outdoor eating, barbecues.* **Accommodation** *18 bedrooms, all with shower en suite, £45 (single £28.50. Children welcome overnight (under-2s free if sharing, 2-8 75% off tariff, 8-14 50%). No dogs. MasterCard,* **VISA**

PORTBALLINTRAE	Sweeney's	FOOD

Tel 01265 732404   Fax 01265 731279   Map 20 C1
6 Seaport Avenue Portballintrae Moyle BT57 8SB

On the sea side of the road, this attractive stone building has its origins in the 18th century when it was built as coaching stables for the nearby Leslie estate. It has now been pleasingly renovated and converted by the current owner, Seymour Sweeney, into a stylish bar and comfortable, informal restaurant. Although the main building is cut off from the view from another similar one on the seaward side (used for accommodation), a conservatory addition gets around the problem for daytime use and the main interior has a cosy open fire and generally welcoming atmosphere (except for pervasive background music in all areas except the conservatory). While gourmet food is not the aim, the kitchen produces a fairly extensive range of snappy modern dishes that should appeal to most age groups – typically, good soup, baked potatoes with various fillings, chicken kebab in pitta bread, confit of duck with creamed lentils or vegetarian leek and mustard crumble. No bookings taken, except for parties. Live music is a regular feature (Mon, Wed, Fri & Sat in summer, Fri & Sat in winter) and there's a late licence until 12.30am when it's playing. Toilet facilities for the disabled. New no-smoking area. *Open 11.30-11, Sun 12.30-2.30, 7-10).* **Bar Food** *12-9.30 summer & holidays (12-2.30, 5-9.30 winter), Sun 12.30-2.30, 7-10. Garden, outdoor eating. Closed 25 Dec. No credit cards.*

We endeavour to be as up-to-date as possible but inevitably some changes to landlords, chefs and other key staff occur after the Guide has gone to press.

PORTGLENONE   Crosskeys Inn   A

Tel 01648 50694   Map 20 D2
Portglenone Ballymena BT42

Follow signs for Randalstown on leaving Portglenone, then lookout for the signs
to Crosskeys to find this charming, 17th-century stone-and-thatch rural inn, which
enjoys an isolated position at a country crossroads. Formerly an old coaching inn and,
until recently, the local post office and general stores, it remains truly unspoilt and
one of the best pub venues for traditional Irish music in Antrim. Eamonn Stinson is
in charge behind the bar, just as his father was before the war, serving a loyal band of
locals and thirsty tourists who track this gem down. The bar is simply adorned and
the adjacent 'kitchen' has a huge fireplace and rustic tables and chairs; the basic back
room is where the musicians gather and the 'impromptu' sessions begin (Wed, Fri,
Sat & Sun eve). No food available. *Open 11-11.30 (Sun 12.30-3, 7-10.30). Patio.*
No credit cards.

Republic of Ireland

Egon Ronay's Jameson Guide Ireland replaces
the Republic of Ireland section in this Guide.
The new edition of the Ireland Guide is
published in March 1997.

ACCEPTED IN MORE HOTELS AND RESTAURANTS THAN MOST PEOPLE EVER HAVE HOT DINNERS.

VISA IS ACCEPTED FOR MORE TRANSACTIONS
WORLDWIDE THAN ANY OTHER CARD.

MAKING LIFE EASIER

Regional Round-Ups

The tinted pages which follow summarise all the entries in the gazetteer (pages 39 to 450) by postal district in London and by region outside London.

ACCEPTED IN MORE HOTELS AND RESTAURANTS THAN MOST PEOPLE EVER HAVE HOT DINNERS.

VISA IS ACCEPTED FOR MORE TRANSACTIONS
WORLDWIDE THAN ANY OTHER CARD.

MAKING LIFE EASIER

London
& Regional Round-Ups

London establishments are summarised in
postal district order.

See the How to Use section (page 10) for a full explanation
of categories, gradings and symbols.

London Pubs by Postal District

See **How To Use This Guide**, on Pages 10-11, for an explanation of our categories (FOOD, B&B, Atmosphere) and symbols.

Location	Establishment	Star	Food	B&B	Atmosphere	Seafood	Beer	Sleep	Family	Waterside	Telephone	Map Ref.
E14	Grapes				◄						0171-987 4396	17 D4
EC1	Cock Tavern		◄								0171-248 2918	16 D3
EC1	The Eagle	★	◄								0171-837 1353	16 C3
EC1	Fox & Anchor		◄								0171-253 4838	16 D3
EC1	The Peasant	★	◄								0171-336 7726	16 D3
EC1	The Hope, Sir Loin Restaurant		◄								0171-250 1442	16 C3
EC1	Thomas Wethered				◄		◄				0171-278 9983	16 D3
EC1	Ye Olde Mitre Tavern		◄		◄						0171-405 4751	16 D3
EC2	Old Dr Butler's Head		◄				◄				0171-606 3504	16 D3
EC3	Lamb Tavern		◄								0171-626 2454	17 D4
EC4	Black Friar				◄		◄				0171-236 5650	17 D4
EC4	Old Bell Tavern				◄		◄				0171-583 0070	17 D4
EC4	Witness Box		◄								0171-353 6427	17 D4

Area	Pub	Telephone	Map Ref						
EC4	Ye Olde Cheshire Cheese	0171-353 6170	17 D4				◄		
N1	Albion	0171-607 7450	16 C2				◄		
N1	Eagle Tavern	0171-253 4715	16 D3		◄		◄		
N1	Marquess Tavern	0171-354 2975	16 D3					◄	
NW1	The Engineer	0171-722 0950	16 C3			♀		◄	★
NW1	The Lansdowne	0171-483 0409	16 C3					◄	★
NW3	Flask	0171-435 4580	16 B2						
NW3	Jack Straw's Castle	0171-435 8885	16 B2		◄		◄		
NW3	Spaniards Inn	0181-455 3276	16 B2		◄		◄		
NW8	Crockers Folly	0171-286 6608	18 B1					◄	
SE1	Anchor	0171-407 1577	17 D4	◄	◄		◄		
SE1	Founders Arms	0171-928 1899	17 D4	◄	◄		◄		
SE1	George Inn	0171-407 2056	17 D4		◄		◄		
SE1	Horniman at Hay's	0171-407 3611	17 D4	◄	◄			◄	
SE5	Phoenix & Firkin	0171-701 8282	17 D5		◄		◄		
SW1	Buckingham Arms	0171-222 3386	19 D4					◄	
SW1	The Grenadier	0171-235 3074	19 C4					◄	
SW1	Morpeth Arms	0171-834 6442	19 D5					◄	
SW1	Nag's Head	0171-235 1135	19 C4					◄	
SW1	Orange Brewery	0171-730 5984	19 C5		◄		◄		
SW1	Star	0171-235 3019	19 C4		◄		◄		
SW3	The Australian	0171-589 3114	19 C5					◄	
SW3	Coopers Arms	0171-376 3120	19 B5			♀		◄	
SW3	Cross Keys	0171-349 9111	19 C6					◄	

Location	Establishment	Star	Food	B&B	Atmosphere	Seafood	Beer	Sleep	Family	Waterside	Telephone	Map Ref.
SW3	Front Page		▲								0171-352 2908	19 B6
SW3	Phene Arms		▲			♢					0171-352 3294	19 B6
SW6	Imperial Arms		▲			♢					0171-736 9179	19 A6
SW6	Jim Thompson's		▲								0171-731 7636	19 A6
SW6	White Horse		▲				▲				0171-736 2115	17 B5
SW10	Chelsea Ram	★	▲								0171-351 4008	19 B6
SW10	Sporting Page		▲								0171-352 6465	19 B6
SW11	The Castle		▲								0171-228 8181	17 B5
SW18	Alma		▲								0181-870 2537	17 B5
SW18	Brewers Inn		▲	▲		♢					0181-874 4128	17 B6
SW18	The Ship		▲		▲	♢				▲	0181-870 9667	17 B5
SW19	Fox & Grapes										0181-946 5599	17 B6
W1	The French House		▲								0171-437 2799	18 D3
W1	The Guinea		▲								0171-499 1210	18 C3
W1	Newman Arms		▲								0171-636 1127	18 D2
W1	O'Conor Don		▲								0171-935 9311	18 C2
W2	The Cow		▲			♢					0171-221 5400	18 A2
W2	Monkey Puzzle				▲						0171-723 0143	18 B2
W2	Prince Bonaparte		▲								0171-229 5912	18 A2
W2	The Westbourne	★	▲		▲						0171-221 1332	18 A2
W4	Bell & Crown									▲	0181-994 4164	17 A5

					Phone	Map ref
W4	City Barge	◄			0181-994 2148	17 A5
W6	Dove	◄	◄		0181-748 5405	17 A4
W8	Britannia	◄			0171-937 1864	19 A4
W8	Churchill Arms	◄	◄		0171-727 4242	18 A3
W8	Windsor Castle				0171-727 8491	19 A4
W9	The Warrington, Ben's Thai	◄	◄		0171-266 3134	18 A1
W11	Ladbroke Arms		◄		0171-727 6648	18 A3
WC1	Cittie of York	◄			0171-242 7670	16 C3
WC1	Lamb	◄			0171-405 0713	16 C3
WC1	Princess Louise	◄	◄	◄	0171-405 8816	16 C3
WC2	Lamb & Flag		◄	◄	0171-497 9504	18 D3
WC2	Opera Tavern		◄		0171-836 7321	17 C4
WC2	Salisbury		◄		0171-836 5863	18 D3

ACCEPTED IN MORE HOTELS AND RESTAURANTS THAN MOST PEOPLE EVER HAVE HOT DINNERS.

VISA IS ACCEPTED FOR MORE TRANSACTIONS
WORLDWIDE THAN ANY OTHER CARD.

MAKING LIFE EASIER

England

Regional Round-Ups

England is divided into the following regions:

Home Counties
Bedfordshire, Berkshire, Buckinghamshire, Essex (inc Barking & Dagenham, Redbridge, Waltham Forest and Havering), Hertfordshire (inc Barnet and Enfield), former Middlesex (Brent, Enfield, Harrow, Hounslow, Hillingdon, Southall) and Surrey (inc Croydon, Sutton, Kingston-upon-Thames and Richmond-upon-Thames)

South of England
Hampshire, Isle of Wight, Kent (inc Bexley and Bromley), East Sussex (inc Brighton) and West Sussex

West Country
Cornwall, Devon, Dorset, Somerset, Wiltshire and the former south part of Avon (Bristol, Bath & North East Somerset and North Somerset)

Midlands/Heart of England
Derbyshire, Gloucestershire, Hereford & Worcester, Leicestershire, Northamptonshire, Nottinghamshire, Oxfordshire, Shropshire, Staffordshire and Warwickshire; plus the north part of former Avon (South Gloucestershire) and the former West Midlands (Birmingham, Coventry, Dudley, Sandwell, Solihull, Wolverhampton and Walsall)

East of England
Cambridgeshire, Lincolnshire (inc North Lincolnshire and North East Lincolnshire - part of south former Humberside), Norfolk and Suffolk

continued over

See the How to Use section (page 10) for a full explanation of categories, gradings and symbols.

North East of England

Former Cleveland (Redcar & Cleveland, Middlesbrough, Stockton-on-Tees, Hartlepool), Durham, north former Humberside (East Riding of Yorkshire and Kingston upon Hull), Northumberland, former Tyne & Wear (Gateshead, Newcastle-upon-Tyne, North Tyneside, South Tyneside, Sunderland), North Yorkshire (inc York), former South Yorkshire (Barnsley, Sheffield, Rotherham and Doncaster) and former West Yorkshire (Bradford, Calderdale, Kirklees, Leeds and Wakefield)

North West of England

Cheshire (inc Wirral, Trafford and Stockport), Cumbria, former Greater Manchester (Wigan, Bolton, Bury, Rochdale, Salford, Manchester, Tameside, Oldham), Merseyside (inc Liverpool, Knowsley, Sefton and St Helens) and Lancashire

See the How to Use section (page 10) for a full explanation of categories, gradings and symbols.

Home Counties

Bedfordshire

Location	Establishment	Star	Food	B&B	Atmosphere	Seafood	Beer	Sleep	Family	Waterside	Telephone	Map Ref.
Bedford	Embankment Hotel			◄						◄	01234 261332	15 E1
Broom	Cock Inn			◄	◄				◄		01767 314411	15a F1
Houghton Conquest	Knife & Cleaver			◄							01234 740387	15a E1
Keysoe	Chequers Inn		◄		◄				◄		01234 708678	15 E1
Little Odell	Mad Dog				◄						01234 720221	15 E1
Odell	Bell									◄	01234 720254	15 E1
Turvey	Three Cranes			◄							01234 881305	15 E1

Berkshire

Location	Establishment	Star	Food	B&B	Atmosphere	Seafood	Beer	Sleep	Family	Waterside	Telephone	Map Ref.
Aldworth	Bell Inn		◄								01635 578272	14a C3
Beenham Village	Six Bells		◄	◄	◄		◄				0118 971 3368	14a C4
Bray-on-Thames	The fish at Bray		◄			♦					01628 781111	15a E3
Cookham Dean	Inn on the Green		◄		◄	♦			◄		01628 482638	15a E3
Cookham Dean	Jolly Farmer		◄						◄		01628 482905	15a E3
Crazies Hill	The Horns				◄						0118 940 1416	15a D3
East Garston	Queens Arms Hotel			◄							01488 648757	14a B4
East Ilsley	Swan			◄					◄		01635 281238	14a C3
Exlade Street	The Highwayman		◄	◄	◄	♦	◄				01491 682020	14a C3
Frilsham	Pot Kiln						◄				01635 201366	14a C4
Hamstead Marshall	White Hart Inn		◄	◄		♦					01488 658201	14a B4

Location	Establishment	Star	Food	B&B	Atmosphere	Seafood	Beer	Sleep	Family	Waterside	Telephone	Map Ref.
Hare Hatch	Queen Victoria		◄								0118 940 2477	15a D3
Highclere	The Yew Tree		◄	◄		◈					01635 253360	14a C4
Kintbury	Dundas Arms		◄	◄		◈				◄	01488 658263	14a B4
Knowl Hill	Bird in Hand			◄				◄			01628 826622	15a D3
Marsh Benham	Rat		◄			◈					01635 582017	14a B4
Sonning	Bull				◄						0118 969 3901	15a D4
Stanford Dingley	Bull Country Inn		◄			◈	◄		◄		0118 974 4409	14a C4
Stanford Dingley	Old Boot		◄			◈					01734 744292	14a C4
West Ilsley	Harrow Inn	★	◄						◄		01635 281260	14a C3
Yattendon	Royal Oak		◄	◄		◈		◄			01635 201325	14a C4

Buckinghamshire

Location	Establishment	Star	Food	B&B	Atmosphere	Seafood	Beer	Sleep	Family	Waterside	Telephone	Map Ref.
Beaconsfield	Greyhound		◄			◈					01494 673823	15a E3
Bellingdon	Bull		◄			◈			◄		01494 758163	15a E2
Bledlow	Lions of Bledlow				◄		◄				01844 343345	15a D2
Bolter End	Peacock		◄			◈					01494 881417	15a D3
Easington	Mole & Chicken		◄			◈					01844 208387	15a D2
Fingest	Chequers Inn				◄						01491 638335	15a D3
Ford	Dinton Hermit		◄			◈					01296 748379	15a D2
Forty Green	Royal Standard of England				◄						01494 673382	15a E3

			Phone	Grid
Great Missenden	The George		01494 862084	15a E2
Ibstone	The Fox		01491 638289	15a D3
Ley Hill	Swan		01494 783075	15a E2
Little Hampden	Rising Sun		01494 488393	15a E2
Long Crendon	The Angel ★		01844 208268	15a D2
Marsh Gibbon	The Greyhound		01869 277365	14a C1
Moulsoe	Carrington Arms		01908 218050	15a E1
Old Amersham	King's Arms		01494 726333	15a E3
Penn Street	Hit or Miss		01494 713109	15a E3
Saunderton	Rose & Crown Inn		01844 345299	15a D2
Stony Stratford	Cock Hotel		01908 567733	15a D1
Turville	Bull & Butcher		01491 638283	15a D3
Waddesdon	Five Arrows Hotel		01296 651727	15a D2
West Wycombe	George & Dragon		01494 464414	15a D3
Whiteleaf	Red Lion		01844 344476	15a D2
Winslow	Bell Hotel		01296 714091	15a D1
Wooburn Common	Chequers Inn		01628 529575	15a E3

Essex

(including Barking & Dagenham, Redbridge, Waltham Forest and Havering)

			Phone	Grid
Burnham-on-Crouch	Ye Olde White Harte		01621 782106	11 C4
Clavering	Cricketers		01799 550442	10 B3
Colchester	Rose & Crown Hotel		01206 866677	10 C3
Dedham	Marlborough Head Hotel		01206 323250	10 C3
Gosfield	Green Man		01787 472746	10 C3
Great Chesterford	Plough		01799 530283	10 B3

Location	Establishment	Star	Food	B&B	Atmosphere	Seafood	Beer	Sleep	Family	Waterside	Telephone	Map Ref.
Great Yeldham	White Hart	★	◄			◊					01787 237250	10 C3
Hastingwood Common	Rainbow & Dove				◄						01279 415419	11 B4
High Roding	Black Lion										01371 872847	11 B4
Horndon-on-the-Hill	Bell Inn & Hill House	★	◄	◄		◊	◄	◄			01375 673154	11 B4
Little Braxted	Green Man		◄								01621 891659	11 C4
Little Canfield	Lion & Lamb		◄		◄				◄		01279 870257	10 B3
Littlebury	Queen's Head			◄			◄		◄		01799 522251	10 B3
Mill Green	Viper						◄				01277 352010	11 B4
Rickling Green	Cricketers Arms		◄	◄	◄				◄		01799 543210	10 B3
Saffron Walden	Eight Bells		◄	◄		◊					01799 522790	10 B3
Saffron Walden	Saffron Hotel		◄	◄							01799 522676	10 B3
Thaxted	Farmhouse Inn										01371 830864	10 B3
Tillingham	Cap & Feathers				◄	◊	◄		◄		01621 779212	11 C4
Toot Hill	Green Man		◄								01992 522255	11 B4

Hertfordshire
(including Barnet)

Location	Establishment	Star	Food	B&B	Atmosphere	Seafood	Beer	Sleep	Family	Waterside	Telephone	Map Ref.
Ayot St Lawrence	Brocket Arms		◄	◄			◄		◄		01438 820250	15a F2
Barley	Fox & Hounds		◄			◊	◄	◄	◄		01763 848459	15 F1
Chenies	Red Lion		◄								01923 282722	15a E2
Chorleywood	Sportsman Hotel		◄	◄					◄		01923 285155	15a E3
Elsenham	Crown		◄						◄		01279 812827	10 B3

		Phone	Grid
St Albans	Rose & Crown	01727 851903	15a F2
Watton at Stone	George & Dragon	01920 830285	15 F1

Surrey

(including Croydon, Sutton, Kingston-upon-Thames and Richmond-upon-Thames)

		Phone	Grid
Albury Heath	King William IV	01483 202685	15a E4
Blackbrook	Plough	01306 886603	15a F4
Chiddingfold	Crown Inn	01428 682255	11 A5
Elstead	Woolpack	01252 703106	15a E4
Grayswood	Wheatsheaf Inn	01428 644440	11 A6
Hascombe	White Horse	01483 208258	11 A5
Hurtmore	The Squirrel	01483 860223	15a E4
Mickleham	King William IV	01372 372590	15a F4
Shamley Green	Red Lion	01483 892202	15a E4
Shepperton	Anchor Hotel	01932 221618	15a F4
Shepperton	King's Head	01932 221910	15a F4
Shepperton	Warren Lodge	01932 242972	15a F4
Thursley	Three Horseshoes	01252 703268	15a E4
Walliswood	Scarlett Arms	01306 627243	11 A5
Windlesham	Brickmakers Arms	01276 472267	15a E4

South of England
Hampshire

Location	Establishment	Star	Food	B&B	Atmosphere	Seafood	Beer	Sleep	Family	Waterside	Telephone	Map Ref.
Alresford	Globe on the Lake		▲			◇			▲	▲	01962 732294	15 D3
Beauworth	Milbury's				▲		▲		▲		01962 771248	15 D3
Bentworth	Sun Inn		▲				▲		▲		01420 562338	15a D4
Boldre	Red Lion				▲						01590 673177	14 C4
Bramdean	Fox Inn		▲			◇					01962 771363	15 D3
Buckler's Hard	Master Builder's House Hotel									▲	01590 616253	15 D4
Buriton	Five Bells		▲	▲		◇	▲				01730 263584	15 D3
Bursledon	Jolly Sailor			▲	▲					▲	01703 405557	15 D4
Cadnam	White Hart		▲			◇					01703 812277	14 C4
Cheriton	Flower Pots Inn		▲	▲			▲				01962 771318	15 D3
Crawley	Fox & Hounds		▲	▲		◇		▲			01962 776285	15 D3
Damerham	Compasses Inn		▲	▲				▲	▲		01725 518231	14 C3
Dummer	The Queen		▲								01256 397367	14a C4
East Meon	Ye Olde George Inn		▲	▲			▲			▲	01730 823481	15 D3
Ellisfield	Fox				▲		▲				01256 381210	14a C4
Emery Down	New Forest Inn		▲	▲					▲		01703 282329	14 C4
Faccombe	Jack Russell Inn		▲	▲		◇		▲	▲	▲	01264 737315	14a B4
Langstone	Royal Oak				▲				▲	▲	01705 483125	15 D4

Location	Name	Phone	Map ref
Linwood	High Corner Inn	01425 473973	14 C4
Longstock	Peat Spade	01264 810612	14 C3
Lower Froyle	Prince of Wales	01420 23102	15a D4
Lower Wield	Yew Tree Inn	01256 389224	14a C4
Micheldever	Dever Arms	01962 774339	15 D3
Odiham	George Hotel	01256 702081	15a D4
Ovington	Bush Inn	01962 732764	15 D3
Priors Dean	White Horse	01420 588387	15 D3
Rockbourne	Rose & Thistle	01725 518236	14 C3
Sherfield English	Hatchet Inn	01794 322487	14 C3
Sparsholt	Plough	01962 776353	15 D3
Steep	Harrow Inn	01730 262685	15 D3
Stratfield Turgis	Wellington Arms	01256 882214	15a D4
Tangley	Fox Inn	01264 730276	14a B4
Testcombe	Mayfly	01264 860283	14 C3
Tichborne	Tichborne Arms	01962 733760	15 D3
Titchfield	Fishermans Rest	01329 842848	15 D4
Well	Chequers	01256 862605	15a D4
Winchester	Wykeham Arms	01962 853834	15 D3

Isle of Wight

Location	Name	Phone	Map ref
Bonchurch	Bonchurch Inn	01983 852611	15 D4
Chale	Clarendon Hotel	01983 730431	15 D4
Rookley	Chequers Inn	01983 840314	15 D4
Seaview	Seaview Hotel	01983 612711	15 D4
Ventnor	Spyglass Inn	01983 855338	15 D4

Kent

(including Bexley and Bromley)

Location	Establishment	Star	Food	B&B	Atmosphere	Seafood	Beer	Sleep	Family	Waterside	Telephone	Map Ref.
Benenden	King William IV		◄								01580 240636	11 C6
Biddenden	Three Chimneys		◄				◄				01580 291472	11 C5
Boughton Aluph	Flying Horse Inn		◄	◄			◄				01233 620914	11 C5
Burham	Golden Eagle		◄								01634 668975	11 B5
Canterbury	Falstaff Hotel			◄							01227 462138	11 C5
Charing	Royal Oak Hotel			◄							01233 712307	11 C5
Chiddingstone	Castle Inn				◄						01892 870247	11 B5
Chilham	White Horse				◄						01227 730355	11 C5
Chilham	Woolpack			◄					◄		01227 730208	11 C5
Chillenden	Griffins Head		◄								01304 840325	11 C5
Cliffe	Black Bull		◄								01634 220893	11 B5
Eastling	Carpenter's Arms		◄	◄		◊					01795 890234	11 C5
Faversham	Albion Tavern		◄			◊					01795 591411	11 C5
Fordcombe	Chafford Arms		◄								01892 740267	11 B5
Goudhurst	Star & Eagle Inn			◄					◄		01580 211512	11 B5
Ightham Common	Harrow Inn	★	◄			◊					01732 885912	11 B5
Ivy Hatch	The Plough	★	◄			◊					01732 810268	11 B5
Lenham	Dog & Bear Hotel			◄					◄		01622 858219	11 C5
Marshside	Gate Inn		◄				◄		◄	◄	01227 860498	11 C5
Newnham	George Inn		◄						◄		01795 890237	11 C5

Town	Establishment								Phone	Map ref
Pluckley	Dering Arms	◄		◡				◄	01233 840371	11 C5
Ringlestone	Ringlestone Inn	◄			◄				01622 859900	11 C5
Selling	White Lion	◄		◡					01227 752211	11 C5
Sevenoaks	Royal Oak	◄	◄					◄	01732 451109	11 B5
Shipbourne	Chaser Inn	◄	◄						01732 810360	11 B5
Smarden	Bell	◄			◄			◄	01233 770283	11 C5
Smarden	Chequers Inn	◄	◄	◡				◄	01233 770217	11 C5
Smarts Hill	Bottle House Inn	◄		◡	◄				01892 870306	11 B5
St Margaret's-at-Cliffe	Cliffe Tavern	◄		◡					01304 852400	11 D5
Stalisfield Green	Plough Inn	◄		◡					01795 890256	11 C5
Tunbridge Wells	Sankeys Cellar Wine Bar	◄		◡					01892 511422	11 B5
Ulcombe	Pepper Box	◄			◄			◄	01622 842558	11 C5
Warren Street	The Harrow	◄	◄			◄			01622 858727	11 C5
Worth	St Crispin Inn		◄		◄	◄			01304 612081	11 D5
Wye	New Flying Horse Inn		◄		◄	◄			01233 812297	11 C5

East Sussex

Town	Establishment								Phone	Map ref
Alciston	Rose Cottage			◄					01323 870377	11 B6
Berwick	Cricketers			◄					01323 870469	11 B6
Blackboys	Blackboys Inn	◄				◡			01825 890283	11 B6
Brighton	Greys	◄				◡			01273 680734	11 B6
Crowborough	White Hart	◄			◄			◄	01892 652367	11 B6
Ewhurst Green	White Dog Inn	◄	◄						01580 830264	11 C6
Firle	Ram Inn	◄	◄		◄			◄	01273 858222	11 B6
Fletching	Griffin Inn	◄	◄		◄	◡		◄	01825 722890	11 B6
Forest Row	Brambletye Hotel	◄							01342 824144	11 B6

Location	Establishment	Star	Food	B&B	Atmosphere	Seafood	Beer	Sleep	Family	Waterside	Telephone	Map Ref.
Horam	Gun Inn		◄			◊			◄		01825 872361	11 B6
Kingston	The Juggs		◄						◄		01273 472523	11 B6
Mayfield	Rose & Crown Inn		◄	◄		◊	◄	◄			01435 872200	11 B6
Old Heathfield	Star Inn		◄			◊					01435 863570	11 B6

West Sussex

Location	Establishment	Star	Food	B&B	Atmosphere	Seafood	Beer	Sleep	Family	Waterside	Telephone	Map Ref.
Burpham	George & Dragon Inn		◄			◊	◄				01903 883131	11 A6
Byworth	Black Horse		◄				◄			◄	01798 342424	11 A6
Chilgrove	White Horse Inn		◄	◄		◊		◄			01243 535219	15 E3
Compton	Coach & Horses		◄	◄		◊	◄				01705 631228	15 D3
Edburton	Tottington Manor		◄			◊		◄			01903 815757	11 B6
Elsted	Three Horseshoes		◄		◄	◊	◄				01730 825746	15 D3
Elsted Marsh	Elsted Inn		◄			◊	◄		◄		01730 813662	15 D3
Fernhurst	Red Lion		◄			◊					01428 653304	11 A6
Fittleworth	The Swan		◄	◄					◄		01798 865429	11 A6
Fulking	Shepherd & Dog		◄		◄		◄				01273 857382	11 B6
Hermitage	Sussex Brewery					◊					01243 371533	15 D4
Lodsworth	Halfway Bridge		◄		◄	◊					01798 861281	11 A6
Lower Beeding	Jeremy's at The Crabtree	★	◄			◊					01403 891257	11 B6
Lurgashall	Noah's Ark										01428 707346	11 A6
Midhurst	Angel Hotel	★	◄	◄		◊		◄			01730 812421	11 A6
Midhurst	Spread Eagle		◄	◄							01730 816911	11 A6

Location	Name	Telephone	Map ref
Nuthurst	Black Horse	01403 891272	11 A6
Oving	Gribble Inn	01243 786893	11 A6
Petworth	Welldiggers Arms	01798 342287	11 A6
Rusper	Star Inn	01293 871264	11 A5
South Harting	Ship Inn	01730 825302	15 D3
South Harting	White Hart	01730 825355	15 D3
Stedham	Hamilton Arms	01730 812555	11 A6
Sutton	White Horse Inn	01798 869221	11 A6
The Haven	The Blue Ship	01403 822709	11 A6
Tillington	Horseguards Inn	01798 342322	11 A6
Warnham	Greets Inn	01403 265047	11 A6
Wineham	Royal Oak	01444 881252	11 B6

West Country

Bristol

Location	Name	Telephone	Map ref
Bristol	Highbury Vaults	0117 973 3203	13 F1

Cornwall

Location	Name	Telephone	Map ref
Charlestown	Pier House Hotel	01726 67955	12 B3
Charlestown	Rashleigh Arms	01726 73635	12 B3
Constantine	Trengilly Wartha Inn	01326 340332	12 B4
Egloshayle	Earl of St Vincent	01208 814807	12 B3
Fowey	King of Prussia	01726 832450	12 C3
Fowey	Ship Inn	01726 833751	12 C3
Gunwalloe	Halzephron Inn ★	01326 240406	12 A4

Location	Establishment	Star	Food	B&B	Atmosphere	Seafood	Beer	Sleep	Family	Waterside	Telephone	Map Ref.
Helford	Shipwrights Arms		▲		▲					▲	01326 231235	12 B4
Kingand	Halfway House Inn		▲	▲					▲	▲	01752 822279	12 C3
Lostwithiel	Royal Oak			▲		◆	▲				01208 872552	12 C3
Ludgvan	White Hart				▲	◆					01736 740574	12 A4
Mithian	Miners Arms		▲			◆			▲		01872 552375	12 B3
Morwenstow	Bush Inn				▲						01288 331242	12 C2
Mousehole	Ship Inn			▲						▲	01736 731234	12 A4
Mylor Bridge	Pandora Inn		▲			◆				▲	01326 372678	12 B3
Padstow	Old Custom House			▲					▲	▲	01841 532359	12 B3
Pelynt	Jubilee Inn			▲					▲		01503 220312	12 C3
Penelewey	Punch Bowl & Ladle				▲						01872 862237	12 B3
Perranuthnoe	Victoria Inn			▲		◆			▲		01736 710309	12 A4
Philleigh	Roseland Inn		▲		▲	◆			▲		01872 580254	12 B3
Polkerris	Rashleigh Inn			▲	▲		▲			▲	01726 813991	12 B3
Port Gaverne	Port Gaverne Hotel			▲				▲		▲	01208 880244	12 B3
Porthleven	Harbour Inn			▲						▲	01326 573876	12 A4
Porthleven	Ship Inn				▲		▲			▲	01326 572841	12 A4
Sennen Cove	Old Success Inn			▲				▲		▲	01736 871232	12 A4
St Agnes	Driftwood Spars Hotel			▲			▲		▲	▲	01872 552428	12 B3
St Austell	White Hart			▲							01726 72100	12 B3
St Kew	St Kew Inn				▲			▲			01208 841259	12 B3
St Mawes	Rising Sun		▲	▲						▲	01326 270233	12 B4

Location	Name								Phone	Map ref
St Mawgan	Falcon Inn				◀			◀	01637 860225	12 B3
Tregadillett	Eliot Arms				◀				01566 772051	12 C3

Devon

Location	Name								Phone	Map ref
Alphington	Double Locks						◀	◀	01392 56947	13 D2
Ashprington	Durant Arms		◆	◀				◀	01803 732240	13 D3
Ashprington	Waterman's Arms	◆	◀				◀	◀	01803 732214	13 D3
Bantham	Sloop Inn	◀						◀	01548 560489	13 D3
Beer	Anchor Inn	◀	◀	◆			◀	◀	01297 20386	13 E2
Blackawton	Normandy Arms	◀	◀						01803 712316	13 D3
Branscombe	Masons Arms	◀	◆		◀			◀	01297 680300	13 E2
Brendon	Stag Hunters Hotel	◀					◀		01598 741222	13 D1
Broadhembury	Drewe Arms ★	◀	◆						01404 841267	13 E2
Butterleigh	Butterleigh Inn			◀					01884 855407	13 E2
Cheriton Bishop	Old Thatch Inn	◀							01647 24204	13 D2
Chillington	Chillington Inn	◀	◆			◀			01548 580244	13 D3
Cockwood	Anchor Inn	◀	◆		◀				01626 890203	13 E3
Cockwood	Ship Inn	◀	◆						01626 890373	13 E3
Coleford	New Inn	◀	◆				◀	◀	01363 84242	13 D2
Cornworthy	Hunters Lodge Inn	◀	◆					◀	01803 732204	13 D3
Cullompton	Manor House Hotel	◀							01884 32281	13 E2
Dalwood	Tuckers Arms	◀	◆						01404 881342	13 E2
Dartington	Cott Inn	◀	◆			◀			01803 863777	13 D3
Dartmouth	Cherub	◀	◆						01803 832571	13 D3
Dartmouth	Royal Castle Hotel	◀					◀	◀	01803 833033	13 D3

Location	Establishment	Star	Food	B&B	Atmosphere	Seafood	Beer	Sleep	Family	Waterside	Telephone	Map Ref.
Doddiscombsleigh	Nobody Inn		◄	◄			◄	◄			01647 252394	13 D3
Harberton	Church House Inn				◄						01803 863707	13 D3
Hatherleigh	George Hotel		◄	◄				◄	◄		01837 810454	13 D2
Hatherleigh	Tally Ho			◄			◄				01837 810306	13 D2
Haytor Vale	Rock Inn		◄	◄		🐟		◄			01364 661305	13 D3
Holne	Church House Inn			◄							01364 631208	13 D3
Horndon	Elephant's Nest		◄						◄		01822 810273	12 C3
Horsebridge	Royal Inn		◄	◄			◄	◄		◄	01822 870214	12 C3
Kingskerswell	Barn Owl Inn		◄	◄		🐟		◄			01803 872130	13 D3
Kingsteignton	Old Rydon Inn	★	◄			🐟			◄		01626 54626	13 D3
Knowstone	Masons Arms		◄			🐟			◄		01398 341231	13 D2
Lifton	Arundell Arms		◄	◄							01566 784666	12 C2
Lower Ashton	Manor Inn		◄	◄		🐟	◄				01647 252304	13 D3
Lydford	Castle Inn		◄	◄		🐟	◄		◄		01822 820242	12 C3
Lynmouth	Rising Sun Hotel			◄				◄	◄	◄	01598 753223	13 D1
Moretonhampstead	White Hart Hotel			◄							01647 440406	13 D2
Newton St Cyres	Crown & Sceptre		◄			🐟			◄	◄	01392 851278	13 D2
Plymouth	China House				◄						01752 260930	12 C3
Rockbeare	Jack in the Green	★	◄			🐟	◄				01404 822240	13 E2
Shaldon	Ness House Hotel		◄	◄					◄	◄	01626 873480	13 D3
South Pool	Millbrook Inn		◄			🐟				◄	01548 531581	13 D3
South Zeal	Oxenham Arms			◄							01837 840244	13 D2

Location	Name	Phone	Map ref
Spreyton	Tom Cobley Tavern	01647 231314	13 D2
Staverton	Sea Trout Inn	01803 762274	13 D3
Stockland	Kings Arms Inn	01404 881361	13 E2
Stokenham	Tradesman's Arms	01548 580313	13 D3
Thelbridge	Thelbridge Cross Inn	01884 860316	13 D2
Torcross	Start Bay Inn	01548 580553	13 D3
Trusham	Cridford Inn	01626 853694	13 D3
Weston	Otter Inn	01404 42594	13 E2
Widecombe-in-the-Moor	Rugglestone Inn	01364 621327	13 D3

Dorset

Location	Name	Phone	Map ref
Abbotsbury	Ilchester Arms	01305 871243	13 F3
Askerswell	Spyway Inn	01308 485250	13 F2
Blandford Forum	Crown Hotel	01258 456626	14 B4
Bridport	Bull Hotel	01308 422878	13 F2
Bridport	George Hotel	01308 423187	13 F2
Buckland Newton	Gaggle of Geese	01300 345249	13 F2
Cerne Abbas	New Inn	01300 341274	13 F2
Cerne Abbas	Red Lion	01300 341441	13 F2
Corfe Castle	Fox	01929 480449	14 B4
Corscombe	Fox Inn	01935 891330	13 F2
Cranborne	Fleur de Lys	01725 517282	14 C4
Dorchester	Kings Arms	01305 265353	13 F2
East Chaldon	Sailors Return	01305 853847	14 B4
Farnham	Museum Hotel	01725 516261	14 C3

Location	Establishment	Star	Food	B&B	Atmosphere	Seafood	Beer	Sleep	Family	Waterside	Telephone	Map Ref.
Loders	Loders Arms		◄			◈					01308 422431	13 E2
Milton Abbas	Hambro Arms		◄	◄		◈					01258 880233	14 B4
Motcombe	Coppleridge Inn		◄	◄		◈		◄			01747 851980	14 B3
Nettlecombe	Marquis of Lorne		◄	◄		◈					01308 485236	13 F2
North Wootton	Three Elms		◄	◄			◄		◄		01935 812881	13 F2
Piddlehinton	Thimble Inn				◄				◄	◄	01300 348270	13 F2
Pimperne	Anvil Hotel			◄							01258 453431	14 B4
Plush	Brace of Pheasants		◄	◄		◈			◄		01300 348357	13 F2
Powerstock	Three Horseshoes Inn		◄	◄		◈		◄	◄		01308 485328	13 F2
Semley	Benett Arms		◄			◈					01747 830221	14 B3
Shave Cross	Shave Cross Inn				◄						01308 868358	13 F2
Shroton	Cricketers		◄			◈	◄				01258 860421	14 B4
Sturminster Newton	Swan Inn			◄							01258 472208	14 B4
Tarrant Monkton	Langton Arms		◄	◄			◄	◄	◄		01258 830225	14 B4
Trent	Rose & Crown		◄			◈			◄		01935 850776	13 F2
West Bexington	Manor Hotel		◄	◄		◈			◄	◄	01308 897785	13 F2
Winkton	Fisherman's Haunt Hotel			◄						◄	01202 484071	14 C4

Somerset

(including North Somerset and Bath & North East Somerset - the former south part of Avon)

Location	Establishment	Star	Food	B&B	Atmosphere	Seafood	Beer	Sleep	Family	Waterside	Telephone	Map Ref.
Appley	The Globe Inn		◄			◈					01823 672327	13 E2
Axbridge	Lamb Inn			◄							01934 732253	13 F1

Location	Establishment		Telephone	Map Ref
Batcombe	Batcombe Inn	★	01749 850359	13 F1
Bathampton	George Inn		01225 425079	13 F1
Beckington	Woolpack Inn	★	01373 831244	14 B3
Bradley Green	Malt Shovel Inn		01278 653432	13 E1
Castle Cary	George Hotel		01963 350761	13 F2
Combe Hay	Wheatsheaf		01225 833504	13 F1
Congresbury	White Hart		01934 833303	13 F1
Cranmore	Strode Arms		01749 880450	13 F1
Croscombe	Bull Terrier		01749 343658	13 F1
East Woodlands	Horse & Groom		01373 462802	14 B3
Exford	Crown Hotel		01643 831554	13 D1
Haselbury Plucknett	Haselbury Inn		01460 72488	13 F2
Kelston	Old Crown Inn		01225 423032	13 F1
Kilve	Hood Arms		01278 741210	13 E1
Kingsdon	Kingsdon Inn		01935 840543	13 F2
Knapp	Rising Sun		01823 490436	13 E2
Langley Marsh	Three Horseshoes		01984 623763	13 E2
Luxborough	Royal Oak		01984 640319	13 E1
Lympsham	Batch Country House Hotel		01934 750371	13 E1
Mells	Talbot Inn		01373 812254	13 F1
Monksilver	Notley Arms	★	01984 656217	13 E2
Montacute	King's Arms Inn		01935 822513	13 F2
North Wootton	Crossways Inn		01749 890237	13 F1
Norton St Philip	George Inn		01373 834224	13 F1
Nunney	George at Nunney		01373 836458	13 F1

Location	Establishment	Star	Food	B&B	Atmosphere	Seafood	Beer	Sleep	Family	Waterside	Telephone	Map Ref.
Over Stratton	Royal Oak				▲				▲		01460 240906	13 F2
Rudge	The Full Moon		▲	▲					▲		01373 830936	14 B3
Shepton Montague	Montague Inn	★	▲	▲		◇	▲	▲			01749 813213	13 F2
Sparkford	Sparkford Inn		▲		▲	◇			▲		01963 440218	13 F2
Stanton Wick	Carpenters Arms		▲	▲		◇			▲		01761 490202	13 F1
Staple Fitzpaine	Greyhound Inn		▲			◇	▲		▲	▲	01823 480277	13 E2
Stoke St Gregory	Rose & Crown		▲	▲		◇					01823 490296	13 E2
West Camel	Walnut Tree		▲	▲		◇		▲			01935 851292	13 F2
West Huntspill	Crossways Inn		▲	▲					▲		01278 783756	13 E1
Winsford	Royal Oak Inn		▲	▲			▲	▲			01643 851455	13 D2
Withypool	Royal Oak Inn		▲	▲				▲			01643 831506	13 D1

Wiltshire

Location	Establishment	Star	Food	B&B	Atmosphere	Seafood	Beer	Sleep	Family	Waterside	Telephone	Map Ref.
Alvediston	Crown Inn		▲								01722 780335	14 B3
Axford	Red Lion Inn		▲	▲		◇					01672 520271	14a A4
Barford St Martin	Barford Inn			▲							01722 742242	14 C3
Bottlesford	Seven Stars		▲			◇			▲		01672 851325	14a A4
Bowden Hill	Rising Sun				▲		▲				01249 730363	14 B2
Box	Bayly's		▲	▲							01225 743622	14 B2
Brinkworth	Three Crowns		▲			◇			▲		01666 510366	14 C2
Broad Chalke	Queen's Head Inn			▲							01722 780344	14 C3
Bromham	Greyhound Inn		▲			◇					01380 850241	14 B3

Location	Name			Phone	Map
Burton	Old House at Home		◆	01454 218227	14 B2
Castle Combe	Castle Inn		◆	01249 783030	14 B2
Castle Combe	White Hart			01249 782295	14 B2
Charlton	Horse & Groom		◆	01666 823904	14 C2
Chicksgrove	Compasses		◆	01722 714318	14 C3
Corsham	Methuen Arms		◆	01249 714867	14 B2
Devizes	Bear Hotel		◆	01380 722444	14 C3
Ebbesbourne Wake	Horseshoes Inn		◆	01722 780474	14 B3
Fonthill Gifford	Beckford Arms		◆	01747 870385	14 B3
Ford	White Hart		◆	01249 782213	14 B2
Hindon	Lamb at Hindon		◆	01747 820573	14 B3
Holt	Old Ham Tree		◆	01225 782581	14 B3
Lacock	George Inn		◆	01249 730263	14 B2
Melksham	King's Arms Hotel		◆	01225 707272	14 B3
North Newnton	Woodbridge Inn	★	◆	01980 630266	14a A4
Nunton	Radnor Arms		◆	01722 329722	14 C3
Pitton	Silver Plough		◆	01722 712266	14 C3
Ramsbury	Bell at Ramsbury		◆	01672 520230	14a A4
Rowde	George & Dragon	★	◆	01380 723053	14 C3
Salisbury	Haunch of Venison			01722 322024	14 C3
Salisbury	King's Arms Hotel		◆	01722 327629	14 C3
Semington	Lamb on the Strand		◆	01380 870263	14 B3
Sherston	Rattlebone Inn			01666 840871	14 B2
Stourton	Spread Eagle Inn		◆	01747 840587	14 B3
Wootton Rivers	Royal Oak		◆	01672 810322	14a A4

Midlands/Heart of England
Derbyshire

Location	Establishment	Star	Food	B&B	Atmosphere	Seafood	Beer	Sleep	Family	Waterside	Telephone	Map Ref.
Ashford-in-the-Water	Ashford Hotel		◄	◄					◄		01629 812725	6 C2
Bamford	Yorkshire Bridge Inn			◄				◄	◄		01433 651361	6 C2
Birch Vale	Sycamore Inn		◄	◄					◄		01663 742715	6 C2
Birch Vale	Waltzing Weasel		◄	◄				◄			01663 743402	6 C2
Birchover	Druid Inn		◄			◊					01629 650302	6 C2
Brassington	Ye Olde Gate			◄	◄						01629 540448	6 C3
Calver	Chequers Inn		◄	◄		◊		◄			01433 630231	6 C2
Castleton	Castle Hotel				◄				◄		01433 620578	6 C2
Derby	Abbey Inn			◄	◄						01332 558297	6 C3
Derby	Ye Olde Dolphin Inn					◊	◄				01332 349115	6 C3
Dronfield	Old Sidings									◄	01246 410023	6 C2
Eyam	Miner's Arms		◄	◄							01433 630853	6 C2
Grindleford	Maynard Arms		◄	◄		◊		◄	◄		01433 630321	6 C2
Hathersage	Hathersage Inn			◄							01433 650259	6 C2
Hope	Poacher's Arms			◄							01433 620380	6 C2
Little Longstone	Packhorse Inn				◄						01629 640471	6 C2
Litton	Red Lion Inn				◄						01298 871458	6 C2
Over Haddon	Lathkil Hotel		◄	◄							01629 812501	6 C2
Tideswell	George			◄							01298 871382	6 C2

Location	Establishment	Phone	Grid
Wardlow	Bull's Head	01298 871431	6 C2
Woolley Moor	White Horse	01246 590319	6 C3

Gloucestershire
(including South Gloucestershire - former north part of Avon)

Location	Establishment	Phone	Grid
Almondsbury	Bowl Inn	01454 612757	13 F1
Amberley	Black Horse	01453 872556	14 B2
Ampney Crucis	Crown of Crucis	01285 851806	14a A2
Andoversford	Kilkeney Inn	01242 820341	14 C1
Aust	Boar's Head	01454 632278	13 F1
Barnsley	The Village Pub	01285 740421	14a A2
Birdlip	The Air Balloon	01452 862541	14 B2
Blockley	Crown Inn & Hotel	01386 700245	14a A1
Broad Campden	Bakers Arms	01386 840515	14a A1
Brockhampton	Craven Arms	01242 820410	14 C1
Chipping Campden	Eight Bells Inn	01386 840371	14a A1
Chipping Campden	Noel Arms	01386 840317	14a A1
Clearwell	Wyndham Arms	01594 833666	14 B2
Coln St Aldwyns	New Inn ★	01285 750651	14a A2
Ewen	Wild Duck Inn	01285 770310	14 C2
Ford	Plough Inn	01386 584215	14a A1
Frampton Mansell	Crown Hotel	01285 760601	14 B2
Great Rissington	The Lamb	01451 820388	14a A2
Gretton	Royal Oak	01242 602477	14 C1
Guiting Power	Ye Olde Inne	01451 850392	14a A1
Kingscote	Hunters Hall	01453 860393	14 B2

Location	Establishment	Star	Food	B&B	Atmosphere	Seafood	Beer	Sleep	Family	Waterside	Telephone	Map Ref.
Little Compton	Red Lion Inn		◀	◀							01608 674397	14a B1
Lower Oddington	The Fox	★	◀			◇					01451 870888	14a A1
Moreton-in-Marsh	Redesdale Arms			◀							01608 650308	14a A1
Northleach	Wheatsheaf Hotel		◀	◀		◇		◀			01451 860244	14a A2
Oddington	Horse & Groom Inn		◀	◀				◀	◀		01451 830584	14a A1
Oldbury-on-Severn	Anchor Inn		◀				◀			◀	01454 413331	13 F1
St Briavels	George Inn			◀							01594 530228	14 B2
Stroud	Old Nelson			◀							01453 765821	14 B2
Tetbury	Calcot Manor, Gunstool Inn		◀			◇			◀		01666 890391	14 B2
Tormarton	Compass Inn										01454 218242	13 F1
Watersley Bottom	New Inn			◀			◀	◀			01453 543659	13 F1
Winchcombe	Old White Lion			◀				◀			01242 603300	14 C1
Woodchester	Ram Inn				◀		◀				01453 873329	14 B2
Woodchester	Woodchester Inn	★				◇					01453 872735	14 B2

Hereford & Worcester

Location	Establishment	Star	Food	B&B	Atmosphere	Seafood	Beer	Sleep	Family	Waterside	Telephone	Map Ref.
Bretforton	Fleece Inn				◀		◀		◀		01386 831173	14a A1
Brimfield	Poppies Restaurant	★	◀	◀		◇		◀			01584 711230	14 A1
Carey	Cottage of Content			◀				◀			01432 840242	14 B1
Dorstone	Pandy Inn		◀			◇		◀			01981 550273	9 D5
Fownhope	Green Man			◀				◀	◀		01432 860243	14 B1
Hay-on-Wye	Old Black Lion		◀	◀		◇	◀	◀	◀		01497 820841	9 D5

Location	Name	Telephone	Map ref
Kempsey	Walter de Cantelupe Inn	01905 820572	14 B1
Knightwick	Talbot Hotel	01886 821235	14 B1
Ledbury	Feathers Hotel	01531 635266	14 B1
Ledbury	Ye Olde Talbot Hotel	01531 632963	14 B1
Leominster	Royal Oak Hotel	01568 612610	14 A1
Little Cowarne	Three Horseshoes	01885 400276	14 B1
Ombersley	King's Arms	01905 620315	14 B1
Pembridge	New Inn	01544 388427	14 A1
Sellack	Loughpool Inn	01989 730236	14 B1
Shobdon	Bateman Arms	01568 708374	14 A1
Upton Bishop	Moody Cow	01989 780470	14 B1
Weobley	Ye Olde Salutation Inn	01544 318443	14 A1
Whitney-on-Wye	Rhydspence Inn	01497 831262	9 D4
Winforton	Sun Inn ★	01544 327677	9 D4
Woolhope	Butcher's Arms	01432 860281	14 B1
Wyre Piddle	Anchor Inn	01386 552799	14 C1

Leicestershire

Location	Name	Telephone	Map ref
Braunston	Blue Ball Inn	01572 722135	7 E4
Braunston	Old Plough	01572 722714	7 E4
Empingham	White Horse	01780 460221	7 E3
Glooston	Old Barn	01858 545215	7 D4
Hallaton	Bewicke Arms	01858 555217	7 D4
Kegworth	Cap & Stocking	01509 674814	7 D3
Leicester	Welford Place	0116 247 0758	7 D4

Location	Establishment	Star	Food	B&B	Atmosphere	Seafood	Beer	Sleep	Family	Waterside	Telephone	Map Ref.
Lyddington	Old White Hart		▲			♦					01572 821703	7 E4
Market Overton	Black Bull		▲			♦					01572 767677	7 E3
Old Dalby	Crown Inn		▲			♦	▲		▲		01664 823134	7 D3
Shardlow	Old Crown		▲			♦	▲			▲	01332 792392	7 D3
Somerby	Old Brewery Inn				▲		▲				01664 454866	7 D3
Stretton	Ram Jam Inn		▲	▲					▲		01780 410776	7 E3
Whitwell	Noel Arms			▲							01780 460334	7 E3

Northamptonshire

Location	Establishment	Star	Food	B&B	Atmosphere	Seafood	Beer	Sleep	Family	Waterside	Telephone	Map Ref.
Blakesley	Bartholomew Arms		▲	▲							01327 860292	15 D1
Castle Ashby	Falcon Hotel		▲	▲				▲			01604 696200	15 E1
East Haddon	Red Lion Hotel		▲	▲		♦	▲		▲		01604 770223	15 D1
Fotheringhay	Falcon Inn		▲				▲				01832 226254	7 E4
Upper Benefield	Wheatsheaf Hotel		▲	▲		♦			▲		01832 205254	7 E4
Woodnewton	White Swan		▲			♦					01780 470381	7 E4

Nottinghamshire

Location	Establishment	Star	Food	B&B	Atmosphere	Seafood	Beer	Sleep	Family	Waterside	Telephone	Map Ref.
Arnold	Burnt Stump		▲		▲				▲		0115 963 1508	7 D3
Colston Bassett	Martins Arms		▲			♦	▲				01949 81361	7 D3
Drakeholes	Griff Inn			▲				▲			01777 817206	7 D2
Elkesley	Robin Hood Inn		▲			♦					01777 838259	7 D2
Nottingham	Lincolnshire Poacher				▲		▲		▲		0115 941 1584	7 D3

Town	Pub	Telephone	Grid ref
Nottingham	Ye Olde Trip to Jerusalem	0115 947 3171	7 D3
Redmile	Peacock Inn	01949 842554	7 D3
Upton	French Horn	01636 812394	7 D3

Oxfordshire

Town	Pub	Telephone	Grid ref
Abingdon	Brewery Tap	01235 521655	14a C3
Adderbury	Red Lion	01295 810269	14a C1
Ardington	Boars Head	01235 833254	14a B3
Aston	Flower Pot	01491 574721	15a D3
Banbury	Ye Olde Reine Deer Inn	01295 264031	14a B1
Barnard Gate	Boot Inn	01865 881231	14a B2
Beckley	Abingdon Arms	01865 351311	14a C2
Bledington	Kings Head Inn ★	01608 658365	14a A1
Blewbury	Blewbury Inn	01235 850496	14a C3
Brightwell Baldwin	Lord Nelson	01491 612497	14a C3
Buckland	Lamb Inn	01367 870484	14a B3
Burcot	Chequers	01865 407771	14a C3
Burford	Inn For All Seasons	01451 844324	14a A2
Burford	Lamb Inn	01993 823155	14a A2
Chadlington	Tite Inn	01608 676475	14a B1
Charlbury	Bell Hotel	01608 810278	14a B2
Charlbury	Bull Inn ★	01608 810689	14a B2
Chislehampton	Coach & Horses	01865 890255	14a C2
Church Enstone	Crown Inn	01608 677262	14a B1
Clanfield	The Plough at Clanfield	01367 810222	14a B2
Clifton	Duke of Cumberland's Head	01869 338534	14a C1

Location	Establishment	Star	Food	B&B	Atmosphere	Seafood	Beer	Sleep	Family	Waterside	Telephone	Map Ref.
Clifton Hampden	Plough Inn		▲					▲	▲		01865 407811	14a C3
Cumnor	Bear & Ragged Staff	★	▲			◊					01865 862329	14a B2
Cumnor	Vine		▲			◊			▲		01865 862567	14a B2
Deddington	Deddington Arms		▲	▲		◊					01869 338364	14a C1
Dorchester-on-Thames	George Hotel			▲							01865 340404	14a C3
Drayton	Roebuck		▲	▲							01295 730542	14a B1
Eynsham	Newlands Inn		▲			◊			▲		01865 881486	14a B2
Freeland	Shepherds Hall Inn			▲					▲		01993 881256	14a B2
Frilford Heath	Dog House Hotel			▲				▲	▲		01865 390830	14a C3
Fyfield	White Hart				▲		▲		▲		01865 390585	14a B2
Godstow	Trout				▲		▲			▲	01865 54485	14a C2
Great Tew	Falkland Arms		▲	▲							01608 683653	14a B1
Hailey	The Bird In Hand		▲	▲				▲	▲		01993 868321	14a B2
Henton	Peacock Hotel			▲			▲	▲			01844 353519	15a D2
Maidensgrove	Five Horseshoes		▲			◊					01491 641282	15a D3
Middleton Stoney	Jersey Arms			▲				▲			01869 343234	14a C1
Nettlebed	White Hart		▲	▲							01491 641245	15a D3
Oxford	The Bear				▲		▲				01865 721783	14a C2
Remenham	Little Angel		▲							▲	01491 574165	15a D3
Roke	Home Sweet Home Inn		▲			◊					01491 838249	14a C3
Satwell	Lamb Inn				▲				▲		01491 628482	15a D3
Shenington	Bell Inn		▲								01295 670274	14a B1

Location	Name	Phone	Map ref
Shipton-under-Wychwood	Lamb Inn	01993 830465	14a B2
Shipton-under-Wychwood	Shaven Crown Hotel	01993 830330	14a B2
Sibford Gower	Wykham Arms	01295 780351	14a B1
Skirmett	Old Crown	01491 638435	15a D3
South Leigh	Mason Arms	01993 702485	14a B2
South Stoke	Perch & Pike	01491 872415	14a C3
Stanton St John	Star Inn	01865 351277	14a C2
Stanton St John	The Talkhouse	01865 351648	14a C2
Steeple Aston	Red Lion	01869 340225	14a C1
Sulgrave	Star Inn	01295 760389	14a C1
Sutton Courtenay	The Fish	01235 848242	14a C3
Thame	Abingdon Arms	01844 260116	15a D2
Watlington	Chequers	01491 612874	15a D3
Weston-on-the-Green	The Chequers	01869 350319	14a C2
Woodstock	Feathers Hotel	01993 812291	14a B2
Wytham	White Hart	01865 244372	14a C2

Shropshire

Location	Name	Phone	Map ref
Brockton	Feathers	01746 785202	6 B4
Heathton	Old Gate Inn	01746 710431	6 B4
Hopton Wafers	Crown Inn	01299 270372	6 B4
Llanfair Waterdine	Red Lion Inn	01547 528214	9 A4
Llanymynech	Bradford Arms	01691 830582	8 D3
Ludlow	Church Inn	01584 872174	6 A4

Location	Establishment	Star	Food	B&B	Atmosphere	Seafood	Beer	Sleep	Family	Waterside	Telephone	Map Ref.
Ludlow	Unicorn Inn		▲	▲		♦		▲		▲	01584 873555	6 A4
Much Wenlock	Talbot Inn		▲	▲		♦		▲			01952 727077	6 B4
Much Wenlock	Wenlock Edge Inn		▲	▲				▲			01746 785403	6 B4
Norton	Hundred House Hotel		▲	▲		♦					01952 730353	6 B4
Picklescott	Bottle & Glass Inn		▲	▲				▲		▲	01694 751345	6 A4
Shifnal	Oddfellows		▲	▲		♦					01952 461517	6 B4

Staffordshire

Location	Establishment	Star	Food	B&B	Atmosphere	Seafood	Beer	Sleep	Family	Waterside	Telephone	Map Ref.
Alstonefield	George Inn				▲						01335 310205	6 C3
Baldwin's Gate	Slater's			▲				▲			01782 680052	6 B3
Cauldon	Yew Tree Inn				▲						01538 308348	6 C3
Cresswell	Izaak Walton Inn		▲	▲							01782 392265	6 B3
Eccleshall	St George Hotel			▲					▲		01785 850300	6 B3
Onecote	Jervis Arms		▲		▲		▲		▲	▲	01538 304206	6 C3
Tatenhill	Horseshoe Inn								▲		01283 564913	6 C3
Tutbury	Ye Olde Dog & Partridge Inn			▲				▲			01283 813030	6 C3
Whitmore	Mainwaring Arms				▲						01782 680851	6 B3

Warwickshire

Location	Establishment	Star	Food	B&B	Atmosphere	Seafood	Beer	Sleep	Family	Waterside	Telephone	Map Ref.
Alderminster	Bell Bistro	▲	▲		♦		▲		▲		01789 450414	14 C1
Ashby St Ledgers	Olde Coach House Inn	▲	▲	▲	♦		▲		▲		01788 890349	15 D1

Location	Pub Name	Telephone	Map Ref
Broom	Broom Tavern	01789 773656	14 C1
Ettington	Houndshill	01789 740267	14 C1
Ilmington	Howard Arms	01608 682226	14a A1
Lowsonford	Fleur de Lys	01564 782431	14 C1
Stratford-upon-Avon	Dirty Duck	01789 297312	14 C1
Wootton Wawen	Bull's Head	01564 792511	14 C1

(Former) West Midlands
(Including Birmingham, Coventry, Dudley, Sandwell, Solihull, Wolverhampton and Walsall)

Location	Pub Name	Telephone	Map Ref
Ansty	Ansty Arms	01203 611817	7 D4
Baginton	Old Mill Inn	01203 303588	6 C4
Coventry	William IV	01203 686394	6 C4
Himley	Crooked House	01384 238583	6 B4
Langley	Brewery Inn	0121-544 6467	6 C4
West Bromwich	Manor House	0121-588 2035	6 C4

East of England
Cambridgeshire

Location	Pub Name	Telephone	Map Ref
Bythorn	White Hart	01832 710226	7 E4
Cambridge	Eagle	01223 301286	15 F1
Cambridge	Free Press	01223 68337	15 F1
Cambridge	Tram Depot	01223 324553	15 F1
Duxford	John Barleycorn	01223 832699	10 B3
Fenstanton	King William IV	01480 462467	15 F1
Fowlmere	Chequers Inn	01763 208369	15 F1
Holywell	Old Ferry Boat Inn	01480 463227	10 B2

Location	Establishment	Star	Food	B&B	Atmosphere	Seafood	Beer	Sleep	Family	Waterside	Telephone	Map Ref.
Horningsea	Plough & Fleece		◄								01223 860795	10 B3
Keyston	Pheasant Inn	★	◄			◊	◄				01832 710241	7 E4
Madingley	Three Horseshoes	★	◄			◊					01954 210221	15 F1
Milton	Jolly Brewers				◄						01223 860585	10 B3
Molesworth	Cross Keys		◄	◄							01832 710283	7 E4
Needingworth	Pike & Eel		◄	◄							01480 463336	10 B2
Newton	Queen's Head		◄								01223 870436	15 F1
St Neots	Chequers Inn		◄						◄		01480 472116	15 E1
St Neots	Eaton Oak		◄	◄					◄		01480 219555	15 E1
Stilton	Bell Inn		◄	◄							01733 241066	7 E4
Sutton Gault	Anchor Inn		◄							◄	01353 778537	10 B2
Swavesey	Trinity Foot		◄			◊		◄			01954 230315	15 F1
Wansford-in-England	The Haycock	★	◄	◄		◊					01780 782223	7 E4

Lincolnshire

(including North Lincolnshire and North East Lincolnshire - part of former South Humberside)

Location	Establishment	Star	Food	B&B	Atmosphere	Seafood	Beer	Sleep	Family	Waterside	Telephone	Map Ref.
Aswarby	Tally Ho		◄	◄							01529 455205	7 E3
Barnoldby-Le-Beck	Ship Inn				◄						01472 822308	7 E2
Collyweston	Cavalier Inn		◄	◄							01780 444288	7 E4
Donington-on-Bain	Black Horse		◄	◄				◄			01507 343640	7 E2
Duddington	Royal Oak Hotel		◄	◄				◄	◄		01780 444267	7 E4
Gedney Dyke	The Chequers		◄			◊	◄				01406 362666	7 F3

Town	Establishment	Phone	Grid
Lincoln	Wig & Mitre	01522 535190	7 E2
Louth	Masons Arms	01507 609525	7 F2
Newton	Red Lion	01529 497256	7 E3
Springthorpe	New Inn	01427 838254	7 E2
Stamford	The George of Stamford	01780 755171	7 E3

Norfolk

Town	Establishment	Phone	Grid
Blickling	Buckinghamshire Arms Hotel	01263 732133	10 C1
Brisley	Bell	01362 668686	10 C1
Burnham Market	Hoste Arms ★	01328 738777	10 C1
Burnham Thorpe	Lord Nelson	01328 738241	10 C1
Cley-next-the-Sea	George & Dragon Hotel	01263 740652	10 C1
East Dereham	Kings Head Hotel	01362 693842	10 C1
Eastgate	Ratcatchers Inn	01603 871430	10 C1
Great Ryburgh	Boar Inn	01328 829212	10 C1
King's Lynn	Tudor Rose	01553 762824	10 B1
Norwich	Adam & Eve	01603 667423	10 C1
Scole	Scole Inn	01379 740481	10 C2
Smallburgh	Crown	01692 536314	10 D1
Snettisham	Rose & Crown	01485 541382	10 B1
Stiffkey	Red Lion	01328 830552	10 C1
Stow Bardolph	Hare Arms	01366 382229	10 B2
Swanton Morley	Darby's	01362 637647	10 C1
Thompson	Chequers Inn	01953 483360	10 C2
Tivetshall St Mary	Old Ram	01379 676794	10 C2

Location	Establishment	Star	Food	B&B	Atmosphere	Seafood	Beer	Sleep	Family	Waterside	Telephone	Map Ref.
Upper Sheringham	Red Lion		◄			◊					01263 825408	10 C1
Warham All Saints	Three Horseshoes		◄	◄		◊	◄				01328 710547	10 C1
Wells-next-the-Sea	Crown Hotel		◄	◄							01328 710209	10 C1
Winterton-on-Sea	Fisherman's Return		◄	◄		◊			◄		01493 393305	10 D1
Wolterton	Saracens Head		◄	◄		◊		◄			01263 768909	10 C1
Woodbastwick	Fur & Feather				◄						01603 720003	10 D1
Suffolk												
Aldeburgh	Ye Olde Cross Keys		◄	◄	◄				◄		0172845 2637	10 D3
Bardwell	Six Bells Country Inn		◄	◄		◊					01359 250820	10 C2
Blyford	Queen's Head		◄	◄		◊					01502 70404	10 D2
Bury St Edmunds	The Nutshell		◄		◄						01284 764867	10 C2
Dunwich	Ship Inn		◄	◄		◊			◄		01728 648219	10 D2
Glemsford	Black Lion		◄								01787 280684	10 C3
Horringer	Beehive		◄			◊			◄		01284 735260	10 C3
Hoxne	Swan		◄								01379 668275	10 C2
Icklingham	Red Lion		◄	◄		◊					01638 717802	10 C2
Ixworth	Pykkerell Inn		◄			◊					01359 230398	10 C2
Lamarsh	Red Lion		◄						◄		01787 227918	10 C3
Lavenham	Angel Inn		◄	◄				◄	◄		01787 247388	10 C3
Long Melford	Bull Hotel		◄	◄							01787 378494	10 C3
Nayland	White Hart	★	◄			◊					01206 263382	10 C3

Location	Establishment		Telephone	Map ref
Pin Mill	Butt & Oyster		01473 780764	10 C3
Ramsholt	Ramsholt Arms		01394 411229	10 D3
Reydon	The Cricketers		01502 723603	10 D2
Snape	Golden Key		01728 688510	10 D3
Southwold	The Crown	★	01502 722275	10 D2
Stoke-by-Nayland	Angel Inn	★	01206 263245	10 C3
Wingfield	De La Pole Arms		01379 384545	10 C2

North East of England

(Former) Cleveland

(including Redcar & Cleveland, Middlesbrough, Stockton-on-Tees, Hartlepool)

Location	Establishment		Telephone	Map ref
Ellerby	Ellerby Hotel		01947 840342	5 E3

Durham

Location	Establishment		Telephone	Map ref
Blanchland	Lord Crewe Arms Hotel		01434 675251	5 D2
Fir Tree	Duke of York		01388 762848	5 D3
Greta Bridge	Morritt Arms Hotel		01833 627232	5 D3
Middleton-in-Teesdale	Teesdale Hotel		01833 640264	5 D3
Romaldkirk	Rose & Crown	★	01833 650213	5 D3
Running Waters	Three Horseshoes Inn		01913 720286	5 E3
Sedgefield	Dun Cow Inn		01740 620894	5 E3

East Riding of Yorkshire and Kingston-upon Hull

(former north part of Humberside)

Location	Establishment		Telephone	Map ref
Low Catton	Gold Cup Inn		01759 371354	7 D1
North Dalton	Star Inn		01377 217688	7 E1
Skidby	Half Moon Inn		01482 843403	7 E1

Northumberland

Location	Establishment	Star	Food	B&B	Atmosphere	Seafood	Beer	Sleep	Family	Waterside	Telephone	Map Ref.
Bamburgh	Lord Crewe Arms			▲							01668 214243	5 D1
Belford	Blue Bell Hotel			▲				▲	▲		01668 213543	5 D1
Carterway Heads	Manor House Inn		▲	▲		◇	▲				01207 255268	5 D3
Chatton	Percy Arms Hotel			▲							01668 215244	5 D1
Corbridge	Angel Inn		▲	▲				▲	▲		01434 632119	5 D2
Craster	Jolly Fisherman			▲	▲				▲	▲	01665 576461	5 E1
Dunstan	Cottage Inn			▲							01665 576658	5 D1
Halwhistle	Milecastle Inn		▲			◇	▲				01434 320682	5 D2
Haydon Bridge	General Havelock Inn		▲			◇					01434 684376	5 D2
Hexham	Dipton Mill Inn		▲				▲				01484 606577	5 D2
Longframlington	Granby Inn		▲	▲		◇					01665 570228	5 D2
Low Newton by the Sea	The Ship -				▲	◇				▲	01665 576262	5 D1
Newton-on-the-Moor	Cook & Barker Inn		▲	▲					▲		01665 575234	5 D2
Rennington	Masons Arms			▲				▲			01665 577275	5 D1
Seahouses	Olde Ship		▲	▲			▲	▲		▲	01665 720200	5 D1
Stannersburn	Pheasant Inn		▲	▲				▲			01434 240382	5 D2
Wall	Hadrian Hotel			▲							01434 681232	5 D2
Warenford	Warenford Lodge	★	▲			◇					01668 213453	5 D1

(Former) Tyne & Wear

(including Gateshead, Newcastle-upon-Tyne, North Tyneside, South Tyneside, Sunderland)

Location	Establishment	Telephone	Map Ref
New York	Shiremoor House Farm	0191-257 6302	5 E2
Newcastle-upon-Tyne	Cooperage	0191-232 8286	5 E2

North Yorkshire

Location	Establishment	Telephone	Map Ref
Asenby	Crab & Lobster	01845 577286	5 E4
Askrigg	King's Arms Hotel	01969 650258	5 D4
Bainbridge	Rose & Crown Hotel	01969 650225	5 D4
Buckden	Buck Inn	01756 760228	5 D4
Carlton-in-Coverdale	Foresters Arms	01969 640272	5 D4
Carthorpe	Fox & Hounds	01845 567433	5 E4
Coxwold	Fauconberg Arms	01347 868214	5 E4
Cray	White Lion	01756 760262	5 D4
Danby	Duke of Wellington	01287 660351	5 E3
Driffield	Bell Hotel	01377 256661	7 E1
East Witton	Blue Lion	01969 624273	5 D4
Elslack	Tempest Arms	01282 842450	6 B1
Goathland	Mallyan Spout	01947 896486	5 F3
Helmsley	Feathers Hotel	01439 770275	5 E4
Hetton	Angel Inn	01756 730263	6 C1
Horton-in-Ribblesdale	Crown Hotel	01729 860209	5 D4
Hovingham	Worsley Arms Hotel	01653 628234	5 E4
Kirkbymoorside	George & Dragon Hotel	01751 433334	5 E4
Linton	Fountaine Inn	01756 752210	6 C1

Location	Establishment	Star	Food	B&B	Atmosphere	Seafood	Beer	Sleep	Family	Waterside	Telephone	Map Ref.
Middleham	Black Swan		◄	◄							01969 622221	5 D4
Moulton	Black Bull Inn		◄			✦					01325 377289	5 E3
Nosterfield	Freemasons Arms		◄			✦					01677 470548	5 E4
Nunnington	Royal Oak		◄			✦					01439 748271	5 E4
Osmotherley	Three Tuns		◄	◄		✦					01609 883301	5 E3
Pickering	The White Swan		◄	◄		✦		◄			01751 472288	5 E4
Pickhill	Nag's Head		◄	◄		✦	◄	◄			01845 567391	5 E4
Reeth	Buck Hotel			◄					◄		01748 884210	5 D3
Ripley	Boar's Head Hotel		◄	◄		✦		◄			01423 771888	6 C1
Rosedale Abbey	Milburn Arms		◄	◄		✦		◄			01751 417312	5 E3
Rosedale Abbey	White Horse Farm Hotel		◄	◄				◄			01751 417239	5 E3
Sawley	Sawley Arms		◄			✦					01765 620642	6 C1
Saxton	Plough Inn	★	◄			✦					01937 557242	7 D1
Starbotton	Fox & Hounds		◄	◄		✦					01756 760269	5 D4
Threshfield	Old Hall Inn		◄				◄	◄	◄		01756 752441	6 C1
Topcliffe	Angel Inn		◄	◄				◄	◄		01845 577237	5 E4
Wass	Wombwell Arms	★	◄	◄				◄			01347 868280	5 E4
Wath-in-Nidderdale	Sportsman's Arms		◄	◄		✦		◄			01423 711306	6 C1
West Witton	Wensleydale Heifer		◄	◄		✦					01969 622322	5 D4
Wigglesworth	Plough Inn		◄	◄					◄		01729 840243	6 B1
Wykeham	Downe Arms Hotel			◄							01723 862471	5 F4

(Former) South Yorkshire
(Barnsley, Sheffield, Rotherham and Doncaster)

Location	Name									Phone	Grid
Cadeby	Cadeby Inn	◀			◀			◀		01709 864009	7 D2
Penistone	Cubley Hall	◀		◈	◀			◀		01226 766086	6 C2

(Former) West Yorkshire
(including Bradford, Calderdale, Kirklees, Leeds and Wakefield)

Location	Name									Phone	Grid
Grange Moor	Kaye Arms	◀		◈	◀			◀		01942 848385	6 C1
Harewood	Harewood Arms		◀			◀				0113 288 6566	6 C1
Haworth	Old White Lion Hotel		◀							01535 642313	6 C1
Heath	King's Arms				◀					01924 377527	6 C1
Holywell Green	Rock Inn Hotel		◀		◀	◀		◀		01422 379721	6 C1
Ledsham	Chequers Inn		◀		◀					01977 683135	7 D1
Leeds	Whitelocks		◀		◀					0113 245 3950	6 C1
Meltham	Will's O'Nat's	◀		◈	◀			◀		01484 850078	6 C2
Ripponden	Old Bridge Inn				◀	◀			◀	01422 822595	6 C1
Shelf	Duke of York		◀			◀				01422 202056	6 C1
Shelley	Three Acres ★	◀	◀	◈		◀				01484 602606	6 C1
Sowerby Bridge	The Hobbit		◀					◀		01422 832202	6 C1
Thornton	Ring O'Bells	◀		◈				◀		01274 832296	6 C1

North West of England
Cheshire
(including Wirral, Trafford and Stockport)

Location	Establishment	Star	Food	B&B	Atmosphere	Seafood	Beer	Sleep	Family	Waterside	Telephone	Map Ref.
Barnston	Fox & Hounds		◀								0151-648 1323	6 A2
Bickley Moss	Cholmondeley Arms		◀	◀		◇			◀		01829 720300	6 B3
Bollington	Church House Inn		◀	◀							01625 574014	6 B2
Brereton Green	Bears Head		◀	◀							01477 535251	6 B2
Broadheath	Old Packet House		◀	◀							0161-929 1331	6 B2
Chester	Ye Olde King's Head			◀							01244 324855	6 A2
Fullers Moor	Copper Mine		◀	◀		◇			◀		01829 782293	6 A3
Higher Burwardsley	The Pheasant		◀	◀		◇		◀	◀		01829 770434	6 A3
Lower Peover	Bells of Peover				◀						01565 722269	6 B2
Macclesfield	Sutton Hall		◀	◀				◀			01260 253211	6 B2
Mellor	Devonshire Arms		◀								0161-427 2563	6 C2
Over Peover	The Dog		◀	◀		◇					01625 861421	6 B2
Stockport	Red Bull		◀								0161-480 2087	6 B2
Strinesdale	Roebuck Inn		◀			◇			◀		0161-624 7819	6 B2
Tarporley	Rising Sun		◀								01829 732423	6 B2
Tarporley	Swan Hotel			◀							01829 733838	6 B2
Tushingham	Blue Bell Inn				◀		◀		◀		01948 662172	6 B3

Cumbria

Location	Name	Telephone	Map Ref
Appleby-in-Westmorland	Royal Oak Inn	01768 351463	5 D3
Armathwaite	Duke's Head Hotel	01697 472226	4 C3
Askham	Punch Bowl Inn	01931 712443	4 C3
Bassenthwaite Lake	Pheasant Inn	01768 776234	4 C3
Beetham	Wheatsheaf	01539 562123	4 C4
Boot	Burnmoor Inn	01946 723224	4 C3
Bowland Bridge	Hare & Hounds	01539 568333	4 C4
Buttermere	Bridge Hotel	01768 770252	4 C3
Cartmel Fell	Masons Arms	01539 568486	4 C4
Casterton	Pheasant Inn	01524 271230	4 C4
Crosthwaite	Punch Bowl	01539 568237	4 C4
Dent	Sun Inn	01539 625208	5 D4
Elterwater	Britannia Inn	015394 37210	4 C3
Eskdale Green	Bower House Inn	01946 723244	4 C3
Gretna	Gretna Chase Hotel	01461 337517	4 C2
Hawkshead	Drunken Duck Inn	015394 36347	4 C3
Hawkshead	Queen's Head Hotel	015394 36271	4 C3
Hesket Newmarket	Old Crown	01697 478288	4 C3
Kirkby Lonsdale	Snooty Fox Tavern	01524 271308	4 C4
Langdale	Three Shires Inn	015394 37215	4 C3
Loweswater	Kirkstile Inn	01900 85219	4 C3
Melmerby	Shepherds Inn	01768 881217	4 C3
Metal Bridge	Metal Bridge Inn	01228 74206	4 C2

Location	Establishment	Star	Food	B&B	Atmosphere	Seafood	Beer	Sleep	Family	Waterside	Telephone	Map Ref.
Ravenstonedale	Black Swan Inn			▲				▲			01539 623204	5 D3
Ravenstonedale	Fat Lamb			▲					▲		01539 623242	5 D3
Scales	White Horse		▲				▲				01768 779241	4 C3
Talkin Village	Blacksmiths Arms		▲	▲							01697 73452	4 C2
Troutbeck	Mortal Man Inn		▲	▲				▲			015394 33193	4 C3
Ulverston	Bay Horse Inn	★	▲	▲				▲			01229 583972	4 C4
Wasdale Head	Wasdale Head Inn			▲			▲	▲		▲	01946 726229	4 C3

Greater Manchester

(including Wigan, Bolton, Bury, Rochdale, Salford, Manchester, Tameside, Oldham)

Location	Establishment	Star	Food	B&B	Atmosphere	Seafood	Beer	Sleep	Family	Waterside	Telephone	Map Ref.
Diggle	Diggle Hotel			▲							01457 872741	6 C2
Manchester	Lass O'Gowrie				▲		▲				0161-273 6932	6 B2
Manchester	Mark Addy		▲							▲	0161-832 4080	6 B2
Manchester	New Ellesmere			▲					▲		0161-728 2791	6 B2
Middleton	Ye Olde Boar's Head				▲						0161-643 3520	6 B2
Saddleworth	Green Ash Hotel			▲				▲			01457 871035	6 C2

Lancashire

Location	Establishment	Star	Food	B&B	Atmosphere	Seafood	Beer	Sleep	Family	Waterside	Telephone	Map Ref.
Blacko	Moorcock Inn		▲			◊			▲		01282 614186	6 B1
Downham	Assheton Arms		▲			◊					01200 441227	6 B1
Goosnargh	Bushells Arms		▲			◊					01772 865235	6 B1
Lydgate	White Hart	★	▲			◊	▲		▲		01457 872566	6 C2

											Phone	Map
Mellor	Millstone Hotel		◄	◄			◁	◄		◄	01254 813333	6 B1
Rochdale	Egerton Arms		◄	◄	◄		◄	◄		◄	01706 46183	6 B1
Whitewell	Inn at Whitewell	★	◄	◄	◄		◁		◄		01200 448222	6 B1
Yealand Conyers	New Inn		◄								01524 732938	4 C4

Merseyside
(including Liverpool, Knowsley, Sefton and St Helens)

											Phone	Map
Liverpool	Philharmonic Dining Rooms			◄							0151-709 1163	6 A2

ACCEPTED IN MORE HOTELS AND RESTAURANTS THAN MOST PEOPLE EVER HAVE HOT DINNERS.

VISA IS ACCEPTED FOR MORE TRANSACTIONS
WORLDWIDE THAN ANY OTHER CARD.

MAKING LIFE EASIER

Scotland
Regional Round-Ups

Scotland is divided into the following regions:

South Scotland
Scottish Borders, Dumfries & Galloway, South Ayrshire, North Ayrshire (inc Isle of Arran), East Ayrshire, Inverclyde, East Renfrewshire, Renfrewshire, City of Glasgow, South Lanarkshire, North Lanarkshire, West Lothian, Midlothian, East Lothian, City of Edinburgh

Central Scotland
Falkirk, East Dunbartonshire, West Dunbartonshire, Fife, Clackmannanshire, Stirling, Dundee City, Angus, Perth & Kinross, Argyll & Bute

North Scotland
Aberdeenshire, Aberdeen City, Moray, Highland, Western Isles, Shetland & Orkney

See the How to Use section (page 10) for a full explanation of categories, gradings and symbols.

South Scotland
Dumfries & Galloway

Location	Establishment	Star	Food	B&B	Atmosphere	Seafood	Beer	Sleep	Family	Waterside	Telephone	Map Ref.
Canonbie	Riverside Inn		▲	▲						▲	01387 371512	4 C2
Kirkcudbright	Selkirk Arms Hotel		▲	▲		◇					01557 330402	4 B3
Moffat	Black Bull			▲					▲		01683 220206	4 C2
New Abbey	Criffel Inn			▲					▲		01387 850305	4 B2
Newton Stewart	Creebridge House Hotel		▲	▲		◇		▲	▲		01671 402121	4 A2
Portpatrick	Crown Hotel		▲	▲		◇			▲	▲	01776 810261	4 A2

Edinburgh & Lothian
(including all former Lothian)

Location	Establishment	Star	Food	B&B	Atmosphere	Seafood	Beer	Sleep	Family	Waterside	Telephone	Map Ref.
Edinburgh	Doric Tavern Wine Bar & Bistro		▲			◇					0131-225 1084	3 C6
Edinburgh	Fishers		▲			◇				▲	0131-554 5666	3 C6
Edinburgh	Tattler		▲			◇	▲				0131-554 9999	3 C6
Edinburgh	Waterfront Wine Bar		▲			◇				▲	0131-554 7427	3 C6
Gifford	Tweeddale Arms		▲	▲					▲		01620 810240	3 D6
Ratho	Bridge Inn		▲						▲	▲	0131-333 1320	3 C6

Glasgow
(including the middle part of former Strathclyde: City of Glasgow, Inverclyde, North & South Lanarks)

Location	Establishment	Star	Food	B&B	Atmosphere	Seafood	Beer	Sleep	Family	Waterside	Telephone	Map Ref.
Castlecary	Castlecary House Hotel			▲							01324 840233	3 C5
Glasgow	Babbity Bowster		▲			◇					0141-552 5055	3 B6
Glasgow	Ubiquitous Chip					◇						

Scottish Borders

		Phone	Map ref
Greenlaw	Castle Inn	01361 810217	3 D6
Innerleithen	Traquair Arms	01896 830229	4 C1
Melrose	Burts Hotel	01896 822285	4 C1
St Boswells	Buccleuch Arms Hotel	01835 822243	4 C1
St Mary's Loch	Tibbie Shiels Inn	01750 42231	4 C1
Swinton	Wheatsheaf Hotel	01890 860257	3 D6
Tweedsmuir	Crook Inn	01899 880272	4 C1

Central Scotland
Argyll & Bute

(including most of former Strathclyde north of the Clyde)

		Phone	Map ref
Ardentinny	Ardentinny Hotel	01369 810209	3 B5
Ardfern	Galley of Lorne Inn	01852 500284	3 B5
Arduaine	Loch Melfort Hotel	01852 200233	3 B5
Clachan Seil	Tigh-an-Truish Inn	01852 300242	3 B5
Clachan Seil	Willowburn Hotel	01852 300276	3 B5
Kilberry	Kilberry Inn ★	01880 770223	3 A6
Loch Eck	Coylet Inn	01369 840426	3 B5
Port Appin	The Pierhouse & Seafood Restaurant	01631 730302	3 B5
Tayvallich	Tayvallich Inn	01546 870282	3 A5

Location	Establishment	Star	Food	B&B	Atmosphere	Seafood	Beer	Sleep	Family	Waterside	Telephone	Map Ref.
Fife												
(including Clackmannanshire and Falkirk)												
Anstruther	Dreel Tavern				◄						01333 310727	3 D5
Crail	Golf Hotel			◄							01333 450206	3 D5
Dysart	Old Rectory Inn		◄			♢				◄	01592 651211	3 C5
Elie	Ship Inn		◄						◄	◄	01333 330246	3 C5
Kirkcaldy	Hoffmans	★	◄						◄		01592 204584	3 C5
Markinch	Town House Hotel		◄	◄		♢			◄		01592 758459	3 C5
Sheriffmuir	Sheriffmuir Inn		◄								01786 823285	3 C5
Stirling												
(including East & West Dunbartonshire)												
Kippen	Cross Keys		◄	◄					◄		01786 870293	3 C5
Strathblane	Kirkhouse Inn			◄				◄			01360 770621	3 B5
(Former) Tayside												
(including Angus, Dundee City and Perth & Kinross)												
Almondbank	Almondbank Inn		◄			♢				◄	01738 583242	3 C5
Burrelton	Burrelton Park Hotel		◄	◄		♢					01828 670206	3 C5
Dundee	Mercantile Bar				◄						01382 225500	3 C5
Glendevon	Tormaukin Hotel		◄	◄		♢					01259 781252	3 C5
Glenfarg	Bein Inn		◄	◄		♢					01577 830216	3 C5
Kenmore	Kenmore Hotel			◄				◄		◄	01887 830205	3 C5
Kilmahog	Lade Inn		◄			♢				◄	01877 330152	3 B5

North Scotland

Aberdeen & Moray
(including former Grampian)

Location	Establishment	Star	Food	B&B	Atmosphere	Seafood	Beer	Sleep	Family	Waterside	Telephone	Map Ref.
Kirkton of Glenisla	Glenisla Hotel		◄			◊			◄		01575 582223	3 C4
Weem	Ailean Chraggan Hotel		◄	◄		◊					01887 820346	3 C4
Aberdeen	Prince of Wales		◄				◄				01224 640597	3 D4
Fochabers	Gordon Arms			◄							01343 820508	2 C3
Kincardine O'Neil	Gordon Arms Hotel		◄	◄							01339 884236	3 D4
Monymusk	Grant Arms Hotel		◄	◄		◊			◄		01467 651226	3 D4
Netherley	Lairhillock Inn		◄						◄		01569 730001	3 D4
Stonehaven	Marine Hotel		◄	◄		◊				◄	01569 762155	3 D4
Turriff	Towie Tavern		◄			◊			◄		01888 511201	2 D3

Highland

Location	Establishment	Star	Food	B&B	Atmosphere	Seafood	Beer	Sleep	Family	Waterside	Telephone	Map Ref.
Applecross	Applecross Inn		◄	◄		◊				◄	01520 744262	2 A3
Ardvasar	Ardvasar Hotel		◄	◄							01471 844223	3 A4
Beauly	Lovat Arms Hotel		◄	◄							01463 782313	2 B3
Carbost	Old Inn		◄	◄						◄	01478 640205	2 A3
Cromarty	Royal Hotel		◄	◄						◄	01381 600217	2 C3
Garve	Inchbae Lodge Hotel		◄	◄				◄	◄	◄	01997 455269	2 B3
Glenelg	Glenelg Inn		◄	◄		◊		◄			01599 522273	3 B4
Kylesku	Kylesku Hotel		◄	◄		◊		◄		◄	01971 502231	2 B2

Location	Name	Phone	Map Ref
Talladale	Loch Maree Hotel	01445 760288	2 B3
Ullapool	Argyll Hotel	01854 612422	2 B2
Ullapool	Ceilidh Place	01854 612103	2 B2
Ullapool	Ferry Boat Inn	01854 612366	2 B2

Islands

(including Orkney, Shetland and Western Isles)

Location	Name	Phone	Map Ref
Busta	Busta House Hotel	01806 522506	2 D1

Wales

Regional Round-Ups

Wales is divided into the following regions:

South Wales
all locations in Carmarthenshire and Pembrokeshire (both part of former Dyfed) plus Bridgend, Rhondda Cynon Taff, Merthyr Tydfil (all in former Mid Glamorgan), Vale of Glamorgan and Cardiff (both in former South Glamorgan), both Swansea and Neath & Port Talbot (in former West Glamorgan) and Monmouthshire, Torfaen, Newport, Caerphilly and Blaenau Gwent (in former Gwent)

Mid Wales
all locations in Powys plus Ceredigion (in former Powys)

North Wales
Conwy, Denbighshire, Flintshire and Wrexham (all in former Clwyd) plus Isle of Anglesey and the new Gwynedd

See the How to Use section (page 10) for a full explanation of categories, gradings and symbols.

South Wales

Carmarthenshire & Pembrokeshire

(including the southern part of former Dyfed)

Location	Establishment	Star	Food	B&B	Atmosphere	Seafood	Beer	Sleep	Family	Waterside	Telephone	Map Ref.
Abergorlech	Black Lion		◄								01558 685271	9 B5
Felindre Farchog	Salutation Inn			◄					◄	◄	01239 820564	9 B5
Landshipping	Stanley Arms		◄			◊				◄	01834 891227	9 A5
Llandovery	King's Head Inn			◄							01550 720393	9 C5
Nevern	Trewern Arms Hotel			◄				◄	◄	◄	01239 820395	9 A5
New Inn	Tate's at Tafarn Newydd										01437 532542	9 B5
Pembroke Ferry	Ferry Inn		◄			◊				◄	01646 682947	9 A5

(Former) Glamorgan

(including former West, Mid and South Glamorgan; Bridgend, Cardiff, Merthyr Tydfil, Neath & Port Talbot)

Location	Establishment	Star	Food	B&B	Atmosphere	Seafood	Beer	Sleep	Family	Waterside	Telephone	Map Ref.
Creigiau	Caesar's Arms		◄			◊					01222 890486	9 C6
East Aberthaw	Blue Anchor Inn		◄			◊	◄				01446 750329	9 C6
Llangynwyd	Olde House Inn				◄				◄		01656 733310	9 C6
Nottage	Rose & Crown			◄							01656 784850	9 C6
Penmark	Six Bells Inn		◄			◊					01446 710229	9 C6

(Former) Gwent

(including Blaenau Gwent, Caerphilly, Monmouthshire, Newport and Torfaen)

Location	Establishment	Star	Food	B&B	Atmosphere	Seafood	Beer	Sleep	Family	Waterside	Telephone	Map Ref.
Abergavenny	Llanwenarth Arms Hotel		◄	◄		◊			◄	◄	01873 810550	9 D5
Bettws Newydd	Black Bear		◄			◊					01873 880701	9 D5

Location	Establishment	Phone	Map Ref
Chepstow	Castle View Hotel	01291 620349	9 D6
Clytha	Clytha Arms	01873 840206	9 D5
Llanfihangel Crucorney	Skirrid Inn	01873 890258	9 D5
Llantrisant	Greyhound Inn	01291 672505	9 D6
Lydart	Gockett Inn	01600 860486	9 D5
Penallt	Boat Inn	01600 712615	14 A2
Raglan	Beaufort Arms Hotel	01291 690412	9 D5
Shirenewton	Carpenters Arms	01291 641231	9 D6
Shirenewton	Tredegar Arms	01291 641274	9 D6
Trellech	Village Green	01600 860119	9 D5
Usk	Three Salmons	01291 672133	9 D5
Whitebrook	Crown at Whitebrook	01600 860254	14 A2

Mid Wales

Cardiganshire/Ceredigion

(including the former northern part of Dyfed)

Location	Establishment	Phone	Map Ref
Cardigan	Black Lion	01239 612532	9 B4
Llanddarog	Butcher's Arms	01267 275330	9 B5
Llangrannog	Ship Inn	01239 654423	9 B4
Llwyndafydd	Crown Inn	01545 560396	9 B4
Pisgah	Halfway Inn	01970 880631	9 C4

Powys

Location	Establishment	Phone	Map Ref
Berriew	Lion Hotel	01686 640452	8 D3
Crickhowell	Bear Hotel	01873 810408	9 D5
Crickhowell	Nantyffin Cider Mill	01873 810775	9 D5

Location	Establishment	Star	Food	B&B	Atmosphere	Seafood	Beer	Sleep	Family	Waterside	Telephone	Map Ref.
Dinas Mawddwy	Dolbrodmaeth Inn		▲	▲				▲	▲		01650 531333	8 C3
Hay-on-Wye	Kilverts		▲	▲		♢		▲	▲		01497 821042	9 D5
Llanfihangel-Nant-Melan	Red Lion Inn		▲	▲		♢		▲	▲		01544 350220	9 D4
Llanfrynach	White Swan		▲								01873 665276	9 C5
Llangattock	Vine Tree		▲			♢					01873 810514	9 D5
Llangorse	Red Lion			▲					▲		01874 658238	9 D5
Llanyre	Bell Country Inn		▲	▲							01597 823959	9 C4
Llowes	Radnor Arms		▲	▲		♢			▲		01497 847460	9 D5
Llyswen	Griffin Inn	★	▲	▲		♢		▲			01874 754241	9 D5
Old Radnor	Harp Inn		▲	▲				▲			01544 350655	9 D4
Pant Mawr	Glansevern Arms Hotel			▲							01686 440240	9 C4
Penybont	Severn Arms Hotel			▲							01597 851224	9 C4
Trecastle	Castle Coaching Inn			▲					▲		01874 636354	9 C5

North Wales
(Former) Clwyd
(including Denbighshire, Flintshire and Wrexham)

Location	Establishment	Star	Food	B&B	Atmosphere	Seafood	Beer	Sleep	Family	Waterside	Telephone	Map Ref.
Afon-Wen	Pwll Gwyn Hotel		▲						▲		01352 720227	8 C2
Babell	Black Lion Inn		▲			♢					01352 720239	8 D1
Bodfari	Dinorben Arms		▲			♢			▲		01745 710309	8 C2
Burton Green	Golden Grove Inn				▲				▲		01244 570445	8 D2
Erbistock	Boat Inn		▲							▲	01978 780143	8 D2

Location	Establishment								Telephone	Map ref
Hanmer	Hanmer Arms Village Hotel	◄						◄	01948 830532	6 A3
Llanarmon D.C.	West Arms Hotel	◄	◄	◇		◄		◄	01691 600665	8 D2
Llangollen	Britannia Inn	◄	◄						01978 860144	8 D2
Llannefydd	Hawk & Buckle Inn	◄	◄			◄			01745 540249	8 C1
Marford	Trevor Arms	◄						◄	01244 570436	8 D2

(Former) Gwynedd
(including Conwy, Isle of Anglesey and the new Gwynedd)

Location	Establishment								Telephone	Map ref
Aberdovey	Penhelig Arms Hotel	◄	◄	◇		◄		◄	01654 767215	8 C3
Beaumaris	Liverpool Arms Hotel	◄	◄	◇		◄		◄	01248 810362	8 B1
Beaumaris	Ye Olde Bull's Head Inn	◄	◄	◇		◄			01248 810329	8 B1
Betws-yn-Rhos	Ffarm Hotel	◄		◇					01492 680287	8 C1
Bontddu	Halfway House	◄							01341 430635	8 C3
Glanwydden	Queen's Head	◄		◇					01492 546570	8 C1
Menai Bridge	Anglesey Arms	◄	◄			◄		◄	01248 712305	8 B2
Penmaenpool	George III Hotel	◄	◄			◄		◄	01341 422525	8 C3
Red Wharf Bay	Ship Inn	◄		◇	◄			◄	01248 852568	8 B1
St George	Kinmel Arms	◄							01745 832207	8 C1
Tremeirchion	Salusbury Arms	◄		◇	◄			◄	01745 710262	8 C1
Tyn-y-Groes	Groes Inn	◄		◇					01492 650545	8 C2

ACCEPTED IN MORE HOTELS AND RESTAURANTS THAN MOST PEOPLE EVER HAVE HOT DINNERS.

VISA IS ACCEPTED FOR MORE TRANSACTIONS WORLDWIDE THAN ANY OTHER CARD.

MAKING LIFE EASIER

Channel Islands & Isle of Man

Regional Round-Ups

See the How to Use section (page 10) for a full explanation of categories, gradings and symbols.

Location	Establishment	Star	Food	B&B	Atmosphere	Seafood	Beer	Sleep	Family	Waterside	Telephone	Map Ref.
Alderney												
St Anne	Georgian House	★	◄	◄		◊		◄			01481 822471	13 F4
Guernsey												
Castel	Hotel Hougue du Pommier		◄	◄		◊		◄			01481 56531	13 E4
Kings Mills	Fleur du Jardin Hotel		◄	◄				◄	◄		01481 57996	13 E4
Le Bourg	Deerhound Inn		◄	◄		◊				◄	01481 38585	13 E4
Pleinmont	Imperial Hotel			◄					◄	◄	01481 64044	13 E4
St Peter Port	Ship & Crown				◄				◄	◄	01481 721368	13 E4
St Peters	Longfrie Inn			◄					◄		01481 63107	13 E4
Herm												
Herm Island	Ship Inn		◄			◊				◄	01481 722159	13 E4
Jersey												
Gorey	Dolphin Hotel		◄	◄						◄	01534 853370	13 F4
St Aubin	Old Court House Inn		◄	◄		◊				◄	01534 46433	13 F4
St Brelade	Old Smugglers Inn		◄						◄		01534 41510	13 F4
St Helier	Tipsy Toad Town House				◄		◄				01534 615000	13 F4
St Lawrence	British Union Hotel		◄						◄		01534 861070	13 F4

									Phone	Map
St Ouen	The Lobster Pot	◄				◄			01534 482888	13 F4
St Peter's Village	Star & Tipsy Toad Brewery		◄		◄		◄	◄	01534 485556	13 F4

Sark

									Phone	Map
Sark	Dixcart Hotel & Bar	◄		◄			◄		01481 832015	13 E4

Isle of Man

									Phone	Map
Peel	Creek Inn	◄		◄				◄	01624 842216	4 A4

ACCEPTED IN MORE HOTELS AND RESTAURANTS THAN MOST PEOPLE EVER HAVE HOT DINNERS.

VISA IS ACCEPTED FOR MORE TRANSACTIONS WORLDWIDE THAN ANY OTHER CARD.

MAKING LIFE EASIER

Northern Ireland

Regional Round-Ups

See the How to Use section (page 10) for a full explanation of categories, gradings and symbols.

(Former) Co Antrim
(including Moyle, Larne, Ballymena, Ballymoney, Belfast City, Antrim, Newtownabbey and Carrickfergus)

Location	Establishment	Star	Food	B&B	Atmosphere	Seafood	Beer	Sleep	Family	Waterside	Telephone	Map Ref.
Ballycastle	House of McDonnell				▲						01265 762975	20 D1
Ballymoney	Old Bank House		▲								01265 663924	20 C1
Belfast	Crown Liquor Saloon				▲						01232 325368	20 D2
Belfast	Kelly's Cellars				▲						01232 324835	20 D2
Carnlough	Londonderry Arms Hotel		▲	▲							01574 885255	20 D1
Cushendall	PJ McCollam				▲						none	20 D1
Portballintrae	Sweeneys		▲								01265 732404	20 C1
Portglenone	Crosskeys Inn		▲		▲						01648 50694	20 D2

(Former) Co Down
(including Ards, Down, Banbridge, Lisburn, Castlereagh and North Down)

Location	Establishment	Star	Food	B&B	Atmosphere	Seafood	Beer	Sleep	Family	Waterside	Telephone	Map Ref.
Crawfordsburn	Old Inn			▲							01247 853255	20 D2
Dundrum	Buck's Head Inn		▲			◊					01396 751868	20 D2
Hillsborough	Hillside Bar	★	▲			◊	▲				01846 682765	20 D2
Hillsborough	Plough Inn		▲			◊					01846 682985	20 D2

(Former) Co Fermanagh

Location	Establishment	Star	Food	B&B	Atmosphere	Seafood	Beer	Sleep	Family	Waterside	Telephone	Map Ref.
Enniskillen	Blakes of the Hollow				▲						01365 322143	20 C2
Irvinestown	The Hollander		▲			◊					01365 621231	20 C2
Kesh	Lusty Beg Island		▲	▲							01365 632032	20 C2

							Phone	Grid
Irvinestown	The Hollander	◄					01365 621231	20 C2
Kesh	Lusty Beg Island	◄	◄	◇			01365 633032	20 C2
(Former) Co Londonderry *(including Coleraine, Derry City, Limavady and Magherafelt)*								
Aghadowey	Brown Trout Golf & Country Inn	◄	◄		◄		01265 868209	20 C1
Coleraine	Salmon Leap Bar	◄					01265 52992	20 C1

ACCEPTED IN MORE HOTELS AND RESTAURANTS THAN MOST PEOPLE EVER HAVE HOT DINNERS.

VISA IS ACCEPTED FOR MORE TRANSACTIONS
WORLDWIDE THAN ANY OTHER CARD.

MAKING LIFE EASIER

Maps

ACCEPTED IN MORE HOTELS AND RESTAURANTS THAN MOST PEOPLE EVER HAVE HOT DINNERS.

VISA IS ACCEPTED FOR MORE TRANSACTIONS
WORLDWIDE THAN ANY OTHER CARD.

MAKING LIFE EASIER

Maps

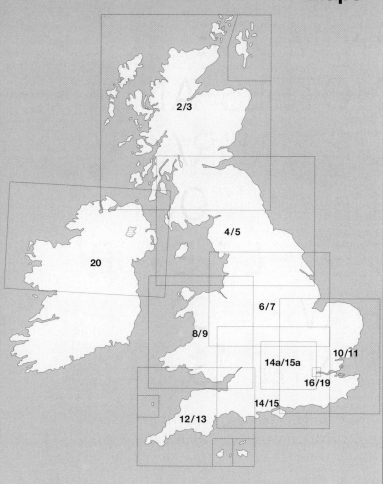

2/3

4/5

20

6/7

8/9

10/11

14a/15a

16/19

14/15

12/13

Motorways	●	Food
Primary Routes	☐	B & B
Other Roads	☑	Food and B & B
County Boundaries	△	Atmosphere

Designed and produced by
European Map Graphics Ltd. Finchampstead, Berks

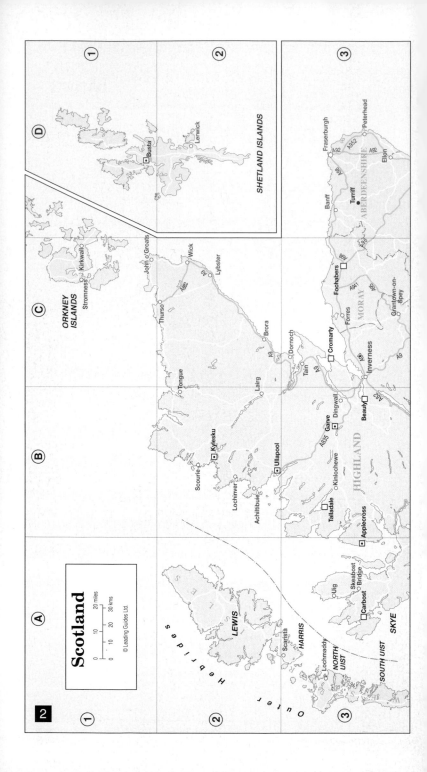

Scotland

© Leading Guides Ltd.

0   10   20   30 kms

0   10   20 miles

ORKNEY ISLANDS

SHETLAND ISLANDS

Outer Hebrides

LEWIS

HARRIS

NORTH UIST

SOUTH UIST

SKYE

HIGHLAND

MORAY

ABERDEENSHIRE

Busta
Lerwick

Stromness
Kirkwall
John o'Groats
Wick
Lybster
Thurso
Brora
Dornoch
Cromarty
Forres
Grantown-on-Spey
Tain
Inverness
Lairg
Dingwall
Beauly
Garve
Tongue
Scourie
Kylesku
Lochinver
Ullapool
Achiltibuie
Kinlochewe
Talladale
Applecross
Uig
Skeabost Bridge
Carbost
Lochmaddy
Scaristla
Fochabers
Banff
Turriff
Fraserburgh
Peterhead
Ellon

A92
A952
A98
A96
A941
A9
A835
A82

2

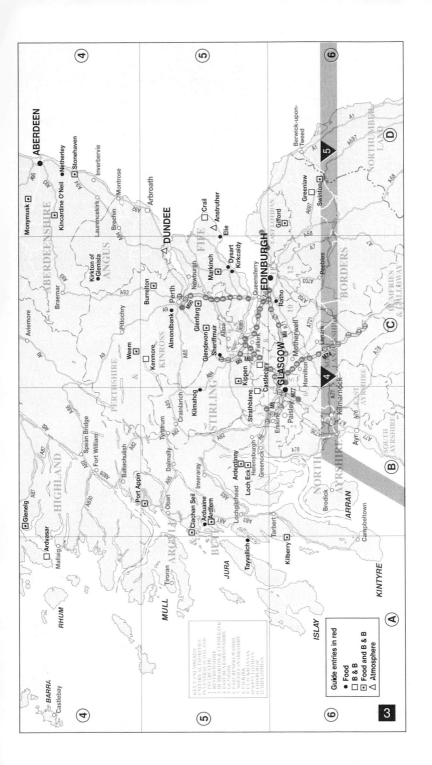

Guide entries in red

● Food
□ B & B
▣ Food and B & B
△ Atmosphere

KEY TO NUMBERED UNITARY AUTHORITIES:
CENTRAL SCOTLAND
1 INVERCLYDE
2 RENFREWSHIRE
3 DUMBARTON & CLYDEBANK
4 EAST RENFREWSHIRE
5 GLASGOW
6 EAST DUNBARTONSHIRE
7 FALKIRK
8 CLACKMANNAN
9 WEST LOTHIAN
10 CITY OF EDINBURGH
11 MIDLOTHIAN

3

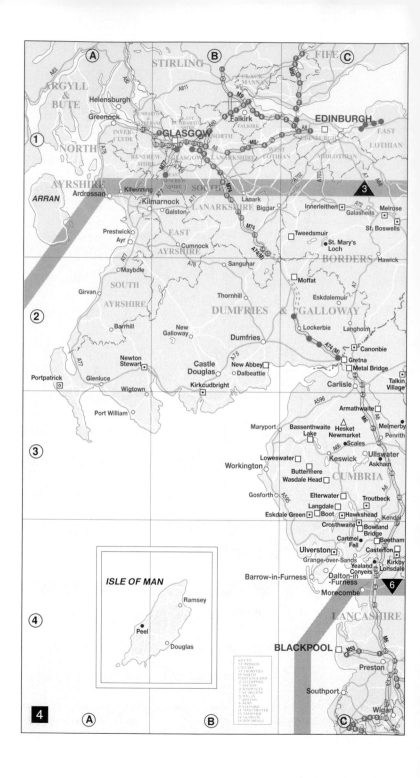

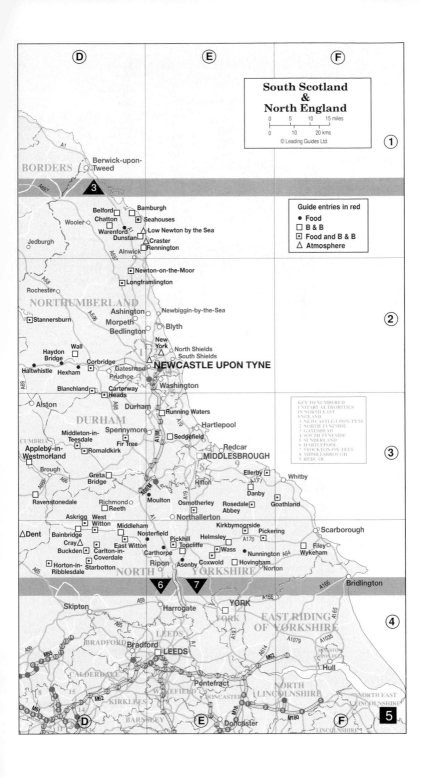

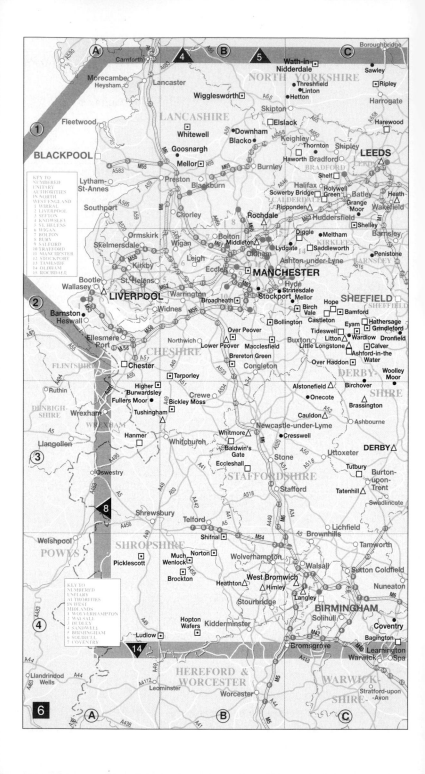

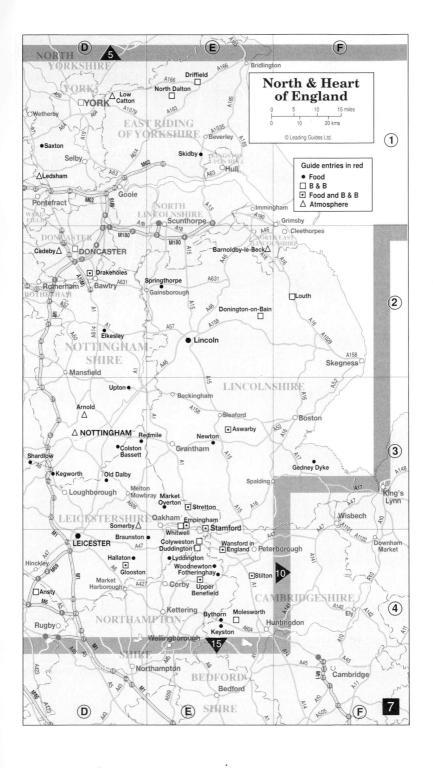

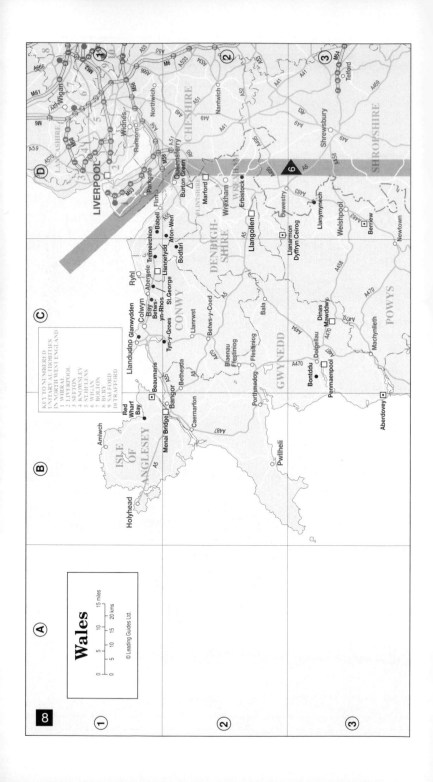

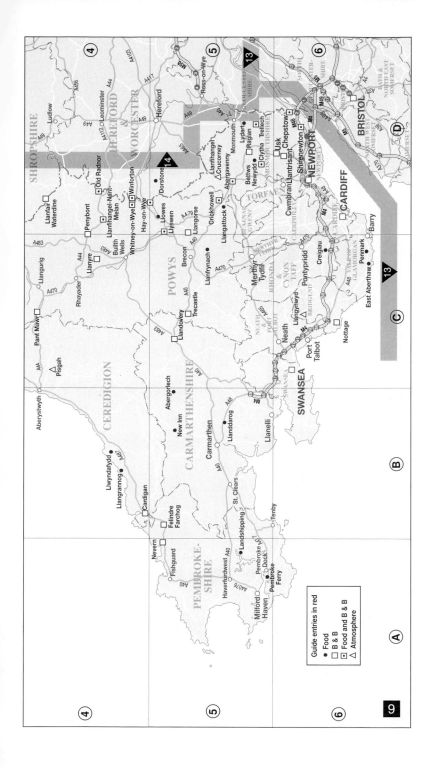

Guide entries in red
● Food
□ B & B
☑ Food and B & B
△ Atmosphere

9

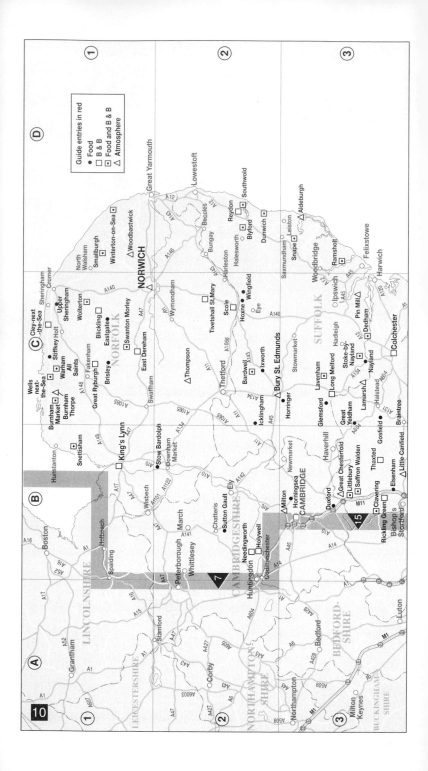

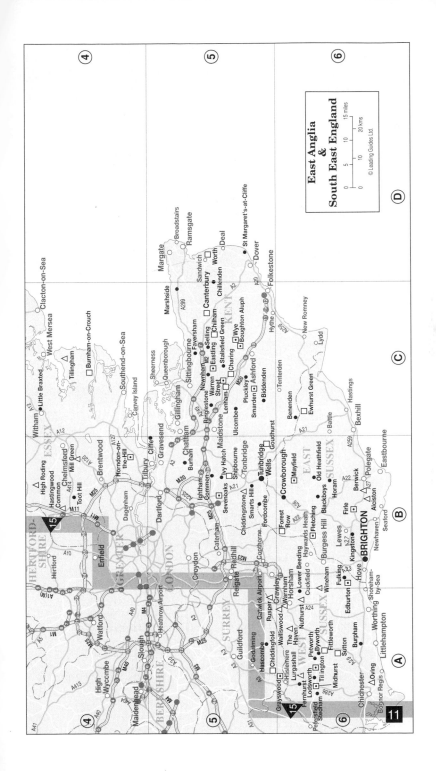

East Anglia
&
South East England

© Leading Guides Ltd.

0   5   10   15 miles

0   10   20 kms

11

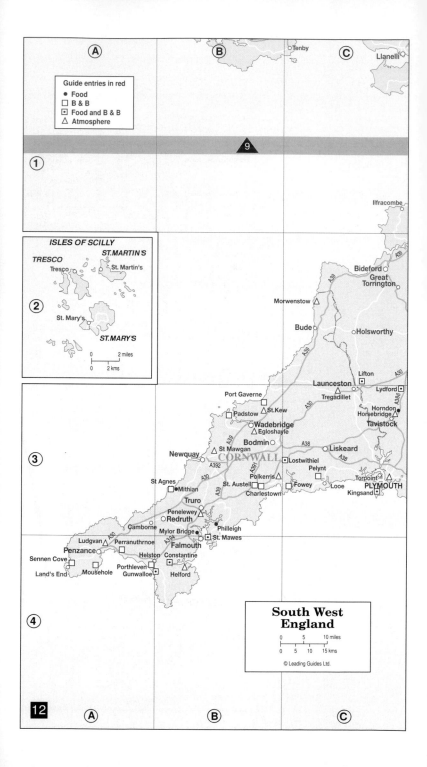

Guide entries in red
● Food
□ B & B
◉ Food and B & B
△ Atmosphere

ISLES OF SCILLY

TRESCO **ST.MARTIN'S**
Tresco △ St. Martin's

St. Mary's

ST.MARY'S

0 ____ 2 miles
0 ____ 2 kms

◉ Tenby Llanelli ○

⑨

①

Ilfracombe ○

② Bideford ○
Great
Torrington ○

Morwenstow △

Bude ○ ○ Holsworthy

Lifton ◉
Launceston ○ Lydford ◉
Tregadillet △
Horndon △
Horsebridge △
Tavistock

Port Gaverne ●
Padstow □ □ St.Kew
● **Wadebridge**
△ Egloshayle
Bodmin ○ Liskeard ●
Newquay ○ △ St Mawgan A38
A392 ◉ Lostwithiel
③ St Agnes Polkerris △ Pelynt
● Mithian St. Austell □□ ◉ Fowey Torpoint △
Truro ○ Charlestown Looe ○ **PLYMOUTH**
Penelewey △ Kingsand ◉
○ **Redruth**
Camborne ○ Philleigh
Mylor Bridge ●
Ludgvan △ ● St. Mawes
Penzance ○ Perranuthrnoe △ **Falmouth**
Sennen Cove □ Helston Constantine
□ Mousehole Porthleven ◉ △
Land's End Gunwalloe ◉ Helford ◉

④

**South West
England**

0 ____ 5 ____ 10 miles
0 ___ 5 ___ 10 ___ 15 kms

© Leading Guides Ltd.

12

Ⓐ   Ⓑ   Ⓒ

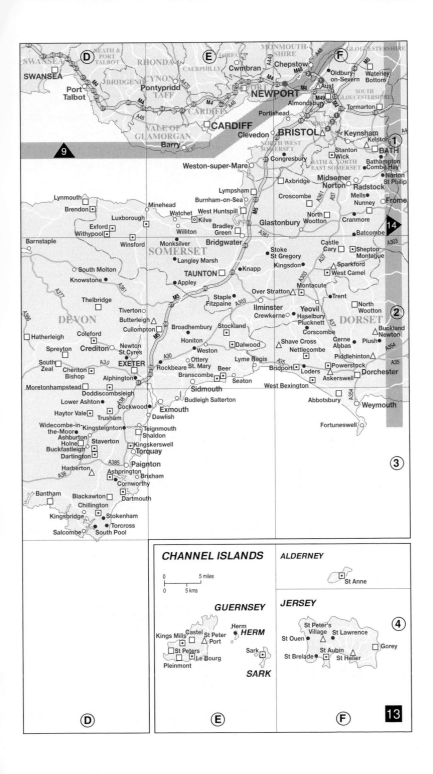

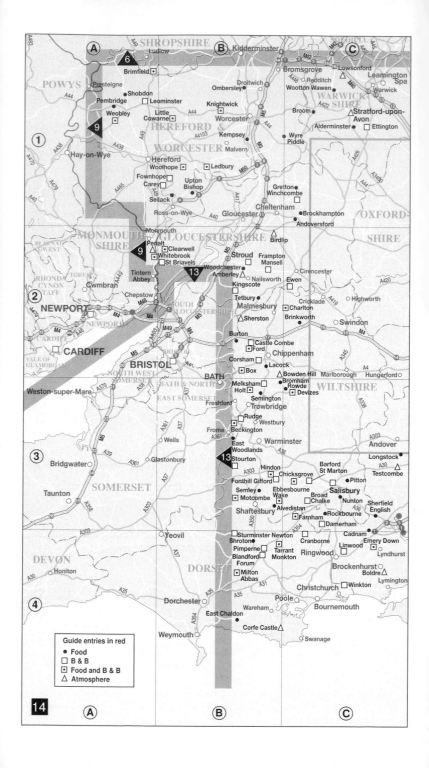

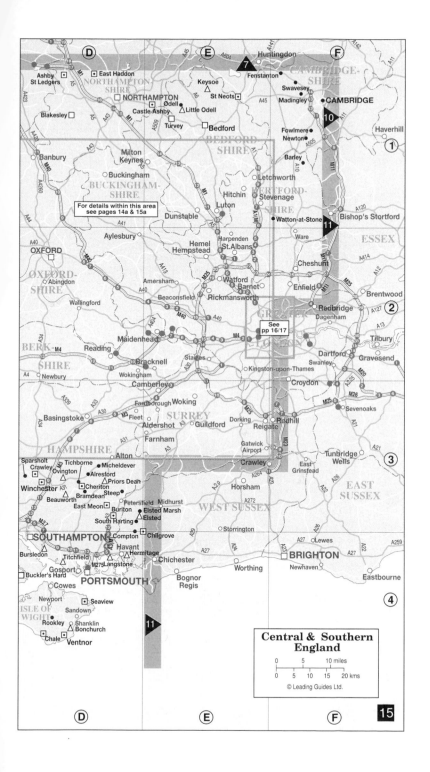

Central & Southern England

0   5   10 miles

0   5   10   15   20 kms

© Leading Guides Ltd.

15

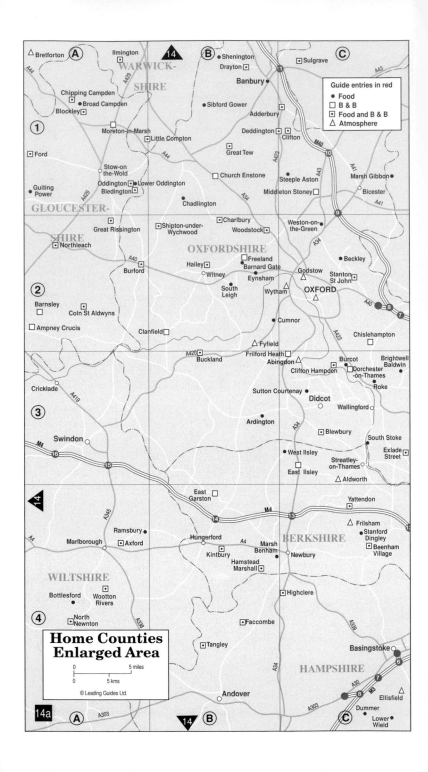

Home Counties
Enlarged Area

0   5 miles
0   5 kms

© Leading Guides Ltd.

Guide entries in red
● Food
□ B & B
☑ Food and B & B
△ Atmosphere

14a

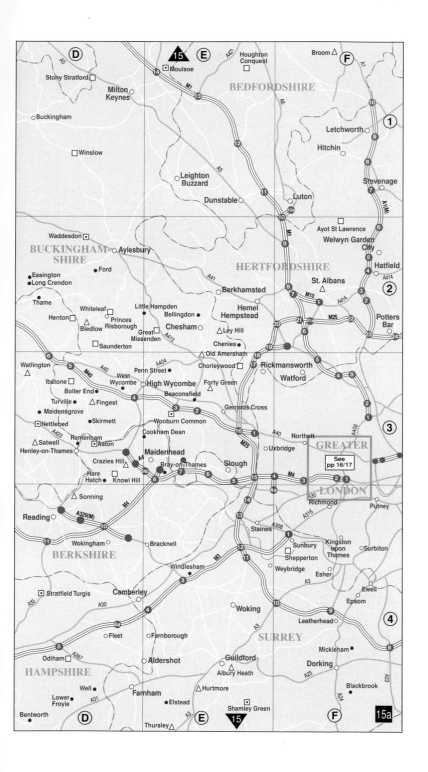

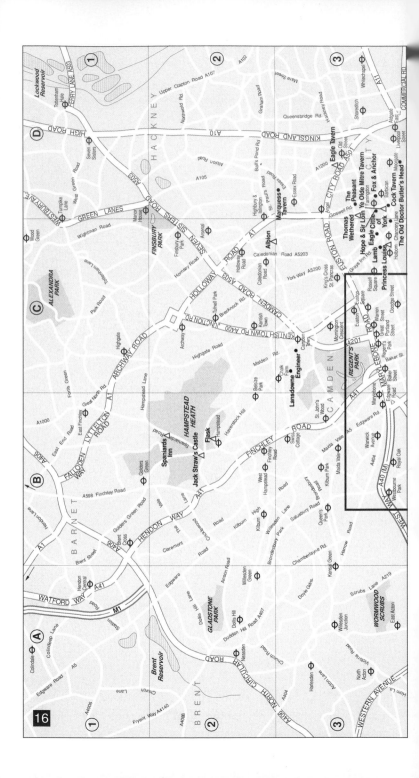

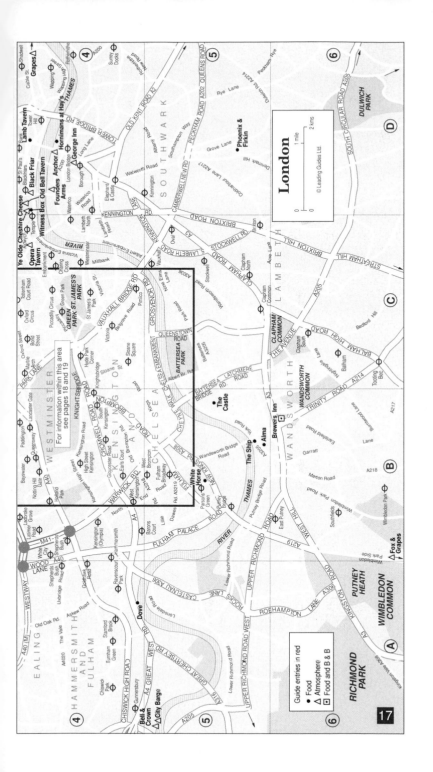

London

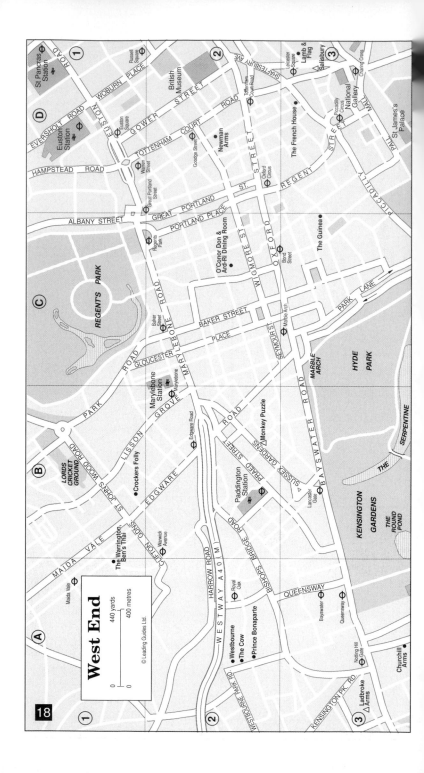

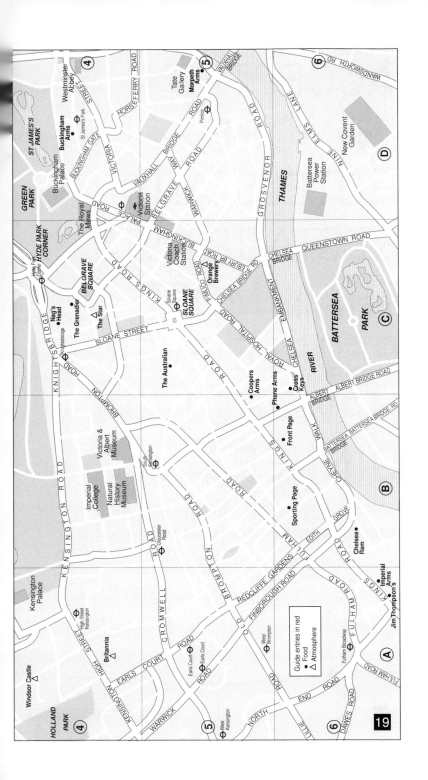

19

ACCEPTED IN MORE HOTELS AND RESTAURANTS THAN MOST PEOPLE EVER HAVE HOT DINNERS.

VISA IS ACCEPTED FOR MORE TRANSACTIONS WORLDWIDE THAN ANY OTHER CARD.

MAKING LIFE EASIER

Index

ACCEPTED IN MORE HOTELS AND RESTAURANTS THAN MOST PEOPLE EVER HAVE HOT DINNERS.

VISA IS ACCEPTED FOR MORE TRANSACTIONS WORLDWIDE THAN ANY OTHER CARD.

MAKING LIFE EASIER

READERS' COMMENTS

Please use this sheet, and the continuation overleaf, to recommend pubs
of **really outstanding quality** and to comment on existing entries.
Complaints about any of the Guide's entries will be treated seriously and passed on to
our inspectorate, but we would like to remind you always to take up your complaint
with the management at the time. We regret that owing to the volume of readers'
communications received each year we will be unable to acknowledge these forms,
but your comments will certainly be seriously considered.

Please post to:
Egon Ronay's Guides, 77 St John Street, London EC1M 4AN

or contact our web site at:
http://www.egon-ronay.infocomint.com

Please use an up-to-date Guide. We publish annually. (Pubs & Inns 1997)

Name and address of establishment   **Your recommendation or complaint**

Name and address of establishment

Your recommendation or complaint

_____   _____

_____   _____

_____   _____

_____   _____

_____   _____

_____   _____

_____   _____

_____   _____

_____   _____

_____   _____

_____   _____

_____   _____

_____   _____

_____   _____

_____   _____

_____   _____

Your name and address *(BLOCK CAPITALS PLEASE)*

_____

_____

_____

_____

_____

_____

READERS' COMMENTS

Please use this sheet, and the continuation overleaf, to recommend pubs
of **really outstanding quality** and to comment on existing entries.
Complaints about any of the Guide's entries will be treated seriously and passed on to
our inspectorate, but we would like to remind you always to take up your complaint
with the management at the time. We regret that owing to the volume of readers'
communications received each year we will be unable to acknowledge these forms,
but your comments will certainly be seriously considered.

Please post to:
Egon Ronay's Guides, 77 St John Street, London EC1M 4AN

or contact our web site at:
http://www.egon-ronay.infocomint.com

Please use an up-to-date Guide. We publish annually. (Pubs & Inns 1997)

Name and address of establishment   **Your recommendation or complaint**

Name and address of establishment

Your recommendation or complaint

_____   _____

_____   _____

_____   _____

_____   _____

_____   _____

_____   _____

_____   _____

_____   _____

_____   _____

_____   _____

_____   _____

_____   _____

_____   _____

_____   _____

_____   _____

Your name and address *(BLOCK CAPITALS PLEASE)*

_____

_____

_____

_____

_____

_____

READERS' COMMENTS

Please use this sheet, and the continuation overleaf, to recommend pubs
of **really outstanding quality** and to comment on existing entries.
Complaints about any of the Guide's entries will be treated seriously and passed on to
our inspectorate, but we would like to remind you always to take up your complaint
with the management at the time. We regret that owing to the volume of readers'
communications received each year we will be unable to acknowledge these forms,
but your comments will certainly be seriously considered.

Please post to:
Egon Ronay's Guides, 77 St John Street, London EC1M 4AN

or contact our web site at:
http://www.egon-ronay.infocomint.com

Please use an up-to-date Guide. We publish annually. (Pubs & Inns 1997)

Name and address of establishment   **Your recommendation or complaint**

Name and address of establishment

Your recommendation or complaint

Your name and address *(BLOCK CAPITALS PLEASE)*

READERS' COMMENTS

Please use this sheet, and the continuation overleaf, to recommend pubs
of **really outstanding quality** and to comment on existing entries.
Complaints about any of the Guide's entries will be treated seriously and passed on to
our inspectorate, but we would like to remind you always to take up your complaint
with the management at the time. We regret that owing to the volume of readers'
communications received each year we will be unable to acknowledge these forms,
but your comments will certainly be seriously considered.

Please post to:
Egon Ronay's Guides, 77 St John Street, London EC1M 4AN

or contact our web site at:
http://www.egon-ronay.infocomint.com

Please use an up-to-date Guide. We publish annually. (Pubs & Inns 1997)

Name and address of establishment   **Your recommendation or complaint**

Name and address of establishment   **Your recommendation or complaint**

_____   _____

_____   _____

_____   _____

_____   _____

_____   _____

_____   _____

_____   _____

_____   _____

_____   _____

_____   _____

_____   _____

_____   _____

_____   _____

_____   _____

_____   _____

Your name and address _(BLOCK CAPITALS PLEASE)_

_____

_____

_____

_____

_____

_____

READERS' COMMENTS

Please use this sheet, and the continuation overleaf, to recommend pubs
of **really outstanding quality** and to comment on existing entries.
Complaints about any of the Guide's entries will be treated seriously and passed on to
our inspectorate, but we would like to remind you always to take up your complaint
with the management at the time. We regret that owing to the volume of readers'
communications received each year we will be unable to acknowledge these forms,
but your comments will certainly be seriously considered.

Please post to:
Egon Ronay's Guides, 77 St John Street, London EC1M 4AN

or contact our web site at:
http://www.egon-ronay.infocomint.com

Please use an up-to-date Guide. We publish annually. (Pubs & Inns 1997)

Name and address of establishment   **Your recommendation or complaint**

Name and address of establishment   **Your recommendation or complaint**

_____   _____

_____   _____

_____   _____

_____   _____

_____   _____

_____   _____

_____   _____

_____   _____

_____   _____

_____   _____

_____   _____

_____   _____

_____   _____

_____   _____

_____   _____

Your name and address *(BLOCK CAPITALS PLEASE)*

_____

_____

_____

_____

_____

_____

READERS' COMMENTS

Please use this sheet, and the continuation overleaf, to recommend pubs
of **really outstanding quality** and to comment on existing entries.
Complaints about any of the Guide's entries will be treated seriously and passed on to
our inspectorate, but we would like to remind you always to take up your complaint
with the management at the time. We regret that owing to the volume of readers'
communications received each year we will be unable to acknowledge these forms,
but your comments will certainly be seriously considered.

Please post to:
Egon Ronay's Guides, 77 St John Street, London EC1M 4AN

or contact our web site at:
http://www.egon-ronay.infocomint.com

Please use an up-to-date Guide. We publish annually. (Pubs & Inns 1997)

Name and address of establishment   **Your recommendation or complaint**

Name and address of establishment

Your recommendation or complaint

_____   _____

_____   _____

_____   _____

_____   _____

_____   _____

_____   _____

_____   _____

_____   _____

_____   _____

_____   _____

_____   _____

_____   _____

_____   _____

_____   _____

_____   _____

Your name and address _(BLOCK CAPITALS PLEASE)_

_____

_____

_____

_____

_____

_____

READERS' COMMENTS

Please use this sheet, and the continuation overleaf, to recommend pubs
of **really outstanding quality** and to comment on existing entries.
Complaints about any of the Guide's entries will be treated seriously and passed on to
our inspectorate, but we would like to remind you always to take up your complaint
with the management at the time. We regret that owing to the volume of readers'
communications received each year we will be unable to acknowledge these forms,
but your comments will certainly be seriously considered.

Please post to:
Egon Ronay's Guides, 77 St John Street, London EC1M 4AN

or contact our web site at:
http://www.egon-ronay.infocomint.com

Please use an up-to-date Guide. We publish annually. (Pubs & Inns 1997)

Name and address of establishment	Your recommendation or complaint

Name and address of establishment **Your recommendation or complaint**

_____   _____

_____   _____

_____   _____

_____   _____

_____   _____

_____   _____

_____   _____

_____   _____

_____   _____

_____   _____

_____   _____

_____   _____

_____   _____

_____   _____

_____   _____

Your name and address _(BLOCK CAPITALS PLEASE)_

_____

_____

_____

_____

_____

_____

READERS' COMMENTS

Please use this sheet, and the continuation overleaf, to recommend pubs
of **really outstanding quality** and to comment on existing entries.
Complaints about any of the Guide's entries will be treated seriously and passed on to
our inspectorate, but we would like to remind you always to take up your complaint
with the management at the time. We regret that owing to the volume of readers'
communications received each year we will be unable to acknowledge these forms,
but your comments will certainly be seriously considered.

Please post to:
Egon Ronay's Guides, 77 St John Street, London EC1M 4AN

or contact our web site at:
http://www.egon-ronay.infocomint.com

Please use an up-to-date Guide. We publish annually. (Pubs & Inns 1997)

Name and address of establishment   **Your recommendation or complaint**

Name and address of establishment   **Your recommendation or complaint**

_____   _____

_____   _____

_____   _____

_____   _____

_____   _____

_____   _____

_____   _____

_____   _____

_____   _____

_____   _____

_____   _____

_____   _____

_____   _____

_____   _____

_____   _____

_____   _____

Your name and address _(BLOCK CAPITALS PLEASE)_

_____

_____

_____

_____

_____

_____

READERS' COMMENTS

Please use this sheet, and the continuation overleaf, to recommend pubs
of **really outstanding quality** and to comment on existing entries.
Complaints about any of the Guide's entries will be treated seriously and passed on to
our inspectorate, but we would like to remind you always to take up your complaint
with the management at the time. We regret that owing to the volume of readers'
communications received each year we will be unable to acknowledge these forms,
but your comments will certainly be seriously considered.

Please post to:
Egon Ronay's Guides, 77 St John Street, London EC1M 4AN

or contact our web site at:
http://www.egon-ronay.infocomint.com

Please use an up-to-date Guide. We publish annually. (Pubs & Inns 1997)

Name and address of establishment   **Your recommendation or complaint**

Name and address of establishment   **Your recommendation or complaint**

————————————————   ————————————————

————————————————   ————————————————

————————————————   ————————————————

————————————————   ————————————————

————————————————   ————————————————

————————————————   ————————————————

————————————————   ————————————————

————————————————   ————————————————

————————————————   ————————————————

————————————————   ————————————————

————————————————   ————————————————

————————————————   ————————————————

————————————————   ————————————————

————————————————   ————————————————

Your name and address *(BLOCK CAPITALS PLEASE)*

————————————————————————————————

————————————————————————————————

————————————————————————————————

————————————————————————————————

————————————————————————————————

————————————————————————————————